11. Format for Bank Reconciliation:

Cash balance according to bank statement		$xxx
Add: Additions by company not on bank statement	$xx	
Bank errors	xx	xx
		$xxx
Deduct: Deductions by company not on bank statement	$xx	
Bank errors	xx	xx
Adjusted balance		$xxx
Cash balance according to company's records		$xxx
Add: Additions by bank not recorded by company	$xx	
Company errors	xx	xx
		$xxx
Deduct: Deductions by bank not recorded by company	$xx	
Company errors	xx	xx
Adjusted balance		$xxx

12. Inventory Costing Methods:

1. First-in, First-out (FIFO)
2. Last-in, First-out (LIFO)
3. Average Cost

13. Interest Computations:

Interest = Face Amount (or Principal) × Rate × Time

14. Methods of Determining Annual Depreciation:

STRAIGHT-LINE: $\frac{\text{Cost} - \text{Estimated Residual Value}}{\text{Estimated Life}}$

DOUBLE-DECLINING-BALANCE: Rate* × Book Value at Beginning of Period

*Rate is commonly twice the straight-line rate (1 ÷ Estimated Life).

15. Adjustments to Net Income (Loss) Using the Indirect Method

	Increase (Decrease)
Net income (loss)	$ XXX
Adjustments to reconcile net income to net cash flow from operating activities:	
Depreciation of fixed assets	XXX
Amortization of intangible assets	XXX
Losses on disposal of assets	XXX
Gains on disposal of assets	(XXX)
Changes in current operating assets and liabilities:	
Increases in noncash current operating assets	(XXX)
Decreases in noncash current operating assets	XXX
Increases in current operating liabilities	XXX
Decreases in current operating liabilities	(XXX)
Net cash flow from operating activities	$ XXX or $(XXX)

16. Contribution Margin Ratio = $\frac{\text{Sales} - \text{Variable Costs}}{\text{Sales}}$

17. Break-E

Unit Contribution Margin

18. Sales (Units) = $\frac{\text{Fixed Costs} + \text{Target Profit}}{\text{Unit Contribution Margin}}$

19. Margin of Safety = $\frac{\text{Sales} - \text{Sales at Break-Even Point}}{\text{Sales}}$

20. Operating Leverage = $\frac{\text{Contribution Margin}}{\text{Income from Operations}}$

21. Variances

$$\text{Direct Materials Price Variance} = \left(\text{Actual Price} - \text{Standard Price}\right) \times \text{Actual Quantity}$$

$$\text{Direct Materials Quantity Variance} = \left(\text{Actual Quantity} - \text{Standard Quantity}\right) \times \text{Standard Price}$$

$$\text{Direct Labor Rate Variance} = \left(\text{Actual Rate per Hour} - \text{Standard Rate per Hour}\right) \times \text{Actual Hours}$$

$$\text{Direct Labor Time Variance} = \left(\text{Actual Direct Labor Hours} - \text{Standard Direct Labor Hours}\right) \times \text{Standard Rate per Hour}$$

$$\text{Variable Factory Overhead Controllable Variance} = \text{Actual Variable Factory Overhead} - \text{Budgeted Variable Factory Overhead}$$

$$\text{Fixed Factory Overhead Volume Variance} = \left(\text{Standard Hours for 100\% of Normal Capacity} - \text{Standard Hours for Actual Units Produced}\right) \times \text{Fixed Factory Overhead Rate}$$

22. Rate of Return on Investment (ROI) = $\frac{\text{Income from Operations}}{\text{Invested Assets}}$

Alternative ROI Computation:

$$\text{ROI} = \frac{\text{Income from Operations}}{\text{Sales}} \times \frac{\text{Sales}}{\text{Invested Assets}}$$

23. Capital Investment Analysis Methods:

1. Methods That Ignore Present Values:
   - A. Average Rate of Return Method
   - B. Cash Payback Method
2. Methods That Use Present Values:
   - A. Net Present Value Method
   - B. Internal Rate of Return Method

24. Average Rate of Return = $\frac{\text{Estimated Average Annual Income}}{\text{Average Investment}}$

25. Present Value Index = $\frac{\text{Total Present Value of Net Cash Flow}}{\text{Amount to Be Invested}}$

26. Present Value Factor for an Annuity of $1 = $\frac{\text{Amount to Be Invested}}{\text{Equal Annual Net Cash Flows}}$

Accounting

24e

Warren | Reeve | Duchac

Australia • Brazil • Japan • Korea • Mexico • Singapore • Spain • United Kingdom • United States

Accounting, 24e

Executive Editors:
Maureen Staudt
Michael Stranz

Senior Project Development Manager:
Linda deStefano

Marketing Specialist:
Courtney Sheldon

Senior Production/Manufacturing Manager:
Donna M. Brown

PreMedia Manager:
Joel Brennecke

Sr. Rights Acquisition Account Manager:
Todd Osborne

Cover Image:
Getty Images*

*Unless otherwise noted, all cover images used by Custom Solutions, a part of Cengage Learning, have been supplied courtesy of Getty Images with the exception of the Earthview cover image, which has been supplied by the National Aeronautics and Space Administration (NASA).

Printed in the United States of America

Accounting, 24th Edition
Warren | Reeve | Duchac

ISBN-13: 978-1-133-36132-9

ISBN-10: 1-133-36132-3

Cengage Learning
5191 Natorp Boulevard
Mason, Ohio 45040
USA

Cengage Learning is a leading provider of customized learning solutions with office locations around the globe, including Singapore, the United Kingdom, Australia, Mexico, Brazil, and Japan. Locate your local office at:
international.cengage.com/region.

Cengage Learning products are represented in Canada by Nelson Education, Ltd.
For your lifelong learning solutions, visit **www.cengage.com/custom.**
Visit our corporate website at **www.cengage.com.**

Brief Table of Contents |

The Author Team

Carl S. Warren

Dr. Carl S. Warren is Professor Emeritus of Accounting at the University of Georgia, Athens. Dr. Warren has taught classes at the University of Georgia, University of Iowa, Michigan State University, and University of Chicago. Professor Warren focused his teaching efforts on principles of accounting and auditing. He received his Ph.D. from Michigan State University and his B.B.A. and M.A. from the University of Iowa. During his career, Dr. Warren published numerous articles in professional journals, including *The Accounting Review, Journal of Accounting Research, Journal of Accountancy, The CPA Journal,* and *Auditing: A Journal of Practice & Theory*. Dr. Warren has served on numerous committees of the American Accounting Association, the American Institute of Certified Public Accountants, and the Institute of Internal Auditors. He has also consulted with numerous companies and public accounting firms. Warren's outside interests include playing handball, golfing, skiing, backpacking, and fly-fishing.

James M. Reeve

Dr. James M. Reeve is Professor Emeritus of Accounting and Information Management at the University of Tennessee. Professor Reeve taught on the accounting faculty for 25 years, after graduating with his Ph.D. from Oklahoma State University. His teaching effort focused on undergraduate accounting principles and graduate education in the Master of Accountancy and Senior Executive MBA programs. Beyond this, Professor Reeve is also very active in the Supply Chain Certification program, which is a major executive education and research effort of the College. His research interests are varied and include work in managerial accounting, supply chain management, lean manufacturing, and information management. He has published over 40 articles in academic and professional journals, including the *Journal of Cost Management, Journal of Management Accounting Research, Accounting Review, Management Accounting Quarterly, Supply Chain Management Review,* and *Accounting Horizons*. He has consulted or provided training around the world for a wide variety of organizations, including Boeing, Procter & Gamble, Norfolk Southern, Hershey Foods, Coca-Cola, and Sony. When not writing books, Professor Reeve plays golf and is involved in faith-based activities.

Jonathan Duchac

Dr. Jonathan Duchac is the Merrill Lynch and Co. Professor of Accounting and Director of the Program in Enterprise Risk Management at Wake Forest University. He earned his Ph.D. in accounting from the University of Georgia and currently teaches introductory and advanced courses in financial accounting. Dr. Duchac has received a number of awards during his career, including the Wake Forest University Outstanding Graduate Professor Award, the T.B. Rose Award for Instructional Innovation, and the University of Georgia Outstanding Teaching Assistant Award. In addition to his teaching responsibilities, Dr. Duchac has served as Accounting Advisor to Merrill Lynch Equity Research, where he worked with research analysts in reviewing and evaluating the financial reporting practices of public companies. He has testified before the U.S. House of Representatives, the Financial Accounting Standards Board, and the Securities and Exchange Commission; and has worked with a number of major public companies on financial reporting and accounting policy issues. In addition to his professional interests, Dr. Duchac is the Treasurer of The Special Children's School of Winston-Salem; a private, nonprofit developmental day school serving children with special needs. Dr. Duchac is an avi long-distance runner, mountain biker, and snow skier. His recent events include th Grandfather Mountain Marathon, the Black Mountain Marathon, the Shut-In Ridge Tra run, and NO MAAM (Nocturnal Overnight Mountain Bike Assault on Mount Mitchell).

A History of Success

For nearly **85** years, *Accounting* has been used effectively to teach generations of businessmen and women. The text has been used by millions of business students. For many, this book provides the only exposure to accounting principles that they will ever receive. As the most successful business textbook of all time, it continues to introduce students to accounting through a variety of time-tested ways.

The previous edition, 23e, started a new journey into learning more about the changing needs of accounting students through a variety of new and innovative research and development methods. Our Blue Sky Workshops brought accounting faculty from all over the country into our book development process in a very direct and creative way. Many of the features and themes present in this text are a result of the collaboration and countless conversations we have had with accounting instructors over the last several years. 24e continues to build on this philosophy and strives to be reflective of the suggestions and feedback we receive from instructors and students on an ongoing basis. We are very happy with the results, and think you will be pleased with the improvements we have made to the text.

The original author of *Accounting*, James McKinsey, could not have imagined the success and influence this text has enjoyed or that his original vision would continue to lead the market into the twenty-first century. As the current authors, we appreciate the responsibility of protecting and enhancing this vision, while continuing to refine it to meet the changing needs of students and instructors. Always in touch with a tradition of excellence but never satisfied with yesterday's success, this edition enthusiastically embraces a changing environment and continues to proudly lead the way. We sincerely thank our many colleagues who have helped to make it happen.

Carl S. Warren

Jonathan Duchac

"The teaching of accounting is no longer designed to train professional accountants only. With the growing complexity of business and the constantly increasing difficulty of the problems of management, it has become essential that everyone who aspires to a position of responsibility should have a knowledge of the fundamental principles of accounting."

—James O. McKinsey, Author, first edition, 1929

New to the 24th Edition

Textbooks continue to play an invaluable role in the teaching and learning environments. Continuing our focus from previous editions, we reached out to accounting instructors in an effort to improve the textbook presentation. Our research informed us of the need to remain current in the areas of emerging topics/trends and to continue to look for ways to make the book more accessible to students. The results of this collaboration with hundreds of accounting instructors are reflected in the following major improvements made to the 24th edition:

International Financial Reporting Standards (IFRS)

IFRS is on the minds of many accounting educators of today. While the future is still unclear, our research indicates a growing need to provide more basic awareness of these standards within the text. We have incorporated some elements of IFRS throughout the text as appropriate to provide this level of awareness, being careful not to encroach upon the core GAAP principles that remain the hallmark focus of the book. These elements include icons that have been placed throughout the financial chapters which point to specific IFRS-related content, outlined with more detail in Appendix D. This table outlines the IFRS impact on the accounting concept.

International Connection

International Connection features highlight IFRS topics from a real-world perspective and appear in Chapters 1, 4, 7, 10, 13, and 16.

International Connection

IFRS FOR STATEMENT OF CASH FLOWS

The statement of cash flows is required under International Financial Reporting Standards (IFRS). The statement of cash flows under IFRS is similar to that reported under U.S. GAAP in that the statement has separate sections for operating, investing, and financing activities. Like U.S. GAAP, IFRS also allow the use of either the indirect or direct method of reporting cash flows from operating activities. IFRS differ from U.S. GAAP in some minor areas, including:

- Interest paid can be reported as either an operating or a financing activity, while interest received can be reported as either an operating or an investing activity. In contrast, U.S. GAAP reports interest paid or received as an operating activity.
- Dividends paid can be reported as either an operating or a financing activity, while dividends received can be reported as either an operating or an investing activity. In contrast, U.S. GAAP reports dividends paid as a financing activity and dividends received as an operating activity.
- Cash flows to pay taxes are reported as a separate line in the operating activities, in contrast to U.S. GAAP, which does not require a separate line disclosure.

* IFRS are further discussed and illustrated on pages 716-716G and in Appendix D.

New to the 24th Edition

Mornin' Joe International

Our authors have prepared statements for Mornin' Joe under IFRS guidelines as a basis for comparison with U.S.-prepared statements. This allows students to see how financial reporting differs under IFRS.

IFRS Training Video and IFRS PowerPoint Presentation

A training video with the voice of our distinguished author, Jim Reeve, will walk an instructor through the nuances of this complex topic. A PowerPoint deck, based on the training video, will allow instructors to customize the presentation for delivery to their students.

The Accounting Equation

A new format has been implemented in Chapter 2 for analyzing transactions. This new format includes the following elements: (1) transaction description, (2) analysis, (3) journal entry, and (4) accounting equation impact. This will help students understand that a transaction ultimately affects the accounting equation—*Assets = Liabilities + Owner's Equity.*

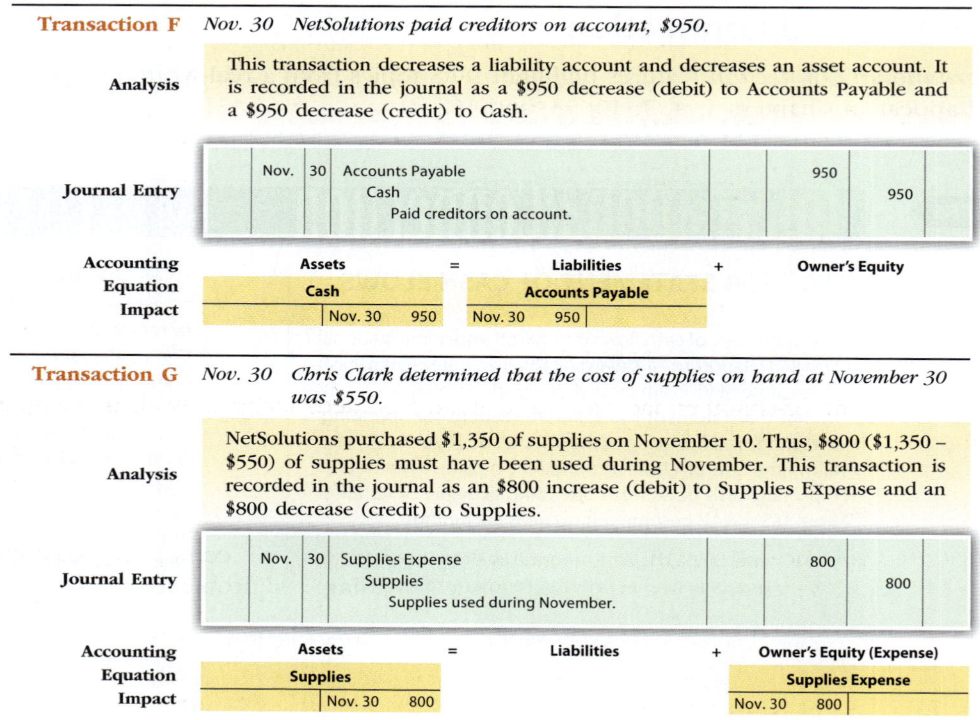

Activity-Based Costing

Pulling from our existing appendix coverage, we have placed in Chapter 25 a thorough discussion of activity-based costing (ABC). ABC is framed in the context of product pricing and profit analysis.

A new uniform method for performing differential analysis is employed for all the differential analysis illustrations and end-of-chapter materials. This approach provides the student a consistent solution grid for solving differential analyses.

Financial Analysis and Interpretation

New Financial Analysis and Interpretation learning objectives have been added to the financial chapters and where appropriate, linked to real-world situations. FAI encourages students to go deeper into the material to analyze accounting information and improve critical thinking skills.

Updated At a Glance

Students prepare for homework and tests by referring to our end-of-chapter grid which outlines learning objectives, linking concept coverage to specific examples. Through our updated At a Glance, students can review the chapter's learning objectives and key learning outcomes. In addition, all the *Example Exercises* and *Practice Exercises* have been indexed so that each learning objective and key outcomes can be viewed.

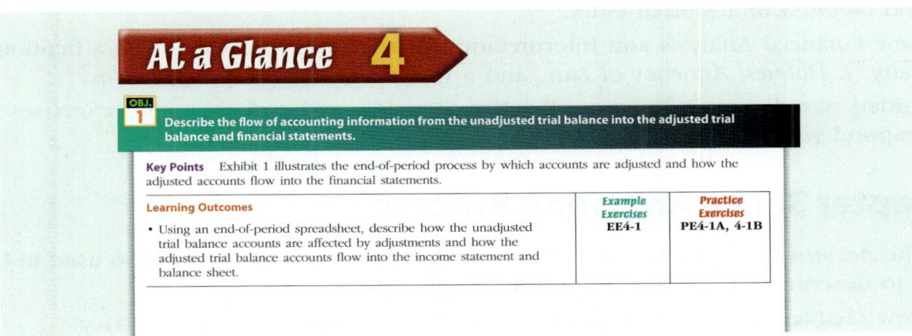

At a Glance 4

OBJ. 1 Describe the flow of accounting information from the unadjusted trial balance into the adjusted trial balance and financial statements.

Key Points Exhibit 1 illustrates the end-of-period process by which accounts are adjusted and how the adjusted accounts flow into the financial statements.

Learning Outcomes	Example Exercises	Practice Exercises
• Using an end-of-period spreadsheet, describe how the unadjusted trial balance accounts are affected by adjustments and how the adjusted trial balance accounts flow into the income statement and balance sheet.	EE4-1	PE4-1A, 4-1B

End-of-Chapter Exercises and Problems

All of our end-of-chapter materials have been updated, using new data, company names, and real-world data.

Test Bank

With the assistance of over fifteen distinguished professors, we completely revamped our test bank. We created more multiple choice, matching, and problem type questions.

Excel Templates

Our Excel templates have been enhanced to allow professors to turn off the "instant feedback" asterisks. Based on the file provided to them, students can complete the spreadsheet and email the file to their instructor. The instructor can then input a code that will automatically grade the student's work. These Excel templates complement end-of-chapter problems. They are located on the companion website (URL) and also within CengageNOW.

Chapter-by-Chapter Enhancements

The following specific content changes can be found in *Accounting, 24e.*

Chapter 1: Introduction to Accounting and Business

- *Google* replaces *Starbucks* in the chapter opening example.
- Proprietorships, partnerships, corporations, and limited liability companies (LLC) are now discussed with the business entity concept.
- Added an International Connection feature to introduce students to IFRS.
- New Financial Analysis and Interpretation (FAI): **Ratio of Liabilities to Owner's Equity** using real-world companies *McDonald's* and *Google.*
- Added new Example Exercise, Practice Exercise, and end-of-chapter exercises to correspond with the new FAI.

Chapter 2: Analyzing Transactions

- A new format has been implemented in Chapter 2 to help students better understand how to analyze and record transactions.
- A table summarizing common transaction terminology has also been added. This table includes common transaction terms and the related accounts that would be debited and credited in a journal entry.
- New Financial Analysis and Interpretation: **Horizontal Analysis** using a fictitious company, *J. Holmes, Attorney at Law*, and a real-world company, *Apple, Inc.*
- Added new Example Exercise, Practice Exercise, and end-of-chapter exercises to correspond with the new FAI.

Chapter 3: The Adjusting Process

- The *Accounting Equation Impact* feature described in Chapter 2 is also used in Chapter 3 to describe and illustrate adjusting entries.
- New chapter opener features *Rhapsody*, an Internet-based music service.
- New Financial Analysis and Interpretation: **Vertical Analysis** continuing with fictitious company, *J. Holmes, Attorney at Law*, and adding a real-world company, *RealNetworks, Inc.*

Chapter 4: Completing the Accounting Cycle

- The Flow of Accounting Information exhibit at the beginning of the chapter has been revised to show the flow of accounting data from the adjusted trial balance directly into the income statement, statement of owner's equity, and balance sheet.
- New Financial Analysis and Interpretation: **Working Capital and Current Ratio** using *Electronic Arts, Inc.* and *Take-Two Interactive Software, Inc.*
- Added new Example Exercise, Practice Exercise, and end-of-chapter exercises to correspond with the new FAI.

Chapter 5: Accounting Systems

- An illustration of a computerized accounting system was updated using the screen shots from Quickbooks® Pro 2010 edition.
- Streamlined discussion of special journals.
- Removed discussion of "Manual Accounting Systems."
- Added a Business Connection feature.

- New Financial Analysis and Interpretation: **Segment Analysis** using real-world company *Intuit, Inc.*
- Added new Example Exercise and Practice Exercise to correspond with the new FAI.

Chapter 6: Accounting for Merchandising Businesses

- The computation of cost of merchandise sold (under the periodic inventory system) has been moved from the beginning of the chapter to an end-of-chapter appendix.
- A new section has been added that summarizes the effects of merchandise transactions on the merchandise inventory account. This is illustrated using a T account for merchandise inventory.
- Moved coverage of "Accounting Systems for Merchandisers" to our online site (www.cengage.com/accounting/warren).
- New Financial Analysis and Interpretation: **Ratio of Net Sales to Assets** using real-world company *Dollar Tree, Inc.*
- Added new Example Exercise and Practice Exercise to correspond with the new FAI.

Chapter 7: Inventories

- New Financial Analysis and Interpretation: **Inventory Turnover and Number of Days, Sales in Inventory** using real-world companies *Best Buy* and *Zales*.
- Added new Example Exercise and Practice Exercise to correspond with the new FAI.

Chapter 8: Sarbanes-Oxley, Internal Control, and Cash

- Updated chapter graphic for better clarity and snapshot comprehension.
- New Financial Analysis and Interpretation: **Ratio of Cash to Monthly Cash Expenses** using real-world company *Evergreen Solar, Inc.*
- Added new Example Exercise and Practice Exercise to correspond with the new FAI.

Chapter 9: Receivables

- New Financial Analysis and Interpretation: **Accounts Receivable Turnover and Number of Days' Sales in Receivables** using real-world company *FedEx*.
- Added new Example Exercise and Practice Exercise to correspond with the new FAI.

Chapter 10: Fixed Assets and Intangible Assets

- Updated many chapter graphics for better clarity and snapshot comprehension.
- New Financial Analysis and Interpretation: **Fixed Asset Turnover Ratio** using real-world company *Starbucks Corporation*.
- Added new Example Exercise and Practice Exercise to correspond with the new FAI.

Chapter 11: Current Liabilities and Payroll

- The example of *Starbucks Corporation* on long-term debt has been replaced by *P.F. Chang's*.
- Updated Wage Bracket Withholding table, based on data from the *2010 Publication 15*.
- Removed discussion of social security cap on withholding (above $100,000).

Chapter-by-Chapter Enhancements

- Updated Business Connection feature to cover *General Motors* and its pension problems.
- New Financial Analysis and Interpretation: **Quick Ratio** using real-world company *TechSolutions, Inc.*
- Added new Example Exercise and Practice Exercise to correspond with the new FAI.

Chapter 12: Accounting for Partnerships and Limited Liability Companies

- *Razor* replaces *AgentBlaze LLC* as the chapter opening example.
- Updated Business Connection feature to Kristen Hall, founding member of the country music group *Sugarland* and her lawsuit.
- New Financial Analysis and Interpretation: **Revenue per Employee** showing *McDonald's* and *Starbucks* to understand evaluation within an industry.
- Added new Example Exercise and Practice Exercise to correspond with the new FAI.
- Eliminated the section on "Errors in Liquidation" to reduce minor redundancy.

Chapter 13: Corporations: Organization, Stock Transactions, and Dividends

- New Financial Analysis and Interpretation: On website they say **JPMorgan Chase & Co. Earnings per Share** using *Hasbro*, *Bank of America Corporation*, and *J.P. Morgan Chase & Co*.
- Added new Example Exercise and Practice Exercise to correspond with the new FAI.

Chapter 14: Long-Term Liabilities: Bonds and Notes

- Updated Business Connection feature on U.S. government debt.
- Updated Business Connection feature to cover *General Motors* bonds.
- Added an Integrity, Objectivity, and Ethics feature to discuss "Liar's Loans."
- New Financial Analysis and Interpretation: **Number of Times Interest Charges Are Earned** using *Under Armour, Inc.*
- Added new Example Exercise and Practice Exercise to correspond with the new FAI.

Chapter 15: Investments and Fair Value Accounting

- Added an Integrity, Objectivity, and Ethics box titled *"Loan Loss Woes"* on mortgage loans called "sub-prime" and "Alt-A" loans.
- Updated Business Connection feature to "Apple's Entrance to Streaming Music."
- Revised "Value and Reporting Investments" to simplify the reading process.
- New Financial Analysis and Interpretation: **Dividend Yield** using *News Corporation*.
- Added new Example Exercise and Practice Exercise to correspond with the new FAI.
- Moved "Accounting for Held-to-Maturity Investments" appendix to www.cengage.com/accounting/warren.

Mornin' Joe

- To expand students' understanding of financial statement preparation outside the United States, the authors took our unique company example, *Mornin' Joe,* and show how it goes international after Chapter 15. They prepared a set of financial statements following IFRS guidelines. To aid in learning, callout features pinpoint the differences between U.S. GAAP and IFRS.

Chapter 16: Statement of Cash Flows

- Updated Business Connection feature to "Cash Crunch!" featuring *Chrysler Group LLC.*
- New Financial Analysis and Interpretation: **Free Cash Flow** using *Research in Motion, Inc.*, maker of BlackBerry® smartphones.
- Added new Example Exercise and Practice Exercise to correspond with the new FAI.

Chapter 17: Financial Statement Analysis

- Real-world financial statement analysis problem uses data from the *Nike, Inc.* 2010 10-K. A portion of Nike's 10-K is located in Appendix C.
- Updated Integrity, Objectivity, and Ethics feature discusses "Chief Financial Officer Bonuses."
- Updated Integrity, Objectivity, and Ethics feature to "Buy Low, Sell High."

Chapter 18: Managerial Accounting Concepts and Principles

- The chapter opener has been modified to feature Paul Stanley of *KISS*. He has a custom guitar built by *Washburn Guitars*.
- Updated Business Connection feature to "Build-to-Order" about *Dell Inc.*

Chapter 19: Job Order Costing

- Updated Business Connection feature to discuss "BMW's Factory Labor Experiment."

Chapter 20: Process Cost Systems

- Updated Business Connection feature entitled "Fridge Pack" to discuss *Alcoa Inc.*

Chapter 21: Cost Behavior and Cost-Volume-Profit Analysis

- Updated Business Connection feature entitled "Breaking Even in the Airline Industry" to discuss the airline industry.
- Added a new Business Connection feature to highlight franchising using real-world companies such as *McDonald's*, *Wendy's*, *Dunkin' Donuts*, and *Fatburger*.

Chapter 22: Budgeting

- Updated Business Connection feature called the "U.S. Federal Budget Deficit."
- Simplified the writing of definitions and other content explanations.

Chapter 23: Performance Evaluation Using Variances from Standard Costs

- Added a new Business Connection feature to highlight *Brinker International*, the operator of popular chains such as *Chili's* and *On the Border*.

Chapter-by-Chapter Enhancements

Chapter 24: Performance Evaluation for Decentralized Operations

- Chapter opener replaces *K2 Sports* with *E.W. Scripps Company*, a conglomerate of media companies.
- Added a new Business Connection feature entitled "Centralized vs. Decentralized Research and Development."

Chapter 25: Differential Analysis, Product Pricing and Activity-Based Costing

- Chapter opener replaces *RealNetworks, Inc.* with *Facebook*.
- The discussion on activity-based costing (ABC) has been moved from the appendix and updated. ABC is framed in the context of product pricing and profit analysis.
- The total cost and variable cost concepts are moved to an appendix. This change simplifies this section to make room for the added ABC material.

Chapter 26: Capital Investment Analysis

- Updated chapter opener with a cleaner writing style.
- Added a new Business Connection feature called "*Avatar:* The Most Expensive Movie Ever Made (and the Most Successful)."

Hallmark Features of Accounting, 24e

Accounting, 24e, is unparalleled in pedagogical innovation. Our constant dialogue with accounting faculty continues to affect how we refine and improve the text to meet the needs of today's students. Our goal is to provide a logical framework and pedagogical system that caters to how students of today study and learn.

Clear Objectives and Key Learning Outcomes To guide students, the authors provide clear chapter objectives and important learning outcomes. All the chapter materials relate back to these key points and outcomes, which keeps students focused on the most important topics and concepts in order to succeed in the course.

Example Exercises Example Exercises reinforce concepts and procedures in a bold, new way. Like a teacher in the classroom, students follow the authors' example to see how to complete accounting applications as they are presented in the text. This feature also provides a list of Practice Exercises that parallel the Example Exercises so students get the practice they need. In addition, the Practice Exercises include references to the chapter Example Exercises so that students can easily cross-reference when completing homework.

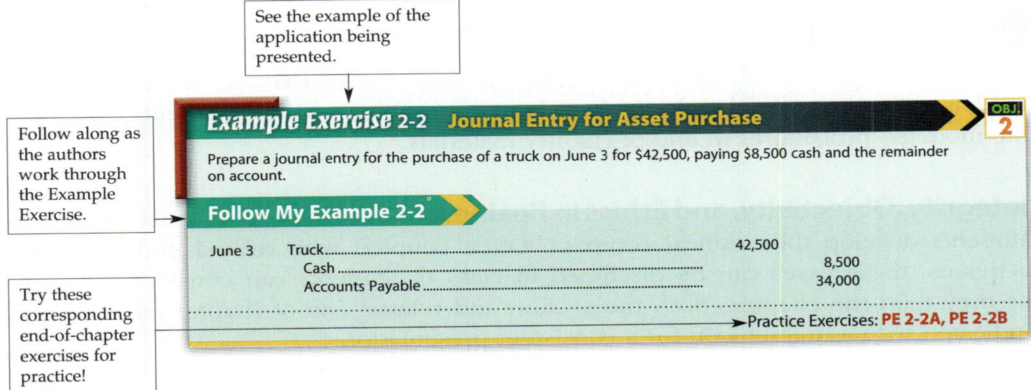

"At a Glance" Chapter Summary At the end of each chapter, the "At a Glance" summary grid ties everything together and helps students stay on track.

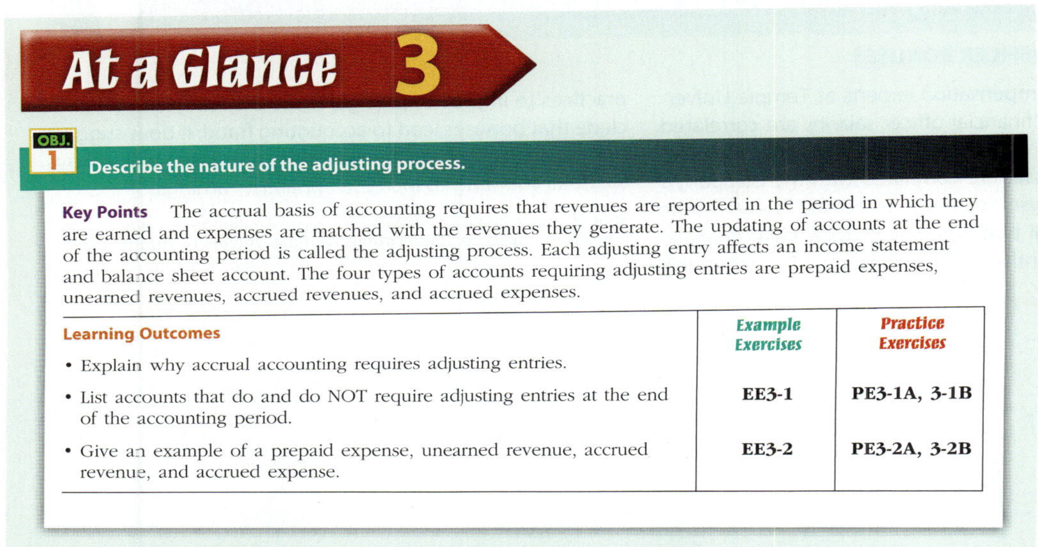

Hallmark Features of Accounting, 24e

CHAPTER 25

facebook

Differential Analysis, Product Pricing, and Activity-Based Costing

Facebook

Many of the decisions that you make depend on comparing the estimated costs of alternatives. The payoff from such comparisons is described in the following report from a University of Michigan study.

Richard Nisbett and two colleagues quizzed Michigan faculty members and university seniors on such questions as how often they walk out on a bad movie, refuse to finish a bad meal, start over on a weak term paper, or abandon a research project that no longer looks promising. They believe that people who cut their losses this way are following sound economic rules: calculating the net benefits of alternative courses of action, writing off past costs that can't be recovered, and weighing the opportunity to use future time and effort more profitably elsewhere.

Among students, those who have learned to use cost-benefit analysis frequently are apt to have far better grades than their Scholastic Aptitude Test scores would have predicted. Again, the more economics courses the students have, the more likely they are to apply cost-benefit analysis outside the classroom.

Dr. Nisbett concedes that for many Americans, cost-benefit rules often appear to conflict with such traditional principles as "never give up" and "waste not, want not."

Managers must also evaluate the costs and benefits of alternative actions. **Facebook**, the largest social networking site in the world, was cofounded by 26-year-old Mark Zuckerberg in 2004. Since then, it has grown to over 350 million users and made Zuckerberg a multibillionaire.

Facebook has plans to grow to over 1 billion users worldwide. Such growth involves decisions about where to expand. For example, expanding the site to new languages and countries involves software programming, marketing, and computer hardware costs. The benefits include adding new users to Facebook.

Analysis of the benefits and costs might lead Facebook to expand in some languages before others. For example, such an analysis might lead Facebook to expand in Spanish before it expands in Tok Pisin (language of Papua New Guinea).

In this chapter, differential analysis, which reports the effects of decisions on total revenues and costs, is discussed. Practical approaches to setting product prices are also described and illustrated. Finally, how production bottlenecks and activity-based costing influence pricing and other decisions are also discussed.

Source: Alan L. Otten, "Economic Perspective Produces Steady Yields," from People Patterns, *The Wall Street Journal*, March 31, 1992, p. B1.

Real-World Chapter Openers Building on the strengths of past editions, these openers continue to relate the accounting and business concepts in the chapter to students' lives. These openers employ examples of real companies and provide invaluable insight into real practice. Several of the openers created especially for this edition focus on interesting companies such as Rhapsody, Razor, E.W. Scripps Company, a diverse media concern, and Facebook.

Continuing Case Study Students follow a fictitious company, **NetSolutions**, throughout Chapters 1–6, which demonstrates a variety of transactions. The continuity of using the same company facilitates student learning especially for Chapters 1–4, which cover the accounting cycle. Also, using the same company allows students to follow the transition of the company from a service business in Chapters 1–4 to a merchandising business in Chapters 5 and 6.

Illustrative Problem and Solution A solved problem models one or more of the chapter's assignment problems so that students can apply the modeled procedures to end-of-chapter materials.

Integrity, Objectivity, and Ethics in Business In each chapter, these cases help students develop their ethical compass. Often coupled with related end-of-chapter activities, these cases can be discussed in class or students can consider the cases as they read the chapter. Both the section and related end-of-chapter materials are indicated with a unique icon for a consistent presentation.

Integrity, Objectivity, and Ethics in Business

CHIEF FINANCIAL OFFICER BONUSES

A recent study by compensation experts at Temple University found that chief financial officer salaries are correlated with the complexity of a company's operations, but chief financial officer bonuses are correlated with the company's ability to meet analysts' earnings forecasts. These results suggest that financial bonuses may provide chief financial officers with an incentive to use questionable accounting practices to improve earnings. While the study doesn't conclude that bonuses lead to accounting fraud, it does suggest that bonuses give chief financial officers a reason to find ways to use accounting to increase apparent earnings.

Source: E. Jelesiewicz, "Today's CFO: More Challenge but Higher Compensation," *News Communications* (Temple University, August 2009).

Business Connection and Comprehensive Real-World Notes Students get a close-up look at how accounting operates in the marketplace through a variety of *Business Connection* boxed features.

Business Connection

AVATAR: THE MOST EXPENSIVE MOVIE EVER MADE (AND THE MOST SUCCESSFUL)

Prior to the release of the blockbuster *Avatar* in December 2009, many were skeptical if the movie's huge $500 million investment would pay off. After all, just to break even the movie would have to perform as one of the top 50 movies of all time. To provide a return that was double the investment, the movie would have to crack the top ten. Many thought this was a tall order, even though James Cameron, the force behind this movie, already had the number one grossing movie of all time: *Titanic*, at $1.8 billion in worldwide box office revenues. Could he do it again? That was the question.

So, how did the film do? Only eight weeks after its release, Avatar had become the number one grossing film of all time, with over $2.2 billion in worldwide box office revenue. Executives at Fox anticipated that the profit might double after the film was released on DVD in the summer of 2010. Needless to say, James Cameron, 20th Century Fox, and other investors are very pleased with their return on this investment.

Sources: Michael Cieply, "A Movie's Budget Pops from the Screen," *New York Times*, November 8, 2009; "Bulk of Avatar Profit Still to Come," *The Age*, February 3, 2010.

Market Leading End-of-Chapter Material Students need to practice accounting so that they can understand and use it. To give students the greatest possible advantage in the real world, *Accounting, 24e*, goes beyond presenting theory and procedure with comprehensive, time-tested, end-of-chapter material.

Online Solutions

South-Western, a division of Cengage Learning, offers a vast array of online solutions to suit your course needs. Choose the product that best meets your classroom needs and course goals. Please check with your Cengage representative for more details or for ordering information.

CengageNow

CengageNOW is a powerful course management and online homework tool that provides robust instructor control and customization to optimize the student learning experience and meet desired outcomes. CengageNOW offers:

- Auto-graded homework (static and algorithmic varieties), test bank, Personalized Study Plan, and eBook are all in one resource.
- Easy-to-use course management options offer flexibility and continuity from one semester to another.
- Different levels of feedback and engaging student resources guide students through material and solidify learning.
- The most robust and flexible assignment options in the industry.
- "Smart Entry" helps eliminate common data entry errors and prevents students from guessing their way through the homework.
- The ability to analyze student work from the gradebook and generate reports on learning outcomes. Each problem is tagged in the Solutions Manual and CengageNOW to AICPA, IMA, AACSB, and ACBSP outcomes so you can measure student performance.

CengageNOW Upgrades:

- Our General Ledger Software is now being offered in a new online format. Your students can solve selected end-of-chapter assignments in a format that emulates commercial general ledger software.
- For a complete list of CengageNOW upgrades, refer to page 6 in the brochure in front of the Instructor Edition.
- New Design: CengageNOW has been redesigned to enhance your experience.

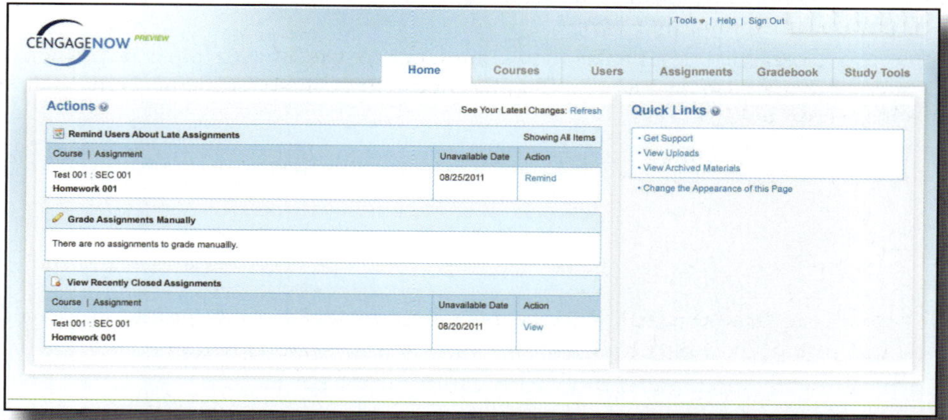

For a CengageNOW demo, visit: www.cengage.com/community/warren

Aplia

Aplia is a premier online homework product that successfully engages students and maximizes the amount of effort they put forth, creating more efficient learners. Aplia's advantages are:

- In addition to static and algorithmic end-of-chapter homework, Aplia offers an **extra problem set** to give you more options!
- Students can receive **unique**, **detailed feedback** and the full solution after each attempt on homework.
- "**Grade It Now**" maximizes student effort on each attempt and ensures students do their own work. Students have three attempts. Each attempt produces an algorithmic variety. The final score is an average of the three attempts.
- "**Smart Entry**" helps eliminate common data entry errors and prevents students from guessing their way through the homework.

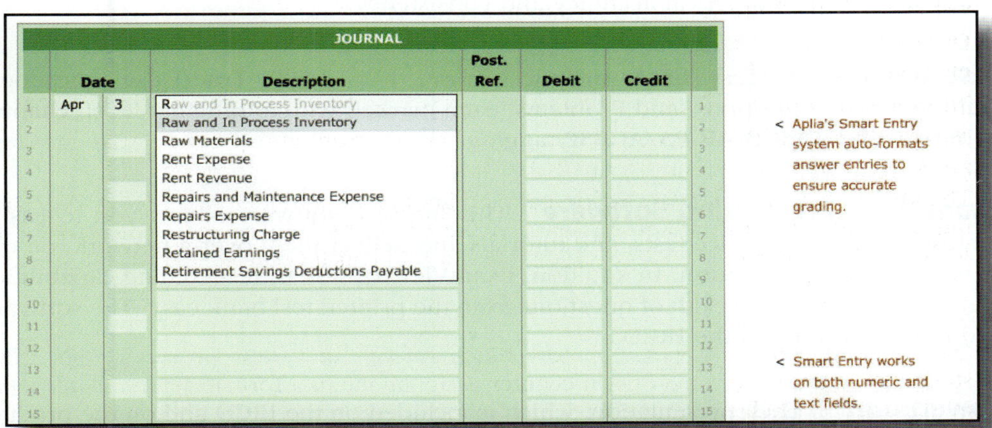

Aplia Upgrades:

- Increased Instructor Control: Instructors now have more options in how they assign materials from the question banks.
- ApliaText: Interactive ApliaText allows students to use eBooks in a new way. This unique flip-book also includes a Chapter Recap that helps students craft their own personal study guide.

For an Aplia demo, visit: www.cengage.com/community/warren

WebTutor™

WebTutor™ on Blackboard® and WebCT®—Improve student grades with online review and test preparation tools in an easy-to-use course cartridge.

Visit www.cengage.com/webtutor for more information.

For the Instructor

When it comes to supporting instructors, South-Western is unsurpassed. *Accounting, 24e*, continues the tradition with powerful print and digital ancillaries aimed at facilitating greater course successes.

Instructor's Manual The Instructor's Manual includes: Brief Synopsis, List of Objectives, Key Terms, Ideas for Class Discussion, Lecture Aids, Demonstration Problems, Group Learning Activities, Exercises and Problems for Reinforcement, and Internet Activities. Suggested Approaches incorporate many modern teaching initiatives, including active learning, collaborative learning, critical thinking, and writing across the curriculum.

Solutions Manual The Solutions Manual contains answers to all exercises, problems, and activities in the text. The solutions are author-written and verified multiple times for numerical accuracy and consistency.

Test Bank The Test Bank includes more than 3,500 True/False questions, Multiple-Choice questions, and Problems, each marked with a difficulty level, chapter objective, and AASCB/AICPA/ACBSP tagging.

ExamView® Pro Testing Software This intuitive software allows you to easily customize exams, practice tests, and tutorials and deliver them over a network, on the Internet, or in printed form. In addition, ExamView comes with searching capabilities that make sorting the wealth of questions from the printed test bank easy. The software and files are found on the IRCD.

PowerPoint® Each presentation, which is included on the IRCD and on the product support site, enhances lectures and simplifies class preparation. Each chapter contains objectives followed by a thorough outline of the chapter that easily provides an entire lecture model. Also, exhibits from the chapter, such as the new Example Exercises, have been recreated as colorful PowerPoint slides to create a powerful, customizable tool.

Instructor Excel® Templates These templates provide the solutions for the problems that have Enhanced Excel® templates for students. Through these files, instructors can see the solutions in the same format as the students. All problems with accompanying templates are marked in the book with an icon and are listed in the information grid in the solutions manual. These templates are available for download on www.cengage.com/accounting/warren or on the IRCD.

Instructor's Resource CD The Instructor's Resource CD includes the PowerPoint® Presentations, Instructor's Manual, Solutions Manual, Test Bank, ExamView®, General Ledger Inspector, and Excel® Template Solutions.

For the Student

Students come to accounting with a variety of learning needs. *Accounting, 24e*, offers a broad range of supplements in both printed form and easy-to-use technology. We continue to refine our entire supplement package around the comments instructors have provided about their courses and teaching needs.

Study Guide This author-written guide provides students Quiz and Test Hints, Matching questions, Fill-in-the-Blank questions (Parts A & B), Multiple-Choice questions, True/False questions, Exercises, and Problems for each chapter.

Working Papers for Exercises and Problems The traditional working papers include problem-specific forms for preparing solutions for Exercises, A & B Problems, the Continuing Problem, and the Comprehensive Problems from the textbook. These forms, with preprinted headings, provide a structure for the problems, which helps students get started and saves them time.

Blank Working Papers These Working Papers are available for completing exercises and problems either from the text or prepared by the instructor. They have no preprinted headings. A guide at the front of the Working Papers tells students which form they will need for each problem and are available online in a .pdf, printable format.

Enhanced Excel® Templates These templates are provided for selected long or complicated end-of-chapter problems and provide assistance to the student as they set up and work the problem. Certain cells are coded to display a red asterisk when an incorrect answer is entered, which helps students stay on track. Selected problems that can be solved using these templates are designated by an icon.

General Ledger Software The CLGL software is now being offered in a new online format. Students can solve selected end-of-chapter assignments in a format that emulates commercial general ledger software. Students make entries into the general journal or special journals, track the posting of the entries to the general ledger, and create financial statements or reports. This gives students important exposure to commercial accounting software, yet in a manner that is more forgiving of student errors. Assignments are automatically graded online.

Product Support Web Site www.cengage.com/accounting/warren This site provides students with a wealth of introductory accounting resources, including quizzing and supplement downloads and access to the Enhanced Excel® Templates.

Acknowledgments

Many of the enhancements made to *Accounting, 24e,* are a direct result of countless conversations we've had with principles of accounting professors and students over the past several years. We want to take this opportunity to thank them for their perspectives and feedback on textbook use. *24e* represents our finest edition yet!

The following instructors are members of our Blue Sky editorial board, whose helpful comments and feedback continue to have a profound impact on the presentation and core themes of this text:

Rick Andrews
Sinclair Community College

Mia Breen
De Anza Community College

Anne M. Cardozo
Broward College

James Cieslak
Cuyahoga Community College

Rebecca A. Foote
Middle Tennessee State University

Gloria Grayless
Sam Houston State University

Robert Gronstal
Metropolitan Community College

Curtis Gustafson
South Dakota State University

Lynn P. Hedge
NHTI—Concord's Community College

Audrey Hunter
Broward College

Phillip Imel
Northern Virginia Community College—Annandale Campus

Christopher Kwak
De Anza College

Bruce W. McClain
Cleveland State University

Jenny Resnick
Santa Monica College

Lawrence A. Roman
Cuyahoga Community College

Robert Smolin
Citrus College

Robert C. Urell
Irvine Valley College

The following students attended our Blue Sky session, providing insights into the life of an accounting student:

Stacy Appleton
Northern Kentucky University

Danny Bradford
Xavier University

Steve Busey
Xavier University

Brandon Butcher
Xavier University

Suzanne Buzek
Xavier University

Jenny Daugherty
Northern Kentucky University

Richard Farmer
Sinclair Community College

Bobby Freking
Xavier University

Steve Latos
Xavier University

Cristi Liska
Northern Kentucky University

Mallory Malinoski
Xavier University

Clare McGrath
Xavier University

Hecia Mpanga
Xavier University

Jessica Nichols
Northern Kentucky University

Oscar Ochieng
Northern Kentucky University

Rick Riva
Sinclair Community College

Max Roberts
Sinclair Community College

Anthony Saxon
Xavier University

The following individuals took the time to participate in surveys, online sessions, content reviews, and test bank revisions:

Bridget Anakwe
Delaware State University

Julia L. Angel
North Arkansas College

Leah Arrington
Northwest Mississippi Community College

Donna T. Ascenzi
Bryant and Stratton College—Syracuse Campus

Ed Bagley
Darton College

James Baker
Harford Community College

Lisa Cooley Banks
University of Michigan

LuAnn Bean
Florida Institute of Technology

Judy Beebe
Western Oregon University

Brenda J. Bindschatel
Green River Community College

Eric D. Bostwick
The University of West Florida

Bryan C. Bouchard
Southern New Hampshire University

Thomas M. Branton
Alvin Community College

Celestino Caicoya
Miami Dade College

John Callister
Cornell University

Deborah Chabaud
Louisiana Technical College

Marilyn G. Ciolino
Delgado Community College

Earl Clay
Cape Cod Community College

Lisa M. Cole
Johnson County Community College

Cori Oliver Crews
Waycross College

Julie Daigle
Ft. Range Community College

Julie Dailey
Central Virginia Community College

John M. Daugherty
Pitt Community College

Becky Davis
East Mississippi Community College

Ginger Dennis
West Georgia Technical College

Scott A. Elza
Wisconsin Indianhead Technical College

Patricia Feller
Nashville State Community College

Mike Foland
Southwestern Illinois College—Belleville

Brenda S. Fowler
Alamance Community College

Jeanne Gerard
Franklin Pierce University

Christopher Gilbert
East Los Angeles College, Montery Park, CA

Mark S. Gleason
Metropolitan State University, St. Paul, Minnesota

Marina Grau
Houston Community College

Judith Grenkowicz
Kirtland Community College

Vicki Greshik
Jamestown College

Lillian S. Grose
Our Lady of Holy Cross College

Denise T. Guest
Germanna Community College

Bruce J. Gunning
Kent State University at East Liverpool

Rosie Hale
Southwest Tennessee Community College

Sara Harris
Arapahoe Community College

Matthew P. Helinski
Northeast Lakeview College

Wanda Hudson
Alabama Southern Community College

Todd A. Jensen
Sierra College

Paul T. Johnson
Mississippi Gulf Coast Community College

Mary Kline
Black Hawk College

Jan Kraft
Northwest College

David W. Krug
Johnson County Community College

Cathy Xanthaky Larson
Middlesex Community College

Brenda G. Lauer
Northeastern Junior College

Ted Lewis
Marshalltown Community College

Marion Loiola
SUNY—Orange County Community College

Ming Lu
Santa Monica College

Don Lucy
Indian River State College

Debbie Luna
El Paso Community College

Anna L. Lusher
Slippery Rock University

Kirk Lynch
Sandhills Community College

Bridgette Mahan
Harold Washington College

Irene Meares
Western New Mexico University

James B. Meir
Cleveland State Community College

John L. Miller
Metropolitan Community College

Peter Moloney
Cerritos College

Janet Morrow
East Central Community College

Pamela G. Needham
Northeast Mississippi Community College

Jeannie M. Neil
Orange Coast College, Costa Mesa, CA

Carolyn Nelson
Coffeyville Community College

Joseph Malino Nicassio
Westmoreland County Community College

Robert L. Osborne
Ohio Dominican University

Scott Paxton
North Idaho College

Ronald Pearson
Bay College

Rachel Pernia
Essex County College

Erick Pifer
Lake Michigan College

Marianne G. Pindar
Lackawanna College

Kenneth J. Plucinski
State University of New York at Fredonia

Debbie Porter
Tidewater Community College

Shirley J. Powell
Arkansas State University—Beebe

Eric M. Primuth
Cuyahoga Community College

Michael Prindle
Grand View University

Rita Pritchett
Brevard Community College

Judy Ramsay
San Jacinto College—North

Patrick Reihing
Nassau Community College

Richard Rickel
South Mountain Community College

Patricia G. Roshto
University of Louisiana—Monroe

Martin Sabo
Community College of Denver

Tracy M. Schmeltzer
Wayne Community College

Dennis C. Shea
Southern New Hampshire University

Acknowledgments

Robert W. Smith (retired)
formerly of Briarcliffe College—Patchogue, NY Campus

Kimberly D. Smith
County College of Morris

Richard Snapp
Olympic College—Bremerton

John L. Stancil
Florida Southern College

Barry Stephens
Bemidji State University

Jeff Strawser
Sam Houston State University

Stacie A. Surowiec
Harford Community College

Eric H. Sussman
UCLA Anderson Graduate School of Management

Bill Talbot
Montgomery College

Kenneth J. Tax
Farmingdale State College (SUNY)

Ronald Tidd
Central Washington University

Erol C. Tucker, Jr.
The Victoria College

Henry Velarde
Malcolm X College

Angela Waits
Gadsden State Community College

Dale Walker
Arkansas State University

Shunda Ware
Atlanta Technical College

Cheryl C. Willingham
Wisconsin Indianhead Technical College

Patrick B. Wilson
Tennessee Board of Regents

Jay E. Wright
New River Community College

The following instructors created content for the supplements that accompany the text:

LuAnn Bean
Florida Institute of Technology

Gary Bower
Community College of Rhode Island

Doug Cloud
Pepperdine University

Ana Cruz & Blanca Ortega
Miami Dade College

Kurt Fredricks
Valencia Community College

Lori Grady
Bucks County Community College

Jose Luis Hortensi
Miami Dade College

Christine Jonick
Gainesville State College

Patti Lopez
Valencia Community College

Don Lucy
Indian River State College

Tracie Nobles
Austin Community College

Craig Pence
Highland Community College

Alice Sineath
Forsyth Technical Community College

Janice Stoudemire
Midlands Technical College

CHAPTER 1

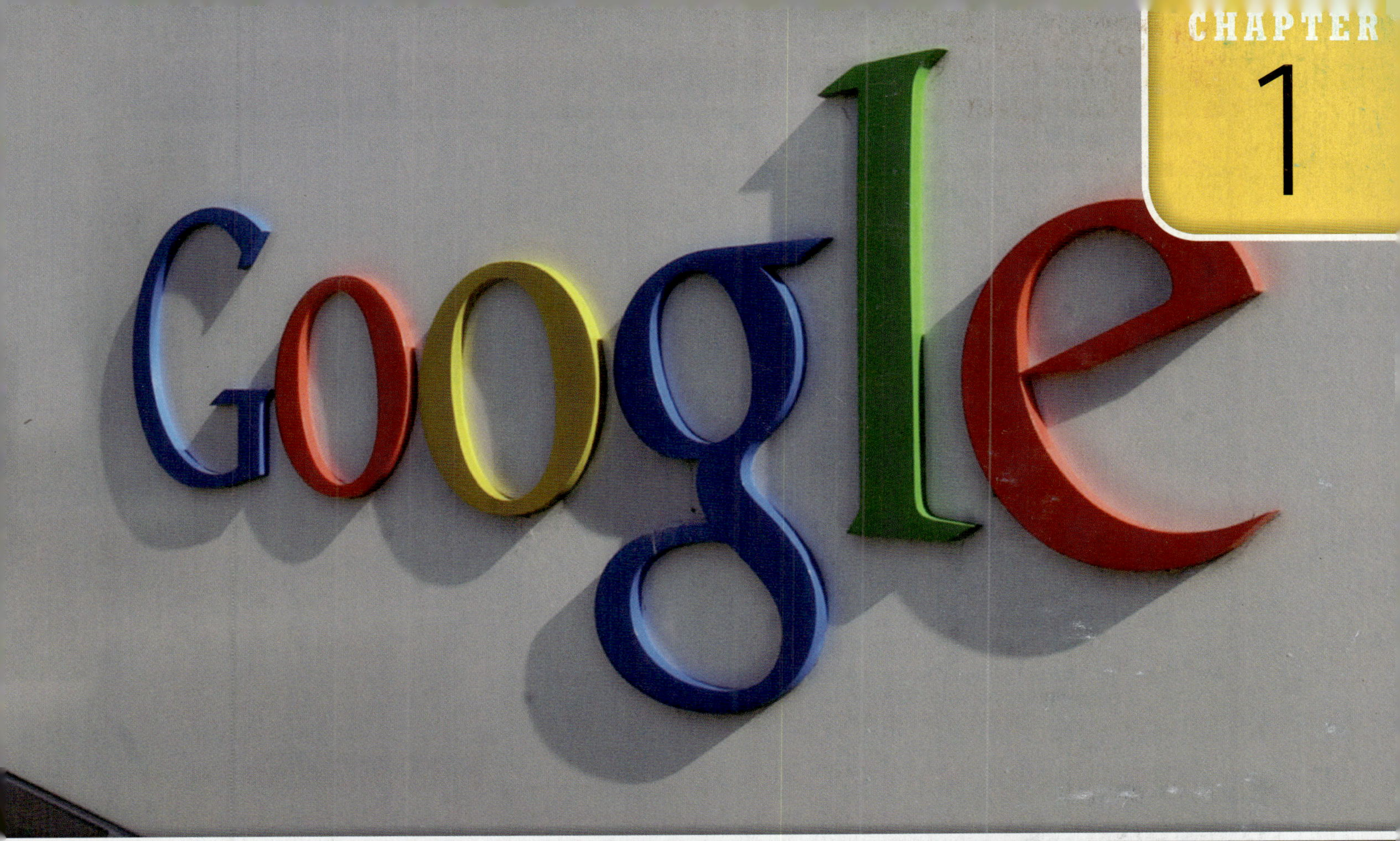

AP Photo/Paul Sakuma

Introduction to Accounting and Business

Google™

When two teams pair up for a game of football, there is often a lot of noise. The band plays, the fans cheer, and fireworks light up the scoreboard. Obviously, the fans are committed and care about the outcome of the game. Just like fans at a football game, the owners of a business want their business to "win" against their competitors in the marketplace. While having your football team win can be a source of pride, winning in the marketplace goes beyond pride and has many tangible benefits. Companies that are winners are better able to serve customers, provide good jobs for employees, and make money for their owners.

One such successful company is **Google**, one of the most visible companies on the Internet. Many of us cannot visit the Web without using Google to power a search. As one writer said, "Google is the closest thing the Web has to an ultimate answer machine." And yet, Google is a free tool—no one asks for your credit card when you use Google's search tools.

Do you think Google has been a successful company? Does it make money? How would you know? Accounting helps to answer these questions. Google's accounting information tells us that Google is a successful company that makes a lot of money, but not from you and me. Google makes its money from advertisers.

This textbook introduces you to accounting, the language of business. Chapter 1 begins by discussing what a business is, how it operates, and the role that accounting plays.

OBJ. 1 Describe the nature of a business, the role of accounting, and ethics in business.

Nature of Business and Accounting

A **business**[1] is an organization in which basic resources (inputs), such as materials and labor, are assembled and processed to provide goods or services (outputs) to customers. Businesses come in all sizes, from a local coffee house to Starbucks, which sells over $10 billion of coffee and related products each year.

The objective of most businesses is to earn a **profit**. Profit is the difference between the amounts received from customers for goods or services and the amounts paid for the inputs used to provide the goods or services. This text focuses on businesses operating to earn a profit. However, many of the same concepts and principles also apply to not-for-profit organizations such as hospitals, churches, and government agencies.

Types of Businesses

Three types of businesses operated for profit include service, merchandising, and manufacturing businesses.

Each type of business and some examples are described below.

Service businesses provide services rather than products to customers.

Delta Air Lines (transportation services)
The Walt Disney Company (entertainment services)

Merchandising businesses sell products they purchase from other businesses to customers.

Wal-Mart (general merchandise)
Amazon.com (Internet books, music, videos)

Manufacturing businesses change basic inputs into products that are sold to customers.

Ford Motor Co. (cars, trucks, vans)
Dell Inc. (personal computers)

1 A complete glossary of terms appears at the end of the text.

The Role of Accounting in Business

The role of accounting in business is to provide information for managers to use in operating the business. In addition, accounting provides information to other users in assessing the economic performance and condition of the business.

Thus, **accounting** can be defined as an information system that provides reports to users about the economic activities and condition of a business. You may think of accounting as the "language of business." This is because accounting is the means by which businesses' financial information is communicated to users.

Note:
Accounting is an information system that provides reports to users about the economic activities and condition of a business.

The process by which accounting provides information to users is as follows:

1. Identify users.
2. Assess users' information needs.
3. Design the accounting information system to meet users' needs.
4. Record economic data about business activities and events.
5. Prepare accounting reports for users.

As illustrated in Exhibit 1, users of accounting information can be divided into two groups: internal users and external users.

EXHIBIT 1

Accounting as an Information System

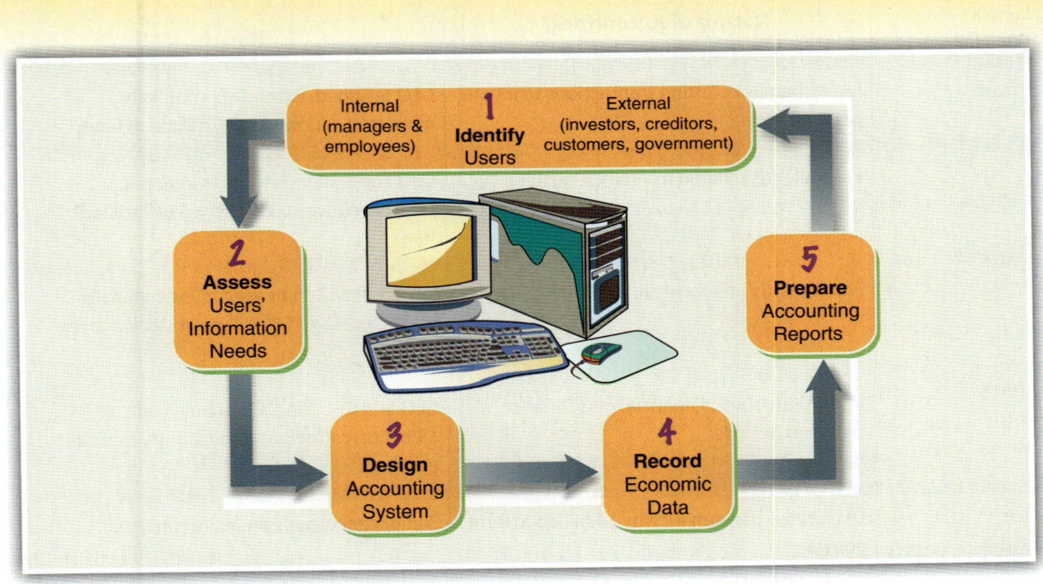

Internal users of accounting information include managers and employees. These users are directly involved in managing and operating the business. The area of accounting that provides internal users with information is called **managerial accounting** or **management accounting**.

The objective of managerial accounting is to provide relevant and timely information for managers' and employees' decision-making needs. Often times, such information is sensitive and is not distributed outside the business. Examples of sensitive information might include information about customers, prices, and plans to expand the business. Managerial accountants employed by a business are employed in **private accounting**.

External users of accounting information include investors, creditors, customers, and the government. These users are not directly involved in managing and operating the business. The area of accounting that provides external users with information is called **financial accounting**.

The objective of financial accounting is to provide relevant and timely information for the decision-making needs of users outside of the business. For example, financial reports on the operations and condition of the business are useful for banks and other creditors in deciding whether to lend money to the business. **General-purpose financial statements** are one type of financial accounting report that is distributed to external users. The term *general-purpose* refers to the wide range of decision-making needs that these reports are designed to serve. Later in this chapter, general-purpose financial statements are described and illustrated.

Role of Ethics in Accounting and Business

The objective of accounting is to provide relevant, timely information for user decision making. Accountants must behave in an ethical manner so that the information they provide users will be trustworthy and, thus, useful for decision making. Managers and employees must also behave in an ethical manner in managing and operating a business. Otherwise, no one will be willing to invest in or loan money to the business.

Ethics are moral principles that guide the conduct of individuals. Unfortunately, business managers and accountants sometimes behave in an unethical manner. A number of managers of the companies listed in Exhibit 2 engaged in accounting or

EXHIBIT 2 Accounting and Business Frauds

Company	Nature of Accounting or Business Fraud	Result
American International Group, Inc. (AIG)	Used sham accounting transactions to inflate performance.	CEO resigned. Executives criminally convicted. AIG paid $126 million in fines.
Computer Associates International, Inc.	Fraudulently inflated its financial results.	CEO and senior executives indicted. Five executives pled guilty. $225 million fine.
Enron	Fraudulently inflated its financial results.	Bankrupcty. Senior executives criminally convicted. Over $60 billion in stock market losses.
Fannie Mae	Improperly shifted financial performance between periods.	CEO and CFO fired. Company made a $9 billion correction to previously reported earnings.
HealthSouth	Overstated performance by $4 billion in false entries.	Senior executives criminally convicted.
Qwest Communications International, Inc.	Improperly recognized $3 billion in false receipts.	CEO and six other executives criminally convicted of "massive financial fraud." $250 million SEC fine.
Satyam Computer Services	Significantly inflated assets and earnings.	Chairman and founder is in jail; investors lost billions.
Terex	Recorded profit prematurely and inflated profits.	Company paid $8 million to Securities and Exchange Commission in settlement.
Tyco International, Ltd.	Failed to disclose secret loans to executives that were subsequently forgiven.	CEO forced to resign and subjected to frozen asset order and criminally convicted.
United Rental	Inflated profits to meet earnings forecasts and analysts expectations.	Vice chairman and chief financial officer indicted for conspiracy, securities fraud, and insider trading.
Xerox Corporation	Recognized $3 billion in revenue prior to when it should have been.	$10 million fine to SEC. Six executives forced to pay $22 million.

business fraud. These ethical violations led to fines, firings, and lawsuits. In some cases, managers were criminally prosecuted, convicted, and sent to prison.

What went wrong for the managers and companies listed in Exhibit 2? The answer normally involved one or both of the following two factors:

Failure of Individual Character. An ethical manager and accountant is honest and fair. However, managers and accountants often face pressures from supervisors to meet company and investor expectations. In many of the cases in Exhibit 2, managers and accountants justified small ethical violations to avoid such pressures. However, these small violations became big violations as the company's financial problems became worse.

Culture of Greed and Ethical Indifference. By their behavior and attitude, senior managers set the company culture. In most of the companies listed in Exhibit 2, the senior managers created a culture of greed and indifference to the truth.

As a result of the accounting and business frauds shown in Exhibit 2, Congress passed new laws to monitor the behavior of accounting and business. For example, the Sarbanes-Oxley Act of 2002 (SOX) was enacted. SOX established a new oversight body for the accounting profession called the Public Company Accounting Oversight Board (PCAOB). In addition, SOX established standards for independence, corporate responsibility, and disclosure.

How does one behave ethically when faced with financial or other types of pressure? Guidelines for behaving ethically are shown in Exhibit 3.[2]

EXHIBIT 3

Guidelines for Ethical Conduct

1. Identify an ethical decision by using your personal ethical standards of honesty and fairness.
2. Identify the consequences of the decision and its effect on others.
3. Consider your obligations and responsibilities to those that will be affected by your decision.
4. Make a decision that is ethical and fair to those affected by it.

Integrity, Objectivity, and Ethics in Business

BERNIE MADOFF

In June 2009, Bernard L. "Bernie" Madoff was sentenced to 150 years in prison for defrauding thousands of investors in one of the biggest frauds in American history. Madoff's fraud started several decades earlier when he began a "Ponzi scheme" in his investment management firm, Bernard L. Madoff Securities LLC.

In a Ponzi scheme, the investment manager uses funds received from new investors to pay a return to existing investors, rather than basing investment returns on the fund's actual performance. As long as the investment manager is able to attract new investors, he or she will have new funds to pay existing investors and continue the fraud. While most Ponzi schemes collapse quickly when the investment manager runs out of new investors, Madoff's reputation, popularity, and personal contacts provided a steady stream of investors which allowed the fraud to survive for decades.

Opportunities for Accountants

Numerous career opportunities are available for students majoring in accounting. Currently, the demand for accountants exceeds the number of new graduates entering the job market. This is partly due to the increased regulation of business caused by the accounting and business frauds shown in Exhibit 2. Also, more and

2 Many companies have ethical standards of conduct for managers and employees. In addition, the Institute of Management Accountants and the American Institute of Certified Public Accountants have professional codes of conduct.

more businesses have come to recognize the importance and value of accounting information.

As indicated earlier, accountants employed by a business are employed in private accounting. Private accountants have a variety of possible career options within a company. Some of these career options are shown in Exhibit 4 along with their starting salaries. Accountants who provide audit services, called auditors, verify the accuracy of financial records, accounts, and systems. As shown in Exhibit 4, several private accounting careers have certification options.

Accountants and their staff who provide services on a fee basis are said to be employed in **public accounting**. In public accounting, an accountant may practice as an individual or as a member of a public accounting firm. Public accountants who have met a state's education, experience, and examination requirements may become **Certified Public Accountants (CPAs)**. CPAs generally perform general accounting,

EXHIBIT 4 **Accounting Career Paths and Salaries**

Accounting Career Track	Description	Career Options	Annual Starting Salaries[1]	Certification
Private Accounting	Accountants employed by companies, government, and not-for-profit entities.	Bookkeeper	$36,125	
		Payroll clerk	$34,875	Certified Payroll Professional (CPP)
		General accountant	$42,000	
		Budget analyst	$44,375	
		Cost accountant	$43,750	Certified Management Accountant (CMA)
		Internal auditor	$48,250	Certified Internal Auditor (CIA)
		Information technology auditor	$56,500	Certified Information Systems Auditor (CISA)
Public Accounting	Accountants employed individually or within a public accounting firm in tax or audit services.	Local firms	$45,063	Certified Public Accountant (CPA)
		National firms	$54,250	Certified Public Accountant (CPA)

Source: Robert Half 2010 Salary Guide (Finance and Accounting), Robert Half International, Inc.
[1]Mean salaries of a reported range. Private accounting salaries are reported for large companies. Salaries may vary by region.

audit, or tax services. As can be seen in Exhibit 4, CPAs have slightly better starting salaries than private accountants. Career statistics indicate, however, that these salary differences tend to disappear over time.

Because all functions within a business use accounting information, experience in private or public accounting provides a solid foundation for a career. Many positions in industry and in government agencies are held by individuals with accounting backgrounds.

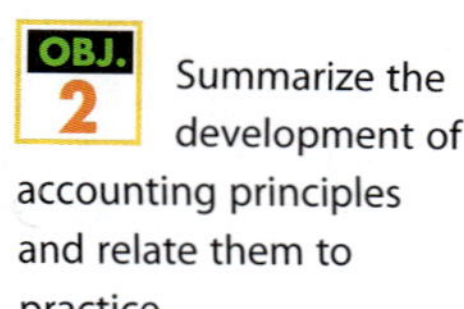

Summarize the development of accounting principles and relate them to practice.

Generally Accepted Accounting Principles

If a company's management could record and report financial data as it saw fit, comparisons among companies would be difficult, if not impossible. Thus, financial accountants follow **generally accepted accounting principles (GAAP)** in preparing reports. These reports allow investors and other users to compare one company to another.

Accounting principles and concepts develop from research, accepted accounting practices, and pronouncements of regulators. Within the United States, the **Financial Accounting Standards Board (FASB)** has the primary responsibility for developing accounting principles. The FASB publishes *Statements of Financial Accounting Standards* as well as *Interpretations* of these Standards. In addition, the **Securities and Exchange Commission (SEC),** an agency of the U.S. government, has authority over the accounting and financial disclosures for companies whose shares of ownership (stock) are traded and sold to the public. The SEC normally accepts the accounting principles set forth by the FASB. However, the SEC may issue *Staff Accounting Bulletins* on accounting matters that may not have been addressed by the FASB.

Many countries outside the United States use generally accepted accounting principles adopted by the **International Accounting Standards Board (IASB)**. The IASB issues *International Financial Reporting Standards (IFRSs)*. Significant differences currently exist between FASB and IASB accounting principles. However, the FASB and IASB are working together to reduce and eliminate these differences into a single set of accounting principles. Such a set of worldwide accounting principles would help facilitate investment and business in an increasingly global economy.

See Appendix D for more information

In this chapter and text, accounting principles and concepts are emphasized. It is by this emphasis on the "why" as well as the "how" that you will gain an understanding of accounting.

IFRS

International Connection

INTERNATIONAL FINANCIAL REPORTING STANDARDS (IFRS)

IFRS are considered to be more "principles-based" than U.S. GAAP, which is considered to be more "rules-based." For example, U.S. GAAP consists of approximately 17,000 pages, which includes numerous industry-specific accounting rules. In contrast, IFRS allow more judgment in deciding how business transactions are recorded. Many believe that the strong regulatory and litigation environment in the United States is the cause for the more rules-based GAAP approach. Regardless, IFRS and GAAP share more in common than differences.*

*Differences between U.S. GAAP and IFRS are further discussed and illustrated in Appendix D.

Business Entity Concept

The **business entity concept** limits the economic data in an accounting system to data related directly to the activities of the business. In other words, the business is viewed as an entity separate from its owners, creditors, or other businesses. For example, the accountant for a business with one owner would record the activities of the business only and would not record the personal activities, property, or debts of the owner.

Note:
Under the business entity concept, the activities of a business are recorded separately from the activities of its owners, creditors, or other businesses.

A business entity may take the form of a proprietorship, partnership, corporation, or limited liability company (LLC). Each of these forms and their major characteristics are listed below.

Form of Business Entity	Characteristics
Proprietorship is owned by one individual.	• 70% of business entities in the United States. • Easy and cheap to organize. • Resources are limited to those of the owner. • Used by small businesses.
Partnership is owned by two or more individuals.	• 10% of business organizations in the United States (combined with limited liability companies). • Combines the skills and resources of more than one person.

(*continued*)

Form of Business Entity	Characteristics
Corporation is organized under state or federal statutes as a separate legal taxable entity.	• Generates 90% of business revenues. • 20% of the business organizations in the United States. • Ownership is divided into shares called stock. • Can obtain large amounts of resources by issuing stock. • Used by large businesses.
Limited liability company (LLC) combines the attributes of a partnership and a corporation.	• 10% of business organizations in the United States (combined with partnerships). • Often used as an alternative to a partnership. • Has tax and legal liability advantages for owners.

The three types of businesses discussed earlier—service, merchandising, and manufacturing—may be organized as proprietorships, partnerships, corporations, or limited liability companies. Because of the large amount of resources required to operate a manufacturing business, most manufacturing businesses such as Ford Motor Company are corporations. Most large retailers such as Wal-Mart and Home Depot are also corporations.

The Cost Concept

Under the **cost concept**, amounts are initially recorded in the accounting records at their cost or purchase price. To illustrate, assume that Aaron Publishers purchased the following building on February 20, 2010, for $150,000:

Price listed by seller on January 1, 2010	$160,000
Aaron Publishers' initial offer to buy on January 31, 2010	140,000
Purchase price on February 20, 2010	150,000
Estimated selling price on December 31, 2012	220,000
Assessed value for property taxes, December 31, 2012	190,000

Under the cost concept, Aaron Publishers records the purchase of the building on February 20, 2010, at the purchase price of $150,000. The other amounts listed above have no effect on the accounting records.

The fact that the building has an estimated selling price of $220,000 on December 31, 2012, indicates that the building has increased in value. However, to use the $220,000 in the accounting records would be to record an illusory or unrealized profit. If Aaron Publishers sells the building on January 9, 2014, for $240,000, a profit of $90,000 ($240,000 – $150,000) is then realized and recorded. The new owner would record $240,000 as its cost of the building.

The cost concept also involves the objectivity and unit of measure concepts. The **objectivity concept** requires that the amounts recorded in the accounting records be based on objective evidence. In exchanges between a buyer and a seller, both try to get the best price. Only the final agreed-upon amount is objective enough to be recorded in the accounting records. If amounts in the accounting records were constantly being revised upward or downward based on offers, appraisals, and opinions, accounting reports could become unstable and unreliable.

The **unit of measure concept** requires that economic data be recorded in dollars. Money is a common unit of measurement for reporting financial data and reports.

Example Exercise 1-1 Cost Concept

OBJ. 2

On August 25, Gallatin Repair Service extended an offer of $125,000 for land that had been priced for sale at $150,000. On September 3, Gallatin Repair Service accepted the seller's counteroffer of $137,000. On October 20, the land was assessed at a value of $98,000 for property tax purposes. On December 4, Gallatin Repair Service was offered $160,000 for the land by a national retail chain. At what value should the land be recorded in Gallatin Repair Service's records?

Follow My Example 1-1

$137,000. Under the cost concept, the land should be recorded at the cost to Gallatin Repair Service.

Practice Exercises: PE 1-1A, PE 1-1B

The Accounting Equation

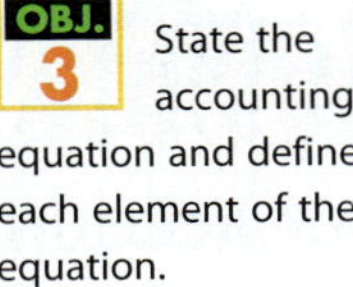

State the accounting equation and define each element of the equation.

The resources owned by a business are its **assets**. Examples of assets include cash, land, buildings, and equipment. The rights or claims to the assets are divided into two types: (1) the rights of creditors and (2) the rights of owners. The rights of creditors are the debts of the business and are called **liabilities**. The rights of the owners are called **owner's equity**. The following equation shows the relationship among assets, liabilities, and owner's equity:

Assets = Liabilities + Owner's Equity

This equation is called the **accounting equation**. Liabilities usually are shown before owner's equity in the accounting equation because creditors have first rights to the assets.

Given any two amounts, the accounting equation may be solved for the third unknown amount. To illustrate, if the assets owned by a business amount to $100,000 and the liabilities amount to $30,000, the owner's equity is equal to $70,000, as shown below.

Assets – Liabilities	=	**Owner's Equity**
$100,000 – $30,000	=	$70,000

Example Exercise 1-2 Accounting Equation

OBJ. 3

John Joos is the owner and operator of You're A Star, a motivational consulting business. At the end of its accounting period, December 31, 2011, You're A Star has assets of $800,000 and liabilities of $350,000. Using the accounting equation, determine the following amounts:

a. Owner's equity, as of December 31, 2011.
b. Owner's equity, as of December 31, 2012, assuming that assets increased by $130,000 and liabilities decreased by $25,000 during 2012.

Follow My Example 1-2

a. Assets = Liabilities + Owner's Equity
$800,000 = $350,000 + Owner's Equity
Owner's Equity = $450,000

b. First, determine the change in Owner's Equity during 2012 as follows:
Assets = Liabilities + Owner's Equity
$130,000 = –$25,000 + Owner's Equity
Owner's Equity = $155,000

Next, add the change in Owner's Equity on December 31, 2011, to arrive at Owner's Equity on December 31, 2012, as shown below.
Owner's Equity on December 31, 2012 = $605,000 = $450,000 + $155,000

Practice Exercises: **PE 1-2A, PE 1-2B**

Business Transactions and the Accounting Equation

Describe and illustrate how business transactions can be recorded in terms of the resulting change in the elements of the accounting equation.

Paying a monthly telephone bill of $168 affects a business's financial condition because it now has less cash on hand. Such an economic event or condition that directly changes an entity's financial condition or its results of operations is a **business transaction**. For example, purchasing land for $50,000 is a business transaction. In contrast, a change in a business's credit rating does not directly affect cash or any other asset, liability, or owner's equity amount.

Business Connection 

THE ACCOUNTING EQUATION

The accounting equation serves as the basic foundation for the accounting systems of all companies. From the smallest business, such as the local convenience store, to the largest business, such as Ford Motor Company, companies use the accounting equation. Some examples taken from recent financial reports of well-known companies are shown below.

Company	Assets*	=	Liabilities	+	Owner's Equity
The Coca-Cola Company	$ 40,519	=	$20,047	+	$20,472
Dell, Inc.	26,500	=	22,229	+	4,271
eBay, Inc.	15,593	=	4,509	+	11,084
Google	31,768	=	3,529	+	28,239
McDonald's	28,462	=	15,079	+	13,383
Microsoft Corporation	77,888	=	38,330	+	39,558
Southwest Airlines Co.	14,308	=	9,355	+	4,953
Wal-Mart	163,429	=	98,144	+	65,285

*Amounts are shown in millions of dollars.

Note:
All business transactions can be stated in terms of changes in the elements of the accounting equation.

All business transactions can be stated in terms of changes in the elements of the accounting equation. How business transactions affect the accounting equation can be illustrated by using some typical transactions. As a basis for illustration, a business organized by Chris Clark is used.

Assume that on November 1, 2011, Chris Clark begins a business that will be known as NetSolutions. The first phase of Chris's business plan is to operate NetSolutions as a service business assisting individuals and small businesses in developing Web pages and installing computer software. Chris expects this initial phase of the business to last one to two years. During this period, Chris plans on gathering information on the software and hardware needs of customers. During the second phase of the business plan, Chris plans to expand NetSolutions into a personalized retailer of software and hardware for individuals and small businesses.

Each transaction during NetSolutions' first month of operations is described in the following paragraphs. The effect of each transaction on the accounting equation is then shown.

Transaction A *Nov. 1, 2011 Chris Clark deposited $25,000 in a bank account in the name of NetSolutions.*

This transaction increases the asset cash (on the left side of the equation) by $25,000. To balance the equation, the owner's equity (on the right side of the equation) increases by the same amount. The equity of the owner is identified using the owner's name and "Capital," such as "Chris Clark, Capital."

The effect of this transaction on NetSolutions' accounting equation is shown below.

Assets	=	Owner's Equity
Cash	=	Chris Clark, Capital
a. 25,000		25,000

Since Chris Clark is the sole owner, NetSolutions is a proprietorship. Also, the accounting equation shown above is only for the business, NetSolutions. Under the business entity concept, Chris Clark's personal assets, such as a home or personal bank account, and personal liabilities are excluded from the equation.

Nov. 5, 2011 NetSolutions paid $20,000 for the purchase of land as a future building site. **Transaction B**

The land is located in a business park with access to transportation facilities. Chris Clark plans to rent office space and equipment during the first phase of the business plan. During the second phase, Chris plans to build an office and a warehouse on the land.

The purchase of the land changes the makeup of the assets, but it does not change the total assets. The items in the equation prior to this transaction and the effect of the transaction are shown below. The new amounts are called *balances.*

	Assets		=	**Owner's Equity**
	Cash	+ Land		Chris Clark, Capital
Bal.	25,000		=	25,000
b.	−20,000	+20,000		
Bal.	5,000	20,000		25,000

Nov. 10, 2011 NetSolutions purchased supplies for $1,350 and agreed to pay the supplier in the near future. **Transaction C**

You have probably used a credit card to buy clothing or other merchandise. In this type of transaction, you received clothing for a promise to pay your credit card bill in the future. That is, you received an asset and incurred a liability to pay a future bill. Net-Solutions entered into a similar transaction by purchasing supplies for $1,350 and agreeing to pay the supplier in the near future. This type of transaction is called a purchase *on account* and is often described as follows: *Purchased supplies on account, $1,350.*

The liability created by a purchase on account is called an **account payable**. Items such as supplies that will be used in the business in the future are called **prepaid expenses**, which are assets. Thus, the effect of this transaction is to increase assets (Supplies) and liabilities (Accounts Payable) by $1,350, as follows:

	Assets			=	**Liabilities**	**+ Owner's Equity**
	Cash	+ Supplies	+ Land	=	Accounts Payable	+ Chris Clark, Capital
Bal.	5,000		20,000			25,000
c.		+1,350			+1,350	
Bal.	5,000	1,350	20,000		1,350	25,000

Nov. 18, 2011 NetSolutions received cash of $7,500 for providing services to customers. **Transaction D**

You may have earned money by painting houses or mowing lawns. If so, you received money for rendering services to a customer. Likewise, a business earns money by selling goods or services to its customers. This amount is called **revenue**.

During its first month of operations, NetSolutions received cash of $7,500 for providing services to customers. The receipt of cash increases NetSolutions' assets and also increases Chris Clark's equity in the business. The revenues of $7,500 are recorded in a Fees Earned column to the right of Chris Clark, Capital. The effect of this transaction is to increase Cash and Fees Earned by $7,500, as shown at the top of the next page.

	Assets			=	Liabilities +	Owner's Equity	
	Cash	+ Supplies +	Land	=	Accounts Payable +	Chris Clark, Capital +	Fees Earned
Bal.	5,000	1,350	20,000		1,350	25,000	
d.	+7,500						+7,500
Bal.	12,500	1,350	20,000		1,350	25,000	7,500

Different terms are used for the various types of revenues. As illustrated above, revenue from providing services is recorded as **fees earned**. Revenue from the sale of merchandise is recorded as **sales**. Other examples of revenue include rent, which is recorded as **rent revenue**, and interest, which is recorded as **interest revenue**.

Instead of receiving cash at the time services are provided or goods are sold, a business may accept payment at a later date. Such revenues are described as *fees earned on account* or *sales on account*. For example, if NetSolutions had provided services on account instead of for cash, transaction (d) would have been described as follows: *Fees earned on account, $7,500.*

In such cases, the firm has an **account receivable**, which is a claim against the customer. An account receivable is an asset, and the revenue is earned and recorded as if cash had been received. When customers pay their accounts, Cash increases and Accounts Receivable decreases.

Transaction E *Nov. 30, 2011 NetSolutions paid the following expenses during the month: wages, $2,125; rent, $800; utilities, $450; and miscellaneous, $275.*

During the month, NetSolutions spent cash or used up other assets in earning revenue. Assets used in this process of earning revenue are called **expenses**. Expenses include supplies used and payments for employee wages, utilities, and other services.

NetSolutions paid the following expenses during the month: wages, $2,125; rent, $800; utilities, $450; and miscellaneous, $275. Miscellaneous expenses include small amounts paid for such items as postage, coffee, and newspapers. The effect of expenses is the opposite of revenues in that expenses reduce assets and owner's equity. Like fees earned, the expenses are recorded in columns to the right of Chris Clark, Capital. However, since expenses reduce owner's equity, the expenses are entered as negative amounts. The effect of this transaction is shown below.

	Assets			=	Liabilities +	Owner's Equity					
	Cash	+ Supplies +	Land	=	Accounts Payable +	Chris Clark, Capital	+ Fees Earned −	Wages Exp. −	Rent Exp. −	Utilities Exp. −	Misc. Exp.
Bal.	12,500	1,350	20,000		1,350	25,000	7,500				
e.	−3,650							−2,125	−800	−450	−275
Bal.	8,850	1,350	20,000		1,350	25,000	7,500	−2,125	−800	−450	−275

Businesses usually record each revenue and expense transaction as it occurs. However, to simplify, NetSolutions' revenues and expenses are summarized for the month in transactions (d) and (e).

Transaction F *Nov. 30, 2011 NetSolutions paid creditors on account, $950.*

When you pay your monthly credit card bill, you decrease the cash in your checking account and decrease the amount you owe to the credit card company. Likewise, when NetSolutions pays $950 to creditors during the month, it reduces assets and liabilities, as shown at the top of the next page.

	Assets			=	Liabilities +	Owner's Equity					
	Cash +	Supplies +	Land	=	Accounts Payable +	Chris Clark, Capital	+ Fees Earned –	Wages Exp. –	Rent Exp. –	Utilities Exp. –	Misc. Exp.
Bal.	8,850	1,350	20,000		1,350	25,000	7,500	–2,125	–800	–450	–275
f.	–950				–950						
Bal.	7,900	1,350	20,000		400	25,000	7,500	–2,125	–800	–450	–275

Paying an amount on account is different from paying an expense. The paying of an expense reduces owner's equity, as illustrated in transaction (e). Paying an amount on account reduces the amount owed on a liability.

Nov. 30, 2011 Chris Clark determined that the cost of supplies on hand at the end of the month was $550. **Transaction G**

The cost of the supplies on hand (not yet used) at the end of the month is $550. Thus, $800 ($1,350 – $550) of supplies must have been used during the month. This decrease in supplies is recorded as an expense, as shown below.

	Assets			=	Liabilities +	Owner's Equity						
	Cash +	Supplies +	Land	=	Accounts Payable +	Chris Clark, Capital	+ Fees Earned –	Wages Exp. –	Rent Exp. –	Supplies Exp. –	Utilities Exp. –	Misc. Exp.
Bal.	7,900	1,350	20,000		400	25,000	7,500	–2,125	–800		–450	–275
g.		–800								–800		
Bal.	7,900	550	20,000		400	25,000	7,500	–2,125	–800	–800	–450	–275

Nov. 30, 2011 Chris Clark withdrew $2,000 from NetSolutions for personal use. **Transaction H**

At the end of the month, Chris Clark withdrew $2,000 in cash from the business for personal use. This transaction is the opposite of an investment in the business by the owner. Withdrawals by the owner should not be confused with expenses. Withdrawals *do not* represent assets or services used in the process of earning revenues. Instead, withdrawals are a distribution of capital to the owner. Owner withdrawals are identified by the owner's name and *Drawing*. For example, Chris Clark's withdrawal is identified as Chris Clark, Drawing. Like expenses, withdrawals are recorded in a column to the right of Chris Clark, Capital. The effect of the $2,000 withdrawal is as follows:

	Assets			=	Liabilities +	Owner's Equity							
	Cash +	Supp. +	Land	=	Accounts Payable +	Chris Clark, Capital –	Chris Clark, Drawing +	Fees Earned –	Wages Exp. –	Rent Exp. –	Supplies Exp. –	Utilities Exp. –	Misc. Exp.
Bal.	7,900	550	20,000		400	25,000		7,500	–2,125	–800	–800	–450	–275
h.	–2,000						–2,000						
Bal.	5,900	550	20,000		400	25,000	–2,000	7,500	–2,125	–800	–800	–450	–275

Summary The transactions of NetSolutions are summarized at the top of the next page. Each transaction is identified by letter, and the balance of each accounting equation element is shown after every transaction.

You should note the following:

1. The effect of every transaction *is an increase or a decrease in one or more of the accounting equation elements.*
2. The two sides of the accounting equation are *always equal.*
3. The owner's equity is *increased by amounts invested by the owner and is decreased by withdrawals by the owner.* In addition, the owner's equity is *increased by revenues* and is *decreased by expenses.*

	Assets			= Liabilities +	Owner's Equity							
	Cash	+ Supp. +	Land	= Accounts Payable +	Chris Clark, Capital	– Chris Clark, Drawing	+ Fees Earned –	Wages Exp.	– Rent Exp. –	Supplies Exp.	– Utilities Exp.	– Misc. Exp.
a.	+25,000				+25,000							
b.	–20,000		+20,000									
Bal.	5,000		20,000		25,000							
c.		+1,350		+1,350								
Bal.	5,000	+1,350	20,000	+1,350	25,000							
d.	+7,500						+7,500					
Bal.	12,500	1,350	20,000	1,350	25,000		7,500					
e.	–3,650							–2,125	–800		–450	–275
Bal.	8,850	1,350	20,000	1,350	25,000		7,500	–2,125	–800		–450	–275
f.	–950			–950								
Bal.	7,900	1,350	20,000	400	25,000		7,500	–2,125	–800		–450	–275
g.		–800								–800		
Bal.	7,900	550	20,000	400	25,000		7,500	–2,125	–800	–800	–450	–275
h.	–2,000					–2,000						
Bal.	5,900	550	20,000	400	25,000	–2,000	7,500	–2,125	–800	–800	–450	–275

The four types of transactions affecting owner's equity are illustrated in Exhibit 5.

EXHIBIT 5

Types of Transactions Affecting Owner's Equity

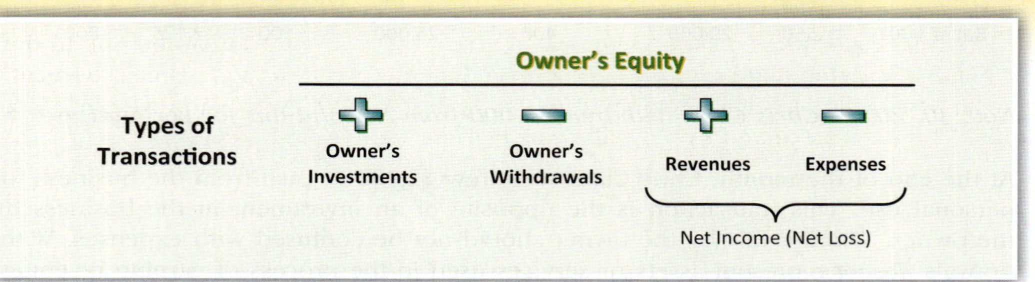

Example Exercise 1-3 Transactions

Salvo Delivery Service is owned and operated by Joel Salvo. The following selected transactions were completed by Salvo Delivery Service during February:

1. Received cash from owner as additional investment, $35,000.
2. Paid creditors on account, $1,800.
3. Billed customers for delivery services on account, $11,250.
4. Received cash from customers on account, $6,740.
5. Paid cash to owner for personal use, $1,000.

Indicate the effect of each transaction on the accounting equation elements (Assets, Liabilities, Owner's Equity, Drawing, Revenue, and Expense). Also, indicate the specific item within the accounting equation element that is affected. To illustrate, the answer to (1) is shown below.

(1) Asset (Cash) increases by $35,000; Owner's Equity (Joel Salvo, Capital) increases by $35,000.

Follow My Example 1-3

(2) Asset (Cash) decreases by $1,800; Liability (Accounts Payable) decreases by $1,800.
(3) Asset (Accounts Receivable) increases by $11,250; Revenue (Delivery Service Fees) increases by $11,250.
(4) Asset (Cash) increases by $6,740; Asset (Accounts Receivable) decreases by $6,740.
(5) Asset (Cash) decreases by $1,000; Drawing (Joel Salvo, Drawing) increases by $1,000.

Practice Exercises: **PE 1-3A, PE 1-3B**

Financial Statements

Describe the financial statements of a proprietorship and explain how they interrelate.

After transactions have been recorded and summarized, reports are prepared for users. The accounting reports providing this information are called **financial statements**. The primary financial statements of a proprietorship are the income statement, the statement of owner's equity, the balance sheet, and the statement of cash flows. The order that the financial statements are prepared and the nature of each statement is described as follows.

Order Prepared	Financial Statement	Description of Statement
1.	**Income statement**	A summary of the revenue and expenses *for a specific period of time*, such as a month or a year.
2.	**Statement of owner's equity**	A summary of the changes in the owner's equity that have occurred *during a specific period of time*, such as a month or a year.
3.	**Balance sheet**	A list of the assets, liabilities, and owner's equity *as of a specific date*, usually at the close of the last day of a month or a year.
4.	**Statement of cash flows**	A summary of the cash receipts and cash payments for a *specific period of time*, such as a month or a year.

The four financial statements and their interrelationships are illustrated in Exhibit 6, on page 17. The data for the statements are taken from the summary of transactions of NetSolutions on page 14.

All financial statements are identified by the name of the business, the title of the statement, and the *date* or *period of time*. The data presented in the income statement, the statement of owner's equity, and the statement of cash flows are for a period of time. The data presented in the balance sheet are for a specific date.

Income Statement

The income statement reports the revenues and expenses for a period of time, based on the **matching concept**. This concept is applied by *matching* the expenses incurred during a period with the revenue that those expenses generated. The excess of the revenue over the expenses is called **net income**, net profit, or **earnings**. If the expenses exceed the revenue, the excess is a **net loss**.

Note:
When revenues exceed expenses, it is referred to as *net income, net profits, or earnings*. When expenses exceed revenues, it is referred to as *net loss*.

The revenue and expenses for NetSolutions were shown in the equation as separate increases and decreases. Net income for a period increases the owner's equity (capital) for the period. A net loss decreases the owner's equity (capital) for the period.

The revenue, expenses, and the net income of $3,050 for NetSolutions are reported in the income statement in Exhibit 6, on page 17. The order in which the expenses are listed in the income statement varies among businesses. Most businesses list expenses in order of size, beginning with the larger items. Miscellaneous expense is usually shown as the last item, regardless of the amount.

Example Exercise 1-4 Income Statement

OBJ. 5

The revenues and expenses of Chickadee Travel Service for the year ended April 30, 2012, are listed below.

Fees earned	$263,200
Miscellaneous expense	12,950
Office expense	63,000
Wages expense	131,700

Prepare an income statement for the current year ended April 30, 2012.

(*Continued*)

Follow My Example 1-4

Chickadee Travel Service
Income Statement
For the Year Ended April 30, 2012

Fees earned		$263,200
Expenses:		
Wages expense	$131,700	
Office expense	63,000	
Miscellaneous expense	12,950	
Total expenses		207,650
Net income		$ 55,550

Practice Exercises: **PE 1-4A, PE 1-4B**

Statement of Owner's Equity

The statement of owner's equity reports the changes in the owner's equity for a period of time. It is prepared *after* the income statement because the net income or net loss for the period must be reported in this statement. Similarly, it is prepared *before* the balance sheet, since the amount of owner's equity at the end of the period must be reported on the balance sheet. Because of this, the statement of owner's equity is often viewed as the connecting link between the income statement and balance sheet.

Three types of transactions affected owner's equity of NetSolutions during November:

1. the original investment of $25,000,
2. the revenue and expenses that resulted in net income of $3,050 for the month, and
3. a withdrawal of $2,000 by the owner.

The preceding information is summarized in the statement of owner's equity in Exhibit 6.

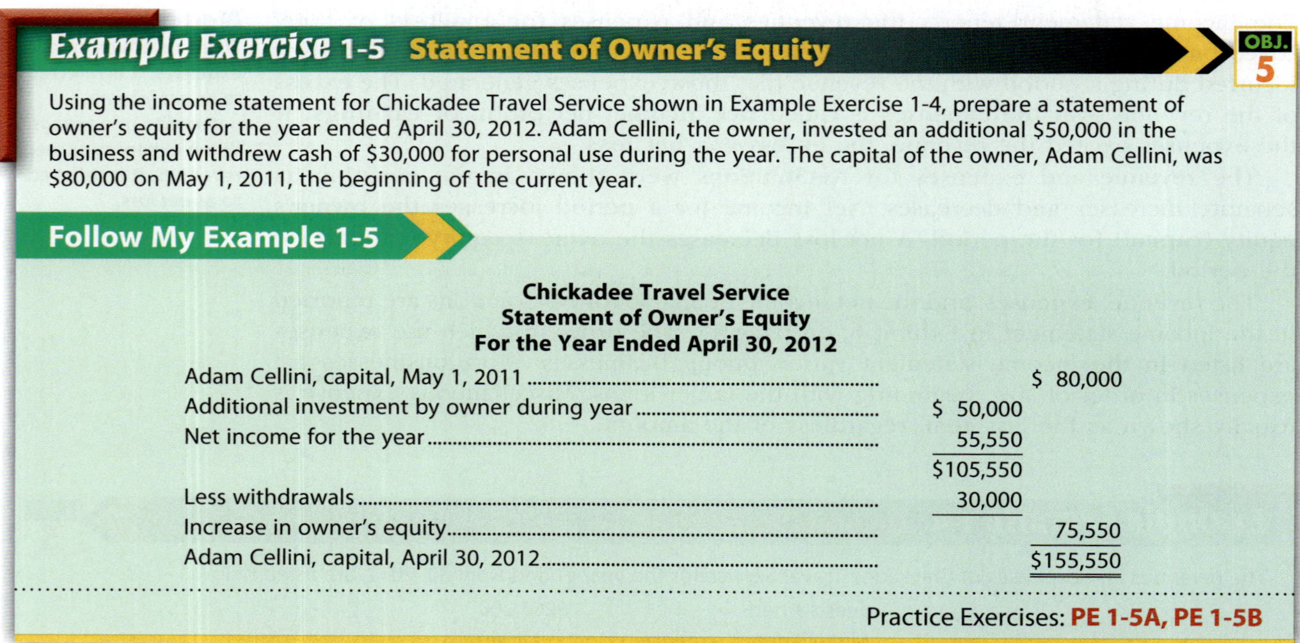

Example Exercise 1-5 Statement of Owner's Equity OBJ. 5

Using the income statement for Chickadee Travel Service shown in Example Exercise 1-4, prepare a statement of owner's equity for the year ended April 30, 2012. Adam Cellini, the owner, invested an additional $50,000 in the business and withdrew cash of $30,000 for personal use during the year. The capital of the owner, Adam Cellini, was $80,000 on May 1, 2011, the beginning of the current year.

Follow My Example 1-5

Chickadee Travel Service
Statement of Owner's Equity
For the Year Ended April 30, 2012

Adam Cellini, capital, May 1, 2011		$ 80,000
Additional investment by owner during year	$ 50,000	
Net income for the year	55,550	
	$105,550	
Less withdrawals	30,000	
Increase in owner's equity		75,550
Adam Cellini, capital, April 30, 2012		$155,550

Practice Exercises: **PE 1-5A, PE 1-5B**

Balance Sheet

The balance sheet in Exhibit 6 reports the amounts of NetSolutions' assets, liabilities, and owner's equity as of November 30, 2011. The asset and liability amounts are taken from the last line of the summary of transactions on page 14. Chris Clark, Capital

EXHIBIT 6

Financial Statements for NetSolutions

NetSolutions
Income Statement
For the Month Ended November 30, 2011

Fees earned		$7,500
Expenses:		
Wages expense	$2,125	
Rent expense	800	
Supplies expense	800	
Utilities expense	450	
Miscellaneous expense	275	
Total expense		4,450
Net income		$3,050

NetSolutions
Statement of Owner's Equity
For the Month Ended November 30 2011

Chris Clark, capital, November 1, 2011		$ 0
Investment on November 1, 2011	$25,000	
Net income for November	3,050	
	$28,050	
Less withdrawals	2,000	
Increase in owner's equity		26,050
Chris Clark, capital, November 30, 2011		$26,050

NetSolutions
Balance Sheet
November 30, 2011

Assets		**Liabilities**	
Cash	$ 5,900	Accounts payable	$ 400
Supplies	550	**Owner's Equity**	
Land	20,000	Chris Clark, capital	26,050
Total assets	$26,450	Total liabilities and owner's equity	$26,450

NetSolutions
Statement of Cash Flows
For the Month Ended November 30, 2011

Cash flows from operating activities:		
Cash received from customers	$ 7,500	
Deduct cash payments for expenses and payments to creditors	4,600	
Net cash flow from operating activities		$ 2,900
Cash flows from investing activities:		
Cash payments for purchase of land		(20,000)
Cash flows from financing activities:		
Cash received as owner's investment	$25,000	
Deduct cash withdrawal by owner	2,000	
Net cash flow from financing activities		23,000
Net cash flow and November 30, 2011, cash balance		$ 5,900

Describe the financial statements of a proprietorship and explain how they interrelate.

Key Points The primary financial statements of a proprietorship are the income statement, the statement of owner's equity, the balance sheet, and the statement of cash flows. The income statement reports a period's net income or net loss, which is also reported on the statement of owner's equity. The ending owner's capital reported on the statement of owner's equity is also reported on the balance sheet. The ending cash balance is reported on the balance sheet and the statement of cash flows.

Learning Outcomes	Example Exercises	Practice Exercises
• List and describe the financial statements of a proprietorship.		
• Prepare an income statement.	EE1-4	PE1-4A, 1-4B
• Prepare a statement of owner's equity.	EE1-5	PE1-5A, 1-5B
• Prepare a balance sheet.	EE1-6	PE1-6A, 1-6B
• Prepare a statement of cash flows.	EE1-7	PE1-7A, 1-7B
• Explain how the financial statements of a proprietorship are interrelated.		

Describe and illustrate the use of the ratio of liabilities to owner's equity in evaluating a company's financial condition.

Key Points A ratio useful in analyzing the ability of a business to pay its creditors is the ratio of liabilities to owner's (stockholders') equity. The lower the ratio of liabilities to owner's equity, the better able the company is to withstand poor business conditions and pay its obligations to creditors.

Learning Outcomes	Example Exercises	Practice Exercises
• Describe the usefulness of the ratio of liabilities to owner's (stockholders') equity.		
• Compute the ratio of liabilities to owner's (stockholders') equity.	EE1-8	PE1-8A, 1-8B

Key Terms

account form (18)
account payable (11)
account receivable (12)
accounting (3)
accounting equation (9)
assets (9)
balance sheet (15)
business (2)
business entity concept (7)
business transaction (9)
Certified Public Accountant (CPA) (6)
corporation (8)
cost concept (8)
earnings (15)
ethics (4)
expenses (12)
fees earned (12)
financial accounting (3)
Financial Accounting Standards Board (FASB) (7)
financial statements (15)
general-purpose financial statements (4)
generally accepted accounting principles (GAAP) (6)
income statement (15)
interest revenue (12)
International Accounting Standards Board (IASB) (7)
liabilities (9)
limited liability company (LLC) (8)
management (or managerial) accounting (3)
manufacturing business (2)
matching concept (15)
merchandising business (2)
net income (or net profit) (15)

net loss (15)
objectivity concept (8)
owner's equity (9)
partnership (7)
prepaid expenses (11)
private accounting (3)
profit (2)
proprietorship (7)
public accounting (6)
ratio of liabilities to owner's (stockholders') equity (21)
rent revenue (12)
revenue (11)
sales (12)
Securities and Exchange Commission (SEC) (7)
service business (2)
statement of cash flows (15)
statement of owner's equity (15)
unit of measure concept (8)

Illustrative Problem

Cecil Jameson, Attorney-at-Law, is a proprietorship owned and operated by Cecil Jameson. On July 1, 2011, Cecil Jameson, Attorney-at-Law, has the following assets and liabilities: cash, $1,000; accounts receivable, $3,200; supplies, $850; land, $10,000; accounts payable, $1,530. Office space and office equipment are currently being rented, pending the construction of an office complex on land purchased last year. Business transactions during July are summarized as follows:

a. Received cash from clients for services, $3,928.
b. Paid creditors on account, $1,055.
c. Received cash from Cecil Jameson as an additional investment, $3,700.
d. Paid office rent for the month, $1,200.
e. Charged clients for legal services on account, $2,025.
f. Purchased supplies on account, $245.
g. Received cash from clients on account, $3,000.
h. Received invoice for paralegal services from Legal Aid Inc. for July (to be paid on August 10), $1,635.
i. Paid the following: wages expense, $850; answering service expense, $250; utilities expense, $325; and miscellaneous expense, $75.
j. Determined that the cost of supplies on hand was $980; therefore, the cost of supplies used during the month was $115.
k. Jameson withdrew $1,000 in cash from the business for personal use.

Instructions

1. Determine the amount of owner's equity (Cecil Jameson's capital) as of July 1, 2011.
2. State the assets, liabilities, and owner's equity as of July 1 in equation form similar to that shown in this chapter. In tabular form below the equation, indicate the increases and decreases resulting from each transaction and the new balances after each transaction.
3. Prepare an income statement for July, a statement of owner's equity for July, and a balance sheet as of July 31, 2011.
4. (Optional). Prepare a statement of cash flows for July.

Solution

1.

Assets – Liabilities = Owner's Equity (Cecil Jameson, capital)
($1,000 + $3,200 + $850 + $10,000) – $1,530 = Owner's Equity (Cecil Jameson, capital)
$15,050 – $1,530 = Owner's Equity (Cecil Jameson, capital)
$13,520 = Owner's Equity (Cecil Jameson, capital)

2.

	Assets				= Liabilities +	Owner's Equity									
	Cash +	Accts. Rec. +	Supp. +	Land =	Accts Pay. +	Cecil Jameson, Capital –	Cecil Jameson, Drawing +	Fees Earned –	Paralegal Exp. –	Rent Exp. –	Wages Exp. –	Utilities Exp. –	Answering Service Exp. –	Supp Exp. –	Misc. Exp.
Bal.	1,000	3,200	850	10,000	1,530	13,520									
a.	+3,928							3,928							
Bal.	4,928	3,200	850	10,000	1,530	13,520		3,928							
b.	–1,055				–1,055										
Bal.	3,873	3,200	850	10,000	475	13,520		3,928							
c.	+3,700					+3,700									
Bal.	7,573	3,200	850	10,000	475	17,220		3,928							
d.	–1,200									–1,200					
Bal.	6,373	3,200	850	10,000	475	17,220		3,928		–1,200					
e.		+ 2,025						+ 2,025							
Bal.	6,373	5,225	850	10,000	475	17,220		5,953		–1,200					
f.			+245		+245										
Bal.	6,373	5,225	1,095	10,000	720	17,220		5,953		–1,200					
g.	+3,000	–3,000													
Bal.	9,373	2,225	1,095	10,000	720	17,220		5,953		–1,200					
h.					+1,635				–1,635						
Bal.	9,373	2,225	1,095	10,000	2,355	17,220		5,953	–1,635	–1,200					
i.	–1,500										–850	–325	–250		–75
Bal.	7,873	2,225	1,095	10,000	2,355	17,220		5,953	–1,635	–1,200	–850	–325	–250		–75
j.			–115											–115	
Bal.	7,873	2,225	980	10,000	2,355	17,220		5,953	–1,635	–1,200	–850	–325	–250	–115	–75
k.	–1,000						–1,000								
Bal.	6,873	2,225	980	10,000	2,355	17,220	–1,000	5,953	–1,635	–1,200	–850	–325	–250	–115	–75

3.

Cecil Jameson, Attorney-at-Law
Income Statement
For the Month Ended July 31, 2011

Fees earned		$5,953
Expenses:		
Paralegal expense	$1,635	
Rent expense	1,200	
Wages expense	850	
Utilities expense	325	
Answering service expense	250	
Supplies expense	115	
Miscellaneous expense	75	
Total expenses		4,450
Net income		$1,503

Cecil Jameson, Attorney-at-Law
Statement of Owner's Equity
For the Month Ended July 31, 2011

Cecil Jameson, capital, July 1, 2011		$13,520
Additional investment by owner	$3,700	
Net income for the month	1,503	
	$5,203	
Less withdrawals	1,000	
Increase in owner's equity		4,203
Cecil Jameson, capital, July 31, 2011		$17,723

(continued)

Cecil Jameson, Attorney-at-Law
Balance Sheet
July 31, 2011

Assets		Liabilities	
Cash	$ 6,873	Accounts payable	$ 2,355
Accounts receivable	2,225	**Owner's Equity**	
Supplies	980	Cecil Jameson, capital	17,723
Land	10,000	Total liabilities and owner's	
Total assets	$20,078	equity	$20,078

4. Optional.

Cecil Jameson, Attorney-at-Law
Statement of Cash Flows
For the Month Ended July 31, 2011

Cash flows from operating activities:		
Cash received from customers	$6,928*	
Deduct cash payments for operating expenses	3,755**	
Net cash flows from operating activities		$3,173
Cash flows from investing activities		—
Cash flows from financing activities:		
Cash received from owner as investment	$3,700	
Deduct cash withdrawals by owner	1,000	
Net cash flows from financing activities		2,700
Net increase in cash during year		$5,873
Cash as of July 1, 2011		1,000
Cash as of July 31, 2011		$6,873

*$6,928 = $3,928 + $3,000
**$3,755 = $1,055 + $1,200 + $1,500

Discussion Questions

1. Name some users of accounting information.
2. What is the role of accounting in business?
3. Why are most large companies like Microsoft, PepsiCo, Caterpillar, and AutoZone organized as corporations?
4. Murray Stoltz is the owner of Ontime Delivery Service. Recently, Murray paid interest of $3,200 on a personal loan of $60,000 that he used to begin the business. Should Ontime Delivery Service record the interest payment? Explain.
5. On October 3, A2Z Repair Service extended an offer of $75,000 for land that had been priced for sale at $90,000. On November 23, A2Z Repair Service accepted the seller's counteroffer of $82,000. Describe how A2Z Repair Service should record the land.
6. a. Land with an assessed value of $400,000 for property tax purposes is acquired by a business for $525,000. Ten years later, the plot of land has an assessed value of $700,000 and the business receives an offer of $1,000,000 for it. Should the monetary amount assigned to the land in the business records now be increased?

   b. Assuming that the land acquired in (a) was sold for $1,000,000, how would the various elements of the accounting equation be affected?

7. Describe the difference between an account receivable and an account payable.
8. A business had revenues of $430,000 and operating expenses of $615,000. Did the business (a) incur a net loss or (b) realize net income?
9. A business had revenues of $825,000 and operating expenses of $708,000. Did the business (a) incur a net loss or (b) realize net income?
10. What particular item of financial or operating data appears on both the income statement and the statement of owner's equity? What item appears on both the balance sheet and the statement of owner's equity? What item appears on both the balance sheet and the statement of cash flows?

Practice Exercises

Learning Objectives	Example Exercises

OBJ. 2 EE 1-1 p. 8

PE 1-1A Cost concept

On June 10, Easy Repair Service extended an offer of $95,000 for land that had been priced for sale at $118,500. On August 2, Easy Repair Service accepted the seller's counteroffer of $105,000. On August 27, the land was assessed at a value of $80,000 for property tax purposes. On April 1, Easy Repair Service was offered $125,000 for the land by a national retail chain. At what value should the land be recorded in Easy Repair Service's records?

OBJ. 2 EE 1-1 p. 8

PE 1-1B Cost concept

On February 7, AAA Repair Service extended an offer of $50,000 for land that had been priced for sale at $65,000. On February 21, AAA Repair Service accepted the seller's counteroffer of $57,500. On April 30, the land was assessed at a value of $40,000 for property tax purposes. On August 30, AAA Repair Service was offered $90,000 for the land by a national retail chain. At what value should the land be recorded in AAA Repair Service's records?

OBJ. 3 EE 1-2 p. 9

PE 1-2A Accounting equation

Shannon Cook is the owner and operator of Galaxy LLC, a motivational consulting business. At the end of its accounting period, December 31, 2011, Galaxy has assets of $800,000 and liabilities of $450,000. Using the accounting equation, determine the following amounts:

a. Owner's equity, as of December 31, 2011.

b. Owner's equity, as of December 31, 2012, assuming that assets increased by $175,000 and liabilities decreased by $60,000 during 2012.

OBJ. 3 EE 1-2 p. 9

PE 1-2B Accounting equation

Jan Petri is the owner and operator of You're the One, a motivational consulting business. At the end of its accounting period, December 31, 2011, You're the One has assets of $575,000 and liabilities of $125,000. Using the accounting equation, determine the following amounts:

a. Owner's equity, as of December 31, 2011.

b. Owner's equity, as of December 31, 2012, assuming that assets increased by $85,000 and liabilities increased by $30,000 during 2012.

OBJ. 4 EE 1-3 p. 14

PE 1-3A Transactions

Queens Delivery Service is owned and operated by Lisa Dewar. The following selected transactions were completed by Queens Delivery Service during June:

1. Received cash from owner as additional investment, $18,000.
2. Paid creditors on account, $1,800.
3. Billed customers for delivery services on account, $12,500.
4. Received cash from customers on account, $6,900.
5. Paid cash to owner for personal use, $4,000.

Indicate the effect of each transaction on the accounting equation elements (Assets, Liabilities, Owner's Equity, Drawing, Revenue, and Expense). Also, indicate the specific item within the accounting equation element that is affected. To illustrate, the answer to (1) is shown below.

(1) Asset (Cash) increases by $18,000; Owner's Equity (Lisa Dewar, Capital) increases by $18,000.

Learning Objectives	Example Exercises

OBJ. 4 EE 1-3 p. 14

PE 1-3B Transactions

Motorcross Delivery Service is owned and operated by Jim Smith. The following selected transactions were completed by Motorcross Delivery Service during February:

1. Received cash from owner as additional investment, $30,000.
2. Paid advertising expense, $1,200.
3. Purchased supplies on account, $450.
4. Billed customers for delivery services on account, $7,500.
5. Received cash from customers on account, $4,900.

Indicate the effect of each transaction on the accounting equation elements (Assets, Liabilities, Owner's Equity, Drawing, Revenue, and Expense). Also, indicate the specific item within the accounting equation element that is affected. To illustrate, the answer to (1) is shown below.

(1) Asset (Cash) increases by $30,000; Owner's Equity (Jim Smith, Capital) increases by $30,000.

OBJ. 5 EE 1-4 p. 16

PE 1-4A Income statement

The revenues and expenses of Dynasty Travel Service for the year ended June 30, 2012, are listed below.

Fees earned	$950,000
Office expense	222,000
Miscellaneous expense	16,000
Wages expense	478,000

Prepare an income statement for the current year ended June 30, 2012.

OBJ. 5 EE 1-4 p. 16

PE 1-4B Income statement

The revenues and expenses of Escape Travel Service for the year ended November 30, 2012, are listed below.

Fees earned	$942,500
Office expense	391,625
Miscellaneous expense	15,875
Wages expense	562,500

Prepare an income statement for the current year ended November 30, 2012.

OBJ. 5 EE 1-5 p. 16

PE 1-5A Statement of owner's equity

Using the income statement for Dynasty Travel Service shown in Practice Exercise 1-4A, prepare a statement of owner's equity for the current year ended June 30, 2012. Nancy Coleman, the owner, invested an additional $60,000 in the business during the year and withdrew cash of $36,000 for personal use. Nancy Coleman, capital as of July 1, 2011, was $250,000.

OBJ. 5 EE 1-5 p. 16

PE 1-5B Statement of owner's equity

Using the income statement for Escape Travel Service shown in Practice Exercise 1-4B, prepare a statement of owner's equity for the current year ended November 30, 2012. Brett Daniels, the owner, invested an additional $45,000 in the business during the year and withdrew cash of $25,000 for personal use. Brett Daniels, capital as of December 1, 2011, was $475,000.

OBJ. 5 EE 1-6 p. 18

PE 1-6A Balance sheet

Using the following data for Dynasty Travel Service as well as the statement of owner's equity shown in Practice Exercise 1-5A, prepare a balance sheet as of June 30, 2012.

Learning Objectives	Example Exercises

Accounts receivable	$ 64,000
Accounts payable	24,000
Cash	156,000
Land	300,000
Supplies	12,000

OBJ. 5 EE 1-6 p. 18

PE 1-6B Balance sheet

Using the following data for Escape Travel Service as well as the statement of owner's equity shown in Practice Exercise 1-5B, prepare a balance sheet as of November 30, 2012.

Accounts receivable	$ 94,375
Accounts payable	52,500
Cash	56,750
Land	362,500
Supplies	6,375

OBJ. 5 EE 1-7 p. 20

PE 1-7A Statement of cash flows

A summary of cash flows for Dynasty Travel Service for the year ended June 30, 2012, is shown below.

Cash receipts:	
Cash received from customers	$920,000
Cash received from additional investment of owner	60,000
Cash payments:	
Cash paid for operating expenses	710,000
Cash paid for land	208,000
Cash paid to owner for personal use	36,000

The cash balance as of July 1, 2011, was $130,000.

Prepare a statement of cash flows for Dynasty Travel Service for the year ended June 30, 2012.

OBJ. 5 EE 1-7 p. 20

PE 1-7B Statement of cash flows

A summary of cash flows for Escape Travel Service for the year ended November 30, 2012, is shown below.

Cash receipts:	
Cash received from customers	$875,000
Cash received from additional investment of owner	45,000
Cash payments:	
Cash paid for operating expenses	912,500
Cash paid for land	67,500
Cash paid to owner for personal use	25,000

The cash balance as of December 1, 2011, was $141,750.

Prepare a statement of cash flows for Escape Travel Service for the year ended November 30, 2012.

OBJ. 6 EE 1-8 p. 22

F·A·I

PE 1-8A Ratio of liabilities to owner's equity

The following data were taken from White Company's balance sheet:

	Dec. 31, 2012	Dec. 31, 2011
Total liabilities	$375,000	$287,500
Total owner's equity	300,000	250,000

a. Compute the ratio of liabilities to owner's equity.

b. Has the creditor's risk increased or decreased from December 31, 2011 to December 31, 2012?

Learning Objectives *Example Exercises*

OBJ. 6 EE 1-8 p. 22

PE 1-8B Ratio of liabilities to owner's equity

The following data were taken from Stone Company's balance sheet:

	Dec. 31, 2012	Dec. 31, 2011
Total liabilities	$340,000	$300,000
Total owner's equity	500,000	400,000

a. Compute the ratio of liabilities to owner's equity.

b. Has the creditor's risk increased or decreased from December 31, 2011 to December 31, 2012?

Exercises

OBJ. 1

EX 1-1 Types of businesses

The following is a list of well-known companies.

1. H&R Block
2. eBay Inc.
3. Wal-Mart Stores, Inc.
4. Ford Motor Company
5. Citigroup
6. Boeing
7. SunTrust
8. Alcoa Inc.
9. Procter & Gamble
10. FedEx
11. Gap Inc.
12. Hilton Hospitality, Inc.
13. CVS
14. Caterpillar
15. The Dow Chemical Company

a. Indicate whether each of these companies is primarily a service, merchandise, or manufacturing business. If you are unfamiliar with the company, use the Internet to locate the company's home page or use the finance Web site of Yahoo (http://finance.yahoo.com).

b. For which of the preceding companies is the accounting equation relevant?

OBJ. 1

EX 1-2 Professional ethics

A fertilizer manufacturing company wants to relocate to Jones County. A report from a fired researcher at the company indicates the company's product is releasing toxic by-products. The company suppressed that report. A later report commissioned by the company shows there is no problem with the fertilizer.

Should the company's chief executive officer reveal the content of the unfavorable report in discussions with Jones County representatives? Discuss.

OBJ. 2

EX 1-3 Business entity concept

Rocky Mountain Sports sells hunting and fishing equipment and provides guided hunting and fishing trips. Rocky Mountain Sports is owned and operated by Mike Weber, a well-known sports enthusiast and hunter. Mike's wife, Susan, owns and operates Madison Boutique, a women's clothing store. Mike and Susan have established a trust fund to finance their children's college education. The trust fund is maintained by National Bank in the name of the children, Kerri and Kyle.

a. For each of the following transactions, identify which of the entities listed should record the transaction in its records.

Entities	
R	Rocky Mountain Sports
B	National Bank Trust Fund
M	Madison Boutique
X	None of the above

1. Susan authorized the trust fund to purchase mutual fund shares.
2. Susan purchased two dozen spring dresses from a Chicago designer for a special spring sale.
3. Mike paid a breeder's fee for an English springer spaniel to be used as a hunting guide dog.
4. Susan deposited a $3,000 personal check in the trust fund at National Bank.
5. Mike paid a local doctor for his annual physical, which was required by the workmen's compensation insurance policy carried by Rocky Mountain Sports.
6. Mike received a cash advance from customers for a guided hunting trip.
7. Susan paid her dues to the YWCA.
8. Susan donated several dresses from inventory for a local charity auction for the benefit of a women's abuse shelter.
9. Mike paid for dinner and a movie to celebrate their fifteenth wedding anniversary.
10. Mike paid for an advertisement in a hunters' magazine.

b. What is a business transaction?

OBJ. 3

✔ Starbucks, $3,046

EX 1-4 Accounting equation

The total assets and total liabilities of Peat's Coffee & Tea Inc. and Starbucks Corporation are shown below.

	Peat's Coffee & Tea (in millions)	Starbucks (in millions)
Assets	$176	$5,577
Liabilities	32	2,531

Determine the owners' equity of each company.

OBJ. 3

✔ Dollar Tree, $1,253

EX 1-5 Accounting equation

The total assets and total liabilities of Dollar Tree Inc. and Target Corporation are shown below.

	Dollar Tree (in millions)	Target Corporation (in millions)
Assets	$2,036	$44,106
Liabilities	783	30,394

Determine the owners' equity of each company.

OBJ. 3

✔ a. 600,000

EX 1-6 Accounting equation

Determine the missing amount for each of the following:

	Assets	=	Liabilities	+	Owner's Equity
a.	×	=	$150,000	+	$450,000
b.	$275,000	=	×	+	50,000
c.	615,000	=	190,000	+	×

OBJ. 3, 4

✔ b. $530,000

EX 1-7 Accounting equation

Todd Olson is the owner and operator of Alpha, a motivational consulting business. At the end of its accounting period, December 31, 2011, Alpha has assets of $800,000 and liabilities of $350,000. Using the accounting equation and considering each case independently, determine the following amounts:

a. Todd Olson, capital, as of December 31, 2011.

b. Todd Olson, capital, as of December 31, 2012, assuming that assets increased by $150,000 and liabilities increased by $70,000 during 2012.

c. Todd Olson, capital, as of December 31, 2012, assuming that assets decreased by $60,000 and liabilities increased by $20,000 during 2012.

d. Todd Olson, capital, as of December 31, 2012, assuming that assets increased by $100,000 and liabilities decreased by $40,000 during 2012.

e. Net income (or net loss) during 2012, assuming that as of December 31, 2012, assets were $975,000, liabilities were $400,000, and there were no additional investments or withdrawals.

OBJ. 3

EX 1-8 Asset, liability, owner's equity items

Indicate whether each of the following is identified with (1) an asset, (2) a liability, or (3) owner's equity:

a. cash
b. wages expense
c. accounts payable
d. fees earned
e. supplies
f. land

OBJ. 4

EX 1-9 Effect of transactions on accounting equation

Describe how the following business transactions affect the three elements of the accounting equation.

a. Invested cash in business.
b. Purchased supplies for cash.
c. Purchased supplies on account.
d. Received cash for services performed.
e. Paid for utilities used in the business.

OBJ. 4

✔ a. (1) increase $250,000

EX 1-10 Effect of transactions on accounting equation

a. A vacant lot acquired for $100,000 is sold for $350,000 in cash. What is the effect of the sale on the total amount of the seller's (1) assets, (2) liabilities, and (3) owner's equity?
b. Assume that the seller owes $75,000 on a loan for the land. After receiving the $350,000 cash in (a), the seller pays the $75,000 owed. What is the effect of the payment on the total amount of the seller's (1) assets, (2) liabilities, and (3) owner's equity?
c. Is it true that a transaction always affects at least two elements (Assets, Liabilities, or Owner's Equity) of the accounting equation? Explain.

OBJ. 4

EX 1-11 Effect of transactions on owner's equity

Indicate whether each of the following types of transactions will either (a) increase owner's equity or (b) decrease owner's equity:

1. owner's investments
2. revenues
3. expenses
4. owner's withdrawals

OBJ. 4

EX 1-12 Transactions

The following selected transactions were completed by Speedy Delivery Service during October:

1. Received cash from owner as additional investment, $30,000.
2. Purchased supplies for cash, $1,500.
3. Paid rent for October, $4,000.
4. Paid advertising expense, $2,500.
5. Received cash for providing delivery services, $18,750.
6. Billed customers for delivery services on account, $41,500.
7. Paid creditors on account, $6,000.
8. Received cash from customers on account, $26,200.
9. Determined that the cost of supplies on hand was $250; therefore, $1,250 of supplies had been used during the month.
10. Paid cash to owner for personal use, $2,000.

Indicate the effect of each transaction on the accounting equation by listing the numbers identifying the transactions, (1) through (10), in a column, and inserting at the right of each number the appropriate letter from the following list:

a. Increase in an asset, decrease in another asset.

b. Increase in an asset, increase in a liability.

c. Increase in an asset, increase in owner's equity.

d. Decrease in an asset, decrease in a liability.

e. Decrease in an asset, decrease in owner's equity.

OBJ. 4

✔ d. $13,200

EX 1-13 Nature of transactions

Jeremy Zabel operates his own catering service. Summary financial data for February are presented in equation form as follows. Each line designated by a number indicates the effect of a transaction on the equation. Each increase and decrease in owner's equity, except transaction (5), affects net income.

	Assets			= Liabilities +	Owner's Equity			
	Cash	+ Supplies +	Land	= Accounts Payable +	Jeremy Zabel, Capital	− Jeremy Zabel, Drawing +	Fees Earned	− Expenses
Bal.	25,000	2,000	75,000	12,000	90,000			
1.	+29,000						29,000	
2.	−20,000		+20,000					
3.	−14,000							−14,000
4.		+1,000		+1,000				
5.	− 2,000					−2,000		
6.	− 7,000			−7,000				
7.		−1800						−1,800
Bal.	11,000	1,200	95,000	6,000	90,000	−2,000	29,000	−15,800

a. Describe each transaction.

b. What is the amount of net decrease in cash during the month?

c. What is the amount of net increase in owner's equity during the month?

d. What is the amount of the net income for the month?

e. How much of the net income for the month was retained in the business?

OBJ. 5

EX 1-14 Net income and owner's withdrawals

The income statement of a proprietorship for the month of December indicates a net income of $120,000. During the same period, the owner withdrew $130,000 in cash from the business for personal use.

Would it be correct to say that the business incurred a net loss of $10,000 during the month? Discuss.

OBJ. 5

✔ Leo: Net income, $60,000

EX 1-15 Net income and owner's equity for four businesses

Four different proprietorships, Aries, Gemini, Leo, and Pisces, show the same balance sheet data at the beginning and end of a year. These data, exclusive of the amount of owner's equity, are summarized as follows:

	Total Assets	Total Liabilities
Beginning of the year	$400,000	$100,000
End of the year	750,000	300,000

On the basis of the above data and the following additional information for the year, determine the net income (or loss) of each company for the year. (*Hint:* First determine the amount of increase or decrease in owner's equity during the year.)

Aries: The owner had made no additional investments in the business and had made no withdrawals from the business.

Gemini: The owner had made no additional investments in the business but had withdrawn $40,000.

Leo: The owner had made an additional investment of $90,000 but had made no withdrawals.

Pisces: The owner had made an additional investment of $90,000 and had withdrawn $40,000.

OBJ. 5

EX 1-16 Balance sheet items

From the following list of selected items taken from the records of Hoosier Appliance Service as of a specific date, identify those that would appear on the balance sheet:

1. Accounts Receivable
2. Cash
3. Fees Earned
4. Land
5. Patsy Adkins, Capital
6. Supplies
7. Supplies Expense
8. Utilities Expense
9. Wages Expense
10. Wages Payable

OBJ. 5

EX 1-17 Income statement items

Based on the data presented in Exercise 1-16, identify those items that would appear on the income statement.

OBJ. 5

✔ Penny Beall, capital, June 30, 2012: $482,000

EX 1-18 Statement of owner's equity

Financial information related to Lost Trail Company, a proprietorship, for the month ended June 30, 2012, is as follows:

Net income for June	$125,000
Penny Beall's withdrawals during June	18,000
Penny Beall's capital, June 1, 2012	375,000

a. Prepare a statement of owner's equity for the month ended June 30, 2012.

b. Why is the statement of owner's equity prepared before the June 30, 2012, balance sheet?

OBJ. 5

✔ Net income: $449,000

EX 1-19 Income statement

Universal Services was organized on October 1, 2012. A summary of the revenue and expense transactions for October follows:

Fees earned	$800,000
Wages expense	270,000
Rent expense	60,000
Supplies expense	9,000
Miscellaneous expense	12,000

Prepare an income statement for the month ended October 31.

OBJ. 5

✔ (a) $45,000

EX 1-20 Missing amounts from balance sheet and income statement data

One item is omitted in each of the following summaries of balance sheet and income statement data for the following four different proprietorships:

	Aquarius	Libra	Scorpio	Taurus
Beginning of the year:				
Assets	$300,000	$500,000	$100,000	(d)
Liabilities	120,000	260,000	76,000	$120,000
End of the year:				
Assets	420,000	700,000	90,000	248,000
Liabilities	110,000	220,000	80,000	136,000
During the year:				
Additional investment in the business	(a)	100,000	10,000	40,000
Withdrawals from the business	25,000	32,000	(c)	60,000
Revenue	190,000	(b)	115,000	112,000
Expenses	80,000	128,000	122,500	128,000

Determine the missing amounts, identifying them by letter. (*Hint:* First determine the amount of increase or decrease in owner's equity during the year.)

OBJ. 5

✔ b. $40,000

EX 1-21 Balance sheets, net income

Financial information related to the proprietorship of Lady Interiors for July and August 2012 is as follows:

	July 31, 2012	August 31, 2012
Accounts payable	$ 90,000	$100,000
Accounts receivable	200,000	240,000
Garth Jacobs, capital	?	?
Cash	80,000	95,000
Supplies	20,000	15,000

a. Prepare balance sheets for Lady Interiors as of July 31 and August 31, 2012.

b. Determine the amount of net income for August, assuming that the owner made no additional investments or withdrawals during the month.

c. Determine the amount of net income for August, assuming that the owner made no additional investments but withdrew $35,000 during the month.

OBJ. 5

EX 1-22 Financial statements

Each of the following items is shown in the financial statements of ExxonMobil Corporation.

1. Accounts payable
2. Cash equivalents
3. Crude oil inventory
4. Equipment
5. Exploration expenses
6. Income taxes payable
7. Investments
8. Long-term debt
9. Marketable securities
10. Notes and loans payable
11. Notes receivable
12. Operating expenses
13. Prepaid taxes
14. Sales
15. Selling expenses

a. Identify the financial statement (balance sheet or income statement) in which each item would appear.

b. Can an item appear on more than one financial statement?

c. Is the accounting equation relevant for ExxonMobil Corporation?

OBJ. 5

EX 1-23 Statement of cash flows

Indicate whether each of the following activities would be reported on the statement of cash flows as (a) an operating activity, (b) an investing activity, or (c) a financing activity:

1. Cash received from fees earned.
2. Cash paid for expenses.
3. Cash paid for land.
4. Cash received as an additional investment by owner.

OBJ. 5

EX 1-24 Statement of cash flows

A summary of cash flows for Absolute Consulting Group for the year ended July 31, 2012, is shown below.

Cash receipts:	
Cash received from customers	$187,500
Cash received from additional investment of owner	40,000
Cash payments:	
Cash paid for operating expenses	127,350
Cash paid for land	30,000
Cash paid to owner for personal use	5,000

The cash balance as of August 1, 2011, was $27,100.

Prepare a statement of cash flows for Absolute Consulting Group for the year ended July 31, 2012.

OBJ. 5

✔ Correct amount of total assets is $88,200.

EX 1-25 Financial statements

Empire Realty, organized May 1, 2012, is owned and operated by Bertram Mitchell. How many errors can you find in the following statements for Empire Realty, prepared after its first month of operations?

Empire Realty
Income Statement
May 31, 2012

Sales commissions		$233,550
Expenses:		
Office salaries expense	$145,800	
Rent expense	49,500	
Automobile expense	11,250	
Miscellaneous expense	3,600	
Supplies expense	1,350	
Total expenses		211,500
Net income		$ 67,050

Bertram Mitchell
Statement of Owner's Equity
May 31, 2011

Bertram Mitchell, capital, May 1, 2012	$ 46,800
Less withdrawals during May	9,000
	$ 37,800
Additional investment during May	11,250
	$ 49,050
Net income for May	67,050
Bertram Mitchell, capital, May 31, 2012	$ 116,100

Balance Sheet
For the Month Ended May 31, 2012

Assets		Liabilities	
Cash	$14,850	Accounts receivable	$ 64,350
Accounts payable	17,100	Supplies	9,000
		Owner's Equity	
		Bertram Mitchell, capital	116,100
Total assets	$31,950	Total liabilities and owner's equity	$189,450

OBJ. 6

EX 1-26 Ratio of liabilities to stockholders' equity

The Home Depot, Inc., is the world's largest home improvement retailer and one of the largest retailers in the United States based on net sales volume. The Home Depot operates over 2,000 Home Depot® stores that sell a wide assortment of building materials and home improvement and lawn and garden products.

The Home Depot reported the following balance sheet data (in millions):

	Feb. 1, 2009	Feb. 3, 2008
Total assets	$41,164	$44,324
Total stockholders' equity	17,777	17,714

a. Determine the total liabilities as of February 1, 2009, and February 3, 2008.

b. Determine the ratio of liabilities to stockholders' equity for 2009 and 2008. Round to two decimal places.

c. What conclusions regarding the margin of protection to the creditors can you draw from (b)?

OBJ. 6

EX 1-27 Ratio of liabilities to stockholders' equity

Lowe's, a major competitor of The Home Depot in the home improvement business, operates over 1,600 stores. For the years ending January 30, 2009, and February 1, 2008, Lowe's reported the following balance sheet data (in millions):

	Jan. 30, 2009	Feb. 1, 2008
Total assets	$32,686	$30,869
Total liabilities	14,631	14,771

a. Determine the total stockholders' equity as of January 30, 2009, and February 1, 2008.

b. Determine the ratio of liabilities to stockholders' equity for 2009 and 2008. Round to two decimal places.

c. What conclusions regarding the margin of protection to the creditors can you draw from (b)?

d. Using the balance sheet data for The Home Depot in Exercise 1-26, how does the ratio of liabilities to stockholders' equity of Lowe's compare to that of The Home Depot?

Problems Series A

OBJ. 4

✔ Cash bal. at end of September: $37,700

PR 1-1A Transactions

On September 1 of the current year, Maria Edsall established a business to manage rental property. She completed the following transactions during September:

a. Opened a business bank account with a deposit of $40,000 from personal funds.

b. Purchased supplies (pens, file folders, and copy paper) on account, $2,200.

c. Received cash from fees earned for managing rental property, $6,000.

d. Paid rent on office and equipment for the month, $2,700.

e. Paid creditors on account, $1,000.

f. Billed customers for fees earned for managing rental property, $5,000.

g. Paid automobile expenses (including rental charges) for month, $600, and miscellaneous expenses, $300.

h. Paid office salaries, $1,900.

i. Determined that the cost of supplies on hand was $1,300; therefore, the cost of supplies used was $900.

j. Withdrew cash for personal use, $1,800.

Instructions

1. Indicate the effect of each transaction and the balances after each transaction, using the following tabular headings:

Assets			= Liabilities +			Owner's Equity					
Cash +	Accounts Receivable +	Supplies =	Accounts Payable +	Maria Edsall, Capital −	Maria Edsall, Drawing +	Fees Earned −	Rent Expense −	Salaries Expense −	Supplies Expense −	Auto Expense −	Misc. Expense

2. Briefly explain why the owner's investment and revenues increased owner's equity, while withdrawals and expenses decreased owner's equity.

3. Determine the net income for September.

4. How much did September's transactions increase or decrease Maria Edsall's capital?

OBJ. 5

✔ 1. Net income: $40,000

PR 1-2A Financial statements

Following are the amounts of the assets and liabilities of New World Travel Agency at December 31, 2012, the end of the current year, and its revenue and expenses for the year. The capital of Kris Taber, owner, was $120,000 on January 1, 2012, the beginning of the current year. During the current year, Kris withdrew $10,000.

Accounts payable	$ 25,000	Rent expense	$45,000
Accounts receivable	60,000	Supplies	5,000
Cash	110,000	Supplies expense	3,000
Fees earned	200,000	Utilities expense	18,000
Miscellaneous expense	4,000	Wages expense	90,000

Instructions

1. Prepare an income statement for the current year ended December 31, 2012.

2. Prepare a statement of owner's equity for the current year ended December 31, 2012.

(Continued)

3. Prepare a balance sheet as of December 31, 2012.
4. What item appears on both the statement of owner's equity and the balance sheet?

OBJ. 5

✔ **1. Net income: $26,400**

PR 1-3A Financial statements

Heidi Fritz established Freedom Financial Services on March 1, 2012. Freedom Financial Services offers financial planning advice to its clients. The effect of each transaction and the balances after each transaction for March are shown below.

	Assets			= Liabilities +	Owner's Equity							
	Cash	+ Accounts Receivable	+ Supplies =	Accounts Payable	+ Heidi Fritz, Capital	– Heidi Fritz, Drawing +	Fees Earned	– Salaries Expense	– Rent Expense	– Auto Expense	– Supplies Expense	– Misc. Expense
a.	+45,000				+45,000							
b.			+6,540	+6,540								
Bal.	45,000		6,540	6,540	45,000							
c.	–1,800			–1,800								
Bal.	43,200		6,540	4,740	45,000							
d.	+84,000						+84,000					
Bal.	127,200		6,540	4,740	45,000		84,000					
e.	–22,500								–22,500			
Bal.	104,700		6,540	4,740	45,000		84,000		–22,500			
f.	–17,100									–13,500		–3,600
Bal.	87,600		6,540	4,740	45,000		84,000		–22,500	–13,500		–3,600
g.	–48,000							–48,000				
Bal.	39,600		6,540	4,740	45,000		84,000	–48,000	–22,500	–13,500		–3,600
h.			–4,500								–4,500	
Bal.	39,600		2,040	4,740	45,000		84,000	–48,000	–22,500	–13,500	–4,500	–3,600
i.		+34,500					+34,500					
Bal.	39,600	34,500	2,040	4,740	45,000		118,500	–48,000	–22,500	–13,500	–4,500	–3,600
j.	–15,000					–15,000						
Bal.	24,600	34,500	2,040	4,740	45,000	–15,000	118,500	–48,000	–22,500	–13,500	–4,500	–3,600

Instructions

1. Prepare an income statement for the month ended March 31, 2012.
2. Prepare a statement of owner's equity for the month ended March 31, 2012.
3. Prepare a balance sheet as of March 31, 2012.
4. (Optional). Prepare a statement of cash flows for the month ending March 31, 2012.

OBJ. 4, 5

✔ **2. Net income: $12,150**

PR 1-4A Transactions; financial statements

On January 1, 2012, Carlton Myers established Vista Realty. Carlton completed the following transactions during the month of January:

a. Opened a business bank account with a deposit of $25,000 from personal funds.
b. Purchased supplies (pens, file folders, paper, etc.) on account, $2,500.
c. Paid creditor on account, $1,600.
d. Earned sales commissions, receiving cash, $25,500.
e. Paid rent on office and equipment for the month, $5,000.
f. Withdrew cash for personal use, $8,000.
g. Paid automobile expenses (including rental charge) for month, $2,500, and miscellaneous expenses, $1,200.
h. Paid office salaries, $3,000.
i. Determined that the cost of supplies on hand was $850; therefore, the cost of supplies used was $1,650.

Instructions

1. Indicate the effect of each transaction and the balances after each transaction, using the following tabular headings:

Assets		= Liabilities +	Owner's Equity							
Cash +	Supplies =	Accounts Payable +	Carlton Myers Capital −	Carlton Myers, Drawing +	Sales Commissions −	Rent Expense −	Office Salaries Expense −	Auto Expense −	Supplies Expense −	Misc. Expense

2. Prepare an income statement for January, a statement of owner's equity for January, and a balance sheet as of January 31.

OBJ. 4, 5

✔ 3. Net income: $14,900

PR 1-5A Transactions; financial statements

Kean Dry Cleaners is owned and operated by Wally Lowman. A building and equipment are currently being rented, pending expansion to new facilities. The actual work of dry cleaning is done by another company at wholesale rates. The assets and the liabilities of the business on March 1, 2012, are as follows: Cash, $15,000; Accounts Receivable, $31,000; Supplies, $3,000; Land, $36,000; Accounts Payable, $13,000. Business transactions during March are summarized as follows:

a. Wally Lowman invested additional cash in the business with a deposit of $28,000 in the business bank account.
b. Paid $14,000 for the purchase of land as a future building site.
c. Received cash from cash customers for dry cleaning revenue, $17,000.
d. Paid rent for the month, $5,000.
e. Purchased supplies on account, $2,500.
f. Paid creditors on account, $12,800.
g. Charged customers for dry cleaning revenue on account, $34,000.
h. Received monthly invoice for dry cleaning expense for March (to be paid on April 10), $13,500.
i. Paid the following: wages expense, $7,500; truck expense, $2,500; utilities expense, $1,300; miscellaneous expense, $2,700.
j. Received cash from customers on account, $28,000.
k. Determined that the cost of supplies on hand was $1,900; therefore, the cost of supplies used during the month was $3,600.
l. Withdrew $8,000 cash for personal use.

Instructions

1. Determine the amount of Wally Lowman's capital as of March 1 of the current year.
2. State the assets, liabilities, and owner's equity as of March 1 in equation form similar to that shown in this chapter. In tabular form below the equation, indicate increases and decreases resulting from each transaction and the new balances after each transaction.
3. Prepare an income statement for March, a statement of owner's equity for March, and a balance sheet as of March 31.
4. (Optional). Prepare a statement of cash flows for March.

OBJ. 5

✔ k. $300,000

PR 1-6A Missing amounts from financial statements

The financial statements at the end of Alpine Realty's first month of operations are as follows:

Alpine Realty
Income Statement
For the Month Ended June 30, 2012

Fees earned		$ (a)
Expenses:		
Wages expense	$120,000	
Rent expense	40,000	
Supplies expense	(b)	
Utilities expense	8,000	
Miscellaneous expense	10,000	
Total expenses		190,000
Net income		$110,000

Alpine Realty
Statement of Owner's Equity
For the Month Ended June 30, 2012

Aaron Gilbert, capital, June 1, 2012		$ (c)
Investment on June 1, 2012	$150,000	
Net income for June	(d)	
	$ (e)	
Less withdrawals	50,000	
Increase in owner's equity		(f)
Aaron Gilbert, capital, June 30, 2012		$ (g)

Alpine Realty
Balance Sheet
June 30, 2012

Assets		**Liabilities**	
Cash	$ 185,000	Accounts payable	$40,000
Supplies	5,000	**Owner's Equity**	
Land	60,000	Aaron Gilbert, capital	(i)
Total assets	$ (h)	Total liabilities and owner's equity	$ (j)

Alpine Realty
Statement of Cash Flows
For the Month Ended June 30, 2012

Cash flows from operating activities:		
Cash received from customers	$ (k)	
Deduct cash payments for expenses and payments to creditors	155,000	
Net cash flow from operating activities		$ (l)
Cash flows from investing activities:		
Cash payments for acquisition of land		(m)
Cash flows from financing activities:		
Cash received as owner's investment	$ (n)	
Deduct cash withdrawal by owner	(o)	
Net cash flow from financing activities		(p)
Net cash flow and June 30, 2012, cash balance		$ (q)

Instructions

By analyzing the interrelationships among the four financial statements, determine the proper amounts for (a) through (q).

Problems Series B

OBJ. 4

✔ Cash bal. at end of January: $73,500

PR 1-1B Transactions

Cody Macedo established an insurance agency on January 1 of the current year and completed the following transactions during January:

a. Opened a business bank account with a deposit of $75,000 from personal funds.
b. Purchased supplies on account, $3,000.
c. Paid creditors on account, $1,000.
d. Received cash from fees earned on insurance commissions, $11,800.
e. Paid rent on office and equipment for the month, $4,000.
f. Paid automobile expenses for month, $600, and miscellaneous expenses, $200.
g. Paid office salaries, $2,500.
h. Determined that the cost of supplies on hand was $1,900; therefore, the cost of supplies used was $1,100.
i. Billed insurance companies for sales commissions earned, $12,500.
j. Withdrew cash for personal use, $5,000.

Instructions

1. Indicate the effect of each transaction and the balances after each transaction, using the following tabular headings:

Assets			= Liabilities +	Owner's Equity							
Cash +	Accounts Receivable +	Supplies =	Accounts Payable +	Cody Macedo, Capital −	Cody Macedo, Drawing +	Fees Earned −	Rent Expense −	Salaries Expense −	Supplies Expense −	Auto Expense −	Misc. Expense

2. Briefly explain why the owner's investment and revenues increased owner's equity, while withdrawals and expenses decreased owner's equity.
3. Determine the net income for January.
4. How much did January's transactions increase or decrease Cody Macedo's capital?

OBJ. 5

✔ **1. Net income: $80,000**

PR 1-2B Financial statements

The amounts of the assets and liabilities of St. Simon Travel Service at June 30, 2012, the end of the current year, and its revenue and expenses for the year are listed below. The capital of Gwen Perez, owner, was $150,000 at July 1, 2011, the beginning of the current year, and the owner withdrew $30,000 during the current year.

Accounts payable	$ 25,000	Supplies	$ 12,000
Accounts receivable	90,000	Supplies expense	10,000
Cash	123,000	Taxes expense	8,000
Fees earned	500,000	Utilities expense	36,000
Miscellaneous expense	11,000	Wages expense	280,000
Rent expense	75,000		

Instructions

1. Prepare an income statement for the current year ended June 30, 2012.
2. Prepare a statement of owner's equity for the current year ended June 30, 2012.
3. Prepare a balance sheet as of June 30, 2012.
4. What item appears on both the income statement and statement of owner's equity?

OBJ. 5

✔ **1. Net income: $91,900**

PR 1-3B Financial statements

Rory Kalur established Computers 4 Less on February 1, 2012. The effect of each transaction and the balances after each transaction for February are shown below.

	Assets			= Liabilities +	Owner's Equity							
	Cash +	Accounts Receivable +	Supplies =	Accounts Payable +	Rory Kalur, Capital −	Rory Kalur, Drawing +	Fees Earned −	Salaries Expense −	Rent Expense −	Auto Expense −	Supplies Expense −	Misc. Expense
a.	+120,000				+120,000							
b.			+10,400	+10,400								
Bal.	120,000		10,400	10,400	120,000							
c.	+118,000						+118,000					
Bal.	238,000		10,400	10,400	120,000		118,000					
d.	−32,000								−32,000			
Bal.	206,000		10,400	10,400	120,000		118,000		−32,000			
e.	−5,000			−5,000								
Bal.	201,000		10,400	5,400	120,000		118,000		−32,000			
f.		+83,000					+83,000					
Bal.	201,000	83,000	10,400	5,400	120,000		201,000		−32,000			
g.	−23,000									−15,500		−7,500
Bal.	178,000	83,000	10,400	5,400	120,000		201,000		−32,000	−15,500		−7,500
h.	−48,000							−48,000				
Bal.	130,000	83,000	10,400	5,400	120,000		201,000	−48,000	−32,000	−15,500		−7,500
i.			−6,100								−6,100	
Bal.	130,000	83,000	4,300	5,400	120,000		201,000	−48,000	−32,000	−15,500	−6,100	−7,500
j.	−30,000					−30,000						
Bal.	100,000	83,000	4,300	5,400	120,000	−30,000	201,000	−48,000	−32,000	−15,500	−6,100	−7,500

Instructions

1. Prepare an income statement for the month ended February 29, 2012.
2. Prepare a statement of owner's equity for the month ended February 29, 2012.
3. Prepare a balance sheet as of February 29, 2012.
4. (Optional). Prepare a statement of cash flows for the month ending February 29, 2012.

OBJ. 4, 5

✔ 2. Net income: $9,300

PR 1-4B Transactions; financial statements

On June 1, 2012, Lindsey Brown established Equity Realty. Lindsey completed the following transactions during the month of June:

a. Opened a business bank account with a deposit of $15,000 from personal funds.
b. Paid rent on office and equipment for the month, $4,000.
c. Paid automobile expenses (including rental charge) for month, $1,200, and miscellaneous expenses, $800.
d. Purchased supplies (pens, file folders, and copy paper) on account, $1,000.
e. Earned sales commissions, receiving cash, $18,500.
f. Paid creditor on account, $600.
g. Paid office salaries, $2,500.
h. Withdrew cash for personal use, $5,000.
i. Determined that the cost of supplies on hand was $300; therefore, the cost of supplies used was $700.

Instructions

1. Indicate the effect of each transaction and the balances after each transaction, using the following tabular headings:

Assets	=	Liabilities +		Owner's Equity													
Cash + Supplies	=	Accounts Payable	+	Lindsey Brown, Capital	–	Lindsey Brown, Drawing	+	Sales Commissions	–	Rent Expense	–	Office Salaries Expense	–	Auto Expense	–	Supplies Expense	– Misc. Expense

2. Prepare an income statement for June, a statement of owner's equity for June, and a balance sheet as of June 30.

OBJ. 4, 5

✔ 3. Net income: $3,700

PR 1-5B Transactions; financial statements

Anny's Dry Cleaners is owned and operated by Anny Brum. A building and equipment are currently being rented, pending expansion to new facilities. The actual work of dry cleaning is done by another company at wholesale rates. The assets and the liabilities of the business on June 1, 2012, are as follows: Cash, $25,000; Accounts Receivable, $30,000; Supplies, $5,000; Land, $50,000; Accounts Payable, $18,000. Business transactions during June are summarized as follows:

a. Anny Brum invested additional cash in the business with a deposit of $15,000 in the business bank account.
b. Purchased land for use as a parking lot, paying cash of $20,000.
c. Paid rent for the month, $3,000.
d. Charged customers for dry cleaning revenue on account, $22,000.
e. Paid creditors on account, $13,000.
f. Purchased supplies on account, $1,000.
g. Received cash from cash customers for dry cleaning revenue, $28,000.
h. Received cash from customers on account, $27,000.
i. Received monthly invoice for dry cleaning expense for June (to be paid on July 10), $21,500.
j. Paid the following: wages expense, $14,000; truck expense, $2,100; utilities expense, $1,800; miscellaneous expense, $1,300.
k. Determined that the cost of supplies on hand was $3,400; therefore, the cost of supplies used during the month was $2,600.
l. Withdrew $1,000 for personal use.

Instructions

1. Determine the amount of Anny Brum's capital as of June 1.
2. State the assets, liabilities, and owner's equity as of June 1 in equation form similar to that shown in this chapter. In tabular form below the equation, indicate increases and decreases resulting from each transaction and the new balances after each transaction.

3. Prepare an income statement for June, a statement of owner's equity for June, and a balance sheet as of June 30.
4. (Optional) Prepare a statement of cash flows for June.

OBJ. 5
✔ i. $130,000

PR 1-6B Missing amounts from financial statements

The financial statements at the end of Cyber Realty's first month of operations are shown below.

Cyber Realty
Income Statement
For the Month Ended October 31, 2012

Fees earned		$250,000
Expenses:		
Wages expense	$ (a)	
Rent expense	30,000	
Supplies expense	11,000	
Utilities expense	9,000	
Miscellaneous expense	3,000	
Total expenses		180,000
Net income		$ (b)

Cyber Realty
Statement of Owner's Equity
For the Month Ended October 31, 2012

Kendra Garcia, capital, October 1, 2012		$ (c)
Investment on October 1, 2012	$ (d)	
Net income for October	(e)	
	$ (f)	
Less withdrawals	(g)	
Increase in owner's equity		(h)
Kendra Garcia, capital, October 31, 2012		$ (i)

Cyber Realty
Balance Sheet
October 31, 2012

Assets		Liabilities	
Cash	$77,000	Accounts payable	$ 30,000
Supplies	8,000	**Owner's Equity**	
Land	(j)	Kendra Garcia, capital	(l)
Total assets	$ (k)	Total liabilities and owner's equity	$ (m)

Cyber Realty
Statement of Cash Flows
For the Month Ended October 31, 2012

Cash flows from operating activities:		
Cash received from customers	$ (n)	
Deduct cash payments for expenses and payments to creditors	158,000	
Net cash flow from operating activities		$ (0)
Cash flows from investing activities:		
Cash payments for acquisition of land		(75,000)
Cash flows from financing activities:		
Cash received as owner's investment	$100,000	
Deduct cash withdrawal by owner	40,000	
Net cash flow from financing activities		(p)
Net cash flow and October 31, 2012, cash balance		$ (q)

Instructions

By analyzing the interrelationships among the four financial statements, determine the proper amounts for (a) through (q).

Continuing Problem

✔ 2. Net income: $1,980

Pat Sharpe enjoys listening to all types of music and owns countless CDs. Over the years, Pat has gained a local reputation for knowledge of music from classical to rap and the ability to put together sets of recordings that appeal to all ages.

During the last several months, Pat served as a guest disc jockey on a local radio station. In addition, Pat has entertained at several friends' parties as the host deejay.

On June 1, 2012, Pat established a proprietorship known as PS Music. Using an extensive collection of music MP3 files, Pat will serve as a disc jockey on a fee basis for weddings, college parties, and other events. During June, Pat entered into the following transactions:

June 1. Deposited $5,000 in a checking account in the name of PS Music.
2. Received $3,600 from a local radio station for serving as the guest disc jockey for June.
2. Agreed to share office space with a local real estate agency, Downtown Realty. PS Music will pay one-fourth of the rent. In addition, PS Music agreed to pay a portion of the salary of the receptionist and to pay one-fourth of the utilities. Paid $750 for the rent of the office.
4. Purchased supplies from City Office Supply Co. for $350. Agreed to pay $100 within 10 days and the remainder by July 5, 2012.
6. Paid $450 to a local radio station to advertise the services of PS Music twice daily for two weeks.
8. Paid $700 to a local electronics store for renting digital recording equipment.
12. Paid $350 (music expense) to Cool Music for the use of its current music demos to make various music sets.
13. Paid City Office Supply Co. $100 on account.
16. Received $500 from a dentist for providing two music sets for the dentist to play for her patients.
22. Served as disc jockey for a wedding party. The father of the bride agreed to pay $1,250 the 1st of July.
25. Received $400 for serving as the disc jockey for a cancer charity ball hosted by the local hospital.
29. Paid $240 (music expense) to Galaxy Music for the use of its library of music demos.
30. Received $900 for serving as PS disc jockey for a local club's monthly dance.
30. Paid Downtown Realty $400 for PS Music's share of the receptionist's salary for June.
30. Paid Downtown Realty $300 for PS Music's share of the utilities for June.
30. Determined that the cost of supplies on hand is $170. Therefore, the cost of supplies used during the month was $180.
30. Paid for miscellaneous expenses, $300.
30. Paid $1,000 royalties (music expense) to National Music Clearing for use of various artists' music during the month.
30. Withdrew $500 of cash from PS Music for personal use.

Instructions

1. Indicate the effect of each transaction and the balances after each transaction, using the following tabular headings:

Assets			= Liabilities +	Owner's Equity										
Cash +	Accts. Rec. +	Supplies =	Accounts Payable +	Pat Sharpe, Capital −	Pat Sharpe, Drawing +	Fees Earned −	Music Exp. −	Office Rent Exp. −	Equipment Rent Exp. −	Advertising Exp. −	Wages Exp. −	Utilities Exp. −	Supplies Exp. −	Misc. Exp.

2. Prepare an income statement for PS Music for the month ended June 30, 2012.
3. Prepare a statement of owner's equity for PS Music for the month ended June 30, 2012.
4. Prepare a balance sheet for PS Music as of June 30, 2012.

Cases & Projects

CP 1-1 Ethics and professional conduct in business

Group Project

Vince Hunt, president of Sabre Enterprises, applied for a $200,000 loan from First National Bank. The bank requested financial statements from Sabre Enterprises as a basis for granting the loan. Vince has told his accountant to provide the bank with a balance sheet. Vince has decided to omit the other financial statements because there was a net loss during the past year.

In groups of three or four, discuss the following questions:

1. Is Vince behaving in a professional manner by omitting some of the financial statements?
2. a. What types of information about their businesses would owners be willing to provide bankers? What types of information would owners not be willing to provide?
   b. What types of information about a business would bankers want before extending a loan?
   c. What common interests are shared by bankers and business owners?

CP 1-2 Net income

On July 1, 2011, Dr. Heather Dewitt established Life Medical, a medical practice organized as a proprietorship. The following conversation occurred the following January between Dr. Dewitt and a former medical school classmate, Dr. Naomi Kennedy, at an American Medical Association convention in Boston.

Dr. Kennedy: Heather, good to see you again. Why didn't you call when you were in Chicago? We could have had dinner together.

Dr. Dewitt: Actually, I never made it to Chicago this year. My husband and kids went up to our Vail condo twice, but I got stuck in Fort Lauderdale. I opened a new consulting practice this July and haven't had any time for myself since.

Dr. Kennedy: I heard about it . . . Life . . . something . . . right?

Dr. Dewitt: Yes, Life Medical. My husband chose the name.

Dr. Kennedy: I've thought about doing something like that. Are you making any money? I mean, is it worth your time?

Dr. Dewitt: You wouldn't believe it. I started by opening a bank account with $40,000, and my December bank statement has a balance of $90,000. Not bad for six months—all pure profit.

Dr. Kennedy: Maybe I'll try it in Chicago! Let's have breakfast together tomorrow and you can fill me in on the details.

Comment on Dr. Dewitt's statement that the difference between the opening bank balance ($40,000) and the December statement balance ($90,000) is pure profit.

CP 1-3 Transactions and financial statements

Jan Martinelli, a junior in college, has been seeking ways to earn extra spending money. As an active sports enthusiast, Jan plays tennis regularly at the Naples Tennis Club, where her family has a membership. The president of the club recently approached Jan with the proposal that she manage the club's tennis courts. Jan's primary duty would be to supervise the operation of the club's four indoor and 10 outdoor courts, including court reservations.

In return for her services, the club would pay Jan $300 per week, plus Jan could keep whatever she earned from lessons and the fees from the use of the ball machine. The club and Jan agreed to a one-month trial, after which both would consider an arrangement for the remaining two years of Jan's college career. On this basis, Jan organized Topspin. During April 2012, Jan managed the tennis courts and entered into the following transactions:

a. Opened a business account by depositing $1,000.
b. Paid $300 for tennis supplies (practice tennis balls, etc.).

c. Paid $200 for the rental of video equipment to be used in offering lessons during April.

d. Arranged for the rental of two ball machines during April for $250. Paid $100 in advance, with the remaining $150 due May 1.

e. Received $1,600 for lessons given during April.

f. Received $500 in fees from the use of the ball machines during April.

g. Paid $800 for salaries of part-time employees who answered the telephone and took reservations while Jan was giving lessons.

h. Paid $225 for miscellaneous expenses.

i. Received $1,200 from the club for managing the tennis courts during April.

j. Determined that the cost of supplies on hand at the end of the month totaled $180; therefore, the cost of supplies used was $120.

k. Withdrew $250 for personal use on April 30.

As a friend and accounting student, you have been asked by Jan to aid her in assessing the venture.

1. Indicate the effect of each transaction and the balances after each transaction, using the following tabular headings:

Assets	=	Liabilities	+	Owner's Equity												
Cash + Supplies	=	Accounts Payable	+	Jan Martinelli, Capital	–	Jan Martinelli, Drawing	+	Service Revenue	–	Salary Expense	–	Rent Expense	–	Supplies Expense	–	Misc. Expense

2. Prepare an income statement for April.
3. Prepare a statement of owner's equity for April.
4. Prepare a balance sheet as of April 30.
5. a. Assume that Jan Martinelli could earn $9 per hour working 30 hours a week as a waitress. Evaluate which of the two alternatives, working as a waitress or operating Topspin, would provide Jan with the most income per month.

   b. Discuss any other factors that you believe Jan should consider before discussing a long-term arrangement with the Naples Tennis Club.

Internet Project

CP 1-4 Certification requirements for accountants

By satisfying certain specific requirements, accountants may become certified as public accountants (CPAs), management accountants (CMAs), or internal auditors (CIAs). Find the certification requirements for one of these accounting groups by accessing the appropriate Internet site listed below.

Site	Description
http://www.ais-cpa.com	This site lists the address and/or Internet link for each state's board of accountancy. Find your state's requirements.
http://www.imanet.org	This site lists the requirements for becoming a CMA.
http://www.theiia.org	This site lists the requirements for becoming a CIA.

CP 1-5 Cash flows

Amazon.com, an Internet retailer, was incorporated and began operation in the mid-90s. On the statement of cash flows, would you expect Amazon.com's net cash flows from operating, investing, and financing activities to be positive or negative for its first three years of operations? Use the following format for your answers, and briefly explain your logic.

	First Year	Second Year	Third Year
Net cash flows from operating activities	negative		
Net cash flows from investing activities			
Net cash flows from financing activities			

Internet Project

CP 1-6 Financial analysis of Enron Corporation

The now defunct Enron Corporation, once headquartered in Houston, Texas, provided products and services for natural gas, electricity, and communications to wholesale and retail customers. Enron's operations were conducted through a variety of subsidiaries and affiliates that involved transporting gas through pipelines, transmitting electricity, and managing energy commodities. The following data was taken from Enron's financial statements:

	In millions
Total revenues	$100,789
Total costs and expenses	98,836
Operating income	1,953
Net income	979
Total assets	65,503
Total liabilities	54,033
Total owners' equity	11,470
Net cash flows from operating activities	4,779
Net cash flows from investing activities	(4,264)
Net cash flows from financing activities	571
Net increase in cash	1,086

The market price of Enron's stock was approximately $83 per share when the prior financial statement data was taken. Before it went bankrupt, Enron's stock sold for $0.22 per share.

Review the preceding financial statement data and search the Internet for articles on Enron Corporation. Briefly explain why Enron's stock dropped so dramatically.

CHAPTER 2

AP Photo/Paul Sakuma

Analyzing Transactions

Apple, Inc.™

Everyday it seems like we get an incredible amount of incoming e-mail messages; you get them from your friends, relatives, subscribed e-mail lists, and even spammers! But how do you organize all of these messages? You might create folders to sort messages by sender, topic, or project. Perhaps you use keyword search utilities. You might even use filters/rules to automatically delete spam or send messages from your best friend to a special folder. In any case, you are organizing information so that it is simple to retrieve and allows you to understand, respond, or refer to the messages.

In the same way that you organize your e-mail, companies develop an organized method for processing, recording, and summarizing financial transactions. For example, **Apple, Inc.**, has a huge volume of financial transactions, resulting from sales of its innovative computers, digital media (iTunes), iPods, iPhones, and iPads. When Apple sells an iPad, a customer has the option of paying with credit card, a debit or check card, an Apple gift card, a financing arrangement, or cash. In order to analyze only the information related to Apple's cash transactions, the company must record or summarize all these similar sales using a single category or "cash" account. Similarly, Apple will record credit card payments for iPads and sales from financing arrangements in different accounts (records).

While Chapter 1 uses the accounting equation (Assets = Liabilities + Owner's Equity) to analyze and record financial transactions, this chapter presents more practical and efficient recording methods that most companies use. In addition, this chapter discusses possible accounting errors that may occur, along with methods to detect and correct them.

Learning Objectives

After studying this chapter, you should be able to:

At a Glance 2 Page 75

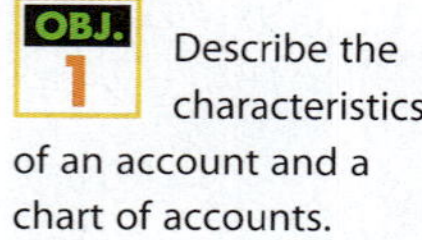

OBJ. 1 Describe the characteristics of an account and a chart of accounts.

Using Accounts to Record Transactions

In Chapter 1, the November transactions for NetSolutions were recorded using the accounting equation format shown in Exhibit 1. However, this format is not efficient or practical for companies that have to record thousands or millions of transactions daily. As a result, accounting systems are designed to show the increases and decreases in each accounting equation element as a separate record. This record is called an **account**.

To illustrate, the Cash column of Exhibit 1 records the increases and decreases in cash. Likewise, the other columns in Exhibit 1 record the increases and decreases in the other accounting equation elements. Each of these columns can be organized into a separate account.

An account, in its simplest form, has three parts.

1. A title, which is the name of the accounting equation element recorded in the account.
2. A space for recording increases in the amount of the element.
3. A space for recording decreases in the amount of the element.

The account form presented below is called a **T account** because it resembles the letter T. The left side of the account is called the *debit* side, and the right side is called the *credit* side.[1]

Title	
Left side *debit*	Right side *credit*

1 The terms *debit* and *credit* are derived from the Latin *debere* and *credere*.

EXHIBIT 1 NetSolutions November Transactions

	Assets			= Liabilities +	Owner's Equity							
	Cash +	Supp. +	Land =	Accounts Payable +	Chris Clark, Capital –	Chris Clark, Drawing +	Fees Earned –	Wages Exp. –	Rent Exp. –	Supplies Exp. –	Utilities Exp. –	Misc. Exp.
a.	+25,000				+25,000							
b.	–20,000		+20,000									
Bal.	5,000		20,000		25,000							
c.		+1,350		+1,350								
Bal.	5,000	1,350	20,000	1,350	25,000							
d.	+7,500						+7,500					
Bal.	12,500	1,350	20,000	1,350	25,000		7,500					
e.	–3,650							–2,125	–800		–450	–275
Bal.	8,850	1,350	20,000	1,350	25,000		7,500	–2,125	–800		–450	–275
f.	–950			–950								
Bal.	7,900	1,350	20,000	400	25,000		7,500	–2,125	–800		–450	–275
g.		–800								–800		
Bal.	7,900	550	20,000	400	25,000		7,500	–2,125	–800	–800	–450	–275
h.	–2,000					–2,000						
Bal.	5,900	550	20,000	400	25,000	–2,000	7,500	–2,125	–800	–800	–450	–275

The amounts shown in the Cash column of Exhibit 1 would be recorded in a cash account as follows:

Note: Amounts entered on the left side of an account are debits, and amounts entered on the right side of an account are credits.

Cash

Debit Side of Account	(a)	25,000	(b)	20,000	Credit Side of Account
	(d)	7,500	(e)	3,650	
			(f)	950	
			(h)	2,000	
	Balance	5,900			

Balance of account → 5,900

Recording transactions in accounts must follow certain rules. For example, increases in assets are recorded on the **debit** (left side) of an account. Likewise, decreases in assets are recorded on the **credit** (right side) of an account. The excess of the debits of an asset account over its credits is the **balance of the account.**

To illustrate, the receipt (increase in Cash) of $25,000 in transaction (a) is entered on the debit (left) side of the cash account shown above. The letter or date of the transaction is also entered into the account. This is done so if any questions later arise related to the entry, the entry can be traced back to the underlying transaction data. In contrast, the payment (decrease in Cash) of $20,000 to purchase land in transaction (b) is entered on the credit (right) side of the account.

The balance of the cash account of $5,900 is the excess of the debits over the credits as shown below.

Debits ($25,000 + $7,500)	$32,500
Less credits ($20,000 + $3,650 + $950 + $2,000)	26,600
Balance of Cash as of November 30, 2011	$ 5,900

The balance of the cash account is inserted in the account, in the Debit column. In this way, the balance is identified as a debit balance.[2] This balance represents NetSolutions' cash on hand as of November 30, 2011. This balance of $5,900 is reported on the November 30, 2011, balance sheet for NetSolutions as shown in Exhibit 6 of Chapter 1.

2 The totals of the debit and credit columns may be shown separately in an account. When this is done, these amounts should be identified in some way so that they are not mistaken for entries or the ending balance of the account.

In an actual accounting system, a more formal account form replaces the T account. Later in this chapter, a four-column account is illustrated. The T account, however, is a simple way to illustrate the effects of transactions on accounts and financial statements. For this reason, T accounts are often used in business to explain transactions.

Each of the columns in Exhibit 1 can be converted into an account form in a similar manner as was done for the Cash column of Exhibit 1. However, as mentioned earlier, recording increases and decreases in accounts must follow certain rules. These rules are discussed after the chart of accounts is described.

Chart of Accounts

A group of accounts for a business entity is called a **ledger**. A list of the accounts in the ledger is called a **chart of accounts**. The accounts are normally listed in the order in which they appear in the financial statements. The balance sheet accounts are listed first, in the order of assets, liabilities, and owner's equity. The income statement accounts are then listed in the order of revenues and expenses.

Assets are resources owned by the business entity. These resources can be physical items, such as cash and supplies, or intangibles that have value. Examples of intangible assets include patent rights, copyrights, and trademarks. Assets also include accounts receivable, prepaid expenses (such as insurance), buildings, equipment, and land.

Liabilities are debts owed to outsiders (creditors). Liabilities are often identified on the balance sheet by titles that include *payable*. Examples of liabilities include accounts payable, notes payable, and wages payable. Cash received before services are delivered creates a liability to perform the services. These future service commitments are called *unearned revenues*. Examples of unearned revenues include magazine subscriptions received by a publisher and tuition received at the beginning of a term by a college.

Owner's equity is the owner's right to the assets of the business after all liabilities have been paid. For a proprietorship, the owner's equity is represented by the balance of the owner's **capital account**. A **drawing** account represents the amount of withdrawals made by the owner.

Revenues are increases in owner's equity as a result of selling services or products to customers. Examples of revenues include fees earned, fares earned, commissions revenue, and rent revenue.

BusinessConnection

THE HIJACKING RECEIVABLE

A company's chart of accounts should reflect the basic nature of its operations. Occasionally, however, transactions take place that give rise to unusual accounts. The following is a story of one such account.

Before strict airport security was implemented across the United States, several airlines experienced hijacking incidents. One such incident occurred when a Southern Airways DC-9 en route from Memphis to Miami was hijacked during a stopover in Birmingham, Alabama. The three hijackers boarded the plane in Birmingham armed with handguns and hand grenades. At gunpoint, the hijackers took the plane, the plane's crew, and the passengers to nine American cities, Toronto, and eventually to Havana, Cuba.

During the long flight, the hijackers demanded a ransom of $10 million. Southern Airways, however, was only able to come up with $2 million. Eventually, the pilot talked the hijackers into settling for the $2 million when the plane landed in Chattanooga for refueling.

Upon landing in Havana, the Cuban authorities arrested the hijackers and, after a brief delay, sent the plane, passengers, and crew back to the United States. The hijackers and $2 million stayed in Cuba.

How did Southern Airways account for and report the hijacking payment in its subsequent financial statements? As you might have analyzed, the initial entry credited Cash for $2 million. The debit was to an account entitled "Hijacking Payment." This account was reported as a type of receivable under "other assets" on Southern's balance sheet. The company maintained that it would be able to collect the cash from the Cuban government and that, therefore, a receivable existed. In fact, Southern Airways was repaid $2 million by the Cuban government, which was, at that time, attempting to improve relations with the United States.

Expenses result from using up assets or consuming services in the process of generating revenues. Examples of expenses include wages expense, rent expense, utilities expense, supplies expense, and miscellaneous expense.

A chart of accounts should meet the needs of a company's managers and other users of its financial statements. The accounts within the chart of accounts are numbered for use as references. A numbering system is normally used, so that new accounts can be added without affecting other account numbers.

Exhibit 2 is NetSolutions' chart of accounts that is used in this chapter. Additional accounts will be introduced in later chapters. In Exhibit 2, each account number has two digits. The first digit indicates the major account group of the ledger in which the account is located. Accounts beginning with 1 represent assets; 2, liabilities; 3, owner's equity; 4, revenue; and 5, expenses. The second digit indicates the location of the account within its group.

Procter & Gamble's account numbers have over 30 digits to reflect P&G's many different operations and regions.

EXHIBIT 2

Chart of Accounts for NetSolutions

Balance Sheet Accounts	Income Statement Accounts
1. Assets	**4. Revenue**
11 Cash	41 Fees Earned
12 Accounts Receivable	**5. Expenses**
14 Supplies	51 Wages Expense
15 Prepaid Insurance	52 Rent Expense
17 Land	54 Utilities Expense
18 Office Equipment	55 Supplies Expense
2. Liabilities	59 Miscellaneous Expense
21 Accounts Payable	
23 Unearned Rent	
3. Owner's Equity	
31 Chris Clark, Capital	
32 Chris Clark, Drawing	

Each of the columns in Exhibit 1 has been assigned an account number in the chart of accounts shown in Exhibit 2. In addition, Accounts Receivable, Prepaid Insurance, Office Equipment, and Unearned Rent have been added. These accounts will be used in recording NetSolutions' December transactions.

Double-Entry Accounting System

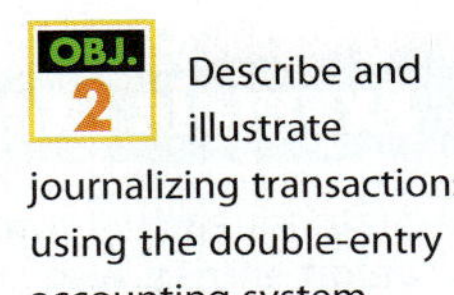

OBJ. 2 Describe and illustrate journalizing transactions using the double-entry accounting system.

All businesses use what is called the **double-entry accounting system**. This system is based on the accounting equation and requires:

1. Every business transaction to be recorded in at least two accounts.
2. The total debits recorded for each transaction to be equal to the total credits recorded.

The double-entry accounting system also has specific **rules of debit and credit** for recording transactions in the accounts.

Balance Sheet Accounts

The debit and credit rules for balance sheet accounts are as follows:

Balance Sheet Accounts

ASSETS Asset Accounts		=	LIABILITIES Liability Accounts		+	OWNER'S EQUITY Owner's Equity Accounts	
Debit for increases (+)	Credit for decreases (–)		Debit for decreases (–)	Credit for increases (+)		Debit for decreases (–)	Credit for increases (+)

Income Statement Accounts

The debit and credit rules for income statement accounts are based on their relationship with owner's equity. As shown on page 55, owner's equity accounts are increased by credits. Since revenues increase owner's equity, revenue accounts are increased by credits and decreased by debits. Since owner's equity accounts are decreased by debits, expense accounts are increased by debits and decreased by credits. Thus, the rules of debit and credit for revenue and expense accounts are as follows:

Income Statement Accounts			
Revenue Accounts		Expense Accounts	
Debit for decreases (−)	Credit for increases (+)	Debit for increases (+)	Credit for decreases (−)

Owner Withdrawals

The debit and credit rules for recording owner withdrawals are based on the effect of owner withdrawals on owner's equity. Since owner's withdrawals decrease owner's equity, the owner's drawing account is increased by debits. Likewise, the owner's drawing account is decreased by credits. Thus, the rules of debit and credit for the owner's drawing account are as follows:

Drawing Account	
Debit for increases (+)	Credit for decreases (−)

Normal Balances

The sum of the increases in an account is usually equal to or greater than the sum of the decreases in the account. Thus, the **normal balance of an account** is either a debit or credit depending on whether increases in the account are recorded as debits or credits. For example, since asset accounts are increased with debits, asset accounts normally have debit balances. Likewise, liability accounts normally have credit balances.

The rules of debit and credit and the normal balances of the various types of accounts are summarized in Exhibit 3. Debits and credits are sometimes abbreviated as Dr. for debit and Cr. for credit.

When an account normally having a debit balance has a credit balance, or vice versa, an error may have occurred or an unusual situation may exist. For example, a credit balance in the office equipment account could result only from an error. This

Example Exercise 2-1 Rules of Debit and Credit and Normal Balances

OBJ. 2

State for each account whether it is likely to have (a) debit entries only, (b) credit entries only, or (c) both debit and credit entries. Also, indicate its normal balance.

1. Amber Saunders, Drawing
2. Accounts Payable
3. Cash
4. Fees Earned
5. Supplies
6. Utilities Expense

Follow My Example 2-1

1. Debit entries only; normal debit balance
2. Debit and credit entries; normal credit balance
3. Debit and credit entries; normal debit balance
4. Credit entries only; normal credit balance
5. Debit and credit entries; normal debit balance
6. Debit entries only; normal debit balance

Practice Exercises: PE 2-1A, PE 2-1B

EXHIBIT 3 Rules of Debit and Credit, Normal Balances of Accounts

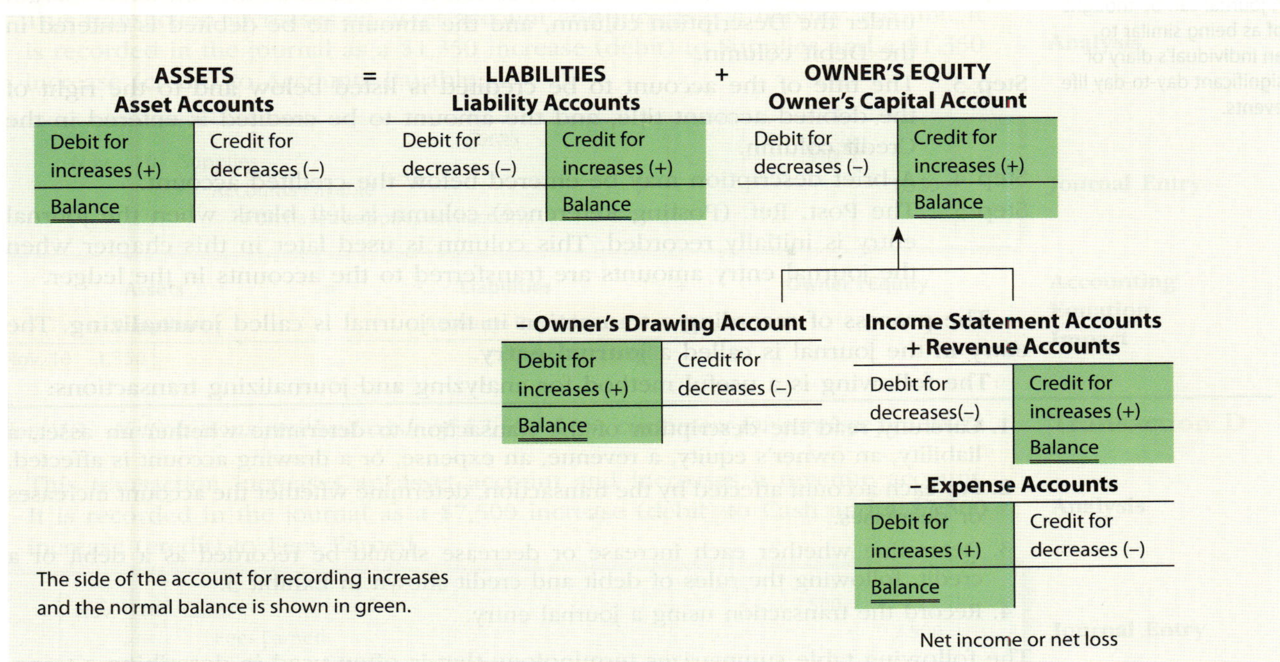

is because a business cannot have more decreases than increases of office equipment. On the other hand, a debit balance in an accounts payable account could result from an overpayment.

Journalizing

Using the rules of debit and credit, transactions are initially entered in a record called a **journal**. In this way, the journal serves as a record of when transactions occurred and were recorded. To illustrate, the November transactions of NetSolutions from Chapter 1 are used.

Nov. 1 Chris Clark deposited $25,000 in a bank account in the name of NetSolutions. **Transaction A**

Analysis

This transaction increases an asset account and increases an owner's equity account. It is recorded in the journal as an increase (debit) to Cash and an increase (credit) to Chris Clark, Capital.

Journal Entry

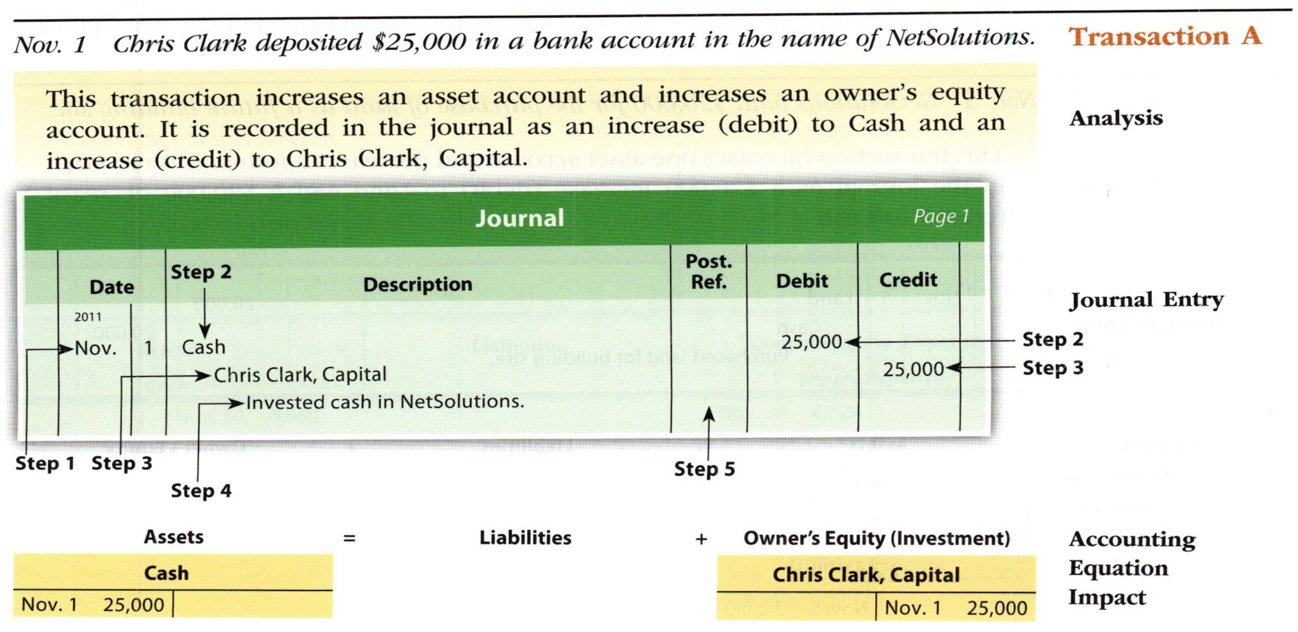

Accounting Equation Impact

Transaction F *Nov. 30 NetSolutions paid creditors on account, $950.*

Analysis

This transaction decreases a liability account and decreases an asset account. It is recorded in the journal as a $950 decrease (debit) to Accounts Payable and a $950 decrease (credit) to Cash.

Journal Entry

Date		Description	Post. Ref.	Debit	Credit
Nov.	30	Accounts Payable		950	
		Cash			950
		Paid creditors on account.			

Accounting Equation Impact

Assets = Liabilities + Owner's Equity

Cash	
	Nov. 30 950

Accounts Payable	
Nov. 30 950	

Transaction G *Nov. 30 Chris Clark determined that the cost of supplies on hand at November 30 was $550.*

Analysis

NetSolutions purchased $1,350 of supplies on November 10. Thus, $800 ($1,350 – $550) of supplies must have been used during November. This transaction is recorded in the journal as an $800 increase (debit) to Supplies Expense and an $800 decrease (credit) to Supplies.

Journal Entry

Date		Description	Post. Ref.	Debit	Credit
Nov.	30	Supplies Expense		800	
		Supplies			800
		Supplies used during November.			

Accounting Equation Impact

Assets = Liabilities + Owner's Equity (Expense)

Supplies	
	Nov. 30 800

Supplies Expense	
Nov. 30 800	

Transaction H *Nov. 30 Chris Clark withdrew $2,000 from NetSolutions for personal use.*

Analysis

This transaction decreases assets and owner's equity. This transaction is recorded in the journal as a $2,000 increase (debit) to Chris Clark, Drawing and a $2,000 decrease (credit) to Cash.

Journal Entry

Journal *Page 2*

Date		Description	Post. Ref.	Debit	Credit
2011					
Nov.	30	Chris Clark, Drawing		2,000	
		Cash			2,000
		Chris Clark withdrew cash for personal use.			

Accounting Equation Impact

Assets = Liabilities + Owner's Equity (Drawing)

Cash	
	Nov. 30 2,000

Chris Clark, Drawing	
Nov. 30 2,000	

Integrity, Objectivity, and Ethics in Business

WILL JOURNALIZING PREVENT FRAUD?

While journalizing transactions reduces the possibility of fraud, it by no means eliminates it. For example, embezzlement can be hidden within the double-entry bookkeeping system by creating fictitious suppliers to whom checks are issued.

Example Exercise 2-2 Journal Entry for Asset Purchase OBJ. 2

Prepare a journal entry for the purchase of a truck on June 3 for $42,500, paying $8,500 cash and the remainder on account.

Follow My Example 2-2

June 3	Truck	42,500	
	Cash		8,500
	Accounts Payable		34,000

Practice Exercises: **PE 2-2A, PE 2-2B**

Posting Journal Entries to Accounts

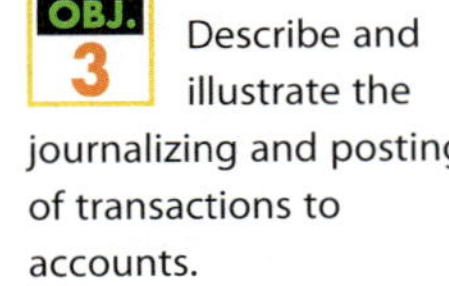

OBJ. 3 Describe and illustrate the journalizing and posting of transactions to accounts.

As illustrated, a transaction is first recorded in a journal. Periodically, the journal entries are transferred to the accounts in the ledger. The process of transferring the debits and credits from the journal entries to the accounts is called **posting**.

The December transactions of NetSolutions are used to illustrate posting from the journal to the ledger. By using the December transactions, an additional review of analyzing and journalizing transactions is provided.

Transaction

Dec. 1 NetSolutions paid a premium of $2,400 for an insurance policy for liability, theft, and fire. The policy covers a one-year period.

Analysis

Advance payments of expenses, such as for insurance premiums, are called prepaid expenses. Prepaid expenses are assets. For NetSolutions, the asset purchased is insurance protection for 12 months. This transaction is recorded as a $2,400 increase (debit) to Prepaid Insurance and a $2,400 decrease (credit) to Cash.

Journal Entry

Date		Description	Post. Ref.	Debit	Credit
Dec.	1	Prepaid Insurance	15	2,400	
		Cash	11		2,400
		Paid premium on one-year policy.			

Accounting Equation Impact

Assets = **Liabilities** + **Owner's Equity**

Cash	**11**
	Dec. 1 2,400

Prepaid Insurance	**15**
Dec. 1 2,400	

The posting of the preceding December 1 transaction is shown in Exhibit 4. Notice that the T account form is not used in Exhibit 4. In practice, the T account is usually replaced with a standard account form similar to that shown in Exhibit 4.

The debits and credits for each journal entry are posted to the accounts in the order in which they occur in the journal. To illustrate, the debit portion of the December 1 journal entry is posted to the prepaid account in Exhibit 4 using the following four steps:

Step 1. The date (Dec. 1) of the journal entry is entered in the Date column of Prepaid Insurance.

EXHIBIT 4 **Diagram of the Recording and Posting of a Debit and a Credit**

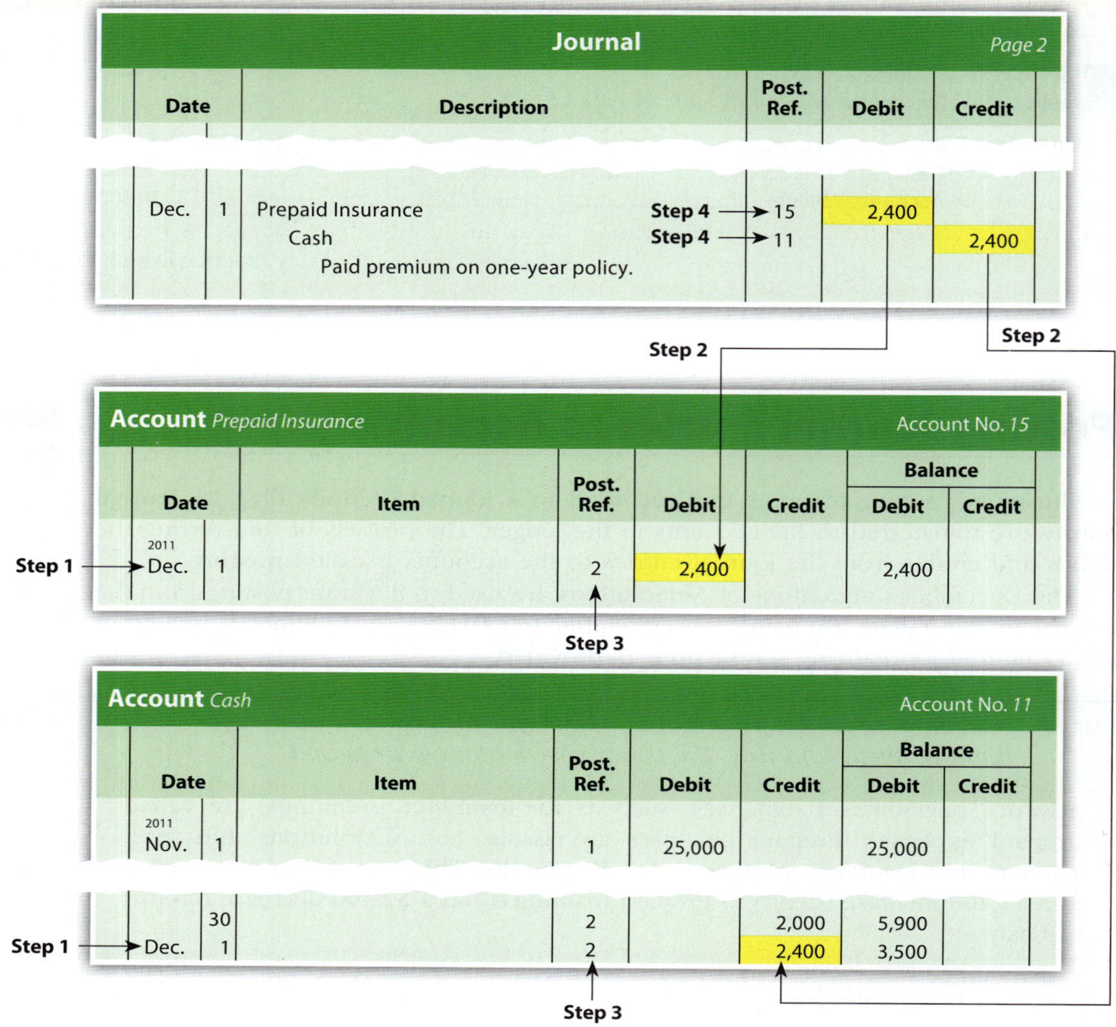

Step 2. The amount (2,400) is entered into the Debit column of Prepaid Insurance.

Step 3. The journal page number (2) is entered in the Posting Reference (Post. Ref.) column of Prepaid Insurance.

Step 4. The account number (15) is entered in the Posting Reference (Post. Ref.) column in the journal.

As shown in Exhibit 4, the credit portion of the December 1 journal entry is posted to the cash account in a similar manner.

The remaining December transactions for NetSolutions are analyzed and journalized in the following paragraphs. These transactions are posted to the ledger in Exhibit 5 on pages 69–70. To simplify, some of the December transactions are stated in summary form. For example, cash received for services is normally recorded on a daily basis. However, only summary totals are recorded at the middle and end of the month for NetSolutions.

Dec. 1 NetSolutions paid rent for December, $800. The company from which NetSolutions is renting its store space now requires the payment of rent on the first of each month, rather than at the end of the month.	**Transaction**

Analysis

The advance payment of rent is an asset, much like the advance payment of the insurance premium in the preceding transaction. However, unlike the insurance premium, this prepaid rent will expire in one month. When an asset is purchased with the expectation that it will be used up in a short period of time, such as a month, it is normal to debit an expense account initially. This avoids having to transfer the balance from an asset account (Prepaid Rent) to an expense account (Rent Expense) at the end of the month. Thus, this transaction is recorded as an $800 increase (debit) to Rent Expense and an $800 decrease (credit) to Cash.

Journal Entry

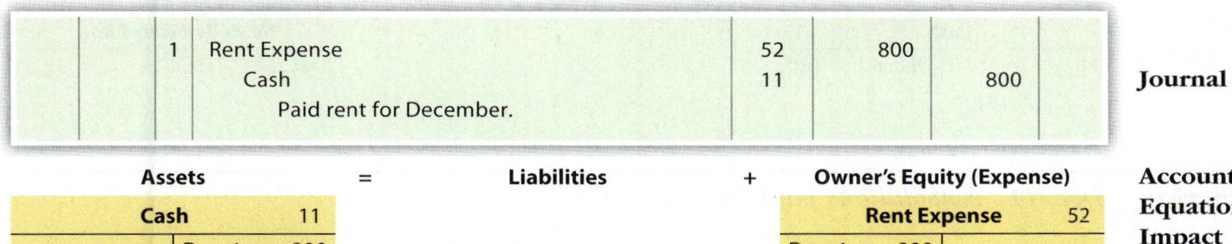

	1	Rent Expense	52	800	
		Cash	11		800
		Paid rent for December.			

Accounting Equation Impact

Assets	=	Liabilities	+	Owner's Equity (Expense)
Cash 11				**Rent Expense** 52
	Dec. 1 800				Dec. 1 800	

Dec. 1 NetSolutions received an offer from a local retailer to rent the land purchased on November 5. The retailer plans to use the land as a parking lot for its employees and customers. NetSolutions agreed to rent the land to the retailer for three months, with the rent payable in advance. NetSolutions received $360 for three months' rent beginning December 1.	**Transaction**

Analysis

By agreeing to rent the land and accepting the $360, NetSolutions has incurred an obligation (liability) to the retailer. This obligation is to make the land available for use for three months and not to interfere with its use. The liability created by receiving the cash in advance of providing the service is called **unearned revenue**. As time passes, the unearned rent liability will decrease and will become revenue. Thus, this transaction is recorded as a $360 increase (debit) to Cash and a $360 increase (credit) to Unearned Rent.

Journal Entry

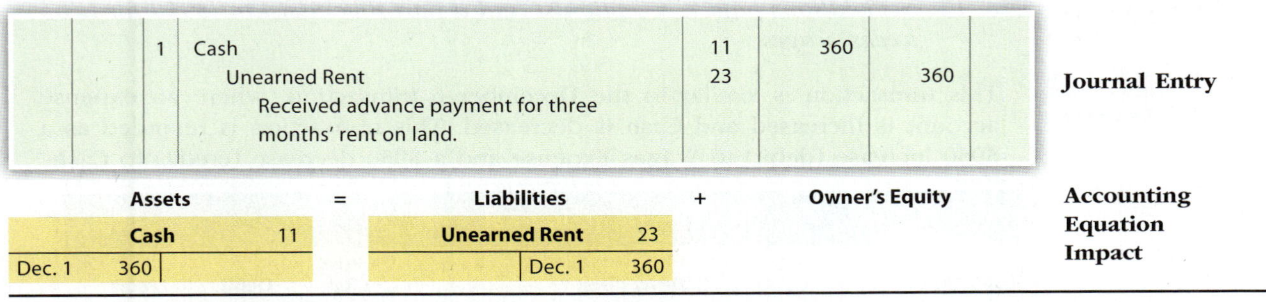

	1	Cash	11	360	
		Unearned Rent	23		360
		Received advance payment for three months' rent on land.			

Accounting Equation Impact

Assets	=	Liabilities	+	Owner's Equity
Cash 11		**Unearned Rent** 23		
Dec. 1 360				Dec. 1 360		

Dec. 4 NetSolutions purchased office equipment on account from Executive Supply Co. for $1,800.	**Transaction**

Analysis

The asset (Office Equipment) and liability accounts (Accounts Payable) increase. This transaction is recorded as a $1,800 increase (debit) to Office Equipment and a $1,800 increase (credit) to Accounts Payable.

Journal Entry

	4	Office Equipment	18	1,800	
		Accounts Payable	21		1,800
		Purchased office equipment on account.			

Accounting Equation Impact

Assets	=	Liabilities	+	Owner's Equity
Office Equipment 18		**Accounts Payable** 21		
Dec. 4 1,800				Dec. 4 1,800		

Transaction *Dec. 6 NetSolutions paid $180 for a newspaper advertisement.*

Analysis

An expense increases and an asset (Cash) decreases. Expense items that are expected to be minor in amount are normally included as part of the miscellaneous expense. This transaction is recorded as a $180 increase (debit) to Miscellaneous Expense and a $180 decrease (credit) to Cash.

Journal Entry

		Description	Post. Ref.	Debit	Credit
	6	Miscellaneous Expense	59	180	
		Cash	11		180
		Paid for newspaper advertisement.			

Accounting Equation Impact

Assets	=	Liabilities	+	Owner's Equity (Expense)
Cash 11: Dec. 6 180 (credit)				**Miscellaneous Exp.** 59: Dec. 6 180 (debit)

Transaction *Dec. 11 NetSolutions paid creditors $400.*

Analysis

A liability (Accounts Payable) and an asset (Cash) decrease. This transaction is recorded as a $400 decrease (debit) to Accounts Payable and a $400 decrease (credit) to Cash.

Journal Entry

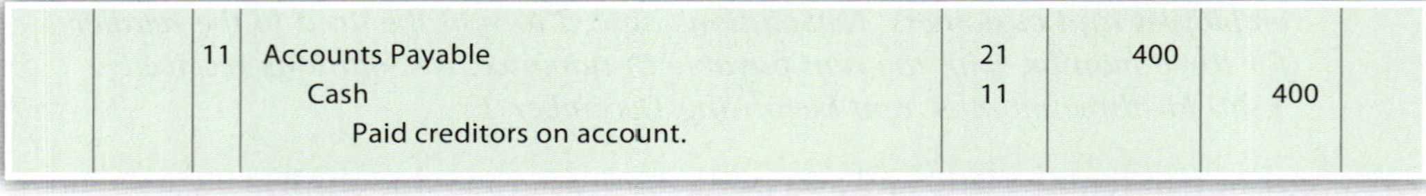

		Description	Post. Ref.	Debit	Credit
	11	Accounts Payable	21	400	
		Cash	11		400
		Paid creditors on account.			

Accounting Equation Impact

Assets	=	Liabilities	+	Owner's Equity
Cash 11: Dec. 11 400 (credit)		**Accounts Payable** 21: Dec. 11 400 (debit)		

Transaction *Dec. 13 NetSolutions paid a receptionist and a part-time assistant $950 for two weeks' wages.*

Analysis

This transaction is similar to the December 6 transaction, where an expense account is increased and Cash is decreased. This transaction is recorded as a $950 increase (debit) to Wages Expense and a $950 decrease (credit) to Cash.

Journal Entry

Journal *Page 3*

Date		Description	Post. Ref.	Debit	Credit
2011					
Dec.	13	Wages Expense	51	950	
		Cash	11		950
		Paid two weeks' wages.			

Accounting Equation Impact

Assets	=	Liabilities	+	Owner's Equity (Expense)
Cash 11: Dec. 13 950 (credit)				**Wages Expense** 51: Dec. 13 950 (debit)

Business Connection

COMPUTERIZED ACCOUNTING SYSTEMS

Computerized accounting systems are widely used by even the smallest of companies. These systems simplify the record keeping process in that transactions are recorded in electronic forms. Forms used to bill customers for services provided are often completed using drop down menus that list services that are normally provided to customers. An auto-complete entry feature may also be used to fill in customer names. For example, type "ca" to display customers with names beginning with "Ca" (Caban, Cahill, Carey, and Caswell). And, to simplify data entry, entries are automatically posted to the ledger accounts when the electronic form is completed.

One popular accounting software package used by small- to medium-sized businesses is QuickBooks®. Some examples of using QuickBooks to record accounting transactions are illustrated and discussed in Chapter 5.

Transaction

Dec. 16 NetSolutions received $3,100 from fees earned for the first half of December.

Analysis

An asset account (Cash) and a revenue account (Fees Earned) increase. This transaction is recorded as a $3,100 increase (debit) to Cash and a $3,100 increase (credit) to Fees Earned.

Journal Entry

	16	Cash	11	3,100	
		Fees Earned	41		3,100
		Received fees from customers.			

Accounting Equation Impact

Assets = Liabilities + Owner's Equity (Revenue)

Cash	11
Dec. 16 3,100	

Fees Earned	41
	Dec. 16 3,100

Transaction

Dec. 16 Fees earned on account totaled $1,750 for the first half of December.

Analysis

When a business agrees that a customer may pay for services provided at a later date, an **account receivable** is created. An account receivable is a claim against the customer. An account receivable is an asset, and the revenue is earned even though no cash has been received. Thus, this transaction is recorded as a $1,750 increase (debit) to Accounts Receivable and a $1,750 increase (credit) to Fees Earned.

Journal Entry

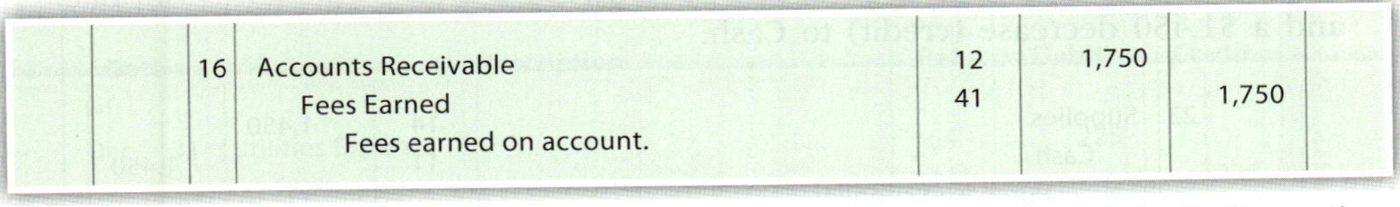

	16	Accounts Receivable	12	1,750	
		Fees Earned	41		1,750
		Fees earned on account.			

Accounting Equation Impact

Assets = Liabilities + Owner's Equity (Revenue)

Accounts Receivable	12
Dec. 16 1,750	

Fees Earned	41
	Dec. 16 1,750

Example Exercise 2-3 Journal Entry for Fees Earned

OBJ. 3

Prepare a journal entry on August 7 for the fees earned on account, $115,000.

Follow My Example 2-3

Aug. 7	Accounts Receivable	115,000	
	Fees Earned		115,000

Practice Exercises: **PE 2-3A, PE 2-3B**

Cash 11

Dec. 31 2,870

Dec. 31 2,870

Impact

Transaction *Dec. 31 Fees earned on account totaled $1,120 for the second half of December.*

Analysis

This is similar to the transaction of December 16. This transaction is recorded as a $1,120 increase (debit) to Accounts Receivable and a $1,120 increase (credit) to Fees Earned.

Journal Entry

31	Accounts Receivable	12	1,120	
	Fees Earned	41		1,120
	Fees earned on account.			

Accounting Equation Impact

Assets = Liabilities + Owner's Equity (Revenue)

Accounts Receivable 12	
Dec. 31 1,120	

Fees Earned 41	
	Dec. 31 1,120

Transaction *Dec. 31 Chris Clark withdrew $2,000 for personal use.*

Analysis

This transaction decreases owner's equity and assets. This transaction is recorded as a $2,000 increase (debit) to Chris Clark, Drawing and a $2,000 decrease (credit) to Cash.

Journal Entry

31	Chris Clark, Drawing	32	2,000	
	Cash	11		2,000
	Chris Clark withdrew cash for personal use.			

Accounting Equation Impact

Assets = Liabilities + Owner's Equity (Drawing)

Cash 11	
	Dec. 31 2,000

Chris Clark, Drawing 32	
Dec. 31 2,000	

Example Exercise 2-4 Journal Entry for Owner's Withdrawal

OBJ. 3

Prepare a journal entry on December 29 for the payment of $12,000 to the owner of Smartstaff Consulting Services, Dominique Walsh, for personal use.

Follow My Example 2-4

Dec. 29	Dominique Walsh, Drawing	12,000	
	Cash		12,000

Practice Exercises: **PE 2-4A, PE 2-4B**

Example Exercise 2-5 Missing Amount from an Account

OBJ. 3

On March 1, the cash account balance was $22,350. During March, cash receipts totaled $241,880 and the March 31 balance was $19,125. Determine the cash payments made during March.

Follow My Example 2-5

Using the following T account, solve for the amount of cash payments (indicated by ? below).

Cash			
Mar. 1 Bal.	22,350	?	Cash payments
Cash receipts	241,880		
Mar. 31 Bal.	19,125		

$19,125 = $22,350 + $241,880 – Cash payments

Cash payments = $22,350 + $241,880 – $19,125 = $245,105

Practice Exercises: **PE 2-5A, PE 2-5B**

Exhibit 5 shows the ledger for NetSolutions after the transactions for both November and December have been posted.

EXHIBIT 5 Ledger NetSolutions

Ledger

Account *Cash* Account No. *11*

Date	Item	Post. Ref.	Debit	Credit	Balance Debit	Balance Credit
2011						
Nov. 1		1	25,000		25,000	
5		1		20,000	5,000	
18		1	7,500		12,500	
30		1		3,650	8,850	
30		1		950	7,900	
30		2		2,000	5,900	
Dec. 1		2		2,400	3,500	
1		2		800	2,700	
1		2	360		3,060	
6		2		180	2,880	
11		2		400	2,480	
13		3		950	1,530	
16		3	3,100		4,630	
20		3		900	3,730	
21		3	650		4,380	
23		3		1,450	2,930	
27		3		1,200	1,730	
31		3		310	1,420	
31		4		225	1,195	
31		4	2,870		4,065	
31		4		2,000	2,065	

Account *Accounts Receivable* Account No. *12*

Date	Item	Post. Ref.	Debit	Credit	Balance Debit	Balance Credit
2011						
Dec. 16		3	1,750		1,750	
21		3		650	1,100	
31		4	1,120		2,220	

Account *Supplies* Account No. *14*

Date	Item	Post. Ref.	Debit	Credit	Balance Debit	Balance Credit
2011						
Nov. 10		1	1,350		1,350	
30		1		800	550	
Dec. 23		3	1,450		2,000	

Account *Prepaid Insurance* Account No. *15*

Date	Item	Post. Ref.	Debit	Credit	Balance Debit	Balance Credit
2011						
Dec. 1		2	2,400		2,400	

Account *Land* Account No. *17*

Date	Item	Post. Ref.	Debit	Credit	Balance Debit	Balance Credit
2011						
Nov. 5		1	20,000		20,000	

Account *Office Equipment* Account No. *18*

Date	Item	Post. Ref.	Debit	Credit	Balance Debit	Balance Credit
2011						
Dec. 4		2	1,800		1,800	

Account *Accounts Payable* Account No. *21*

Date	Item	Post. Ref.	Debit	Credit	Balance Debit	Balance Credit
2011						
Nov. 10		1		1,350		1,350
30		1	950			400
Dec. 4		2		1,800		2,200
11		2	400			1,800
20		3	900			900

Account *Unearned Rent* Account No. *23*

Date	Item	Post. Ref.	Debit	Credit	Balance Debit	Balance Credit
2011						
Dec. 1		2		360		360

Account *Chris Clark, Capital* Account No. *31*

Date	Item	Post. Ref.	Debit	Credit	Balance Debit	Balance Credit
2011						
Nov. 1		1		25,000		25,000

Account *Chris Clark, Drawing* Account No. *32*

Date	Item	Post. Ref.	Debit	Credit	Balance Debit	Balance Credit
2011						
Nov. 30		2	2,000		2,000	
Dec. 31		4	2,000		4,000	

(continued)

EXHIBIT 5 **Ledger NetSolutions *(concluded)***

Account *Fees Earned* — Account No. *41*

Date	Item	Post. Ref.	Debit	Credit	Balance Debit	Balance Credit
2011						
Nov. 18		1		7,500		7,500
Dec. 16		3		3,100		10,600
16		3		1,750		12,350
31		4		2,870		15,220
31		4		1,120		16,340

Account *Wages Expense* — Account No. *51*

Date	Item	Post. Ref.	Debit	Credit	Balance Debit	Balance Credit
2011						
Nov. 30		1	2,125		2,125	
Dec. 13		3	950		3,075	
27		3	1,200		4,275	

Account *Rent Expense* — Account No. *52*

Date	Item	Post. Ref.	Debit	Credit	Balance Debit	Balance Credit
2011						
Nov. 30		1	800		800	
Dec. 1		2	800		1,600	

Account *Utilities Expense* — Account No. *54*

Date	Item	Post. Ref.	Debit	Credit	Balance Debit	Balance Credit
2011						
Nov. 30		1	450		450	
Dec. 31		3	310		760	
31		4	225		985	

Account *Supplies Expense* — Account No. *55*

Date	Item	Post. Ref.	Debit	Credit	Balance Debit	Balance Credit
2011						
Nov. 30		1	800		800	

Account *Miscellaneous Expense* — Account No. *59*

Date	Item	Post. Ref.	Debit	Credit	Balance Debit	Balance Credit
2011						
Nov. 30		1	275		275	
Dec. 6		2	180		455	

OBJ. 4 Prepare an unadjusted trial balance and explain how it can be used to discover errors.

Trial Balance

Errors may occur in posting debits and credits from the journal to the ledger. One way to detect such errors is by preparing a **trial balance**. Double-entry accounting requires that debits must always equal credits. The trial balance verifies this equality. The steps in preparing a trial balance are as follows:

Step 1. List the name of the company, the title of the trial balance, and the date the trial balance is prepared.
Step 2. List the accounts from the ledger and enter their debit or credit balance in the Debit or Credit column of the trial balance.
Step 3. Total the Debit and Credit columns of the trial balance.
Step 4. Verify that the total of the Debit column equals the total of the Credit column.

The trial balance for NetSolutions as of December 31, 2011, is shown in Exhibit 6. The account balances in Exhibit 6 are taken from the ledger shown in Exhibit 5. Before a trial balance is prepared, each account balance in the ledger must be determined. When the standard account form is used as in Exhibit 5, the balance of each account appears in the balance column on the same line as the last posting to the account.

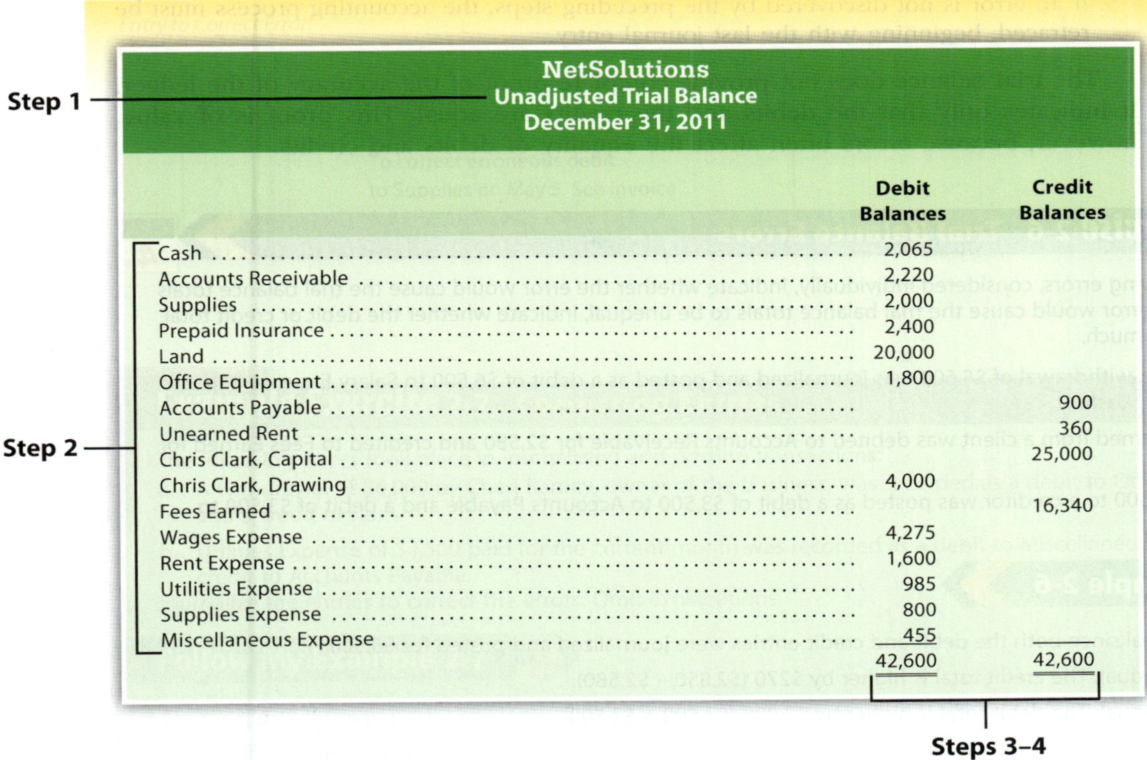

NetSolutions
Unadjusted Trial Balance
December 31, 2011

	Debit Balances	Credit Balances
Cash	2,065	
Accounts Receivable	2,220	
Supplies	2,000	
Prepaid Insurance	2,400	
Land	20,000	
Office Equipment	1,800	
Accounts Payable		900
Unearned Rent		360
Chris Clark, Capital		25,000
Chris Clark, Drawing	4,000	
Fees Earned		16,340
Wages Expense	4,275	
Rent Expense	1,600	
Utilities Expense	985	
Supplies Expense	800	
Miscellaneous Expense	455	
	42,600	42,600

EXHIBIT 6

Trial Balance

The trial balance shown in Exhibit 6 is titled an **unadjusted trial balance**. This is to distinguish it from other trial balances that will be prepared in later chapters. These other trial balances include an adjusted trial balance and a post-closing trial balance.[3]

Errors Affecting the Trial Balance

If the trial balance totals are not equal, an error has occurred. In this case, the error must be found and corrected. A method useful in discovering errors is as follows:

1. If the difference between the Debit and Credit column totals is 10, 100, or 1,000, an error in addition may have occurred. In this case, re-add the trial balance column totals. If the error still exists, recompute the account balances.
2. If the difference between the Debit and Credit column totals can be evenly divisible by 2, the error may be due to the entering of a debit balance as a credit balance, or vice versa. In this case, review the trial balance for account balances of one-half the difference that may have been entered in the wrong column. For example, if the Debit column total is $20,640 and the Credit column total is $20,236, the difference of $404 ($20,640 – $20,236) may be due to a credit account balance of $202 that was entered as a debit account balance.
3. If the difference between the Debit and Credit column totals is evenly divisible by 9, trace the account balances back to the ledger to see if an account balance was incorrectly copied from the ledger. Two common types of copying errors are transpositions and slides. A **transposition** occurs when the order of the digits is copied incorrectly, such as writing $542 as $452 or $524. In a **slide**, the entire number is copied incorrectly one or more spaces to the right or the left, such as writing $542.00 as $54.20 or $5,420.00. In both cases, the resulting error will be evenly divisible by 9.
4. If the difference between the Debit and Credit column totals is not evenly divisible by 2 or 9, review the ledger to see if an account balance in the amount of the error has been omitted from the trial balance. If the error is not discovered, review the journal postings to see if a posting of a debit or credit may have been omitted.

3 The adjusted trial balance is discussed in Chapter 3, and the post-closing trial balance is discussed in Chapter 4.

OBJ. 2 Describe and illustrate journalizing transactions using the double-entry accounting system.

Key Points Transactions are initially entered in a record called a journal. The rules of debit and credit for recording increases or decreases in accounts are shown in Exhibit 3. Each transaction is recorded so that the sum of the debits is always equal to the sum of the credits. The normal balance of an account is indicated by the side of the account (debit or credit) that receives the increases.

Learning Outcomes	Example Exercises	Practice Exercises
• Indicate the normal balance of an account.	EE2-1	PE2-1A, 2-1B
• Journalize transactions using the rules of debit and credit.	EE2-2	PE2-2A, 2-2B

OBJ. 3 Describe and illustrate the journalizing and posting of transactions to accounts.

Key Points Transactions are journalized and posted to the ledger using the rules of debit and credit. The debits and credits for each journal entry are posted to the accounts in the order in which they occur in the journal.

Learning Outcomes	Example Exercises	Practice Exercises
• Journalize transactions using the rules of debit and credit.	EE2-3	PE2-3A, 2-3B
• Given other account data, determine the missing amount of an account entry.	EE2-4	PE2-4A, 2-4B
• Post journal entries to a standard account.	EE2-5	PE2-5A, 2-5B
• Post journal entries to a T account.		

OBJ. 4 Prepare an unadjusted trial balance and explain how it can be used to discover errors.

Key Points A trial balance is prepared by listing the accounts from the ledger and their balances. The totals of the Debit column and Credit column of the trial balance must be equal. If the two totals are not equal, an error has occurred. Errors may occur even though the trial balance totals are equal. Such errors may require a correcting journal entry.

Learning Outcomes	Example Exercises	Practice Exercises
• Prepare an unadjusted trial balance.		
• Discover errors that cause unequal totals in the trial balance.	EE2-6	PE2-6A, 2-6B
• Prepare correcting journal entries for various errors.	EE2-7	PE2-7A, 2-7B

Describe and illustrate the use of horizontal analysis in evaluating a company's performance and financial condition.

Key Points In horizontal analysis, the amount of each item on a current financial statement is compared with the same item on an earlier statement. The increase or decrease in the *amount* of the item is computed together with the *percent* of increase or decrease. When two statements are being compared, the earlier statement is used as the base for computing the amount and the percent of change.

Learning Outcomes	Example Exercises	Practice Exercises
• Describe horizontal analysis.		
• Prepare a horizontal analysis report of a financial statement.	EE2-8	PE2-8A, 2-8B

Key Terms

account (52)
account receivable (65)
assets (54)
balance of the account (53)
capital account (54)
chart of accounts (54)
correcting journal entry (72)
credit (53)
debit (53)
double-entry accounting system (55)
drawing (54)
expenses (55)
horizontal analysis (73)
journal (57)
journal entry (58)
journalizing (58)
ledger (54)
liabilities (54)
normal balance of an account (56)
owner's equity (54)
posting (61)
revenues (54)
rules of debit and credit (55)
slide (71)
T account (52)
transposition (71)
trial balance (70)
unadjusted trial balance (71)
unearned revenue (63)

Illustrative Problem

J. F. Outz, M.D., has been practicing as a cardiologist for three years. During April 2011, Outz completed the following transactions in her practice of cardiology:

Apr. 1. Paid office rent for April, $800.
3. Purchased equipment on account, $2,100.
5. Received cash on account from patients, $3,150.
8. Purchased X-ray film and other supplies on account, $245.
9. One of the items of equipment purchased on April 3 was defective. It was returned with the permission of the supplier, who agreed to reduce the account for the amount charged for the item, $325.
12. Paid cash to creditors on account, $1,250.

Apr. 17. Paid cash for renewal of a six-month property insurance policy, $370.

20. Discovered that the balances of the cash account and the accounts payable account as of April 1 were overstated by $200. A payment of that amount to a creditor in March had not been recorded. Journalize the $200 payment as of April 20.

24. Paid cash for laboratory analysis, $545.

27. Paid cash from business bank account for personal and family expenses, $1,250.

30. Recorded the cash received in payment of services (on a cash basis) to patients during April, $1,720.

30. Paid salaries of receptionist and nurses, $1,725.

30. Paid various utility expenses, $360.

30. Recorded fees charged to patients on account for services performed in April, $5,145.

30. Paid miscellaneous expenses, $132.

Outz's account titles, numbers, and balances as of April 1 (all normal balances) are listed as follows: Cash, 11, $4,123; Accounts Receivable, 12, $6,725; Supplies, 13, $290; Prepaid Insurance, 14, $465; Equipment, 18, $19,745; Accounts Payable, 22, $765; J. F. Outz, Capital, 31, $30,583; J. F. Outz, Drawing, 32, $0; Professional Fees, 41, $0; Salary Expense, 51, $0; Rent Expense, 53, $0; Laboratory Expense, 55, $0; Utilities Expense, 56, $0; Miscellaneous Expense, 59, $0.

Instructions

1. Open a ledger of standard four-column accounts for Dr. Outz as of April 1. Enter the balances in the appropriate balance columns and place a check mark (✓) in the Posting Reference column. (*Hint:* Verify the equality of the debit and credit balances in the ledger before proceeding with the next instruction.)
2. Journalize each transaction in a two-column journal.
3. Post the journal to the ledger, extending the month-end balances to the appropriate balance columns after each posting.
4. Prepare an unadjusted trial balance as of April 30.

Solution 1., 2., and 3.

Journal Page 27

Date	Description	Post. Ref.	Debit	Credit
2011				
Apr. 1	Rent Expense	53	800	
	Cash	11		800
	Paid office rent for April.			
3	Equipment	18	2,100	
	Accounts Payable	22		2,100
	Purchased equipment on account.			
5	Cash	11	3,150	
	Accounts Receivable	12		3,150
	Received cash on account.			
8	Supplies	13	245	
	Accounts Payable	22		245
	Purchased supplies.			
9	Accounts Payable	22	325	
	Equipment	18		325
	Returned defective equipment.			
12	Accounts Payable	22	1,250	
	Cash	11		1,250
	Paid creditors on account.			
17	Prepaid Insurance	14	370	
	Cash	11		370
	Renewed six-month property policy.			
20	Accounts Payable	22	200	
	Cash	11		200
	Recorded March payment to creditor.			

Journal Page 28

Date	Description	Post. Ref.	Debit	Credit
2011				
Apr. 24	Laboratory Expense	55	545	
	Cash	11		545
	Paid for laboratory analysis.			
27	J. F. Outz, Drawing	32	1,250	
	Cash	11		1,250
	J. F. Outz withdrew cash for personal use.			
30	Cash	11	1,720	
	Professional Fees	41		1,720
	Received fees from patients.			
30	Salary Expense	51	1,725	
	Cash	11		1,725
	Paid salaries.			
30	Utilities Expense	56	360	
	Cash	11		360
	Paid utilities.			
30	Accounts Receivable	12	5,145	
	Professional Fees	41		5,145
	Recorded fees earned on account.			
30	Miscellaneous Expense	59	132	
	Cash	11		132
	Paid expenses.			

Account *Cash* Account No. *11*

					Balance	
Date	Item	Post. Ref.	Debit	Credit	Debit	Credit
2011						
Apr. 1	Balance	✓			4,123	
1		27		800	3,323	
5		27	3,150		6,473	
12		27		1,250	5,223	
17		27		370	4,853	
20		27		200	4,653	
24		28		545	4,108	
27		28		1,250	2,858	
30		28	1,720		4,578	
30		28		1,725	2,853	
30		28		360	2,493	
30		28		132	2,361	

Account *Accounts Receivable* Account No. *12*

					Balance	
Date	Item	Post. Ref.	Debit	Credit	Debit	Credit
2011						
Apr. 1	Balance	✓			6,725	
5		27		3,150	3,575	
30		28	5,145		8,720	

Account *Supplies* Account No. *13*

					Balance	
Date	Item	Post. Ref.	Debit	Credit	Debit	Credit
2011						
Apr. 1	Balance	✓			290	
8		27	245		535	

Account *Prepaid Insurance* — Account No. *14*

Date	Item	Post. Ref.	Debit	Credit	Balance Debit	Balance Credit
2011						
Apr. 1	Balance	✓			465	
17		27	370		835	

Account *Equipment* — Account No. *18*

Date	Item	Post. Ref.	Debit	Credit	Balance Debit	Balance Credit
2011						
Apr. 1	Balance	✓			19,745	
3		27	2,100		21,845	
9		27		325	21,520	

Account *Accounts Payable* — Account No. *22*

Date	Item	Post. Ref.	Debit	Credit	Balance Debit	Balance Credit
2011						
Apr. 1	Balance	✓				765
3		27		2,100		2,865
8		27		245		3,110
9		27	325			2,785
12		27	1,250			1,535
20		27	200			1,335

Account *J. F. Outz, Capital* — Account No. *31*

Date	Item	Post. Ref.	Debit	Credit	Balance Debit	Balance Credit
2011						
Apr. 1	Balance	✓				30,583

Account *J. F. Qutz, Drawing* — Account No. *32*

Date	Item	Post. Ref.	Debit	Credit	Balance Debit	Balance Credit
2011						
Apr. 27		28	1,250		1,250	

Account *Professional Fees* — Account No. *41*

Date	Item	Post. Ref.	Debit	Credit	Balance Debit	Balance Credit
2011						
Apr. 30		28		1,720		1,720
30		28		5,145		6,865

Account *Salary Expense* — Account No. *51*

Date	Item	Post. Ref.	Debit	Credit	Balance Debit	Balance Credit
2011						
Apr. 30		28	1,725		1,725	

Account *Rent Expense* — Account No. *53*

Date	Item	Post. Ref.	Debit	Credit	Balance Debit	Balance Credit
2011						
Apr. 1		27	800		800	

Account *Laboratory Expense* — Account No. *55*

Date	Item	Post. Ref.	Debit	Credit	Balance Debit	Balance Credit
2011						
Apr. 24		28	545		545	

Account *Utilities Expanse* — Account No. *56*

Date	Item	Post. Ref.	Debit	Credit	Balance Debit	Balance Credit
2011						
Apr. 30		28	360		360	

Account *Miscellaneous Expense* — Account No. *59*

Date	Item	Post. Ref.	Debit	Credit	Balance Debit	Balance Credit
2011						
Apr. 30		28	132		132	

4.

J. F. Outz, M.D.
Unadjusted Trial Balance
April 30, 2011

	Debit Balances	Credit Balances
Cash	2,361	
Accounts Receivable	8,720	
Supplies	535	
Prepaid Insurance	835	
Equipment	21,520	
Accounts Payable		1,335
J. F. Outz, Capital		30,583
J. F. Outz, Drawing	1,250	
Professional Fees		6,865
Salary Expense	1,725	
Rent Expense	800	
Laboratory Expense	545	
Utilities Expense	360	
Miscellaneous Expense	132	
	38,783	38,783

Discussion Questions

1. What is the difference between an account and a ledger?
2. Do the terms *debit* and *credit* signify increase or decrease or can they signify either? Explain.
3. Weir Company adheres to a policy of depositing all cash receipts in a bank account and making all payments by check. The cash account as of December 31 has a credit balance of $3,190, and there is no undeposited cash on hand. (a) Assuming no errors occurred during journalizing or posting, what caused this unusual balance? (b) Is the $3,190 credit balance in the cash account an asset, a liability, owner's equity, a revenue, or an expense?
4. Resource Services Company performed services in February for a specific customer, for a fee of $11,250. Payment was received the following March. (a) Was the revenue earned in February or March? (b) What accounts should be debited and credited in (1) February and (2) March?
5. If the two totals of a trial balance are equal, does it mean that there are no errors in the accounting records? Explain.
6. Assume that a trial balance is prepared with an account balance of $21,740 listed as $2,174 and an account balance of $4,500 listed as $5,400. Identify the transposition and the slide.
7. Assume that when a purchase of supplies of $3,100 for cash was recorded, both the debit and the credit were journalized and posted as $1,300. (a) Would this error cause the trial balance to be out of balance? (b) Would the trial balance be out of balance if the $3,100 entry had been journalized correctly but the credit to Cash had been posted as $1,300?
8. Assume that Timberline Consulting erroneously recorded the payment of $9,000 of owner withdrawals as a debit to Salary Expense. (a) How would this error affect the equality of the trial balance? (b) How would this error affect the income statement, statement of owner's equity, and balance sheet?
9. Assume that Western Realty Co. borrowed $200,000 from Mountain First Bank and Trust. In recording the transaction, Western erroneously recorded the receipt as a debit to Cash, $200,000, and a credit to Fees Earned, $200,000. (a) How would this error affect the equality of the trial balance? (b) How would this error affect the income statement, statement of owner's equity, and balance sheet?
10. Checking accounts are the most common form of deposits for banks. Assume that Village Storage has a checking account at Camino Savings Bank. What type of account (asset, liability, owner's equity, revenue, expense, drawing) does the account balance of $8,750 represent from the viewpoint of (a) Village Storage and (b) Camino Savings Bank?

Practice Exercises

Learning Objectives	Example Exercises	
OBJ. 2	EE 2-1 p. 56	**PE 2-1A Rules of debit and credit and normal balances**

State for each account whether it is likely to have (a) debit entries only, (b) credit entries only, or (c) both debit and credit entries. Also, indicate its normal balance.

1. Accounts Receivable
2. Commissions Earned
3. Notes Payable
4. Paul Howe, Capital
5. Rent Revenue
6. Wages Expense

OBJ. 2 EE 2-1 p. 56

PE 2-1B Rules of debit and credit and normal balances

State for each account whether it is likely to have (a) debit entries only, (b) credit entries only, or (c) both debit and credit entries. Also, indicate its normal balance.

1. Accounts Payable
2. Cash
3. Malissa Wahl, Drawing
4. Miscellaneous Expense
5. Insurance Expense
6. Fees Earned

OBJ. 2 EE 2-2 p. 61

PE 2-2A Journal entry for asset purchase

Prepare a journal entry for the purchase of office equipment on March 4 for $27,150, paying $5,000 cash and the remainder on account.

OBJ. 2 EE 2-2 p. 61

PE 2-2B Journal entry for asset purchase

Prepare a journal entry for the purchase of office supplies on August 7 for $4,000, paying $1,000 cash and the remainder on account.

OBJ. 3 EE 2-3 p. 65

PE 2-3A Journal entry for fees earned

Prepare a journal entry on September 6 for fees earned on account, $8,000.

OBJ. 3 EE 2-3 p. 65

PE 2-3B Journal entry for fees earned

Prepare a journal entry on May 29 for cash received for services rendered, $5,000.

OBJ. 3 EE 2-4 p. 68

PE 2-4A Journal entry for owner's withdrawal

Prepare a journal entry on December 22 for the withdrawal of $10,000 by Jason Von Pentz for personal use.

OBJ. 3 EE 2-4 p. 68

PE 2-4B Journal entry for owner's withdrawal

Prepare a journal entry on February 3 for the withdrawal of $7,500 by Allene Collette for personal use.

Learning Objectives	Example Exercises

OBJ. 3 EE 2-5 p. 68

PE 2-5A Missing amount from an account

On June 1, the cash account balance was $17,200. During June, cash payments totaled $178,300, and the June 30 balance was $23,900. Determine the cash receipts during June.

OBJ. 3 EE 2-5 p. 68

PE 2-5B Missing amount from an account

On October 1, the supplies account balance was $900. During October, supplies of $2,750 were purchased, and $1,025 of supplies were on hand as of October 31. Determine supplies expense for October.

OBJ. 4 EE 2-6 p. 72

PE 2-6A Trial balance errors

For each of the following errors, considered individually, indicate whether the error would cause the trial balance totals to be unequal. If the error would cause the trial balance totals to be unequal, indicate whether the debit or credit total is higher and by how much.

a. The payment of an insurance premium of $4,800 for a two-year policy was debited to Prepaid Insurance for $4,800 and credited to Cash for $8,400.

b. A payment of $318 on account was debited to Accounts Payable for $381 and credited to Cash for $381.

c. A purchase of supplies on account for $1,200 was debited to Supplies for $1,200 and debited to Accounts Payable for $1,200.

OBJ. 4 EE 2-6 p. 72

PE 2-6B Trial balance errors

For each of the following errors, considered individually, indicate whether the error would cause the trial balance totals to be unequal. If the error would cause the trial balance totals to be unequal, indicate whether the debit or credit total is higher and by how much.

a. The payment of cash for the purchase of office equipment of $15,000 was debited to Land for $15,000 and credited to Cash for $15,000.

b. The payment of $5,200 on account was debited to Accounts Payable for $520 and credited to Cash for $5,200.

c. The receipt of cash on account of $1,270 was recorded as a debit to Cash for $1,720 and a credit to Accounts Receivable for $1,270.

OBJ. 4 EE 2-7 p. 73

PE 2-7A Correcting entries

The following errors took place in journalizing and posting transactions:

a. Advertising expense of $2,700 paid for the current month was recorded as a debit to Miscellaneous Expense and a credit to Advertising Expense.

b. The payment of $3,950 from a customer on account was recorded as a debit to Cash and a credit to Accounts Payable.

Journalize the entries to correct the errors. Omit explanations.

OBJ. 4 EE 2-7 p. 73

PE 2-7B Correcting entries

The following errors took place in journalizing and posting transactions:

a. The receipt of $5,800 for services rendered was recorded as a debit to Accounts Receivable and a credit to Fees Earned.

b. The purchase of supplies of $1,800 on account was recorded as a debit to Office Equipment and a credit to Supplies.

Journalize the entries to correct the errors. Omit explanations.

OBJ. 5 EE 2-8 p. 75

PE 2-8A Horizontal analysis

Two income statements for Boyer Company are shown on the following page.

Learning Objectives | Example Exercises

Boyer Company
Income Statements
For Years Ended December 31

	2012	2011
Fees earned	$315,000	$300,000
Operating expenses	176,400	180,000
Net income	$138,600	$120,000

Prepare a horizontal analysis of Boyer Company's income statements.

OBJ. 5 EE 2-8 p. 75

PE 2-8B Horizontal analysis

Two income statements for Hitt Company are shown below.

Hitt Company
Income Statements
For Years Ended December 31

	2012	2011
Fees earned	$937,500	$750,000
Operating expenses	612,500	500,000
Net income	$325.000	$250,000

Prepare a horizontal analysis of Hitt Company's income statements.

Exercises

OBJ. 1

EX 2-1 Chart of accounts

The following accounts appeared in recent financial statements of Continental Airlines:

Accounts Payable	Flight Equipment
Air Traffic Liability	Landing Fees (Expense)
Aircraft Fuel Expense	Passenger Revenue
Cargo and Mail Revenue	Purchase Deposits for Flight Equipment
Commissions (Expense)	Spare Parts and Supplies

Identify each account as either a balance sheet account or an income statement account. For each balance sheet account, identify it as an asset, a liability, or owner's equity. For each income statement account, identify it as a revenue or an expense.

OBJ. 1

EX 2-2 Chart of accounts

Innerscape Interiors is owned and operated by Jean Cartier, an interior decorator. In the ledger of Innerscape Interiors, the first digit of the account number indicates its major account classification (1—assets, 2—liabilities, 3—owner's equity, 4—revenues, 5—expenses). The second digit of the account number indicates the specific account within each of the preceding major account classifications.

Match each account number with its most likely account in the list below. The account numbers are 11, 12, 13, 21, 31, 32, 41, 51, 52, and 53.

Accounts Payable	Jean Cartier, Drawing
Accounts Receivable	Land
Cash	Miscellaneous Expense
Fees Earned	Supplies Expense
Jean Cartier, Capital	Wages Expense

OBJ. 1

EX 2-3 Chart of accounts

Alpha School is a newly organized business that teaches people how to inspire and influence others. The list of accounts to be opened in the general ledger is as follows:

Accounts Payable	Miscellaneous Expense
Accounts Receivable	Prepaid Insurance
Cash	Rent Expense
Equipment	Supplies
Fees Earned	Supplies Expense
Jan Pulver, Capital	Unearned Rent
Jan Pulver, Drawing	Wages Expense

List the accounts in the order in which they should appear in the ledger of Alpha School and assign account numbers. Each account number is to have two digits: the first digit is to indicate the major classification (1 for assets, etc.), and the second digit is to identify the specific account within each major classification (11 for Cash, etc.).

OBJ. 1,2

EX 2-4 Rules of debit and credit

The following table summarizes the rules of debit and credit. For each of the items (a) through (l), indicate whether the proper answer is a debit or a credit.

	Increase	Decrease	Normal Balance
Balance sheet accounts:			
Asset	(a)	Credit	(b)
Liability	Credit	(c)	(d)
Owner's equity:			
Capital	Credit	(e)	(f)
Drawing	(g)	(h)	(i)
Income statement accounts:			
Revenue	Credit	(j)	(k)
Expense	(l)	Credit	Debit

OBJ. 2

EX 2-5 Normal entries for accounts

During the month, Iris Labs Co. has a substantial number of transactions affecting each of the following accounts. State for each account whether it is likely to have (a) debit entries only, (b) credit entries only, or (c) both debit and credit entries.

1. Accounts Payable
2. Accounts Receivable
3. Cash
4. Fees Earned
5. Insurance Expense
6. Nicki Swanson, Drawing
7. Utilities Expense

OBJ. 1,2

EX 2-6 Normal balances of accounts

Identify each of the following accounts of Advanced Services Co. as asset, liability, owner's equity, revenue, or expense, and state in each case whether the normal balance is a debit or a credit.

a. Accounts Payable
b. Accounts Receivable
c. Barbara Mallary, Capital
d. Barbara Mallary, Drawing
e. Cash
f. Fees Earned
g. Office Equipment
h. Rent Expense
i. Supplies
j. Wages Expense

OBJ. 2

EX 2-7 Transactions

Chalet Co. has the following accounts in its ledger: Cash; Accounts Receivable; Supplies; Office Equipment; Accounts Payable; Andee Freese, Capital; Andee Freese, Drawing; Fees Earned; Rent Expense; Advertising Expense; Utilities Expense; Miscellaneous Expense.

Journalize the following selected transactions for October 2012 in a two-column journal. Journal entry explanations may be omitted.

Oct. 1. Paid rent for the month, $2,000.
2. Paid advertising expense, $900.
5. Paid cash for supplies, $1,300.
6. Purchased office equipment on account, $16,000.
10. Received cash from customers on account, $6,700.
15. Paid creditor on account, $1,200.
27. Paid cash for repairs to office equipment, $600.
30. Paid telephone bill for the month, $180.
31. Fees earned and billed to customers for the month, $26,800.
31. Paid electricity bill for the month, $400.
31. Withdrew cash for personal use, $3,000.

OBJ. 2,3

EX 2-8 Journalizing and posting

On February 3, 2012, Wilco Co. purchased $3,250 of supplies on account. In Wilco Co.'s chart of accounts, the supplies account is No. 15, and the accounts payable account is No. 21.

a. Journalize the February 3, 2012, transaction on page 19 of Wilco Co.'s two-column journal. Include an explanation of the entry.

b. Prepare a four-column account for Supplies. Enter a debit balance of $975 as of February 1, 2012. Place a check mark (✓) in the Posting Reference column.

c. Prepare a four-column account for Accounts Payable. Enter a credit balance of $13,150 as of February 1, 2012. Place a check mark (✓) in the Posting Reference column.

d. Post the February 3, 2012, transaction to the accounts.

e. Do the rules of debit and credit apply to all companies?

OBJ. 2,3

EX 2-9 Transactions and T accounts

The following selected transactions were completed during August of the current year:

1. Billed customers for fees earned, $35,700.
2. Purchased supplies on account, $2,000.
3. Received cash from customers on account, $26,150.
4. Paid creditors on account, $800.

a. Journalize the above transactions in a two-column journal, using the appropriate number to identify the transactions. Journal entry explanations may be omitted.

b. Post the entries prepared in (a) to the following T accounts: Cash, Supplies, Accounts Receivable, Accounts Payable, Fees Earned. To the left of each amount posted in the accounts, place the appropriate number to identify the transactions.

c. Assume that the unadjusted trial balance on August 31 shows a credit balance for Accounts Receivable. Does this credit balance mean an error has occurred?

OBJ. 1,2,3

EX 2-10 Cash account balance

During the month, Lathers Co. received $400,000 in cash and paid out $290,000 in cash.

a. Do the data indicate that Lathers Co. had net income of $110,000 during the month? Explain.

b. If the balance of the cash account is $185,000 at the end of the month, what was the cash balance at the beginning of the month?

OBJ. 1,2,3

✓ c. $284,175

EX 2-11 Account balances

a. During October, $90,000 was paid to creditors on account, and purchases on account were $125,000. Assuming the October 31 balance of Accounts Payable was $40,000, determine the account balance on October 1.

b. On May 1, the accounts receivable account balance was $25,000. During May, $240,000 was collected from customers on account. Assuming the May 31 balance was $36,000, determine the fees billed to customers on account during May.

c. On November 1, the cash account balance was $18,275. During November, cash receipts totaled $279,100 and the November 30 balance was $13,200. Determine the cash payments made during November.

OBJ. 1,2

EX 2-12 Capital account balance

As of January 1, Brenda Cikan, Capital, had a credit balance of $125,000. During the year, withdrawals totaled $7,000, and the business incurred a net loss of $130,000.

a. Compute the balance of Brenda Cikan, Capital, as of the end of the year.

b. Assuming that there have been no recording errors, will the balance sheet prepared at December 31 balance? Explain.

OBJ. 1,2

EX 2-13 Identifying transactions

Southwest Tours Co. is a travel agency. The nine transactions recorded by Southwest Tours during May 2012, its first month of operations, are indicated in the following T accounts:

Cash

	Debit		Credit
(1)	40,000	(2)	2,000
(7)	10,000	(3)	3,600
		(4)	2,700
		(6)	9,000
		(9)	4,000

Equipment

	Debit		Credit
(3)	18,000		

Mickey O'Dell, Drawing

	Debit		Credit
(9)	4,000		

Accounts Receivable

	Debit		Credit
(5)	18,500	(7)	10,000

Accounts Payable

	Debit		Credit
(6)	9,000	(3)	14,400

Service Revenue

	Debit		Credit
		(5)	18,500

Supplies

	Debit		Credit
(2)	2,000	(8)	1,050

Mickey O'Dell, Capital

	Debit		Credit
		(1)	40,000

Operating Expenses

	Debit		Credit
(4)	2,700		
(8)	1,050		

Indicate for each debit and each credit: (a) whether an asset, liability, owner's equity, drawing, revenue, or expense account was affected and (b) whether the account was increased (+) or decreased (–). Present your answers in the following form, with transaction (1) given as an example:

	Account Debited		Account Credited	
Transaction	Type	Effect	Type	Effect
(1)	asset	+	owner's equity	+

OBJ. 1,2

EX 2-14 Journal entries

Based upon the T accounts in Exercise 2-13, prepare the nine journal entries from which the postings were made. Journal entry explanations may be omitted.

OBJ. 4

✔ Total Debit column: $63,900

EX 2-15 Trial balance

Based upon the data presented in Exercise 2-13, (a) prepare an unadjusted trial balance, listing the accounts in their proper order. (b) Based upon the unadjusted trial balance, determine the net income or net loss.

OBJ. 4

✔ Total of Credit column: $491,400

EX 2-16 Trial balance

The accounts in the ledger of Diva Co. as of July 31, 2012, are listed in alphabetical order as follows. All accounts have normal balances. The balance of the cash account has been intentionally omitted.

Accounts Payable	$ 28,000	Notes Payable	$ 50,000
Accounts Receivable	40,000	Prepaid Insurance	6,400
Cash	?	Rent Expense	36,000
Cheryl Sievert, Capital	49,900	Supplies	4,000
Cheryl Sievert, Drawing	25,000	Supplies Expense	9,000
Fees Earned	350,000	Unearned Rent	13,500
Insurance Expense	6,000	Utilities Expense	18,000
Land	125,000	Wages Expense	195,000
Miscellaneous Expense	12,000		

Prepare an unadjusted trial balance, listing the accounts in their normal order and inserting the missing figure for cash.

OBJ. 4

EX 2-17 Effect of errors on trial balance

Indicate which of the following errors, each considered individually, would cause the trial balance totals to be unequal:

a. A fee of $15,000 earned and due from a client was not debited to Accounts Receivable or credited to a revenue account, because the cash had not been received.

b. A receipt of $6,000 from an account receivable was journalized and posted as a debit of $6,000 to Cash and a credit of $6,000 to Fees Earned.

c. A payment of $1,200 to a creditor was posted as a debit of $1,200 to Accounts Payable and a debit of $1,200 to Cash.

d. A payment of $10,000 for equipment purchased was posted as a debit of $1,000 to Equipment and a credit of $1,000 to Cash.

e. Payment of a cash withdrawal of $10,000 was journalized and posted as a debit of $1,000 to Salary Expense and a credit of $10,000 to Cash.

Indicate which of the preceding errors would require a correcting entry.

OBJ. 4

✔ Total of Credit column: $225,000

EX 2-18 Errors in trial balance

The following preliminary unadjusted trial balance of Seats-For-You Co., a sports ticket agency, does not balance:

Seats-For-You Co.
Unadjusted Trial Balance
March 31, 2012

	Debit Balances	Credit Balances
Cash	98,000	
Accounts Receivable	17,800	
Prepaid Insurance		9,000
Equipment	7,500	
Accounts Payable		16,500
Unearned Rent		11,600
Gina Ness, Capital	81,700	
Gina Ness, Drawing	13,000	
Service Revenue		125,000
Wages Expense		60,000
Advertising Expense	11,300	
Miscellaneous Expense		15,400
	229,300	237,500

When the ledger and other records are reviewed, you discover the following: (1) the debits and credits in the cash account total $98,000 and $82,500, respectively; (2) a billing of $8,000 to a customer on account was not posted to the accounts receivable account; (3) a payment of $3,600 made to a creditor on account was not posted to the accounts payable account; (4) the balance of the unearned rent account is $5,400; (5) the correct balance of the equipment account is $75,000; and (6) each account has a normal balance.

Prepare a corrected unadjusted trial balance.

OBJ. 4

EX 2-19 Effect of errors on trial balance

The following errors occurred in posting from a two-column journal:

1. A credit of $7,150 to Accounts Payable was not posted.
2. An entry debiting Accounts Receivable and crediting Fees Earned for $11,000 was not posted.
3. A debit of $1,000 to Accounts Payable was posted as a credit.
4. A debit of $800 to Supplies was posted twice.
5. A debit of $900 to Cash was posted to Miscellaneous Expense.
6. A credit of $360 to Cash was posted as $630.
7. A debit of $9,420 to Wages Expense was posted as $9,240.

Considering each case individually (i.e., assuming that no other errors had occurred), indicate: (a) by "yes" or "no" whether the trial balance would be out of balance; (b) if answer to (a) is "yes," the amount by which the trial balance totals would differ; and (c) whether the Debit or Credit column of the trial balance would have the larger total. Answers should be presented in the following form, with error (1) given as an example:

	(a)	(b)	(c)
Error	**Out of Balance**	**Difference**	**Larger Total**
1.	yes	$7,150	debit

OBJ. 4

✔ Total of Credit column: $750,000

EX 2-20 Errors in trial balance

Identify the errors in the following trial balance. All accounts have normal balances.

Bluefin Co.
Unadjusted Trial Balance
For the Month Ending August 31, 2012

	Debit Balances	Credit Balances
Cash	45,000	
Accounts Receivable		98,400
Prepaid Insurance	21,600	
Equipment	300,000	
Accounts Payable	11,100	
Salaries Payable		7,500
Ken Frye, Capital		259,200
Ken Frye, Drawing		36,000
Service Revenue		472,200
Salary Expense	196,860	
Advertising Expense		43,200
Miscellaneous Expense	8,940	
	916,500	916,500

OBJ. 4

EX 2-21 Entries to correct errors

The following errors took place in journalizing and posting transactions:

a. Rent of $12,500 paid for the current month was recorded as a debit to Rent Expense and a credit to Prepaid Rent.

b. A withdrawal of $7,500 by Trent Benedict, owner of the business, was recorded as a debit to Wages Expense and a credit to Cash.

Journalize the entries to correct the errors. Omit explanations.

OBJ. 4

EX 2-22 Entries to correct errors

The following errors took place in journalizing and posting transactions:

a. Cash of $12,975 received on account was recorded as a debit to Fees Earned and a credit to Cash.

b. A $3,200 purchase of supplies for cash was recorded as a debit to Supplies Expense and a credit to Accounts Payable.

Journalize the entries to correct the errors. Omit explanations.

OBJ. 5

EX 2-23 Horizontal analysis of income statement

The following data (in millions) is taken from the financial statements of Target Corporation.

	2009	2008
Net sales (revenues)	$64,948	$63,367
Total operating expenses	60,546	58,095

a. For Target Corporation, comparing 2009 with 2008, determine the amount of change in millions and the percent of change for:

1. Net sales (revenues)
2. Total operating expenses

b. What conclusions can you draw from your analysis of the net sales and the total operating expenses?

OBJ. 5

EX 2-24 Horizontal analysis of income statement

The following data were adapted from the financial statements of Kmart Corporation, prior to its filing for bankruptcy:

	In millions	
For years ending January 31	**2000**	**1999**
Sales	$ 37,028	$ 35,925
Cost of sales (expense)	(29,658)	(28,111)
Selling, general, and administrative expenses	(7,415)	(6,514)
Operating income (loss)	$ (45)	$ 1,300

a. Prepare a horizontal analysis for the income statement showing the amount and percent of change in each of the following:

1. Sales
2. Cost of sales
3. Selling, general, and administrative expenses
4. Operating income (loss)

b. Comment on the results of your horizontal analysis in part (a).

Problems Series A

OBJ. 1,2,3,4

✔ 3. Total of Debit column: $78,350

PR 2-1A Entries into T accounts and trial balance

Leila Durkin, an architect, opened an office on May 1, 2012. During the month, she completed the following transactions connected with her professional practice:

a. Transferred cash from a personal bank account to an account to be used for the business, $30,000.
b. Paid May rent for office and workroom, $3,500.
c. Purchased used automobile for $25,000, paying $5,000 cash and giving a note payable for the remainder.
d. Purchased office and computer equipment on account, $9,000.
e. Paid cash for supplies, $1,200.
f. Paid cash for annual insurance policies, $2,400.
g. Received cash from client for plans delivered, $8,150.
h. Paid cash for miscellaneous expenses, $300.
i. Paid cash to creditors on account, $2,500.
j. Paid installment due on note payable, $400.
k. Received invoice for blueprint service, due in June, $1,200.
l. Recorded fee earned on plans delivered, payment to be received in June, $12,900.
m. Paid salary of assistant, $1,800.
n. Paid gas, oil, and repairs on automobile for May, $600.

Instructions

1. Record the above transactions directly in the following T accounts, without journalizing: Cash; Accounts Receivable; Supplies; Prepaid Insurance; Automobiles; Equipment; Notes Payable; Accounts Payable; Leila Durkin, Capital; Professional Fees; Rent Expense; Salary Expense; Blueprint Expense; Automobile Expense; Miscellaneous Expense. To the left of the amount entered in the accounts, place the appropriate letter to identify the transaction.
2. Determine account balances of the T accounts. Accounts containing a single entry only (such as Prepaid Insurance) do not need a balance.
3. Prepare an unadjusted trial balance for Leila Durkin, Architect, as of May 31, 2012.
4. Determine the net income or net loss for May.

OBJ. 1,2,3,4

✔ 4. c. $8,550

PR 2-2A Journal entries and trial balance

On October 1, 2012, Faith Schultz established Heavenly Realty, which completed the following transactions during the month:

a. Faith Schultz transferred cash from a personal bank account to an account to be used for the business, $20,000.
b. Paid rent on office and equipment for the month, $3,750.
c. Purchased supplies on account, $1,100.
d. Paid creditor on account, $400.
e. Earned sales commissions, receiving cash, $16,750.
f. Paid automobile expenses (including rental charge) for month, $1,000, and miscellaneous expenses, $700.
g. Paid office salaries, $2,150.
h. Determined that the cost of supplies used was $600.
i. Withdrew cash for personal use, $1,000.

Instructions

1. Journalize entries for transactions (a) through (i), using the following account titles: Cash; Supplies; Accounts Payable; Faith Schultz, Capital; Faith Schultz, Drawing; Sales Commissions; Rent Expense; Office Salaries Expense; Automobile Expense; Supplies Expense; Miscellaneous Expense. Explanations may be omitted.
2. Prepare T accounts, using the account titles in (1). Post the journal entries to these accounts, placing the appropriate letter to the left of each amount to identify the transactions. Determine the account balances, after all posting is complete. Accounts containing only a single entry do not need a balance.
3. Prepare an unadjusted trial balance as of October 31, 2012.
4. Determine the following:
   a. Amount of total revenue recorded in the ledger.
   b. Amount of total expenses recorded in the ledger.
   c. Amount of net income for October.
5. Determine the increase or decrease in owner's equity for October.

OBJ. 1,2,3,4

✔ 3. Total of Credit column: $66,500

PR 2-3A Journal entries and trial balance

On April 1, 2012, Kathleen Alvarez established an interior decorating business, Intrex Designs. During the month, Kathleen completed the following transactions related to the business:

Apr. 1. Kathleen transferred cash from a personal bank account to an account to be used for the business, $17,000.
2. Paid rent for period of April 2 to end of month, $3,400.
6. Purchased office equipment on account, $10,000.
8. Purchased a used truck for $21,000, paying $2,000 cash and giving a note payable for the remainder.
10. Purchased supplies for cash, $1,800.
12. Received cash for job completed, $13,000.

Apr. 15. Paid annual premiums on property and casualty insurance, $1,800.

23. Recorded jobs completed on account and sent invoices to customers, $9,000.

24. Received an invoice for truck expenses, to be paid in April, $1,000.

Enter the following transactions on Page 2 of the two-column journal.

29. Paid utilities expense, $1,500.

29. Paid miscellaneous expenses, $750.

30. Received cash from customers on account, $7,800.

30. Paid wages of employees, $4,000.

30. Paid creditor a portion of the amount owed for equipment purchased on April 6, $2,500.

30. Withdrew cash for personal use, $2,000.

Instructions

1. Journalize each transaction in a two-column journal beginning on Page 1, referring to the following chart of accounts in selecting the accounts to be debited and credited. (Do not insert the account numbers in the journal at this time.) Explanations may be omitted.

11 Cash	31 Kathleen Alvarez, Capital
12 Accounts Receivable	32 Kathleen Alvarez, Drawing
13 Supplies	41 Fees Earned
14 Prepaid Insurance	51 Wages Expense
16 Equipment	53 Rent Expense
18 Truck	54 Utilities Expense
21 Notes Payable	55 Truck Expense
22 Accounts Payable	59 Miscellaneous Expense

2. Post the journal to a ledger of four-column accounts, inserting appropriate posting references as each item is posted. Extend the balances to the appropriate balance columns after each transaction is posted.
3. Prepare an unadjusted trial balance for Intrex Designs as of April 30, 2012.
4. Determine the excess of revenues over expenses for April.
5. Can you think of any reason why the amount determined in (4) might not be the net income for April?

OBJ. 1,2,3,4

✔ 4. Total of Debit column: $259,600

PR 2-4A Journal entries and trial balance

Utopia Realty acts as an agent in buying, selling, renting, and managing real estate. The unadjusted trial balance on October 31, 2012, is shown below.

Utopia Realty
Unadjusted Trial Balance
October 31, 2012

		Debit Balances	Credit Balances
11	Cash	13,150	
12	Accounts Receivable	30,750	
13	Prepaid Insurance	1,500	
14	Office Supplies	900	
16	Land	—	
21	Accounts Payable		7,000
22	Unearned Rent		—
23	Notes Payable		—
31	Ian Rogstad, Capital		23,000
32	Ian Rogstad, Drawing	1,000	
41	Fees Earned		120,000
51	Salary and Commission Expense	74,100	
52	Rent Expense	15,000	
53	Advertising Expense	8,900	
54	Automobile Expense	2,750	
59	Miscellaneous Expense	1,950	
		150,000	150,000

The following business transactions were completed by Utopia Realty during November 2012:

Nov. 1. Paid rent on office for month, $5,000.
2. Purchased office supplies on account, $1,300.
5. Paid annual insurance premiums, $3,600.
10. Received cash from clients on account, $25,000.
15. Purchased land for a future building site for $90,000, paying $10,000 in cash and giving a note payable for the remainder.
17. Paid creditors on account, $4,500.
20. Returned a portion of the office supplies purchased on November 2, receiving full credit for their cost, $200.
23. Paid advertising expense, $2,000.

Enter the following transactions on Page 19 of the two-column journal.

27. Discovered an error in computing a commission; received cash from the salesperson for the overpayment, $1,000.
28. Paid automobile expense (including rental charges for an automobile), $1,500.
29. Paid miscellaneous expenses, $450.
30. Recorded revenue earned and billed to clients during the month, $30,000.
30. Paid salaries and commissions for the month, $7,500.
30. Withdrew cash for personal use, $1,000.
30. Rented land purchased on November 15 to local merchants association for use as a parking lot in December and January, during a street rebuilding program; received advance payment of $3,000.

Instructions

1. Record the November 1, 2010, balance of each account in the appropriate balance column of a four-column account, write *Balance* in the item section, and place a check mark (✓) in the Posting Reference column.
2. Journalize the transactions for November in a two-column journal beginning on Page 18. Journal entry explanations may be omitted.
3. Post to the ledger, extending the account balance to the appropriate balance column after each posting.
4. Prepare an unadjusted trial balance of the ledger as of November 30, 2012.
5. Assume that the November 30 transaction for salaries and commissions should have been $5,700. (a) Why did the unadjusted trial balance in (4) balance? (b) Journalize the correcting entry. (c) Is this error a transposition or slide?

OBJ. 4

✔ **7. Total of Debit column: $43,338.10**

PR 2-5A Errors in trial balance

If the working papers correlating with this textbook are not used, omit Problem 2-5A.

The following records of A-Aall Electronic Repair are presented in the working papers:

- Journal containing entries for the period May 1–31.
- Ledger to which the May entries have been posted.
- Preliminary trial balance as of May 31, which does not balance.

Locate the errors, supply the information requested, and prepare a corrected trial balance according to the following instructions. The balances recorded in the accounts as of May 1 and the entries in the journal are correctly stated. If it is necessary to correct any posted amounts in the ledger, a line should be drawn through the erroneous figure and the correct amount inserted above. Corrections or notations may be inserted on the preliminary trial balance in any manner desired. It is not necessary to complete all of the instructions if equal trial balance totals can be obtained earlier. However, the requirements of instructions (6) and (7) should be completed in any event.

Instructions

1. Verify the totals of the preliminary trial balance, inserting the correct amounts in the schedule provided in the working papers.

(Continued)

2. Compute the difference between the trial balance totals.
3. Compare the listings in the trial balance with the balances appearing in the ledger, and list the errors in the space provided in the working papers.
4. Verify the accuracy of the balance of each account in the ledger, and list the errors in the space provided in the working papers.
5. Trace the postings in the ledger back to the journal, using small check marks to identify items traced. Correct any amounts in the ledger that may be necessitated by errors in posting, and list the errors in the space provided in the working papers.
6. Journalize as of May 31 the payment of $100 for advertising expense. The bill had been paid on May 31 but was inadvertently omitted from the journal. Post to the ledger. (Revise any amounts necessitated by posting this entry.)
7. Prepare a new unadjusted trial balance.

OBJ. 4

✔ 1. Total of Debit column: $1,400,000

PR 2-6A Corrected trial balance

Imperial Carpet has the following unadjusted trial balance as of March 31, 2012.

Imperial Carpet
Unadjusted Trial Balance
March 31, 2012

	Debit Balances	Credit Balances
Cash	38,200	
Accounts Receivable	81,000	
Supplies	16,690	
Prepaid Insurance	3,600	
Equipment	392,000	
Notes Payable		200,000
Accounts Payable		54,000
Leonardo Pepin, Capital		254,300
Leonardo Pepin, Drawing	116,000	
Fees Earned		858,900
Wages Expense	490,000	
Rent Expense	112,600	
Advertising Expense	50,400	
Miscellaneous Expense	10,200	
	1,310,690	508,300

The debit and credit totals are not equal as a result of the following errors:

a. The balance of cash was understated by $12,000.
b. A cash receipt of $13,900 was posted as a debit to Cash of $19,300.
c. A debit of $15,000 to Accounts Receivable was not posted.
d. A return of $90 of defective supplies was erroneously posted as a $900 credit to Supplies.
e. An insurance policy acquired at a cost of $2,500 was posted as a credit to Prepaid Insurance.
f. The balance of Notes Payable was understated by $35,200.
g. A credit of $7,600 in Accounts Payable was overlooked when determining the balance of the account.
h. A debit of $10,000 for a withdrawal by the owner was posted as a credit to Leonardo Pepin, Capital.
i. The balance of $116,200 in Rent Expense was entered as $112,600 in the trial balance.
j. Gas, Electricity, and Water Expense, with a balance of $48,300 was omitted from the trial balance.

Instructions

1. Prepare a corrected unadjusted trial balance as of March 31, 2012.
2. Does the fact that the unadjusted trial balance in (1) is balanced mean that there are no errors in the accounts? Explain.

Problems Series B

OBJ. 1,2,3

✔ 3. Total of Debit column: $74,700

PR 2-1B Entries into T accounts and trial balance

April Layton, an architect, opened an office on June 1, 2012. During the month, she completed the following transactions connected with her professional practice:

a. Transferred cash from a personal bank account to an account to be used for the business, $25,000.
b. Purchased used automobile for $24,000, paying $5,000 cash and giving a note payable for the remainder.
c. Paid June rent for office and workroom, $2,000.
d. Paid cash for supplies, $1,450.
e. Purchased office and computer equipment on account, $8,000.
f. Paid cash for annual insurance policies on automobile and equipment, $3,600.
g. Received cash from a client for plans delivered, $10,500.
h. Paid cash to creditors on account, $1,750.
i. Paid cash for miscellaneous expenses, $600.
j. Received invoice for blueprint service, due in July, $1,500.
k. Recorded fee earned on plans delivered, payment to be received in July, $12,800.
l. Paid salary of assistant, $1,600.
m. Paid cash for miscellaneous expenses, $200.
n. Paid installment due on note payable, $350.
o. Paid gas, oil, and repairs on automobile for June, $550.

Instructions

1. Record the above transactions directly in the following T accounts, without journalizing: Cash; Accounts Receivable; Supplies; Prepaid Insurance; Automobiles; Equipment; Notes Payable; Accounts Payable; April Layton, Capital; Professional Fees; Rent Expense; Salary Expense; Blueprint Expense; Automobile Expense; Miscellaneous Expense. To the left of each amount entered in the accounts, place the appropriate letter to identify the transaction.
2. Determine account balances of the T accounts. Accounts containing a single entry only (such as Prepaid Insurance) do not need a balance.
3. Prepare an unadjusted trial balance for April Layton, Architect, as of June 30, 2012.
4. Determine the net income or net loss for June.

OBJ. 1,2,3,4

✔ 4. c. $5,500

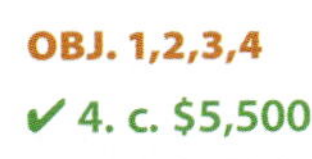

PR 2-2B Journal entries and trial balance

On March 1, 2012, Mitch Quade established Marine Realty, which completed the following transactions during the month:

a. Mitch Quade transferred cash from a personal bank account to an account to be used for the business, $18,000.
b. Purchased supplies on account, $1,200.
c. Earned sales commissions, receiving cash, $14,000.
d. Paid rent on office and equipment for the month, $3,000.
e. Paid creditor on account, $750.
f. Withdrew cash for personal use, $2,000.
g. Paid automobile expenses (including rental charge) for month, $1,500, and miscellaneous expenses, $400.
h. Paid office salaries, $2,800.
i. Determined that the cost of supplies used was $800.

Instructions

1. Journalize entries for transactions (a) through (i), using the following account titles: Cash; Supplies; Accounts Payable; Mitch Quade, Capital; Mitch Quade, Drawing; Sales Commissions; Rent Expense; Office Salaries Expense; Automobile Expense; Supplies Expense; Miscellaneous Expense. Journal entry explanations may be omitted.

(Continued)

2. Prepare T accounts, using the account titles in (1). Post the journal entries to these accounts, placing the appropriate letter to the left of each amount to identify the transactions. Determine the account balances, after all posting is complete. Accounts containing only a single entry do not need a balance.
3. Prepare an unadjusted trial balance as of March 31, 2012.
4. Determine the following:
   a. Amount of total revenue recorded in the ledger.
   b. Amount of total expenses recorded in the ledger.
   c. Amount of net income for March.
5. Determine the increase or decrease in owner's equity for March

---

OBJ. 1,2,3,4

✔ 3. Total of Credit column: $64,500

PR 2-3B Journal entries and trial balance

On July 1, 2012, Kim Wheeler established an interior decorating business, Aztec Designs. During the month, Kim completed the following transactions related to the business:

July 1. Kim transferred cash from a personal bank account to an account to be used for the business, $21,000.
4. Paid rent for period of July 4 to end of month, $2,750.
10. Purchased a used truck for $18,000, paying $4,000 cash and giving a note payable for the remainder.
13. Purchased equipment on account, $9,000.
14. Purchased supplies for cash, $1,500.
15. Paid annual premiums on property and casualty insurance, $3,600.
15. Received cash for job completed, $12,000.

Enter the following transactions on Page 2 of the two-column journal.

21. Paid creditor a portion of the amount owed for equipment purchased on July 13, $2,000.
24. Recorded jobs completed on account and sent invoices to customers, $9,800.
26. Received an invoice for truck expenses, to be paid in August, $700.
27. Paid utilities expense, $1,000.
27. Paid miscellaneous expenses, $300.
29. Received cash from customers on account, $4,600.
30. Paid wages of employees, $2,800.
31. Withdrew cash for personal use, $2,500.

Instructions

1. Journalize each transaction in a two-column journal beginning on Page 1, referring to the following chart of accounts in selecting the accounts to be debited and credited. (Do not insert the account numbers in the journal at this time.) Journal entry explanations may be omitted.

11 Cash	31 Kim Wheeler, Capital
12 Accounts Receivable	32 Kim Wheeler, Drawing
13 Supplies	41 Fees Earned
14 Prepaid Insurance	51 Wages Expense
16 Equipment	53 Rent Expense
18 Truck	54 Utilities Expense
21 Notes Payable	55 Truck Expense
22 Accounts Payable	59 Miscellaneous Expense

2. Post the journal to a ledger of four-column accounts, inserting appropriate posting references as each item is posted. Extend the balances to the appropriate balance columns after each transaction is posted.
3. Prepare an unadjusted trial balance for Aztec Designs as of July 31, 2012.
4. Determine the excess of revenues over expenses for July.
5. Can you think of any reason why the amount determined in (4) might not be the net income for July?

OBJ. 1,2,3,4

✔ 4. Total of Debit column: $575,400

PR 2-4B Journal entries and trial balance

Prime Time Realty acts as an agent in buying, selling, renting, and managing real estate. The unadjusted trial balance on July 31, 2012, is shown below.

Prime Time Realty
Unadjusted Trial Balance
July 31, 2012

		Debit Balances	Credit Balances
11	Cash	30,000	
12	Accounts Receivable	57,200	
13	Prepaid Insurance	7,200	
14	Office Supplies	1,600	
16	Land	—	
21	Accounts Payable		12,000
22	Unearned Rent		—
23	Notes Payable		—
31	Sandy Ulrich, Capital		50,000
32	Sandy Ulrich, Drawing	25,600	
41	Fees Earned		338,000
51	Salary and Commission Expense	220,000	
52	Rent Expense	28,000	
53	Advertising Expense	18,400	
54	Automobile Expense	9,000	
59	Miscellaneous Expense	3,000	
		400,000	400,000

The following business transactions were completed by Prime Time Realty during August 2012:

Aug. 1. Purchased office supplies on account, $1,800.
2. Paid rent on office for month, $5,000.
3. Received cash from clients on account, $40,000.
5. Paid annual insurance premiums, $6,000.
9. Returned a portion of the office supplies purchased on August 1, receiving full credit for their cost, $400.
17. Paid advertising expense, $5,500.
23. Paid creditors on account, $7,000

Enter the following transactions on Page 19 of the two-column journal.

29. Paid miscellaneous expenses, $500.
30. Paid automobile expense (including rental charges for an automobile), $2,500.
31. Discovered an error in computing a commission; received cash from the salesperson for the overpayment, $8,000.
31. Paid salaries and commissions for the month, $18,000.
31. Recorded revenue earned and billed to clients during the month, $112,000.
31. Purchased land for a future building site for $75,000, paying $10,000 in cash and giving a note payable for the remainder.
31. Withdrew cash for personal use, $12,000.
31. Rented land purchased on August 31 to a local university for use as a parking lot during football season (September, October, and November); received advance payment of $4,000.

Instructions

1. Record the August 1 balance of each account in the appropriate balance column of a four-column account, write *Balance* in the item section, and place a check mark (✓) in the Posting Reference column.
2. Journalize the transactions for August in a two-column journal beginning on Page 18. Journal entry explanations may be omitted.
3. Post to the ledger, extending the account balance to the appropriate balance column after each posting.

(Continued)

Anwar keeps notes of all receipts and expenses in a shoe box. An examination of Anwar's shoe box records for June revealed the following:

June 1. Transferred $3,500 from personal bank account to be used to operate the caddy service.
1. Paid rent expense to Mission Valley Golf and Country Club, $700.
2. Paid for golf supplies (practice balls, etc.), $800.
3. Arranged for the rental of 25 regular (pulling) golf carts and 10 gasoline-driven carts for $3,000 per month. Paid $500 in advance, with the remaining $2,500 due June 20.
7. Purchased supplies, including gasoline, for the golf carts on account, $600. Mission Valley Golf and Country Club has agreed to allow Anwar to store the gasoline in one of its fuel tanks at no cost.
15. Received cash for services from June 1–15, $4,150.
17. Paid cash to creditors on account, $600.
20. Paid remaining rental on golf carts, $2,500.
22. Purchased supplies, including gasoline, on account, $400.
25. Accepted IOUs from customers on account, $1,800.
28. Paid miscellaneous expenses, $350.
30. Received cash for services from June 16–30, $6,350.
30. Paid telephone and electricity (utilities) expenses, $340.
30. Paid wages of part-time employees, $850.
30. Received cash in payment of IOUs on account, $1,200.
30. Determined the amount of supplies on hand at the end of June, $500.

Anwar has asked you several questions concerning his financial affairs to date, and he has asked you to assist with his record keeping and reporting of financial data.

a. To assist Anwar with his record keeping, prepare a chart of accounts that would be appropriate for AA Caddy Service.

b. Prepare an income statement for June in order to help Anwar assess the profitability of AA Caddy Service. For this purpose, the use of T accounts may be helpful in analyzing the effects of each June transaction.

c. Based on Anwar's records of receipts and payments, compute the amount of cash on hand on June 30. For this purpose, a T account for cash may be useful.

d. A count of the cash on hand on June 30 totaled $8,390. Briefly discuss the possible causes of the difference between the amount of cash computed in (c) and the actual amount of cash on hand.

Internet Project

CP 2-6 Opportunities for accountants

The increasing complexity of the current business and regulatory environment has created an increased demand for accountants who can analyze business transactions and interpret their effects on the financial statements. In addition, a basic ability to analyze the effects of transactions is necessary to be successful in all fields of business as well as in other disciplines, such as law. To better understand the importance of accounting in today's environment, search the Internet or your local newspaper for job opportunities. One possible Internet site is **http://www.careerbuilder.com.** Then do one of the following:

1. Print a listing of one or two ads for accounting jobs. Alternatively, bring to class one or two newspaper ads for accounting jobs.
2. Print a listing of one or two ads for nonaccounting jobs for which some knowledge of accounting is preferred or necessary. Alternatively, bring to class one or two newspaper ads for such jobs.

CHAPTER 3

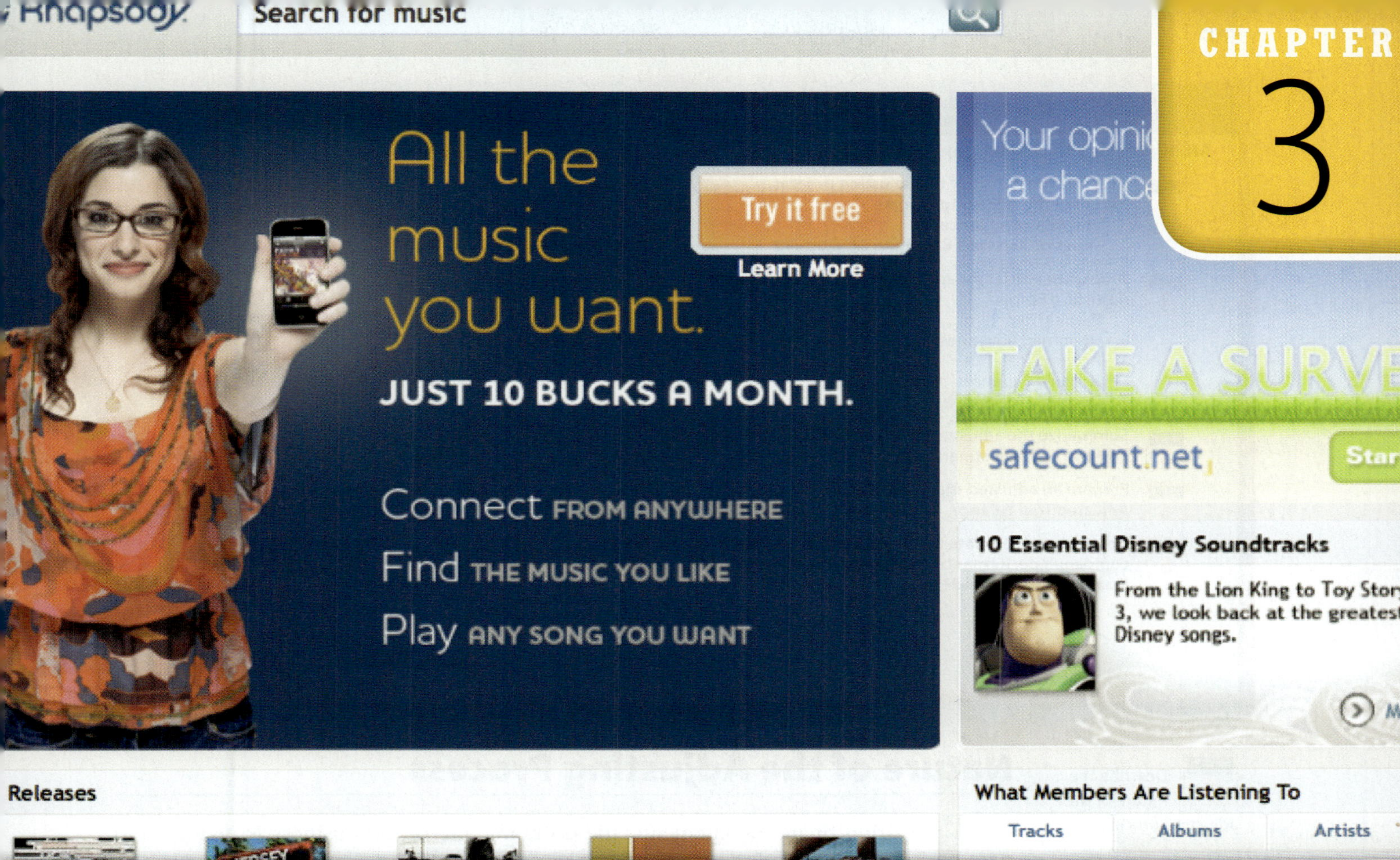

The Adjusting Process

Rhapsody

Do you subscribe to an Internet-based music service such as **Rhapsody®**? Rhapsody began by providing digital music to its subscribers through Internet audio streaming. You can subscribe to "Rhapsody Premier" for $10.00 per month and listen to music by New Boyz, Coldplay, Flo Rida, or Carrie Underwood. Rhapsody, which is partially owned by RealNetworks®, has also expanded its services to include games and video content.

When should a company such as RealNetworks record revenue from its subscriptions? Subscription revenue is recorded when it is earned. Subscriptions revenue is earned when the service has been delivered to the customer. However, in many cases cash is received before the service is delivered. For example, the subscription to "Rhapsody Premier" is paid at the beginning of the month. In this case, the cash received represents unearned revenue. As time passes and the services are delivered, the unearned revenue becomes earned and thus, becomes revenue. As a result, companies like RealNetworks must update their accounting records for items such as unearned subscriptions before preparing their financial statements. For example, RealNetworks reported in its financial statements that it had unearned (deferred) revenue of approximately $33 million as of December 31, 2009.

This chapter describes and illustrates the process by which companies update their accounting records before preparing financial statements. This discussion includes the adjustments for unearned revenues made at the end of the accounting period.

Learning Objectives

After studying this chapter, you should be able to:

OBJ. 1 Describe the nature of the adjusting process.

Nature of the Adjusting Process

When preparing financial statements, the economic life of the business is divided into time periods. This **accounting period concept** requires that revenues and expenses be reported in the proper period. To determine the proper period, accountants use generally accepted accounting principles (GAAP), which requires the **accrual basis of accounting**.

Under the accrual basis of accounting, revenues are reported on the income statement in the period in which they are earned. For example, revenue is reported when the services are provided to customers. Cash may or may not be received from customers during this period. The accounting concept supporting this reporting of revenues is called the **revenue recognition concept**.

Under the accrual basis, expenses are reported in the same period as the revenues to which they relate. For example, utility expenses incurred in December are reported as an expense and matched against December's revenues even though the utility bill may not be paid until January. The accounting concept supporting reporting revenues and related expenses in the same period is called the **matching concept**, or **matching principle**. By matching revenues and expenses, net income or loss for the period is properly reported on the income statement.

American Airlines uses the accrual basis of accounting. Revenues are recognized when passengers take flights, not when the passenger makes the reservation or pays for the ticket.

Although GAAP requires the accrual basis of accounting, some businesses use the **cash basis of accounting**. Under the cash basis of accounting, revenues and expenses are reported on the income statement in the period in which cash is received or paid. For example, fees are recorded when cash is received from clients; likewise, wages are recorded when cash is paid to employees. The net income (or net loss) is the difference between the cash receipts (revenues) and the cash payments (expenses).

Small service businesses may use the cash basis, because they have few receivables and payables. For example, attorneys, physicians, and real estate agents often use the cash basis. For them, the cash basis provides financial statements similar to those of the accrual basis. For most large businesses, however, the cash basis will not provide accurate financial statements for user needs. For this reason, the accrual basis is used in this text.

The Adjusting Process

At the end of the accounting period, many of the account balances in the ledger are reported in the financial statements without change. For example, the balances of the cash and land accounts are normally the amount reported on the balance sheet.

Some accounts, however, require updating for the following reasons:[1]

1. Some expenses are not recorded daily. For example, the daily use of supplies would require many entries with small amounts. Also, the amount of supplies on hand on a day-to-day basis is normally not needed.
2. Some revenues and expenses are incurred as time passes rather than as separate transactions. For example, rent received in advance (unearned rent) expires and becomes revenue with the passage of time. Likewise, prepaid insurance expires and becomes an expense with the passage of time.
3. Some revenues and expenses may be unrecorded. For example, a company may have provided services to customers that it has not billed or recorded at the end of the accounting period. Likewise, a company may not pay its employees until the next accounting period even though the employees have earned their wages in the current period.

The analysis and updating of accounts at the end of the period before the financial statements are prepared is called the **adjusting process**. The journal entries that bring the accounts up to date at the end of the accounting period are called **adjusting entries**. All adjusting entries affect at least one income statement account and one balance sheet account. Thus, an adjusting entry will *always* involve a revenue or an expense account *and* an asset or a liability account.

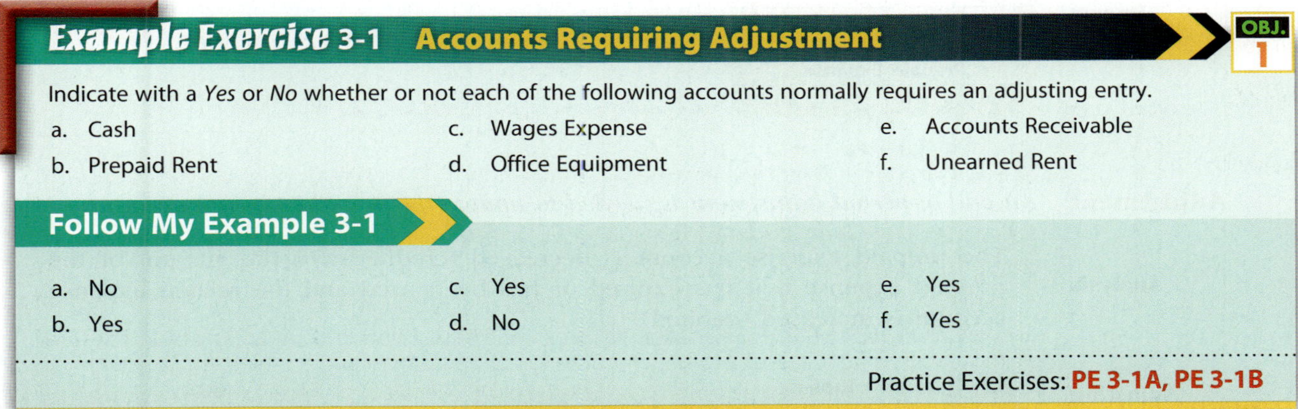

Example Exercise 3-1 Accounts Requiring Adjustment OBJ. 1

Indicate with a *Yes* or *No* whether or not each of the following accounts normally requires an adjusting entry.

a. Cash
b. Prepaid Rent
c. Wages Expense
d. Office Equipment
e. Accounts Receivable
f. Unearned Rent

Follow My Example 3-1

a. No
b. Yes
c. Yes
d. No
e. Yes
f. Yes

Practice Exercises: **PE 3-1A, PE 3-1B**

Types of Accounts Requiring Adjustment

Four basic types of accounts require adjusting entries as shown below.

1. Prepaid expenses
2. Unearned revenues
3. Accrued revenues
4. Accrued expenses

Prepaid expenses are the advance payment of *future* expenses and are recorded as assets when cash is paid. Prepaid expenses become expenses over time or during normal operations. To illustrate, the following transaction of NetSolutions from Chapter 2 is used.

Dec. 1 NetSolutions paid $2,400 as a premium on a one-year insurance policy.

On December 1, the cash payment of $2,400 was recorded as a debit to Prepaid Insurance and credit to Cash for $2,400. At the end of December, only $200 ($2,400 divided by 12 months) of the insurance premium is expired and has become an expense. The remaining $2,200 of prepaid insurance will become an expense in future months. Thus, the $200 is insurance expense of December and should be recorded with an adjusting entry.

1 Under the cash basis of accounting, accounts do not require adjusting. This is because transactions are recorded only when cash is received or paid. Thus, the matching concept is not used under the cash basis.

Other examples of prepaid expenses include supplies, prepaid advertising, and prepaid interest.

Exhibit 1 summarizes the nature of prepaid expenses.

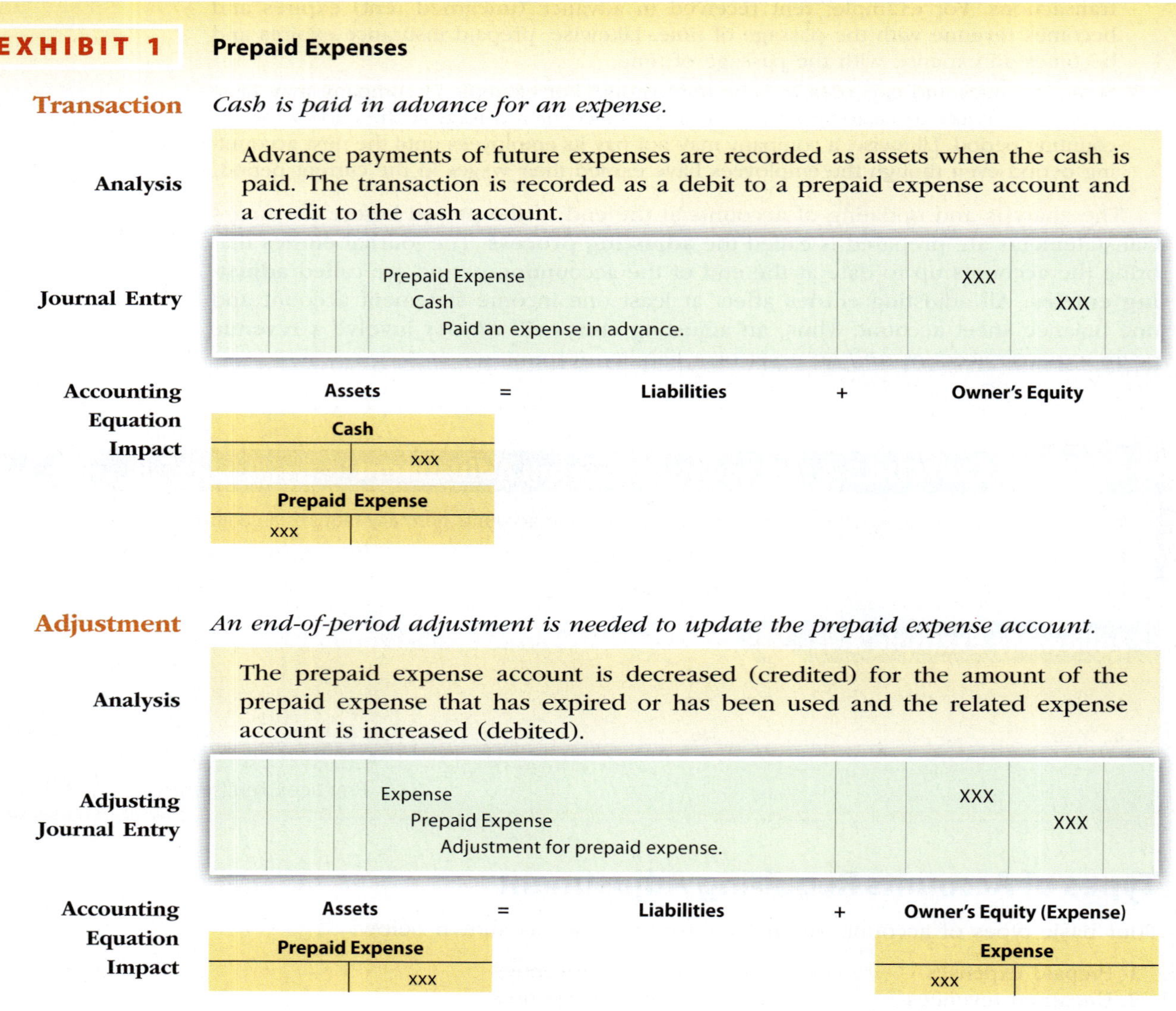

Unearned revenues are the advance receipt of *future* revenues and are recorded as liabilities when cash is received. Unearned revenues become earned revenues over time or during normal operations. To illustrate, the following December 1 transaction of NetSolutions is used.

Dec. 1	NetSolutions received $360 from a local retailer to rent land for three months.

On December 1, the cash receipt of $360 was recorded as a debit to Cash and a credit to Unearned Rent for $360. At the end of December, $120 ($360 divided by 3 months) of the unearned rent has been earned. The remaining $240 will become rent revenue in future months. Thus, the $120 is rent revenue of December and should be recorded with an adjusting entry.

Other examples of unearned revenues include tuition received in advance by a school, an annual retainer fee received by an attorney, premiums received in advance by an insurance company, and magazine subscriptions received in advance by a publisher.

Exhibit 2 summarizes the nature of unearned revenues.

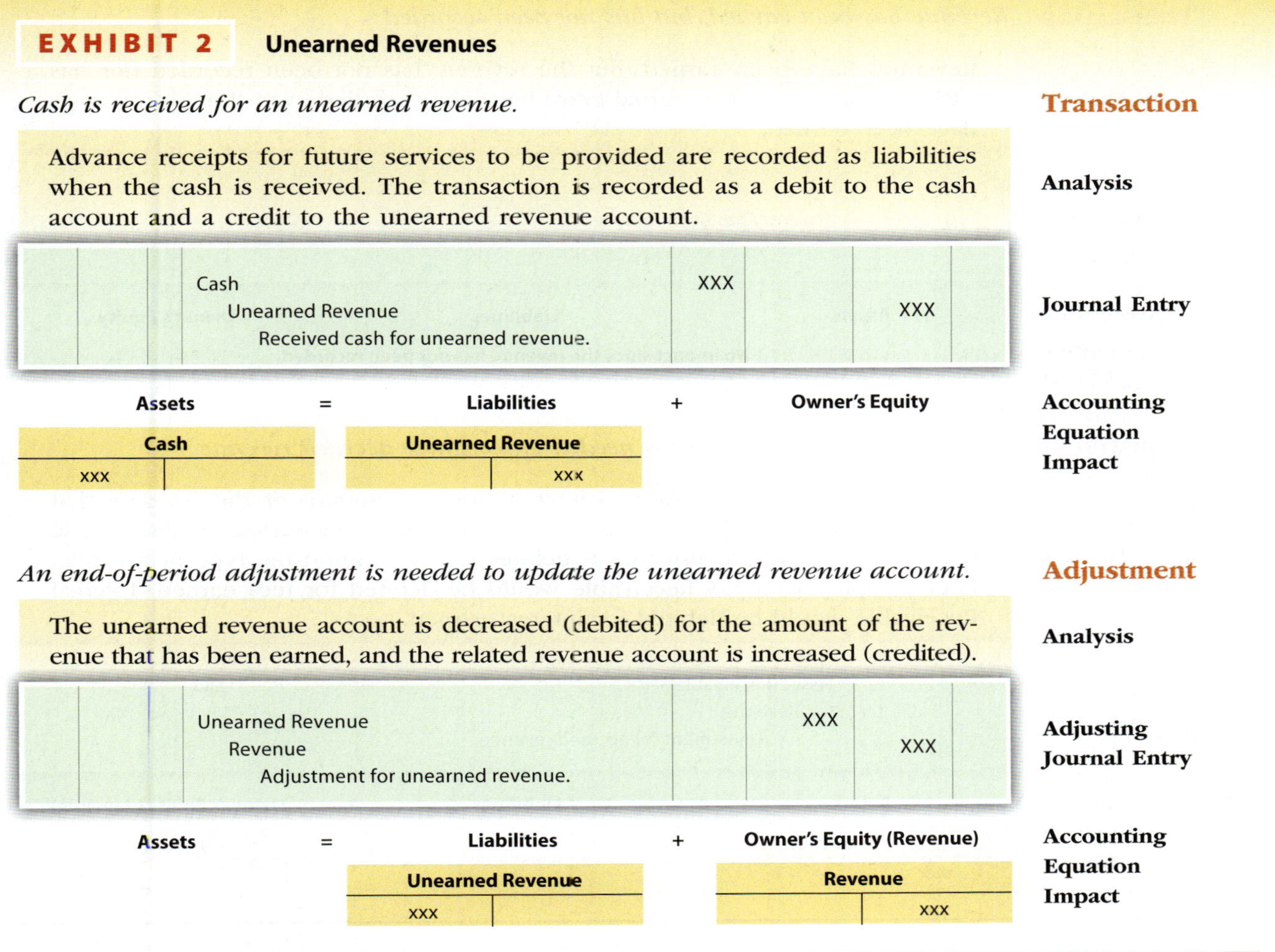

EXHIBIT 2 Unearned Revenues

Cash is received for an unearned revenue. — **Transaction**

Analysis: Advance receipts for future services to be provided are recorded as liabilities when the cash is received. The transaction is recorded as a debit to the cash account and a credit to the unearned revenue account.

Journal Entry

		Debit	Credit
Cash		XXX	
Unearned Revenue			XXX
Received cash for unearned revenue.			

Accounting Equation Impact

Assets = Liabilities + Owner's Equity

Cash	
XXX	

Unearned Revenue	
	XXX

An end-of-period adjustment is needed to update the unearned revenue account. — **Adjustment**

Analysis: The unearned revenue account is decreased (debited) for the amount of the revenue that has been earned, and the related revenue account is increased (credited).

Adjusting Journal Entry

		Debit	Credit
Unearned Revenue		XXX	
Revenue			XXX
Adjustment for unearned revenue.			

Accounting Equation Impact

Assets = Liabilities + Owner's Equity (Revenue)

Unearned Revenue	
XXX	

Revenue	
	XXX

Accrued revenues are unrecorded revenues that have been earned and for which cash has yet to be received. Fees for services that an attorney or a doctor has provided but not yet billed are accrued revenues. To illustrate, the following example involving NetSolutions and one of its customers is used.

Dec. 15 NetSolutions signed an agreement with Dankner Co. under which NetSolutions will bill Dankner Co. on the fifteenth of each month for services rendered at the rate of $20 per hour.

From December 16–31, NetSolutions provided 25 hours of service to Dankner Co. Although the revenue of $500 (25 hours × $20) has been earned, it will not be billed until January 15. Likewise, cash of $500 will not be received until Dankner pays its bill. Thus, the $500 of accrued revenue and the $500 of fees earned should be recorded with an adjusting entry on December 31.

Other examples of accrued revenues include accrued interest on notes receivable and accrued rent on property rented to others.

Exhibit 3 summarizes the nature of accrued revenues.

EXHIBIT 3 **Accrued Revenues**

Transaction *Revenue has been earned, but has not been recorded.*

Analysis

Revenues have been earned, but the revenue has not been recorded nor has cash been received. No journal entry has been recorded even though revenues have been earned.

Journal Entry

		No entry has been recorded.			

Accounting Equation Impact

Assets = Liabilities + Owner's Equity

No impact since the revenue has not been recorded.

Adjustment *An end-of-period adjustment is needed to recognize accrued revenue.*

Analysis

An asset account is increased (debited) for the amount of the revenue that has been earned, and the related revenue account is increased (credited). The type of receivable account that is debited depends upon the type of revenue. For example, Accounts Receivable would be debited for fees earned. Interest Receivable would be debited for interest earned.

Adjusting Journal Entry

		Asset (Receivable)		XXX	
		Revenue			XXX
		Adjustment for accrued revenue.			

Accounting Equation Impact

Assets = Liabilities + Owner's Equity (Revenue)

______ Receivable	
XXX	

Revenue	
	XXX

Accrued expenses are unrecorded expenses that have been incurred and for which cash has yet to be paid. Wages owed to employees at the end of a period but not yet paid are an accrued expense. To illustrate, the following example involving NetSolutions and its employees is used.

Dec. 31	NetSolutions owes its employees wages of $250 for Monday and Tuesday, December 30 and 31.

NetSolutions paid wages of $950 on December 13 and $1,200 on December 27, 2011. These payments covered the biweekly pay periods that ended on those days. As of December 31, 2011, NetSolutions owes its employees wages of $250 for Monday and Tuesday, December 30 and 31. The wages of $250 will be paid on January 10, 2012; however, they are an expense of December. Thus, $250 of accrued wages should be recorded with an adjusting entry on December 31.

Other examples of accrued expenses include accrued interest on notes payable and accrued taxes.

Exhibit 4 summarizes the nature of accrued expenses.

EXHIBIT 4 Accrued Expenses

Transaction

An expense has been incurred, but has not been recorded.

Analysis

An expense has been incurred, but the expense has not been recorded nor has cash been paid. No journal entry has been recorded even though an expense has been incurred.

Journal Entry

No entry has been recorded.

Accounting Equation Impact

Assets	=	Liabilities	+	Owner's Equity

No impact since the expense has not been recorded.

Adjustment

An end-of-period adjustment is needed to recognize the accrued expense.

Analysis

An expense account is increased (debited) for the amount of the expense that has been incurred and the related liability account is increased (credited). The liability account that is credited depends upon the type of expense. For example, Wages Payable would be credited for wages expense. Interest Payable would be credited for interest expense.

Adjusting Journal Entry

Expense	XXX	
Liability (Payable)		XXX
Adjustment for accrued expense.		

Accounting Equation Impact

Assets	=	Liabilities	+	Owner's Equity (Expense)
		______ Payable		Expense
		Cr. XXX		Dr. XXX

As illustrated in Exhibit 4, accrued revenues are earned revenues that are unrecorded. The cash receipts for accrued revenues are normally received in the next accounting period. Accrued expenses are expenses that have been incurred, but are unrecorded. The cash payments for accrued expenses are normally paid in the next accounting period.

Prepaid expenses and unearned revenues are sometimes referred to as *deferrals*. This is because the recording of the related expense or revenue is deferred to a future period. Accrued revenues and accrued expenses are sometimes referred to as *accruals*. This is because the related revenue or expense should be recorded or accrued in the current period.

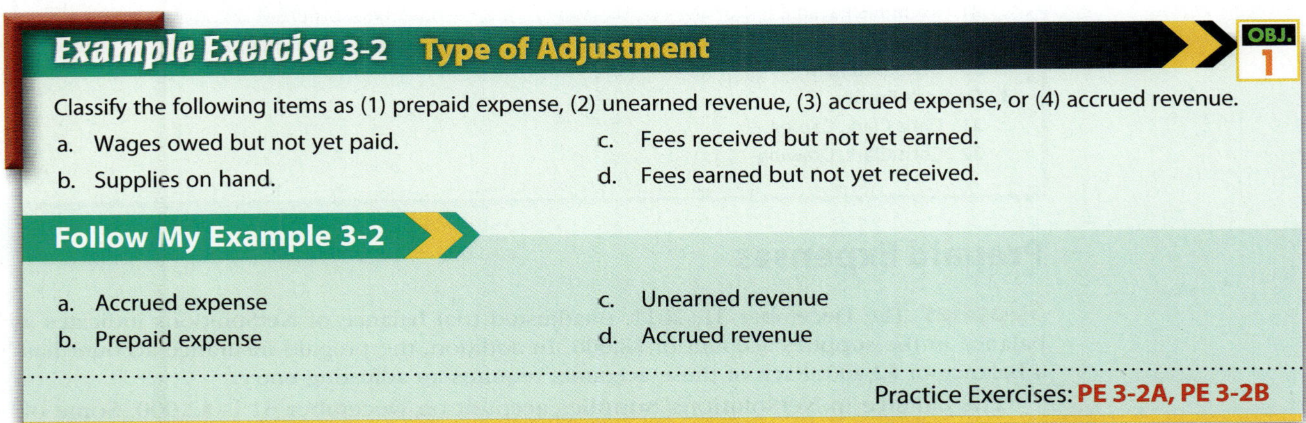

Example Exercise 3-2 Type of Adjustment OBJ. 1

Classify the following items as (1) prepaid expense, (2) unearned revenue, (3) accrued expense, or (4) accrued revenue.

a. Wages owed but not yet paid.
b. Supplies on hand.
c. Fees received but not yet earned.
d. Fees earned but not yet received.

Follow My Example 3-2

a. Accrued expense
b. Prepaid expense
c. Unearned revenue
d. Accrued revenue

Practice Exercises: **PE 3-2A, PE 3-2B**

Journalize entries for accounts requiring adjustment.

Adjusting Entries

To illustrate adjusting entries, the December 31, 2011, unadjusted trial balance of NetSolutions shown in Exhibit 5 is used. An expanded chart of accounts for NetSolutions is shown in Exhibit 6. The additional accounts used in this chapter are shown in color. The rules of debit and credit shown in Exhibit 3 of Chapter 2 are used to record the adjusting entries.

EXHIBIT 5

Unadusted Trial Balance for NetSolutions

NetSolutions
Unadusted Trial Balance
December 31, 2011

	Debit Balances	Credit Balances
Cash	2,065	
Accounts Receivable	2,220	
Supplies	2,000	
Prepaid Insurance	2,400	
Land	20,000	
Office Equipment	1,800	
Accounts Payable		900
Unearned Rent		360
Chris Clark, Capital		25,000
Chris Clark, Drawing	4,000	
Fees Earned		16,340
Wages Expense	4,275	
Rent Expense	1,600	
Utilities Expense	985	
Supplies Expense	800	
Miscellaneous Expense	455	
	42,600	42,600

EXHIBIT 6

Expanded Chart of Accounts for NetSolutions

Balance Sheet Accounts	Income Statement Accounts
1. Assets	**4. Revenue**
11 Cash	41 Fees Earned
12 Accounts Receivable	42 Rent Revenue
14 Supplies	**5. Expenses**
15 Prepaid Insurance	51 Wages Expense
17 Land	52 Rent Expense
18 Office Equipment	53 Depreciation Expense
19 Accumulated Depreciation—Office Equipment	54 Utilities Expense
2. Liabilities	55 Supplies Expense
21 Accounts Payable	56 Insurance Expense
22 Wages Payable	59 Miscellaneous Expense
23 Unearned Rent	
3. Owner's Equity	
31 Chris Clark, Capital	
32 Chris Clark, Drawing	

Prepaid Expenses

Supplies The December 31, 2011, unadjusted trial balance of NetSolutions indicates a balance in the supplies account of $2,000. In addition, the prepaid insurance account has a balance of $2,400. Each of these accounts requires an adjusting entry.

The balance in NetSolutions' supplies account on December 31 is $2,000. Some of these supplies (CDs, paper, envelopes, etc.) were used during December, and some are still on hand (not used). If either amount is known, the other can be determined. It is normally easier to determine the cost of the supplies on hand at the end of the month than to record daily supplies used.

Assuming that on December 31 the amount of supplies on hand is $760, the amount to be transferred from the asset account to the expense account is $1,240, computed as follows:

Supplies available during December (balance of account)	$2,000
Supplies on hand, December 31	760
Supplies used (amount of adjustment)	$1,240

At the end of December, the supplies expense account is increased (debited) for $1,240, and the supplies account is decreased (credited) for $1,240 to record the supplies used during December. The adjusting journal entry and T accounts for Supplies and Supplies Expense are as follows:

Journal *Page 5*

Date		Description	Post. Ref.	Debit	Credit
2011 Dec.	31	Supplies Expense	55	1,240	
		Supplies	14		1,240
		Supplies used ($2,000 – $760).			

Adjusting Journal Entry

Assets = Liabilities + Owner's Equity (Expense)

Supplies		14	
Bal.	2,000	Dec. 31	1,240
Adj. Bal.	760		

Supplies Expense		55
Bal.	800	
Dec. 31	1,240	
Adj. Bal.	2,040	

Accounting Equation Impact

The adjusting entry is shown in color in the T accounts to separate it from other transactions. After the adjusting entry is recorded and posted, the supplies account has a debit balance of $760. This balance is an asset that will become an expense in a future period.

Prepaid Insurance The debit balance of $2,400 in NetSolutions' prepaid insurance account represents a December 1 prepayment of insurance for 12 months. At the end of December, the insurance expense account is increased (debited), and the prepaid insurance account is decreased (credited) by $200, the insurance for one month. The adjusting journal entry and T accounts for Prepaid Insurance and Insurance Expense are as follows:

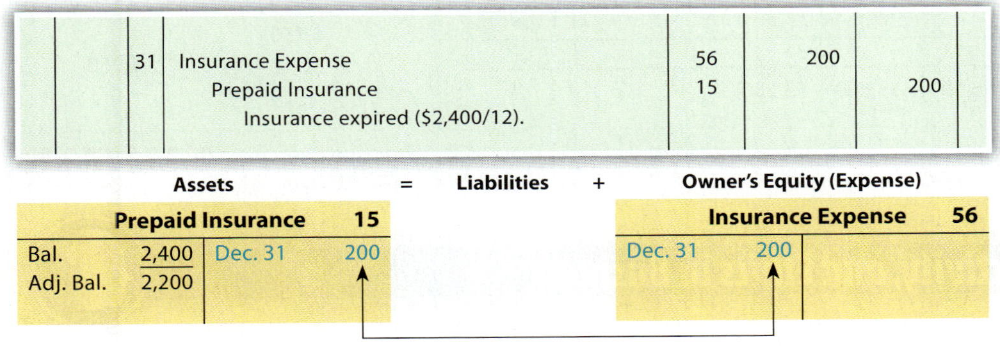

	31	Insurance Expense	56	200	
		Prepaid Insurance	15		200
		Insurance expired ($2,400/12).			

Adjusting Journal Entry

Assets = Liabilities + Owner's Equity (Expense)

Prepaid Insurance		15	
Bal.	2,400	Dec. 31	200
Adj. Bal.	2,200		

Insurance Expense		56
Dec. 31	200	

Accounting Equation Impact

After the adjusting entry is recorded and posted, the prepaid insurance account has a debit balance of $2,200. This balance is an asset that will become an expense in future periods. The insurance expense account has a debit balance of $200, which is an expense of the current period.

If the preceding adjustments for supplies ($1,240) and insurance ($200) are not recorded, the financial statements prepared as of December 31 will be misstated. On the income statement, Supplies Expense and Insurance Expense will be understated by a total of $1,440 ($1,240 + $200), and net income will be overstated by $1,440. On the balance sheet, Supplies and Prepaid Insurance will be overstated by a total of $1,440. Since net income increases owner's equity, Chris Clark, Capital will also be overstated by $1,440 on the balance sheet. The effects of omitting these adjusting entries on the income statement and balance sheet are as follows:

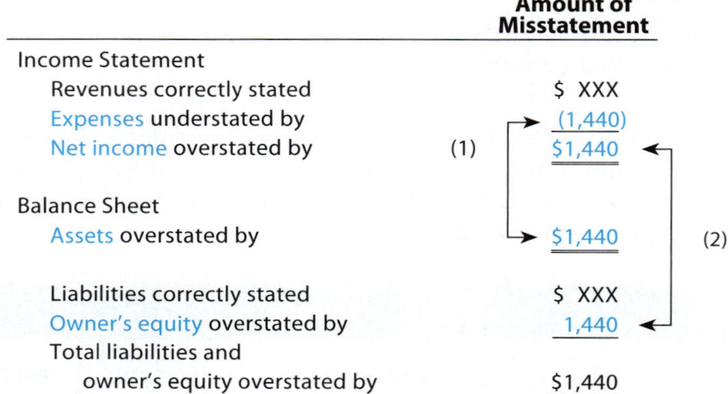

		Amount of Misstatement	
Income Statement			
Revenues correctly stated		$ XXX	
Expenses understated by		(1,440)	
Net income overstated by	(1)	$1,440	
Balance Sheet			
Assets overstated by		$1,440	(2)
Liabilities correctly stated		$ XXX	
Owner's equity overstated by		1,440	
Total liabilities and owner's equity overstated by		$1,440	

Arrow (1) indicates the effect of the understated expenses on assets. Arrow (2) indicates the effect of the overstated net income on owner's equity.

Payments for prepaid expenses are sometimes made at the beginning of the period in which they will be *entirely used or consumed*. To illustrate, the following December 1 transaction of NetSolutions is used.

Dec. 1 NetSolutions paid rent of $800 for the month.

On December 1, the rent payment of $800 represents Prepaid Rent. However, the Prepaid Rent expires daily, and at the end of December there will be no asset left. In such cases, the payment of $800 is recorded as Rent Expense rather than as Prepaid Rent. In this way, no adjusting entry is needed at the end of the period.[2]

Example Exercise 3-3 Adjustment for Prepaid Expense

OBJ. 2

The prepaid insurance account had a beginning balance of $6,400 and was debited for $3,600 of premiums paid during the year. Journalize the adjusting entry required at the end of the year assuming the amount of unexpired insurance related to future periods is $3,250.

Follow My Example 3-3

Insurance Expense	6,750	
Prepaid Insurance		6,750
Insurance expired ($6,400 + $3,600 – $3,250).		

Practice Exercises: **PE 3-3A, PE 3-3B**

Integrity, Objectivity, and Ethics in Business

FREE ISSUE

Office supplies are often available to employees on a "free issue" basis. This means that employees do not have to "sign" for the release of office supplies but merely obtain the necessary supplies from a local storage area as needed. Just because supplies are easily available, however, doesn't mean they can be taken for personal use. There are many instances where employees have been terminated for taking supplies home for personal use.

2 An alternative treatment of recording the cost of supplies, rent, and other prepayments of expenses is discussed in an appendix that can be downloaded from the book's companion Web site (**academic.cengage.com/accounting/warren**).

Unearned Revenues

The December 31 unadjusted trial balance of NetSolutions indicates a balance in the unearned rent account of $360. This balance represents the receipt of three months' rent on December 1 for December, January, and February. At the end of December, one months' rent has been earned. Thus, the unearned rent account is decreased (debited) by $120, and the rent revenue account is increased (credited) by $120. The $120 represents the rental revenue for one month ($360/3). The adjusting journal entry and T accounts are shown below.

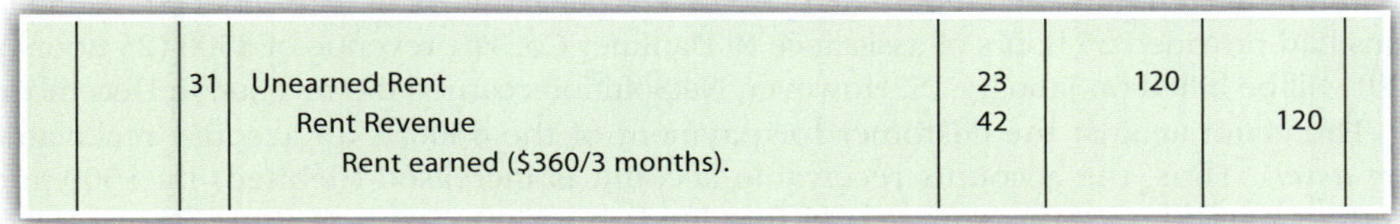

	31	Unearned Rent	23	120	
		Rent Revenue	42		120
		Rent earned ($360/3 months).			

Adjusting Journal Entry

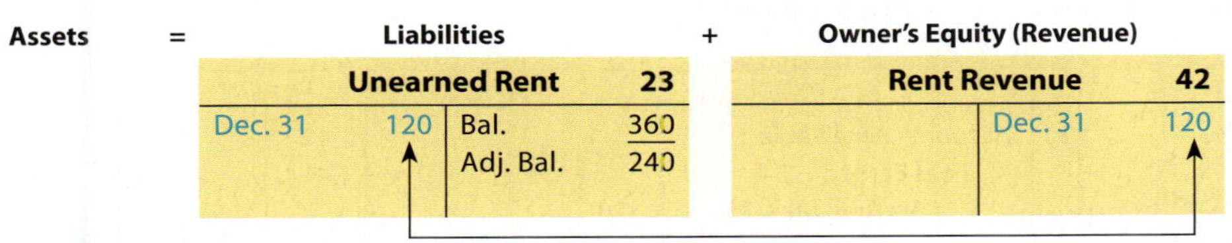

Assets = Liabilities + Owner's Equity (Revenue)

Unearned Rent		23	
Dec. 31	120	Bal.	360
		Adj. Bal.	240

Rent Revenue		42	
		Dec. 31	120

Accounting Equation Impact

Best Buy sells extended warranty contracts with terms between 12 and 36 months. The receipts from sales of these contracts are reported as unearned revenue on Best Buy's balance sheet. Revenue is recorded as the contracts expire.

After the adjusting entry is recorded and posted, the unearned rent account has a credit balance of $240. This balance is a liability that will become revenue in a future period. Rent Revenue has a balance of $120, which is revenue of the current period.[3]

If the preceding adjustment of unearned rent and rent revenue is not recorded, the financial statements prepared on December 31 will be misstated. On the income statement, Rent Revenue and the net income will be understated by $120. On the balance sheet, Unearned Rent will be overstated by $120, and Chris Clark, Capital will be understated by $120. The effects of omitting this adjusting entry are shown below.

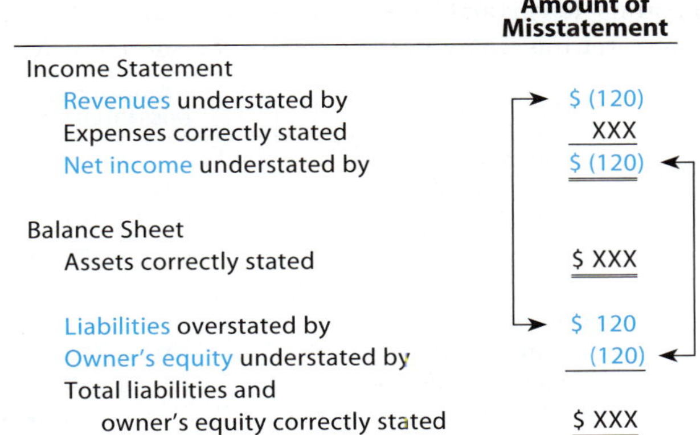

	Amount of Misstatement
Income Statement	
Revenues understated by	$ (120)
Expenses correctly stated	XXX
Net income understated by	$ (120)
Balance Sheet	
Assets correctly stated	$ XXX
Liabilities overstated by	$ 120
Owner's equity understated by	(120)
Total liabilities and owner's equity correctly stated	$ XXX

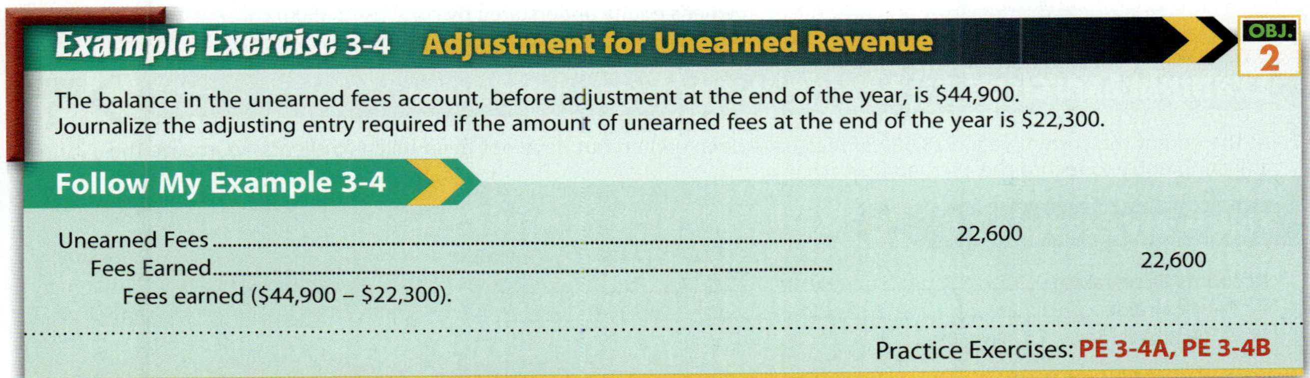

Example Exercise 3-4 Adjustment for Unearned Revenue OBJ. 2

The balance in the unearned fees account, before adjustment at the end of the year, is $44,900. Journalize the adjusting entry required if the amount of unearned fees at the end of the year is $22,300.

Follow My Example 3-4

Unearned Fees	22,600	
Fees Earned		22,600
Fees earned ($44,900 – $22,300).		

Practice Exercises: **PE 3-4A, PE 3-4B**

3 An alternative treatment of recording revenues received in advance of their being earned is discussed in an appendix that can be downloaded from the book's companion Web site (**academic.cengage.com/accounting/warren**).

Accrued Revenues

RadioShack Corporation is engaged in consumer electronics retailing. RadioShack accrues revenue for finance charges and late payment charges related to its credit operations.

During an accounting period, some revenues are recorded only when cash is received. Thus, at the end of an accounting period, there may be revenue that has been earned *but has not been recorded*. In such cases, the revenue is recorded by increasing (debiting) an asset account and increasing (crediting) a revenue account.

To illustrate, assume that NetSolutions signed an agreement with Dankner Co. on December 15. The agreement provides that NetSolutions will answer computer questions and render assistance to Dankner Co.'s employees. The services will be billed to Dankner Co. on the fifteenth of each month at a rate of $20 per hour. As of December 31, NetSolutions had provided 25 hours of assistance to Dankner Co. The revenue of $500 (25 hours × $20) will be billed on January 15. However, NetSolutions earned the revenue in December.

The claim against the customer for payment of the $500 is an account receivable (*an asset*). Thus, the accounts receivable account is increased (debited) by $500 and the fees earned account is increased (credited) by $500. The adjusting journal entry and T accounts are shown below.

Adjusting Journal Entry

Accounting Equation Impact

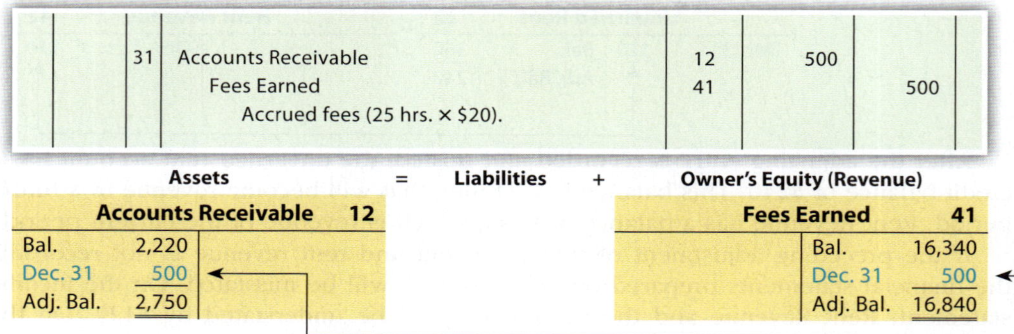

	31	Accounts Receivable	12	500	
		Fees Earned	41		500
		Accrued fees (25 hrs. × $20).			

Assets = Liabilities + Owner's Equity (Revenue)

Accounts Receivable 12		
Bal.	2,220	
Dec. 31	500	
Adj. Bal.	2,750	

Fees Earned 41		
	Bal.	16,340
	Dec. 31	500
	Adj. Bal.	16,840

If the adjustment for the accrued revenue ($500) is not recorded, Fees Earned and the net income will be understated by $500 on the income statement. On the balance sheet, Accounts Receivable and Chris Clark, Capital will be understated by $500. The effects of omitting this adjusting entry are shown below.

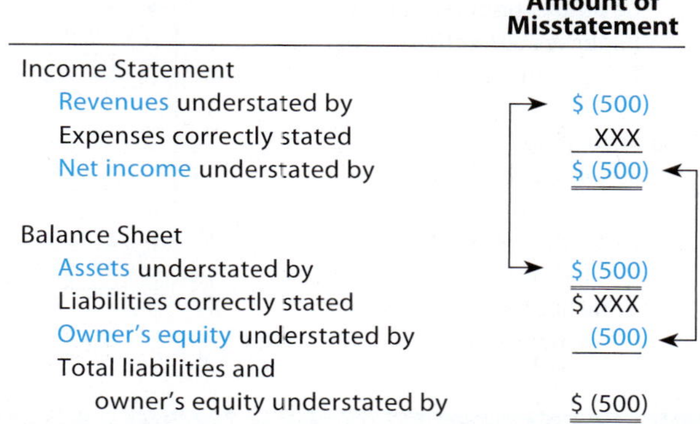

	Amount of Misstatement
Income Statement	
Revenues understated by	$ (500)
Expenses correctly stated	XXX
Net income understated by	$ (500)
Balance Sheet	
Assets understated by	$ (500)
Liabilities correctly stated	$ XXX
Owner's equity understated by	(500)
Total liabilities and owner's equity understated by	$ (500)

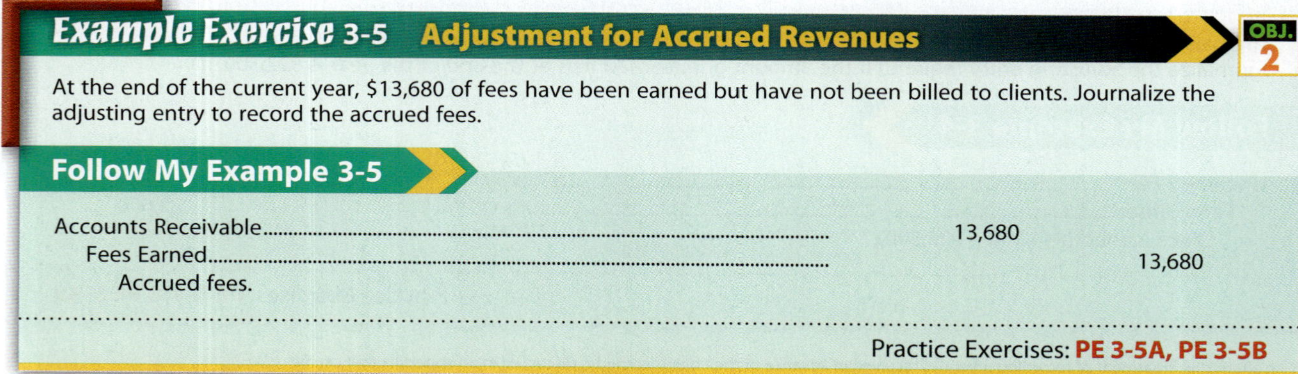

Example Exercise 3-5 Adjustment for Accrued Revenues OBJ. 2

At the end of the current year, $13,680 of fees have been earned but have not been billed to clients. Journalize the adjusting entry to record the accrued fees.

Follow My Example 3-5

Accounts Receivable	13,680	
Fees Earned		13,680
Accrued fees.		

Practice Exercises: PE 3-5A, PE 3-5B

Accrued Expenses

Some types of services used in earning revenues are paid for *after* the service has been performed. For example, wages expense is used hour by hour, but is paid only daily, weekly, biweekly, or monthly. At the end of the accounting period, the amount of such *accrued* but unpaid items is an expense and a liability.

For example, if the last day of the employees' pay period is not the last day of the accounting period, an accrued expense (wages expense) and the related liability (wages payable) must be recorded by an adjusting entry. This adjusting entry is necessary so that expenses are properly matched to the period in which they were incurred in earning revenue.

To illustrate, NetSolutions pays its employees biweekly. During December, NetSolutions paid wages of $950 on December 13 and $1,200 on December 27. These payments covered pay periods ending on those days as shown in Exhibit 7.

EXHIBIT 7

Accrued Wages

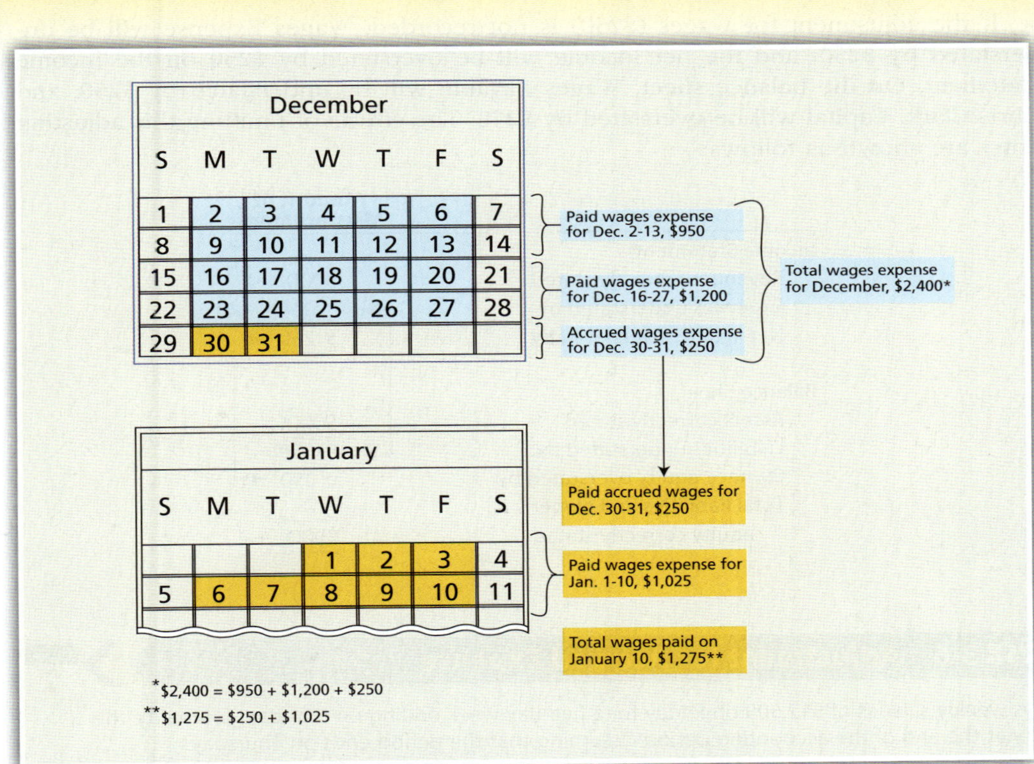

As of December 31, NetSolutions owes $250 of wages to employees for Monday and Tuesday, December 30 and 31. Thus, the wages expense account is increased (debited) by $250 and the wages payable account is increased (credited) by $250. The adjusting journal entry and T accounts are shown below.

Adjusting Journal Entry

	31	Wages Expense	51	250	
		Wages Payable	22		250
		Accrued wages.			

Accounting Equation Impact

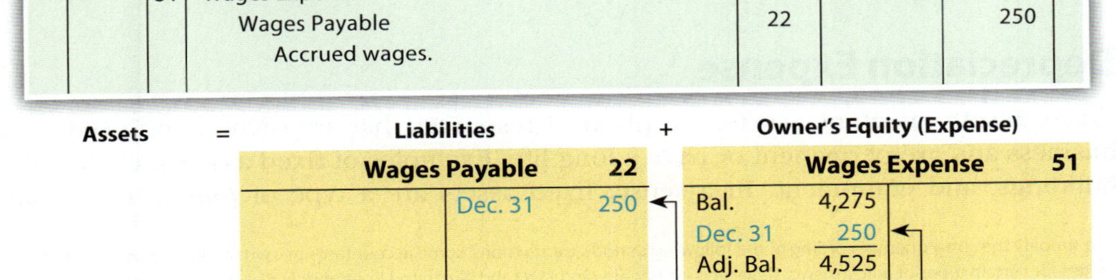

Callaway Golf Company, a manufacturer of such innovative golf clubs as the "Big Bertha" driver, reports accrued warranty expense on its balance sheet.

After the adjusting entry is recorded and posted, the debit balance of the wages expense account is $4,525. This balance of $4,525 is the wages expense for two months, November and December. The credit balance of $250 in Wages Payable is the liability for wages owed on December 31.

As shown in Exhibit 7, NetSolutions paid wages of $1,275 on January 10. This payment includes the $250 of accrued wages recorded on December 31. Thus, on January 10, the wages payable account is decreased (debited) by $250. Also, the wages expense account is increased (debited) by $1,025 ($1,275 – $250), which is the wages expense for January 1–10. Finally, the cash account is decreased (credited) by $1,275. The journal entry for the payment of wages on January 10 is shown below.[4]

Jan	10	Wages Expense	51	1,025	
		Wages Payable	22	250	
		Cash	11		1,275

If the adjustment for wages ($250) is not recorded, Wages Expense will be understated by $250, and the net income will be overstated by $250 on the income statement. On the balance sheet, Wages Payable will be understated by $250, and Chris Clark, Capital will be overstated by $250. The effects of omitting this adjusting entry are shown as follows:

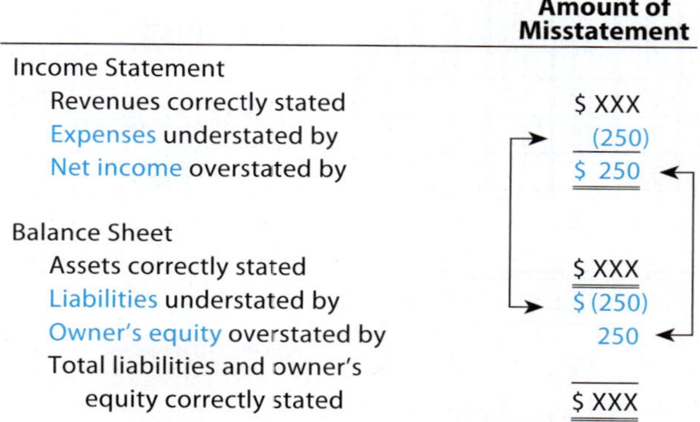

	Amount of Misstatement
Income Statement	
Revenues correctly stated	$ XXX
Expenses understated by	(250)
Net income overstated by	$ 250
Balance Sheet	
Assets correctly stated	$ XXX
Liabilities understated by	$ (250)
Owner's equity overstated by	250
Total liabilities and owner's equity correctly stated	$ XXX

Example Exercise 3-6 Adjustment for Accrued Expense OBJ. 2

Sanregret Realty Co. pays weekly salaries of $12,500 on Friday for a five-day week ending on that day. Journalize the necessary adjusting entry at the end of the accounting period, assuming that the period ends on Thursday.

Follow My Example 3-6

Salaries Expense	10,000	
Salaries Payable		10,000
Accrued salaries [($12,500/5 days) × 4 days].		

Practice Exercises: **PE 3-6A, PE 3-6B**

Depreciation Expense

Fixed assets, or **plant assets**, are physical resources that are owned and used by a business and are permanent or have a long life. Examples of fixed assets include land, buildings, and equipment. In a sense, fixed assets are a type of *long-term* prepaid

4 To simplify the subsequent recording of the following period's transactions, some accountants use what is known as reversing entries for certain types of adjustments. Reversing entries are discussed and illustrated in Appendix B at the end of the textbook.

Business Connection

FORD MOTOR COMPANY WARRANTIES

Ford Motor Company provides warranties on the vehicles that it sells. For example, Ford offers "bumper-to-bumper" coverage in the United States for five years or 60,000 miles on its Ford brand. A bumper-to-bumper warranty normally implies that every part of a new car will be repaired or replaced if it is defective during the term of the warranty.

When Ford sells a new car, it estimates the future warranty costs that it will incur on the vehicle and accrues a warranty expense. Accruals for estimated warranty costs are based on historical warranty claim experience, which is adjusted for changes such as offering new types of vehicles. For example, Ford adjusted its warranty costs when it began selling its new fuel efficient Ford Escape Hybrid. The Ford Escape Hybrid has a gas-electric engine that automatically shuts off when the vehicle is stopped. The Escape also uses an electric motor to assist in accelerating or when the vehicle is coasting or slowing down.

Ford's warranty cost accruals (in millions) for the years ended December 31, 2009 and 2008 are as follows:

	2009	2008
Beginning balance	$ 3,346	$ 4,209
Payments during the year	(2,481)	(2,747)
Warranties issued during year	2,233	2,122
Other	121	(238)
Ending balance of accrued warranties	$ 3,219	$ 3,346

expense. However, because of their unique nature and long life, they are discussed separately from other prepaid expenses.

Fixed assets, such as office equipment, are used to generate revenue much like supplies are used to generate revenue. Unlike supplies, however, there is no visible reduction in the quantity of the equipment. Instead, as time passes, the equipment loses its ability to provide useful services. This decrease in usefulness is called **depreciation**.

All fixed assets, except land, lose their usefulness and, thus, are said to **depreciate**. As a fixed asset depreciates, a portion of its cost should be recorded as an expense. This periodic expense is called **depreciation expense**.

The adjusting entry to record depreciation expense is similar to the adjusting entry for supplies used. The depreciation expense account is increased (debited) for the amount of depreciation. However, the fixed asset account is not decreased (credited). This is because both the original cost of a fixed asset and the depreciation recorded since its purchase are reported on the balance sheet. Instead, an account entitled **Accumulated Depreciation** is increased (credited).

Accumulated depreciation accounts are called **contra accounts**, or **contra asset accounts**. This is because accumulated depreciation accounts are deducted from their related fixed asset accounts on the balance sheet. The normal balance of a contra account is opposite to the account from which it is deducted. Since the normal balance of a fixed asset account is a debit, the normal balance of an accumulated depreciation account is a credit.

Lowe's Companies, Inc., reported land, buildings, and store equipment at a cost of over $18 billion and accumulated depreciation of over $4.1 billion.

The normal titles for fixed asset accounts and their related contra asset accounts are as follows:

Fixed Asset Account	Contra Asset Account
Land	None—Land is not depreciated.
Buildings	Accumulated Depreciation—Buildings
Store Equipment	Accumulated Depreciation—Store Equipment
Office Equipment	Accumulated Depreciation—Office Equipment

The December 31, 2011, unadjusted trial balance of NetSolutions (Exhibit 5) indicates that NetSolutions owns two fixed assets: land and office equipment. Land does not depreciate; however, an adjusting entry is recorded for the depreciation of the office equipment for December. Assume that the office equipment depreciates $50 during December. The depreciation expense account is increased (debited) by $50, and the accumulated depreciation—office equipment account is increased (credited) by $50.[5] The adjusting journal entry and T accounts are shown below.

Adjusting Journal Entry

Accounting Equation Impact

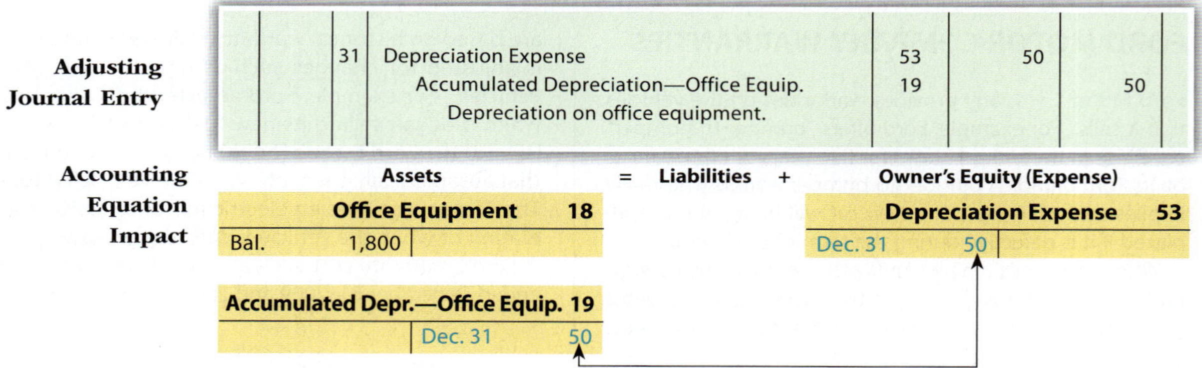

	Date	Description	Post. Ref.	Debit	Credit
	31	Depreciation Expense	53	50	
		Accumulated Depreciation—Office Equip.	19		50
		Depreciation on office equipment.			

After the adjusting journal entry is recorded and posted, the office equipment account still has a debit balance of $1,800. This is the original cost of the office equipment that was purchased on December 4. The accumulated depreciation—office equipment account has a credit balance of $50. The difference between these two balances is the cost of the office equipment that has not yet been depreciated. This amount, called the **book value of the asset** (or **net book value**), is computed as shown below.

Book Value of Asset = Cost of the Asset – Accumulated Depreciation of Asset
Book Value of Office Equipment = Cost of Office Equipment – Accumulated Depre. of Office Equipment
Book Value of Office Equipment = $1,800 – $50
Book Value of Office Equipment = $1,750

The office equipment and its related accumulated depreciation are reported on the December 31, 2011, balance sheet as follows:

Office equipment	$1,800	
Less accumulated depreciation	50	$1,750

The market value of a fixed asset usually differs from its book value. This is because depreciation is an *allocation* method, not a *valuation* method. That is, depreciation allocates the cost of a fixed asset to expense over its estimated life. Depreciation does not measure changes in market values, which vary from year to year. Thus, on December 31, 2011, the market value of NetSolutions' office equipment could be more or less than $1,750.

If the adjustment for depreciation ($50) is not recorded, Depreciation Expense on the income statement will be understated by $50, and the net income will be overstated by $50. On the balance sheet, the book value of Office Equipment and Chris Clark, Capital will be overstated by $50. The effects of omitting the adjustment for depreciation are shown below.

	Amount of Misstatement
Income Statement	
Revenues correctly stated	$ XX
Expenses understated by	(50)
Net income overstated by	$ 50
Balance Sheet	
Assets overstated by	$ 50
Liabilities correctly stated	$ XX
Owner's equity overstated by	50
Total liabilities and owner's equity overstated by	$ 50

5 Methods of computing depreciation expense are described and illustrated in Chapter 10.

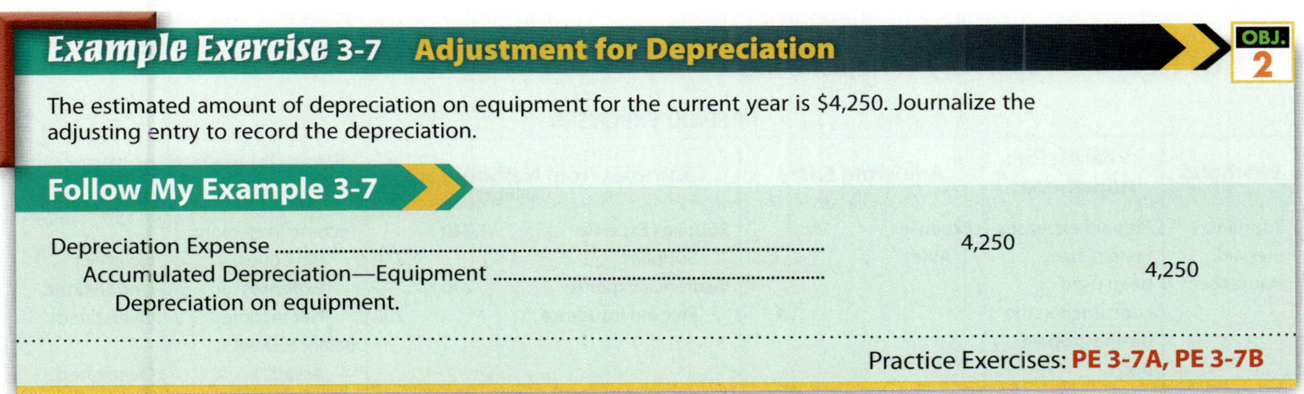

Example Exercise 3-7 Adjustment for Depreciation OBJ. 2

The estimated amount of depreciation on equipment for the current year is $4,250. Journalize the adjusting entry to record the depreciation.

Follow My Example 3-7

Depreciation Expense	4,250	
Accumulated Depreciation—Equipment		4,250
Depreciation on equipment.		

Practice Exercises: **PE 3-7A, PE 3-7B**

Summary of Adjustment Process

OBJ. 3 Summarize the adjustment process.

A summary of the basic types of adjusting entries is shown in Exhibit 8 on page 120.

The adjusting entries for NetSolutions are shown in Exhibit 9 on page 121. The adjusting entries are dated as of the last day of the period. However, because collecting the adjustment data requires time, the entries are usually recorded at a later date. An explanation is normally included with each adjusting entry.

NetSolutions' adjusting entries are posted to the ledger shown in Exhibit 10 on pages 122–123. The adjustments are shown in color in Exhibit 10 to distinguish them from other transactions.

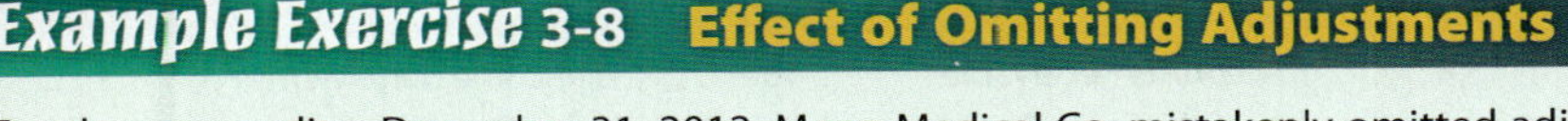

Example Exercise 3-8 Effect of Omitting Adjustments OBJ. 3

For the year ending December 31, 2012, Mann Medical Co. mistakenly omitted adjusting entries for (1) $8,600 of unearned revenue that was earned, (2) earned revenue that was not billed of $12,500, and (3) accrued wages of $2,900. Indicate the combined effect of the errors on (a) revenues, (b) expenses, and (c) net income for the year ended December 31, 2012.

Follow My Example 3-8

a. Revenues were understated by $21,100 ($8,600 + $12,500).
b. Expenses were understated by $2,900.
c. Net income was understated by $18,200 ($8,600 + $12,500 – $2,900).

Practice Exercises: **PE 3-8A, PE 3-8B**

EXHIBIT 8 **Summary of Adjustments**

Examples	Reason for Adjustment	Adjusting Entry	Examples from NetSolutions	Financial Statement Impact if Adjusting Entry Is Omitted
PREPAID EXPENSES				
Supplies, prepaid insurance	Prepaid expenses (assets) have been used or consumed in the business operations.	Expense Dr. Asset Cr.	Supplies Expense 1,240 Supplies 1,240 Insurance Expense 200 Prepaid Insurance 200	Income Statement: Revenues: No effect Expenses: Understated Net income: Overstated Balance Sheet: Assets: Overstated Liabilities: No effect Owner's equity (capital): Overstated
UNEARNED REVENUES				
Unearned rent, magazine subscriptions received in advance, fees received in advance of services	Cash received before the services have been provided is recorded as a liability. Some services have been provided to customer before the end of the accounting period.	Liability Dr. Revenue Cr.	Unearned Rent 120 Rent Revenue 120	Income Statement: Revenues: Understated Expenses: No effect Net income: Understated Balance Sheet: Assets: No effect Liabilities: Overstated Owner's equity (capital): Understated
ACCRUED REVENUES				
Services performed but not billed, interest to be received	Services have been provided to the customer, but have not been billed or recorded. Interest has been earned, but has not been received or recorded.	Asset Dr. Revenue Cr.	Accounts Receivable 500 Fees Earned 500	Income Statement: Revenues: Understated Expenses: No effect Net income: Understated Balance Sheet: Assets: Understated Liabilities: No effect Owner's equity (capital): Understated
ACCRUED EXPENSES				
Wages or salaries incurred but not paid, interest incurred but not paid	Expenses have been incurred, but have not been paid or recorded.	Expense Dr. Liability Cr.	Wages Expense 250 Wages Payable 250	Income Statement: Revenues: No effect Expenses: Understated Net income: Overstated Balance Sheet: Assets: No effect Liabilities: Understated Owner's equity (capital): Overstated
DEPRECIATION				
Depreciation of equipment and buildings	Fixed assets depreciate as they are used or consumed in the business operations.	Expense Dr. Contra Asset Cr.	Depreciation Expense 50 Accum. Depreciation—Office Equipment 50	Income Statement: Revenues: No effect Expenses: Understated Net income: Overstated Balance Sheet: Assets: Overstated Liabilities: No effect Owner's equity (capital): Overstated

EXHIBIT 9

Adjusting Entries—NetSolutions

Journal — *Page 5*

Date		Description	Post. Ref.	Debit	Credit
		Adjusting Entries			
2011 Dec	31	Supplies Expense	55	1,240	
		Supplies	14		1,240
		Supplies used ($2,000 – $760).			
	31	Insurance Expense	56	200	
		Prepaid Insurance	15		200
		Insurance expired ($2,400/12 months).			
	31	Unearned Rent	23	120	
		Rent Revenue	42		120
		Rent earned ($360/3 months).			
	31	Accounts Receivable	12	500	
		Fees Earned	41		500
		Accrued fees (25 hrs. × $20).			
	31	Wages Expense	51	250	
		Wages Payable	22		250
		Accrued wages.			
	31	Depreciation Expense	53	50	
		Accum. Depreciation—Office Equipment	19		50
		Depreciation on office equipment.			

An accountant may check whether all adjustments have been made by comparing current period adjustments with those of the prior period.

BusinessConnection

MICROSOFT CORPORATION

Microsoft Corporation develops, manufactures, licenses, and supports a wide range of computer software products, including Windows Vista, Windows 7, Windows XP, Word, Excel, and the Xbox® gaming system. When Microsoft sells its products, it incurs an obligation to support its software with technical support and periodic updates. As a result, not all the revenue is earned on the date of sale; some of the revenue on the date of sale is unearned. The portion of revenue related to support services, such as updates and technical support, is earned as time passes and support is provided to customers. Thus, each year Microsoft makes adjusting entries transferring some of its unearned revenue to revenue. The following excerpts were taken from Microsoft's financial statements:

> The percentage of revenue recorded as unearned . . . ranges from approximately 15% to 25% of the sales price for Windows XP Home, approximately 5% to 15% of the sales price for Windows XP Professional, . . .
>
> Unearned Revenue:

	June 30, 2009	June 30, 2008
Unearned revenue (in millions)	$14,284	$15,297

During the year ending June 30, 2010, Microsoft expects to record over $13,003 million of unearned revenue as revenue. At the same time, Microsoft will record additional unearned revenue from current period sales.

Source: Taken from Microsoft's June 30, 2009, annual report.

EXHIBIT 10 Ledger with Adjusting Entries—NetSolutions

Account *Cash* Account No. *11*

Date	Item	Post. Ref.	Debit	Credit	Balance Debit	Balance Credit
2011						
Nov. 1		1	25,000		25,000	
5		1		20,000	5,000	
18		1	7,500		12,500	
30		1		3,650	8,850	
30		1		950	7,900	
30		2		2,000	5,900	
Dec. 1		2		2,400	3,500	
1		2		800	2,700	
1		2	360		3,060	
6		2		180	2,880	
11		2		400	2,480	
13		3		950	1,530	
16		3	3,100		4,630	
20		3		900	3,730	
21		3	650		4,380	
23		3		1,450	2,930	
27		3		1,200	1,730	
31		3		310	1,420	
31		4		225	1,195	
31		4	2,870		4,065	
31		4		2,000	2,065	

Account *Accounts Receivable* Account No. *12*

Date	Item	Post. Ref.	Debit	Credit	Balance Debit	Balance Credit
2011						
Dec. 16		3	1,750		1,750	
21		3		650	1,100	
31		4	1,120		2,220	
31	Adjusting	5	500		2,720	

Account *Supplies* Account No. *14*

Date	Item	Post. Ref.	Debit	Credit	Balance Debit	Balance Credit
2011						
Nov. 10		1	1,350		1,350	
30		1		800	550	
Dec. 23		3	1,450		2,000	
31	Adjusting	5		1,240	760	

Account *Prepaid Insurance* Account No. *15*

Date	Item	Post. Ref.	Debit	Credit	Balance Debit	Balance Credit
2011						
Dec. 1		2	2,400		2,400	
31	Adjusting	5		200	2,200	

Account *Land* Account No. *17*

Date	Item	Post. Ref.	Debit	Credit	Balance Debit	Balance Credit
2011						
Nov. 5		1	20,000		20,000	

Account *Office Equipment* Account No. *18*

Date	Item	Post. Ref.	Debit	Credit	Balance Debit	Balance Credit
2011						
Dec. 4		2	1,800		1,800	

Account *Accum. Depr.—Office Equip.* Account No. *19*

Date	Item	Post. Ref.	Debit	Credit	Balance Debit	Balance Credit
2011						
Dec. 1	Adjusting	5		50		50

Account *Accounts Payable* Account No. *21*

Date	Item	Post. Ref.	Debit	Credit	Balance Debit	Balance Credit
2011						
Nov. 10		1		1,350		1,350
30		1	950			400
Dec. 4		2		1,800		2,200
11		2	400			1,800
20		3	900			900

Account *Wages Payable* Account No. *22*

Date	Item	Post. Ref.	Debit	Credit	Balance Debit	Balance Credit
2011						
Dec. 31	Adjusting	5		250		250

Account *Unearned Rent* Account No. *23*

Date	Item	Post. Ref.	Debit	Credit	Balance Debit	Balance Credit
2011						
Dec. 1		2		360		360
31	Adjusting	5	120			240

Account *Chris Clark, Capital* Account No. *31*

Date	Item	Post. Ref.	Debit	Credit	Balance Debit	Balance Credit
2011						
Nov. 1		1		25,000		25,000

EXHIBIT 10 **Ledger with Adjusting Entries—NetSolutions (*Concluded*)**

Account *Chris Clark, Drawing* — Account No. *32*

Date	Item	Post. Ref.	Debit	Credit	Balance Debit	Balance Credit
2011						
Nov. 30		2	2,000		2,000	
Dec. 31		4	2,000		4,000	

Account *Fees Earned* — Account No. *41*

Date	Item	Post. Ref.	Debit	Credit	Balance Debit	Balance Credit
2011						
Nov. 18		1		7,500		7,500
Dec. 16		3		3,100		10,600
16		3		1,750		12,350
31		4		2,870		15,220
31		4		1,120		16,340
31	Adjusting	5		500		16,840

Account *Rent Revenue* — Account No. *42*

Date	Item	Post. Ref.	Debit	Credit	Balance Debit	Balance Credit
2011						
Dec. 31	Adjusting	5		120		120

Account *Wages Expense* — Account No. *51*

Date	Item	Post. Ref.	Debit	Credit	Balance Debit	Balance Credit
2011						
Nov. 30		1	2,125		2,125	
Dec. 13		3	950		3,075	
27		3	1,200		4,275	
31	Adjusting	5	250		4,525	

Account *Rent Expense* — Account No. *52*

Date	Item	Post. Ref.	Debit	Credit	Balance Debit	Balance Credit
2011						
Nov. 30		1	800		800	
Dec. 1		2	800		1,600	

Account *Depreciation Expense* — Account No. *53*

Date	Item	Post. Ref.	Debit	Credit	Balance Debit	Balance Credit
2011						
Dec. 31	Adjusting	5	50		50	

Account *Utilities Expense* — Account No. *54*

Date	Item	Post. Ref.	Debit	Credit	Balance Debit	Balance Credit
2011						
Nov. 30		1	450		450	
Dec. 31		3	310		760	
31		4	225		985	

Account *Supplies Expense* — Account No. *55*

Date	Item	Post. Ref.	Debit	Credit	Balance Debit	Balance Credit
2011						
Nov. 30		1	800		800	
Dec. 31	Adjusting	5	1,240		2,040	

Account *Insurance Expense* — Account No. *56*

Date	Item	Post. Ref.	Debit	Credit	Balance Debit	Balance Credit
2011						
Dec. 31	Adjusting	5	200		200	

Account *Miscellaneous Expense* — Account No. *59*

Date	Item	Post. Ref.	Debit	Credit	Balance Debit	Balance Credit
2011						
Nov. 30		1	275		275	
Dec. 6		2	180		455	

Adjusted Trial Balance

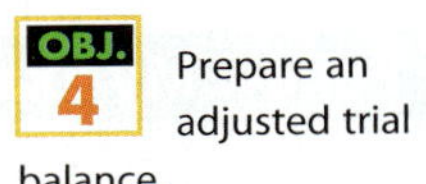

Prepare an adjusted trial balance.

After the adjusting entries are posted, an **adjusted trial balance** is prepared. The adjusted trial balance verifies the equality of the total debit and credit balances before the financial statements are prepared. If the adjusted trial balance does not balance, an error has occurred. However, as discussed in Chapter 2, errors may occur even though the adjusted trial balance totals agree. For example, if an adjusting entry were omitted, the adjusted trial balance totals would still agree.

Exhibit 11 shows the adjusted trial balance for NetSolutions as of December 31, 2011. Chapter 4 discusses how financial statements, including a classified balance sheet, are prepared from an adjusted trial balance.

EXHIBIT 11

Adjusted Trial Balance

NetSolutions
Adjusted Trial Balance
December 31, 2011

	Debit Balances	Credit Balances
Cash	2,065	
Accounts Receivable	2,720	
Supplies	760	
Prepaid Insurance	2,200	
Land	20,000	
Office Equipment	1,800	
Accumulated Depreciation—Office Equipment		50
Accounts Payable		900
Wages Payable		250
Unearned Rent		240
Chris Clark, Capital		25,000
Chris Clark, Drawing	4,000	
Fees Earned		16,840
Rent Revenue		120
Wages Expense	4,525	
Rent Expense	1,600	
Depreciation Expense	50	
Utilities Expense	985	
Supplies Expense	2,040	
Insurance Expense	200	
Miscellaneous Expense	455	
	43,400	43,400

Example Exercise 3-9 Effect of Errors on Adjusted Trial Balance

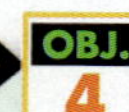

For each of the following errors, considered individually, indicate whether the error would cause the adjusted trial balance totals to be unequal. If the error would cause the adjusted trial balance totals to be unequal, indicate whether the debit or credit total is higher and by how much.

a. The adjustment for accrued fees of $5,340 was journalized as a debit to Accounts Payable for $5,340 and a credit to Fees Earned of $5,340.

b. The adjustment for depreciation of $3,260 was journalized as a debit to Depreciation Expense for $3,620 and a credit to Accumulated Depreciation for $3,260.

Follow My Example 3-9

a. The totals are equal even though the debit should have been to Accounts Receivable instead of Accounts Payable.

b. The totals are unequal. The debit total is higher by $360 ($3,620 – $3,260).

Practice Exercises: PE 3-9A, PE 3-9B

Financial Analysis and Interpretation: Vertical Analysis

F·A·I

OBJ. 5 Describe and illustrate the use of vertical analysis in evaluating a company's performance and financial condition.

Comparing each item in a financial statement with a total amount from the same statement is useful in analyzing relationships within the financial statement. **Vertical analysis** is the term used to describe such comparisons.

In vertical analysis of a balance sheet, each asset item is stated as a percent of the total assets. Each liability and owner's equity item is stated as a percent of total liabilities and owner's equity. In vertical analysis of an income statement, each item is stated as a percent of revenues or fees earned.

Vertical analysis is also useful for analyzing changes in financial statements over time. To illustrate, a vertical analysis of two years of income statements for J. Holmes, Attorney-at-Law, is shown below.

J. Holmes, Attorney-at-Law
Income Statements
For the Years Ended December 31, 2012 and 2011

	2012		2011	
	Amount	Percent	Amount	Percent
Fees earned	$187,500	100.0%	$150,000	100.0%
Operating expenses:				
Wages expense	$ 60,000	32.0%*	$ 45,000	30.0%**
Rent expense	15,000	8.0	12,000	8.0
Utilities expense	12,500	6.7	9,000	6.0
Supplies expense	2,700	1.4	3,000	2.0
Miscellaneous expense	2,300	1.2	1,800	1.2
Total operating expenses	$ 92,500	49.3%	$ 70,800	47.2%
Net income	$ 95,000	50.7%	$ 79,200	52.8%

*Rounded to one decimal place.
**$45,000 ÷ $150,000

The preceding vertical analysis indicates both favorable and unfavorable trends affecting the income statement of J. Holmes, Attorney-at-Law. The increase in wages expense of 2% (32.0% – 30.0%) is an unfavorable trend, as is the increase in utilities expense of 0.7% (6.7% – 6.0%). A favorable trend is the decrease in supplies expense of 0.6% (2.0% – 1.4%). Rent expense and miscellaneous expense as a percent of fees earned were constant. The net result of these trends is that net income decreased as a percent of fees earned from 52.8% to 50.7%.

The analysis of the various percentages shown for J. Holmes, Attorney-at-Law, can be enhanced by comparisons with industry averages. Such averages are published by trade associations and financial information services. Any major differences between industry averages should be investigated.

Vertical analysis of operating income taken from two years of income statements for RealNetworks is shown below.

RealNetworks
Income Statements
For the Years Ended December 31, 2009 and 2008

	2009		2008	
	Amount	Percent	Amount	Percent
Revenues	$562,264*	100.0%	$604,810	100.0%
Expenses:				
Cost of revenues	$ 222,142	39.5%	$233,244	38.6%
Selling expenses	199,148	35.4	256,135	42.3
Administrative expenses	79,164	14.1	69,981	11.6
Other expenses (net)	299,048	53.2	332,855	55.0
Total operating expenses	$799,502	142.2%	$892,215	147.5%
Operating income (loss)	$(237,238)	(42.2)%	$ (287,405)	(47.5)%

*In millions

The preceding analysis indicates that RealNetworks experienced an operating loss of 42.2% of revenues in 2009. The analysis indicates that the cost of revenues was comparable across both years. Selling expenses decreased from 42.3% to 35.4%, while administrative expenses increased from 11.6% to 14.1%. The major cause of the losses in 2009 and 2008 was due to the other expenses, which were 53.2% and 55.0% of revenues for 2009 and 2008, respectively. The cause of these other expenses should be investigated. An examination of RealNetworks' annual report indicates that a large portion of these expenses was caused by the loss in value of some of its long-term assets due to the depressed economic conditions of the last several years.

Example Exercise 3-10 Vertical Analysis

OBJ. 5

Two income statements for Fortson Company are shown below.

Fortson Company
Income Statements
For the Years Ended December 31, 2012 and 2011

	2012	2011
Fees earned	$425,000	$375,000
Operating expenses	263,500	210,000
Operating income	$161,500	$165,000

a. Prepare a vertical analysis of Fortson Company's income statements.

b. Does the vertical analysis indicate a favorable or unfavorable trend?

Follow My Example 3-10

a.

Fortson Company
Income Statements
For the Years Ended December 31, 2012 and 2011

	2012		2011	
	Amount	Percent	Amount	Percent
Fees earned	$425,000	100%	$375,000	100%
Operating expenses	263,500	62	210,000	56
Operating income	$161,500	38%	$165,000	44%

b. An unfavorable trend of increasing operating expenses and decreasing operating income is indicated.

Practice Exercises: PE 3-10A, PE 3-10B

At a Glance 3

Describe the nature of the adjusting process.

Key Points The accrual basis of accounting requires that revenues are reported in the period in which they are earned and expenses are matched with the revenues they generate. The updating of accounts at the end of the accounting period is called the adjusting process. Each adjusting entry affects an income statement and balance sheet account. The four types of accounts requiring adjusting entries are prepaid expenses, unearned revenues, accrued revenues, and accrued expenses.

Learning Outcomes	Example Exercises	Practice Exercises
• Explain why accrual accounting requires adjusting entries.		
• List accounts that do and do NOT require adjusting entries at the end of the accounting period.	EE3-1	PE3-1A, 3-1B
• Give an example of a prepaid expense, unearned revenue, accrued revenue, and accrued expense.	EE3-2	PE3-2A, 3-2B

Journalize entries for accounts requiring adjustment.

Key Points At the end of the period, adjusting entries are needed for prepaid expenses, unearned revenues, accrued revenues, and accrued expenses. In addition, an adjusting entry is necessary to record depreciation on fixed assets.

Learning Outcomes	Example Exercises	Practice Exercises
• Prepare an adjusting entry for a prepaid expense.	EE3-3	PE3-3A, 3-3B
• Prepare an adjusting entry for an unearned revenue.	EE3-4	PE3-4A, 3-4B
• Prepare an adjusting entry for an accrued revenue.	EE3-5	PE3-5A, 3-5B
• Prepare an adjusting entry for an accrued expense.	EE3-6	PE3-6A, 3-6B
• Prepare an adjusting entry for depreciation expense.	EE3-7	PE3-7A, 3-7B

Summarize the adjustment process.

Key Points A summary of adjustments, including the type of adjustment, reason for the adjustment, the adjusting entry, and the effect of omitting an adjustment on the financial statements, is shown in Exhibit 8.

Learning Outcomes	Example Exercises	Practice Exercises
• Determine the effect on the income statement and balance sheet of omitting an adjusting entry for prepaid expense, unearned revenue, accrued revenue, accrued expense, and depreciation.	EE3-8	PE3-8A, 3-8B

Prepare an adjusted trial balance.

Key Points After all the adjusting entries have been posted, the equality of the total debit balances and total credit balances is verified by an adjusted trial balance.

Learning Outcomes	Example Exercises	Practice Exercises
• Prepare an adjusted trial balance.		
• Determine the effect of errors on the equality of the adjusted trial balance.	EE3-9	PE3-9A, 3-9B

Describe and illustrate the use of vertical analysis in evaluating a company's performance and financial condition.

Key Points Comparing each item on a financial statement with a total amount from the same statement is called vertical analysis. On the balance sheet, each asset is expressed as a percent of total assets and each liability and owner's equity is expressed as a percent of total liabilities and owner's equity. On the income statement, each revenue and expense is expressed as a percent of total revenues or fees earned.

Learning Outcomes	Example Exercises	Practice Exercises
• Describe vertical analysis.		
• Prepare a vertical analysis report of a financial statement.	EE3-10	PE3-10A, 3-10B

Key Terms

accounting period concept (104)
accrual basis of accounting (104)
accrued expenses (108)
accrued revenues (107)
Accumulated Depreciation (117)
adjusted trial balance (123)
adjusting entries (105)
adjusting process (105)
book value of the asset (or net book value) (118)
cash basis of accounting (104)
contra accounts (or contra asset accounts) (117)
depreciate (117)
depreciation (117)
depreciation expense (117)
fixed assets (or plant assets) (116)
matching concept (or matching principle) (104)
prepaid expenses (105)
revenue recognition concept (104)
unearned revenues (106)
vertical analysis (125)

Illustrative Problem

Three years ago, T. Roderick organized Harbor Realty. At July 31, 2012, the end of the current year, the unadjusted trial balance of Harbor Realty appears as shown below.

Harbor Realty
Unadjusted Trial Balance
July 31, 2012

	Debit Balances	Credit Balances
Cash	3,425	
Accounts Receivable	7,000	
Supplies	1,270	
Prepaid Insurance	620	
Office Equipment	51,650	
Accumulated Depreciation—Office Equipment		9,700
Accounts Payable		925
Wages Payable		0
Unearned Fees		1,250
T. Roderick, Capital		29,000
T. Roderick, Drawing	5,200	
Fees Earned		59,125
Wages Expense	22,415	
Depreciation Expense	0	
Rent Expense	4,200	
Utilities Expense	2,715	
Supplies Expense	0	
Insurance Expense	0	
Miscellaneous Expense	1,505	
	100,000	100,000

The data needed to determine year-end adjustments are as follows:

a. Supplies on hand at July 31, 2012, $380.
b. Insurance premiums expired during the year, $315.
c. Depreciation of equipment during the year, $4,950.
d. Wages accrued but not paid at July 31, 2012, $440.

e. Accrued fees earned but not recorded at July 31, 2012, $1,000.

f. Unearned fees on July 31, 2012, $750.

Instructions

1. Prepare the necessary adjusting journal entries. Include journal entry explanations.
2. Determine the balance of the accounts affected by the adjusting entries, and prepare an adjusted trial balance.

Solution

1.

Journal

Date		Description	Post. Ref.	Debit	Credit
2012					
July	31	Supplies Expense		890	
		Supplies			890
		Supplies used ($1,270 – $380).			
	31	Insurance Expense		315	
		Prepaid Insurance			315
		Insurance expired.			
	31	Depreciation Expense		4,950	
		Accumulated Depreciation—Office Equipment			4,950
		Depreciation expense.			
	31	Wages Expense		440	
		Wages Payable			440
		Accrued wages.			
	31	Accounts Receivable		1,000	
		Fees Earned			1,000
		Accrued fees.			
	31	Unearned Fees		500	
		Fees Earned			500
		Fees earned ($1,250 – $750).			

2.

Harbor Realty
Adjusted Trial Balance
July 31, 2012

	Debit Balances	Credit Balances
Cash	3,425	
Accounts Receivable	8,000	
Supplies	380	
Prepaid Insurance	305	
Office Equipment	51,650	
Accumulated Depreciation—Office Equipment		14,650
Accounts Payable		925
Wages Payable		440
Unearned Fees		750
T. Roderick, Capital		29,000
T. Roderick, Drawing	5,200	
Fees Earned		60,625
Wages Expense	22,855	
Depreciation Expense	4,950	
Rent Expense	4,200	
Utilities Expense	2,715	
Supplies Expense	890	
Insurance Expense	315	
Miscellaneous Expense	1,505	
	106,390	106,390

Discussion Questions

1. How are revenues and expenses reported on the income statement under (a) the cash basis of accounting and (b) the accrual basis of accounting?
2. Is the matching concept related to (a) the cash basis of accounting or (b) the accrual basis of accounting?
3. Why are adjusting entries needed at the end of an accounting period?
4. What is the difference between *adjusting entries* and *correcting entries*?
5. Identify the four different categories of adjusting entries frequently required at the end of an accounting period.
6. If the effect of the debit portion of an adjusting entry is to increase the balance of an asset account, which of the following statements describes the effect of the credit portion of the entry?
   a. Increases the balance of a revenue account.
   b. Increases the balance of an expense account.
   c. Increases the balance of a liability account.
7. If the effect of the credit portion of an adjusting entry is to increase the balance of a liability account, which of the following statements describes the effect of the debit portion of the entry?
   a. Increases the balance of a revenue account.
   b. Increases the balance of an expense account.
   c. Increases the balance of an asset account.
8. Does every adjusting entry have an effect on determining the amount of net income for a period? Explain.
9. On November 1 of the current year, a business paid the November rent on the building that it occupies. (a) Do the rights acquired at November 1 represent an asset or an expense? (b) What is the justification for debiting Rent Expense at the time of payment?
10. (a) Explain the purpose of the two accounts: Depreciation Expense and Accumulated Depreciation. (b) What is the normal balance of each account? (c) Is it customary for the balances of the two accounts to be equal in amount? (d) In what financial statements, if any, will each account appear?

Practice Exercises

Learning Objectives	Example Exercises	
OBJ. 1	EE 3-1 p. 105	**PE 3-1A Accounts requiring adjustment**

PE 3-1A Accounts requiring adjustment (OBJ. 1; EE 3-1 p. 105)

Indicate with a Yes or No whether or not each of the following accounts normally requires an adjusting entry.

a. Accumulated Depreciation
b. Albert Stucky, Drawing
c. Office Equipment
d. Salaries Payable
e. Supplies
f. Unearned Rent

PE 3-1B Accounts requiring adjustment (OBJ. 1; EE 3-1 p. 105)

Indicate with a Yes or No whether or not each of the following accounts normally requires an adjusting entry.

a. Building
b. Cash
c. Interest Expense
d. Miscellaneous Expense
e. Pam Ingersoll, Capital
f. Prepaid Insurance

PE 3-2A Type of adjustment (OBJ. 1; EE 3-2 p. 109)

Classify the following items as (1) prepaid expense, (2) unearned revenue, (3) accrued revenue, or (4) accrued expense.

a. Cash received for services not yet rendered
b. Insurance paid
c. Rent revenue earned but not received
d. Salaries owed but not yet paid

PE 3-2B Type of adjustment (OBJ. 1; EE 3-2 p. 109)

Classify the following items as (1) prepaid expense, (2) unearned revenue, (3) accrued revenue, or (4) accrued expense.

a. Cash received for use of land next month
b. Fees earned but not received
c. Rent expense owed but not yet paid
d. Supplies on hand

PE 3-3A Adjustment for prepaid expense (OBJ. 2; EE 3-3 p. 112)

The supplies account had a beginning balance of $2,400 and was debited for $3,975 for supplies purchased during the year. Journalize the adjusting entry required at the end of the year assuming the amount of supplies on hand is $1,375.

PE 3-3B Adjustment for prepaid expense (OBJ. 2; EE 3-3 p. 112)

The prepaid insurance account had a beginning balance of $7,200 and was debited for $4,800 of premiums paid during the year. Journalize the adjusting entry required at the end of the year assuming the amount of unexpired insurance related to future periods is $8,000.

PE 3-4A Adjustment for unearned revenue (OBJ. 2; EE 3-4 p. 113)

The balance in the unearned fees account, before adjustment at the end of the year, is $178,900. Journalize the adjusting entry required assuming the amount of unearned fees at the end of the year is $18,650.

PE 3-4B Adjustment for unearned revenue (OBJ. 2; EE 3-4 p. 113)

On August 1, 2012, Treadwell Co. received $10,500 for the rent of land for 12 months. Journalize the adjusting entry required for unearned rent on December 31, 2012.

PE 3-5A Adjustment for accrued revenues (OBJ. 2; EE 3-5 p. 114)

At the end of the current year, $11,600 of fees have been earned but have not been billed to clients. Journalize the adjusting entry to record the accrued fees.

Granite Appliance Repairs
Income Statement
For the Year Ended July 31, 2012

Service revenue		$225,000
Less: Rent paid	$62,400	
Wages paid	49,500	
Supplies paid	14,000	
Utilities paid	13,000	
Insurance paid	7,200	
Miscellaneous payments	18,200	164,300
Net income		$ 60,700

Granite Appliance Repairs
Balance Sheet
July 31, 2012

Assets	
Cash	$ 31,800
Amounts due from customers	37,500
Truck	110,700
Total assets	$180,000
Equities	
Owner's capital	$180,000

After reviewing the financial statements, the loan officer at the bank asked your brother if he used the accrual basis of accounting for revenues and expenses. Your brother responded that he did and that is why he included an account for "Amounts Due from Customers." The loan officer then asked whether or not the accounts were adjusted prior to the preparation of the statements. Your brother answered that they had not been adjusted.

a. Why do you think the loan officer suspected that the accounts had not been adjusted prior to the preparation of the statements?

b. Indicate possible accounts that might need to be adjusted before an accurate set of financial statements could be prepared.

CP 3-5 Codes of ethics

Obtain a copy of your college or university's student code of conduct. In groups of three or four, answer the following questions:

1. Compare this code of conduct with the accountant's Codes of Professional Conduct, which is linked to the text Web site at **www.cengage.com/accounting/warren**.
2. One of your classmates asks you for permission to copy your homework, which your instructor will be collecting and grading for part of your overall term grade. Although your instructor has not stated whether one student may or may not copy another student's homework, is it ethical for you to allow your classmate to copy your homework? Is it ethical for your classmate to copy your homework?

CHAPTER 4

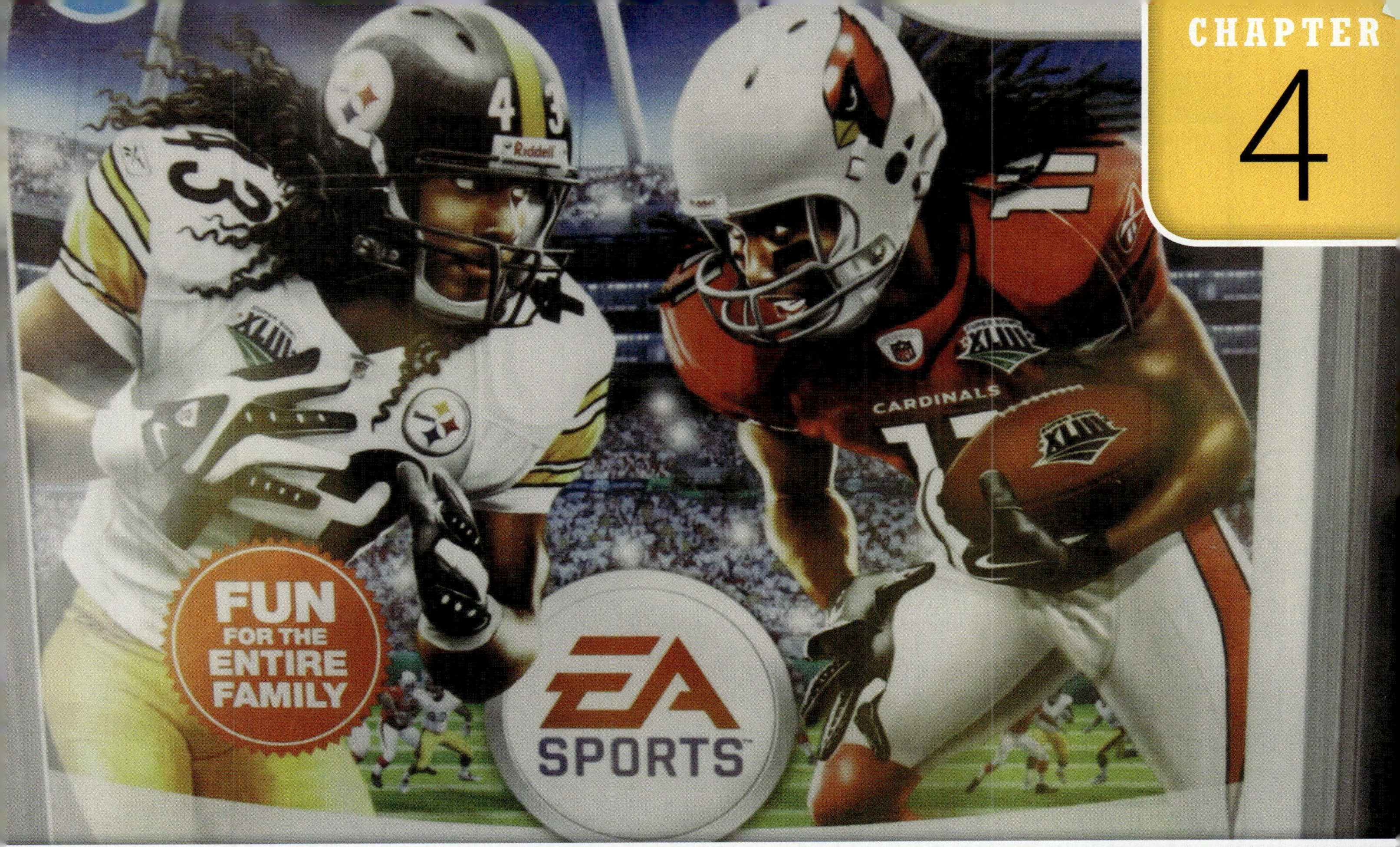

AP Photo/Paul Sakuma

Completing the Accounting Cycle

Electronic Arts Inc.

Most of us have had to file a personal tax return. At the beginning of the year, you estimate your upcoming income and decide whether you need to increase your payroll tax withholdings or perhaps pay estimated taxes. During the year, you earn income and enter into tax-related transactions, such as making charitable contributions. At the end of the year, your employer sends you a tax withholding information (W-2) form, and you collect the tax records needed for completing your yearly tax forms. As the next year begins, you start the cycle all over again.

Businesses also go through a cycle of activities. For example, **Electronic Arts Inc.**, the world's largest developer and marketer of electronic game software, begins its cycle by developing new or revised game titles, such as Madden NFL Football®, Need for Speed®, The Sims®, and The Lord of the Rings®. These games are marketed and sold throughout the year. During the year, operating transactions of the business are recorded. For Electronic Arts, such transactions include the salaries of game developers, advertising expenditures, costs for producing and packaging games, and game revenues. At the end of the year, financial statements are prepared that summarize the operating activities for the year. Electronic Arts publishes these statements on its Web site at **http:// investor.ea.com**. Finally, before the start of the next year, the accounts are readied for recording the operations of the next year.

In Chapter 1, the initial cycle for NetSolutions began with Chris Clark's investment in the business on November 1, 2011. The cycle continued with recording NetSolutions' transactions for November and December, as we discussed and illustrated in Chapters 1 and 2. In Chapter 3, the cycle continued when the adjusting entries for the two months ending December 31, 2011, were recorded. In this chapter, the cycle is completed for NetSolutions by preparing financial statements and getting the accounts ready for recording transactions of the next period.

Learning Objectives

After studying this chapter, you should be able to:	Example Exercises	Page
OBJ. 1 Describe the flow of accounting information from the unadjusted trial balance into the adjusted trial balance and financial statements.		
Flow of Accounting Information	EE 4-1	152
OBJ. 2 Prepare financial statements from adjusted account balances.		
Financial Statements		
Income Statement		
Statement of Owner's Equity	EE 4-2	154
Balance Sheet	EE 4-3	155–156
OBJ. 3 Prepare closing entries.		
Closing Entries		
Journalizing and Posting Closing Entries	EE 4-4	159
Post-Closing Trial Balance		
OBJ. 4 Describe the accounting cycle.		
Accounting Cycle	EE 4-5	162
OBJ. 5 Illustrate the accounting cycle for one period.		
Illustration of the Accounting Cycle		
OBJ. 6 Explain what is meant by the fiscal year and the natural business year.		
Fiscal Year		
OBJ. 7 Describe and illustrate the use of working capital and the current ratio in evaluating a company's financial condition.		
Financial Analysis and Interpretation: Working Capital and Current Ratio	EE 4-6	175–176

At a Glance 4 Page 176D

OBJ. 1 Describe the flow of accounting information from the unadjusted trial balance into the adjusted trial balance and financial statements.

Flow of Accounting Information

The process of adjusting the accounts and preparing financial statements is one of the most important in accounting. Using the **NetSolutions** illustration from Chapters 1–3, the end-of-period spreadsheet and flow of accounting data in adjusting accounts and preparing financial statements are summarized in Exhibit 1.

The end-of-period spreadsheet in Exhibit 1 begins with the unadjusted trial balance. The unadjusted trial balance verifies that the total of the debit balances equals the total of the credit balances. If the trial balance totals are unequal, an error has occurred. Any errors must be found and corrected before the end-of-period process can continue.

Many companies use Microsoft's Excel® software to prepare end-of-period spreadsheets.

The adjustments for NetSolutions from Chapter 3 are shown in the Adjustments columns of the spreadsheet. Cross-referencing (by letters) the debit and credit of each adjustment is useful in reviewing the effect of the adjustments on the unadjusted account balances. The adjustments are normally entered in the order in which the data are assembled. If the titles of the accounts to be adjusted do not appear in the unadjusted trial balance, the accounts are inserted in their proper order in the Account Title column. The total of the Adjustments columns verifies that the total debits equal the total credits for the adjusting entries. The total of the Debit column must equal the total of the Credit column.

The adjustments in the spreadsheet are added to or subtracted from the amounts in the Unadjusted Trial Balance columns to arrive at the amounts inserted in the Adjusted Trial Balance columns. In this way, the Adjusted Trial Balance columns of the spreadsheet illustrate the effect of the adjusting entries on the unadjusted accounts. The totals of the Adjusted Trial Balance columns verify that the totals of the debit and credit balances are equal after adjustment.

EXHIBIT 1

End-of-Period Spreadsheet and Flow of Accounting Data, NetSolutions

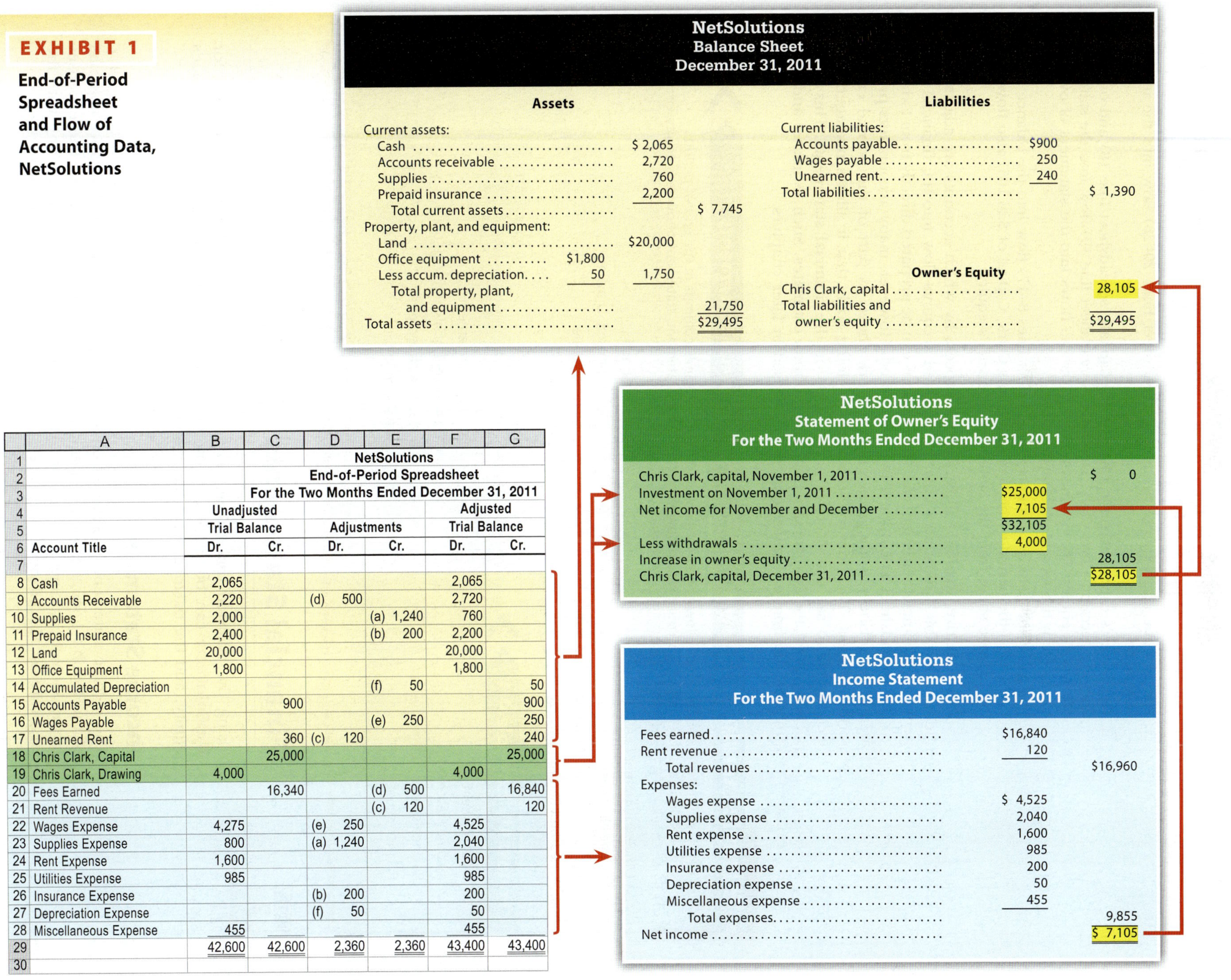

	A	B	C	D	E	F	G
1				NetSolutions			
2				End-of-Period Spreadsheet			
3				For the Two Months Ended December 31, 2011			
4		Unadjusted				Adjusted	
5		Trial Balance		Adjustments		Trial Balance	
6	Account Title	Dr.	Cr.	Dr.	Cr.	Dr.	Cr.
7							
8	Cash	2,065				2,065	
9	Accounts Receivable	2,220		(d) 500		2,720	
10	Supplies	2,000			(a) 1,240	760	
11	Prepaid Insurance	2,400			(b) 200	2,200	
12	Land	20,000				20,000	
13	Office Equipment	1,800				1,800	
14	Accumulated Depreciation				(f) 50		50
15	Accounts Payable		900				900
16	Wages Payable				(e) 250		250
17	Unearned Rent		360	(c) 120			240
18	Chris Clark, Capital		25,000				25,000
19	Chris Clark, Drawing	4,000				4,000	
20	Fees Earned		16,340		(d) 500		16,840
21	Rent Revenue				(c) 120		120
22	Wages Expense	4,275		(e) 250		4,525	
23	Supplies Expense	800		(a) 1,240		2,040	
24	Rent Expense	1,600				1,600	
25	Utilities Expense	985				985	
26	Insurance Expense			(b) 200		200	
27	Depreciation Expense			(f) 50		50	
28	Miscellaneous Expense	455				455	
29		42,600	42,600	2,360	2,360	43,400	43,400
30							

NetSolutions
Balance Sheet
December 31, 2011

Assets			
Current assets:			
Cash		$ 2,065	
Accounts receivable		2,720	
Supplies		760	
Prepaid insurance		2,200	
Total current assets			$ 7,745
Property, plant, and equipment:			
Land		$20,000	
Office equipment	$1,800		
Less accum. depreciation	50	1,750	
Total property, plant, and equipment			21,750
Total assets			$29,495

Liabilities		
Current liabilities:		
Accounts payable	$900	
Wages payable	250	
Unearned rent	240	
Total liabilities		$ 1,390
Owner's Equity		
Chris Clark, capital		28,105
Total liabilities and owner's equity		$29,495

NetSolutions
Statement of Owner's Equity
For the Two Months Ended December 31, 2011

Chris Clark, capital, November 1, 2011		$ 0
Investment on November 1, 2011	$25,000	
Net income for November and December	7,105	
	$32,105	
Less withdrawals	4,000	
Increase in owner's equity		28,105
Chris Clark, capital, December 31, 2011		$28,105

NetSolutions
Income Statement
For the Two Months Ended December 31, 2011

Fees earned	$16,840	
Rent revenue	120	
Total revenues		$16,960
Expenses:		
Wages expense	$ 4,525	
Supplies expense	2,040	
Rent expense	1,600	
Utilities expense	985	
Insurance expense	200	
Depreciation expense	50	
Miscellaneous expense	455	
Total expenses		9,855
Net income		$ 7,105

Exhibit 1 also illustrates the flow of accounts from the adjusted trial balance into the financial statements as follows:

1. The revenue and expense accounts (spreadsheet lines 20–28) flow into the income statement.
2. The owner's capital account, Chris Clark, Capital, (spreadsheet line 18) and owner's drawing account, Chris Clark, Drawing, (spreadsheet line 19) flow into the statement of owner's equity. The net income of $7,105 also flows into the statement of owner's equity from the income statement.
3. The asset and liability accounts (spreadsheet lines 8–17) flow into the balance sheet. The end-of-the-period owner's equity (Chris Clark, Capital of $28,105) also flows into the balance sheet from the statement of owner's equity.

To summarize, Exhibit 1 illustrates the process by which accounts are adjusted. In addition, Exhibit 1 illustrates how the adjusted accounts flow into the financial statements. The financial statements for NetSolutions can be prepared directly from Exhibit 1.

The spreadsheet in Exhibit 1 is not required. However, many accountants prepare such a spreadsheet, sometimes called a work sheet, as part of the normal end-of-period process. The primary advantage in doing so is that it allows managers and accountants to see the effect of adjustments on the financial statements. This is especially useful for adjustments that depend upon estimates. Such estimates and their effect on the financial statements are discussed in later chapters.[1]

Example Exercise 4-1 Flow of Accounts into Financial Statements

OBJ. 1

The balances for the accounts listed below appear in the Adjusted Trial Balance columns of the end-of-period spreadsheet. Indicate whether each account would flow into the income statement, statement of owner's equity, or balance sheet.

1. Office Equipment
2. Utilities Expense
3. Accumulated Depreciation—Equipment
4. Unearned Rent
5. Fees Earned
6. Doug Johnson, Drawing
7. Rent Revenue
8. Supplies

Follow My Example 4-1

1. Balance sheet
2. Income statement
3. Balance sheet
4. Balance sheet
5. Income statement
6. Statement of owner's equity
7. Income statement
8. Balance sheet

Practice Exercises: **PE 4-1A, PE 4-1B**

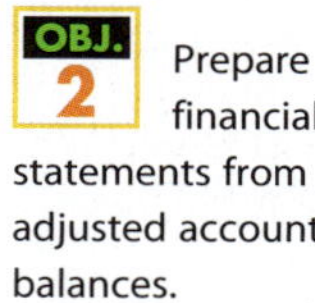

Prepare financial statements from adjusted account balances.

Financial Statements

Using the adjusted trial balance shown in Exhibit 1, the financial statements for **NetSolutions** can be prepared. The income statement, the statement of owner's equity, and the balance sheet are shown in Exhibit 2.

Income Statement

The income statement is prepared directly from the Adjusted Trial Balance columns of the Exhibit 1 spreadsheet, beginning with fees earned of $16,840. The expenses in the income statement in Exhibit 2 are listed in order of size, beginning with the larger items. Miscellaneous expense is the last item, regardless of its amount.

1 The appendix to this chapter describes and illustrates how to prepare an end-of-period spreadsheet (work sheet) that includes financial statement columns.

EXHIBIT 2 **Financial Statements, NetSolutions**

NetSolutions
Income Statement
For the Two Months Ended December 31, 2011

Fees earned	$16,840	
Rent revenue	120	
Total revenues		$16,960
Expenses:		
Wages expense	$ 4,525	
Supplies expense	2,040	
Rent expense	1,600	
Utilities expense	985	
Insurance expense	200	
Depreciation expense	50	
Miscellaneous expense	455	
Total expenses		9,855
Net income		$ 7,105

NetSolutions
Statement of Owner's Equity
For the Two Months Ended December 31, 2011

Chris Clark, capital, November 1, 2011		$ 0
Investment on November 1, 2011	$25,000	
Net income for November and December	7,105	
	$32,105	
Less withdrawals	4,000	
Increase in owner's equity		28,105
Chris Clark, capital, December 31, 2011		$28,105

NetSolutions
Balance Sheet
December 31, 2011

Assets				**Liabilities**		
Current assets:				Current liabilities:		
Cash		$ 2,065		Accounts payable	$900	
Accounts receivable		2,720		Wages payable	250	
Supplies		760		Unearned rent	240	
Prepaid insurance		2,200		Total liabilities		$ 1,390
Total current assets			$ 7,745			
Property, plant, and equipment:						
Land		$20,000				
Office equipment	$1,800					
Less accum. depreciation	50	1,750		**Owner's Equity**		
Total property, plant, and equipment			21,750	Chris Clark, capital		28,105
Total assets			$29,495	Total liabilities and owner's equity		$29,495

31	Adjusting	5	250		4,525		Dec. 6		2	180		455	
31	Closing	6		4,525	—	—	31	Closing	6		455	—	—

(continued)

EXHIBIT 6 Ledger, NetSolutions

EXHIBIT 17 Ledger, Kelly Consulting

Ledger

Account *Cash* — Account No. *11*

Date	Item	Post. Ref.	Debit	Credit	Balance Debit	Balance Credit
2012						
Apr. 1		1	13,100		13,100	
1		1		4,800	8,300	
2		1		1,800	6,500	
4		1	5,000		11,500	
6		1	1,800		13,300	
10		1		120	13,180	
12		1		1,200	11,980	
14		1		750	11,230	
17		2	6,250		17,480	
18		2		800	16,680	
24		2	3,850		20,530	
26		2	5,600		26,130	
27		2		750	25,380	
29		2		130	25,250	
30		2		200	25,050	
30		2	3,050		28,100	
30		2		6,000	22,100	

Account *Accounts Receivable* — Account No. *12*

Date	Item	Post. Ref.	Debit	Credit	Balance Debit	Balance Credit
2012						
Apr. 1		1	3,000		3,000	
6		1		1,800	1,200	
12		1	4,200		5,400	
20		2	2,100		7,500	
26		2		5,600	1,900	
30		2	1,500		3,400	

Account *Supplies* — Account No. *14*

Date	Item	Post. Ref.	Debit	Credit	Balance Debit	Balance Credit
2012						
Apr. 1		1	1,400		1,400	
18		2	800		2,200	
30	Adjusting	3		850	1,350	

Account *Prepaid Rent* — Account No. *15*

Date	Item	Post. Ref.	Debit	Credit	Balance Debit	Balance Credit
2012						
Apr. 1		1	4,800		4,800	
30	Adjusting	3		1,600	3,200	

Account *Prepaid Insurance* — Account No. *16*

Date	Item	Post. Ref.	Debit	Credit	Balance Debit	Balance Credit
2012						
Apr. 2		1	1,800		1,800	
30	Adjusting	3		300	1,500	

Account *Office Equipment* — Account No. *18*

Date	Item	Post. Ref.	Debit	Credit	Balance Debit	Balance Credit
2012						
Apr. 1		1	12,500		12,500	
5		1	2,000		14,500	

Account *Accumulated Depreciation* — Account No. *19*

Date	Item	Post. Ref.	Debit	Credit	Balance Debit	Balance Credit
2012						
Apr. 30	Adjusting	3		330		330

Account *Accounts Payable* — Account No. *21*

Date	Item	Post. Ref.	Debit	Credit	Balance Debit	Balance Credit
2012						
Apr. 5		1		2,000		2,000
12		1	1,200			800

Account *Salaries Payable* — Account No. *22*

Date	Item	Post. Ref.	Debit	Credit	Balance Debit	Balance Credit
2012						
Apr. 30	Adjusting	3		120		120

Account *Unearned Fees* — Account No. *23*

Date	Item	Post. Ref.	Debit	Credit	Balance Debit	Balance Credit
2012						
Apr. 4		1		5,000		5,000
30	Adjusting	3	2,500			2,500

Account *Kelly Pitney, Capital* — Account No. *31*

Date	Item	Post. Ref.	Debit	Credit	Balance Debit	Balance Credit
2012						
Apr. 1		1		30,000		30,000
30	Closing	4		18,300		48,300
30	Closing	4	6,000			42,300

EXHIBIT 17 Ledger, Kelly Consulting (*concluded*)

Account *Kelly Pitney, Drawing* — Account No. *32*

Date	Item	Post. Ref.	Debit	Credit	Balance Debit	Balance Credit
2012 Apr. 30		2	6,000		6,000	
30	Closing	4		6,000	—	—

Account *Income Summary* — Account No. *33*

Date	Item	Post. Ref.	Debit	Credit	Balance Debit	Balance Credit
2012 Apr. 30	Closing	4		23,450		23,450
30	Closing	4	5,150			18,300
30	Closing	4	18,300		—	—

Account *Fees Earned* — Account No. *41*

Date	Item	Post. Ref.	Debit	Credit	Balance Debit	Balance Credit
2012 Apr. 12		1		4,200		4,200
17		2		6,250		10,450
20		2		2,100		12,550
24		2		3,850		16,400
30		2		3,050		19,450
30		2		1,500		20,950
30	Adjusting	3		2,500		23,450
30	Closing	4	23,450		—	—

Account *Salary Expense* — Account No. *51*

Date	Item	Post. Ref.	Debit	Credit	Balance Debit	Balance Credit
2012 Apr. 14		1	750		750	
27		2	750		1,500	
30	Adjusting	3	120		1,620	
30	Closing	4		1,620	—	—

Account *Rent Expense* — Account No. *52*

Date	Item	Post. Ref.	Debit	Credit	Balance Debit	Balance Credit
2012 Apr. 30	Adjusting	3	1,600		1,600	
30	Closing	4		1,600	—	—

Account *Supplies Expense* — Account No. *53*

Date	Item	Post. Ref.	Debit	Credit	Balance Debit	Balance Credit
2012 Apr. 30	Adjusting	3	850		850	
30	Closing	4		850	—	—

Account *Depreciation Expense* — Account No. *54*

Date	Item	Post. Ref.	Debit	Credit	Balance Debit	Balance Credit
2012 Apr. 30	Adjusting	3	330		330	
30	Closing	4		330	—	—

Account *Insurance Expense* — Account No. *55*

Date	Item	Post. Ref.	Debit	Credit	Balance Debit	Balance Credit
2012 Apr. 30	Adjusting	3	300		300	
30	Closing	4		300	—	—

Account *Miscellaneous Expense* — Account No. *59*

Date	Item	Post. Ref.	Debit	Credit	Balance Debit	Balance Credit
2012 Apr. 10		1	120		120	
29		2	130		250	
30		2	200		450	
30	Closing	4		450	—	—

Fiscal Year

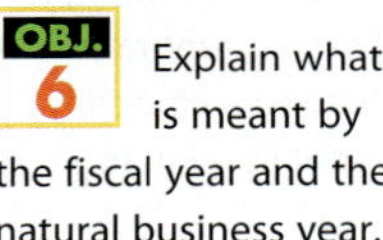

Explain what is meant by the fiscal year and the natural business year.

The annual accounting period adopted by a business is known as its **fiscal year**. Fiscal years begin with the first day of the month selected and end on the last day of the following twelfth month. The period most commonly used is the calendar year. Other periods are not unusual, especially for businesses organized as corporations. For example, a corporation may adopt a fiscal year that ends when business activities have reached the lowest point in its annual operating cycle. Such a fiscal

Percentage of Companies with Fiscal Years Ending in:			
January	5%	July	2%
February	2	August	3
March	3	September	6
April	2	October	3
May	3	November	2
June	6	December	63

Source: *Accounting Trends & Techniques*, 63rd edition, 2009 (New York: American Institute of Certified Public Accountants).

year is called the **natural business year**. At the low point in its operating cycle, a business has more time to analyze the results of operations and to prepare financial statements.

Because companies with fiscal years often have highly seasonal operations, investors and others should be careful in interpreting partial-year reports for such companies. That is, you should expect the results of operations for these companies to vary significantly throughout the fiscal year.

The financial history of a business may be shown by a series of balance sheets and income statements for several fiscal years. If the life of a business is expressed by a line moving from left to right, the series of balance sheets and income statements may be graphed as follows:

Financial History of a Business

Income Statement for the year ended Dec. 31, 2010 →

Balance Sheet Dec. 31, 2010

Income Statement for the year ended Dec. 31, 2011 →

Balance Sheet Dec. 31, 2011

Income Statement for the year ended Dec. 31, 2012 →

Balance Sheet Dec. 31, 2012

Business Connection

CHOOSING A FISCAL YEAR

CVS Caremark Corporation (CVS) operates over 7,000 pharmacies throughout the United States and fills more than one billion prescriptions annually. CVS recently chose December 31 as its fiscal year-end described as follows:

.... our Board of Directors approved a change in our fiscal year-end ... to December 31 of each year to better reflect our position in the health care ... industry.

In contrast, most large retailers such as Walmart and Target use fiscal years ending January 31, when their operations are the slowest following the December holidays.

Financial Analysis and Interpretation: Working Capital and Current Ratio

OBJ. 7 Describe and illustrate the use of working capital and the current ratio in evaluating a company's financial condition.

The ability to convert assets into cash is called **liquidity**, while the ability of a business to pay its debts is called **solvency**. Two financial measures for evaluating a business's short-term liquidity and solvency are working capital and the current ratio.

Working capital is the excess of the current assets of a business over its current liabilities, as shown below.

$$\text{Working Capital} = \text{Current Assets} - \text{Current Liabilities}$$

Current assets are more liquid than long-term assets. Thus, an increase in a company's current assets increases or improves its liquidity. An increase in working capital increases or improves liquidity in the sense that current assets are available for uses other than paying current liabilities.

A positive working capital implies that the business is able to pay its current liabilities and is solvent. Thus, an increase in working capital increases or improves a company's solvency.

To illustrate, NetSolutions' working capital at the end of 2011 is $675 as computed below. This amount of working capital implies that NetSolutions is able to pay its current liabilities.

$$\begin{aligned}\text{Working Capital} &= \text{Current Assets} - \text{Current Liabilities}\\ &= \$7{,}745 - \$1{,}390\\ &= \$6{,}355\end{aligned}$$

The **current ratio** is another means of expressing the relationship between current assets and current liabilities. The current ratio is computed by dividing current assets by current liabilities, as shown below.

$$\text{Current Ratio} = \frac{\text{Current Assets}}{\text{Current Liabilities}}$$

To illustrate, the current ratio for NetSolutions at the end of 2011 is 1.5, computed as follows:

$$\begin{aligned}\text{Current Ratio} &= \frac{\text{Current Assets}}{\text{Current Liabilities}}\\ &= \frac{\$7{,}745}{\$1{,}390}\\ &= 5.6 \text{ (Rounded)}\end{aligned}$$

The current ratio is more useful than working capital in making comparisons across companies or with industry averages. To illustrate, the following data (in millions) were taken from the financial statements of Electronic Arts Inc. and Take-Two Interactive Software, Inc.

	Electronic Arts		Take-Two	
	Mar. 31, 2009	Mar. 31, 2008	Oct. 31, 2009	Oct. 31, 2008
Current assets	$3,120	$3,925	$628	$724
Current liabilities	1,136	1,299	354	365
Working capital	$1,984	$2,626	$274	$359
Current ratio	2.75	3.02	1.77	1.98
Operating income (loss)	($3,120 ÷ $1,136)	($3,925 ÷ $1,299)	($628 ÷ $354)	($724 ÷ $365)

Electronic Arts is larger than Take-Two and has 2009 working capital of $1,984 as compared to Take-Two's 2009 working capital of $274. Such size differences make comparisons across companies difficult. In contrast, the current ratio allows comparability across companies.

To illustrate, Electronic Arts has over seven times more working capital ($1,984) than does Take Two ($274). However, by using the current ratio the changes in liquidity of both companies can be directly compared. Specifically, Electronic Arts' current ratio declined from 3.02 to 2.75, or 0.27. Take Two's current ratio also declined from 1.98 to 1.77, or 0.21. Thus, both companies experienced a small decline in their liquidity in 2009.

Example Exercise 4-6 Working Capital and Current Ratio

OBJ. 7

Two income statements for Fortson Company are shown below.

	2012	2011
Current assets	$310,500	$262,500
Current liabilities	172,500	150,000

a. Determine the working capital and current ratio for 2012 and 2011.

b. Does the change in the current ratio from 2011 to 2012 indicate a favorable or an unfavorable trend?

(continued)

Follow My Example 4-6

a.

	2012	2011
Current assets	$310,500	$262,500
Current liabilities	172,500	150,000
Working capital	$138,000	$112,500
Current ratio	1.80	1.75
	($310,500 ÷ $172,500)	($262,500 ÷ $150,000)

b. The change from 1.75 to 1.80 indicates a favorable trend.

Practice Exercises: **PE 4-6A, PE 4-6B**

APPENDIX 1

End-of-Period Spreadsheet (Work Sheet)

Accountants often use working papers for analyzing and summarizing data. Such working papers are not a formal part of the accounting records. This is in contrast to the chart of accounts, the journal, and the ledger, which are essential parts of an accounting system. Working papers are usually prepared by using a computer spreadsheet program such as Microsoft's Excel.™

The end-of-period spreadsheet shown in Exhibit 1 is a working paper used to summarize adjusting entries and their effects on the accounts. As illustrated in the chapter, the financial statements for **NetSolutions** can be prepared directly from the spreadsheet's Adjusted Trial Balance columns.

Some accountants prefer to expand the end-of-period spreadsheet shown in Exhibit 1 to include financial statement columns. Exhibits 18 through 22 illustrate the step-by-step process of how to prepare this expanded spreadsheet. As a basis for illustration, NetSolutions is used.

Step 1. Enter the Title

The spreadsheet is started by entering the following data:

1. Name of the business: *NetSolutions*
2. Type of working paper: *End-of-Period Spreadsheet*
3. The period of time: *For the Two Months Ended December 31, 2011*

Exhibit 18 shows the preceding data entered for NetSolutions.

Step 2. Enter the Unadjusted Trial Balance

Enter the unadjusted trial balance on the spreadsheet. The spreadsheet in Exhibit 18 shows the unadjusted trial balance for NetSolutions at December 31, 2011.

Step 3. Enter the Adjustments

The adjustments for NetSolutions from Chapter 3 are entered in the Adjustments columns, as shown in Exhibit 19. Cross-referencing (by letters) the debit and credit of each adjustment is useful in reviewing the spreadsheet. It is also helpful for identifying the adjusting entries that need to be recorded in the journal. This cross-referencing process is sometimes referred to as *keying* the adjustments.

The adjustments are normally entered in the order in which the data are assembled. If the titles of the accounts to be adjusted do not appear in the unadjusted trial balance, the accounts are inserted in their proper order in the Account Title column.

The adjusting entries for NetSolutions that are entered in the Adjustments columns are as follows:

(a) **Supplies**. The supplies account has a debit balance of $2,000. The cost of the supplies on hand at the end of the period is $760. The supplies expense for December is the difference between the two amounts, or $1,240 ($2,000 – $760). The adjustment is entered as (1) $1,240 in the Adjustments Debit column on the same line as Supplies Expense and (2) $1,240 in the Adjustments Credit column on the same line as Supplies.

(b) **Prepaid Insurance**. The prepaid insurance account has a debit balance of $2,400. This balance represents the prepayment of insurance for 12 months beginning December 1. Thus, the insurance expense for December is $200 ($2,400 ÷ 12). The adjustment is entered as (1) $200 in the Adjustments Debit column on the same line as Insurance Expense and (2) $200 in the Adjustments Credit column on the same line as Prepaid Insurance.

(c) **Unearned Rent**. The unearned rent account had a credit balance of $360. This balance represents the receipt of three months' rent, beginning with December. Thus, the rent revenue for December is $120 ($360 ÷ 3). The adjustment is entered as (1) $120 in the Adjustments Debit column on the same line as Unearned Rent and (2) $120 in the Adjustments Credit column on the same line as Rent Revenue.

Turn Exhibit 19

(d) **Accrued Fees**. Fees accrued at the end of December but not recorded total $500. This amount is an increase in an asset and an increase in revenue. The adjustment is entered as (1) $500 in the Adjustments Debit column on the same line as Accounts Receivable and (2) $500 in the Adjustments Credit column on the same line as Fees Earned.

(e) **Wages**. Wages accrued but not paid at the end of December total $250. This amount is an increase in expenses and an increase in liabilities. The adjustment is entered as (1) $250 in the Adjustments Debit column on the same line as Wages Expense and (2) $250 in the Adjustments Credit column on the same line as Wages Payable.

(f) **Depreciation**. Depreciation of the office equipment is $50 for December. The adjustment is entered as (1) $50 in the Adjustments Debit column on the same line as Depreciation Expense and (2) $50 in the Adjustments Credit column on the same line as Accumulated Depreciation.

After the adjustments have been entered, the Adjustments columns are totaled to verify the equality of the debits and credits. The total of the Debit column must equal the total of the Credit column.

Step 4. Enter the Adjusted Trial Balance

The adjusted trial balance is entered by combining the adjustments with the unadjusted balances for each account. The adjusted amounts are then extended to the Adjusted Trial Balance columns, as shown in Exhibit 20.

To illustrate, the cash amount of $2,065 is extended to the Adjusted Trial Balance Debit column since no adjustments affected Cash. Accounts Receivable has an initial balance of $2,220 and a debit adjustment of $500. Thus, $2,720 ($2,220 + $500) is entered in the Adjusted Trial Balance Debit column for Accounts Receivable. The same process continues until all account balances are extended to the Adjusted Trial Balance columns.

Turn Exhibit 20

After the accounts and adjustments have been extended, the Adjusted Trial Balance columns are totaled to verify the equality of debits and credits. The total of the Debit column must equal the total of the Credit column.

Step 5. Extend the Accounts to the Income Statement and Balance Sheet Columns

Turn Exhibit 21

The adjusted trial balance amounts are extended to the Income Statement and Balance Sheet columns. The amounts for revenues and expenses are extended to the Income Statement column. The amounts for assets, liabilities, owner's capital, and drawing are extended to the Balance Sheet columns.[3]

3 The balances of the owner's capital and drawing accounts are extended to the Balance Sheet columns because the spreadsheet does not have separate Statement of Owner's Equity columns.

EXHIBIT 22 Completed Spreadsheet (Work Sheet) with Net Income Shown

1				NetSolutions							
2				End-of-Period Spreadsheet (Work Sheet)							
3				For the Two Months Ended December 31, 2011							
4		Unadjusted				Adjusted					
5		Trial Balance		Adjustments		Trial Balance		Income Statement		Balance Sheet	
6	Account Title	Dr.	Cr.	Dr.	Cr.	Dr.	Cr.	Dr.	Cr.	Dr.	Cr.
7											
8	Cash	2,065									
9	Accounts Receivable	2,220		(d) 500							
10	Supplies	2,000			(a) 1,240						
11	Prepaid Insurance	2,400			(b) 200						
12	Land	20,000									
13	Office Equipment	1,800									
14	Accumulated Depreciation				(f) 50						
15	Accounts Payable		900								
16	Wages Payable				(e) 250						
17	Unearned Rent		360	(c) 120							
18	Chris Clark, Capital		25,000								
19	Chris Clark, Drawing	4,000									
20	Fees Earned		16,340		(d) 500						
21	Rent Revenue				(c) 120						
22	Wages Expense	4,275		(e) 250							
23	Supplies Expense	800		(a) 1,240							
24	Rent Expense	1,600									
25	Utilities Expense	985									
26	Insurance Expense			(b) 200							
27	Depreciation Expense			(f) 50							
28	Miscellaneous Expense	455									
29		42,600	42,600	2,360	2,360			9,855	16,960	33,545	26,440
30	Net income							7,105			7,105
31								16,960	16,960	33,545	33,545
32											

The adjustments on the spreadsheet (work sheet) are used in preparing the adjusting journal entries.

The difference between the Income Statement column totals is the net income (or net loss) for the period. The difference between the Balance Sheet column totals is also the net income (or net loss) for the period.

The first account listed in the Adjusted Trial Balance columns is Cash with a debit balance of $2,065. Cash is an asset, is listed on the balance sheet, and has a debit balance. Therefore, $2,065 is extended to the Balance Sheet Debit column. The Fees Earned balance of $16,840 is extended to the Income Statement Credit column. The same process continues until all account balances have been extended to the proper columns, as shown in Exhibit 21.

Turn Exhibit 21

Step 6. Total the Income Statement and Balance Sheet Columns, Compute the Net Income or Net Loss, and Complete the Spreadsheet

After the account balances are extended to the Income Statement and Balance Sheet columns, each of the columns is totaled. The difference between the two Income Statement column totals is the amount of the net income or the net loss for the period. This difference (net income or net loss) will also be the difference between the two Balance Sheet column totals.

If the Income Statement Credit column total (total revenue) is greater than the Income Statement Debit column total (total expenses), the difference is the net income. If the Income Statement Debit column total is greater than the Income Statement Credit column total, the difference is a net loss.

As shown in Exhibit 22, the total of the Income Statement Credit column is $16,960, and the total of the Income Statement Debit column is $9,855. Thus, the net income for NetSolutions is $7,105 as shown below.

Turn Exhibit 22

Total of Income Statement Credit column (revenues)	$16,960
Total of Income Statement Debit column (expenses)	9,855
Net income (excess of revenues over expenses)	$ 7,105

The amount of the net income, $7,105, is entered in the Income Statement Debit column and the Balance Sheet Credit column. *Net income* is also entered in the Account Title column. Entering the net income of $7,105 in the Balance Sheet Credit column has the effect of transferring the net balance of the revenue and expense accounts to the owner's capital account.

If there was a net loss instead of net income, the amount of the net loss would be entered in the Income Statement Credit column and the Balance Sheet Debit column. *Net loss* would also be entered in the Account Title column.

After the net income or net loss is entered on the spreadsheet, the Income Statement and Balance Sheet columns are totaled. The totals of the two Income Statement columns must now be equal. The totals of the two Balance Sheet columns must also be equal.

Preparing the Financial Statements from the Spreadsheet

The spreadsheet can be used to prepare the income statement, the statement of owner's equity, and the balance sheet shown in Exhibit 2. The income statement is normally prepared directly from the spreadsheet. The expenses are listed in the income statement in Exhibit 2 in order of size, beginning with the larger items. Miscellaneous expense is the last item, regardless of its amount.

The first item normally presented on the statement of owner's equity is the balance of the owner's capital account at the beginning of the period. The amount listed as owner's capital in the spreadsheet, however, is not always the account balance at the beginning of the period. The owner may have invested additional assets in the business during the period. Thus, for the beginning balance and any additional investments, it is necessary to refer to the capital account in the ledger. These amounts, along with the net income (or net loss) and the drawing amount shown in the spreadsheet, are used to determine the ending capital account balance.

The balance sheet can be prepared directly from the spreadsheet columns except for the ending balance of owner's capital. The ending balance of owner's capital is taken from the statement of owner's equity.

When a spreadsheet is used, the adjusting and closing entries are normally not journalized or posted until after the spreadsheet and financial statements have been prepared. The data for the adjusting entries are taken from the Adjustments columns of the spreadsheet. The data for the first two closing entries are taken from the Income Statement columns of the spreadsheet. The amount for the third closing entry is the net income or net loss appearing at the bottom of the spreadsheet. The amount for the fourth closing entry is the drawing account balance that appears in the Balance Sheet Debit column of the spreadsheet.

At a Glance 4

Describe the flow of accounting information from the unadjusted trial balance into the adjusted trial balance and financial statements.

Key Points Exhibit 1 illustrates the end-of-period process by which accounts are adjusted and how the adjusted accounts flow into the financial statements.

Learning Outcomes	Example Exercises	Practice Exercises
• Using an end-of-period spreadsheet, describe how the unadjusted trial balance accounts are affected by adjustments and how the adjusted trial balance accounts flow into the income statement and balance sheet.	EE4-1	PE4-1A, 4-1B

OBJ. 2

Prepare financial statements from adjusted account balances.

Key Points Using the end-of-period spreadsheet shown in Exhibit 1, the income statement and balance sheet for NetSolutions can be prepared. The statement of owner's equity is prepared by referring to transactions that have been posted to owner's capital accounts in the ledger. A classified balance sheet has sections for current assets; property, plant, and equipment; current liabilities; long-term liabilities; and owner's equity.

Learning Outcomes	Example Exercises	Practice Exercises
• Describe how the net income or net loss from the period can be determined from an end-of-period spreadsheet.		
• Prepare an income statement, statement of owner's equity, and a balance sheet.	EE4-2	PE4-2A, 4-2B
• Indicate how accounts would be reported on a classified balance sheet.	EE4-3	PE4-3A, 4-3B

Prepare closing entries.

Key Points Four entries are required in closing the temporary accounts. The first entry closes the revenue accounts to Income Summary. The second entry closes the expense accounts to Income Summary. The third entry closes the balance of Income Summary (net income or net loss) to the owner's capital account. The fourth entry closes the drawing account to the owner's capital account.

After the closing entries have been posted to the ledger, the balance in the capital account agrees with the amount reported on the statement of owner's equity and balance sheet. In addition, the revenue, expense, and drawing accounts will have zero balances.

Learning Outcomes	Example Exercises	Practice Exercises
• Prepare the closing entry for revenues.	EE4-4	PE4-4A, 4-4B
• Prepare the closing entry for expenses.	EE4-4	PE4-4A, 4-4B
• Prepare the closing entry for transferring the balance of Income Summary to the owner's capital account.	EE4-4	PE4-4A, 4-4B
• Prepare the closing entry for the owner's drawing account.	EE4-4	PE4-4A, 4-4B

Describe the accounting cycle.

Key Points The 10 basic steps of the accounting cycle are as follows:

1. Transactions are analyzed and recorded in the journal.
2. Transactions are posted to the ledger.
3. An unadjusted trial balance is prepared.
4. Adjustment data are assembled and analyzed.
5. An optional end-of-period spreadsheet is prepared.
6. Adjusting entries are journalized and posted to the ledger.
7. An adjusted trial balance is prepared.
8. Financial statements are prepared.
9. Closing entries are journalized and posted to the ledger.
10. A post-closing trial balance is prepared.

Learning Outcomes	Example Exercises	Practice Exercises
• List the 10 steps of the accounting cycle.		
• Determine whether any steps are out of order in a listing of accounting cycle steps.		
• Determine whether there are any missing steps in a listing of accounting cycle steps.	EE4-5	PE4-5A, 4-5B

Illustrate the accounting cycle for one period.

Key Points The complete accounting cycle for Kelly Consulting for the month of April is described and illustrated on pages 163–173.

Learning Outcomes

• Complete the accounting cycle for a period from beginning to end.

Explain what is meant by the fiscal year and the natural business year.

Key Points The annual accounting period adopted by a business is its fiscal year. A company's fiscal year that ends when business activities have reached the lowest point in its annual operating cycle is called the natural business year.

Learning Outcomes

- Explain why companies use a fiscal year that is different from the calendar year.

Describe and illustrate the use of working capital and the current ratio in evaluating a company's financial condition.

Key Points The ability to convert assets into cash is called liquidity, while the ability of a business to pay its debts is called solvency. Two financial measures for evaluating a business's short-term liquidity and solvency are working capital and the current ratio. Working capital is computed by subtracting current liabilities from current assets. An excess of current assets over current liabilities implies that the business is able to pay its current liabilities. The current ratio is computed by dividing current assets by current liabilities. The current ratio is more useful than working capital in making comparisons across companies or with industry averages.

Learning Outcomes	Example Exercises	Practice Exercises
• Define liquidity and solvency.		
• Compute working capital.	EE4-6	PE4-6A, 4-6B
• Compute the current ratio.	EE4-6	PE4-6A, 4-6B

Key Terms

accounting cycle (162)
clearing account (157)
closing entries (156)
closing process (156)
closing the books (156)
current assets (155)
current liabilities (155)
current ratio (175)
fiscal year (173)
fixed (plant) assets (155)
Income Summary (157)
liquidity (174)
long-term liabilities (155)
natural business year (174)
notes receivable (155)
real (permanent) accounts (156)
solvency (174)
temporary (nominal) accounts (156)
working capital (174)

Illustrative Problem

Three years ago, T. Roderick organized Harbor Realty. At July 31, 2012, the end of the current fiscal year, the following end-of-period spreadsheet was prepared:

	A	B	C	D	E	F	G
1		Harbor Realty					
2		End-of-Period Spreadsheet					
3		For the Year Ended July 31, 2012					
4		Unadjusted				Adjusted	
5		Trial Balance		Adjustments		Trial Balance	
6	Account Title	Dr.	Cr.	Dr.	Cr.	Dr.	Cr.
7							
8	Cash	3,425				3,425	
9	Accounts Receivable	7,000		(e) 1,000		8,000	
10	Supplies	1,270			(a) 890	380	
11	Prepaid Insurance	620			(b) 315	305	
12	Office Equipment	51,650				51,650	
13	Accum. Depreciation		9,700		(c) 4,950		14,650
14	Accounts Payable		925				925
15	Unearned Fees		1,250	(f) 500			750
16	Wages Payable				(d) 440		440
17	T. Roderick, Capital		29,000				29,000
18	T. Roderick, Drawing	5,200				5,200	
19	Fees Earned		59,125		(e) 1,000		60,625
20					(f) 500		
21	Wages Expense	22,415		(d) 440		22,855	
22	Depreciation Expense			(c) 4,950		4,950	
23	Rent Expense	4,200				4,200	
24	Utilities Expense	2,715				2,715	
25	Supplies Expense			(a) 890		890	
26	Insurance Expense			(b) 315		315	
27	Miscellaneous Expense	1,505				1,505	
28		100,000	100,000	8,095	8,095	106,390	106,390
29							

Instructions

1. Prepare an income statement, a statement of owner's equity (no additional investments were made during the year), and a balance sheet.
2. On the basis of the data in the end-of-period spreadsheet, journalize the closing entries.

Solution

1.

Harbor Realty
Income Statement
For the Year Ended July 31, 2012

Fees earned		$60,625
Expenses:		
Wages expense	$22,855	
Depreciation expense	4,950	
Rent expense	4,200	
Utilities expense	2,715	
Supplies expense	890	
Insurance expense	315	
Miscellaneous expense	1,505	
Total expenses		37,430
Net income		$23,195

Harbor Realty
Statement of Owner's Equity
For the Year Ended July 31, 2012

T. Roderick, capital, August 1, 2011		$29,000
Net income for the year	$23,195	
Less withdrawals	5,200	
Increase in owner's equity		17,995
T. Roderick, capital, July 31, 2012		$46,995

Harbor Realty
Balance Sheet
July 31, 2012

Assets			Liabilities		
Current assets:			Current liabilities:		
Cash	$ 3,425		Accounts payable	$925	
Accounts receivable	8,000		Unearned fees	750	
Supplies	380		Wages payable	440	
Prepaid insurance	305		Total liabilities		$ 2,115
Total current assets		$12,110			
Property, plant, and equipment:					
Office equipment	$51,650				
Less accum. depreciation	14,650		**Owner's Equity**		
Total property, plant, and equipment		37,000	T. Roderick, capital		46,995
Total assets		$49,110	Total liabilities and owner's equity		$49,110

2.

Journal					Page
Date		Description	Post. Ref.	Debit	Credit
		Closing Entries			
2012 July	31	Fees Earned		60,625	
		Income Summary			60,625
	31	Income Summary		37,430	
		Wages Expense			22,855
		Depreciation Expense			4,950
		Rent Expense			4,200
		Utilities Expense			2,715
		Supplies Expense			890
		Insurance Expense			315
		Miscellaneous Expense			1,505
	31	Income Summary		23,195	
		T. Roderick, Capital			23,195
	31	T. Roderick, Capital		5,200	
		T. Roderick, Drawing			5,200

Discussion Questions

1. Why do some accountants prepare an end-of-period spreadsheet?
2. Describe the nature of the assets that compose the following sections of a balance sheet: (a) current assets, (b) property, plant, and equipment.
3. What is the difference between a current liability and a long-term liability?
4. What types of accounts are referred to as temporary accounts?
5. Why are closing entries required at the end of an accounting period?
6. What is the difference between adjusting entries and closing entries?
7. What is the purpose of the post-closing trial balance?
8. (a) What is the most important output of the accounting cycle? (b) Do all companies have an accounting cycle? Explain.
9. What is the natural business year?
10. The fiscal years for several well-known companies are as follows:

Company	Fiscal Year Ending	Company	Fiscal Year Ending
Sears	January 30	Home Depot	January 31
JCPenney	January 30	Tiffany & Co.	January 31
Target Corp.	January 30	Limited Brands, Inc.	January 31

What general characteristic shared by these companies explains why they do not have fiscal years ending December 31?

Practice Exercises

Learning Objectives	Example Exercises
OBJ. 1	EE 4-1 p. 152

PE 4-1A Flow of accounts into financial statements

The balances for the accounts listed below appear in the Adjusted Trial Balance columns of the end-of-period spreadsheet. Indicate whether each account would flow into the income statement, statement of owner's equity, or balance sheet.

1. Accounts Receivable
2. Depreciation Expense—Equipment
3. Jean Kehler, Capital
4. Office Equipment
5. Rent Revenue
6. Supplies Expense
7. Unearned Revenue
8. Wages Payable

OBJ. 1 EE 4-1 p. 152

PE 4-1B Flow of accounts into financial statements

The balances for the accounts listed below appear in the Adjusted Trial Balance columns of the end-of-period spreadsheet. Indicate whether each account would flow into the income statement, statement of owner's equity, or balance sheet.

1. Accumulated Depreciation—Building
2. Cash
3. Fees Earned
4. Insurance Expense
5. Prepaid Rent
6. Supplies
7. Vincent Schafer, Drawing
8. Wages Expense

OBJ. 2 EE 4-2 p. 154

PE 4-2A Statement of owner's equity

Judy Flint owns and operates Derby Advertising Services. On January 1, 2011, Judy Flint, Capital had a balance of $290,000. During the year, Judy invested an additional $100,000 and withdrew $40,000. For the year ended December 31, 2011, Derby Advertising Services reported a net income of $93,750. Prepare a statement of owner's equity for the year ended December 31, 2011.

OBJ. 2 EE 4-2 p. 154

PE 4-2B Statement of owner's equity

Mavis Curry owns and operates A2Z Delivery Services. On January 1, 2011, Mavis Curry, Capital had a balance of $600,000. During the year, Mavis made no additional investments and withdrew $45,000. For the year ended December 31, 2011, A2Z Delivery Services reported a net loss of $13,500. Prepare a statement of owner's equity for the year ended December 31, 2011.

OBJ. 2 EE 4-3 p. 155

PE 4-3A Classified balance sheet

The following accounts appear in an adjusted trial balance of Pilot Consulting. Indicate whether each account would be reported in the (a) current asset; (b) property, plant, and equipment; (c) current liability; (d) long-term liability; or (e) owner's equity section of the December 31, 2011, balance sheet of Pilot Consulting.

1. Building
2. Marty Ramsey, Capital
3. Notes Payable (due in 2017)
4. Prepaid Rent
5. Salaries Payable
6. Supplies
7. Taxes Payable
8. Unearned Service Fees

Learning Objectives	Example Exercises
OBJ. 2	EE 4-3 p. 155

PE 4-3B Classified balance sheet

The following accounts appear in an adjusted trial balance of F-18 Consulting. Indicate whether each account would be reported in the (a) current asset; (b) property, plant, and equipment; (c) current liability; (d) long-term liability; or (e) owner's equity section of the December 31, 2011, balance sheet of F-18 Consulting.

1. Accounts Payable
2. Accounts Receivable
3. Accumulated Depreciation—Building
4. Cash
5. Jess Garza, Capital
6. Note Payable (due in 2018)
7. Supplies
8. Wages Payable

OBJ. 3 EE 4-4 p. 159

PE 4-4A Closing entries

After the accounts have been adjusted at October 31, the end of the fiscal year, the following balances were taken from the ledger of Silver Gate Delivery Services Co.:

Mira Craig, Capital	$800,000
Mira Craig, Drawing	125,000
Fees Earned	700,000
Wages Expense	400,000
Rent Expense	75,000
Supplies Expense	16,000
Miscellaneous Expense	5,000

Journalize the four entries required to close the accounts.

OBJ. 3 EE 4-4 p. 159

PE 4-4B Closing entries

After the accounts have been adjusted at June 30, the end of the fiscal year, the following balances were taken from the ledger of Hillcrest Landscaping Co.:

Bryan Orr, Capital	$275,000
Bryan Orr, Drawing	25,000
Fees Earned	400,000
Wages Expense	280,000
Rent Expense	40,000
Supplies Expense	3,000
Miscellaneous Expense	12,000

Journalize the four entries required to close the accounts.

OBJ. 4 EE 4-5 p. 162

PE 4-5A Accounting cycle

From the following list of steps in the accounting cycle, identify what two steps are missing.

a. Transactions are analyzed and recorded in the journal.
b. An unadjusted trial balance is prepared.
c. Adjustment data are assembled and analyzed.
d. An optional end-of-period spreadsheet is prepared.
e. Adjusting entries are journalized and posted to the ledger.
f. An adjusted trial balance is prepared.
g. Closing entries are journalized and posted to the ledger.
h. A post-closing trial balance is prepared.

OBJ. 4 EE 4-5 p. 162

PE 4-5B Accounting cycle

From the following list of steps in the accounting cycle, identify what two steps are missing.

a. Transactions are analyzed and recorded in the journal.
b. Transactions are posted to the ledger.

Learning Objectives | Example Exercises

c. An unadjusted trial balance is prepared.
d. An optional end-of-period spreadsheet is prepared.
e. Adjusting entries are journalized and posted to the ledger.
f. An adjusted trial balance is prepared.
g. Financial statements are prepared.
h. A post-closing trial balance is prepared.

OBJ. 7 EE 4-6 p. 175

F·A·I

PE 4-6A Working capital and current ratio

The following balance sheet data for Mayer Company are shown below.

	2012	2011
Current assets	$840,000	$1,430,000
Current liabilities	600,000	550,000

a. Determine the working capital and current ratio for 2012 and 2011.
b. Does the change in the current ratio from 2011 to 2012 indicate a favorable or an unfavorable trend?

OBJ. 7 EE 4-6 p. 175

F·A·I

PE 4-6B Working capital and current ratio

The following balance sheet data for Finn Company are shown below.

	2012	2011
Current assets	$288,000	$171,000
Current liabilities	120,000	90,000

a. Determine the working capital and current ratio for 2012 and 2011.
b. Does the change in the current ratio from 2011 to 2012 indicate a favorable or an unfavorable trend?

Exercises

OBJ. 1, 2

EX 4-1 Flow of accounts into financial statements

The balances for the accounts listed below appear in the Adjusted Trial Balance columns of the end-of-period spreadsheet. Indicate whether each account would flow into the income statement, statement of owner's equity, or balance sheet.

1. Accounts Payable
2. Accounts Receivable
3. Cash
4. Dora Kovar, Drawing
5. Fees Earned
6. Supplies
7. Unearned Rent
8. Utilities Expense
9. Wages Expense
10. Wages Payable

OBJ. 1, 2

EX 4-2 Classifying accounts

Balances for each of the following accounts appear in an adjusted trial balance. Identify each as (a) asset, (b) liability, (c) revenue, or (d) expense.

1. Accounts Receivable
2. Equipment
3. Fees Earned
4. Insurance Expense
5. Prepaid Advertising
6. Prepaid Rent
7. Rent Revenue
8. Salary Expense
9. Salary Payable
10. Supplies
11. Supplies Expense
12. Unearned Rent

OBJ. 1, 2

EX 4-3 Financial statements from the end-of-period spreadsheet

Pacifica Consulting is a consulting firm owned and operated by Tara Milsap. The end-of-period spreadsheet shown below was prepared for the year ended August 31, 2012.

	A	B	C	D	E	F	G
1		Pacifica Consulting					
2		End-of-Period Spreadsheet					
3		For the Year Ended August 31, 2012					
4		Unadjusted				Adjusted	
5		Trial Balance		Adjustments		Trial Balance	
6	Account Title	Dr.	Cr.	Dr.	Cr.	Dr.	Cr.
7							
8	Cash	9,500				9,500	
9	Accounts Receivable	22,500				22,500	
10	Supplies	2,400			(a) 2,000	400	
11	Office Equipment	18,500				18,500	
12	Accumulated Depreciation		2,500		(b) 1,200		3,700
13	Accounts Payable		6,100				6,100
14	Salaries Payable				(c) 300		300
15	Tara Milsap, Capital		22,600				22,600
16	Tara Milsap, Drawing	3,000				3,000	
17	Fees Earned		43,800				43,800
18	Salary Expense	17,250		(c) 300		17,550	
19	Supplies Expense			(a) 2,000		2,000	
20	Depreciation Expense			(b) 1,200		1,200	
21	Miscellaneous Expense	1,850				1,850	
22		75,000	75,000	3,500	3,500	76,500	76,500
23							

Based on the preceding spreadsheet, prepare an income statement, statement of owner's equity, and balance sheet for Pacifica Consulting.

OBJ. 1, 2

EX 4-4 Financial statements from the end-of-period spreadsheet

Three Winds Consulting is a consulting firm owned and operated by Gabriel Brull. The following end-of-period spreadsheet was prepared for the year ended June 30, 2012.

	A	B	C	D	E	F	G
1		Three Winds Consulting					
2		End-of-Period Spreadsheet					
3		For the Year Ended June 30, 2012					
4		Unadjusted				Adjusted	
5		Trial Balance		Adjustments		Trial Balance	
6	Account Title	Dr.	Cr.	Dr.	Cr.	Dr.	Cr.
7							
8	Cash	7,500				7,500	
9	Accounts Receivable	23,500				23,500	
10	Supplies	3,000			(a) 2,400	600	
11	Office Equipment	30,500				30,500	
12	Accumulated Depreciation		4,500		(b) 800		5,300
13	Accounts Payable		3,300				3,300
14	Salaries Payable				(c) 500		500
15	Gabriel Brull, Capital		32,200				32,200
16	Gabriel Brull, Drawing	2,000				2,000	
17	Fees Earned		60,000				60,000
18	Salary Expense	32,000		(c) 500		32,500	
19	Supplies Expense			(a) 2,400		2,400	
20	Depreciation Expense			(b) 800		800	
21	Miscellaneous Expense	1,500				1,500	
22		100,000	100,000	3,700	3,700	101,300	101,300
23							

Based on the preceding spreadsheet, prepare an income statement, statement of owner's equity, and balance sheet for Three Winds Consulting.

OBJ. 2

✔ Net income, $89,600

EX 4-5 Income statement

The following account balances were taken from the adjusted trial balance for On-Time Messenger Service, a delivery service firm, for the current fiscal year ended April 30, 2012:

Depreciation Expense	$ 6,400	Rent Expense	$ 48,400
Fees Earned	340,000	Salaries Expense	171,040
Insurance Expense	1,200	Supplies Expense	2,200
Miscellaneous Expense	2,600	Utilities Expense	18,560

Prepare an income statement.

OBJ. 2

✔ Net loss, $36,600

EX 4-6 Income statement; net loss

The following revenue and expense account balances were taken from the ledger of Graphics Services Co. after the accounts had been adjusted on February 29, 2012, the end of the current fiscal year:

Depreciation Expense	$ 9,000	Service Revenue	$250,000
Insurance Expense	4,000	Supplies Expense	3,000
Miscellaneous Expense	5,000	Utilities Expense	14,600
Rent Expense	36,000	Wages Expense	215,000

Prepare an income statement.

OBJ. 2

Internet Project

✔ a. Net income: $98

EX 4-7 Income statement

FedEx Corporation had the following revenue and expense account balances (in millions) at its fiscal year-end of May 31, 2009:

Depreciation	$1,975	Purchased Transportation	$ 4,534
Fuel	3,811	Rentals and Landing Fees	2,429
Maintenance and Repairs	1,898	Revenues	35,497
Other Expense (Income) Net	6,406	Salaries and Employee Benefits	13,767
Provision for Income Taxes	579		

a. Prepare an income statement.

b. Compare your income statement with the related income statement that is available at the FedEx Corporation Web site, which is linked to the text's Web site at **academic.cengage.com/accounting/warren.** What similarities and differences do you see?

OBJ. 2

✔ Lisa DuBois, capital, Oct. 31, 2012: $635,000

EX 4-8 Statement of owner's equity

Fouts Systems Co. offers its services to residents in the Chicago area. Selected accounts from the ledger of Fouts Systems Co. for the current fiscal year ended October 31, 2012, are as follows:

Lisa DuBois, Capital

Oct. 31	20,000	Nov. 1 (2011)	550,000
		Oct. 31	105,000

Lisa DuBois, Drawing

Jan. 31	5,000	Oct. 31	20,000
Apr. 30	5,000		
July 31	5,000		
Oct. 31	5,000		

Income Summary

Oct. 31	375,000	Oct. 31	480,000
31	105,000		

Prepare a statement of owner's equity for the year.

OBJ. 2

✔ Erica Kilty, capital, June 30, 2012: $346,500

EX 4-9 Statement of owner's equity; net loss

Selected accounts from the ledger of Balboa Sports for the current fiscal year ended June 30, 2012, are as follows:

Erica Kilty, Capital

June 30	42,000	July 1 (2011)	398,500
30	10,000		

Erica Kilty, Drawing

Sept. 30	2,500	June 30	10,000
Dec. 31	2,500		
May 31	2,500		
June 30	2,500		

Income Summary			
June 30	402,000	June 30	360,000
		30	42,000

Prepare a statement of owner's equity for the year.

OBJ. 2

EX 4-10 Classifying assets

Identify each of the following as (a) a current asset or (b) property, plant, and equipment:

1. Accounts receivable
2. Building
3. Cash
4. Equipment
5. Prepaid Insurance
6. Supplies

OBJ. 2

EX 4-11 Balance sheet classification

At the balance sheet date, a business owes a mortgage note payable of $480,000, the terms of which provide for monthly payments of $2,500.

Explain how the liability should be classified on the balance sheet.

OBJ. 2

✔ Total assets: $750,000

EX 4-12 Balance sheet

My-Best Weight Co. offers personal weight reduction consulting services to individuals. After all the accounts have been closed on November 30, 2012, the end of the current fiscal year, the balances of selected accounts from the ledger of My-Best Weight Co. are as follows:

Accounts Payable	$ 34,500	Land	$400,000
Accounts Receivable	83,120	Prepaid Insurance	19,200
Accumulated Depreciation—Equipment	103,900	Prepaid Rent	12,000
Blanca Tierney, Capital	692,000	Salaries Payable	13,500
Cash	?	Supplies	2,080
Equipment	300,000	Unearned Fees	10,000

Prepare a classified balance sheet that includes the correct balance for Cash.

OBJ. 2

✔ Corrected balance sheet, total assets: $525,000

EX 4-13 Balance sheet

List the errors you find in the following balance sheet. Prepare a corrected balance sheet.

Poshe Services Co.
Balance Sheet
For the Year Ended May 31, 2012

Assets			**Liabilities**		
Current assets:			Current liabilities:		
Cash	$ 14,000		Accounts receivable	$ 32,500	
Accounts payable	24,000		Accum. depr.—building	155,000	
Supplies	6,500		Accum. depr.—equipment	25,000	
Prepaid insurance	12,000		Net income	135,000	
Land	180,000		Total liabilities		$347,500
Total current assets		$236,500			
Property, plant, and equipment:			**Owner's Equity**		
Building	$375,000		Wages payable	$ 2,500	
Equipment	85,000		Hector Delgado, capital	498,500	
Total property, plant, and equipment		612,000	Total owner's equity		501,000
Total assets		$848,500	Total liabilities and owner's equity		$848,500

OBJ. 3

EX 4-14 Identifying accounts to be closed

From the list at the top of the next page, identify the accounts that should be closed to Income Summary at the end of the fiscal year:

a. Accounts Payable
b. Accumulated Depreciation—Equipment
c. Depreciation Expense—Equipment
d. Equipment
e. Fauzi Hanna, Capital
f. Fauzi Hanna, Drawing
g. Fees Earned
h. Land
i. Supplies
j. Supplies Expense
k. Wages Expense
l. Wages Payable

OBJ. 3

EX 4-15 Closing entries

Prior to its closing, Income Summary had total debits of $815,000 and total credits of $1,280,000.

Briefly explain the purpose served by the income summary account and the nature of the entries that resulted in the $815,000 and the $1,280,000.

OBJ. 3

EX 4-16 Closing entries with net income

After all revenue and expense accounts have been closed at the end of the fiscal year, Income Summary has a debit of $315,000 and a credit of $449,500. At the same date, Faye Barnes, Capital has a credit balance of $750,000, and Faye Barnes, Drawing has a balance of $40,000. (a) Journalize the entries required to complete the closing of the accounts. (b) Determine the amount of Faye Barnes, Capital at the end of the period.

OBJ. 3

EX 4-17 Closing entries with net loss

Imex Services Co. offers its services to individuals desiring to improve their personal images. After the accounts have been adjusted at March 31, the end of the fiscal year, the following balances were taken from the ledger of Imex Services Co.

Margo Hoskins, Capital	$300,000	Rent Expense	$40,000
Margo Hoskins, Drawing	15,000	Supplies Expense	20,000
Fees Earned	180,000	Miscellaneous Expense	7,500
Wages Expense	90,000		

Journalize the four entries required to close the accounts.

OBJ. 3

EX 4-18 Identifying permanent accounts

Which of the following accounts will usually appear in the post-closing trial balance?

a. Accounts Payable
b. Accumulated Depreciation
c. Anthony Adams, Capital
d. Anthony Adams, Drawing
e. Cash
f. Depreciation Expense
g. Fees Earned
h. Office Equipment
i. Salaries Expense
j. Salaries Payable
k. Supplies

OBJ. 3

✔ Correct column totals, $129,500

EX 4-19 Post-closing trial balance

An accountant prepared the following post-closing trial balance:

Gypsy Treasures Co.
Post-Closing Trial Balance
March 31, 2012

	Debit Balances	Credit Balances
Cash	18,000	
Accounts Receivable	31,000	
Supplies		5,500
Equipment		75,000
Accumulated Depreciation—Equipment	19,000	
Accounts Payable	11,000	
Salaries Payable		1,000
Unearned Rent	6,000	
Leticia Aloni, Capital	92,500	
	177,500	81,500

Prepare a corrected post-closing trial balance. Assume that all accounts have normal balances and that the amounts shown are correct.

OBJ. 4

EX 4-20 Steps in the accounting cycle

Rearrange the following steps in the accounting cycle in proper sequence:

a. Financial statements are prepared.
b. An adjusted trial balance is prepared.
c. Adjustment data are asssembled and analyzed.
d. Adjusting entries are journalized and posted to the ledger.
e. Closing entries are journalized and posted to the ledger.
f. An unadjusted trial balance is prepared.
g. Transactions are posted to the ledger.
h. Transactions are analyzed and recorded in the journal.
i. An optional end-of-period spreadsheet (work sheet) is prepared.
j. A post-closing trial balance is prepared.

OBJ. 7

EX 4-21 Working capital and current ratio

The following data (in thousands) were taken from recent financial statements of Under Armour, Inc.:

	December 31	
	2008	2007
Current assets	$396,423	$322,245
Current liabilities	113,110	95,699

a. Compute the working capital and the current ratio as of December 31, 2008 and 2007. Round to two decimal places.
b. What conclusions concerning the company's ability to meet its financial obligations can you draw from part (a)?

OBJ. 7

EX 4-22 Working capital and current ratio

The following data (in thousands) were taken from recent financial statements of Starbucks Corporation:

	Sept. 27, 2009	Sept. 28, 2008
Current assets	$2,035,800	$1,748,000
Current liabilities	1,581,000	2,189,700

a. Compute the working capital and the current ratio as of September 27, 2009, and September 28, 2008. Round to two decimal places.
b. What conclusions concerning the company's ability to meet its financial obligations can you draw from part (a)?

Appendix

EX 4-23 Completing an end-of-period spreadsheet (work sheet)

List (a) through (j) in the order they would be performed in preparing and completing an end-of-period spreadsheet (work sheet).

a. Add the Debit and Credit columns of the Unadjusted Trial Balance columns of the spreadsheet (work sheet) to verify that the totals are equal.
b. Add the Debit and Credit columns of the Balance Sheet and Income Statement columns of the spreadsheet (work sheet) to verify that the totals are equal.
c. Add or deduct adjusting entry data to trial balance amounts, and extend amounts to the Adjusted Trial Balance columns.

(Continued)

d. Add the Debit and Credit columns of the Adjustments columns of the spreadsheet (work sheet) to verify that the totals are equal.
e. Add the Debit and Credit columns of the Balance Sheet and Income Statement columns of the spreadsheet (work sheet) to determine the amount of net income or net loss for the period.
f. Add the Debit and Credit columns of the Adjusted Trial Balance columns of the spreadsheet (work sheet) to verify that the totals are equal.
g. Enter the adjusting entries into the spreadsheet (work sheet), based on the adjustment data.
h. Enter the amount of net income or net loss for the period in the proper Income Statement column and Balance Sheet column.
i. Enter the unadjusted account balances from the general ledger into the Unadjusted Trial Balance columns of the spreadsheet (work sheet).
j. Extend the adjusted trial balance amounts to the Income Statement columns and the Balance Sheet columns.

✔ Total debits of Adjustments column: $27

Appendix
EX 4-24 Adjustment data on an end-of-period spreadsheet (work sheet)

Zeidman Security Services Co. offers security services to business clients. The trial balance for Zeidman Security Services Co. has been prepared on the end-of-period spreadsheet (work sheet) for the year ended July 31, 2012, shown below.

Zeidman Security Services Co.
End-of-Period Spreadsheet (Work Sheet)
For the Year Ended July 31, 2012

	Unadjusted Trial Balance		Adjustments		Adjusted Trial Balance	
Account Title	**Dr.**	**Cr.**	**Dr.**	**Cr.**	**Dr.**	**Cr.**
Cash	12					
Accounts Receivable	80					
Supplies	8					
Prepaid Insurance	12					
Land	100					
Equipment	40					
Accum. Depr.—Equipment		4				
Accounts Payable		36				
Wages Payable		0				
Alex Zeidman, Capital		170				
Alex Zeidman, Drawing	8					
Fees Earned		90				
Wages Expense	20					
Rent Expense	12					
Insurance Expense	0					
Utilities Expense	6					
Supplies Expense	0					
Depreciation Expense	0					
Miscellaneous Expense	2					
	300	300				

The data for year-end adjustments are as follows:

a. Fees earned, but not yet billed, $9.
b. Supplies on hand, $3.
c. Insurance premiums expired, $8.
d. Depreciation expense, $4.
e. Wages accrued, but not paid, $1.

Enter the adjustment data, and place the balances in the Adjusted Trial Balance columns.

✔ Net income: $41

Appendix
EX 4-25 Completing an end-of-period spreadsheet (work sheet)

Zeidman Security Services Co. offers security services to business clients. Complete the following end-of-period spreadsheet (work sheet) for Zeidman Security Services Co.

Zeidman Security Services Co.
End-of-Period Spreadsheet (Work Sheet)
For the Year Ended July 31, 2012

	Adjusted Trial Balance		Income Statement		Balance Sheet	
Account Title	**Dr.**	**Cr.**	**Dr.**	**Cr.**	**Dr.**	**Cr.**
Cash	12					
Accounts Receivable	89					
Supplies	3					
Prepaid Insurance	4					
Land	100					
Equipment	40					
Accum. Depr.—Equipment		8				
Accounts Payable		36				
Wages Payable		1				
Alex Zeidman, Capital		170				
Alex Zeidman, Drawing	8					
Fees Earned		99				
Wages Expense	21					
Rent Expense	12					
Insurance Expense	8					
Utilities Expense	6					
Supplies Expense	5					
Depreciation Expense	4					
Miscellaneous Expense	2					
	314	314				
Net income (loss)						

✔ Alex Zeidman, capital, July 31, 2012: $203

Appendix
EX 4-26 Financial statements from an end-of-period spreadsheet (work sheet)

Based on the data in Exercise 4-25, prepare an income statement, statement of owner's equity, and balance sheet for Zeidman Security Services Co.

Appendix
EX 4-27 Adjusting entries from an end-of-period spreadsheet (work sheet)

Based on the data in Exercise 4-24, prepare the adjusting entries for Zeidman Security Services Co.

Appendix
EX 4-28 Appendix: Closing entries from an end-of-period spreadsheet (work sheet)

Based on the data in Exercise 4-25, prepare the closing entries for Zeidman Security Services Co.

Problems Series A

OBJ. 1, 2, 3

✔ 3. Total assets: $239,500

PR 4-1A Financial statements and closing entries

Beacon Company maintains and repairs warning lights, such as those found on radio towers and lighthouses. Beacon Company prepared the end-of-period spreadsheet shown on the next page at October 31, 2012, the end of the current fiscal year:

Instructions

1. Prepare an income statement for the year ended October 31.
2. Prepare a statement of owner's equity for the year ended October 31. No additional investments were made during the year.
3. Prepare a balance sheet as of October 31.
4. Based upon the end-of-period spreadsheet, journalize the closing entries.

(Continued)

5. Prepare a post-closing trial balance.

	A	B	C	D	E	F	G
1	Beacon Company						
2	End-of-Period Spreadsheet						
3	For the Year Ended October 31, 2012						
4		Unadjusted				Adjusted	
5		Trial Balance		Adjustments		Trial Balance	
6	Account Title	Dr.	Cr.	Dr.	Cr.	Dr.	Cr.
7	Cash	5,800				5,800	
8	Accounts Receivable	18,900		(a) 3,300		22,200	
9	Prepaid Insurance	4,200			(b) 2,500	1,700	
10	Supplies	2,730			(c) 1,730	1,000	
11	Land	98,000				98,000	
12	Building	200,000				200,000	
13	Accum. Depr.—Building		100,300		(d) 1,600		101,900
14	Equipment	101,000				101,000	
15	Accum. Depr.—Equipment		85,100		(e) 3,200		88,300
16	Accounts Payable		5,700				5,700
17	Salaries & Wages Payable				(f) 1,800		1,800
18	Unearned Rent		2,100	(g) 1,000			1,100
19	Neil Shepard, Capital		103,100				103,100
20	Neil Shepard, Drawing	10,000				10,000	
21	Fees Revenue		303,700		(a) 3,300		307,000
22	Rent Revenue				(g) 1,000		1,000
23	Salaries & Wages Expense	113,100		(f) 1,800		114,900	
24	Advertising Expense	21,700				21,700	
25	Utilities Expense	11,400				11,400	
26	Repairs Expense	8,850				8,850	
27	Depr. Exp.—Equipment			(e) 3,200		3,200	
28	Insurance Expense			(b) 2,500		2,500	
29	Supplies Expense			(c) 1,730		1,730	
30	Depr. Exp.—Building			(d) 1,600		1,600	
31	Misc. Expense	4,320				4,320	
32		600,000	600,000	15,130	15,130	609,900	609,900
33							

OBJ. 2, 3

✔ **1. Tom Wagner, capital, June 30: $284,300**

PR 4-2A Financial statements and closing entries

Info-Mart Company is an investigative services firm that is owned and operated by Tom Wagner. On June 30, 2012, the end of the current fiscal year, the accountant for Info-Mart Company prepared an end-of-period spreadsheet, a part of which is shown below.

	A	F	G
1	Info-Mart Company		
2	End-of-Period Spreadsheet		
3	For the Year Ended June 30, 2012		
4		Adjusted	
5		Trial Balance	
6	Account Title	Dr.	Cr.
7	Cash	20,000	
8	Accounts Receivable	47,200	
9	Supplies	7,500	
10	Prepaid Insurance	4,800	
11	Building	270,500	
12	Accumulated Depreciation—Building		55,200
13	Accounts Payable		6,000
14	Salaries Payable		1,500
15	Unearned Rent		3,000
16	Tom Wagner, Capital		255,300
17	Tom Wagner, Drawing	50,000	
18	Service Fees		500,000
19	Rent Revenue		25,000
20	Salaries Expense	350,000	
21	Rent Expense	62,500	
22	Supplies Expense	12,000	
23	Depreciation Expense—Equipment	6,000	
24	Utilities Expense	4,400	
25	Repairs Expense	3,200	
26	Insurance Expense	2,800	
27	Miscellaneous Expense	5,100	
28		846,000	846,000

Instructions

1. Prepare an income statement, statement of owner's equity (no additional investments were made during the year), and a balance sheet.
2. Journalize the entries that were required to close the accounts at June 30.
3. If Tom Wagner, Capital decreased $75,000 after the closing entries were posted, and the withdrawals remained the same, what was the amount of net income or net loss?

OBJ. 2, 3

✔ 2. Net income: $39,300

PR 4-3A T accounts, adjusting entries, financial statements, and closing entries; optional end-of-period spreadsheet (work sheet)

The unadjusted trial balance of Launderland at November 30, 2012, the end of the current fiscal year, is shown below.

Launderland
Unadjusted Trial Balance
November 30, 2012

	Debit Balances	Credit Balances
Cash	9,000	
Laundry Supplies	20,900	
Prepaid Insurance	9,600	
Laundry Equipment	290,000	
Accumulated Depreciation		150,400
Accounts Payable		11,800
Gene Halsey, Capital		105,600
Gene Halsey, Drawing	8,400	
Laundry Revenue		232,200
Wages Expense	97,000	
Rent Expense	40,000	
Utilities Expense	19,700	
Miscellaneous Expense	5,400	
	500,000	500,000

The data needed to determine year-end adjustments are as follows:

a. Laundry supplies on hand at November 30 are $5,000.
b. Insurance premiums expired during the year are $6,400.
c. Depreciation of equipment during the year is $7,000.
d. Wages accrued but not paid at November 30 are $1,500.

Instructions

1. For each account listed in the unadjusted trial balance, enter the balance in a T account. Identify the balance as "November 30 Bal." In addition, add T accounts for Wages Payable, Depreciation Expense, Laundry Supplies Expense, Insurance Expense, and Income Summary.
2. **Optional:** Enter the unadjusted trial balance on an end-of-period spreadsheet (work sheet) and complete the spreadsheet. Add the accounts listed in part (1) as needed.
3. Journalize and post the adjusting entries. Identify the adjustments by "Adj." and the new balances as "Adj. Bal."
4. Prepare an adjusted trial balance.
5. Prepare an income statement, a statement of owner's equity (no additional investments were made during the year), and a balance sheet.
6. Journalize and post the closing entries. Identify the closing entries by "Clos."
7. Prepare a post-closing trial balance.

OBJ. 2, 3

✔ 4. Net income: $22,350

PR 4-4A Ledger accounts, adjusting entries, financial statements, and closing entries; optional end-of-period spreadsheet (work sheet)

If the working papers correlating with this textbook are not used, omit Problem 4-4A.

The ledger and trial balance of Wizard Services Co. as of July 31, 2012, the end of the first month of its current fiscal year, are presented in the working papers.

Data needed to determine the necessary adjusting entries are as follows:

a. Service revenue accrued at July 31 is $1,000.
b. Supplies on hand at July 31 are $3,900.
c. Insurance premiums expired during July are $1,100.
d. Depreciation of the building during July is $1,400.
e. Depreciation of equipment during July is $900.
f. Unearned rent at July 31 is $700.
g. Wages accrued at July 31 are $100.

Instructions

1. **Optional:** Complete the end-of-period spreadsheet (work sheet) using the adjustment data shown above.
2. Journalize and post the adjusting entries, inserting balances in the accounts affected.
3. Prepare an adjusted trial balance.
4. Prepare an income statement, a statement of owner's equity, and a balance sheet.
5. Journalize and post the closing entries. Indicate closed accounts by inserting a line in both Balance columns opposite the closing entry. Insert the new balance of the capital account.
6. Prepare a post-closing trial balance.

OBJ. 2, 3

✔ 5. Net income: $63,700

PR 4-5A Ledger accounts, adjusting entries, financial statements, and closing entries; optional spreadsheet (work sheet)

The unadjusted trial balance of Bruno's Hauling at February 29, 2012, the end of the current year, is shown below.

Bruno's Hauling
Unadjusted Trial Balance
February 29, 2012

		Debit Balances	Credit Balances
11	Cash	5,000	
13	Supplies	12,000	
14	Prepaid Insurance	3,600	
16	Equipment	110,000	
17	Accumulated Depreciation—Equipment		25,000
18	Trucks	60,000	
19	Accumulated Depreciation—Trucks		15,000
21	Accounts Payable		4,000
31	Bruno Shelton, Capital		71,000
32	Bruno Shelton, Drawing	15,000	
41	Service Revenue		160,000
51	Wages Expense	45,000	
53	Rent Expense	10,600	
54	Truck Expense	9,000	
59	Miscellaneous Expense	4,800	
		275,000	275,000

The data needed to determine year-end adjustments are as follows:

a. Supplies on hand at February 29 are $1,000.
b. Insurance premiums expired during year are $2,400.
c. Depreciation of equipment during year is $8,000.
d. Depreciation of trucks during year is $5,000.
e. Wages accrued but not paid at February 29 are $500.

Instructions

1. For each account listed in the trial balance, enter the balance in the appropriate Balance column of a four-column account and place a check mark (✓) in the Posting Reference column.

2. **Optional:** Enter the unadjusted trial balance on an end-of-period spreadsheet (work sheet) and complete the spreadsheet. Add the accounts listed in part (3) as needed.
3. Journalize and post the adjusting entries, inserting balances in the accounts affected. Record the adjusting entries on Page 26 of the journal. The following additional accounts from Bruno's Hauling's chart of accounts should be used: Wages Payable, 22; Supplies Expense, 52; Depreciation Expense—Equipment, 55; Depreciation Expense—Trucks, 56; Insurance Expense, 57.
4. Prepare an adjusted trial balance.
5. Prepare an income statement, a statement of owner's equity (no additional investments were made during the year), and a balance sheet.
6. Journalize and post the closing entries. Record the closing entries on Page 27 of the journal. (Income Summary is account #33 in the chart of accounts.) Indicate closed accounts by inserting a line in both Balance columns opposite the closing entry.
7. Prepare a post-closing trial balance.

OBJ. 4, 5

✔ 8. Net income: $23,500

PR 4-6A Complete accounting cycle

For the past several years, Shane Banovich has operated a part-time consulting business from his home. As of October 1, 2012, Shane decided to move to rented quarters and to operate the business, which was to be known as Epic Consulting, on a full-time basis. Epic Consulting entered into the following transactions during October:

Oct. 1. The following assets were received from Shane Banovich: cash, $12,000; accounts receivable, $6,000; supplies, $1,500; and office equipment, $9,000. There were no liabilities received.

1. Paid three months' rent on a lease rental contract, $4,800.

2. Paid the premiums on property and casualty insurance policies, $3,000.

4. Received cash from clients as an advance payment for services to be provided and recorded it as unearned fees, $4,000.

5. Purchased additional office equipment on account from Office Station Co., $2,000.

6. Received cash from clients on account, $3,500.

10. Paid cash for a newspaper advertisement, $400.

12. Paid Office Station Co. for part of the debt incurred on October 5, $1,000.

12. Recorded services provided on account for the period October 1–12, $6,000.

14. Paid part-time receptionist for two weeks' salary, $1,000.

Record the following transactions on Page 2 of the journal.

17. Recorded cash from cash clients for fees earned during the period October 1–17, $7,500.

18. Paid cash for supplies, $750.

20. Recorded services provided on account for the period October 13–20, $5,200.

24. Recorded cash from cash clients for fees earned for the period October 17–24, $3,700.

26. Received cash from clients on account, $5,500.

27. Paid part-time receptionist for two weeks' salary, $1,000.

29. Paid telephone bill for October, $250.

31. Paid electricity bill for October, $300.

31. Recorded cash from cash clients for fees earned for the period October 25–31, $2,800.

31. Recorded services provided on account for the remainder of October, $3,000.

31. Shane withdrew $8,000 for personal use.

Instructions

1. Journalize each transaction in a two-column journal starting on Page 1, referring to the following chart of accounts in selecting the accounts to be debited and credited. (Do not insert the account numbers in the journal at this time.)

11 Cash	31 Shane Banovich, Capital
12 Accounts Receivable	32 Shane Banovich, Drawing
14 Supplies	41 Fees Earned
15 Prepaid Rent	51 Salary Expense
16 Prepaid Insurance	52 Rent Expense
18 Office Equipment	53 Supplies Expense
19 Accumulated Depreciation	54 Depreciation Expense
21 Accounts Payable	55 Insurance Expense
22 Salaries Payable	59 Miscellaneous Expense
23 Unearned Fees	

2. Post the journal to a ledger of four-column accounts.
3. Prepare an unadjusted trial balance.
4. At the end of October, the following adjustment data were assembled. Analyze and use these data to complete parts (5) and (6).
   a. Insurance expired during October is $250.
   b. Supplies on hand on October 31 are $700.
   c. Depreciation of office equipment for October is $300.
   d. Accrued receptionist salary on October 31 is $250.
   e. Rent expired during October is $1,600.
   f. Unearned fees on October 31 are $1,800.
5. **Optional:** Enter the unadjusted trial balance on an end-of-period spreadsheet (work sheet) and complete the spreadsheet.
6. Journalize and post the adjusting entries. Record the adjusting entries on Page 3 of the journal.
7. Prepare an adjusted trial balance.
8. Prepare an income statement, a statement of owner's equity, and a balance sheet.
9. Prepare and post the closing entries. (Income Summary is account #33 in the chart of accounts.) Record the closing entries on Page 4 of the journal. Indicate closed accounts by inserting a line in both the Balance columns opposite the closing entry.
10. Prepare a post-closing trial balance.

Problems Series B

OBJ. 1, 2, 3

✔ 3. Total assets: $290,175

PR 4-1B Financial statements and closing entries

DNA 4 U Company offers legal consulting advice to prison inmates. DNA 4 U Company prepared the end-of-period spreadsheet at the top of the following page at April 30, 2012, the end of the current fiscal year.

Instructions

1. Prepare an income statement for the year ended April 30.
2. Prepare a statement of owner's equity for the year ended April 30. No additional investments were made during the year.
3. Prepare a balance sheet as of April 30.
4. On the basis of the end-of-period spreadsheet, journalize the closing entries.
5. Prepare a post-closing trial balance.

	A	B	C	D	E	F	G
1	DNA 4U Company						
2	End-of-Period Spreadsheet						
3	For the Year Ended April 30, 2012						
4		Unadjusted				Adjusted	
5		Trial Balance		Adjustments		Trial Balance	
6	Account Title	Dr.	Cr.	Dr.	Cr.	Dr.	Cr.
7	Cash	5,100				5,100	
8	Accounts Receivable	12,750		(a) 1,250		14,000	
9	Prepaid Insurance	3,600			(b) 1,200	2,400	
10	Supplies	2,025			(c) 1,400	625	
11	Land	80,000				80,000	
12	Building	200,000				200,000	
13	Accum. Depr.—Building		90,000		(d) 2,500		92,500
14	Equipment	140,000				140,000	
15	Accum. Depr.—Equipment		54,450		(e) 5,000		59,450
16	Accounts Payable		9,750				9,750
17	Sal. & Wages Payable				(f) 1,900		1,900
18	Unearned Rent		4,500	(g) 3,000			1,500
19	Luis Cortes, Capital		311,300				311,300
20	Luis Cortes, Drawing	20,000				20,000	
21	Fees Revenue		280,000		(a) 1,250		281,250
22	Rent Revenue				(g) 3,000		3,000
23	Salaries & Wages Expense	145,100		(f) 1,900		147,000	
24	Advertising Expense	86,800				86,800	
25	Utilities Expense	30,000				30,000	
26	Travel Expense	18,750				18,750	
27	Depr. Exp.—Equipment			(e) 5,000		5,000	
28	Depr. Exp.—Building			(d) 2,500		2,500	
29	Supplies Expense			(c) 1,400		1,400	
30	Insurance Expense			(b) 1,200		1,200	
31	Misc. Expense	5,875				5,875	
32		750,000	750,000	16,250	16,250	760,650	760,650
33							

OBJ. 2, 3

✔ 1. Lee Mather, capital, July 31: $468,000

PR 4-2B Financial statements and closing entries

Mather Services Company is a financial planning services firm owned and operated by Lee Mather. As of July 31, 2012, the end of the current fiscal year, the accountant for Mather Services Company prepared an end-of-period spreadsheet (work sheet), part of which is shown below.

	A	F	G
1	Mather Services Company		
2	End-of-Period Spreadsheet		
3	For the Year Ended July 31, 2012		
4		Adjusted	
5		Trial Balance	
6	Account Title	Dr.	Cr.
7	Cash	11,000	
8	Accounts Receivable	28,150	
9	Supplies	6,350	
10	Prepaid Insurance	9,500	
11	Land	100,000	
12	Buildings	360,000	
13	Accumulated Depreciation—Buildings		117,200
14	Equipment	260,000	
15	Accumulated Depreciation—Equipment		151,700
16	Accounts Payable		33,300
17	Salaries Payable		3,300
18	Unearned Rent		1,500
19	Lee Mather, Capital		407,000
20	Lee Mather, Drawing	25,000	
21	Service Fees		475,000
22	Rent Revenue		5,000
23	Salaries Expense	325,000	
24	Depreciation Expense—Equipment	17,500	
25	Rent Expense	15,500	
26	Supplies Expense	9,000	
27	Utilities Expense	8,500	
28	Depreciation Expense—Buildings	6,600	
29	Repairs Expense	3,450	
30	Insurance Expense	3,000	
31	Miscellaneous Expense	5,450	
32		1,194,000	1,194,000

Instructions

1. Prepare an income statement, a statement of owner's equity (no additional investments were made during the year), and a balance sheet.
2. Journalize the entries that were required to close the accounts at July 31.
3. If the balance of Lee Mather, Capital increased $40,000 after the closing entries were posted, and the withdrawals remained the same, what was the amount of net income or net loss?

OBJ. 2, 3

✔ 2. Net income: $30,640

PR 4-3B T accounts, adjusting entries, financial statements, and closing entries; optional end-of-period spreadsheet (work sheet)

The unadjusted trial balance of Laundry Basket at January 31, 2012, the end of the current fiscal year, is shown below.

Laundry Basket
Unadjusted Trial Balance
January 31, 2012

	Debit Balances	Credit Balances
Cash	3,480	
Laundry Supplies	9,000	
Prepaid Insurance	5,760	
Laundry Equipment	130,800	
Accumulated Depreciation		49,200
Accounts Payable		7,440
Stacy Martinell, Capital		45,360
Stacy Martinell, Drawing	2,400	
Laundry Revenue		198,000
Wages Expense	85,800	
Rent Expense	43,200	
Utilities Expense	16,320	
Miscellaneous Expense	3,240	
	300,000	300,000

The data needed to determine year-end adjustments are as follows:

a. Wages accrued but not paid at January 31 are $900.
b. Depreciation of equipment during the year is $7,000.
c. Laundry supplies on hand at January 31 are $2,100.
d. Insurance premiums expired during the year are $4,000.

Instructions

1. For each account listed in the unadjusted trial balance, enter the balance in a T account. Identify the balance as "Jan. 31 Bal." In addition, add T accounts for Wages Payable, Depreciation Expense, Laundry Supplies Expense, Insurance Expense, and Income Summary.
2. **Optional:** Enter the unadjusted trial balance on an end-of-period spreadsheet (work sheet) and complete the spreadsheet. Add the accounts listed in part (1) as needed.
3. Journalize and post the adjusting entries. Identify the adjustments by "Adj." and the new balances as "Adj. Bal."
4. Prepare an adjusted trial balance.
5. Prepare an income statement, a statement of owner's equity (no additional investments were made during the year), and a balance sheet.
6. Journalize and post the closing entries. Identify the closing entries by "Clos."
7. Prepare a post-closing trial balance.

OBJ. 2

✔ 4. Net income: $22,150

PR 4-4B Ledger accounts, adjusting entries, financial statements, and closing entries; optional end-of-period spreadsheet (work sheet)

If the working papers correlating with this textbook are not used, omit Problem 4-4B.

The ledger and trial balance of Sweetwater Services Co. as of July 31, 2012, the end of the first month of its current fiscal year, are presented in the working papers.

Data needed to determine the necessary adjusting entries are as follows:

a. Service revenue accrued at July 31 is $1,500.
b. Supplies on hand at July 31 are $3,800.
c. Insurance premiums expired during July are $1,200.
d. Depreciation of the building during July is $1,400.
e. Depreciation of equipment during July is $1,100.
f. Unearned rent at July 31 is $900.
g. Wages accrued but not paid at July 31 are $200.

Instructions

1. **Optional:** Complete the end-of-period spreadsheet (work sheet) using the adjustment data shown on the previous page.
2. Journalize and post the adjusting entries, inserting balances in the accounts affected.
3. Prepare an adjusted trial balance.
4. Prepare an income statement, a statement of owner's equity, and a balance sheet.
5. Journalize and post the closing entries. Indicate closed accounts by inserting a line in both Balance columns opposite the closing entry. Insert the new balance of the capital account.
6. Prepare a post-closing trial balance.

OBJ. 2, 3

✔ 5. Net income: $35,150

PR 4-5B Ledger accounts, adjusting entries, financial statements, and closing entries; optional end-of-period spreadsheet (work sheet)

The unadjusted trial balance of Oak and Brass Interiors at December 31, 2012, the end of the current year, is shown below.

Oak and Brass Interiors
Unadjusted Trial Balance
December 31, 2012

		Debit Balances	Credit Balances
11	Cash	3,100	
13	Supplies	6,000	
14	Prepaid Insurance	7,500	
16	Equipment	90,000	
17	Accumulated Depreciation—Equipment		12,000
18	Trucks	50,000	
19	Accumulated Depreciation—Trucks		27,100
21	Accounts Payable		4,500
31	Sally Kriebel, Capital		66,400
32	Sally Kriebel, Drawing	3,000	
41	Service Revenue		140,000
51	Wages Expense	72,000	
52	Rent Expense	7,600	
53	Truck Expense	5,350	
59	Miscellaneous Expense	5,450	
		250,000	250,000

The data needed to determine year-end adjustments are as follows:

a. Supplies on hand at December 31 are $1,750.
b. Insurance premiums expired during the year are $2,000.
c. Depreciation of equipment during the year is $5,000.
d. Depreciation of trucks during the year is $2,200.
e. Wages accrued but not paid at December 31 are $1,000.

Instructions

1. For each account listed in the unadjusted trial balance, enter the balance in the appropriate Balance column of a four-column account and place a check mark (✓) in the Posting Reference column.
2. **Optional:** Enter the unadjusted trial balance on an end-of-period spreadsheet (work sheet) and complete the spreadsheet. Add the accounts listed in part (3) as needed.
3. Journalize and post the adjusting entries, inserting balances in the accounts affected. Record the adjusting entries on Page 26 of the journal. The following additional accounts from Oak and Brass Interiors' chart of accounts should be used: Wages Payable, 22; Depreciation Expense—Equipment, 54; Supplies Expense, 55; Depreciation Expense—Trucks, 56; Insurance Expense, 57.
4. Prepare an adjusted trial balance.
5. Prepare an income statement, a statement of owner's equity (no additional investments were made during the year), and a balance sheet.

(Continued)

6. Journalize and post the closing entries. Record the closing entries on Page 27 of the journal. (Income Summary is account #33 in the chart of accounts.) Indicate closed accounts by inserting a line in both Balance columns opposite the closing entry.
7. Prepare a post-closing trial balance.

OBJ. 4, 5

✔ 8. Net income: $35,150

PR 4-6B Complete accounting cycle

For the past several years, Abby Brown has operated a part-time consulting business from her home. As of June 1, 2012, Abby decided to move to rented quarters and to operate the business, which was to be known as Square One Consulting, on a full-time basis. Square One Consulting entered into the following transactions during June:

June 1. The following assets were received from Abby Brown: cash, $30,000; accounts receivable, $7,500; supplies, $2,000; and office equipment, $15,000. There were no liabilities received.

1. Paid three months' rent on a lease rental contract, $6,000.

2. Paid the premiums on property and casualty insurance policies, $3,600.

4. Received cash from clients as an advance payment for services to be provided and recorded it as unearned fees, $5,000.

5. Purchased additional office equipment on account from Office Depot Co., $6,000.

6. Received cash from clients on account, $4,000.

10. Paid cash for a newspaper advertisement, $200.

12. Paid Office Depot Co. for part of the debt incurred on June 5, $1,200.

12. Recorded services provided on account for the period June 1–12, $13,000.

14. Paid part-time receptionist for two weeks' salary, $1,500.

Record the following transactions on Page 2 of the journal.

17. Recorded cash from cash clients for fees earned during the period June 1–16, $9,000.

18. Paid cash for supplies, $1,400.

20. Recorded services provided on account for the period June 13–20, $8,500.

24. Recorded cash from cash clients for fees earned for the period June 17–24, $6,300.

26. Received cash from clients on account, $12,100.

27. Paid part-time receptionist for two weeks' salary, $1,500.

29. Paid telephone bill for June, $150.

30. Paid electricity bill for June, $400.

30. Recorded cash from cash clients for fees earned for the period June 25–30, $3,900.

30. Recorded services provided on account for the remainder of June, $2,500.

30. Abby withdrew $10,000 for personal use.

Instructions

1. Journalize each transaction in a two-column journal starting on Page 1, referring to the following chart of accounts in selecting the accounts to be debited and credited. (Do not insert the account numbers in the journal at this time.)

11 Cash	31 Abby Brown, Capital
12 Accounts Receivable	32 Abby Brown, Drawing
14 Supplies	41 Fees Earned
15 Prepaid Rent	51 Salary Expense
16 Prepaid Insurance	52 Supplies Expense
18 Office Equipment	53 Rent Expense
19 Accumulated Depreciation	54 Depreciation Expense
21 Accounts Payable	55 Insurance Expense
22 Salaries Payable	59 Miscellaneous Expense
23 Unearned Fees	

2. Post the journal to a ledger of four-column accounts.
3. Prepare an unadjusted trial balance.
4. At the end of June, the following adjustment data were assembled. Analyze and use these data to complete parts (5) and (6).
   a. Insurance expired during June is $200.
   b. Supplies on hand on June 30 are $600.
   c. Depreciation of office equipment for June is $250.
   d. Accrued receptionist salary on June 30 is $350.
   e. Rent expired during June is $2,500.
   f. Unearned fees on June 30 are $3,200.
5. **Optional:** Enter the unadjusted trial balance on an end-of-period spreadsheet (work sheet) and complete the spreadsheet.
6. Journalize and post the adjusting entries. Record the adjusting entries on Page 3 of the journal.
7. Prepare an adjusted trial balance.
8. Prepare an income statement, a statement of owner's equity, and a balance sheet.
9. Prepare and post the closing entries. Record the closing entries on Page 4 of the journal. (Income Summary is account #33 in the chart of accounts.) Indicate closed accounts by inserting a line in both the Balance columns opposite the closing entry.
10. Prepare a post-closing trial balance.

Continuing Problem

✔ 2. Net income: $6,210

The unadjusted trial balance of PS Music as of July 31, 2012, along with the adjustment data for the two months ended July 31, 2012, are shown in Chapter 3.

Based upon the adjustment data, the adjusted trial balance shown below was prepared.

PS Music
Adjusted Trial Balance
July 31, 2012

	Debit Balances	Credit Balances
Cash	10,510	
Accounts Receivable	4,750	
Supplies	400	
Prepaid Insurance	2,475	
Office Equipment	6,000	
Accumulated Depreciation—Office Equipment		75
Accounts Payable		7,080
Wages Payable		170
Unearned Revenue		3,600
Pat Sharpe, Capital		9,000
Pat Sharpe, Drawing	2,000	
Fees Earned		21,950
Wages Expense	2,970	
Office Rent Expense	2,550	
Equipment Rent Expense	1,300	
Utilities Expense	1,060	
Music Expense	3,610	
Advertising Expense	1,450	
Supplies Expense	1,030	
Insurance Expense	225	
Depreciation Expense	75	
Miscellaneous Expense	1,470	
	41,875	41,875

CP 4-3 Financial statements

Assume that you recently accepted a position with Frontier National Bank as an assistant loan officer. As one of your first duties, you have been assigned the responsibility of evaluating a loan request for $150,000 from Icancreateart.com, a small proprietorship. In support of the loan application, Tess Ramey, owner, submitted a "Statement of Accounts" (trial balance) for the first year of operations ended July 31, 2012.

Icancreateart.com
Statement of Accounts
July 31, 2012

Cash	5,000	
Billings Due from Others	40,000	
Supplies (chemicals, etc.)	7,500	
Building	122,300	
Equipment	25,000	
Amounts Owed to Others		11,000
Investment in Business		74,000
Service Revenue		215,000
Wages Expense	75,000	
Utilities Expense	10,000	
Rent Expense	8,000	
Insurance Expense	6,000	
Other Expenses	1,200	
	300,000	300,000

1. Explain to Tess Ramey why a set of financial statements (income statement, statement of owner's equity, and balance sheet) would be useful to you in evaluating the loan request.
2. In discussing the "Statement of Accounts" with Tess Ramey, you discovered that the accounts had not been adjusted at July 31. Analyze the "Statement of Accounts" and indicate possible adjusting entries that might be necessary before an accurate set of financial statements could be prepared.
3. Assuming that an accurate set of financial statements will be submitted by Tess Ramey in a few days, what other considerations or information would you require before making a decision on the loan request?

Internet Project

CP 4-4 Compare balance sheets

Group Project

In groups of three or four, compare the balance sheets of two different companies, and present to the class a summary of the similarities and differences of the two companies. You may obtain the balance sheets you need from one of the following sources:

1. Your school or local library.
2. The investor relations department of each company.
3. The company's Web site on the Internet.
4. EDGAR (Electronic Data Gathering, Analysis, and Retrieval), the electronic archives of financial statements filed with the Securities and Exchange Commission.

SEC documents can be retrieved using the EdgarScan™ service at **http://sec.gov.** To obtain annual report information, click on "Search for Company Filing," click on "Companies & Other Filers," type in the company name, and then click on "Find Companies." Click on the CIK related to the company name, search for Form 10-K, and click on "Retrieve Selected Findings." Finally, click on the "html" for the latest period and the related document.

CHAPTER 5

xland/Jupiter Images

Accounting Systems

Intuit Inc.

Whether you realize it or not, you likely interact with accounting systems. For example, your bank statement is a type of accounting system. When you make a deposit, the bank records an addition to your cash; when you withdraw cash, the bank records a reduction in your cash. Such a simple accounting system works well for a person with just a few transactions per month. However, over time, you may find that your financial affairs will become more complex and involve many different types of transactions, including investments and loan payments. At this point, relying on your bank statement may not be sufficient for managing your financial affairs. Personal financial planning software, such as **Intuit**'s Quicken, can be useful when your financial affairs become more complex.

What happens if you decide to begin a small business? Transactions expand to include customers, vendors, and employees. As a result, the accounting system will need to adjust to this complexity. Thus, many small businesses will use small-business accounting software, such as Intuit's QuickBooks, as their first accounting system. As a business grows, more sophisticated accounting systems will be needed. Companies such as **SAP**, **Oracle**, **Microsoft**, and **Sage Software, Inc.**, offer accounting system solutions for businesses that become larger with more complex accounting needs.

Accounting systems used by large and small businesses employ the basic principles of the accounting cycle discussed in the previous chapters. However, these accounting systems include features that simplify the recording and summary process. In this chapter, we will discuss these simplifying procedures as they apply to both manual and computerized systems.

Learning Objectives

After studying this chapter, you should be able to:	Example Exercises	Page
OBJ. 1 Define and describe an accounting system.		
Basic Accounting Systems		
OBJ. 2 Journalize and post transactions in a manual accounting system that uses subsidiary ledgers and special journals.		
Manual Accounting Systems		
Subsidiary Ledgers		
Special Journals		
Revenue Journal	EE 5-1	211
Cash Receipts Journal		
Accounts Receivable Control Account and Subsidiary Ledger	EE 5-2	214
Purchases Journal	EE 5-3	216
Cash Payments Journal		
Accounts Payable Control Account and Subsidiary Ledger	EE 5-4	219
OBJ. 3 Describe and illustrate the use of a computerized accounting system.		
Computerized Accounting Systems		
OBJ. 4 Describe the basic features of e-commerce.		
E-Commerce		
OBJ. 5 Use segment analysis in evaluating the operating performance of a company.		
Financial Analysis and Interpretation: Segment Analysis	EE 5-5	225

At a Glance 5 Page 225

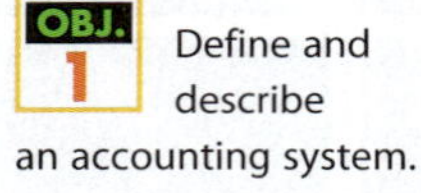

Define and describe an accounting system.

Basic Accounting Systems

In Chapters 1–4, an accounting system for NetSolutions was described and illustrated. An **accounting system** is the methods and procedures for collecting, classifying, summarizing, and reporting a business's financial and operating information. Most accounting systems, however, are more complex than NetSolutions'. For example, Southwest Airlines's accounting system not only records basic transaction data, but also records data on such items as ticket reservations, credit card collections, frequent-flier mileage, and aircraft maintenance.

As a business grows and changes, its accounting system also changes in a three-step process. This three-step process is as follows:

Step 1. *Analyze* user information needs.
Step 2. *Design* the system to meet the user needs.
Step 3. *Implement* the system.

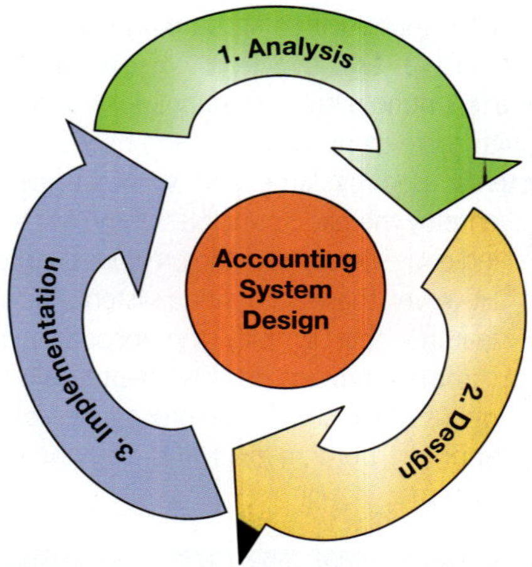

For NetSolutions, our analysis determined that Chris Clark needed financial statements for the new business. We designed the system, using a basic manual system that included a chart of accounts, a two-column journal, and a general ledger. Finally, we implemented the system to record transactions and prepare financial statements.

Once a system has been implemented, input from users is used to analyze and improve the system. For example, in later chapters, NetSolutions expands its chart of accounts to record more complex transactions.

The accounting system design consists of:

1. internal controls and
2. information processing methods.

Internal controls are the policies and procedures that protect assets from misuse, ensure that business information is accurate, and ensure that laws and regulations are being followed. Internal controls are discussed in Chapter 8.

Processing methods are the means by which the accounting system collects, summarizes, and reports accounting information. These methods may be either *manual* or *computerized*. In the following sections, manual accounting systems that use special journals and subsidiary ledgers are described and illustrated. This is followed by a discussion of computerized accounting systems.

Manual Accounting Systems

OBJ. 2 Journalize and post transactions in a manual accounting system that uses subsidiary ledgers and special journals.

Accounting systems are manual or computerized. Understanding a manual accounting system is useful in identifying relationships between accounting data and reports. Also, most computerized systems use principles from manual systems.

In prior chapters, the transactions for NetSolutions were manually recorded in an all-purpose (two-column) journal. The journal entries were then posted individually to the accounts in the ledger. Such a system is simple to use and easy to understand when there are a small number of transactions. However, when a business has a large number of *similar* transactions, using an all-purpose journal is inefficient and impractical. In such cases, subsidiary ledgers and special journals are useful.

Subsidiary Ledgers

A large number of individual accounts with a common characteristic can be grouped together in a separate ledger called a **subsidiary ledger**. The primary ledger, which contains all of the balance sheet and income statement accounts, is then called the **general ledger**. Each subsidiary ledger is represented in the general ledger by a summarizing account, called a **controlling account**. The sum of the balances of the accounts in a subsidiary ledger must equal the balance of the related controlling account. Thus, a subsidiary ledger is a secondary ledger that supports a controlling account in the general ledger.

Two of the most common subsidiary ledgers are as follows:

1. Accounts receivable subsidiary ledger
2. Accounts payable subsidiary ledger

The **accounts receivable subsidiary ledger**, or *customers ledger*, lists the individual customer accounts in alphabetical order. The controlling account in the general ledger that summarizes the debits and credits to the individual customer accounts is Accounts Receivable.

The **accounts payable subsidiary ledger**, or *creditors ledger*, lists individual creditor accounts in alphabetical order. The related controlling account in the general ledger is Accounts Payable.

The relationship between the general ledger and the accounts receivable and accounts payable subsidiary ledgers is illustrated in Exhibit 1.

Many businesses use subsidiary ledgers for other accounts in addition to Accounts Receivable and Accounts Payable. For example, businesses often use an equipment subsidiary ledger to keep track of each item of equipment purchased, its cost, location, and other data.

Special Journals

One method of processing transactions more efficiently in a manual system is to use special journals. **Special journals** are designed to record a single kind of

EXHIBIT 2 Revenue Journal

Revenue Journal *Page 35*

Date		Invoice No.	Account Debited	Post. Ref.	Accts. Rec. Dr. Fees Earned Cr.
2012					
Mar.	2	615	Accessories By Claire		2,200
	6	616	RapZone		1,750
	18	617	Web Cantina		2,650
	27	618	Accessories By Claire		3,000
	31				9,600

3. Account Debited column: *Accessories By Claire*
4. Accts. Rec. Dr./Fees Earned Cr. column: *2,200*

The process of posting from a revenue journal, shown in Exhibit 3, is as follows:

1. Each transaction is posted individually to a customer account in the accounts receivable subsidiary ledger. Postings to customer accounts should be made on a regular basis. In this way, the customer's account will show a current balance. Since the balances in the customer accounts are usually debit balances, the three-column account form is shown in Exhibit 3.

   To illustrate, Exhibit 3 shows the posting of the $2,200 debit to Accessories By Claire in the accounts receivable subsidiary ledger. After the posting, Accessories By Claire has a debit balance of $2,200.

2. To provide a trail of the entries posted to the subsidiary and general ledger, the source of these entries is indicated in the Posting Reference column of each account by inserting the letter R (for revenue journal) and the page number of the revenue journal.

   To illustrate, Exhibit 3 shows that after $2,200 is posted to Accessories By Claire's account, R35 is inserted into the Post. Ref. column of the account.

3. To indicate that the transaction has been posted to the accounts receivable subsidiary ledger, a check mark (✓) is inserted in the Post. Ref. column of the revenue journal, as shown in Exhibit 3.

   To illustrate, Exhibit 3 shows that a check mark (✓) has been inserted in the Post. Ref. column next to Accessories By Claire in the revenue journal to indicate that the $2,200 has been posted.

4. A single monthly total is posted to Accounts Receivable and Fees Earned in the general ledger. This total is equal to the sum of the month's debits to the individual accounts in the subsidiary ledger. It is posted in the general ledger as a debit to Accounts Receivable and a credit to Fees Earned, as shown in Exhibit 3. The accounts receivable account number (12) and the fees earned account number (41) are then inserted below the total in the revenue journal to indicate that the posting is completed.

   To illustrate, Exhibit 3 shows the monthly total of $9,600 was posted as a debit to Accounts Receivable (12) and as a credit to Fees Earned (41).

Exhibit 3 illustrates the efficiency gained by using the revenue journal rather than the general journal. Specifically, all of the transactions for fees earned during the month are posted to the general ledger only once—at the end of the month.

EXHIBIT 3 Revenue Journal and Postings

Revenue Journal *Page 35*

Date		Invoice No.	Account Debited	Post. Ref.	Accts. Rec. Dr. Fees Earned Cr.
2012					
Mar.	2	615	Accessories By Claire	✓	2,200
	6	616	RapZone	✓	1,750
	18	617	Web Cantina	✓	2,650
	27	618	Accessories By Claire	✓	3,000
	31				9,600
					(12) (41)

General Ledger

Account *Accounts Receivable* Account No. *12*

Date		Item	Post. Ref.	Debit	Credit	Balance Debit	Balance Credit
2012							
Mar.	1	Balance	✓			3,400	
	31		R35	9,600		13,000	

Account *Fees Earned* Account No. *41*

Date		Item	Post. Ref.	Debit	Credit	Balance Debit	Balance Credit
2012							
Mar.	31		R35		9,600		9,600

Accounts Receivable Subsidiary Ledger

Name: *Accessories By Claire*

Date		Item	Post. Ref.	Debit	Credit	Balance
2012						
Mar.	2		R35	2,200		2,200
	27		R35	3,000		5,200

Name: *RapZone*

Date		Item	Post. Ref.	Debit	Credit	Balance
2012						
Mar.	6		R35	1,750		1,750

Name: *Web Cantina*

Date		Item	Post. Ref.	Debit	Credit	Balance
2012						
Mar.	1	Balance	✓			3,400
	18		R35	2,650		6,050

Example Exercise 5-1 Revenue Journal

OBJ. 2

The following revenue transactions occurred during December:

Dec. 5. Issued Invoice No. 302 to Butler Company for services provided on account, $5,000.
9. Issued Invoice No. 303 to JoJo Enterprises for services provided on account, $2,100.
15. Issued Invoice No. 304 to Double D Inc. for services provided on account, $3,250.

Record these transactions in a revenue journal as illustrated in Exhibit 2.

Follow My Example 5-1

REVENUE JOURNAL

Date	Invoice No.	Account Debited	Post. Ref.	Accts. Rec. Dr. Fees Earned Cr.
Dec. 5	302	Butler Company		5,000
9	303	JoJo Enterprises		2,100
15	304	Double D Inc.		3,250

Practice Exercises: PE 5-1A, PE 5-1B

column of the cash receipts journal. Also, at the end of ... entered below the Other Accounts Cr. column to indicate that no further action is needed.

EXHIBIT 6 Cash Payments Journal and Postings

Cash Payments Journal — Page 7

Date		Ck. No.	Account Debited	Post. Ref.	Other Accounts Dr.	Accounts Payable Dr.	Cash Cr.
2012							
Mar.	2	150	Rent Expense	52	1,600		1,600
	15	151	Grayco Supplies	✓		1,230	1,230
	21	152	Jewett Business Systems	✓		2,800	2,800
	22	153	Donnelly Supplies	✓		420	420
	30	154	Utilities Expense	54	1,050		1,050
	31	155	Howard Supplies	✓		600	600
	31				2,650	5,050	7,700
					(✓)	(21)	(11)

General Ledger

Account *Cash* — Account No. *11*

Date		Item	Post. Ref.	Debit	Credit	Balance Debit	Balance Credit
2012							
Mar.	1	Balance	✓			6,200	
	31		CR14	7,750		13,950	
	31		CP7		7,700	6,250	

Account *Accounts Payable* — Account No. 21

Date		Item	Post. Ref.	Debit	Credit	Balance Debit	Balance Credit
2012							
Mar.	1	Balance	✓				1,230
	31		P11		6,230		7,460
	31		CP7	5,050			2,410

Account *Rent Expense* — Account No. 52

Date		Item	Post. Ref.	Debit	Credit	Balance Debit	Balance Credit
2012							
Mar.	2		CP7	1,600		1,600	

Account *Utilities Expense* — Account No. 54

Date		Item	Post. Ref.	Debit	Credit	Balance Debit	Balance Credit
2012							
Mar.	30		CP7	1,050		1,050	

Accounts Payable Subsidiary Ledger

Name: *Donnelly Supplies*

Date		Item	Post. Ref.	Debit	Credit	Balance
2012						
Mar.	7		P11		420	420
	19		P11		1,450	1,870
	22		CP7	420		1,450

Name: *Grayco Supplies*

Date		Item	Post. Ref.	Debit	Credit	Balance
2012						
Mar.	1	Balance	✓			1,230
	15		CP7	1,230		—

Name: *Howard Supplies*

Date		Item	Post. Ref.	Debit	Credit	Balance
2012						
Mar.	3		P11		600	600
	27		P11		960	1,560
	31		CP7	600		960

Name: *Jewett Business Systems*

Date		Item	Post. Ref.	Debit	Credit	Balance
2012						
Mar.	12		P11		2,800	2,800
	21		CP7	2,800		—

4. A single monthly total of the Accounts Payable Dr. column is posted to the accounts payable general ledger account. This is the total cash paid on account and is posted as a debit to Accounts Payable. The accounts payable account number (21) is then inserted below the Accounts Payable Dr. column to indicate that the posting is complete. *To illustrate, Exhibit 6 shows the monthly total of $5,050 was posted as a debit to Accounts Payable (21).*

5. A single monthly total of the Cash Cr. column is posted to the cash general ledger account. This is the total cash payments during the month and is posted as a credit to Cash. The cash account number (11) is then inserted below the Cash Cr. column to indicate that the posting is complete.
   To illustrate, Exhibit 6 shows the monthly total of $7,700 was posted as a credit to Cash (11).
6. The accounts listed in the Other Accounts Dr. column are posted on a regular basis as a separate debit to each account. The account number is then inserted in the Post. Ref. column to indicate that the posting is complete. Because accounts in the Other Accounts Dr. column are posted individually, a check mark is placed below the column total at the end of the month to show that no further action is needed.
   To illustrate, Exhibit 6 shows that $1,600 was posted as a debit to Rent Expense (52) and $1,050 was posted as a debit to Utilities Expense (54) in the general ledger. The account numbers (52 and 54, respectively) were entered in the Post. Ref. column of the cash payments journal. Also, at the end of the month, a check mark (✓) is entered below the Other Accounts Dr. column to indicate that no further action is needed.

Accounts Payable Control Account and Subsidiary Ledger

After all posting has been completed for the month, the balances in the accounts payable subsidiary ledger should be totaled. This total should then be compared with the balance of the accounts payable controlling account in the general ledger. If the controlling account and the subsidiary ledger do not agree, an error has occurred. Before proceeding, the error must be located and corrected.

The total of NetSolutions' accounts payable subsidiary ledger is $2,410. This total agrees with the balance of its accounts payable control account on March 31, 2012, as shown below.

Accounts Payable (Control)

Balance, March 1, 2012	$1,230
Total credits (from purchases journal)	6,230
Total debits (from cash payments journal)	(5,050)
Balance, March 31, 2012	$2,410

NetSolutions
Accounts Payable Creditor Balances
March 31, 2012

Donnelly Supplies	$1,450
Grayco Supplies	0
Howard Supplies	960
Jewett Business Systems	0
Total	$2,410

Equal credit balances

Example Exercise 5-4 Accounts Payable Subsidiary Ledger

OBJ. 2

The debits and credits from two transactions are presented in the following creditor's (supplier's) account:

NAME *Lassiter Services Inc.*
ADDRESS *301 St. Bonaventure Ave.*

Date	Item	Post. Ref.	Debit	Credit	Balance
Aug. 1	Balance				320
12	Invoice No. 101	CP36	200		120
22	Invoice No. 106	P16		140	260

Describe each transaction and the source of each posting.

Follow My Example 5-4

Aug. 12. Paid $200 to Lassiter Services Inc. on account (Invoice No. 101). Amount posted from page 36 of the cash payments journal.

22. Purchased $140 of services on account from Lassiter Services Inc. itemized on Invoice No. 106. Amount posted from page 16 of the purchases journal.

Practice Exercises: PE 5-4A, PE 5-4B

OBJ. 2 Journalize and post transactions in a manual accounting system that uses subsidiary ledgers and special journals.

Key Points Subsidiary ledgers may be used to maintain separate records for customers and creditors (vendors). A controlling account in the general ledger summarizes the subsidiary ledger accounts. The sum of the subsidiary ledger account balances must agree with the balance in the related controlling account.

Learning Outcomes	Example Exercises	Practice Exercises
• Prepare a revenue journal and post services provided on account to individual customer accounts and the column total to the corresponding general ledger accounts.	EE5-1	PE5-1A, 5-1B
• Prepare a cash receipts journal and post collections on account to individual customer accounts. Post Other Accounts column entries individually and special column totals to the corresponding general ledger accounts.	EE5-2	PE5-2A, 5-2B
• Prepare a purchases journal and post amounts owed to individual creditor accounts. Post Other Accounts column entries individually and special column totals to the corresponding general ledger accounts.	EE5-3	PE5-3A, 5-3B
• Prepare a cash payments journal and post the amounts paid to individual creditor accounts. Post Other Accounts column entries individually and special column totals to the corresponding general ledger accounts.	EE5-4	PE5-4A, 5-4B

OBJ. 3 Describe and illustrate the use of a computerized accounting system.

Key Points Computerized accounting systems are similar to manual systems. The main advantages of a computerized accounting system are the simultaneous recording and posting of transactions, high degree of accuracy, and timeliness of reporting.

Learning Outcomes	Example Exercises	Practice Exercises
• Differentiate between a manual and a computerized accounting system.		
• Illustrate revenue and cash receipts transactions using QuickBooks.		

OBJ. 4 Describe the basic features of e-commerce.

Key Points Using the Internet to perform business transactions is termed e-commerce. B2C e-commerce involves Internet transactions between a business and consumer, while B2B e-commerce involves Internet transactions between businesses. More elaborate e-commerce involves planning and coordinating suppliers, customers, and product design.

Learning Outcomes	Example Exercises	Practice Exercises
• Define e-commerce and describe the major trends in e-commerce.		

Use segment analysis in evaluating the operating performance of a company.

Key Points Businesses may be segmented by region, by product or service, or by type of customer. Segment revenues can be analyzed using horizontal and vertical analyses. Such analyses are useful to management for evaluating the causes of business performance.

Learning Outcomes	Example Exercises	Practice Exercises
• Prepare horizontal and vertical analyses for business segments.	EE5-5	PE5-5A, 5-5B

Key Terms

accounting system (206)
accounts payable subsidiary ledger (207)
accounts receivable subsidiary ledger (207)
cash payments journal (217)
cash receipts journal (212)
controlling account (207)
e-commerce (223)
general journal (208)
general ledger (207)
internal controls (207)
invoice (209)
purchases journal (214)
revenue journal (209)
special journals (207)
subsidiary ledger (207)

Illustrative Problem

Selected transactions of O'Malley Co. for the month of May are as follows:

a. May 1. Issued Check No. 1001 in payment of rent for May, $1,200.
b. 2. Purchased office supplies on account from McMillan Co., $3,600.
c. 4. Issued Check No. 1003 in payment of freight charges on the supplies purchased on May 2, $320.
d. 8. Provided services on account to Waller Co., Invoice No. 51, $4,500.
e. 9. Issued Check No. 1005 for office supplies purchased, $450.
f. 10. Received cash for office supplies sold to employees at cost, $120.
g. 11. Purchased office equipment on account from Fender Office Products, $15,000.
h. 12. Issued Check No. 1010 in payment of the supplies purchased from McMillan Co. on May 2, $3,600.
i. 16. Provided services on account to Riese Co., Invoice No. 58, $8,000.
j. 18. Received $4,500 from Waller Co. in payment of May 8 invoice.
k. 20. Invested additional cash in the business, $10,000.
l. 25. Provided services for cash, $15,900.
m. 30. Issued Check No. 1040 for withdrawal of cash for personal use, $1,000.
n. 30. Issued Check No. 1041 in payment of electricity and water invoices, $690.

o. May 30. Issued Check No. 1042 in payment of office and sales salaries for May, $15,800.

p. 31. Journalized adjusting entries from the work sheet prepared for the fiscal year ended May 31.

O'Malley Co. maintains a revenue journal, a cash receipts journal, a purchases journal, a cash payments journal, and a general journal. In addition, accounts receivable and accounts payable subsidiary ledgers are used.

Instructions

1. Indicate the journal in which each of the preceding transactions, (a) through (p), would be recorded.
2. Indicate whether an account in the accounts receivable or accounts payable subsidiary ledgers would be affected for each of the preceding transactions.
3. Journalize transactions (b), (c), (d), (h), and (j) in the appropriate journals.

Solution

1. Journal	2. Subsidiary Ledger
a. Cash payments journal	
b. Purchases journal	Accounts payable ledger
c. Cash payments journal	
d. Revenue journal	Accounts receivable ledger
e. Cash payments journal	
f. Cash receipts journal	
g. Purchases journal	Accounts payable ledger
h. Cash payments journal	Accounts payable ledger
i. Revenue journal	Accounts receivable ledger
j. Cash receipts journal	Accounts receivable ledger
k. Cash receipts journal	
l. Cash receipts journal	
m. Cash payments journal	
n. Cash payments journal	
o. Cash payments journal	
p. General journal	

3.

Transaction (b):

Purchases Journal

Date		Account Credited	Post. Ref.	Accounts Payable Cr.	Office Supplies Dr.	Other Accounts Dr.	Post. Ref.	Amount
May	2	McMillan Co.		3,600	3,600			

Transactions (c) and (h):

Cash Payments Journal

Date		Ck. No.	Account Debited	Post. Ref.	Other Accounts Dr.	Accounts Payable Dr.	Cash Cr.
May	4	1003	Freight Expense		320		320
	12	1010	McMillan Co.			3,600	3,600

Transaction (d):

Revenue Journal					
Date		Invoice No.	Account Debited	Post. Ref.	Accts. Rec. Dr. Fees Earned Cr.
May	8	51	Waller Co.		4,500

Transaction (j):

Cash Receipts Journal						
Date		Account Credited	Post. Ref.	Other Accounts Cr.	Accounts Receivable Cr.	Cash Dr.
May	18	Waller Co.			4,500	4,500

Discussion Questions

1. Why would a company maintain separate accounts receivable ledgers for each customer, as opposed to maintaining a single accounts receivable ledger for all customers?
2. What are the major advantages of the use of special journals?
3. In recording 400 fees earned on account during a single month, how many times will it be necessary to write Fees Earned (a) if each transaction, including fees earned, is recorded individually in a two-column general journal; (b) if each transaction for fees earned is recorded in a revenue journal?
4. How many postings to Fees Earned for the month would be needed in Discussion Question 3 if the procedure described in (a) had been used; if the procedure described in (b) had been used?
5. During the current month, the following errors occurred in recording transactions in the purchases journal or in posting from it.
   a. An invoice for $1,875 of supplies from Kelly Co. was recorded as having been received from Kelley Co., another supplier.
   b. A credit of $420 to Blackstone Company was posted as $240 in the subsidiary ledger.
   c. An invoice for equipment of $4,800 was recorded as $4,000.
   d. The Accounts Payable column of the purchases journal was overstated by $3,600.

   How will each error come to the bookkeeper's attention, other than by chance discovery?
6. Assuming the use of a two-column general journal, a purchases journal, and a cash payments journal as illustrated in this chapter, indicate the journal in which each of the following transactions should be recorded:
   a. Purchase of office supplies on account.
   b. Purchase of supplies for cash.
   c. Purchase of store equipment on account.
   d. Payment of cash on account to creditor.
   e. Payment of cash for office supplies.
7. What is an electronic form, and how is it used in a computerized accounting system?
8. Do computerized systems use controlling accounts to verify the accuracy of the subsidiary accounts?
9. What happens to the special journal in a computerized accounting system that uses electronic forms?
10. How would e-commerce improve the revenue/collection cycle?

Practice Exercises

Learning Objectives | Example Exercises

OBJ. 2 EE 5-1 p. 211

PE 5-1A Revenue journal

The following revenue transactions occurred during October:

Oct. 7. Issued Invoice No. 121 to Darcy Co. for services provided on account, $320.
17. Issued Invoice No. 122 to Triple A Inc. for services provided on account, $470.
21. Issued Invoice No. 123 to Whaley Co. for services provided on account, $530.

Record these three transactions into the following revenue journal format:

REVENUE JOURNAL

Date	Invoice No.	Account Debited	Post. Ref.	Accts. Rec. Dr. Fees Earned Cr.

OBJ. 2 EE 5-1 p. 211

PE 5-1B Revenue journal

The following revenue transactions occurred during May:

May 6. Issued Invoice No. 78 to Lemon Co. for services provided on account, $1,240.
9. Issued Invoice No. 79 to Hitchcock Inc. for services provided on account, $3,420.
19. Issued Invoice No. 80 to Conrad Inc. for services provided on account, $1,470.

Record these three transactions into the following revenue journal format:

REVENUE JOURNAL

Date	Invoice No.	Account Debited	Post. Ref.	Accts. Rec. Dr. Fees Earned Cr.

OBJ. 2 EE 5-2 p. 214

PE 5-2A Accounts receivable subsidiary ledger

The debits and credits from two transactions are presented in the following customer account:

NAME *Signal Communications Inc.*
ADDRESS *76 Oak Ridge Rd.*

Date	Item	Post. Ref.	Debit	Credit	Balance
June 1	Balance	✓			280
20	Invoice 579	CR106		95	185
28	Invoice 527	R92	75		260

Describe each transaction and the source of each posting.

OBJ. 2 EE 5-2 p. 214

PE 5-2B Accounts receivable subsidiary ledger

The debits and credits from two transactions are presented in the following customer account:

NAME *Mobility Products Inc.*
ADDRESS *46 W. Main St.*

Date	Item	Post. Ref.	Debit	Credit	Balance
Sept. 1	Balance	✓			1,200
8	Invoice 119	R24	840		2,040
17	Invoice 106	CR46		590	1,450

Describe each transaction and the source of each posting.

Learning Objectives	Example Exercises
OBJ. 2	EE 5-3 p. 216

PE 5-3A Purchases journal

The following purchase transactions occurred during August for Elegance Catering Service:

Aug. 11. Purchased party supplies for $390, on account from Party Zone Supplies Inc.
14. Purchased party supplies for $290, on account from Fun 4 All Supplies Inc.
29. Purchased office furniture for $3,560, on account from Office Space Inc.

Record these transactions in the following purchases journal format:

PURCHASES JOURNAL

Date	Accounts Credited	Post. Ref.	Accounts Payable Cr.	Office Supplies Dr.	Other Account Dr.	Post. Ref.	Amount

OBJ. 2 EE 5-3 p. 216

PE 5-3B Purchases journal

The following purchase transactions occurred during December for Rehoboth Inc.:

Dec. 6. Purchased office supplies for $415, on account from Supply Hut Inc.
14. Purchased office equipment for $1,950, on account from Zell Computer Inc.
19. Purchased office supplies for $450, on account from Supply Hut Inc.

Record these transactions in the following purchases journal format:

PURCHASES JOURNAL

Date	Accounts Credited	Post. Ref.	Accounts Payable Cr.	Office Supplies Dr.	Other Account Dr.	Post. Ref.	Amount

OBJ. 2 EE 5-4 p. 219

PE 5-4A Accounts payable subsidiary ledger

The debits and credits from two transactions are presented in the following supplier's (creditor's) account:

NAME *Newton Computer Services Inc.*
ADDRESS *2199 Technology Place*

Date	Item	Post. Ref.	Debit	Credit	Balance
Nov. 1	Balance				9,400
11	Invoice 75	P8		2,790	12,190
21	Invoice 43	CP46	6,550		5,640

Describe each transaction and the source of each posting.

OBJ. 2 EE 5-4 p. 219

PE 5-4B Accounts payable subsidiary ledger

The debits and credits from two transactions are presented in the following supplier's (creditor's) account:

NAME *Daisy Inc.*
ADDRESS *5000 Grand Ave.*

Date	Item	Post. Ref.	Debit	Credit	Balance
Feb. 1	Balance				92
11	Invoice 122	CP71	79		13
20	Invoice 139	P55		57	70

Describe each transaction and the source of each posting.

OBJ. 5 EE 5-5 p. 225

PE 5-5A Segment analysis

Harrow Company does business in two customer segments, Retail and Wholesale. The following annual revenue information was determined from the accounting system's invoice information:

Learning Objectives *Example Exercises*

	2012	2011
Retail	$ 80,000	$ 75,000
Wholesale	120,000	140,000
Total revenue	$200,000	$215,000

Prepare a horizontal and vertical analysis of the segments. Round to one decimal place.

OBJ. 5 EE 5-5 p. 225

PE 5-5B Segment analysis

Outdoor Country, Inc. does business in two product segments, Camping and Fishing. The following annual revenue information was determined from the accounting system's invoice information:

	2012	2011
Camping	$250,000	$280,000
Fishing	100,000	60,000
Total revenue	$350,000	$340,000

Prepare a horizontal and vertical analysis of the segments. Round to one decimal place.

Exercises

OBJ. 2

EX 5-1 Identify postings from revenue journal

Using the following revenue journal for Gamma Services Inc., identify each of the posting references, indicated by a letter, as representing (1) posting to general ledger accounts or (2) posting to subsidiary ledger accounts.

REVENUE JOURNAL

Date	Invoice No.	Account Debited	Post. Ref.	Accounts Rec. Dr. Fees Earned Cr.
2012				
June 1	112	Hazmat Safety Co.	(a)	$2,625
10	113	Masco Co.	(b)	980
18	114	Eco-Systems	(c)	1,600
27	115	Nero Enterprises	(d)	1,240
30				$6,445
				(e)

OBJ. 2

✔ d. Total accounts receivable, $6,975

EX 5-2 Accounts receivable ledger

Based on the data presented in Exercise 5-1, assume that the beginning balances for the customer accounts were zero, except for Nero Enterprises, which had a $530 beginning balance. In addition, there were no collections during the period.

a. Set up a T account for Accounts Receivable and T accounts for the four accounts needed in the customer ledger.

b. Post to the T accounts.

c. Determine the balance in the accounts.

d. Prepare a listing of the accounts receivable subsidiary ledger account balances as of June 30, 2012.

OBJ. 2

EX 5-3 Identify journals

Assuming the use of a two-column (all-purpose) general journal, a revenue journal, and a cash receipts journal as illustrated in this chapter, indicate the journal in which each of the following transactions should be recorded:

a. Sale of office supplies on account, at cost, to a neighboring business.

b. Receipt of cash from sale of office equipment.

c. Closing of drawing account at the end of the year.
d. Providing services for cash.
e. Receipt of cash refund from overpayment of taxes.
f. Adjustment to record accrued salaries at the end of the year.
g. Receipt of cash for rent.
h. Receipt of cash on account from a customer.
i. Providing services on account.
j. Investment of additional cash in the business by the owner.

OBJ. 2

EX 5-4 Identify journals

Assuming the use of a two-column (all-purpose) general journal, a purchases journal, and a cash payments journal as illustrated in this chapter, indicate the journal in which each of the following transactions should be recorded:

a. Purchase of an office computer on account.
b. Purchase of services on account.
c. Purchase of office supplies on account.
d. Adjustment to prepaid rent at the end of the month.
e. Adjustment to record accrued salaries at the end of the period.
f. Purchase of office supplies for cash.
g. Advance payment of a one-year fire insurance policy on the office.
h. Purchase of office equipment for cash.
i. Adjustment to prepaid insurance at the end of the month.
j. Adjustment to record depreciation at the end of the month.
k. Payment of six months' rent in advance.

OBJ. 2

EX 5-5 Identify transactions in accounts receivable ledger

The debits and credits from three related transactions are presented in the following customer's account taken from the accounts receivable subsidiary ledger.

NAME *Casey By Design*
ADDRESS *1319 Elm Street*

Date	Item	Post. Ref.	Debit	Credit	Balance
2012					
Feb. 3		R44	740		740
6		J11		80	660
16		CR81		660	—

Describe each transaction, and identify the source of each posting.

OBJ. 2

EX 5-6 Prepare journal entries in a revenue journal

Madison Services Company had the following transactions during the month of April:

Apr. 2. Issued Invoice No. 201 to Triple Play Corp. for services rendered on account, $345.
3. Issued Invoice No. 202 to Mid States Inc. for services rendered on account, $410.
14. Issued Invoice No. 203 to Triple Play Corp. for services rendered on account, $110.
25. Issued Invoice No. 204 to Parker Co. for services rendered on account, $830.
28. Collected Invoice No. 201 from Triple Play Corp.

a. Prepare a revenue journal with the following headings to record the April revenue transactions for Madison Services Company.

(Continued)

REVENUE JOURNAL

Date	Invoice No.	Account Debited	Post. Ref.	Accts. Rec. Dr. Fees Earned Cr.

b. What is the total amount posted to the accounts receivable and fees earned accounts from the revenue journal for April?

c. What is the April 30 balance of the Triple Play Corp. customer account assuming a zero balance on April 1?

OBJ. 2, 3

EX 5-7 Posting a revenue journal

The revenue journal for Tech-Aid Consulting Inc. is shown below. The accounts receivable control account has a July 1, 2012, balance of $805 consisting of an amount due from Astro Star Co. There were no collections during July.

REVENUE JOURNAL — Page 12

Date	Invoice No.	Account Debited	Post. Ref.	Accts. Rec. Dr. Fees Earned Cr.
2012				
July 4	355	Borman Co.		1,960
9	356	Life Star Inc.		3,220
14	357	Astro Star Co.		1,490
22	359	Borman Co.		2,650
				9,320

a. Prepare a T account for the accounts receivable customer accounts.

b. Post the transactions from the revenue journal to the customer accounts, and determine their ending balances.

c. Prepare T accounts for the accounts receivable and fees earned accounts. Post control totals to the two accounts, and determine the ending balances.

d. Prepare a schedule of the customer account balances to verify the equality of the sum of the customer account balances and the accounts receivable account balance.

e. How might a computerized system differ from a revenue journal in recording revenue transactions?

OBJ. 2

✔ Accounts Receivable balance, May 31, $5,490

EX 5-8 Accounts receivable subsidiary ledger

The revenue and cash receipts journals for Amazon Productions Inc. are shown below. The accounts receivable control account has a May 1, 2012, balance of $3,910, consisting of an amount due from Bishop Studios Inc.

REVENUE JOURNAL — Page 16

Date	Invoice No.	Account Debited	Post. Ref.	Accts. Rec. Dr. Fees Earned Cr.
2012				
May 6	1	Chandler Broadcasting Co.	✓	1,250
14	2	Gold Coast Media Inc.	✓	5,700
22	3	Chandler Broadcasting Co.	✓	2,200
27	4	Bishop Studios Inc.	✓	1,250
28	5	Amber Communications Inc.	✓	2,040
30				12,440
				(12) (41)

CASH RECEIPTS JOURNAL — Page 36

Date	Account Credited	Post. Ref.	Fees Earned Cr.	Accts. Rec. Cr.	Cash Dr.
2012					
May 6	Bishop Studios Inc.	✓	—	3,910	3,910
11	Fees Earned		3,200		3,200
18	Chandler Broadcasting Co	✓	—	1,250	1,250
28	Gold Coast Media Inc.	✓	—	5,700	5,700
30			3,200	10,860	14,060
			(41)	(12)	(11)

Prepare a listing of the accounts receivable subsidiary ledger account balances and verify that the total agrees with the ending balance of the accounts receivable account.

OBJ. 2

EX 5-9 Revenue and cash receipts journals

Transactions related to revenue and cash receipts completed by Main Line Inc. during the month of August 2012 are as follows:

Aug. 2. Issued Invoice No. 512 to Boston Co., $780.
4. Received cash from CMI Inc., on account, for $195.
8. Issued Invoice No. 513 to Gabriel Co., $275.
12. Issued Invoice No. 514 to Dockers Inc., $690.
19. Received cash from Dockers Inc., on account, $525.
22. Issued Invoice No. 515 to Electronic Central Inc., $150.
27. Received cash from Marshall Inc. for services provided, $115.
29. Received cash from Boston Co. for invoice of August 2.
31. Received cash from McCleary Co. for services provided, $65.

Prepare a single-column revenue journal and a cash receipts journal to record these transactions. Use the following column headings for the cash receipts journal: Fees Earned Cr., Accounts Receivable Cr., and Cash Dr. Place a check mark (✓) in the Post. Ref. column to indicate when the accounts receivable subsidiary ledger should be posted.

OBJ. 2
✔ Revenue journal total, $10,160

EX 5-10 Revenue and cash receipts journals

Essential Paris, Inc. has $2,290 in the December 1 balance of the accounts receivable account consisting of $940 from Chrystal Co. and $1,350 from Venus Co. Transactions related to revenue and cash receipts completed by Essential Paris, Inc. during the month of December 2012 are as follows:

Dec. 3. Issued Invoice No. 622 for services provided to Palace Corp., $1,920.
5. Received cash from Chrystal Co., on account, for $940.
8. Issued Invoice No. 623 for services provided to Sunstream Aviation Inc., $3,450.
12. Received cash from Venus Co., on account, for $1,350.
18. Issued Invoice No. 624 for services provided to Amex Services Inc., $2,600.
23. Received cash from Palace Corp. for Invoice No. 622.
28. Issued Invoice No. 625 to Venus Co., on account, for $2,190.
30. Received cash from Rogers Co. for services provided, $80.

a. Prepare a single-column revenue journal and a cash receipts journal to record these transactions. Use the following column headings for the cash receipts journal: Fees Earned Cr., Accounts Receivable Cr., and Cash Dr. Place a check mark (✓) in the Post. Ref. column to indicate when the accounts receivable subsidiary ledger should be posted.
b. Prepare a listing of the accounts receivable subsidiary ledger account balances and verify that the total of the accounts receivable subsidiary ledger equals the balance of the accounts receivable account on December 31, 2012.
c. Why does Essential Paris use a subsidiary ledger for accounts receivable?

OBJ. 2

EX 5-11 Identify postings from purchases journal

Using the following purchases journal, identify each of the posting references, indicated by a letter, as representing (1) a posting to a general ledger account, (2) a posting to a subsidiary ledger account, or (3) that no posting is required.

PURCHASES JOURNAL — Page 49

Date	Account Credited	Post. Ref.	Accounts Payable Cr.	Store Supplies Dr.	Office Supplies Dr.	Other Accounts Dr.	Post. Ref.	Amount
2012								
Mar. 4	Arrow Supply Co.	(a)	4,000		4,000			
6	Coastal Equipment Co.	(b)	5,325			Warehouse Equipment	(c)	5,325
9	Thorton Products	(d)	1,875	1,600	275			
14	Office Warehouse	(e)	2,200			Office Equipment	(f)	2,200
20	Office Warehouse	(g)	6,000			Store Equipment	(h)	6,000
25	Monroe Supply Co.	(i)	2,740	2,740				
30			22,140	4,340	4,275			13,525
			(j)	(k)	(l)			(m)

OBJ. 2

EX 5-12 Identify postings from cash payments journal

Using the following cash payments journal, identify each of the posting references, indicated by a letter, as representing (1) a posting to a general ledger account, (2) a posting to a subsidiary ledger account, or (3) that no posting is required.

CASH PAYMENTS JOURNAL — Page 46

Date	Ck. No.	Account Debited	Post. Ref.	Other Accounts Dr.	Accounts Payable Dr.	Cash Cr.
2012						
Aug. 3	611	Energy Systems Co.	(a)		4,000	4,000
5	612	Utilities Expense	(b)	310		310
10	613	Prepaid Rent	(c)	3,200		3,200
16	614	Flowers to Go, Inc.	(d)		1,250	1,250
19	615	Advertising Expense	(e)	640		640
22	616	Office Equipment	(f)	3,600		3,600
25	617	Office Supplies	(g)	250		250
26	618	Echo Co.	(h)		5,500	5,500
31	619	Salaries Expense	(i)	1,750		1,750
31				9,750	10,750	20,500
				(j)	(k)	(l)

OBJ. 2

EX 5-13 Identify transactions in accounts payable ledger account

The debits and credits from three related transactions are presented in the following creditor's account taken from the accounts payable ledger.

NAME *Apex Performance Co.*
ADDRESS *101 W. Stratford Ave.*

Date	Item	Post. Ref.	Debit	Credit	Balance
2012					
Mar. 6		P44		12,000	12,000
11		J12	400		11,600
16		CP23	11,600		—

Describe each transaction, and identify the source of each posting.

OBJ. 2

EX 5-14 Prepare journal entries in a purchases journal

Sentry Security Company had the following transactions during the month of January:

Jan. 4. Purchased office supplies from Office Universe Inc. on account, $550.
9. Purchased office equipment on account from Tek Village, Inc., $2,300.
16. Purchased office supplies from Office Universe Inc. on account, $90.
21. Purchased office supplies from Paper-to-Go Inc. on account, $170.
27. Paid invoice on January 4 purchase from Office Universe Inc.

a. Prepare a purchases journal with the following headings to record the January purchase transactions for Sentry Security Company.

PURCHASES JOURNAL

Date	Account Credited	Post. Ref.	Accts. Payable Cr.	Office Supplies Dr.	Other Accounts Dr.	Post. Ref.	Amount

b. What is the total amount posted to the accounts payable and office supplies accounts from the purchases journal for January?

c. What is the January 31 balance of the Office Universe Inc. creditor account assuming a zero balance on January 1?

OBJ. 2, 3

✔ d. Total, $4,215

EX 5-15 Posting a purchases journal

The purchases journal for Crystal View Window Cleaners Inc. is shown below. The accounts payable account has a January 1, 2012, balance of $365 of an amount due from Little Co. There were no payments made on creditor invoices during January.

PURCHASES JOURNAL Page *16*

Date		Account Credited	Post. Ref.	Accts. Payable Cr.	Cleaning Supplies Dr.	Other Accounts Dr.	Post. Ref.	Amount
2012								
Jan.	4	Kleen-Mate Supplies Inc.		570	570			
	15	Little Co.		250	250			
	19	Office Mate Inc.		2,700		Office Equipment		2,700
	26	Kleen-Mate Supplies Inc.		330	330			
	31			3,850	1,150			2,700

a. Prepare a T account for the accounts payable creditor accounts.

b. Post the transactions from the purchases journal to the creditor accounts, and determine their ending balances.

c. Prepare T accounts for the accounts payable control and cleaning supplies accounts. Post control totals to the two accounts, and determine their ending balances.

d. Prepare a schedule of the creditor account balances to verify the equality of the sum of the creditor account balances and the accounts payable account balance.

e. How might a computerized accounting system differ from the use of a purchases journal in recording purchase transactions?

OBJ. 2

✔ Accts. Pay., June 30, $15,860

EX 5-16 Accounts payable subsidiary ledger

The cash payments and purchases journals for Out of Eden Landscaping Co. are shown below. The accounts payable control account has a June 1, 2012, balance of $2,450, consisting of an amount owed to Augusta Sod Co.

CASH PAYMENTS JOURNAL Page *31*

Date		Ck. No.	Account Debited	Post. Ref.	Other Accounts Dr.	Accounts Payable Dr.	Cash Cr.
2012							
June	4	203	Augusta Sod Co	✓		2,450	2,450
	5	204	Utilities Expense	54	410		410
	15	205	Kopp Lumber Co.	✓		5,135	5,135
	24	206	Schott's Fertilizer	✓		820	820
	30				410	8,405	8,815
					(✓)	(21)	(11)

PURCHASES JOURNAL Page *22*

Date		Account Credited	Post. Ref.	Accounts Payable Cr.	Landscaping Supplies Dr.	Other Accounts Dr	Post. Ref.	Amount
2012								
June	3	Kopp Lumber Co.	✓	5,135	5,135			
	7	Concrete Equipment Co.	✓	2,650		Equipment	18	2,650
	14	Schott's Fertilizer	✓	820	820			
	24	Augusta Sod Co.	✓	6,010	6,010			
	29	Kopp Lumber Co.	✓	7,200	7,200			
	30			21,815	19,165			2,650
				(21)	(14)			(✓)

(Continued)

Prepare a schedule of the accounts payable subsidiary ledger balances, and determine that the total agrees with the ending balance of the accounts payable account.

OBJ. 2

✔ Purchases journal, Accts. Pay., Total, $815

EX 5-17 Purchases and cash payments journals

Transactions related to purchases and cash payments completed by Marion Cleaning Services Inc. during the month of August 2012 are as follows:

Aug. 1. Issued Check No. 57 to Liquid Klean Supplies Inc. in payment of account, $275.
3. Purchased cleaning supplies on account from Sani-Fresh Products Inc., $160.
8. Issued Check No. 58 to purchase equipment from Carson Equipment Sales, $2,400.
12. Purchased cleaning supplies on account from Porter Products Inc., $250.
15. Issued Check No. 59 to Abbott Laundry Service in payment of account, $120.
18. Purchased supplies on account from Liquid Klean Supplies Inc., $265.
20. Purchased laundry services from Abbott Laundry Service on account, $140.
26. Issued Check No. 60 to Sani-Fresh Products Inc. in payment of August 3 invoice.
31. Issued Check No. 61 in payment of salaries, $5,200.

Prepare a purchases journal and a cash payments journal to record these transactions. The forms of the journals are similar to those illustrated in the text. Place a check mark (✓) in the Post. Ref. column to indicate when the accounts payable subsidiary ledger should be posted. Marion Cleaning Services Inc. uses the following accounts:

Cash	11
Cleaning Supplies	14
Equipment	18
Accounts Payable	21
Salary Expense	51
Laundry Service Expense	53

OBJ. 2

EX 5-18 Purchases and cash payments journals

Happy Tails Inc. has a September 1 accounts payable balance of $525, which consists of $340 due Labradore Inc. and $185 due Meow Mart Inc. Transactions related to purchases and cash payments completed by Happy Tails Inc. during the month of September 2012 are as follows:

Sept. 4. Purchased pet supplies from Best Friend Supplies Inc. on account, $230.
6. Issued Check No. 345 to Labradore Inc. in payment of account, $340.
13. Purchased pet supplies from Poodle Pals Inc., $660.
18. Issued Check No. 346 to Meow Mart Inc. in payment of account, $185.
19. Purchased office equipment from Office Helper Inc. on account, $2,250.
23. Issued Check No. 347 to Best Friend Supplies Inc. in payment of account from purchase made on September 4.
27. Purchased pet supplies from Meow Mart Inc. on account, $350.
30. Issued Check No. 348 to Sanders Inc. for cleaning expenses, $50.

a. Prepare a purchases journal and a cash payments journal to record these transactions. The forms of the journals are similar to those used in the text. Place a check mark (✓) in the Post. Ref. column to indicate when the accounts payable subsidiary ledger should be posted. Happy Tails Inc. uses the following accounts:

Cash	11
Office Equipment	13
Pet Supplies	14
Accounts Payable	21
Cleaning Expense	54

b. Prepare a listing of accounts payable subsidiary ledger balances on September 30, 2012. Verify that the total of the accounts payable subsidiary ledger balances equals the balance of the accounts payable control account on September 30, 2012.

c. Why does Happy Tails use a subsidiary ledger for accounts payable?

OBJ. 2

EX 5-19 Error in accounts payable ledger and accounts payable subsidiary ledger

After Gold Rush Assay Services Inc. had completed all postings for March in the current year (2012), the sum of the balances in the following accounts payable ledger did not agree with the $37,900 balance of the controlling account in the general ledger.

NAME *C. D. Greer and Son*
ADDRESS *972 S. Tenth Street*

Date	Item	Post. Ref.	Debit	Credit	Balance
2012					
Mar. 17		P30		3,750	3,750
27		P31		12,000	15,750

NAME *Chester Chemical Supplies Inc.*
ADDRESS *1170 Mattis Avenue*

Date	Item	Post. Ref.	Debit	Credit	Balance
2012					
Mar. 1	Balance	✓			8,300
9		P30		6,200	14,000
12		J7	300		13,700
20		CP23	5,800		7,900

NAME *Cutler and Powell*
ADDRESS *717 Elm Street*

Date	Item	Post. Ref.	Debit	Credit	Balance
2012					
Mar. 1	Balance	✓			6,100
18		CP23	6,100		—
29		P31		7,800	7,800

NAME *Montana Minerals Co.*
ADDRESS *1240 W. Main Street*

Date	Item	Post. Ref.	Debit	Credit	Balance
2012					
Mar. 1	Balance	✓			4,750
10		CP22	4,750		—
17		P30		3,700	3,700
25		J7	900		1,800

NAME *Valley Power*
ADDRESS *915 E. Walnut Street*

Date	Item	Post. Ref.	Debit	Credit	Balance
2012					
Mar. 5		P30		3,150	3,150

Assuming that the controlling account balance of $37,900 has been verified as correct, (a) determine the error(s) in the preceding accounts and (b) prepare a listing of accounts payable subsidiary ledger balances (from the corrected accounts payable subsidiary ledger).

OBJ. 2

EX 5-20 Identify postings from special journals

ViewPoint Consulting Company makes most of its sales and purchases on credit. It uses the five journals described in this chapter (revenue, cash receipts, purchases, cash payments, and general journals). Identify the journal most likely used in recording the postings for selected transactions indicated by letter in the T accounts on the following page:

Cash

a.	10,940	b.	6,500

Prepaid Rent

		e.	1,200

Accounts Receivable

c.	11,790	a.	10,940

Accounts Payable

b.	6,500	d.	7,400

Office Supplies

d.	7,400		

Fees Earned

		c.	11,790

Rent Expense

e.	1,200		

OBJ. 2

EX 5-21 Cash receipts journal

The following cash receipts journal headings have been suggested for a small service firm. List the errors you find in the headings.

CASH RECEIPTS JOURNAL Page *12*

Date	Account Credited	Post. Ref.	Fees Earned Cr.	Accts. Rec. Cr.	Cash Cr.	Other Accounts Dr.

OBJ. 3

EX 5-22 Computerized accounting systems

Most computerized accounting systems use electronic forms to record transaction information, such as the invoice form illustrated at the top of Exhibit 7.

a. Identify the key input fields (spaces) in an electronic invoice form.

b. What accounts are posted from an electronic invoice form?

c. Why aren't special journal totals posted to control accounts at the end of the month in an electronic accounting system?

OBJ. 3, 4

EX 5-23 Computerized accounting systems and e-commerce

Apple Corporation's iTunes® provides digital products, such as music, video, and software, which can be downloaded to portable devices such as iPhone® and iPod®. Purchases made on iTunes are made with a credit card that is on file with the credit card processing company. Such transactions are considered cash transactions. Once the purchase is made, the consumer can download the requested digital product to their portable device for their enjoyment and the charge will show up on their credit card bill.

a. What kind of e-commerce application is described by Apple iTunes?

b. Assume you purchased 12 songs for $1 each on iTunes. Provide the journal entry generated by Apple's e-commerce application.

c. If a special journal were used, what type of special journal would be used to record this sales transaction?

d. If an electronic form were used, what type of electronic form would be used to record this sales transaction?

e. How might you expect revenues to be recorded for a B2C e-commerce transaction?

OBJ. 4

EX 5-24 E-commerce

For each of the following companies, determine if their e-commerce strategy is primarily business-to-consumer (B2C), business-to-business (B2B), or both. Use the Internet to investigate each company's site in conducting your research.

a. Amazon.com

b. Dell Inc.

c. Dupont

d. Intuit Inc.

e. L.L. Bean, Inc.

f. W.W. Grainger, Inc.

OBJ. 5

EX 5-25 Segment revenue horizontal analysis

Starbucks Corporation reported the following geographical segment revenues for fiscal years 2009 and 2008:

	2009 (in millions)	2008 (in millions)
United States	$7,104	$ 7,532
International	1,920	2,103
Global consumer products	750	748
Total revenues	$9,774	$10,383

a. Prepare a horizontal analysis of the segment data using 2008 as the base year.

b. Prepare a vertical analysis of the segment data.

c. What conclusions can be drawn from your analyses?

OBJ. 5

EX 5-26 Segment revenue vertical analysis

News Corporation is one of the world's largest entertainment companies that includes Twentieth Century Fox films, Fox Broadcasting, Fox News, the FX, and various satellite, cable, and publishing properties. The company provided revenue disclosures by its major product segments in the notes to its financial statements as follows:

Major Product Segments	For the Year Ended June 30, 2009 (in millions)
Filmed Entertainment	$ 5,936
Television	4,602
Cable Network Programming	5,580
Direct Broadcast Satellite Television	3,760
Magazines and Inserts	1,168
Newspapers and Information Services	5,858
Book Publishing	1,141
Other	2,378
Total revenues	$30,423

a. Provide a vertical analysis of the product segment revenues.

b. Are the revenues of News Corporation diversified or concentrated within a product segment? Explain.

OBJ. 5

EX 5-27 Segment revenue horizontal and vertical analyses

The comparative regional segment revenues for McDonald's Corporation is as follows:

	2009 (in millions)	2008 (in millions)
United States	$ 7,943.8	$ 8,078.3
Europe	9,273.8	9,922.9
APMEA*	4,337.0	4,230.8
Other Countries & Corporate	1,190.1	1,290.4
Total revenues	$22,744.7	$23,522.4

*APMEA = Asia/Pacific, Middle East, Africa

a. Provide a horizontal analysis of the regional segment revenues using 2008 as the base year. Round whole percents to one digit.

b. Provide a vertical analysis of the regional segment revenues for both years. Round whole percents to one digit.

c. What conclusions can be drawn from your analyses?

Problems Series A

OBJ. 2, 3

✔ 1. Revenue journal, total fees earned, $830

PR 5-1A Revenue journal; accounts receivable and general ledgers

Newton Learning Centers was established on October 20, 2012, to provide educational services. The services provided during the remainder of the month are as follows:

Oct. 21. Issued Invoice No. 1 to J. Dunlop for $60 on account.
22. Issued Invoice No. 2 to K. Todd for $255 on account.
24. Issued Invoice No. 3 to T. Patrick for $55 on account.
25. Provided educational services, $100, to K. Todd in exchange for educational supplies.
27. Issued Invoice No. 4 to F. Mintz for $150 on account.
30. Issued Invoice No. 5 to D. Chase for $135 on account.
30. Issued Invoice No. 6 to K. Todd for $105 on account.
31. Issued Invoice No. 7 to T. Patrick for $70 on account.

Instructions

1. Journalize the transactions for October, using a single-column revenue journal and a two-column general journal. Post to the following customer accounts in the accounts receivable ledger, and insert the balance immediately after recording each entry: D. Chase; J. Dunlop; F. Mintz; T. Patrick; K. Todd.
2. Post the revenue journal and the general journal to the following accounts in the general ledger, inserting the account balances only after the last postings:

   12 Accounts Receivable
   13 Supplies
   41 Fees Earned

3. a. What is the sum of the balances of the accounts in the subsidiary ledger at October 31?
   b. What is the balance of the controlling account at October 31?
4. Assume Newton Learning Centers began using a computerized accounting system to record the sales transactions on November 1. What are some of the benefits of the computerized system over the manual system?

OBJ. 2, 3

✔ 3. Total cash receipts, $32,870

PR 5-2A Revenue and cash receipts journals; accounts receivable and general ledgers

Transactions related to revenue and cash receipts completed by Aspen Architects Co. during the period June 2–30, 2012, are as follows:

June 2. Issued Invoice No. 793 to Nickle Co., $4,900.
5. Received cash from Mendez Co. for the balance owed on its account.
6. Issued Invoice No. 794 to Preston Co., $1,760.
13. Issued Invoice No. 795 to Shilo Co., $2,630.
Post revenue and collections to the accounts receivable subsidiary ledger.
15. Received cash from Preston Co. for the balance owed on June 1.
16. Issued Invoice No. 796 to Preston Co., $5,500.
Post revenue and collections to the accounts receivable subsidiary ledger.
19. Received cash from Nickle Co. for the balance due on invoice of June 2.
20. Received cash from Preston Co. for invoice of June 6.
22. Issued Invoice No. 797 to Mendez Co., $7,240.
25. Received $2,000 note receivable in partial settlement of the balance due on the Shilo Co. account.
30. Recorded cash fees earned, $12,350.
Post revenue and collections to the accounts receivable subsidiary ledger.

Instructions

1. Insert the following balances in the general ledger as of June 1:

11	Cash	$11,350
12	Accounts Receivable	13,860
14	Notes Receivable	6,000
41	Fees Earned	—

2. Insert the following balances in the accounts receivable subsidiary ledger as of June 1:

Mendez Co.	$7,970
Nickle Co.	—
Preston Co.	5,890
Shilo Co.	—

3. Prepare a single-column revenue journal (p. 40) and a cash receipts journal (p. 36). Use the following column headings for the cash receipts journal: Fees Earned Cr., Accounts Receivable Cr., and Cash Dr. The Fees Earned column is used to record cash fees. Insert a check mark (✓) in the Post. Ref. column when recording cash fees.
4. Using the two special journals and the two-column general journal (p. 1), journalize the transactions for June. Post to the accounts receivable subsidiary ledger, and insert the balances at the points indicated in the narrative of transactions. Determine the balance in the customer's account before recording a cash receipt.
5. Total each of the columns of the special journals, and post the individual entries and totals to the general ledger. Insert account balances after the last posting.
6. Determine that the subsidiary ledger agrees with the controlling account in the general ledger.
7. Why would an automated system omit postings to a control account as performed in step 5 for Accounts Receivable?

OBJ. 2, 4

✔ 5b. Total accounts payable credit, $14,195

PR 5-3A Purchases, accounts payable account, and accounts payable ledger

English Garden Landscaping designs and installs landscaping. The landscape designers and office staff use office supplies, while field supplies (rock, bark, etc.) are used in the actual landscaping. Purchases on account completed by English Garden Landscaping during January 2012 are as follows:

Jan. 2. Purchased office supplies on account from Meade Co., $350.
5. Purchased office equipment on account from Peach Computers Co., $3,150.
9. Purchased office supplies on account from Executive Office Supply Co., $290.
13. Purchased field supplies on account from Yamura Co., $1,140.
14. Purchased field supplies on account from Naples Co., $2,680.
17. Purchased field supplies on account from Yamura Co., $1,050.
24. Purchased field supplies on account from Naples Co., $3,240.
29. Purchased office supplies on account from Executive Office Supply Co., $260.
31. Purchased field supplies on account from Naples Co., $1,000.

Instructions

1. Insert the following balances in the general ledger as of January 1:

14	Field Supplies	$ 5,920
15	Office Supplies	750
18	Office Equipment	12,300
21	Accounts Payable	1,035

2. Insert the following balances in the accounts payable subsidiary ledger as of January 1:

Executive Office Supply Co.	$340
Meade Co.	695
Naples Co.	—
Peach Computers Co.	—
Yamura Co.	—

3. Journalize the transactions for January, using a purchases journal (p. 30) similar to the one illustrated in this chapter. Prepare the purchases journal with columns for Accounts

(Continued)

Payable, Field Supplies, Office Supplies, and Other Accounts. Post to the creditor accounts in the accounts payable subsidiary ledger immediately after each entry.

4. Post the purchases journal to the accounts in the general ledger.
5. a. What is the sum of the balances in the subsidiary ledger at January 31?
   b. What is the balance of the controlling account at January 31?
6. What type of e-commerce application would be used to plan and coordinate suppliers?

OBJ. 2

✔ 1. Total cash payments, $93,615

PR 5-4A Purchases and cash payments journals; accounts payable and general ledgers

Green Mountain Water Testing Service was established on November 16, 2012. Green Mountain uses field equipment and field supplies (chemicals and other supplies) to analyze water for unsafe contaminants in streams, lakes, and ponds. Transactions related to purchases and cash payments during the remainder of November are as follows:

Nov. 16. Issued Check No. 1 in payment of rent for the remainder of November, $1,700.
16. Purchased field supplies on account from Hydro Supply Co., $4,380.
16. Purchased field equipment on account from Test-Rite Equipment Co., $16,900.
17. Purchased office supplies on account from Best Office Supply Co., $375.
19. Issued Check No. 2 in payment of field supplies, $2,560, and office supplies, $300.

Post the journals to the accounts payable subsidiary ledger.

23. Purchased office supplies on account from Best Office Supply Co., $580.
23. Issued Check No. 3 to purchase land, $45,000.
24. Issued Check No. 4 to Hydro Supply Co. in payment of invoice, $4,380.
26. Issued Check No. 5 to Test-Rite Equipment Co. in payment of invoice, $16,900.

Post the journals to the accounts payable subsidiary ledger.

30. Acquired land in exchange for field equipment having a cost of $8,000.
30. Purchased field supplies on account from Hydro Supply Co., $5,900.
30. Issued Check No. 6 to Best Office Supply Co. in payment of invoice, $375.
30. Purchased the following from Test-Rite Equipment Co. on account: field supplies, $900, and field equipment, $3,700.
30. Issued Check No. 7 in payment of salaries, $22,400.

Post the journals to the accounts payable subsidiary ledger.

Instructions

1. Journalize the transactions for November. Use a purchases journal and a cash payments journal, similar to those illustrated in this chapter, and a two-column general journal. Use debit columns for Field Supplies, Office Supplies, and Other Accounts in the purchases journal. Refer to the following partial chart of accounts:

11	Cash	19	Land
14	Field Supplies	21	Accounts Payable
15	Office Supplies	61	Salary Expense
17	Field Equipment	71	Rent Expense

At the points indicated in the narrative of transactions, post to the following accounts in the accounts payable subsidiary ledger:

Best Office Supply Co.
Hydro Supply Co.
Test-Rite Equipment Co.

2. Post the individual entries (Other Accounts columns of the purchases journal and the cash payments journal and both columns of the general journal) to the appropriate general ledger accounts.
3. Total each of the columns of the purchases journal and the cash payments journal, and post the appropriate totals to the general ledger. (Because the problem does not include transactions related to cash receipts, the cash account in the ledger will have a credit balance.)
4. Sum the balances of the accounts payable subsidiary ledger.
5. Why might Green Mountain consider using a subsidiary ledger for the field equipment?

OBJ. 2

✔ 2. Total cash receipts, $58,160

PR 5-5A All journals and general ledger; trial balance

The transactions completed by Sure N' Safe Courier Company during July 2012, the first month of the fiscal year, were as follows:

July 1. Issued Check No. 610 for July rent, $7,500.
2. Issued Invoice No. 940 to Capps Co., $2,680.
3. Received check for $6,700 from Trimble Co. in payment of account.
5. Purchased a vehicle on account from Browning Transportation, $34,600.
6. Purchased office equipment on account from Austin Computer Co., $5,200.
6. Issued Invoice No. 941 to Dawar Co., $5,970.
9. Issued Check No. 611 for fuel expense, $900.
10. Received check from Sing Co. in payment of $3,980 invoice.
10. Issued Check No. 612 for $1,040 to Office To Go Inc. in payment of invoice.
10. Issued Invoice No. 942 to Joy Co., $2,640.
11. Issued Check No. 613 for $3,670 to Essential Supply Co. in payment of account.
11. Issued Check No. 614 for $725 to Porter Co. in payment of account.
12. Received check from Capps Co. in payment of $2,680 invoice.
13. Issued Check No. 615 to Browning Transportation in payment of $34,600 balance.
16. Issued Check No. 616 for $42,100 for cash purchase of a vehicle.
16. Cash fees earned for July 1–16, $18,900.
17. Issued Check No. 617 for miscellaneous administrative expense, $750.
18. Purchased maintenance supplies on account from Essential Supply Co., $1,950.
19. Purchased the following on account from McClain Co.: maintenance supplies, $1,900; office supplies, $470.
20. Issued Check No. 618 in payment of advertising expense, $2,350.
20. Used $4,000 maintenance supplies to repair delivery vehicles.
23. Purchased office supplies on account from Office To Go Inc., $600.
24. Issued Invoice No. 943 to Sing Co., $7,000.
24. Issued Check No. 619 to J. Bourne as a personal withdrawal, $3,000.
25. Issued Invoice No. 944 to Dawar Co., $6,450.
25. Received check for $4,500 from Trimble Co. in payment of balance.
26. Issued Check No. 620 to Austin Computer Co. in payment of $5,200 invoice of July 6.
30. Issued Check No. 621 for monthly salaries as follows: driver salaries, $18,900; office salaries, $8,300.
31. Cash fees earned for July 17–31, $21,400.
31. Issued Check No. 622 in payment for office supplies, $800.

Instructions

1. Enter the following account balances in the general ledger as of July 1:

11	Cash	$167,900	32	J. Bourne, Drawing	—
12	Accounts Receivable	15,180	41	Fees Earned	—
14	Maintenance Supplies	10,850	51	Driver Salaries Expense	—
15	Office Supplies	4,900	52	Maintenance Supplies Exp.	—
16	Office Equipment	28,500	53	Fuel Expense	—
17	Accum. Depr.—Office Equip.	6,900	61	Office Salaries Expense	—
18	Vehicles	95,900	62	Rent Expense	—
19	Accum. Depr.—Vehicles	14,700	63	Advertising Expense	—
21	Accounts Payable	5,435	64	Miscellaneous Administrative Expense	—
31	J. Bourne, Capital	296,195			

(Continued)

2. Journalize the transactions for July 2012, using the following journals similar to those illustrated in this chapter: cash receipts journal (p. 31), purchases journal (p. 37, with columns for Accounts Payable, Maintenance Supplies, Office Supplies, and Other Accounts), single-column revenue journal (p. 35), cash payments journal (p. 34), and two-column general journal (p. 1). Assume that the daily postings to the individual accounts in the accounts payable ledger and the accounts receivable ledger have been made.
3. Post the appropriate individual entries to the general ledger.
4. Total each of the columns of the special journals, and post the appropriate totals to the general ledger; insert the account balances.
5. Prepare a trial balance.

Problems Series B

OBJ. 2, 3

✔ 1. Revenue journal, total fees earned, $2,320

PR 5-1B Revenue journal; accounts receivable and general ledgers

Sentinel Security Services was established on March 15, 2012, to provide security services. The services provided during the remainder of the month are listed below.

Mar. 18. Issued Invoice No. 1 to Murphy Co. for $410 on account.
20. Issued Invoice No. 2 to Qwik-Mart Co. for $290 on account.
24. Issued Invoice No. 3 to Goforth Co. for $625 on account.
27. Issued Invoice No. 4 to Carson Co. for $510 on account.
28. Issued Invoice No. 5 to Amber Waves Co. for $100 on account.
28. Provided security services, $90, to Qwik-Mart Co. in exchange for supplies.
30. Issued Invoice No. 6 to Qwik-Mart Co. for $140 on account.
31. Issued Invoice No. 7 to Goforth Co. for $245 on account.

Instructions

1. Journalize the transactions for March, using a single-column revenue journal and a two-column general journal. Post to the following customer accounts in the accounts receivable ledger, and insert the balance immediately after recording each entry: Amber Waves Co.; Carson Co.; Goforth Co.; Murphy Co.; Qwik-Mart Co.
2. Post the revenue journal to the following accounts in the general ledger, inserting the account balances only after the last postings:

   12 Accounts Receivable
   14 Supplies
   41 Fees Earned

3. a. What is the sum of the balances of the accounts in the subsidiary ledger at March 31?
   b. What is the balance of the controlling account at March 31?
4. Assume Sentinel Security Services began using a computerized accounting system to record the sales transactions on April 1. What are some of the benefits of the computerized system over the manual system?

OBJ. 2, 3

✔ 3. Total cash receipts, $7,690

PR 5-2B Revenue and cash receipts journals; accounts receivable and general ledgers

Transactions related to revenue and cash receipts completed by Pinnacle Engineering Services during the period April 2–30, 2012, are as follows:

Apr. 2. Issued Invoice No. 717 to Yee Co., $950.
3. Received cash from Auto-Flex Co. for the balance owed on its account.
7. Issued Invoice No. 718 to Park Development Co., $530.
10. Issued Invoice No. 719 to Ridge Communities, $2,350.
Post revenue and collections to the accounts receivable subsidiary ledger.

Apr. 14. Received cash from Park Development Co. for the balance owed on April 1.

16. Issued Invoice No. 720 to Park Development Co., $325.

Post revenue and collections to the accounts receivable subsidiary ledger.

18. Received cash from Yee Co. for the balance due on invoice of April 2.

20. Received cash from Park Development Co. for invoice of April 7.

23. Issued Invoice No. 721 to Auto-Flex Co., $790.

30. Recorded cash fees earned, $3,950.

30. Received office equipment of $1,500 in partial settlement of balance due on the Ridge Communities account.

Post revenue and collections to the accounts receivable subsidiary ledger.

Instructions

1. Insert the following balances in the general ledger as of April 1:

11	Cash	$18,340
12	Accounts Receivable	2,260
18	Office Equipment	34,700
41	Fees Earned	—

2. Insert the following balances in the accounts receivable subsidiary ledger as of April 1:

Auto-Flex Co.	$1,460
Park Development Co.	800
Ridge Communities	—
Yee Co.	—

3. Prepare a single-column revenue journal (p. 40) and a cash receipts journal (p. 36). Use the following column headings for the cash receipts journal: Fees Earned Cr., Accounts Receivable Cr., and Cash Dr. The Fees Earned column is used to record cash fees. Insert a check mark (✓) in the Post. Ref. column when recording cash fees.
4. Using the two special journals and the two-column general journal (p. 1), journalize the transactions for April. Post to the accounts receivable subsidiary ledger, and insert the balances at the points indicated in the narrative of transactions. Determine the balance in the customer's account before recording a cash receipt.
5. Total each of the columns of the special journals, and post the individual entries and totals to the general ledger. Insert account balances after the last posting.
6. Determine that the subsidiary ledger agrees with the controlling account in the general ledger.
7. Why would an automated system omit postings to a control account as performed in step 5 for Accounts Receivable?

OBJ. 2, 4

✔ 5a. Total accounts payable credit, $27,370

PR 5-3B Purchases, accounts payable account, and accounts payable ledger

True Plumb Surveyors provides survey work for construction projects. The office staff use office supplies, while surveying crews use field supplies. Purchases on account completed by True Plumb Surveyors during August 2012 are as follows:

Aug. 1. Purchased field supplies on account from Wendell Co., $2,670.

3. Purchased office supplies on account from Lassiter Co., $290.

8. Purchased field supplies on account from Ready Supplies, $3,900.

12. Purchased field supplies on account from Wendell Co., $2,950.

15. Purchased office supplies on account from J-Mart Co., $400.

19. Purchased office equipment on account from Accu-Vision Supply Co., $7,350.

23. Purchased field supplies on account from Ready Supplies, $2,140.

26. Purchased office supplies on account from J-Mart Co., $205.

30. Purchased field supplies on account from Ready Supplies, $2,750.

Instructions

1. Insert the following balances in the general ledger as of August 1:

14	Field Supplies	$ 6,200
15	Office Supplies	1,490
18	Office Equipment	19,400
21	Accounts Payable	4,715

2. Insert the following balances in the accounts payable subsidiary ledger as of August 1:

Accu-Vision Supply Co.	$3,600
J-Mart Co.	690
Lassiter Co.	425
Ready Supplies	—
Wendell Co.	—

3. Journalize the transactions for August, using a purchases journal (p. 30) similar to the one illustrated in this chapter. Prepare the purchases journal with columns for Accounts Payable, Field Supplies, Office Supplies, and Other Accounts. Post to the creditor accounts in the accounts payable ledger immediately after each entry.
4. Post the purchases journal to the accounts in the general ledger.
5. a. What is the sum of the balances in the subsidiary ledger at August 31?
   b. What is the balance of the controlling account at August 31?
6. What type of e-commerce application would be used to plan and coordinate suppliers?

OBJ. 2

✔ 1. Total cash payments, $265,000

PR 5-4B Purchases and cash payments journals; accounts payable and general ledgers

Texas Tea Exploration Co. was established on July 15, 2012, to provide oil-drilling services. Texas Tea uses field equipment (rigs and pipe) and field supplies (drill bits and lubricants) in its operations. Transactions related to purchases and cash payments during the remainder of July are as follows:

July 16. Issued Check No. 1 in payment of rent for the remainder of July, $6,000.
16. Purchased field equipment on account from Petro Services Inc., $26,400.
17. Purchased field supplies on account from Culver Supply Co., $8,750.
18. Issued Check No. 2 in payment of field supplies, $3,150, and office supplies, $500.
20. Purchased office supplies on account from A-One Office Supply Co., $1,200.
Post the journals to the accounts payable subsidiary ledger.
24. Issued Check No. 3 to Petro Services Inc., in payment of July 16 invoice.
26. Issued Check No. 4 to Culver Supply Co. in payment of July 17 invoice.
28. Issued Check No. 5 to purchase land, $190,000.
28. Purchased office supplies on account from A-One Office Supply Co., $2,970.
Post the journals to the accounts payable subsidiary ledger.
30. Purchased the following from Petro Services Inc. on account: field supplies, $22,980 and office equipment, $4,200.
30. Issued Check No. 6 to A-One Office Supply Co. in payment of July 20 invoice.
30. Purchased field supplies on account from Culver Supply Co., $10,200.
31. Issued Check No. 7 in payment of salaries, $29,000.
31. Rented building for one year in exchange for field equipment having a cost of $14,000.
Post the journals to the accounts payable subsidiary ledger.

Instructions

1. Journalize the transactions for July. Use a purchases journal and a cash payments journal, similar to those illustrated in this chapter, and a two-column general journal. Set debit columns for Field Supplies, Office Supplies, and Other Accounts in the purchases journal. Refer to the following partial chart of accounts:

11	Cash	18	Office Equipment
14	Field Supplies	19	Land
15	Office Supplies	21	Accounts Payable
16	Prepaid Rent	61	Salary Expense
17	Field Equipment	71	Rent Expense

At the points indicated in the narrative of transactions, post to the following subsidiary accounts in the accounts payable ledger:

A-One Office Supply Co.
Culver Supply Co.
Petro Services Inc.

2. Post the individual entries (Other Accounts columns of the purchases journal and the cash payments journal; both columns of the general journal) to the appropriate general ledger accounts.
3. Total each of the columns of the purchases journal and the cash payments journal, and post the appropriate totals to the general ledger. (Because the problem does not include transactions related to cash receipts, the cash account in the ledger will have a credit balance.)
4. Sum the balances of the accounts payable subsidiary ledger.
5. Why might Texas Tea consider using a subsidiary ledger for the field equipment?

OBJ. 2

✔ 2. Total cash receipts, $84,390

PR 5-5B All journals and general ledger; trial balance

The transactions completed by By Tomorrow Express Company during May 2012, the first month of the fiscal year, were as follows:

May 1. Issued Check No. 205 for May rent, $1,500.
2. Purchased a vehicle on account from McIntyre Sales Co., $23,700.
3. Purchased office equipment on account from Office Mate Inc., $640.
5. Issued Invoice No. 91 to Martin Co., $6,000.
6. Received check for $6,890 from Chavez Co. in payment of invoice.
7. Issued Invoice No. 92 to Trent Co., $8,650.
9. Issued Check No. 206 for fuel expense, $710.
10. Received check for $9,500 from Sajeev Co. in payment of invoice.
10. Issued Check No. 207 to Office City in payment of $500 invoice.
10. Issued Check No. 208 to Bastille Co. in payment of $1,450 invoice.
11. Issued Invoice No. 93 to Jarvis Co., $6,900.
11. Issued Check No. 209 to Porter Co. in payment of $375 invoice.
12. Received check for $6,000 from Martin Co. in payment of invoice.
13. Issued Check No. 210 to McIntyre Sales Co. in payment of $23,700 invoice.
16. Cash fees earned for May 1–16, $24,600.
16. Issued Check No. 211 for purchase of a vehicle, $24,000.
17. Issued Check No. 212 for miscellaneous administrative expense, $4,360.
18. Purchased maintenance supplies on account from Bastille Co., $1,790.
18. Received check for rent revenue on office space, $2,500.
19. Purchased the following on account from Master Supply Co.: maintenance supplies, $2,500, and office supplies, $2,000.
20. Issued Check No. 213 in payment of advertising expense, $7,810.
20. Used maintenance supplies with a cost of $4,200 to repair vehicles.
21. Purchased office supplies on account from Office City, $790.
24. Issued Invoice No. 94 to Sajeev Co., $8,000.
25. Received check for $12,500 from Chavez Co. in payment of invoice.

May 25. Issued Invoice No. 95 to Trent Co., $5,900.
26. Issued Check No. 214 to Office Mate Inc. in payment of $640 invoice.
27. Issued Check No. 215 to J. Wu as a personal withdrawal, $3,500.
30. Issued Check No. 216 in payment of driver salaries, $29,300.
31. Issued Check No. 217 in payment of office salaries, $19,400.
31. Issued Check No. 218 for office supplies, $560.
31. Cash fees earned for May 17–31, $22,400.

Instructions

1. Enter the following account balances in the general ledger as of May 1:

11	Cash	$ 65,200	32	J. Wu, Drawing	—
12	Accounts Receivable	28,890	41	Fees Earned	—
14	Maintenance Supplies	7,240	42	Rent Revenue	—
15	Office Supplies	3,690	51	Driver Salaries Expense	—
16	Office Equipment	17,300	52	Maintenance Supplies Expense	—
17	Accum. Depr.—Office Equip.	4,250	53	Fuel Expense	—
18	Vehicles	62,400	61	Office Salaries Expense	—
19	Accum. Depr.—Vehicles	17,800	62	Rent Expense	—
21	Accounts Payable	2,325	63	Advertising Expense	—
31	J. Wu, Capital	160,345	64	Miscellaneous Administrative Exp.	—

2. Journalize the transactions for May 2012, using the following journals similar to those illustrated in this chapter: single-column revenue journal (p. 35), cash receipts journal (p. 31), purchases journal (p. 37, with columns for Accounts Payable, Maintenance Supplies, Office Supplies, and Other Accounts), cash payments journal (p. 34), and two-column general journal (p. 1). Assume that the daily postings to the individual accounts in the accounts payable ledger and the accounts receivable ledger have been made.
3. Post the appropriate individual entries to the general ledger.
4. Total each of the columns of the special journals, and post the appropriate totals to the general ledger; insert the account balances.
5. Prepare a trial balance.

Cases & Projects

CP 5-1 Ethics and professional conduct in business

E-Biz Financial, Inc., provides accounting applications for business customers on the Internet for a monthly subscription. E-Biz Financial customers run their accounting system on the Internet; thus, the business data and accounting software reside on the servers of E-Biz Financial, Inc. The senior management of E-Biz believes that once a customer begins to use E-Biz Financial it would be very difficult to cancel the service. That is, customers are "locked in" because it would be difficult to move the business data from E-Biz Financial to another accounting application, even though the customers own their own data. Therefore, E-Biz Financial has decided to entice customers with an initial low monthly price that is half of the normal monthly rate for the first year of services. After a year, the price will be increased to the regular monthly rate. E-Biz Financial management believes that customers will have to accept the full price because customers will be "locked in" after one year of use.

a. Discuss whether the half-price offer is an ethical business practice.
b. Discuss whether customer "lock in" is an ethical business practice.

CP 5-2 Manual vs. computerized accounting systems

The following conversation took place between Merit Construction Co.'s bookkeeper, Dan Essex, and the accounting supervisor, Sarah Nelson:

Sarah: Dan, I'm thinking about bringing in a new computerized accounting system to replace our manual system. I guess this will mean that you will need to learn how to do computerized accounting.

Dan: What does computerized accounting mean?

Sarah: I'm not sure, but you'll need to prepare for this new way of doing business.

Dan: I'm not so sure we need a computerized system. I've been looking at some of the sample reports from the software vendor. It looks to me as if the computer will not add much to what we are already doing.

Sarah: What do you mean?

Dan: Well, look at these reports. This Sales by Customer Report looks like our revenue journal, and the Deposit Detail Report looks like our cash receipts journal. Granted, the computer types them, so they look much neater than my special journals, but I don't see that we're gaining much from this change.

Sarah: Well, surely there's more to it than nice-looking reports. I've got to believe that a computerized system will save us time and effort someplace.

Dan: I don't see how. We still need to key in transactions into the computer. If anything, there may be more work when it's all said and done.

Do you agree with Dan? Why might a computerized environment be preferred over the manual system?

CP 5-3 Accounts receivable and accounts payable

A subsidiary ledger is used for accounts receivable and accounts payable. Thus, transactions that are made "on account" are posted to the individual customer or vendor accounts.

a. Why do companies use subsidiary ledgers for accounts payable and accounts receivable?

b. Identify another account that may benefit from using a subsidiary ledger.

CP 5-4 Design of accounting systems

For the past few years, your client, Professional Health Services (PHS), has operated a small medical practice. PHS's current annual revenues are $945,000. Because the accountant has been spending more and more time each month recording all transactions in a two-column journal and preparing the financial statements, PHS is considering improving the accounting system by adding special journals and subsidiary ledgers. PHS has asked you to help with this project and has compiled the following information:

Type of Transaction	Estimated Frequency per Month
Fees earned on account	240
Purchase of medical supplies on account	190
Cash receipts from patients on account	175
Cash payments on account	160
Cash receipts from patients at time services provided	120
Purchase of office supplies on account	35
Purchase of magazine subscriptions on account	5
Purchase of medical equipment on account	4
Cash payments for office salaries	3
Cash payments for utilities expense	3

1. Briefly discuss the circumstances under which special journals would be used in place of a two-column (all-purpose) journal. Include in your answer your recommendations for PHS's medical practice.
2. Assume that PHS has decided to use a revenue journal and a purchases journal. Design the format for each journal, giving special consideration to the needs of the medical practice.
3. Which subsidiary ledgers would you recommend for the medical practice?

Internet Project

CP 5-5 Internet-based accounting systems

Internet-based accounting software is a recent trend in business computing. Major software firms such as Oracle, SAP, and NetSuites are running their core products on the Internet. NetSuite Inc. is one of the most popular small business Internet-based accounting systems.

Go to the text's Web site at **academic.cengage.com/accounting/warren** and click on the link to the NetSuite Inc. site. Read about the product from the site, and prepare a memo to management, defining Internet-based accounting. Also, outline the advantages and disadvantages of Internet-based accounting compared to running software on a company's internal computer network.

Internet Project

CP 5-6 SCM and CRM

Group Project

The two leading software application providers for supply chain management (SCM) and customer relationship management (CRM) software are I2 Technologies and Salesforce.com, respectively. In groups of two or three, go to the Web site for each company (linked to the text's Web site at **academic.cengage.com/accounting/warren**) and list the functions provided by each company's application.

CHAPTER 6

san Van Etten

Accounting for Merchandising Businesses

Dollar Tree Stores, Inc.

When you are low on cash but need to pick up party supplies, housewares, or other consumer items, where do you go? Many shoppers are turning to **Dollar Tree Stores, Inc.**, the nation's largest single price point dollar retailer with over 3,400 stores in 48 states. For the fixed price of $1 on merchandise in its stores, Dollar Tree has worked hard providing "new treasures" every week for the entire family.

Despite the fact that items cost only $1, the accounting for a merchandiser, like Dollar Tree, is more complex than for a service company. This is because a service company sells only services and has no inventory. With Dollar Tree's locations and merchandise, the company must design its accounting system to not only record the receipt of goods for resale, but also to keep track of what merchandise is available for sale as well as where the merchandise is located. In addition, Dollar Tree must record the sales and costs of the goods sold for each of its stores. Finally, Dollar Tree must record such data as delivery costs, merchandise discounts, and merchandise returns.

This chapter focuses on the accounting principles and concepts for a merchandising business. In doing so, the basic differences between merchandiser and service company activities are highlighted. The financial statements of a merchandising business and accounting for merchandise transactions are also described and illustrated.

Learning Objectives

OBJ. 1 Distinguish between the activities and financial statements of service and merchandising businesses.

Nature of Merchandising Businesses

The activities of a service business differ from those of a merchandising business. These differences are illustrated in the following condensed income statements:

Service Business	
Fees earned	$XXX
Operating expenses	–XXX
Net income	$XXX

Merchandising Business	
Sales	$XXX
Cost of merchandise sold	–XXX
Gross profit	$XXX
Operating expenses	–XXX
Net income	$XXX

The revenue activities of a service business involve providing services to customers. On the income statement for a service business, the revenues from services are reported as *fees earned*. The operating expenses incurred in providing the services are subtracted from the fees earned to arrive at *net income*.

In contrast, the revenue activities of a merchandising business involve the buying and selling of merchandise. A merchandising business first purchases merchandise to sell to its customers. When this merchandise is sold, the revenue is reported as sales, and its cost is recognized as an expense. This expense is called the **cost of merchandise sold**. The cost of merchandise sold is subtracted from sales to arrive at gross profit. This amount is called **gross profit** because it is the profit *before* deducting operating expenses.

Merchandise on hand (not sold) at the end of an accounting period is called **merchandise inventory**. Merchandise inventory is reported as a current asset on the balance sheet.

Example Exercise 6-1 Gross Profit OBJ. 1

During the current year, merchandise is sold for $250,000 cash and for $975,000 on account. The cost of the merchandise sold is $735,000. What is the amount of the gross profit?

Follow My Example 6-1

The gross profit is $490,000 ($250,000 + $975,000 – $735,000).

Practice Exercises: **PE 6-1A, PE 6-1B**

The Operating Cycle

The operations of a merchandising business involve the purchase of merchandise for sale (purchasing), the sale of the products to customers (sales), and the receipt of cash from customers (collection). This overall process is referred to as the *operating cycle*. Thus, the operating cycle begins with spending cash, and it ends with receiving cash from customers. The operating cycle for a merchandising business is shown to the right.

Operating cycles for retailers are usually shorter than for manufacturers because retailers purchase goods in a form ready for sale to the customer. Of course, some retailers will have shorter operating cycles than others because of the nature of their products. For example, a jewelry store or an automobile dealer normally has a longer operating cycle than a consumer electronics store or a grocery store.

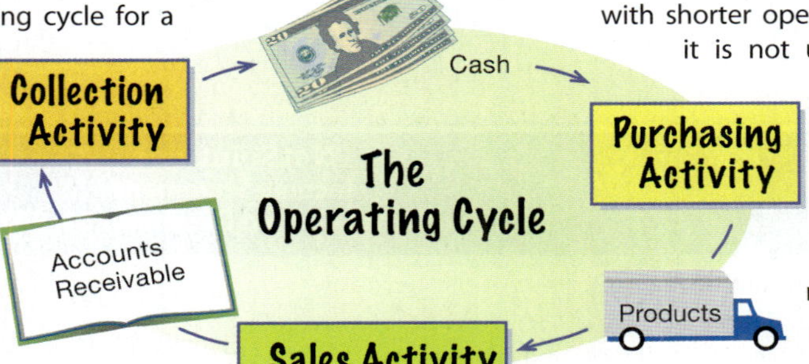

Businesses with longer operating cycles normally have higher profit margins on their products than businesses with shorter operating cycles. For example, it is not unusual for jewelry stores to price their jewelry at 30%–50% above cost. In contrast, grocery stores operate on very small profit margins, often below 5%. Grocery stores make up the difference by selling their products more quickly.

Financial Statements for a Merchandising Business

OBJ. 2 Describe and illustrate the financial statements of a merchandising business.

This section illustrates the financial statements for **NetSolutions** after it becomes a retailer of computer hardware and software. During 2011, Chris Clark implemented the second phase of NetSolutions' business plan. In doing so, Chris notified clients that beginning July 1, 2012, NetSolutions would no longer offer consulting services. Instead, it would become a retailer.

NetSolutions' business strategy is to offer personalized service to individuals and small businesses who are upgrading or purchasing new computer systems. NetSolutions' personal service includes a no-obligation, on-site assessment of the customer's computer needs. By providing personalized service and follow-up, Chris feels that NetSolutions can compete effectively against such retailers as Best Buy and Office Depot, Inc.

Multiple-Step Income Statement

The 2013 income statement for NetSolutions is shown in Exhibit 1.[1] This form of income statement, called a **multiple-step income statement**, contains several sections, subsections, and subtotals.

1 The NetSolutions income statement for 2013 is used because it allows a better illustration of the computation of the cost of merchandise sold in the appendix to this chapter.

Revenue from Sales This section of the multiple-step income statement consists of sales, sales returns and allowances, sales discounts, and net sales. This section, as shown in Exhibit 1, is as follows:

Revenue from sales:			
Sales		$720,185	
Less: Sales returns and allowances	$6,140		
Sales discounts	5,790	11,930	
Net sales			$708,255

Sales is the total amount charged customers for merchandise sold, including cash sales and sales on account. During 2013, NetSolutions sold merchandise of $720,185 for cash or on account.

Sales returns and allowances are granted by the seller to customers for damaged or defective merchandise. In such cases, the customer may either return the merchandise or accept an allowance from the seller. NetSolutions reported $6,140 of sales returns and allowances during 2013.

Sales discounts are granted by the seller to customers for early payment of amounts owed. For example, a seller may offer a customer a 2% discount on a sale of $10,000 if the customer pays within 10 days. If the customer pays within the 10-day period, the seller receives cash of $9,800, and the buyer receives a discount of $200 ($10,000 × 2%). NetSolutions reported $5,790 of sales discounts during 2013.

EXHIBIT 1

Multiple-Step Income Statement

NetSolutions
Income Statement
For the Year Ended December 31, 2013

Revenue from sales:			
Sales		$720,185	
Less: Sales returns and allowances	$ 6,140		
Sales discounts	5,790	11,930	
Net sales			$708,255
Cost of merchandise sold			525,305
Gross profit			$182,950
Operating expenses:			
Selling expenses:			
Sales salaries expense	$53,430		
Advertising expense	10,860		
Depreciation expense—store equipment	3,100		
Delivery expense	2,800		
Miscellaneous selling expense	630		
Total selling expenses		$ 70,820	
Administrative expenses:			
Office salaries expense	$21,020		
Rent expense	8,100		
Depreciation expense—office equipment	2,490		
Insurance expense	1,910		
Office supplies expense	610		
Miscellaneous administrative expense	760		
Total administrative expenses		34,890	
Total operating expenses			105,710
Income from operations			$ 77,240
Other income and expense:			
Rent revenue		$ 600	
Interest expense		(2,440)	(1,840)
Net income			$ 75,400

Net sales is determined by subtracting sales returns and allowances and sales discounts from sales. As shown in Exhibit 1, NetSolutions reported $708,255 of net sales during 2013. Some companies report only net sales and report sales, sales returns and allowances, and sales discounts in notes to the financial statements.

Cost of Merchandise Sold As shown in Exhibit 1, NetSolutions reported cost of merchandise sold of $525,305 during 2013. The cost of merchandise sold is the cost of merchandise sold to customers. Merchandise costs consist of all the costs of acquiring the merchandise and readying it for sale, such as purchase and freight costs. Recording these costs is described and illustrated later in this chapter.

For many merchandising businesses, the cost of merchandise sold is usually the largest expense. For example, the approximate percentage of cost of merchandise sold to sales is 63% for JCPenney and 66% for The Home Depot.

Two systems of accounting for recording and reporting the cost of merchandise sold are:

1. Periodic inventory system
2. Perpetual inventory system

Under the **periodic inventory system**, the inventory records do not show the amount available for sale or the amount sold during the period. Instead, the cost of merchandise sold and the merchandise on hand are determined at the end of the period by physically counting the inventory. The periodic inventory system is described and illustrated in the appendix to this chapter.

Under the **perpetual inventory system**, each purchase and sale of merchandise is recorded in the inventory and the cost of merchandise sold accounts. As a result, the amounts of merchandise available for sale and sold are continuously (perpetually) updated in the inventory records. Because many retailers use computerized systems, the perpetual inventory system is widely used.

Under a perpetual inventory system, the cost of merchandise sold is reported as a single line on the income statement. An example of such reporting is illustrated in Exhibit 1 for NetSolutions. Because of its wide use, the perpetual inventory system is used in the remainder of this chapter.

Retailers, such as Best Buy, Sears Holding Corporation, and Walmart, and grocery store chains, such as Winn-Dixie Stores, Inc. and Kroger, use bar codes and optical scanners as part of their computerized inventory systems.

Gross Profit Gross profit is computed by subtracting the cost of merchandise sold from net sales, as shown below.

Net sales	$708,255
Cost of merchandise sold	525,305
Gross profit	$182,950

As shown above and in Exhibit 1, NetSolutions has gross profit of $182,950 in 2013.

Income from Operations **Income from operations**, sometimes called operating income, is determined by subtracting operating expenses from gross profit. Operating expenses are normally classified as either selling expenses or administrative expenses.

Selling expenses are incurred directly in the selling of merchandise. Examples of selling expenses include sales salaries, store supplies used, depreciation of store equipment, delivery expense, and advertising.

Administrative expenses, sometimes called **general expenses**, are incurred in the administration or general operations of the business. Examples of administrative expenses include office salaries, depreciation of office equipment, and office supplies used.

Each selling and administrative expense may be reported separately as shown in Exhibit 1. However, many companies report selling, administrative, and operating expenses as single line items as shown below for NetSolutions.

See Appendix D for more information

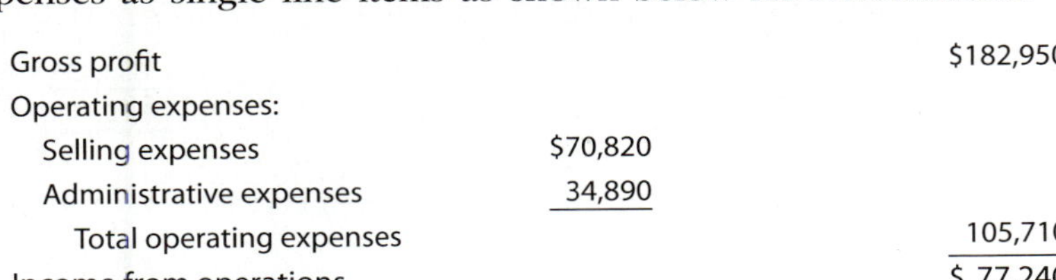

Gross profit		$182,950
Operating expenses:		
Selling expenses	$70,820	
Administrative expenses	34,890	
Total operating expenses		105,710
Income from operations		$ 77,240

Other Income and Expense Other income and expense items are not related to the primary operations of the business. **Other income** is revenue from sources other than the primary operating activity of a business. Examples of other income include income from interest, rent, and gains resulting from the sale of fixed assets. **Other expense** is an expense that cannot be traced directly to the normal operations of the business. Examples of other expenses include interest expense and losses from disposing of fixed assets.

Other income and other expense are offset against each other on the income statement. If the total of other income exceeds the total of other expense, the difference is added to income from operations to determine net income. If the reverse is true, the difference is subtracted from income from operations. The other income and expense items of NetSolutions are reported as shown below and in Exhibit 1.

Income from operations		$77,240
Other income and expense:		
Rent revenue	$ 600	
Interest expense	(2,440)	(1,840)
Net income		$75,400

Single-Step Income Statement

An alternate form of income statement is the **single-step income statement.** As shown in Exhibit 2, the income statement for NetSolutions deducts the total of all expenses *in one step* from the total of all revenues.

The single-step form emphasizes total revenues and total expenses in determining net income. A criticism of the single-step form is that gross profit and income from operations are not reported.

Statement of Owner's Equity

The statement of owner's equity for NetSolutions is shown in Exhibit 3. This statement is prepared in the same manner as for a service business.

Balance Sheet

The balance sheet may be presented with assets on the left-hand side and the liabilities and owner's equity on the right-hand side. This form of the balance sheet is called the **account form.** The balance sheet may also be presented in a downward sequence in

EXHIBIT 2

Single-Step Income Statement

NetSolutions
Income Statement
For the Year Ended December 31, 2013

Revenues:		
Net sales		$708,255
Rent revenue		600
Total revenues		$708,855
Expenses:		
Cost of merchandise sold	$525,305	
Selling expenses	70,820	
Administrative expenses	34,890	
Interest expense	2,440	
Total expenses		633,455
Net income		$ 75,400

EXHIBIT 3

Statement of Owner's Equity for Merchandising Business

NetSolutions
Statement of Owner's Equity
For the Year Ended December 31, 2013

Chris Clark, capital, January 1, 2013		$153,800
Net income for the year	$75,400	
Less withdrawals	18,000	
Increase in owner's equity		57,400
Chris Clark, capital, December 31, 2013		$211,200

three sections. This form of balance sheet is called the **report form.** The report form of balance sheet for NetSolutions is shown in Exhibit 4. In Exhibit 4, merchandise inventory is reported as a current asset and the current portion of the note payable of $5,000 is reported as a current liability.

EXHIBIT 4

Report Form of Balance Sheet

NetSolutions
Balance Sheet
December 31, 2013

Assets			
Current assets:			
Cash		$52,950	
Accounts receivable		91,080	
Merchandise inventory		62,150	
Office supplies		480	
Prepaid insurance		2,650	
Total current assets			$209,310
Property, plant, and equipment:			
Land		$20,000	
Store equipment	$27,100		
Less accumulated depreciation	5,700	21,400	
Office equipment	$15,570		
Less accumulated depreciation	4,720	10,850	
Total property, plant, and equipment			52,250
Total assets			$261,560
Liabilities			
Current liabilities:			
Accounts payable		$22,420	
Note payable (current portion)		5,000	
Salaries payable		1,140	
Unearned rent		1,800	
Total current liabilities			$ 30,360
Long-term liabilities:			
Note payable (final payment due 2023)			20,000
Total liabilities			$ 50,360
Owner's Equity			
Chris Clark, capital			211,200
Total liabilities and owner's equity			$261,560

Business Connection

H&R BLOCK VERSUS THE HOME DEPOT

H&R Block is a service business that primarily offers tax planning and preparation to its customers. The Home Depot is a large home improvement retailer. The differences in the operations of a service and merchandise business are illustrated in their income statements, as shown below.

H&R Block
Condensed Income Statement
For the Year Ending April 30, 2009
(in millions)

Revenue	$4,084
Operating expenses	3,245
Operating income	$ 839
Other expense (net)	28
Income before taxes	$ 811
Income taxes	326
Net income	$ 485

As discussed in a later chapter, corporations are subject to income taxes. Thus, the income statements of H&R Block and The Home Depot report "income taxes" as a deduction from "income before income taxes" in arriving at net income. This is in contrast to a proprietorship such as NetSolutions, which is not subject to income taxes.

The Home Depot
Condensed Income Statement
For the Year Ending February 1, 2009
(in millions)

Net sales	$71,288
Cost of merchandise sold	47,298
Gross profit	$23,990
Operating expenses	19,631
Operating income	$ 4,359
Other expense (net)	821
Income before taxes	$ 3,538
Income taxes	1,278
Net income	$ 2,260

OBJ. 3 Describe and illustrate the accounting for merchandise transactions including:

- sale of merchandise
- purchase of merchandise
- freight
- sales taxes and trade discounts
- dual nature of merchandising transactions

Merchandising Transactions

The prior section described and illustrated the financial statements of a merchandising business, **NetSolutions**. This section describes and illustrates the recording of merchandise transactions, including the use of a chart of accounts for a merchandising business.

Chart of Accounts for a Merchandising Business

The chart of accounts for a merchandising business should reflect the elements of the financial statements. The chart of accounts for NetSolutions is shown in Exhibit 5. The accounts related to merchandising transactions are shown in color.

As shown in Exhibit 5, NetSolutions' chart of accounts consists of three-digit account numbers. The first digit indicates the major financial statement classification (1 for assets, 2 for liabilities, and so on). The second digit indicates the subclassification (e.g., 11 for current assets, 12 for noncurrent assets). The third digit identifies the specific account (e.g., 110 for Cash, 123 for Store Equipment). Using a three-digit numbering system makes it easier to add new accounts as they are needed.

Sales Transactions

Merchandise transactions are recorded using the rules of debit and credit that we described and illustrated in Chapter 2. Exhibit 3, shown on page 57 of Chapter 2, summarizes these rules.

Special journals may be used, or transactions may be entered, recorded, and posted using a computerized accounting system. To simplify, a two-column general journal is used in this chapter.

EXHIBIT 5

Chart of Accounts for NetSolutions, a Merchandising Business

Balance Sheet Accounts	Income Statement Accounts
100 Assets	400 Revenues
110 Cash	410 Sales
112 Accounts Receivable	411 Sales Returns and Allowances
115 Merchandise Inventory	412 Sales Discounts
116 Office Supplies	500 Costs and Expenses
117 Prepaid Insurance	510 Cost of Merchandise Sold
120 Land	520 Sales Salaries Expense
123 Store Equipment	521 Advertising Expense
124 Accumulated Depreciation—Store Equipment	522 Depreciation Expense—Store Equipment
125 Office Equipment	523 Delivery Expense
126 Accumulated Depreciation—Office Equipment	529 Miscellaneous Selling Expense
200 Liabilities	530 Office Salaries Expense
210 Accounts Payable	531 Rent Expense
211 Salaries Payable	532 Depreciation Expense—Office Equipment
212 Unearned Rent	533 Insurance Expense
215 Notes Payable	534 Office Supplies Expense
300 Owner's Equity	539 Misc. Administrative Expense
310 Chris Clark, Capital	600 Other Income
311 Chris Clark, Drawing	610 Rent Revenue
312 Income Summary	700 Other Expense
	710 Interest Expense

Cash Sales A business may sell merchandise for cash. Cash sales are normally entered (rung up) on a cash register and recorded in the accounts. To illustrate, assume that on January 3, NetSolutions sells merchandise for $1,800. These cash sales are recorded as follows:

Journal *Page 25*

Date		Description	Post. Ref.	Debit	Credit
2013 Jan.	3	Cash		1,800	
		Sales			1,800
		To record cash sales.			

Using the perpetual inventory system, the cost of merchandise sold and the decrease in merchandise inventory are also recorded. In this way, the merchandise inventory account indicates the amount of merchandise on hand (not sold).

To illustrate, assume that the cost of merchandise sold on January 3 is $1,200. The entry to record the cost of merchandise sold and the decrease in the merchandise inventory is as follows:

Date		Description	Post. Ref.	Debit	Credit
Jan.	3	Cost of Merchandise Sold		1,200	
		Merchandise Inventory			1,200
		To record the cost of merchandise sold.			

Sales may be made to customers using credit cards such as MasterCard or VISA. Such sales are recorded as cash sales. This is because these sales are normally processed by a clearing-house that contacts the bank that issued the card. The issuing bank then electronically transfers cash directly to the retailer's bank account.[2] Thus, the retailer normally receives cash within a few days of making the credit card sale.

If the customers in the preceding sales had used MasterCards to pay for their purchases, the sales would be recorded exactly as shown in the preceding entry. Any processing fees charged by the clearing-house or issuing bank are periodically recorded as an expense. This expense is normally reported on the income statement as an administrative expense. To illustrate, assume that NetSolutions paid credit card processing fees of $48 on January 31. These fees would be recorded as follows:

Jan.	31	Credit Card Expense		48	
		Cash			48
		To record service charges on credit card sales for the month.			

A retailer may accept MasterCard or VISA but not American Express. Why? American Express Co.'s service fees are normally higher than MasterCard's or VISA's. As a result, some retailers choose not to accept American Express cards. The disadvantage of this practice is that the retailer may lose customers to competitors who do accept American Express cards.

Instead of using MasterCard or VISA, a customer may use a credit card that is not issued by a bank. For example, a customer might use an American Express card. If the seller uses a clearing-house, the clearing-house will collect the receivable and transfer the cash to the retailer's bank account similar to the way it would have if the customer had used MasterCard or VISA. Large businesses, however, may not use a clearing-house. In such cases, nonbank credit card sales must first be reported to the card company before cash is received. Thus, a receivable is created with the nonbank credit card company. However, since most retailers use clearing-houses to process both bank and nonbank credit cards, all credit card sales will be recorded as cash sales.

Sales on Account A business may sell merchandise on account. The seller records such sales as a debit to Accounts Receivable and a credit to Sales. An example of an entry for a NetSolutions sale on account of $510 follows. The cost of merchandise sold was $280.

Jan.	12	Accounts Receivable—Sims Co.		510	
		Sales			510
		Invoice No. 7172.			
	12	Cost of Merchandise Sold		280	
		Merchandise Inventory			280
		Cost of merch. sold on Invoice No. 7172.			

Sales Discounts The terms of a sale are normally indicated on the **invoice** or bill that the seller sends to the buyer. An example of a sales invoice for NetSolutions is shown in Exhibit 6.

The terms for when payments for merchandise are to be made are called the **credit terms.** If payment is required on delivery, the terms are *cash* or *net cash*. Otherwise, the buyer is allowed an amount of time, known as the **credit period,** in which to pay.

The credit period usually begins with the date of the sale as shown on the invoice. If payment is due within a stated number of days after the invoice date, such as 30 days, the terms are *net 30 days*. These terms may be written as *n/30*.[3] If payment

2 CyberSource is one of the major credit card clearing-houses. For a more detailed description of how credit card sales are processed, see the following CyberSource Web page: **http://www.cybersource.com/products_and_services/global_payment_services/credit_card_processing/howitworks.xml**.

3 The word *net* as used here does not have the usual meaning of a number after deductions have been subtracted, as in *net income*.

NetSolutions 5101 Washington Ave. Cincinnati, OH 45227-5101			106-8
Invoice			Made in U.S.A.
SOLD TO Omega Technologies 1000 Matrix Blvd. San Jose, CA. 95116-1000		**CUSTOMER'S ORDER NO. & DATE** 412 Jan. 4, 2013	
DATE SHIPPED Jan. 7, 2013	**HOW SHIPPED AND ROUTE** US Express Trucking Co.	**TERMS** 2/10, n/30	**INVOICE DATE** Jan. 7, 2013
FROM Cincinnati	**F.O.B.** Cincinnati		
QUANTITY	**DESCRIPTION**	**UNIT PRICE**	**AMOUNT**
10	3COM Wireless PC Card	150.00	1,500.00

EXHIBIT 6

Invoice

is due by the end of the month in which the sale was made, the terms are written as *n/eom*.

To encourage the buyer to pay before the end of the credit period, the seller may offer a discount. For example, a seller may offer a 2% discount if the buyer pays within 10 days of the invoice date. If the buyer does not take the discount, the total amount is due within 30 days. These terms are expressed as *2/10, n/30* and are read as *2% discount if paid within 10 days, net amount due within 30 days*. The credit terms of 2/10, n/30 are summarized in Exhibit 7, using the invoice in Exhibit 6.

Discounts taken by the buyer for early payment are recorded as sales discounts by the seller. Managers usually want to know the amount of the sales discounts for a period. For this reason, sales discounts are recorded in a separate sales discounts account, which is a *contra* (or *offsetting*) account to Sales.

To illustrate, assume that NetSolutions receives $1,470 on January 17 for the invoice shown in Exhibit 6. Since the invoice was paid within the discount period (10 days), the buyer deducted $30 ($1,500 × 2%) from the invoice amount. NetSolutions would record the receipt of the cash as follows:

Jan.	17	Cash		1,470	
		Sales Discounts		30	
		Accounts Receivable—Omega Technologies			1,500
		Collection on Invoice No. 106-8, less 2% discount.			

Sales Returns and Allowances Merchandise sold may be returned to the seller (sales return). In other cases, the seller may reduce the initial selling price (sales allowance). This might occur if the merchandise is defective, damaged during shipment, or does not meet the buyer's expectations.

If the return or allowance is for a sale on account, the seller usually issues the buyer a **credit memorandum**, often called a **credit memo**. A credit memo authorizes

EXHIBIT 7

Credit Terms

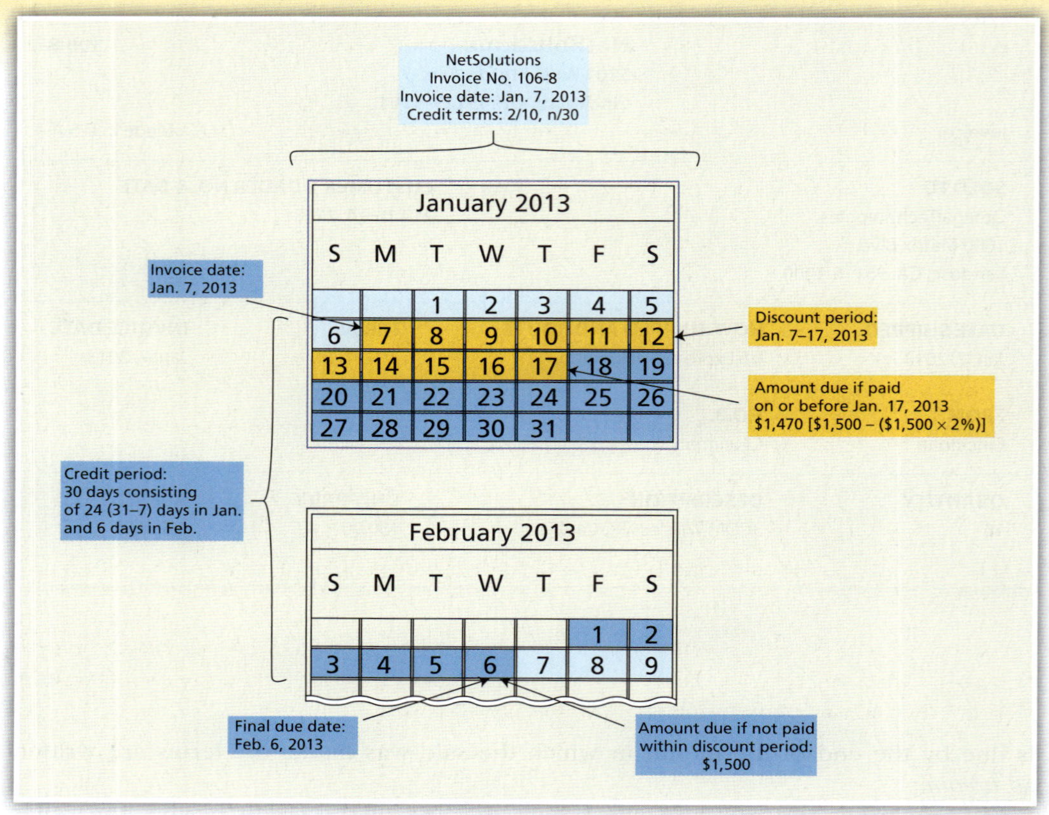

a credit to (decreases) the buyer's account receivable. A credit memo indicates the amount and reason for the credit. An example of a credit memo issued by NetSolutions is shown in Exhibit 8.

Like sales discounts, sales returns and allowances reduce sales revenue. Also, returns often result in additional shipping and handling expenses. Thus, managers usually want to know the amount of returns and allowances for a period. For this reason, sales returns and allowances are recorded in a separate sales returns and allowances account, which is a *contra* (or *offsetting*) account to Sales.

The seller debits Sales Returns and Allowances for the amount of the return or allowance. If the sale was on account, the seller credits Accounts Receivable. Using a perpetual inventory system, the seller must also debit (increase) Merchandise Inventory and decrease (credit) Cost of Merchandise Sold for the cost of the returned merchandise.

EXHIBIT 8

Credit Memo

NetSolutions
5101 Washington Ave.
Cincinnati, OH 45227-5101

No. 32

CREDIT MEMO

TO
Krier Company
7608 Melton Avenue
Los Angeles, CA 90025-3942

DATE
January 13, 2013

WE CREDIT YOUR ACCOUNT AS FOLLOWS

1 Graphic Video Card 225.00

To illustrate, the credit memo shown in Exhibit 8 is used. The selling price of the merchandise returned in Exhibit 8 is $225. Assuming that the cost of the merchandise returned is $140, the sales return and allowance would be recorded as follows:

Jan.	13	Sales Returns and Allowances		225	
		Accounts Receivable—Krier Company			225
		Credit Memo No. 32.			
	13	Merchandise Inventory		140	
		Cost of Merchandise Sold			140
		Cost of merchandise returned, Credit Memo No. 32.			

A buyer may pay for merchandise and then later return it. In this case, the seller may do one of the following:

1. Issue a credit that is applied against the buyer's other receivables.
2. Issue a cash refund.

If the credit is applied against the buyer's other receivables, the seller records the credit with entries similar to those shown above. If cash is refunded, the seller debits Sales Returns and Allowances and credits Cash.

Example Exercise 6-2 Sales Transactions

OBJ. 3

Journalize the following merchandise transactions:

a. Sold merchandise on account, $7,500 with terms 2/10, n/30. The cost of the merchandise sold was $5,625.
b. Received payment less the discount.

Follow My Example 6-2

a.	Accounts Receivable	7,500	
	Sales		7,500
	Cost of Merchandise Sold	5,625	
	Merchandise Inventory		5,625
b.	Cash	7,350	
	Sales Discounts	150	
	Accounts Receivable		7,500

Practice Exercises: PE 6-2A, PE 6-2B

Integrity, Objectivity, and Ethics in Business

THE CASE OF THE FRAUDULENT PRICE TAGS

One of the challenges for a retailer is policing its sales return policy. There are many ways in which customers can unethically or illegally abuse such policies. In one case, a couple was accused of attaching **Marshalls**' store price tags to cheaper merchandise bought or obtained elsewhere. The couple then returned the cheaper goods and received the substantially higher refund amount. Company security officials discovered the fraud and had the couple arrested after they had allegedly bilked the company for over $1 million.

Purchase Transactions

Under the perpetual inventory system, cash purchases of merchandise are recorded as follows:

Journal					Page 24
Date		Description	Post. Ref.	Debit	Credit
2013 Jan.	3	Merchandise Inventory		2,510	
		Cash			2,510
		Purchased inventory from Bowen Co.			

Purchases of merchandise on account are recorded as follows:

Date		Description	Post. Ref.	Debit	Credit
Jan.	4	Merchandise Inventory		9,250	
		Accounts Payable—Thomas Corporation			9,250
		Purchased inventory on account.			

Purchases Discounts A buyer may receive a discount from the seller (sales discount) for early payment of the amount owed. From the buyer's perspective, such discounts are called **purchases discounts**.

Purchases discounts taken by a buyer reduce the cost of the merchandise purchased. Even if the buyer has to borrow to pay within a discount period, it is normally to the buyer's advantage to do so. For this reason, accounting systems are normally designed so that all available discounts are taken.

To illustrate, assume that NetSolutions purchased merchandise from Alpha Technologies as follows:

Invoice Date	Invoice Amount	Terms
March 12	$3,000	2/10, n/30

The last day of the discount period is March 22 (March 12 + 10 days). Assume that in order to pay the invoice on March 22, NetSolutions borrows $2,940, which is $3,000 less the discount of $60 ($3,000 × 2%). If we also assume an annual interest rate of 6% and a 360-day year, the interest on the loan of $2,940 for the remaining 20 days of the credit period is $9.80 ($2,940 × 6% × 20/360).

The net savings to NetSolutions of taking the discount is $50.20, computed as follows:

Discount of 2% on $3,000	$60.00
Interest for 20 days at a rate of 6% on $2,940	9.80
Savings from taking the discount	$50.20

The savings can also be seen by comparing the interest rate on the money *saved* by taking the discount and the interest rate on the money *borrowed* to take the discount. The interest rate on the money saved in the prior example is estimated by converting 2% for 20 days to a yearly rate, as follows:

$$2\% \times \frac{360 \text{ days}}{20 \text{ days}} = 2\% \times 18 = 36\%$$

NetSolutions borrowed $2,940 at 6% to take the discount. If NetSolutions does not take the discount, it *pays* an estimated interest rate of 36% for using the $2,940 for the remaining 20 days of the credit period. Thus, buyers should normally take all available purchase discounts.

Under the perpetual inventory system, the buyer initially debits Merchandise Inventory for the amount of the invoice. When paying the invoice within the discount period, the buyer credits Merchandise Inventory for the amount of the discount. In this way, Merchandise Inventory shows the *net* cost to the buyer.

To illustrate, NetSolutions would record the Alpha Technologies invoice and its payment at the end of the discount period as follows:

Mar.	12	Merchandise Inventory		3,000	
		Accounts Payable—Alpha Technologies			3,000
	22	Accounts Payable—Alpha Technologies		3,000	
		Cash			2,940
		Merchandise Inventory			60

Assume that NetSolutions does not take the discount, but instead pays the invoice on April 11. In this case, NetSolutions would record the payment on April 11 as follows:

Apr.	11	Accounts Payable--Alpha Technologies		3,000	
		Cash			3,000

Purchases Returns and Allowances A buyer may receive an allowance for merchandise that is returned (purchases return) or a price allowance (purchases allowance) for damaged or defective merchandise. From a buyer's perspective, such sales returns and allowances are called **purchases returns and allowances**. In both cases, the buyer normally sends the seller a debit memorandum.

A **debit memorandum**, often called a **debit memo**, is shown in Exhibit 9. A debit memo informs the seller of the amount the buyer proposes to *debit* to the account payable due the seller. It also states the reasons for the return or the request for the price allowance.

The buyer may use the debit memo as the basis for recording the return or allowance or wait for approval from the seller (creditor). In either case, the buyer debits Accounts Payable and credits Merchandise Inventory.

EXHIBIT 9

Debit Memo

NetSolutions
5101 Washington Ave.
Cincinnati, OH 45227-5101

No. 18

DEBIT MEMO

TO
Maxim Systems
7519 East Wilson Ave.
Seattle, WA 98101-7519

DATE
March 7, 2013

WE DEBITED YOUR ACCOUNT AS FOLLOWS

10	Server Network Interface Cards, your invoice No. 7291, are being returned via parcel post. Our order specified No. 825X.	@90.00	900.00

To illustrate, NetSolutions records the return of the merchandise indicated in the debit memo in Exhibit 9 as follows:

Mar.	7	Accounts Payable—Maxim Systems	900	
		Merchandise Inventory		900
		Debit Memo No. 18.		

A buyer may return merchandise or be granted a price allowance before paying an invoice. In this case, the amount of the debit memo is deducted from the invoice. The amount is deducted before the purchase discount is computed.

To illustrate, assume the following data concerning a purchase of merchandise by NetSolutions on May 2:

May 2. Purchased $5,000 of merchandise on account from Delta Data Link, terms 2/10, n/30.
4. Returned $3,000 of the merchandise purchased on March 2.
12. Paid for the purchase of May 2 less the return and discount.

NetSolutions would record these transactions as follows:

May	2	Merchandise Inventory	5,000	
		Accounts Payable—Delta Data Link		5,000
		Purchased merchandise.		
	4	Accounts Payable—Delta Data Link	3,000	
		Merchandise Inventory		3,000
		Returned portion of merch. purchased.		
	12	Accounts Payable—Delta Data Link	2,000	
		Cash		1,960
		Merchandise Inventory		40
		Paid invoice [($5,000 – $3,000) × 2% = $40; $2,000 – $40 = $1,960].		

Example Exercise 6-3 Purchase Transactions OBJ. 3

Rofles Company purchased merchandise on account from a supplier for $11,500, terms 2/10, n/30. Rofles Company returned $3,000 of the merchandise and received full credit.

a. If Rofles Company pays the invoice within the discount period, what is the amount of cash required for the payment?
b. Under a perpetual inventory system, what account is credited by Rofles Company to record the return?

Follow My Example 6-3

a. $8,330. Purchase of $11,500 less the return of $3,000 less the discount of $170 [($11,500 – $3,000) × 2%].
b. Merchandise Inventory

Practice Exercises: **PE 6-3A, PE 6-3B**

Freight

Purchases and sales of merchandise often involve freight. The terms of a sale indicate when ownership (title) of the merchandise passes from the seller to the buyer. This point determines whether the buyer or the seller pays the freight costs.[4]

The ownership of the merchandise may pass to the buyer when the seller delivers the merchandise to the freight carrier. In this case, the terms are said to be **FOB (free on board) shipping point**. This term means that the buyer pays the freight costs from the shipping point to the final destination. Such costs are part of the buyer's total cost of purchasing inventory and are added to the cost of the inventory by debiting Merchandise Inventory.

Note:
The buyer bears the freight costs if the shipping terms are FOB shipping point.

To illustrate, assume that on June 10, NetSolutions purchased merchandise as follows:

June 10. Purchased merchandise from Magna Data, $900, terms FOB shipping point.
10. Paid freight of $50 on June 10 purchase from Magna Data.

Sometimes FOB shipping point and FOB destination are expressed in terms of a specific location at which the title to the merchandise passes to the buyer. For example, if Toyota Motor Corporation's assembly plant in Osaka, Japan, sells automobiles to a dealer in Chicago, FOB shipping point is expressed as FOB Osaka. Likewise, FOB destination is expressed as FOB Chicago.

NetSolutions would record these two transactions as follows:

June	10	Merchandise Inventory		900	
		Accounts Payable—Magna Data			900
		Purchased merchandise, terms FOB shipping point.			
	10	Merchandise Inventory		50	
		Cash			50
		Paid shipping cost on merchandise purchased.			

The ownership of the merchandise may pass to the buyer when the buyer receives the merchandise. In this case, the terms are said to be **FOB (free on board) destination**. This term means that the seller pays the freight costs from the shipping point to the buyer's final destination. When the seller pays the delivery charges, the seller debits Delivery Expense or Freight Out. Delivery Expense is reported on the seller's income statement as a selling expense.

Note:
The seller bears the freight costs if the shipping terms are FOB destination.

To illustrate, assume that NetSolutions sells merchandise as follows:

June 15. Sold merchandise to Kranz Company on account, $700, terms FOB destination. The cost of the merchandise sold is $480.
15. NetSolutions pays freight of $40 on the sale of June 15.

NetSolutions records the sale, the cost of the sale, and the freight cost as follows:

June	15	Accounts Receivable—Kranz Company		700	
		Sales			700
		Sold merchandise, terms FOB destination.			
	15	Cost of Merchandise Sold		480	
		Merchandise Inventory			480
		Recorded cost of merchandise sold to Kranz Company.			
	15	Delivery Expense		40	
		Cash			40
		Paid shipping cost on merch. sold.			

4 The passage of title also determines whether the buyer or seller must pay other costs, such as the cost of insurance, while the merchandise is in transit.

The seller may prepay the freight, even though the terms are FOB shipping point. The seller will then add the freight to the invoice. The buyer debits Merchandise Inventory for the total amount of the invoice, including the freight. Any discount terms would not apply to the prepaid freight.

To illustrate, assume that NetSolutions sells merchandise as follows:

June 20. Sold merchandise to Planter Company on account, $800, terms FOB shipping point. NetSolutions paid freight of $45, which was added to the invoice. The cost of the merchandise sold is $360.

NetSolutions records the sale, the cost of the sale, and the freight as follows:

June	20	Accounts Receivable—Planter Company		800	
		Sales			800
		Sold merch., terms FOB shipping point.			
	20	Cost of Merchandise Sold		360	
		Merchandise Inventory			360
		Recorded cost of merchandise sold to Planter Company.			
	20	Accounts Receivable—Planter Company		45	
		Cash			45
		Prepaid shipping cost on merch. sold.			

Shipping terms, the passage of title, and whether the buyer or seller is to pay the freight costs are summarized in Exhibit 10.

EXHIBIT 10 Freight Terms

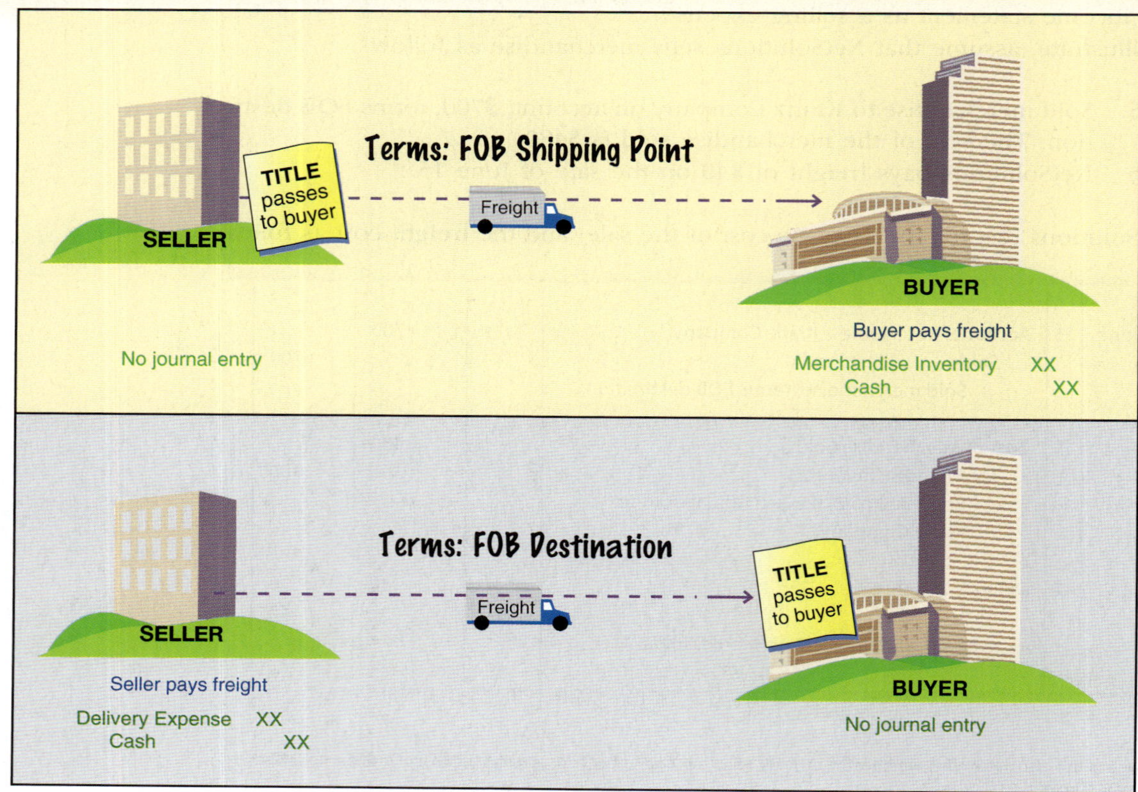

Example Exercise 6-4 Freight Terms

OBJ. 3

Determine the amount to be paid in full settlement of each of invoices (a) and (b), assuming that credit for returns and allowances was received prior to payment and that all invoices were paid within the discount period.

	Merchandise	Freight Paid by Seller	Freight Terms	Returns and Allowances
a.	$4,500	$200	FOB shipping point, 1/10, n/30	$ 800
b.	5,000	60	FOB destination, 2/10, n/30	2,500

Follow My Example 6-4

a. $3,863. Purchase of $4,500 less return of $800 less the discount of $37 [($4,500 – $800) × 1%] plus $200 of shipping.

b. $2,450. Purchase of $5,000 less return of $2,500 less the discount of $50 [($5,000 – $2,500) × 2%].

Practice Exercises: **PE 6-4A, PE 6-4B**

Summary: Recording Merchandise Inventory

Recording merchandise inventory transactions under the perpetual inventory system has been described and illustrated in the preceding sections. These transactions involved purchases, purchases discounts, purchases returns and allowances, freight, sales, and sales returns from customers. Exhibit 11 summarizes how these transactions are recorded in T account form.

EXHIBIT 11

Recording Merchandise Inventory

Merchandise Inventory

Debit		Credit	
Purchases of merchandise for sale	XXX	Purchases discounts	XXX
Freight for merchandise purchased FOB shipping point	XXX	Purchases returns and allowances	XXX
Merchandise returned from customer	XXX	Cost of merchandise sold	XXX

Cost of Merchandise Sold

Debit		Credit	
Cost of merchandise sold	XXX	Merchandise returned from customer	XXX

Sales Taxes and Trade Discounts

Sales of merchandise often involve sales taxes. Also, the seller may offer buyers trade discounts.

Sales Taxes Almost all states levy a tax on sales of merchandise.[5] The liability for the sales tax is incurred when the sale is made.

5 Businesses that purchase merchandise for resale to others are normally exempt from paying sales taxes on their purchases. Only final buyers of merchandise normally pay sales taxes.

At the time of a cash sale, the seller collects the sales tax. When a sale is made on account, the seller charges the tax to the buyer by debiting Accounts Receivable. The seller credits the sales account for the amount of the sale and credits the tax to Sales Tax Payable. For example, the seller would record a sale of $100 on account, subject to a tax of 6%, as follows:

Aug.	12	Accounts Receivable—Lemon Co.		106	
		Sales			100
		Sales Tax Payable			6
		Invoice No. 339.			

On a regular basis, the seller pays to the taxing authority (state) the amount of the sales tax collected. The seller records such a payment as follows:

Sept.	15	Sales Tax Payable		2,900	
		Cash			2,900
		Payment for sales taxes collected during August.			

Business Connection

SALES TAXES

While there is no federal sales tax, most states have enacted state-wide sales taxes. In addition, many states allow counties and cities to collect a "local option" sales taxes. Delaware, Montana, New Hampshire, and Oregon have no state or local sales taxes. Tennessee (9.4%), California (9.15%), Washington (8.75%), and Louisiana (8.75%) have the highest average combined rates (including state and local option taxes). Several towns in Tuscaloosa County, Alabama, have the highest combined rates in the United States of 11%, while Chicago, Illinois, has the highest combined city rate of 10.25%.

What about companies that sell merchandise through the Internet? The general rule is that if the company ships merchandise to a customer in a state where the company does not have a physical location, no sales tax is due. For example, a customer in Montana who purchases merchandise online from a New York retailer (and no physical location in Montana) does not have to pay sales tax to either Montana or New York.

Source: The Sales Tax Clearinghouse at **www.thestc.com/FAQ.stm** (accessed May 6, 2010).

Trade Discounts Wholesalers are companies that sell merchandise to other businesses rather than to the public. Many wholesalers publish sales catalogs. Rather than updating their catalogs, wholesalers may publish price updates. These updates may include large discounts from the catalog list prices. In addition, wholesalers often offer special discounts to government agencies or businesses that order large quantities. Such discounts are called **trade discounts**.

Sellers and buyers do not normally record the list prices of merchandise and trade discounts in their accounts. For example, assume that an item has a list price of $1,000 and a 40% trade discount. The seller records the sale of the item at $600 [$1,000 less the trade discount of $400 ($1,000 × 40%)]. Likewise, the buyer records the purchase at $600.

Dual Nature of Merchandise Transactions

Each merchandising transaction affects a buyer and a seller. In the following illustration, the same transactions for a seller and buyer are recorded. In this example, the seller is Scully Company and the buyer is Burton Co.

Transaction	Scully Company (Seller)			Burton Co. (Buyer)		
July 1. Scully Company sold merchandise on account to Burton Co., $7,500, terms FOB shipping point, n/45. The cost of the merchandise sold was $4,500.	Accounts Receivable—Burton Co.	7,500		Merchandise Inventory	7,500	
	Sales		7,500	Accounts Payable—Scully Co.		7,500
	Cost of Merchandise Sold	4,500				
	Merchandise Inventory		4,500			
July 2. Burton Co. paid freight of $150 on July 1 purchase from Scully Company.	No journal entry.			Merchandise Inventory	150	
				Cash		150
July 5. Scully Company sold merchandise on account to Burton Co., $5,000, terms FOB destination, n/30. The cost of the merchandise sold was $3,500.	Accounts Receivable—Burton Co.	5,000		Merchandise Inventory	5,000	
	Sales		5,000	Accounts Payable—Scully Co.		5,000
	Cost of Merchandise Sold	3,500				
	Merchandise Inventory		3,500			
July 7. Scully Company paid freight of $250 for delivery of merchandise sold to Burton Co. on July 5.	Delivery Expense	250		No journal entry.		
	Cash		250			
July 13. Scully Company issued Burton Co. a credit memo for merchandise returned, $1,000. The merchandise had been purchased by Burton Co. on account on July 5. The cost of the merchandise returned was $700.	Sales Returns and Allowances	1,000		Accounts Payable—Scully Co.	1,000	
	Accounts Receivable—Burton Co.		1,000	Merchandise Inventory		1,000
	Merchandise Inventory	700				
	Cost of Merchandise Sold		700			
July 15. Scully Company received payment from Burton Co. for purchase of July 5.	Cash	4,000		Accounts Payable—Scully Co.	4,000	
	Accounts Receivable—Burton Co.		4,000	Cash		4,000
July 18. Scully Company sold merchandise on account to Burton Co.,$12,000, terms FOB shipping point, 2/10, n/eom. Scully Company prepaid freight of $500, which was added to the invoice. The cost of the merchandise sold was $7,200.	Accounts Receivable—Burton Co.	12,000		Merchandise Inventory	12,500	
	Sales		12,000	Accounts Payable—Scully Co.		12,500
	Accounts Receivable—Burton Co.	500				
	Cash		500			
	Cost of Merchandise Sold	7,200				
	Merchandise Inventory		7,200			
July 28. Scully Company received payment from Burton Co. for purchase of July 18, less discount (2% × $12,000).	Cash	12,260		Accounts Payable—Scully Co.	12,500	
	Sales Discounts	240		Merchandise Inventory		240
	Accounts Receivable—Burton Co.		12,500	Cash		12,260

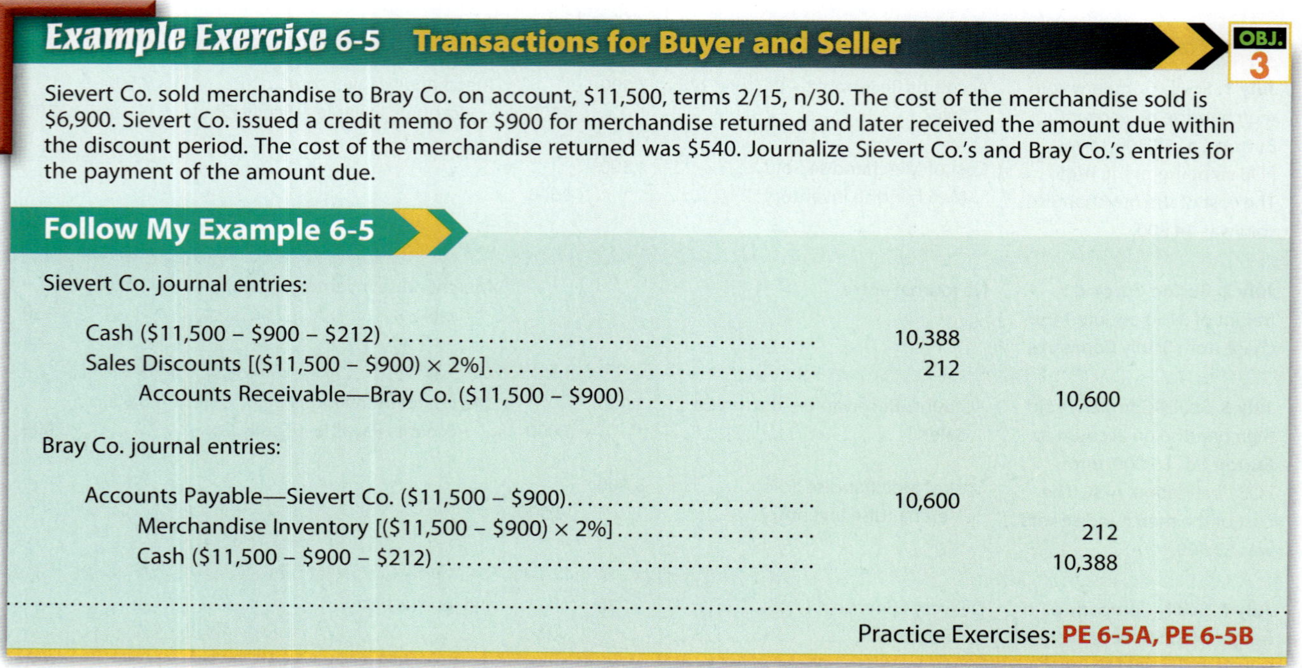

Example Exercise 6-5 Transactions for Buyer and Seller OBJ. 3

Sievert Co. sold merchandise to Bray Co. on account, $11,500, terms 2/15, n/30. The cost of the merchandise sold is $6,900. Sievert Co. issued a credit memo for $900 for merchandise returned and later received the amount due within the discount period. The cost of the merchandise returned was $540. Journalize Sievert Co.'s and Bray Co.'s entries for the payment of the amount due.

Follow My Example 6-5

Sievert Co. journal entries:

Cash ($11,500 – $900 – $212)	10,388	
Sales Discounts [($11,500 – $900) × 2%]	212	
Accounts Receivable—Bray Co. ($11,500 – $900)		10,600

Bray Co. journal entries:

Accounts Payable—Sievert Co. ($11,500 – $900)	10,600	
Merchandise Inventory [($11,500 – $900) × 2%]		212
Cash ($11,500 – $900 – $212)		10,388

Practice Exercises: PE 6-5A, PE 6-5B

OBJ. 4 Describe the adjusting and closing process for a merchandising business.

The Adjusting and Closing Process

Thus far, the chart of accounts and the recording of transactions for a merchandising business have been described and illustrated. The preparation of financial statements for **NetSolutions** has also been illustrated. In the remainder of this chapter, the adjusting and closing process for a merchandising business will be described. In this discussion, the focus will be on the elements of the accounting cycle that differ from those of a service business.

Adjusting Entry for Inventory Shrinkage

Under the perpetual inventory system, the merchandise inventory account is continually updated for purchase and sales transactions. As a result, the balance of the merchandise inventory account is the amount of merchandise available for sale at that point in time. However, retailers normally experience some loss of inventory due to shoplifting, employee theft, or errors. Thus, the physical inventory on hand at the end of the accounting period is usually less than the balance of Merchandise Inventory. This difference is called **inventory shrinkage** or **inventory shortage**.

To illustrate, NetSolutions' inventory records indicate the following on December 31, 2013:

	Dec. 31, 2013
Account balance of Merchandise Inventory	$63,950
Physical merchandise inventory on hand	62,150
Inventory shrinkage	$ 1,800

At the end of the accounting period, inventory shrinkage is recorded by the following adjusting entry:

		Adjusting Entry			
Dec.	31	Cost of Merchandise Sold		1,800	
		Merchandise Inventory			1,800
		Inventory shrinkage ($63,950 – $62,150).			

After the preceding entry is recorded, the balance of Merchandise Inventory agrees with the physical inventory on hand at the end of the period. Since inventory shrinkage cannot be totally eliminated, it is considered a normal cost of operations. If, however, the amount of the shrinkage is unusually large, it may be disclosed separately on the income statement. In such cases, the shrinkage may be recorded in a separate account, such as Loss from Merchandise Inventory Shrinkage.[6]

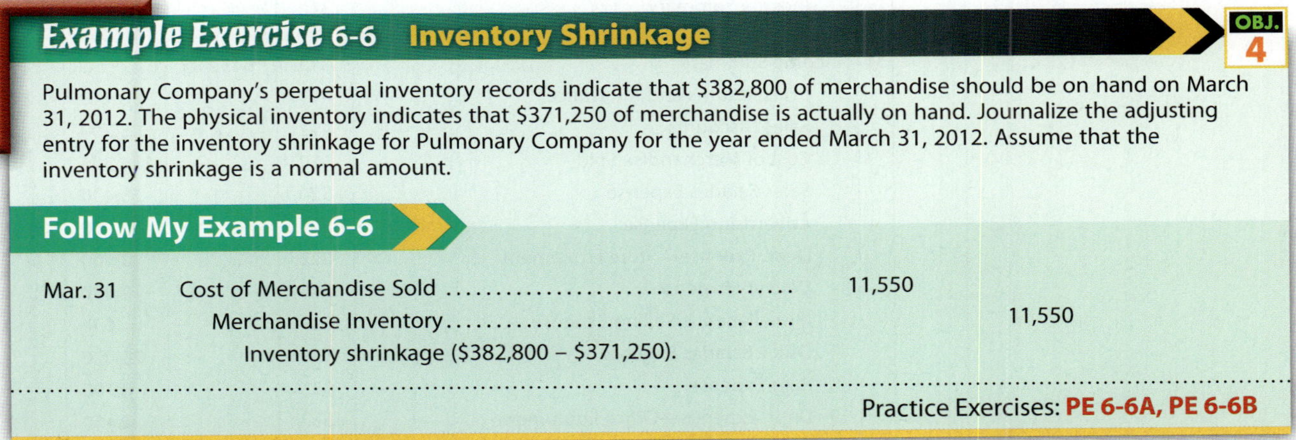

Example Exercise 6-6 Inventory Shrinkage OBJ. 4

Pulmonary Company's perpetual inventory records indicate that $382,800 of merchandise should be on hand on March 31, 2012. The physical inventory indicates that $371,250 of merchandise is actually on hand. Journalize the adjusting entry for the inventory shrinkage for Pulmonary Company for the year ended March 31, 2012. Assume that the inventory shrinkage is a normal amount.

Follow My Example 6-6

Mar. 31	Cost of Merchandise Sold	11,550	
	Merchandise Inventory		11,550
	Inventory shrinkage ($382,800 – $371,250).		

Practice Exercises: **PE 6-6A, PE 6-6B**

Closing Entries

The closing entries for a merchandising business are similar to those for a service business. The four closing entries for a merchandising business are as follows:

1. Debit each temporary account with a credit balance, such as Sales, for its balance and credit Income Summary.
2. Credit each temporary account with a debit balance, such as the various expenses, and credit Income Summary. Since Sales Returns and Allowances, Sales Discounts, and Cost of Merchandise Sold are temporary accounts with debit balances, they are credited for their balances.
3. Debit Income Summary for the amount of its balance (net income) and credit the owner's capital account. The accounts debited and credited are reversed if there is a net loss.
4. Debit the owner's capital account for the balance of the drawing account and credit the drawing account.

The four closing entries for NetSolutions are shown at the top of the following page.

NetSolutions' income summary account after the closing entries have been posted is as follows:

Account *Income Summary* — Account No. *312*

Date		Item	Post. Ref.	Debit	Credit	Balance Debit	Balance Credit
2013 Dec.	31	Revenues	29		720,785		720,785
	31	Expenses	29	645,385			75,400
	31	Net income	29	75,400		—	—

After the closing entries are posted to the accounts, a post-closing trial balance is prepared. The only accounts that should appear on the post-closing trial balance are the asset, contra asset, liability, and owner's capital accounts with balances. These are the same accounts that appear on the end-of-period balance sheet. If the two totals of the trial balance columns are not equal, an error has occurred that must be found and corrected.

6 The adjusting process for a merchandising business may be aided by preparing an end-of-period spreadsheet (work sheet). An end-of-period spreadsheet (work sheet) for a merchandising business is described and illustrated in an online appendix at **cengage.com/accounting/warren**.

Journal Page 29

Date		Item	Post. Ref.	Debit	Credit
		Closing Entries			
2013 Dec.	31	Sales	410	720,185	
		Rent Revenue	610	600	
		Income Summary	312		720,785
	31	Income Summary	312	645,385	
		Sales Returns and Allowances	411		6,140
		Sales Discounts	412		5,790
		Cost of Merchandise Sold	510		525,305
		Sales Salaries Expense	520		53,430
		Advertising Expense	521		10,860
		Depr. Expense—Store Equipment	522		3,100
		Delivery Expense	523		2,800
		Miscellaneous Selling Expense	529		630
		Office Salaries Expense	530		21,020
		Rent Expense	531		8,100
		Depr. Expense—Office Equipment	532		2,490
		Insurance Expense	533		1,910
		Office Supplies Expense	534		610
		Misc. Administrative Expense	539		760
		Interest Expense	710		2,440
	31	Income Summary	312	75,400	
		Chris Clark, Capital	310		75,400
	31	Chris Clark, Capital	310	18,000	
		Chris Clark, Drawing	311		18,000

F·A·I

OBJ. 5 Describe and illustrate the use of the ratio of net sales to assets in evaluating a company's operating performance.

Financial Analysis and Interpretation: Ratio of Net Sales to Assets

The **ratio of net sales to assets** measures how effectively a business is using its assets to generate sales. A high ratio indicates an effective use of assets. The assets used in computing the ratio may be the total assets at the end of the year, the average of the total assets at the beginning and end of the year, or the average of the monthly assets. For our purposes, the average of the total assets at the beginning and end of the year is used.

The ratio of net sales to assets is computed as follows:

$$\text{Ratio of Net Sales to Assets} = \frac{\text{Net Sales}}{\text{Average Total Assets}}$$

To illustrate the use of this ratio, the following data (in millions) were taken from the annual reports of Dollar Tree, Inc.:

	For Years Ended	
	January 31, 2009	February 2, 2008
Total revenues (net sales)	$4,645	$4,243
Total assets:		
Beginning of year	1,788	1,873
End of year	2,036	1,788

The ratios of net sales to assets for each year are as follows:

	For Years Ended	
	January 31, 2009	February 2, 2008
Ratio of net sales to assets	2.43	2.32
	$4,645/[($1,788 + $2,036)/2]	$4,243/[($1,873 + $1,788)/2]

Based on the preceding ratios, Dollar Tree improved its ratio of net sales to assets from 2.32 in 2008 to 2.43 in 2009. Thus, Dollar Tree improved the utilization of its assets to generate sales in 2009.

Using the ratio of net sales to assets for comparisons to competitors and with industry averages could also be beneficial in interpreting Dollar Tree's use of its assets. For example, the following data (in millions) were taken from the annual reports of Dollar General Corporation for the year ended January 30, 2009:

	For Year Ended January 30, 2009
Total revenues (net sales)	$10,458
Total assets:	
Beginning of year	8,656
End of year	8,889

Dollar General's ratio of net sales to assets for 2009 is as follows:

	For Year Ended January 30, 2009
Ratio of net sales to assets	1.19
	$10,458/[($8,656 + $8,889)/2]

Comparing Dollar General's 2009 ratio of 1.19 to Dollar Tree's 2009 ratio of 2.43 implies Dollar Tree is using its assets more efficiently than Dollar General.

Example Exercise 6-7 Ratio of Net Sales to Assets

OBJ. 5

The following financial statement data for the years ending December 31, 2012 and 2011, for Gilbert Company are shown below.

	2012	2011
Net sales	$1,305,000	$962,500
Total assets:		
Beginning of year	840,000	700,000
End of year	900,000	840,000

a. Determine the ratio of net sales to assets for 2012 and 2011.

b. Does the change in the current ratio from 2011 to 2012 indicate a favorable or an unfavorable trend?

Follow My Example 6-7

a.

	2012	2011
Ratio of net sales to assets	1.50	1.25
	$1,305,000/[($840,000 + $900,000)/2]	$962,500/[($840,000 + $700,000)/2]

b. The change from 1.25 to 1.50 indicates a favorable trend in using assets to generate sales.

Practice Exercises: PE 6-7A, PE 6-7B

Integrity, Objectivity, and Ethics in Business

THE COST OF EMPLOYEE THEFT

One survey reported that the 22 largest U.S. retail store chains have lost over $6 billion to shoplifting and employee theft. The stores apprehended over 900,000 shoplifters and dishonest employees and recovered more than $182 million from these thieves. Approximately 1 out of every 30 employees was apprehended for theft from his or her employer. Each dishonest employee stole approximately 7 times the amount stolen by shoplifters ($969 vs. $136).

Source: Jack L. Hayes International, 21st Annual Retail Theft Survey, 2009.

APPENDIX

The Periodic Inventory System

Throughout this chapter, the perpetual inventory system was used to record purchases and sales of merchandise. Not all merchandise businesses, however, use the perpetual inventory system. For example, small merchandise businesses, such as a local hardware store, may use a manual accounting system. A manual perpetual inventory system is time consuming and costly to maintain. In this case, the periodic inventory system may be used.

Cost of Merchandise Sold Using the Periodic Inventory System

In the periodic inventory system, sales are recorded in the same manner as in the perpetual inventory system. However, cost of merchandise sold is not recorded on the date of sale. Instead, cost of merchandise sold is determined at the end of the period as shown in Exhibit 12 for **NetSolutions**.

EXHIBIT 12

Determining Cost of Merchandise Sold Using the Periodic System

Merchandise inventory, January 1, 2013			$ 59,700
Purchases		$521,980	
Less: Purchases returns and allowances	$9,100		
Purchases discounts	2,525	11,625	
Net purchases		$510,355	
Add freight in		17,400	
Cost of merchandise purchased			527,755
Merchandise available for sale			$587,455
Less merchandise inventory, December 31, 2013			62,150
Cost of merchandise sold			$525,305

Chart of Accounts Under the Periodic Inventory System

The chart of accounts under a periodic inventory system is shown in Exhibit 13. The accounts used to record transactions under the periodic inventory system are highlighted in Exhibit 13.

EXHIBIT 13

Chart of Accounts Under the Periodic Inventory System

Balance Sheet Accounts	Income Statement Accounts
100 Assets	400 Revenues
110 Cash	410 Sales
111 Notes Receivable	411 Sales Returns and Allowances
112 Accounts Receivable	412 Sales Discounts
115 Merchandise Inventory	500 Costs and Expenses
116 Office Supplies	510 Purchases
117 Prepaid Insurance	511 Purchases Returns and Allowances
120 Land	512 Purchases Discounts
123 Store Equipment	513 Freight In
124 Accumulated Depreciation—Store Equipment	520 Sales Salaries Expense
125 Office Equipment	521 Advertising Expense
126 Accumulated Depreciation—Office Equipment	522 Depreciation Expense—Store Equipment
200 Liabilities	523 Delivery Expense
210 Accounts Payable	529 Miscellaneous Selling Expense
211 Salaries Payable	530 Office Salaries Expense
212 Unearned Rent	531 Rent Expense
215 Notes Payable	532 Depreciation Expense—Office Equipment
300 Owner's Equity	533 Insurance Expense
310 Chris Clark, Capital	534 Office Supplies Expense
311 Chris Clark, Drawing	539 Misc. Administrative Expense
312 Income Summary	600 Other Income
	610 Rent Revenue
	700 Other Expense
	710 Interest Expense

Recording Merchandise Transactions Under the Periodic Inventory System

Using the periodic inventory system, purchases of inventory are not recorded in the merchandise inventory account. Instead, purchases, purchases discounts, and purchases returns and allowances accounts are used. In addition, the sales of merchandise are not recorded in the inventory account. Thus, there is no detailed record of the amount of inventory on hand at any given time. At the end of the period, a physical count of merchandise inventory on hand is taken. This physical count is used to determine the cost of merchandise sold as shown in Exhibit 12.

The use of purchases, purchases discounts, purchases returns and allowances, and freight in accounts are described below.

Purchases Purchases of inventory are recorded in a purchases account rather than in the merchandise inventory account. Purchases is debited for the invoice amount of a purchase.

Purchases Discounts Purchases discounts are normally recorded in a separate purchases discounts account. The balance of the purchases discounts account is reported as a deduction from Purchases for the period. Thus, Purchases Discounts is a contra (or offsetting) account to Purchases.

Purchases Returns and Allowances Purchases returns and allowances are recorded in a similar manner as purchases discounts. A separate purchases returns and allowances account is used to record returns and allowances. Purchases returns and allowances are reported as a deduction from Purchases for the period. Thus, Purchases Returns and Allowances is a contra (or offsetting) account to Purchases.

Freight In When merchandise is purchased FOB shipping point, the buyer pays for the freight. Under the periodic inventory system, freight paid when purchasing merchandise FOB shipping point is debited to Freight In, Transportation In, or a similar account.

The preceding periodic inventory accounts and their effect on the cost of merchandise purchased are summarized below.

Account	Entry to Increase	Normal Balance	Effect on Cost of Merchandise Purchased
Purchases	Debit	Debit	Increases
Purchases Discounts	Credit	Credit	Decreases
Purchases Returns and Allowances	Credit	Credit	Decreases
Freight In	Debit	Debit	Increases

Exhibit 14 illustrates the recording of merchandise transactions using the periodic system. As a review, Exhibit 14 also illustrates how each transaction would have been recorded using the perpetual system.

EXHIBIT 14 **Transactions Using the Periodic and Perpetual Inventory Systems**

Transaction	Periodic Inventory System			Perpetual Inventory System		
June 5. Purchased $30,000 of merchandise on account, terms 2/10, n/30.	Purchases	30,000		Merchandise Inventory	30,000	
	Accounts Payable		30,000	Accounts Payable		30,000
June 8. Returned merchandise purchased on account on June 5, $500.	Accounts Payable	500		Accounts Payable	500	
	Purchases Returns and Allowances		500	Merchandise Inventory		500
June 15. Paid for purchase of June 5, less return of $500 and discount of $590 [($30,000 – $500) × 2%].	Accounts Payable	29,500		Accounts Payable	29,500	
	Cash		28,910	Cash		28,910
	Purchases Discounts		590	Merchandise Inventory		590
June 18. Sold merchandise on account, $12,500, 1/10, n/30. The cost of the merchandise sold was $9,000.	Accounts Receivable	12,500		Accounts Receivable	12,500	
	Sales		12,500	Sales		12,500
				Cost of Merchandise Sold	9,000	
				Merchandise Inventory		9,000
June 21. Received merchandise returned on account, $4,000. The cost of the merchandise returned was $2,800.	Sales Returns and Allowances	4,000		Sales Returns and Allowances	4,000	
	Accounts Receivable		4,000	Accounts Receivable		4,000
				Merchandise Inventory	2,800	
				Cost of Merchandise Sold		2,800
June 22. Purchased merchandise, $15,000, terms FOB shipping point, 2/15, n/30, with prepaid freight of $750 added to the invoice.	Purchases	15,000		Merchandise Inventory	15,750	
	Freight In	750		Accounts Payable		15,750
	Accounts Payable		15,750			
June 28. Received $8,415 as payment on account from June 18 sale less return of June 21 and less discount of $85 [($12,500 – $4,000) × 1%].	Cash	8,415		Cash	8,415	
	Sales Discounts	85		Sales Discounts	85	
	Accounts Receivable		8,500	Accounts Receivable		8,500
June 29. Received $19,600 from cash sales. The cost of the merchandise sold was $13,800.	Cash	19,600		Cash	19,600	
	Sales		19,600	Sales		19,600
				Cost of Merchandise Sold	13,800	
				Merchandise Inventory		13,800

Adjusting Process Under the Periodic Inventory System

The adjusting process is the same under the periodic and perpetual inventory systems except for the inventory shrinkage adjustment. The ending merchandise inventory is determined by a physical count under both systems.

Under the perpetual inventory system, the ending inventory physical count is compared to the balance of Merchandise Inventory. The difference is the amount of inventory shrinkage. The inventory shrinkage is then recorded as a debit to Cost of Merchandise Sold and a credit to Merchandise Inventory.

Under the periodic inventory system, the merchandise inventory account is not kept up to date for purchases and sales. As a result, the inventory shrinkage cannot be directly determined. Instead, any inventory shrinkage is included indirectly in the computation of cost of merchandise sold as shown in Exhibit 12. This is a major disadvantage of the periodic inventory system. That is, under the periodic inventory system, inventory shrinkage is not separately determined.

Financial Statements Under the Periodic Inventory System

The financial statements are similar under the perpetual and periodic inventory systems. When the multiple-step format of income statement is used, cost of merchandise sold may be reported as shown in Exhibit 12.

Closing Entries Under the Periodic Inventory System

The closing entries differ in the periodic inventory system in that there is no cost of merchandise sold account to close to Income Summary. Instead, the purchases, purchases discounts, purchases returns and allowances, and freight in accounts are closed to Income Summary. In addition, the merchandise inventory account is adjusted to the end-of-period physical inventory count during the closing process.

The four closing entries under the periodic inventory system are as follows:

1. Debit each temporary account with a credit balance, such as Sales, for its balance and credit Income Summary. Since Purchases Discounts and Purchases Returns and Allowances are temporary accounts with credit balances, they are debited for their balances. In addition, Merchandise Inventory is debited for its end-of-period balance based on the end-of-period physical inventory.
2. Credit each temporary account with a debit balance, such as the various expenses, and debit Income Summary. Since Sales Returns and Allowances, Sales Discounts, Purchases, and Freight In are temporary accounts with debit balances, they are credited for their balances. In addition, Merchandise Inventory is credited for its balance as of the beginning of the period.
3. Debit Income Summary for the amount of its balance (net income) and credit the owner's capital account. The accounts debited and credited are reversed if there is a net loss.
4. Debit the owner's capital account for the balance of the drawing account and credit the drawing account.

The four closing entries for NetSolutions under the periodic inventory system are shown on the next page.

Journal

Date		Item	Post. Ref.	Debit	Credit
2013		Closing Entries			
Dec.	31	Merchandise Inventory	115	62,150	
		Sales	410	720,185	
		Purchases Returns and Allowances	511	9,100	
		Purchases Discounts	512	2,525	
		Rent Revenue	610	600	
		Income Summary	312		794,560
	31	Income Summary	312	719,160	
		Merchandise Inventory	115		59,700
		Sales Returns and Allowances	411		6,140
		Sales Discounts	412		5,790
		Purchases	510		521,980
		Freight In	513		17,400
		Sales Salaries Expense	520		53,430
		Advertising Expense	521		10,860
		Depreciation Expense—Store Equipment	522		3,100
		Delivery Expense	523		2,800
		Miscellaneous Selling Expense	529		630
		Office Salaries Expense	530		21,020
		Rent Expense	531		8,100
		Depreciation Expense—Office Equipment	532		2,490
		Insurance Expense	533		1,910
		Office Supplies Expense	534		610
		Miscellaneous Administrative Expense	539		760
		Interest Expense	710		2,440
	31	Income Summary	312	75,400	
		Chris Clark, Capital	310		75,400
	31	Chris Clark, Capital	310	18,000	
		Chris Clark, Drawing	311		18,000

In the first closing entry, Merchandise Inventory is debited for $62,150. This is the ending physical inventory count on December 31, 2013. In the second closing entry, Merchandise Inventory is credited for its January 1, 2013, balance of $59,700. In this way, the closing entries highlight the importance of the beginning and ending balances of Merchandise Inventory in determining cost of merchandise sold, as shown in Exhibit 12. After the closing entries are posted, Merchandise Inventory will have a balance of $62,150. This is the amount reported on the December 31, 2013, balance sheet.

In the preceding closing entries, the periodic accounts are highlighted in color. Under the perpetual inventory system, the highlighted periodic inventory accounts are replaced by the cost of merchandise sold account.

At a Glance 6

Distinguish between the activities and financial statements of service and merchandising businesses.

Key Points Merchandising businesses purchase merchandise for selling to customers.

On a merchandising business's income statement, revenue from selling merchandise is reported as sales. The cost of the merchandise sold is subtracted from sales to arrive at gross profit. The operating expenses are subtracted from gross profit to arrive at net income. Merchandise inventory, which is merchandise not sold, is reported as a current asset on the balance sheet.

Learning Outcomes	Example Exercises	Practice Exercises
• Describe how the activities of a service and a merchandising business differ.		
• Describe the differences between the income statements of a service and a merchandising business.		
• Compute gross profit.	EE6-1	PE6-1A, 6-1B
• Describe how merchandise inventory is reported on the balance sheet.		

Describe and illustrate the financial statements of a merchandising business.

Key Points The multiple-step income statement of a merchandiser reports sales, sales returns and allowances, sales discounts, and net sales. The cost of the merchandise sold is subtracted from net sales to determine the gross profit. Operating income is determined by subtracting selling and administrative expenses from gross profit. Net income is determined by adding or subtracting the net of other income and expense. The income statement may also be reported in a single-step form.

The statement of owner's equity is similar to that for a service business.

The balance sheet reports merchandise inventory at the end of the period as a current asset.

Learning Outcomes	Example Exercises	Practice Exercises
• Prepare a multiple-step income statement for a merchandising business.		
• Prepare a single-step income statement.		
• Prepare a statement of owner's equity for a merchandising business.		
• Prepare a balance sheet for a merchandising business.		

Describe and illustrate the accounting for merchandise transactions including:

- sale of merchandise
- purchase of merchandise
- freight
- sales taxes and trade discounts
- dual nature of merchandising transactions

Key Points The chart of accounts for a merchandising business (NetSolutions) is shown in Exhibit 5. Sales of merchandise for cash or on account are recorded as sales. The cost of merchandise sold and the reduction in merchandise inventory are also recorded at the time of sale. Discounts for early payment of sales on account are recorded as sales discounts. Price adjustments and returned merchandise are recorded as sales returns and allowances.

Purchases of merchandise for cash or on account are recorded as merchandise inventory. Discounts for early payment of purchases on account are recorded as purchases discounts. Price adjustments or returned merchandise are recorded as purchases returns and allowances.

When merchandise is shipped FOB shipping point, the buyer pays the freight and debits Merchandise Inventory. When merchandise is shipped FOB destination, the seller pays the freight and debits Delivery Expense or Freight Out.

The liability for sales tax is incurred when the sale is made and is recorded by the seller as a credit to the sales tax payable account. Trade discounts are discounts off the list price of merchandise.

Each merchandising transaction affects a buyer and a seller.

Learning Outcomes	Example Exercises	Practice Exercises
• Prepare journal entries to record sales of merchandise for cash or using a credit card.		
• Prepare journal entries to record sales of merchandise on account.	EE6-2	PE6-2A, 6-2B
• Prepare journal entries to record sales discounts and sales returns and allowances.	EE6-2	PE6-2A, 6-2B
• Prepare journal entries to record the purchase of merchandise for cash.		
• Prepare journal entries to record the purchase of merchandise on account.	EE6-3	PE6-3A, 6-3B
• Prepare journal entries to record purchases discounts and purchases returns and allowances.	EE6-3	PE6-3A, 6-3B
• Prepare journal entries for freight from the point of view of the buyer and seller.		
• Determine the total cost of the purchase of merchandise under differing freight terms.	EE6-4	PE6-4A, 6-4B
• Prepare journal entries for the collection and payment of sales taxes by the seller.		
• Determine the cost of merchandise purchased when a trade discount is offered by the seller.		
• Record the same merchandise transactions for the buyer and seller.	EE6-5	PE6-5A, 6-5B

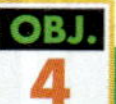

Describe the adjusting and closing process for a merchandising business.

Key Points The normal adjusting entry for inventory shrinkage is to debit Cost of Merchandise Sold and credit Merchandise Inventory.

The closing entries for a merchandising business are similar to those for a service business except that the cost of merchandise sold, sales discounts, and sales returns and allowances accounts are also closed to Income Summary.

Learning Outcomes	Example Exercises	Practice Exercises
• Prepare the adjusting journal entry for inventory shrinkage.	EE6-6	PE6-6A, 6-6B
• Prepare the closing entries for a merchandising business.		

OBJ. 5

Describe and illustrate the use of the ratio of net sales to assets in evaluating a company's operating performance.

Key Points The ratio of net sales to assets measures how effectively a business is using its assets to generate sales. A high ratio indicates an effective use of assets. Using the average of the total assets at the beginning and end of the year, the ratio is computed as follows:

$$\text{Ratio of Net Sales to Assets} = \frac{\text{Net Sales}}{\text{Average Total Assets}}$$

Learning Outcomes	Example Exercises	Practice Exercises
• Interpret a high ratio of net sales to assets.		
• Compute the ratio of net sales to assets.	EE6-7	PE6-7A, 6-7B

Key Terms

account form (258)
administrative expenses (general expenses) (257)
cost of merchandise sold (254)
credit memorandum (credit memo) (263)
credit period (262)
credit terms (262)
debit memorandum (debit memo) (267)
FOB (free on board) destination (269)
FOB (free on board) shipping point (269)
gross profit (254)
income from operations (operating income) (257)
inventory shrinkage (inventory shortage) (274)
invoice (262)
merchandise inventory (254)
multiple-step income statement (255)
net sales (257)
other expense (258)
other income (258)
periodic inventory system (257)
perpetual inventory system (257)
purchases discounts (266)
purchases returns and allowances (267)
ratio of net sales to assets (276)
report form (259)
sales (256)
sales discounts (256)
sales returns and allowances (256)
selling expenses (257)
single-step income statement (258)
trade discounts (272)

Illustrative Problem

The following transactions were completed by Montrose Company during May of the current year. Montrose Company uses a perpetual inventory system.

May 3. Purchased merchandise on account from Floyd Co., $4,000, terms FOB shipping point, 2/10, n/30, with prepaid freight of $120 added to the invoice.

5. Purchased merchandise on account from Kramer Co., $8,500, terms FOB destination, 1/10, n/30.

6. Sold merchandise on account to C. F. Howell Co., list price $4,000, trade discount 30%, terms 2/10, n/30. The cost of the merchandise sold was $1,125.

8. Purchased office supplies for cash, $150.

10. Returned merchandise purchased on May 5 from Kramer Co., $1,300.

13. Paid Floyd Co. on account for purchase of May 3, less discount.

May 14. Purchased merchandise for cash, $10,500.

15. Paid Kramer Co. on account for purchase of May 5, less return of May 10 and discount.

16. Received cash on account from sale of May 6 to C. F. Howell Co., less discount.

19. Sold merchandise on MasterCard credit cards, $2,450. The cost of the merchandise sold was $980.

22. Sold merchandise on account to Comer Co., $3,480, terms 2/10, n/30. The cost of the merchandise sold was $1,400.

24. Sold merchandise for cash, $4,350. The cost of the merchandise sold was $1,750.

25. Received merchandise returned by Comer Co. from sale on May 22, $1,480. The cost of the returned merchandise was $600.

31. Paid a service processing fee of $140 for MasterCard sales.

Instructions

1. Journalize the preceding transactions.
2. Journalize the adjusting entry for merchandise inventory shrinkage, $3,750.

Solution

1.	May	3	Merchandise Inventory	4,120	
			Accounts Payable—Floyd Co.		4,120
		5	Merchandise Inventory	8,500	
			Accounts Payable—Kramer Co.		8,500
		6	Accounts Receivable—C. F. Howell Co.	2,800	
			Sales		2,800
			[$4,000 – (30% × $4,000)]		
		6	Cost of Merchandise Sold	1,125	
			Merchandise Inventory		1,125
		8	Office Supplies	150	
			Cash		150
		10	Accounts Payable—Kramer Co.	1,300	
			Merchandise Inventory		1,300
		13	Accounts Payable—Floyd Co.	4,120	
			Merchandise Inventory		80
			Cash		4,040
			[$4,000 – (2% × $4,000) + $120]		
		14	Merchandise Inventory	10,500	
			Cash		10,500
		15	Accounts Payable—Kramer Co.	7,200	
			Merchandise Inventory		72
			Cash		7,128
			[($8,500 – $1,300) × 1% = $72; $8,500 – $1,300 – $72 = $7,128]		
		16	Cash	2,744	
			Sales Discounts	56	
			Accounts Receivable—C. F. Howell Co.		2,800
		19	Cash	2,450	
			Sales		2,450
		19	Cost of Merchandise Sold	980	
			Merchandise Inventory		980
		22	Accounts Receivable—Comer Co.	3,480	
			Sales		3,480
		22	Cost of Merchandise Sold	1,400	
			Merchandise Inventory		1,400
		24	Cash	4,350	
			Sales		4,350

	May 24	Cost of Merchandise Sold	1,750	
		Merchandise Inventory		1,750
	25	Sales Returns and Allowances	1,480	
		Accounts Receivable—Comer Co.		1,480
	25	Merchandise Inventory	600	
		Cost of Merchandise Sold		600
	31	Credit Card Expense	140	
		Cash		140
2.	May 31	Cost of Merchandise Sold	3,750	
		Merchandise Inventory		3,750
		Inventory shrinkage.		

Discussion Questions

1. What distinguishes a merchandising business from a service business?
2. Can a business earn a gross profit but incur a net loss? Explain.
3. Name at least three accounts that would normally appear in the chart of accounts of a merchandising business but would not appear in the chart of accounts of a service business.
4. How are sales to customers using MasterCard and VISA recorded?
5. The credit period during which the buyer of merchandise is allowed to pay usually begins with what date?
6. What is the meaning of (a) 1/15, n/60; (b) n/30; (c) n/eom?
7. What is the nature of (a) a credit memo issued by the seller of merchandise, (b) a debit memo issued by the buyer of merchandise?
8. Who bears the freight when the terms of sale are (a) FOB shipping point, (b) FOB destination?
9. Mountain Gear Inc., which uses a perpetual inventory system, experienced a normal inventory shrinkage of $21,950. What accounts would be debited and credited to record the adjustment for the inventory shrinkage at the end of the accounting period?
10. Assume that Mountain Gear Inc. in Discussion Question 9 experienced an abnormal inventory shrinkage of $263,750. Mountain Gear Inc. has decided to record the abnormal inventory shrinkage so that it would be separately disclosed on the income statement. What account would be debited for the abnormal inventory shrinkage?

Practice Exercises

Learning Objectives	Example Exercises

OBJ. 1 EE 6-1 p. 255

PE 6-1A Gross profit

During the current year, merchandise is sold for $275,000 cash and $990,000 on account. The cost of the merchandise sold is $950,000. What is the amount of the gross profit?

OBJ. 1 EE 6-1 p. 255

PE 6-1B Gross profit

During the current year, merchandise is sold for $40,000 cash and $415,000 on account. The cost of the merchandise sold is $360,000. What is the amount of the gross profit?

OBJ. 3 EE 6-2 p. 265

PE 6-2A Sales transactions

Journalize the following merchandise transactions:

a. Sold merchandise on account, $29,000 with terms 2/10, n/30. The cost of the merchandise sold was $21,750.

b. Received payment less the discount.

OBJ. 3 EE 6-2 p. 265

PE 6-2B Sales transactions

Journalize the following merchandise transactions:

a. Sold merchandise on account, $60,000 with terms 1/10, n/30. The cost of the merchandise sold was $40,000.

b. Received payment less the discount.

OBJ. 3 EE 6-3 p. 268

PE 6-3A Purchase transactions

MR Tile Company purchased merchandise on account from a supplier for $9,000, terms 2/10, n/30. MR Tile Company returned $1,500 of the merchandise and received full credit.

a. If MR Tile Company pays the invoice within the discount period, what is the amount of cash required for the payment?

b. Under a perpetual inventory system, what account is credited by MR Tile Company to record the return?

OBJ. 3 EE 6-3 p. 268

PE 6-3B Purchase transactions

Piedmont Company purchased merchandise on account from a supplier for $30,000, terms 1/10, n/30. Piedmont Company returned $4,000 of the merchandise and received full credit.

a. If Piedmont Company pays the invoice within the discount period, what is the amount of cash required for the payment?

b. Under a perpetual inventory system, what account is debited by Piedmont Company to record the return?

OBJ. 3 EE 6-4 p. 271

PE 6-4A Freight terms

Determine the amount to be paid in full settlement of each of invoices (a) and (b), assuming that credit for returns and allowances was received prior to payment and that all invoices were paid within the discount period.

Learning Objectives	Example Exercises

	Merchandise	Freight Paid by Seller	Freight Terms	Returns and Allowances
a.	$120,000	$5,000	FOB shipping point, 1/10, n/30	$15,000
b.	90,000	1,000	FOB destination, 2/10, n/30	2,000

OBJ. 3 EE 6-4 p. 271

PE 6-4B Freight terms

Determine the amount to be paid in full settlement of each of invoices (a) and (b), assuming that credit for returns and allowances was received prior to payment and that all invoices were paid within the discount period.

	Merchandise	Freight Paid by Seller	Freight Terms	Returns and Allowances
a.	$20,000	$500	FOB destination, 1/10, n/30	$2,000
b.	18,000	250	FOB shipping point, 2/10, n/30	1,000

OBJ. 3 EE 6-5 p. 274

PE 6-5A Transactions for buyer and seller

Storall Co. sold merchandise to Bunting Co. on account, $8,000, terms 2/15, n/30. The cost of the merchandise sold is $3,000. Storall Co. issued a credit memo for $1,000 for merchandise returned and later received the amount due within the discount period. The cost of the merchandise returned was $400. Journalize Storall Co.'s and Bunting Co.'s entries for the payment of the amount due.

OBJ. 3 EE 6-5 p. 274

PE 6-5B Transactions for buyer and seller

SPA Co. sold merchandise to Boyd Co. on account, $25,000, terms FOB shipping point, 2/10, n/30. The cost of the merchandise sold is $16,000. SPA Co. paid freight of $675 and later received the amount due within the discount period. Journalize SPA Co.'s and Boyd Co.'s entries for the payment of the amount due.

OBJ. 4 EE 6-6 p. 275

PE 6-6A Inventory shrinkage

House of Clean Company's perpetual inventory records indicate that $375,000 of merchandise should be on hand on June 30, 2012. The physical inventory indicates that $366,500 of merchandise is actually on hand. Journalize the adjusting entry for the inventory shrinkage for House of Clean Company for the year ended June 30, 2012. Assume that the inventory shrinkage is a normal amount.

OBJ. 4 EE 6-6 p. 275

PE 6-6B Inventory shrinkage

Zurich Company's perpetual inventory records indicate that $1,380,000 of merchandise should be on hand on August 31, 2012. The physical inventory indicates that $1,315,900 of merchandise is actually on hand. Journalize the adjusting entry for the inventory shrinkage for Zurich Company for the year ended August 31, 2012. Assume that the inventory shrinkage is a normal amount.

OBJ. 5 EE 6-7 p. 277

F·A·I

PE 6-7A Ratio of net sales to assets

The following financial statement data for years ending December 31 for Foodworks Company are shown below.

	2012	2011
Net sales	$880,000	$787,500
Total assets:		
Beginning of year	500,000	375,000
End of year	600,000	500,000

a. Determine the ratio of net sales to assets for 2012 and 2011.

b. Does the change in the ratio of net sales to assets from 2011 to 2012 indicate a favorable or an unfavorable trend?

CHAPTER 7

Ryan McVay/Digital Vision/Getty Images

Inventories

Best Buy

Assume that in September you purchased a Sony HDTV plasma television from **Best Buy**. At the same time, you purchased a Denon surround sound system for $399.99. You liked your surround sound so well that in November you purchased an identical Denon system on sale for $349.99 for your bedroom TV. Over the holidays, you moved to a new apartment and in the process of unpacking discovered that one of the Denon surround sound systems was missing. Luckily, your renters/homeowners insurance policy will cover the theft, but the insurance company needs to know the cost of the system that was stolen.

The Denon systems were identical. However, to respond to the insurance company, you will need to identify which system was stolen. Was it the first system, which cost $399.99, or was it the second system, which cost $349.99? Whichever assumption you make may determine the amount that you receive from the insurance company.

Merchandising businesses such as Best Buy make similar assumptions when identical merchandise is purchased at different costs. For example, Best Buy may have purchased thousands of Denon surround sound systems over the past year at different costs. At the end of a period, some of the Denon systems will still be in inventory, and some will have been sold. But which costs relate to the sold systems, and which costs relate to the Denon systems still in inventory? Best Buy's assumption about inventory costs can involve large dollar amounts and, thus, can have a significant impact on the financial statements. For example, Best Buy reported $4,753 million of inventory on February 28, 2009, and net income of $1,003 million for the year.

This chapter discusses such issues as how to determine the cost of merchandise in inventory and the cost of merchandise sold. However, this chapter begins by discussing the importance of control over inventory.

Learning Objectives

After studying this chapter, you should be able to:

At a Glance 7 Page 333

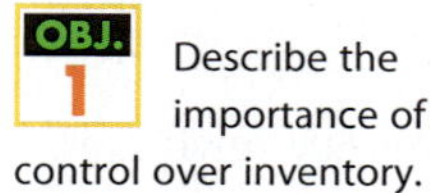

Describe the importance of control over inventory.

Control of Inventory

Two primary objectives of control over inventory are as follows:[1]

1. Safeguarding the inventory from damage or theft.
2. Reporting inventory in the financial statements.

Safeguarding Inventory

Controls for safeguarding inventory begin as soon as the inventory is ordered. The following documents are often used for inventory control:

Purchase order
Receiving report
Vendor's invoice

The **purchase order** authorizes the purchase of the inventory from an approved vendor. As soon as the inventory is received, a receiving report is completed. The **receiving report** establishes an initial record of the receipt of the inventory. To make

1 Additional controls used by businesses are described and illustrated in Chapter 8, "Sarbanes-Oxley, Internal Control, and Cash."

sure the inventory received is what was ordered, the receiving report is compared with the company's purchase order. The price, quantity, and description of the item on the purchase order and receiving report are then compared to the vendor's invoice. If the receiving report, purchase order, and vendor's invoice agree, the inventory is recorded in the accounting records. If any differences exist, they should be investigated and reconciled.

Recording inventory using a perpetual inventory system is also an effective means of control. The amount of inventory is always available in the **subsidiary inventory ledger**. This helps keep inventory quantities at proper levels. For example, comparing inventory quantities with maximum and minimum levels allows for the timely reordering of inventory and prevents ordering excess inventory.

Finally, controls for safeguarding inventory should include security measures to prevent damage and customer or employee theft. Some examples of security measures include the following:

1. Storing inventory in areas that are restricted to only authorized employees.
2. Locking high-priced inventory in cabinets.
3. Using two-way mirrors, cameras, security tags, and guards.

Best Buy uses scanners to screen customers as they leave the store for merchandise that has not been purchased. In addition, Best Buy stations greeters at the store's entrance to keep customers from bringing in bags that can be used to shoplift merchandise.

Reporting Inventory

A **physical inventory** or count of inventory should be taken near year-end to make sure that the quantity of inventory reported in the financial statements is accurate. After the quantity of inventory on hand is determined, the cost of the inventory is assigned for reporting in the financial statements. Most companies assign costs to inventory using one of three inventory cost flow assumptions. If a physical count is not possible or inventory records are not available, the inventory cost may be estimated as described in the appendix at the end of this chapter.

Inventory Cost Flow Assumptions

OBJ. 2 Describe three inventory cost flow assumptions and how they impact the income statement and balance sheet.

An accounting issue arises when identical units of merchandise are acquired at different unit costs during a period. In such cases, when an item is sold, it is necessary to determine its cost using a cost flow assumption and related inventory cost flow method. Three common cost flow assumptions and related inventory cost flow methods are shown below.

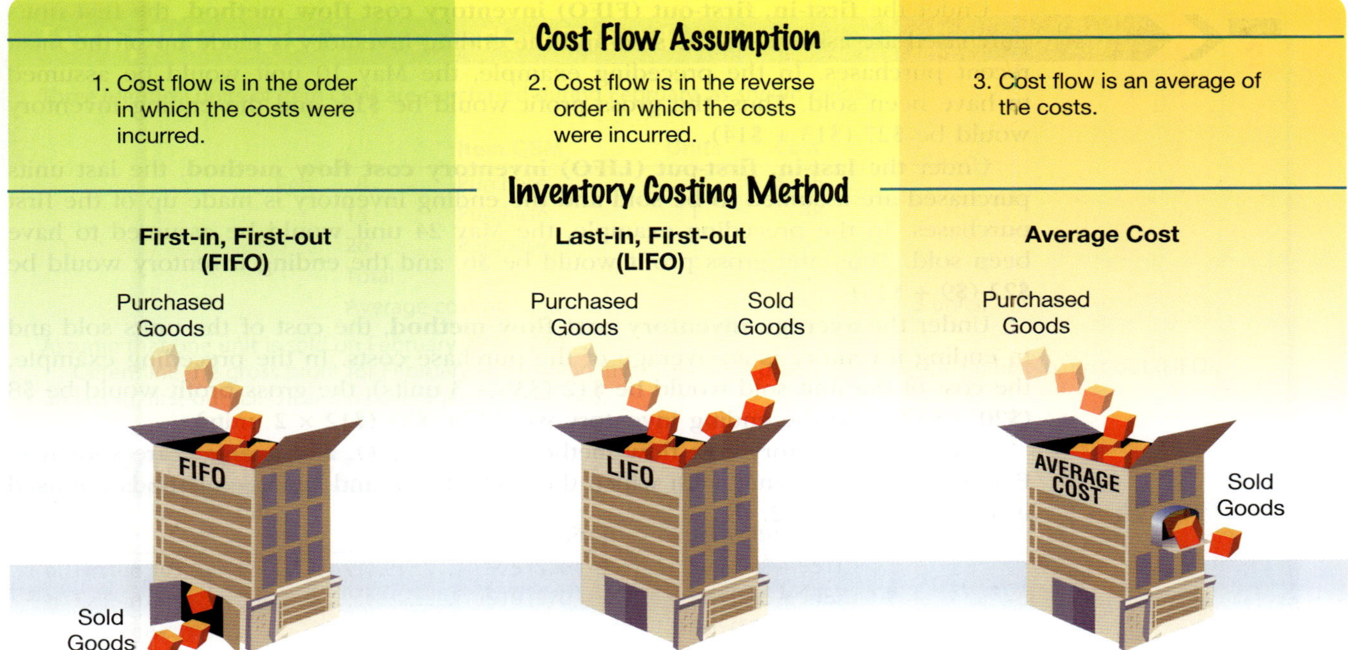

OBJ. 3 Determine the cost of inventory under the perpetual inventory system, using the FIFO, LIFO, and average cost methods.

Inventory Costing Methods Under a Perpetual Inventory System

As illustrated in the prior section, when identical units of an item are purchased at different unit costs, an inventory cost flow method must be used. This is true regardless of whether the perpetual or periodic inventory system is used.

In this section, the FIFO, LIFO, and average cost methods are illustrated under a perpetual inventory system. For purposes of illustration, the data for Item 127B are used, as shown below.

Although e-tailers, such as eToys Direct, Inc., Amazon.com, and Furniture.com, Inc., don't have retail stores, they still take possession of inventory in warehouses. Thus, they must account for inventory as illustrated in this chapter.

		Item 127B	Units	Cost
Jan.	1	Inventory	100	$20
	4	Sale at $30 per unit	70	
	10	Purchase	80	21
	22	Sale at $30 per unit	40	
	28	Sale at $30 per unit	20	
	30	Purchase	100	22

First-In, First-Out Method

When the FIFO method is used, costs are included in cost of merchandise sold in the order in which they were purchased. This is often the same as the physical flow of the merchandise. Thus, the FIFO method often provides results that are about the same as those that would have been obtained using the specific identification method. For example, grocery stores shelve milk and other perishable products by expiration dates. Products with early expiration dates are stocked in front. In this way, the oldest products (earliest purchases) are sold first.

To illustrate, Exhibit 3 shows use of FIFO under a perpetual inventory system for Item 127B. The journal entries and the subsidiary inventory ledger for Item 127B are shown in Exhibit 3 as follows:

1. The beginning balance on January 1 is $2,000 (100 units at a unit cost of $20).
2. On January 4, 70 units were sold at a price of $30 each for sales of $2,100 (70 units × $30). The cost of merchandise sold is $1,400 (70 units at a unit cost of $20). After the sale, there remains $600 of inventory (30 units at a unit cost of $20).

EXHIBIT 3 **Entries and Perpetual Inventory Account (FIFO)**

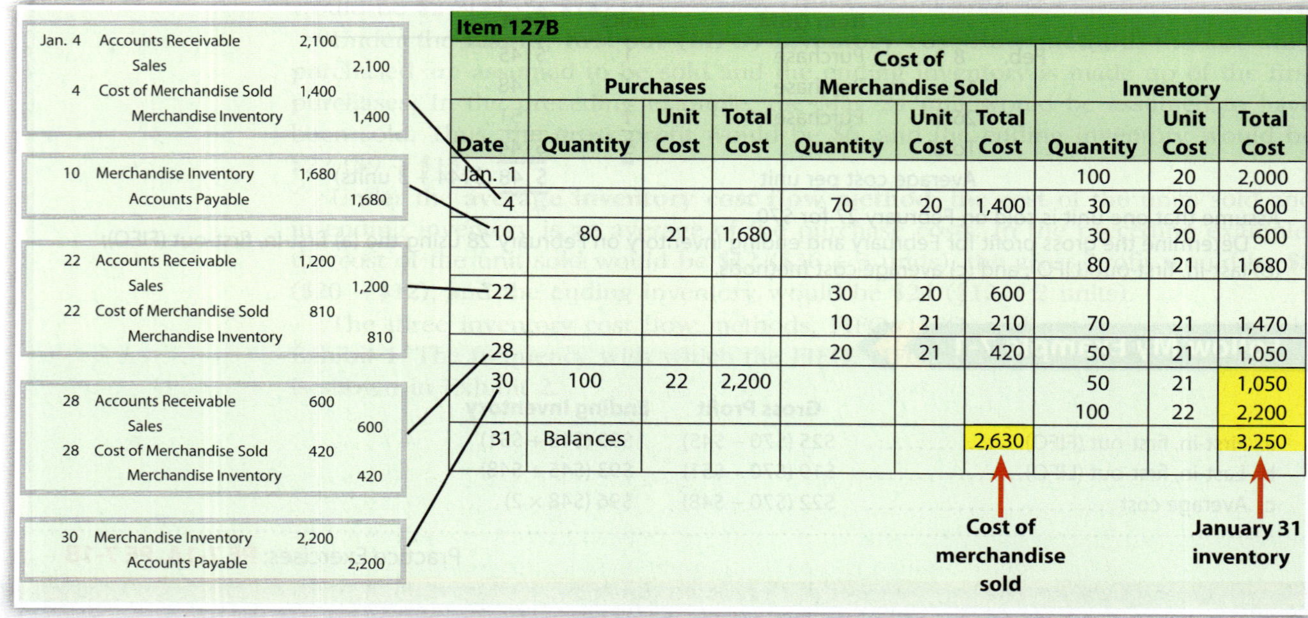

Jan. 4	Accounts Receivable	2,100	
	Sales		2,100
4	Cost of Merchandise Sold	1,400	
	Merchandise Inventory		1,400
10	Merchandise Inventory	1,680	
	Accounts Payable		1,680
22	Accounts Receivable	1,200	
	Sales		1,200
22	Cost of Merchandise Sold	810	
	Merchandise Inventory		810
28	Accounts Receivable	600	
	Sales		600
28	Cost of Merchandise Sold	420	
	Merchandise Inventory		420
30	Merchandise Inventory	2,200	
	Accounts Payable		2,200

Item 127B

	Purchases			Cost of Merchandise Sold			Inventory		
Date	Quantity	Unit Cost	Total Cost	Quantity	Unit Cost	Total Cost	Quantity	Unit Cost	Total Cost
Jan. 1							100	20	2,000
4				70	20	1,400	30	20	600
10	80	21	1,680				30	20	600
							80	21	1,680
22				30	20	600			
				10	21	210	70	21	1,470
28				20	21	420	50	21	1,050
30	100	22	2,200				50	21	1,050
							100	22	2,200
31	Balances					2,630			3,250

3. On January 10, $1,680 is purchased (80 units at a unit cost of $21). After the purchase, the inventory is reported on two lines, $600 (30 units at a unit cost of $20) from the beginning inventory and $1,680 (80 units at a unit cost of $21) from the January 10 purchase.
4. On January 22, 40 units are sold at a price of $30 each for sales of $1,200 (40 units × $30). Using FIFO, the cost of merchandise sold of $810 consists of $600 (30 units at a unit cost of $20) from the beginning inventory plus $210 (10 units at a unit cost of $21) from the January 10 purchase. After the sale, there remains $1,470 of inventory (70 units at a unit cost of $21) from the January 10 purchase.
5. The January 28 sale and January 30 purchase are recorded in a similar manner.
6. The ending balance on January 31 is $3,250. This balance is made up of two layers of inventory as follows:

	Date of Purchase	Quantity	Unit Cost	Total Cost
Layer 1:	Jan. 10	50	$21	$1,050
Layer 2:	Jan. 30	100	22	2,200
Total		150		$3,250

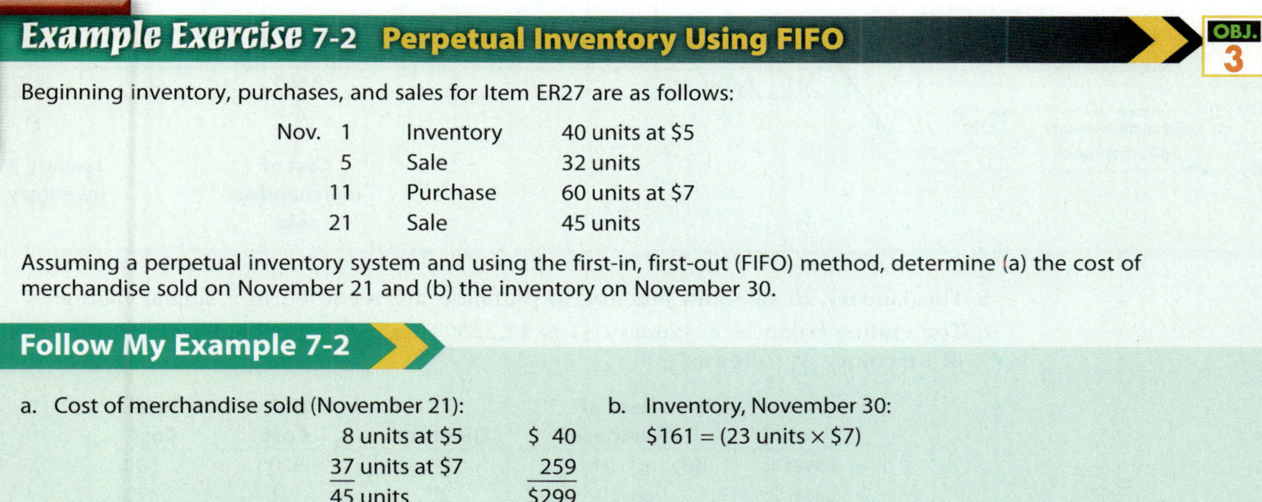

Example Exercise 7-2 Perpetual Inventory Using FIFO OBJ. 3

Beginning inventory, purchases, and sales for Item ER27 are as follows:

Nov. 1	Inventory	40 units at $5
5	Sale	32 units
11	Purchase	60 units at $7
21	Sale	45 units

Assuming a perpetual inventory system and using the first-in, first-out (FIFO) method, determine (a) the cost of merchandise sold on November 21 and (b) the inventory on November 30.

Follow My Example 7-2

a. Cost of merchandise sold (November 21):

8 units at $5	$ 40
37 units at $7	259
45 units	$299

b. Inventory, November 30:
$161 = (23 units × $7)

Practice Exercises: **PE 7-2A, PE 7-2B**

Last-In, First-Out Method

See Appendix D for more information

When the LIFO method is used, the cost of the units sold is the cost of the most recent purchases. The LIFO method was originally used in those rare cases where the units sold were taken from the most recently purchased units. However, for tax purposes, LIFO is now widely used even when it does not represent the physical flow of units. The tax impact of LIFO is discussed later in this chapter.

To illustrate, Exhibit 4 shows the use of LIFO under a perpetual inventory system for Item 127B. The journal entries and the subsidiary inventory ledger for Item 127B are shown in Exhibit 4 as follows:

1. The beginning balance on January 1 is $2,000 (100 units at a unit of cost of $20).
2. On January 4, 70 units were sold at a price of $30 each for sales of $2,100 (70 units × $30). The cost of merchandise sold is $1,400 (70 units at a unit cost of $20). After the sale, there remains $600 of inventory (30 units at a unit cost of $20).
3. On January 10, $1,680 is purchased (80 units at a unit cost of $21). After the purchase, the inventory is reported on two lines, $600 (30 units at a unit cost of $20) from the beginning inventory and $1,680 (80 units at $21 per unit) from the January 10 purchase.
4. On January 22, 40 units are sold at a price of $30 each for sales of $1,200 (40 units × $30). Using LIFO, the cost of merchandise sold is $840 (40 units at unit cost of $21) from the January 10 purchase. After the sale, there remains $1,440 of inventory consisting of $600 (30 units at a unit cost of $20) from the beginning inventory and $840 (40 units at a unit cost of $21) from the January 10 purchase.

EXHIBIT 4 **Entries and Perpetual Inventory Account (LIFO)**

Jan. 4	Accounts Receivable	2,100	
	Sales		2,100
4	Cost of Merchandise Sold	1,400	
	Merchandise Inventory		1,400
10	Merchandise Inventory	1,680	
	Accounts Payable		1,680
22	Accounts Receivable	1,200	
	Sales		1,200
22	Cost of Merchandise Sold	840	
	Merchandise Inventory		840
28	Accounts Receivable	600	
	Sales		600
28	Cost of Merchandise Sold	420	
	Merchandise Inventory		420
30	Merchandise Inventory	2,200	
	Accounts Payable		2,200

Item 127B

	Purchases			Cost of Merchandise Sold			Inventory		
Date	**Quantity**	**Unit Cost**	**Total Cost**	**Quantity**	**Unit Cost**	**Total Cost**	**Quantity**	**Unit Cost**	**Total Cost**
Jan. 1							100	20	2,000
4				70	20	1,400	30	20	600
10	80	21	1,680				30	20	600
							80	21	1,680
22				40	21	840	30	20	600
							40	21	840
28				20	21	420	30	20	600
							20	21	420
30	100	22	2,200				30	20	600
							20	21	420
							100	22	2,200
31	Balances					2,660			3,220

Cost of merchandise sold **January 31 inventory**

5. The January 28 sale and January 30 purchase are recorded in a similar manner.
6. The ending balance on January 31 is $3,220. This balance is made up of three layers of inventory as follows:

	Date of Purchase	Quantity	Unit Cost	Total Cost
Layer 1:	Beg. inv. (Jan. 1)	30	$20	$ 600
Layer 2:	Jan. 10	20	21	420
Layer 3:	Jan. 30	100	22	2,200
Total		150		$3,220

When the LIFO method is used, the subsidiary inventory ledger is sometimes maintained in units only. The units are converted to dollars when the financial statements are prepared at the end of the period.

Example Exercise 7-3 Perpetual Inventory Using LIFO

OBJ. 3

Beginning inventory, purchases, and sales for Item ER27 are as follows:

Nov.	1	Inventory	40 units at $5
	5	Sale	32 units
	11	Purchase	60 units at $7
	21	Sale	45 units

Assuming a perpetual inventory system and using the last-in, first-out (LIFO) method, determine (a) the cost of the merchandise sold on November 21 and (b) the inventory on November 30.

Follow My Example 7-3

a. Cost of merchandise sold (November 21):
$315 = (45 units × $7)

b. Inventory, November 30:

8 units at $5	$ 40
15 units at $7	105
23 units	$145

Practice Exercises: **PE 7-3A, PE 7-3B**

IFRS

International Connection

INTERNATIONAL FINANCIAL REPORTING STANDARDS (IFRS)

IFRS permit the first-in, first-out and average cost methods but prohibit the last-in, first-out (LIFO) method for determining inventory costs. Since LIFO is used in the United States, adoption of IFRS could have a significant impact on many U.S. companies. For example, Caterpillar Inc. uses LIFO and reported that its inventories would have been $3,003 million higher in 2009 if FIFO had been used. Since Caterpillar reported profits of only $895 million in 2009, the adoption of IFRS would have resulted in a loss in 2009 if IFRS and FIFO had been used.*

* Differences between U.S. GAAP and IFRS are further discussed and illustrated in Appendix D.

Average Cost Method

When the average cost method is used in a perpetual inventory system, an average unit cost for each item is computed each time a purchase is made. This unit cost is used to determine the cost of each sale until another purchase is made and a new average is computed. This technique is called a *moving average.* Since the average cost method is rarely used in a perpetual inventory system, it is not illustrated.

Computerized Perpetual Inventory Systems

A perpetual inventory system may be used in a manual accounting system. However, if there are many inventory transactions, such a system is costly and time consuming. In most cases, perpetual inventory systems are computerized.

Computerized perpetual inventory systems are useful to managers in controlling and managing inventory. For example, fast-selling items can be reordered before the stock runs out. Sales patterns can also be analyzed to determine when to mark down merchandise or when to restock seasonal merchandise. Finally, inventory data can be used in evaluating advertising campaigns and sales promotions.

Inventory Costing Methods Under a Periodic Inventory System

OBJ. 4 Determine the cost of inventory under the periodic inventory system, using the FIFO, LIFO, and average cost methods.

When the periodic inventory system is used, only revenue is recorded each time a sale is made. No entry is made at the time of the sale to record the cost of the merchandise sold. At the end of the accounting period, a physical inventory is taken to determine the cost of the inventory and the cost of the merchandise sold.[2]

Like the perpetual inventory system, a cost flow assumption must be made when identical units are acquired at different unit costs during a period. In such cases, the FIFO, LIFO, or average cost method is used.

First-In, First-Out Method

To illustrate the use of the FIFO method in a periodic inventory system, we use the same data for Item 127B as in the perpetual inventory example. The beginning inventory entry and purchases of Item 127B in January are as follows:

Jan. 1	Inventory	100 units at	$20	$2,000
10	Purchase	80 units at	21	1,680
30	Purchase	100 units at	22	2,200
Available for sale during month		280		$5,880

2 Determining the cost of merchandise sold using the periodic system was illustrated in the appendix to Chapter 6.

The physical count on January 31 shows that 150 units are on hand. Using the FIFO method, the cost of the merchandise on hand at the end of the period is made up of the most recent costs. The cost of the 150 units in ending inventory on January 31 is determined as follows:

Most recent costs, January 30 purchase	100 units at	$22	$2,200
Next most recent costs, January 10 purchase	50 units at	$21	1,050
Inventory, January 31	150 units		$3,250

Deducting the cost of the January 31 inventory of $3,250 from the cost of merchandise available for sale of $5,880 yields the cost of merchandise sold of $2,630, as shown below.

Beginning inventory, January 1	$2,000
Purchases ($1,680 + $2,200)	3,880
Cost of merchandise available for sale in January	$5,880
Less ending inventory, January 31	3,250
Cost of merchandise sold	$2,630

The $3,250 cost of the ending merchandise inventory on January 31 is made up of the most recent costs. The $2,630 cost of merchandise sold is made up of the beginning inventory and the earliest costs. Exhibit 5 shows the relationship of the cost of merchandise sold for January and the ending inventory on January 31.

EXHIBIT 5

First-In, First-Out Flow of Costs

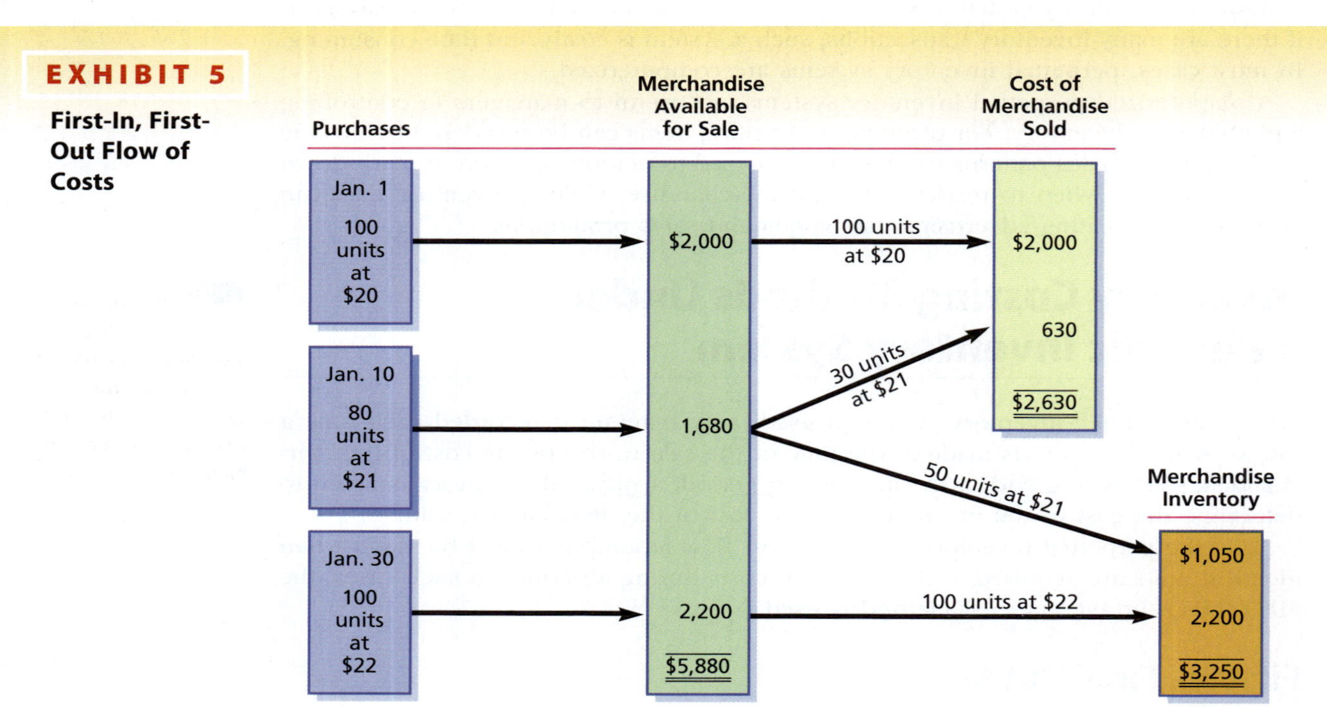

Last-In, First-Out Method

See Appendix D for more information

When the LIFO method is used, the cost of merchandise on hand at the end of the period is made up of the earliest costs. Based on the same data as in the FIFO example, the cost of the 150 units in ending inventory on January 31 is determined as follows:

Beginning inventory, January 1	100 units at	$20	$2,000
Next earliest costs, January 10	50 units at	$21	1,050
Inventory, January 31	150 units		$3,050

Deducting the cost of the January 31 inventory of $3,050 from the cost of merchandise available for sale of $5,880 yields the cost of merchandise sold of $2,830, as shown below.

Beginning inventory, January 1	$2,000
Purchases ($1,680 + $2,200)	3,880
Cost of merchandise available for sale in January	$5,880
Less ending inventory, January 31	3,050
Cost of merchandise sold	$2,830

The $3,050 cost of the ending merchandise inventory on January 31 is made up of the earliest costs. The $2,830 cost of merchandise sold is made up of the most recent costs. Exhibit 6 shows the relationship of the cost of merchandise sold for January and the ending inventory on January 31.

EXHIBIT 6

Last-In, First-Out Flow of Costs

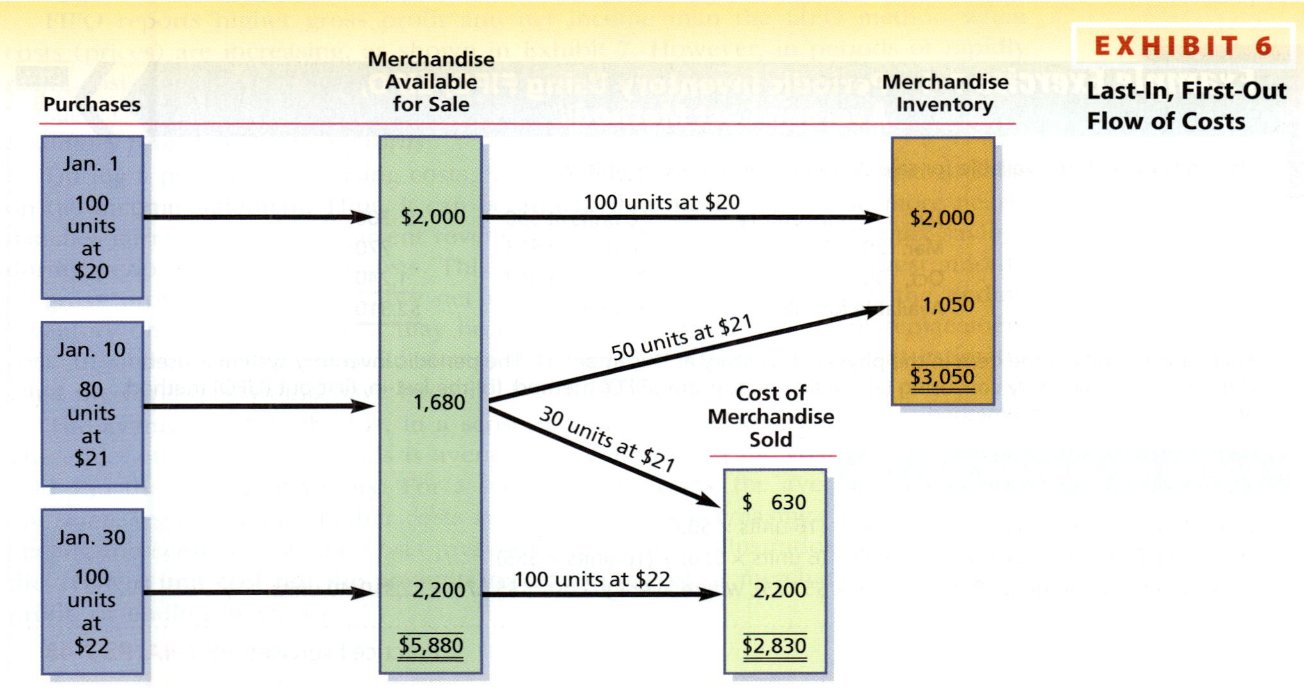

Average Cost Method

The average cost method is sometimes called the *weighted average method*. The average cost method uses the average unit cost for determining cost of merchandise sold and the ending merchandise inventory. If purchases are relatively uniform during a period, the average cost method provides results that are similar to the physical flow of goods.

The weighted average unit cost is determined as follows:

$$\text{Average Unit Cost} = \frac{\text{Total Cost of Units Available for Sale}}{\text{Units Available for Sale}}$$

324 Chapter 7 Inventories

Integrity, Objectivity, and Ethics in Business

WHERE'S THE BONUS?

Managers are often given bonuses based on reported earnings numbers. This can create a conflict. LIFO can improve the value of the company through lower taxes. However, in periods of rising costs (prices), LIFO also produces a lower earnings number and, therefore, lower management bonuses. Ethically, managers should select accounting procedures that will maximize the value of the firm, rather than their own compensation. Compensation specialists can help avoid this ethical dilemma by adjusting the bonus plan for the accounting procedure differences.

Describe and illustrate the reporting of merchandise inventory in the financial statements.

Reporting Merchandise Inventory in the Financial Statements

Cost is the primary basis for valuing and reporting inventories in the financial statements. However, inventory may be valued at other than cost in the following cases:

1. The cost of replacing items in inventory is below the recorded cost.
2. The inventory cannot be sold at normal prices due to imperfections, style changes, or other causes.

Valuation at Lower of Cost or Market

See Appendix D for more information

If the cost of replacing inventory is lower than its recorded purchase cost, the **lower-of-cost-or-market (LCM) method** is used to value the inventory. *Market,* as used in *lower of cost or market,* is the cost to replace the inventory. The market value is based on normal quantities that would be purchased from suppliers.

The lower-of-cost-or-market method can be applied in one of three ways. The cost, market price, and any declines could be determined for the following:

1. Each item in the inventory.
2. Each major class or category of inventory.
3. Total inventory as a whole.

The amount of any price decline is included in the cost of merchandise sold. This, in turn, reduces gross profit and net income in the period in which the price declines occur. This matching of price declines to the period in which they occur is the primary advantage of using the lower-of-cost-or-market method.

To illustrate, assume the following data for 400 identical units of Item A in inventory on December 31, 2012:

Unit purchased cost	$10.25
Replacement cost on December 31, 2012	9.50

Since Item A could be replaced at $9.50 a unit, $9.50 is used under the lower-of-cost-or-market method.

Exhibit 8 illustrates applying the lower-of-cost-or-market method to each inventory item (A, B, C, and D). As applied on an item-by-item basis, the total lower-of-cost-or-market is $15,070, which is a market decline of $450 ($15,520 − $15,070). This market decline of $450 is included in the cost of merchandise sold.

In Exhibit 8, Items A, B, C, and D could be viewed as a class of inventory items. If the lower-of-cost-or-market method is applied to the class, the inventory would be valued at $15,472, which is a market decline of $48 ($15,520 − $15,472). Likewise, if Items A, B, C, and D make up the total inventory, the lower-of-cost-or-market method as applied to the total inventory would be the same amount, $15,472.

	A	B	C	D	E	F	G
1			Unit	Unit		Total	
2		Inventory	Cost	Market			Lower
3	Item	Quantity	Price	Price	Cost	Market	of C or M
4	A	400	$10.25	$ 9.50	$ 4,100	$ 3,800	$ 3,800
5	B	120	22.50	24.10	2,700	2,892	2,700
6	C	600	8.00	7.75	4,800	4,650	4,650
7	D	280	14.00	14.75	3,920	4,130	3,920
8	Total				$15,520	$15,472	$15,070
9							

EXHIBIT 8

Determining Inventory at Lower of Cost or Market

Example Exercise 7-5 Lower-of-Cost-or-Market Method

OBJ. 6

On the basis of the following data, determine the value of the inventory at the lower of cost or market. Apply lower of cost or market to each inventory item as shown in Exhibit 8.

Item	Inventory Quantity	Unit Cost Price	Unit Market Price
C17Y	10	$ 39	$40
B563	7	110	98

Follow My Example 7-5

	A	B	C	D	E	F	G
1			Unit	Unit		Total	
2		Inventory	Cost	Market			Lower
3	Item	Quantity	Price	Price	Cost	Market	of C or M
4	C17Y	10	$ 39	$ 40	$ 390	$ 400	$ 390
5	B563	7	110	98	770	686	686
6	Total				$1,160	$1,086	$1,076
7							

Practice Exercises: **PE 7-5A, PE 7-5B**

Valuation at Net Realizable Value

Merchandise that is out of date, spoiled, or damaged can often be sold only at a price below its original cost. Such merchandise should be valued at its **net realizable value**. Net realizable value is determined as follows:

Net Realizable Value = Estimated Selling Price – Direct Costs of Disposal

Direct costs of disposal include selling expenses such as special advertising or sales commissions. To illustrate, assume the following data about an item of damaged merchandise:

Original cost	$1,000
Estimated selling price	800
Selling expenses	150

The merchandise should be valued at its net realizable value of $650 as shown below.

Net Realizable Value = $800 – $150 = $650

Business Connection

INVENTORY WRITE-DOWNS

Worthington Industries, Inc., is a diversified metal processing company that manufactures metal products, such as metal framing and pressure cylinders. During the year ended May 31, 2009, the company experienced rapidly changing business conditions. Due to the global financial crisis and recession, steel prices underwent a severe and rapid decline. As a result, the company recorded an inventory write-down of $105 million and an overall net loss of $108 million for the year.

Merchandise Inventory on the Balance Sheet

See Appendix D for more information

Merchandise inventory is usually reported in the Current Assets section of the balance sheet. In addition to this amount, the following are reported:

1. The method of determining the cost of the inventory (FIFO, LIFO, or average)
2. The method of valuing the inventory (cost or the lower of cost or market)

The financial statement reporting for the topics covered in Chapters 7–15 are illustrated using excerpts from the financial statements of Mornin' Joe. Mornin' Joe is a fictitious company that offers drip and espresso coffee in a coffeehouse setting. The complete financial statements of Mornin' Joe are illustrated at the end of Chapter 15 (pages 713–716).

The balance sheet presentation for merchandise inventory for Mornin' Joe is as follows:

Mornin' Joe
Balance Sheet
December 31, 2012

Current assets:		
Cash and cash equivalents		$235,000
Trading investments (at cost)	$420,000	
Plus valuation allowance on trading investments	45,000	465,000
Accounts receivable	$305,000	
Less allowance for doubtful accounts	12,300	292,700
Merchandise inventory—at lower of cost (first-in, first-out method) or market		120,000

It is not unusual for a large business to use different costing methods for segments of its inventories. Also, a business may change its inventory costing method. In such cases, the effect of the change and the reason for the change are disclosed in the financial statements.

Effect of Inventory Errors on the Financial Statements

Any errors in merchandise inventory will affect the balance sheet and income statement. Some reasons that inventory errors may occur include the following:

1. Physical inventory on hand was miscounted.
2. Costs were incorrectly assigned to inventory. For example, the FIFO, LIFO, or average cost method was incorrectly applied.
3. Inventory in transit was incorrectly included or excluded from inventory.
4. Consigned inventory was incorrectly included or excluded from inventory.

Inventory errors often arise from merchandise that is in transit at year-end. As discussed in Chapter 6, shipping terms determine when the title to merchandise passes. When goods are purchased or sold *FOB shipping point*, title passes to the buyer when the goods are shipped. When the terms are *FOB destination*, title passes to the buyer when the goods are received.

To illustrate, assume that SysExpress ordered the following merchandise from American Products:

Date ordered:	December 27, 2011
Amount:	$10,000
Terms:	FOB shipping point, 2/10, n/30
Date shipped by seller:	December 30
Date delivered:	January 3, 2012

When SysExpress counts its physical inventory on December 31, 2011, the merchandise is still in transit. In such cases, it would be easy for SysExpress to not include the $10,000 of merchandise in its December 31 physical inventory. However, since the merchandise was purchased *FOB shipping point*, SysExpress owns the merchandise. Thus, it should be included in the ending December 31 inventory even though it is not on hand. Likewise, any merchandise *sold* by SysExpress *FOB destination* is still SysExpress's inventory even if it is in transit to the buyer on December 31.

Inventory errors often arise from **consigned inventory**. Manufacturers sometimes ship merchandise to retailers who act as the manufacturer's selling agent. The manufacturer, called the **consignor**, retains title until the goods are sold. Such merchandise is said to be shipped *on consignment* to the retailer, called the **consignee**. Any unsold merchandise at year-end is a part of the manufacturer's (consignor's) inventory, even though the merchandise is in the hands of the retailer (consignee). At year-end, it would be easy for the retailer (consignee) to incorrectly include the consigned merchandise in its physical inventory. Likewise, the manufacturer (consignor) should include consigned inventory in its physical inventory even though the inventory is not on hand.

Income Statement Effects Inventory errors will misstate the income statement amounts for cost of merchandise sold, gross profit, and net income. The effects of inventory errors on the current period's income statement are summarized in Exhibit 9.

EXHIBIT 9

Effect of Inventory Errors on Current Period's Income Statement

	Income Statement Effect		
Inventory Error	**Cost of Merchandise Sold**	**Gross Profit**	**Net Income**
Beginning inventory is:			
Understated	*Understated*	*Overstated*	*Overstated*
Overstated	*Overstated*	*Understated*	*Understated*
Ending inventory is:			
Understated	*Overstated*	*Understated*	*Understated*
Overstated	*Understated*	*Overstated*	*Overstated*

To illustrate, the income statements of SysExpress shown in Exhibit 10 are used.[5] On December 31, 2011, assume that SysExpress incorrectly records its physical inventory as $50,000 instead of the correct amount of $60,000. Thus, the December 31, 2011, inventory is understated by $10,000 ($60,000 – $50,000). As a result, the cost of merchandise sold is overstated by $10,000. The gross profit and the net income for the year will also be understated by $10,000.

The December 31, 2011, merchandise inventory becomes the January 1, 2012, inventory. Thus, the beginning inventory for 2012 is understated by $10,000. As a result, the cost of merchandise sold is understated by $10,000 for 2012. The gross profit and net income for 2012 will be overstated by $10,000.

As shown in Exhibit 10, since the ending inventory of one period is the beginning inventory of the next period, the effects of inventory errors carry forward to the next period. Specifically, if uncorrected, the effects of inventory errors reverse themselves

5 The effect of inventory errors will be illustrated using the periodic system. This is because it is easier to see the impact of inventory errors on the income statement using the periodic system. The effect of inventory errors would be the same under the perpetual inventory system.

EXHIBIT 10 **Effects of Inventory Errors on Two Years' Income Statements**

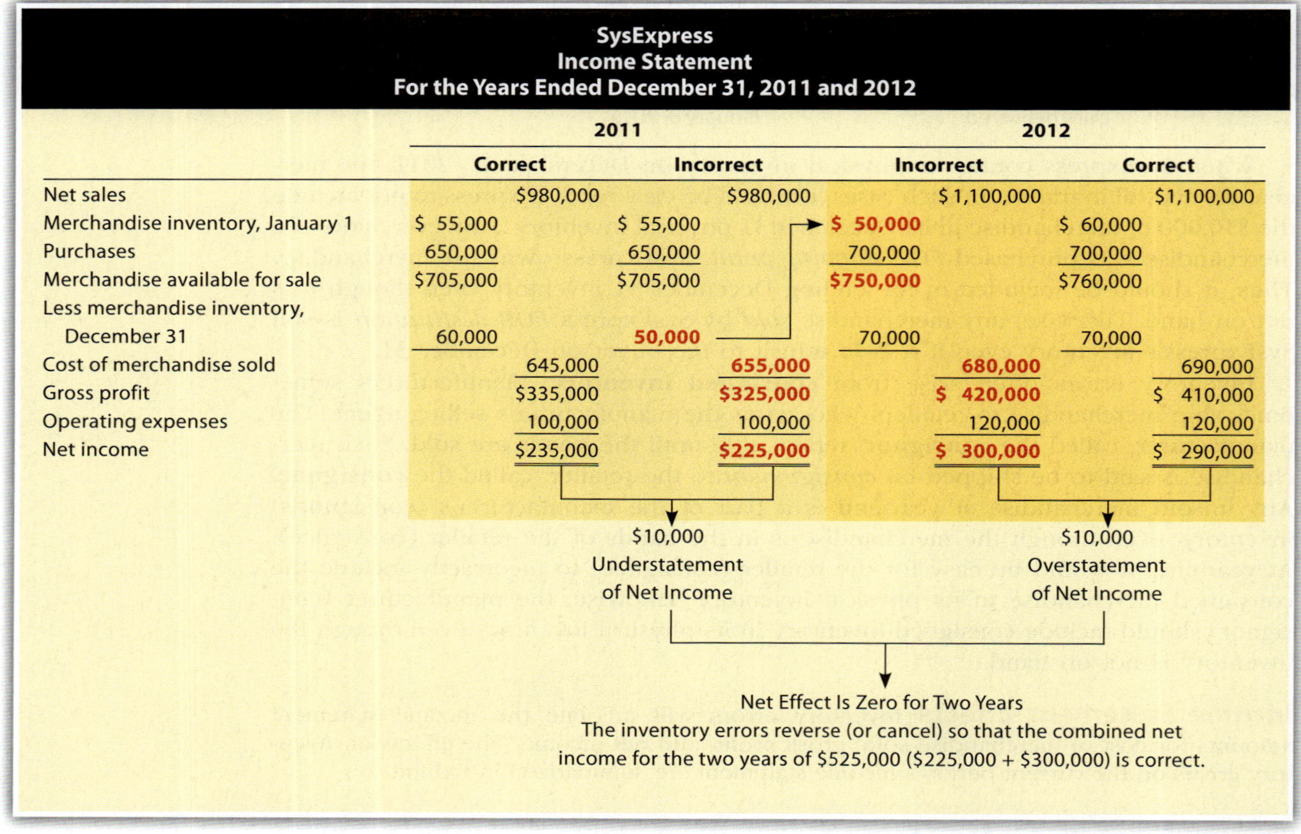

SysExpress
Income Statement
For the Years Ended December 31, 2011 and 2012

	2011		2012	
	Correct	**Incorrect**	**Incorrect**	**Correct**
Net sales	$980,000	$980,000	$1,100,000	$1,100,000
Merchandise inventory, January 1	$ 55,000	$ 55,000	$ 50,000	$ 60,000
Purchases	650,000	650,000	700,000	700,000
Merchandise available for sale	$705,000	$705,000	$750,000	$760,000
Less merchandise inventory, December 31	60,000	50,000	70,000	70,000
Cost of merchandise sold	645,000	655,000	680,000	690,000
Gross profit	$335,000	$325,000	$ 420,000	$ 410,000
Operating expenses	100,000	100,000	120,000	120,000
Net income	$235,000	$225,000	$ 300,000	$ 290,000

in the next period. In Exhibit 10, the combined net income for the two years of $525,000 is correct even though the 2011 and 2012 income statements were incorrect.

Balance Sheet Effects Inventory errors misstate the merchandise inventory, current assets, total assets, and owner's equity on the balance sheet. The effects of inventory errors on the current period's balance sheet are summarized in Exhibit 11.

EXHIBIT 11 **Effect of Inventory Errors on Current Period's Balance Sheet**

	Balance Sheet Effect			
Ending Inventory Error	**Merchandise Inventory**	**Current Assets**	**Total Assets**	**Owner's Equity (Capital)**
Understated	*Understated*	*Understated*	*Understated*	*Understated*
Overstated	*Overstated*	*Overstated*	*Overstated*	*Overstated*

For the SysExpress illustration shown in Exhibit 10, the December 31, 2011, ending inventory was understated by $10,000. As a result, the merchandise inventory, current assets, and total assets would be understated by $10,000 on the December 31, 2011, balance sheet. Because the ending physical inventory is understated, the cost of merchandise sold for 2011 will be overstated by $10,000. Thus, the gross profit and the net income for 2011 are understated by $10,000. Since the net income is closed to owner's equity (capital) at the end of the period, the owner's equity on the December 31, 2011, balance sheet is also understated by $10,000.

As discussed above, inventory errors reverse themselves within two years. As a result, the balance sheet will be correct as of December 31, 2012. Using the SysExpress illustration from Exhibit 10, these effects are summarized on the next page.

	Amount of Misstatement	
Balance Sheet:	December 31, 2011	December 31, 2012
Merchandise inventory overstated (understated)	$(10,000)	Correct
Current assets overstated (understated)	(10,000)	Correct
Total assets overstated (understated)	(10,000)	Correct
Owner's equity overstated (understated)	(10,000)	Correct
Income Statement:	2011	2012
Cost of merchandise sold overstated (understated)	$ 10,000	$(10,000)
Gross profit overstated (understated)	(10,000)	10,000
Net income overstated (understated)	(10,000)	10,000

Example Exercise 7-6 Effect of Inventory Errors

OBJ. 6

Zula Repair Shop incorrectly counted its December 31, 2012, inventory as $250,000 instead of the correct amount of $220,000. Indicate the effect of the misstatement on Zula's December 31, 2012, balance sheet and income statement for the year ended December 31, 2012.

Follow My Example 7-6

	Amount of Misstatement Overstatement (Understatement)
Balance Sheet:	
Merchandise inventory overstated	$ 30,000
Current assets overstated	30,000
Total assets overstated	30,000
Owner's equity overstated	30,000
Income Statement:	
Cost of merchandise sold understated	$(30,000)
Gross profit overstated	30,000
Net income overstated	30,000

Practice Exercises: PE 7-6A, PE 7-6B

Business Connection

RAPID INVENTORY AT COSTCO

Costco Wholesale Corporation operates over 500 membership warehouses that offer members low prices on a limited selection of nationally branded and selected private label products. Costco emphasizes high sales volumes and rapid inventory turnover. This enables Costco to operate profitably at lower gross margins than traditional wholesalers, discount retailers, and supermarkets. In addition, Costco's rapid inventory turnover allows it to conserve its working capital, as described below.

Because of our high sales volume and rapid inventory turnover, we generally have the opportunity to sell and be paid for inventory before we are required to pay ... our merchandise vendors.... As sales increase and inventory turnover becomes more rapid, a greater percentage of inventory is financed through payment terms provided by suppliers rather than by our working capital.

© Don Ryan/AP Images

Source: Costco Wholesale Corporation, Annual Report on Form 10-K for the fiscal year ended August 31, 2009.

OBJ. 2

Describe three inventory cost flow assumptions and how they impact the income statement and balance sheet.

Key Points The three common inventory cost flow assumptions used in business are the (1) first-in, first-out method (FIFO); (2) last-in, first-out method (LIFO); and (3) average cost method. The cost flow assumption affects the income statement and balance sheet.

Learning Outcomes	Example Exercises	Practice Exercises
• Describe the FIFO, LIFO, and average cost flow methods.		
• Describe how choice of a cost flow method affects the income statement and balance sheet.	EE7-1	PE7-1A, 7-1B

Determine the cost of inventory under the perpetual inventory system, using the FIFO, LIFO, and average cost methods.

Key Points In a perpetual inventory system, the number of units and the cost of each type of merchandise are recorded in a subsidiary inventory ledger, with a separate account for each type of merchandise.

Learning Outcomes	Example Exercises	Practice Exercises
• Determine the cost of inventory and cost of merchandise sold using a perpetual inventory system under the FIFO method.	EE7-2	PE7-2A, 7-2B
• Determine the cost of inventory and cost of merchandise sold using a perpetual inventory system under the LIFO method.	EE7-3	PE7-3A, 7-3B

Determine the cost of inventory under the periodic inventory system, using the FIFO, LIFO, and average cost methods.

Key Points In a periodic inventory system, a physical inventory is taken to determine the cost of the inventory and the cost of merchandise sold.

Learning Outcomes	Example Exercises	Practice Exercises
• Determine the cost of inventory and cost of merchandise sold using a periodic inventory system under the FIFO method.	EE7-4	PE7-4A, 7-4B
• Determine the cost of inventory and cost of merchandise sold using a periodic inventory system under the LIFO method.	EE7-4	PE7-4A, 7-4B
• Determine the cost of inventory and cost of merchandise sold using a periodic inventory system under the average cost method.	EE7-4	PE7-4A, 7-4B

Compare and contrast the use of the three inventory costing methods.

Key Points The three inventory costing methods will normally yield different amounts for (1) the ending inventory, (2) the cost of merchandise sold for the period, and (3) the gross profit (and net income) for the period.

Learning Outcomes	Example Exercises	Practice Exercises
• Indicate which inventory cost flow method will yield the highest and lowest ending inventory and net income during periods of increasing prices.		
• Indicate which inventory cost flow method will yield the highest and lowest ending inventory and net income during periods of decreasing prices.		

Describe and illustrate the reporting of merchandise inventory in the financial statements.

Key Points The lower of cost or market is used to value inventory. Inventory that is out of date, spoiled, or damaged is valued at its net realizable value.

Merchandise inventory is usually presented in the Current Assets section of the balance sheet, following receivables. The method of determining the cost and valuing the inventory is reported.

Errors in reporting inventory based on the physical inventory will affect the balance sheet and income statement.

Learning Outcomes	Example Exercises	Practice Exercises
• Determine inventory using lower of cost or market.	EE7-5	PE7-5A, 7-5B
• Illustrate the use of net realizable value for spoiled or damaged inventory.		
• Prepare the Current Assets section of the balance sheet that includes inventory.		
• Determine the effect of inventory errors on the balance sheet and income statement.	EE7-6	PE7-6A, 7-6B

Describe and illustrate the inventory turnover and the number of days' sales in inventory in analyzing the efficiency and effectiveness of inventory management.

Key Points Two measures to analyze the efficiency and effectiveness of inventory management are (1) inventory turnover and (2) number of days' sales in inventory

Learning Outcomes	Example Exercises	Practice Exercises
• Describe the use of inventory turnover and number of days' sales in inventory in analyzing how well a company manages inventory.		
• Compute the inventory turnover.	EE7-7	PE7-7A, 7-7B
• Compute the number of days' sales in inventory.	EE7-7	PE7-7A, 7-7B

Key Terms

average inventory cost flow method (314)
consigned inventory (327)
consignee (327)
consignor (327)
first-in, first-out (FIFO) inventory cost flow method (314)
gross profit method (333)
inventory turnover (330)
last-in, first-out (LIFO) inventory cost flow method (314)
lower-of-cost-or-market (LCM) method (324)
net realizable value (325)
number of days' sales in inventory (330)
physical inventory (313)
purchase order (312)
receiving report (312)
retail inventory method (332)
specific identification inventory cost flow method (314)
subsidiary inventory ledger (313)

Illustrative Problem

Stewart Co.'s beginning inventory and purchases during the year ended December 31, 2012, were as follows:

		Unit	Units Cost	Total Cost
January 1	Inventory	1,000	$50.00	$ 50,000
March 10	Purchase	1,200	52.50	63,000
June 25	Sold 800 units			
August 30	Purchase	800	55.00	44,000
October 5	Sold 1,500 units			
November 26	Purchase	2,000	56.00	112,000
December 31	Sold 1,000 units			
Total		5,000		$269,000

Instructions

1. Determine the cost of inventory on December 31, 2012, using the perpetual inventory system and each of the following inventory costing methods:
   a. first-in, first-out
   b. last-in, first-out

2. Determine the cost of inventory on December 31, 2012, using the periodic inventory system and each of the following inventory costing methods:
   a. first-in, first-out
   b. last-in, first-out
   c. average cost

3. Appendix: Assume that during the fiscal year ended December 31, 2012, sales were $290,000 and the estimated gross profit rate was 40%. Estimate the ending inventory at December 31, 2012, using the gross profit method.

Solution

1. a. First-in, first-out method: $95,200
   b. Last-in, first-out method: $91,000 ($35,000 + $56,000)

2. a. First-in, first-out method:
   1,700 units at $56 = $95,200

   b. Last-in, first-out method:

1,000 units at $50.00	$50,000
700 units at $52.50	36,750
1,700 units	$86,750

1. a. First-in, first-out method: $95,200

Date	Purchases			Cost of Merchandise Sold			Inventory		
	Quantity	Unit Cost	Total Cost	Quantity	Unit Cost	Total Cost	Quantity	Unit Cost	Total Cost
2012									
Jan. 1							1,000	50.00	50,000
Mar. 10	1,200	52.50	63,000				1,000	50.00	50,000
							1,200	52.50	63,000
June 25				800	50.00	40,000	200	50.00	10,000
							1,200	52.50	63,000
Aug. 30	800	55.00	44,000				200	50.00	10,000
							1,200	52.50	63,000
							800	55.00	44,000
Oct. 5				200	50.00	10,000	700	55.00	38,500
				1,200	52.50	63,000			
				100	55.00	5,500			
Nov. 26	2,000	56.00	112,000				700	55.00	38,500
							2,000	56.00	112,000
Dec. 31				700	55.00	38,500	1,700	56.00	95,200
				300	56.00	16,800			
31	Balances					173,800			95,200

b. Last-in, first-out method: $91,000 ($35,000 + $56,000)

Date	Purchases			Cost of Merchandise Sold			Inventory		
	Quantity	Unit Cost	Total Cost	Quantity	Unit Cost	Total Cost	Quantity	Unit Cost	Total Cost
2012									
Jan. 1							1,000	50.00	50,000
Mar. 10	1,200	52.50	63,000				1,000	50.00	50,000
							1,200	52.50	63,000
June 25				800	52.50	42,000	1,000	50.00	50,000
							400	52.50	21,000
Aug. 30	800	55.00	44,000				1,000	50.00	50,000
							400	52.50	21,000
							800	55.00	44,000
Oct. 5				800	55.00	44,000	700	50.00	35,000
				400	52.50	21,000			
				300	50.00	15,000			
Nov. 26	2,000	56.00	112,000				700	50.00	35,000
							2,000	56.00	112,000
Dec. 31				1,000	56.00	56,000	700	50.00	35,000
							1,000	56.00	56,000
31	Balances					178,000			91,000

c. Average cost method:

Average cost per unit: $269,000/5,000 units = $53.80

Inventory, December 31, 2012: 1,700 units at $53.80 = $91,460

3. Appendix:

Merchandise inventory, January 1, 2012		$ 50,000
Purchases (net)		219,000
Merchandise available for sale		$269,000
Sales (net)	$290,000	
Less estimated gross profit ($290,000 × 40%)	116,000	
Estimated cost of merchandise sold		174,000
Estimated merchandise inventory, December 31, 2012		$ 95,000

Discussion Questions

1. Before inventory purchases are recorded, the receiving report should be reconciled to what documents?
2. Why is it important to periodically take a physical inventory when using a perpetual inventory system?
3. Do the terms *FIFO* and *LIFO* refer to techniques used in determining quantities of the various classes of merchandise on hand? Explain.
4. If merchandise inventory is being valued at cost and the price level is decreasing, which of the three methods of costing—FIFO, LIFO, or average cost—will yield (a) the highest inventory cost, (b) the lowest inventory cost, (c) the highest gross profit, and (d) the lowest gross profit?
5. Which of the three methods of inventory costing—FIFO, LIFO, or average cost—will in general yield an inventory cost most nearly approximating current replacement cost?
6. If inventory is being valued at cost and the price level is steadily rising, which of the three methods of costing—FIFO, LIFO, or average cost—will yield the lowest annual income tax expense? Explain.
7. Because of imperfections, an item of merchandise cannot be sold at its normal selling price. How should this item be valued for financial statement purposes?
8. The inventory at the end of the year was understated by $23,950. (a) Did the error cause an overstatement or an understatement of the gross profit for the year? (b) Which items on the balance sheet at the end of the year were overstated or understated as a result of the error?
9. X-mas Co. sold merchandise to Mistletoe Company on October 31, FOB shipping point. If the merchandise is in transit on October 31, the end of the fiscal year, which company would report it in its financial statements? Explain.
10. A manufacturer shipped merchandise to a retailer on a consignment basis. If the merchandise is unsold at the end of the period, in whose inventory should the merchandise be included?

Practice Exercises

Learning Objectives	Example Exercises

OBJ. 2 EE 7-1 p. 315

PE 7-1A Cost flow methods

Three identical units of Item K113 are purchased during July, as shown below.

		Item JC07	Units	Cost	
July	9	Purchase	1	$160	
	17	Purchase	1	168	
	26	Purchase	1	176	
	Total		3	$504	
	Average cost per unit			$168	($504 ÷ 3 units)

Assume that one unit is sold on July 31 for $225.

Determine the gross profit for July and ending inventory on July 31 using the (a) first-in, first-out (FIFO); (b) last-in, first-out (LIFO); and (c) average cost methods.

OBJ. 2 EE 7-1 p. 315

PE 7-1B Cost flow methods

Three identical units of Item ZE9 are purchased during April, as shown below.

		Item WH4	Units	Cost	
Apr.	2	Purchase	1	$10	
	12	Purchase	1	12	
	23	Purchase	1	14	
	Total		3	$36	
	Average cost per unit			$12	($36 ÷ 3 units)

Assume that one unit is sold on April 27 for $29.

Determine the gross profit for April and ending inventory on April 30 using the (a) first-in, first-out (FIFO); (b) last-in, first-out (LIFO); and (c) average cost methods.

OBJ. 3 EE 7-2 p. 317

PE 7-2A Perpetual inventory using FIFO

Beginning inventory, purchases, and sales for Item B901 are as follows:

Aug.	1	Inventory	50 units at $80
	9	Sale	30 units
	13	Purchase	40 units at $85
	28	Sale	25 units

Assuming a perpetual inventory system and using the first-in, first-out (FIFO) method, determine (a) the cost of merchandise sold on August 28 and (b) the inventory on August 31.

OBJ. 3 EE 7-2 p. 317

PE 7-2B Perpetual inventory using FIFO

Beginning inventory, purchases, and sales for Item CSW15 are as follows:

Mar.	1	Inventory	100 units at $15
	7	Sale	88 units
	15	Purchase	125 units at $18
	24	Sale	75 units

Assuming a perpetual inventory system and using the first-in, first-out (FIFO) method, determine (a) the cost of merchandise sold on March 24 and (b) the inventory on March 31.

CHAPTER 8

Kemie Guaida/iStockphoto Inc.

Sarbanes-Oxley, Internal Control, and Cash

eBay Inc.

Controls are a part of your everyday life. At one extreme, laws are used to limit your behavior. For example, speed limits are designed to control your driving for traffic safety. In addition, you are also affected by many nonlegal controls. For example, you can keep credit card receipts in order to compare your transactions to the monthly credit card statement. Comparing receipts to the monthly statement is a control designed to catch mistakes made by the credit card company. In addition, banks give you a personal identification number (PIN) as a control against unauthorized access to your cash if you lose your automated teller machine (ATM) card. Dairies use freshness dating on their milk containers as a control to prevent the purchase or sale of soured milk. As you can see, you use and encounter controls every day.

Just as there are many examples of controls throughout society, businesses must also implement controls to help guide the behavior of their managers, employees, and customers. For example, **eBay Inc.** maintains an Internet-based marketplace for the sale of goods and services. Using eBay's online platform, buyers and sellers can browse, buy, and sell a wide variety of items including antiques and used cars. However, in order to maintain the integrity and trust of its buyers and sellers, eBay must have controls to ensure that buyers pay for their items and sellers don't misrepresent their items or fail to deliver sales. One such control eBay uses is a feedback forum that establishes buyer and seller reputations. A prospective buyer or seller can view the member's reputation and feedback comments before completing a transaction. Dishonest or unfair trading can lead to a negative reputation and even suspension or cancellation of the member's ability to trade on eBay.

This chapter discusses controls that can be included in accounting systems to provide reasonable assurance that the financial statements are relia[ble]. Controls to discover and prevent errors to a bank [ac]count are also discussed. This chapter begins by [dis]cussing the Sarbanes-Oxley Act of 2002 and its i[mpact] on controls and financial reporting.

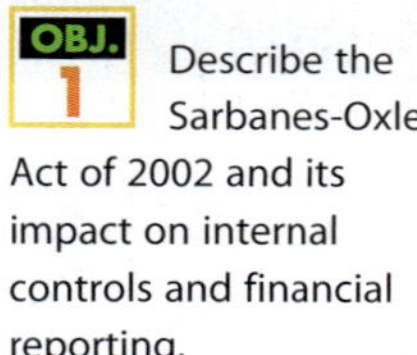

Describe the Sarbanes-Oxley Act of 2002 and its impact on internal controls and financial reporting.

Sarbanes-Oxley Act of 2002

During the financial scandals of the early 2000s, stockholders, creditors, and other investors lost billions of dollars.[1] As a result, the U.S. Congress passed the **Sarbanes-Oxley Act of 2002**. This act, often referred to as *Sarbanes-Oxley*, is one of the most important laws affecting U.S. companies in recent history. The purpose of Sarbanes-Oxley is to restore public confidence and trust in the financial reporting of companies.

Sarbanes-Oxley applies only to companies whose stock is traded on public exchanges, referred to as *publicly held companies*. However, Sarbanes-Oxley highlighted the importance of assessing the financial controls and reporting of all companies. As a result, companies of all sizes have been influenced by Sarbanes-Oxley.

Sarbanes-Oxley emphasizes the importance of effective internal control.[2] **Internal control** is defined as the procedures and processes used by a company to:

1. Safeguard its assets.
2. Process information accurately.
3. Ensure compliance with laws and regulations.

Sarbanes-Oxley requires companies to maintain effective internal controls over the recording of transactions and the preparing of financial statements. Such controls are important because they deter fraud and prevent misleading financial statements as shown on the next page.

1 Exhibit 2 in Chapter 1 briefly summarizes these scandals.

2 Sarbanes-Oxley also has important implications for corporate governance and the regulation of the public accounting profession. This chapter, however, focuses on the internal control implications of Sarbanes-Oxley.

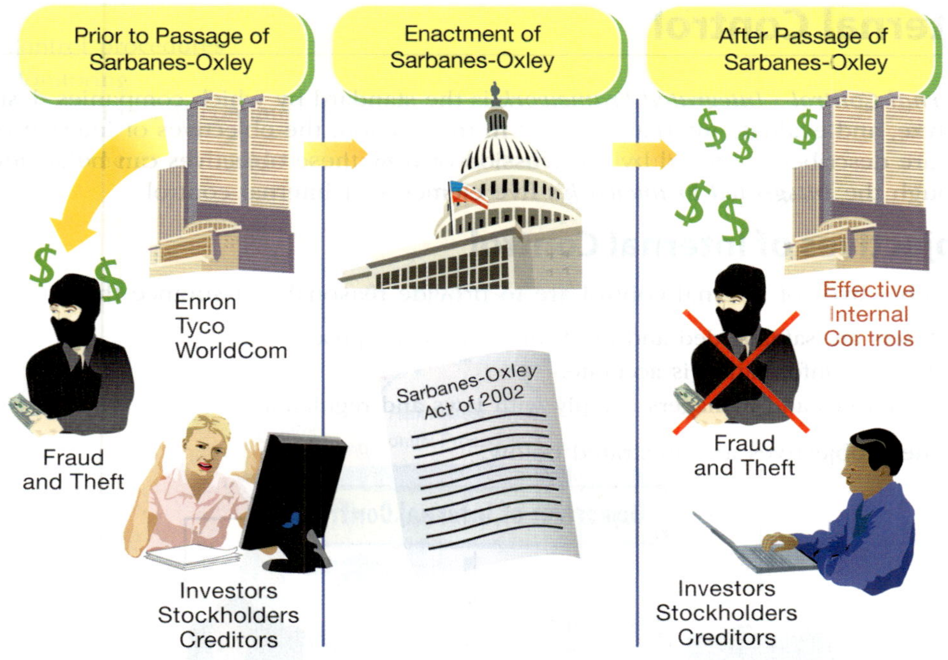

Sarbanes-Oxley also requires companies and their independent accountants to report on the effectiveness of the company's internal controls.[3] These reports are required to be filed with the company's annual 10-K report with the Securities and Exchange Commission. Companies are also encouraged to include these reports in their annual reports to stockholders. An example of such a report by the management of Nike is shown in Exhibit 1.

EXHIBIT 1

Sarbanes-Oxley Report of Nike

Management's Annual Report on Internal Control Over Financial Reporting

Management is responsible for establishing and maintaining adequate internal control over financial reporting . . . , Under the supervision and with the participation of our Chief Executive Officer and Chief Financial Officer, our management conducted an evaluation of the effectiveness of our internal control over financial reporting based upon the framework in *Internal Control—Integrated Framework* issued by the Committee of Sponsoring Organizations of the Treadway Commission. Based on that evaluation, our management concluded that our internal control over financial reporting is effective as of May 31, 2009. . . .

PricewaterhouseCoopers LLP, an independent registered public accounting firm, has audited . . . management's assessment of the effectiveness of our internal control over financial reporting . . . and . . . the effectiveness of our internal control over financial reporting . . . as stated in their report. . . .

MARK G. PARKER
Chief Executive Officer and President

DONALD W. BLAIR
Chief Financial Officer

Exhibit 1 indicates that Nike based its evaluation of internal controls on *Internal Control—Integrated Framework*, which was issued by the Committee of Sponsoring Organizations (COSO) of the Treadway Commission. This framework is the standard by which companies design, analyze, and evaluate internal controls. For this reason, this framework is used as the basis for discussing internal controls.

Information on *Internal Control—Integrated Framework* can be found on COSO's Web site at **http://www.coso.or**

3 These reporting requirements are required under Section 404 of the act. As a result, these requirements and reports are often referred to as 404 requirements and 404 reports.

A bank makes credit entries (issues credit memos) for the following:

1. Deposits made by electronic funds transfer (EFT)
2. Collections of note receivable for the company
3. Proceeds for a loan made to the company by the bank
4. Interest earned on the company's account
5. Correction (if any) of bank errors

A bank makes debit entries (issues debit memos) for the following:

1. Payments made by electronic funds transfer (EFT)
2. Service charges
3. Customer checks returned for not sufficient funds
4. Correction (if any) of bank errors

Customers' checks returned for not sufficient funds, called *NSF checks*, are customer checks that were initially deposited, but were not paid by the customer's bank. Since the company's bank credited the customer's check to the company's account when it was deposited, the bank debits the company's account (issues a debit memo) when the check is returned without payment.

The reason for a credit or debit memo entry is indicated on the bank statement. Exhibit 5 identifies the following types of credit and debit memo entries:

EC: Error correction to correct bank error
NSF: Not sufficient funds check
SC: Service charge
ACH: Automated clearing house entry for electronic funds transfer
MS: Miscellaneous item such as collection of a note receivable on behalf of the company or receipt of a loan by the company from the bank

The above list includes the notation "ACH" for electronic funds transfers. ACH is a network for clearing electronic funds transfers among individuals, companies, and banks.[7] Because electronic funds transfers may be either deposits or payments, ACH entries may indicate either a debit or credit entry to the company's account. Likewise, entries to correct bank errors and miscellaneous items may indicate a debit or credit entry to the company's account.

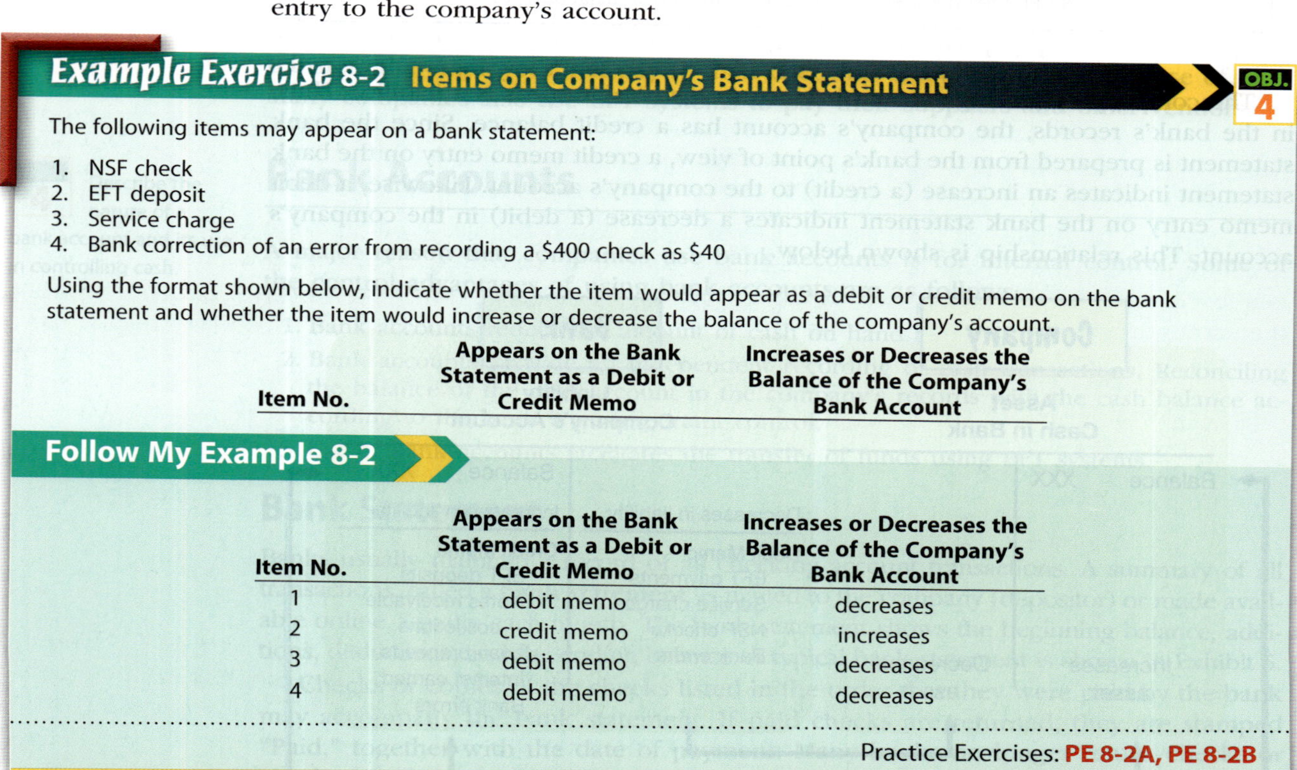

Example Exercise 8-2 Items on Company's Bank Statement OBJ. 4

The following items may appear on a bank statement:

1. NSF check
2. EFT deposit
3. Service charge
4. Bank correction of an error from recording a $400 check as $40

Using the format shown below, indicate whether the item would appear as a debit or credit memo on the bank statement and whether the item would increase or decrease the balance of the company's account.

Item No.	Appears on the Bank Statement as a Debit or Credit Memo	Increases or Decreases the Balance of the Company's Bank Account

Follow My Example 8-2

Item No.	Appears on the Bank Statement as a Debit or Credit Memo	Increases or Decreases the Balance of the Company's Bank Account
1	debit memo	decreases
2	credit memo	increases
3	debit memo	decreases
4	debit memo	decreases

Practice Exercises: **PE 8-2A, PE 8-2B**

7 For further information on ACH, go to **http://www.nacha.org/**. Click on "About Us," and then click on "Intro to NACHA".

Using the Bank Statement as a Control Over Cash

The bank statement is a primary control that a company uses over cash. A company uses the bank's statement as a control by comparing the company's recording of cash transactions to those recorded by the bank.

The cash balance shown by a bank statement is usually different from the company's cash balance, as shown in Exhibit 6.

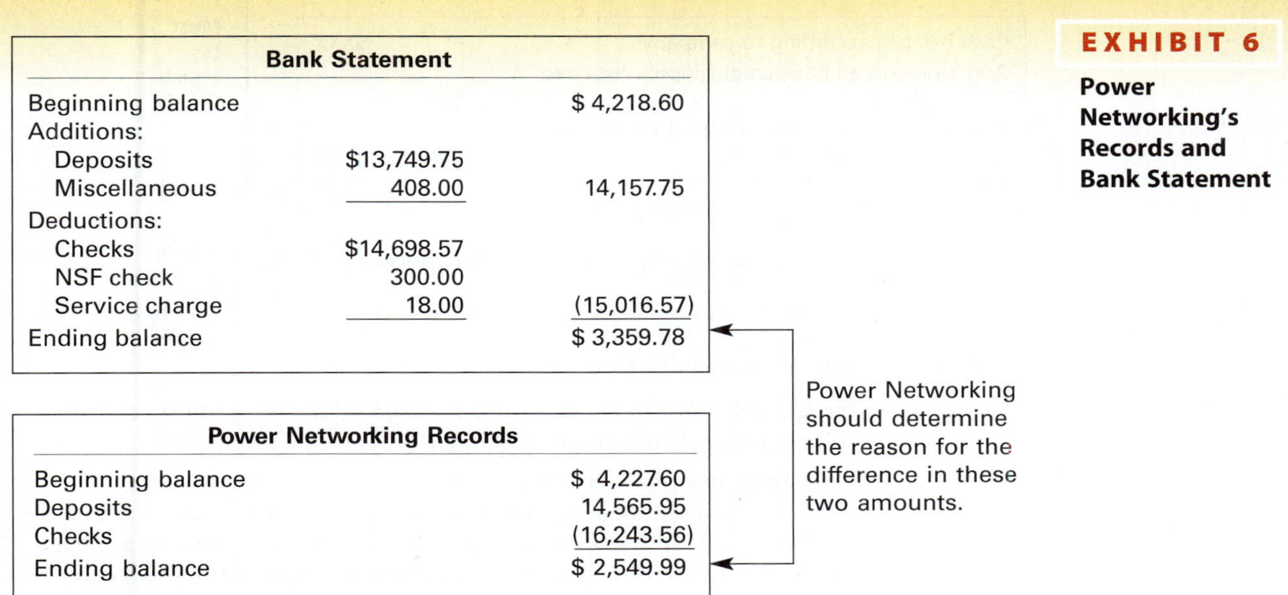

EXHIBIT 6

Power Networking's Records and Bank Statement

Bank Statement		
Beginning balance		$ 4,218.60
Additions:		
Deposits	$13,749.75	
Miscellaneous	408.00	14,157.75
Deductions:		
Checks	$14,698.57	
NSF check	300.00	
Service charge	18.00	(15,016.57)
Ending balance		$ 3,359.78

Power Networking Records	
Beginning balance	$ 4,227.60
Deposits	14,565.95
Checks	(16,243.56)
Ending balance	$ 2,549.99

Power Networking should determine the reason for the difference in these two amounts.

Differences between the company and bank balance may arise because of a delay by either the company or bank in recording transactions. For example, there is normally a time lag of one or more days between the date a check is written and the date that it is paid by the bank. Likewise, there is normally a time lag between when the company mails a deposit to the bank (or uses the night depository) and when the bank receives and records the deposit.

Differences may also arise because the bank has debited or credited the company's account for transactions that the company will not know about until the bank statement is received. Finally, differences may arise from errors made by either the company or the bank. For example, the company may incorrectly post to Cash a check written for $4,500 as $450. Likewise, a bank may incorrectly record the amount of a check.

Bank Reconciliation

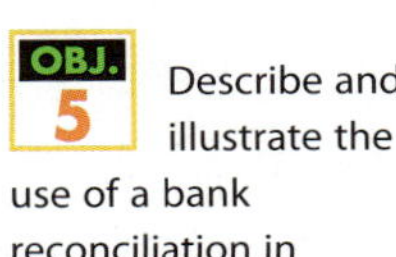

Describe and illustrate the use of a bank reconciliation in controlling cash.

A **bank reconciliation** is an analysis of the items and amounts that result in the cash balance reported in the bank statement to differ from the balance of the cash account in the ledger. The adjusted cash balance determined in the bank reconciliation is reported on the balance sheet.

A bank reconciliation is usually divided into two sections as follows:

1. The *bank section* begins with the cash balance according to the bank statement and ends with the *adjusted balance*.
2. The *company section* begins with the cash balance according to the company's records and ends with the *adjusted balance*.

The *adjusted balance* from bank and company sections must be equal. The format of the bank reconciliation is shown below.

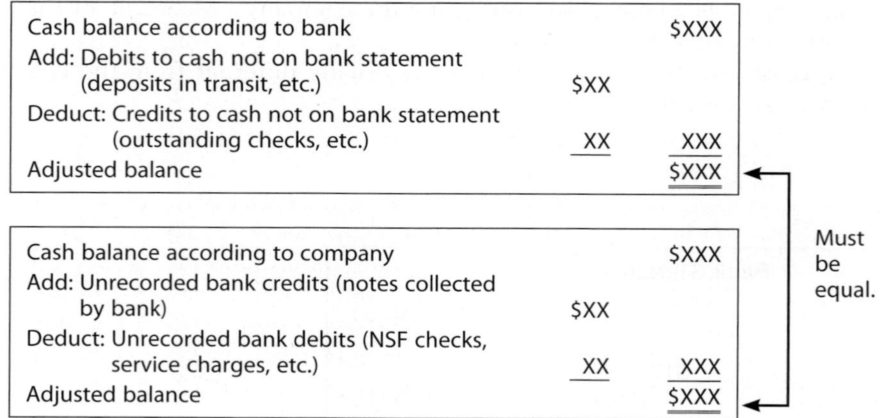
Cash balance according to bank		$XXX
Add: Debits to cash not on bank statement (deposits in transit, etc.)	$XX	
Deduct: Credits to cash not on bank statement (outstanding checks, etc.)	XX	XXX
Adjusted balance		$XXX

Cash balance according to company		$XXX
Add: Unrecorded bank credits (notes collected by bank)	$XX	
Deduct: Unrecorded bank debits (NSF checks, service charges, etc.)	XX	XXX
Adjusted balance		$XXX

A bank reconciliation is prepared using the following steps:

Bank Section of Reconciliation

Step 1. Enter the *Cash balance according to bank* from the ending cash balance according to the bank statement.

Step 2. *Add deposits not recorded by the bank.*
Identify deposits not recorded by the bank by comparing each deposit listed on the bank statement with unrecorded deposits appearing in the preceding period's reconciliation and with the current period's deposits.
Examples: Deposits in transit at the end of the period.

Step 3. *Deduct outstanding checks that have not been paid by the bank.*
Identify outstanding checks by comparing paid checks with outstanding checks appearing on the preceding period's reconciliation and with recorded checks.
Examples: Outstanding checks at the end of the period.

Step 4. Determine the *Adjusted balance* by adding Step 2 and deducting Step 3.

Company Section of Reconciliation

Step 5. Enter the *Cash balance according to company* from the ending cash balance in the ledger.

Step 6. *Add credit memos that have not been recorded.*
Identify the bank credit memos that have not been recorded by comparing the bank statement credit memos to entries in the journal.
Examples: A note receivable and interest that the bank has collected for the company.

Step 7. *Deduct debit memos that have not been recorded.*
Identify the bank debit memos that have not been recorded by comparing the bank statement debit memos to entries in the journal.
Examples: Customers' not sufficient funds (NSF) checks; bank service charges.

Step 8. Determine the *Adjusted balance* by adding Step 6 and deducting Step 7.

Step 9. Verify that the adjusted balances determined in Steps 4 and 8 are equal.

The adjusted balances in the bank and company sections of the reconciliation must be equal. If the balances are not equal, an item has been overlooked and must be found.

Sometimes, the adjusted balances are not equal because either the company or the bank has made an error. In such cases, the error is often discovered by comparing the amount of each item (deposit and check) on the bank statement with that in the company's records.

Any bank or company errors discovered should be added or deducted from the bank or company section of the reconciliation depending on the nature of the error. For example, assume that the bank incorrectly recorded a company check for $50 as $500. This bank error of $450 ($500 – $50) would be added to the bank balance in the bank section of the reconciliation. In addition, the bank would be notified of the error so that it could be corrected. On the other hand, assume that the company recorded a deposit of $1,200 as $2,100. This company error of $900 ($2,100 – $1,200) would be deducted from the cash balance in the company section of the bank reconciliation. The company would later correct the error using a journal entry.

To illustrate, the bank statement for Power Networking in Exhibit 5 on page 367 is used. This bank statement shows a balance of $3,359.78 as of July 31. The cash balance in Power Networking's ledger on the same date is $2,549.99. Using the preceding steps, the following reconciling items were identified:

Step 2. Deposit of July 31, not recorded on bank statement: $816.20

Step 3. Outstanding checks:

Check No. 812	$1,061.00
Check No. 878	435.39
Check No. 883	48.60
Total	$1,544.99

Step 6. Note receivable of $400 plus interest of $8 collected by bank not recorded in the journal as indicated by a credit memo of $408.

Step 7. Check from customer (Thomas Ivey) for $300 returned by bank because of insufficient funds (NSF) as indicated by a debit memo of $300.00.
Bank service charges of $18, not recorded in the journal as indicated by a debit memo of $18.00.

In addition, an error of $9 was discovered. This error occurred when Check No. 879 for $732.26 to Taylor Co., on account, was recorded in the company's journal as $723.26.

The bank reconciliation, based on the Exhibit 5 bank statement and the preceding reconciling items, is shown in Exhibit 7.

The company's records do not need to be updated for any items in the *bank section* of the reconciliation. This section begins with the cash balance according to the bank statement. However, the bank should be notified of any errors that need to be corrected.

The company's records do need to be updated for any items in the *company section* of the bank reconciliation. The company's records are updated using journal entries. For example, journal entries should be made for any unrecorded bank memos and any company errors.

The journal entries for Power Networking, based on the bank reconciliation shown in Exhibit 7, are as follows:

July	31	Cash		408	
		Notes Receivable			400
		Interest Revenue			8
	31	Accounts Receivable—Thomas Ivey		300	
		Miscellaneous Expense		18	
		Accounts Payable—Taylor Co.		9	
		Cash			327

EXHIBIT 7 **Bank Reconciliation for Power Networking**

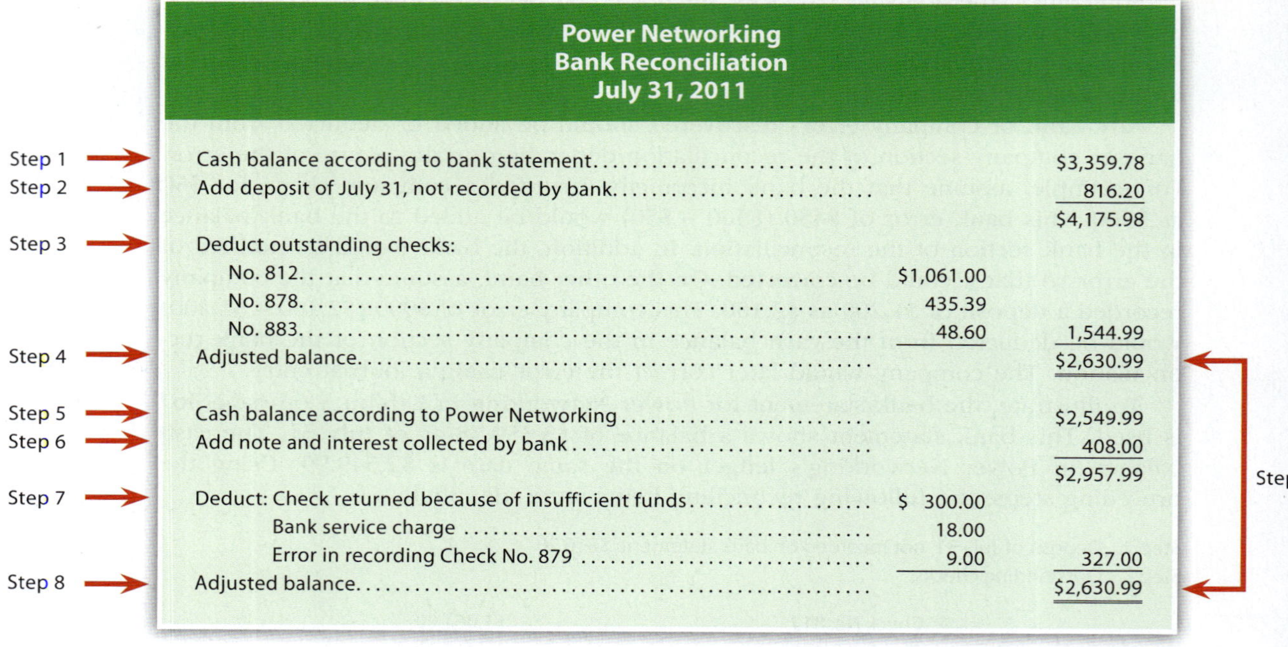

Power Networking
Bank Reconciliation
July 31, 2011

Step			
Step 1	Cash balance according to bank statement		$3,359.78
Step 2	Add deposit of July 31, not recorded by bank		816.20
			$4,175.98
Step 3	Deduct outstanding checks:		
	No. 812	$1,061.00	
	No. 878	435.39	
	No. 883	48.60	1,544.99
Step 4	Adjusted balance		$2,630.99
Step 5	Cash balance according to Power Networking		$2,549.99
Step 6	Add note and interest collected by bank		408.00
			$2,957.99
Step 7	Deduct: Check returned because of insufficient funds	$ 300.00	
	Bank service charge	18.00	
	Error in recording Check No. 879	9.00	327.00
Step 8	Adjusted balance		$2,630.99

After the preceding journal entries are recorded and posted, the cash account will have a debit balance of $2,630.99. This cash balance agrees with the adjusted balance shown on the bank reconciliation. This is the amount of cash on July 31 and is the amount that is reported on Power Networking's July 31 balance sheet.

Businesses may reconcile their bank accounts in a slightly different format from that shown in Exhibit 7. Regardless, the objective is to control cash by reconciling the company's records with the bank statement. In doing so, any errors or misuse of cash may be detected.

To enhance internal control, the bank reconciliation should be prepared by an employee who does not take part in or record cash transactions. Otherwise, mistakes may occur, and it is more likely that cash will be stolen or misapplied. For example, an employee who handles cash and also reconciles the bank statement could steal a cash deposit, omit the deposit from the accounts, and omit it from the reconciliation.

Bank reconciliations are also an important part of computerized systems where deposits and checks are stored in electronic files and records. Some systems use computer software to determine the difference between the bank statement and company cash balances. The software then adjusts for deposits in transit and outstanding checks. Any remaining differences are reported for further analysis.

Example Exercise 8-3 Bank Reconciliation — OBJ. 5

The following data were gathered to use in reconciling the bank account of Photo Op:

Balance per bank	$14,500
Balance per company records	13,875
Bank service charges	75
Deposit in transit	3,750
NSF check	800
Outstanding checks	5,250

a. What is the adjusted balance on the bank reconciliation?

b. Journalize any necessary entries for Photo Op based on the bank reconciliation.

(continued)

Follow My Example 8-3

a. $13,000, as shown below.
Bank section of reconciliation: $14,500 + $3,750 – $5,250 = $13,000
Company section of reconciliation: $13,875 – $75 – $800 = $13,000

b.

Accounts Receivable	800	
Miscellaneous Expense	75	
Cash		875

Practice Exercises: **PE 8-3A, PE 8-3B**

Integrity, Objectivity, and Ethics in Business

BANK ERROR IN YOUR FAVOR

You may sometime have a bank error in your favor, such as a misposted deposit. Such errors are not a case of "found money," as in the Monopoly® game. Bank control systems quickly discover most errors and make automatic adjustments. Even so, you have a legal responsibility to report the error and return the money to the bank.

Special-Purpose Cash Funds

OBJ. 6 Describe the accounting for special-purpose cash funds.

A company often has to pay small amounts for such items as postage, office supplies, or minor repairs. Although small, such payments may occur often enough to total a significant amount. Thus, it is desirable to control such payments. However, writing a check for each small payment is not practical. Instead, a special cash fund, called a **petty cash fund**, is used.

A petty cash fund is established by estimating the amount of payments needed from the fund during a period, such as a week or a month. A check is then written and cashed for this amount. The money obtained from cashing the check is then given to an employee, called the *petty cash custodian*. The petty cash custodian disburses monies from the fund as needed. For control purposes, the company may place restrictions on the maximum amount and the types of payments that can be made from the fund. Each time money is paid from petty cash, the custodian records the details on a petty cash receipts form.

The petty cash fund is normally replenished at periodic intervals, when it is depleted, or reaches a minimum amount. When a petty cash fund is replenished, the accounts debited are determined by summarizing the petty cash receipts. A check is then written for this amount, payable to Petty Cash.

To illustrate, assume that a petty cash fund of $500 is established on August 1. The entry to record this transaction is as follows:

Aug.	1	Petty Cash		500	
		Cash			500

The only time Petty Cash is debited is when the fund is initially established, as shown in the preceding entry, or when the fund is being increased. The only time Petty Cash is credited is when the fund is being decreased.

OBJ. 2 Describe and illustrate the objectives and elements of internal control.

Key Points The objectives of internal control are to provide reasonable assurance that (1) assets are safeguarded and used for business purposes, (2) business information is accurate, and (3) laws and regulations are complied with. The elements of internal control are the control environment, risk assessment, control procedures, monitoring, and information and communication.

Learning Outcomes	Example Exercises	Practice Exercises
• List the objectives of internal control.		
• List the elements of internal control.		
• Describe each element of internal control and factors influencing each element.	EE8-1	PE8-1A, 8-1B

OBJ. 3 Describe and illustrate the application of internal controls to cash.

Key Points A cash register is a control for protecting cash received in over-the-counter sales. A remittance advice is a control for cash received through the mail. Separating the duties of handling cash and recording cash is also a control. A voucher system is a control system for cash payments. Many companies use electronic funds transfers for cash receipts and cash payments.

Learning Outcomes	Example Exercises	Practice Exercises
• Describe and give examples of controls for cash received from cash sales, cash received in the mail, and cash received by EFT.		
• Describe and give examples of controls for cash payments made using a voucher system and cash payments made by EFT.		

OBJ. 4 Describe the nature of a bank account and its use in controlling cash.

Key Points Bank accounts control cash by reducing the amount of cash on hand and facilitating the transfer of cash between businesses and locations. In addition, the bank statement allows a business to reconcile the cash transactions recorded in the accounting records to those recorded by the bank.

Learning Outcomes	Example Exercises	Practice Exercises
• Describe how the use of bank accounts helps control cash.		
• Describe a bank statement and provide examples of items that appear on a bank statement as debit and credit memos.	EE8-2	PE8-2A, 8-2B

OBJ. 5 Describe and illustrate the use of a bank reconciliation in controlling cash.

Key Points A bank reconciliation is prepared using nine steps as summarized on page 370. The items in the company section of a bank reconciliation must be journalized on the company's records.

Learning Outcomes	Example Exercises	Practice Exercises
• Describe a bank reconciliation.		
• Prepare a bank reconciliation.	EE8-3	PE8-3A, 8-3B
• Journalize any necessary entries on the company's records based on the bank reconciliation.	EE8-3	PE8-3A, 8-3B

OBJ. 6 Describe the accounting for special-purpose cash funds.

Key Points Special-purpose cash funds, such as a petty cash fund or travel funds, are used by businesses to meet specific needs. Each fund is established by cashing a check for the amount of cash needed. At periodic intervals, the fund is replenished and the disbursements recorded.

Learning Outcomes	Example Exercises	Practice Exercises
• Describe the use of special-purpose cash funds.		
• Journalize the entry to establish a petty cash fund.	EE8-4	PE8-4A, 8-4B
• Journalize the entry to replenish a petty cash fund.	EE8-4	PE8-4A, 8-4B

OBJ. 7 Describe and illustrate the reporting of cash and cash equivalents in the financial statements.

Key Points Cash is listed as the first asset in the Current assets section of the balance sheet. Companies that have invested excess cash in highly liquid investments usually report *Cash and cash equivalents* on the balance sheet.

Learning Outcomes	Example Exercises	Practice Exercises
• Describe the reporting of cash and cash equivalents in the financial statements.		
• Illustrate the reporting of cash and cash equivalents in the financial statements.		

OBJ. 8 Describe and illustrate the use of the ratio of cash to monthly cash expenses to assess the ability of a company to continue in business.

Key Points The ratio of cash to monthly cash expenses is useful for assessing how long a company can continue to operate without (1) additional financing or (2) generating positive cash flows from operations.

Learning Outcomes	Example Exercises	Practice Exercises
• Describe the use of the ratio of cash to monthly cash expenses.		
• Compute the ratio of cash to monthly cash expenses.	EE8-5	PE 8-5A, 8-5B

Key Terms

bank reconciliation (369)
bank statement (366)
cash (363)
cash equivalents (374)
cash short and over account (364)
compensating balance (375)
control environment (359)
electronic funds transfer (EFT) (365)
elements of internal control (358)
employee fraud (358)
internal control (356)
petty cash fund (373)
ratio of cash to monthly cash expenses (375)
Sarbanes-Oxley Act of 2002 (356)
special-purpose funds (374)
voucher (366)
voucher system (366)

Illustrative Problem

The bank statement for Urethane Company for June 30, 2011, indicates a balance of $9,143.11. All cash receipts are deposited each evening in a night depository, after banking hours. The accounting records indicate the following summary data for cash receipts and payments for June:

Cash balance as of June 1	$ 3,943.50
Total cash receipts for June	28,971.60
Total amount of checks issued in June	28,388.85

Comparing the bank statement and the accompanying canceled checks and memos with the records reveals the following reconciling items:

a. The bank had collected for Urethane Company $1,030 on a note left for collection. The face amount of the note was $1,000.

b. A deposit of $1,852.21, representing receipts of June 30, had been made too late to appear on the bank statement.

c. Checks outstanding totaled $5,265.27.

d. A check drawn for $139 had been incorrectly charged by the bank as $157.

e. A check for $30 returned with the statement had been recorded in the company's records as $240. The check was for the payment of an obligation to Avery Equipment Company for the purchase of office supplies on account.

f. Bank service charges for June amounted to $18.20.

Instructions

1. Prepare a bank reconciliation for June.
2. Journalize the entries that should be made by Urethane Company.

Solution

1.

Urethane Company
Bank Reconciliation
June 30, 2011

Cash balance according to bank statement		$ 9,143.11
Add: Deposit of June 30 not recorded by bank	$1,852.21	
Bank error in charging check as $157 instead of $139	18.00	1,870.21
		$11,013.32
Deduct: Outstanding checks		5,265.27
Adjusted balance		$ 5,748.05
Cash balance according to company's records		$ 4,526.25*
Add: Proceeds of note collected by bank, including $30 interest	$1,030.00	
Error in recording check	210.00	1,240.00
		$ 5,766.25
Deduct: Bank service charges		18.20
Adjusted balance		$ 5,748.05

*$3,943.50 + $28,971.60 – $28,388.85

2.

June	30	Cash		1,240.00	
		Notes Receivable			1,000.00
		Interest Revenue			30.00
		Accounts Payable—Avery Equipment Company			210.00
	30	Miscellaneous Administrative Expense		18.20	
		Cash			18.20

Discussion Questions

1. (a) Name and describe the five elements of internal control. (b) Is any one element of internal control more important than another?
2. Why should the employee who handles cash receipts not have the responsibility for maintaining the accounts receivable records? Explain.
3. The ticket seller at a movie theater doubles as a ticket taker for a few minutes each day while the ticket taker is on a break. Which control procedure of a business's system of internal control is violated in this situation?
4. Why should the responsibility for maintaining the accounting records be separated from the responsibility for operations? Explain.
5. Assume that Peggy Gyger, accounts payable clerk for Patmen Inc., stole $193,750 by paying fictitious invoices for goods that were never received. The clerk set up accounts in the names of the fictitious companies and cashed the checks at a local bank. Describe a control procedure that would have prevented or detected the fraud.
6. Before a voucher for the purchase of merchandise is approved for payment, supporting documents should be compared to verify the accuracy of the liability. Give an example of supporting documents for the purchase of merchandise.
7. The balance of Cash is likely to differ from the bank statement balance. What two factors are likely to be responsible for the difference?
8. What is the purpose of preparing a bank reconciliation?
9. Smyrna Inc. has a petty cash fund of $900. (a) Since the petty cash fund is only $900, should Smyrna Inc. implement controls over petty cash? (b) What controls, if any, could be used for the petty cash fund?
10. (a) How are cash equivalents reported in the financial statements? (b) What are some examples of cash equivalents?

Practice Exercises

Learning Objectives	Example Exercises

OBJ. 2 EE 8-1 p. 363

PE 8-1A Internal control elements

Identify each of the following as relating to (a) the control environment, (b) control procedures, or (c) information and communication.

1. Separating related operations
2. Report of internal auditors
3. Management's philosophy and operating style

OBJ. 2 EE 8-1 p. 363

PE 8-1B Internal control elements

Identify each of the following as relating to (a) the control environment, (b) control procedures, or (c) monitoring.

1. Personnel policies
2. Safeguarding inventory in a locked warehouse
3. Hiring of external auditors to review the adequacy of controls

OBJ. 4 EE 8-2 p. 368

PE 8-2A Items on company's bank statement

The following items may appear on a bank statement:

1. EFT payment
2. Note collected for company
3. Bank correction of an error from recording a $7,200 deposit as $2,700
4. Service charge

Using the format shown below, indicate whether each item would appear as a debit or credit memo on the bank statement and whether the item would increase or decrease the balance of the company's account.

Item No.	Appears on the Bank Statement as a Debit or Credit Memo	Increases or Decreases the Balance of the Company's Bank Account

OBJ. 4 EE 8-2 p. 368

PE 8-2B Items on company's bank statement

The following items may appear on a bank statement:

1. NSF check
2. Bank correction of an error from posting another customer's check to the company's account
3. Loan proceeds
4. EFT deposit

Using the format shown below, indicate whether each item would appear as a debit or credit memo on the bank statement and whether the item would increase or decrease the balance of the company's account.

Item No.	Appears on the Bank Statement as a Debit or Credit Memo	Increases or Decreases the Balance of the Company's Bank Account

Learning Objectives | *Example Exercises*

OBJ. 5 EE 8-3 *p. 372*

PE 8-3A Bank reconciliation

The following data were gathered to use in reconciling the bank account of Azalea Company:

Balance per bank	$25,500
Balance per company records	27,475
Bank service charges	75
Deposit in transit	7,500
NSF check	3,400
Outstanding checks	9,000

a. What is the adjusted balance on the bank reconciliation?

b. Journalize any necessary entries for Azalea Company based on the bank reconciliation.

OBJ. 5 EE 8-3 *p. 372*

PE 8-3B Bank reconciliation

The following data were gathered to use in reconciling the bank account of Bradford Company:

Balance per bank	$17,400
Balance per company records	5,765
Bank service charges	125
Deposit in transit	3,000
Note collected by bank with $360 interest	9,360
Outstanding checks	5,400

a. What is the adjusted balance on the bank reconciliation?

b. Journalize any necessary entries for Bradford Company based on the bank reconciliation.

OBJ. 6 EE 8-4 *p. 374*

PE 8-4A Petty cash fund

Prepare journal entries for each of the following:

a. Issued a check to establish a petty cash fund of $800.

b. The amount of cash in the petty cash fund is $225. Issued a check to replenish the fund, based on the following summary of petty cash receipts: repair expense, $450 and miscellaneous selling expense, $75. Record any missing funds in the cash short and over account.

OBJ. 6 EE 8-4 *p. 374*

PE 8-4B Petty cash fund

Prepare journal entries for each of the following:

a. Issued a check to establish a petty cash fund of $750.

b. The amount of cash in the petty cash fund is $325. Issued a check to replenish the fund, based on the following summary of petty cash receipts: store supplies, $300 and miscellaneous selling expense, $100. Record any missing funds in the cash short and over account.

OBJ. 8 EE 8-5 *p. 376*

F·A·I

PE 8-5A Ratio of cash to monthly cash expenses

Financial data for Hauser Company are shown below.

	For Year Ending December 31, 2012
Cash on December 31, 2012	$ 58,800
Cash flow from operations	(72,000)

a. Compute the ratio of cash to monthly cash expenses.

b. Interpret the results computed in (a).

OBJ. 8 EE 8-5 *p. 376*

F·A·I

PE 8-5B Ratio of cash to monthly cash expenses

Financial data for Preston Company are shown below.

	For Year Ending December 31, 2012
Cash on December 31, 2012	$ 184,800
Cash flow from operations	(158,400)

a. Compute the ratio of cash to monthly cash expenses.

b. Interpret the results computed in (a).

Exercises

OBJ. 1

EX 8-1 Sarbanes-Oxley internal control report

Using Wikpedia (**www.wikpedia.com**), look up the entry for Sarbanes-Oxley Act. Look over the table of contents and find the section that describes Section 404.

What does Section 404 require of management's internal control report?

OBJ. 2, 3

EX 8-2 Internal controls

Joan Whalen has recently been hired as the manager of Jittery Coffee Shop. Jittery Coffee Shop is a national chain of franchised coffee shops. During her first month as store manager, Joan encountered the following internal control situations:

a. Since only one employee uses the cash register, that employee is responsible for counting the cash at the end of the shift and verifying that the cash in the drawer matches the amount of cash sales recorded by the cash register. Joan expects each cashier to balance the drawer to the penny *every* time—no exceptions.

b. Joan caught an employee putting a case of 400 single-serving tea bags in her car. Not wanting to create a scene, Joan smiled and said, "I don't think you're putting those tea bags on the right shelf. Don't they belong inside the coffee shop?" The employee returned the tea bags to the stockroom.

c. Jittery Coffee Shop has one cash register. Prior to Joan's joining the coffee shop, each employee working on a shift would take a customer order, accept payment, and then prepare the order. Joan made one employee on each shift responsible for taking orders and accepting the customer's payment. Other employees prepare the orders.

State whether you agree or disagree with Joan's method of handling each situation and explain your answer.

OBJ. 2, 3

EX 8-3 Internal controls

Meridian Clothing is a retail store specializing in women's clothing. The store has established a liberal return policy for the holiday season in order to encourage gift purchases. Any item purchased during November and December may be returned through January 31, with a receipt, for cash or exchange. If the customer does not have a receipt, cash will still be refunded for any item under $50. If the item is more than $50, a check is mailed to the customer.

Whenever an item is returned, a store clerk completes a return slip, which the customer signs. The return slip is placed in a special box. The store manager visits the return counter approximately once every two hours to authorize the return slips. Clerks are instructed to place the returned merchandise on the proper rack on the selling floor as soon as possible.

This year, returns at Meridian Clothing have reached an all-time high. There are a large number of returns under $50 without receipts.

a. How can sales clerks employed at Meridian Clothing use the store's return policy to steal money from the cash register?

b. What internal control weaknesses do you see in the return policy that make cash thefts easier?

c. Would issuing a store credit in place of a cash refund for all merchandise returned without a receipt reduce the possibility of theft? List some advantages and disadvantages of issuing a store credit in place of a cash refund.

d. Assume that Meridian Clothing is committed to the current policy of issuing cash refunds without a receipt. What changes could be made in the store's procedures regarding customer refunds in order to improve internal control?

OBJ. 2, 3

EX 8-4 Internal controls for bank lending

Evergreen Bank provides loans to businesses in the community through its Commercial Lending Department. Small loans (less than $250,000) may be approved by an individual loan officer, while larger loans (greater than $250,000) must be approved by a board of loan officers. Once a loan is approved, the funds are made available to the loan applicant under agreed-upon terms. The president of Evergreen Bank has instituted a policy whereby he has the individual authority to approve loans up to $10,000,000. The president believes that this policy will allow flexibility to approve loans to valued clients much quicker than under the previous policy.

As an internal auditor of Evergreen Bank, how would you respond to this change in policy?

OBJ. 2, 3

EX 8-5 Internal controls

One of the largest losses in history from unauthorized securities trading involved a securities trader for the French bank, Societe Generale. The trader was able to circumvent internal controls and create over $7 billion in trading losses in six months. The trader apparently escaped detection by using knowledge of the bank's internal control systems learned from a previous back-office monitoring job. Much of this monitoring involved the use of software to monitor trades. In addition, traders were usually kept to tight trading limits. Apparently, these controls failed in this case.

What general weaknesses in Societe Generale's internal controls contributed to the occurrence and size of the losses?

OBJ. 2, 3

EX 8-6 Internal controls

An employee of JHT Holdings, Inc., a trucking company, was responsible for resolving roadway accident claims under $25,000. The employee created fake accident claims and wrote settlement checks of between $5,000 and $25,000 to friends or acquaintances acting as phony "victims." One friend recruited subordinates at his place of work to cash some of the checks. Beyond this, the JHT employee also recruited lawyers, who he paid to represent both the trucking company and the fake victims in the bogus accident settlements. When the lawyers cashed the checks, they allegedly split the money with the corrupt JHT employee. This fraud went undetected for two years.

Why would it take so long to discover such a fraud?

OBJ. 2, 3

EX 8-7 Internal controls

Frog Sound Co. discovered a fraud whereby one of its front office administrative employees used company funds to purchase goods, such as computers, digital cameras, compact disk players, and other electronic items for her own use. The fraud was discovered when employees noticed an increase in delivery frequency from vendors and the use of unusual vendors. After some investigation, it was discovered that the employee would alter the description or change the quantity on an invoice in order to explain the cost on the bill.

What general internal control weaknesses contributed to this fraud?

OBJ. 2, 3

EX 8-8 Financial statement fraud

A former chairman, CFO, and controller of Donnkenny, Inc., an apparel company that makes sportswear for Pierre Cardin and Victoria Jones, pleaded guilty to financial statement fraud. These managers used false journal entries to record fictitious sales, hid inventory in public warehouses so that it could be recorded as "sold," and required sales orders to be backdated so that the sale could be moved back to an earlier period. The combined effect of these actions caused $25 million out of $40 million in quarterly sales to be phony.

a. Why might control procedures listed in this chapter be insufficient in stopping this type of fraud?

b. How could this type of fraud be stopped?

OBJ. 2, 3

EX 8-9 Internal control of cash receipts

The procedures used for over-the-counter receipts are as follows. At the close of each day's business, the sales clerks count the cash in their respective cash drawers, after which they determine the amount recorded by the cash register and prepare the memo cash form, noting any discrepancies. An employee from the cashier's office counts the cash, compares the total with the memo, and takes the cash to the cashier's office.

a. Indicate the weak link in internal control.

b. How can the weakness be corrected?

OBJ. 2, 3

EX 8-10 Internal control of cash receipts

Mel Lane works at the drive-through window of Bison Burgers. Occasionally, when a drive-through customer orders, Mel fills the order and pockets the customer's money. He does not ring up the order on the cash register.

Identify the internal control weaknesses that exist at Bison Burgers, and discuss what can be done to prevent this theft.

OBJ. 2, 3

EX 8-11 Internal control of cash receipts

The mailroom employees send all remittances and remittance advices to the cashier. The cashier deposits the cash in the bank and forwards the remittance advices and duplicate deposit slips to the Accounting Department.

a. Indicate the weak link in internal control in the handling of cash receipts.

b. How can the weakness be corrected?

OBJ. 2, 3

EX 8-12 Entry for cash sales; cash short

The actual cash received from cash sales was $27,943, and the amount indicated by the cash register total was $28,000. Journalize the entry to record the cash receipts and cash sales.

OBJ. 2, 3

EX 8-13 Entry for cash sales; cash over

The actual cash received from cash sales was $13,590, and the amount indicated by the cash register total was $13,540. Journalize the entry to record the cash receipts and cash sales.

OBJ. 2, 3

EX 8-14 Internal control of cash payments

Signs-A-Rama Co. is a small merchandising company with a manual accounting system. An investigation revealed that in spite of a sufficient bank balance, a significant amount of available cash discounts had been lost because of failure to make timely payments. In addition, it was discovered that the invoices for several purchases had been paid twice.

Outline procedures for the payment of vendors' invoices, so that the possibilities of losing available cash discounts and of paying an invoice a second time will be minimized.

OBJ. 2, 3

EX 8-15 Internal control of cash payments

Digit Tech Company, a communications equipment manufacturer, recently fell victim to a fraud scheme developed by one of its employees. To understand the scheme, it is necessary to review Digit Tech's procedures for the purchase of services.

The purchasing agent is responsible for ordering services (such as repairs to a photocopy machine or office cleaning) after receiving a service requisition from an authorized manager. However, since no tangible goods are delivered, a receiving report is not prepared. When the Accounting Department receives an invoice billing Digit Tech for a service call, the accounts payable clerk calls the manager who requested the service in order to verify that it was performed.

The fraud scheme involves Loretta Trent, the manager of plant and facilities. Loretta arranged for her uncle's company, Laser Systems, to be placed on Digit Tech's approved vendor list. Loretta did not disclose the family relationship.

On several occasions, Loretta would submit a requisition for services to be provided by Laser Systems. However, the service requested was really not needed, and it was never performed. Laser Systems would bill Digit Tech for the service and then split the cash payment with Loretta.

Explain what changes should be made to Digit Tech's procedures for ordering and paying for services in order to prevent such occurrences in the future.

OBJ. 5

EX 8-16 Bank reconciliation

Identify each of the following reconciling items as: (a) an addition to the cash balance according to the bank statement, (b) a deduction from the cash balance according to the bank statement, (c) an addition to the cash balance according to the company's records, or (d) a deduction from the cash balance according to the company's records. (None of the transactions reported by bank debit and credit memos have been recorded by the company.)

1. Bank service charges, $120.
2. Check of a customer returned by bank to company because of insufficient funds, $4,200.
3. Check for $240 incorrectly recorded by the company as $420.
4. Check for $1,000 incorrectly charged by bank as $10,000.
5. Deposit in transit, $24,950.
6. Outstanding checks, $18,100.
7. Note collected by bank, $15,600.

OBJ. 5

EX 8-17 Entries based on bank reconciliation

Which of the reconciling items listed in Exercise 8-16 require an entry in the company's accounts?

OBJ. 5

✔ Adjusted balance: $16,000

EX 8-18 Bank reconciliation

The following data were accumulated for use in reconciling the bank account of Maplewood Co. for July:

1. Cash balance according to the company's records at July 31, $15,600.
2. Cash balance according to the bank statement at July 31, $16,230.
3. Checks outstanding, $3,180.
4. Deposit in transit, not recorded by bank, $2,950.
5. A check for $270 in payment of an account was erroneously recorded in the check register as $720.
6. Bank debit memo for service charges, $50.

a. Prepare a bank reconciliation, using the format shown in Exhibit 7.

b. If the balance sheet were prepared for Maplewood Co. on July 31, what amount should be reported for cash?

c. Must a bank reconciliation always balance (reconcile)?

OBJ. 5

EX 8-19 Entries for bank reconciliation

Using the data presented in Exercise 8-18, journalize the entry or entries that should be made by the company.

OBJ. 5

EX 8-20 Entries for note collected by bank

Accompanying a bank statement for O'Fallon Company is a credit memo for $21,200, representing the principal ($20,000) and interest ($1,200) on a note that had been collected by the bank. The company had been notified by the bank at the time of the collection, but had made no entries. Journalize the entry that should be made by the company to bring the accounting records up to date.

OBJ. 5

✔ Adjusted balance: $14,000

EX 8-21 Bank reconciliation

An accounting clerk for Muskegon Co. prepared the following bank reconciliation:

Muskegon Co.
Bank Reconciliation
May 31, 2012

Cash balance according to company's records		$ 5,110
Add: Outstanding checks	$2,500	
Error by Muskegon Co. in recording Check No. 2219 as $810 instead of $180	630	
Note for $8,000 collected by bank, including interest	8,320	11,450
		$16,560
Deduct: Deposit in transit on May 31	$5,200	
Bank service charges	60	5,260
Cash balance according to bank statement		$11,300

a. From the data in the above bank reconciliation, prepare a new bank reconciliation for Muskegon Co., using the format shown in the illustrative problem.

b. If a balance sheet were prepared for Muskegon Co. on May 31, 2012, what amount should be reported for cash?

OBJ. 5

✔ Corrected adjusted balance: $13,000

EX 8-22 Bank reconciliation

Identify the errors in the following bank reconciliation:

Alma Co.
Bank Reconciliation
For the Month Ended November 30, 2012

Cash balance according to bank statement			$12,090
Add outstanding checks:			
No. 915		$ 850	
960		615	
964		850	
965		775	3,090
			$15,180
Deduct deposit of November 30, not recorded by bank			4,000
Adjusted balance			$11,180
Cash balance according to company's records			$ 4,430
Add: Proceeds of note collected by bank:			
Principal	$5,000		
Interest	200	$5,200	
Service charges		30	5,230
			$ 9,660
Deduct: Check returned because of insufficient funds		$1,100	
Error in recording November 23 deposit of $6,100 as $1,600		4,500	5,600
Adjusted balance			$ 4,060

OBJ. 2, 3, 5

EX 8-23 Using bank reconciliation to determine cash receipts stolen

Lasting Impressions Co. records all cash receipts on the basis of its cash register tapes. Lasting Impressions Co. discovered during April 2012 that one of its sales clerks had stolen an undetermined amount of cash receipts when she took the daily deposits to the bank. The following data have been gathered for April:

Cash in bank according to the general ledger	$ 8,900
Cash according to the April 30, 2012, bank statement	20,500
Outstanding checks as of April 30, 2012	6,800
Bank service charge for April	100
Note receivable, including interest collected by bank in April	10,400

No deposits were in transit on April 30.

a. Determine the amount of cash receipts stolen by the sales clerk.

b. What accounting controls would have prevented or detected this theft?

OBJ. 6

EX 8-24 Petty cash fund entries

Journalize the entries to record the following:

a. Check No. 6300 is issued to establish a petty cash fund of $1,200.

b. The amount of cash in the petty cash fund is now $200. Check No. 6527 is issued to replenish the fund, based on the following summary of petty cash receipts: office supplies, $650; miscellaneous selling expense, $230; miscellaneous administrative expense, $90. (Since the amount of the check to replenish the fund plus the balance in the fund do not equal $1,200, record the discrepancy in the cash short and over account.)

OBJ. 7

EX 8-25 Variation in cash flows

Mattel, Inc., designs, manufactures, and markets toy products worldwide. Mattel's toys include Barbie™ fashion dolls and accessories, Hot Wheels™, and Fisher-Price brands. For a recent year, Mattel reported the following net cash flows from operating activities (in thousands):

First quarter ending March 31	$ (214,807)
Second quarter ending June 30	(135,003)
Third quarter ending September 30	31,003
Fourth quarter December 31	1,102,915

Explain why Mattel reported negative net cash flows from operating activities during the first two quarters, a small positive net cash flow in the third quarter, and a large positive cash flow for the fourth quarter with overall net positive cash flow for the year.

OBJ. 8

EX 8-26 Cash to monthly cash expenses ratio

During 2012, Pierport Inc. has monthly cash expenses of $400,000. On December 31, 2012, the cash balance is $3,600,000.

a. Compute the ratio of cash to monthly cash expenses.

b. Based on (a), what are the implications for Pierport Inc.?

OBJ. 8

EX 8-27 Cash to monthly cash expenses ratio

Delta Air Lines, one of the world's largest airlines, provides passenger and cargo services throughout the United States and the world. Delta reported the following financial data (in millions) for the year ended December 31, 2008:

Net cash flows from operating activities	$(1,7 07)
Cash and cash equivalents, December 31, 2008	4,255

a. Determine the monthly cash expenses. Round to one decimal place.

b. Determine the ratio of cash to monthly cash expenses. Round to one decimal place.

c. Based on your analysis, do you believe that Delta will remain in business?

OBJ. 8

EX 8-28 Cash to monthly cash expenses ratio

Allos Therapeutics, Inc., is a biopharmaceutical company that develops drugs for the treatment of cancer. Allos Therapeutics reported the following financial data (in thousands) for the years ending December 31, 2008, 2007, and 2006.

	For Years Ending December 31		
	2008	2007	2006
Cash and cash equivalents	$ 30,696	$ 16,103	$ 10,437
Net cash flows from operations	(42,850)	(30,823)	(25,147)

a. Determine the monthly cash expenses for 2008, 2007, and 2006. Round to one decimal place.

b. Determine the ratio of cash to monthly cash expenses as of December 31, 2008, 2007, and 2006. Round to one decimal place.

c. Based on (a) and (b), comment on Allos Therapeutics' ratio of cash to monthly operating expenses for 2008, 2007, and 2006.

Problems Series A

OBJ. 2, 3

PR 8-1A Evaluating internal control of cash

The following procedures were recently installed by Pine Creek Company:

a. Along with petty cash expense receipts for postage, office supplies, etc., several post-dated employee checks are in the petty cash fund.

b. After necessary approvals have been obtained for the payment of a voucher, the treasurer signs and mails the check. The treasurer then stamps the voucher and supporting documentation as paid and returns the voucher and supporting documentation to the accounts payable clerk for filing.

c. At the end of each day, all cash receipts are placed in the bank's night depository.

d. The accounts payable clerk prepares a voucher for each disbursement. The voucher along with the supporting documentation is forwarded to the treasurer's office for approval.

e. At the end of each day, an accounting clerk compares the duplicate copy of the daily cash deposit slip with the deposit receipt obtained from the bank.

f. The bank reconciliation is prepared by the cashier, who works under the supervision of the treasurer.

g. All mail is opened by the mail clerk, who forwards all cash remittances to the cashier. The cashier prepares a listing of the cash receipts and forwards a copy of the list to the accounts receivable clerk for recording in the accounts.

h. At the end of the day, cash register clerks are required to use their own funds to make up any cash shortages in their registers.

Instructions

Indicate whether each of the procedures of internal control over cash represents (1) a strength or (2) a weakness. For each weakness, indicate why it exists.

OBJ. 3, 6

PR 8-2A Transactions for petty cash, cash short and over

Picasso Restoration Company completed the following selected transactions during August 2012:

Aug. 1. Established a petty cash fund of $750.

10. The cash sales for the day, according to the cash register records, totaled $9,780. The actual cash received from cash sales was $9,800.

31. Petty cash on hand was $240. Replenished the petty cash fund for the following disbursements, each evidenced by a petty cash receipt:

Aug. 3. Store supplies, $251.

7. Express charges on merchandise sold, $60 (Delivery Expense).

9. Office supplies, $20.

13. Office supplies, $30.

19. Postage stamps, $11 (Office Supplies).

21. Repair to office file cabinet lock, $40 (Miscellaneous Administrative Expense).

Aug. 22. Postage due on special delivery letter, $18 (Miscellaneous Administrative Expense).
24. Express charges on merchandise sold, $50 (Delivery Expense).
30. Office supplies, $15.
31. The cash sales for the day, according to the cash register records, totaled $11,200. The actual cash received from cash sales was $11,130.
31. Decreased the petty cash fund by $100.

Instructions

Journalize the transactions.

OBJ. 5

✔ 1. Adjusted balance: $11,400

PR 8-3A Bank reconciliation and entries

The cash account for Online Medical Co. at June 30, 2012, indicated a balance of $9,375. The bank statement indicated a balance of $10,760 on June 30, 2012. Comparing the bank statement and the accompanying canceled checks and memos with the records revealed the following reconciling items:

a. Checks outstanding totaled $3,900.
b. A deposit of $4,000, representing receipts of June 30, had been made too late to appear on the bank statement.
c. The bank had collected $2,100 on a note left for collection. The face of the note was $2,000.
d. A check for $550 returned with the statement had been incorrectly recorded by Online Medical Co. as $500. The check was for the payment of an obligation to Hirsch Co. for the purchase on account.
e. A check drawn for $60 had been erroneously charged by the bank as $600.
f. Bank service charges for June amounted to $25.

Instructions

1. Prepare a bank reconciliation.
2. Journalize the necessary entries. The accounts have not been closed.
3. If a balance sheet were prepared for Online Medical Co. on June 30, 2012, what amount should be reported as cash?

OBJ. 5

✔ 1. Adjusted balance: $23,750

PR 8-4A Bank reconciliation and entries

The cash account for Bravo Bike Co. at May 1, 2012, indicated a balance of $15,085. During May, the total cash deposited was $75,100 and checks written totaled $69,750. The bank statement indicated a balance of $25,460 on May 31. Comparing the bank statement, the canceled checks, and the accompanying memos with the records revealed the following reconciling items:

a. Checks outstanding totaled $11,360.
b. A deposit of $9,200, representing receipts of May 31, had been made too late to appear on the bank statement.
c. The bank had collected for Bravo Bike Co. $4,725 on a note left for collection. The face of the note was $4,500.
d. A check for $490 returned with the statement had been incorrectly charged by the bank as $940.
e. A check for $410 returned with the statement had been recorded by Bravo Bike Co. as $140. The check was for the payment of an obligation to Portage Co. on account.
f. Bank service charges for July amounted to $40.
g. A check for $1,100 from Elkhart Co. was returned by the bank because of insufficient funds.

Instructions

1. Prepare a bank reconciliation as of May 31.
2. Journalize the necessary entries. The accounts have not been closed.
3. If a balance sheet were prepared for Bravo Bike Co. on May 31, 2012, what amount should be reported as cash?

OBJ. 5

✔ 1. Adjusted balance: $13,900.50

PR 8-5A Bank reconciliation and entries

Oneida Furniture Company deposits all cash receipts each Wednesday and Friday in a night depository, after banking hours. The data required to reconcile the bank statement as of June 30 have been taken from various documents and records and are reproduced as follows. The sources of the data are printed in capital letters. All checks were written for payments on account.

CASH ACCOUNT:

Balance as of June 1	$9,317.40
CASH RECEIPTS FOR MONTH OF JUNE	$9,524.16

DUPLICATE DEPOSIT TICKETS:

Date and amount of each deposit in June:

Date	Amount	Date	Amount	Date	Amount
June 1	$1,080.50	June 10	$ 896.61	June 22	$ 897.34
3	854.17	15	882.95	24	942.71
8	845.00	17	1,607.64	30	1,517.24

CHECKS WRITTEN:

Number and amount of each check issued in June:

Check No.	Amount	Check No.	Amount	Check No.	Amount
740	$237.50	747	Void	754	$ 449.75
741	495.15	748	$450.90	755	272.75
742	501.90	749	640.13	756	113.95
743	671.30	750	276.77	757	407.95
744	560.88	751	299.37	758	259.60
745	117.25	752	537.01	759	901.50
746	298.66	753	380.95	760	486.39
Total amount of checks issued in June					$8,359.66

BANK RECONCILIATION FOR PRECEDING MONTH:

Oneida Furniture Company
Bank Reconciliation
May 31, 20—

Cash balance according to bank statement		$ 9,447.20
Add deposit for May 31, not recorded by bank		690.25
		$10,137.45
Deduct outstanding checks:		
No. 731	$162.15	
736	345.95	
738	251.40	
739	60.55	820.05
Adjusted balance		$ 9,317.40
Cash balance according to company's records		$ 9,352.50
Deduct service charges		35.10
Adjusted balance		$ 9,317.40

JUNE BANK STATEMENT:

AMERICAN NATIONAL BANK OF CHICAGO
MEMBER FDIC
CHICAGO, IL 60603 (312)441-1239

ONEIDA FURNITURE COMPANY

	PAGE	1
	ACCOUNT NUMBER	
	FROM 6/01/20–	TO 6/30/20–
	BALANCE	9,447.20
9	DEPOSITS	8,691.77
20	WITHDRAWALS	8,014.37
4	OTHER DEBITS AND CREDITS	3,370.00CR
	NEW BALANCE	13,494.60

CHECKS AND OTHER DEBITS				DEPOSITS	DATE	BALANCE
No.731	162.15	No.736	345.95	690.25	6/01	9,629.35
No.739	60.55	No.740	237.50	1,080.50	6/02	10,411.80
No.741	495.15	No.742	501.90	854.17	6/04	10,268.92
No.743	671.30	No.744	506.88	840.50	6/09	9,931.24
No.745	117.25	No.746	298.66	MS 3,500.00	6/09	13,015.33
No.748	450.90	No.749	640.13	MS 210.00	6/09	12,134.30
No.750	276.77	No.751	299.37	896.61	6/11	12,454.77
No.752	537.01	No.753	380.95	882.95	6/16	12,419.76
No.754	449.75	No.755	272.75	1,606.74	6/18	13,304.00
No.757	407.95	No.759	901.50	897.34	6/23	12,891.89
				942.71	6/25	13,834.60
		NSF	300.00		6/28	13,534.60
		SC	40.00		6/30	13,494.60

EC — ERROR CORRECTION
MS — MISCELLANEOUS
NSF — NOT SUFFICIENT FUNDS
OD — OVERDRAFT
PS — PAYMENT STOPPED
SC — SERVICE CHARGE

* * * * * * * * *

THE RECONCILEMENT OF THIS STATEMENT WITH YOUR RECORDS IS ESSENTIAL.
ANY ERROR OR EXCEPTION SHOULD BE REPORTED IMMEDIATELY.

Instructions

1. Prepare a bank reconciliation as of June 30. If errors in recording deposits or checks are discovered, assume that the errors were made by the company. Assume that all deposits are from cash sales. All checks are written to satisfy accounts payable.
2. Journalize the necessary entries. The accounts have not been closed.
3. What is the amount of Cash that should appear on the balance sheet as of June 30?
4. Assume that a canceled check for $270 has been incorrectly recorded by the bank as $720. Briefly explain how the error would be included in a bank reconciliation and how it should be corrected.

Problems Series B

OBJ. 2, 3

PR 8-1B Evaluate internal control of cash

The following procedures were recently installed by The Blind Shop:

a. At the end of a shift, each cashier counts the cash in his or her cash register, unlocks the cash register record, and compares the amount of cash with the amount on the record to determine cash shortages and overages.

b. Checks received through the mail are given daily to the accounts receivable clerk for recording collections on account and for depositing in the bank.

c. Each cashier is assigned a separate cash register drawer to which no other cashier has access.

d. Vouchers and all supporting documents are perforated with a PAID designation after being paid by the treasurer.

e. All sales are rung up on the cash register, and a receipt is given to the customer. All sales are recorded on a record locked inside the cash register.

f. Disbursements are made from the petty cash fund only after a petty cash receipt has been completed and signed by the payee.

g. The bank reconciliation is prepared by the cashier.

Instructions

Indicate whether each of the procedures of internal control over cash represents (1) a strength or (2) a weakness. For each weakness, indicate why it exists.

OBJ. 3, 6

PR 8-2B Transactions for petty cash, cash short and over

Cedar Springs Company completed the following selected transactions during November 2012:

Nov. 1. Established a petty cash fund of $850.

12. The cash sales for the day, according to the cash register records, totaled $16,100. The actual cash received from cash sales was $16,175.

30. Petty cash on hand was $70. Replenished the petty cash fund for the following disbursements, each evidenced by a petty cash receipt:

    Nov. 2. Store supplies, $100.

    10. Express charges on merchandise purchased, $260 (Merchandise Inventory).

    14. Office supplies, $125.

    15. Office supplies, $80.

    18. Postage stamps, $70 (Office Supplies).

    20. Repair to fax, $35 (Miscellaneous Administrative Expense).

    21. Repair to office door lock, $15 (Miscellaneous Administrative Expense).

    22. Postage due on special delivery letter, $40 (Miscellaneous Administrative Expense).

    28. Express charges on merchandise purchased, $40 (Merchandise Inventory).

30. The cash sales for the day, according to the cash register records, totaled $19,415. The actual cash received from cash sales was $19,350.

30. Increased the petty cash fund by $150.

Instructions

Journalize the transactions.

OBJ. 5

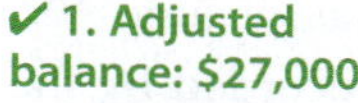

✔ 1. Adjusted balance: $27,000

PR 8-3B Bank reconciliation and entries

The cash account for Ambulance Systems at February 29, 2012, indicated a balance of $20,580. The bank statement indicated a balance of $24,750 on February 29, 2012. Comparing the bank statement and the accompanying canceled checks and memos with the records reveals the following reconciling items:

a. Checks outstanding totaled $9,300.

b. A deposit of $12,000, representing receipts of February 29, had been made too late to appear on the bank statement.

c. The bank had collected $6,240 on a note left for collection. The face of the note was $6,000.

d. A check for $140 returned with the statement had been incorrectly recorded by Ambulance Systems as $410. The check was for the payment of an obligation to Holland Co. for the purchase of office supplies on account.

e. A check drawn for $725 had been incorrectly charged by the bank as $275.

f. Bank service charges for February amounted to $90.

Instructions

1. Prepare a bank reconciliation.
2. Journalize the necessary entries. The accounts have not been closed.
3. If a balance sheet were prepared for Ambulance Systems on February 29, 2012, what amount should be reported as cash?

OBJ. 5

✔ 1. Adjusted balance: $30,175

PR 8-4B Bank reconciliation and entries

The cash account for South Bay Sports Co. on April 1, 2012, indicated a balance of $35,025. During April, the total cash deposited was $83,150, and checks written totaled $90,000. The bank statement indicated a balance of $34,345 on April 30, 2012. Comparing the bank statement, the canceled checks, and the accompanying memos with the records revealed the following reconciling items:

a. Checks outstanding totaled $7,700.

b. A deposit of $3,800, representing receipts of April 30, had been made too late to appear on the bank statement.

c. A check for $960 had been incorrectly charged by the bank as $690.

d. A check for $150 returned with the statement had been recorded by South Bay Sports Co. as $1,500. The check was for the payment of an obligation to Jones Co. on account.

e. The bank had collected for South Bay Sports Co. $2,600 on a note left for collection. The face of the note was $2,500.

f. Bank service charges for June amounted to $50.

g. A check for $1,900 from Valley Schools Academy was returned by the bank because of insufficient funds.

Instructions

1. Prepare a bank reconciliation as of April 30.
2. Journalize the necessary entries. The accounts have not been closed.
3. If a balance sheet were prepared for South Bay Sports Co. on April 30, 2012, what amount should be reported as cash?

OBJ. 5

✔ 1. Adjusted balance: $11,200.00

PR 8-5B Bank reconciliation and entries

La Casa Interiors deposits all cash receipts each Wednesday and Friday in a night depository, after banking hours. The data required to reconcile the bank statement as of July 31 have been taken from various documents and records and are reproduced as follows. The sources of the data are printed in capital letters. All checks were written for payments on account.

BANK RECONCILIATION FOR PRECEDING MONTH (DATED JUNE 30):		
Cash balance according to bank statement		$ 9,422.80
Add deposit of June 30, not recorded by bank		780.80
		$10,203.60
Deduct outstanding checks:		
No. 580	$310.10	
No. 602	85.50	
No. 612	92.50	
No. 613	137.50	625.60
Adjusted balance		$ 9,578.00
Cash balance according to company's records		$ 9,605.70
Deduct service charges		27.70
Adjusted balance		$ 9,578.00
CASH ACCOUNT:		
Balance as of July 1		$ 9,578.00
CHECKS WRITTEN:		
Number and amount of each check issued in July:		

Check No.	Amount	Check No.	Amount	Check No.	Amount
614	$243.50	621	$309.50	628	$ 837.70
615	350.10	622	Void	629	329.90
616	279.90	623	Void	630	882.80
617	395.50	624	707.01	631	1,081.56
618	435.40	625	185.63	632	325.40
619	320.10	626	550.03	633	310.08
620	238.87	627	318.73	634	241.71
Total amount of checks issued in July					$8,343.42

CASH RECEIPTS FOR MONTH OF JULY 6,247.12

DUPLICATE DEPOSIT TICKETS:

Date and amount of each deposit in July:

Date	Amount	Date	Amount	Date	Amount
July 2	$569.50	July 12	$580.70	July 23	$731.45
5	701.80	16	600.10	26	601.50
9	812.94	19	701.26	31	947.87

JULY BANK STATEMENT:

MEMBER FDIC

AMERICAN NATIONAL BANK OF DETROIT

DETROIT, MI 48201-2500 (313)933-8547

PAGE 1

ACCOUNT NUMBER

FROM 7/01/20– TO 7/31/20–

LA CASA INTERIORS

	BALANCE	9,422.80
9	DEPOSITS	6,086.35
20	WITHDRAWALS	8,237.41
4	OTHER DEBITS AND CREDITS	3,685.00CR
	NEW BALANCE	10,956.74

CHECKS AND OTHER DEBITS					DEPOSITS	DATE	BALANCE
No.580	310.10	No.612	92.50		780.80	07/01	9,801.00
No.602	85.50	No.614	243.50		569.50	07/03	10,041.50
No.615	350.10	No.616	279.90		701.80	07/06	10,113.30
No.617	395.50	No.618	435.40		819.24	07/11	10,101.64
No.619	320.10	No.620	238.87		580.70	07/13	10,123.37
No.621	309.50	No.624	707.01		MS 4,000.00	07/14	13,106.86
No.625	158.63	No.626	550.03		MS 160.00	07/14	12,558.20
No.627	318.73	No.629	329.90		600.10	07/17	12,509.67
No.630	882.80	No.631	1,081.56	NSF 450.00		07/20	10,095.31
No.628	837.70	No.633	310.08		701.26	07/21	9,648.79
					731.45	07/24	10,380.24
					601.50	07/28	10,981.74
		SC	25.00			07/31	10,956.74

EC — ERROR CORRECTION
MS — MISCELLANEOUS
NSF — NOT SUFFICIENT FUNDS
OD — OVERDRAFT
PS — PAYMENT STOPPED
SC — SERVICE CHARGE

* * *

THE RECONCILEMENT OF THIS STATEMENT WITH YOUR RECORDS IS ESSENTIAL. ANY ERROR OR EXCEPTION SHOULD BE REPORTED IMMEDIATELY.

Instructions

1. Prepare a bank reconciliation as of July 31. If errors in recording deposits or checks are discovered, assume that the errors were made by the company. Assume that all deposits are from cash sales. All checks are written to satisfy accounts payable.
2. Journalize the necessary entries. The accounts have not been closed.
3. What is the amount of Cash that should appear on the balance sheet as of July 31?
4. Assume that a canceled check for $325 has been incorrectly recorded by the bank as $3,250. Briefly explain how the error would be included in a bank reconciliation and how it should be corrected.

Cases & Projects

CP 8-1 Ethics and professional conduct in business

During the preparation of the bank reconciliation for Regal Concepts Co., Misty Watts, the assistant controller, discovered that Windsor National Bank incorrectly recorded a $15,750 check written by Regal Concepts Co. as $1,575. Misty has decided not to notify the bank but wait for the bank to detect the error. Misty plans to record the $14,175 error as Other Income if the bank fails to detect the error within the next three months.

Discuss whether Misty is behaving in a professional manner.

CP 8-2 Internal controls

The following is an excerpt from a conversation between two sales clerks, Craig Rice and Jill Allen. Craig and Jill are employed by Ogden Electronics, a locally owned and operated electronics retail store.

Craig: Did you hear the news?

Jill: What news?

Craig: Kate and Steve were both arrested this morning.

Jill: What? Arrested? You're putting me on!

Craig: No, really! The police arrested them first thing this morning. Put them in handcuffs, read them their rights—the whole works. It was unreal!

Jill: What did they do?

Craig: Well, apparently they were filling out merchandise refund forms for fictitious customers and then taking the cash.

Jill: I guess I never thought of that. How did they catch them?

Craig: The store manager noticed that returns were twice that of last year and seemed to be increasing. When he confronted Kate, she became flustered and admitted to taking the cash, apparently over $10,000 in just three months. They're going over the last six months' transactions to try to determine how much Steve stole. He apparently started stealing first.

Suggest appropriate control procedures that would have prevented or detected the theft of cash.

CP 8-3 Internal controls

The following is an excerpt from a conversation between the store manager of Dozier Brothers Grocery Stores, Amy Blankenship, and Mike Ulrich, president of Dozier Brothers Grocery Stores.

Mike: Amy, I'm concerned about this new scanning system.

Amy: What's the problem?

Mike: Well, how do we know the clerks are ringing up all the merchandise?

Amy: That's one of the strong points about the system. The scanner automatically rings up each item, based on its bar code. We update the prices daily, so we're sure that the sale is rung up for the right price.

Mike: That's not my concern. What keeps a clerk from pretending to scan items and then simply not charging his friends? If his friends were buying 10-15 items, it would be easy for the clerk to pass through several items with his finger over the bar code or just pass the merchandise through the scanner with the wrong side showing. It would look normal for anyone observing. In the old days, we at least could hear the cash register ringing up each sale.

Amy: I see your point.

Suggest ways that Dozier Brothers Grocery Stores could prevent or detect the theft of merchandise as described.

CP 8-4 Ethics and professional conduct in business

Eric Inman and Darcy Getz are both cash register clerks for Farmer John's Markets. Nancy McNeil is the store manager for Farmer John's Markets. The following is an excerpt of a conversation between Eric and Darcy:

Eric: Darcy, how long have you been working for Farmer John's Markets?

Darcy: Almost five years this June. You just started two weeks ago . . . right?

Eric: Yes. Do you mind if I ask you a question?

Darcy: No, go ahead.

Eric: What I want to know is, have they always had this rule that if your cash register is short at the end of the day, you have to make up the shortage out of your own pocket?

Darcy: Yes, as long as I've been working here.

Eric: Well, it's the pits. Last week I had to pay in almost $25.

Darcy: It's not that big a deal. I just make sure that I'm not short at the end of the day.

Eric: How do you do that?

Darcy: I just shortchange a few customers early in the day. There are a few jerks that deserve it anyway. Most of the time, their attention is elsewhere and they don't think to check their change.

Eric: What happens if you're over at the end of the day?

Darcy: Nancy lets me keep it as long as it doesn't get to be too large. I've not been short in over a year. I usually clear about $10 to $15 extra per day.

 Discuss this case from the viewpoint of proper controls and professional behavior.

CP 8-5 Bank reconciliation and internal control

The records of Diamondale Company indicate a May 31 cash balance of $10,550, which includes undeposited receipts for May 30 and 31. The cash balance on the bank statement as of May 31 is $8,575. This balance includes a note of $5,000 plus $200 interest collected by the bank but not recorded in the journal. Checks outstanding on May 31 were as follows: No. 670, $900; No. 679, $750; No. 690, $1,650; No. 1148, $225; No. 1149, $300; and No. 1151, $600.

On May 3, the cashier resigned, effective at the end of the month. Before leaving on May 31, the cashier prepared the following bank reconciliation:

Cash balance per books, May 31		$10,550
Add outstanding checks:		
No. 1148	$225	
1149	300	
1151	600	1,025
		$11,575
Less undeposited receipts		3,000
Cash balance per bank, May 31		$ 8,575
Deduct unrecorded note with interest		5,200
True cash, May 31		$ 3,375

Calculator Tape of Outstanding Checks:
0*
225+
300+
600+
1,025*

Subsequently, the owner of Diamondale Company discovered that the cashier had stolen an unknown amount of undeposited receipts, leaving only $1,000 to be deposited on May 31. The owner, a close family friend, has asked your help in determining the amount that the former cashier has stolen.

1. Determine the amount the cashier stole from Diamondale Company. Show your computations in good form.
2. How did the cashier attempt to conceal the theft?
3. a. Identify two major weaknesses in internal controls, which allowed the cashier to steal the undeposited cash receipts.
   b. Recommend improvements in internal controls, so that similar types of thefts of undeposited cash receipts can be prevented.

CP 8-6 Observe internal controls over cash

Group Project

Select a business in your community and observe its internal controls over cash receipts and cash payments. The business could be a bank or a bookstore, restaurant, department store, or other retailer. In groups of three or four, identify and discuss the similarities and differences in each business's cash internal controls.

CP 8-7 Cash to monthly cash expenses ratio

OccuLogix, Inc., is a health care company that specializes in developing diagnostic devices for eye disease. OccuLogix reported the following data (in thousands) for the years ending December 31, 2008, 2007, and 2006:

	For Years Ending December 31		
	2008	2007	2006
Cash and cash equivalents	$ 2,565	$ 2,236	$ 5,741
Net cash flows from operations	(9,434)	(17,217)	(14,548)

1. Determine the monthly cash expenses for 2008, 2007, and 2006. Round to one decimal place.
2. Determine the ratio of cash to monthly cash expenses as of December 31, 2008, 2007, and 2006. Round to one decimal place.
3. Based on (1) and (2), comment on OccuLogix's ratio of cash to monthly operating expenses for 2008, 2007, and 2006.

CHAPTER 9

ik Isakson/Tetra Images/Jupiter Images

Receivables

Oakley, Inc.

The sale and purchase of merchandise involves the exchange of goods for cash. However, the point at which cash actually changes hands varies with the transaction. Consider transactions by **Oakley, Inc.**, a worldwide leader in the design, development, manufacture, and distribution of premium sunglasses, goggles, prescription eyewear, apparel, footwear, and accessories. Not only does the company sell its products through three different company-owned retail chains, but it also has approximately 10,000 independent distributors.

If you were to buy a pair of sunglasses at an Oakley Vault, which is one of the company's retail outlet stores, you would have to pay cash or use a credit card to pay for the glasses before you left the store. However, Oakley allows its distributors to purchase sunglasses "on account." These sales on account are recorded as receivables due from the distributors.

As an individual, you also might build up a trusted financial history with a local company or department store that would allow you to purchase merchandise on account. Like Oakley's distributors, your purchase on account would be recorded as an account receivable. Such credit transactions facilitate sales and are a significant current asset for many businesses.

This chapter describes common classifications of receivables, illustrates how to account for uncollectible receivables, and demonstrates the reporting of receivables on the balance sheet.

Learning Objectives

At a Glance 9 Page 419

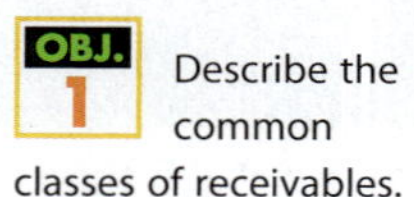

OBJ. 1 Describe the common classes of receivables.

Classification of Receivables

The receivables that result from sales on account are normally accounts receivable or notes receivable. The term **receivables** includes all money claims against other entities, including people, companies, and other organizations. Receivables are usually a significant portion of the total current assets.

Accounts Receivable

The most common transaction creating a receivable is selling merchandise or services on account (on credit). The receivable is recorded as a debit to Accounts Receivable. Such **accounts receivable** are normally collected within a short period, such as 30 or 60 days. They are classified on the balance sheet as a current asset.

An annual report of La-Z-Boy Incorporated reported that receivables made up over 46% of La-Z-Boy's current assets.

Notes Receivable

Notes receivable are amounts that customers owe for which a formal, written instrument of credit has been issued. If notes receivable are expected to be collected within a year, they are classified on the balance sheet as a current asset.

Notes are often used for credit periods of more than 60 days. For example, an automobile dealer may require a down payment at the time of sale and accept a note or a series of notes for the remainder. Such notes usually provide for monthly payments.

Notes may also be used to settle a customer's account receivable. Notes and accounts receivable that result from sales transactions are sometimes called *trade receivables*. In this chapter, all notes and accounts receivable are from sales transactions.

Other Receivables

Other receivables include interest receivable, taxes receivable, and receivables from officers or employees. Other receivables are normally reported separately on the balance sheet. If they are expected to be collected within one year, they are classified as current assets. If collection is expected beyond one year, they are classified as noncurrent assets and reported under the caption *Investments*.

Uncollectible Receivables

OBJ. 2 Describe the accounting for uncollectible receivables.

In prior chapters, the accounting for sales of merchandise or services on account (on credit) was described and illustrated. A major issue that has not yet been discussed is that some customers will not pay their accounts. That is, some accounts receivable will be uncollectible.

Companies may shift the risk of uncollectible receivables to other companies. For example, some retailers do not accept sales on account, but will only accept cash or credit cards. Such policies shift the risk to the credit card companies.

Companies may also sell their receivables. This is often the case when a company issues its own credit card. For example, Macy's and JCPenney issue their own credit cards. Selling receivables is called *factoring* the receivables. The buyer of the receivables is called a *factor*. An advantage of factoring is that the company selling its receivables immediately receives cash for operating and other needs. Also, depending on the factoring agreement, some of the risk of uncollectible accounts is shifted to the factor.

Regardless of how careful a company is in granting credit, some credit sales will be uncollectible. The operating expense recorded from uncollectible receivables is called **bad debt expense**, *uncollectible accounts expense*, or *doubtful accounts expense.*

There is no general rule for when an account becomes uncollectible. Some indications that an account may be uncollectible include the following:

1. The receivable is past due.
2. The customer does not respond to the company's attempts to collect.
3. The customer files for bankruptcy.
4. The customer closes its business.
5. The company cannot locate the customer.

Adams, Stevens & Bradley, Ltd. is a collection agency that operates on a contingency basis. That is, its fees are based on what it collects.

If a customer doesn't pay, a company may turn the account over to a collection agency. After the collection agency attempts to collect payment, any remaining balance in the account is considered worthless.

The two methods of accounting for uncollectible receivables are as follows:

1. The **direct write-off method** records bad debt expense only when an account is determined to be worthless.
2. The **allowance method** records bad debt expense by estimating uncollectible accounts at the end of the accounting period.

The direct write-off method is often used by small companies and companies with few receivables.[1] Generally accepted accounting principles (GAAP), however, require companies with a large amount of receivables to use the allowance method. As a result, most well-known companies such as General Electric, Pepsi, Intel, and FedEx use the allowance method.

Direct Write-Off Method for Uncollectible Accounts

OBJ. 3 Describe the direct write-off method of accounting for uncollectible receivables.

Under the direct write-off method, Bad Debt Expense is not recorded until the customer's account is determined to be worthless. At that time, the customer's account receivable is written off.

1 The direct write-off method is also required for federal income tax purposes.

To illustrate, assume that a $4,200 account receivable from D. L. Ross has been determined to be uncollectible. The entry to write off the account is as follows:

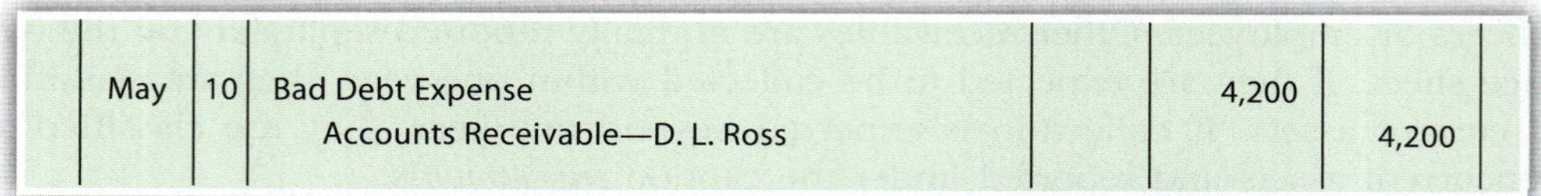

May	10	Bad Debt Expense	4,200	
		Accounts Receivable—D. L. Ross		4,200

An account receivable that has been written off may be collected later. In such cases, the account is reinstated by an entry that reverses the write-off entry. The cash received in payment is then recorded as a receipt on account.

To illustrate, assume that the D. L. Ross account of $4,200 written off on May 10 is later collected on November 21. The reinstatement and receipt of cash is recorded as follows:

Nov.	21	Accounts Receivable—D. L. Ross	4,200	
		Bad Debt Expense		4,200
	21	Cash	4,200	
		Accounts Receivable—D. L. Ross		4,200

The direct write-off method is used by businesses that sell most of their goods or services for cash or through the acceptance of MasterCard or VISA, which are recorded as cash sales. In such cases, receivables are a small part of the current assets and any bad debt expense is small. Examples of such businesses are a restaurant, a convenience store, and a small retail store.

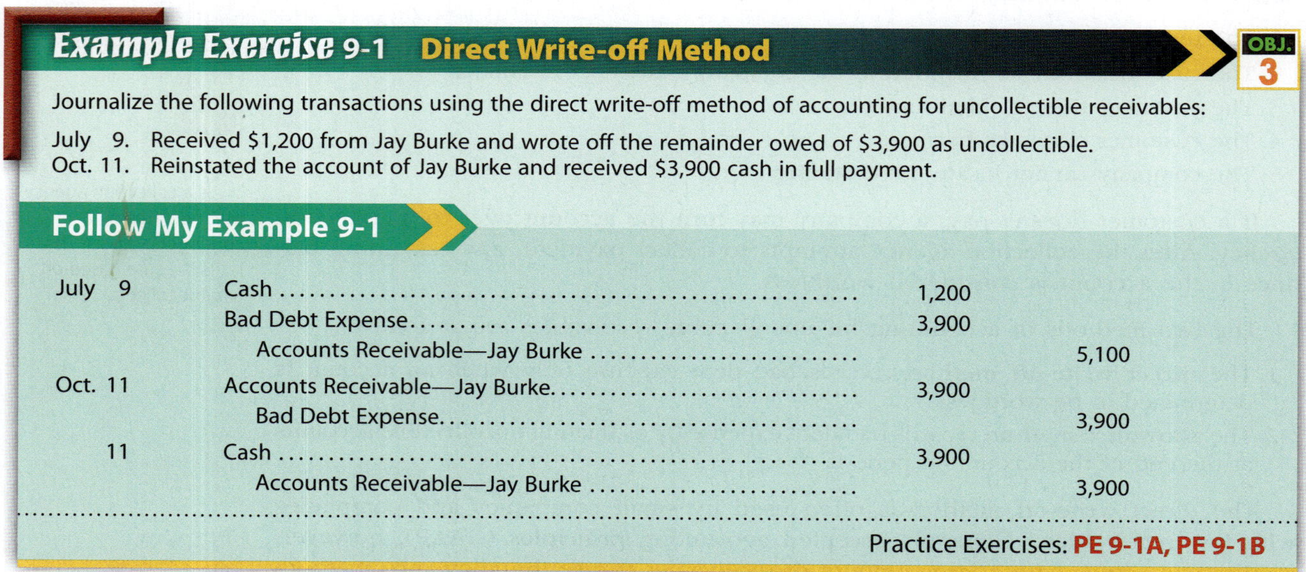

Example Exercise 9-1 Direct Write-off Method OBJ. 3

Journalize the following transactions using the direct write-off method of accounting for uncollectible receivables:

July 9. Received $1,200 from Jay Burke and wrote off the remainder owed of $3,900 as uncollectible.
Oct. 11. Reinstated the account of Jay Burke and received $3,900 cash in full payment.

Follow My Example 9-1

July 9	Cash	1,200	
	Bad Debt Expense	3,900	
	Accounts Receivable—Jay Burke		5,100
Oct. 11	Accounts Receivable—Jay Burke	3,900	
	Bad Debt Expense		3,900
11	Cash	3,900	
	Accounts Receivable—Jay Burke		3,900

Practice Exercises: PE 9-1A, PE 9-1B

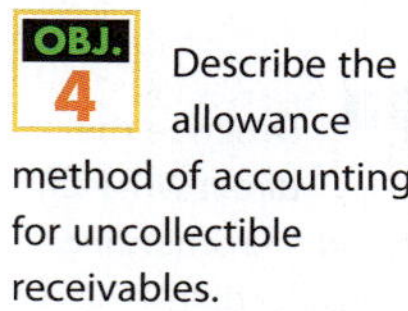

Describe the allowance method of accounting for uncollectible receivables.

Allowance Method for Uncollectible Accounts

The allowance method estimates the uncollectible accounts receivable at the end of the accounting period. Based on this estimate, Bad Debt Expense is recorded by an adjusting entry.

To illustrate, assume that ExTone Company began operations August 1. As of the end of its accounting period on December 31, 2011, ExTone has an accounts receivable balance of $200,000. This balance includes some past due accounts. Based on industry averages, ExTone estimates that $30,000 of the December 31 accounts receivable will be uncollectible. However, on December 31, ExTone doesn't know which customer accounts will be uncollectible. Thus, specific customer accounts cannot be decreased or credited. Instead, a contra asset account, **Allowance for Doubtful Accounts**, is credited for the estimated bad debts.

Using the $30,000 estimate, the following adjusting entry is made on December 31:

2011 Dec.	31	Bad Debt Expense		30,000	
		Allowance for Doubtful Accounts			30,000
		Uncollectible accounts estimate.			

The preceding adjusting entry affects the income statement and balance sheet. On the income statement, the $30,000 of Bad Debt Expense will be matched against the related revenues of the period. On the balance sheet, the value of the receivables is reduced to the amount that is expected to be collected or realized. This amount, $170,000 ($200,000 – $30,000), is called the **net realizable value** of the receivables.

Note:
The adjusting entry reduces receivables to their net realizable value and matches the uncollectible expense with revenues.

After the preceding adjusting entry is recorded, Accounts Receivable still has a debit balance of $200,000. This balance is the total amount owed by customers on account on December 31 as supported by the accounts receivable subsidiary ledger. The accounts receivable contra account, Allowance for Doubtful Accounts, has a credit balance of $30,000.

Integrity, Objectivity, and Ethics in Business

SELLER BEWARE

A company in financial distress will still try to purchase goods and services on account. In these cases, rather than "buyer beware," it is more like "seller beware." Sellers must be careful in advancing credit to such companies, because trade creditors have low priority for cash payments in the event of bankruptcy. To help suppliers, third-party services specialize in evaluating court actions and payment decisions of financially distressed companies.

Write-Offs to the Allowance Account

When a customer's account is identified as uncollectible, it is written off against the allowance account. This requires the company to remove the specific accounts receivable and an equal amount from the allowance account.

To illustrate, on January 21, 2012, John Parker's account of $6,000 with ExTone Company is written off as follows:

2012 Jan.	21	Allowance for Doubtful Accounts		6,000	
		Accounts Receivable—John Parker			6,000

At the end of a period, Allowance for Doubtful Accounts will normally have a balance. This is because Allowance for Doubtful Accounts is based on an estimate. As a result, the total write-offs to the allowance account during the period will rarely equal the balance of the account at the beginning of the period. The allowance account will have a credit balance at the end of the period if the write-offs during the period are less than the beginning balance. It will have a debit balance if the write-offs exceed the beginning balance.

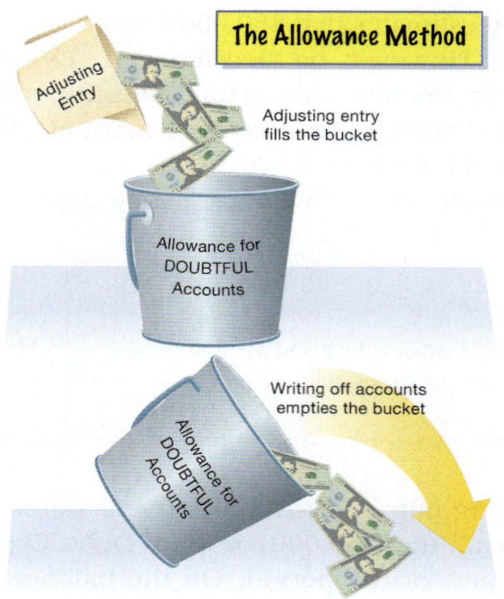

To illustrate, assume that during 2012 ExTone Company writes off $26,750 of uncollectible accounts, including the $6,000 account of John Parker recorded on January 21. Allowance for Doubtful Accounts will have a credit balance of $3,250 ($30,000 – $26,750), as shown below.

ALLOWANCE FOR DOUBTFUL ACCOUNTS

				Jan. 1	Balance	30,000
Total accounts written off $26,750	Jan.	21	6,000			
	Feb.	2	3,900			
	⋮		⋮			
				Dec. 31	Unadjusted balance	3,250

If ExTone Company had written off $32,100 in accounts receivable during 2012, Allowance for Doubtful Accounts would have a debit balance of $2,100, as shown below.

ALLOWANCE FOR DOUBTFUL ACCOUNTS

				Jan. 1	Balance	30,000
Total accounts written off $32,100	Jan.	21	6,000			
	Feb.	2	3,900			
	⋮		⋮			
Dec. 31	Unadjusted balance		2,100			

The allowance account balances (credit balance of $3,250 and debit balance of $2,100) in the preceding illustrations are *before* the end-of-period adjusting entry. After the end-of-period adjusting entry is recorded, Allowance for Doubtful Accounts should always have a credit balance.

An account receivable that has been written off against the allowance account may be collected later. Like the direct write-off method, the account is reinstated by an entry that reverses the write-off entry. The cash received in payment is then recorded as a receipt on account.

To illustrate, assume that Nancy Smith's account of $5,000 which was written off on April 2 is collected later on June 10. ExTone Company records the reinstatement and the collection as follows:

June	10	Accounts Receivable—Nancy Smith	5,000	
		Allowance for Doubtful Accounts		5,000
	10	Cash	5,000	
		Accounts Receivable—Nancy Smith		5,000

Example Exercise 9-2 Allowance Method

OBJ. 4

Journalize the following transactions using the allowance method of accounting for uncollectible receivables.

July 9. Received $1,200 from Jay Burke and wrote off the remainder owed of $3,900 as uncollectible.
Oct. 11. Reinstated the account of Jay Burke and received $3,900 cash in full payment.

Follow My Example 9-2

July 9	Cash	1,200	
	Allowance for Doubtful Accounts	3,900	
	Accounts Receivable—Jay Burke		5,100
Oct. 11	Accounts Receivable—Jay Burke	3,900	
	Allowance for Doubtful Accounts		3,900
11	Cash	3,900	
	Accounts Receivable—Jay Burke		3,900

Practice Exercises: PE 9-2A, PE 9-2B

Estimating Uncollectibles

The allowance method requires an estimate of uncollectible accounts at the end of the period. This estimate is normally based on past experience, industry averages, and forecasts of the future.

The two methods used to estimate uncollectible accounts are as follows:

1. Percent of sales method.
2. Analysis of receivables method.

Percent of Sales Method Since accounts receivable are created by credit sales, uncollectible accounts can be estimated as a percent of credit sales. If the portion of credit sales to sales is relatively constant, the percent may be applied to total sales or net sales.

Business Connection

ALLOWANCE PERCENTAGES ACROSS COMPANIES

The percent of the allowance for doubtful accounts to total accounts receivable will vary across companies and industries. For example, the following percentages were computed from recent annual reports:

HCA's higher percent of allowance for doubtful accounts to total accounts receivable is due in part because Medicare reimbursements are often less than the amounts billed patients.

Company	Industry	Percent of Allowance for Doubtful Accounts to Total Accounts Receivable
Apple Inc.	Computer/technology products	1.5%
Deere & Company	Farm machinery & equipment	17.1
Delta Air Lines	Transportation services	2.8
HCA Inc.	Health services	59.0
Sears	Retail	4.8

To illustrate, assume the following data for ExTone Company on December 31, 2012, before any adjustments:

Balance of Accounts Receivable	$ 240,000
Balance of Allowance for Doubtful Accounts	3,250 (Cr.)
Total credit sales	3,000,000
Bad debt as a percent of credit sales	¾%

Bad Debt Expense of $22,500 is estimated as follows:

Bad Debt Expense = Credit Sales × Bad Debt as a Percent of Credit Sales
Bad Debt Expense = $3,000,000 × ¾% = $22,500

The adjusting entry for uncollectible accounts on December 31, 2012, is as follows:

Dec.	31	Bad Debt Expense	22,500	
		Allowance for Doubtful Accounts		22,500
		Uncollectible accounts estimate ($3,000,000 × ¾% = $22,500).		

After the adjusting entry is posted to the ledger, Bad Debt Expense will have an adjusted balance of $22,500. Allowance for Doubtful Accounts will have an adjusted balance of $25,750 ($3,250 + $22,500). Both T accounts are shown below.

BAD DEBT EXPENSE

Dec. 31	Adjusting entry	22,500	
Dec. 31	Adjusted balance	22,500	

ALLOWANCE FOR DOUBTFUL ACCOUNTS

			Jan. 1	Balance	30,000
Total accounts written off $26,750	Jan. 21	6,000			
	Feb. 2	3,900			
	⋮	⋮			
			Dec. 31	Unadjusted balance	3,250
			Dec. 31	Adjusting entry	22,500
			Dec. 31	Adjusted balance	25,750

Under the percent of sales method, the amount of the adjusting entry is the amount estimated for Bad Debt Expense. This estimate is credited to whatever the unadjusted balance is for Allowance for Doubtful Accounts.

Note:
The estimate based on sales is added to any balance in Allowance for Doubtful Accounts.

To illustrate, assume that in the preceding example the unadjusted balance of Allowance for Doubtful Accounts on December 31, 2012, had been a $2,100 debit balance instead of a $3,250 credit balance. The adjustment would still have been $22,500. However, the December 31, 2012, ending adjusted balance of Allowance for Doubtful Accounts would have been $20,400 ($22,500 – $2,100).

Example Exercise 9-3 Percent of Sales Method

OBJ. 4

At the end of the current year, Accounts Receivable has a balance of $800,000; Allowance for Doubtful Accounts has a credit balance of $7,500; and net sales for the year total $3,500,000. Bad debt expense is estimated at ½ of 1% of net sales.

Determine (a) the amount of the adjusting entry for uncollectible accounts; (b) the adjusted balances of Accounts Receivable, Allowance for Doubtful Accounts, and Bad Debt Expense; and (c) the net realizable value of accounts receivable.

Follow My Example 9-3

a. $17,500 ($3,500,000 × 0.005)

	Adjusted Balance
b. Accounts Receivable	$800,000
Allowance for Doubtful Accounts ($7,500 + $17,500)	25,000
Bad Debt Expense	17,500

c. $775,000 ($800,000 – $25,000)

Practice Exercises: PE 9-3A, PE 9-3B

Analysis of Receivables Method The analysis of receivables method is based on the assumption that the longer an account receivable is outstanding, the less likely that it will be collected. The analysis of receivables method is applied as follows:

Step 1. The due date of each account receivable is determined.

Step 2. The number of days each account is past due is determined. This is the number of days between the due date of the account and the date of the analysis.

Step 3. Each account is placed in an aged class according to its days past due. Typical aged classes include the following:

- Not past due
- 1–30 days past due
- 31–60 days past due
- 61–90 days past due
- 91–180 days past due
- 181–365 days past due
- Over 365 days past due

Step 4. The totals for each aged class are determined.

Step 5. The total for each aged class is multiplied by an estimated percentage of uncollectible accounts for that class.

Step 6. The estimated total of uncollectible accounts is determined as the sum of the uncollectible accounts for each aged class.

The preceding steps are summarized in an aging schedule, and this overall process is called **aging the receivables**.

To illustrate, assume that ExTone Company uses the analysis of receivables method instead of the percent of sales method. ExTone prepared an aging schedule for its accounts receivable of $240,000 as of December 31, 2012, as shown in Exhibit 1.

EXHIBIT 1 **Aging of Receivables Schedule, December 31, 2012**

		A	B	C	D	E	F	G	H	I
	1			Not	Days Past Due					
	2			Past						Over
	3	Customer	Balance	Due	1–30	31–60	61–90	91–180	181–365	365
Steps 1–3	4	Ashby & Co.	1,500			1,500				
	5	B. T. Barr	6,100					3,500	2,600	
	6	Brock Co.	4,700	4,700						
	21									
	22	Saxon Woods Co.	600					600		
Step 4 →	23	Total	240,000	125,000	64,000	13,100	8,900	5,000	10,000	14,000
Step 5 →	24	Percent uncollectible		2%	5%	10%	20%	30%	50%	80%
Step 6 →	25	Estimate of uncollectible accounts	26,490	2,500	3,200	1,310	1,780	1,500	5,000	11,200

Assume that ExTone Company sold merchandise to Saxon Woods Co. on August 29 with terms 2/10, n/30. Thus, the due date (Step 1) of Saxon Woods' account is September 28, as shown below.

Credit terms, net	30 days
Less: Aug. 29 to Aug. 31	2 days
Days in September	28 days

As of December 31, Saxon Woods' account is 94 days past due (Step 2), as shown below.

Number of days past due in September	2 days (30 – 28)
Number of days past due in October	31 days
Number of days past due in November	30 days
Number of days past due in December	31 days
Total number of days past due	94 days

Exhibit 1 shows that the $600 account receivable for Saxon Woods Co. was placed in the 91–180 days past due class (Step 3).

The total for each of the aged classes is determined (Step 4). Exhibit 1 shows that $125,000 of the accounts receivable are not past due, while $64,000 are 1–30 days past due. ExTone Company applies a different estimated percentage of uncollectible accounts to the totals of each of the aged classes (Step 5). As shown in Exhibit 1, the percent is 2% for accounts not past due, while the percent is 80% for accounts over 365 days past due.

The sum of the estimated uncollectible accounts for each aged class (Step 6) is the estimated uncollectible accounts on December 31, 2012. This is the desired adjusted balance for Allowance for Doubtful Accounts. For ExTone Company, this amount is $26,490, as shown in Exhibit 1.

Comparing the estimate of $26,490 with the unadjusted balance of the allowance account determines the amount of the adjustment for Bad Debt Expense. For ExTone, the unadjusted balance of the allowance account is a credit balance of $3,250. The amount to be added to this balance is therefore $23,240 ($26,490 – $3,250). The adjusting entry is as follows:

Note:
The estimate based on receivables is compared to the balance in the allowance account to determine the amount of the adjusting entry.

Dec.	31	Bad Debt Expense	23,240	
		Allowance for Doubtful Accounts		23,240
		Uncollectible accounts estimate ($26,490 – $3,250).		

After the preceding adjusting entry is posted to the ledger, Bad Debt Expense will have an adjusted balance of $23,240. Allowance for Doubtful Accounts will have an adjusted balance of $26,490, and the net realizable value of the receivables is $213,510 ($240,000 – $26,490). Both T accounts are shown below.

BAD DEBT EXPENSE

Dec. 31	Adjusting entry	23,240			
Dec. 31	Adjusted balance	23,240			

ALLOWANCE FOR DOUBTFUL ACCOUNTS

			Dec. 31	Unadjusted balance	3,250
			Dec. 31	Adjusting entry	23,240
			Dec. 31	Adjusted balance	26,490

Under the analysis of receivable method, the amount of the adjusting entry is the amount that will yield an adjusted balance for Allowance for Doubtful Accounts equal to that estimated by the aging schedule.

To illustrate, if the unadjusted balance of the allowance account had been a debit balance of $2,100, the amount of the adjustment would have been $28,590 ($26,490 + $2,100). In this case, Bad Debt Expense would have an adjusted balance of $28,590. However, the adjusted balance of Allowance for Doubtful Accounts would still have been $26,490. After the adjusting entry is posted, both T accounts are shown below.

BAD DEBT EXPENSE

Dec. 31	Adjusting entry	28,590			
Dec. 31	Adjusted balance	28,590			

ALLOWANCE FOR DOUBTFUL ACCOUNTS

Dec. 31	Unadjusted balance	2,100			
			Dec. 31	Adjusting entry	28,590
			Dec. 31	Adjusted balance	26,490

Example Exercise 9-4 Analysis of Receivables Method

OBJ. 4

At the end of the current year, Accounts Receivable has a balance of $800,000; Allowance for Doubtful Accounts has a credit balance of $7,500; and net sales for the year total $3,500,000. Using the aging method, the balance of Allowance for Doubtful Accounts is estimated as $30,000.

Determine (a) the amount of the adjusting entry for uncollectible accounts; (b) the adjusted balances of Accounts Receivable, Allowance for Doubtful Accounts, and Bad Debt Expense; and (c) the net realizable value of accounts receivable.

Follow My Example 9-4

a. $22,500 ($30,000 – $7,500)

		Adjusted Balance
b.	Accounts Receivable	$800,000
	Allowance for Doubtful Accounts	30,000
	Bad Debt Expense	22,500

c. $770,000 ($800,000 – $30,000)

Practice Exercises: PE 9-4A, PE 9-4B

Comparing Estimation Methods Both the percent of sales and analysis of receivables methods estimate uncollectible accounts. However, each method has a slightly different focus and financial statement emphasis.

Under the percent of sales method, Bad Debt Expense is the focus of the estimation process. The percent of sales method places more emphasis on matching revenues and expenses and, thus, emphasizes the income statement. That is, the amount of the adjusting entry is based on the estimate of Bad Debt Expense for the period. Allowance for Doubtful Accounts is then credited for this amount.

Under the analysis of receivables method, Allowance for Doubtful Accounts is the focus of the estimation process. The analysis of receivables method places more emphasis on the net realizable value of the receivables and, thus, emphasizes the balance sheet. That is, the amount of the adjusting entry is the amount that will yield an adjusted balance for Allowance for Doubtful Accounts equal to that estimated by the aging schedule. Bad Debt Expense is then debited for this amount.

Exhibit 2 summarizes these differences between the percent of sales and the analysis of receivables methods. Exhibit 2 also shows the results of the ExTone Company illustration for the percent of sales and analysis of receivables methods. The amounts shown in Exhibit 2 assume an unadjusted credit balance of $3,250 for Allowance for

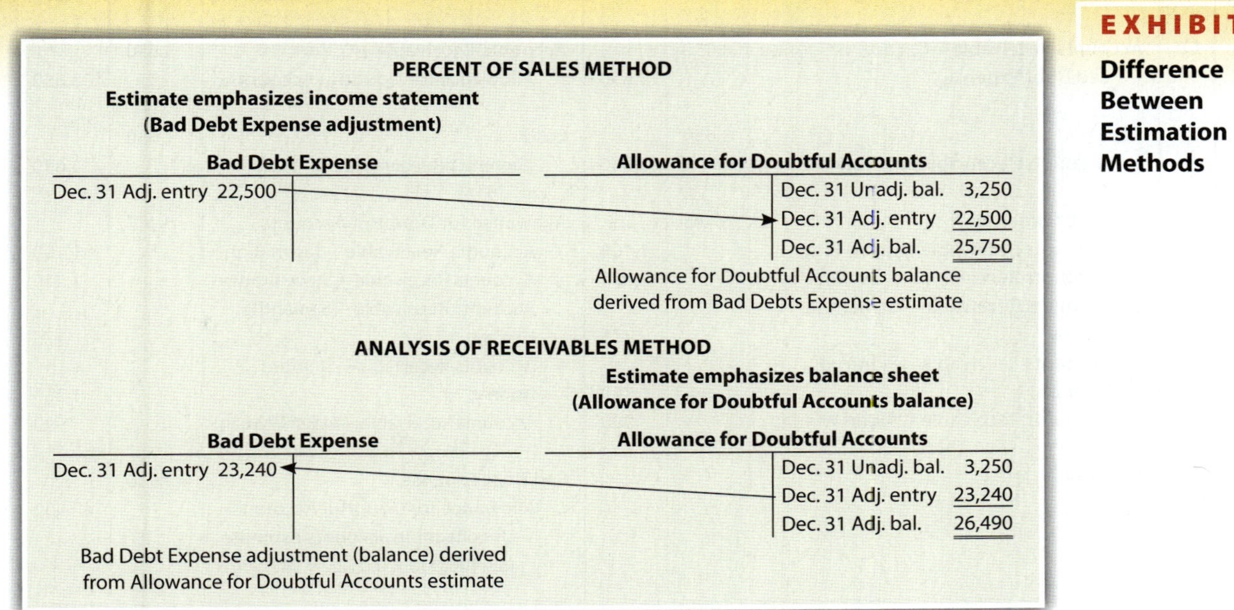

EXHIBIT 2

Difference Between Estimation Methods

Doubtful Accounts. While the methods normally yield different amounts for any one period, over several periods the amounts should be similar.

OBJ. 5 Compare the direct write-off and allowance methods of accounting for uncollectible accounts.

Comparing Direct Write-Off and Allowance Methods

Journal entries for the direct write-off and allowance methods are illustrated and compared in this section. As a basis for illustration, the following transactions, taken from the records of Hobbs Co. for the year ending December 31, 2011, are used:

Mar. 1. Wrote off account of C. York, $3,650.

Apr. 12. Received $2,250 as partial payment on the $5,500 account of Cary Bradshaw. Wrote off the remaining balance as uncollectible.

June 22. Received the $3,650 from C. York, which had been written off on March 1. Reinstated the account and recorded the cash receipt.

Sept. 7. Wrote off the following accounts as uncollectible (record as one journal entry):

Jason Bigg	$1,100	Stanford Noonan	$1,360
Steve Bradey	2,220	Aiden Wyman	990
Samantha Neeley	775		

Dec. 31. Hobbs Company uses the percent of credit sales method of estimating uncollectible expenses. Based on past history and industry averages, 1.25% of credit sales are expected to be uncollectible. Hobbs recorded $3,400,000 of credit sales during 2011.

Exhibit 3 illustrates the journal entries for Hobbs Company using the direct write-off and allowance methods. Using the direct write-off method, there is no adjusting entry on December 31 for uncollectible accounts. In contrast, the allowance method records an adjusting entry for estimated uncollectible accounts of $42,500.

EXHIBIT 3 Comparing Direct Write-Off and Allowance Methods

		Direct Write-Off Method			Allowance Method		
2011 Mar.	1	Bad Debt Expense	3,650		Allowance for Doubtful Accounts	3,650	
		Accounts Receivable—C. York		3,650	Accounts Receivable—C. York		3,650
Apr.	12	Cash	2,250		Cash	2,250	
		Bad Debt Expense	3,250		Allowance for Doubtful Accounts	3,250	
		Accounts Receivable—Cary Bradshaw		5,500	Accounts Receivable—Cary Bradshaw		5,500
June	22	Accounts Receivable—C. York	3,650		Accounts Receivable—C. York	3,650	
		Bad Debt Expense		3,650	Allowance for Doubtful Accounts		3,650
	22	Cash	3,650		Cash	3,650	
		Accounts Receivable—C. York		3,650	Accounts Receivable—C. York		3,650
Sept.	7	Bad Debt Expense	6,445		Allowance for Doubtful Accounts	6,445	
		Accounts Receivable—Jason Bigg		1,100	Accounts Receivable—Jason Bigg		1,100
		Accounts Receivable—Steve Bradey		2,220	Accounts Receivable—Steve Bradey		2,220
		Accounts Receivable—Samantha Neeley		775	Accounts Receivable—Samantha Neeley		775
		Accounts Receivable—Stanford Noonan		1,360	Accounts Receivable—Stanford Noonan		1,360
		Accounts Receivable—Aiden Wyman		990	Accounts Receivable—Aiden Wyman		990
Dec.	31	No Entry			Bad Debt Expense	42,500	
					Allowance for Doubtful Accounts		42,500
					Uncollectible accounts estimate ($3,400,000 × 0.0125 = $42,500).		

The primary differences between the direct write-off and allowance methods are summarized below.

	Direct Write-Off Method	Allowance Method
Bad debt expense is recorded	When the specific customer accounts are determined to be uncollectible.	Using estimate based on (1) a percent of sales or (2) an analysis of receivables.
Allowance account	No allowance account is used.	The allowance account is used.
Primary users	Small companies and companies with few receivables.	Large companies and those with a large amount of receivables.

Notes Receivable

OBJ. 6 Describe the accounting for notes receivable.

A note has some advantages over an account receivable. By signing a note, the debtor recognizes the debt and agrees to pay it according to its terms. Thus, a note is a stronger legal claim.

Characteristics of Notes Receivable

A promissory note is a written promise to pay the face amount, usually with interest, on demand or at a date in the future.[2] Characteristics of a promissory note are as follows:

1. The *maker* is the party making the promise to pay.
2. The *payee* is the party to whom the note is payable.
3. The *face amount* is the amount for which the note is written on its face.
4. The *issuance date* is the date a note is issued.
5. The *due date* or *maturity date* is the date the note is to be paid.
6. The *term* of a note is the amount of time between the issuance and due dates.
7. The *interest rate* is that rate of interest that must be paid on the face amount for the term of the note.

Exhibit 4 illustrates a promissory note. The maker of the note is Selig Company, and the payee is Pearland Company. The face value of the note is $2,000, and the issuance date is March 16, 2011. The term of the note is 90 days, which results in a due date of June 14, 2011, as shown below.

Days in March	31 days
Minus issuance date of note	16
Days remaining in March	15 days
Add days in April	30
Add days in May	31
Add days in June (due date of June 14)	14
Term of note	90 days

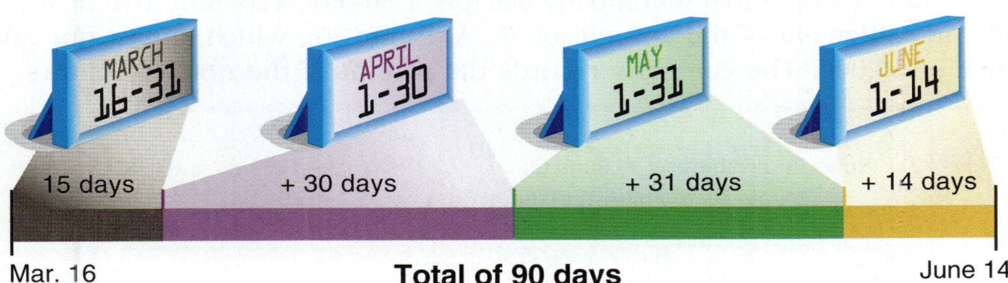

In Exhibit 4, the term of the note is 90 days and has an interest rate of 10%.

2 You may see references to noninterest-bearing notes. Such notes are not widely used and carry an assumed or implicit interest rate.

EXHIBIT 4 Promissory Note

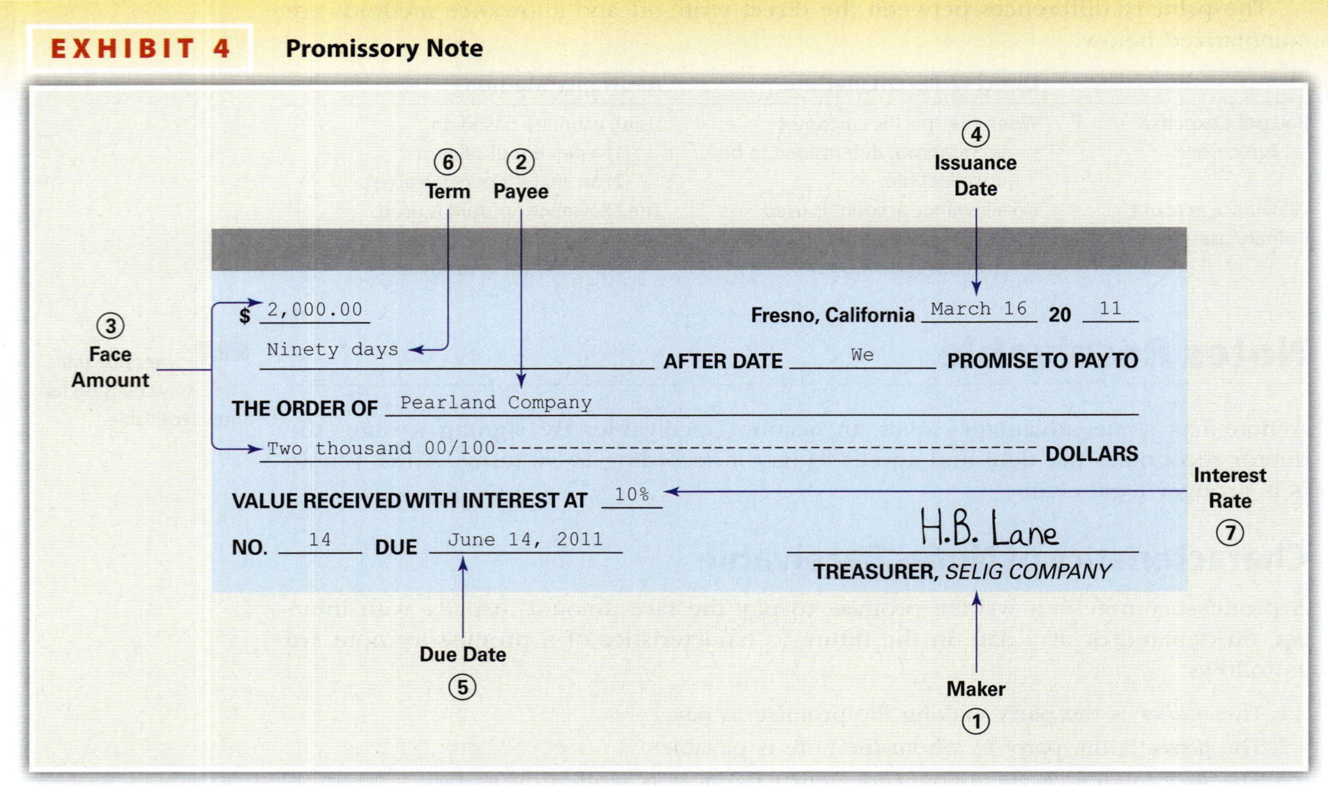

The interest on a note is computed as follows:

Interest = Face Amount × Interest Rate × (Term/360 days)

The interest rate is stated on an annual (yearly) basis, while the term is expressed as days. Thus, the interest on the note in Exhibit 4 is computed as follows:

Interest = $2,000 × 10% × (90/360) = $50

To simplify, 360 days per year will be used. In practice, companies such as banks and mortgage companies use the exact number of days in a year, 365.

The **maturity value** is the amount that must be paid at the due date of the note, which is the sum of the face amount and the interest. The maturity value of the note in Exhibit 4 is $2,050 ($2,000 + $50).

Accounting for Notes Receivable

A promissory note may be received by a company from a customer to replace an account receivable. In such cases, the promissory note is recorded as a note receivable.[3]

To illustrate, assume that a company accepts a 30-day, 12% note dated November 21, 2012, in settlement of the account of W. A. Bunn Co., which is past due and has a balance of $6,000. The company records the receipt of the note as follows:

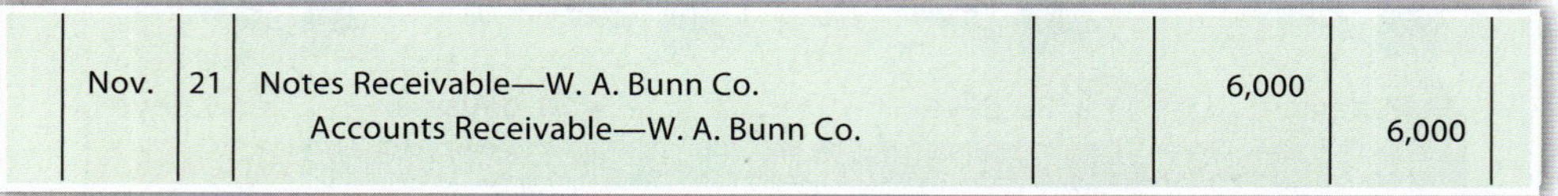

Nov.	21	Notes Receivable—W. A. Bunn Co.		6,000	
		Accounts Receivable—W. A. Bunn Co.			6,000

3 The accounting for notes payable is described and illustrated in Chapter 14.

At the due date, the company records the receipt of $6,060 ($6,000 face amount plus $60 interest) as follows:

Dec.	21	Cash	6,060	
		Notes Receivable—W. A. Bunn Co.		6,000
		Interest Revenue		60
		[$6,060 = $6,000 + ($6,000 × 12% × 30/360)].		

If the maker of a note fails to pay the note on the due date, the note is a **dishonored note receivable**. A company that holds a dishonored note transfers the face amount of the note plus any interest due back to an accounts receivable account. For example, assume that the $6,000, 30-day, 12% note received from W. A. Bunn Co. and recorded on November 21 is dishonored. The company holding the note transfers the note and interest back to the customer's account as follows:

Dec.	21	Accounts Receivable—W. A. Bunn Co.	6,060	
		Notes Receivable—W. A. Bunn Co.		6,000
		Interest Revenue		60

The company has earned the interest of $60, even though the note is dishonored. If the account receivable is uncollectible, the company will write off $6,060 against Allowance for Doubtful Accounts.

A company receiving a note should record an adjusting entry for any accrued interest at the end of the period. For example, assume that Crawford Company issues a $4,000, 90-day, 12% note dated December 1, 2012, to settle its account receivable. If the accounting period ends on December 31, the company receiving the note would record the following entries:

2012 Dec.	1	Notes Receivable—Crawford Company	4,000	
		Accounts Receivable—Crawford Company		4,000
	31	Interest Receivable	40	
		Interest Revenue		40
		Accrued interest ($4,000 × 12% × 30/360).		
2013 Mar.	1	Cash	4,120	
		Notes Receivable—Crawford Company		4,000
		Interest Receivable		40
		Interest Revenue		80
		Total interest of $120 ($4,000 × 12% × 90/360).		

The interest revenue account is closed at the end of each accounting period. The amount of interest revenue is normally reported in the Other Income section of the income statement.

Example Exercise 9-5 Note Receivable

OBJ. 6

Same Day Surgery Center received a 120-day, 6% note for $40,000, dated March 14 from a patient on account.

a. Determine the due date of the note.
b. Determine the maturity value of the note.
c. Journalize the entry to record the receipt of the payment of the note at maturity.

(continued)

Follow My Example 9-6

a. Accounts receivable turnover:

	2012	2011
Average accounts receivable:		
($550,000 + $640,000)/2	$595,000	
($400,000 + $550,000)/2		$475,000
Accounts receivable turnover:		
$4,284,000/$595,000	7.2	
$3,040,000/$475,000		6.4

b. Number of days' sales in receivables:

	2012	2011
Average daily sales:		
$4,284,000/365 days	$11,737	
$3,040,000/365 days		$8,329
Number of days' sales in receivables:		
$595,000/$11,737	50.7 days	
$475,000/$8,329		57.0 days

c. The increase in the accounts receivable turnover from 6.4 to 7.2 and the decrease in the number of days' sales in receivables from 57.0 days to 50.7 days indicate favorable trends in the efficiency of collecting accounts receivable.

Practice Exercises: **PE 9-6A, PE 9-6B**

The number of days' sales in receivables confirms that FedEx's efficiency in collecting accounts receivable has remained the same during 2009 and 2008. Generally, the efficiency in collecting accounts receivable has improved when the accounts receivable turnover increases or the number of days' sales in receivables decreases.

Business Connection

DELTA AIR LINES

Delta Air Lines is a major air carrier that services cities throughout the United States and the world. In its operations, Delta generates accounts receivable as reported in the following note to its financial statements:

Our accounts receivable are generated largely from the sale of passenger airline tickets and cargo transportation services. The majority of these sales are processed through major credit card companies, resulting in accounts receivable... We also have receivables from the sale of mileage credits under our SkyMiles and WorldPerks Programs to participating airlines and nonairline businesses such as credit card companies, hotels, and car rental agencies. We believe the credit risk associated with these receivables is minimal and that the allowance for uncollectible accounts that we have provided is appropriate.

© AP Photo/Ric Feld

In its December 31, 2008, balance sheet, Delta reported the following accounts receivable (in millions):

	Dec. 31, 2009	Dec. 31, 2008
Current Assets:		
...		
Accounts receivable, net of an allowance for uncollectible accounts of $47 at December 31, 2009 and $42 at December 31, 2008	$1,353	$1,513

At a Glance 9

OBJ. 1 Describe the common classes of receivables.

Key Points *Receivables* includes all money claims against other entities. Receivables are normally classified as accounts receivable, notes receivable, or other receivables.

Learning Outcomes	Example Exercises	Practice Exercises
• Define the term *receivables*.		
• List some common classifications of receivables.		

OBJ. 2 Describe the accounting for uncollectible receivables.

Key Points The operating expense recorded from uncollectible receivables is called *bad debt expense*. The two methods of accounting for uncollectible receivables are the direct write-off method and the allowance method.

Learning Outcomes	Example Exercises	Practice Exercises
• Describe how a company may shift the risk of uncollectible receivables to other companies.		
• List factors that indicate an account receivable is uncollectible		
• Describe two methods of accounting for uncollectible accounts receivable.		

OBJ. 3 Describe the direct write-off method of accounting for uncollectible receivables.

Key Points Under the direct write-off method, the entry to write off an account debits Bad Debt Expense and credits Accounts Receivable. Neither an allowance account nor an adjusting entry is needed at the end of the period.

Learning Outcomes	Example Exercises	Practice Exercises
• Prepare journal entries to write off an account using the direct write-off method.	EE9-1	PE9-1A, 9-1B
• Prepare journal entries for the reinstatement and collection of an account previously written off.	EE9-1	PE9-1A, 9-1B

OBJ. 4 Describe the allowance method of accounting for uncollectible receivables.

Key Points Under the allowance method, an adjusting entry is made for uncollectible accounts. When an account is determined to be uncollectible, it is written off against the allowance account. The allowance account normally has a credit balance after the adjusting entry has been posted and is a contra asset account.

The estimate of uncollectibles may be based on a percent of sales or an analysis of receivables. Exhibit 2 compares and contrasts these two methods..

Learning Outcomes	Example Exercises	Practice Exercises
• Prepare journal entries to write off an account using the allowance method.	EE9-2	PE9-2A, 9-2B
• Prepare journal entries for the reinstatement and collection of an account previously written off.	EE9-2	PE9-2A, 9-2B
• Determine the adjustment, bad debt expense, and net realizable value of accounts receivable using the percent of sales method.	EE9-3	PE9-3A, 9-3B
• Determine the adjustment, bad debt expense, and net realizable value of accounts receivable using the analysis of receivables method.	EE9-4	PE9-4A, 9-4B

OBJ. 5 Compare the direct write-off and allowance methods of accounting for uncollectible accounts.

Key Points Exhibit 3 illustrates the differences between the direct write-off and allowance methods of accounting for uncollectible accounts.

Learning Outcomes	Example Exercises	Practice Exercises
• Describe the differences in accounting for uncollectible accounts under the direct write-off and allowance methods.		
• Record journal entries using the direct write-off and allowance methods.		

OBJ. 6 Describe the accounting for notes receivable.

Key Points A note received to settle an account receivable is recorded as a debit to Notes Receivable and a credit to Accounts Receivable. When a note is paid at maturity, Cash is debited, Notes Receivable is credited, and Interest Revenue is credited. If the maker of a note fails to pay, the dishonored note is recorded by debiting an accounts receivable account for the amount due from the maker of the note.

Learning Outcomes	Example Exercises	Practice Exercises
• Describe the characteristics of a note receivable.		
• Determine the due date and maturity value of a note receivable.	EE9-5	PE9-5A, 9-5B
• Prepare journal entries for the receipt of the payment of a note receivable.	EE9-5	PE9-5A, 9-5B
• Prepare a journal entry for the dishonored note receivable.		

Describe the reporting of receivables on the balance sheet.

Key Points All receivables that are expected to be realized in cash within a year are reported in the Current Assets section of the balance sheet. In addition to the allowance for doubtful accounts, additional receivable disclosures include the market (fair) value and unusual credit risks.

Learning Outcomes	Example Exercises	Practice Exercises
• Describe how receivables are reported in the Current Assets section of the balance sheet.		
• Describe disclosures related to receivables that should be reported in the financial statements.		

Describe and illustrate the use of accounts receivable turnover and number of days' sales in receivables to evaluate a company's efficiency in collecting its receivables.

Key Points Two financial measures that are especially useful in evaluating efficiency in collecting receivables are (1) the accounts receivable turnover and (2) the number of days' sales in receivables. Generally, the efficiency in collecting accounts receivable has improved when the accounts receivable turnover increases or there is a decrease in the number of days' sales in receivables.

Learning Outcomes	Example Exercises	Practice Exercises
• Describe two measures of the efficiency of managing receivables.		
• Compute and interpret the accounts receivable turnover and number of days' sales in receivables.	EE9-6	PE9-6A, 9-6B

Key Terms

accounts receivable (402)
accounts receivable turnover (417)
aging the receivables (409)
Allowance for Doubtful Accounts (405)
allowance method (403)
bad debt expense (403)
direct write-off method (403)
dishonored note receivable (415)
maturity value (414)
net realizable value (405)
notes receivable (402)
number of days' sales in receivables (417)
receivables (402)

Illustrative Problem

Ditzler Company, a construction supply company, uses the allowance method of accounting for uncollectible accounts receivable. Selected transactions completed by Ditzler Company are as follows:

Feb.	1.	Sold merchandise on account to Ames Co., $8,000. The cost of the merchandise sold was $4,500.
Mar.	15.	Accepted a 60-day, 12% note for $8,000 from Ames Co. on account.
Apr.	9.	Wrote off a $2,500 account from Dorset Co. as uncollectible.
	21.	Loaned $7,500 cash to Jill Klein, receiving a 90-day, 14% note.
May	14.	Received the interest due from Ames Co. and a new 90-day, 14% note as a renewal of the loan. (Record both the debit and the credit to the notes receivable account.)
June	13.	Reinstated the account of Dorset Co., written off on April 9, and received $2,500 in full payment.
July	20.	Jill Klein dishonored her note.
Aug.	12.	Received from Ames Co. the amount due on its note of May 14.
	19.	Received from Jill Klein the amount owed on the dishonored note, plus interest for 30 days at 15%, computed on the maturity value of the note.
Dec.	16.	Accepted a 60-day, 12% note for $12,000 from Global Company on account.
	31.	It is estimated that 3% of the credit sales of $1,375,000 for the year ended December 31 will be uncollectible.

Instructions

1. Journalize the transactions.
2. Journalize the adjusting entry to record the accrued interest on December 31 on the Global Company note.

Solution

1.

Feb.	1	Accounts Receivable—Ames Co.		8,000.00	
		Sales			8,000.00
	1	Cost of Merchandise Sold		4,500.00	
		Merchandise Inventory			4,500.00
Mar.	15	Notes Receivable—Ames Co.		8,000.00	
		Accounts Receivable—Ames Co.			8,000.00
Apr.	9	Allowance for Doubtful Accounts		2,500.00	
		Accounts Receivable—Dorset Co.			2,500.00
	21	Notes Receivable—Jill Klein		7,500.00	
		Cash			7,500.00
May	14	Notes Receivable—Ames Co.		8,000.00	
		Cash		160.00	
		Notes Receivable—Ames Co.			8,000.00
		Interest Revenue			160.00
June	13	Accounts Receivable—Dorset Co.		2,500.00	
		Allowance for Doubtful Accounts			2,500.00
	13	Cash		2,500.00	
		Accounts Receivable—Dorset Co.			2,500.00
July	20	Accounts Receivable—Jill Klein		7,762.50	
		Notes Receivable—Jill Klein			7,500.00
		Interest Revenue			262.50
Aug.	12	Cash		8,280.00	
		Notes Receivable—Ames Co.			8,000.00
		Interest Revenue			280.00
	19	Cash		7,859.53	
		Accounts Receivable—Jill Klein			7,762.50
		Interest Revenue			97.03
		($7,762.50 × 15% × 30/360).			
Dec.	16	Notes Receivable—Global Company		12,000.00	
		Accounts Receivable—Global Company			12,000.00
	31	Bad Debt Expense		41,250.00	
		Allowance for Doubtful Accounts			41,250.00
		Uncollectible accounts estimate			
		($1,375,000 × 3%).			

2.

Dec.	31	Interest Receivable		60.00	
		Interest Revenue			60.00
		Accrued interest			
		($12,000 × 12% × 15/360).			

Discussion Questions

1. What are the three classifications of receivables?
2. Elite Hardware is a small hardware store in the rural township of Rexburg that rarely extends credit to its customers in the form of an account receivable. The few customers that are allowed to carry accounts receivable are long-time residents of Rexburg and have a history of doing business at Elite Hardware. What method of accounting for uncollectible receivables should Elite Hardware use? Why?
3. What kind of an account (asset, liability, etc.) is Allowance for Doubtful Accounts, and is its normal balance a debit or a credit?
4. After the accounts are adjusted and closed at the end of the fiscal year, Accounts Receivable has a balance of $471,200 and Allowance for Doubtful Accounts has a balance of $27,500. Describe how the accounts receivable and the allowance for doubtful accounts are reported on the balance sheet.
5. A firm has consistently adjusted its allowance account at the end of the fiscal year by adding a fixed percent of the period's net sales on account. After seven years, the balance in Allowance for Doubtful Accounts has become very large in relationship to the balance in Accounts Receivable. Give two possible explanations.
6. Which of the two methods of estimating uncollectibles provides for the most accurate estimate of the current net realizable value of the receivables?
7. Calypso Company issued a note receivable to Kearny Company. (a) Who is the payee? (b) What is the title of the account used by Kearny Company in recording the note?
8. If a note provides for payment of principal of $150,000 and interest at the rate of 4%, will the interest amount to $6,000? Explain.
9. The maker of a $60,000, 5%, 90-day note receivable failed to pay the note on the due date of April 30. What accounts should be debited and credited by the payee to record the dishonored note receivable?
10. The note receivable dishonored in Discussion Question 9 is paid on May 30 by the maker, plus interest for 30 days, 8%. What entry should be made to record the receipt of the payment?

Practice Exercises

Learning Objectives	Example Exercises

OBJ. 3 **EE 9-1** *p. 404*

PE 9-1A Direct write-off method

Journalize the following transactions using the direct write-off method of accounting for uncollectible receivables:

Jan. 17. Received $250 from Ian Kearns and wrote off the remainder owed of $750 as uncollectible.

Apr. 6. Reinstated the account of Ian Kearns and received $750 cash in full payment.

OBJ. 3 **EE 9-1** *p. 404*

PE 9-1B Direct write-off method

Journalize the following transactions using the direct write-off method of accounting for uncollectible receivables:

July 7. Received $500 from Betty Williams and wrote off the remainder owed of $2,000 as uncollectible.

Nov. 13. Reinstated the account of Betty Williams and received $2,000 cash in full payment.

OBJ. 4 **EE 9-2** *p. 407*

PE 9-2A Allowance method

Journalize the following transactions using the allowance method of accounting for uncollectible receivables:

Jan. 17. Received $250 from Ian Kearns and wrote off the remainder owed of $750 as uncollectible.

Apr. 6. Reinstated the account of Ian Kearns and received $750 cash in full payment.

OBJ. 4 **EE 9-2** *p. 407*

PE 9-2B Allowance method

Journalize the following transactions using the allowance method of accounting for uncollectible receivables:

July 7. Received $500 from Betty Williams and wrote off the remainder owed of $2,000 as uncollectible.

Nov. 13. Reinstated the account of Betty Williams and received $2,000 cash in full payment.

OBJ. 4 **EE 9-3** *p. 408*

PE 9-3A Percent of sales method

At the end of the current year, Accounts Receivable has a balance of $325,000; Allowance for Doubtful Accounts has a credit balance of $3,900; and net sales for the year total $4,500,000. Bad debt expense is estimated at ½ of 1% of net sales.

Determine (a) the amount of the adjusting entry for uncollectible accounts; (b) the adjusted balances of Accounts Receivable, Allowance for Doubtful Accounts, and Bad Debt Expense; and (c) the net realizable value of accounts receivable.

OBJ. 4 **EE 9-3** *p. 408*

PE 9-3B Percent of sales method

At the end of the current year, Accounts Receivable has a balance of $2,500,000; Allowance for Doubtful Accounts has a debit balance of $9,000; and net sales for the year total $32,000,000. Bad debt expense is estimated at ¼ of 1% of net sales.

Determine (a) the amount of the adjusting entry for uncollectible accounts; (b) the adjusted balances of Accounts Receivable, Allowance for Doubtful Accounts, and Bad Debt Expense; and (c) the net realizable value of accounts receivable.

Learning Objectives	Example Exercises

OBJ. 4 EE 9-4 p. 411

PE 9-4A Analysis of receivables method

At the end of the current year, Accounts Receivable has a balance of $325,000; Allowance for Doubtful Accounts has a credit balance of $3,900; and net sales for the year total $4,500,000. Using the aging method, the balance of Allowance for Doubtful Accounts is estimated as $25,000.

Determine (a) the amount of the adjusting entry for uncollectible accounts; (b) the adjusted balances of Accounts Receivable, Allowance for Doubtful Accounts, and Bad Debt Expense; and (c) the net realizable value of accounts receivable.

OBJ. 4 EE 9-4 p. 411

PE 9-4B Analysis of receivables method

At the end of the current year, Accounts Receivable has a balance of $2,500,000; Allowance for Doubtful Accounts has a debit balance of $9,000; and net sales for the year total $32,000,000. Using the aging method, the balance of Allowance for Doubtful Accounts is estimated as $76,000.

Determine (a) the amount of the adjusting entry for uncollectible accounts; (b) the adjusted balances of Accounts Receivable, Allowance for Doubtful Accounts, and Bad Debt Expense; and (c) the net realizable value of accounts receivable.

OBJ. 6 EE 9-5 p. 415

PE 9-5A Note receivable

Vista Supply Company received a 30-day, 4% note for $90,000, dated September 8 from a customer on account.

a. Determine the due date of the note.

b. Determine the maturity value of the note.

c. Journalize the entry to record the receipt of the payment of the note at maturity.

OBJ. 6 EE 9-5 p. 415

PE 9-5B Note receivable

Gorilla Supply Company received a 120-day, 5% note for $150,000, dated March 27 from a customer on account.

a. Determine the due date of the note.

b. Determine the maturity value of the note.

c. Journalize the entry to record the receipt of the payment of the note at maturity.

OBJ. 8 EE 9-6 p. 417

F·A·I

PE 9-6A Accounts receivable turnover and number of days' sales in receivables

Financial statement data for years ending December 31 for Blum Company are shown below.

	2012	2011
Net sales	$2,430,000	$1,920,000
Accounts receivable:		
Beginning of year	180,000	120,000
End of year	225,000	180,000

a. Determine the accounts receivable turnover for 2012 and 2011.

b. Determine the number of days' sales in receivables for 2012 and 2011. Round to one decimal place.

c. Does the change in accounts receivable turnover and the number of days' sales in receivables from 2011 to 2012 indicate a favorable or an unfavorable trend?

OBJ. 8 EE 9-6 p. 417

F·A·I

PE 9-6B Accounts receivable turnover and number of days' sales in receivables

Financial statement data for years ending December 31 for Sherick Company are shown below.

	2012	2011
Net sales	$4,514,000	$4,200,000
Accounts receivable:		
Beginning of year	280,000	320,000
End of year	330,000	280,000

a. Determine the accounts receivable turnover for 2012 and 2011.

b. Determine the number of days' sales in receivables for 2012 and 2011. Round to one decimal place.

c. Does the change in accounts receivable turnover and the number of days' sales in receivables from 2011 to 2012 indicate a favorable or an unfavorable trend?

Exercises

OBJ. 1

EX 9-1 Classifications of receivables

Boeing is one of the world's major aerospace firms, with operations involving commercial aircraft, military aircraft, missiles, satellite systems, and information and battle management systems. As of December 31, 2009, Boeing had $3,090 million of receivables involving U.S. government contracts and $1,206 million of receivables involving commercial aircraft customers, such as Delta Air Lines and United Airlines.

Should Boeing report these receivables separately in the financial statements, or combine them into one overall accounts receivable amount? Explain.

OBJ. 2
✔ a. 20.9%

EX 9-2 Nature of uncollectible accounts

The MGM Mirage owns and operates casinos including the MGM Grand and the Bellagio in Las Vegas, Nevada. As of December 31, 2009, The MGM Mirage reported accounts and notes receivable of $465,580,000 and allowance for doubtful accounts of $97,106,000. Johnson & Johnson manufactures and sells a wide range of health care products including Band-Aids and Tylenol. As of December 31, 2009, Johnson & Johnson reported accounts receivable of $9,979,000,000 and allowance for doubtful accounts of $333,000,000.

a. Compute the percentage of the allowance for doubtful accounts to the accounts and notes receivable as of December 31, 2009, for The MGM Mirage. Round to one decimal place.

b. Compute the percentage of the allowance for doubtful accounts to the accounts receivable as of December 31, 2009, for Johnson & Johnson. Round to one decimal place.

c. Discuss possible reasons for the difference in the two ratios computed in (a) and (b).

OBJ. 3

EX 9-3 Entries for uncollectible accounts, using direct write-off method

Journalize the following transactions in the accounts of Cecena Medical Co., a medical equipment company that uses the direct write-off method of accounting for uncollectible receivables:

Feb. 13. Sold merchandise on account to Dr. Ben Katz, $120,000. The cost of the merchandise sold was $72,000.

May 4. Received $90,000 from Dr. Ben Katz and wrote off the remainder owed on the sale of February 13 as uncollectible.

Nov. 19. Reinstated the account of Dr. Ben Katz that had been written off on May 4 and received $30,000 cash in full payment.

OBJ. 4

EX 9-4 Entries for uncollectible receivables, using allowance method

Journalize the following transactions in the accounts of Metromark Company, a restaurant supply company that uses the allowance method of accounting for uncollectible receivables:

Feb. 11. Sold merchandise on account to Dakota Co., $29,000. The cost of the merchandise sold was $17,400.

Apr. 15. Received $7,500 from Dakota Co. and wrote off the remainder owed on the sale of February 11 as uncollectible.

Sept. 3. Reinstated the account of Dakota Co. that had been written off on April 15 and received $21,500 cash in full payment.

OBJ. 3, 4

EX 9-5 Entries to write off accounts receivable

Acropolis Company, a computer consulting firm, has decided to write off the $12,950 balance of an account owed by a customer, Aaron Guzman. Journalize the entry to record the write-off, assuming that (a) the direct write-off method is used and (b) the allowance method is used.

OBJ. 4
✔ a. $80,000
✔ b. $82,000

EX 9-6 Providing for doubtful accounts

At the end of the current year, the accounts receivable account has a debit balance of $1,275,000 and net sales for the year total $16,000,000. Determine the amount of the adjusting entry to provide for doubtful accounts under each of the following assumptions:

a. The allowance account before adjustment has a debit balance of $5,000. Bad debt expense is estimated at ½ of 1% of net sales.

b. The allowance account before adjustment has a debit balance of $5,000. An aging of the accounts in the customer ledger indicates estimated doubtful accounts of $77,000.

c. The allowance account before adjustment has a credit balance of $7,500. Bad debt expense is estimated at ¼ of 1% of net sales.

d. The allowance account before adjustment has a credit balance of $7,500. An aging of the accounts in the customer ledger indicates estimated doubtful accounts of $43,500.

OBJ. 4

✔ Alpha Auto, 77 days

EX 9-7 Number of days past due

Honest Abe's Auto Supply distributes new and used automobile parts to local dealers throughout the Northeast. Honest Abe's credit terms are n/30. As of the end of business on July 31, the following accounts receivable were past due:

Account	Due Date	Amount
Alpha Auto	May 15	$ 9,000
Best Auto	July 8	3,000
Downtown Repair	March 18	7,500
Lucky's Auto Repair	June 1	5,000
Pit Stop Auto	June 3	750
Sally's	April 12	13,000
Trident Auto	May 31	1,500
Washburn Repair & Tow	March 2	1,500

Determine the number of days each account is past due.

OBJ. 4

EX 9-8 Aging of receivables schedule

The accounts receivable clerk for Quigley Industries prepared the following partially completed aging of receivables schedule as of the end of business on November 30:

	A	B	C	D	E	F	G
1			Not	Days Past Due			
2			Past				Over
3	Customer	Balance	Due	1–30	31–60	61–90	90
4	Able Brothers Inc.	3,000	3,000				
5	Accent Company	4,500		4,500			
21	Zumpano Company	5,000			5,000		
22	Subtotals	830,000	500,000	180,000	80,000	45,000	25,000

The following accounts were unintentionally omitted from the aging schedule and not included in the subtotals above:

Customer	Balance	Due Date
Beltran Industries	$12,000	July 10
Doodle Company	8,000	September 20
La Corp Inc.	17,000	October 17
VIP Sales Company	10,000	November 4
We-Go Company	23,000	December 21

a. Determine the number of days past due for each of the preceding accounts.

b. Complete the aging-of-receivables schedule by adding the omitted accounts to the bottom of the schedule and updating the totals.

OBJ. 4

✔ $68,130

EX 9-9 Estimating allowance for doubtful accounts

Quigley Industries has a past history of uncollectible accounts, as shown below. Estimate the allowance for doubtful accounts, based on the aging of receivables schedule you completed in Exercise 9-8.

Age Class	Percent Uncollectible
Not past due	1%
1–30 days past due	4
31–60 days past due	15
61–90 days past due	35
Over 90 days past due	60

OBJ. 4

EX 9-10 Adjustment for uncollectible accounts

Using data in Exercise 9-9, assume that the allowance for doubtful accounts for Quigley Industries has a credit balance of $14,280 before adjustment on November 30. Journalize the adjusting entry for uncollectible accounts as of November 30.

OBJ. 4

EX 9-11 Estimating doubtful accounts

Imperial Bikes Co. is a wholesaler of motorcycle supplies. An aging of the company's accounts receivable on December 31, 2012, and a historical analysis of the percentage of uncollectible accounts in each age category are as follows:

Age Interval	Balance	Percent Uncollectible
Not past due	$600,000	¼%
1–30 days past due	120,000	2
31–60 days past due	60,000	3
61–90 days past due	45,000	10
91–180 days past due	26,000	40
Over 180 days past due	24,000	75
	$875,000	

Estimate what the proper balance of the allowance for doubtful accounts should be as of December 31, 2012.

OBJ. 4

EX 9-12 Entry for uncollectible accounts

Using the data in Exercise 9-11, assume that the allowance for doubtful accounts for Imperial Bikes Co. had a debit balance of $1,400 as of December 31, 2012.

Journalize the adjusting entry for uncollectible accounts as of December 31, 2012.

OBJ. 5

✔ c. $14,900 higher

EX 9-13 Entries for bad debt expense under the direct write-off and allowance methods

The following selected transactions were taken from the records of Aprilla Company for the first year of its operations ending December 31, 2012:

Jan. 27. Wrote off account of C. Knoll, $6,000.

Feb. 17. Received $1,000 as partial payment on the $3,000 account of Joni Lester. Wrote off the remaining balance as uncollectible.

Mar. 3. Received $6,000 from C. Knoll, which had been written off on January 27. Reinstated the account and recorded the cash receipt.

Dec. 31. Wrote off the following accounts as uncollectible (record as one journal entry):

Jason Short	$4,500
Kim Snider	1,500
Sue Pascall	1,100
Tracy Lane	3,500
Randy Pape	500

31. If necessary, record the year-end adjusting entry for uncollectible accounts.

a. Journalize the transactions for 2012 under the direct write-off method.

b. Journalize the transactions for 2012 under the allowance method. Aprilla Company uses the percent of credit sales method of estimating uncollectible accounts expense. Based on past history and industry averages, 1¾% of credit sales are expected to be uncollectible. Aprilla Company recorded $1,600,000 of credit sales during 2012.

c. How much higher (lower) would Aprilla Company's net income have been under the direct write-off method than under the allowance method?

OBJ. 5

✔ c. $200 higher

EX 9-14 Entries for bad debt expense under the direct write-off and allowance methods

The following selected transactions were taken from the records of Silhouette Company for the year ending December 31, 2012:

Mar. 4. Wrote off account of Myron Rimando, $7,500.

May 19. Received $2,000 as partial payment on the $10,000 account of Shirley Mason. Wrote off the remaining balance as uncollectible.

Aug. 7. Received the $7,500 from Myron Rimando, which had been written off on March 4. Reinstated the account and recorded the cash receipt.

Dec. 31. Wrote off the following accounts as uncollectible (record as one journal entry):

Brandon Peele	$ 5,000
Clyde Stringer	9,000
Ned Berry	13,000
Mary Adams	2,000
Gina Bowers	4,500

Dec. 31. If necessary, record the year-end adjusting entry for uncollectible accounts.

a. Journalize the transactions for 2012 under the direct write-off method.

b. Journalize the transactions for 2012 under the allowance method, assuming that the allowance account had a beginning balance of $45,000 on January 1, 2012, and the company uses the analysis of receivables method. Silhouette Company prepared the following aging schedule for its accounts receivable:

Aging Class (Number of Days Past Due)	Receivables Balance on December 31	Estimated Percent of Uncollectible Accounts
0–30 days	$300,000	1%
31–60 days	80,000	4
61–90 days	20,000	15
91–120 days	10,000	40
More than 120 days	40,000	80
Total receivables	$450,000	

c. How much higher (lower) would Silhouette's 2012 net income have been under the direct write-off method than under the allowance method?

OBJ. 5

EX 9-15 Effect of doubtful accounts on net income

During its first year of operations, Filippi's Plumbing Supply Co. had net sales of $4,800,000, wrote off $65,000 of accounts as uncollectible using the direct write-off method, and reported net income of $375,000. Determine what the net income would have been if the allowance method had been used, and the company estimated that 1½% of net sales would be uncollectible.

OBJ. 5

✔ b. $19,500 credit balance

EX 9-16 Effect of doubtful accounts on net income

Using the data in Exercise 9-15, assume that during the second year of operations Filippi's Plumbing Supply Co. had net sales of $5,500,000, wrote off $70,000 of accounts as uncollectible using the direct write-off method, and reported net income of $450,000.

a. Determine what net income would have been in the second year if the allowance method (using 1½% of net sales) had been used in both the first and second years.

b. Determine what the balance of the allowance for doubtful accounts would have been at the end of the second year if the allowance method had been used in both the first and second years.

OBJ. 5

✔ c. $16,000 higher

EX 9-17 Entries for bad debt expense under the direct write-off and allowance methods

Spangler Company wrote off the following accounts receivable as uncollectible for the first year of its operations ending December 31, 2012:

Customer	Amount
Will Boyette	$10,000
Stan Frey	8,000
Tammy Imes	5,000
Shana Wagner	6,000
Total	$29,000

a. Journalize the write-offs for 2012 under the direct write-off method.

b. Journalize the write-offs for 2012 under the allowance method. Also, journalize the adjusting entry for uncollectible accounts. The company recorded $3,000,000 of credit sales during 2012. Based on past history and industry averages, 1½% of credit sales are expected to be uncollectible.

c. How much higher (lower) would Spangler Company's 2012 net income have been under the direct write-off method than under the allowance method?

OBJ. 5

EX 9-18 Entries for bad debt expense under the direct write-off and allowance methods

Magnetics International wrote off the following accounts receivable as uncollectible for the year ending December 31, 2012:

Customer	Amount
Trey Betts	$15,500
Cheryl Carson	9,000
Irene Harris	29,700
Renee Putman	3,100
Total	$57,300

The company prepared the following aging schedule for its accounts receivable on December 31, 2012:

Aging Class (Number of Days Past Due)	Receivables Balance on December 31	Estimated Percent of Uncollectible Accounts
0–30 days	$600,000	1%
31–60 days	150,000	2
61–90 days	75,000	18
91–120 days	50,000	30
More than 120 days	60,000	50
Total receivables	$935,000	

a. Journalize the write-offs for 2012 under the direct write-off method.

b. Journalize the write-offs and the year-end adjusting entry for 2012 under the allowance method, assuming that the allowance account had a beginning balance of $55,000 on January 1, 2012, and the company uses the analysis of receivables method.

c. How much higher (lower) would Magnetics International's 2012 net income have been under the allowance method than under the direct write-off method?

OBJ. 6

✔ a. Aug. 13, $600

EX 9-19 Determine due date and interest on notes

Determine the due date and the amount of interest due at maturity on the following notes:

	Date of Note	Face Amount	Interest Rate	Term of Note
a.	May 15	$40,000	6%	90 days
b.	March 20	15,000	4	60 days
c.	May 19	24,000	3	60 days
d.	October 1	10,500	8	60 days
e.	August 30	18,000	5	120 days

OBJ. 6

✔ b. $91,350

EX 9-20 Entries for notes receivable

Oregon Interior Decorators issued a 90-day, 6% note for $90,000, dated April 9, to Corvallis Furniture Company on account.

a. Determine the due date of the note.

b. Determine the maturity value of the note.

c. Journalize the entries to record the following: (1) receipt of the note by Corvallis Furniture and (2) receipt of payment of the note at maturity.

OBJ. 6

EX 9-21 Entries for notes receivable

The series of seven transactions recorded in the following T accounts were related to a sale to a customer on account and the receipt of the amount owed. Briefly describe each transaction.

CASH

Debit		Credit	
(7)	40,602		

NOTES RECEIVABLE

Debit		Credit	
(5)	40,000	(6)	40,000

ACCOUNTS RECEIVABLE

Debit		Credit	
(1)	50,000	(3)	10,000
(6)	40,400	(5)	40,000
		(7)	40,400

SALES RETURNS AND ALLOWANCES

Debit		Credit	
(3)	10,000		

MERCHANDISE INVENTORY

Debit		Credit	
(4)	6,000	(2)	30,000

COST OF MERCHANDISE SOLD

Debit		Credit	
(2)	30,000	(4)	6,000

SALES

Debit		Credit	
		(1)	50,000

INTEREST REVENUE

Debit		Credit	
		(6)	400
		(7)	202

OBJ. 6

EX 9-22 Entries for notes receivable, including year-end entries

The following selected transactions were completed by Zip-Up Co., a supplier of zippers for clothing:

2011

Dec. 10. Received from Point Loma Clothing & Bags Co., on account, a $36,000, 90-day, 4% note dated December 10.

31. Recorded an adjusting entry for accrued interest on the note of December 10.

31. Recorded the closing entry for interest revenue.

2012

Mar. 9. Received payment of note and interest from Point Loma Clothing & Bags Co.

Journalize the transactions.

OBJ. 6

EX 9-23 Entries for receipt and dishonor of note receivable

Journalize the following transactions of Frankenstein Productions:

May 3. Received a $150,000, 120-day, 6% note dated May 3 from Sunrider Co. on account.

Aug. 31. The note is dishonored by Sunrider Co.

Oct. 30. Received the amount due on the dishonored note plus interest for 60 days at 9% on the total amount charged to Sunrider Co. on August 31.

OBJ. 4, 6

EX 9-24 Entries for receipt and dishonor of notes receivable

Journalize the following transactions in the accounts of Jamba Co., which operates a riverboat casino:

Mar. 1. Received an $80,000, 60-day, 6% note dated March 1 from Tomekia Co. on account.

18. Received a $75,000, 60-day, 8% note dated March 18 from Mystic Co. on account.

Apr. 30. The note dated March 1 from Tomekia Co. is dishonored, and the customer's account is charged for the note, including interest.

May 17. The note dated March 18 from Mystic Co. is dishonored, and the customer's account is charged for the note, including interest.

July 29. Cash is received for the amount due on the dishonored note dated March 1 plus interest for 90 days at 8% on the total amount debited to Tomekia Co. on April 30.

Aug. 23. Wrote off against the allowance account the amount charged to Mystic Co. on May 17 for the dishonored note dated March 18.

OBJ. 7

EX 9-25 Receivables on the balance sheet

List any errors you can find in the following partial balance sheet:

Tulips Company
Balance Sheet
December 31, 2012

Assets		
Current assets:		
Cash		$138,000
Notes receivable	$400,000	
Less interest receivable	20,000	380,000
Accounts receivable	$795,000	
Plus allowance for doubtful accounts	14,500	809,500

OBJ. 8

✔ a. 2009: 8.6

EX 9-26 Accounts receivable turnover and days' sales in receivables

Polo Ralph Lauren Corporation designs, markets, and distributes a variety of apparel, home decor, accessory, and fragrance products. The company's products include such brands as Polo by Ralph Lauren, Ralph Lauren Purple Label, Ralph Lauren, Polo Jeans Co., and Chaps. Polo Ralph Lauren reported the following (in thousands):

	For the Period Ending	
	March 29, 2009	**March 29, 2008**
Net sales	$5,018,900	$4,880,100
Accounts receivable	576,700	585,000

Assume that accounts receivable (in millions) were $511,900 at the beginning of the 2008 fiscal year.

a. Compute the accounts receivable turnover for 2009 and 2008. Round to one decimal place.

b. Compute the days' sales in receivables for 2009 and 2008. Round to one decimal place.

c. What conclusions can be drawn from these analyses regarding Ralph Lauren's efficiency in collecting receivables?

OBJ. 8

✔a. 2009: 8.7

EX 9-27 Accounts receivable turnover and days' sales in receivables

H.J. Heinz Company was founded in 1869 at Sharpsburg, Pennsylvania, by Henry J. Heinz. The company manufactures and markets food products throughout the world, including ketchup, condiments and sauces, frozen food, pet food, soups, and tuna. For the fiscal years 2009 and 2008, H.J. Heinz reported the following (in thousands):

	Year Ending	
	April 29, 2009	April 30, 2008
Net sales	$10,148,082	$10,070,778
Accounts receivable	1,171,797	1,161,481

Assume that the accounts receivable (in thousands) were $996,852 at the beginning of fiscal year 2008.

a. Compute the accounts receivable turnover for 2009 and 2008. Round to one decimal place.

b. Compute the days' sales in receivables at the end of 2009 and 2008. Round to one decimal place.

c. What conclusions can be drawn from these analyses regarding Heinz's efficiency in collecting receivables?

OBJ. 8

EX 9-28 Accounts receivable turnover and days' sales in receivables

The Limited Brands Inc. sells women's clothing and personal health care products through specialty retail stores including Victoria's Secret and Bath & Body Works stores. The Limited Brands reported the following (in millions):

	For the Period Ending	
	Jan. 31, 2010	Jan. 31, 2009
Net sales	$8,632	$9,043
Accounts receivable	249	313

Assume that accounts receivable (in millions) were $355 at the beginning of fiscal year 2009.

a. Compute the accounts receivable turnover for 2010 and 2009. Round to one decimal place.

b. Compute the day's sales in receivables for 2010 and 2009. Round to one decimal place.

c. What conclusions can be drawn from these analyses regarding The Limited Brands' efficiency in collecting receivables?

OBJ. 8

EX 9-29 Accounts receivable turnover

Use the data in Exercises 9-27 and 9-28 to analyze the accounts receivable turnover ratios of H.J. Heinz Company and The Limited Brands Inc.

a. Compute the average accounts receivable turnover ratio for The Limited Brands Inc. and H.J. Heinz Company for the years shown in Exercises 9-27 and 9-28.

b. Does The Limited Brands or H.J. Heinz Company have the higher average accounts receivable turnover ratio?

c. Explain the logic underlying your answer in (b).

Problems Series A

OBJ. 4

✔ 3. $1,140,000

PR 9-1A Entries related to uncollectible accounts

The following transactions were completed by Axiom Management Company during the current fiscal year ended December 31:

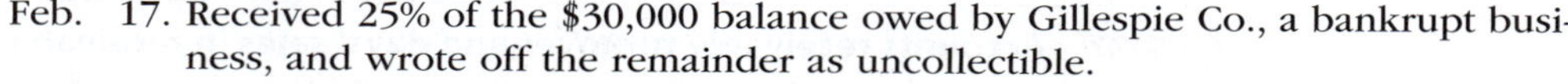

Feb. 17. Received 25% of the $30,000 balance owed by Gillespie Co., a bankrupt business, and wrote off the remainder as uncollectible.

Apr. 11. Reinstated the account of Colleen Bertram, which had been written off in the preceding year as uncollectible. Journalized the receipt of $4,250 cash in full payment of Colleen's account.

July 6. Wrote off the $9,000 balance owed by Covered Wagon Co., which has no assets.

Nov. 20. Reinstated the account of Dugan Co., which had been written off in the preceding year as uncollectible. Journalized the receipt of $5,900 cash in full payment of the account.

Dec. 31. Wrote off the following accounts as uncollectible (compound entry): Kipp Co., $3,000; Moore Co., $4,000; Butte Distributors, $8,000; Parker Towers, $6,700.

31. Based on an analysis of the $1,200,000 of accounts receivable, it was estimated that $60,000 will be uncollectible. Journalized the adjusting entry.

Instructions

1. Record the January 1 credit balance of $40,000 in a T account for Allowance for Doubtful Accounts.
2. Journalize the transactions. Post each entry that affects the following selected T accounts and determine the new balances:

   Allowance for Doubtful Accounts

   Bad Debt Expense
3. Determine the expected net realizable value of the accounts receivable as of December 31.
4. Assuming that instead of basing the provision for uncollectible accounts on an analysis of receivables, the adjusting entry on December 31 had been based on an estimated expense of ¾ of 1% of the net sales of $7,500,000 for the year, determine the following:
   a. Bad debt expense for the year.
   b. Balance in the allowance account after the adjustment of December 31.
   c. Expected net realizable value of the accounts receivable as of December 31.

OBJ. 4

✔ 3. $111,095

PR 9-2A Aging of receivables; estimating allowance for doubtful accounts

Angler's Dream Company supplies flies and fishing gear to sporting goods stores and outfitters throughout the western United States. The accounts receivable clerk for Angler's Dream prepared the following partially completed aging of receivables schedule as of the end of business on December 31, 2011:

	A	B	C	D	E	F	G	H
1			Not	Days Past Due				
2			Past					
3	Customer	Balance	Due	1–30	31–60	61–90	91–120	Over 120
4	AAA Fishery	20,000	20,000					
5	Blue Ribbon Flies	7,500			7,500			
30	Z Fish Co.	4,000		4,000				
31	Subtotals	1,060,000	500,000	315,000	120,000	40,000	25,000	60,000

The following accounts were unintentionally omitted from the aging schedule:

Customer	Due Date	Balance
Antelope Sports & Flies	June 21, 2011	$ 3,000
Big Hole Flies	Aug. 30, 2011	6,500
Charlie's Fish Co.	Sept. 8, 2011	12,000
Deschutes Sports	Oct. 20, 2011	4,000
Green River Sports	Nov. 7, 2011	3,500
Smith River Co.	Nov. 28, 2011	1,500
Wild Trout Company	Dec. 5, 2011	5,000
Wolfe Sports	Jan. 7, 2012	4,500

CHAPTER 10

AP Photo/W. A. Harewood

Fixed Assets and Intangible Assets

Fatburger Inc.

Do you remember purchasing your first car? You probably didn't buy your first car like you would buy a CD. Purchasing a new or used car is expensive. In addition, you would drive (use) the car for the next 3–5 years or longer. As a result, you might spend hours or weeks considering different makes and models, safety ratings, warranties, and operating costs before deciding on the final purchase.

Like buying her first car, Lovie Yancey spent a lot of time before deciding to open her first restaurant. In 1952, she created the biggest, juiciest hamburger that anyone had ever seen. She called it a Fatburger. The restaurant initially started as a 24-hour operation to cater to the schedules of professional musicians. As a fan of popular music and its performers, Yancey played rhythm and blues, jazz, and blues recordings for her customers. Fatburger's popularity with entertainers was illustrated when its name was used in a 1992 rap by Ice Cube. "Two in the mornin' got the Fatburger," Cube said, in "It Was a Good Day," a track on his *Predator* album.

The demand for this incredible burger was such that, in 1980, Ms. Yancey decided to offer Fatburger franchise opportunities. In 1990, with the goal of expanding Fatburger throughout the world, **Fatburger Inc.** purchased the business from Ms. Yancey. Today, Fatburger has grown to a multi-restaurant chain with owners and investors such as talk show host Montel Williams, former Cincinnati Bengals' tackle Willie Anderson, comedian David Spade, and musicians Cher, Janet Jackson, and Pharrell.

So, how much would it cost you to open a Fatburger restaurant? On average, the total investment begins at over $700,000 per restaurant. Thus, in starting a Fatburger restaurant, you would be making a significant investment that would affect your life for years to come.

This chapter discusses the accounting for investments in fixed assets such as those used to open a Fatburger restaurant. How to determine the portion of the fixed asset that becomes an expense over time is also discussed. Finally, the accounting for the disposal of fixed assets and accounting for intangible assets such as patents and copyrights are discussed.

Define, classify, and account for the cost of fixed assets.

Nature of Fixed Assets

Fixed assets are long-term or relatively permanent assets such as equipment, machinery, buildings, and land. Other descriptive titles for fixed assets are *plant assets* or *property, plant, and equipment*. Fixed assets have the following characteristics:

1. They exist physically and, thus, are *tangible* assets.
2. They are owned and used by the company in its normal operations.
3. They are not offered for sale as part of normal operations.

Exhibit 1 shows the percent of fixed assets to total assets for some select companies. As shown in Exhibit 1, fixed assets are often a significant portion of the total assets of a company.

EXHIBIT 1 **Fixed Assets as a Percent of Total Assets—Selected Companies**

	Fixed Assets as a Percent of Total Assets
Alcoa Inc.	47%
ExxonMobil Corporation	53
Ford Motor Company	25
Kroger	57
Office Depot Inc.	30
United Parcel Service, Inc.	57
Verizon Communications	43
Walgreen Co.	43
Wal-Mart	59

Classifying Costs

See Appendix D for more information

A cost that has been incurred may be classified as a fixed asset, an investment, or an expense. Exhibit 2 shows how to determine the proper classification of a cost and how it should be recorded. As shown in Exhibit 2, classifying a cost involves the following steps:

Step 1. Is the purchased item long-lived?

If *yes*, the item is recorded as an asset on the balance sheet, either as a fixed asset or an investment. Proceed to Step 2.

If *no*, the item is classified and recorded as an *expense*.

Step 2. Is the asset used in normal operations?

If *yes*, the asset is classified and recorded as a *fixed asset*.

If *no*, the asset is classified and recorded as an *investment*.

Items that are classified and recorded as fixed assets include land, buildings, or equipment. Such assets normally last more than a year and are used in the normal operations. However, standby equipment for use during peak periods or when other equipment breaks down is still classified as a fixed asset even though it is not used very often. In contrast, fixed assets that have been abandoned or are no longer used in operations are not classified as fixed assets.

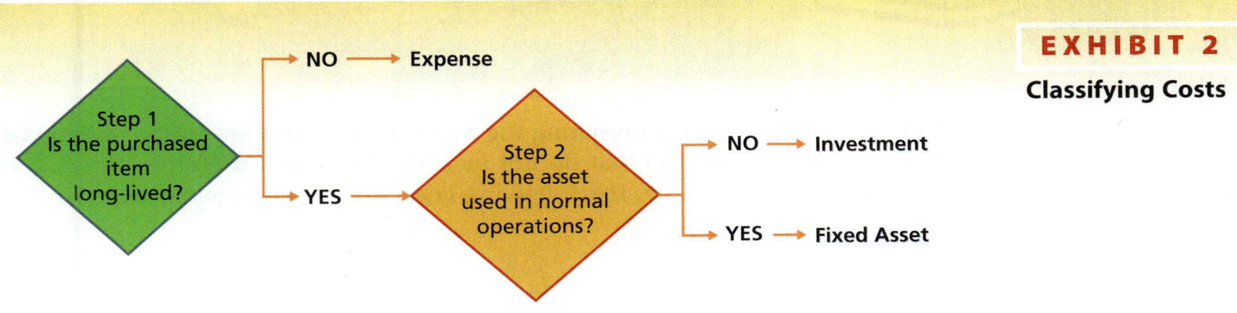

EXHIBIT 2

Classifying Costs

Although fixed assets may be sold, they should not be offered for sale as part of normal operations. For example, cars and trucks offered for sale by an automotive dealership are not fixed assets of the dealership. On the other hand, a tow truck used in the normal operations of the dealership is a fixed asset of the dealership.

Investments are long-lived assets that are not used in the normal operations and are held for future resale. Such assets are reported on the balance sheet in a section entitled *Investments*. For example, undeveloped land acquired for future resale would be classified and reported as an investment, not land.

The Cost of Fixed Assets

In addition to purchase price, costs of acquiring fixed assets include all amounts spent getting the asset in place and ready for use. For example, freight costs and the costs of installing equipment are part of the asset's total cost.

Exhibit 3 summarizes some of the common costs of acquiring fixed assets. These costs are recorded by debiting the related fixed asset account, such as Land,[1] Building, Land Improvements, or Machinery and Equipment.

EXHIBIT 3 **Costs of Acquiring Fixed Assets**

Building

- Architects' fees
- Engineers' fees
- Insurance costs incurred during construction
- Interest on money borrowed to finance construction
- Walkways to and around the building
- Sales taxes
- Repairs (purchase of existing building)
- Reconditioning (purchase of existing building)
- Modifying for use
- Permits from government agencies

Machinery & Equipment

- Sales taxes
- Freight
- Installation
- Repairs (purchase of used equipment)
- Reconditioning (purchase of used equipment)
- Insurance while in transit
- Assembly
- Modifying for use
- Testing for use
- Permits from government agencies

Land

- Purchase price
- Sales taxes
- Permits from government agencies
- Broker's commissions
- Title fees
- Surveying fees
- Delinquent real estate taxes
- Removing unwanted building less any salvage
- Grading and leveling
- Paving a public street bordering the land

Only costs necessary for preparing the fixed asset for use are included as a cost of the asset. Unnecessary costs that do not increase the asset's usefulness are recorded as an expense. For example, the following costs are included as an expense:

1. Vandalism
2. Mistakes in installation
3. Uninsured theft
4. Damage during unpacking and installing
5. Fines for not obtaining proper permits from governmental agencies

A company may incur costs associated with constructing a fixed asset such as a new building. The direct costs incurred in the construction, such as labor and

1 As discussed here, land is assumed to be used only as a location or site and not for its mineral deposits or other natural resources.

materials, should be capitalized as a debit to an account entitled Construction in Progress. When the construction is complete, the costs are reclassified by crediting Construction in Progress and debiting the proper fixed asset account such as Building. For some companies, construction in progress can be significant.

Intel Corporation reported in a recent annual report construction in progress of $2.7 billion, which was 16% of its total fixed assets.

See Appendix D for more information

Capital and Revenue Expenditures

Once a fixed asset has been acquired and placed in service, costs may be incurred for ordinary maintenance and repairs. In addition, costs may be incurred for improving an asset or for extraordinary repairs that extend the asset's useful life. Costs that benefit only the current period are called **revenue expenditures**. Costs that improve the asset or extend its useful life are **capital expenditures**.

Ordinary Maintenance and Repairs Costs related to the ordinary maintenance and repairs of a fixed asset are recorded as an expense of the current period. Such expenditures are *revenue expenditures* and are recorded as increases to Repairs and Maintenance Expense. For example, $300 paid for a tune-up of a delivery truck is recorded as follows:

		Repairs and Maintenance Expense		300	
		Cash			300

Asset Improvements After a fixed asset has been placed in service, costs may be incurred to improve the asset. For example, the service value of a delivery truck might be improved by adding a $5,500 hydraulic lift to allow for easier and quicker loading of cargo. Such costs are *capital expenditures* and are recorded as increases to the fixed asset account. In the case of the hydraulic lift, the expenditure is recorded as follows:

		Delivery Truck		5,500	
		Cash			5,500

Because the cost of the delivery truck has increased, depreciation for the truck would also change over its remaining useful life.

Extraordinary Repairs After a fixed asset has been placed in service, costs may be incurred to extend the asset's useful life. For example, the engine of a forklift that is near the end of its useful life may be overhauled at a cost of $4,500, extending its useful life by eight years. Such costs are *capital expenditures* and are recorded as a decrease in an accumulated depreciation account. In the case of the forklift, the expenditure is recorded as follows:

		Accumulated Depreciation—Forklift		4,500	
		Cash			4,500

Integrity, Objectivity, and Ethics in Business

CAPITAL CRIME

One of the largest alleged accounting frauds in history involved the improper accounting for capital expenditures. WorldCom, the second largest telecommunications company in the United States at the time, improperly treated maintenance expenditures on its telecommunications network as capital expenditures. As a result, the company had to restate its prior years' earnings downward by nearly $4 billion to correct this error. The company declared bankruptcy within months of disclosing the error, and the CEO was sentenced to 25 years in prison.

Because the forklift's remaining useful life has changed, depreciation for the forklift would also change based on the new book value of the forklift.

The accounting for revenue and capital expenditures is summarized below.

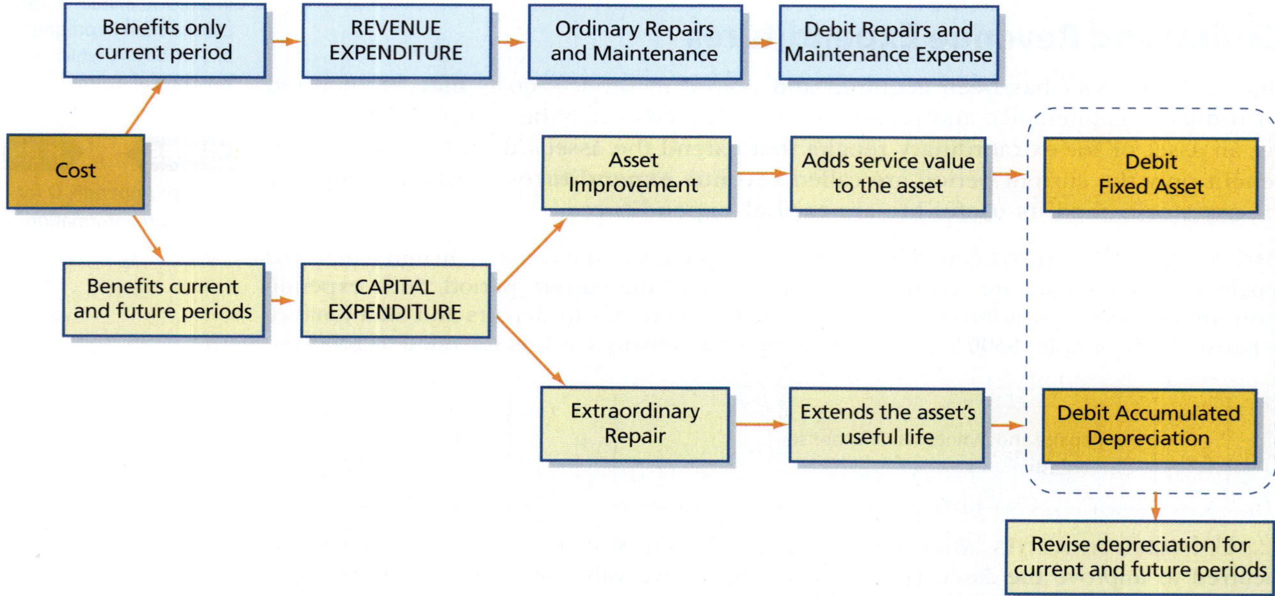

Example Exercise 10-1 Capital and Revenue Expenditures

OBJ. 1

On June 18, GTS Co. paid $1,200 to upgrade a hydraulic lift and $45 for an oil change for one of its delivery trucks. Journalize the entries for the hydraulic lift upgrade and oil change expenditures.

Follow My Example 10-1

June 18	Delivery Truck	1,200	
	Cash		1,200
18	Repairs and Maintenance Expense	45	
	Cash		45

Practice Exercises: **PE 10-1A, PE 10-1B**

Leasing Fixed Assets

A *lease* is a contract for the use of an asset for a period of time. Leases are often used in business. For example, automobiles, computers, medical equipment, buildings, and airplanes are often leased.

The two parties to a lease contract are as follows:

1. The *lessor* is the party who owns the asset.
2. The *lessee* is the party to whom the rights to use the asset are granted by the lessor.

Delta Air Lines leases facilities, aircraft, and equipment using both capital and operating leases.

Under a lease contract, the lessee pays rent on a periodic basis for the lease term. The lessee accounts for a lease contract in one of two ways depending on how the lease contract is classified. A lease contract can be classified as either a:

1. *Capital lease* or
2. *Operating lease*

A **capital lease** is accounted for as if the lessee has purchased the asset. The lessee debits an asset account for the fair market value of the asset and credits a long-term lease liability account. The asset is then written off as an expense (amortized) over the life of the capital lease. The accounting for capital leases is discussed in more advanced accounting texts.

An **operating lease** is accounted for as if the lessee is renting the asset for the lease term. The lessee records operating lease payments by debiting *Rent Expense* and crediting *Cash*. The lessee's future lease obligations are not recorded in the accounts. However, such obligations are disclosed in notes to the financial statements.

The asset rentals described in earlier chapters of this text were accounted for as operating leases. To simplify, all leases are assumed to be operating leases throughout this text.

Accounting for Depreciation

Compute depreciation, using the following methods: straight-line method, units-of-production method, and double-declining-balance method.

Over time, fixed assets, with the exception of land, lose their ability to provide services. Thus, the costs of fixed assets such as equipment and buildings should be recorded as an expense over their useful lives. This periodic recording of the cost of fixed assets as an expense is called **depreciation**. Because land has an unlimited life, it is not depreciated.

The adjusting entry to record depreciation debits *Depreciation Expense* and credits a *contra asset* account entitled *Accumulated Depreciation* or *Allowance for Depreciation*. The use of a contra asset account allows the original cost to remain unchanged in the fixed asset account.

Note:
The adjusting entry to record depreciation debits Depreciation Expense and credits Accumulated Depreciation.

Depreciation can be caused by physical or functional factors.

1. *Physical depreciation* factors include wear and tear during use or from exposure to weather.
2. *Functional depreciation* factors include obsolescence and changes in customer needs that cause the asset to no longer provide services for which it was intended. For example, equipment may become obsolete due to changing technology.

Two common misunderstandings that exist about *depreciation* as used in accounting include:

1. Depreciation does not measure a decline in the market value of a fixed asset. Instead, depreciation is an allocation of a fixed asset's cost to expense over the asset's useful life. Thus, the book value of a fixed asset (cost less accumulated depreciation) usually does not agree with the asset's market value. This is justified in accounting because a fixed asset is for use in a company's operations rather than for resale.
2. Depreciation does not provide cash to replace fixed assets as they wear out. This misunderstanding may occur because depreciation, unlike most expenses, does not require an outlay of cash when it is recorded.

Factors in Computing Depreciation Expense

Three factors determine the depreciation expense for a fixed asset. These three factors are as follows:

1. The asset's initial cost
2. The asset's expected useful life
3. The asset's estimated residual value

The initial *cost* of a fixed asset is determined using the concepts discussed and illustrated earlier in this chapter.

The *expected useful life* of a fixed asset is estimated at the time the asset is placed into service. Estimates of expected useful lives are available from industry trade associations. The Internal Revenue Service also publishes guidelines for useful lives, which may be helpful for financial reporting purposes. However, it is not uncommon for different companies to use a different useful life for similar assets.

The **residual value** of a fixed asset at the end of its useful life is estimated at the time the asset is placed into service. Residual value is sometimes referred to as *scrap* *value, salvage value*, or *trade-in value*. The difference between a fixed asset's initial cost and its residual value is called the asset's *depreciable cost*. The depreciable cost is the amount of the asset's cost that is allocated over its useful life as depreciation expense. If a fixed asset has no residual value, then its entire cost should be allocated to depreciation.

Exhibit 4 shows the relationship between depreciation expense and a fixed asset's initial cost, expected useful life, and estimated residual value.

EXHIBIT 4

Depreciation Expense Factors

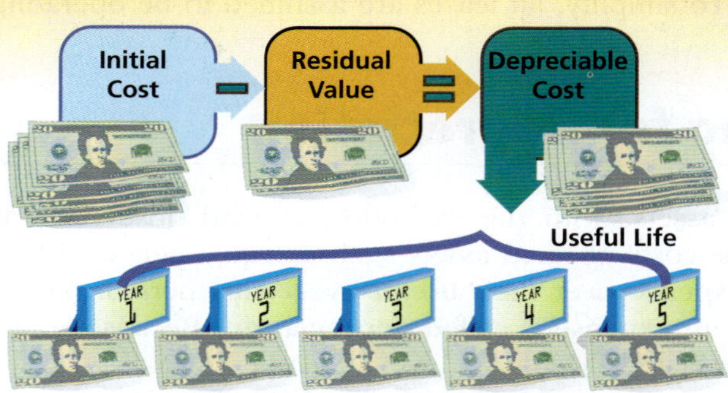

For an asset placed into or taken out of service during the first half of a month, many companies compute depreciation on the asset for the entire month. That is, the asset is treated as having been purchased or sold on the first day of *that* month. Likewise, purchases and sales during the second half of a month are treated as having occurred on the first day of the *next* month. To simplify, this practice is used in this chapter.

The three depreciation methods used most often are as follows:[2]

1. Straight-line depreciation
2. Units-of-production depreciation
3. Double-declining-balance depreciation

Exhibit 5 shows how often these methods are used in financial statements.

EXHIBIT 5

Use of Depreciation Methods

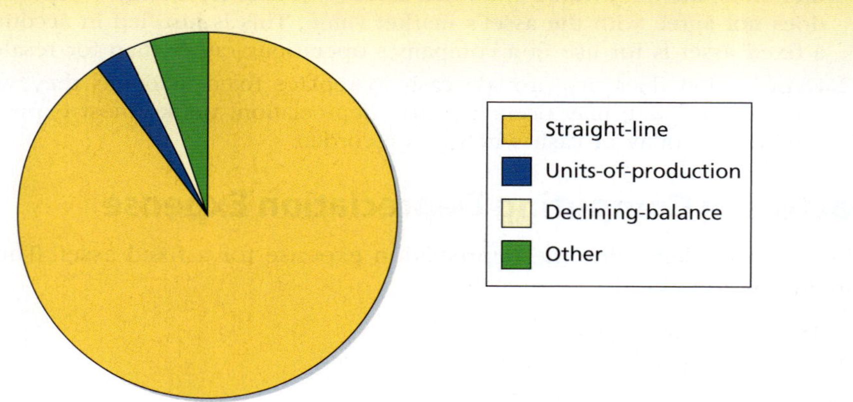

Source: *Accounting Trends & Techniques*, 63rd ed., American Institute of Certified Public Accountants, New York, 2009.

It is not necessary for a company to use only one method of computing depreciation for all of its fixed assets. For example, a company may use one method for depreciating equipment and another method for depreciating buildings.

2 Another method not often used today, called the *sum-of-the-years-digits method*, is described and illustrated in an online appendix located at **www.cengage.com/accounting/warren**.

A company may also use different methods for determining income and property taxes.

Straight-Line Method

The **straight-line method** provides for the same amount of depreciation expense for each year of the asset's useful life. As shown in Exhibit 5, the straight-line method is by far the most widely used depreciation method.

To illustrate, assume that equipment was purchased on January 1 as follows:

Initial cost	$24,000
Expected useful life	5 years
Estimated residual value	$2,000

The annual straight-line depreciation of $4,400 is computed below.

$$\text{Annual Depreciation} = \frac{\text{Cost} - \text{Residual Value}}{\text{Useful Life}} = \frac{\$24{,}000 - \$2{,}000}{5 \text{ Years}} = \$4{,}400$$

If an asset is used for only part of a year, the annual depreciation is prorated. For example, assume that the preceding equipment was purchased and placed into service on October 1. The depreciation for the year ending December 31 would be **$1,100**, computed as follows:

$$\textit{First-Year Partial Depreciation} = \$4{,}400 \times 3/12 = \$1{,}100$$

The computation of straight-line depreciation may be simplified by converting the annual depreciation to a percentage of depreciable cost.[3] The straight-line percentage is determined by dividing 100% by the number of years of expected useful life, as shown below.

Expected Years of Useful Life	Straight-Line Percentage
5 years	20% (100%/5)
8 years	12.5% (100%/8)
10 years	10% (100%/10)
20 years	5% (100%/20)
25 years	4% (100%/25)

For the preceding equipment, the annual depreciation of $4,400 can be computed by multiplying the depreciable cost of $22,000 by 20% (100%/5).

Example Exercise 10-2 Straight-Line Depreciation

OBJ. 2

Equipment acquired at the beginning of the year at a cost of $125,000 has an estimated residual value of $5,000 and an estimated useful life of 10 years. Determine (a) the depreciable cost, (b) the straight-line rate, and (c) the annual straight-line depreciation.

Follow My Example 10-2

a. $120,000 ($125,000 – $5,000)

b. 10% = 1/10

c. $12,000 ($120,000 × 10%), or ($120,000/10 years)

Practice Exercises: PE 10-2A, PE 10-2B

3 The depreciation rate may also be expressed as a fraction. For example, the annual straight-line rate for an asset with a three-year useful life is 1/3.

4 Real estate is in either a 27½-year or a 31½-year class and is depreciated by the straight-line method.

(Continued)

Compute depreciation, using the following methods: straight-line method, units-of- production method, and double-declining-balance method.

Key Points All fixed assets except land should be depreciated over time. Three factors are considered in determining depreciation: (1) the fixed asset's initial cost, (2) the useful life of the asset, and (3) the residual value of the asset.

2. What method yields the highest depreciation expense for 2011?
3. What method yields the most depreciation over the four-year life of the equipment?

OBJ. 2

✔ a. 2010, $17,325

PR 10-3B Depreciation by three methods; partial years

Helix Company purchased tool sharpening equipment on April 1, 2010, for $72,000. The equipment was expected to have a useful life of three years, or 9,000 operating hours, and a residual value of $2,700. The equipment was used for 2,400 hours during 2010, 4,000 hours in 2011, 2,000 hours in 2012, and 600 hours in 2013.

Instructions

Determine the amount of depreciation expense for the years ended December 31, 2010, 2011, 2012, and 2013, by (a) the straight-line method, (b) the units-of-production method, and (c) the double-declining-balance method.

OBJ. 2, 3

✔ 1. b. Year 1, $36,000 depreciation expense

PR 10-4B Depreciation by two methods; sale of fixed asset

New tire retreading equipment, acquired at a cost of $72,000 at the beginning of a fiscal year, has an estimated useful life of four years and an estimated residual value of $5,400. The manager requested information regarding the effect of alternative methods on the amount of depreciation expense each year. On the basis of the data presented to the manager, the double-declining-balance method was selected.

In the first week of the fourth year, the equipment was sold for $13,750.

Instructions

1. Determine the annual depreciation expense for each of the estimated four years of use, the accumulated depreciation at the end of each year, and the book value of the equipment at the end of each year by (a) the straight-line method and (b) the double-declining-balance method. The following columnar headings are suggested for each schedule:

Year	Depreciation Expense	Accumulated Depreciation, End of Year	Book Value, End of Year

2. Journalize the entry to record the sale.
3. Journalize the entry to record the sale, assuming that the equipment sold for $3,700 instead of $13,750.

OBJ. 1, 2, 3

PR 10-5B Transactions for fixed assets, including sale

The following transactions, adjusting entries, and closing entries were completed by McHenry Furniture Co. during a three-year period. All are related to the use of delivery equipment. The double-declining-balance method of depreciation is used.

2010

Jan. 4. Purchased a used delivery truck for $54,000, paying cash.

Feb. 24. Paid garage $275 for changing the oil, replacing the oil filter, and tuning the engine on the delivery truck.

Dec. 31. Recorded depreciation on the truck for the fiscal year. The estimated useful life of the truck is eight years, with a residual value of $12,000 for the truck.

2011

Jan. 3. Purchased a new truck for $60,000, paying cash.

Mar. 7. Paid garage $300 to tune the engine and make other minor repairs on the used truck.

Apr. 30 Sold the used truck for $35,000. (Record depreciation to date in 2011 for the truck.)

Dec. 31. Record depreciation for the new truck. It has an estimated residual value of $16,000 and an estimated life of 10 years.

2012

July 1. Purchased a new truck for $64,000, paying cash.

Oct. 7. Sold the truck purchased January 3, 2011, for $45,000. (Record depreciation for the year.)

Dec. 31. Recorded depreciation on the remaining truck. It has an estimated residual value of $17,500 and an estimated useful life of 10 years.

Instructions

Journalize the transactions and the adjusting entries.

OBJ. 4, 5

✔ b. $45,000

PR 10-6B Amortization and depletion entries

Data related to the acquisition of timber rights and intangible assets during the current year ended December 31 are as follows:

a. On December 31, the company determined that $1,800,000 of goodwill was impaired.

b. Governmental and legal costs of $900,000 were incurred on June 30 in obtaining a patent with an estimated economic life of 10 years. Amortization is to be for one-half year.

c. Timber rights on a tract of land were purchased for $1,560,000 on February 4. The stand of timber is estimated at 12,000,000 board feet. During the current year, 3,200,000 board feet of timber were cut and sold.

Instructions

1. Determine the amount of the amortization, depletion, or impairment for the current year for each of the foregoing items.
2. Journalize the adjusting entries to record the amortization, depletion, or impairment for each item.

Cases & Projects

CP 10-1 Ethics and professional conduct in business

Rosa Salinas, CPA, is an assistant to the controller of Zebra Consulting Co. In her spare time, Rosa also prepares tax returns and performs general accounting services for clients. Frequently, Rosa performs these services after her normal working hours, using Zebra Consulting Co.'s computers and laser printers. Occasionally, Rosa's clients will call her at the office during regular working hours.

Discuss whether Rosa is performing in a professional manner.

CP 10-2 Financial vs. tax depreciation

The following is an excerpt from a conversation between two employees of Omni Technologies, Jay Bach and Cora Hardaway. Jay is the accounts payable clerk, and Cora is the cashier.

Jay: Cora, could I get your opinion on something?

Cora: Sure, Jay.

Jay: Do you know Jo, the fixed assets clerk?

Cora: I know who she is, but I don't know her real well. Why?

Jay: Well, I was talking to her at lunch last Monday about how she liked her job, etc. You know, the usual . . . and she mentioned something about having to keep two sets of books . . . one for taxes and one for the financial statements. That can't be good accounting, can it? What do you think?

Cora: Two sets of books? It doesn't sound right.

Jay: It doesn't seem right to me either. I was always taught that you had to use generally accepted accounting principles. How can there be two sets of books? What can be the difference between the two?

How would you respond to Jay and Cora if you were Jo?

CP 10-3 Effect of depreciation on net income

Atlas Construction Co. specializes in building replicas of historic houses. Paul Raines, president of Atlas Construction, is considering the purchase of various items of equipment on July 1, 2010, for $500,000. The equipment would have a useful life of five years and no residual value. In the past, all equipment has been leased. For tax purposes, Paul is considering depreciating the equipment by the straight-line method. He discussed the matter with his CPA and learned that, although the straight-line method could be elected, it was to his advantage to use the Modified Accelerated Cost Recovery System (MACRS) for tax purposes. He asked for your advice as to which method to use for tax purposes.

1. Compute depreciation for each of the years (2010, 2011, 2012, 2013, 2014, and 2015) of useful life by (a) the straight-line method and (b) MACRS. In using the straight-line method, one-half year's depreciation should be computed for 2010 and 2015. Use the MACRS rates presented on page 457.
2. Assuming that income before depreciation and income tax is estimated to be $900,000 uniformly per year and that the income tax rate is 40%, compute the net income for each of the years 2010, 2011, 2012, 2013, 2014, and 2015 if (a) the straight-line method is used and (b) MACRS is used.
3. What factors would you present for Paul's consideration in the selection of a depreciation method?

Internet Project

CP 10-4 Applying for patents, copyrights, and trademarks

Group Project

Go to the Internet and review the procedures for applying for a patent, a copyright, and a trademark. You may find information available on Wikipedia (Wikipedia.org) useful for this purpose. Prepare a brief written summary of these procedures.

CP 10-5 Fixed asset turnover: three industries

The following table shows the revenues and average net fixed assets for a recent fiscal year for three different companies from three different industries: retailing, manufacturing, and communications.

	Revenues (in millions)	Average Net Fixed Assets (in millions)
Wal-Mart	$405,607	$96,335
Occidental Petroleum Corporation	15,403	32,856
Comcast Corporation	34,256	24,034

a. For each company, determine the fixed asset turnover ratio. Round to two decimal places.

b. Explain Wal-Mart's ratio relative to the other two companies.

Photo/Tom Gannam

CHAPTER 11

Current Liabilities and Payroll

Panera Bread

Buying goods on credit is probably as old as business itself. In fact, the ancient Babylonians were lending money to support trade as early as 1300 B.C. The use of credit makes transactions more convenient and improves buying power. For *individuals*, the most common form of short-term credit is a credit card. Credit cards allow individuals to purchase items before they are paid for, while removing the need for individuals to carry large amounts of cash. They also provide documentation of purchases through a monthly credit card statement.

Short-term credit is also used by *businesses* to make purchasing items for manufacture or resale more convenient. Short-term credit also gives a business control over the payment for goods and services. For example, **Panera Bread**, a chain of bakery-cafés located throughout the United States, uses short-term trade credit, or accounts payable, to purchase ingredients for making bread products in its bakeries. Short-term trade credit gives Panera control over cash payments by separating the purchase function from the payment function. Thus, the employee responsible for purchasing the bakery ingredients is separated from the employee responsible for paying for the purchase. This separation of duties can help prevent unauthorized purchases or payments.

In addition to accounts payable, a business like Panera Bread can also have current liabilities related to payroll, payroll taxes, employee benefits, short-term notes, unearned revenue, and contingencies. This chapter discusses each of these types of current liabilities.

Learning Objectives

OBJ. 1 Describe and illustrate current liabilities related to accounts payable, current portion of long-term debt, and notes payable.

Current Liabilities

When a company or a bank advances *credit,* it is making a loan. The company or bank is called a *creditor* (or *lender*). The individuals or companies receiving the loan are called *debtors* (or *borrowers*).

Debt is recorded as a liability by the debtor. *Long-term liabilities* are debts due beyond one year. Thus, a 30-year mortgage used to purchase property is a long-term liability. *Current liabilities* are debts that will be paid out of current assets and are due within one year.

Three types of current liabilities are discussed in this section—accounts payable, the current portion of long-term debt, and short-term notes payable.

Accounts Payable

Accounts payable transactions have been described and illustrated in earlier chapters. These transactions involved a variety of purchases on account, including the purchase of merchandise and supplies. For most companies, accounts payable is the largest current liability. Exhibit 1 shows the accounts payable balance as a percent of total current liabilities for a number of companies.

EXHIBIT 1

Accounts Payable as a Percent of Total Current Liabilities

Company	Accounts Payable as a Percent of Total Current Liabilities
Alcoa Inc.	36%
AT&T	57
Gap Inc.	47
IBM	17
Rite Aid Corp.	55
Chevron Corp.	52

Current Portion of Long-Term Debt

Long-term liabilities are often paid back in periodic payments, called *installments*. Such installments that are due *within* the coming year are classified as a current liability. The installments due *after* the coming year are classified as a long-term liability.

To illustrate, The Coca-Cola Company reported the following debt payments schedule in its December 31, 2009, annual report to shareholders:

Fiscal year ending	
2010	$ 51,000,000
2011	573,000,000
2012	153,000,000
2013	178,000,000
2014	912,000,000
Thereafter	3,243,000,000
Total principal payments	$5,110,000,000

The debt of $51,000,000 due in 2010 would be reported as a current liability on the December 31, 2009, balance sheet. The remaining debt of $5,059,000,000 ($5,110,000,000 – $51,000,000) would be reported as a long-term liability on the balance sheet.

Short-Term Notes Payable

Notes may be issued to purchase merchandise or other assets. Notes may also be issued to creditors to satisfy an account payable created earlier.[1]

To illustrate, assume that Nature's Sunshine Company issued a 90-day, 12% note for $1,000, dated August 1, 2011, to Murray Co. for a $1,000 overdue account. The entry to record the issuance of the note is as follows:

				Debit	Credit
Aug.	1	Accounts Payable—Murray Co.		1,000	
		Notes Payable			1,000
		Issued a 90-day, 12% note on account.			

When the note matures, the entry to record the payment of $1,000 plus $30 interest ($1,000 × 12% × 90/360) is as follows:

				Debit	Credit
Oct.	30	Notes Payable		1,000	
		Interest Expense		30	
		Cash			1,030
		Paid principal and interest due on note.			

1 The accounting for notes received to satisfy an account receivable was described and illustrated in Chapter 9, Receivables.

The interest expense is reported in the Other Expense section of the income statement for the year ended December 31, 2011. The interest expense account is closed at December 31.

Each note transaction affects a debtor (borrower) and creditor (lender). The following illustration shows how the same transactions are recorded by the debtor and creditor. In this illustration, the debtor (borrower) is Bowden Co., and the creditor (lender) is Coker Co.

	Bowden Co. (Borrower)			Coker Co. (Creditor)		
May 1. Bowden Co. purchased merchandise on account from Coker Co., $10,000, 2/10, n/30. The merchandise cost Coker Co. $7,500.	Merchandise Inventory	10,000		Accounts Receivable	10,000	
	Accounts Payable		10,000	Sales		10,000
				Cost of Merchandise Sold	7,500	
				Merchandise Inventory		7,500
May 31. Bowden Co. issued a 60-day, 12% note for $10,000 to Coker Co. on account.	Accounts Payable	10,000		Notes Receivable	10,000	
	Notes Payable		10,000	Accounts Receivable		10,000
July 30. Bowden Co. paid Coker Co. the amount due on the note of May 31. Interest: $10,000 × 12% × 60/360.	Notes Payable	10,000		Cash	10,200	
	Interest Expense	200		Interest Revenue		200
	Cash		10,200	Notes Receivable		10,000

A company may also borrow from a bank by issuing a note. To illustrate, assume that on September 19 Iceburg Company borrowed cash from First National Bank by issuing a $4,000, 90-day, 15% note to the bank. The entry to record the issuance of the note and the cash proceeds is as follows:

Sept.	19	Cash	4,000	
		Notes Payable		4,000
		Issued a 90-day, 15% note to First National Bank.		

On the due date of the note (December 18), Iceburg Company owes First National Bank $4,000 plus interest of $150 ($4,000 × 15% × 90/360). The entry to record the payment of the note is as follows:

Dec.	18	Notes Payable	4,000	
		Interest Expense	150	
		Cash		4,150
		Paid principal and interest due on note.		

In some cases, a *discounted note* may be issued rather than an interest-bearing note. A discounted note has the following characteristics:

1. The interest rate on the note is called the *discount rate*.
2. The amount of interest on the note, called the *discount*, is computed by multiplying the discount rate times the face amount of the note.
3. The debtor (borrower) receives the face amount of the note less the discount, called the *proceeds*.
4. The debtor must repay the face amount of the note on the due date.

To illustrate, assume that on August 10, Cary Company issues a $20,000, 90-day discounted note to Western National Bank. The discount rate is 15%, and the amount of the discount is $750 ($20,000 × 15% × 90/360). Thus, the proceeds received by Cary Company are $19,250. The entry by Cary Company is as follows:

Date		Description		Debit	Credit
Aug.	10	Cash		19,250	
		Interest Expense		750	
		Notes Payable			20,000
		Issued a 90-day discounted note to Western National Bank at a 15% discount rate.			

The entry when Cary Company pays the discounted note on November 8 is as follows:[2]

Date		Description		Debit	Credit
Nov.	8	Notes Payable		20,000	
		Cash			20,000
		Paid note due.			

Other current liabilities that have been discussed in earlier chapters include accrued expenses, unearned revenue, and interest payable. The accounting for wages and salaries, termed *payroll accounting*, is discussed next.

Example Exercise 11-1 Proceeds from Notes Payable OBJ. 1

On July 1, Bella Salon Company issued a 60-day note with a face amount of $60,000 to Delilah Hair Products Company for merchandise inventory.

a. Determine the proceeds of the note, assuming the note carries an interest rate of 6%.

b. Determine the proceeds of the note, assuming the note is discounted at 6%.

Follow My Example 11-1

a. $60,000

b. $59,400 [$60,000 – ($60,000 × 6% × 60/360)]

Practice Exercises: **PE 11-1A, PE 11-1B**

Payroll and Payroll Taxes

OBJ. 2 Determine employer liabilities for payroll, including liabilities arising from employee earnings and deductions from earnings.

In accounting, **payroll** refers to the amount paid to employees for services they provided during the period. A company's payroll is important for the following reasons:

1. Payroll and related payroll taxes significantly affect the net income of most companies.
2. Payroll is subject to federal and state regulations.
3. Good employee morale requires payroll to be paid timely and accurately.

Liability for Employee Earnings

Salary usually refers to payment for managerial and administrative services. Salary is normally expressed in terms of a month or a year. *Wages* usually refers to payment for employee manual labor. The rate of wages is normally stated on an hourly or a weekly basis. The salary or wage of an employee may be increased by bonuses, commissions, profit sharing, or cost-of-living adjustments.

Note: **Employee salaries and wages are expenses to an employer.**

2 If the accounting period ends before a discounted note is paid, an adjusting entry should record the prepaid (deferred) interest that is not yet an expense. This deferred interest would be deducted from Notes Payable in the Current Liabilities section of the balance sheet.

Companies engaged in interstate commerce must follow the Fair Labor Standards Act. This act, sometimes called the Federal Wage and Hour Law, requires employers to pay a minimum rate of 1½ times the regular rate for all hours worked in excess of 40 hours per week. Exemptions are provided for executive, administrative, and some supervisory positions. Increased rates for working overtime, nights, or holidays are common, even when not required by law. These rates may be as much as twice the regular rate.

To illustrate computing an employee's earnings, assume that John T. McGrath is a salesperson employed by McDermott Supply Co. McGrath's regular rate is $34 per hour, and any hours worked in excess of 40 hours per week are paid at 1½ times the regular rate. McGrath worked 42 hours for the week ended December 27. His earnings of **$1,462** for the week are computed as follows:

Earnings at regular rate (40 hrs. × $34)	$1,360
Earnings at overtime rate [2 hrs. × ($34 × 1½)]	102
Total earnings	$1,462

Deductions from Employee Earnings

The total earnings of an employee for a payroll period, including any overtime pay, are called **gross pay**. From this amount is subtracted one or more *deductions* to arrive at the **net pay**. Net pay is the amount paid the employee. The deductions normally include federal, state, and local income taxes, medical insurance, and pension contributions.

Income Taxes Employers normally withhold a portion of employee earnings for payment of the employees' federal income tax. Each employee authorizes the amount to be withheld by completing an "Employee's Withholding Allowance Certificate," called a W-4. Exhibit 2 is the W-4 form submitted by John T. McGrath.

On the W-4, an employee indicates marital status and the number of withholding allowances. A single employee may claim one withholding allowance. A married employee may claim an additional allowance for a spouse. An employee may also claim an allowance for each dependent other than a spouse. Each allowance reduces the federal income tax withheld from the employee's pay. Exhibit 2 indicates that John T. McGrath is single and, thus, claimed one withholding allowance.

The federal income tax withheld depends on each employee's gross pay and W-4 allowance. Withholding tables issued by the Internal Revenue Service (IRS) are used to determine amounts to withhold. Exhibit 3 is an example of an IRS wage withholding table for a single person who is paid weekly.[3]

EXHIBIT 2

Employee's Withholding Allowance Certificate (W-4 Form)

Cut here and give Form W-4 to your employer. Keep the top part for your records.

Form **W-4** — Department of the Treasury, Internal Revenue Service

Employee's Withholding Allowance Certificate

► Whether you are entitled to claim a certain number of allowances or exemption from withholding is subject to review by the IRS. Your employer may be required to send a copy of this form to the IRS.

OMB No. 1545-0074 — **2011**

1 Type or print your first name and middle initial. John T. | Last name McGrath | 2 Your social security number 381 : 48 : 9120

Home address (number and street or rural route) 1830 4th Street | 3 ☒ Single ☐ Married ☐ Married, but withhold at higher Single rate. Note. If married, but legally separated, or spouse is a nonresident alien, check the "Single" box.

City or town, state, and ZIP code Clinton, Iowa 52732-6142 | 4 If your last name differs from that shown on your social security card, check here. You must call 1-800-772-1213 for a replacement card. ► ☐

5 Total number of allowances you are claiming (from line **H** above **or** from the applicable worksheet on page 2) | 5 | 1

6 Additional amount, if any, you want withheld from each paycheck . . . . | 6 | $

7 I claim exemption from withholding for 2010, and I certify that I meet **both** of the following conditions for exemption.
- Last year I had a right to a refund of **all** federal income tax withheld because I had **no** tax liability **and**
- This year I expect a refund of **all** federal income tax withheld because I expect to have **no** tax liability.

If you meet both conditions, write "Exempt" here . . . . ► | 7 |

Under penalties of perjury, I declare that I have examined this certificate and to the best of my knowledge and belief, it is true, correct, and complete.

Employee's signature (Form is not valid unless you sign it.) ► *John T. McGrath* Date ► June 2, 2010

8 Employer's name and address (Employer: Complete lines 8 and 10 only if sending to the IRS.) | 9 Office code (optional) | 10 Employer identification number (EIN)

For Privacy Act and Paperwork Reduction Act Notice, see page 2. Cat. No. 10220Q Form **W-4** (2011)

3 IRS withholding tables are also available for married employees and for pay periods other than weekly.

In Exhibit 3, each row is the employee's wages after deducting the employee's withholding allowances. Each year, the amount of the standard withholding allowance is determined by the IRS. For ease of computation and because this amount changes each year, we assume that the standard withholding allowance to be deducted in Exhibit 3 for a single person paid weekly is $70.[4] Thus, if two withholding allowances are claimed, $140 ($70 × 2) is deducted.

To illustrate, John T. McGrath made $1,462 for the week ended December 27. McGrath's W-4 claims one withholding allowance of $70. Thus, the wages used in determining McGrath's withholding bracket in Exhibit 3 are $1,392 ($1,462 – $70).

After the person's withholding wage bracket has been computed, the federal income tax to be withheld is determined as follows:

Step 1. Locate the proper withholding wage bracket in Exhibit 3.

McGrath's wages after deducting one standard IRS withholding allowance are $1,392 ($1,462 – $70). Therefore, the wage bracket for McGrath is $1,302–$1,624.

Step 2. Compute the withholding for the proper wage bracket using the directions in the two right-hand columns in Exhibit 3.

For McGrath's wage bracket, the withholding is computed as "$234.60. plus 27% of the excess over $1,302." Hence, McGrath's withholding is $258.90, as shown below.

Initial withholding from wage bracket	*$234.60*
Plus [27% × ($1,392 – $1,302)]	*24.30*
Total withholding	*$258.90*

EXHIBIT 3 **Wage Bracket Withholding Table**

Table for Percentage Method of Withholding WEEKLY Payroll Period

(a) SINGLE person (including head of household)—

If the amount of wages (after subtracting withholding allowances) is:		The amount of income tax to withhold is:	
Not over $116		$0	
Over—	**But not over—**		**of excess over—**
$116	—$200	10%	—$116
$200	—$693	$8.40 plus 15%	—$200
$693	—$1,302	$82.35 plus 25%	—$693
$1,302	—$1,624	$234.60 plus 27%	—$1,302
$1,624	—$1,687	$321.54 plus 30%	—$1,624
$1,687	—$3,344	$340.44 plus 28%	—$1,687
$3,344	—$7,225	$804.40 plus 33%	—$3,344
$7,225		$2,085.13 plus 35%	—$7,225

← McGrath wage bracket

Source: Publication 15, *Employer's Tax Guide*, Internal Revenue Service, 2010.

Residents of New York City must pay federal, state, and city income taxes.

Employers may also be required to withhold state or city income taxes. The amounts to be withheld are determined on state-by-state and city-by-city bases.

Example Exercise 11-2 Federal Income Tax Withholding OBJ. 2

Karen Dunn's weekly gross earnings for the present week were $2,250. Dunn has two exemptions. Using the wage bracket withholding table in Exhibit 3 with a $70 standard withholding allowance for each exemption, what is Dunn's federal income tax withholding?

(continued)

4 The actual IRS standard withholding allowance changes every year and was $70.19 for 2010.

Follow My Example 11-2

Total wage payment		$ 2,250
One allowance (provided by IRS)	$70	
Multiplied by allowances claimed on Form W-4	× 2	140
Amount subject to withholding		$ 2,110
Initial withholding from wage bracket in Exhibit 3		$340.44
Plus additional withholding: 28% of excess over $1,687		118.44*
Federal income tax withholding		$458.88

*28% × ($2,110 – $1,687)

Practice Exercises: **PE 11-2A, PE 11-2B**

FICA Tax Employers are required by the Federal Insurance Contributions Act (FICA) to withhold a portion of the earnings of each employee. The **FICA tax** withheld contributes to the following two federal programs:

1. *Social security*, which provides payments for retirees, survivors, and disability insurance.
2. *Medicare*, which provides health insurance for senior citizens.

The amount withheld from each employee is based on the employee's earnings *paid* in the *calendar* year. The withholding tax rates and maximum earnings subject to tax are often revised by Congress.[5] To simplify, this chapter assumes the following rates and earnings subject to tax:

1. Social security: 6% on all earnings
2. Medicare: 1.5% on all earnings

To illustrate, assume that John T. McGrath's earnings for the week ending December 27 are $1,462 and the total FICA tax to be withheld is **$109.65**, as shown below.

Earnings subject to 6% social security tax	$1,462	
Social security tax rate	× 6%	
Social security tax		$ 87.72
Earnings subject to 1.5% Medicare tax	$1,462	
Medicare tax rate	× 1.5%	
Medicare tax		21.93
Total FICA tax		$109.65

Other Deductions Employees may choose to have additional amounts deducted from their gross pay. For example, an employee may authorize deductions for retirement savings, for charitable contributions, or life insurance. A union contract may also require the deduction of union dues.

Computing Employee Net Pay

Gross earnings less payroll deductions equals *net pay*, sometimes called *take-home pay*. Assuming that John T. McGrath authorized deductions for retirement savings and

5 As of January 1, 2010, the social security tax rate was 6.2% and the Medicare tax rate was 1.45%. Earnings subject to the social security tax are limited to an annual threshold amount, but for text examples and problems, assume all accumulated annual earnings are below this threshold and subject to the tax.

for a United Fund contribution, McGrath's net pay for the week ended December 27 is $1,068.45, as shown below.

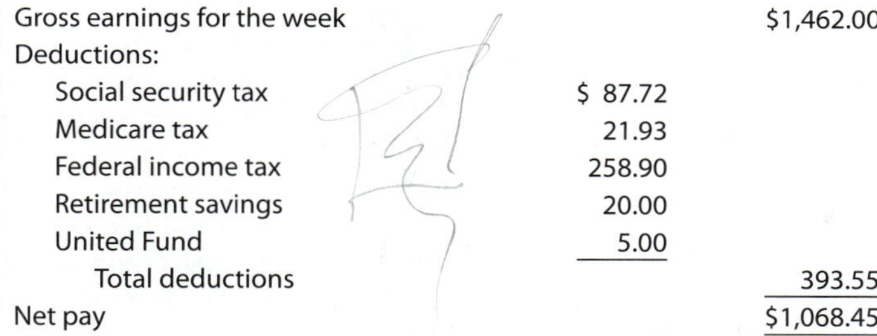

Gross earnings for the week		$1,462.00
Deductions:		
Social security tax	$ 87.72	
Medicare tax	21.93	
Federal income tax	258.90	
Retirement savings	20.00	
United Fund	5.00	
Total deductions		393.55
Net pay		$1,068.45

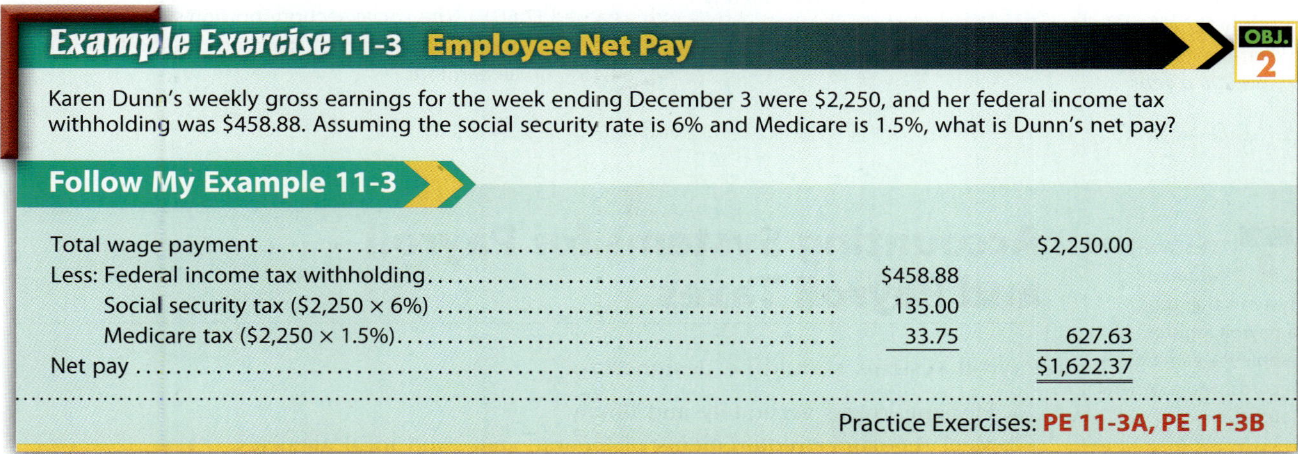

Example Exercise 11-3 Employee Net Pay OBJ. 2

Karen Dunn's weekly gross earnings for the week ending December 3 were $2,250, and her federal income tax withholding was $458.88. Assuming the social security rate is 6% and Medicare is 1.5%, what is Dunn's net pay?

Follow My Example 11-3

Total wage payment		$2,250.00
Less: Federal income tax withholding	$458.88	
Social security tax ($2,250 × 6%)	135.00	
Medicare tax ($2,250 × 1.5%)	33.75	627.63
Net pay		$1,622.37

Practice Exercises: **PE 11-3A, PE 11-3B**

Liability for Employer's Payroll Taxes

Employers are subject to the following payroll taxes for amounts paid their employees:

1. *FICA Tax*: Employers must match the employee's FICA tax contribution.
2. *Federal Unemployment Compensation Tax (FUTA)*: This employer tax provides for temporary payments to those who become unemployed. The tax collected by the federal government is allocated among the states for use in state programs rather than paid directly to employees. Congress often revises the FUTA tax rate and maximum earnings subject to tax.
3. *State Unemployment Compensation Tax (SUTA)*: This employer tax also provides temporary payments to those who become unemployed. The FUTA and SUTA programs are closely coordinated, with the states distributing the unemployment checks.[6] SUTA tax rates and earnings subject to tax vary by state.[7]

The preceding employer taxes are an operating expense of the company. Exhibit 4 summarizes the responsibility for employee and employer payroll taxes.

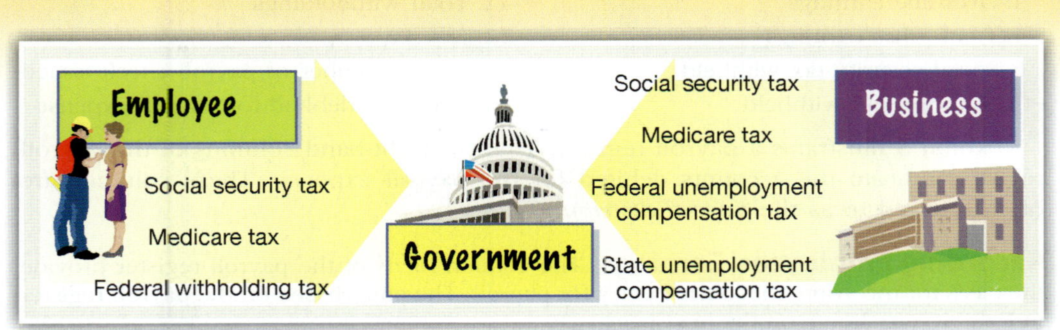

EXHIBIT 4
Responsibility for Tax Payments

6 This rate may be reduced to 0.8% for credits for state unemployment compensation tax.

7 As of January 1, 2010, the maximum state rate credited against the federal unemployment rate was 5.4% of the first $7,000 of each employee's earnings during a calendar year.

Business Connection

THE MOST YOU WILL EVER PAY

In 1936, the Social Security Board described how the tax was expected to affect a worker's pay, as follows:

The taxes called for in this law will be paid both by your employer and by you. For the next 3 years you will pay maybe 15 cents a week, maybe 25 cents a week, maybe 30 cents or more, according to what you earn. That is to say, during the next 3 years, beginning January 1, 1937, you will pay 1 cent for every dollar you earn, and at the same time your employer will pay 1 cent for every dollar you earn, up to $3,000 a year. . . .

. . . Beginning in 1940 you will pay, and your employer will pay, 1½ cents for each dollar you earn, up to $3,000 a year . . . and then beginning in 1943, you will pay 2 cents, and so will your employer, for every dollar you earn for the next three years. After that, you and your employer will each pay half a cent more for 3 years, and finally, beginning in 1949, . . . you and your employer will each pay 3 cents on each dollar you earn, up to $3,000 a year. That is the most you will ever pay.

The rate on January 1, 2010, was 7.65 cents per dollar earned (7.65%). The social security portion was 6.20% on the first $106,800 of earnings. The Medicare portion was 1.45% on all earnings.

Source: Arthur Lodge, "That Is the Most You Will Ever Pay," *Journal of Accountancy*, October 1985, p. 44.

OBJ. 3 Describe payroll accounting systems that use a payroll register, employee earnings records, and a general journal.

Accounting Systems for Payroll and Payroll Taxes

Payroll systems should be designed to:

1. Pay employees accurately and timely.
2. Meet regulatory requirements of federal, state, and local agencies.
3. Provide useful data for management decision-making needs.

Although payroll systems differ among companies, the major elements of most payroll systems are:

1. Payroll register
2. Employee's earnings record
3. Payroll checks

Payroll Register

The **payroll register** is a multicolumn report used for summarizing the data for each payroll period. Although payroll registers vary by company, a payroll register normally includes the following columns:

1. Employee name
2. Total hours worked
3. Regular earnings
4. Overtime earnings
5. Total gross earnings
6. Social security tax withheld
7. Medicare tax withheld
8. Federal income tax withheld
9. Retirement savings withheld
10. Miscellaneous items withheld
11. Total withholdings
12. Net pay
13. Check number of payroll check issued
14. Accounts debited for payroll expense

Exhibit 5 illustrates a payroll register. The two right-hand columns of the payroll register indicate the accounts debited for the payroll expense. These columns are often referred to as the *payroll distribution*.

Recording Employees' Earnings The column totals of the payroll register provide the basis for recording the journal entry for payroll. The entry based on the payroll register in Exhibit 5 is shown on the next page.

Note:
Payroll taxes become a liability to the employer when the payroll is paid.

Recording and Paying Payroll Taxes Payroll taxes are recorded as liabilities when the payroll is *paid* to employees. In addition, employers compute and report payroll taxes on a *calendar-year* basis, which may differ from the company's fiscal year.

Dec.	27	Sales Salaries Expense		11,122.00	
		Office Salaries Expense		2,780.00	
		Social Security Tax Payable			834.12
		Medicare Tax Payable			208.53
		Employees Federal Income Tax Payable			3,332.00
		Retirement Savings Deductions Payable			680.00
		United Fund Deductions Payable			520.00
		Salaries Payable			8,327.35
		Payroll for week ended December 27.			

Example Exercise 11-4 Journalize Period Payroll

OBJ. 3

The payroll register of Chen Engineering Services indicates $900 of social security withheld and $225 of Medicare tax withheld on total salaries of $15,000 for the period. Federal withholding for the period totaled $2,925.

Provide the journal entry for the period's payroll.

Follow My Example 11-4

Salaries Expense	15,000	
Social Security Tax Payable		900
Medicare Tax Payable		225
Employees Federal Withholding Tax Payable		2,925
Salaries Payable		10,950

Practice Exercises: **PE 11-4A, PE 11-4B**

On December 27, McDermott Supply has the following payroll data:

Sales salaries	$11,122
Office salaries owed	2,780
Wages owed employees on December 27	$13,902
Wages subject to payroll taxes:	
Social security tax (6%)	$13,902
Medicare tax (1.5%)	13,902
State (5.4%) and federal (0.8%) unemployment compensation tax	2,710

Employers must match the employees' social security and Medicare tax contributions. In addition, the employer must pay state unemployment compensation tax (SUTA) of 5.4% and federal unemployment compensation tax (FUTA) of 0.8%. When payroll is paid on December 27, these payroll taxes are computed as follows:

Social security tax	$ 834.12 ($13,902 × 6%, and from Social Security Tax column of Exhibit 5)
Medicare tax	208.53 ($13,902 × 1.5%, and from Medicare Tax column of Exhibit 5)
SUTA	146.34 ($2,710 × 5.4%)
FUTA	21.68 ($2,710 × 0.8%)
Total payroll taxes	$1,210.67

The entry to journalize the payroll tax expense for Exhibit 5 is shown below.

Dec.	27	Payroll Tax Expense		1,210.67	
		Social Security Tax Payable			834.12
		Medicare Tax Payable			208.53
		State Unemployment Tax Payable			146.34
		Federal Unemployment Tax Payable			21.68
		Payroll taxes for week ended December 27.			

EXHIBIT 5 Payroll Register

			Earnings			
	Employee Name	Total Hours	Regular	Overtime	Total	
1	Abrams, Julie S.	40	500.00		500.00	1
2	Elrod, Fred G.	44	392.00	58.80	450.80	2
3	Gomez, Jose C.	40	840.00		840.00	3
4	McGrath, John T.	42	1,360.00	102.00	1,462.00	4
25	Wilkes, Glenn K.	40	480.00		480.00	25
26	Zumpano, Michael W.	40	600.00		600.00	26
27	Total		13,328.00	574.00	13,902.00	27
28						28

The preceding entry records a liability for each payroll tax. When the payroll taxes are paid, an entry is recorded debiting the payroll tax liability accounts and crediting Cash.

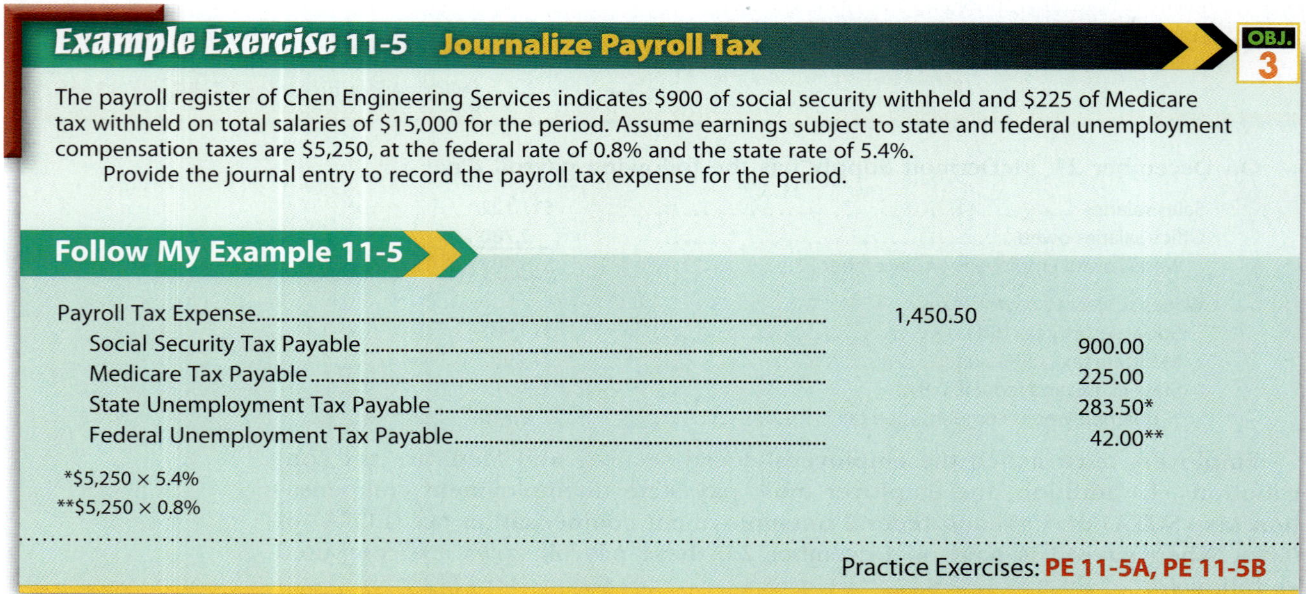

Example Exercise 11-5 Journalize Payroll Tax OBJ. 3

The payroll register of Chen Engineering Services indicates $900 of social security withheld and $225 of Medicare tax withheld on total salaries of $15,000 for the period. Assume earnings subject to state and federal unemployment compensation taxes are $5,250, at the federal rate of 0.8% and the state rate of 5.4%.

Provide the journal entry to record the payroll tax expense for the period.

Follow My Example 11-5

Payroll Tax Expense	1,450.50	
Social Security Tax Payable		900.00
Medicare Tax Payable		225.00
State Unemployment Tax Payable		283.50*
Federal Unemployment Tax Payable		42.00**

*$5,250 × 5.4%
**$5,250 × 0.8%

Practice Exercises: **PE 11-5A, PE 11-5B**

Employee's Earnings Record

Each employee's earnings to date must be determined at the end of each payroll period. This total is necessary for computing the employee's social security tax withholding and the employer's payroll taxes. Thus, detailed payroll records must be kept for each employee. This record is called an **employee's earnings record**.

Exhibit 6, on pages 502–503, shows a portion of John T. McGrath's employee's earnings record. An employee's earnings record and the payroll register are interrelated. For example, McGrath's earnings record for December 27 can be traced to the fourth line of the payroll register in Exhibit 5.

As shown in Exhibit 6, an employee's earnings record has quarterly and yearly totals. These totals are used for tax, insurance, and other reports. For example, one such report is the Wage and Tax Statement, commonly called a *W-2*. This form is

EXHIBIT 5 (Concluded)

	Deductions Withheld						Paid		Accounts Debited		
	Social Security Tax	Medicare Tax	Federal Income Tax	Retirement Savings	Misc.	Total	Net Pay	Check No.	Sales Salaries Expense	Office Salaries Expense	
1	30.00	7.50	74.00	20.00	UF 10.00	141.50	358.50	6857	500.00		1
2	27.05	6.76	62.00		UF 50.00	145.81	304.99	6858		450.80	2
3	50.40	12.60	131.00	25.00	UF 10.00	229.00	611.00	6859	840.00		3
4	87.72	21.93	258.90	20.00	UF 5.00	393.55	1,068.45	6860	1,462.00		4
25	28.80	7.20	69.00	10.00		115.00	365.00	6880	480.00		25
26	36.00	9.00	79.00	5.00	UF 2.00	131.00	469.00	6881		600.00	26
27	834.12	208.53	3,332.00	680.00	UF 520.00	5,574.65	8,327.35		11,122.00	2,780.00	27
28											28

Miscellaneous Deductions: UF—United Fund

provided annually to each employee as well as to the Social Security Administration. The W-2 shown below is based on John T. McGrath's employee's earnings record shown in Exhibit 6.

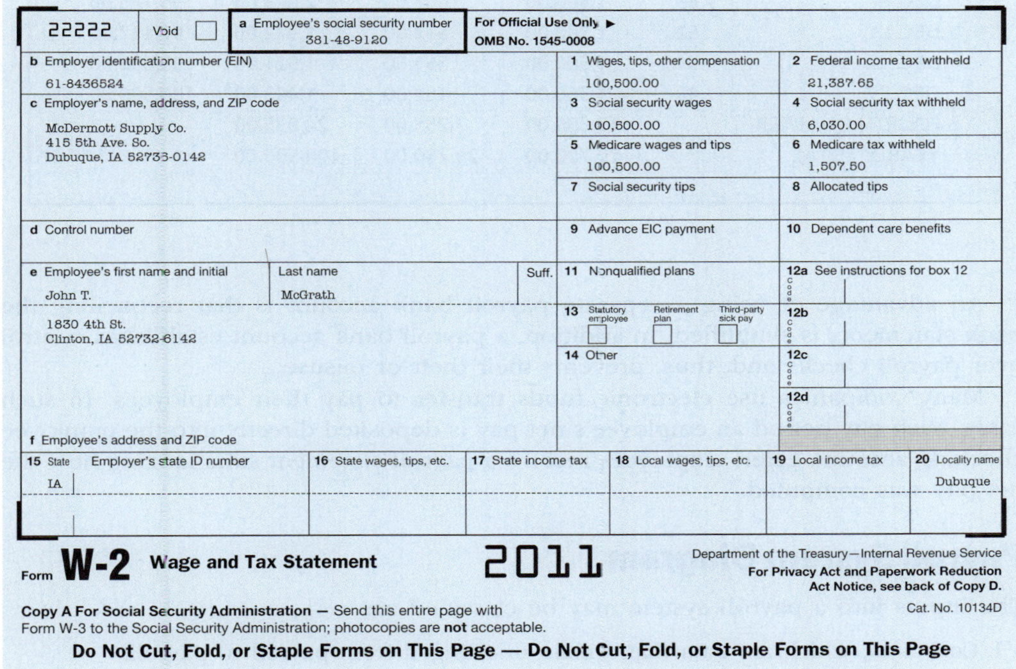

22222 Void ☐ | a Employee's social security number 381-48-9120 | For Official Use Only ▶ OMB No. 1545-0008

b Employer identification number (EIN) 61-8436524

1 Wages, tips, other compensation 100,500.00

2 Federal income tax withheld 21,387.65

c Employer's name, address, and ZIP code
McDermott Supply Co.
415 5th Ave. So.
Dubuque, IA 52733-0142

3 Social security wages 100,500.00

4 Social security tax withheld 6,030.00

5 Medicare wages and tips 100,500.00

6 Medicare tax withheld 1,507.50

7 Social security tips

8 Allocated tips

d Control number

9 Advance EIC payment

10 Dependent care benefits

e Employee's first name and initial John T. | Last name McGrath | Suff.

11 Nonqualified plans

12a See instructions for box 12

1830 4th St.
Clinton, IA 52732-6142

13 Statutory employee ☐ Retirement plan ☐ Third-party sick pay ☐

12b

14 Other

12c

12d

f Employee's address and ZIP code

15 State	Employer's state ID number	16 State wages, tips, etc.	17 State income tax	18 Local wages, tips, etc.	19 Local income tax	20 Locality name
IA						Dubuque

Form **W-2** Wage and Tax Statement 2011

Department of the Treasury—Internal Revenue Service
For Privacy Act and Paperwork Reduction Act Notice, see back of Copy D.
Cat. No. 10134D

Copy A For Social Security Administration — Send this entire page with Form W-3 to the Social Security Administration; photocopies are **not** acceptable.

Do Not Cut, Fold, or Staple Forms on This Page — Do Not Cut, Fold, or Staple Forms on This Page

Payroll Checks

Companies may pay employees, especially part-time employees, by issuing *payroll checks*. Each check includes a detachable statement showing how the net pay was computed. Exhibit 7, on page 504, illustrates a payroll check for John T. McGrath.

Most companies issuing payroll checks use a special payroll bank account. In such cases, payroll is processed as follows:

1. The total net pay for the period is determined from the payroll register.
2. The company authorizes an electronic funds transfer (EFT) from its regular bank account to the special payroll bank account for the total net pay.
3. Individual payroll checks are written from the payroll account.
4. The numbers of the payroll checks are inserted in the payroll register.

EXHIBIT 6

Employee's Earnings Record

John T. McGrath 1830 4th St. Clinton, IA 52732-6142		PHONE: 555-3148
SINGLE	NUMBER OF WITHHOLDING ALLOWANCES: 1	PAY RATE: $1,360.00 Per Week
OCCUPATION: Salesperson		EQUIVALENT HOURLY RATE: $34

			Earnings				
	Period Ending	Total Hours	Regular Earnings	Overtime Earnings	Total Earnings	Total	
42	SEPT. 27	53	1,360.00	663.00	2,023.00	75,565.00	42
43	THIRD QUARTER		17,680.00	7,605.00	25,285.00		43
44	OCT. 4	51	1,360.00	561.00	1,921.00	77,486.00	44
50	NOV. 15	50	1,360.00	510.00	1,870.00	89,382.00	50
51	NOV. 22	53	1,360.00	663.00	2,023.00	91,405.00	51
52	NOV. 29	47	1,360.00	357.00	1,717.00	93,122.00	52
53	DEC. 6	53	1,360.00	663.00	2,023.00	95,145.00	53
54	DEC.13	52	1,360.00	612.00	1,972.00	97,117.00	54
55	DEC. 20	51	1,360.00	561.00	1,921.00	99,038.00	55
56	DEC. 27	42	1,360.00	102.00	1,462.00	100,500.00	56
57	FOURTH QUARTER		17,680.00	7,255.00	24,935.00		57
58	YEARLY TOTAL		70,720.00	29,780.00	100,500.00		58

An advantage of using a separate payroll bank account is that reconciling the bank statements is simplified. In addition, a payroll bank account establishes control over payroll checks and, thus, prevents their theft or misuse.

Many companies use electronic funds transfer to pay their employees. In such cases, each pay period an employee's net pay is deposited directly into the employee checking account. Later, employees receive a payroll statement summarizing how the net pay was computed.

Payroll System Diagram

The inputs into a payroll system may be classified as:

1. Constants, which are data that remain unchanged from payroll to payroll.

   Examples: Employee names, social security numbers, marital status, number of income tax withholding allowances, rates of pay, tax rates, and withholding tables.

2. Variables, which are data that change from payroll to payroll.

   Examples: Number of hours or days worked for each employee, accrued days of sick leave, vacation credits, total earnings to date, and total taxes withheld.

In a computerized accounting system, constants are stored within a payroll file. The variables are input each pay period by a payroll clerk. In some systems, employees swipe their identification (ID) cards when they report for and leave work. In such cases, the hours worked by each employee are automatically updated.

A computerized payroll system also maintains electronic versions of the payroll register and employee earnings records. Payroll system outputs, such as payroll checks, EFTs, and tax records, are automatically produced each pay period.

EXHIBIT 6 (Concluded)

SOC. SEC. NO.: 381-48-9120	EMPLOYEE NO.: 814
DATE OF BIRTH: February 15, 1982	
DATE EMPLOYMENT TERMINATED:	

	Deductions							Paid		
	Social Security Tax	Medicare Tax	Federal Income Tax	Retirement Savings	Other		Total	Net Amount	Check No.	
42	121.38	30.35	429.83	20.00			601.56	1,421.44	6175	42
43	1,517.10	379.28	5,391.71	260.00	UF	40.00	7,588.09	17,696.91		43
44	115.26	28.82	401.27	20.00			565.35	1,355.65	6225	44
50	112.20	28.05	386.99	20.00			547.24	1,322.76	6530	50
51	121.38	30.35	429.83	20.00			601.56	1,421.44	6582	51
52	103.02	25.76	344.15	20.00			492.93	1,224.07	6640	52
53	121.38	30.35	429.83	20.00	UF	5.00	606.56	1,416.44	6688	53
54	118.32	29.58	415.55	20.00			583.45	1,388.55	6743	54
55	115.26	28.82	401.27	20.00			565.35	1,355.65	6801	55
56	87.72	21.93	258.90	20.00	UF	5.00	393.55	1,068.45	6860	56
57	1,496.10	374.03	5,293.71	260.00	UF	15.00	7,438.84	17,496.16		57
58	6,030.00	1,507.50	21,387.65	1,040.00	UF	100.00	30,065.15	70,434.85		58

Internal Controls for Payroll Systems

The cash payment controls described in Chapter 8, *Sarbanes-Oxley, Internal Control, and Cash*, also apply to payrolls. Some examples of payroll controls include the following:

1. If a check-signing machine is used, blank payroll checks and access to the machine should be restricted to prevent their theft or misuse.
2. The hiring and firing of employees should be properly authorized and approved in writing.
3. All changes in pay rates should be properly authorized and approved in writing.
4. Employees should be observed when arriving for work to verify that employees are "checking in" for work only once and only for themselves. Employees may "check in" for work by using a time card or by swiping their employee ID card.
5. Payroll checks should be distributed by someone other than employee supervisors.
6. A special payroll bank account should be used.

Integrity, Objectivity, and Ethics in Business

$8 MILLION FOR 18 MINUTES OF WORK

Computer system controls can be very important in issuing payroll checks. In one case, a Detroit schoolteacher was paid $4,015,625 after deducting $3,884,375 in payroll deductions for 18 minutes of overtime work. The error was caused by a computer glitch when the teacher's employee identification number was substituted incorrectly in the "hourly wage" field and wasn't caught by the payroll software. After six days, the error was discovered and the money was returned. "One of the things that came with (the software) is a fail-safe that prevents that. It doesn't work," a financial officer said. The district has since installed a program to flag any paycheck exceeding $10,000.

Source: Associated Press, September 27, 2002.

EXHIBIT 7
Payroll Check

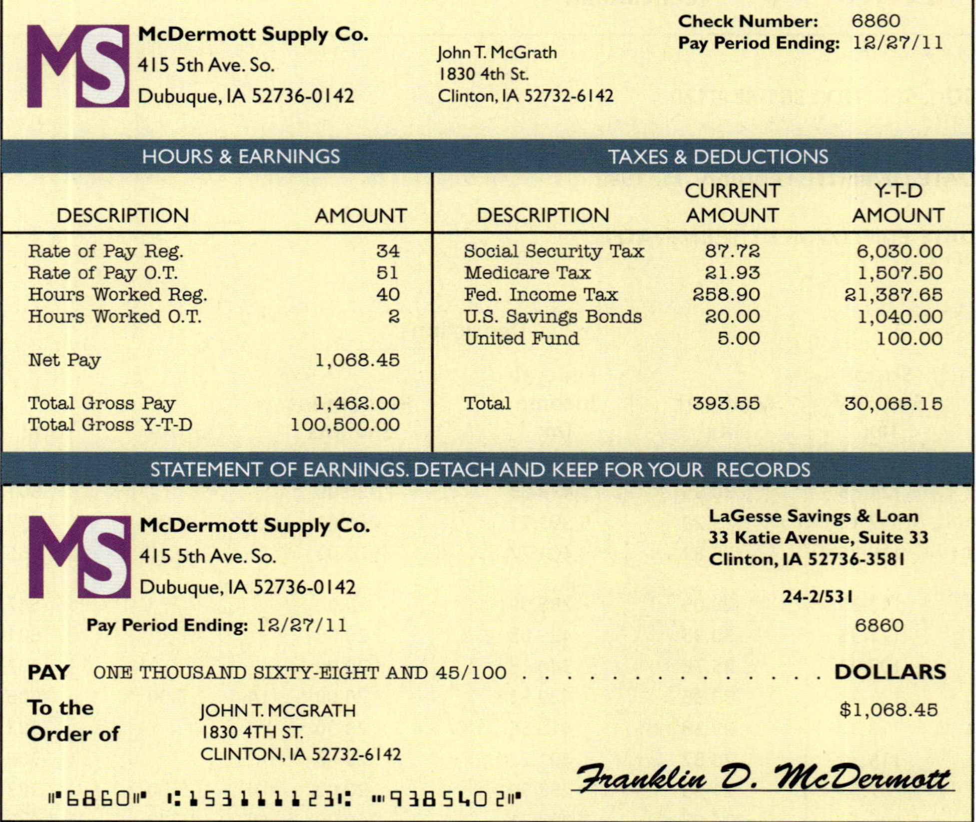

McDermott Supply Co.
415 5th Ave. So.
Dubuque, IA 52736-0142

John T. McGrath
1830 4th St.
Clinton, IA 52732-6142

Check Number: 6860
Pay Period Ending: 12/27/11

HOURS & EARNINGS		TAXES & DEDUCTIONS		
DESCRIPTION	AMOUNT	DESCRIPTION	CURRENT AMOUNT	Y-T-D AMOUNT
Rate of Pay Reg.	34	Social Security Tax	87.72	6,030.00
Rate of Pay O.T.	51	Medicare Tax	21.93	1,507.50
Hours Worked Reg.	40	Fed. Income Tax	258.90	21,387.65
Hours Worked O.T.	2	U.S. Savings Bonds	20.00	1,040.00
		United Fund	5.00	100.00
Net Pay	1,068.45			
Total Gross Pay	1,462.00	Total	393.55	30,065.15
Total Gross Y-T-D	100,500.00			

STATEMENT OF EARNINGS. DETACH AND KEEP FOR YOUR RECORDS

McDermott Supply Co.
415 5th Ave. So.
Dubuque, IA 52736-0142

LaGesse Savings & Loan
33 Katie Avenue, Suite 33
Clinton, IA 52736-3581

24-2/531

Pay Period Ending: 12/27/11

6860

PAY ONE THOUSAND SIXTY-EIGHT AND 45/100 . . . . DOLLARS

To the Order of JOHN T. MCGRATH
1830 4TH ST.
CLINTON, IA 52732-6142

$1,068.45

Franklin D. McDermott

⑈6860⑈ ⑆153111123⑆ ⑈938540 2⑈

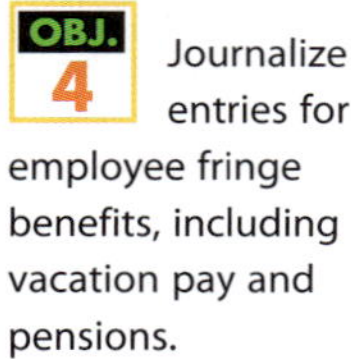

Journalize entries for employee fringe benefits, including vacation pay and pensions.

Employees' Fringe Benefits

Many companies provide their employees benefits in addition to salary and wages earned. Such **fringe benefits** may include vacation, medical, and retirement benefits.

The cost of employee fringe benefits is recorded as an expense by the employer. To match revenues and expenses, the estimated cost of fringe benefits is recorded as an expense during the period in which the employees earn the benefits.

Vacation Pay

Note:
Vacation pay becomes the employer's liability as the employee earns vacation rights.

Most employers provide employees vacations, sometimes called *compensated absences*. The liability to pay for employee vacations could be accrued as a liability at the end of each pay period. However, many companies wait and record an adjusting entry for accrued vacation at the end of the year.

To illustrate, assume that employees earn one day of vacation for each month worked. The estimated vacation pay for the year ending December 31 is $325,000. The adjusting entry for the accrued vacation is shown below.

Dec.	31	Vacation Pay Expense	325,000	
		Vacation Pay Payable		325,000
		Accrued vacation pay for the year.		

Employees may be required to take all their vacation time within one year. In such cases, any accrued vacation pay will be paid within one year. Thus, the vacation pay payable is reported as a current liability on the balance sheet. If employees are allowed to accumulate their vacation pay, the estimated vacation pay payable that will *not* be taken within a year is reported as a long-term liability.

When employees take vacations, the liability for vacation pay is decreased by debiting Vacation Pay Payable. Salaries or Wages Payable and the other related payroll accounts for taxes and withholdings are credited.

Pensions

A **pension** is a cash payment to retired employees. Pension rights are accrued by employees as they work, based on the employer's pension plan. Two basic types of pension plans are:

1. Defined contribution plan
2. Defined benefit plan

In a **defined contribution plan**, the company invests contributions on behalf of the employee during the employee's working years. Normally, the employee and employer contribute to the plan. The employee's pension depends on the total contributions and the investment returns earned on those contributions.

One of the more popular defined contribution plans is the 401k plan. Under this plan, employees contribute a portion of their gross pay to investments, such as mutual funds. A 401k plan offers employees two advantages.

1. The employee contribution is deducted before taxes.
2. The contributions and related earnings are not taxed until withdrawn at retirement.

In most cases, the employer matches some portion of the employee's contribution. The employer's cost is debited to *Pension Expense*. To illustrate, assume that Heaven Scent Perfumes Company contributes 10% of employee monthly salaries to an employee 401k plan. Assuming $500,000 of monthly salaries, the journal entry to record the monthly contribution is shown below.

Dec.	31	Pension Expense		50,000	
		Cash			50,000
		Contributed 10% of monthly salaries to pension plan.			

In a **defined benefit plan**, the company pays the employee a fixed annual pension based on a formula. The formula is normally based on such factors as the employee's years of service, age, and past salary.

Annual Pension = 1.5% × Years of Service × Highest 3-Year Average Salary

In a defined benefit plan, the employer is obligated to pay for (fund) the employee's future pension benefits. As a result, many companies are replacing their defined benefit plans with defined contribution plans.

The pension cost of a defined benefit plan is debited to *Pension Expense*. Cash is credited for the amount contributed (funded) by the employer. Any unfunded amount is credited to *Unfunded Pension Liability*.

To illustrate, assume that the defined benefit plan of Hinkle Co. requires an annual pension cost of $80,000. This annual contribution is based on estimates of Hinkle's future pension liabilities. On December 31, Hinkle Co. pays $60,000 to the pension fund. The entry to record the payment and unfunded liability is shown below.

Dec.	31	Pension Expense	80,000	
		Cash		60,000
		Unfunded Pension Liability		20,000
		Annual pension cost and contribution.		

If the unfunded pension liability is to be paid within one year, it is reported as a current liability on the balance sheet. Any portion of the unfunded pension liability that will be paid beyond one year is a long-term liability.

The accounting for pensions is complex due to the uncertainties of estimating future pension liabilities. These estimates depend on such factors as employee life expectancies, employee turnover, expected employee compensation levels, and investment income on pension contributions. Additional accounting and disclosures related to pensions are covered in advanced accounting courses.

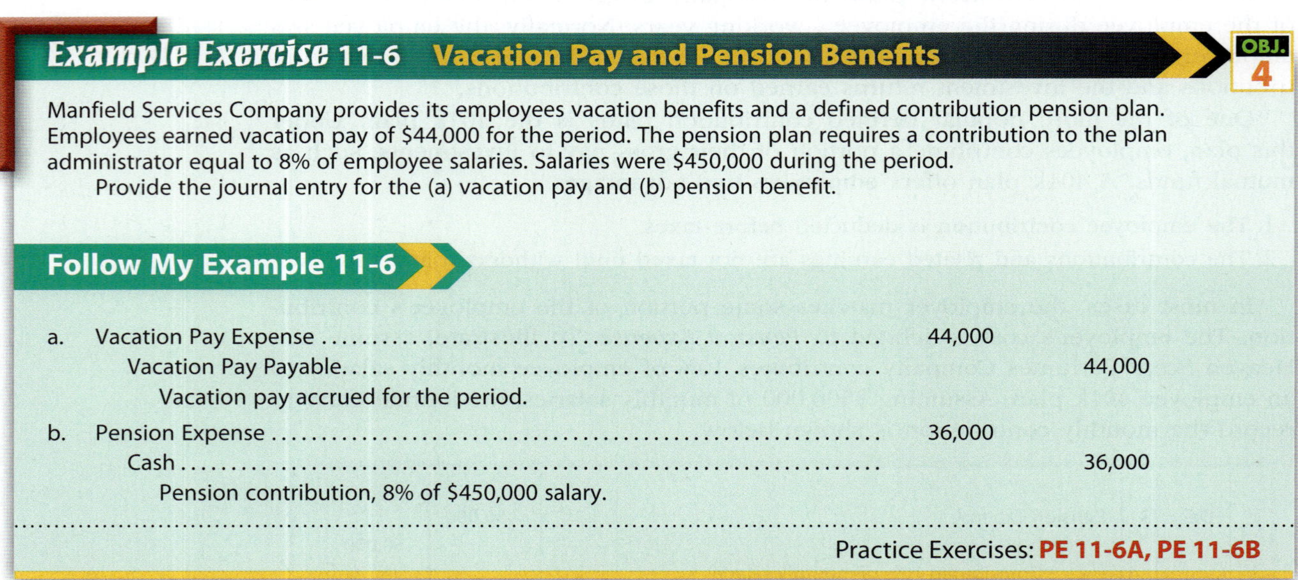

Example Exercise 11-6 Vacation Pay and Pension Benefits OBJ. 4

Manfield Services Company provides its employees vacation benefits and a defined contribution pension plan. Employees earned vacation pay of $44,000 for the period. The pension plan requires a contribution to the plan administrator equal to 8% of employee salaries. Salaries were $450,000 during the period.

Provide the journal entry for the (a) vacation pay and (b) pension benefit.

Follow My Example 11-6

a.	Vacation Pay Expense	44,000	
	Vacation Pay Payable		44,000
	Vacation pay accrued for the period.		
b.	Pension Expense	36,000	
	Cash		36,000
	Pension contribution, 8% of $450,000 salary.		

Practice Exercises: **PE 11-6A, PE 11-6B**

Postretirement Benefits Other than Pensions

Employees may earn rights to other postretirement benefits from their employer. Such benefits may include dental care, eye care, medical care, life insurance, tuition assistance, tax services, and legal services.

The accounting for other postretirement benefits is similar to that of defined benefit pension plans. The estimate of the annual benefits expense is recorded by debiting *Postretirement Benefits Expense*. If the benefits are fully funded, Cash is credited for the same amount. If the benefits are not fully funded, a postretirement benefits plan liability account is also credited.

The financial statements should disclose the nature of the postretirement benefit liabilities. These disclosures are usually included as notes to the financial statements. Additional accounting and disclosures for postretirement benefits are covered in advanced accounting courses.

Current Liabilities on the Balance Sheet

Accounts payable, the current portion of long-term debt, notes payable, and any other debts that are due within one year are reported as current liabilities on the balance sheet. The balance sheet presentation of current liabilities for Mornin' Joe is as shown on the next page.

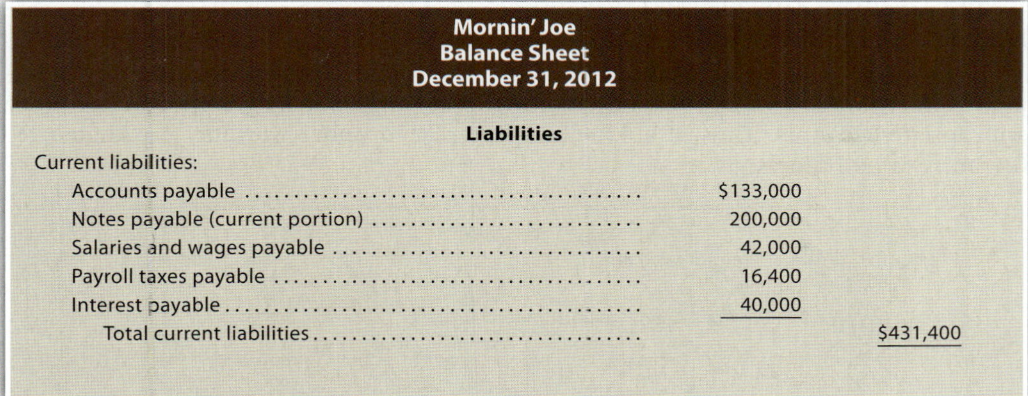

Mornin' Joe
Balance Sheet
December 31, 2012

Liabilities

Current liabilities:		
Accounts payable	$133,000	
Notes payable (current portion)	200,000	
Salaries and wages payable	42,000	
Payroll taxes payable	16,400	
Interest payable	40,000	
Total current liabilities		$431,400

Business Connection

GENERAL MOTORS PENSION PROBLEMS

In June 2009, General Motors Company, the world's second-largest automaker, filed for bankruptcy. The company's troubles began decades earlier when the company agreed to provide employees with large pension benefits instead of giving them wage increases. While this strategy was initially successful, by the mid-1990s large numbers of employees began to retire, and the increasing pension costs began to put a financial strain on the company. In 2003, the company issued $18.5 billion in debt to fund its growing unfunded pension liability, but this only provided a temporary fix. From 1993 to 2007, General Motors spent $103 billion on pension and health care benefits for retirees, and the company had 4.61 retired union employees for every one active union employee. By June 2009, the combination of growing pension obligations and deteriorating sales forced the company into bankruptcy.

Source: R. Lowenstein, "Siphoning GM's Future," *The New York Times*, July 10, 2008.

Contingent Liabilities

OBJ. 5 Describe the accounting treatment for contingent liabilities and journalize entries for product warranties.

Some liabilities may arise from past transactions if certain events occur in the future. These *potential* liabilities are called **contingent liabilities**.

The accounting for contingent liabilities depends on the following two factors:

1. Likelihood of occurring: Probable, reasonably possible, or remote
2. Measurement: Estimable or not estimable

The likelihood that the event creating the liability occurring is classified as *probable*, *reasonably possible*, or *remote*. The ability to estimate the potential liability is classified as *estimable* or *not estimable*.

Probable and Estimable

If a contingent liability is *probable* and the amount of the liability can be *reasonably estimated*, it is recorded and disclosed. The liability is recorded by debiting an expense and crediting a liability.

To illustrate, assume that during June a company sold a product for $60,000 that includes a 36-month warranty for repairs. The average cost of repairs over the warranty period is 5% of the sales price. The entry to record the estimated product warranty expense for June is as shown below.

June	30	Product Warranty Expense		3,000	
		Product Warranty Payable			3,000
		Warranty expense for June, 5% × $60,000.			

The estimated costs of warranty work on new car sales are a contingent liability for Ford Motor Company.

The preceding entry records warranty expense in the same period in which the sale is recorded. In this way, warranty expense is matched with the related revenue (sales).

If the product is repaired under warranty, the repair costs are recorded by debiting *Product Warranty Payable* and crediting *Cash, Supplies, Wages Payable*, or other appropriate accounts. Thus, if a $200 part is replaced under warranty on August 16, the entry is as follows:

Aug.	16	Product Warranty Payable		200	
		Supplies			200
		Replaced defective part under warranty.			

Example Exercise 11-7 Estimated Warranty Liability

OBJ. 5

Cook-Rite Co. sold $140,000 of kitchen appliances during August under a six-month warranty. The cost to repair defects under the warranty is estimated at 6% of the sales price. On September 11, a customer required a $200 part replacement plus $90 of labor under the warranty.

Provide the journal entry for (a) the estimated warranty expense on August 31 and (b) the September 11 warranty work.

Follow My Example 11-7

a.	Product Warranty Expense	8,400	
	Product Warranty Payable		8,400
	To record warranty expense for August, 6% × $140,000.		
b.	Product Warranty Payable	290	
	Supplies		200
	Wages Payable		90
	Replaced defective part under warranty.		

Practice Exercises: **PE 11-7A, PE 11-7B**

Probable and Not Estimable

A contingent liability may be probable, but cannot be estimated. In this case, the contingent liability is disclosed in the notes to the financial statements. For example, a company may have accidentally polluted a local river by dumping waste products. At the end of the period, the cost of the cleanup and any fines may not be able to be estimated.

Reasonably Possible

A contingent liability may be only possible. For example, a company may have lost a lawsuit for infringing on another company's patent rights. However, the verdict is under appeal and the company's lawyers feel that the verdict will be reversed or significantly reduced. In this case, the contingent liability is disclosed in the notes to the financial statements.

Remote

A contingent liability may be remote. For example, a ski resort may be sued for injuries incurred by skiers. In most cases, the courts have found that a skier accepts the risk of injury when participating in the activity. Thus, unless the ski resort is grossly negligent, the resort will not incur a liability for ski injuries. In such cases, no disclosure needs to be made in the notes to the financial statements.

The accounting treatment of contingent liabilities is summarized in Exhibit 8.

Common examples of contingent liabilities disclosed in notes to the financial statements are litigation, environmental matters, guarantees, and contingencies from the sale of receivables.

EXHIBIT 8 Accounting Treatment of Contingent Liabilities

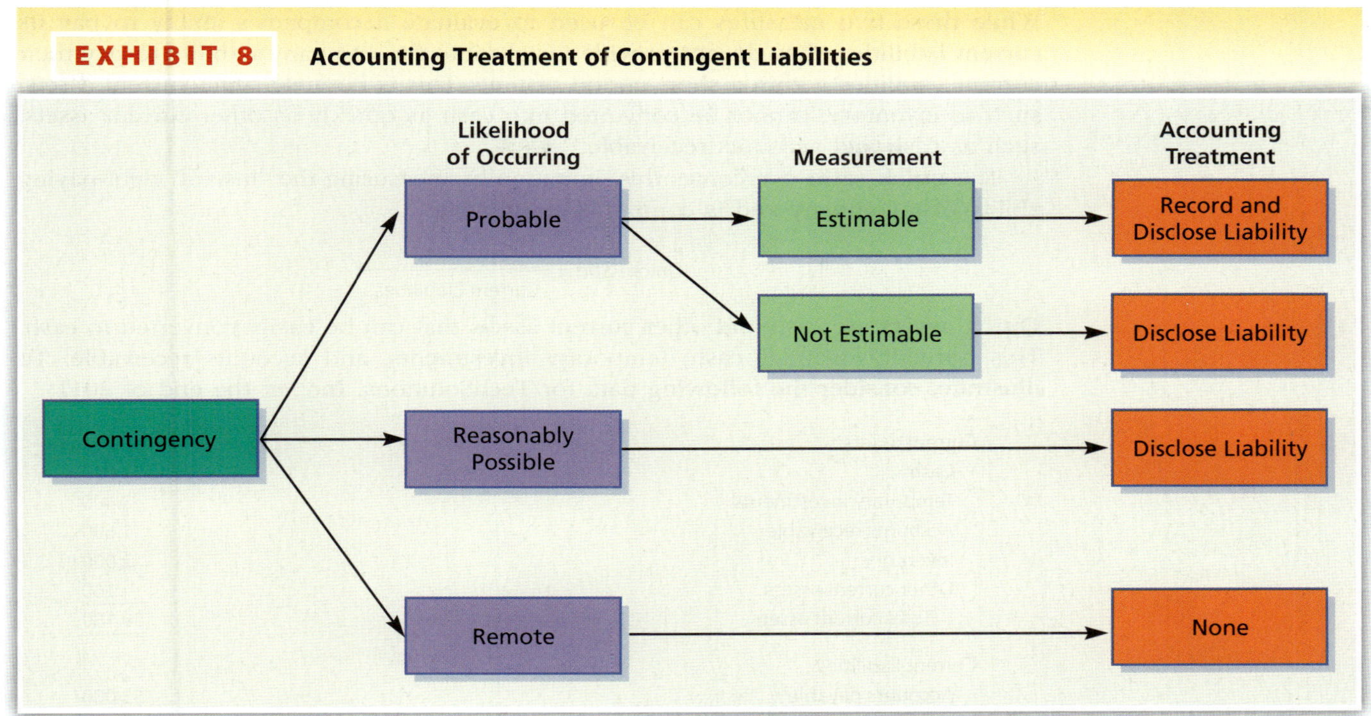

An example of a contingent liability disclosure from a recent annual report of Google Inc. is shown below.

> *We have also had copyright claims filed against us alleging that features of certain of our products and services, including Google Web Search, Google News, Google Video, Google Image Search, Google Book Search and YouTube, infringe their rights. Adverse results in these lawsuits may include awards of substantial monetary damages, costly royalty or licensing agreements or orders preventing us from offering certain functionalities, and may also result in a change in our business practices, which could result in a loss of revenue for us or otherwise harm our business. . . .*
>
> *Although the results of litigation and claims cannot be predicted with certainty, we believe that the final outcome of the matters discussed above will not have a material adverse effect on our business . . .*

Professional judgment is necessary in distinguishing between classes of contingent liabilities. This is especially the case when distinguishing between probable and reasonably possible contingent liabilities.

Financial Analysis and Interpretation: Quick Ratio

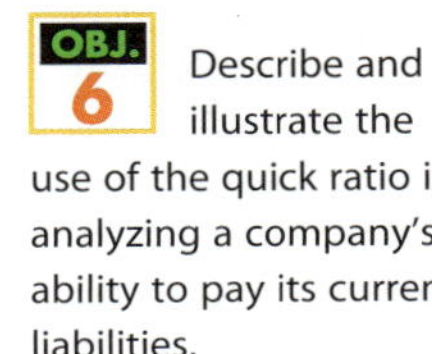

Describe and illustrate the use of the quick ratio in analyzing a company's ability to pay its current liabilities.

Current position analysis helps creditors evaluate a company's ability to pay its current liabilities. This analysis is based on the following three measures:

1. Working capital
2. Current ratio
3. Quick ratio

Working capital and the current ratio were discussed in Chapter 4, and are computed as follows:

$$\text{Working Capital} = \text{Current Assets} - \text{Current Liabilities}$$

$$\text{Current Ratio} = \frac{\text{Current Assets}}{\text{Current Liabilities}}$$

While these two measures can be used to evaluate a company's ability to pay its current liabilities, they do not provide insight into the company's ability to pay their current liabilities within a short period of time. This is because some current assets, such as inventory, cannot be converted into cash as quickly as other current assets, such as cash and accounts receivable.

The **quick ratio** overcomes this limitation by measuring the "instant" debt-paying ability of a company and is computed as follows:

$$\text{Quick Ratio} = \frac{\text{Quick Assets}}{\text{Current Liabilities}}$$

Quick assets are cash and other current assets that can be easily converted to cash. This normally includes cash, temporary investments, and accounts receivable. To illustrate, consider the following data for TechSolutions, Inc., at the end of 2011:

Current assets:	
Cash	$2,020
Temporary investments	3,400
Accounts receivable	1,600
Inventory	2,000
Other current assets	160
Total current assets	$9,180
Current liabilities:	
Accounts payable	$3,000
Other current liabilities	2,400
Total current liabilities	$5,400
Working capital (current assets – current liabilities)	$3,780
Current ratio (current assets/current liabilities)	1.7

The quick ratio for TechSolutions, Inc., is computed as follows:

$$\text{Quick Ratio} = \frac{\$2{,}020 + \$3{,}400 + \$1{,}600}{\$5{,}400} = 1.3$$

The quick ratio of 1.3 indicates that the company has more than enough quick assets to pay its current liabilities in a short period of time. A quick ratio below 1.0 would indicate that the company does not have enough quick assets to cover its current liabilities.

Like the current ratio, the quick ratio is particularly useful in making comparisons across companies. To illustrate, the following selected balance sheet data (excluding ratios) were taken from the 2008 financial statements of Panera Bread Company and Starbucks Corporation (in thousands):

	Panera Bread	Starbucks
Current assets:		
Cash and cash equivalents	$ 74,710	$ 599,800
Temporary investments	2,400	66,300
Accounts receivable	35,079	557,600
Inventory	11,959	664,900
Other current assets	14,265	147,200
Total current assets	$138,413	$2,035,800
Current liabilities:		
Accounts payable	$114,014	$1,192,100
Other current liabilities	—	388,900
Total current liabilities	$114,014	$1,581,000
Working capital (current assets – current liabilities)	$ 24,399	$ 454,800
Current ratio (current assets/current liabilities)	1.2	1.3
Quick ratio (quick assets/current liabilities)*	1.0	0.8

*The quick ratio for each company is computed as follows:
Panera Bread: ($74,710 + $2,400 + $35,079)/$114,014 = 1.0
Starbucks: ($599,800 + $66,300 + $557,600)/$1,581,000 = 0.8

Starbucks is larger than Panera Bread and has over 18 times the amount of working capital. Such size differences make working capital comparisons between companies difficult. In contrast, the current and quick ratios provide better comparisons across companies. In this example, Panera Bread has a slightly lower current ratio than Starbucks. However, Starbucks' 0.8 quick ratio reveals that it does not have enough quick assets to cover its current liabilities, while Panera Bread's quick ratio of 1.0 indicates that the company has just enough quick assets to meet its current liabilities.

Example Exercise 11-8 Quick Ratio

OBJ. 6

Sayer Company reported the following current assets and current liabilities for the years ended December 31, 2012 and 2011:

	2012	2011
Cash	$1,250	$1,000
Temporary investments	1,925	1,650
Accounts receivable	1,775	1,350
Inventory	1,900	1,700
Accounts payable	2,750	2,500

a. Compute the quick ratio for 2012 and 2011.

b. Interpret the company's quick ratio across the two time periods.

Follow My Example 11-8

a. December 31, 2012:
Quick Ratio = Quick Assets/Current Liabilities
Quick Ratio = ($1,250 + $1,925 + $1,775)/$2,750
Quick Ratio = 1.8

December 31, 2011:
Quick Ratio = Quick Assets/Current Liabilities
Quick Ratio = ($1,000 + $1,650 + $1,350)/$2,500
Quick Ratio = 1.6

b. The quick ratio of Sayer Company has improved from 1.6 in 2011 to 1.8 in 2012. This increase is the result of a large increase in the three types of quick assets (cash, temporary investments, and accounts receivable) compared to a relatively smaller increase in the current liability, accounts payable.

Practice Exercises: **PE 11-8A, PE 11-8B**

At a Glance 11

Describe and illustrate current liabilities related to accounts payable, current portion of long-term debt, and notes payable.

Key Points Current liabilities are obligations that are to be paid out of current assets and are due within a short time, usually within one year. The three primary types of current liabilities are accounts payable, notes payable, and current portion of long-term debt.

Learning Outcomes	Example Exercises	Practice Exercises
• Identify and define the most frequently reported current liabilities on the balance sheet.		
• Determine the interest from interest-bearing and discounted notes payable.	EE11-1	PE11-1A, 11-1B

Determine employer liabilities for payroll, including liabilities arising from employee earnings and deductions from earnings.

Key Points An employer's liability for payroll is determined from employee total earnings, including overtime pay. From this amount, employee deductions are subtracted to arrive at the net pay to be paid to each employee. Most employers also incur liabilities for payroll taxes, such as social security tax, Medicare tax, federal unemployment compensation tax, and state unemployment compensation tax.

Learning Outcomes	Example Exercises	Practice Exercises
• Compute the federal withholding tax from a wage bracket withholding table.	EE11-2	PE11-2A, 11-2B
• Compute employee net pay, including deductions for social security and Medicare tax.	EE11-3	PE11-3A, 11-3B

OBJ. 3

Describe payroll accounting systems that use a payroll register, employee earnings records, and a general journal.

Key Points The payroll register is used in assembling and summarizing the data needed for each payroll period. The payroll register is supported by a detailed payroll record for each employee, called an *employee's earnings record.*

Learning Outcomes	Example Exercises	Practice Exercises
• Journalize the employee's earnings, net pay, and payroll liabilities from the payroll register.	EE11-4	PE11-4A, 11-4B
• Journalize the payroll tax expense.	EE11-5	PE11-5A, 11-5B
• Describe elements of a payroll system, including the employee's earnings record, payroll checks, and internal controls.		

OBJ. 4 Journalize entries for employee fringe benefits, including vacation pay and pensions.

Key Points Fringe benefits are expenses of the period in which the employees earn the benefits. Fringe benefits are recorded by debiting an expense account and crediting a liability account.

Learning Outcomes	Example Exercises	Practice Exercises
• Journalize vacation pay.	EE11-6	PE11-6A, 11-6B
• Distinguish and journalize defined contribution and defined benefit pension plans.	EE11-6	PE11-6A, 11-6B

OBJ. 5 Describe the accounting treatment for contingent liabilities and journalize entries for product warranties.

Key Points A contingent liability is a potential obligation that results from a past transaction but depends on a future event. The accounting for contingent liabilities is summarized in Exhibit 8.

Learning Outcomes	Example Exercises	Practice Exercises
• Describe the accounting for contingent liabilities.		
• Journalize estimated warranty obligations and services granted under warranty.	EE11-7	PE11-7A, 11-7B

OBJ. 6 Describe and illustrate the use of the quick ratio in analyzing a company's ability to pay its current liabilities.

Key Points The quick ratio is a measure of a company's ability to pay current liabilities within a short period of time. The quick ratio is computed by dividing quick assets by current liabilities. Quick assets include cash, temporary investments, accounts receivable, and other current assets that can be easily converted into cash. A quick ratio exceeding 1.0 is usually desirable.

Learning Outcomes	Example Exercises	Practice Exercises
• Describe the quick ratio.		
• Compute and evaluate the quick ratio.	EE11-8	PE11-8A, 11-8B

Key Terms

contingent liabilities (507)
current position analysis (509)
defined benefit plan (505)
defined contribution plan (505)
employee's earnings record (500)
FICA tax (496)
fringe benefits (504)
gross pay (494)
net pay (494)
payroll (493)
payroll register (498)
pension (505)
quick assets (510)
quick ratio (510)

Illustrative Problem

Selected transactions of Taylor Company, completed during the fiscal year ended December 31, are as follows:

Mar. 1. Purchased merchandise on account from Kelvin Co., $20,000.

Apr. 10. Issued a 60-day, 12% note for $20,000 to Kelvin Co. on account.

June 9. Paid Kelvin Co. the amount owed on the note of April 10.

Aug. 1. Issued a $50,000, 90-day note to Harold Co. in exchange for a building. Harold Co. discounted the note at 15%.

Oct. 30. Paid Harold Co. the amount due on the note of August 1.

Dec. 27. Journalized the entry to record the biweekly payroll. A summary of the payroll record follows:

Salary distribution:		
Sales	$63,400	
Officers	36,600	
Office	10,000	$110,000
Deductions:		
Social security tax	$ 6,600	
Medicare tax	1,650	
Federal income tax withheld	17,600	
State income tax withheld	4,950	
Savings bond deductions	850	
Medical insurance deductions	1,120	32,770
Net amount		$ 77,230

27. Journalized the entry to record payroll taxes for social security and Medicare from the biweekly payroll.

30. Issued a check in payment of liabilities for employees' federal income tax of $17,600, social security tax of $13,200, and Medicare tax of $3,300.

31. Issued a check for $9,500 to the pension fund trustee to fully fund the pension cost for December.

31. Journalized an entry to record the employees' accrued vacation pay, $36,100.

31. Journalized an entry to record the estimated accrued product warranty liability, $37,240.

Instructions

Journalize the preceding transactions.

Solution

				Debit	Credit
Mar.	1	Merchandise Inventory		20,000	
		Accounts Payable—Kelvin Co.			20,000
Apr.	10	Accounts Payable—Kelvin Co.		20,000	
		Notes Payable			20,000
June	9	Notes Payable		20,000	
		Interest Expense		400	
		Cash			20,400
Aug.	1	Building		48,125	
		Interest Expense		1,875	
		Notes Payable			50,000
Oct.	30	Notes Payable		50,000	
		Cash			50,000
Dec.	27	Sales Salaries Expense		63,400	
		Officers Salaries Expense		36,600	
		Office Salaries Expense		10,000	
		Social Security Tax Payable			6,600
		Medicare Tax Payable			1,650
		Employees Federal Income Tax Payable			17,600
		Employees State Income Tax Payable			4,950
		Bond Deductions Payable			850
		Medical Insurance Payable			1,120
		Salaries Payable			77,230
	27	Payroll Tax Expense		8,250	
		Social Security Tax Payable			6,600
		Medicare Tax Payable			1,650
	30	Employees Federal Income Tax Payable		17,600	
		Social Security Tax Payable		13,200	
		Medicare Tax Payable		3,300	
		Cash			34,100
	31	Pension Expense		9,500	
		Cash			9,500
		Fund pension cost.			
	31	Vacation Pay Expense		36,100	
		Vacation Pay Payable			36,100
		Accrue vacation pay.			
	31	Product Warranty Expense		37,240	
		Product Warranty Payable			37,240
		Accrue warranty expense.			

Discussion Questions

1. Does a discounted note payable provide credit without interest? Discuss.
2. Employees are subject to taxes withheld from their paychecks.
   a. List the federal taxes withheld from most employee paychecks.
   b. Give the title of the accounts credited by amounts withheld.
3. Why are deductions from employees' earnings classified as liabilities for the employer?
4. For each of the following payroll-related taxes, indicate whether they generally apply to (a) employees only, (b) employers only, or (c) both employees and employers:
   1. Federal income tax
   2. Medicare tax
   3. Social security tax
   4. Federal unemployment compensation tax
   5. State unemployment compensation tax
5. What are the principal reasons for using a special payroll checking account?
6. Explain how a payroll system that is properly designed and operated tends to ensure that wages paid are based on hours actually worked.
7. To match revenues and expenses properly, should the expense for employee vacation pay be recorded in the period during which the vacation privilege is earned or during the period in which the vacation is taken? Discuss.
8. Identify several factors that influence the future pension obligation of an employer under a defined benefit pension plan.
9. When should the liability associated with a product warranty be recorded? Discuss.
10. General Motors Corporation reported $7.0 billion of product warranties in the Current Liabilities section of a recent balance sheet. How would costs of repairing a defective product be recorded?

Practice Exercises

Learning Objectives	Example Exercises	
OBJ. 1	EE 11-1 p. 493	**PE 11-1A Proceeds from notes payable**

On September 1, Rongo Co. issued a 45-day note with a face amount of $80,000 to Simone Co. for merchandise inventory.

a. Determine the proceeds of the note, assuming the note carries an interest rate of 8%.

b. Determine the proceeds of the note, assuming the note is discounted at 8%.

OBJ. 1 EE 11-1 p. 493

PE 11-1B Proceeds from notes payable

On February 1, Tectronic Co. issued a 60-day note with a face amount of $120,000 to Tokai Warehouse Co. for cash.

a. Determine the proceeds of the note, assuming the note carries an interest rate of 9%.

b. Determine the proceeds of the note, assuming the note is discounted at 9%.

OBJ. 2 EE 11-2 p. 495

PE 11-2A Federal income tax withholding

Bob Tappert's weekly gross earnings for the present week were $1,600. Tappert has one exemption. Using the wage bracket withholding table in Exhibit 3 with a $70 standard withholding allowance for each exemption, what is Tappert's federal income tax withholding?

OBJ. 2 EE 11-2 p. 495

PE 11-2B Federal income tax withholding

John Wolfe's weekly gross earnings for the present week were $2,200. Wolfe has two exemptions. Using the wage bracket withholding table in Exhibit 3 with a $70 standard withholding allowance for each exemption, what is Wolfe's federal income tax withholding?

OBJ. 2 EE 11-3 p. 497

PE 11-3A Employee net pay

Bob Tappert's weekly gross earnings for the week ending December 18 were $1,600, and his federal income tax withholding was $296.16. Assuming the social security rate is 6% and Medicare is 1.5% of all earnings, what is Tappert's net pay?

OBJ. 2 EE 11-3 p. 497

PE 11-3B Employee net pay

John Wolfe's weekly gross earnings for the week ending September 5 were $2,200, and his federal income tax withholding was $444.88. Assuming the social security rate is 6% and Medicare is 1.5% of all earnings, what is Wolfe's net pay?

OBJ. 3 EE 11-4 p. 499

PE 11-4A Journalize period payroll

The payroll register of Gregory Communications Co. indicates $4,080 of social security withheld and $1,020 of Medicare tax withheld on total salaries of $68,000 for the period. Federal withholding for the period totaled $13,464.

Provide the journal entry for the period's payroll.

OBJ. 3 EE 11-4 p. 499

PE 11-4B Journalize period payroll

The payroll register of Russert Construction Co. indicates $18,000 of social security withheld and $4,500 of Medicare tax withheld on total salaries of $300,000 for the period.

Learning Objectives *Example Exercises*

Retirement savings withheld from employee paychecks were $18,000 for the period. Federal withholding for the period totaled $59,400.

Provide the journal entry for the period's payroll.

OBJ. 3 EE 11-5 *p. 500*

PE 11-5A Journalize payroll tax

The payroll register of Gregory Communications Co. indicates $4,080 of social security withheld and $1,020 of Medicare tax withheld on total salaries of $68,000 for the period. Assume earnings subject to state and federal unemployment compensation taxes are $12,500, at the federal rate of 0.8% and the state rate of 5.4%.

Provide the journal entry to record the payroll tax expense for the period.

OBJ. 3 EE 11-5 *p. 500*

PE 11-5B Journalize payroll tax

The payroll register of Russert Construction Co. indicates $18,000 of social security withheld and $4,500 of Medicare tax withheld on total salaries of $300,000 for the period. Assume earnings subject to state and federal unemployment compensation taxes are $13,000, at the federal rate of 0.8% and the state rate of 5.4%.

Provide the journal entry to record the payroll tax expense for the period.

OBJ. 4 EE 11-6 *p. 506*

PE 11-6A Vacation pay and pension benefits

Lutes Company provides its employees with vacation benefits and a defined contribution pension plan. Employees earned vacation pay of $25,500 for the period. The pension plan requires a contribution to the plan administrator equal to 8% of employee salaries. Salaries were $340,000 during the period.

Provide the journal entry for the (a) vacation pay and (b) pension benefit.

OBJ. 4 EE 11-6 *p. 506*

PE 11-6B Vacation pay and pension benefits

Wang Equipment Company provides its employees vacation benefits and a defined benefit pension plan. Employees earned vacation pay of $42,000 for the period. The pension formula calculated a pension cost of $273,000. Only $210,000 was contributed to the pension plan administrator.

Provide the journal entry for the (a) vacation pay and (b) pension benefit.

OBJ. 5 EE 11-7 *p. 508*

PE 11-7A Estimated warranty liability

Zinn Co. sold $500,000 of equipment during May under a one-year warranty. The cost to repair defects under the warranty is estimated at 5% of the sales price. On October 10, a customer required a $100 part replacement, plus $65 of labor under the warranty.

Provide the journal entry for (a) the estimated warranty expense on May 31 and (b) the October 10 warranty work.

OBJ. 5 EE 11-7 *p. 508*

PE 11-7B Estimated warranty liability

Caldwell Industries sold $410,000 of consumer electronics during August under a nine-month warranty. The cost to repair defects under the warranty is estimated at 4% of the sales price. On October 15, a customer was given $110 cash under terms of the warranty.

Provide the journal entry for (a) the estimated warranty expense on August 31 and (b) the October 15 cash payment.

OBJ. 6 EE 11-8 *p. 511*

F·A·I

PE 11-8A Quick ratio

Grangel Company reported the following current assets and liabilities for December 31, 2012 and 2011:

Learning Objectives | Example Exercises

	Dec. 31, 2012	Dec. 31, 2011
Cash	$ 620	$ 560
Temporary investments	1,330	1,250
Accounts receivable	850	830
Inventory	1,000	1,000
Accounts payable	2,800	2,200

a. Compute the quick ratio for December 31, 2012 and 2011.

b. Interpret the company's quick ratio. Is the quick ratio improving or declining?

OBJ. 6 EE 11-8 p. 511

PE 11-8B Quick ratio

Tappert Company reported the following current assets and liabilities for December 31, 2012 and 2011:

	Dec. 31, 2012	Dec. 31, 2011
Cash	$ 990	$ 860
Temporary investments	1,910	1,500
Accounts receivable	1,600	1,280
Inventory	2,000	1,400
Accounts payable	3,000	2,800

a. Compute the quick ratio for December 31, 2012 and 2011.

b. Interpret the company's quick ratio. Is the quick ratio improving or declining?

Exercises

OBJ. 1

✔ Total current liabilities, $782,500

EX 11-1 Current liabilities

New Wave Co. sold 10,000 annual subscriptions of *Game Life* for $75 during December 2012. These new subscribers will receive monthly issues, beginning in January 2013. In addition, the business had taxable income of $550,000 during the first calendar quarter of 2013. The federal tax rate is 40%. A quarterly tax payment will be made on April 7, 2013.

Prepare the Current Liabilities section of the balance sheet for New Wave Co. on March 31, 2013.

OBJ. 1

EX 11-2 Entries for discounting notes payable

TKR Enterprises issues a 30-day note for $570,000 to Sweeney Industries for merchandise inventory. Sweeney Industries discounts the note at 8%.

a. Journalize TKR Enterprises' entries to record:
   1. the issuance of the note.
   2. the payment of the note at maturity.

b. Journalize Sweeney Industries' entries to record:
   1. the receipt of the note.
   2. the receipt of the payment of the note at maturity.

OBJ. 1

EX 11-3 Evaluate alternative notes

A borrower has two alternatives for a loan: (1) issue a $180,000, 45-day, 10% note or (2) issue a $180,000, 45-day note that the creditor discounts at 10%.

a. Calculate the amount of the interest expense for each option.

b. Determine the proceeds received by the borrower in each situation.

c. Which alternative is more favorable to the borrower? Explain.

OBJ. 1

EX 11-4 Entries for notes payable

A business issued a 45-day, 6% note for $80,000 to a creditor on account. Journalize the entries to record (a) the issuance of the note and (b) the payment of the note at maturity, including interest.

OBJ. 1

EX 11-5 Entries for discounted note payable

A business issued a 30-day note for $72,000 to a creditor on account. The note was discounted at 7%. Journalize the entries to record (a) the issuance of the note and (b) the payment of the note at maturity.

OBJ. 1

EX 11-6 Fixed asset purchases with note

On June 30, Beahm Management Company purchased land for $250,000 and a building for $350,000, paying $300,000 cash and issuing an 8% note for the balance, secured by a mortgage on the property. The terms of the note provide for 20 semiannual payments of $15,000 on the principal plus the interest accrued from the date of the preceding payment. Journalize the entry to record (a) the transaction on June 30, (b) the payment of the first installment on December 31, and (c) the payment of the second installment the following June 30.

OBJ. 1

EX 11-7 Current portion of long-term debt

Burger King Holdings, Inc., the operator and franchisor of Burger King restaurants, reported the following information about its long-term debt in the notes to a recent financial statement:

Long-term debt is comprised of the following:

	June 30	
	2009	**2008**
Notes payable	$823,100,000	$876,200,000
Less current portion	(67,500,000)	(7,400,000)
Long-term debt	$755,600,000	$868,800,000

a. How much of the notes payable was disclosed as a current liability on the June 30, 2009, balance sheet?

b. How much did the total current liabilities change between 2008 and 2009 as a result of the current portion of long-term debt?

c. If Burger King did not issue additional notes payable during 2010, what would be the total notes payable on June 30, 2010?

OBJ. 2

✔ b. Net pay, 2,725.75

EX 11-8 Calculate payroll

An employee earns $60 per hour and 1.5 times that rate for all hours in excess of 40 hours per week. Assume that the employee worked 55 hours during the week, Assume further that the social security tax rate was 6.0%, the Medicare tax rate was 1.5%, and federal income tax to be withheld was $743.

a. Determine the gross pay for the week.

b. Determine the net pay for the week.

OBJ. 2

✔ Administrator net pay, $1,776.92

EX 11-9 Calculate payroll

Donohue Professional Services has three employees—a consultant, a computer programmer, and an administrator. The following payroll information is available for each employee:

	Consultant	Computer Programmer	Administrator
Regular earnings rate	$2,800 per week	$30 per hour	$42 per hour
Overtime earnings rate	Not applicable	1.5 times hourly rate	2 times hourly rate
Number of withholding allowances	3	2	1

For the current pay period, the computer programmer worked 60 hours and the administrator worked 50 hours. The federal income tax withheld for all three employees, who are single, can be determined from the wage bracket withholding table in Exhibit 3 in the chapter. Assume further that the social security tax rate was 6.0%, the Medicare tax rate was 1.5%, and one withholding allowance is $70.

Determine the gross pay and the net pay for each of the three employees for the current pay period.

OBJ. 2, 3

✔ a. (3) Total earnings, $900,000

EX 11-10 Summary payroll data

In the following summary of data for a payroll period, some amounts have been intentionally omitted:

Earnings:	
1. At regular rate	?
2. At overtime rate	$135,000
3. Total earnings	?
Deductions:	
4. Social security tax	54,000
5. Medicare tax	13,500
6. Income tax withheld	225,000
7. Medical insurance	31,500
8. Union dues	?
9. Total deductions	335,250
10. Net amount paid	564,750
Accounts debited:	
11. Factory Wages	475,000
12. Sales Salaries	?
13. Office Salaries	200,000

a. Calculate the amounts omitted in lines (1), (3), (8), and (12).

b. Journalize the entry to record the payroll accrual.

c. Journalize the entry to record the payment of the payroll.

OBJ. 3

✔ a. $85,000

EX 11-11 Payroll tax entries

According to a summary of the payroll of Brooks Industries Co., $1,100,000 was subject to the 6.0% social security tax and the 1.5% Medicare tax. Also, $50,000 was subject to state and federal unemployment taxes.

a. Calculate the employer's payroll taxes, using the following rates: state unemployment, 4.2%; federal unemployment, 0.8%.

b. Journalize the entry to record the accrual of payroll taxes.

OBJ. 3

EX 11-12 Payroll entries

The payroll register for Robinson Company for the week ended November 18 indicated the following:

Salaries	$1,300,000
Social security tax withheld	61,100
Medicare tax withheld	19,500
Federal income tax withheld	260,000

In addition, state and federal unemployment taxes were calculated at the rate of 5.2% and 0.8%, respectively, on $240,000 of salaries.

a. Journalize the entry to record the payroll for the week of November 18.

b. Journalize the entry to record the payroll tax expense incurred for the week of November 18.

OBJ. 3

EX 11-13 Payroll entries

Faber Company had gross wages of $110,000 during the week ended June 17. The amount of wages subject to social security tax was $110,000, while the amount of wages subject to federal and state unemployment taxes was $15,000. Tax rates are as follows:

Social security	6.0%
Medicare	1.5%
State unemployment	5.4%
Federal unemployment	0.8%

The total amount withheld from employee wages for federal taxes was $22,000.

a. Journalize the entry to record the payroll for the week of June 17.

b. Journalize the entry to record the payroll tax expense incurred for the week of June 17.

OBJ. 3

EX 11-14 Payroll internal control procedures

Big Dave's Pizza is a pizza restaurant specializing in the sale of pizza by the slice. The store employs 10 full-time and 15 part-time workers. The store's weekly payroll averages $5,600 for all 25 workers.

Big Dave's Pizza uses a personal computer to assist in preparing paychecks. Each week, the store's accountant collects employee time cards and enters the hours worked into the payroll program. The payroll program calculates each employee's pay and prints a paycheck. The accountant uses a check-signing machine to sign the paychecks. Next, the restaurant's owner authorizes the transfer of funds from the restaurant's regular bank account to the payroll account.

For the week of June 11, the accountant accidentally recorded 200 hours worked instead of 40 hours for one of the full-time employees.

Does Big Dave's Pizza have internal controls in place to catch this error? If so, how will this error be detected?

OBJ. 3

EX 11-15 Internal control procedures

Matt's Bikes is a small manufacturer of specialty bicycles. The company employs 18 production workers and four administrative persons. The following procedures are used to process the company's weekly payroll:

a. Whenever an employee receives a pay raise, the supervisor must fill out a wage adjustment form, which is signed by the company president. This form is used to change the employee's wage rate in the payroll system.

b. All employees are required to record their hours worked by clocking in and out on a time clock. Employees must clock out for lunch break. Due to congestion around the time clock area at lunch time, management has not objected to having one employee clock in and out for an entire department.

c. Whenever a salaried employee is terminated, Personnel authorizes Payroll to remove the employee from the payroll system. However, this procedure is not required when an hourly worker is terminated. Hourly employees only receive a paycheck if their time cards show hours worked. The computer automatically drops an employee from the payroll system when that employee has six consecutive weeks with no hours worked.

d. Paychecks are signed by using a check-signing machine. This machine is located in the main office so that it can be easily accessed by anyone needing a check signed.

e. Matt's Bikes maintains a separate checking account for payroll checks. Each week, the total net pay for all employees is transferred from the company's regular bank account to the payroll account.

State whether each of the procedures is appropriate or inappropriate after considering the principles of internal control. If a procedure is inappropriate, describe the appropriate procedure.

OBJ. 4

EX 11-16 Accrued vacation pay

A business provides its employees with varying amounts of vacation per year, depending on the length of employment. The estimated amount of the current year's vacation pay is $61,200.

a. Journalize the adjusting entry required on January 31, the end of the first month of the current year, to record the accrued vacation pay.

b. How is the vacation pay reported on the company's balance sheet? When is this amount removed from the company's balance sheet?

OBJ. 4

EX 11-17 Pension plan entries

Wren Co. operates a chain of gift shops. The company maintains a defined contribution pension plan for its employees. The plan requires quarterly installments to be paid to the funding agent, Whims Funds, by the fifteenth of the month following the end of each quarter. Assume that the pension cost is $141,500 for the quarter ended March 31.

a. Journalize the entries to record the accrued pension liability on March 31 and the payment to the funding agent on April 15.

b. How does a defined contribution plan differ from a defined benefit plan?

OBJ. 4

EX 11-18 Defined benefit pension plan terms

In a recent year's financial statements, Procter & Gamble showed an unfunded pension liability of $3,706 million and a periodic pension cost of $341 million.

Explain the meaning of the $3,706 million unfunded pension liability and the $341 million periodic pension cost.

OBJ. 5

EX 11-19 Accrued product warranty

Parker Products Co. warrants its products for one year. The estimated product warranty is 3% of sales. Assume that sales were $442,000 for September. In October, a customer received warranty repairs requiring $110 of parts and $86 of labor.

a. Journalize the adjusting entry required at September 30, the end of the first month of the current fiscal year, to record the accrued product warranty.

b. Journalize the entry to record the warranty work provided in October.

OBJ. 5

EX 11-20 Accrued product warranty

General Motors Corporation disclosed estimated product warranty payable for comparative years as follows:

	(in millions)	
	12/31/08	12/31/07
Current estimated product warranty payable	$3,792	$4,655
Noncurrent estimated product warranty payable	4,699	4,960
Total	$8,491	$9,615

GM's sales were $177,594 million in 2007 and decreased to $147,732 million in 2008. Assume that the total paid on warranty claims during 2008 was $5,000 million.

a. Why are short- and long-term estimated warranty liabilities separately disclosed?

b. Provide the journal entry for the 2008 product warranty expense.

c. What two conditions must be met in order for a product warranty liability to be reported in the financial statements?

OBJ. 5

EX 11-21 Contingent liabilities

Several months ago, Reiltz Industries, Inc. experienced a hazardous materials spill at one of its plants. As a result, the Environmental Protection Agency (EPA) fined the company $570,000. The company is contesting the fine. In addition, an employee is seeking $560,000 in damages related to the spill. Lastly, a homeowner has sued the company for $364,000. The homeowner lives 35 miles from the plant, but believes that the incident has reduced the home's resale value by $364,000.

Reiltz's legal counsel believes that it is probable that the EPA fine will stand. In addition, counsel indicates that an out-of-court settlement of $238,000 has recently been reached with the employee. The final papers will be signed next week. Counsel believes that the homeowner's case is much weaker and will be decided in favor of Reiltz. Other litigation related to the spill is possible, but the damage amounts are uncertain.

a. Journalize the contingent liabilities associated with the hazardous materials spill. Use the account "Damage Awards and Fines" to recognize the expense for the period.

b. Prepare a note disclosure relating to this incident.

OBJ. 6
✔ a. 2012: 1.0
F·A·I

EX 11-22 Quick ratio

CCB Co. had the following current assets and liabilities for two comparative years:

	Dec. 31, 2012	Dec. 31, 2011
Current assets:		
Cash	$ 506,000	$ 524,000
Accounts receivable	354,000	364,000
Inventory	240,000	200,000
Total current assets	$1,100,000	$1,088,000
Current liabilities:		
Current portion of long-term debt	$ 160,000	$ 120,000
Accounts payable	265,000	220,000
Accrued and other current liabilities	435,000	400,000
Total current liabilities	$ 860,000	$ 740,000

a. Determine the quick ratio for December 31, 2012 and 2011.

b. Interpret the change in the quick ratio between the two balance sheet dates.

OBJ. 6
✔ a. Apple, 2.4

EX 11-23 Quick ratio

The current assets and current liabilities for Apple Computer, Inc., and Dell Inc. are shown as follows at the end of a recent fiscal period:

	Apple Computer, Inc. (in millions) Sept. 26, 2009	Dell Inc. (in millions) Jan. 29, 2010
Current assets:		
Cash and cash equivalents	$ 5,263	$10,635
Short-term investments	18,201	373
Accounts receivable	4,496	8,543
Inventories	455	1,051
Other current assets*	3,140	3,643
Total current assets	$31,555	$24,245
Current liabilities:		
Accounts payable	$ 9,453	$15,257
Accrued and other current liabilities	2,053	3,703
Total current liabilities	$11,506	$18,960

*These represent prepaid expense and other nonquick current assets.

a. Determine the quick ratio for both companies.

b. Interpret the quick ratio difference between the two companies.

Problems Series A

OBJ. 1, 5

PR 11-1A Liability transactions

The following items were selected from among the transactions completed by Isis Co. during the current year:

Feb 15. Purchased merchandise on account from Viper Co., $260,000, terms n/30.

Mar. 17. Issued a 45-day, 5% note for $260,000 to Viper Co., on account.

May 1. Paid Viper Co. the amount owed on the note of March 17.

June 15. Borrowed $300,000 from Ima Bank, issuing a 60-day, 9% note.

July 21. Purchased tools by issuing a $240,000, 60-day note to Charger Co., which discounted the note at the rate of 7%.

Aug. 14. Paid Ima Bank the interest due on the note of June 15 and renewed the loan by issuing a new 30-day, 10% note for $300,000. (Journalize both the debit and credit to the notes payable account.)

Sept. 13. Paid Ima Bank the amount due on the note of August 14.

19. Paid Charger Co. the amount due on the note of July 21.

Dec. 1. Purchased office equipment from Challenger Co. for $235,000, paying $35,000 and issuing a series of ten 7.5% notes for $20,000 each, coming due at 30-day intervals.

12. Settled a product liability lawsuit with a customer for $121,600, payable in January. Isis accrued the loss in a litigation claims payable account.

31. Paid the amount due Challenger Co. on the first note in the series issued on December 1.

Instructions

1. Journalize the transactions.
2. Journalize the adjusting entry for each of the following accrued expenses at the end of the current year: (a) product warranty cost, $26,240; (b) interest on the nine remaining notes owed to Challenger Co.

OBJ. 2, 3

✔ 1. (b) Dr. Payroll Tax Expense, $42,465

PR 11-2A Entries for payroll and payroll taxes

The following information about the payroll for the week ended December 30 was obtained from the records of Arnsparger Equipment Co.:

Salaries:		Deductions:	
Sales salaries	$270,000	Income tax withheld	$ 95,920
Warehouse salaries	142,000	Social security tax withheld	32,700
Office salaries	133,000	Medicare tax withheld	8,175
	$545,000	U.S. savings bonds	11,990
		Group insurance	9,810
			$158,595

Tax rates assumed:

Social security, 6%

Medicare, 1.5%

State unemployment (employer only), 4.5%

Federal unemployment (employer only), 0.8%

Instructions

1. Assuming that the payroll for the last week of the year is to be paid on December 31, journalize the following entries:
   a. December 30, to record the payroll.
   b. December 30, to record the employer's payroll taxes on the payroll to be paid on December 31. Of the total payroll for the last week of the year, $30,000 is subject to unemployment compensation taxes.

(continued)

2. Assuming that the payroll for the last week of the year is to be paid on January 5 of the following fiscal year, journalize the following entries:
   a. December 30, to record the payroll.
   b. January 5, to record the employer's payroll taxes on the payroll to be paid on January 5. Since it is a new fiscal year, all $545,000 in salaries is subject to unemployment compensation taxes.

OBJ. 2, 3

✔ 2. (e) $32,274

PR 11-3A Wage and tax statement data on employer FICA tax

Courtside Concepts Co. began business on January 2, 2011. Salaries were paid to employees on the last day of each month, and social security tax, Medicare tax, and federal income tax were withheld in the required amounts. An employee who is hired in the middle of the month receives half the monthly salary for that month. All required payroll tax reports were filed, and the correct amount of payroll taxes was remitted by the company for the calendar year. Early in 2012, before the Wage and Tax Statements (Form W-2) could be prepared for distribution to employees and for filing with the Social Security Administration, the employees' earnings records were inadvertently destroyed.

None of the employees resigned or were discharged during the year, and there were no changes in salary rates. The social security tax was withheld at the rate of 6.0% and Medicare tax at the rate of 1.5% on salary. Data on dates of employment, salary rates, and employees' income taxes withheld, which are summarized as follows, were obtained from personnel records and payroll records:

Employee	Date First Employed	Monthly Salary	Monthly Income Tax Withheld
Garnett	Jan. 2	$ 4,400	$ 706
Kidd	Oct. 1	7,200	1,442
J. O'Neal	Apr. 16	3,600	506
Bryant	Nov. 1	3,000	356
S. O'Neal	Jan. 16	12,800	3,012
Marbury	Dec. 1	5,000	856
Duncan	Feb. 1	11,200	2,564

Instructions

1. Calculate the amounts to be reported on each employee's Wage and Tax Statement (Form W-2) for 2011, arranging the data in the following form:

Employee	Gross Earnings	Federal Income Tax Withheld	Social Security Tax Withheld	Medicare Tax Withheld

2. Calculate the following employer payroll taxes for the year: (a) social security; (b) Medicare; (c) state unemployment compensation at 4.6% on the first $10,000 of each employee's earnings; (d) federal unemployment compensation at 0.8% on the first $10,000 of each employee's earnings; (e) total.

OBJ. 2, 3

✔ 3. Dr. Payroll Tax Expense, $1,002.93

PR 11-4A Payroll register

If the working papers correlating with this textbook are not used, omit Problem 11-4A. The payroll register for Knapp Co. for the week ended September 14, 2012, is presented in the working papers.

Instructions

1. Journalize the entry to record the payroll for the week.
2. Journalize the entry to record the issuance of the checks to employees.
3. Journalize the entry to record the employer's payroll taxes for the week. Assume the following tax rates: state unemployment, 3.6%; federal unemployment, 0.8%. Of the earnings, $2,000 is subject to unemployment taxes.
4. Journalize the entry to record a check issued on September 17 to Fourth National Bank in payment of employees' income taxes, $2,062.17, social security taxes, $1,463.88, and Medicare taxes, $365.98.

OBJ. 2, 3

✔ 1. Total net amount payable, $11,180.93

PR 11-5A Payroll register

The following data for Throwback Industries, Inc. relate to the payroll for the week ended December 7, 2012:

Employee	Hours Worked	Hourly Rate	Weekly Salary	Federal Income Tax	U.S. Savings Bonds
Blanda	48	$44.00		$526.24	$ 45
Dawson	42	38.00		351.31	50
Fouts	44	46.00		402.04	55
Griese	36	32.00		241.92	65
Namath	45	40.00		399.00	0
Marino			$2,200	528.00	44
Staubach	35	29.00		152.25	110
Starr			2,450	539.00	102
Unitas	41	38.00		315.40	0

Employees Marino and Starr are office staff, and all of the other employees are sales personnel. All sales personnel are paid 1½ times the regular rate for all hours in excess of 40 hours per week. The social security tax rate is 6.0%, and Medicare tax is 1.5% of each employee's annual earnings. The next payroll check to be used is No. 625.

Instructions

1. Prepare a payroll register for Throwback Industries, Inc. for the week ended December 7, 2012. Use the following columns for the payroll register: Name, Total Hours, Regular Earnings, Overtime Earnings, Total Earnings, Social Security Tax, Medicare Tax, Federal Income Tax, U.S. Savings Bonds, Total Deductions, Net Pay, Ck. No., Sales Salaries Expense, and Office Salaries Expense.
2. Journalize the entry to record the payroll sales for the week.

OBJ. 2, 3, 4

PR 11-6A Payroll accounts and year-end entries

The following accounts, with the balances indicated, appear in the ledger of Quinn Co. on December 1 of the current year:

Account	Balance	Account	Balance
311 Salaries Payable	—	318 Bond Deductions Payable	$ 4,200
312 Social Security Tax Payable	$10,830	319 Medical Insurance Payable	33,000
313 Medicare Tax Payable	2,850	511 Operations Salaries Expense	1,150,000
314 Employees Federal Income Tax Payable	17,575	611 Officers Salaries Expense	750,000
315 Employees State Income Tax Payable	17,100	612 Office Salaries Expense	190,000
316 State Unemployment Tax Payable	1,800	619 Payroll Tax Expense	163,680
317 Federal Unemployment Tax Payable	600		

The following transactions relating to payroll, payroll deductions, and payroll taxes occurred during December:

Dec. 2. Issued Check No. 210 for $4,200 to Ace Bank to purchase U.S. savings bonds for employees.

5. Issued Check No. 211 to Ace Bank for $31,255 in payment of $10,830 of social security tax, $2,850 of Medicare tax, and $17,575 of employees' federal income tax due.

16. Journalized the entry to record the biweekly payroll. A summary of the payroll record follows:

Salary distribution:		
Operations	$52,200	
Officers	34,100	
Office	8,650	$94,950
Deductions:		
Social security tax	$ 5,697	
Medicare tax	1,424	
Federal income tax withheld	17,566	
State income tax withheld	4,273	
Savings bond deductions	2,100	
Medical insurance deductions	5,500	36,560
Net amount		$58,390

Dec. 16. Issued Check No. 220 in payment of the net amount of the biweekly payroll.

16. Journalized the entry to record payroll taxes on employees' earnings of December 16: social security tax, $5,697; Medicare tax, $1,424; state unemployment tax, $450; federal unemployment tax, $150.

19. Issued Check No. 224 to Ace Bank for $31,048, in payment of $11,394 of social security tax, $2,848 of Medicare tax, and $17,566 of employees' federal income tax due.

19. Issued Check No. 229 to Blackwood Insurance Company for $33,000, in payment of the semiannual premium on the group medical insurance policy.

30. Journalized the entry to record the biweekly payroll. A summary of the payroll record follows:

Salary distribution:		
Operations	$51,400	
Officers	34,100	
Office	8,400	$93,900
Deductions:		
Social security tax	$ 5,634	
Medicare tax	1,409	
Federal income tax withheld	17,184	
State income tax withheld	4,226	
Savings bond deductions	2,100	30,553
Net amount		$63,347

30. Issued Check No. 341 in payment of the net amount of the biweekly payroll.

30. Journalized the entry to record payroll taxes on employees' earnings of December 30: social security tax, $5,634; Medicare tax, $1,409; state unemployment tax, $225; federal unemployment tax, $75.

30. Issued Check No. 243 for $25,599 to State Department of Revenue in payment of employees' state income tax due on December 31.

30. Issued Check No. 245 to Ace Bank for $4,200 to purchase U.S. savings bonds for employees.

31. Paid $50,000 to the employee pension plan. The annual pension cost is $65,000. (Record both the payment and unfunded pension liability.)

Instructions

1. Journalize the transactions.
2. Journalize the following adjusting entries on December 31:
   a. Salaries accrued: operations salaries, $5,140; officers salaries, $3,410; office salaries, $840. The payroll taxes are immaterial and are not accrued.
   b. Vacation pay, $17,500.

Problems Series B

OBJ. 1, 5

PR 11-1B Liability transactions

The following items were selected from among the transactions completed by Javelin, Inc. during the current year:

Mar. 1. Borrowed $80,000 from Nova Company, issuing a 30-day, 9% note for that amount.

15. Purchased equipment by issuing a $180,000, 180-day note to Shelby Manufacturing Co., which discounted the note at the rate of 7.5%.

31. Paid Nova Company the interest due on the note of March 1 and renewed the loan by issuing a new 60-day, 9% note for $80,000. (Record both the debit and credit to the notes payable account.)

May 30. Paid Nova Company the amount due on the note of March 31.

July 6. Purchased merchandise on account from Pacer Co., $56,000, terms, n/30.

Aug. 5. Issued a 45-day, 8% note for $56,000 to Pacer Co., on account.

Sept. 11. Paid Shelby Manufacturing Co. the amount due on the note of March 15.

19. Paid Pacer Co. the amount owed on the note of August 5.

Nov. 16. Purchased store equipment from Gremlin Co. for $190,000, paying $40,000 and issuing a series of fifteen 6% notes for $10,000 each, coming due at 30-day intervals.

Dec. 16. Paid the amount due Gremlin Co. on the first note in the series issued on November 16.

21. Settled a personal injury lawsuit with a customer for $55,250, to be paid in January. Javelin, Inc. accrued the loss in a litigation claims payable account.

Instructions

1. Journalize the transactions.
2. Journalize the adjusting entry for each of the following accrued expenses at the end of the current year:
   a. Product warranty cost, $13,520.
   b. Interest on the 14 remaining notes owed to Gremlin Co.

OBJ. 2, 3

✔ 1. (b) Dr. Payroll Tax Expense, $67,248

PR 11-2B Entries for payroll and payroll taxes

The following information about the payroll for the week ended December 30 was obtained from the records of Dart Co.:

Salaries:		Deductions:	
Sales salaries	$546,000	Income tax withheld	$172,480
Warehouse salaries	116,000	Social security tax withheld	52,800
Office salaries	218,000	Medicare tax withheld	13,200
	$880,000	U.S. savings bonds	26,400
		Group insurance	39,600
			$304,480

Tax rates assumed:

Social security, 6%

Medicare, 1.5%

State unemployment (employer only), 4.0%

Federal unemployment (employer only), 0.8%

Instructions

1. Assuming that the payroll for the last week of the year is to be paid on December 31, journalize the following entries:
   a. December 30, to record the payroll.
   b. December 30, to record the employer's payroll taxes on the payroll to be paid on December 31. Of the total payroll for the last week of the year, $26,000 is subject to unemployment compensation taxes.
2. Assuming that the payroll for the last week of the year is to be paid on January 4 of the following fiscal year, journalize the following entries:
   a. December 30, to record the payroll.
   b. January 4, to record the employer's payroll taxes on the payroll to be paid on January 4. Since it is a new fiscal year, all $880,000 in salaries is subject to unemployment compensation taxes.

OBJ. 2, 3

✔ 2. (e) $23,977.00

PR 11-3B Wage and tax statement data and employer FICA tax

Diamond Industries, Inc., began business on January 2, 2011. Salaries were paid to employees on the last day of each month, and social security tax, Medicare tax, and federal income tax were withheld in the required amounts. An employee who is hired in the middle of the month receives half the monthly salary for that month. All required payroll tax reports were filed, and the correct amount of payroll taxes was remitted by the company for the calendar year. Early in 2012, before the Wage and Tax Statements

(Form W-2) could be prepared for distribution to employees and for filing with the Social Security Administration, the employees' earnings records were inadvertently destroyed.

None of the employees resigned or were discharged during the year, and there were no changes in salary rates. The social security tax was withheld at the rate of 6.0% and Medicare tax at the rate of 1.5% on salary. Data on dates of employment, salary rates, and employees' income taxes withheld, which are summarized as follows, were obtained from personnel records and payroll records:

Employee	Date First Employed	Monthly Salary	Monthly Income Tax Withheld
Beltran	Jan. 1	$ 4,300	$ 681
Jeter	Apr. 16	11,000	2,508
Lee	Aug. 1	7,800	1,612
Rodriguez	Nov. 16	3,000	356
Santana	Mar. 1	6,120	1,145
Ramirez	May 16	3,840	566
Ordonez	Dec. 1	4,000	606

Instructions

1. Calculate the amounts to be reported on each employee's Wage and Tax Statement (Form W-2) for 2011, arranging the data in the following form:

Employee	Gross Earnings	Federal Income Tax Withheld	Social Security Tax Withheld	Medicare Tax Withheld

2. Calculate the following employer payroll taxes for the year: (a) social security; (b) Medicare; (c) state unemployment compensation at 4.4% on the first $9,000 of each employee's earnings; (d) federal unemployment compensation at 0.8% on the first $9,000 of each employee's earnings; (e) total.

OBJ. 2, 3

✔ 3. Dr. Payroll Tax Expense, $1,188.61

PR 11-4B Payroll register

If the working papers correlating with this textbook are not used, omit Problem 11-4B.

The payroll register for Ritchie Manufacturing Co. for the week ended September 14, 2012, is presented in the working papers.

Instructions

1. Journalize the entry to record the payroll for the week.
2. Journalize the entry to record the issuance of the checks to employees.
3. Journalize the entry to record the employer's payroll taxes for the week. Assume the following tax rates: state unemployment, 3.4%; federal unemployment, 0.8%. Of the earnings, $2,200 is subject to unemployment taxes.
4. Journalize the entry to record a check issued on September 17 to Second National Bank in payment of employees' income taxes, $2,464.97, social security taxes, $1,753.92, and Medicare taxes, $438.50.

OBJ. 2, 3

✔ 1. Total net amount payable, $9,583.80

PR 11-5B Payroll register

The following data for Gridiron Industries, Inc., relate to the payroll for the week ended December 7, 2012:

Employee	Hours Worked	Hourly Rate	Weekly Salary	Federal Income Tax	U.S. Savings Bonds
Aikman	50	$26.00		$328.90	$45
Csonka			$3,400	731.00	0
Dickerson	35	28.00		186.20	38
Elway	44	34.00		328.44	30
Harris	38	22.00		175.56	45
Motley			2,000	480.00	68
Nagurski	45	26.00		185.25	0
Sanders	45	27.00		282.15	45
Swann	42	25.00		215.00	0

Employees Csonka and Motley are office staff, and all of the other employees are sales personnel. All sales personnel are paid 1½ times the regular rate for all hours in excess of 40 hours per week. The social security tax rate is 6.0% of each employee's annual earnings, and Medicare tax is 1.5% of each employee's annual earnings. The next payroll check to be used is No. 328.

Instructions

1. Prepare a payroll register for Gridiron Industries, Inc., for the week ended December 7, 2012. Use the following columns for the payroll register: Name, Total Hours, Regular Earnings, Overtime Earnings, Total Earnings, Social Security Tax, Medicare Tax, Federal Income Tax, U.S. Savings Bonds, Total Deductions, Net Pay, Ck. No., Sales Salaries Expense, and Office Salaries Expense.
2. Journalize the entry to record the payroll sales for the week.

OBJ. 2, 3, 4

PR 11-6B Payroll accounts and year-end entries

The following accounts, with the balances indicated, appear in the ledger of Codigo Co. on December 1 of the current year:

111	Salaries Payable	—	118	Bond Deductions Payable	$ 2,520
112	Social Security Tax Payable	$ 6,847	119	Medical Insurance Payable	2,800
113	Medicare Tax Payable	1,763	411	Sales Salaries Expense	778,000
114	Employees Federal Income Tax Payable	10,873	511	Officers Salaries Expense	375,000
115	Employees State Income Tax Payable	9,874	611	Office Salaries Expense	140,000
116	State Unemployment Tax Payable	1,400	618	Payroll Tax Expense	104,610
117	Federal Unemployment Tax Payable	400			

The following transactions relating to payroll, payroll deductions, and payroll taxes occurred during December:

Dec. 1. Issued Check No. 615 to Canal Insurance Company for $2,800, in payment of the semiannual premium on the group medical insurance policy.

1. Issued Check No. 616 to Green Bank for $19,483, in payment for $6,847 of social security tax, $1,763 of Medicare tax, and $10,873 of employees' federal income tax due.

2. Issued Check No. 617 for $2,520 to Green Bank to purchase U.S. savings bonds for employees.

12. Journalized the entry to record the biweekly payroll. A summary of the payroll record follows:

Salary distribution:		
Sales	$35,300	
Officers	17,000	
Office	6,300	$58,600
Deductions:		
Social security tax	$ 3,516	
Medicare tax	879	
Federal income tax withheld	10,431	
State income tax withheld	2,637	
Savings bond deductions	1,260	
Medical insurance deductions	467	19,190
Net amount		$39,410

12. Issued Check No. 622 in payment of the net amount of the biweekly payroll.

12. Journalized the entry to record payroll taxes on employees' earnings of December 12: social security tax, $3,516; Medicare tax, $879; state unemployment tax, $350; federal unemployment tax, $100.

15. Issued Check No. 630 to Green Bank for $18,635, in payment for $7,032 of social security tax, $1,758 of Medicare tax, and $10,431 of employees' federal income tax due.

(Continued)

CP 11-3 Ethics and professional conduct in business

Gloria Seuss was discussing summer employment with Ella Kitt, president of Hotel California Construction Service:

Ella: I'm glad that you're thinking about joining us for the summer. We could certainly use the help.

Gloria: Sounds good. I enjoy outdoor work, and I could use the money to help with next year's school expenses.

Ella: I've got a plan that can help you out on that. As you know, I'll pay you $14 per hour, but in addition, I'd like to pay you with cash. Since you're only working for the summer, it really doesn't make sense for me to go to the trouble of formally putting you on our payroll system. In fact, I do some jobs for my clients on a strictly cash basis, so it would be easy to just pay you that way.

Gloria: Well, that's a bit unusual, but I guess money is money.

Ella: Yeah, not only that, it's tax-free!

Gloria: What do you mean?

Ella: Didn't you know? Any money that you receive in cash is not reported to the IRS on a W-2 form; therefore, the IRS doesn't know about the income—hence, it's the same as tax-free earnings.

a. Why does Ella Kitt want to conduct business transactions using cash (not check or credit card)?

b. How should Gloria respond to Ella's suggestion?

Internet Project

CP 11-4 Payroll forms

Group Project

Payroll accounting involves the use of government-supplied forms to account for payroll taxes. Three common forms are the W-2, Form 940, and Form 941. Form a team with three of your classmates and retrieve copies of each of these forms. They may be obtained from a local IRS office, a library, or downloaded from the Internet at **http://www.irs.gov** (go to forms and publications).

Briefly describe the purpose of each of the three forms.

Internet Project

CP 11-5 Contingent liabilities

Altria Group, Inc., has over 12 pages dedicated to describing contingent liabilities in the notes to recent financial statements. These pages include extensive descriptions of multiple contingent liabilities. Use the Internet to research Altria Group, Inc., at **http://www.altria.com**.

a. What are the major business units of Altria Group?

b. Based on your understanding of this company, why would Altria Group require 11 pages of contingency disclosure?

CHAPTER 12

ris Hondros/Newsmakers/Getty Images

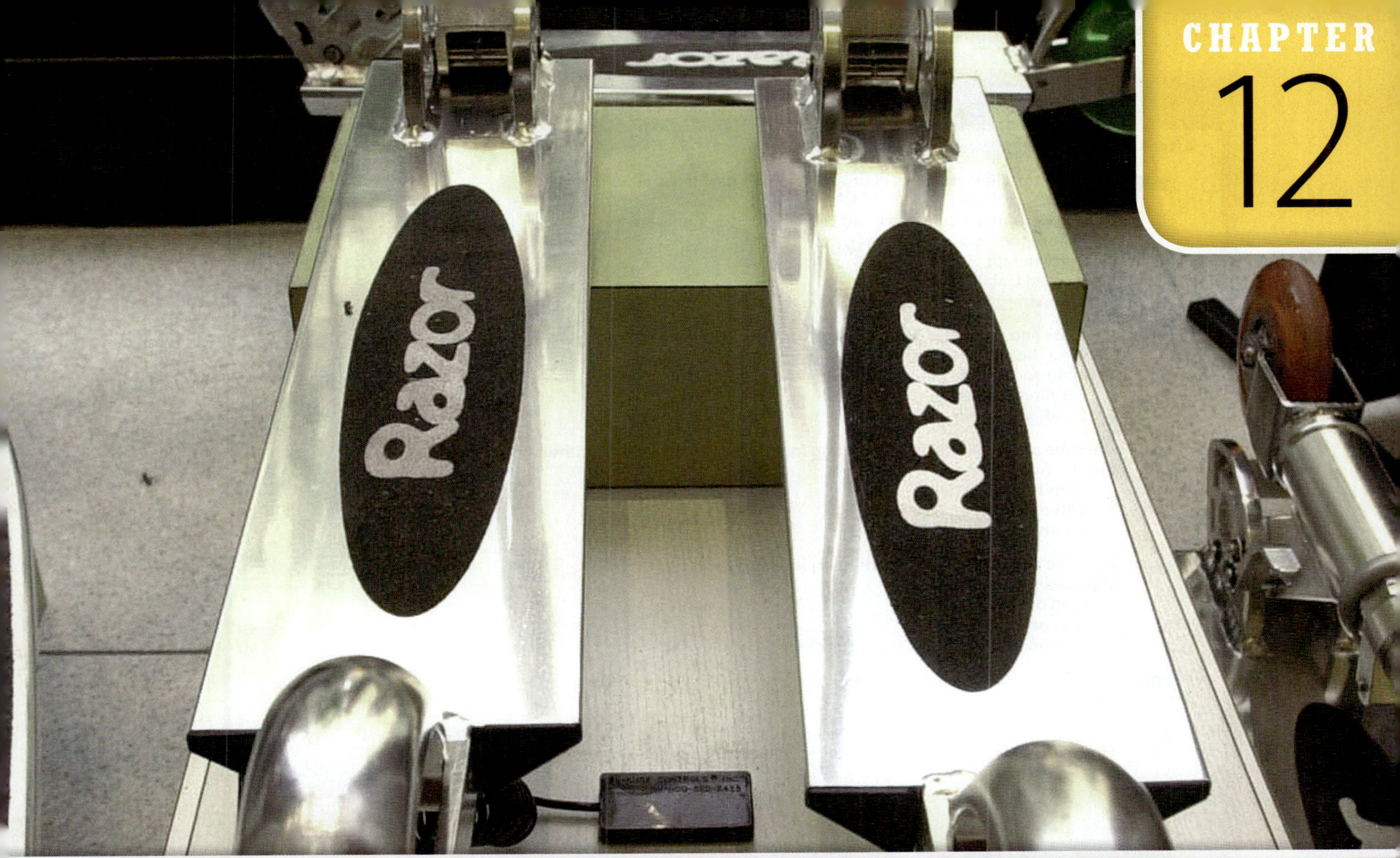

Accounting for Partnerships and Limited Liability Companies

Razor USA, LLC

Most good ideas begin as the solution to a problem, such as with Gino Tsai. Gino's legs got tired as he walked around his Taiwanese bicycle factory. As a result, Gino spent five years designing what is now known as the Razor scooter. Little did he know that his new, lightweight foldable scooter would be used by people of all ages, as well as being an Xtreme sport for youth. Today the Razor scooter, along with other Razor products, are sold worldwide by **Razor USA, LLC**. The letters "LLC" stand for limited liability company. Unlike sole proprietorships illustrated in prior chapters, a LLC is a business form that normally has multiple owners.

The entity form chosen by a business has an important impact on the owners' legal liability, taxation, and ability to raise money. The four major forms of business entities discussed in this text are the proprietorship, partnership, limited liability company, and corporation. Proprietorships have been discussed in prior chapters. Partnerships and limited liability companies will be discussed in this chapter, and corporations will be introduced in the next chapter.

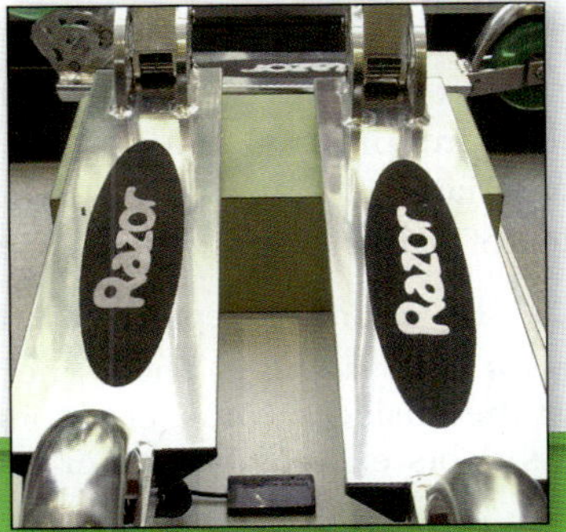

Learning Objectives

After studying this chapter, you should be able to:

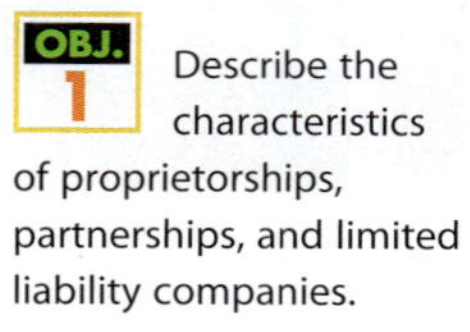

Describe the characteristics of proprietorships, partnerships, and limited liability companies.

Proprietorships, Partnerships, and Limited Liability Companies

The four most common legal forms for organizing and operating a business are as follows:

1. Proprietorship
2. Corporation
3. Partnership
4. Limited liability company

In this section, the characteristics of proprietorships, partnerships, and limited liability companies are described. The characteristics of corporations are described in Chapter 13.

Proprietorships

The **Internal Revenue Service (IRS)** estimates that proprietorships file 70% of business tax returns, but earn only 5% of all business revenues.

A proprietorship is a company owned by a single individual. The most common type of proprietorships are professional service providers, such as lawyers, architects, realtors, and physicians.

Characteristics of proprietorships include the following:

1. *Simple to form.* There are no legal restrictions or forms to file.
2. *No limitation on legal liability.* The owner is personally liable for any debts or legal claims against the business. Thus, creditors can take the personal assets of the owner if the business debts exceed the owner's investment in the company.

3. *Not taxable.* For federal income tax purposes, a proprietorship is not taxed. Instead, the proprietorship's income or loss is "passed through" to the owner's individual income tax return.[1]
4. *Limited life.* When the owner dies or retires, the proprietorship ceases to exist.
5. *Limited ability to raise capital (funds).* The ability to raise capital (funds) is limited to what the owner can provide from personal resources or through borrowing.

Partnerships

A **partnership** is an association of two or more persons who own and manage a business for profit.[2] Partnerships are less widely used than proprietorships.

Characteristics of a partnership include the following:

1. *Moderately complex to form.* A partnership requires only an agreement between two or more persons to organize. However, the **partnership agreement**, sometimes called the *articles of partnership*, includes matters such as amounts to be invested, limits on withdrawals, distributions of income and losses, and admission and withdrawal of partners. Thus, an attorney is often used in forming a partnership.
2. *No limitation on legal liability.* The partners are personally liable for any debts or legal claims against the partnership. Therefore, creditors can take the personal assets of the partners if the business debts exceed the partners' investment in the business.
3. *Not taxable.* For federal income tax purposes, a partnership is not taxed. Instead, the partnership's income or loss is "passed through" to the partners' individual income tax returns. However, partnerships must still report revenues, expenses, and income or loss annually to the Internal Revenue Service.
4. *Limited life.* When a partner dies or retires, the partnership ceases to exist. Likewise, the admission of a new partner dissolves the old partnership, and a new partnership must be formed if operations are to continue.
5. *Limited ability to raise capital (funds).* The ability to raise capital (funds) for the partnership is limited to what the partners can provide from personal resources or through borrowing.

Note:
A partnership is a nontaxable entity that has a limited life and unlimited liability.

In addition to those characteristics, some unique aspects of partnerships are:

1. *Co-ownership of partnership property.* The property invested in a partnership by a partner becomes the joint property of all the partners. When a partnership is dissolved, each partner's share of the partnership assets is the balance in their capital account.
2. *Mutual agency.* Each partner is an agent of the partnership and may act on behalf of the entire partnership. Thus, any liabilities created by one partner become liabilities of all the partners.
3. *Participation in income.* Net income and net loss are distributed among the partners according to their partnership agreement. If the partnership agreement does not provide for distribution of income and losses, then income and losses are divided equally among the partners.

Business Connection

BREAKING UP IS HARD TO DO

In August 7, 2008, Kristen Hall, founding member of the country music group Sugarland, filed a lawsuit against her other two band members. Kristen felt entitled to one-third of the profits the band earned on its double platinum album, *Enjoy the Ride*, after she left the band to pursue a song-writing career. However, the band did not have a formal partnership agreement and, thus, there was no way to easily determine what she should receive. Without a partnership agreement, the case will be decided using Georgia partnership law. This dispute and related lawsuit might have been avoided by a formal partnership agreement.

1 The proprietor's statement of income is included on Schedule C of the individual 1040 tax return.

2 The definition of a partnership is included in the Uniform Partnership Act, which has been adopted by most states.

A partnership may be organized as a limited partnership. A *limited partnership* is a unique legal form that provides partners who are not involved in the operations of the partnership with limited liability. In such a form, at least one *general partner* operates the partnership and has unlimited liability. The remaining partners are considered *limited partners*.

Limited Liability Companies

A **limited liability company (LLC)** is a form of legal entity that provides limited liability to its owners, but is treated as a partnership for tax purposes. The LLC is a relatively new form of business entity that has become widely used for small companies. LLCs, which may be owned by one or more persons or entities, are designed to overcome some of the disadvantages of a partnership.

Many companies have joint ventures organized as LLCs. For example, Walt Disney Company has a 42% interest in A&E Television Networks, LLC.

Characteristics of an LLC include the following:

1. *Moderately complex to form.* An LLC requires an agreement among the owners who are called members. The *operating agreement*, sometimes called *articles of organization*, includes matters such as amounts to be invested, limits on withdrawals, distributions of income and losses, and admission and withdrawal of members. An attorney is normally used in forming an LCC.
2. *Limited legal liability.* The members have *limited liability* even if they are active in the company. Thus, the members' personal assets are legally protected against creditor claims made against the LLC. That is, only the members' investments in the company are subject to claims of creditors.
3. *Not taxable.* An LLC may elect to be treated as a partnership for tax purposes. In this way, income passes through the LLC and is taxed on the individual members' tax returns.[3]
4. *Unlimited life.* Most LLC operating agreements specify continuity of life for the LLC, even when a member withdraws or new members join the LLC.
5. *Moderate ability to raise capital (funds).* Because of their limited liability, LLCs are attractive to many investors, thus allowing for greater access to capital (funds) than is normally the case in a partnership.

An LLC may elect to operate as a *member-managed* or a *manager-managed* company. In a member-managed LLC, individual members may legally bind the LLC, like partners bind a partnership. In a manager-managed LLC, only authorized members may legally bind the LLC. Thus, in a manager-managed LLC, members may share in the income of the LLC without concern for managing the company. As a result, manager-managed LLCs are attractive to many investors.

Comparing Proprietorships, Partnerships, and Limited Liability Companies

Exhibit 1 summarizes the characteristics of proprietorships, partnerships, and limited liability companies.

EXHIBIT 1 **Characteristics of Proprietorships, Partnerships, and Limited Liability Companies**

Organizational Form	Complexity of Formation	Legal Liability	Taxation	Limitation on Life of Entity	Access to Capital
Proprietorship	Simple	No limitation	Nontaxable (pass-through) entity	Limited	Limited
Partnership	Moderate	No limitation	Nontaxable (pass-through) entity	Limited	Limited
Limited Liability Company	Moderate	Limited liability	Nontaxable (pass-through) entity by election	Unlimited	Moderate

3 An LLC may also be taxed as a separate entity. However, doing so would remove these tax benefits, making this a less common election.

Business Connection

ORGANIZATIONAL FORMS IN THE ACCOUNTING INDUSTRY

The four major accounting firms, KPMG LLP, Ernst & Young, PricewaterhouseCoopers, and Deloitte & Touche, all began as partnerships. This form was legally required due to the theory of mutual agency. That is, the partnership form was thought to create public trust by requiring all partners to be jointly liable and responsible for each other's judgments. In addition, investment in the partnerships was limited to practicing accountants. This prevented any pressures from outside investors affecting professional decisions.

As these firms grew and the risk increased, all of these firms were allowed to change, by law, to limited liability partnerships (LLPs). Thus, while remaining a partnership, the liability of the partners was limited to their investment in the firm. The LLP form is very similar to an LLC, except that investment is restricted to professionals.

Forming and Dividing Income of a Partnership

OBJ. 2 Describe and illustrate the accounting for forming a partnership and for dividing the net income and net loss of a partnership.

Most of the day-to-day accounting for a partnership or an LLC is similar to that illustrated in earlier chapters. However, the formation, division of net income or net loss, dissolution, and liquidation of partnerships and LLCs give rise to unique transactions.

In the remainder of this chapter, the unique transactions for partnerships and LLCs are described and illustrated. The accounting for an LLC is the same as a partnership, except that the terms "member" and "members' equity" are used rather than "partner" or "owners' capital." For this reason, the journal entries for an LLC are shown alongside the partnership entries.

Forming a Partnership

In forming a partnership, the investments of each partner are recorded in separate entries. The assets contributed by a partner are debited to the partnership asset accounts. If any liabilities are assumed by the partnership, the partnership liability accounts are credited. The partner's capital account is credited for the net amount.

To illustrate, assume that Joseph Stevens and Earl Foster, owners of competing hardware stores, agree to combine their businesses in a partnership. Stevens agrees to contribute the following:

Cash	$ 7,200	Office equipment	$2,500
Accounts receivable	16,300	Allowance for doubtful accounts	1,500
Merchandise inventory	28,700	Accounts payable	2,600
Store equipment	5,400		

The entry to record the assets and liabilities contributed by Stevens is as follows:

LLC

Cash	*7,200*	
Accounts Receivable	*16,300*	
Merchandise Inventory	*28,700*	
Store Equipment	*5,400*	
Office Equipment	*2,500*	
Allowance for Doubtful Accounts		*1,500*
Accounts Payable		*2,600*
Joseph Stevens, Member Equity		*56,000*

Apr.	1	Cash		7,200	
		Accounts Receivable		16,300	
		Merchandise Inventory		28,700	
		Store Equipment		5,400	
		Office Equipment		2,500	
		Allowance for Doubtful Accounts			1,500
		Accounts Payable			2,600
		Joseph Stevens, Capital			56,000

In the preceding entry, the noncash assets are recorded at values agreed upon by the partners. These values are normally based on current market values. As a result, the book value of the assets contributed by the partners normally differs from that recorded by the new partnership.

To illustrate, the store equipment contributed by Stevens may have had a book value of $3,500 in Stevens' ledger (cost of $10,000 less accumulated depreciation of $6,500). However, the store equipment is recorded at its current market value of $5,400 in the preceding entry. The contributions of Foster would be recorded in an entry similar to the entry for Stevens.

Example Exercise 12-1 Journalize Partner's Original Investment

OBJ. 2

Reese Howell contributed equipment, inventory, and $34,000 cash to a partnership. The equipment had a book value of $23,000 and a market value of $29,000. The inventory had a book value of $60,000, but only had a market value of $15,000, due to obsolescence. The partnership also assumed a $12,000 note payable owed by Howell that was used originally to purchase the equipment.

Provide the journal entry for Howell's contribution to the partnership.

Follow My Example 12-1

Cash	34,000	
Inventory	15,000	
Equipment	29,000	
Notes Payable		12,000
Reese Howell, Capital		66,000

Practice Exercises: PE 12-1A, PE 12-1B

Dividing Income

Income or losses of the partnership are divided *equally* if no partnership agreement exists or the partnership agreement does not specify how the division is to occur. Most partnership agreements, however, do specify how income or losses are to be divided.

Common methods of dividing partnership income are based on:

1. Services of the partners
2. Services and investments of the partners

Dividing Income—Services of Partners One method of dividing partnership income is based on the services provided by each partner to the partnership. These services are often recognized by partner salary allowances. Such allowances reflect differences in partners' abilities and time devoted to the partnership. Since partners are not employees, such allowances are recorded as divisions of net income and are credited to the partners' capital accounts.

To illustrate, assume that the partnership agreement of Jennifer Stone and Crystal Mills provides for the following:

	Monthly Salary Allowance
Jennifer Stone	$5,000
Crystal Mills	4,000
Remaining net income:	Divided Equally

The division of income may be reported at the bottom of the partnership income statement. Using this format, the division of $150,000 of net income would be reported on the bottom of the partnership income statement as follows:

Net income $150,000

Division of net income:

	J. Stone	C. Mills	Total
Annual salary allowance	$ 60,000	$ 48,000	$ 108,000
Remaining income	21,000	21,000	42,000
Net income	$81,000	$69,000	$150,000

The division of net income may also be reported as a separate statement accompanying the balance sheet and the income statement or in a statement of partnership capital.

The net income division is recorded as a closing entry, even if the partners do not withdraw the amounts of their salary allowances. The entry for closing Income Summary and dividing net income is as follows:

LLC

Income Summary	*150,000*	
Jennifer Stone, Member Equity		*81,000*
Crystal Mills, Member Equity		*69,000*

Dec.	31	Income Summary		150,000	
		Jennifer Stone, Capital			81,000
		Crystal Mills, Capital			69,000

If Stone and Mills withdraw their salary allowances monthly, the withdrawals are debited to their drawing accounts. At the end of the year, the drawing account debit balances of $60,000 and $48,000 are then closed to the partners' capital accounts.

Dividing Income—Services of Partners and Investments A partnership agreement may divide income not only based upon services, but also based upon the amount invested by each partner. In doing so, the partnership may pay interest on the capital balance of each partner. In this way, partners with more invested in the partnership are rewarded by receiving more of the partnership income. One such method of dividing partnership income would be as follows:

1. Partner salary allowances
2. Interest on capital investments
3. Any remaining income equally

To illustrate, assume that the partnership agreement for Stone and Mills provides for the following:

1.

	Monthly Salary Allowance
Jennifer Stone	$5,000
Crystal Mills	4,000

2. Interest of 12% on each partner's capital balance as of January 1.

Capital, Jennifer Stone, January 1	$160,000
Capital, Crystal Mills, January 1	120,000

3. Remaining income: Divided Equally

The $150,000 net income for the year is divided as follows:

Net income.......... **$150,000**

Division of net income:

	J. Stone	C. Mills	Total
Annual salary allowance	$ 60,000	$ 48,000	$ 108,000
Interest allowance	19,200[1]	14,400[2]	33,600
Remaining income	4,200	4,200	8,400
Net income	**$83,400**	**$66,600**	**$150,000**

[1]12% × $160,000
[2]12% × $120,000

The entry for closing Income Summary and dividing net income is as follows:

LLC

Income Summary	*150,000*	
Jennifer Stone, Member Equity		*83,400*
Crystal Mills, Member Equity		*66,600*

Dec.	31	Income Summary		150,000	
		Jennifer Stone, Capital			83,400
		Crystal Mills, Capital			66,600

Integrity, Objectivity, and Ethics in Business

TYRANNY OF THE MAJORITY

Some partnerships involve the contribution of money by one partner and the contribution of effort and expertise by another. This can create a conflict between the two partners, since one works and the other doesn't. Without a properly developed partnership agreement, the working partner could take income in the form of a salary allowance, leaving little for the investor partner. Thus, partnership agreements often require all partners to agree on salary allowances provided to working partners.

Dividing Income—Allowances Exceed Net Income In the preceding example, the net income is $150,000. The total of the salary ($108,000) and interest ($33,600) allowances is $141,600. Thus, the net income exceeds the salary and interest allowances. In some cases, however, the net income may be less than the total of the allowances. In this case, the remaining net income to divide is a *negative* amount. This negative amount is divided among the partners as though it were a net loss.

To illustrate, assume the same salary and interest allowances as in the preceding example, but that the net income is $100,000. In this case, the total of the allowances of $141,600 exceeds the net income by $41,600 ($100,000 − $141,600). This amount is divided equally between Stone and Mills. Thus, $20,800 ($41,600/2) is deducted from each partner's share of the allowances. The final division of net income between Stone and Mills is shown below.

Net income.......... $100,000

Division of net income:

	J. Stone	C. Mills	Total
Annual salary allowance	$ 60,000	$ 48,000	$ 108,000
Interest allowance	19,200	14,400	33,600
Total	$ 79,200	$ 62,400	$ 141,600
Deduct excess of allowances over income	20,800	20,800	41,600
Net income	$58,400	$41,600	$100,000

The entry for closing Income Summary and dividing net income is as follows:[4]

LLC

Income Summary	*100,000*	
Jennifer Stone, Member Equity		*58,400*
Crystal Mills, Member Equity		*41,600*

Dec.	31	Income Summary		100,000	
		Jennifer Stone, Capital			58,400
		Crystal Mills, Capital			41,600

Example Exercise 12-2 Dividing Partnership Net Income

Steve Prince and Chelsy Bernard formed a partnership, dividing income as follows:

1. Annual salary allowance to Prince of $42,000.
2. Interest of 9% on each partner's capital balance on January 1.
3. Any remaining net income divided equally.

Prince and Bernard had $20,000 and $150,000 in their January 1 capital balances, respectively. Net income for the year was $240,000.

How much net income should be distributed to Prince?

(Continued)

4 In the event of a net loss, the amount deducted from the total allowances would be the "excess of allowances over loss" or the sum of the net loss and the allowances, divided according to the sharing ratio.

Follow My Example 12-2

	Steve Prince	Chelsy Bernard	Total
Annual salary	$ 42,000	$ 0	$ 42,000
Interest	1,800[1]	13,500[2]	15,300
Remaining income	91,350[3]	91,350	182,700
Total distributed to Prince	$135,150	$104,850	$240,000

[1] $20,000 × 9%
[2] $150,000 × 9%
[3] ($240,000 – $42,000 – $15,300) × 50%

Practice Exercises: **PE 12-2A, PE 12-2B**

Partner Admission and Withdrawal

Describe and illustrate the accounting for partner admission and withdrawal.

Many partnerships provide for admitting new partners and for partner withdrawals by amending the existing partnership agreement. In this way, the company may continue operating without having to form a new partnership and prepare a new partnership agreement.

Admitting a Partner

As shown in Exhibit 2, a person may be admitted to a partnership by either of the following:

1. Purchasing an interest from one or more of the existing partners
2. Contributing assets to the partnership

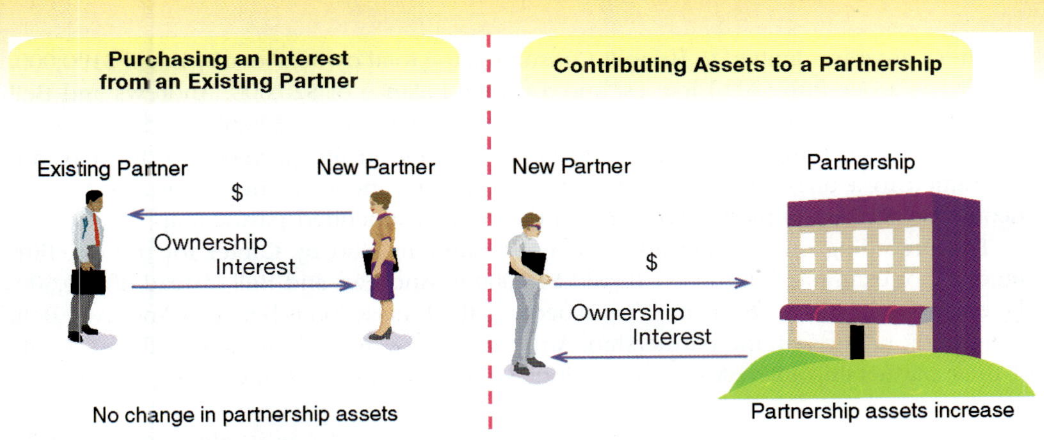

EXHIBIT 2
Two Methods for Admitting a Partner

When a new partner is admitted by *purchasing an interest* from one or more of the existing partners, the total assets and the total owners' equity of the partnership are not affected. The capital (equity) of the new partner is recorded by transferring capital (equity) from the existing partners.

When a new partner is admitted by *contributing assets* to the partnership, the total assets and the total owners' equity of the partnership are increased. The capital (equity) of the new partner is recorded as the amount of assets contributed to the partnership by the new partner.

Purchasing an Interest from Existing Partners When a new partner is admitted by purchasing an interest from one or more of the existing partners, the transaction is between the new and existing partners acting as individuals. The admission of the new partner is recorded by transferring owners' equity amounts from the capital accounts of the selling partners to the capital account of the new partner.

To illustrate, assume that on June 1 Tom Andrews and Nathan Bell each sell one-fifth of their partnership equity of Bring It Consulting to Joe Canter for $10,000 in cash. On June 1, the partnership has net assets of $100,000 and both existing partners have capital balances of $50,000 each. This transaction is between Andrews, Bell, and Canter. The only entry required by Bring It Consulting is to record the transfer of capital (equity) from Andrews and Bell to Canter, as shown below.

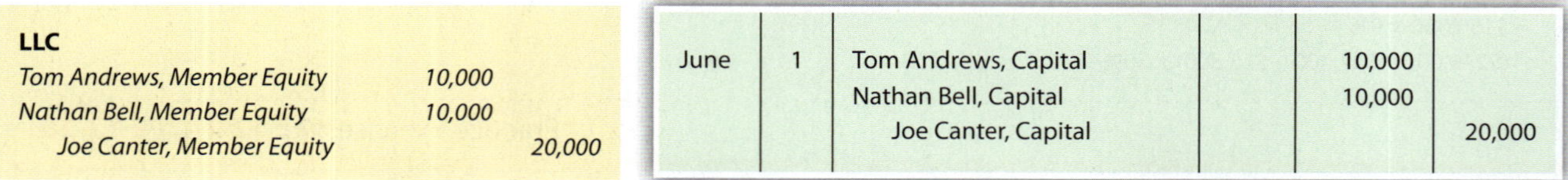

LLC		
Tom Andrews, Member Equity	*10,000*	
Nathan Bell, Member Equity	*10,000*	
Joe Canter, Member Equity		*20,000*

June	1	Tom Andrews, Capital		10,000	
		Nathan Bell, Capital		10,000	
		Joe Canter, Capital			20,000

The effect of the transaction on the partnership accounts is shown in the following diagram:

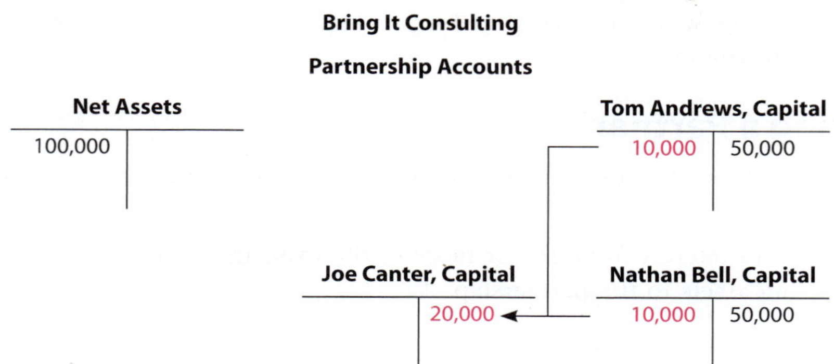

After Canter is admitted to Bring It Consulting, the total owners' equity is still $100,000. Canter has a one-fifth (20%) interest and a capital balance of $20,000. Andrews and Bell each own two-fifths (40%) interest and have capital balances of $40,000 each.

Even though Canter has a one-fifth (20%) interest in the partnership, he may not be entitled to a one-fifth share of the partnership net income. The division of the net income or net loss is made according to the new or amended partnership agreement.

The preceding entry is not affected by the amount paid by Canter for the one-fifth interest. For example, if Canter had paid $15,000 to Andrews and Bell instead of $10,000, the entry would still be the same. This is because the transaction is between Andrews, Bell, and Canter, rather than the partnership. Any gain or loss by Andrews and Bell on the sale of their partnership interest is theirs as individuals and does not affect the partnership.

Contributing Assets to a Partnership When a new partner is admitted by contributing assets to the partnership, the total assets and the total owners' equity of the partnership are increased. This is because the transaction is between the new partner and the partnership.

To illustrate, assume that instead of purchasing a one-fifth ownership in Bring It Consulting directly from Tom Andrews and Nathan Bell, Joe Canter contributes $20,000 cash to Bring It Consulting for ownership equity of $20,000. The entry to record this transaction is as follows:

LLC		
Cash	*20,000*	
Joe Canter, Member Equity		*20,000*

June	1	Cash		20,000	
		Joe Canter, Capital			20,000

The effect of the transaction on the partnership accounts is shown in the following diagram:

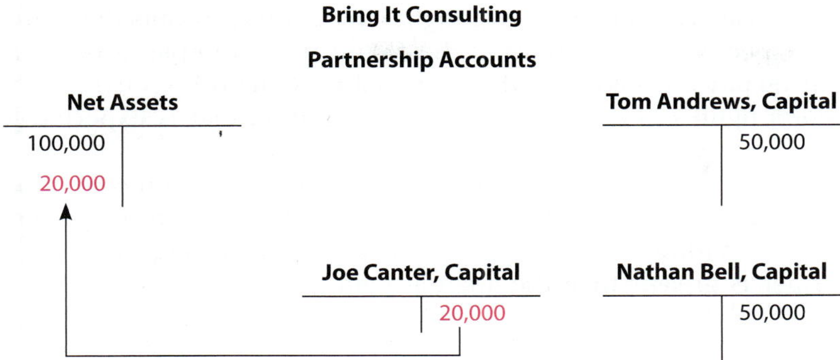

After the admission of Canter, the net assets and total owners' equity of Bring It Consulting increase to $120,000, of which Joe Canter has a $20,000 interest. In contrast, in the prior example, the net assets and total owners' equity of Bring It Consulting did not change from $100,000.

Revaluation of Assets Before a new partner is admitted, the balances of a partnership's asset accounts should be stated at current values. If necessary, the accounts should be adjusted. Any net adjustment (increase or decrease) in asset values is divided among the capital accounts of the existing partners similar to the division of income.

To illustrate, assume that in the preceding example the balance of the merchandise inventory account is $14,000 and the current replacement value is $17,000. If Andrews and Bell share net income equally, the revaluation is recorded as follows:

LLC		
Merchandise Inventory	*3,000*	
Tom Andrews, Member Equity		*1,500*
Nathan Bell, Member Equity		*1,500*

June	1	Merchandise Inventory		3,000	
		Tom Andrews, Capital			1,500
		Nathan Bell, Capital			1,500

Failure to adjust the partnership accounts for current values before admission of a new partner may result in the new partner sharing in asset gains or losses that arose in prior periods.

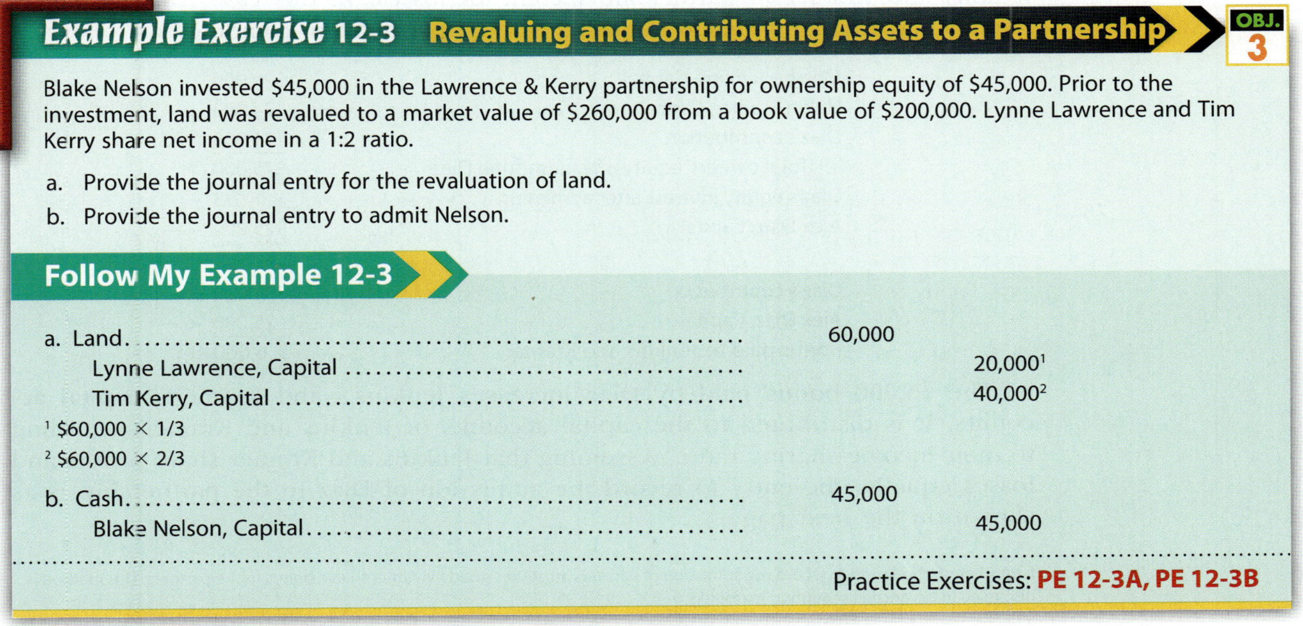

Example Exercise 12-3 Revaluing and Contributing Assets to a Partnership OBJ. 3

Blake Nelson invested $45,000 in the Lawrence & Kerry partnership for ownership equity of $45,000. Prior to the investment, land was revalued to a market value of $260,000 from a book value of $200,000. Lynne Lawrence and Tim Kerry share net income in a 1:2 ratio.

a. Provide the journal entry for the revaluation of land.
b. Provide the journal entry to admit Nelson.

Follow My Example 12-3

a. Land	60,000	
Lynne Lawrence, Capital		20,000[1]
Tim Kerry, Capital		40,000[2]

[1] $60,000 × 1/3
[2] $60,000 × 2/3

b. Cash	45,000	
Blake Nelson, Capital		45,000

Practice Exercises: **PE 12-3A, PE 12-3B**

Partner Bonuses A new partner may pay existing partners a bonus to join a partnership. In other cases, existing partners may pay a new partner a bonus to join the partnership.

Bonuses are usually paid because of higher than normal profits the new or existing partners are expected to contribute in the future. For example, a new partner may bring special qualities or skills to the partnership. Celebrities such as actors, musicians, or sports figures often provide name recognition that is expected to increase a partnership's profits.

Partner bonuses are illustrated in Exhibit 3. Existing partners receive a bonus when the ownership interest received by the new partner is less than the amount paid. In contrast, the new partner receives a bonus when the ownership interest received by the new partner is greater than the amount paid.

EXHIBIT 3

Partner Bonuses

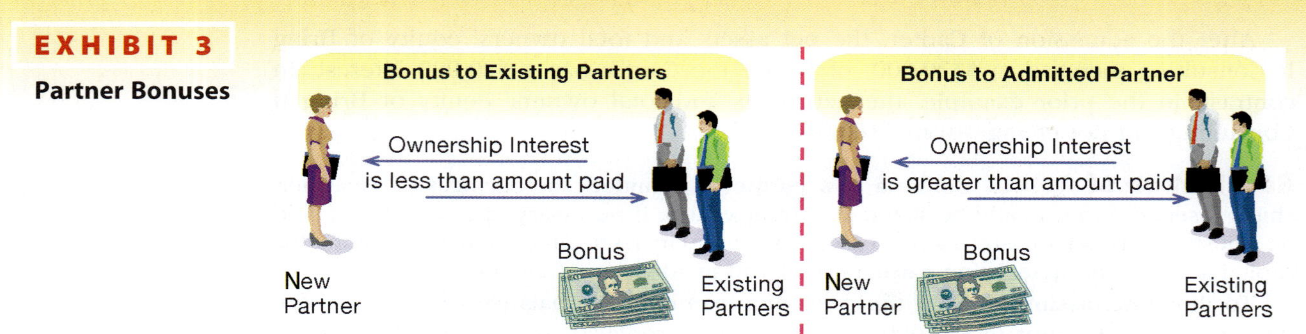

To illustrate, assume that on March 1 the partnership of Marsha Jenkins and Helen Kramer is considering a new partner, Alex Diaz. After the assets of the partnership have been adjusted to current market values, the capital balances of Jenkins and Kramer are as follows:

Marsha Jenkins, Capital	$20,000
Helen Kramer, Capital	24,000
Total owners' equity *before* admitting Diaz	$44,000

Jenkins and Kramer agree to admit Diaz to the partnership for $31,000. In return, Diaz will receive a one-third equity in the partnership and will share equally with Jenkins and Kramer in partnership income or losses. In this case, Diaz is paying Jenkins and Kramer a $6,000 bonus to join the partnership, computed as follows:

Marsha Jenkins, Capital	$20,000
Helen Kramer, Capital	24,000
Diaz's contribution	31,000
Total owners' equity *after* admitting Diaz	$75,000
Diaz's equity interest after admission	× 1/3
Alex Diaz, Capital	$25,000
Diaz's contribution	$31,000
Alex Diaz, Capital	25,000
Bonus paid to Jenkins and Kramer	$ 6,000

The $6,000 bonus paid by Diaz increases Jenkins's and Kramer's capital accounts. It is distributed to the capital accounts of Jenkins and Kramer according to their income-sharing ratio.[5] Assuming that Jenkins and Kramer share profits and losses equally, the entry to record the admission of Diaz to the partnership is as shown on the next page:

5 Another method used to record the admission of partners attributes goodwill rather than a bonus to the partners. This method is discussed in advanced accounting textbooks.

LLC		
Cash	*31,000*	
Alex Diaz, Member Equity		*25,000*
Marsha Jenkins, Member Equity		*3,000*
Helen Kramer, Member Equity		*3,000*

Mar.	1	Cash		31,000	
		Alex Diaz, Capital			25,000
		Marsha Jenkins, Capital			3,000
		Helen Kramer, Capital			3,000

Existing partners may agree to pay the new partner a bonus to join a partnership. To illustrate, assume that after adjusting assets to market values, the capital balances of Janice Cowen and Steve Dodd are as follows:

Janice Cowen, Capital	$ 80,000
Steve Dodd, Capital	40,000
Total owners' equity *before* admitting Chou	$120,000

Cowen and Dodd agree to admit Ellen Chou to the partnership on June 1 for an investment of $30,000. In return, Chou will receive a one-fourth equity interest in the partnership and will share in one-fourth of the profits and losses. In this case, Cowen and Dodd are paying Chou a $7,500 bonus to join the partnership, computed as follows:

Janice Cowen, Capital	$ 80,000
Steve Dodd, Capital	40,000
Chou's contribution	30,000
Total owners' equity *after* admitting Chou	$150,000
Chou's equity interest after admission	× ¼
Ellen Chou, Capital	$ 37,500
Ellen Chou, Capital	$ 37,500
Chou's contribution	30,000
Bonus paid to Chou	$ 7,500

The $7,500 bonus paid to Chou decreases Cowen's and Dodd's capital accounts. It is distributed to the capital accounts of Cowen and Dodd according to their income-sharing ratio. Assuming that the income-sharing ratio of Cowen and Dodd was 2:1 before the admission of Chou, the entry to record the admission of Chou to the partnership is as follows:

LLC		
Cash	*30,000*	
Janice Cowen, Member Equity	*5,000[1]*	
Steve Dodd, Member Equity	*2,500[2]*	
Ellen Chou, Member Equity		*37,500*

June	1	Cash		30,000	
		Janice Cowen, Capital		5,000[1]	
		Steve Dodd, Capital		2,500[2]	
		Ellen Chou, Capital			37,500

[1] $7,500 × 2/3
[2] $7,500 × 1/3

Example Exercise 12-4 Partner Bonus

OBJ. 3

Lowman has a capital balance of $45,000 after adjusting assets to fair market value. Conrad contributes $26,000 to receive a 30% interest in a new partnership with Lowman.

Determine the amount and recipient of the partner bonus.

Follow My Example 12-4

Equity of Lowman	$45,000
Conrad's contribution	26,000
Total equity after admitting Conrad	$71,000
Conrad's equity interest	× 30%
Conrad's equity after admission	$21,300
Conrad's contribution	$26,000
Conrad's equity after admission	21,300
Bonus paid to Lowman	$ 4,700

Practice Exercises: **PE 12-4A, PE 12-4B**

Withdrawal of a Partner

A partner generally cannot withdraw without permission of the remaining partners, nor can a partner be forced to withdraw by the other partners. In this sense, a partnership is like a marriage, "for better or for worse."

A partner may retire or withdraw from a partnership. In such cases, the withdrawing partner's interest is normally sold to the:

1. Existing partners or
2. Partnership

If the *existing partners* purchase the withdrawing partner's interest, the purchase and sale of the partnership interest is between the partners as individuals. The only entry on the partnership's records is to debit the capital account of the partner withdrawing and to credit the capital account of the partner or partners buying the additional interest.

If the *partnership purchases* the withdrawing partner's interest, the assets and the owners' equity of the partnership are reduced by the purchase price. Before the purchase, the asset accounts should be adjusted to current values. The net amount of any adjustment should be divided among the capital accounts of the partners according to their income-sharing ratio.

The entry to record the purchase debits the capital account of the withdrawing partner and credits Cash for the amount of the purchase. If not enough partnership cash is available to pay the withdrawing partner, a liability may be created (credited) for the amount owed the withdrawing partner.

Death of a Partner

When a partner dies, the partnership accounts should be closed as of the date of death. The net income for the current period should then be determined and divided among the partners' capital accounts. The asset accounts should also be adjusted to current values and the amount of any adjustment divided among the capital accounts of the partners.

After the income is divided and any assets revalued, an entry is recorded to close the deceased partner's capital account. The entry debits the deceased partner's capital account for its balance and credits a liability account, which is payable to the deceased's estate. The remaining partner or partners may then decide to continue the business or liquidate it.

Describe and illustrate the accounting for liquidating a partnership.

Liquidating Partnerships

When a partnership goes out of business, it sells the assets, pays the creditors, and distributes the remaining cash or other assets to the partners. This winding-up process is called the **liquidation** of the partnership. Although *liquidating* refers to the payment of liabilities, it includes the entire winding-up process.

When the partnership goes out of business and the normal operations are discontinued, the accounts should be adjusted and closed. The only accounts remaining open will be the asset, contra asset, liability, and owners' equity accounts.

The liquidation process is illustrated in Exhibit 4. The steps in the liquidation process are as follows:

Step 1. Sell the partnership assets. This step is called **realization.**

Step 2. Distribute any gains or losses from realization to the partners based on their income-sharing ratio.

Step 3. Pay the claims of creditors using the cash from step 1 realization.

Step 4. Distribute the remaining cash to the partners based on the balances in their capital accounts.

Note:
In liquidation, cash is distributed to partners according to their capital balances.

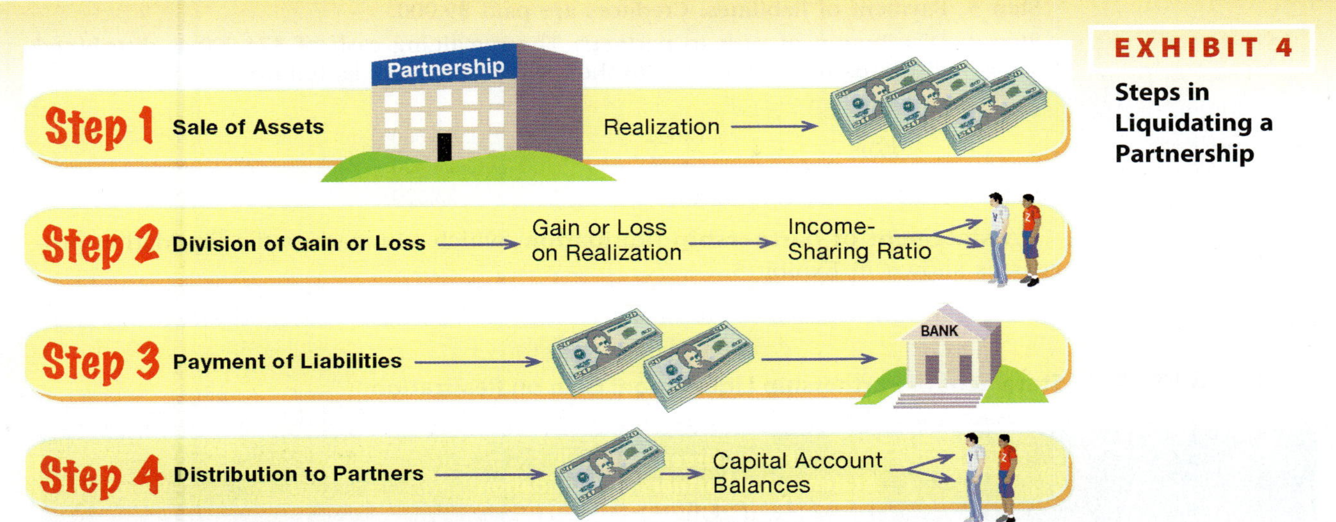

EXHIBIT 4

Steps in Liquidating a Partnership

To illustrate, assume that Farley, Green, and Hall decide to liquidate their partnership. On April 9, after discontinuing business operations of the partnership and closing the accounts, the following trial balance is prepared:

Farley, Green, and Hall
Post-Closing Trial Balance
April 9, 2012

	Debit Balances	Credit Balances
Cash	11,000	
Noncash Assets	64,000	
Liabilities		9,000
Jean Farley, Capital		22,000
Brad Green, Capital		22,000
Alice Hall, Capital		22,000
	75,000	75,000

Farley, Green, and Hall share income and losses in a ratio of 5:3:2 (50%, 30%, 20%). To simplify, assume that all noncash assets are sold in a single transaction and that all liabilities are paid at one time. In addition, Noncash Assets and Liabilities will be used as account titles in place of the various asset, contra asset, and liability accounts.

Gain on Realization

Assume that Farley, Green, and Hall sell all noncash assets for $72,000. Thus, a gain of $8,000 ($72,000 – $64,000) is realized. The partnership is liquidated during April as follows:

Step 1. Sale of assets: $72,000 is realized from sale of all the noncash assets.

Step 2. Division of gain: The gain of $8,000 is distributed to Farley, Green, and Hall in the income-sharing ratio of 5:3:2. Thus, the partner capital accounts are credited as follows:

Farley	$4,000 ($8,000 × 50%)
Green	2,400 ($8,000 × 30%)
Hall	1,600 ($8,000 × 20%)

Step 3. Payment of liabilities: Creditors are paid $9,000.

Step 4. Distribution of cash to partners: The remaining cash of $74,000 is distributed to the partners according to their capital balances as follows:

Farley	$26,000
Green	24,400
Hall	23,600

A **statement of partnership liquidation**, which summarizes the liquidation process, is shown in Exhibit 5.

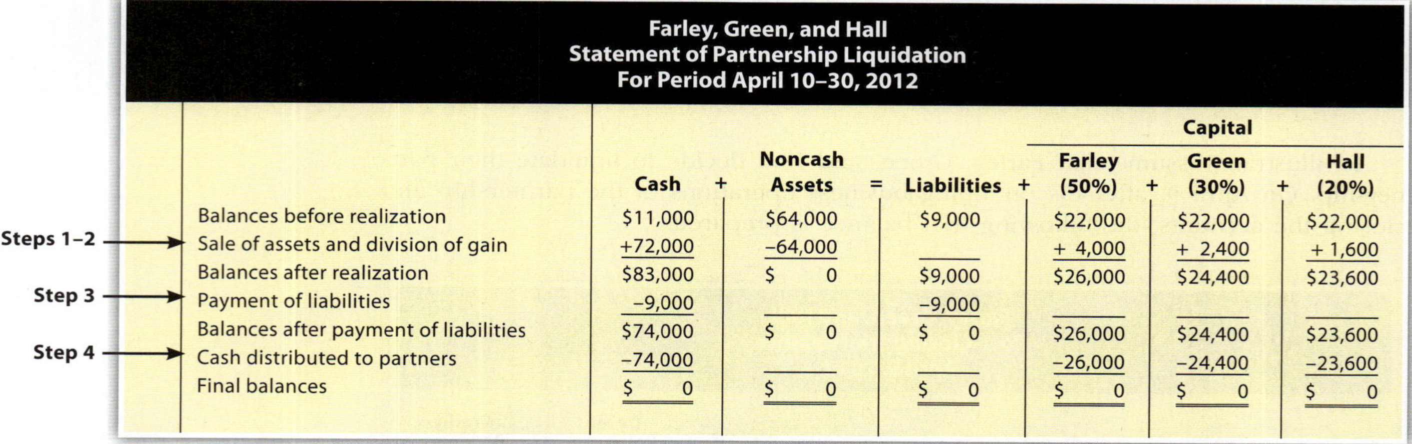

EXHIBIT 5 **Statement of Partnership Liquidation: Gain on Realization**

Farley, Green, and Hall
Statement of Partnership Liquidation
For Period April 10–30, 2012

		Cash +	Noncash Assets =	Liabilities +	Capital Farley (50%) +	Capital Green (30%) +	Capital Hall (20%)
	Balances before realization	$11,000	$64,000	$9,000	$22,000	$22,000	$22,000
Steps 1–2 →	Sale of assets and division of gain	+72,000	−64,000		+ 4,000	+ 2,400	+ 1,600
	Balances after realization	$83,000	$ 0	$9,000	$26,000	$24,400	$23,600
Step 3 →	Payment of liabilities	−9,000		−9,000			
	Balances after payment of liabilities	$74,000	$ 0	$ 0	$26,000	$24,400	$23,600
Step 4 →	Cash distributed to partners	−74,000			−26,000	−24,400	−23,600
	Final balances	$ 0	$ 0	$ 0	$ 0	$ 0	$ 0

The entries to record the steps in the liquidating process are as follows:

Sale of assets (Step 1):

LLC		
Cash	*72,000*	
Noncash Assets		*64,000*
Gain on Realization		*8,000*

		Cash	72,000	
		Noncash Assets		64,000
		Gain on Realization		8,000

Division of gain (Step 2):

LLC		
Gain on Realization	*8,000*	
Jean Farley, Member Equity		*4,000*
Brad Green, Member Equity		*2,400*
Alice Hall, Member Equity		*1,600*

		Gain on Realization	8,000	
		Jean Farley, Capital		4,000
		Brad Green, Capital		2,400
		Alice Hall, Capital		1,600

Payment of liabilities (Step 3):

LLC		
Liabilities	*9,000*	
Cash		*9,000*

		Liabilities	9,000	
		Cash		9,000

Distribution of cash to partners (Step 4):

Jean Farley, Capital		26,000	
Brad Green, Capital		24,400	
Alice Hall, Capital		23,600	
Cash			74,000

LLC

Jean Farley, Member Equity	*26,000*	
Brad Green, Member Equity	*24,400*	
Alice Hall, Member Equity	*23,600*	
Cash		*74,000*

As shown in Exhibit 5, *the cash is distributed to the partners based on the balances of their capital accounts.* These balances are determined after the gain on realization has been divided among the partners and the liabilities paid. The *income-sharing ratio should not be used as a basis for distributing the cash to partners.*

Loss on Realization

Assume that Farley, Green, and Hall sell all noncash assets for $44,000. Thus, a loss of $20,000 ($64,000 – $44,000) is realized. The liquidation of the partnership is as follows:

Step 1. Sale of assets: $44,000 is realized from the sale of all the noncash assets.

Step 2. Division of loss: The loss of $20,000 is distributed to Farley, Green, and Hall in the income-sharing ratio of 5:3:2. Thus, the partner capital accounts are debited as follows:

Farley	$10,000 ($20,000 × 50%)
Green	6,000 ($20,000 × 30%)
Hall	4,000 ($20,000 × 20%)

Step 3. Payment of liabilities: Creditors are paid $9,000.

Step 4. Distribution of cash to partners: The remaining cash of $46,000 is distributed to the partners according to their capital balances as follows:

Farley	$12,000
Green	16,000
Hall	18,000

The steps in liquidating the partnership are summarized in the statement of partnership liquidation shown in Exhibit 6.

EXHIBIT 6 Statement of Partnership Liquidation: Loss on Realization

Farley, Green, and Hall
Statement of Partnership Liquidation
For Period April 10–30, 2012

		Cash	+	Noncash Assets	=	Liabilities	+	Capital Farley (50%)	+	Capital Green (30%)	+	Capital Hall (20%)
	Balances before realization	$11,000		$64,000		$9,000		$22,000		$22,000		$22,000
Steps 1–2 →	Sale of assets and division of loss	+44,000		–64,000				–10,000		– 6,000		– 4,000
	Balances after realization	$55,000		$ 0		$9,000		$12,000		$16,000		$18,000
Step 3 →	Payment of liabilities	–9,000				–9,000						
	Balances after payment of liabilities	$46,000		$ 0		$ 0		$12,000		$16,000		$18,000
Step 4 →	Cash distributed to partners	–46,000						–12,000		–16,000		–18,000
	Final balances	$ 0		$ 0		$ 0		$ 0		$ 0		$ 0

The entries to liquidate the partnership are as follows:

Sale of assets (Step 1):

LLC

Cash	*44,000*	
Loss on Realization	*20,000*	
Noncash Assets		*64,000*

	Cash		44,000	
	Loss on Realization		20,000	
	Noncash Assets			64,000

Division of loss (Step 2):

LLC

Jean Farley, Member Equity	*10,000*	
Brad Green, Member Equity	*6,000*	
Alice Hall, Member Equity	*4,000*	
Loss on Realization		*20,000*

	Jean Farley, Capital		10,000	
	Brad Green, Capital		6,000	
	Alice Hall, Capital		4,000	
	Loss on Realization			20,000

Payment of liabilities (Step 3):

LLC

Liabilities	*9,000*	
Cash		*9,000*

	Liabilities		9,000	
	Cash			9,000

Distribution of cash to partners (Step 4):

LLC

Jean Farley, Member Equity	*12,000*	
Brad Green, Member Equity	*16,000*	
Alice Hall, Member Equity	*18,000*	
Cash		*46,000*

	Jean Farley, Capital		12,000	
	Brad Green, Capital		16,000	
	Alice Hall, Capital		18,000	
	Cash			46,000

Example Exercise 12-5 Liquidating Partnerships

OBJ. 4

Prior to liquidating their partnership, Todd and Gentry had capital accounts of $50,000 and $100,000, respectively. Prior to liquidation, the partnership had no other cash assets than what was realized from the sale of assets. These assets were sold for $220,000. The partnership had $20,000 of liabilities. Todd and Gentry share income and losses equally. Determine the amount received by Gentry as a final distribution from the liquidation of the partnership.

Follow My Example 12-5

Gentry's equity prior to liquidation		$100,000
Realization of asset sale	$220,000	
Book value of assets ($50,000 + $100,000 + $20,000)	170,000	
Gain on liquidation	$ 50,000	
Gentry's share of gain (50% × $50,000)		25,000
Gentry's cash distribution		$125,000

Practice Exercises: **PE 12-5A, PE 12-5B**

Loss on Realization—Capital Deficiency

The share of a loss on realization may be greater than the balance in a partner's capital account. The resulting debit balance in the capital account is called a **deficiency**. It represents a claim of the partnership against the partner.

To illustrate, assume that Farley, Green, and Hall sell all noncash assets for $10,000. Thus, a loss of $54,000 ($64,000 – $10,000) is realized. The liquidation of the partnership is as follows:

Step 1. Sale of assets: $10,000 is realized from the sale of all the noncash assets.

Step 2. Division of loss: The loss of $54,000 is distributed to Farley, Green, and Hall in the income-sharing ratio of 5:3:2. The partner capital accounts are debited as follows:

Farley	$27,000 ($54,000 × 50%)
Green	16,200 ($54,000 × 30%)
Hall	10,800 ($54,000 × 20%)

Step 3. Payment of liabilities: Creditors are paid $9,000.

Step 4. Distribution of cash to partners: The share of the loss allocated to Farley, $27,000 (50% × $54,000), exceeds the $22,000 balance in her capital account. This $5,000 deficiency represents an amount that Farley owes the partnership. Assuming that Farley pays the deficiency, the cash of $17,000 is distributed to the partners according to their capital balances as follows:

Farley	$ 0
Green	5,800
Hall	11,200

The steps in liquidating the partnership are summarized in the statement of partnership liquidation shown in Exhibit 7.

The entries to liquidate the partnership are as follows:

Sale of assets (Step 1):

LLC		
Cash	*10,000*	
Loss on Realization	*54,000*	
Noncash Assets		*64,000*

	Cash		10,000	
	Loss on Realization		54,000	
	Noncash Assets			64,000

EXHIBIT 7 Statement of Partnership Liquidation: Loss on Realization—Capital Deficiency

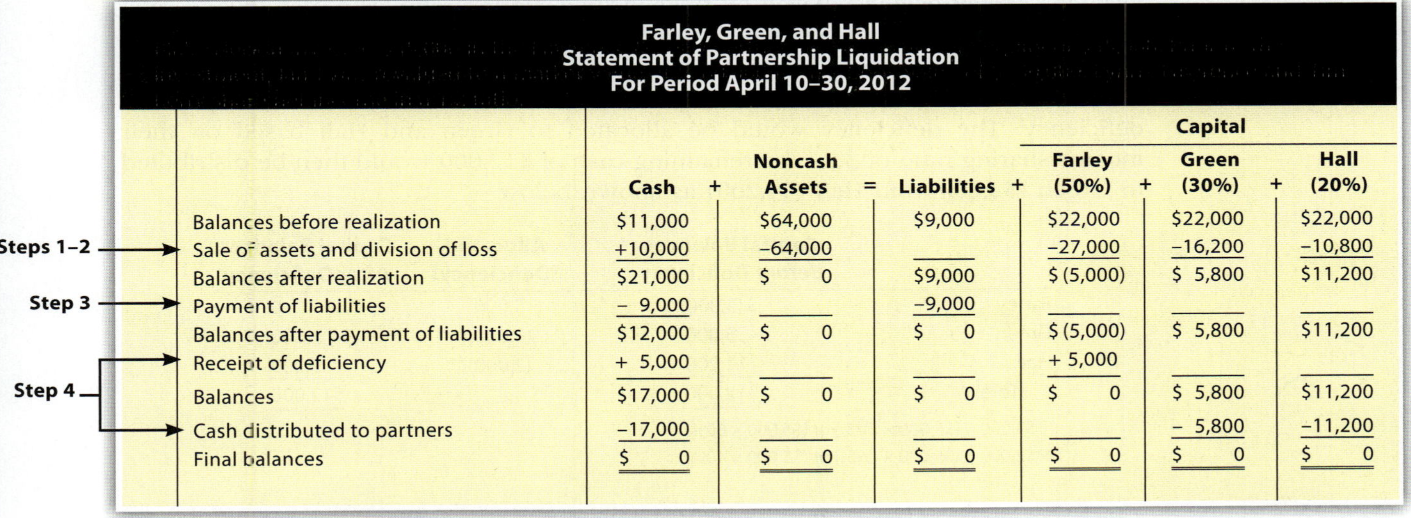

Farley, Green, and Hall
Statement of Partnership Liquidation
For Period April 10–30, 2012

		Cash	+	Noncash Assets	=	Liabilities	+	Capital: Farley (50%)	+	Capital: Green (30%)	+	Capital: Hall (20%)
	Balances before realization	$11,000		$64,000		$9,000		$22,000		$22,000		$22,000
Steps 1–2 →	Sale of assets and division of loss	+10,000		–64,000				–27,000		–16,200		–10,800
	Balances after realization	$21,000		$ 0		$9,000		$ (5,000)		$ 5,800		$11,200
Step 3 →	Payment of liabilities	– 9,000				–9,000						
	Balances after payment of liabilities	$12,000		$ 0		$ 0		$ (5,000)		$ 5,800		$11,200
Step 4 →	Receipt of deficiency	+ 5,000						+ 5,000				
	Balances	$17,000		$ 0		$ 0		$ 0		$ 5,800		$11,200
Step 4 →	Cash distributed to partners	–17,000								– 5,800		–11,200
	Final balances	$ 0		$ 0		$ 0		$ 0		$ 0		$ 0

Division of loss (Step 2):

LLC		
Jean Farley, Member Equity	*27,000*	
Brad Green, Member Equity	*16,200*	
Alice Hall, Member Equity	*10,800*	
Loss on Realization		*54,000*

	Jean Farley, Capital		27,000	
	Brad Green, Capital		16,200	
	Alice Hall, Capital		10,800	
	Loss on Realization			54,000

Payment of liabilities (Step 3):

LLC		
Liabilities	*9,000*	
Cash		*9,000*

	Liabilities		9,000	
	Cash			9,000

Receipt of deficiency (Step 4):

LLC		
Cash	*5,000*	
Jean Farley, Member Equity		*5,000*

	Cash		5,000	
	Jean Farley, Capital			5,000

Distribution of cash to partners (Step 4):

LLC		
Brad Green, Member Equity	*5,800*	
Alice Hall, Member Equity	*11,200*	
Cash		*17,000*

	Brad Green, Capital		5,800	
	Alice Hall, Capital		11,200	
	Cash			17,000

If the deficient partner does not pay the partnership their deficiency, there will not be sufficient partnership cash to pay the remaining partners in full. Any uncollected deficiency becomes a loss to the partnership and is divided among the remaining partners' capital balances based on their income-sharing ratio. The cash balance will then equal the sum of the capital account balances. The cash can then be distributed to the remaining partners, based on the balances of their capital accounts.

To illustrate, assume that in the preceding example Farley could not pay her deficiency. The deficiency would be allocated to Green and Hall based on their income-sharing ratio of 3:2. The remaining cash of $12,000 would then be distributed to Green ($2,800) and Hall ($9,200) as shown below.

	Capital Balances *Before* Deficiency	Allocated (Deficiency)	Capital Balances *After* Deficiency
Farley	$ (5,000)	$ 5,000	$ 0
Green	5,800	(3,000)*	2,800
Hall	11,200	(2,000)**	9,200
Total	$12,000		$12,000

*$3,000 = [$5,000 × (3/5)] or ($5,000 × 60%)

**$2,000 = [$5,000 × (2/5)] or ($5,000 × 40%)

The entries to allocate Farley's deficiency and distribute the cash are as follows:

Allocation of deficiency (Step 4):

LLC		
Brad Green, Member Equity	*3,000*	
Alice Hall, Member Equity	*2,000*	
Jean Farley, Member Equity		*5,000*

	Brad Green, Capital		3,000	
	Alice Hall, Capital		2,000	
	Jean Farley, Capital			5,000

Distribution of cash to partners (Step 4):

LLC		
Brad Green, Member Equity	*2,800*	
Alice Hall, Member Equity	*9,200*	
Cash		*12,000*

	Brad Green, Capital		2,800	
	Alice Hall, Capital		9,200	
	Cash			12,000

Example Exercise 12-6 Liquidating Partnerships—Deficiency OBJ. 4

Prior to liquidating their partnership, Short and Bain had capital accounts of $20,000 and $80,000, respectively. The partnership assets were sold for $40,000. The partnership had no liabilities. Short and Bain share income and losses equally.

a. Determine the amount of Short's deficiency.
b. Determine the amount distributed to Bain, assuming Short is unable to satisfy the deficiency.

Follow My Example 12-6

a. Short's equity prior to liquidation		$ 20,000
Realization of asset sale	$ 40,000	
Book value of assets ($20,000 + $80,000)	100,000	
Loss on liquidation	$ 60,000	
Short's share of loss (50% × $60,000)		30,000
Short's deficiency		$(10,000)

b. $40,000. $80,000 – $30,000 share of loss – $10,000 Short deficiency.

Practice Exercises: PE 12-6A, PE 12-6B

Statement of Partnership Equity

OBJ. 5 Prepare the statement of partnership equity.

Reporting changes in partnership capital accounts is similar to that for a proprietorship. The primary difference is that there is a capital account for each partner. The changes in partner capital accounts for a period of time are reported in a **statement of partnership equity**.

Exhibit 8 illustrates a statement of partnership equity for Investors Associates, a partnership of Dan Cross and Kelly Baker. Each partner's capital account is shown as a separate column. The partner capital accounts may change due to capital additions, net income, or withdrawals.

The equity reporting for an LLC is similar to that of a partnership. Instead of a statement of partnership capital, a statement of members' equity is prepared. The **statement of members' equity** reports the changes in member equity for a period.

EXHIBIT 8

Statement of Partnership Equity

Investors Associates Statement of Partnership Equity For the Year Ended December 31, 2012			
	Dan Cross, Capital	**Kelly Baker, Capital**	**Total Partnership Capital**
Balance, January 1, 2012	$245,000	$365,000	$610,000
Capital additions	50,000		50,000
Net income for the year	40,000	80,000	120,000
Less partner withdrawals	(5,000)	(45,000)	(50,000)
Balance, December 31, 2012	$330,000	$400,000	$730,000

The statement is similar to Exhibit 8, except that the columns represent member equity rather than partner equity.

Financial Analysis and Interpretation: Revenue per Employee

OBJ. 6 Analyze and interpret employee efficiency.

Many partnerships and LLCs operate as service-oriented enterprises. This is the case for many professions, such as medical, advertising, and accounting. The performance of such firms can be measured by the amount of net income per partner, as illustrated in this chapter. Another measure used to assess the performance of a service-oriented business is revenue per employee.

Revenue per employee is a measure of the efficiency of the business in generating revenues. It is computed as follows:

$$\text{Revenue per Employee} = \frac{\text{Revenue}}{\text{Number of Employees}}$$

In a partnership, the number of partners may be included with employees or partners may be evaluated separately. Generally, the higher the revenue per employee the more efficient the company is in generating revenue from its employees. In evaluating revenue per employee, changes over time as well as comparisons with industry averages are often used.

To illustrate comparisons over time, assume Washburn & Lovett, CPAs, has the following information for two years:

	2013	**2012**
Revenues	$220,000,000	$180,000,000
Number of employees	1,600	1,500

For Washburn & Lovett, the revenue per employee ratio is computed for 2013 and 2012 as follows:

$$\text{Revenue per employee, 2013: } \frac{\$220{,}000{,}000}{1{,}600 \text{ employees}} = \$137{,}500 \text{ per employee}$$

$$\text{Revenue per employee, 2012: } \frac{\$180{,}000{,}000}{1{,}500 \text{ employees}} = \$120{,}000 \text{ per employee}$$

Washburn & Lovett increased revenues by $40,000,000 ($220,000,000 – $180,000,000), or 22.2% ($40,000,000/$180,000,000) from 2012 to 2013. The number of employees increased by 100, or 6.7% (100 employees/1,500 employees) between the two years. Thus, the firm increased revenues at a rate faster than the increase in employees. As a result, the revenue per employee improved from $120,000 to $137,500 between the two years, suggesting improved efficiency in generating revenues.

To illustrate comparison within an industry, the revenue per employee for Starbucks and McDonald's for a recent year are as computed below.

$$\text{Starbucks: } \frac{\$10{,}383{,}000{,}000}{172{,}000 \text{ employees}} = \$60{,}366 \text{ per employee}$$

$$\text{McDonald's: } \frac{\$23{,}500{,}000{,}000}{400{,}000 \text{ employees}} = \$58{,}750 \text{ per employee}$$

The difference in the preceding ratios is small enough to conclude that Starbucks and McDonald's are equally efficient in their ability to generate revenue per employee.

The importance of comparing revenue per employee within an industry is further illustrated by comparing Apple, Inc., and Dell Inc. The revenue per employee for Apple, Inc., is $1,014,969. In contrast, Dell has revenue per employee of $756,700. Thus, Apple has higher revenue per employee efficiency than does Dell.

Finally, you should note that comparisons across industries are often misleading. For example, Apple's revenue per employee of $1,014,969 is much higher than Starbucks' $60,366. However, Apple is a much different company than Starbucks; thus, this comparison is misleading. McDonald's is a better comparison for Starbucks, as is Dell for Apple.

Example Exercise 12-7 Revenue per Employee

OBJ. 6

AccuTax, CPAs earned $4,200,000 during 2012 using 20 employees. During 2013, the firm grew revenues to $4,560,000 and expanded the staff to 24 employees.

a. Determine the revenue per employee for each year.
b. Interpret the results.

Follow My Example 12-7

a. 2012: $\frac{\$4{,}200{,}000}{20 \text{ employees}} = \$210{,}000 \text{ per employee}$

2013: $\frac{\$4{,}560{,}000}{24 \text{ employees}} = \$190{,}000 \text{ per employee}$

b. While AccuTax grew revenues by $360,000 ($4,560,000 – $4,200,000), or 8.6% ($360,000/$4,200,000), the number of employees expanded by 4, or 20% (4/20). The growth in revenue was less than the growth in the number of employees; thus, the revenue per employee declined between the two years. The firm was less efficient in generating revenues from its employees in 2013.

Practice Exercises: **PE 12-7A, PE 12-7B**

At a Glance 12

Describe the characteristics of proprietorships, partnerships, and limited liability companies.

Key Points The advantages and disadvantages of proprietorships, partnerships, and limited liability companies are summarized in Exhibit 1.

Learning Outcomes	Example Exercises	Practice Exercises
• Identify the advantages and disadvantages of proprietorships, partnerships, and limited liability companies.		

Describe and illustrate the accounting for forming a partnership and for dividing the net income and net loss of a partnership.

Key Points When a partnership is formed, accounts are debited for contributed assets and credited for assumed liabilities, and the partner's capital account is credited for the net amount. The net income of a partnership may be divided among the partners on the basis of services rendered, interest earned on the capital account balance, and the income-sharing ratio.

Learning Outcomes	Example Exercises	Practice Exercises
• Journalize the initial formation of a partnership and establish partner capital.	EE12-1	PE12-1A, 12-1B
• Determine and journalize the income distributed to each partner.	EE12-2	PE12-2A, 12-2B

Describe and illustrate the accounting for partner admission and withdrawal.

Key Points Partnership assets should be restated to current values prior to admission or withdrawal of a partner. A new partner may be admitted into a partnership by either purchasing an interest from an existing partner or by purchasing an interest directly from the partnership.

Learning Outcomes	Example Exercises	Practice Exercises
• Prepare for partner admission by revaluing assets to approximate current values.	EE12-3	PE12-3A, 12-3B
• Distinguish between partner admission through purchase from an existing partner or purchase from the partnership.	EE12-3	PE12-3A, 12-3B
• Determine partner bonuses.	EE12-4	PE12-4A, 12-4B

Describe and illustrate the accounting for liquidating a partnership.

Key Points A partnership is liquidated by the (1) sale of partnership assets (realization), (2) distribution of gain or loss on realization to the partners, (3) payments to creditors, and (4) distribution of the remaining cash to partners according to their capital account balances. A partner may be deficient when the amount of loss distribution exceeds the capital balance.

Learning Outcomes	Example Exercises	Practice Exercises
• Apply the four steps of liquidating a partnership for either gain or loss on realization.	EE12-5	PE12-5A, 12-5B
• Apply the four steps of partnership liquidation when there is a partner deficiency.	EE12-6	PE12-6A, 12-6B

Prepare the statement of partnership equity.

Key Points A statement of partnership equity reports the changes in partnership equity from capital additions, net income, and withdrawals.

Learning Outcomes	Example Exercises	Practice Exercises
• Prepare a statement of partnership equity.		

Analyze and interpret employee efficiency.

Key Points The revenue per employee ratio is calculated as the total annual revenues divided by the total employees. This ratio measures the total revenue earned by each employee, and thus, is a measure of the efficiency of each employee in revenue terms. The ratio is often used to measure efficiency trends over time and across similar firms.

Learning Outcomes	Example Exercises	Practice Exercises
• Analyze and interpret the revenue per employee ratio.	EE12-7	PE12-7A, 12-7B

Key Terms

deficiency (555)
limited liability company (LLC) (540)
liquidation (550)
partnership (539)
partnership agreement (539)
realization (550)
revenue per employee (558)
statement of members' equity (557)
statement of partnership equity (557)
statement of partnership liquidation (552)

Illustrative Problem

Radcliffe, Sonders, and Towers, who share in income and losses in the ratio of 2:3:5, decided to discontinue operations as of April 30, 2012, and liquidate their partnership. After the accounts were closed on April 30, 2012, the following trial balance was prepared:

Radcliffe, Sonders, and Towers
Post-Closing Trial Balance
April 30, 2012

	Debit Balances	Credit Balances
Cash	5,900	
Noncash Assets	109,900	
Liabilities		26,800
Radcliffe, Capital		14,600
Sonders, Capital		27,900
Towers, Capital		46,500
	115,800	115,800

Between May 1 and May 18, the noncash assets were sold for $27,400, and the liabilities were paid.

Instructions

1. Assuming that the partner with the capital deficiency pays the entire amount owed to the partnership, prepare a statement of partnership liquidation.

2. Journalize the entries to record (a) the sale of the assets, (b) the division of loss on the sale of the assets, (c) the payment of the liabilities, (d) the receipt of the deficiency, and (e) the distribution of cash to the partners.

Solution

1.

Radcliffe, Sonders, and Towers
Statement of Partnership Liquidation
For Period May 1–18, 2012

	Cash	+	Noncash Assets	=	Liabilities	+	Capital Radcliffe (20%)	+	Capital Sonders (30%)	+	Capital Towers (50%)
Balances before realization	$ 5,900		$109,000		$26,800		$14,600		$27,900		$46,500
Sale of assets and division of loss	+27,400		−109,000				−16,500		−24,750		−41,250
Balances after realization	$33,300		$ 0		$26,800		$ (1,900)		$ 3,150		$ 5,250
Payment of liabilities	−26,800				−26,800						
Balances after payment of liabilities	$ 6,500		$ 0		$ 0		$ (1,900)		$ 3,150		$ 5,250
Receipt of deficiency	+ 1,900						+ 1,900				
Balances	$ 8,400		$ 0		$ 0		$ 0		$ 3,150		$ 5,250
Cash distributed to partners	−8,400								− 3,150		− 5,250
Final balances	$ 0		$ 0		$ 0		$ 0		$ 0		$ 0

2.a.

	Debit	Credit
Cash	27,400	
Loss on Realization	82,500	
Noncash Assets		109,900

b.

	Debit	Credit
Radcliffe, Capital	16,500	
Sonders, Capital	24,750	
Towers, Capital	41,250	
Loss on Realization		82,500

c.

	Debit	Credit
Liabilities	26,800	
Cash		26,800

d.

	Debit	Credit
Cash	1,900	
Radcliffe, Capital		1,900

e.

	Sonders, Capital		3,150	
	Towers, Capital		5,250	
	Cash			8,400

Discussion Questions

1. What are the main advantages of (a) proprietorships, (b) partnerships, and (c) limited liability companies?
2. What are the disadvantages of a partnership over a limited liability company form of organization for a profit-making business?
3. Emilio Alvarez and Graciela Zavala joined together to form a partnership. Is it possible for them to lose a greater amount than the amount of their investment in the partnership? Explain.
4. What are the major features of a partnership agreement for a partnership, or an operating agreement for a limited liability company?
5. Josiah Barlow, Patty DuMont, and Owen Maholic are contemplating the formation of a partnership. According to the partnership agreement, Barlow is to invest $60,000 and devote one-half time, DuMont is to invest $40,000 and devote three-fourths time, and Maholic is to make no investment and devote full time. Would Maholic be correct in assuming that, since he is not contributing any assets to the firm, he is risking nothing? Explain.
6. During the current year, Marsha Engles withdrew $4,000 monthly from the partnership of Engles and Cox Water Management Consultants. Is it possible that her share of partnership net income for the current year might be more or less than $48,000? Explain.
7. a. What accounts are debited and credited to record a partner's cash withdrawal in lieu of salary?
   b. The articles of partnership provide for a salary allowance of $6,000 per month to partner C. If C withdrew only $4,000 per month, would this affect the division of the partnership net income?
   c. At the end of the fiscal year, what accounts are debited and credited to record the division of net income among partners?
8. Explain the difference between the admission of a new partner to a partnership (a) by purchase of an interest from another partner and (b) by contribution of assets to the partnership.
9. Why is it important to state all partnership assets in terms of current prices at the time of the admission of a new partner?
10. Why might a partnership pay a bonus to a newly admitted partner?

Practice Exercises

Learning Objectives	Example Exercises

OBJ. 2 **EE 12-1** p. 542

PE 12-1A Journalize partner's original investment

Brittany Adams contributed a patent, accounts receivable, and $61,000 cash to a partnership. The patent had a book value of $56,000. However, the technology covered by the patent appeared to have significant market potential. Thus, the patent was appraised at $240,000. The accounts receivable control account was $78,000, with an allowance for doubtful accounts of $4,000. The partnership also assumed a $15,000 account payable from Adams.

Provide the journal entry for Adams' contribution to the partnership.

OBJ. 2 **EE 12-1** p. 542

PE 12-1B Journalize partner's original investment

Kevin LaRoche contributed land, inventory, and $28,000 cash to a partnership. The land had a book value of $65,000 and a market value of $135,000. The inventory had a book value of $60,000 and a market value of $51,000. The partnership also assumed a $50,000 note payable owed by LaRoche that was used originally to purchase the land.

Provide the journal entry for LaRoche's contribution to the partnership.

OBJ. 2 **EE 12-2** p. 544

PE 12-2A Dividing partnership net income

Cody Paulson and Hannah O'Brien formed a partnership, dividing income as follows:

1. Annual salary allowance to Paulson of $26,000.
2. Interest of 5% on each partner's capital balance on January 1.
3. Any remaining net income divided to Paulson and O'Brien, 2:1.

Paulson and O'Brien had $50,000 and $120,000, respectively, in their January 1 capital balances. Net income for the year was $33,000.

How much net income should be distributed to Paulson?

OBJ. 2 **EE 12-2** p. 544

PE 12-2B Dividing partnership net income

Alex Conyers and Shaunika Stevens formed a partnership, dividing income as follows:

1. Annual salary allowance to Stevens of $45,000.
2. Interest of 8% on each partner's capital balance on January 1.
3. Any remaining net income divided equally.

Conyers and Stevens had $50,000 and $160,000, respectively, in their January 1 capital balances. Net income for the year was $200,000.

How much net income should be distributed to Stevens?

OBJ. 3 **EE 12-3** p. 547

PE 12-3A Revaluing and contributing assets to a partnership

Antoine Dodd purchased one-half of Kyle Bryan's interest in the Rich and Bryan partnership for $24,000. Prior to the investment, land was revalued to a market value of $110,000 from a book value of $84,000. Zach Rich and Kyle Bryan share net income equally. Bryan had a capital balance of $25,000 prior to these transactions.

a. Provide the journal entry for the revaluation of land.

b. Provide the journal entry to admit Dodd.

Learning Objectives	Example Exercises

OBJ. 3 EE 12-3 p. 547

PE 12-3B Revaluing and contributing assets to a partnership

Naseef Asad invested $75,000 in the Lionel and Morehouse partnership for ownership equity of $75,000. Prior to the investment, equipment was revalued to a market value of $57,000 from a book value of $33,000. Justin Lionel and Courtney Morehouse share net income in a 2:1 ratio.

a. Provide the journal entry for the revaluation of equipment.

b. Provide the journal entry to admit Asad.

OBJ. 3 EE 12-4 p. 549

PE 12-4A Partner bonus

Sharpe has a capital balance of $300,000 after adjusting assets to fair market value. Rojas contributes $250,000 to receive a 60% interest in a new partnership with Sharpe.

Determine the amount and recipient of the partner bonus.

OBJ. 3 EE 12-4 p. 549

PE 12-4B Partner bonus

Joshi has a capital balance of $80,000 after adjusting assets to fair market value. Costas contributes $40,000 to receive a 40% interest in a new partnership with Joshi.

Determine the amount and recipient of the partner bonus.

OBJ. 4 EE 12-5 p. 554

PE 12-5A Liquidating partnerships

Prior to liquidating their partnership, Fowler and Ericson had capital accounts of $26,000 and $40,000, respectively. Prior to liquidation, the partnership had no cash assets other than what was realized from the sale of assets. These partnership assets were sold for $86,000. The partnership had $12,000 of liabilities. Fowler and Ericson share income and losses equally. Determine the amount received by Fowler as a final distribution from liquidation of the partnership.

OBJ. 4 EE 12-5 p. 554

PE 12-5B Liquidating partnerships

Prior to liquidating their partnership, Quinn and Kestor had capital accounts of $200,000 and $120,000, respectively. Prior to liquidation, the partnership had no cash assets other than what was realized from the sale of assets. These partnership assets were sold for $240,000. The partnership had $30,000 of liabilities. Quinn and Kestor share income and losses equally. Determine the amount received by Quinn as a final distribution from liquidation of the partnership.

OBJ. 4 EE 12-6 p. 557

PE 12-6A Liquidating partnerships—deficiency

Prior to liquidating their partnership, Jolly and Haines had capital accounts of $80,000 and $45,000, respectively. The partnership assets were sold for $30,000. The partnership had no liabilities. Jolly and Haines share income and losses equally.

a. Determine the amount of Haines' deficiency.

b. Determine the amount distributed to Jolly, assuming Haines is unable to satisfy the deficiency.

OBJ. 4 EE 12-6 p. 557

PE 12-6B Liquidating partnerships—deficiency

Prior to liquidating their partnership, Chow and Fuentes had capital accounts of $85,000 and $165,000, respectively. The partnership assets were sold for $45,000. The partnership had no liabilities. Chow and Fuentes share income and losses equally.

a. Determine the amount of Chow's deficiency.

b. Determine the amount distributed to Fuentes, assuming Chow is unable to satisfy the deficiency.

Learning Objectives *Example Exercises*

OBJ. 6 EE 12-7 p. 559

PE 12-7A Revenue per employee

Aaron and Rogers, CPAs earned $12,600,000 during 2012 using 90 employees. During 2013, the firm grew revenues to $14,400,000 and expanded the staff to 96 employees.

a. Determine the revenue per employee for each year.

b. Interpret the results.

OBJ. 6 EE 12-7 p. 559

PE 12-7B Revenue per employee

TechSystems, Architects earned $3,600,000 during 2012 using 20 employees. During 2013, the firm reduced revenues to $3,200,000 and reduced the staff to 16 employees.

a. Determine the revenue per employee for each year.

b. Interpret the results.

Exercises

OBJ. 2

EX 12-1 Record partner's original investment

Amber Moss and Latoya Pell decide to form a partnership by combining the assets of their separate businesses. Moss contributes the following assets to the partnership: cash, $15,000; accounts receivable with a face amount of $159,000 and an allowance for doubtful accounts of $9,700; merchandise inventory with a cost of $100,000; and equipment with a cost of $155,000 and accumulated depreciation of $100,000.

The partners agree that $6,000 of the accounts receivable are completely worthless and are not to be accepted by the partnership, that $11,400 is a reasonable allowance for the uncollectibility of the remaining accounts, that the merchandise inventory is to be recorded at the current market price of $91,450, and that the equipment is to be valued at $62,500.

Journalize the partnership's entry to record Moss's investment.

OBJ. 2

EX 12-2 Record partner's original investment

Jessica Kimble and Carlos Segura form a partnership by combining assets of their former businesses. The following balance sheet information is provided by Kimble, sole proprietorship:

Cash		$ 50,000
Accounts receivable	$100,000	
Less: Allowance for doubtful accounts	5,900	94,100
Land		180,000
Equipment	$ 70,000	
Less: Accumulated depreciation—equipment	43,000	27,000
Total assets		$351,100
Accounts payable		$ 22,500
Notes payable		80,000
Jessica Kimble, capital		248,600
Total liabilities and owner's equity		$351,100

Kimble obtained appraised values for the land and equipment as follows:

Land	$284,000
Equipment	19,000

An analysis of the accounts receivable indicated that the allowance for doubtful accounts should be increased to $7,000.

Journalize the partnership's entry for Kimble's investment.

OBJ. 2
✔ b. Wyatt, $315,000

EX 12-3 Dividing partnership income

Jennifer Wyatt and Megan Truett formed a partnership, investing $330,000 and $110,000, respectively. Determine their participation in the year's net income of $420,000 under each of the following independent assumptions: (a) no agreement concerning division of net income; (b) divided in the ratio of original capital investment; (c) interest at the rate of 8% allowed on original investments and the remainder divided in the ratio of 2:3; (d) salary allowances of $50,000 and $70,000, respectively, and the balance divided equally; (e) allowance of interest at the rate of 8% on original investments, salary allowances of $50,000 and $70,000, respectively, and the remainder divided equally.

OBJ. 2
✔ c. Wyatt, $76,320

EX 12-4 Dividing partnership income

Determine the income participation of Wyatt and Truett, according to each of the five assumptions as to income division listed in Exercise 12-3 if the year's net income is $160,000.

OBJ. 2

EX 12-5 Dividing partnership net loss

Ashley Adams and Michael Rovell formed a partnership in which the partnership agreement provided for salary allowances of $45,000 and $35,000, respectively. Determine the division of a $30,000 net loss for the current year.

OBJ. 2

EX 12-6 Negotiating income-sharing ratio

Sixty-year-old Mary Filmore retired from her computer consulting business in Boston and moved to Florida. There she met 27-year-old Emily Wright, who had just graduated from Eldon Community College with an associate degree in computer science. Mary and Emily formed a partnership called F&W Computer Consultants. Mary contributed $35,000 for startup costs and devoted one-half time to the business. Emily devoted full time to the business. The monthly drawings were $2,000 for Mary and $4,000 for Emily.

At the end of the first year of operations, the two partners disagreed on the division of net income. Mary reasoned that the division should be equal. Although she devoted only one-half time to the business, she contributed all of the startup funds. Emily reasoned that the income-sharing ratio should be 2:1 in her favor because she devoted full time to the business and her monthly drawings were twice those of Mary.

a. Can you identify any flaws in the partners' reasoning regarding the income-sharing ratio?

b. How could an income-sharing agreement resolve this dispute?

OBJ. 2
✔ a. Richards, $85,200

EX 12-7 Dividing LLC income

Joshua Richards and Taylor Clark formed a limited liability company with an operating agreement that provided a salary allowance of $60,000 and $50,000 to each member, respectively. In addition, the operating agreement specified an income-sharing ratio of 3:2. The two members withdrew amounts equal to their salary allowances.

a. Determine the division of $152,000 net income for the year.

b. Provide journal entries to close the (1) income summary and (2) drawing accounts for the two members.

c. If the net income were less than the sum of the salary allowances, how would income be divided between the two members of the LLC?

OBJ. 2, 5
✔ a. Nelson, $269,890

EX 12-8 Dividing LLC net income and statement of members' equity

Macro Media, LLC, has three members: WLKT Partners, Amanda Nelson, and Daily Sentinel Newspaper, LLC. On January 1, 2012, the three members had equity of $250,000, $50,000, and $140,000, respectively. WLKT Partners contributed an additional $50,000 to Macro Media, LLC, on June 1, 2012. Amanda Nelson received an annual salary allowance of $88,700 during 2012. The members' equity accounts are also credited with 10% interest on each member's January 1 capital balance. Any remaining income is to be shared in the ratio of 4:3:3 among the three members. The net income for Macro Media, LLC, for 2012 was $720,000. Amounts equal to the salary and interest allowances were withdrawn by the members.

a. Determine the division of income among the three members.
b. Prepare the journal entry to close the net income and withdrawals to the individual member equity accounts.
c. Prepare a statement of members' equity for 2012.
d. What are the advantages of an income-sharing agreement for the members of this LLC?

OBJ. 2

EX 12-9 Partner income and withdrawal journal entries

The notes to the annual report for KPMG LLP (U.K.) indicated the following policies regarding the partners' capital:

> *The allocation of profits to those who were partners during the financial year occurs following the finalization of the annual financial statements. During the year, partners receive monthly drawings and, from time to time, additional profit distributions. Both the monthly drawings and profit distributions represent payments on account of current-year profits and are reclaimable from partners until profits have been allocated.*

Assume that the partners draw £40 million per month for 2012 and the net income for the year is £600 million. Journalize the partner capital and partner drawing control accounts in the following requirements:

a. Provide the journal entry for the monthly partner drawing for January.
b. Provide the journal entry to close the income summary account at the end of the year.
c. Provide the journal entry to close the drawing account at the end of the year.
d. Why would partner drawings be considered "reclaimable" until profits have been allocated?

OBJ. 3

EX 12-10 Admitting new partners

Lily Yuan and Kayla Dunn are partners who share in the income equally and have capital balances of $180,000 and $62,500, respectively. Yuan, with the consent of Dunn, sells one-third of her interest to Rachel Burnett. What entry is required by the partnership if the sales price is (a) $40,000? (b) $80,000?

OBJ. 3

✔ b. Faber, $120,000

EX 12-11 Admitting new partners who buy an interest and contribute assets

The capital accounts of Jonathan Faber and Faheem Ahmad have balances of $150,000 and $110,000, respectively. Lauren Wells and Rachel Lee are to be admitted to the partnership. Wells buys one-fifth of Faber's interest for $35,000 and one-fourth of Ahmad's interest for $25,000. Lee contributes $70,000 cash to the partnership, for which she is to receive an ownership equity of $70,000.

a. Journalize the entries to record the admission of (1) Wells and (2) Lee.
b. What are the capital balances of each partner after the admission of the new partners?

OBJ. 3

✔ b. Rivas, $65,000

EX 12-12 Admitting new partner who contributes assets

After the tangible assets have been adjusted to current market prices, the capital accounts of Brandon Newman and Latrell Osbourne have balances of $75,000 and $125,000, respectively. Juan Rivas is to be admitted to the partnership, contributing $50,000 cash to the partnership, for which he is to receive an ownership equity of $65,000. All partners share equally in income.

a. Journalize the entry to record the admission of Rivas, who is to receive a bonus of $15,000.
b. What are the capital balances of each partner after the admission of the new partner?
c. Why are tangible assets adjusted to current market prices, prior to admitting a new partner?

OBJ. 3

EX 12-13 Admitting new partner with bonus

Andrew Hall and Brian Li formed a partnership to provide landscaping services. Hall and Li shared profits and losses equally. After all the tangible assets have been adjusted to current market prices, the capital accounts of Andrew Hall and Brian Li have balances of $54,000 and $71,000, respectively. Kristin Lane has expertise with using the computer to prepare landscape designs, cost estimates, and renderings. Hall and Li deem these skills useful; thus, Lane is admitted to the partnership at a 30% interest for a purchase price of $35,000.

a. Determine the recipient and amount of the partner bonus.

b. Provide the journal entry to admit Lane into the partnership.

c. Why would a bonus be paid in this situation?

OBJ. 3

✔ b. (2) Bonus paid to Mann, $15,000

EX 12-14 Admitting a new LLC member with bonus

HealthSource, LLC, consists of two doctors, Drew and Moore, who share in all income and losses according to a 2:3 income-sharing ratio. Dr. Mann has been asked to join the LLC. Prior to admitting Mann, the assets of HealthSource were revalued to reflect their current market values. The revaluation resulted in medical equipment being increased by $35,000. Prior to the revaluation, the equity balances for Drew and Moore were $201,000 and $289,000, respectively.

a. Provide the journal entry for the asset revaluation.

b. Provide the journal entry for the bonus under the following independent situations:

1. Mann purchased a 30% interest in HealthSource, LLC, for $285,000.
2. Mann purchased a 25% interest in HealthSource, LLC, for $155,000.

OBJ. 3

✔ b. (1) Bonus paid to Jenkins, $11,000

EX 12-15 Admitting new partner with bonus

J. Witt and K. Torres are partners in Whole Earth Consultants. Witt and Torres share income equally. L. Jenkins will be admitted to the partnership. Prior to the admission, equipment was revalued downward by $12,000. The capital balances of each partner are $106,000 and $141,000, respectively, prior to the revaluation.

a. Provide the journal entry for the asset revaluation.

b. Provide the journal entry for Jenkins' admission under the following independent situations:

1. Jenkins purchased a 20% interest for $45,000.
2. Jenkins purchased a 30% interest for $135,000.

OBJ. 2, 3, 5

✔ Wilson capital, Dec. 31, 2012, $191,700

EX 12-16 Partner bonuses, statement of partners' equity

The partnership of Angel Investor Associates began operations on January 1, 2012, with contributions from two partners as follows:

Scott Wilson	$120,000
Michael Goforth	80,000

The following additional partner transactions took place during the year:

1. In early January, Lance McGinnis is admitted to the partnership by contributing $50,000 cash for a 20% interest.
2. Net income of $250,000 was earned in 2012. In addition, Scott Wilson received a salary allowance of $45,000 for the year. The three partners agree to an income-sharing ratio equal to their capital balances after admitting McGinnis.
3. The partners' withdrawals are equal to half of the increase in their capital balances from salary allowance and income.

Prepare a statement of partnership equity for the year ended December 31, 2012.

OBJ. 3

EX 12-17 Withdrawal of partner

David Winner is to retire from the partnership of Winner and Associates as of March 31, the end of the current fiscal year. After closing the accounts, the capital balances of the partners are as follows: David Winner, $210,000; Alexis Richards, $125,000; and Marcus Williams, $140,000. They have shared net income and net losses in the ratio of 3:2:2. The partners agree that the merchandise inventory should be increased by $32,000, and the allowance for doubtful accounts should be increased by $4,000. Winner agrees to accept a note for $150,000 in partial settlement of his ownership equity. The remainder of his claim is to be paid in cash. Richards and Williams are to share equally in the net income or net loss of the new partnership.

Journalize the entries to record (a) the adjustment of the assets to bring them into agreement with current market prices and (b) the withdrawal of Winner from the partnership.

OBJ. 2, 3, 5

✔ a. 2:3

EX 12-18 Statement of members' equity, admitting new member

The statement of members' equity for Bonanza, LLC, is shown below.

Bonanza, LLC
Statement of Members' Equity
For the Years Ended December 31, 2012 and 2013

	Idaho Properties, LLC, Member Equity	Silver Holdings, LLC, Member Equity	Justin Thomas Member Equity	Total Members' Equity
Members' equity, December 31, 2011	$552,000	$420,500		$ 972,500
Net income	128,000	192,000		320,000
Members' equity, December 31, 2012	$680,000	$612,500		$1,292,500
Thomas contribution, January 1, 2013	8,000	12,000	$250,000	270,000
Net income	90,000	225,000	135,000	450,000
Less member withdrawals	(32,000)	(48,000)	(50,000)	(130,000)
Members' equity, December 31, 2013	$746,000	$801,500	$335,000	$1,882,500

a. What was the income-sharing ratio in 2012?
b. What was the income-sharing ratio in 2013?
c. How much cash did Justin Thomas contribute to Bonanza, LLC, for his interest?
d. Why do the member equity accounts of Idaho Properties, LLC, and Silver Holdings, LLC, have positive entries for Justin Thomas' contribution?
e. What percentage interest of Bonanza did Justin Thomas acquire?
f. Why are withdrawals less than net income?

OBJ. 4

✔ a. $6,000 loss

EX 12-19 Distribution of cash upon liquidation

Lyle and Fisher are partners, sharing gains and losses equally. They decide to terminate their partnership. Prior to realization, their capital balances are $15,000 and $7,000, respectively. After all noncash assets are sold and all liabilities are paid, there is a cash balance of $16,000.

a. What is the amount of a gain or loss on realization?
b. How should the gain or loss be divided between Lyle and Fisher?
c. How should the cash be divided between Lyle and Fisher?

OBJ. 4

✔ Mason, $40,000

EX 12-20 Distribution of cash upon liquidation

Daniel Mason and Srini Kumar, with capital balances of $34,000 and $36,000, respectively, decide to liquidate their partnership. After selling the noncash assets and paying the liabilities, there is $82,000 of cash remaining. If the partners share income and losses equally, how should the cash be distributed?

OBJ. 4
✔ b. $79,500

EX 12-21 Liquidating partnerships—capital deficiency

Gifford, Lawrence, and Ma share equally in net income and net losses. After the partnership sells all assets for cash, divides the losses on realization, and pays the liabilities, the balances in the capital accounts are as follows: Gifford, $32,000 Cr.; Lawrence, $62,500 Cr.; Ma, $15,000 Dr.

a. What term is applied to the debit balance in Ma's capital account?

b. What is the amount of cash on hand?

c. Journalize the transaction that must take place for Gifford and Lawrence to receive cash in the liquidation process equal to their capital account balances.

OBJ. 4
✔ a. Deacon, $650

EX 12-22 Distribution of cash upon liquidation

Deacon, Raines, and Francis arranged to import and sell orchid corsages for a university dance. They agreed to share equally the net income or net loss of the venture. Deacon and Raines advanced $300 and $450 of their own respective funds to pay for advertising and other expenses. After collecting for all sales and paying creditors, the partnership has $1,800 in cash.

a. How should the money be distributed?

b. Assuming that the partnership has only $600 instead of $1,800, do any of the three partners have a capital deficiency? If so, how much?

OBJ. 4

EX 12-23 Liquidating partnerships—capital deficiency

Arnold, Peters, and Suzuki are partners sharing income 3:2:1. After the firm's loss from liquidation is distributed, the capital account balances were: Arnold, $18,000 Dr.; Peters, $75,000 Cr.; and Suzuki, $55,000 Cr. If Arnold is personally bankrupt and unable to pay any of the $18,000, what will be the amount of cash received by Peters and Suzuki upon liquidation?

OBJ. 4

EX 12-24 Statement of partnership liquidation

After closing the accounts on July 1, prior to liquidating the partnership, the capital account balances of Jessup, King, and Oliver are $70,000, $43,000, and $22,000, respectively. Cash, noncash assets, and liabilities total $62,000, $108,000, and $35,000, respectively. Between July 1 and July 29, the noncash assets are sold for $90,000, the liabilities are paid, and the remaining cash is distributed to the partners. The partners share net income and loss in the ratio of 3:2:1. Prepare a statement of partnership liquidation for the period July 1–29, 2012.

OBJ. 4

EX 12-25 Statement of LLC liquidation

Hall, Lang, and Das are members of Evergreen Sales, LLC, sharing income and losses in the ratio of 2:2:1, respectively. The members decide to liquidate the limited liability company. The members' equity prior to liquidation and asset realization on May 1, 2012, are as follows:

Hall	$37,000
Lang	40,000
Das	18,000
Total	$95,000

In winding up operations during the month of May, noncash assets with a book value of $107,000 are sold for $123,000, and liabilities of $25,000 are satisfied. Prior to realization, Evergreen Sales has a cash balance of $13,000.

a. Prepare a statement of LLC liquidation.

b. Provide the journal entry for the final cash distribution to members.

c. What is the role of the income- and loss-sharing ratio in liquidating a LLC?

OBJ. 2, 5

✔ b. Menendez, Capital, Dec. 31, $89,000

EX 12-26 Partnership entries and statement of partners' equity

The capital accounts of Gary Menendez and Melissa Breeden have balances of $75,000 and $55,000, respectively, on January 1, 2012, the beginning of the current fiscal year. On April 10, Menendez invested an additional $12,000. During the year, Menendez and Breeden withdrew $44,000 and $35,000, respectively, and net income for the year was $92,000. The articles of partnership make no reference to the division of net income.

a. Journalize the entries to close (1) the income summary account and (2) the drawing accounts.

b. Prepare a statement of partners' equity for the current year for the partnership of Menendez and Breeden.

OBJ. 6

EX 12-27 Revenue per professional staff

The accounting firm of Deloitte & Touche is the largest international accounting firm in the world as ranked by total revenues. For the last two years, Deloitte & Touche reported the following for its U.S. operations:

	2009	2008
Revenue (in billions)	$26.1	$27.4
Number of professional staff (including partners)	139,760	133,100

a. For 2009 and 2008, determine the revenue per professional staff. Round to the nearest thousand dollars.

b. Interpret the trend between the two years.

OBJ. 6

EX 12-28 Revenue per employee

Commerical Cleaning Services, LLC, provides cleaning services for office buildings. The firm has 10 members in the LLC, which did not change between 2012 and 2013. During 2013, the business terminated two commercial contracts. The following revenue and employee information is provided:

	2013	2012
Revenues (in thousands)	$20,000	$22,400
Number of employees (excluding members)	160	200

a. For 2013 and 2012, determine the revenue per employee (excluding members).

b. Interpret the trend between the two years.

Problems Series A

OBJ. 2

✔ 3. Cole net income, $47,200

PR 12-1A Entries and balance sheet for partnership

On August 1, 2012, Wardell Cole and Marva Landers form a partnership. Cole agrees to invest $15,600 in cash and merchandise inventory valued at $62,400. Landers invests certain business assets at valuations agreed upon, transfers business liabilities, and contributes sufficient cash to bring her total capital to $60,000. Details regarding the book values of the business assets and liabilities, and the agreed valuations, follow:

	Landers' Ledger Balance	Agreed-Upon Valuation
Accounts Receivable	$25,300	$23,700
Allowance for Doubtful Accounts	1,500	1,900
Equipment	92,300	57,900
Accumulated Depreciation—Equipment	35,600	
Accounts Payable	20,000	20,000
Notes Payable	30,000	30,000

The partnership agreement includes the following provisions regarding the division of net income: interest on original investments at 10%, salary allowances of $22,500 (Cole) and $30,400 (Landers), and the remainder equally.

Instructions

1. Journalize the entries to record the investments of Cole and Landers in the partnership accounts.
2. Prepare a balance sheet as of August 1, 2012, the date of formation of the partnership of Cole and Landers.
3. After adjustments and the closing of revenue and expense accounts at July 31, 2013, the end of the first full year of operations, the income summary account has a credit balance of $100,500, and the drawing accounts have debit balances of $25,000 (Cole) and $30,400 (Landers). Journalize the entries to close the income summary account and the drawing accounts at July 31, 2013.

OBJ. 2

✔ 1. f. Dyer net income, $41,600

PR 12-2A Dividing partnership income

Dyer and Salinas have decided to form a partnership. They have agreed that Dyer is to invest $120,000 and that Salinas is to invest $40,000. Dyer is to devote one-half time to the business and Salinas is to devote full time. The following plans for the division of income are being considered:

a. Equal division.
b. In the ratio of original investments.
c. In the ratio of time devoted to the business.
d. Interest of 12% on original investments and the remainder equally.
e. Interest of 12% on original investments, salary allowances of $32,000 to Dyer and $64,000 to Salinas, and the remainder equally.
f. Plan (e), except that Salinas is also to be allowed a bonus equal to 20% of the amount by which net income exceeds the total salary allowances.

Instructions

For each plan, determine the division of the net income under each of the following assumptions: (1) net income of $108,000 and (2) net income of $150,000. Present the data in tabular form, using the following columnar headings:

	$108,000		$150,000	
Plan	**Dyer**	**Salinas**	**Dyer**	**Salinas**

OBJ. 2, 5

✔ 2. Dec. 31 capital—Adkins, $85,000

PR 12-3A Financial statements for partnership

The ledger of Aiden Durant and Jasmine Adkins, attorneys-at-law, contains the following accounts and balances after adjustments have been recorded on December 31, 2012:

Aiden, Durant, Adkins
Trial Balance
December 31, 2012

	Debit Balances	Credit Balances
Cash	42,000	
Accounts Receivable	42,300	
Supplies	1,500	
Land	100,000	
Building	108,100	
Accumulated Depreciation—Building		62,500
Office Equipment	46,000	
Accumulated Depreciation—Office Equipment		19,400
Accounts Payable		29,800
Salaries Payable		3,200
Aiden Durant, Capital		100,000
Aiden Durant, Drawing	45,000	

Jasmine Adkins, Capital		60,000
Jasmine Adkins, Drawing	65,000	
Professional Fees		364,500
Salary Expense	146,000	
Depreciation Expense—Building	14,500	
Property Tax Expense	9,000	
Heating and Lighting Expense	7,200	
Supplies Expense	5,200	
Depreciation Expense—Office Equipment	4,500	
Miscellaneous Expense	3,100	
	639,400	639,400

The balance in Adkins' capital account includes an additional investment of $10,000 made on August 10, 2012.

Instructions

1. Prepare an income statement for 2012, indicating the division of net income. The articles of partnership provide for salary allowances of $40,000 to Durant and $50,000 to Adkins, allowances of 10% on each partner's capital balance at the beginning of the fiscal year, and equal division of the remaining net income or net loss.
2. Prepare a statement of partners' equity for 2012.
3. Prepare a balance sheet as of the end of 2012.

OBJ. 3

✔ 3. Total assets, $282,500

PR 12-4A Admitting new partner

Tosio Kato and Angela Gordon have operated a successful firm for many years, sharing net income and net losses equally. Tricia McCay is to be admitted to the partnership on May 1 of the current year, in accordance with the following agreement:

a. Assets and liabilities of the old partnership are to be valued at their book values as of April 30, except for the following:
   - Accounts receivable amounting to $2,400 are to be written off, and the allowance for doubtful accounts is to be increased to 5% of the remaining accounts.
   - Merchandise inventory is to be valued at $63,200.
   - Equipment is to be valued at $141,900.

b. McCay is to purchase $60,000 of the ownership interest of Gordon for $65,000 cash and to contribute another $35,000 cash to the partnership for a total ownership equity of $95,000.

The post-closing trial balance of Kato and Gordon as of April 30 is as follows:

Kato and Gordon
Post-Closing Trial Balance
April 30, 2012

	Debit Balances	Credit Balances
Cash	6,000	
Accounts Receivable	38,400	
Allowance for Doubtful Accounts		1,400
Merchandise Inventory	59,000	
Prepaid Insurance	2,200	
Equipment	165,000	
Accumulated Depreciation—Equipment		51,700
Accounts Payable		9,500
Notes Payable		40,000
Tosio Kato, Capital		90,000
Angela Gordon, Capital		78,000
	270,600	270,600

Instructions

1. Journalize the entries as of April 30 to record the revaluations, using a temporary account entitled Asset Revaluations. The balance in the accumulated depreciation account is to be eliminated. After journalizing the revaluations, close the balance of the asset revaluations account to the capital accounts of Tosio Kato and Angela Gordon.
2. Journalize the additional entries to record McCay's entrance to the partnership on May 1, 2012.
3. Present a balance sheet for the new partnership as of May 1, 2012.

OBJ. 4

PR 12-5A Statement of partnership liquidation

After the accounts are closed on July 3, 2012, prior to liquidating the partnership, the capital accounts of Rebecca Adams, Austin Cooper, and Ricardo Ruiz are $22,400, $5,300, and $31,900, respectively. Cash and noncash assets total $8,800 and $68,800, respectively. Amounts owed to creditors total $18,000. The partners share income and losses in the ratio of 2:1:1. Between July 3 and July 29, the noncash assets are sold for $33,200, the partner with the capital deficiency pays his deficiency to the partnership, and the liabilities are paid.

Instructions

1. Prepare a statement of partnership liquidation, indicating (a) the sale of assets and division of loss, (b) the payment of liabilities, (c) the receipt of the deficiency (from the appropriate partner), and (d) the distribution of cash.
2. Assume the partner with the capital deficiency declares bankruptcy and is unable to pay the deficiency. Journalize the entries to (a) allocate the partner's deficiency and (b) distribute the remaining cash.

OBJ. 4

PR 12-6A Statement of partnership liquidation

On October 1, 2012, the firm of Sams, Price, and Ladd decided to liquidate their partnership. The partners have capital balances of $54,000, $77,000, and $12,000, respectively. The cash balance is $26,000, the book values of noncash assets total $155,000, and liabilities total $38,000. The partners share income and losses in the ratio of 2:2:1.

Instructions

1. Prepare a statement of partnership liquidation, covering the period October 1–30 2012, for each of the following independent assumptions:
   a. All of the noncash assets are sold for $212,000 in cash, the creditors are paid, and the remaining cash is distributed to the partners.
   b. All of the noncash assets are sold for $70,000 in cash, the creditors are paid, the partner with the debit capital balance pays the amount owed to the firm, and the remaining cash is distributed to the partners.
2. Assume the partner with the capital deficiency in part (b) above declares bankruptcy and is unable to pay the deficiency. Journalize the entries to (a) allocate the partner's deficiency and (b) distribute the remaining cash.

Problems Series B

OBJ. 2

✔ 3. Harber net income, $56,900

PR 12-1B Entries and balance sheet for partnership

On June 1, 2011, Anne Harber and Heather Lamb form a partnership. Harber agrees to invest $16,000 cash and merchandise inventory valued at $42,000. Lamb invests certain business assets at valuations agreed upon, transfers business liabilities, and contributes sufficient cash to bring her total capital to $80,000. Details regarding the book values of the business assets and liabilities, and the agreed valuations, follow:

	Lamb's Ledger Balance	Agreed-Upon Balance
Accounts Receivable	$21,400	$19,400
Allowance for Doubtful Accounts	1,000	1,300
Merchandise Inventory	24,300	25,900
Equipment	44,000	34,000
Accumulated Depreciation—Equipment	14,000	
Accounts Payable	7,000	7,000
Notes Payable	5,000	5,000

The partnership agreement includes the following provisions regarding the division of net income: interest of 10% on original investments, salary allowances of $36,000 (Harber) and $22,000 (Lamb), and the remainder equally.

Instructions

1. Journalize the entries to record the investments of Harber and Lamb in the partnership accounts.
2. Prepare a balance sheet as of June 1, 2011, the date of formation of the partnership of Harber and Lamb.
3. After adjustments and the closing of revenue and expense accounts at May 31, 2012, the end of the first full year of operations, the income summary account has a credit balance of $102,000, and the drawing accounts have debit balances of $40,000 (Harber) and $25,000 (Lamb). Journalize the entries to close the income summary account and the drawing accounts at May 31, 2012.

OBJ. 2

✔ 1. f. Snyder net income, $128,900

PR 12-2B Dividing partnership income

Tim Snyder and Jay Wise have decided to form a partnership. They have agreed that Snyder is to invest $30,000 and that Wise is to invest $40,000. Snyder is to devote full time to the business, and Wise is to devote one-half time. The following plans for the division of income are being considered:

a. Equal division.

b. In the ratio of original investments.

c. In the ratio of time devoted to the business.

d. Interest of 10% on original investments and the remainder in the ratio of 3:2.

e. Interest of 10% on original investments, salary allowances of $34,000 to Snyder and $17,000 to Wise, and the remainder equally.

f. Plan (e), except that Snyder is also to be allowed a bonus equal to 20% of the amount by which net income exceeds the total salary allowances.

Instructions

For each plan, determine the division of the net income under each of the following assumptions: (1) net income of $210,000 and (2) net income of $84,000. Present the data in tabular form, using the following columnar headings:

	$210,000		$84,000	
Plan	Snyder	Wise	Snyder	Wise

OBJ. 2, 5

✔ 2. Dec. 31 capital—Hoffman, $201,200

PR 12-3B Financial statements for partnerships

The ledger of Jin Ding and Paul Hoffman, attorneys-at-law, contains the following accounts and balances after adjustments have been recorded on December 31, 2012:

Ding and Hoffman
Trial Balance
December 31, 2012

	Debit Balances	Credit Balances
Cash	26,900	
Accounts Receivable	41,300	
Supplies	6,700	
Land	140,000	
Building	160,000	
Accumulated Depreciation—Building		52,000
Office Equipment	62,000	
Accumulated Depreciation—Office Equipment		21,300
Accounts Payable		3,400
Salaries Payable		5,200
Jin Ding, Capital		130,000
Jin Ding, Drawing	50,000	
Paul Hoffman, Capital		170,000
Paul Hoffman, Drawing	60,000	
Professional Fees		583,200
Salary Expense	315,700	
Depreciation Expense—Building	75,000	
Heating and Lighting Expense	11,900	
Depreciation Expense—Office Equipment	6,700	
Property Tax Expense	3,500	
Supplies Expense	3,400	
Miscellaneous Expense	2,000	
	965,100	965,100

The balance in Hoffman's capital account includes an additional investment of $20,000 made on April 5, 2012.

Instructions

1. Prepare an income statement for the current fiscal year, indicating the division of net income. The articles of partnership provide for salary allowances of $60,000 to Ding and $75,000 to Hoffman, allowances of 12% on each partner's capital balance at the beginning of the fiscal year, and equal division of the remaining net income or net loss.
2. Prepare a statement of partners' equity for 2012.
3. Prepare a balance sheet as of the end of 2012.

OBJ. 3

✔ 3. Total assets, $227,300

PR 12-4B Admitting new partner

Anthony Simpson and Shawna Ryder have operated a successful firm for many years, sharing net income and net losses equally. Blaine Evans is to be admitted to the partnership on June 1 of the current year, in accordance with the following agreement:

a. Assets and liabilities of the old partnership are to be valued at their book values as of May 31, except for the following:
   - Accounts receivable amounting to $3,400 are to be written off, and the allowance for doubtful accounts is to be increased to 5% of the remaining accounts.
   - Merchandise inventory is to be valued at $64,300.
   - Equipment is to be valued at $88,000.

b. Evans is to purchase $32,000 of the ownership interest of Ryder for $37,500 cash and to contribute $40,000 cash to the partnership for a total ownership equity of $72,000.

The post-closing trial balance of Simpson and Ryder as of May 31 follows.

Simpson and Ryder
Post-Closing Trial Balance
May 31, 2012

	Debit Balances	Credit Balances
Cash	14,400	
Accounts Receivable	21,400	
Allowance for Doubtful Accounts		500
Merchandise Inventory	58,600	
Prepaid Insurance	3,500	
Equipment	97,000	
Accumulated Depreciation—Equipment		25,700
Accounts Payable		14,700
Notes Payable		12,000
Anthony Simpson, Capital		80,000
Shawna Ryder, Capital		62,000
	194,900	194,900

Instructions

1. Journalize the entries as of May 31 to record the revaluations, using a temporary account entitled Asset Revaluations. The balance in the accumulated depreciation account is to be eliminated. After journalizing the revaluations, close the balance of the asset revaluations account to the capital accounts of Anthony Simpson and Shawna Ryder.
2. Journalize the additional entries to record Evans' entrance to the partnership on May 31, 2012.
3. Present a balance sheet for the new partnership as of June 1, 2012.

OBJ. 4

PR 12-5B Statement of partnership liquidation

After the accounts are closed on September 10, 2012, prior to liquidating the partnership, the capital accounts of Randy Campbell, Ken Thayer, and Linda Tipton are $38,000, $6,400, and $28,500, respectively. Cash and noncash assets total $17,700 and $64,200, respectively. Amounts owed to creditors total $9,000. The partners share income and losses in the ratio of 1:1:2. Between September 10 and September 30, the noncash assets are sold for $35,000, the partner with the capital deficiency pays his or her deficiency to the partnership, and the liabilities are paid.

Instructions

1. Prepare a statement of partnership liquidation, indicating (a) the sale of assets and division of loss, (b) the payment of liabilities, (c) the receipt of the deficiency (from the appropriate partner), and (d) the distribution of cash.
2. Assume the partner with the capital deficiency declares bankruptcy and is unable to pay the deficiency. Journalize the entries to (a) allocate the partner's deficiency and (b) distribute the remaining cash.

OBJ. 4

PR 12-6B Statement of partnership liquidation

On June 3, 2012, the firm of Lyon, Malone, and Chen decided to liquidate their partnership. The partners have capital balances of $12,000, $76,000, and $104,000, respectively. The cash balance is $19,000, the book values of noncash assets total $218,000, and liabilities total $45,000. The partners share income and losses in the ratio of 1:2:2.

Instructions

1. Prepare a statement of partnership liquidation, covering the period June 3–29, 2012, for each of the following independent assumptions:
   a. All of the noncash assets are sold for $272,000 in cash, the creditors are paid, and the remaining cash is distributed to the partners.
   b. All of the noncash assets are sold for $105,000 in cash, the creditors are paid, the partner with the debit capital balance pays the amount owed to the firm, and the remaining cash is distributed to the partners.
2. Assume the partner with the capital deficiency in part (b) above declares bankruptcy and is unable to pay the deficiency. Journalize the entries to (a) allocate the partner's deficiency and (b) distribute the remaining cash.

Cases & Projects

CP 12-1 Partnership agreement

Colin Maples, M.D., and Daniel Graham, M.D., are sole owners of two medical practices that operate in the same medical building. The two doctors agree to combine assets and liabilities of the two businesses to form a partnership. The partnership agreement calls for dividing income equally between the two doctors. After several months, the following conversation takes place between the two doctors:

Maples: I've noticed that your patient load has dropped over the last couple of months. When we formed our partnership, we were seeing about the same number of patients per week. However, now our patient records show that you have been seeing about half as many patients as I have. Are there any issues that I should be aware of?

Graham: There's nothing going on. When I was working on my own, I was really putting in the hours. One of the reasons I formed this partnership was to enjoy life a little more and scale back a little bit.

Maples: I see. Well, I find that I'm working as hard as I did when I was on my own, yet making less than I did previously. Essentially, you're sharing in half of my billings and I'm sharing in half of yours. Since you are working much less than I am, I end up on the short end of the bargain.

Graham: Well, I don't know what to say. An agreement is an agreement. The partnership is based on a 50/50 split. That's what a partnership is all about.

Maples: If that's so, then it applies equally well on the effort end of the equation as on the income end.

Discuss whether Graham is acting in an ethical manner. How could Maples renegotiate the partnership agreement to avoid this dispute?

CP 12-2 Dividing partnership income

Jerry Graves and Bonnie Moss decide to form a partnership. Graves will contribute $300,000 to the partnership, while Moss will contribute only $30,000. However, Moss will be responsible for running the day-to-day operations of the partnership, which are anticipated to require about 45 hours per week. In contrast, Graves will only work five hours per week for the partnership. The two partners are attempting to determine a formula for dividing partnership net income. Graves believes the partners should divide income in the ratio of 7:3, favoring Graves, since Graves provides the majority of the capital. Moss believes the income should be divided 7:3, favoring Moss, since Moss provides the majority of effort in running the partnership business.

How would you advise the partners in developing a method for dividing income?

CP 12-3 Revenue per employee

The following table shows key operating statistics for the four largest public accounting firms:

	U.S. Net Revenues (in millions)	No. of Partners	No. of Professional Staff
Deloitte & Touche	$10,980	2,949	32,857
Ernst & Young	8,232	2,350	20,250
PricewaterhouseCoopers	7,578	2,198	22,100
KPMG LLP	5,679	1,818	16,564

Source: The 2009 *Accounting Today* Top 100 Firms.

a. Determine the revenue per partner and revenue per professional staff for each firm. Round to the nearest dollar.

b. Interpret the differences between the firms in terms of your answer in (a) and the table information.

CP 12-4 Partnership agreement

Karen Pratt has agreed to invest $200,000 into an LLC with Jennifer Stahl and Don Keene. Stahl and Keene will not invest any money, but will provide effort and expertise to the LLC. Stahl and Keene have agreed that the net income of the LLC should be divided so that Pratt is to receive a 10% preferred return on her capital investment prior to any remaining income being divided equally among the partners. In addition, Stahl and Keene have suggested that the operating agreement be written so that all matters are settled by majority vote, with each partner having a one-third voting interest in the LLC.

If you were providing Karen Pratt counsel, what might you suggest in forming the final agreement?

CP 12-5 Information on LLC

Group Project

In an assigned group or individually (if so assigned), go to the Web site for Chrysler Group LLC at **http://www.chryslergroupllc.com.** Using this Web site and other Internet information about Chrysler Group LLC, answer the following questions:

a. Briefly describe the business of Chrysler Group LLC.

b. When was Chrysler Group LLC formed?

c. Describe the membership structure of Chrysler Group LLC.

d. Is Chrysler Group LLC a public company?

by permission of Hasbro

CHAPTER 13

Corporations: Organization, Stock Transactions, and Dividends

Hasbro

If you purchase a share of stock from **Hasbro**, you own a small interest in the company. You may request a Hasbro stock certificate as an indication of your ownership.

As you may know, Hasbro is one of the world's largest toy manufacturers and produces popular children's toys such as G.I. Joe, Play-Doh, Tonka toys, Mr. Potato Head, and NERF. In addition, Hasbro manufactures family entertainment products such as Monopoly, Scrabble, and Trivial Pursuit under the Milton Bradley and Parker Brothers labels. In fact, the stock certificate of Hasbro has a picture of Mr. Monopoly, the Monopoly game icon, printed on it.

Purchasing a share of stock from Hasbro may be a great gift idea for the "hard-to-shop-for person." However, a stock certificate represents more than just a picture that you can frame. In fact, the stock certificate is a document that reflects legal ownership of the future financial prospects of Hasbro. In addition, as a shareholder, it represents your claim against the assets and earnings of the corporation.

If you are purchasing Hasbro stock as an investment, you should analyze Hasbro's financial statements and management's plans for the future. For example, Hasbro has a unique relationship with Disney that allows it to produce and sell licensed Disney products. Should this Disney relationship affect how much you are willing to pay for the stock? Also, you might want to know if Hasbro plans to pay cash dividends or whether management is considering issuing additional shares of stock.

This chapter describes and illustrates the nature of corporations including the accounting for stock and dividends. This discussion will aid you in making decisions such as whether or not to buy Hasbro stock.

Learning Objectives

After studying this chapter, you should be able to:

At a Glance 13 Page 602

OBJ. 1 Describe the nature of the corporate form of organization.

Nature of a Corporation

Most large businesses are organized as corporations. As a result, corporations generate more than 90% of the total business dollars in the United States. In contrast, most small businesses are organized as proprietorships, partnerships, or limited liability companies.

Characteristics of a Corporation

A corporation was defined in the Dartmouth College case of 1819, in which Chief Justice Marshall of the U.S. Supreme Court stated: "A corporation is an artificial being, invisible, intangible, and existing only in contemplation of the law."

A *corporation* is a legal entity, distinct and separate from the individuals who create and operate it. As a legal entity, a corporation may acquire, own, and dispose of property in its own name. It may also incur liabilities and enter into contracts. Most importantly, it can sell shares of ownership, called **stock**. This characteristic gives corporations the ability to raise large amounts of capital.

The **stockholders** or *shareholders* who own the stock own the corporation. They can buy and sell stock without affecting the corporation's operations or continued existence. Corporations whose shares of stock are traded in public markets are called *public corporations*. Corporations whose shares are not traded publicly are usually owned by a small group of investors and are called *nonpublic* or *private corporations*.

The stockholders of a corporation have *limited liability*. This means that creditors usually may not go beyond the assets of the corporation to satisfy their claims. Thus, the financial loss that a stockholder may suffer is limited to the amount invested.

The stockholders control a corporation by electing a *board of directors*. This board meets periodically to establish corporate policies. It also selects the chief executive officer (CEO) and other major officers to manage the corporation's day-to-day affairs. Exhibit 1 shows the organizational structure of a corporation.

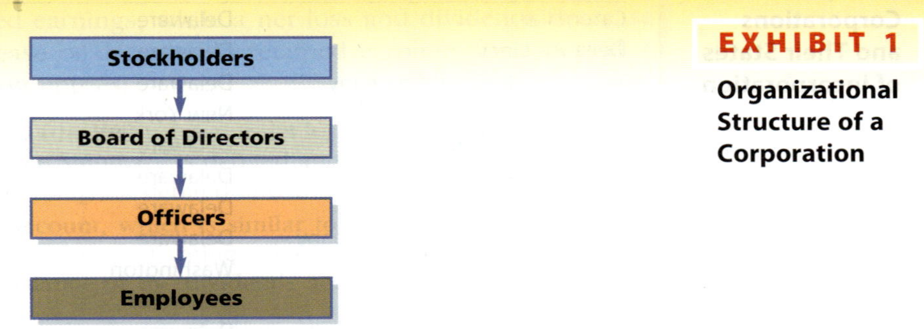

EXHIBIT 1

Organizational Structure of a Corporation

As a separate entity, a corporation is subject to taxes. For example, corporations must pay federal income taxes on their income.[1] Thus, corporate income that is distributed to stockholders in the form of *dividends* has already been taxed. In turn, stockholders must pay income taxes on the dividends they receive. This *double taxation* of corporate earnings is a major disadvantage of the corporate form. The advantages and disadvantages of the corporate form are listed in Exhibit 2.

Note: Corporations have a separate legal existence, transferable units of ownership, and limited stockholder liability.

EXHIBIT 2 **Advantages and Disadvantages of the Corporate Form**

Advantages	Explanation
Separate legal existence	A corporation exists separately from its owners.
Continuous life	A corporation's life is separate from its owners; therefore, it exists indefinitely.
Raising large amounts of capital	The corporate form is suited for raising large amounts of money from shareholders.
Ownership rights are easily transferable	A corporation sells shares of ownership, called *stock*. The stockholders of a public company can transfer their shares of stock to other stockholders through stock markets, such as the New York Stock Exchange.
Limited liability	A corporation's creditors usually may not go beyond the assets of the corporation to satisfy their claims. Thus, the financial loss that a stockholder may suffer is limited to the amount invested.
Disadvantages	**Explanation**
Owner is separate from management	Stockholders control management through a board of directors. The board of directors should represent shareholder interests; however, the board is often more closely tied to management than to shareholders. As a result, the board of directors and management may not always behave in the best interests of stockholders.
Double taxation of dividends	As a separate legal entity, a corporation is subject to taxation. Thus, net income distributed as dividends will be taxed once at the corporation level, and then again at the individual level.
Regulatory costs	Corporations must satisfy many requirements such as those required by the Sarbanes-Oxley Act of 2002.

Forming a Corporation

The first step in forming a corporation is to file an *application of incorporation* with the state. State incorporation laws differ, and corporations often organize in those states with the more favorable laws. For this reason, more than half of the largest companies are incorporated in Delaware. Exhibit 3 lists some corporations, their states of incorporation, and the location of their headquarters.

After the application of incorporation has been approved, the state grants a *charter* or *articles of incorporation*. The articles of incorporation formally create the corporation.[2]

1 A majority of states also require corporations to pay income taxes.

2 The articles of incorporation may also restrict a corporation's activities in certain areas, such as owning certain types of real estate, conducting certain types of business activities, or purchasing its own stock.

When only one class of stock is issued, it is called common stock. Each share of common stock has equal rights.

CHAPTER 14

der Armour®/PRNewsFoto/AP Photos Publicity

Long-Term Liabilities: Bonds and Notes

Under Armour®

Most of us don't have enough money in our bank accounts to buy a house or a car by simply writing a check. Just imagine if you had to save the entire purchase price of a house before you could buy it! To help us make these types of purchases, banks will typically lend us the money, as long as we agree to repay the loan with interest in smaller future payments. Loans such as this, or long-term debt, allow us to purchase assets such as houses and cars today, which benefit us over the long term.

The use of debt can also help a business reach its objectives. Most businesses have to borrow money in order to acquire assets that they will use to generate income. For example, **Under Armour®**, a maker of performance athletic clothing, uses debt to acquire assets that it needs to manufacture and sell its products. Since it began in 1995, the company has used long-term debt to transform itself from a small business to a leading athletic wear company. The company now sells products in over 8,000 retail stores across the world. In addition, Under Armour® products are used by a number of teams in the National Football League, Major League Baseball, the National Hockey League, and in Olympic sports.

While debt can help companies like Under Armour® grow to achieve financial success, too much debt can be a financial burden that may even lead to bankruptcy. Just like individuals, businesses must manage debt wisely. In this chapter, we will discuss the nature of, accounting for, analysis of, and investments in long-term debt.

Learning Objectives

After studying this chapter, you should be able to:

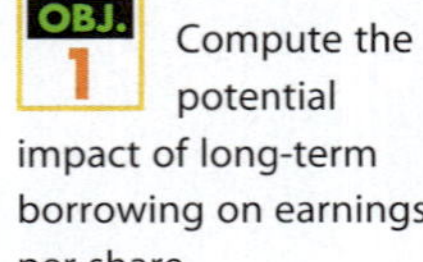

Compute the potential impact of long-term borrowing on earnings per share.

Financing Corporations

Corporations finance their operations using the following sources:

1. Short-term debt, such as purchasing goods or services on account.
2. Long-term debt, such as issuing bonds or notes payable.
3. Equity, such as issuing common or preferred stock.

Short-term debt including the purchase of goods and services on account and the issuance of short-term notes payable was discussed in Chapter 11, while issuing equity in the form of common or preferred stock was discussed in Chapter 13. This chapter focuses on the use of long-term debt such as bonds and notes payable to finance a company's operations.

A **bond** is a form of an interest-bearing note. Like a note, a bond requires periodic interest payments with the face amount to be repaid at the maturity date. As creditors of the corporation, bondholder claims on the corporation's assets rank ahead of stockholders.

To illustrate the effects of long-term financing, assume Huckadee Corporation is considering the following plans to issue debt and equity:

	Plan 1		Plan 2		Plan 3	
	Amount	Percent	Amount	Percent	Amount	Percent
Issue 12% bonds	—	0%	—	0%	$2,000,000	50%
Issue 9% preferred stock, $50 par value	—	0	$2,000,000	50	1,000,000	25
Issue common stock, $10 par value	$4,000,000	100	2,000,000	50	1,000,000	25
Total amount of financing	$4,000,000	100%	$4,000,000	100%	$4,000,000	100%

Each of the preceding plans finances some of the corporation's operations by issuing common stock. However, the percentage financed by common stock varies from 100% (Plan 1) to 25% (Plan 3). In deciding among financing plans, the effect on earnings per share is often considered.

Earnings per share (EPS) measures the income earned by each share of common stock. It is computed as follows:[1]

$$\text{Earnings per Share} = \frac{\text{Net Income} - \text{Preferred Dividends}}{\text{Number of Common Shares Outstanding}}$$

To illustrate, assume the following data for Huckadee Corporation:

1. Earnings before interest and income taxes are $800,000.
2. The tax rate is 40%.
3. All bonds or stocks are issued at their par or face amount.

The effect of the preceding financing plans on Huckadee's net income and earnings per share is shown in Exhibit 1.

EXHIBIT 1

Effect of Alternative Financing Plans—$800,000 Earnings

	Plan 1	Plan 2	Plan 3
12% bonds	—	—	$2,000,000
Preferred 9% stock, $50 par	—	$2,000,000	1,000,000
Common stock, $10 par	$4,000,000	2,000,000	1,000,000
Total	$4,000,000	$4,000,000	$4,000,000
Earnings before interest and income tax	$ 800,000	$ 800,000	$ 800,000
Deduct interest on bonds	—	—	240,000
Income before income tax	$ 800,000	$ 800,000	$ 560,000
Deduct income tax	320,000	320,000	224,000
Net income	$ 480,000	$ 480,000	$ 336,000
Dividends on preferred stock	—	180,000	90,000
Available for dividends on common stock	$ 480,000	$ 300,000	$ 246,000
Shares of common stock outstanding	÷ 400,000	÷ 200,000	÷ 100,000
Earnings per share on common stock	$ 1.20	$ 1.50	$ 2.46

Exhibit 1 indicates that Plan 3 yields the highest earnings per share on common stock and, thus, is the most attractive for common stockholders. If the estimated earnings are more than $800,000, the difference between the earnings per share to common stockholders under Plans 1 and 3 is even greater.[2]

If smaller earnings occur, however, Plans 1 and 2 become more attractive to common stockholders. To illustrate, Exhibit 2 shows the effect on earnings per share if estimated earnings are $440,000 rather than $800,000 as estimated in Exhibit 1.

EXHIBIT 2

Effect of Alternative Financing Plans—$440,000 Earnings

	Plan 1	Plan 2	Plan 3
12% bonds	—	—	$2,000,000
Preferred 9% stock, $50 par	—	$2,000,000	1,000,000
Common stock, $10 par	$4,000,000	2,000,000	1,000,000
Total	$4,000,000	$4,000,000	$4,000,000
Earnings before interest and income tax	$ 440,000	$ 440,000	$ 440,000
Deduct interest on bonds	—	—	240,000
Income before income tax	$ 440,000	$ 440,000	$ 200,000
Deduct income tax	176,000	176,000	80,000
Net income	$ 264,000	$ 264,000	$ 120,000
Dividends on preferred stock	—	180,000	90,000
Available for dividends on common stock	$ 264,000	$ 84,000	$ 30,000
Shares of common stock outstanding	÷ 400,000	÷ 200,000	÷ 100,000
Earnings per share on common stock	$ 0.66	$ 0.42	$ 0.30

1 Earnings per share is also discussed in the *Financial Analysis and Interpretation* section of Chapter 13 and in Chapter 17.

2 The higher earnings per share under Plan 3 is due to a finance concept known as *leverage*. This concept is discussed further in Chapter 17.

In addition to earnings per share, the corporation should consider other factors in deciding among the financing plans. For example, if bonds are issued, the interest and the face value of the bonds at maturity must be paid. If these payments are not made, the bondholders could seek court action and force the company into bankruptcy. In contrast, a corporation is not legally obligated to pay dividends on preferred or common stock.

Example Exercise 14-1 Alternative Financing Plans

OBJ. 1

Gonzales Co. is considering the following alternative plans for financing its company:

	Plan 1	Plan 2
Issue 10% bonds (at face value)	—	$2,000,000
Issue common stock, $10 par	$3,000,000	1,000,000

Income tax is estimated at 40% of income.

Determine the earnings per share of common stock under the two alternative financing plans, assuming income before bond interest and income tax is $750,000.

Follow My Example 14-1

	Plan 1	Plan 2
Earnings before bond interest and income tax	$750,000	$750,000
Bond interest	0	200,000[2]
Balance	$750,000	$550,000
Income tax	300,000[1]	220,000[3]
Net income	$450,000	$330,000
Dividends on preferred stock	0	0
Earnings available for common stock	$450,000	$330,000
Number of common shares	÷300,000	÷100,000
Earnings per share on common stock	$ 1.50	$ 3.30

[1]$750,000 × 40% [2]$2,000,000 × 10% [3]$550,000 × 40%

Practice Exercises: PE 14-1A, PE 14-1B

Describe the characteristics and terminology of bonds payable.

Nature of Bonds Payable

Corporate bonds normally differ in face amount, interest rates, interest payment dates, and maturity dates. Bonds also differ in other ways such as whether corporate assets are pledged in support of the bonds.

Bond Characteristics and Terminology

The underlying contract between the company issuing bonds and the bondholders is called a **bond indenture** or *trust indenture*. A bond issue is normally divided into a number of individual bonds. The face amount of each bond is call the principal. This is the amount that must be repaid on the dates the bonds mature. The principal is usually $1,000, or a multiple of $1,000. The interest on bonds may be payable annually, semiannually, or quarterly. Most bonds pay interest semiannually.

Dow Chemical Company's 8.55% bonds, maturing in 2019, sold for 119.753 on January 19, 2010.

When all bonds of an issue mature at the same time, they are called *term bonds*. If the bonds mature over several dates, they are called *serial bonds*. For example, one-tenth of an issue of $1,000,000 bonds, or $100,000, may mature 16 years from the issue date, another $100,000 in the 17th year, and so on.

Bonds that may be exchanged for other securities, such as common stock, are called *convertible bonds*. Bonds that a corporation reserves the right to redeem before their maturity are called *callable bonds*. Bonds issued on the basis of the general credit of the corporation are called *debenture bonds*.

Proceeds from Issuing Bonds

When a corporation issues bonds, the proceeds received for the bonds depend on:

1. The face amount of the bonds, which is the amount due at the maturity date.
2. The interest rate on the bonds.
3. The market rate of interest for similar bonds.

The face amount and the interest rate on the bonds are identified in the bond indenture. The interest rate to be paid on the face amount of the bond is called the **contract rate** or *coupon rate.*

The **market rate of interest**, sometimes called the **effective rate of interest**, is the rate determined from sales and purchases of similar bonds. The market rate of interest is affected by a variety of factors, including investors' expectations of current and future economic conditions.

By comparing the market and contract rates of interest, it can be determined whether the bonds will sell for more than, less than, or at their face amount, as shown below.

If the market rate equals the contract rate, bonds will sell at the **face amount**.

If the market rate is greater than the contract rate, the bonds will sell for less than their face value. The face amount of the bonds less the selling price is called a **discount**. A bond sells at a discount because buyers are not willing to pay the full face amount for bonds whose contract rate is lower than the market rate.

If the market rate is less than the contract rate, the bonds will sell for more than their face value. The selling price of the bonds less the face amount is called a **premium**. A bond sells at a premium because buyers are willing to pay more than the face amount for bonds whose contract rate is higher than the market rate.

The price of a bond is quoted as a percentage of the bond's face value. For example, a $1,000 bond quoted at 98 could be purchased or sold for $980 ($1,000 × 0.98). Likewise, bonds quoted at 109 could be purchased or sold for $1,090 ($1,000 × 1.09).

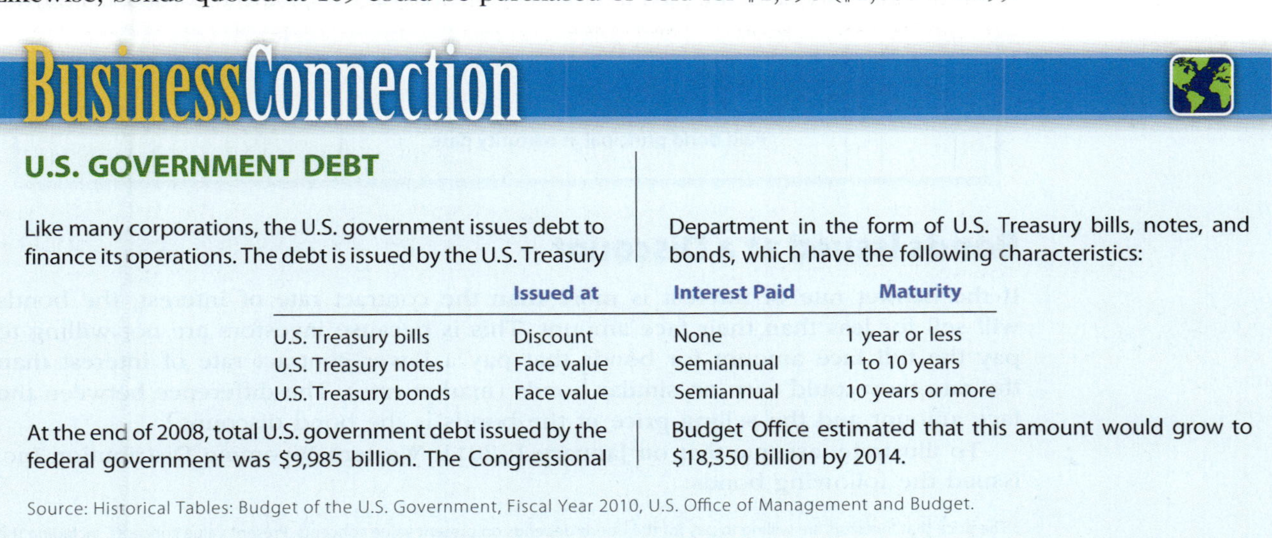
BusinessConnection

U.S. GOVERNMENT DEBT

Like many corporations, the U.S. government issues debt to finance its operations. The debt is issued by the U.S. Treasury Department in the form of U.S. Treasury bills, notes, and bonds, which have the following characteristics:

	Issued at	Interest Paid	Maturity
U.S. Treasury bills	Discount	None	1 year or less
U.S. Treasury notes	Face value	Semiannual	1 to 10 years
U.S. Treasury bonds	Face value	Semiannual	10 years or more

At the end of 2008, total U.S. government debt issued by the federal government was $9,985 billion. The Congressional Budget Office estimated that this amount would grow to $18,350 billion by 2014.

Source: Historical Tables: Budget of the U.S. Government, Fiscal Year 2010, U.S. Office of Management and Budget.

Journalize entries for bonds payable.

Accounting for Bonds Payable

Bonds may be issued at their face amount, a discount, or a premium. When bonds are issued at less or more than their face amount, the discount or premium must be amortized over the life of the bonds. At the maturity date, the face amount must be repaid. In some situations, a corporation may redeem bonds before their maturity date by repurchasing them from investors.

Bonds Issued at Face Amount

If the market rate of interest is equal to the contract rate of interest, the bonds will sell for their face amount or a price of 100. To illustrate, assume that on January 1, 2011, Eastern Montana Communications Inc. issued the following bonds:

Face amount	$100,000
Contract rate of interest	12%
Interest paid semiannually on June 30 and December 31.	
Term of bonds	5 years
Market rate of interest	12%

Since the contract rate of interest and the market rate of interest are the same, the bonds will sell at their face amount. The entry to record the issuance of the bonds is as follows:

Date		Account	Debit	Credit
2011 Jan.	1	Cash	100,000	
		Bonds Payable		100,000
		Issued $100,000 bonds payable at face amount.		

Every six months (on June 30 and December 31) after the bonds are issued, interest of $6,000 ($100,000 × 12% × ½) is paid. The first interest payment on June 30, 2011, is recorded as follows:

Date		Account	Debit	Credit
2011 June	30	Interest Expense	6,000	
		Cash		6,000
		Paid six months' interest on bonds.		

At the maturity date, the payment of the principal of $100,000 is recorded as follows:

Date		Account	Debit	Credit
2015 Dec.	31	Bonds Payable	100,000	
		Cash		100,000
		Paid bond principal at maturity date.		

Bonds Issued at a Discount

If the market rate of interest is more than the contract rate of interest, the bonds will sell for less than their face amount. This is because investors are not willing to pay the full face amount for bonds that pay a lower contract rate of interest than the rate they could earn on similar bonds (market rate). The difference between the face amount and the selling price of the bonds is the bond discount.[3]

To illustrate, assume that on January 1, 2011, Western Wyoming Distribution Inc. issued the following bonds:

3 The price that investors are willing to pay for the bonds depends on present value concepts. Present value concepts, including the computation of bond prices, are described and illustrated in Appendix 1 at the end of this chapter.

Face amount	$100,000
Contract rate of interest	12%
Interest paid semiannually on June 30 and December 31.	
Term of bonds	5 years
Market rate of interest	13%

Note:
Bonds will sell at a discount when the market rate of interest is higher than the contract rate.

Since the contract rate of interest is less than the market rate of interest, the bonds will sell at less than their face amount. Assuming the bonds sell for $96,406, the entry to record the issuance of the bonds is as follows:

2011 Jan.	1	Cash		96,406	
		Discount on Bonds Payable		3,594	
		Bonds Payable			100,000
		Issued $100,000 bonds at discount.			

The $96,406 may be viewed as the amount investors are willing to pay for bonds that have a lower contract rate of interest (12%) than the market rate (13%). The discount is the market's way of adjusting the contract rate of interest to the higher market rate of interest.

The account, Discount on Bonds Payable, is a contra account to Bonds Payable and has a normal debit balance. It is subtracted from Bonds Payable to determine the carrying amount (or book value) of the bonds payable. Thus, after the preceding entry, the carrying amount of the bonds payable is $96,406 ($100,000 – $3,594).

Example Exercise 14-2 Issuing Bonds at a Discount

OBJ. 3

On the first day of the fiscal year, a company issues a $1,000,000, 6%, five-year bond that pays semiannual interest of $30,000 ($1,000,000 × 6% × ½), receiving cash of $936,420. Journalize the entry to record the issuance of the bonds.

Follow My Example 14-2

Cash	936,420	
Discount on Bonds Payable	63,580	
Bonds Payable		1,000,000

Practice Exercises: PE 14-2A, PE 14-2B

Amortizing a Bond Discount

A bond discount must be amortized to interest expense over the life of the bond. The entry to amortize a bond discount is shown below.

		Interest Expense		XXX	
		Discount on Bonds Payable			XXX

The preceding entry may be made annually as an adjusting entry, or it may be combined with the semiannual interest payment. In the latter case, the entry would be as follows:

		Interest Expense		XXX	
		Discount on Bonds Payable			XXX
		Cash (amount of semiannual interest)			XXX

The two methods of computing the amortization of a bond discount are:

1. *Straight-line method*
2. *Effective interest rate method,* sometimes called the *interest method*

The **effective interest rate method** is required by generally accepted accounting principles. However, the straight-line method may be used if the results do not differ significantly from the interest method. The straight-line method is used in this chapter. The effective interest rate method is described and illustrated in Appendix 2 at the end of this chapter.

The straight-line method provides equal amounts of amortization. To illustrate, amortization of the Western Wyoming Distribution bond discount of $3,594 is computed below.

Discount on bonds payable	$3,594
Term of bonds	5 years
Semiannual amortization	$359.40 ($3,594/10 periods)

The combined entry to record the first interest payment and the amortization of the discount is as follows:

2011					
June	30	Interest Expense		6,359.40	
		Discount on Bonds Payable			359.40
		Cash			6,000.00
		Paid semiannual interest and amortized 1/10 of bond discount.			

The preceding entry is made on each interest payment date. Thus, the amount of the semiannual interest expense on the bonds ($6,359.40) remains the same over the life of the bonds.

The effect of the discount amortization is to increase the interest expense from $6,000.00 to $6,359.40 on every semiannual interest payment date. In effect, this increases the contract rate of interest from 12% to a rate of interest that approximates the market rate of 13%. In addition, as the discount is amortized, the carrying amount of the bonds increases until it equals the face amount of the bonds on the maturity date.

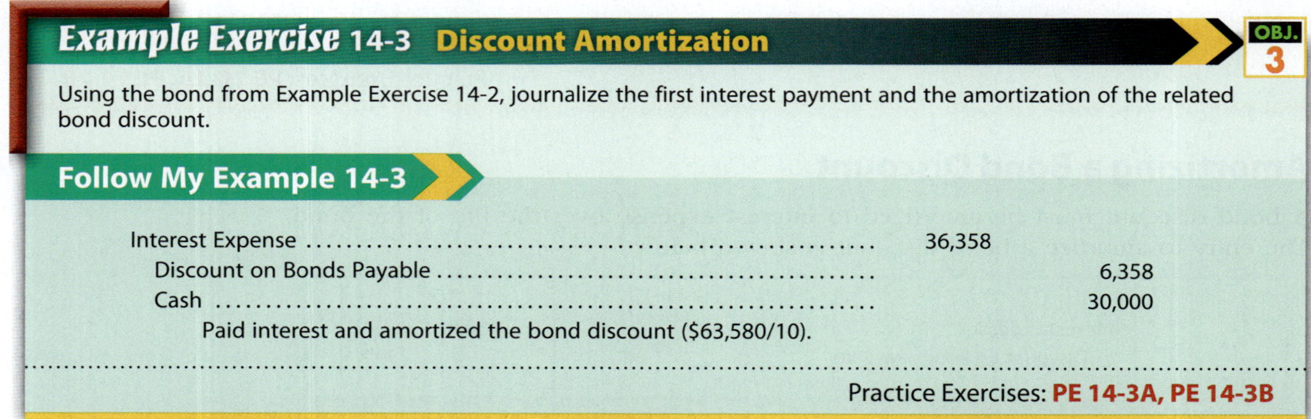

Example Exercise 14-3 Discount Amortization OBJ. 3

Using the bond from Example Exercise 14-2, journalize the first interest payment and the amortization of the related bond discount.

Follow My Example 14-3

Interest Expense	36,358	
Discount on Bonds Payable		6,358
Cash		30,000
Paid interest and amortized the bond discount ($63,580/10).		

Practice Exercises: PE 14-3A, PE 14-3B

Note: Bonds will sell at a premium when the market rate of interest is less than the contract rate.

Bonds Issued at a Premium

If the market rate of interest is less than the contract rate of interest, the bonds will sell for more than their face amount. This is because investors are willing to pay more for bonds that pay a higher contract rate of interest than the rate they could earn on similar bonds (market rate).

To illustrate, assume that on January 1, 2011, Northern Idaho Transportation Inc. issued the following bonds:

Face amount	$100,000
Contract rate of interest	12%
Interest paid semiannually on June 30 and December 31.	
Term of bonds	5 years
Market rate of interest	11%

Since the contract rate of interest is more than the market rate of interest, the bonds will sell at more than their face amount. Assuming the bonds sell for $103,769, the entry to record the issuance of the bonds is as follows:

2011					
Jan.	1	Cash		103,769	
		Bonds Payable			100,000
		Premium on Bonds Payable			3,769
		Issued $100,000 bonds at a premium.			

The $3,769 premium may be viewed as the extra amount investors are willing to pay for bonds that have a higher contract rate of interest (12%) than the market rate (11%). The premium is the market's way of adjusting the contract rate of interest to the lower market rate of interest.

The account, Premium on Bonds Payable, has a normal credit balance. It is added to Bonds Payable to determine the carrying amount (or book value) of the bonds payable. Thus, after the preceding entry, the carrying amount of the bonds payable is $103,769 ($100,000 + $3,769).

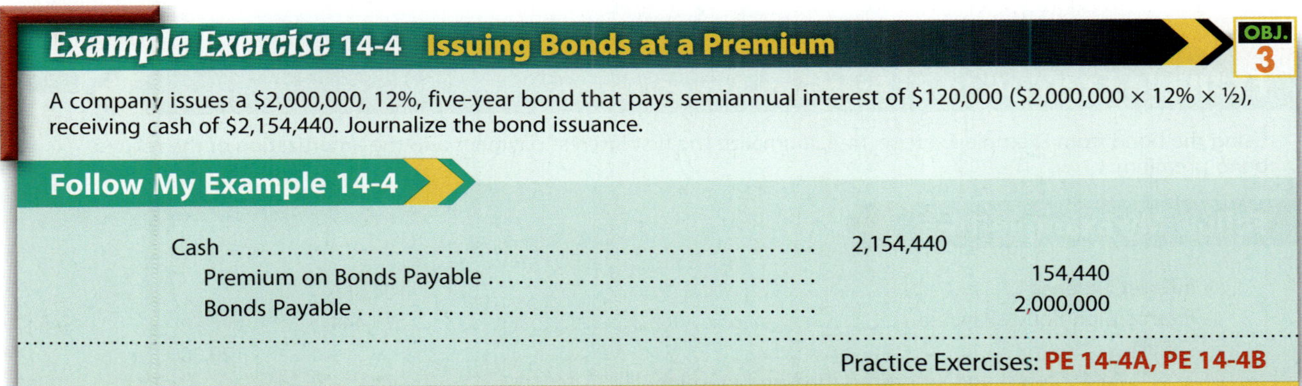
Example Exercise 14-4 Issuing Bonds at a Premium OBJ. 3

A company issues a $2,000,000, 12%, five-year bond that pays semiannual interest of $120,000 ($2,000,000 × 12% × ½), receiving cash of $2,154,440. Journalize the bond issuance.

Follow My Example 14-4

Cash	2,154,440	
Premium on Bonds Payable		154,440
Bonds Payable		2,000,000

Practice Exercises: **PE 14-4A, PE 14-4B**

Amortizing a Bond Premium

Like bond discounts, a bond premium must be amortized over the life of the bond. The amortization can be computed using either the straight-line or the effective interest rate method. The entry to amortize a bond premium is shown below.

		Premium on Bonds Payable		XXX	
		Interest Expense			XXX

The preceding entry may be made annually as an adjusting entry, or it may be combined with the semiannual interest payment. In the latter case, it would be:

		Interest Expense		XXX	
		Premium on Bonds Payable		XXX	
		Cash (amount of semiannual interest)			XXX

To illustrate, amortization of the preceding premium of $3,769 is computed using the straight-line method as shown below.

Premium on bonds payable..................	$3,769
Term of bonds...............................	5 years
Semiannual amortization.....................	$376.90 ($3,769/10 periods)

The combined entry to record the first interest payment and the amortization of the discount is as follows:

2011					
June	30	Interest Expense		5,623.10	
		Premium on Bonds Payable		376.90	
		Cash			6,000.00
		Paid semiannual interest and amortized 1/10 of bond discount.			

The preceding entry is made on each interest payment date. Thus, the amount of the semiannual interest expense ($5,623.10) on the bonds remains the same over the life of the bonds.

The effect of the premium amortization is to decrease the interest expense from $6,000.00 to $5,623.10. In effect, this decreases the rate of interest from 12% to a rate of interest that approximates the market rate of 11%. In addition, as the premium is amortized, the carrying amount of the bonds decreases until it equals the face amount of bonds on the maturity date.

Example Exercise 14-5 Premium Amortization

OBJ. 3

Using the bond from Example Exercise 14-4, journalize the first interest payment and the amortization of the related bond premium.

Follow My Example 14-5

Interest Expense	104,556	
Premium on Bonds Payable	15,444	
Cash..		120,000
Paid interest and amortized the bond premium ($154,440/10).		

Practice Exercises: PE 14-5A, PE 14-5B

Business Connection

GENERAL MOTORS BONDS

In June 2009, after years of losses and weakening financial condition, General Motors Corporation, maker of Chevrolet, Saturn, Pontiac, and Saab cars and trucks, was forced to file for bankruptcy. As part of the bankruptcy and restructuring plan, the U.S. government made a multibillion-dollar cash investment in the company in exchange for 60% of the restructured company's common stock. In addition, General Motors' bondholders were forced to exchange their bonds for the remaining common shares in the restructured company, which were worth only a fraction of the bonds' face value. Bondholders also lost the security of interest payments and repayment of the bonds' face value at maturity.

Source: C. Isidore, "GM Bankruptcy: End of an Era," *CNNMoney.com*, June 2, 2009.

Bond Redemption

A corporation may redeem or call bonds before they mature. This is often done when the market rate of interest declines below the contract rate of interest. In such cases, the corporation may issue new bonds at a lower interest rate and use the proceeds to redeem the original bond issue.

Callable bonds can be redeemed by the issuing corporation within the period of time and at the price stated in the bond indenture. Normally, the call price is above the face value. A corporation may also redeem its bonds by purchasing them on the open market.[4]

A corporation usually redeems its bonds at a price different from the carrying amount (or book value) of the bonds. The **carrying amount** of bonds payable is the face amount of the bonds less any unamortized discount or plus any unamortized premium. A gain or loss may be realized on a bond redemption as follows:

1. A *gain* is recorded if the price paid for redemption is below the bond carrying amount.
2. A *loss* is recorded if the price paid for the redemption is above the carrying amount.

Gains and losses on the redemption of bonds are reported in the *Other income (loss)* section of the income statement.

To illustrate, assume that on June 30, 2011, a corporation has the following bond issue:

Face amount of bonds	$100,000
Premium on bonds payable	4,000

On June 30, 2011, the corporation redeemed one-fourth ($25,000) of these bonds in the market for $24,000. The entry to record the redemption is as follows:

2011 June	30	Bonds Payable		25,000	
		Premium on Bonds Payable		1,000	
		Cash			24,000
		Gain on Redemption of Bonds			2,000
		Redeemed $25,000 bonds for $24,000.			

In the preceding entry, only the portion of the premium related to the redeemed bonds ($4,000 × 25% = $1,000) is written off. The difference between the carrying amount of the bonds redeemed, $26,000 ($25,000 + $1,000), and the redemption price, $24,000, is recorded as a gain.

Assume that the corporation calls the remaining $75,000 of outstanding bonds, which are held by a private investor, for $79,500 on July 1, 2011. The entry to record the redemption is as follows:

2011 July	1	Bonds Payable		75,000	
		Premium on Bonds Payable		3,000	
		Loss on Redemption of Bonds		1,500	
		Cash			79,500
		Redeemed $75,000 bonds for $79,500.			

Example Exercise 14-6 Redemption of Bonds Payable

OBJ. 3

A $500,000 bond issue on which there is an unamortized discount of $40,000 is redeemed for $475,000. Journalize the redemption of the bonds.

(Continued)

4 Some bond indentures require the corporation issuing the bonds to transfer cash to a special cash fund, called a *sinking fund*, over the life of the bond. Such funds help assure investors that there will be adequate cash to pay the bonds at their maturity date.

Follow My Example 14-6

Bonds Payable	500,000	
Loss on Redemption of Bonds	15,000	
Discount on Bonds Payable		40,000
Cash		475,000

Practice Exercises: **PE 14-6A, PE 14-6B**

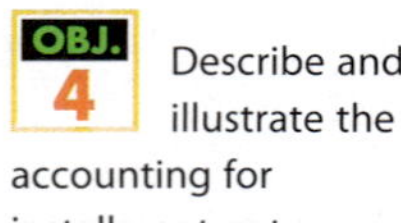
Describe and illustrate the accounting for installment notes.

Installment Notes

Corporations often finance their operations by issuing bonds payable. As an alternative, corporations may issue installment notes. An **installment note** is a debt that requires the borrower to make equal periodic payments to the lender for the term of the note. Unlike bonds, each note payment includes the following:

1. Payment of a portion of the amount initially borrowed, called the *principal*
2. Payment of interest on the outstanding balance

Individuals typically use mortgage notes when buying a house or car.

At the end of the note's term, the principal will have been repaid in full.

Installment notes are often used to purchase specific assets such as equipment, and are often secured by the purchased asset. When a note is secured by an asset, it is called a **mortgage note**. If the borrower fails to pay a mortgage note, the lender has the right to take possession of the pledged asset and sell it to pay off the debt. Mortgage notes are typically issued by an individual bank.

Issuing an Installment Note

When an installment note is issued, an entry is recorded debiting Cash and crediting Notes Payable. To illustrate, assume that Lewis Company issues the following installment note to City National Bank on January 1, 2010.

Principal amount of note	$24,000
Interest rate	6%
Term of note	5 years
Annual payments	$5,698[5]

The entry to record the issuance of the note is as follows:

2010					
Jan.	1	Cash		24,000	
		Notes Payable			24,000
		Issued installment note for cash.			

Annual Payments

The preceding note payable requires Lewis Company to repay the principal and interest in equal payments of $5,698 beginning December 3, 2010, for each of the next five years. Unlike bonds, however, each installment note payment includes an interest and principal component.

The interest portion of an installment note payment is computed by multiplying the interest rate by the carrying amount (book value) of the note at the beginning of the period. The principal portion of the payment is then computed as the difference between the total installment note payment (cash paid) and the interest component. These computations are illustrated in Exhibit 3 as follows:

5 The amount of the annual payment is calculated by using the present value concepts discussed in Appendix 1. The annual payment of $5,698 is computed by dividing the $24,000 loan amount by the present value of an annuity of $1 for 5 periods at 6% (4.21236) from Exhibit 5 (rounded to the nearest dollar).

EXHIBIT 3 Amortization of Installment Notes

	A	B	C	D	E
For the Year Ending	January 1 Carrying Amount	Note Payment (cash paid)	Interest Expense (6% of January 1 Note Carrying Amount)	Decrease in Notes Payable (B – C)	December 31 Carrying Amount (A – D)
December 31, 2010	$24,000	$ 5,698	$ 1,440 (6% of $24,000)	$ 4,258	$19,742
December 31, 2011	19,742	5,698	1,185 (6% of $19,742)	4,513	15,229
December 31, 2012	15,229	5,698	914 (6% of $15,229)	4,784	10,445
December 31, 2013	10,445	5,698	627 (6% of $10,445)	5,071	5,374
December 31, 2014	5,374	5,698	324* (6% of $5,374)	5,374	0
		$28,490	$4,490	$24,000	

*Rounded ($5,374 – $5,698).

1. The January 1, 2010, carrying value (Column A) equals the amount borrowed from the bank. The January 1 balance in the following years equals the December 31 balance from the prior year.
2. The note payment (Column B) remains constant at $5,698, the annual cash payments required by the bank.
3. The interest expense (Column C) is computed at 6% of the installment note carrying amount at the beginning of each year. As a result, the interest expense decreases each year.
4. Notes payable decreases each year by the amount of the principal repayment (Column D). The principal repayment is computed by subtracting the interest expense (Column C) from the total payment (Column B). The principal repayment (Column D) increases each year as the interest expense decreases (Column C).
5. The carrying amount on December 31 (Column E) of the note decreases from $24,000, the initial amount borrowed, to $0 at the end of the five years.

The entry to record the first payment on December 31, 2010, is as follows:

2010				
Dec.	31	Interest Expense	1,440	
		Notes Payable	4,258	
		Cash		5,698
		Paid principal and interest on installment note.		

The entry to record the second payment on December 31, 2011, is as follows:

2011				
Dec.	31	Interest Expense	1,185	
		Notes Payable	4,513	
		Cash		5,698
		Paid principal and interest on installment note.		

As the prior entries show, the cash payment is the same in each year. The interest and principal repayment, however, change each year. This is because the carrying amount (book value) of the note decreases each year as principal is repaid, which decreases the interest component the next period.

The entry to record the final payment on December 31, 2014, is as follows:

2014				
Dec.	31	Interest Expense	324	
		Notes Payable	5,374	
		Cash		5,698
		Paid principal and interest on installment note.		

After the final payment, the carrying amount on the note is zero, indicating that the note has been paid in full. Any assets that secure the note would then be released by the bank.

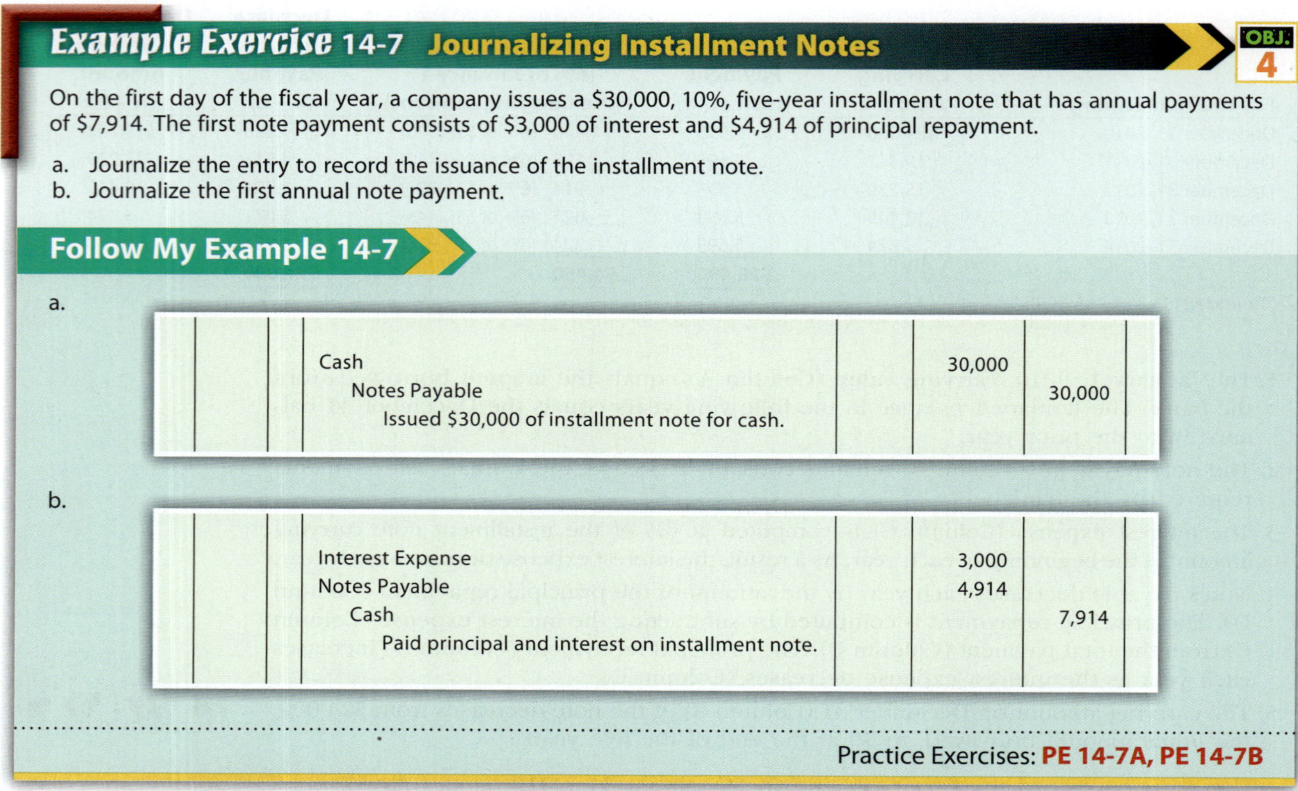

Example Exercise 14-7 Journalizing Installment Notes

OBJ. 4

On the first day of the fiscal year, a company issues a $30,000, 10%, five-year installment note that has annual payments of $7,914. The first note payment consists of $3,000 of interest and $4,914 of principal repayment.

a. Journalize the entry to record the issuance of the installment note.
b. Journalize the first annual note payment.

Follow My Example 14-7

a.

		Cash	30,000	
		Notes Payable		30,000
		Issued $30,000 of installment note for cash.		

b.

		Interest Expense	3,000	
		Notes Payable	4,914	
		Cash		7,914
		Paid principal and interest on installment note.		

Practice Exercises: **PE 14-7A, PE 14-7B**

Integrity, Objectivity, and Ethics in Business

LIAR'S LOANS

One of the main causes of the 2008 financial crisis was a widespread inability of homeowners to repay their home mortgages. While the weak economy contributed to these problems, many mortgage defaults were the result of unethical lending practices in the form of "stated income" or "liar's" loans. In a conventional home mortgage, lenders base the amount of a loan on the borrower's income, expenses, and total assets. These amounts are verified by reviewing the borrower's tax returns, bank statements, and payroll records. Liar's loans, however, based the amount of the loan on the borrower's "stated income," without verifying it through sources such as tax returns, W-2 statements, or payroll records. Without independent verification, borrowers often falsified or lied about their "stated income" in order to obtain a larger loan than they were qualified for. Once in their homes, many of these borrowers were unable to make their loan payments, causing them to default on their home mortgages.

OBJ. 5 Describe and illustrate the reporting of long-term liabilities including bonds and notes payable.

Reporting Long-Term Liabilities

Bonds payable and notes payable are reported as liabilities on the balance sheet. Any portion of the bonds or notes that is due within one year is reported as a current liability. Any remaining bonds or notes are reported as a long-term liability.

Any unamortized premium is reported as an addition to the face amount of the bonds. Any unamortized discount is reported as a deduction from the face amount of the bonds. A description of the bonds and notes should also be reported either on the face of the financial statements or in the accompanying notes.

The reporting of bonds and notes payable for Mornin' Joe is shown below.

Mornin' Joe Balance Sheet December 31, 2012		
Current liabilities:		
Accounts payable	$133,000	
Notes payable (current portion)	200,000	
Salaries and wages payable	42,000	
Payroll taxes payable	16,400	
Interest payable	40,000	
Total current liabilities		$ 431,400
Long-term liabilities:		
Bonds payable, 8%, due December 31, 2030	$500,000	
Less unamortized discount	16,000	$ 484,000
Notes payable		1,400,000
Total long-term liabilities		$1,884,000
Total liabilities		$2,315,400

Financial Analysis and Interpretation: Number of Times Interest Charges Are Earned

OBJ. 6 Describe and illustrate how the number of times interest charges are earned is used to evaluate a company's financial condition.

As we have discussed, the assets of a company are subject to the (1) claims of creditors and (2) the rights of owners. As creditors, bondholders are primarily concerned with the company's ability to make its periodic interest payments and repay the face amount of the bonds at maturity.

Analysts assess the risk that bondholders will not receive their interest payments by computing the **number of times interest charges are earned** during the year as follows:

$$\text{Number of Times Interest Charges Are Earned} = \frac{\text{Income Before Income Tax} + \text{Interest Expense}}{\text{Interest Expense}}$$

This ratio computes the number of times interest payments could be paid out of current period earnings, measuring the company's ability to make its interest payments. Because interest payments reduce income tax expense, the ratio is computed using income before tax.

To illustrate, the following data were taken from the 2008 annual report of Under Armour, Inc. (in thousands):

Interest expense	$ 850
Income before income tax	69,900

The number of times interest charges are earned for Under Armour, Inc., is computed as follows:

$$\text{Number of Times Interest Charges Are Earned} = \frac{\$69{,}900 + \$850}{\$850} = 83.24$$

Compare this to the number of times interest charges are earned for Southwest Airlines (an airline), and Verizon Communications (a telecommunications company) shown on the next page (in thousands):

	Under Armour	Southwest Airlines	Verizon Communications
Interest expense	$850	$105,000	$1,819,000
Income before income tax expense	$69,900	$278,000	$9,759,000
Number of times interest charges are earned	83.24	3.65	6.37

Under Armour's number of times interest charges are earned is 83.24, indicating that the company generates enough income before taxes to pay (cover) its interest payments 83.24 times. As a result, debtholders have extremely good protection in the event of an earnings decline. Compare this to Southwest Airlines, which only generates enough income before taxes to pay (cover) its interest payments 3.65 times. A small decrease in Southwest Airlines' earnings could jeopardize the payment of interest. Verizon Communications falls in between, with a ratio of 6.37.

Example Exercise 14-8 Number of Times Interest Charges Are Earned

Harris Industries reported the following on the company's income statement in 2012 and 2011:

	2012	2011
Interest expense	$ 200,000	$180,000
Income before income tax expense	1,000,000	720,000

a. Determine the number of times interest charges were earned for 2012 and 2011. Round to one decimal place.
b. Is the number of times interest charges are earned improving or declining?

Follow My Example 14-8

a. 2012:

$$\text{Number of times interest charges are earned: } 6.0 = \frac{\$1,000,000 + \$200,000}{\$200,000}$$

2011:

$$\text{Number of times interest charges are earned: } 5.0 = \frac{\$720,000 + \$180,000}{\$180,000}$$

b. The number of times interest charges are earned has increased from 5.0 in 2011 to 6.0 in 2012. Thus, the debtholders have improved confidence in the company's ability to make its interest payments.

Practice Exercises: **PE 14-8A, PE 14-8B**

APPENDIX 1

Present Value Concepts and Pricing Bonds Payable

When a corporation issues bonds, the price that investors are willing to pay for the bonds depends on the following:

1. The face amount of the bonds, which is the amount due at the maturity date.
2. The periodic interest to be paid on the bonds.
3. The market rate of interest.

An investor determines how much to pay for the bonds by computing the present value of the bond's future cash receipts, using the market rate of interest. A bond's future cash receipts include its face value at maturity and the periodic interest payments.

Present Value Concepts

The concept of present value is based on the time value of money. The *time value of money concept* recognizes that cash received today is worth more than the same amount of cash to be received in the future.

To illustrate, what would you rather have: $1,000 today or $1,000 one year from now? You would rather have the $1,000 today because it could be invested to earn interest. For example, if the $1,000 could be invested to earn 10% per year, the $1,000 will accumulate to $1,100 ($1,000 plus $100 interest) in one year. In this sense, you can think of the $1,000 in hand today as the **present value** of $1,100 to be received a year from today. This present value is illustrated below.

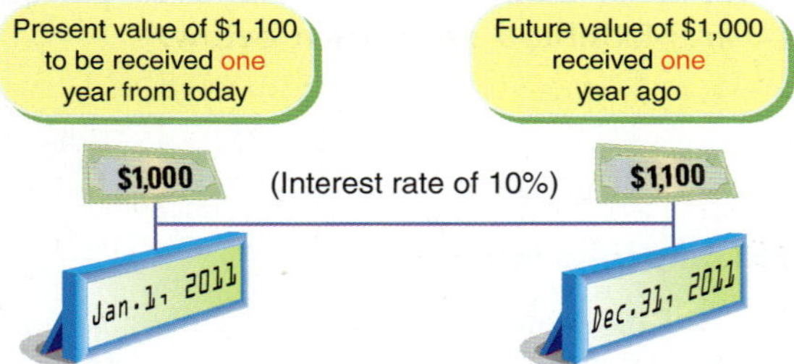

A related concept to present value is **future value**. To illustrate, using the preceding example, the $1,100 to be received on December 31, 2011, is the *future value* of $1,000 on January 1, 2011, assuming an interest rate of 10%.

Present Value of an Amount

To illustrate the present value of an amount, assume that $1,000 is to be received in one year. If the market rate of interest is 10%, the present value of the $1,000 is $909.09 ($1,000/1.10). This present value is illustrated below.

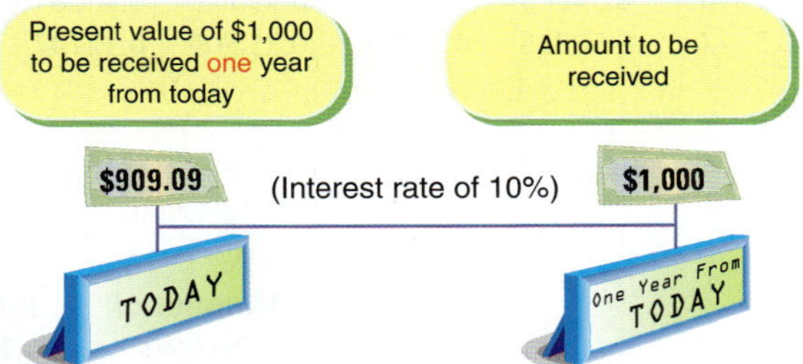

If the $1,000 is to be received in two years, with interest of 10% compounded at the end of the first year, the present value is $826.45 ($909.09/1.10).[6] This present value is illustrated below.

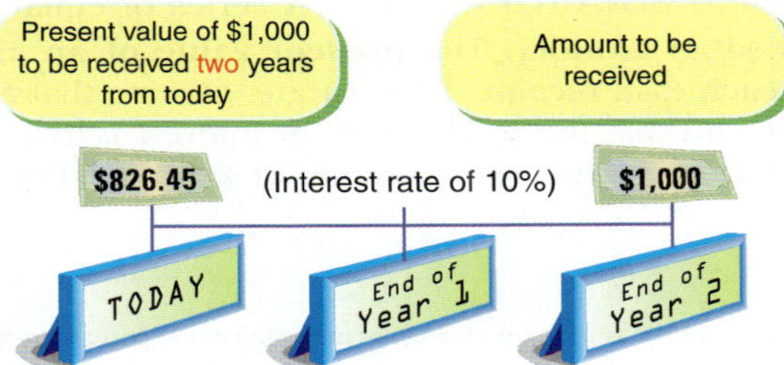

6 Note that the future value of $826.45 in two years, at an interest rate of 10% compounded annually, is $1,000.

Spreadsheet software with built-in present value functions can be used to calculate present values.

The present value of an amount to be received in the future can be determined by a series of divisions such as illustrated on the previous page. In practice, however, it is easier to use a table of present values.

The *present value of $1* table is used to find the present value factor for $1 to be received after a number of periods in the future. The amount to be received is then multiplied by this factor to determine its present value.

To illustrate, Exhibit 4 is a partial table of the present value of $1.[7] Exhibit 4 indicates that the present value of $1 to be received in two years with a market rate of interest of 10% a year is 0.82645. Multiplying $1,000 to be received in two years by 0.82645 yields $826.45 ($1,000 × 0.82645). This amount is the same amount computed earlier. In Exhibit 4, the Periods column represents the number of compounding periods, and the percentage columns represent the compound interest rate per period. Thus, the present value factor from Exhibit 4 for 12% for five years is 0.56743. If the interest is compounded semiannually, the interest rate is 6% (12% divided by 2), and the number of periods is 10 (5 years × 2 times per year). Thus, the present value factor from Exhibit 4 for 6% and 10 periods is 0.55840. Some additional examples using Exhibit 4 are shown below.

EXHIBIT 4 **Present Value of $1 at Compound Interest**

Periods	5%	5½%	6%	6½%	7%	10%	11%	12%	13%	14%
1	0.95238	0.94787	0.94340	0.93897	0.93458	0.90909	0.90090	0.89286	0.88496	0.87719
2	0.90703	0.89845	0.89000	0.88166	0.87344	0.82645	0.81162	0.79719	0.78315	0.76947
3	0.86384	0.85161	0.83962	0.82785	0.81630	0.75132	0.73119	0.71178	0.69305	0.67497
4	0.82270	0.80722	0.79209	0.77732	0.76290	0.68301	0.65873	0.63552	0.61332	0.59208
5	0.78353	0.76513	0.74726	0.72988	0.71299	0.62092	0.59345	0.56743	0.54276	0.51937
6	0.74622	0.72525	0.70496	0.68533	0.66634	0.56447	0.53464	0.50663	0.48032	0.45559
7	0.71068	0.68744	0.66506	0.64351	0.62275	0.51316	0.48166	0.45235	0.42506	0.39964
8	0.67684	0.65160	0.62741	0.60423	0.58201	0.46651	0.43393	0.40388	0.37616	0.35056
9	0.64461	0.61763	0.59190	0.56735	0.54393	0.42410	0.39092	0.36061	0.33288	0.30751
10	0.61391	0.58543	0.55840	0.53273	0.50835	0.38554	0.35218	0.32197	0.29459	0.26974

	Number of Periods	Interest Rate	Present Value of $1 Factor from Exhibit 4
10% for *two* years compounded *annually*	2	10%	0.82645
10% for *two* years compounded *semiannually*	4	5%	0.82270
10% for *three* years compounded *semiannually*	6	5%	0.74622
12% for *five* years compounded *semiannually*	10	6%	0.55840

Present Value of the Periodic Receipts A series of equal cash receipts spaced equally in time is called an **annuity**. The **present value of an annuity** is the sum of the present values of each cash receipt. To illustrate, assume that $100 is to be received annually for two years and that the market rate of interest is 10%. Using Exhibit 4, the present value of the receipt of the two amounts of $100 is $173.55, as shown on the next page.

7 To simplify the illustrations and homework assignments, the tables presented in this chapter are limited to 10 periods for a small number of interest rates, and the amounts are carried to only five decimal places. Computer programs are available for determining present value factors for any number of interest rates, decimal places, or periods. More complete interest tables are presented in Appendix A of the text.

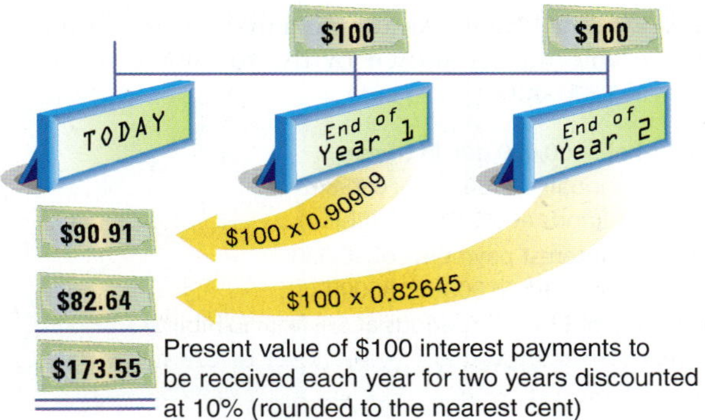

Instead of using present value of $1 tables to determine the present value of each cash flow separately, such as Exhibit 4, the present value of an annuity can be computed in a single step. Using a value from the present value of an annuity of $1 table in Exhibit 5, the present value of the entire annuity can be calculated by multiplying the equal cash payment times the appropriate present value of an annuity of $1.

EXHIBIT 5 **Present Value of an Annuity of $1 at Compound Interest**

Periods	5%	5½%	6%	6½%	7%	10%	11%	12%	13%	14%
1	0.95238	0.94787	0.94340	0.93897	0.93458	0.90909	0.90090	0.89286	0.88496	0.87719
2	1.85941	1.84632	1.83339	1.82063	1.80802	1.73554	1.71252	1.69005	1.66810	1.64666
3	2.72325	2.69793	2.67301	2.64848	2.62432	2.48685	2.44371	2.40183	2.36115	2.32163
4	3.54595	3.50515	3.46511	3.42580	3.38721	3.16987	3.10245	3.03735	2.97447	2.91371
5	4.32948	4.27028	4.21236	4.15568	4.10020	3.79079	3.69590	3.60478	3.51723	3.43308
6	5.07569	4.99553	4.91732	4.84101	4.76654	4.35526	4.23054	4.11141	3.99755	3.88867
7	5.78637	5.68297	5.58238	5.48452	5.38929	4.86842	4.71220	4.56376	4.42261	4.28830
8	6.46321	6.33457	6.20979	6.08875	5.97130	5.33493	5.14612	4.96764	4.79677	4.63886
9	7.10782	6.95220	6.80169	6.65610	6.51523	5.75902	5.53705	5.32825	5.13166	4.94637
10	7.72174	7.53763	7.36009	7.18883	7.02358	6.14457	5.88923	5.65022	5.42624	5.21612

To illustrate, the present value of $100 to be received at the end of each of the next two years at 10% compound interest per period is $173.55 ($100 × 1.73554). This amount is the same amount computed above using the present value of $1.

Pricing Bonds

The selling price of a bond is the sum of the present values of:

1. The face amount of the bonds due at the maturity date
2. The periodic interest to be paid on the bonds

The market rate of interest is used to compute the present value of both the face amount and the periodic interest.

To illustrate the pricing of bonds, assume that Southern Utah Communications Inc. issued the following bond on January 1, 2011:

Face amount	$100,000
Contract rate of interest	12%
Interest paid semiannually on June 30 and December 31.	
Term of bonds	5 years

Market Rate of Interest of 12% Assuming a market rate of interest of 12%, the bonds would sell for their face amount. As shown by the following present value computations, the bonds would sell for $100,000.

Present value of face amount of $100,000 due in 5 years, at 12% compounded semiannually: $100,000 × 0.55840 (present value of $1 for 10 periods at 6% from Exhibit 4)	$ 55,840
Present value of 10 semiannual interest payments of $6,000, at 12% compounded semiannually: $6,000 × 7.36009 (present value of an annuity of $1 for 10 periods at 6% from Exhibit 5)	44,160
Total present value of bonds	$100,000

Market Rate of Interest of 13% Assuming a market rate of interest of 13%, the bonds would sell at a discount. As shown by the following present value computations, the bonds would sell for $96,406.[8]

Present value of face amount of $100,000 due in 5 years, at 13% compounded semiannually: $100,000 × 0.53273 (present value of $1 for 10 periods at 6½% from Exhibit 4)	$53,273
Present value of 10 semiannual interest payments of $6,000, at 13% compounded semiannually: $6,000 × 7.18883 (present value of an annuity of $1 for 10 periods at 6½% from Exhibit 5)	43,133
Total present value of bonds	$96,406

Market Rate of Interest of 11% Assuming a market rate of interest of 11%, the bonds would sell at a premium. As shown by the following present value computations, the bonds would sell for $103,769.

Present value of face amount of $100,000 due in 5 years, at 11% compounded semiannually: $100,000 × 0.58543 (present value of $1 for 10 periods at 5½% from Exhibit 4)	$ 58,543
Present value of 10 semiannual interest payments of $6,000, at 11% compounded semiannually: $6,000 × 7.53763 (present value of an annuity of $1 for 10 periods at 5½% from Exhibit 5)	45,226
Total present value of bonds	$103,769

As shown above, the selling price of the bond varies with the present value of the bond's face amount at maturity, interest payments, and the market rate of interest.

APPENDIX 2

Effective Interest Rate Method of Amortization

The effective interest rate method of amortization provides for a constant *rate* of interest over the life of the bonds. As the discount or premium is amortized, the carrying amount of the bonds changes. As a result, interest expense also changes each period. This is in contrast to the straight-line method, which provides for a constant *amount* of interest expense each period.

The interest rate used in the effective interest rate method of amortization, sometimes called the *interest method*, is the market rate on the date the bonds are issued. The carrying amount of the bonds is multiplied by this interest rate to determine the interest expense for the period. The difference between the interest expense and the interest payment is the amount of discount or premium to be amortized for the period.

8 Some corporations issue bonds called **zero-coupon bonds** that provide for only the payment of the face amount at maturity. Such bonds sell for large discounts. In this example, such a bond would sell for $53,273, which is the present value of the face amount.

Amortization of Discount by the Interest Method

To illustrate, the following data taken from the chapter illustration of issuing bonds at a discount are used:

Face value of 12%, 5-year bonds, interest compounded semiannually	$100,000
Present value of bonds at effective (market) rate of interest of 13%	96,406
Discount on bonds payable	$ 3,594

Exhibit 6 illustrates the interest method for the preceding bonds. Exhibit 6 begins with six columns. The first column is not lettered. The remaining columns are lettered A through E. The exhibit was then prepared as follows:

Step 1. List the interest payments dates in the first column, which for the preceding bond are 10 interest payment dates (semiannual interest over five years). Also, list on the first line the initial amount of discount in Column D and the initial carrying amount (selling price) of the bonds in Column E.

Step 2. List in Column A the semiannual interest payments, which for the preceding bond is $6,000 ($100,000 × 6%).

Step 3. Compute the interest expense in Column B by multiplying the bond carrying amount at the beginning of each period times 6½%, which is the effective interest (market) rate.

Step 4. Compute the discount to be amortized each period in Column C by subtracting the interest payment in Column A ($6,000) from the interest expense for the period shown in Column B.

Step 5. Compute the remaining unamortized discount by subtracting the amortized discount in Column C for the period from the unamortized discount at the beginning of the period in Column D.

Step 6. Compute the bond carrying amount at the end of the period by subtracting the unamortized discount at the end of the period in Column D from the face amount of the bonds ($100,000).

Steps 3–6 are repeated for each interest payment.

As shown in Exhibit 6, the interest expense increases each period as the carrying amount of the bond increases. Also, the unamortized discount decreases each period to zero at the maturity date. Finally, the carrying amount of the bonds increases from $96,406 to $100,000 (the face amount) at maturity.

EXHIBIT 6 **Amortization of Discount on Bonds Payable**

Interest Payment Date	A Interest Paid (6% of Face Amount)	B Interest Expense (6½% of Bond Carrying Amount)	C Discount Amortization (B – A)	D Unamortized Discount (D – C)	E Bond Carrying Amount ($100,000 – D)
				$3,594	$ 96,406
June 30, 2011	$6,000	$6,266 (6½% of $96,406)	$266	3,328	96,672
Dec. 31, 2011	6,000	6,284 (6½% of $96,672)	284	3,044	96,956
June 30, 2012	6,000	6,302 (6½% of $96,956)	302	2,742	97,258
Dec. 31, 2012	6,000	6,322 (6½% of $97,258)	322	2,420	97,580
June 30, 2013	6,000	6,343 (6½% of $97,580)	343	2,077	97,923
Dec. 31, 2013	6,000	6,365 (6½% of $97,923)	365	1,712	98,288
June 30, 2014	6,000	6,389 (6½% of $98,288)	389	1,323	98,677
Dec. 31, 2014	6,000	6,414 (6½% of $98,677)	414	909	99,091
June 30, 2015	6,000	6,441 (6½% of $99,091)	441	468	99,532
Dec. 31, 2015	6,000	6,470 (6½% of $99,532)	468*	—	100,000

*Cannot exceed unamortized discount.

The entry to record the first interest payment on June 30, 2011, and the related discount amortization is as follows:

2011				
June	30	Interest Expense	6,266	
		Discount on Bonds Payable		266
		Cash		6,000
		Paid semiannual interest and amortized bond discount for 1/2 year.		

If the amortization is recorded only at the end of the year, the amount of the discount amortized on December 31, 2011, would be $550. This is the sum of the first two semiannual amortization amounts ($266 and $284) from Exhibit 6.

Amortization of Premium by the Interest Method

To illustrate, the following data taken from the chapter illustration of issuing bonds at a premium are used:

Present value of bonds at effective (market) rate of interest of 11%	$103,769
Face value of 12%, 5-year bonds, interest compounded semiannually	100,000
Premium on bonds payable	$ 3,769

Exhibit 7 illustrates the interest method for the preceding bonds. Exhibit 7 begins with six columns. The first column is not lettered. The remaining columns are lettered A through E. The exhibit was then prepared as follows:

Step 1. List the number of interest payments in the first column, which for the preceding bond are 10 interest payments (semiannual interest over 5 years). Also, list on the first line the initial amount of premium in Column D and the initial carrying amount of the bonds in Column E.

Step 2. List in Column A the semiannual interest payments, which for the preceding bond is $6,000 ($100,000 × 6%).

Step 3. Compute the interest expense in Column B by multiplying the bond carrying amount at the beginning of each period times 5½%, which is the effective interest (market) rate.

Step 4. Compute the premium to be amortized each period in Column C by subtracting the interest expense for the period shown in Column B from the interest payment in Column A ($6,000).

EXHIBIT 7 **Amortization of Premium on Bonds Payable**

Interest Payment Date	A Interest Paid (6% of Face Amount)	B Interest Expense (5½% of Bond Carrying Amount)	C Premium Amortization (A – B)	D Unamortized Premium (D – C)	E Bond Carrying Amount ($100,000 + D)
				$3,769	$103,769
June 30, 2011	$6,000	$5,707 (5½% of $103,769)	$293	3,476	103,476
Dec. 31, 2011	6,000	5,691 (5½% of $103,476)	309	3,167	103,167
June 30, 2012	6,000	5,674 (5½% of $103,167)	326	2,841	102,841
Dec. 31, 2012	6,000	5,656 (5½% of $102,841)	344	2,497	102,497
June 30, 2013	6,000	5,637 (5½% of $102,497)	363	2,134	102,134
Dec. 31, 2013	6,000	5,617 (5½% of $102,134)	383	1,751	101,751
June 30, 2014	6,000	5,596 (5½% of $101,751)	404	1,347	101,347
Dec. 31, 2014	6,000	5,574 (5½% of $101,347)	426	921	100,921
June 30, 2015	6,000	5,551 (5½% of $100,921)	449	472	100,472
Dec. 31, 2015	6,000	5,526 (5½% of $100,472)	472*	—	100,000

*Cannot exceed unamortized premium.

Step 5. Compute the remaining unamortized premium by subtracting the amortized premium in Column C for the period from the unamortized premium at the beginning of the period in Column D.

Step 6. Compute the bond carrying amount at the end of the period in Column D by adding the unamortized premium at the end of the period to the face amount of the bonds ($100,000).

Steps 3–6 are repeated for each interest payment.

As shown in Exhibit 7, the interest expense decreases each period as the carrying amount of the bond decreases. Also, the unamortized premium decreases each period to zero at the maturity date. Finally, the carrying amount of the bonds decreases from $103,769 to $100,000 (the face amount) at maturity.

The entry to record the first interest payment on June 30, 2011, and the related premium amortization is as follows:

2011					
June	30	Interest Expense		5,707	
		Premium on Bonds Payable		293	
		Cash			6,000
		Paid semiannual interest and amortized bond premium for ½ year.			

If the amortization is recorded only at the end of the year, the amount of the premium amortized on December 31, 2011, would be $602. This is the sum of the first two semiannual amortization amounts ($293 and $309) from Exhibit 7.

At a Glance 14

OBJ. 1 Compute the potential impact of long-term borrowing on earnings per share.

Key Points Corporations can finance their operations by issuing short-term debt, long-term debt, or equity. One of the many factors that influence a corporation's decision on whether it should issue long-term debt or equity is the effect each alternative has on earnings per share.

Learning Outcomes	Example Exercises	Practice Exercises
• Define the concept of a bond.		
• Calculate and compare the effect of alternative long-term financing plans on earnings per share.	EE14-1	PE14-1A, 14-1B

OBJ. 2 Describe the characteristics and terminology of bonds payable.

Key Points A corporation that issues bonds enters into a contract, or bond indenture.

When a corporation issues bonds, the price that buyers are willing to pay for the bonds depends on (1) the face amount of the bonds, (2) the periodic interest to be paid on the bonds, and (3) the market rate of interest.

Learning Outcomes	Example Exercises	Practice Exercises
• Define the characteristics of a bond.		
• Describe the various types of bonds.		
• Describe the factors that determine the price of a bond.		

Journalize entries for bonds payable.

Key Points The journal entry for issuing bonds payable debits Cash and credits Bonds Payable. Any difference between the face amount of the bonds and the selling price is debited to Discount on Bonds Payable or credited to Premium on Bonds Payable when the bonds are issued. The discount or premium on bonds payable is amortized to interest expense over the life of the bonds.

At the maturity date, the entry to record the repayment of the face value of a bond is a debit to Bonds Payable and a credit to Cash.

When a corporation redeems bonds before they mature, Bonds Payable is debited for the face amount of the bonds, the premium (discount) on bonds payable account is debited (credited) for its unamoritized balance, Cash is credited, and any gain or loss on the redemption is recorded.

Learning Outcomes	Example Exercises	Practice Exercises
• Journalize the issuance of bonds at face value and the payment of periodic interest.		
• Journalize the issuance of bonds at a discount.	EE14-2	PE14-2A, 14-2B
• Journalize the amortization of a bond discount.	EE14-3	PE14-3A, 14-3B
• Journalize the issuance of bonds at a premium.	EE14-4	PE14-4A, 14-4B
• Journalize the amortization of a bond premium.	EE14-5	PE14-5A, 14-5B
• Describe bond redemptions.		
• Journalize the redemption of bonds payable.	EE14-6	PE14-6A, 14-6B

Describe and illustrate the accounting for installment notes.

Key Points An installment note requires the borrower to make equal periodic payments to the lender for the term of the note. Unlike bonds, the annual payment in an installment note consists of both principal and interest. The journal entry for the annual payment debits Interest Expense and Notes Payable and credits Cash for the amount of the payment. After the final payment, the carrying amount on the note is zero.

Learning Outcomes	Example Exercises	Practice Exercises
• Define the characteristics of an installment note.		
• Journalize the issuance of installment notes.	EE14-7	PE14-7A, 14-7B
• Journalize the annual payment for an installment note.		

Describe and illustrate the reporting of long-term liabilities including bonds and notes payable.

Key Points Bonds payable and notes payable are usually reported as long-term liabilities. If the balance sheet date is within one year, they are reported as a current liability. A discount on bonds should be reported as a deduction from the related bonds payable. A premium on bonds should be reported as an addition to related bonds payable.

Learning Outcome	Example Exercises	Practice Exercises
• Illustrate the balance sheet presentation of bonds payable and notes payable.		

OBJ. 6

Describe and illustrate how the number of times interest charges are earned is used to evaluate a company's financial condition.

Key Points The number of times interest charges are earned measures the risk to bondholders that a company will not be able to make its interest payments. It is computed by dividing income before income tax plus interest expense by interest expense. This ratio measures the number of times interest payments could be paid (covered) by current period earnings.

Learning Outcomes	Example Exercises	Practice Exercises
• Describe and compute the number of times interest charges are earned.	EE14-8	PE14-8A, 14-8B
• Interpret the number of times interest charges are earned.		

Key Terms

bond (626)
bond indenture (628)
carrying amount (635)
contract rate (629)
discount (629)
earnings per share (EPS) (627)
effective interest rate method (632)
effective rate of interest (629)
face amount (629)
installment note (636)
market rate of interest (629)
mortgage notes (636)
number of times interest charges are earned (639)
premium (629)

Illustrative Problem

The fiscal year of Russell Inc., a manufacturer of acoustical supplies, ends December 31. Selected transactions for the period 2011 through 2018, involving bonds payable issued by Russell Inc., are as follows:

2011

June 30. Issued $2,000,000 of 25-year, 7% callable bonds dated June 30, 2011, for cash of $1,920,000. Interest is payable semiannually on June 30 and December 31.

Dec. 31. Paid the semiannual interest on the bonds.

31. Recorded straight-line amortization of $1,600 of discount on the bonds.

31. Closed the interest expense account.

2012

June 30. Paid the semiannual interest on the bonds.

Dec. 31. Paid the semiannual interest on the bonds.

31. Recorded straight-line amortization of $3,200 of discount on the bonds.

31. Closed the interest expense account.

2018

June 30. Recorded the redemption of the bonds, which were called at 101.5. The balance in the bond discount account is $57,600 after the payment of interest and amortization of discount have been recorded. (Record the redemption only.)

Instructions

1. Journalize entries to record the preceding transactions.
2. Determine the amount of interest expense for 2011 and 2012.
3. Determine the carrying amount of the bonds as of December 31, 2012.

Solution

1.

Date			Account	Dr.	Cr.
2011					
June	30		Cash	1,920,000	
			Discount on Bonds Payable	80,000	
			Bonds Payable		2,000,000
Dec.	31		Interest Expense	70,000	
			Cash		70,000
	31		Interest Expense	1,600	
			Discount on Bonds Payable		1,600
			Amortization of discount from July 1 to December 31.		
	31		Income Summary	71,600	
			Interest Expense		71,600
2012					
June	30		Interest Expense	70,000	
			Cash		70,000
Dec.	31		Interest Expense	70,000	
			Cash		70,000
	31		Interest Expense	3,200	
			Discount on Bonds Payable		3,200
			Amortization of discount from January 1 to December 31.		
	31		Income Summary	143,200	
			Interest Expense		143,200
2018					
June	30		Bonds Payable	2,000,000	
			Loss on Redemption of Bonds Payable	87,600	
			Discount on Bonds Payable		57,600
			Cash		2,030,000

2. a. 2011: $71,600 = $70,000 + $1,600

   b. 2012: $143,200 = $70,000 + $70,000 + $3,200

3.

Initial carrying amount of bonds	$1,920,000
Discount amortized on December 31, 2011	1,600
Discount amortized on December 31, 2012	3,200
Carrying amount of bonds, December 31, 2012	$1,924,800

Discussion Questions

1. Describe the two distinct obligations incurred by a corporation when issuing bonds.
2. Explain the meaning of each of the following terms as they relate to a bond issue: (a) convertible, (b) callable, and (c) debenture.
3. If you asked your broker to purchase for you a 12% bond when the market interest rate for such bonds was 11%, would you expect to pay more or less than the face amount for the bond? Explain.
4. A corporation issues $18,000,000 of 10% bonds to yield interest at the rate of 8%. (a) Was the amount of cash received from the sale of the bonds greater or less than $18,000,000? (b) Identify the following terms related to the bond issue: (1) face amount, (2) market or effective rate of interest, (3) contract rate of interest, and (4) maturity amount.
5. If bonds issued by a corporation are sold at a premium, is the market rate of interest greater or less than the contract rate?
6. The following data relate to a $200,000,000, 5% bond issued for a selected semiannual interest period:

Bond carrying amount at beginning of period	$216,221,792
Interest paid during period	5,000,000
Interest expense allocable to the period	4,864,990

(a) Were the bonds issued at a discount or at a premium? (b) What is the unamortized amount of the discount or premium account at the beginning of the period? (c) What account was debited to amortize the discount or premium?

7. Bonds Payable has a balance of $3,500,000 and Discount on Bonds Payable has a balance of $125,000. If the issuing corporation redeems the bonds at 97, is there a gain or loss on the bond redemption?
8. What is a mortgage note?
9. Fleeson Company needs additional funds to purchase equipment for a new production facility and is considering either issuing bonds payable or borrowing the money from a local bank in the form of an installment note. How does an installment note differ from a bond payable?
10. How would a bond payable be reported on the balance sheet if: (a) it is payable within one year and (b) it is payable beyond one year?

Practice Exercises

Learning Objectives	Example Exercises

OBJ. 1 EE 14-1 p. 628

PE 14-1A Alternative financing plans

Baker Co. is considering the following alternative financing plans:

	Plan 1	Plan 2
Issue 5% bonds (at face value)	$3,000,000	$1,500,000
Issue preferred $4 stock, $25 par	—	2,500,000
Issue common stock, $40 par	3,000,000	2,000,000

Income tax is estimated at 40% of income.

Determine the earnings per share of common stock, assuming income before bond interest and income tax is $1,000,000.

OBJ. 1 EE 14-1 p. 628

PE 14-1B Alternative financing plans

Fly Co. is considering the following alternative financing plans:

	Plan 1	Plan 2
Issue 12% bonds (at face value)	$10,000,000	$5,000,000
Issue preferred $1.75 stock, $20 par	—	8,000,000
Issue common stock, $20 par	10,000,000	7,000,000

Income tax is estimated at 40% of income.

Determine the earnings per share of common stock, assuming income before bond interest and income tax is $2,000,000.

OBJ. 3 EE 14-2 p. 631

PE 14-2A Issuing bonds at a discount

On the first day of the fiscal year, a company issues a $4,000,000, 10%, 10-year bond that pays semiannual interest of $200,000 ($4,000,000 × 10% × ½), receiving cash of $3,760,992. Journalize the bond issuance.

OBJ. 3 EE 14-2 p. 631

PE 14-2B Issuing bonds at a discount

On the first day of the fiscal year, a company issues a $1,500,000, 9%, five-year bond that pays semiannual interest of $67,500 ($1,500,000 × 9% × ½), receiving cash of $1,334,398. Journalize the bond issuance.

OBJ. 3 EE 14-3 p. 632

PE 14-3A Discount amortization

Using the bond from Practice Exercise 14-2A, journalize the first interest payment and the amortization of the related bond discount. Round to the nearest dollar.

OBJ. 3 EE 14-3 p. 632

PE 14-3B Discount amortization

Using the bond from Practice Exercise 14-2B, journalize the first interest payment and the amortization of the related bond discount. Round to the nearest dollar.

OBJ. 3 EE 14-4 p. 633

PE 14-4A Issuing bonds at a premium

A company issues a $2,000,000, 9%, five-year bond that pays semiannual interest of $90,000 ($2,000,000 × 9% × ½), receiving cash of $2,166,332. Journalize the bond issuance.

OBJ. 3 EE 14-4 p. 633

PE 14-4B Issuing bonds at a premium

A company issues a $6,000,000, 12%, five-year bond that pays semiannual interest of $360,000 ($6,000,000 × 12% × ½), receiving cash of $6,463,304. Journalize the bond issuance.

Learning Objectives	Example Exercises

OBJ. 3 EE 14-5 p. 634

PE 14-5A Premium amortization

Using the bond from Practice Exercise 14-4A, journalize the first interest payment and the amortization of the related bond premium. Round to the nearest dollar.

OBJ. 3 EE 14-5 p. 634

PE 14-5B Premium amortization

Using the bond from Practice Exercise 14-4B, journalize the first interest payment and the amortization of the related bond premium. Round to the nearest dollar.

OBJ. 3 EE 14-6 p. 635

PE 14-6A Redemption of bonds payable

An $800,000 bond issue on which there is an unamortized discount of $60,000 is redeemed for $760,000. Journalize the redemption of the bonds.

OBJ. 3 EE 14-6 p. 635

PE 14-6B Redemption of bonds payable

A $450,000 bond issue on which there is an unamortized premium of $25,000 is redeemed for $441,000. Journalize the redemption of the bonds.

OBJ. 4 EE 14-7 p. 638

PE 14-7A Journalizing installment notes

On the first day of the fiscal year, a company issues $100,000, 8%, six-year installment notes that have annual payments of $21,632. The first note payment consists of $8,000 of interest and $13,632 of principal repayment.

a. Journalize the entry to record the issuance of the installment notes.

b. Journalize the first annual note payment.

OBJ. 4 EE 14-7 p. 638

PE 14-7B Journalizing installment notes

On the first day of the fiscal year, a company issues $55,000, 9%, five-year installment notes that have annual payments of $14,140. The first note payment consists of $4,950 of interest and $9,190 of principal repayment.

a. Journalize the entry to record the issuance of the installment notes.

b. Journalize the first annual note payment.

OBJ. 6 EE 14-8 p. 640

PE 14-8A Number of times interest charges are earned

Katula Company reported the following on the company's income statement in 2012 and 2011:

	2012	2011
Interest expense	$ 250,000	$ 275,000
Income before income tax expense	3,100,000	4,400,000

a. Determine the number of times interest charges were earned for 2011 and 2012. Round to one decimal place.

b. Is the number of times interest charges are earned improving or declining?

OBJ. 6 EE 14-8 p. 640

PE 14-8B Number of times interest charges are earned

Marsh Products, Inc., reported the following on the company's income statement in 2012 and 2011:

	2012	2011
Interest expense	$ 420,000	$ 375,000
Income before income tax expense	4,200,000	3,000,000

a. Determine the number of times interest charges were earned for 2011 and 2012. Round to one decimal place.

b. Is the number of times interest charges are earned improving or declining?

Exercises

OBJ. 1
✔ a. $1.30

EX 14-1 Effect of financing on earnings per share

Kelton Co., which produces and sells skiing equipment, is financed as follows:

Bonds payable, 8% (issued at face amount)	$20,000,000
Preferred $2 stock, $10 par	20,000,000
Common stock, $25 par	20,000,000

Income tax is estimated at 40% of income.

Determine the earnings per share of common stock, assuming that the income before bond interest and income tax is (a) $10,000,000, (b) $12,000,000, and (c) $14,000,000.

OBJ. 1

EX 14-2 Evaluate alternative financing plans

Based on the data in Exercise 14-1, what factors other than earnings per share should be considered in evaluating these alternative financing plans?

OBJ. 1

EX 14-3 Corporate financing

The financial statements for Nike, Inc., are presented in Appendix C at the end of the text. What is the major source of financing for Nike?

OBJ. 3

EX 14-4 Bond price

Procter and Gamble's 4.7% bonds due in 2019 were reported as selling for 104.797.

Were the bonds selling at a premium or at a discount? Why is Proctor & Gamble able to sell its bonds at this price?

OBJ. 3

EX 14-5 Entries for issuing bonds

Austin Co. produces and distributes semiconductors for use by computer manufacturers. Austin Co. issued $15,000,000 of 12-year, 12% bonds on May 1 of the current year, with interest payable on May 1 and November 1. The fiscal year of the company is the calendar year. Journalize the entries to record the following selected transactions for the current year:

May 1. Issued the bonds for cash at their face amount.

Nov. 1. Paid the interest on the bonds.

Dec. 31. Recorded accrued interest for two months.

OBJ. 3
✔ b. $2,867,977

EX 14-6 Entries for issuing bonds and amortizing discount by straight-line method

On the first day of its fiscal year, Keller Company issued $25,000,000 of five–year, 10% bonds to finance its operations of producing and selling home improvement products. Interest is payable semiannually. The bonds were issued at a market (effective) interest rate of 12%, resulting in Keller Company receiving cash of $23,160,113.

a. Journalize the entries to record the following:
   1. Sale of the bonds.
   2. First semiannual interest payment. (Amortization of discount is to be recorded annually.)
   3. Second semiannual interest payment.
   4. Amortization of discount at the end of the first year, using the straight-line method. (Round to the nearest dollar.)

b. Determine the amount of the bond interest expense for the first year.

c. Explain why the company was able to issue the bonds for only $23,160,113 rather than for the face amount of $25,000,000.

OBJ. 2, 3

EX 14-7 Entries for issuing bonds and amortizing premium by straight-line method

McCool Corporation wholesales repair products to equipment manufacturers. On April 1, 2010, McCool Corporation issued $30,000,000 of five-year, 10% bonds at a market (effective) interest rate of 8%, receiving cash of $32,446,500. Interest is payable semiannually on April 1 and October 1. Journalize the entries to record the following:

a. Sale of bonds on April 1, 2012.

b. First interest payment on October 1, 2012, and amortization of bond premium for six months, using the straight-line method. (Round to the nearest dollar.)

c. Explain why the company was able to issue the bonds for $32,446,500 rather than for the face amount of $30,000,000.

OBJ. 3

EX 14-8 Entries for issuing and calling bonds; loss

Dillip Corp., a wholesaler of office equipment, issued $45,000,000 of 10-year, 10% callable bonds on March 1, 2012, with interest payable on March 1 and September 1. The fiscal year of the company is the calendar year. Journalize the entries to record the following selected transactions:

2012

Mar. 1. Issued the bonds for cash at their face amount.

Sept. 1. Paid the interest on the bonds.

2016

Sept. 1. Called the bond issue at 103, the rate provided in the bond indenture. (Omit entry for payment of interest.)

OBJ. 3

EX 14-9 Entries for issuing and calling bonds; gain

Fogel Corp. produces and sells renewable energy equipment. To finance its operations, Fogel Corp. issued $32,000,000 of 20-year, 11% callable bonds on January 1, 2012, with interest payable on January 1 and July 1. The fiscal year of the company is the calendar year. Journalize the entries to record the following selected transactions:

2012

Jan. 1. Issued the bonds for cash at their face amount.

July 1. Paid the interest on the bonds.

2018

July 1. Called the bond issue at 97, the rate provided in the bond indenture. (Omit entry for payment of interest.)

OBJ. 4

EX 14-10 Entries for issuing installment note transactions

On the first day of the fiscal year, Harris Company borrowed $65,000 by giving a 10-year, 6% installment note to Cuba Bank. The note requires annual payments of $8,832, with the first payment occurring on the last day of the fiscal year. The first payment consists of interest of $3,900 and principal repayment of $4,932.

a. Journalize the entries to record the following:

   1. Issued the installment note for cash on the first day of the fiscal year.

   2. Paid the first annual payment on the note.

b. Explain how the notes payable would be reported on the balance sheet at the end of the first year.

OBJ. 4

EX 14-11 Entries for issuing installment note transactions

On January 1, 2012, Averill Company issued a $120,000, 8-year, 10% installment note from Deacon Bank. The note requires annual payments of $22,493, beginning on December 31, 2012. Journalize the entries to record the following:

2012

Jan. 1. Issued the notes for cash at their face amount.

Dec. 31. Paid the annual payment on the note, which consisted of interest of $12,000 and principal of $10,493.

2017

Dec. 31. Paid the annual payment on the note, which consisted of interest of $5,594 and principal of $16,899.

OBJ. 4

EX 14-12 Entries for issuing installment note transactions

On January 1, 2012, Daan Company obtained a $28,000, four-year, 9% installment note from Poklers Bank. The note requires annual payments of $8,642, beginning on December 31, 2012.

a. Prepare an amortization table for this installment note, similar to the one presented in Exhibit 3.

b. Journalize the entries for the issuance of the note and the four annual note payments.

c. Describe how the annual note payment would be reported in the 2012 income statement.

OBJ. 5

EX 14-13 Reporting bonds

At the beginning of the current year, two bond issues (Putnam Industries 5% 10-year bonds and Rucker Corporation 6% five-year bonds) were outstanding. During the year, the Putnam Industries bonds were redeemed and a significant loss on the redemption of bonds was reported as an extraordinary item on the income statement. At the end of the year, the Rucker Corporation bonds were reported as a noncurrent liability. The maturity date on the Rucker Corporation bonds was early in the following year.

Identify the flaws in the reporting practices related to the two bond issues.

OBJ. 6

F·A·I

EX 14-14 Number of times interest charges are earned

The following data were taken from recent annual reports of Southwest Airlines, which operates a low-fare airline service to over 50 cities in the United States.

	Current Year	Preceding Year
Interest expense	$105,000,000	$69,000,000
Income before income tax	278,000,000	1,058,000

a. Determine the number of times interest charges were earned for the current and preceding years. Round to one decimal place.

b. What conclusions can you draw?

OBJ. 6

F·A·I

EX 14-15 Number of times interest charges are earned

Quansi, Inc., reported the following on the company's income statement in 2012 and 2011:

	2012	2011
Interest expense	$ 10,000,000	$ 12,500,000
Income before income tax expense	240,000,000	375,000,000

a. Determine the number of times interest charges were earned for 2011 and 2012. Round to one decimal place.

b. Is the number of times interest charges are earned improving or declining?

OBJ. 6

EX 14-16 Number of times interest charges are earned

Vixeron Company reported the following on the company's income statement for 2012 and 2011:

	2012	2011
Interest expense	$3,000,000	$3,000,000
Income before income tax	1,200,000	3,600,000

a. Determine the number of times interest charges were earned for 2011 and 2012. Round to one decimal place.

b. What conclusions can you draw?

Appendix 1
EX 14-17 Present value of amounts due

Determine the present value of $750,000 to be received in three years, using an interest rate of 12%, compounded annually.

a. Use the present value table in Exhibit 4.

b. Why is the present value less than the $750,000 to be received in the future?

Appendix 1
EX 14-18 Present value of an annuity

Determine the present value of $150,000 to be received at the end of each of four years, using an interest rate of 7%, compounded annually, as follows:

a. By successive computations, using the present value table in Exhibit 4.

b. By using the present value table in Exhibit 5.

c. Why is the present value of the four $150,000 cash receipts less than the $600,000 to be received in the future?

✔ $79,077,130

Appendix 1
EX 14-19 Present value of an annuity

On January 1, 2012, you win $110,000,000 in the state lottery. The $110,000,000 prize will be paid in equal installments of $11,000,000 over 10 years. The payments will be made on December 31 of each year, beginning on December 31, 2012. If the current interest rate is 6.5%, determine the present value of your winnings. Use the present value tables in Appendix A.

Appendix 1
EX 14-20 Present value of an annuity

Assume the same data as in Appendix 1 Exercise 14–19, except that the current interest rate is 13%.

Will the present value of your winnings using an interest rate of 13% be one-half the present value of your winnings using an interest rate of 6.5%? Why or why not?

Appendix 1
EX 14-21 Present value of bonds payable; discount

Baliga Co. produces and sells high-quality audio equipment. To finance its operations, Baliga Co. issued $18,000,000 of five-year, 8% bonds with interest payable semiannually at a market (effective) interest rate of 10%. Determine the present value of the bonds payable, using the present value tables in Exhibits 4 and 5. Round to the nearest dollar.

✔ $86,030,076

Appendix 1
EX 14-22 Present value of bonds payable; premium

Herbst Co. issued $80,000,000 of five-year, 13% bonds with interest payable semiannually, at a market (effective) interest rate of 11%. Determine the present value of the bonds payable, using the present value tables in Exhibits 4 and 5. Round to the nearest dollar.

✔ b. $3,396,512

Appendix 2
EX 14-23 Amortize discount by interest method

On the first day of its fiscal year, Ramsey Company issued $35,000,000 of 10-year, 9% bonds to finance its operations. Interest is payable semiannually. The bonds were issued at a market (effective) interest rate of 11%, resulting in Ramsey Company receiving cash of $30,817,399. The company uses the interest method.

a. Journalize the entries to record the following:

1. Sale of the bonds.
2. First semiannual interest payment, including amortization of discount. Round to the nearest dollar.

(continued)

3. Second semiannual interest payment, including amortization of discount. Round to the nearest dollar.

b. Compute the amount of the bond interest expense for the first year.

c. Explain why the company was able to issue the bonds for only $30,817,399 rather than for the face amount of $35,000,000.

✔ b. $1,879,754

Appendix 2

EX 14-24 Amortize premium by interest method

Knight Corporation wholesales auto parts to auto manufacturers. On March 1, 2012, Knight Corporation issued $17,500,000 of five-year, 12% bonds at a market (effective) interest rate of 10%, receiving cash of $18,851,252. Interest is payable semiannually. Knight Corporation's fiscal year begins on March 1. The company uses the interest method.

a. Journalize the entries to record the following:
   1. Sale of the bonds.
   2. First semiannual interest payment, including amortization of premium. Round to the nearest dollar.
   3. Second semiannual interest payment, including amortization of premium. Round to the nearest dollar.

b. Determine the bond interest expense for the first year.

c. Explain why the company was able to issue the bonds for $18,851,252 rather than for the face amount of $17,500,000.

✔ a. $53,680,315
✔ c. $295,932

Appendix 1 and Appendix 2

EX 14-25 Compute bond proceeds, amortizing premium by interest method, and interest expense

Evans Co. produces and sells motorcycle parts. On the first day of its fiscal year, Evans Co. issued $50,000,000 of five-year, 14% bonds at a market (effective) interest rate of 12%, with interest payable semiannually. Compute the following, presenting figures used in your computations.

a. The amount of cash proceeds from the sale of the bonds. Use the tables of present values in Exhibits 4 and 5. Round to the nearest dollar.

b. The amount of premium to be amortized for the first semiannual interest payment period, using the interest method. Round to the nearest dollar.

c. The amount of premium to be amortized for the second semiannual interest payment period, using the interest method. Round to the nearest dollar.

d. The amount of the bond interest expense for the first year.

✔ a. $53,530,290
✔ b. $479,469

Appendix 1 and Appendix 2

EX 14-26 Compute bond proceeds, amortizing discount by interest method, and interest expense

Lewis Co. produces and sells aviation equipment. On the first day of its fiscal year, Lewis Co. issued $60,000,000 of five-year, 10% bonds at a market (effective) interest rate of 13%, with interest payable semiannually. Compute the following, presenting figures used in your computations.

a. The amount of cash proceeds from the sale of the bonds. Use the tables of present values in Exhibits 4 and 5. Round to the nearest dollar.

b. The amount of discount to be amortized for the first semiannual interest payment period, using the interest method. Round to the nearest dollar.

c. The amount of discount to be amortized for the second semiannual interest payment period, using the interest method. Round to the nearest dollar.

d. The amount of the bond interest expense for the first year.

Problems Series A

OBJ. 1

✔ 1. Plan 3: $5.35

PR 14-1A Effect of financing on earnings per share

Three different plans for financing a $200,000,000 corporation are under consideration by its organizers. Under each of the following plans, the securities will be issued at their par or face amount, and the income tax rate is estimated at 40% of income.

	Plan 1	Plan 2	Plan 3
11% bonds	—	—	$100,000,000
Preferred 5% stock, $40 par	—	$100,000,000	50,000,000
Common stock, $25 par	$200,000,000	100,000,000	50,000,000
Total	$200,000,000	$200,000,000	$200,000,000

Instructions

1. Determine for each plan the earnings per share of common stock, assuming that the income before bond interest and income tax is $30,000,000.
2. Determine for each plan the earnings per share of common stock, assuming that the income before bond interest and income tax is $16,000,000.
3. Discuss the advantages and disadvantages of each plan.

OBJ. 2, 3

✔ 3. $1,439,986

PR 14-2A Bond discount, entries for bonds payable transactions

On July 1, 2012, Bliss Industries Inc. issued $24,000,000 of 20-year, 11% bonds at a market (effective) interest rate of 14%, receiving cash of $19,200,577. Interest on the bonds is payable semiannually on December 31 and June 30. The fiscal year of the company is the calendar year.

Instructions

1. Journalize the entry to record the amount of cash proceeds from the sale of the bonds.
2. Journalize the entries to record the following:
   a. The first semiannual interest payment on December 31, 2012, and the amortization of the bond discount, using the straight-line method. (Round to the nearest dollar.)
   b. The interest payment on June 30, 2013, and the amortization of the bond discount, using the straight-line method. (Round to the nearest dollar.)
3. Determine the total interest expense for 2012.
4. Will the bond proceeds always be less than the face amount of the bonds when the contract rate is less than the market rate of interest?
5. (Appendix 1) Compute the price of $19,200,577 received for the bonds by using the tables of present value in Appendix A at the end of the text. (Round to the nearest dollar.)

OBJ. 2, 3

✔ 3. $7,677,935

PR 14-3A Bond premium, entries for bonds payable transactions

Fabulator, Inc. produces and sells fashion clothing. On July 1, 2012, Fabulator, Inc. issued $120,000,000 of 20-year, 14% bonds at a market (effective) interest rate of 11%, receiving cash of $148,882,608. Interest on the bonds is payable semiannually on December 31 and June 30. The fiscal year of the company is the calendar year.

Instructions

1. Journalize the entry to record the amount of cash proceeds from the sale of the bonds.
2. Journalize the entries to record the following:
   a. The first semiannual interest payment on December 31, 2012, and the amortization of the bond premium, using the straight-line method. (Round to the nearest dollar.)
   b. The interest payment on June 30, 2013, and the amortization of the bond premium, using the straight-line method. (Round to the nearest dollar.)
3. Determine the total interest expense for 2012.
4. Will the bond proceeds always be greater than the face amount of the bonds when the contract rate is greater than the market rate of interest?

(continued)

5. (Appendix 1) Compute the price of $148,882,608 received for the bonds by using the tables of present value in Appendix A at the end of the text. (Round to the nearest dollar.)

OBJ. 3, 4

✔ 3. $58,236,896

PR 14-4A Entries for bonds payable and installment note transactions

The following transactions were completed by Simmons Inc., whose fiscal year is the calendar year:

2012

July 1. Issued $64,000,000 of 10-year, 12% callable bonds dated July 1, 2012, at a market (effective) rate of 14%, receiving cash of $57,219,878. Interest is payable semiannually on December 31 and June 30.

Oct. 1. Borrowed $320,000 as a five-year, 6% installment note from Ibis Bank. The note requires annual payments of $75,967, with the first payment occurring on September 30, 2013.

Dec. 31. Accrued $4,800 of interest on the installment note. The interest is payable on the date of the next installment note payment.

31. Paid the semiannual interest on the bonds. The bond discount is amortized annually in a separate journal entry.

31. Recorded bond discount amortization of $339,006, which was determined using the straight-line method.

31. Closed the interest expense account.

2013

June 30. Paid the semiannual interest on the bonds.

Sept. 30. Paid the annual payment on the note, which consisted of interest of $19,200 and principal of $56,767.

Dec. 31. Accrued $3,948 of interest on the installment note. The interest is payable on the date of the next installment note payment.

31. Paid the semiannual interest on the bonds. The bond discount is amortized annually in a separate journal entry.

31. Recorded bond discount amortization of $678,012, which was determined using the straight-line method.

31. Closed the interest expense account.

2014

June 30. Recorded the redemption of the bonds, which were called at 98. The balance in the bond discount account is $5,424,098 after payment of interest and amortization of discount have been recorded. (Record the redemption only.)

Sept. 30. Paid the second annual payment on the note, which consisted of interest of $15,794 and principal of $60,173.

Instructions

1. Journalize the entries to record the foregoing transactions.
2. Indicate the amount of the interest expense in (a) 2012 and (b) 2013.
3. Determine the carrying amount of the bonds as of December 31, 2013.

✔ 3. $1,344,040

Appendix 1 and Appendix 2

PR 14-5A Bond discount, entries for bonds payable transactions, interest method of amortizing bond discount

On July 1, 2012, Bliss Industries, Inc. issued $24,000,000 of 20-year, 11% bonds at a market (effective) interest rate of 14%, receiving cash of $19,200,577. Interest on the bonds is payable semiannually on December 31 and June 30. The fiscal year of the company is the calendar year.

Instructions

1. Journalize the entry to record the amount of cash proceeds from the sale of the bonds.
2. Journalize the entries to record the following:

a. The first semiannual interest payment on December 31, 2012, and the amortization of the bond discount, using the interest method. (Round to the nearest dollar.)

b. The interest payment on June 30, 2013, and the amortization of the bond discount, using the interest method. (Round to the nearest dollar.)

3. Determine the total interest expense for 2012.

✔ 3. $8,188,543

Appendix 1 and Appendix 2

PR 14-6A Bond premium, entries for bonds payable transactions, interest method of amortizing bond discount

Fabulator, Inc. produces and sells fashion clothing. On July 1, 2012, Fabulator, Inc. issued $120,000,000 of 20-year, 14% bonds at a market (effective) interest rate of 11%, receiving cash of $148,882,608. Interest on the bonds is payable semiannually on December 31 and June 30. The fiscal year of the company is the calendar year.

Instructions

1. Journalize the entry to record the amount of cash proceeds from the sale of the bonds.
2. Journalize the entries to record the following:
   a. The first semiannual interest payment on December 31, 2012, and the amortization of the bond discount, using the interest method. (Round to the nearest dollar.)
   b. The interest payment on June 30, 2013, and the amortization of the bond discount, using the interest method. (Round to the nearest dollar.)
3. Determine the total interest expense for 2012.

Problems Series B

OBJ. 1

✔ 1. Plan 3: $4.75

PR 14-1B Effect of financing on earnings per share

Three different plans for financing a $40,000,000 corporation are under consideration by its organizers. Under each of the following plans, the securities will be issued at their par or face amount, and the income tax rate is estimated at 40% of income.

	Plan 1	Plan 2	Plan 3
10% bonds	—	—	$20,000,000
Preferred $2.50 stock, $50 par	—	$20,000,000	10,000,000
Common stock, $25 par	$40,000,000	20,000,000	10,000,000
Total	$40,000,000	$40,000,000	$40,000,000

Instructions

1. Determine for each plan the earnings per share of common stock, assuming that the income before bond interest and income tax is $6,000,000.
2. Determine for each plan the earnings per share of common stock, assuming that the income before bond interest and income tax is $3,200,000.
3. Discuss the advantages and disadvantages of each plan.

OBJ. 2, 3

✔ 3. $2,100,119

PR 14-2B Bond discount, entries for bonds payable transactions

On July 1, 2012, Hallo Corporation, a wholesaler of communication equipment, issued $34,000,000 of 20-year, 12% bonds at a market (effective) interest rate of 13%, receiving cash of $31,595,241. Interest on the bonds is payable semiannually on December 31 and June 30. The fiscal year of the company is the calendar year.

Instructions

1. Journalize the entry to record the amount of cash proceeds from the sale of the bonds.
2. Journalize the entries to record the following:
   a. The first semiannual interest payment on December 31, 2012, and the amortization of the bond discount, using the straight-line method. (Round to the nearest dollar.)

(continued)

   b. The interest payment on June 30, 2013, and the amortization of the bond discount, using the straight-line method. (Round to the nearest dollar.)
3. Determine the total interest expense for 2012.
4. Will the bond proceeds always be less than the face amount of the bonds when the contract rate is less than the market rate of interest?
5. (Appendix 1) Compute the price of $31,595,241 received for the bonds by using the tables of present value in Appendix A at the end of the text. (Round to the nearest dollar.)

OBJ. 2, 3

✔ 3. $803,316

PR 14-3B Bond premium, entries for bonds payable transactions

Buddie Corporation produces and sells baseball gloves. On July 1, 2012, Buddie Corporation issued $12,500,000 of 10-year, 14% bonds at a market (effective) interest rate of 12%, receiving cash of $13,933,680. Interest on the bonds is payable semiannually on December 31 and June 30. The fiscal year of the company is the calendar year.

Instructions

1. Journalize the entry to record the amount of cash proceeds from the sale of the bonds.
2. Journalize the entries to record the following:
   a. The first semiannual interest payment on December 31, 2012, and the amortization of the bond premium, using the straight-line method. (Round to the nearest dollar.)
   b. The interest payment on June 30, 2013, and the amortization of the bond premium, using the straight-line method. (Round to the nearest dollar.)
3. Determine the total interest expense for 2012.
4. Will the bond proceeds always be greater than the face amount of the bonds when the contract rate is greater than the market rate of interest?
5. (Appendix 1) Compute the price of $13,933,680 received for the bonds by using the tables of present value in Appendix A at the end of the text. (Round to the nearest dollar.)

OBJ. 3, 4

✔ 3. $48,673,530

PR 14-4B Entries for bonds payable and installment note transactions

The following transactions were completed by Wilkerson Inc., whose fiscal year is the calendar year:

2012

July 1. Issued $42,000,000 of 10-year, 13% callable bonds dated July 1, 2012, at a market (effective) rate of 10%, receiving cash of $49,851,213. Interest is payable semiannually on December 31 and June 30.

Oct. 1. Borrowed $510,000 as a six-year, 9% installment note from Challenger Bank. The note requires annual payments of $113,689, with the first payment occurring on September 30, 2013.

Dec. 31. Accrued $11,475 of interest on the installment note. The interest is payable on the date of the next installment note payment.

31. Paid the semiannual interest on the bonds. The bond discount is amortized annually in a separate journal entry.

31. Recorded bond premium amortization of $392,561, which was determined using the straight-line method.

31. Closed the interest expense account.

2013

June 30. Paid the semiannual interest on the bonds.

Sept. 30. Paid the annual payment on the note, which consisted of interest of $45,900 and principal of $67,789.

Dec. 31. Accrued $9,950 of interest on the installment note. The interest is payable on the date of the next installment note payment.

Dec. 31. Paid the semiannual interest on the bonds. The bond discount is amortized annually in a separate journal entry.

31. Recorded bond premium amortization of $785,122, which was determined using the straight-line method.

31. Closed the interest expense account.

2014

June 30. Recorded the redemption of the bonds, which were called at 102. The balance in the bond premium account is $6,280,969 after payment of interest and amortization of premium have been recorded. (Record the redemption only.)

Sept. 30. Paid the second annual payment on the note, which consisted of interest of $39,799 and principal of $73,890.

Instructions

1. Journalize the entries to record the foregoing transactions.
2. Indicate the amount of the interest expense in (a) 2012 and (b) 2013.
3. Determine the carrying amount of the bonds as of December 31, 2013.

✔ 3. $2,053,691

Appendix 1 and Appendix 2

PR 14-5B Bond discount, entries for bonds payable transactions, interest method of amortizing bond discount

On July 1, 2012, Hallo Corporation, a wholesaler of communication equipment, issued $34,000,000 of 20-year, 12% bonds at a market (effective) interest rate of 13%, receiving cash of $31,595,241. Interest on the bonds is payable semiannually on December 31 and June 30. The fiscal year of the company is the calendar year.

Instructions

1. Journalize the entry to record the amount of cash proceeds from the sale of the bonds.
2. Journalize the entries to record the following:
   a. The first semiannual interest payment on December 31, 2012, and the amortization of the bond discount, using the interest method. (Round to the nearest dollar.)
   b. The interest payment on June 30, 2013, and the amortization of the bond discount, using the interest method. (Round to the nearest dollar.)
3. Determine the total interest expense for 2012.

✔ 3. $836,021

Appendix 1 and Appendix 2

PR 14-6B Bond premium, entries for bonds payable transactions, interest method of amortizing bond premium

Buddie Corporation produces and sells baseball gloves. On July 1, 2012, Buddie Corporation issued $12,500,000 of 10-year, 14% bonds at a market (effective) interest rate of 12%, receiving cash of $13,933,680. Interest on the bonds is payable semiannually on December 31 and June 30. The fiscal year of the company is the calendar year.

Instructions

1. Journalize the entry to record the amount of cash proceeds from the sale of the bonds.
2. Journalize the entries to record the following:
   a. The first semiannual interest payment on December 31, 2012, and the amortization of the bond premium, using the interest method. (Round to the nearest dollar.)
   b. The interest payment on June 30, 2013, and the amortization of the bond premium, using the interest method. (Round to the nearest dollar.)
3. Determine the total interest expense for 2012.

Cases & Projects

CP 14-1 General Electric bond issuance

General Electric Capital, a division of General Electric, uses long-term debt extensively. In a recent year, GE Capital issued $11 billion in long-term debt to investors, then within days filed legal documents to prepare for another $50 billion long-term debt issue. As a result of the $50 billion filing, the price of the initial $11 billion offering declined (due to higher risk of more debt).

> *Bill Gross, a manager of a bond investment fund, "denounced a 'lack in candor' related to GE's recent debt deal. 'It was the most recent and most egregious example of how bondholders are mistreated.' Gross argued that GE was not forthright when GE Capital recently issued $11 billion in bonds, one of the largest issues ever from a U.S. corporation. What bothered Gross is that three days after the issue the company announced its intention to sell as much as $50 billion in additional debt, warrants, preferred stock, guarantees, letters of credit and promissory notes at some future date."*

In your opinion, did GE Capital act unethically by selling $11 billion of long-term debt without telling those investors that a few days later it would be filing documents to prepare for another $50 billion debt offering?

Source: Jennifer Ablan, "Gross Shakes the Bond Market; GE Calms It, a Bit," *Barron's,* March 25, 2002.

CP 14-2 Ethics and professional conduct in business

Juicy Energy Industries develops and produces bio mass, an alternative energy source. The company has an outstanding $10,000,000, 30-year, 10% bond issue dated July 1, 2007. The bond issue is due June 30, 2037. Some bond indentures require the corporation issuing the bonds to transfer cash to a special cash fund, called a sinking fund, over the life of the bond. Such funds help assure investors that there will be adequate cash to pay the bonds at their maturity date.

The bond indenture requires a bond sinking fund, which has a balance of $1,200,000 as of July 1, 2012. The company is currently experiencing a shortage of funds due to a recent acquisition. Dillip Fogel, the company's treasurer, is considering using the funds from the bond sinking fund to cover payroll and other bills that are coming due at the end of the month. Dillip's brother-in-law is a trustee in a sinking fund, who has indicated willingness to allow Dillip to use the funds from the sinking fund to temporarily meet the company's cash needs.

Discuss whether Dillip's proposal is appropriate.

CP 14-3 Present values

Bailey Mills recently won the jackpot in the New Jersey lottery while he was visiting his parents. When he arrived at the lottery office to collect his winnings, he was offered the following three payout options:

a. Receive $40,000,000 in cash today.

b. Receive $10,000,000 today and $3,600,000 per year for 10 years, with the first payment being received one year from today.

c. Receive $5,000,000 per year for 20 years, with the first payment being received one year from today.

Assuming that the effective rate of interest is 10%, which payout option should Bailey select? Explain your answer and provide any necessary supporting calculations.

CP 14-4 Preferred stock vs. bonds

Accusport Inc. has decided to expand its operations to owning and operating golf courses. The following is an excerpt from a conversation between the chief executive officer, Tucker Thorup, and the vice president of finance, Don Clark.

Tucker: Don, have you given any thought to how we're going to finance the acquisition of Knotty Pines Golf Course?

Don: Well, the two basic options, as I see it, are to issue either preferred stock or bonds. The equity market is a little depressed right now. The rumor is that the Federal Reserve Bank's going to increase the interest rates either this month or next.

Tucker: Yes, I've heard the rumor. The problem is that we can't wait around to see what's going to happen. We'll have to move on this next week if we want any chance to complete the acquisition of Knotty Pines Golf Course.

Don: Well, the bond market is strong right now. Maybe we should issue debt this time around.

Tucker: That's what I would have guessed as well. Knotty Pines Golf Course's financial statements look pretty good, except for the volatility of its income and cash flows. But that's characteristic of the industry.

Discuss the advantages and disadvantages of issuing preferred stock versus bonds.

CP 14-5 Financing business expansion

You hold a 25% common stock interest in the family-owned business, a construction equipment company. Your sister, who is the manager, has proposed an expansion of plant facilities at an expected cost of $10,000,000. Two alternative plans have been suggested as methods of financing the expansion. Each plan is briefly described as follows:

Plan 1. Issue $10,000,000 of 20-year, 10% notes at face amount.

Plan 2. Issue an additional 200,000 shares of $10 par common stock at $20 per share, and $6,000,000 of 20-year, 10% notes at face amount.

The balance sheet as of the end of the previous fiscal year is as follows:

Thacker, Inc.
Balance Sheet
December 31, 2012

Assets	
Current assets	$ 6,000,000
Property, plant, and equipment	9,000,000
Total assets	$15,000,000
Liabilities and Stockholders' Equity	
Liabilities	$ 4,500,000
Common stock, $10	1,600,000
Paid-in capital in excess of par	200,000
Retained earnings	8,700,000
Total liabilities and stockholders' equity	$15,000,000

Net income has remained relatively constant over the past several years. The expansion program is expected to increase yearly income before bond interest and income tax from $800,000 in the previous year to $1,500,000 for this year. Your sister has asked you, as the company treasurer, to prepare an analysis of each financing plan.

1. Prepare a table indicating the expected earnings per share on the common stock under each plan. Assume an income tax rate of 40%. Round to the nearest cent.
2. a. Discuss the factors that should be considered in evaluating the two plans.
   b. Which plan offers the greater benefit to the present stockholders? Give reasons for your opinion.

CP 14-6 Number of times interest charges are earned

The following financial data were taken from the financial statements of Williams-Sonoma, Inc.

	Fiscal Year		
	2009	2008	2007
Interest expense	$ 1,480	$ 2,099	$ 2,125
Earnings before taxes	41,953	316,340	337,186

1. What is the number of times interest charges are earned for Williams-Sonoma in 2009, 2008, and 2007? (Round your answers to one decimal place.)
2. Evaluate this ratio for Williams-Sonoma.

CHAPTER 15

red Prouser/Reuters/Landov

Investments and Fair Value Accounting

News Corporation

You invest cash to earn more cash. For example, you could deposit cash in a bank account to earn interest. You could also invest cash in preferred or common stocks and in corporate or U.S. government notes and bonds.

Preferred and common stock can be purchased through a stock exchange, such as the **New York Stock Exchange (NYSE)**. Preferred stock is purchased primarily with the expectation of earning dividends. Common stock is purchased with the expectation of earning dividends or realizing gains from a price increase in the stock.

Corporate and U.S. government bonds can also be purchased through a bond exchange. Bonds are purchased with the primary expectation of earning interest revenue.

Companies make investments for many of the same reasons that you would as an individual. For example, **News Corporation**, a diversified media company, which produces such popular television shows as *The Simpsons* and *American Idol*, has invested $150 million of available cash in stocks and bonds. These investments are held by News Corporation for interest, dividends, and expected price increases.

Unlike most individuals, however, companies also purchase significant amounts of the outstanding common stock of other companies for strategic reasons. For example, News Corporation invested in 32% of the Hulu, an online video joint venture with other major media companies.

Investments in debt and equity securities give rise to a number of accounting issues. These issues are described and illustrated in this chapter.

At a Glance 15

Describe why companies invest in debt and equity securities.

Key Points Cash can be used to (1) invest in current operations, (2) invest to earn additional revenue in marketable securities, or (3) invest in marketable securities for strategic reasons.

Learning Outcomes	Example Exercises	Practice Exercises
• Describe the ways excess cash is used by a business.		
• Describe the purpose of temporary investments.		
• Describe the strategic purpose of long-term investments.		

Describe and illustrate the accounting for debt investments.

Key Points The accounting for debt investments includes recording the purchase, interest revenue, and sale of the debt. Both the purchase and sale date may include accrued interest.

Learning Outcomes	Example Exercises	Practice Exercises
• Prepare journal entries to record the purchase of a debt investment, including accrued interest.	EE15-1	PE15-1A, 15-1B
• Prepare journal entries for interest revenue from debt investments.	EE15-1	PE15-1A, 15-1B
• Prepare journal entries to record the sale of a debt investment at a gain or loss.	EE15-1	PE15-1A, 15-1B

Describe and illustrate the accounting for equity investments.

Key Points The accounting for equity investments differs depending on the degree of control. Accounting for investments of less than 20% of the outstanding stock (no control) of the investee includes recording the purchase of stock, receipt of dividends, and sale of stock at a gain or loss. Influential investments of 20%–50% of the outstanding stock of an investee are accounted for under the *equity method*. An investment for more than 50% of the outstanding stock of an investee is treated as a *business combination* and accounted for using *consolidated financial statements*.

Learning Outcomes	Example Exercises	Practice Exercises
• Describe the accounting for less than 20%, 20%–50%, and greater than 50% investments.		
• Prepare journal entries to record the purchase of a stock investment.	EE15-2	PE15-2A, 15-2B
• Prepare journal entries for receipt of dividends.	EE15-2	PE15-2A, 15-2B
• Prepare journal entries for the sale of a stock investment at a gain or loss.	EE15-2	PE15-2A, 15-2B
• Prepare journal entries for the equity earnings of an equity method investee.	EE15-3	PE15-3A, 15-3B
• Prepare journal entries for the dividends received from an equity method investee.	EE15-3	PE15-3A, 15-3B
• Describe a business combination, parent company, and subsidiary company.		
• Describe consolidated financial statements.		

OBJ. 4 Describe and illustrate valuing and reporting investments in the financial statements.

Key Points Debt and equity securities are classified as (1) trading securities, (2) available-for-sale securities, and (3) held-to-maturity securities for reporting and valuation purposes. *Trading securities* are valued at *fair value*, with unrealized gains and losses reported on the income statement. *Available-for-sale securities* are debt and equity securities that are not classified as trading or held-to-maturity. Available-for-sale securities are reported at fair value with unrealized gains or losses reported in the Stockholders' Equity section of the balance sheet. *Held-to-maturity* investments are debt securities that are intended to be held until their maturity date. Held-to-maturity debt investments are valued at amortized cost.

Learning Outcomes	Example Exercises	Practice Exercises
• Describe trading securities, held-to-maturity securities, and available-for-sale securities.		
• Prepare journal entries to record the change in the fair value of a trading security portfolio.	**EE15-4**	**PE15-4A, 15-4B**
• Describe and illustrate the reporting of trading securities on the balance sheet.		
• Prepare journal entries to record the change in fair value of an available-for-sale security portfolio.	**EE15-5**	**PE15-5A, 15-5B**
• Describe and illustrate the reporting of available-for-sale securities on the balance sheet.		
• Describe the accounting for held-to-maturity debt securities.		

OBJ. 5 Describe fair value accounting and its implications for the future.

Key Points There is a trend toward fair value accounting in generally accepted accounting principles (GAAP). Fair value provides relevance at the sacrifice of objectivity for assets without established market prices.

Learning Outcomes	Example Exercises	Practice Exercises
• Describe the reasons why there is a trend toward fair value accounting.		
• Describe the disadvantages of fair value accounting.		
• Describe how fair value accounting impacts the balance sheet and income statement.		
• Describe the future of fair value accounting.		

OBJ. 6 Describe and illustrate the computation of dividend yield.

Key Points The dividend yield measures the cash return from common dividends as a percent of the market price. The ratio is computed as dividends per share of common stock divided by the market price per share of common stock.

Learning Outcomes	Example Exercises	Practice Exercises
• Compute dividend yield.	**EE15-6**	**PE15-6A, 15-6B**
• Describe how dividend yield measures the return to stockholders from dividends.		

Key Terms

accumulated other comprehensive income (687)
available-for-sale securities (679)
business combination (676)
comprehensive income (686)
consolidated financial statements (676)
cost method (673)
debt securities (669)
dividend yield (685)
equity method (674)
equity securities (669)
fair value (677)
held-to-maturity securities (681)
investee (672)
investments (669)
investor (672)
other comprehensive income (686)
parent company (676)
subsidiary company (676)
trading securities (677)
unrealized gain or loss (677)

Illustrative Problem

The following selected investment transactions were completed by Rosewell Company during 2012, its first year of operations:

2012

Jan. 11. Purchased 800 shares of Bryan Company stock as an available-for-sale security at $23 per share plus an $80 brokerage commission.

Feb. 6. Purchased $40,000 of 8% U.S. Treasury bonds at par value plus accrued interest for 36 days. The bonds pay interest on January 1 and July 1. The bonds were classified as held-to-maturity securities.

Mar. 3. Purchased 1,900 shares of Cohen Company stock as a trading security at $48 per share plus a $152 brokerage commission.

Apr. 5. Purchased 2,400 shares of Lyons Inc. stock as an available-for-sale security at $68 per share plus a $120 brokerage commission.

May 12. Purchased 200,000 shares of Myers Company at $37 per share plus an $8,000 brokerage commission. Myers Company has 800,000 common shares issued and outstanding. The equity method was used for this investment.

July 1. Received semiannual interest on bonds purchased on February 6.

Aug. 29. Sold 1,200 shares of Cohen Company stock at $61 per share less a $90 brokerage commission.

Oct. 5. Received an $0.80-per-share dividend on Bryan Company stock.

Nov. 11. Received a $1.10-per-share dividend on Myers Company stock.

16. Purchased 3,000 shares of Morningside Company stock as a trading security for $52 per share plus a $150 brokerage commission.

Dec. 31. Accrued interest on February 6 bonds.

31. Myers Company earned $1,200,000 during the year. Rosewell recorded its share of Myers Company earnings using the equity method.

31. Prepared adjusting entries for the portfolios of trading and available-for-sale securities based upon the following fair values (stock prices):

Bryan Company	$21
Cohen Company	43
Lyons Inc.	88
Myers Company	40
Morningside Company	45

Instructions

1. Journalize the preceding transactions.
2. Prepare the balance sheet disclosure for Rosewell Company's investments on December 31, 2012. Assume held-to-maturity investments are classified as noncurrent assets.

Solution

1.

Date		Account	Post. Ref.	Debit	Credit
2012 Jan.	11	Available-for-Sale Investments—Bryan Company		18,480*	
		Cash			18,480
		*(800 shares × $23 per share) + $80			

Date		Account	Post. Ref.	Debit	Credit
Feb.	6	Investments—U.S. Treasury Bonds		40,000	
		Interest Receivable		320*	
		Cash			40,320
		*$40,000 × 8% × (36 days/360 days)			

Date		Account	Post. Ref.	Debit	Credit
Mar.	3	Trading Investments—Cohen Company		91,352*	
		Cash			91,352
		*(1,900 shares × $48 per share) + $152			

Date		Account	Post. Ref.	Debit	Credit
Apr.	5	Available-for-Sale Investments—Lyons Inc.		163,320*	
		Cash			163,320
		*(2,400 shares × $68 per share) + $120			

Date		Account	Post. Ref.	Debit	Credit
May	12	Investment in Myers Company		7,408,000*	
		Cash			7,408,000
		*(200,000 shares × $37 per share) + $8,000			

Date		Account	Post. Ref.	Debit	Credit
July	1	Cash		1,600*	
		Interest Receivable			320
		Interest Revenue			1,280
		*$40,000 × 8% × ½			

Date		Account	Post. Ref.	Debit	Credit
Aug.	29	Cash		73,110*	
		Trading Investments—Cohen Company			57,696**
		Gain on Sale of Investments			15,414
		*(1,200 shares × $61 per share) – $90			
		**1,200 shares × ($91,352/1,900 shares)			

			Debit	Credit
2012 Oct.	5	Cash	640	
		Dividend Revenue		640
		*800 shares × $0.80 per share		

			Debit	Credit
Nov.	11	Cash	220,000	
		Investment in Myers Company Stock		220,000
		*200,000 shares × $1.10 per share		

			Debit	Credit
Nov.	16	Trading Investments—Morningside Company	156,150*	
		Cash		156,150
		*(3,000 shares × $52 per share) + $150		

			Debit	Credit
Dec.	31	Interest Receivable	1,600	
		Interest Revenue		1,600
		Accrue interest, $40,000 × 8% × ½.		

			Debit	Credit
Dec.	31	Investment in Myers Company Stock	300,000	
		Income of Myers Company		300,000
		Record equity income, $1,200,000 × (200,000 shares/800,000 shares).		

			Debit	Credit
Dec.	31	Unrealized Loss on Trading Investments	24,706	
		Valuation Allowance for Trading Investments		24,706
		Record decease in fair value of trading investments, $165,100 –$189,806.		

Name	**Number of Shares**	**Total Cost**	**Total Fair Value**
Cohen Company	700	$ 33,656	$ 30,100*
Morningside Company	3,000	156,150	135,000**
Total		$189,806	$165,100

*700 shares × $43 per share
**3,000 shares × $45 per share

Note: Myers Company is valued using the equity method; thus, the fair value is not used.

			Debit	Credit
Dec.	31	Valuation Allowance for Available-for-Sale Investments	46,200	
		Unrealized Gain (Loss) on Available-for-Sale Investments		46,200
		Record increase in fair value of available-for-sale investments, $228,000 – $181,800.		

Name	Number of Shares	Total Cost	Total Fair Value
Bryan Company	800	$ 18,480	$ 16,800*
Lyons Inc.	2,400	163,320	211,200**
Total		$181,800	$228,000

*800 shares × $21 per share
**2,400 shares × $88 per share

2.

Rosewell Company
Balance Sheet (Selected)
December 31, 2012

Current assets:		
Cash		$ XXX,XXX
Trading investments (at cost)	$189,806	
Less valuation allowance for trading investments	24,706	
Trading investments at fair value		165,100
Available-for-sale investments (at cost)	$181,800	
Plus valuation allowance for available-for-sale investments	46,200	
Available-for-sale investments at fair value		228,000
Noncurrent investments:		
Held-to-maturity investments		$ 40,000
Investments in Myers Company (equity method)		7,488,000
Stockholders' equity:		
Common stock		$ XX,XXX
Paid-in capital in excess of par value		XXX,XXX
Retained earnings		XXX,XXX
Plus unrealized gain (loss) on available-for-sale investments		46,200
Total stockholders' equity		$ XXX,XXX

Discussion Questions

1. Why might a business invest in another company's stock?
2. Why would there be a gain or loss on the sale of a bond investment?
3. When is using the cost method the appropriate accounting for equity investments?
4. How does the accounting for a dividend received differ between the cost method and the equity method?
5. If an investor owns more than 50% of an investee, how is this treated on the investor's financial statements?
6. What is the major difference in the accounting for a portfolio of trading securities and a portfolio of available-for-sale securities?
7. If Valuation Allowance for Trading Investments has a credit balance, how is it treated on the balance sheet?
8. How would a debit balance in Unrealized Gain (Loss) on Available-for-Sale Investments be disclosed in the financial statements?
9. What is the evidence of the trend toward fair value accounting?
10. What are some potential disadvantages of fair value accounting?

Practice Exercises

Learning Objectives | *Example Exercises*

OBJ. 2 EE 15-1 *p. 672*

PE 15-1A Bond transactions

Journalize the entries to record the following selected bond investment transactions for Capital Trust:

a. Purchased for cash $250,000 of Belmont City 4% bonds at 100 plus accrued interest of $1,500.

b. Received first semiannual interest.

c. Sold $80,000 of the bonds at 97 plus accrued interest of $500.

OBJ. 2 EE 15-1 *p. 672*

PE 15-1B Bond transactions

Journalize the entries to record the following selected bond investment transactions for Jennings Products:

a. Purchased for cash $40,000 of Tech Grove, Inc. 6% bonds at 100 plus accrued interest of $850.

b. Received first semiannual interest.

c. Sold $15,000 of the bonds at 102 plus accrued interest of $150.

OBJ. 3 EE 15-2 *p. 674*

PE 15-2A Stock transactions

On February 12, 5,000 shares of Mid-Ex Company are acquired at a price of $24 per share plus a $200 brokerage fee. On April 22, a $0.36-per-share dividend was received on the Mid-Ex Company stock. On May 10, 4,000 shares of the Mid-Ex Company stock were sold for $31 per share less a $160 brokerage fee. Prepare the journal entries for the original purchase, dividend, and sale.

OBJ. 3 EE 15-2 *p. 674*

PE 15-2B Stock transactions

On August 15, 1,600 shares of Birch Company are acquired at a price of $44 per share plus a $160 brokerage fee. On September 10, a $0.75-per-share dividend was received on the Birch Company stock. On October 5, 500 shares of the Birch Company stock were sold for $35 per share less a $50 brokerage fee. Prepare the journal entries for the original purchase, dividend, and sale.

OBJ. 3 EE 15-3 *p. 676*

PE 15-3A Equity method

On January 2, THT Company acquired 40% of the outstanding stock of First Alert Company for $155,000. For the year ending December 31, First Alert Company earned income of $42,000 and paid dividends of $12,000. Prepare the entries for THT Company for the purchase of the stock, share of First Alert income, and dividends received from First Alert Company.

OBJ. 3 EE 15-3 *p. 676*

PE 15-3B Equity method

On January 2, Bassett Company acquired 30% of the outstanding stock of Nassim Company for $400,000. For the year ending December 31, Nassim Company earned income of $110,000 and paid dividends of $46,000. Prepare the entries for Bassett Company for the purchase of the stock, share of Nassim income, and dividends received from Nassim Company.

Learning Objectives	Example Exercises

OBJ. 4 EE 15-4 p. 678

PE 15-4A Valuing trading securities at fair value

On January 1, 2012, Valuation Allowance for Trading Investments had a zero balance. On December 31, 2012, the cost of the trading securities portfolio was $105,800 and the fair value was $101,600. Prepare the December 31, 2012, adjusting journal entry to record the unrealized gain or loss on trading investments.

OBJ. 4 EE 15-4 p. 678

PE 15-4B Valuing trading securities at fair value

On January 1, 2012, Valuation Allowance for Trading Investments had a zero balance. On December 31, 2012, the cost of the trading securities portfolio was $33,200, and the fair value was $39,500. Prepare the December 31, 2012, adjusting journal entry to record the unrealized gain or loss on trading investments.

OBJ. 4 EE 15-5 p. 681

PE 15-5A Valuing available-for-sale securities at fair value

On January 1, 2012, Valuation Allowance for Available-for-Sale Securities had a zero balance. On December 31, 2012, the cost of the available-for-sale securities was $62,400, and the fair value was $56,900. Prepare the adjusting entry to record the unrealized gain or loss for available-for-sale securities on December 31, 2012.

OBJ. 4 EE 15-5 p. 681

PE 15-5B Valuing available-for-sale securities at fair value

On January 1, 2012, Valuation Allowance for Available-for-Sale Securities had a zero balance. On December 31, 2012, the cost of the available-for-sale securities was $7,600, and the fair value was $9,500. Prepare the adjusting entry to record the unrealized gain or loss for available-for-sale securities on December 31, 2012.

OBJ. 6 EE 15-6 p. 686

F·A·I

PE 15-6A Dividend yield

On September 25, 2012, Lucas Corporation had a market price per share of common stock of $8. For the previous year, Lucas paid an annual dividend of $0.16. Compute the dividend yield for Lucas Corporation.

OBJ. 6 EE 15-6 p. 686

PE 15-6B Dividend yield

On June 12, 2012, Mid State Power and Electric Company had a market price per share of common stock of $48. For the previous year, Mid State paid an annual dividend of $2.88. Compute the dividend yield for Mid State Power and Electric Company.

Exercises

OBJ. 2

EX 15-1 Entries for investment in bonds, interest, and sale of bonds

Dristol Company acquired $56,000 Reynolds Company, 4.5% bonds on April 1, 2012, at par value. Interest is paid semiannually on April 1 and October 1. On October 1, 2012, Dristol sold $20,000 of the bonds for 99.

Journalize entries to record the following:

a. The initial acquisition of the bonds on April 1.

b. The semiannual interest received on October 1.

c. The sale of the bonds on October 1.

d. The accrual of $637 interest on December 31, 2012.

OBJ. 2

EX 15-2 Entries for investments in bonds, interest, and sale of bonds

Jupiter Investments acquired $40,000 Carlisle Corp., 9% bonds at par value on September 1, 2012. The bonds pay interest on September 1 and March 1. On March 1, 2013, Jupiter sold $40,000 par value Carlisle Corp. bonds at 103.

Journalize the entries to record the following:

a. The initial acquisition of the Carlisle Corp. bonds on September 1, 2012.

b. The adjusting entry for four months of accrued interest earned on the Carlisle Corp. bonds on December 31, 2012.

c. The receipt of semiannual interest on March 1, 2013.

d. The sale of $10,000 Carlisle Corp. bonds on March 1, 2013, at 103.

OBJ. 2

✔ Dec. 1, Loss on sale of investments, $220

EX 15-3 Entries for investment in bonds, interest, and sale of bonds

Afton Co. purchased $24,000 of 4%, 10-year Davis County bonds on July 12, 2012, directly from the county at par value. The bonds pay semiannual interest on May 1 and November 1. On December 1, 2012, Afton Co. sold $6,000 of the Davis County bonds at 98 plus $20 accrued interest, less a $100 brokerage commission.

Provide the journal entries for:

a. the purchase of the bonds on July 12, plus 72 days of accrued interest.

b. semiannual interest on November 1.

c. sale of the bonds on December 1.

d. adjusting entry for accrued interest of $120 on December 31, 2012.

OBJ. 2

✔ Sept. 5, Loss on sale of investments, $720

EX 15-4 Entries for investment in bonds, interest, and sale of bonds

The following bond investment transactions were completed during 2012 by Mission Company:

Jan. 21. Purchased 50, $1,000 par value government bonds at 100 plus 20 days' accrued interest. The bonds pay 4.5% annual interest on June 30 and January 1.

June 30. Received semiannual interest on bond investment.

Sept. 5. Sold 24, $1,000 par value bonds at 97 plus $201 accrued interest.

a. Journalize the entries for these transactions.

b. Provide the December 31, 2012, adjusting journal entry for semiannual interest earned from the bond coupon.

OBJ. 2

EX 15-5 Interest on bond investments

On May 1, 2012, Todd Company purchased $66,000 of 5%, 12-year Lincoln Company bonds at par plus two months' accrued interest. The bonds pay interest on March 1 and September 1. On October 1, 2012, Todd Company sold $24,000 of the Lincoln Company bonds acquired on May 1, plus one month accrued interest. On December 31, 2012, four months' interest was accrued for the remaining bonds.

Determine the interest earned by Todd Company on Lincoln Company bonds for 2012.

OBJ. 3

✔ c. Gain on sale of investments, $5,625

EX 15-6 Entries for investment in stock, receipt of dividends, and sale of shares

On February 17, Walters Corporation acquired 4,000 shares of the 100,000 outstanding shares of Lycore Co. common stock at $22.50 plus commission charges of $200. On July 11, a cash dividend of $0.80 per share was received. On December 4, 1,000 shares were sold at $28.30, less commission charges of $125.

Record the entries for (a) the purchase of stock, (b) the receipt of dividends, and (c) the sale of 1,000 shares.

OBJ. 3

✔ June 3, Loss on sale of investments, $4,097

EX 15-7 Entries for investment in stock, receipt of dividends, and sale of shares

The following equity investment-related transactions were completed by Kindle Company in 2012:

Jan. 12. Purchased 1,400 shares of Inskip Company for a price of $48.90 per share plus a brokerage commission of $112.

Apr. 10. Received a quarterly dividend of $0.22 per share on the Inskip Company investment.

June 3. Sold 900 shares for a price of $44.50 per share less a brokerage commission of $65.

Journalize the entries for these transactions.

OBJ. 3

✔ Nov. 14, Dividend revenue, $60

EX 15-8 Entries for stock investments, dividends, and sale of stock

Archway Tech Corp. manufactures surveying equipment. Journalize the entries to record the following selected equity investment transactions completed by Archway during 2012:

Feb. 2. Purchased for cash 800 shares of Parr Inc. stock for $28 per share plus a $120 brokerage commission.

Apr. 16. Received dividends of $0.12 per share on Parr Inc. stock.

June 17. Purchased 600 shares of Parr Inc. stock for $33 per share plus a $150 brokerage commission.

Aug. 19. Sold 1,000 shares of Parr Inc. stock for $41 per share less a $200 brokerage commission. Archway assumes that the first investments purchased are the first investments sold.

Nov. 14. Received dividends of $0.15 per share on Parr Inc. stock.

OBJ. 3

EX 15-9 Entries for stock investments, dividends, and sale of stock

Hombolt Industries, Inc. buys and sells investments as part of its ongoing cash management. The following investment transactions were completed during the year:

Feb. 6. Acquired 500 shares of Randolph Co. stock for $112 per share plus a $125 brokerage commission.

Apr. 21. Acquired 1,400 shares of Sterling Co. stock for $28 per share plus a $98 commission.

Aug. 15. Sold 200 shares of Randolph Co. stock for $124 per share less an $80 brokerage commission.

Sept. 8. Sold 500 shares of Sterling Co. stock for $22.50 per share less a $70 brokerage commission.

Oct. 31. Received dividends of $0.26 per share on Randolph Co. stock.

Journalize the entries for these transactions.

OBJ. 3

EX 15-10 Equity method for stock investment

At a total cost of $660,000, Penn Corporation acquired 60,000 shares of Teller Corp. common stock as a long-term investment. Penn Corporation uses the equity method of accounting for this investment. Teller Corp. has 200,000 shares of common stock outstanding, including the shares acquired by Penn Corporation.

Journalize the entries by Penn Corporation to record the following information:

a. Teller Corp. reports net income of $940,000 for the current period.

b. A cash dividend of $2.50 per common share is paid by Teller Corp. during the current period.

c. Why is the equity method appropriate for the Teller Corp. investment?

OBJ. 3

✔ b. $3,786,300

EX 15-11 Equity method for stock investment

On January 15, 2012, Outdoor Life Inc. purchased 94,500 shares of Escape Tours Inc. directly from one of the founders for a price of $38 per share. Escape Tours has 225,000 shares outstanding, including the Outdoor Life shares. On July 2, 2012, Escape Tours paid $230,000 in total dividends to its shareholders. On December 31, 2012, Escape Tours reported a net income of $695,000 for the year. Outdoor Life uses the equity method in accounting for its investment in Escape Tours.

a. Provide the Outdoor Life Inc. journal entries for the transactions involving its investment in Escape Tours Inc. during 2012.

b. Determine the December 31, 2012, balance of Investment in Escape Tours Inc. Stock.

OBJ. 3

EX 15-12 Equity method for stock investment with loss

On January 10, 2012, Badger Co. purchased 30% of the outstanding stock of Crest Co. for $123,000. Crest paid total dividend to all shareholders of $15,000 on July 15. Crest had a net loss of $25,000 for 2012.

a. Journalize Badger's purchase of the stock, receipt of dividend, and adjusting entry for the equity loss in Crest Co. stock.

b. Compute the balance of Investment in Crest Co. Stock for December 31, 2012.

c. How does valuing an investment under the equity method differ from valuing an investment at fair value?

OBJ. 3

EX 15-13 Equity method for stock investment

Jarvis Company's balance sheet disclosed its long-term investment in Moss Company under the equity method for comparative years as follows:

	Dec. 31, 2013	Dec. 31, 2012
Investment in Moss Company stock (in millions)	$105	$116

In addition, the 2013 Jarvis Company income statement disclosed equity earnings in the Moss Company investment as $15 million. Jarvis Company neither purchased nor sold Moss Company stock during 2013. The fair value of Moss Company stock investment on December 31, 2013, was $125 million.

Explain the change in the Investment in Moss Company Stock balance sheet account from December 31, 2012, to December 31, 2013.

OBJ. 4

✔ g. $6,000

EX 15-14 Missing statement items, trading investments

KVS Capital, Inc., makes investments in trading securities. Selected income statement items for the years ended December 31, 2012 and 2013, plus selected items from comparative balance sheets, are as follows:

KVS Capital, Inc.
Selected Income Statement Items
For the Years Ended December 31, 2012 and 2013

	2012	2013
Operating income	a.	e.
Unrealized gain (loss)	b.	$(3,000)
Net income	c.	19,000

KVS Capital, Inc.
Selected Balance Sheet Items
December 31, 2011, 2012, and 2013

	Dec. 31, 2011	Dec. 31, 2012	Dec. 31, 2013
Trading investments, at cost	$123,000	$146,000	$172,000
Valuation allowance for trading investments	(4,000)	9,000	g.
Trading investments, at fair value	d.	f.	h.
Retained earnings	$156,000	$192,000	i.

There were no dividends.

Determine the missing lettered items.

OBJ. 3, 4

EX 15-15 Fair value journal entries, trading investments

The investments of Giving Tree, Inc. include a single investment: 9,000 shares of Cardio Solutions, Inc. common stock purchased on March 3, 2012, for $22 per share including brokerage commission. These shares were classified as trading securities. As of the December 31, 2012, balance sheet date, the share price increased to $29 per share.

a. Journalize the entries to acquire the investment on March 3, and record the adjustment to fair value on December 31, 2012.

b. How is the unrealized gain or loss for trading investments disclosed on the financial statements?

OBJ. 3, 4

EX 15-16 Fair value journal entries, trading investments

Acorn Bancorp Inc. purchased a portfolio of trading securities during 2012. The cost and fair value of this portfolio on December 31, 2012, was as follows:

Name	Number of Shares	Total Cost	Total Fair Value
Apex, Inc.	1,200	$16,000	$17,500
Evans Company	700	23,000	19,000
Quaker Company	300	9,000	8,600
Total		$48,000	$45,100

On April 3, 2013, Acorn Bancorp Inc. purchased 500 shares of Luke, Inc., at $36 per share plus a $100 brokerage fee.

Provide the journal entries to record the following:

a. The adjustment of the trading security portfolio to fair value on December 31, 2012.

b. The April 3, 2013, purchase of Luke, Inc., stock.

OBJ. 3, 4

✔ a. Dec. 31, 2012, Unrealized gain on trading investments, $12,600

EX 15-17 Fair value journal entries, trading investments

First Guarantee Financial, Inc., purchased the following trading securities during 2012, its first year of operations:

Name	Number of Shares	Cost
B&T Transportation, Inc.	3,400	$ 74,200
Citrus Foods, Inc.	1,500	26,500
Stuart Housewares, Inc.	800	45,200
Total		$145,900

88400
28500
41600
25850

The market price per share for the trading security portfolio on December 31, 2012, was as follows:

	Market Price per Share Dec. 31, 2012
B&T Transportation, Inc.	$26
Citrus Foods, Inc.	19
Stuart Housewares, Inc.	52

a. Provide the journal entry to adjust the trading security portfolio to fair value on December 31, 2012.

b. Assume the market prices of the portfolio were the same on December 31, 2013, as they were on December 31, 2012. What would be the journal entry to adjust the portfolio to fair value?

OBJ. 4

EX 15-18 Financial statement disclosure, trading investments

The income statement for Tri-Con, Inc., for the year ended December 31, 2012, was as follows:

Tri-Con, Inc.
Income Statement (selected items)
For the Year Ended December 31, 2012

Income from operations	$148,000
Gain on sale of investments	12,000
Less unrealized loss on trading investments	34,000
Net income	$126,000

The balance sheet dated December 31, 2011, showed a Retained Earnings balance of $614,000. During 2012, the company purchased trading investments for the first time at a cost of $166,000. In addition, trading investments with a cost of $45,000 were sold at a gain during 2012. The company paid $35,000 in dividends during 2012.

a. Determine the December 31, 2012, Retained Earnings balance.

b. Provide the December 31, 2012, balance sheet disclosure for Trading Investments.

OBJ. 4
✔ f. ($9,000)

EX 15-19 Missing statement items, available-for-sale securities

Oceanic Airways makes investments in available-for-sale securities. Selected income statement items for the years ended December 31, 2012 and 2013, plus selected items from comparative balance sheets, are as follows:

Oceanic Airways
Selected Income Statement Items
For the Years Ended December 31, 2012 and 2013

	2012	2013
Operating income	a.	g.
Gain (loss) from sale of investments	$4,000	$ (8,000)
Net income (loss)	b.	(15,000)

Oceanic Airways
Selected Balance Sheet Items
December 31, 2011, 2012, and 2013

	Dec. 31, 2011	Dec. 31, 2012	Dec. 31, 2013
Assets			
Available-for-sale investments, at cost	$ 78,000	$ 68,000	$95,000
Valuation allowance for available-for-sale investments	6,000	(9,000)	h.
Available-for-sale investments, at fair value	c.	e.	i.
Stockholders' Equity			
Unrealized gain (loss) on available-for- sale investments	d.	f.	(11,000)
Retained earnings	$151,000	$201,000	j.

There were no dividends.
Determine the missing lettered items.

OBJ. 3, 4

EX 15-20 Fair value journal entries, available-for-sale investments

The investments of Macon, Inc. include a single investment: 8,000 shares of Pacific Wave, Inc. common stock purchased on August 10, 2012, for $8 per share including brokerage commission. These shares were classified as available-for-sale securities. As of the December 31, 2012, balance sheet date, the share price declined to $6 per share.

a. Journalize the entries to acquire the investment on August 10, and record the adjustment to fair value on December 31, 2012.

b. How is the unrealized gain or loss for available-for-sale investments disclosed on the financial statements?

OBJ. 3, 4

EX 15-21 Fair value journal entries, available-for-sale investments

Arnott Inc. purchased a portfolio of available-for-sale securities in 2012, its first year of operations. The cost and fair value of this portfolio on December 31, 2012, was as follows:

Name	Number of Shares	Total Cost	Total Fair Value
Jasper, Inc.	600	$ 9,000	$10,500
Parker Corp.	900	21,000	23,400
Smithfield Corp.	1,800	32,500	31,900
Total		$62,500	$65,800

On May 10, 2013, Arnott purchased 900 shares of Violet Inc. at $42 per share plus a $125 brokerage fee.

a. Provide the journal entries to record the following:
   1. The adjustment of the available-for-sale security portfolio to fair value on December 31, 2012.
   2. The May 10, 2013, purchase of Violet Inc. stock.

b. How are unrealized gains and losses treated differently for available-for-sale securities than for trading securities?

OBJ. 3, 4

EX 15-22 Fair value journal entries, available-for-sale investments

Cumberland, Inc., purchased the following available-for-sale securities during 2012, its first year of operations:

Name	Number of Shares	Cost
Abbotford Electronics, Inc.	1,500	$ 42,500
Ryan Co.	400	28,200
Sharon Co.	2,200	66,100
Total		$136,800

The market price per share for the available-for-sale security portfolio on December 31, 2012, was as follows:

	Market Price per Share Dec. 31, 2012
Abbotford Electronics, Inc.	$22
Ryan Co.	65
Sharon Co.	32

a. Provide the journal entry to adjust the available-for-sale security portfolio to fair value on December 31, 2012.

b. Describe the income statement impact from the December 31, 2012, journal entry.

OBJ. 4

EX 15-23 Balance sheet presentation of available-for-sale investments

During 2012, its first year of operations, Newton Company purchased two available-for-sale investments as follows:

Security	Shares Purchased	Cost
Starlight Products, Inc.	700	$31,000
Reynolds Co.	1,900	41,000

Assume that as of December 31, 2012, the Starlight Products, Inc., stock had a market value of $55 per share and the Reynolds Co. stock had a market value of $18 per share. Newton Company had net income of $250,000, and paid no dividends for the year ending December 31, 2012.

a. Prepare the Current Assets section of the balance sheet presentation for the available-for-sale investments.

b. Prepare the Stockholders' Equity section of the balance sheet to reflect the earnings and unrealized gain (loss) for the available-for-sale investments.

OBJ. 4

EX 15-24 Balance sheet presentation of available-for-sale investments

During 2012, Norcross Corporation held a portfolio of available-for-sale securities having a cost of $175,000. There were no purchases or sales of investments during the year. The market values at the beginning and end of the year were $215,000 and $150,000, respectively. The net income for 2012 was $110,000, and no dividends were paid during the year. The Stockholders' Equity section of the balance sheet was as follows on December 31, 2011:

Norcross Corporation
Stockholders' Equity
December 31, 2011

Common stock	$ 50,000
Paid-in capital in excess of par value	350,000
Retained earnings	265,000
Unrealized gain (loss) on available-for- sale investments	40,000
Total	$705,000

Prepare the Stockholders' Equity section of the balance sheet for December 31, 2012.

Appendix
EX 15-25 Comprehensive income

On April 23, 2012, Frost Co. purchased 1,500 shares of Apex, Inc., for $88 per share including the brokerage commission. The Apex investment was classified as an available-for-sale security. On December 31, 2012, the fair value of Apex, Inc., was $101 per share. The net income of Frost Co. was $60,000 for 2012.

Compute the comprehensive income for Frost Co. for the year ended December 31, 2012.

Appendix
EX 15-26 Comprehensive income

On December 31, 2011, Memphis Co. had the following available-for-sale investment disclosure within the Current Assets section of the balance sheet:

Available-for-sale investments (at cost)	$105,000
Plus valuation allowance for available-for-sale investments	15,000
Available-for-sale investments (at fair value)	$120,000

There were no purchases or sales of available-for-sale investments during 2012. On December 31, 2012, the fair value of the available-for-sale investment portfolio was $94,000. The net income of Memphis Co. was $150,000 for 2012.

Compute the comprehensive income for Memphis Co. for the year ended December 31, 2012.

OBJ. 6

EX 15-27 Dividend yield

At the market close on February 19, 2010, McDonald's Corporation had a closing stock price of $64.74. In addition, McDonald's Corporation had a dividend per share of $2.05 over the previous year.

Determine McDonald's Corporation's dividend yield. (Round to one decimal place.)

OBJ. 6

✔ a. Dec. 31, 2008, 2.37%

EX 15-28 Dividend yield

The market price for Microsoft Corporation closed at $19.40 and $30.48 on December 31, 2008, and 2009, respectively. The dividends per share were $0.46 for 2008 and $0.52 for 2009.

a. Determine the dividend yield for Microsoft on December 31, 2008, and 2009. (Round percentages to two decimal places.)

b. Interpret these measures.

OBJ. 6

EX 15-29 Dividend yield

eBay Inc. developed a Web-based marketplace at **http://www.ebay.com**, in which individuals can buy and sell a variety of items. eBay also acquired PayPal, an online payments system that allows businesses and individuals to send and receive online payments securely. In a recent annual report, eBay published the following dividend policy:

We have never paid cash dividends on our stock and currently anticipate that we will continue to retain any future earnings for the foreseeable future.

Given eBay's dividend policy, why would an investor be attracted to its stock?

Problems Series A

OBJ. 2, 4

PR 15-1A Debt investment transactions, available-for-sale valuation

Fleet Inc. is an athletic footware company that began operations on January 1, 2012. The following transactions relate to debt investments acquired by Fleet Inc., which has a fiscal year ending on December 31:

2012

Mar. 1. Purchased $36,000 of Madison Co. 5%, 10-year bonds at face value plus accrued interest of $150. The bonds pay interest semiannually on February 1 and August 1.

Apr. 16. Purchased $45,000 of Westville 4%, 15-year bonds at face value plus accrued interest of $75. The bonds pay interest semiannually on April 1 and October 1.

Aug. 1. Received semiannual interest on the Madison Co. bonds.

Sept. 1. Sold $12,000 of Madison Co. bonds at 98 plus accrued interest of $50.

Oct. 1. Received semiannual interest on Westville bonds.

Dec. 31. Accrued $500 interest on Madison Co. bonds.

31. Accrued $450 interest on Westville bonds.

2013

Feb. 1. Received semiannual interest on the Madison Co. bonds.

Apr. 1. Received semiannual interest on the Westville bonds.

Instructions

1. Journalize the entries to record these transactions.
2. If the bond portfolio was classified as available-for-sale, what impact would this have on financial statement disclosure?

OBJ. 3, 4

PR 15-2A Stock investment transactions, trading securities

Heritage Insurance Co. is a regional insurance company that began operations on January 1, 2012. The following transactions relate to trading securities acquired by Heritage Insurance Co., which has a fiscal year ending on December 31:

2012

Feb. 21. Purchased 4,000 shares of Astor Inc. as a trading security at $30 per share plus a brokerage commission of $600.

Mar. 9. Purchased 800 shares of Millsaps Inc. as a trading security at $41 per share plus a brokerage commission of $160.

May 3. Sold 600 shares of Astor Inc. for $27.50 per share less an $80 brokerage commission.

June 8. Received an annual dividend of $0.22 per share on Astor Inc. stock.

Dec. 31. The portfolio of trading securities was adjusted to fair values of $32 and $30 per share for Astor Inc. and Millsaps Inc., respectively.

2013

May 21. Purchased 2,000 shares of Essex Inc. as a trading security at $21 per share plus a $200 brokerage commission.

June 11. Received an annual dividend of $0.25 per share on Astor Inc. stock.

Aug. 16. Sold 400 shares of Essex Inc. for $25 per share less an $80 brokerage commission.

Dec. 31. The portfolio of trading securities had a cost of $169,230 and fair value of $170,560, requiring a debit balance in Valuation Allowance for Trading Investments of $1,330 ($170,560 − $169,230). Thus, the credit balance from December 31, 2012, is to be adjusted to the new balance.

Instructions

1. Journalize the entries to record these transactions.
2. Prepare the investment-related current asset balance sheet disclosures for Heritage Insurance Co. on December 31, 2013.
3. How are unrealized gains or losses on trading investments disclosed on the financial statements of Heritage Insurance Co.?

OBJ. 3, 4

PR 15-3A Stock investment transactions, equity method and available-for-sale securities

White Way Inc. produces and sells theater set designs and costumes. The company began operations on January 1, 2012. The following transactions relate to securities acquired by White Way Inc., which has a fiscal year ending on December 31:

2012

Jan. 10. Purchased 8,000 shares of Lott Inc. as an available-for-sale security at $14 per share, including the brokerage commission.

Mar. 10. Received the regular cash dividend of $0.12 per share on Lott Inc. stock.

Sept. 9. Lott Inc. stock was split two for one. The regular cash dividend of $0.06 per share was received on the stock after the stock split.

Oct. 16. Sold 2,000 shares of Lott Inc. stock at $5 per share, less a brokerage commission of $100.

Dec. 31. Lott Inc. is classified as an available-for-sale investment and is adjusted to a fair value of $8.50 per share. Use the valuation allowance for available-for-sale investments account in making the adjustment.

2013

Jan. 5. Purchased an influential interest in Stage Hand Inc. for $235,000 by purchasing 50,000 shares directly from the estate of the founder of Stage Hand Inc. There are 200,000 shares of Stage Hand Inc. stock outstanding.

Mar. 9. Received the regular cash divided of $0.07 per share on Lott Inc. stock.

Sept. 10. Received the regular cash dividend of $0.07 per share plus an extra dividend of $0.03 per share on Lott Inc. stock.

Dec. 31. Received $21,500 of cash dividends on Stage Hand Inc. stock. Stage Hand Inc. reported net income of $136,000 in 2013. White Way Inc. uses the equity method of accounting for its investment in Stage Hand Inc.

31. Lott Inc. is classified as an available-for-sale investment and is adjusted to a fair value of $8 per share. Use the valuation allowance for available-for-sale investments account in making the adjustment for the decrease in fair value from $8.50 to $8.00 per share.

Instructions

1. Journalize the entries to record these transactions.
2. Prepare the investment-related asset and stockholders' equity balance sheet disclosures for White Way Inc. on December 31, 2013, assuming the Retained Earnings balance on December 31, 2013, is $310,000.

OBJ. 2, 3, 4

✔ h. $(4,500)

PR 15-4A Investment reporting

Luminous Publishing, Inc., is a book publisher. The comparative unclassified balance sheets for December 31, 2013 and 2012 are provided below. Selected missing balances are shown by letters.

Luminous Publishing, Inc.
Balance Sheet
December 31, 2013 and 2012

	Dec. 31, 2013	Dec. 31, 2012
Cash	$178,000	$157,000
Accounts receivable (net)	106,000	98,000
Available-for-sale investments (at cost)—Note 1	a.	53,400
Less valuation allowance for available-for-sale investments	b.	3,900
Available-for-sale investments (fair value)	$ c.	$ 49,500
Interest receivable	$ d.	—
Investment in Quest Co. stock—Note 2	e.	$ 55,000
Office equipment (net)	90,000	95,000
Total assets	$ f.	$454,500
Accounts payable	$ 56,900	$ 51,400
Common stock	50,000	50,000
Excess of issue price over par	160,000	160,000
Retained earnings	g.	197,000
Less unrealized gain (loss) on available-for-sale investments	h.	3,900
Total liabilities and stockholders' equity	$ i.	$454,500

Note 1. Investments are classified as available for sale. The investments at cost and fair value on December 31, 2012, are as follows:

	No. of Shares	Cost per Share	Total Cost	Total Fair Value
Barns Co. Stock	1,600	$12	$19,200	$17,500
Dynasty Co. Stock	900	38	34,200	32,000
			$53,400	$49,500

Note 2. The investment in Quest Co. stock is an equity method investment representing 32% of the outstanding shares of Quest Co.

The following selected investment transactions occurred during 2013:

May 5. Purchased 2,200 shares of Gypsy, Inc., at $22 per share including brokerage commission. Gypsy, Inc., is classified as an available-for-sale security.

Sept. 1. Purchased $30,000 of Norton Co. 5%, 10-year bonds at 100. The bonds are classified as available for sale. The bonds pay interest on September 1 and March 1.

9. Dividends of $9,000 are received on the Quest Co. investment.

Dec. 31. Quest Co. reported a total net income of $80,000 for 2013. Luminous recorded equity earnings for its share of Quest Co. net income.

31. Accrued four months of interest on the Norton bonds.

31. Adjusted the available-for-sale investment portfolio to fair value using the following fair value per-share amounts:

Available-for-Sale Investments	Fair Value
Barns Co. stock	$11 per share
Dynasty Co. stock	$33 per share
Gypsy Inc. stock	$23 per share
Norton Co. bonds	98 per $100 of face value

Dec. 31. Closed the Luminous Publishing Inc. net income of $114,000 for 2013. Luminous paid no dividends during 2013.

Instructions

Determine the missing letters in the unclassified balance sheet. Provide appropriate supporting calculations.

Problems Series B

OBJ. 2, 4

PR 15-1B Debt investment transactions, available-for-sale valuation

Savers Mart Inc. is a general merchandise retail company that began operations on January 1, 2012. The following transactions relate to debt investments acquired by Savers Mart Inc., which has a fiscal year ending on December 31:

2012

May 1. Purchased $80,000 of Northridge City 4.5%, 10-year bonds at face value plus accrued interest of $600. The bonds pay interest semiannually on March 1 and September 1.

June 16. Purchased $38,000 of Hancock Co. 6%, 12-year bonds at face value plus accrued interest of $95. The bonds pay interest semiannually on June 1 and December 1.

Sept. 1. Received semiannual interest on the Northridge City bonds.

Oct. 1. Sold $24,000 of Northridge City bonds at 102 plus accrued interest of $90.

Dec. 1. Received semiannual interest on Hancock Co. bonds.

31. Accrued $840 interest on Northridge City bonds.

31. Accrued $190 interest on Hancock Co. bonds.

2013

Mar. 1. Received semiannual interest on the Northridge City bonds.

June 1. Received semiannual interest on the Hancock Co. bonds.

Instructions

1. Journalize the entries to record these transactions.
2. If the bond portfolio was classified as available-for-sale, what impact would this have on financial statement disclosure?

OBJ. 3, 4

PR 15-2B Stock investment transactions, trading securities

Ophir Investments Inc. is a regional investment company that began operations on January 1, 2012. The following transactions relate to trading securities acquired by Ophir Investments Inc., which has a fiscal year ending on December 31:

2012

Feb. 3. Purchased 2,000 shares of Mapco Inc. as a trading security at $42 per share plus a brokerage commission of $500.

Mar. 23. Purchased 1,400 shares of Swift Inc. as a trading security at $23 per share plus a brokerage commission of $210.

May 19. Sold 500 shares of Mapco Inc. for $46 per share less an $80 brokerage commission.

June 12. Received an annual dividend of $0.14 per share on Mapco stock.

Dec. 31. The portfolio of trading securities was adjusted to fair values of $40 and $29 per share for Mapco Inc. and Swift Inc., respectively.

2013

Apr. 9. Purchased 900 shares of Corvair Inc. as a trading security at $62 per share plus a $90 brokerage commission.

June 15. Received an annual dividend of $0.16 per share on Mapco Inc. stock.

Aug. 30. Sold 200 shares of Corvair Inc. for $51 per share less a $60 brokerage commission.

Dec. 31. The portfolio of trading securities had a cost of $139,255 and fair value of $133,470, requiring a credit balance in Valuation Allowance for Trading Investments of $5,785 ($139,255 − $133,470). Thus, the debit balance from December 31, 2012, is to be adjusted to the new balance.

Instructions

1. Journalize the entries to record these transactions.
2. Prepare the investment-related current asset balance sheet disclosures for Ophir Investments Inc. on December 31, 2013.
3. How are unrealized gains or losses on trading investments disclosed on the financial statements of Ophir Investments Inc.?

OBJ. 3, 4

PR 15-3B Stock investment transactions, equity method and available-for-sale securities

Samson Products, Inc., is a wholesaler of men's hair products. The company began operations on January 1, 2012. The following transactions relate to securities acquired by Samson Products, Inc., which has a fiscal year ending on December 31:

2012

Jan. 3. Purchased 5,000 shares of Merlin Inc. as an available-for-sale investment at $22 per share, including the brokerage commission.

July 8. Merlin Inc. stock was split two for one. The regular cash dividend of $0.40 per share was received on the stock after the stock split.

Oct. 19. Sold 1,200 shares of Merlin Inc. stock at $13 per share, less a brokerage commission of $50.

Dec. 12. Received the regular cash dividend of $0.40 per share.

31. Merlin Inc. is classified as an available-for-sale investment and is adjusted to a fair value of $9.50 per share. Use the valuation allowance for available-for-sale investments account in making the adjustment.

2013

Jan. 5. Purchased an influential interest in Juarez Co. for $540,000 by purchasing 60,000 shares directly from the estate of the founder of Juarez. There are 150,000 shares of Juarez Co. stock outstanding.

July 9. Received the regular cash divided of $0.50 per share on Merlin Inc. stock.

Dec. 8. Received the regular cash dividend of $0.50 per share plus an extra dividend of $0.05 per share on Merlin Inc. stock.

Dec. 31. Received $21,000 of cash dividends on Juarez Co. stock. Juarez Co. reported net income of $96,000 in 2013. Samson Products uses the equity method of accounting for its investment in Juarez Co.

31. Merlin Inc. is classified as an available-for-sale investment and is adjusted to a fair value of $10 per share. Use the valuation allowance for available-for-sale investments account in making the adjustment for the increase in fair value from $9.50 to $10 per share.

Instructions

1. Journalize the entries to record the preceding transactions.
2. Prepare the investment-related asset and stockholders' equity balance sheet disclosures for Samson Products, Inc., on December 31, 2013, assuming the Retained Earnings balance on December 31, 2013, is $395,000.

OBJ. 2, 3, 4

✔ b. $250

PR 15-4B Investment reporting

Guardian Devices, Inc., manufactures and sells commercial and residential security equipment. The comparative unclassified balance sheets for December 31, 2013 and 2012 are provided below. Selected missing balances are shown by letters.

Guardian Devices, Inc.
Balance Sheet
December 31, 2013 and 2012

	Dec. 31, 2013	Dec. 31, 2012
Cash	$104,000	$ 98,000
Accounts receivable (net)	71,000	67,500
Available-for-sale investments (at cost)—Note 1	a.	36,000
Plus valuation allowance for available-for-sale investments	b.	6,000
Available-for-sale investments (fair value)	$ c.	$ 42,000
Interest receivable	$ d.	—
Investment in Omaha Co. stock—Note 2	e.	$ 62,000
Office equipment (net)	60,000	65,000
Total assets	$ f.	$334,500
Accounts payable	$ 56,900	$ 45,100
Common stock	50,000	50,000
Excess of issue price over par	160,000	160,000
Retained earnings	g.	73,400
Plus unrealized gain (loss) on available-for-sale investments	h.	6,000
Total liabilities and stockholders' equity	$ i.	$334,500

Note 1. Investments are classified as available for sale. The investments at cost and fair value on December 31, 2012, are as follows:

	No. of Shares	Cost per Share	Total Cost	Total Fair Value
Tyndale Inc. Stock	600	$24	$14,400	$17,000
UR-Smart Inc. Stock	1,200	18	21,600	25,000
			$36,000	$42,000

Note 2. The Investment in Omaha Co. stock is an equity method investment representing 32% of the outstanding shares of Omaha Co.

The following selected investment transactions occurred during 2013:

Apr. 21. Purchased 500 shares of Walton Winery, Inc., at $25 including brokerage commission. Walton Winery is classified as an available-for-sale security.

Sept. 9. Dividends of $7,500 are received on the Omaha Co. investment.

Oct. 1. Purchased $15,000 of Yokohama Co. 6%, 10-year bonds at 100. The bonds are classified as available for sale. The bonds pay interest on October 1 and April 1.

Dec. 31. Omaha Co. reported a total net income of $50,000 for 2013. Guardian recorded equity earnings for its share of Omaha Co. net income.

Dec. 31. Accrued interest for three months on Yokohama bonds purchased on October 1.

31. Adjusted the available-for-sale investment portfolio to fair value using the following fair value per-share amounts:

Available-for-Sale Investments	Fair Value
Tyndale Inc. stock	$26 per share
UR-Smart, Inc., stock	$15 per share
Walton Winery, Inc., stock	$30 per share
Yokohama Co. bonds	101 per $100 of face value

31. Closed the Guardian Devices, Inc., net income of $28,925 for 2013. Guardian paid no dividends during 2013.

Instructions

Determine the missing letters in the unclassified balance sheet. Provide appropriate supporting calculations.

Comprehensive Problem 4

Selected transactions completed by Everyday Products Inc. during the fiscal year ending December 31, 2012, were as follows:

a. Issued 12,500 shares of $25 par common stock at $32, receiving cash.

b. Issued 2,000 shares of $100 par preferred 5% stock at $105, receiving cash.

c. Issued $400,000 of 10-year, 6% bonds at 105, with interest payable semiannually.

d. Declared a quarterly dividend of $0.45 per share on common stock and $1.25 per share on preferred stock. On the date of record, 85,000 shares of common stock were outstanding, no treasury shares were held, and 17,000 shares of preferred stock were outstanding.

e. Paid the cash dividends declared in (d).

f. Purchased 5,500 shares of Kress Corp. at $22 per share, plus a $275 brokerage commission. The investment is classified as an available-for-sale investment.

g. Purchased 6,500 shares of treasury common stock at $35 per share.

h. Purchased 36,000 shares of Lifecare Co. stock directly from the founders for $18 per share. Lifecare has 112,500 shares issued and outstanding. Everyday Products Inc. treated the investment as an equity method investment.

i. Declared a 2% stock dividend on common stock and a $1.25 quarterly cash dividend per share on preferred stock. On the date of declaration, the market value of the common stock was $40 per share. On the date of record, 85,000 shares of common stock had been issued, 6,500 shares of treasury common stock were held, and 17,000 shares of preferred stock had been issued.

j. Issued the stock certificates for the stock dividends declared in (h) and paid the cash dividends to the preferred stockholders.

k. Received $24,500 dividend from Lifecare Co. investment in (h).

l. Purchased $62,000 of Nordic Wear Inc. 10-year, 6% bonds, directly from the issuing company at par value, plus accrued interest of $550. The bonds are classifed as a held-to-maturity long-term investment.

m. Sold, at $42 per share, 2,600 shares of treasury common stock purchased in (g).

n. Received a dividend of $0.65 per share from the Kress Corp. investment in (f).

o. Sold 500 shares of Kress Corp. at $26.50, including commission.

p. Recorded the payment of semiannual interest on the bonds issued in (c) and the amortization of the premium for six months. The amortization was determined using the straight-line method.

q. Accrued interest for three months on the Nordic Wear Inc. bonds purchased in (l).

r. Lifecare Co. recorded total earnings of $205,000. Everyday Products recorded equity earnings for its share of Lifecare Co. net income.

s. The fair value for Kress Corp. stock was $18.50 per share on December 31, 2012. The investment is adjusted to fair value using a valuation allowance account. Assume Valuation Allowance for Available-for-Sale Investments had a beginning balance of zero.

Instructions

1. Journalize the selected transactions.
2. After all of the transactions for the year ended December 31, 2012, had been posted [including the transactions recorded in part (1) and all adjusting entries], the data below and on the following page were taken from the records of Everyday Products Inc.
   a. Prepare a multiple-step income statement for the year ended December 31, 2012, concluding with earnings per share. In computing earnings per share, assume that the average number of common shares outstanding was 84,000 and preferred dividends were $85,000. (Round earnings per share to the nearest cent.)
   b. Prepare a retained earnings statement for the year ended December 31, 2012.
   c. Prepare a balance sheet in report form as of December 31, 2012.

Income statement data:	
Advertising expense	$ 125,000
Cost of merchandise sold	3,650,000
Delivery expense	29,000
Depreciation expense—office buildings and equipment	26,000
Depreciation expense—store buildings and equipment	95,000
Dividend revenue	3,575
Gain on sale of investment	2,225
Income from Lifecare Co. investment	65,600
Income tax expense	128,500
Interest expense	19,000
Interest revenue	1,800
Miscellaneous administrative expense	7,500
Miscellaneous selling expense	13,750
Office rent expense	50,000
Office salaries expense	165,000
Office supplies expense	10,000
Sales	5,145,000
Sales commissions	182,000
Sales salaries expense	365,000
Store supplies expense	22,000

Retained earnings and balance sheet data:	
Accounts payable	$ 195,000
Accounts receivable	543,000
Accumulated depreciation—office buildings and equipment	1,580,000
Accumulated depreciation—store buildings and equipment	4,126,000
Allowance for doubtful accounts	8,150
Available-for-sale investments (at cost)	110,250
Bonds payable, 6%, due 2022	400,000
Cash	240,000
Common stock, $25 par (400,000 shares authorized; 86,570 shares issued, 82,670 outstanding)	2,164,250
Dividends:	
Cash dividends for common stock	155,120
Cash dividends for preferred stock	85,000
Stock dividends for common stock	62,800
Goodwill	510,000
Income tax payable	40,000
Interest receivable	930
Investment in Lifecare Co. stock (equity method)	689,100
Investment in Nordic Wear Inc. bonds (long term)	62,000

Merchandise inventory (December 31, 2012), at lower of cost (FIFO) or market	$ 780,000
Office buildings and equipment	4,320,000
Paid-in capital from sale of treasury stock	18,200
Paid-in capital in excess of par—common stock	842,000
Paid-in capital in excess of par—preferred stock	150,000
Preferred 5% stock, $100 par (30,000 shares authorized; 17,000 shares issued)	1,700,000
Premium on bonds payable	19,000
Prepaid expenses	26,500
Retained earnings, January 1, 2012	8,708,150
Store buildings and equipment	12,560,000
Treasury stock (3,900 shares of common stock at cost of $35 per share)	136,500
Unrealized gain (loss) on available-for-sale investments	(17,750)
Valuation allowance for available-for-sale investments	(17,750)

Cases & Projects

CP 15-1 Benefits of fair value

On August 16, 1997, Parson Corp. purchased 20 acres of land for $500,000. The land has been held for a future plant site until the current date, December 31, 2012. On December 5, 2012, Overland, Inc., purchased 20 acres of land for $3,000,000 to be used for a distribution center. The Overland land is located next to the Parson Corp. land. Thus, both Parson Corp. and Overland, Inc., own nearly identical pieces of land.

1. What are the valuations of land on the balance sheets of Parson Corp. and Overland, Inc., using generally accepted accounting principles?
2. How might fair value accounting aid comparability when evaluating these two companies?

CP 15-2 International fair value accounting

International Accounting Standard No. 16 provides companies the option of valuing property, plant, and equipment at either historical cost or fair value. If fair value is selected, then the property, plant, and equipment must be revalued periodically to fair value. Under fair value, if there is an increase in the value of the property, plant, and equipment over the reporting period, then the increase is credited to stockholders' equity. However, if there is a decrease in fair value, then the decrease is reported as an expense for the period.

1. Why do International Accounting Standards influence U.S. GAAP?
2. What would be some of the disadvantages of using fair value accounting for property, plant, and equipment?
3. How is the international accounting treatment for changes in fair value for property, plant, and equipment similar to investments?

CP 15-3 Ethics and fair value measurement

Financial assets include stocks and bonds. These are fairly simple securities that can often be valued using quoted market prices. However, Wall Street has created many complex and exotic securities that do not have quoted market prices. These complex securities must still be valued on the balance sheet at fair value. Generally accepted accounting principles require that the reporting entity use assumptions in valuing investments when market prices or critical valuation inputs are unobservable.

What are the ethical considerations in making subjective valuations of complex and exotic investments?

CP 15-4 Warren Buffett and "look-through" earnings

Berkshire Hathaway, the investment holding company of Warren Buffett, reports its "less than 20% ownership" investments according to generally accepted accounting principles. However, it also provides additional disclosures that it terms "look-through" earnings.

Warren Buffett states,

Many of these companies (in the less than 20% owned category) pay out relatively small proportions of their earnings in dividends. This means that only a small proportion of their earning power is recorded in our own current operating earnings. But, while our reported operating earnings reflect only the dividends received from such companies, our economic well-being is determined by their earnings, not their dividends.

The value to Berkshire Hathaway of retained earnings (of our investees) is not determined by whether we own 100%, 50%, 20%, or 1% of the businesses in which they reside.... Our perspective on such "forgotten-but-not-gone" earnings is simple: the way they are accounted for is of no importance, but their ownership and subsequent utilization is all-important. We care not whether the auditors hear a tree fall in the forest; we do care who owns the tree and what's next done with it.

I believe the best way to think about our earnings is in terms of "look-through" results, calculated as follows: Take $250 million, which is roughly our share of the operating earnings retained by our investees (<20% ownership holdings); subtract... incremental taxes we would have owed had that $250 million been paid to us in dividends; then add the remainder, $220 million, to our reported earnings of $371 million. Thus our, "look-through" earnings were about $590 million.

Source: Warren Buffett, *The Essays of Warren Buffett: Lessons for Corporate America*, edited by Lawrence A. Cunningham, pp. 180–183 (excerpted).

1. What are "look-through" earnings?
2. Why does Warren Buffett favor "look-through" earnings?

Internet Project

CP 15-5 Reporting investments

Group Project

In groups of three or four, find the latest annual report for Microsoft Corporation. The annual report can be found on the company's Web site at **http://www.microsoft.com/msft/default.mspx.**

The notes to the financial statements include details of Microsoft's investments. Find the notes that provide details of its investments (Note 4) and the income from its investments (Note 3).

From these disclosures, answer the following questions:

1. What is the total cost of investments?
2. What is the fair value (recorded value) of investments?
3. What is the total unrealized gain from investments?
4. What is the total unrealized loss from investments?
5. What percent of total investments (at fair value) are:
   a. Cash and equivalents
   b. Short-term investments
   c. Equity and other investments (long term)
6. What was the total combined dividend and interest revenue?
7. What was the recognized net gain or loss from sale of investments?

Financial Statements for Mornin' Joe

The financial statements of Mornin' Joe are provided in the following pages. Mornin' Joe is a fictitious coffeehouse chain featuring drip and espresso coffee in a café setting. The financial statements of Mornin' Joe are provided to illustrate the complete financial statements of a corporation using the terms, formats, and reporting illustrated throughout this text. In addition, excerpts of the Mornin' Joe financial statements are used to illustrate the financial reporting presentation for the topics discussed in Chapters 7–15. Thus, you can refer to the complete financial statements shown here or the excerpts in Chapters 7–15. A set of real world financial statements by Nike, Inc., is provided in Appendix C.

Mornin' Joe
Income Statement
For the Year Ended December 31, 2012

Revenue from sales:			
Sales		$5,450,000	
Less: Sales returns and allowances	$ 26,500		
Sales discounts	21,400	47,900	
Net sales			$5,402,100
Cost of merchandise sold			2,160,000
Gross profit			$3,242,100
Operating expenses			
Selling expenses:			
Wages expense	$825,000		
Advertising expense	678,900		
Depreciation expense—buildings	124,300		
Miscellaneous selling expense	26,500		
Total selling expenses		$1,654,700	
Administrative expenses:			
Office salaries expense	$325,000		
Rent expense	425,600		
Payroll tax expense	110,000		
Depreciation expense—office equipment	68,900		
Bad debt expense	14,000		
Amortization expense	10,500		
Total administrative expenses		954,000	
Total operating expenses			2,608,700
Income from operations			$ 633,400
Other income and expense:			
Interest revenue		$ 18,000	
Interest expense		(136,000)	
Loss on disposal of fixed asset		(23,000)	
Unrealized gain on trading investments		5,000	
Equity income in AM Coffee		57,000	(79,000)
Income before income taxes			$ 554,400
Income tax expense			132,800
Net income			$ 421,600
Basic earnings per share [($421,600 − $30,000)/44,000 shares issued and outstanding]			$ 8.90

Mornin' Joe International

Mornin' Joe is planning to expand operations to various places around the world. Financing for this expansion will come from foreign banks. While financial statements prepared under U.S. GAAP may be appropriate for U.S. operations, financial statements prepared for foreign bankers should be prepared using international accounting standards.

The European Union (EU) has developed accounting standards similar in structure to U.S. standards. Its accounting standards board is called the International Accounting Standards Board (IASB). The IASB issues accounting standards that are termed *International Financial Reporting Standards* (IFRS). The intent of the IASB is to create a set of financial standards that can be used by public companies worldwide, not just in the EU.

Currently, the EU countries and over 100 other countries around the world have adopted or are planning to adopt IFRS. As a result, there are efforts under way to converge U.S. GAAP with IFRS so as to harmonize accounting standards around the world.

The following pages illustrate the financial statements of Mornin' Joe International using IFRS. This illustration highlights reporting and terminology differences between IFRS and U.S. GAAP. Differences in recording transactions under IFRS and U.S. GAAP are discussed in Appendix D and in various International Connection boxes throughout the text.

The following Mornin' Joe International financial statements are simplified and illustrate only portions of IFRS that are appropriate for introductory accounting. The financial statements are presented in euros (€) for demonstration purposes only. The euro is the standard currency of the European Union. The euro is translated at a 1:1 ratio from the dollar to simplify comparisons. Throughout the illustration, call-outs and end notes to each statement are used to highlight the differences between financial statements prepared under IFRS and under U.S. GAAP.

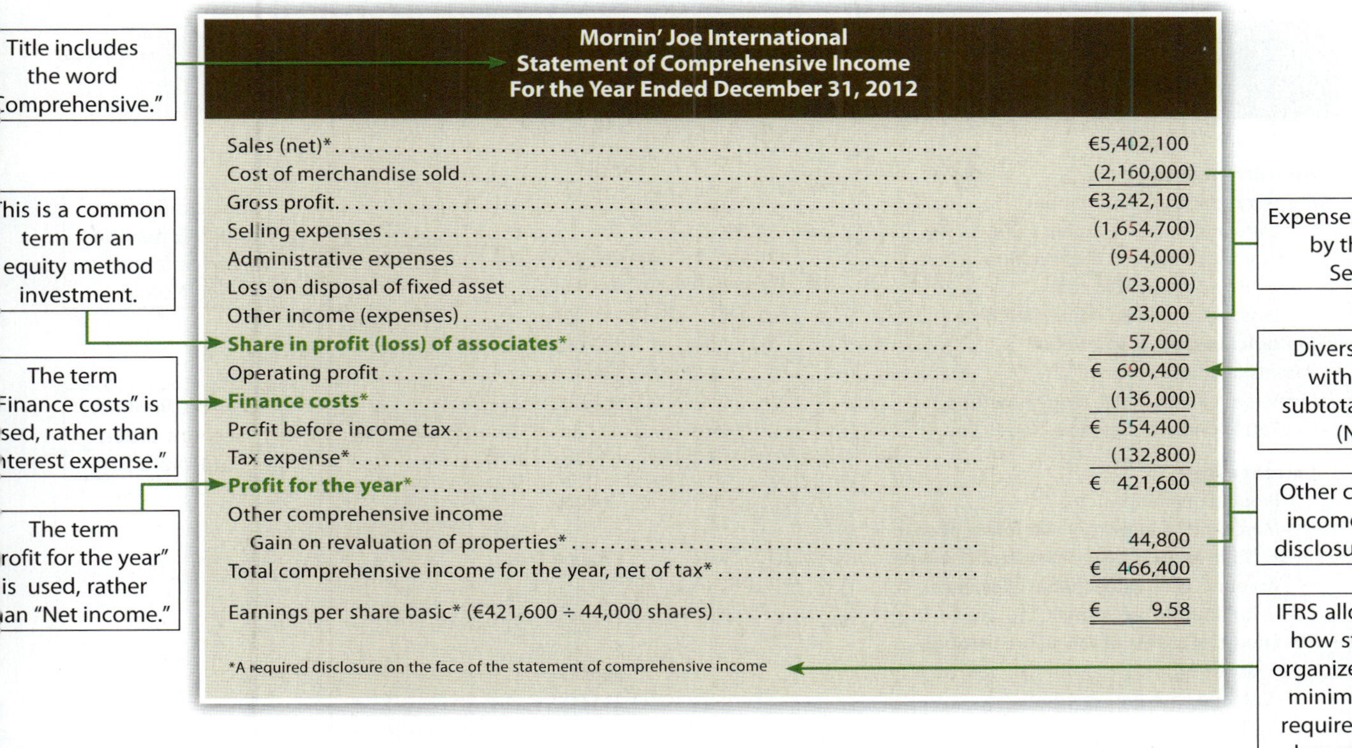

Mornin' Joe International
Statement of Comprehensive Income
For the Year Ended December 31, 2012

Sales (net)*	€5,402,100
Cost of merchandise sold	(2,160,000)
Gross profit	€3,242,100
Selling expenses	(1,654,700)
Administrative expenses	(954,000)
Loss on disposal of fixed asset	(23,000)
Other income (expenses)	23,000
Share in profit (loss) of associates*	57,000
Operating profit	€ 690,400
Finance costs*	(136,000)
Profit before income tax	€ 554,400
Tax expense*	(132,800)
Profit for the year*	€ 421,600
Other comprehensive income	
Gain on revaluation of properties*	44,800
Total comprehensive income for the year, net of tax*	€ 466,400
Earnings per share basic* (€421,600 ÷ 44,000 shares)	€ 9.58

*A required disclosure on the face of the statement of comprehensive income

1. IFRS statements are often more summarized than U.S. GAAP statements. To compensate, IFRS requires specific disclosures on the face of the financial statements (denoted *) and additional disclosures in the footnotes to the financial statements. Since additions and subtractions are grouped together in sections of IFRS statements, parentheses are used to indicate subtractions.
2. Expenses in an IFRS income statement are classified by either their nature or function. The nature of an expense is how the expense would naturally be recorded in a journal entry reflecting the economic benefit received for that expense. Examples include salaries, depreciation, advertising, and utilities. The function of an expense identifies the purpose of the expense, such as a selling expense or an administrative expense.

   IFRS does not permit the natural and functional classifications to be mixed together on the same statement. That is, all expenses must be classified by either nature or function. However, if a functional classification of expenses is used, a footnote to the income statement must show the natural classification of expenses. To illustrate, because Mornin' Joe International uses the functional classification of expenses in its income statement, it must also show the following natural classification of expenses in a footnote:

Cost of product	€2,100,000	The cost of product purchased for resale
Employee benefits expense	1,260,000	Required natural disclosure
Depreciation and amortization expense	203,700	Required natural disclosure
Rent expense	425,600	
Advertising expense	678,900	
Other expenses	58,500	
Total natural expenses	€4,726,700	

3. IFRS provides flexibility with regard to line items, headings, and subtotals on the income statement. There is less flexibility under U.S. GAAP for public companies.
4. IFRS requires the reporting of other comprehensive income (see appendix to Chapter 15) either on the income statement (illustrated) or in a separate statement. In contrast, other comprehensive income is often disclosed on the statement of changes in stockholders' equity under U.S. GAAP. For Mornin' Joe International, other comprehensive income consists of the restatement of café locations to fair value (see Note 6 for more details).

Preferred title for the "Balance Sheet."

Mornin' Joe International
Statement of Financial Position
December 31, 2012

Assets			
Noncurrent assets			
Property, plant, and equipment*			
Land and buildings at fair value	€4,180,000		
Less: Accumulated depreciation	375,200	€3,804,800	
Office equipment at cost	€ 350,000		
Less: Accumulated depreciation	102,000	248,000	
Biological assets at fair value*		320,000	
Patents at amortized cost*		140,000	
Investment in *AM Coffee* (equity method)*		565,000	
Total noncurrent assets			€5,077,800
Current assets			
Prepaid insurance		€ 24,000	
Merchandise inventory—**at lower of cost (first-in, first-out) or realizable value***		120,000	
Accounts receivable (net of allowance for doubtful accounts)*		292,700	
Financial assets at fair value through profit or loss*		465,000	
Cash and cash equivalents*		235,000	
Total current assets			1,136,700
Total assets*			€6,214,500
Equity attributable to owners			
Preferred 10% stock, $50 par (6,000 shares authorized and issued)*		€ 300,000	
Common stock, $20 par (50,000 shares authorized, 45,000 shares issued)*		900,000	
Share premium*		1,500,000	
Reserves*		(1,200)	
Retained earnings*		1,200,300	
Total equity attributable to owners*			€3,899,100
Liabilities			
Noncurrent liabilities*			
Bonds payable, 8%, due December 31, 2030 (net of discount)		€ 484,000	
Notes payable		1,400,000	
Total noncurrent liabilities			€1,884,000
Current liabilities			
Accounts payable*		€ 133,000	
Loans*		200,000	
Employee provisions*		58,400	
Interest payable		40,000	
Total current liabilities			431,400
Total liabilities*			€2,315,400
Total equity and liabilities*			€6,214,500

*Required disclosures. Footnotes provide additional subclassification detail.

"Biological assets" are a required disclosure at fair value. See Note 7.

Subclassifications of PP&E may be valued at fair value. See Note 6.

Reverse liquidity account order. See Note 5.

Inventory valuation. See Note 8.

International terminology for "Trading investments." Same accounting treatment.

International terminology for "Excess of issue price over par."

Other comprehensive items and treasury stock. See Note 9.

Equities listed first, then liabilities. See Note 5.

Noncurrent liabilities listed prior to current liabilities.

Employee provisions are wages, salaries, and payroll taxes payable. See Note 10.

5. Under IFRS, there is no standard format for the balance sheet (statement of financial position). A typical format for European Union companies is to begin the asset section of the balance sheet with noncurrent assets. This is followed by current assets listed in reverse order of liquidity. That is, the asset side of the balance sheet is reported

in reverse order of liquidity from least liquid to most liquid. Listing noncurrent assets first emphasizes the going concern nature of the entity.

The liability and owners' equity side of the balance sheet is also reported differently than under U.S. GAAP. Specifically, owners' equity is reported first followed by noncurrent liabilities and current liabilities. Listing equity first emphasizes the going concern nature of the entity and the long-term financial interest of the owners in the business.

6. Under IFRS, property, plant, and equipment (PP&E) may be measured at historical cost or fair value. If fair value is used, the revaluation must be for similar classifications of PP&E, but need not be for all PP&E. This departs from U.S. GAAP which requires PP&E to be measured at historical cost. Mornin' Joe International restated its Land and Buildings to fair value since the café sites have readily available real estate market prices. Land and buildings are included together because their fair values are not separable. The office equipment remains at historical cost since its does not have a readily available market price. The increase in fair value is recorded by reducing accumulated depreciation and recognizing the gain as other comprehensive income. This element of other comprehensive income is accumulated in stockholders' equity under the heading Property revaluation reserve.* This treatment is similar (with different titles) to the U.S. GAAP treatment of unrealized gains (losses) from available-for-sale securities. For Mornin' Joe International, there is an increase in the property revaluation reserve of €44,800. This amount is the only difference between Mornin' Joe's U.S. GAAP net income, total assets, and total stockholders' equity and Mornin' Joe International's IFRS total comprehensive income, total assets, and total stockholders' equity.
7. Mornin' Joe International recently acquired a coffee plantation. This is an example of a biological asset. IFRS requires separate reporting of biological assets (principally agricultural assets) at fair value.
8. Inventories are valued at lower of cost or market; however, "market" is defined as net realizable value under IFRS. U.S. GAAP defines "market" as replacement cost under most conditions. In addition, IFRS prohibits LIFO cost valuation.
9. Under IFRS, some elements of other comprehensive income and owner's equity are often aggregated under the term "reserves." In contrast, under U.S. GAAP "reserve" is used to identify a liability. IFRS also does not require separate disclosure of treasury stock as does U.S. GAAP. Specifically, treasury stock may be reported as a reduction of a reserve, a reduction of a stock premium, or as a separate item.
10. The term "provision" is used to denote a liability under IFRS, whereas this term often indicates an expense under U.S. GAAP. For example, "Provision for income taxes" means "Income tax expense" under U.S. GAAP, whereas it would mean "Income taxes payable" under IFRS.

* The term "property revaluation surplus" is also used.

Mornin' Joe International
Statement of Changes in Equity
For the Year Ended December 31, 2012

	Preferred Stock	Common Stock	Share Premium	Reserves: Property Revaluation Reserve	Reserves: Reserve for Own Shares	Retained Earnings	Total Equity Attributable to Owners
Balance, January 1, 2012	€300,000	€800,000	€1,325,000	€ 0	(€36,000)	€ 852,700	€3,241,700
Profit for the year						421,600	421,600
Other comprehensive income							
Property revaluation (gain)				44,800			44,800
Total comprehensive income				€44,800		€ 421,600	€ 466,400
Contributions by and distributions to owners							
Dividends on preferred stock						(30,000)	(30,000)
Dividends on common stock						(44,000)	(44,000)
Issuance of additional common stock		100,000	175,000				275,000
Purchase of own shares					(10,000)		(10,000)
Total contributions and distributions to owners	€ 0	€100,000	€ 175,000	€ 0	(€10,000)	(€ 74,000)	€ 191,000
Balance, December 31, 2012	€300,000	€900,000	€1,500,000	€44,800	(€46,000)	€1,200,300	€3,899,100

"Reserves", see Notes 9 and 11.

11. The statement of changes in equity under IFRS is similar to U.S. GAAP. For example, both IFRS and GAAP include other comprehensive income items and total comprehensive income disclosures in the statement of changes in equity. In this illustration, treasury stock is included as part a reserve (Reserve for Own Shares). As discussed in Note 9, under U.S. GAAP the term "reserve" denotes a liability.

Discussion Questions

1. Contrast U.S. GAAP income statement terms with their differing IFRS terms, starting with the name of the statement.
2. What is the difference between classifying an expense by nature or function?
3. If a functional expense classification is used for the statement of comprehensive income, what must also be disclosed?
4. What is an example of "Other comprehensive income"? How would it be reported on the statement of comprehensive income?
5. How is the term "provision" used differently under IFRS than under U.S. GAAP?
6. What are two main differences in inventory valuation under IFRS compared to U.S. GAAP?
7. What is a "biological asset"?
8. What is the most significant IFRS departure from U.S. GAAP for valuing property, plant, and equipment?
9. What is a "share premium"?
10. How is the term "reserve" used under IFRS, and how does it differ from its meaning under U.S. GAAP?
11. How is treasury stock reported under IFRS? How does this differ from its treatment under U.S. GAAP?

IFRS Activity 1

IFRS

Unilever Group is a global company that markets a wide variety of products, including Lever® soap, Breyer's® ice cream, and Hellman's® mayonnaise. The income statement and statement of comprehensive income for the Dutch company, Unilever Group is shown below.

Unilever Group Consolidated Income Statement For the Year Ended December 31, 2009 (in millions of euros)	
Turnover	€39,823
Operating profit	5,020
After (charging)/crediting:	
Restructuring	(897)
Business disposals, impairments, other	29
Net finance costs	(593)
Finance income	75
Finance costs	(504)
Pensions and similar obligations	(164)
Share of net profit/(loss) of joint ventures	111
Share of net profit/(loss) of associates	4
Other income from non-current investments	374
Profit before taxation	€ 4,916
Taxation	(1,257)
Net profit	€ 3,659
Earnings per share—basic	€ 1.21
Earnings per share—diluted	€ 1.17

Consolidated Statement of Comprehensive Income For the Year Ended December 31, 2009	
Fair value gains (losses), net of tax	€ 65
Actuarial gains (losses) on pensions, net of tax	18
Currency retranslation gains (losses), net of tax	396
Net income (expense) recognized directly into equity	€ 519
Net profit	3,659
Total comprehensive income	€4,178

a. What do you think is meant by "turnover"?

b. How does Unilever's income statement presentation differ significantly from that of Mornin' Joe?

c. How is the total for net finance costs presented differently than would be typically found under U.S. GAAP?

d. What are two ways in which other comprehensive income items can be disclosed under IFRS, and how does this differ from U.S. GAAP?

IFRS Activity 2

The following is the consolidated statement of financial position for LVMH, a French company that markets the Louis Vuitton® and Moët Hennessy® brands.

LVMH
Statement of Financial Position
December 31, 2009
(in millions of euros)

Assets	
Brands and other intangible assets—net	€ 8,697
Goodwill—net	4,270
Property, plant, and equipment—net	6,140
Investment in associates	213
Non-current available for sale financial assets	540
Other non-current assets	750
Deferred tax	521
Non-current assets	€21,131
Inventories	€ 5,644
Trade accounts receivable	1,455
Income taxes receivable	217
Other current assets	1,213
Cash and cash equivalents	2,446
Current assets	€10,975
TOTAL ASSETS	€32,106
Liabilities and Equity	
Share capital	€ 147
Share premium	1,763
Treasury shares	(929)
Revaluation reserves	871
Other reserves	10,684
Net profit, group share	1,755
Equity, group share	€13,796
Minority interests	989
Total equity	€14,785
Long-term borrowings	€ 4,077
Provisions	990
Deferred tax	3,117
Other non-current liabilities	3,089
Total non-current liabilities	€11,273
Short-term borrowings	1,708
Trade accounts payable	1,911
Income taxes payable	221
Provisions	334
Other current liabilities	1,874
Total current liabilities	€ 6,048
TOTAL LIABILITIES AND EQUITY	€32,106

a. Identify presentation differences between the balance sheet of LVMH and a balance sheet prepared under U.S. GAAP. Use the Mornin' Joe balance sheet on page 714 as an example of a U.S. GAAP balance sheet. (Ignore minority interests.)

b. Compare the terms used in this balance sheet with the terms used by Mornin' Joe (page 714), using the table below.

LVMH Term	U.S. GAAP Term as Used by Mornin' Joe
Statement of financial position	
Share capital	
Share premium	
Other reserves	
Provisions	

c. What does the "Revaluation reserves" in the equity section of the balance sheet represent?

IFRS Activity 3

IFRS

Under U.S. GAAP, LIFO is an acceptable inventory method. Listed below is financial statement information for three companies that use LIFO. All table numbers are in millions of dollars.

	LIFO Inventory	FIFO Inventory (from footnotes)	Impact on Net Income from Using LIFO Rather than FIFO (from footnotes)	Total Current Assets	Net Income as Reported
ExxonMobil	$11,553	$28,653	$207	$55,235	$19,280
Kroger	4,902	5,705	(49)	7,450	70
Ford Motor*	5,450	6,248	33	40,560	1,212

*Autos and trucks only

Assume these companies adopted IFRS, and thus were required to use FIFO, rather than LIFO. Prepare a table with the following columns as shown below.

(1) Difference between FIFO and LIFO inventory valuation.

(2) Revised IFRS net income using FIFO.

(3) Difference between FIFO and LIFO inventory valuation as a percent of total current assets.

(4) Revised IFRS net income as a percent of the reported net income.

(1)	(2)	(3)	(4)
FIFO less LIFO	IFRS Net Income	(FIFO less LIFO) / Total Current Assets	IFRS Net Income Col. (2) / Reported Net Income

a. Complete the table.

b. For which company would a change to IFRS for inventory valuation have the largest percentage impact on total current assets (Col. 3)?

c. For which company would a change to IFRS for inventory valuation have the largest percentage impact on net income (Col. 4)?

d. Why might Kroger have a negative impact on net income from using LIFO, while the other two companies have a positive impact on net income from using LIFO?

CHAPTER 16

AP Photo/Elaine Thompson

Statement of Cash Flows

Jones Soda Co.

Suppose you were to receive $100 from an event. Would it make a difference what the event was? Yes, it would! If you received $100 for your birthday, then it's a gift. If you received $100 as a result of working part time for a week, then it's the result of your effort. If you received $100 as a loan, then it's money that you will have to pay back in the future. If you received $100 as a result of selling your iPod, then it's the result of giving up something tangible. Thus, $100 received can be associated with different types of events, and these events have different meanings to you, and different implications for your future. You would much rather receive a $100 gift than take out a $100 loan. Likewise, company stakeholders view inflows and outflows of cash differently depending on their source.

Companies are required to report information about the events causing a change in cash over a period of time. This information is reported in the statement of cash flows. One such company is **Jones Soda Co.** Jones began in the late 1980s as an alternative beverage company, known for its customer-provided labels, unique flavors, and support for extreme sports. You have probably seen Jones Soda at **Barnes & Noble**, **Panera Bread**, or **Starbucks**, or maybe sampled some of its unique flavors, such as Fufu Berry®, Blue Bubblegum®, or Lemon Drop®. As with any company, cash is important to Jones Soda. Without cash, Jones would be unable to expand its brands, distribute its product, support extreme sports, or provide a return for its owners. Thus, its managers are concerned about the sources and uses of cash.

In previous chapters, we have used the income statement, balance sheet, statement of retained earnings, and other information to analyze the effects of management decisions on a business's financial position and operating performance. In this chapter, we focus on the events causing a change in cash by presenting the preparation and use of the statement of cash flows.

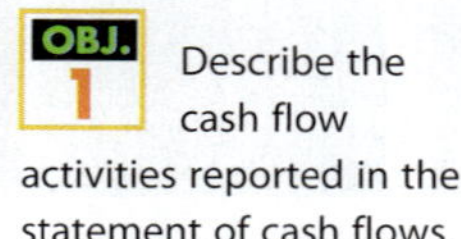

Describe the cash flow activities reported in the statement of cash flows.

Reporting Cash Flows

The **statement of cash flows** reports a company's cash inflows and outflows for a period.[1] The statement of cash flows provides useful information about a company's ability to do the following:

1. Generate cash from operations
2. Maintain and expand its operating capacity
3. Meet its financial obligations
4. Pay dividends

The statement of cash flows is used by managers in evaluating past operations and in planning future investing and financing activities. It is also used by external users such as investors and creditors to assess a company's profit potential and ability to pay its debt and pay dividends.

The statement of cash flows reports three types of cash flow activities as follows:

Cash flows from operating activities are cash flows from transactions that affect the net income of the company.

Example: Purchase and sale of merchandise by a retailer.

Cash flows from investing activities are cash flows from transactions that affect investments in the noncurrent assets of the company.

Example: Purchase and sale of fixed assets, such as equipment and buildings.

1 As used in this chapter, *cash* refers to cash and cash equivalents. Examples of cash equivalents include short-term, highly liquid investments, such as money market accounts, bank certificates of deposit, and U.S. Treasury bills.

Cash flows from financing activities are cash flows from transactions that affect the debt and equity of the company.

Example: Issuing or retiring equity and debt securities.

The cash flows are reported in the statement of cash flows as follows:

Cash flows from operating activities	$XXX
Cash flows from investing activities	XXX
Cash flows from financing activities	XXX
Net increase or decrease in cash for the period	$XXX
Cash at the beginning of the period	XXX
Cash at the end of the period	$XXX

The ending cash on the statement of cash flows equals the cash reported on the company's balance sheet at the end of the year.

Exhibit 1 illustrates the sources (increases) and uses (decreases) of cash by each of the three cash flow activities. A *source* of cash causes the cash flow to increase and is called a *cash inflow*. A *use* of cash causes cash flow to decrease and is called *cash outflow*.

Note:
The statement of cash flows reports cash flows from operating, investing, and financing activities.

EXHIBIT 1
Cash Flows

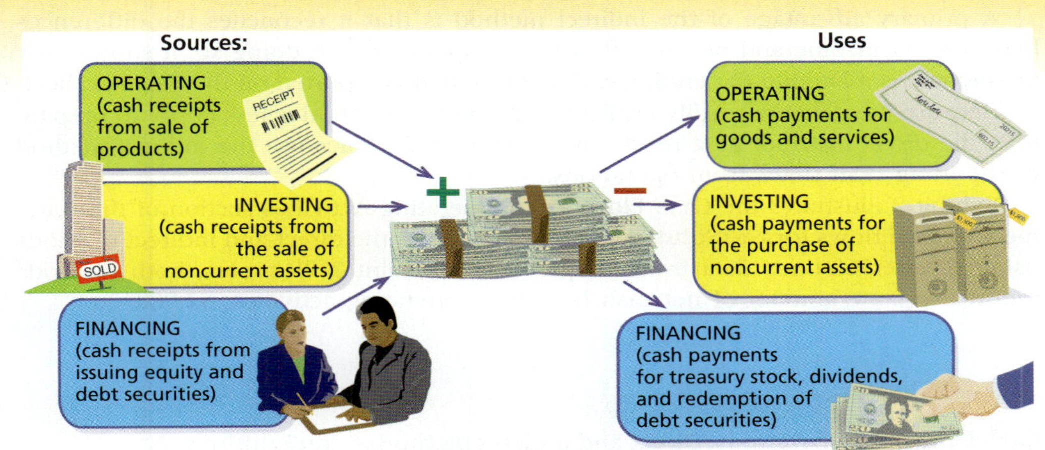

Cash Flows from Operating Activities

Cash flows from operating activities is the cash inflow or outflow from a company's day-to-day operations. Companies may select one of two alternative methods for reporting cash flows from operating activities in the statement of cash flows:

1. The direct method
2. The indirect method

Both methods result in the same amount of cash flows from operating activities. They differ in the way they report cash flow from operating activities as discussed below.

The **direct method** reports operating cash inflows (receipts) and cash outflows (payments) as follows:

Cash flows from operating activities:		
Cash received from customers		$XXX
Less: Cash payments for merchandise	$XXX	
Cash payments for operating expenses	XXX	
Cash payments for interest	XXX	
Cash payments for income taxes	XXX	XXX
Net cash flows from operating activities		$XXX

The primary operating cash inflow is cash received from customers. The primary operating cash outflows are cash payments for merchandise, operating expenses, interest, and income tax payments. The cash received from operating activities less the cash payments for operating activities is the net cash flow from operating activities.

The primary advantage of the direct method is that it *directly* reports cash receipts and cash payments in the statement of cash flows. Its primary disadvantage is that these data may not be readily available in the accounting records. Thus, the direct method is normally more costly to prepare and, as a result, is used by less than 1% of companies.[2]

The **indirect method** reports cash flows from operating activities by beginning with net income and adjusting it for revenues and expenses that do not involve the receipt or payment of cash as follows:

Cash flows from operating activities:		
Net income	$XXX	
Adjustments to reconcile net income to net cash flow from operating activities	XXX	
Net cash flow from operating activities		$XXX

The adjustments to reconcile net income to net cash flow from operating activities include such items as depreciation and gains or losses on fixed assets. Changes in current operating assets and liabilities such as accounts receivable or accounts payable are also added or deducted depending on their effect on cash flows. In effect, these additions and deductions adjust net income, which is reported on an accrual accounting basis, to cash flows from operating activities, which uses a cash basis.

A primary advantage of the indirect method is that it reconciles the differences between net income and net cash flows from operations. In doing so, it shows how net income is related to the ending cash balance that is reported on the balance sheet.

Because the data are readily available, the indirect method is less costly to prepare than the direct method. As a result, over 99% of companies use the indirect method of reporting cash flows from operations.

Exhibit 2 illustrates the Cash Flows from Operating Activities section of the statement of cash flows for **NetSolutions**. Exhibit 2 shows the direct and indirect methods using the NetSolutions data from Chapter 1. As Exhibit 2 illustrates, both methods report the same amount of net cash flow from operating activities, $2,900.

EXHIBIT 2 **Cash Flow from Operations: Direct and Indirect Methods—NetSolutions**

Direct Method

Cash flows from operating activities:	
Cash received from customers	$7,500
Deduct cash payments for expenses and payments to creditors	4,600
Net cash flow from operating activities	$2,900

Indirect Method

Cash flows from operating activities:	
Net income	$3,050
Add increase in accounts payable	400
	$3,450
Deduct increase in supplies	550
Net cash flow from operating activities	$2,900

the same

Cash Flows from Investing Activities

In October 2008, the U.S. government invested $250 billion of cash into U.S. banks to help stabilize the financial system.

Cash flows from investing activities show the cash inflows and outflows related to changes in a company's long-term assets. Cash flows from investing activities are reported on the statement of cash flows as follows:

Cash flows from investing activities:		
Cash inflows from investing activities	$XXX	
Less cash used for investing activities	XXX	
Net cash flows from investing activities		$XXX

2 *Accounting Trends & Techniques*, AICPA, 2008 edition.

Cash inflows from investing activities normally arise from selling fixed assets, investments, and intangible assets. Cash outflows normally include payments to purchase fixed assets, investments, and intangible assets.

Cash Flows from Financing Activities

Cash flows from financing activities show the cash inflows and outflows related to changes in a company's long-term liabilities and stockholders' equity. Cash flows from financing activities are reported on the statement of cash flows as follows:

Cash flows from financing activities:		
Cash inflows from financing activities	$XXX	
Less cash used for financing activities	XXX	
Net cash flows from financing activities		$XXX

Cash inflows from financing activities normally arise from issuing long-term debt or equity securities. For example, issuing bonds, notes payable, preferred stock, and common stock creates cash inflows from financing activities. Cash outflows from financing activities include paying cash dividends, repaying long-term debt, and acquiring treasury stock.

Noncash Investing and Financing Activities

A company may enter into transactions involving investing and financing activities that do not *directly* affect cash. For example, a company may issue common stock to retire long-term debt. Although this transaction does not directly affect cash, it does eliminate future cash payments for interest and for paying the bonds when they mature. Because such transactions *indirectly* affect cash flows, they are reported in a separate section of the statement of cash flows. This section usually appears at the bottom of the statement of cash flows.

In fiscal 2009, Apple, Inc., generated $10.1 billion in cash flow from operating activities.

Example Exercise 16-1 Classifying Cash Flows

OBJ. 1

Identify whether each of the following would be reported as an operating, investing, or financing activity in the statement of cash flows.

a. Purchase of patent
b. Payment of cash dividend
c. Disposal of equipment
d. Cash sales
e. Purchase of treasury stock
f. Payment of wages expense

Follow My Example 16-1

a. Investing
b. Financing
c. Investing
d. Operating
e. Financing
f. Operating

Practice Exercises: PE 16-1A, PE 16-1B

No Cash Flow per Share

Cash flow per share is sometimes reported in the financial press. As reported, cash flow per share is normally computed as *cash flow from operations per share*. However, such reporting may be misleading because of the following:

1. Users may misinterpret cash flow per share as the per-share amount available for dividends. This would not be the case if the cash generated by operations is required for repaying loans or for reinvesting in the business.
2. Users may misinterpret cash flow per share as equivalent to (or better than) earnings per share.

For these reasons, the financial statements, including the statement of cash flows, should not report cash flow per share.

The net income of $108,000 reported by Rundell Inc. does not equal the cash flows from operating activities for the period. This is because net income is determined using the accrual method of accounting.

Prepare a statement of cash flows, using the indirect method.

Key Points The indirect method reports cash flow from operating activities by adjusting net income for revenues and expenses that do not involve the receipt or payment of cash. Noncash expenses such as depreciation are added back to net income. Gains and losses on the disposal of assets are added to or deducted from net income. Changes in current operating assets and liabilities are added to or subtracted from net income depending on their effect on cash. Cash flow from investing activities and cash flow from financing activities are reported below cash flow from operating activities in the statement of cash flows.

Learning Outcomes	Example Exercises	Practice Exercises
• Determine cash flow from operating activities under the indirect method by adjusting net income for noncash expenses and gains and losses from asset disposals.	EE16-2	PE16-2A, 16-2B
• Determine cash flow from operating activities under the indirect method by adjusting net income for changes in current operating assets and liabilities.	EE16-3	PE16-3A, 16-3B
• Prepare the Cash Flows from Operating Activities section of the statement of cash flows using the indirect method.	EE16-4	PE16-4A, 16-4B
• Prepare the Cash Flows from Investing Activities and Cash Flows from Financing Activities sections of the statement of cash flows.	EE16-5	PE16-5A, 16-5B

Prepare a statement of cash flows, using the direct method.

Key Points The amount of cash flows from operating activities is the same under both the direct and indirect methods, but the manner in which cash flow from operating activities is reported is different. The direct method reports cash flows from operating activities by major classes of operating cash receipts and cash payments. The difference between the major classes of total operating cash receipts and total operating cash payments is the net cash flow from operating activities. The Cash Flows from Investing and Financing Activities sections of the statement are the same under both the direct and indirect methods.

Learning Outcomes	Example Exercises	Practice Exercises
• Prepare the cash flows from operating activities and the remainder of the statement of cash flows under the direct method.	EE16-6 EE16-7	PE16-6A, 16-6B PE16-7A, 16-7B

Describe and illustrate the use of free cash flow in evaluating a company's cash flow.

Key Points Free cash flow measures the operating cash flow available for company use after purchasing the fixed assets that are necessary to maintain current productive capacity. It is calculated by subtracting these fixed asset purchases from cash flow from operating activities. A company with strong free cash flow is able to fund internal growth, retire debt, pay dividends, and enjoy financial flexibility. A company with weak free cash flow has much less financial flexibility for such activities.

Learning Outcomes	Example Exercises	Practice Exercises
• Describe free cash flow.		
• Calculate and evaluate free cash flow.	EE16-8	PE16-8A, 16-8B

Key Terms

cash flow per share (721)
cash flows from financing activities (719)
cash flows from investing activities (718)
cash flows from operating activities (718)
direct method (719)
free cash flow (737)
indirect method (720)
statement of cash flows (718)

Illustrative Problem

The comparative balance sheet of Dowling Company for December 31, 2012 and 2011, is as follows:

Dowling Company
Comparative Balance Sheet
December 31, 2012 and 2011

	2012	2011
Assets		
Cash	$ 140,350	$ 95,900
Accounts receivable (net)	95,300	102,300
Inventories	165,200	157,900
Prepaid expenses	6,240	5,860
Investments (long-term)	35,700	84,700
Land	75,000	90,000
Buildings	375,000	260,000
Accumulated depreciation—buildings	(71,300)	(58,300)
Machinery and equipment	428,300	428,300
Accumulated depreciation—machinery and equipment	(148,500)	(138,000)
Patents	58,000	65,000
Total assets	$1,159,290	$1,093,660
Liabilities and Stockholders' Equity		
Accounts payable (merchandise creditors)	$ 43,500	$ 46,700
Accrued expenses payable (operating expenses)	14,000	12,500
Income taxes payable	7,900	8,400
Dividends payable	14,000	10,000
Mortgage note payable, due 2023	40,000	0
Bonds payable	150,000	250,000
Common stock, $30 par	450,000	375,000
Excess of issue price over par—common stock	66,250	41,250
Retained earnings	373,640	349,810
Total liabilities and stockholders' equity	$1,159,290	$1,093,660

The income statement for Dowling Company is shown here.

Dowling Company Income Statement For the Year Ended December 31, 2012		
Sales		$1,100,000
Cost of merchandise sold		710,000
Gross profit		$ 390,000
Operating expenses:		
Depreciation expense	$ 23,500	
Patent amortization	7,000	
Other operating expenses	196,000	
Total operating expenses		226,500
Income from operations		$ 163,500
Other income:		
Gain on sale of investments	$ 11,000	
Other expense:		
Interest expense	26,000	(15,000)
Income before income tax		$ 148,500
Income tax expense		50,000
Net income		$ 98,500

An examination of the accounting records revealed the following additional information applicable to 2012:

a. Land costing $15,000 was sold for $15,000.

b. A mortgage note was issued for $40,000.

c. A building costing $115,000 was constructed.

d. 2,500 shares of common stock were issued at $40 in exchange for the bonds payable.

e. Cash dividends declared were $74,670.

Instructions

1. Prepare a statement of cash flows, using the indirect method of reporting cash flows from operating activities.
2. Prepare a statement of cash flows, using the direct method of reporting cash flows from operating activities.

Solution

1.

Dowling Company Statement of Cash Flows—Indirect Method For the Year Ended December 31, 2012			
Cash flows from operating activities:			
Net income		$ 98,500	
Adjustments to reconcile net income to net cash flow from operating activities:			
Depreciation		23,500	
Amortization of patents		7,000	
Gain on sale of investments		(11,000)	
Changes in current operating assets and liabilities:			
Decrease in accounts receivable		7,000	
Increase in inventories		(7,300)	
Increase in prepaid expenses		(380)	
Decrease in accounts payable		(3,200)	
Increase in accrued expenses payable		1,500	
Decrease in income taxes payable		(500)	
Net cash flow from operating activities			$115,120
Cash flows from investing activities:			
Cash received from sale of:			
Investments	$60,000[1]		
Land	15,000	$ 75,000	
Less: Cash paid for construction of building		115,000	
Net cash flow used for investing activities			(40,000)
Cash flows from financing activities:			
Cash received from issuing mortgage note payable		$ 40,000	
Less: Cash paid for dividends		70,670[2]	
Net cash flow used for financing activities			(30,670)
Increase in cash			$ 44,450
Cash at the beginning of the year			95,900
Cash at the end of the year			$140,350
Schedule of Noncash Investing and Financing Activities:			
Issued common stock to retire bonds payable			$100,000

[1] $60,000 = $11,000 gain + $49,000 (decrease in investments)

[2] $70,670 = $74,670 – $4,000 (increase in dividends)

2.

Dowling Company
Statement of Cash Flows—Direct Method
For the Year Ended December 31, 2012

Cash flows from operating activities:			
Cash received from customers[1]		$1,107,000	
Deduct: Cash paid for merchandise[2]	$720,500		
Cash paid for operating expenses[3]	194,880		
Cash paid for interest expense	26,000		
Cash paid for income tax[4]	50,500	991,880	
Net cash flow from operating activities			$115,120
Cash flows from investing activities:			
Cash received from sale of:			
Investments	$ 60,000[5]		
Land	15,000	$ 75,000	
Less: Cash paid for construction of building		115,000	
Net cash flow used for investing activities			(40,000)
Cash flows from financing activities:			
Cash received from issuing mortgage note payable		$ 40,000	
Less: Cash paid for dividends[6]		70,670	
Net cash flow used for financing activities			(30,670)
Increase in cash			$ 44,450
Cash at the beginning of the year			95,900
Cash at the end of the year			$140,350
Schedule of Noncash Investing and Financing Activities:			
Issued common stock to retire bonds payable			$100,000
Schedule Reconciling Net Income with Cash Flows from Operating Activities[7]			

Computations:

[1]$1,100,000 + $7,000 = $1,107,000
[2]$710,000 + $3,200 + $7,300 = $720,500
[3]$196,000 + $380 – $1,500 = $194,880
[4]$50,000 + $500 = $50,500
[5]$60,000 = $11,000 gain + $49,000 (decrease in investments)
[6]$74,670 + $10,000 – $14,000 = $70,670
[7]The content of this schedule is the same as the Operating Activities section of part (1) of this solution and is not reproduced here for the sake of brevity.

Discussion Questions

1. What is the principal disadvantage of the direct method of reporting cash flows from operating activities?
2. What are the major advantages of the indirect method of reporting cash flows from operating activities?
3. A corporation issued $1,000,000 of common stock in exchange for $1,000,000 of fixed assets. Where would this transaction be reported on the statement of cash flows?
4. A retail business, using the accrual method of accounting, owed merchandise creditors (accounts payable) $240,000 at the beginning of the year and $265,000 at the end of the year. How would the $25,000 increase be used to adjust net income in determining the amount of cash flows from operating activities by the indirect method? Explain.
5. If salaries payable was $75,000 at the beginning of the year and $40,000 at the end of the year, should $35,000 be added to or deducted from income to determine the amount of cash flows from operating activities by the indirect method? Explain.
6. A long-term investment in bonds with a cost of $800,000 was sold for $910,000 cash. (a) What was

the gain or loss on the sale? (b) What was the effect of the transaction on cash flows? (c) How should the transaction be reported in the statement of cash flows if cash flows from operating activities are reported by the indirect method?

7. A corporation issued $10,000,000 of 20-year bonds for cash at 102. How would the transaction be reported on the statement of cash flows?

8. Fully depreciated equipment costing $25,000 was discarded. What was the effect of the transaction on cash flows if (a) $10,000 cash is received, (b) no cash is received?

9. For the current year, Bearings Company decided to switch from the indirect method to the direct method for reporting cash flows from operating activities on the statement of cash flows. Will the change cause the amount of net cash flow from operating activities to be (a) larger, (b) smaller, or (c) the same as if the indirect method had been used? Explain.

10. Name five common major classes of operating cash receipts or operating cash payments presented on the statement of cash flows when the cash flows from operating activities are reported by the direct method.

decreased $7,400 over the year. Determine the amount of cash received from customers.

Appendices

A Interest Tables

B Reversing Entries

C Nike, Inc., 2010 Annual Report

D International Financial Reporting Standards

Appendix A

Interest Tables

Present Value of $1 at Compound Interest Due in *n* Periods

Periods	5%	5.5%	6%	6.5%	7%	8%
1	0.95238	0.94787	0.94334	0.93897	0.93458	0.92593
2	0.90703	0.89845	0.89000	0.88166	0.87344	0.85734
3	0.86384	0.85161	0.83962	0.82785	0.81630	0.79383
4	0.82270	0.80722	0.79209	0.77732	0.76290	0.73503
5	0.78353	0.76513	0.74726	0.72988	0.71290	0.68058
6	0.74622	0.72525	0.70496	0.68533	0.66634	0.63017
7	0.71068	0.68744	0.66506	0.64351	0.62275	0.58349
8	0.67684	0.65160	0.62741	0.60423	0.58201	0.54027
9	0.64461	0.61763	0.59190	0.56735	0.54393	0.50025
10	0.61391	0.58543	0.55840	0.53273	0.50835	0.46319
11	0.58468	0.55491	0.52679	0.50021	0.47509	0.42888
12	0.55684	0.52598	0.49697	0.46968	0.44401	0.39711
13	0.53032	0.49856	0.46884	0.44102	0.41496	0.36770
14	0.50507	0.47257	0.44230	0.41410	0.38782	0.34046
15	0.48102	0.44793	0.41726	0.38883	0.36245	0.31524
16	0.45811	0.42458	0.39365	0.36510	0.33874	0.29189
17	0.43630	0.40245	0.37136	0.34281	0.31657	0.27027
18	0.41552	0.38147	0.35034	0.32189	0.29586	0.25025
19	0.39573	0.36158	0.33051	0.30224	0.27651	0.23171
20	0.37689	0.34273	0.31180	0.28380	0.25842	0.21455
21	0.35894	0.32486	0.29416	0.26648	0.24151	0.19866
22	0.34185	0.30793	0.27750	0.25021	0.22571	0.18394
23	0.32557	0.29187	0.26180	0.23494	0.21095	0.17032
24	0.31007	0.27666	0.24698	0.22060	0.19715	0.15770
25	0.29530	0.26223	0.23300	0.20714	0.18425	0.14602
26	0.28124	0.24856	0.21981	0.19450	0.17211	0.13520
27	0.26785	0.23560	0.20737	0.18263	0.16093	0.12519
28	0.25509	0.22332	0.19563	0.17148	0.15040	0.11591
29	0.24295	0.21168	0.18456	0.16101	0.14056	0.10733
30	0.23138	0.20064	0.17411	0.15119	0.13137	0.09938
31	0.22036	0.19018	0.16426	0.14196	0.12277	0.09202
32	0.20987	0.18027	0.15496	0.13329	0.11474	0.08520
33	0.19987	0.17087	0.14619	0.12516	0.10724	0.07889
34	0.19036	0.16196	0.13791	0.11752	0.10022	0.07304
35	0.18129	0.15352	0.13010	0.11035	0.09366	0.06764
40	0.14205	0.11746	0.09722	0.08054	0.06678	0.04603
45	0.11130	0.08988	0.07265	0.05879	0.04761	0.03133
50	0.08720	0.06877	0.05429	0.04291	0.03395	0.02132

Present Value of $1 at Compound Interest Due in *n* Periods

Periods	9%	10%	11%	12%	13%	14%
1	0.91743	0.90909	0.90090	0.89286	0.88496	0.87719
2	0.84168	0.82645	0.81162	0.79719	0.78315	0.76947
3	0.77218	0.75132	0.73119	0.71178	0.69305	0.67497
4	0.70842	0.68301	0.65873	0.63552	0.61332	0.59208
5	0.64993	0.62092	0.59345	0.56743	0.54276	0.51937
6	0.59627	0.56447	0.53464	0.50663	0.48032	0.45559
7	0.54703	0.51316	0.48166	0.45235	0.42506	0.39964
8	0.50187	0.46651	0.43393	0.40388	0.37616	0.35056
9	0.46043	0.42410	0.39092	0.36061	0.33288	0.30751
10	0.42241	0.38554	0.35218	0.32197	0.29459	0.26974
11	0.38753	0.35049	0.31728	0.28748	0.26070	0.23662
12	0.35554	0.31863	0.28584	0.25668	0.23071	0.20756
13	0.32618	0.28966	0.25751	0.22917	0.20416	0.18207
14	0.29925	0.26333	0.23199	0.20462	0.18068	0.15971
15	0.27454	0.23939	0.20900	0.18270	0.15989	0.14010
16	0.25187	0.21763	0.18829	0.16312	0.14150	0.12289
17	0.23107	0.19784	0.16963	0.14564	0.12522	0.10780
18	0.21199	0.17986	0.15282	0.13004	0.11081	0.09456
19	0.19449	0.16351	0.13768	0.11611	0.09806	0.08295
20	0.17843	0.14864	0.12403	0.10367	0.08678	0.07276
21	0.16370	0.13513	0.11174	0.09256	0.07680	0.06383
22	0.15018	0.12285	0.10067	0.08264	0.06796	0.05599
23	0.13778	0.11168	0.09069	0.07379	0.06014	0.04911
24	0.12640	0.10153	0.08170	0.06588	0.05323	0.04308
25	0.11597	0.09230	0.07361	0.05882	0.04710	0.03779
26	0.10639	0.08390	0.06631	0.05252	0.04168	0.03315
27	0.09761	0.07628	0.05974	0.04689	0.03689	0.02908
28	0.08955	0.06934	0.05382	0.04187	0.03264	0.02551
29	0.08216	0.06304	0.04849	0.03738	0.02889	0.02237
30	0.07537	0.05731	0.04368	0.03338	0.02557	0.01963
31	0.06915	0.05210	0.03935	0.02980	0.02262	0.01722
32	0.06344	0.04736	0.03545	0.02661	0.02002	0.01510
33	0.05820	0.04306	0.03194	0.02376	0.01772	0.01325
34	0.05331	0.03914	0.02878	0.02121	0.01568	0.01162
35	0.04899	0.03558	0.02592	0.01894	0.01388	0.01019
40	0.03184	0.02210	0.01538	0.01075	0.00753	0.00529
45	0.02069	0.01372	0.00913	0.00610	0.00409	0.00275
50	0.01345	0.00852	0.00542	0.00346	0.00222	0.00143

Present Value of Ordinary Annuity of $1 per Period

Periods	5%	5.5%	6%	6.5%	7%	8%
1	0.95238	0.94787	0.94340	0.93897	0.93458	0.92593
2	1.85941	1.84632	1.83339	1.82063	1.80802	1.78326
3	2.72325	2.69793	2.67301	2.64848	2.62432	2.57710
4	3.54595	3.50515	3.46511	3.42580	3.38721	3.31213
5	4.32948	4.27028	4.21236	4.15568	4.10020	3.99271
6	5.07569	4.99553	4.91732	4.84101	4.76654	4.62288
7	5.78637	5.68297	5.58238	5.48452	5.38923	5.20637
8	6.46321	6.33457	6.20979	6.08875	5.97130	5.74664
9	7.10782	6.95220	6.80169	6.65610	6.51523	6.24689
10	7.72174	7.53763	7.36009	7.18883	7.02358	6.71008
11	8.30641	8.09254	7.88688	7.68904	7.49867	7.13896
12	8.86325	8.61852	8.38384	8.15873	7.94269	7.53608
13	9.39357	9.11708	8.85268	8.59974	8.35765	7.90378
14	9.89864	9.58965	9.29498	9.01384	8.74547	8.22424
15	10.37966	10.03758	9.71225	9.40267	9.10791	8.55948
16	10.83777	10.46216	10.10590	9.76776	9.44665	8.85137
17	11.27407	10.86461	10.47726	10.11058	9.76322	9.12164
18	11.68959	11.24607	10.82760	10.43247	10.05909	9.37189
19	12.08532	11.60765	11.15812	10.73471	10.33560	9.60360
20	12.46221	11.95038	11.46992	11.01851	10.59401	9.81815
21	12.82115	12.27524	11.76408	11.28498	10.83553	10.01680
22	13.16300	12.58317	12.04158	11.53520	11.06124	10.20074
23	13.48857	12.87504	12.30338	11.77014	11.27219	10.37106
24	13.79864	13.15170	12.55036	11.99074	11.46933	10.52876
25	14.09394	13.41393	12.78336	12.19788	11.65358	10.67478
26	14.37518	13.66250	13.00317	12.39237	11.82578	10.80998
27	14.64303	13.89810	13.21053	12.57500	11.98671	10.93516
28	14.89813	14.12142	13.40616	12.74648	12.13711	11.05108
29	15.14107	14.33310	13.59072	12.90749	12.27767	11.15841
30	15.37245	14.53375	13.76483	13.05868	12.40904	11.25778
31	15.59281	14.72393	13.92909	13.20063	12.53181	11.34980
32	15.80268	14.90420	14.08404	13.33393	12.64656	11.43500
33	16.00255	15.07507	14.23023	13.45909	12.75379	11.51389
34	16.19290	15.23703	14.36814	13.57661	12.85401	11.58693
35	16.37420	15.39055	14.49825	13.68696	12.94767	11.65457
40	17.15909	16.04612	15.04630	14.14553	13.33171	11.92461
45	17.77407	16.54773	15.45583	14.48023	13.60552	12.10840
50	18.25592	16.93152	15.76186	14.72452	13.80075	12.23348

Present Value of Ordinary Annuity of $1 per Period

Periods	9%	10%	11%	12%	13%	14%
1	0.91743	0.90909	0.90090	0.89286	0.88496	0.87719
2	1.75911	1.73554	1.71252	1.69005	1.66810	1.64666
3	2.53130	2.48685	2.44371	2.40183	2.36115	2.32163
4	3.23972	3.16986	3.10245	3.03735	2.97447	2.91371
5	3.88965	3.79079	3.69590	3.60478	3.51723	3.43308
6	4.48592	4.35526	4.23054	4.11141	3.99755	3.88867
7	5.03295	4.86842	4.71220	4.56376	4.42261	4.28830
8	5.53482	5.33493	5.14612	4.96764	4.79677	4.63886
9	5.99525	5.75902	5.53705	5.32825	5.13166	4.94637
10	6.41766	6.14457	5.88923	5.65022	5.42624	5.21612
11	6.80519	6.49506	6.20652	5.93770	5.68694	5.45273
12	7.16072	6.81369	6.49236	6.19437	5.91765	5.66029
13	7.48690	7.10336	6.74987	6.42355	6.12181	5.84236
14	7.78615	7.36669	6.96187	6.62817	6.30249	6.00207
15	8.06069	7.60608	7.19087	6.81086	6.46238	6.14217
16	8.31256	7.82371	7.37916	6.97399	6.60388	6.26506
17	8.54363	8.02155	7.54879	7.11963	6.72909	6.37286
18	8.75562	8.20141	7.70162	7.24967	6.83991	6.46742
19	8.95012	8.36492	7.83929	7.36578	6.93797	6.55037
20	9.12855	8.51356	7.96333	7.46944	7.02475	6.62313
21	9.29224	8.64869	8.07507	7.56200	7.10155	6.68696
22	9.44242	8.77154	8.17574	7.64465	7.16951	6.74294
23	9.58021	8.88322	8.26643	7.71843	7.22966	6.79206
24	9.70661	8.98474	8.34814	7.78432	7.28288	6.83514
25	9.82258	9.07704	8.42174	7.84314	7.32998	6.87293
26	9.92897	9.16094	8.48806	7.89566	7.37167	6.90608
27	10.02658	9.23722	8.54780	7.94255	7.40856	6.93515
28	10.11613	9.30657	8.60162	7.98442	7.44120	6.96066
29	10.19828	9.36961	8.65011	8.02181	7.47009	6.98304
30	10.27365	9.42691	8.69379	8.05518	7.49565	7.00266
31	10.34280	9.47901	8.73315	8.08499	7.51828	7.01988
32	10.40624	9.52638	8.76860	8.11159	7.53830	7.03498
33	10.46444	9.56943	8.80054	8.13535	7.55602	7.04823
34	10.51784	9.60858	8.82932	8.15656	7.57170	7.05985
35	10.56682	9.64416	8.85524	8.17550	7.58557	7.07005
40	10.75736	9.77905	8.95105	8.24378	7.63438	7.10504
45	10.88118	9.86281	9.00791	8.28252	7.66086	7.12322
50	10.96168	9.91481	9.04165	8.30450	7.67524	7.13266

Appendix B

Reversing Entries

Some of the adjusting entries recorded at the end of the accounting period affect transactions that occur in the next period. In such cases, a reversing entry may be used to simplify the recording of the next period's transactions.

To illustrate, an adjusting entry for accrued wages expense affects the first payment of wages in the next period. Without using a reversing entry, Wages Payable must be debited for the accrued wages at the end of the preceding period. In addition, Wages Expense must also be debited for only that portion of the payroll that is an expense of the current period.

Using a reversing entry, however, simplifies the analysis and recording of the first wages payment in the next period. As the term implies, a *reversing entry* is the exact opposite of the related adjusting entry. The amounts and accounts are the same as the adjusting entry, but the debits and credits are reversed.

Reversing entries are illustrated by using the accrued wages for **NetSolutions** presented in Chapter 3. These data are summarized in Exhibit 1.

EXHIBIT 1

Accrued Wages

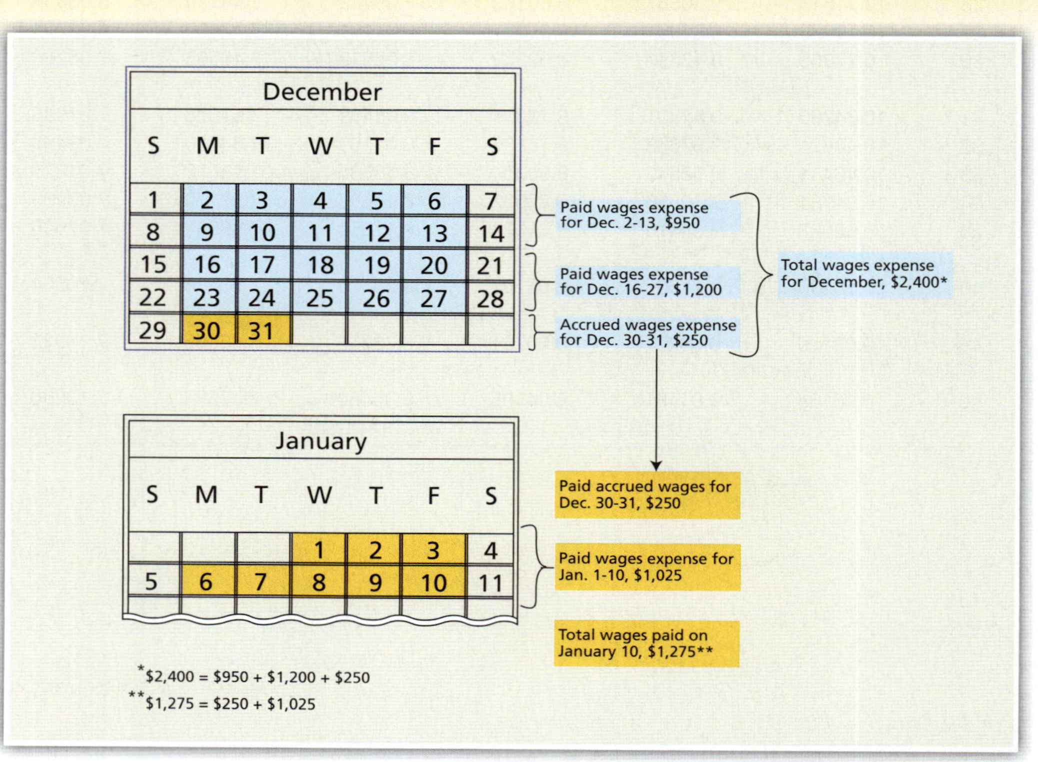

The adjusting entry for the accrued wages of December 30 and 31 is as follows:

2011					
Dec.	31	Wages Expense	51	250	
		Wages Payable	22		250
		Accrued wages.			

After the adjusting entry is recorded, Wages Expense will have a debit balance of $4,525 ($4,275 + $250), as shown on the top of page B-3. Wages Payable will have a credit balance of $250, as shown on page B-3.

After the closing entries are recorded, Wages Expense will have a zero balance. However, since Wages Payable is a liability account, it is not closed. Thus, Wages Payable will have a credit balance of $250 as of January 1, 2012.

Without recording a reversing entry, the payment of the $1,275 payroll on January 10 would be recorded as follows:

2012					
Jan.	10	Wages Payable	22	250	
		Wages Expense	51	1,025	
		Cash	11		1,275

As shown above, to record the January 10 payroll correctly Wages Payable must be debited for $250. This means that the employee who records the January 10 payroll must refer to the December 31, 2011, adjusting entry or to the ledger to determine the amount to debit Wages Payable.

Because the January 10 payroll is not recorded in the normal manner, there is a greater chance that an error may occur. This chance of error is reduced by recording a reversing entry as of the first day of the next period. For example, the reversing entry for the accrued wages expense would be recorded on January 1, 2012, as follows:

2012					
Jan.	1	Wages Payable	22	250	
		Wages Expense	51		250
		Reversing entry.			

The preceding reversing entry transfers the $250 liability from Wages Payable to the credit side of Wages Expense. The nature of the $250 is unchanged—it is still a liability. However, because of its unusual nature, an explanation is written under the reversing entry.

When the payroll is paid on January 10, the following entry is recorded:

Jan.	10	Wages Expense	51	1,275	
		Cash	11		1,275

After the January 10 payroll is recorded, Wages Expense has a debit balance of $1,025. This is the wages expense for the period January 1–10, 2012.

Wages Payable and Wages Expense after posting the adjusting, closing, and reversing entries are shown on the next page.

Account *Wages Payable* — Account No. *22*

Date		Item	Post. Ref.	Debit	Credit	Balance Debit	Balance Credit
2011							
Dec.	31	Adjusting	5		250		250
2012							
Jan.	1	Reversing	7	250		—	—

Account *Wages Expense* — Account No. *51*

Date		Item	Post. Ref.	Debit	Credit	Balance Debit	Balance Credit
2011							
Nov.	30		1	2,125		2,125	
Dec.	13		3	950		3,075	
	27		3	1,200		4,275	
	31	Adjusting	5	250		4,525	
	31	Closing	6		4,525	—	—
2012							
Jan.	1	Reversing	7		250		250
	10		7	1,275		1,025	

In addition to accrued expenses (accrued liabilities), reversing entries are also used for accrued revenues (accrued assets). To illustrate, the reversing entry for NetSolutions' accrued fees earned as of December 31, 2011, is as follows:

Jan.	1	Fees Earned	41	500	
		Accounts Receivable	12		500
		Reversing entry.			

The use of reversing entries is optional. However, in computerized accounting systems, data entry employees often input routine accounting entries. In such cases, reversing entries may be useful in avoiding errors.

EX B-1 Adjusting and reversing entries

On the basis of the following data, (a) journalize the adjusting entries at December 31, the end of the current fiscal year, and (b) journalize the reversing entries on January 1, the first day of the following year.

1. Sales salaries are uniformly $21,000 for a five-day workweek, ending on Friday. The last payday of the year was Friday, December 26.
2. Accrued fees earned but not recorded at December 31, $33,750.

EX B-2 Adjusting and reversing entries

On the basis of the following data, (a) journalize the adjusting entries at June 30, the end of the current fiscal year, and (b) journalize the reversing entries on July 1, the first day of the following year.

1. Wages are uniformly $48,000 for a five-day workweek, ending on Friday. The last payday of the year was Friday, June 27.
2. Accrued fees earned but not recorded at June 30, $23,900.

EX B-3 Entries posted to the wages expense account

Portions of the wages expense account of a business are shown below.

a. Indicate the nature of the entry (payment, adjusting, closing, reversing) from which each numbered posting was made.

b. Journalize the complete entry from which each numbered posting was made.

Account ***Wages Expense*** **Account No. 53**

Date	Item	Post. Ref.	Dr.	Cr.	Balance Dr.	Balance Cr.
2011						
Dec. 26	(1)	125	32,000		1,600,000	
31	(2)	126	19,200		1,619,200	
31	(3)	127		1,619,200	—	—
2012						
Jan. 1	(4)	128		19,200		19,200
2	(5)	129	32,000		12,800	

EX B-4 Entries posted to the salaries expense account

Portions of the salaries expense account of a business are shown below.

Account ***Salaries Expense*** **Account No. 53**

Date	Item	Post. Ref.	Dr.	Cr.	Balance Dr.	Balance Cr.
2011						
Dec. 27	(1)	29	18,500		897,800	
31	(2)	30	7,400		905,200	
31	(3)	31		905,200	—	—
2012						
Jan. 1	(4)	32		7,400		7,400
2	(5)	33	18,500		11,100	

a. Indicate the nature of the entry (payment, adjusting, closing, reversing) from which each numbered posting was made.

b. Journalize the complete entry from which each numbered posting was made.

Appendix C

NIKE INC (NKE)

ONE BOWERMAN DR
BEAVERTON, OR, 97005–6453
503–671–3173
www.nikebiz.com

10–K

Annual report pursuant to section 13 and 15(d)
Filed on 7/20/2010
Filed Period 5/31/2010

Table of Contents

An Internal Audit department reviews the results of its work with the Audit Committee of the Board of Directors, presently consisting of three outside directors. The Audit Committee is responsible for the appointment of the independent registered public accounting firm and reviews with the independent registered public accounting firm, management and the internal audit staff, the scope and the results of the annual examination, the effectiveness of the accounting control system and other matters relating to the financial affairs of NIKE as they deem appropriate. The independent registered public accounting firm and the internal auditors have full access to the Committee, with and without the presence of management, to discuss any appropriate matters.

Management's Annual Report on Internal Control Over Financial Reporting

Management is responsible for establishing and maintaining adequate internal control over financial reporting, as such term is defined in Rule 13a–15(f) and Rule 15d–15(f) of the Securities Exchange Act of 1934, as amended. Internal control over financial reporting is a process designed to provide reasonable assurance regarding the reliability of financial reporting and the preparation of the financial statements for external purposes in accordance with generally accepted accounting principles in the United States of America. Internal control over financial reporting includes those policies and procedures that: (i) pertain to the maintenance of records that, in reasonable detail, accurately and fairly reflect the transactions and dispositions of assets of the company; (ii) provide reasonable assurance that transactions are recorded as necessary to permit preparation of financial statements in accordance with generally accepted accounting principles, and that receipts and expenditures of the company are being made only in accordance with authorizations of our management and directors; and (iii) provide reasonable assurance regarding prevention or timely detection of unauthorized acquisition, use or disposition of assets of the company that could have a material effect on the financial statements.

While "reasonable assurance" is a high level of assurance, it does not mean absolute assurance. Because of its inherent limitations, internal control over financial reporting may not prevent or detect every misstatement and instance of fraud. Controls are susceptible to manipulation, especially in instances of fraud caused by the collusion of two or more people, including our senior management. Also, projections of any evaluation of effectiveness to future periods are subject to the risk that controls may become inadequate because of changes in conditions, or that the degree of compliance with the policies or procedures may deteriorate.

Under the supervision and with the participation of our Chief Executive Officer and Chief Financial Officer, our management conducted an evaluation of the effectiveness of our internal control over financial reporting based upon the framework in *Internal Control — Integrated Framework* issued by the Committee of Sponsoring Organizations of the Treadway Commission (COSO). Based on the results of our evaluation, our management concluded that our internal control over financial reporting was effective as of May 31, 2010.

PricewaterhouseCoopers LLP, an independent registered public accounting firm, has audited (1) the consolidated financial statements and (2) the effectiveness of our internal control over financial reporting as of May 31, 2010, as stated in their report herein.

Mark G. Parker
Chief Executive Officer and President

Donald W. Blair
Chief Financial Officer

Table of Contents

REPORT OF INDEPENDENT REGISTERED PUBLIC ACCOUNTING FIRM

To the Board of Directors and
Shareholders of NIKE, Inc.:

In our opinion, the consolidated financial statements listed in the index appearing under Item 15(a)(1) present fairly, in all material respects, the financial position of NIKE, Inc. and its subsidiaries at May 31, 2010 and 2009, and the results of their operations and their cash flows for each of the three years in the period ended May 31, 2010 in conformity with accounting principles generally accepted in the United States of America. In addition, in our opinion, the financial statement schedule listed in the appendix appearing under Item 15(a)(2) presents fairly, in all material respects, the information set forth therein when read in conjunction with the related consolidated financial statements. Also in our opinion, the Company maintained, in all material respects, effective internal control over financial reporting as of May 31, 2010, based on criteria established in *Internal Control — Integrated Framework* issued by the Committee of Sponsoring Organizations of the Treadway Commission (COSO). The Company's management is responsible for these financial statements and financial statement schedule, for maintaining effective internal control over financial reporting and for its assessment of the effectiveness of internal control over financial reporting, included in Management's Annual Report on Internal Control Over Financial Reporting appearing under Item 8. Our responsibility is to express opinions on these financial statements, on the financial statement schedule, and on the Company's internal control over financial reporting based on our integrated audits. We conducted our audits in accordance with the standards of the Public Company Accounting Oversight Board (United States). Those standards require that we plan and perform the audits to obtain reasonable assurance about whether the financial statements are free of material misstatement and whether effective internal control over financial reporting was maintained in all material respects. Our audits of the financial statements included examining, on a test basis, evidence supporting the amounts and disclosures in the financial statements, assessing the accounting principles used and significant estimates made by management, and evaluating the overall financial statement presentation. Our audit of internal control over financial reporting included obtaining an understanding of internal control over financial reporting, assessing the risk that a material weakness exists, and testing and evaluating the design and operating effectiveness of internal control based on the assessed risk. Our audits also included performing such other procedures as we considered necessary in the circumstances. We believe that our audits provide a reasonable basis for our opinions.

A company's internal control over financial reporting is a process designed to provide reasonable assurance regarding the reliability of financial reporting and the preparation of financial statements for external purposes in accordance with generally accepted accounting principles. A company's internal control over financial reporting includes those policies and procedures that (i) pertain to the maintenance of records that, in reasonable detail, accurately and fairly reflect the transactions and dispositions of the assets of the company; (ii) provide reasonable assurance that transactions are recorded as necessary to permit preparation of financial statements in accordance with generally accepted accounting principles, and that receipts and expenditures of the company are being made only in accordance with authorizations of management and directors of the company; and (iii) provide reasonable assurance regarding prevention or timely detection of unauthorized acquisition, use, or disposition of the company's assets that could have a material effect on the financial statements.

Because of its inherent limitations, internal control over financial reporting may not prevent or detect misstatements. Also, projections of any evaluation of effectiveness to future periods are subject to the risk that controls may become inadequate because of changes in conditions, or that the degree of compliance with the policies or procedures may deteriorate.

/s/ PricewaterhouseCoopers LLP

Portland, Oregon
July 20, 2010

Table of Contents

NIKE, INC.

CONSOLIDATED STATEMENTS OF INCOME

	Year Ended May 31,		
	2010	2009	2008
	(In millions, except per share data)		
Revenues	$19,014.0	$19,176.1	$18,627.0
Cost of sales	10,213.6	10,571.7	10,239.6
Gross margin	8,800.4	8,604.4	8,387.4
Selling and administrative expense	6,326.4	6,149.6	5,953.7
Restructuring charges (Note 16)	—	195.0	—
Goodwill impairment (Note 4)	—	199.3	—
Intangible and other asset impairment (Note 4)	—	202.0	—
Interest expense (income), net (Notes 6, 7 and 8)	6.3	(9.5)	(77.1)
Other (income) expense, net (Notes 17 and 18)	(49.2)	(88.5)	7.9
Income before income taxes	2,516.9	1,956.5	2,502.9
Income taxes (Note 9)	610.2	469.8	619.5
Net income	$ 1,906.7	$ 1,486.7	$ 1,883.4
Basic earnings per common share (Notes 1 and 12)	$ 3.93	$ 3.07	$ 3.80
Diluted earnings per common share (Notes 1 and 12)	$ 3.86	$ 3.03	$ 3.74
Dividends declared per common share	$ 1.06	$ 0.98	$ 0.875

The accompanying notes to consolidated financial statements are an integral part of this statement.

Table of Contents

NIKE, INC.

CONSOLIDATED BALANCE SHEETS

	May 31, 2010	May 31, 2009
	(In millions)	
ASSETS		
Current assets:		
Cash and equivalents	$ 3,079.1	$ 2,291.1
Short–term investments (Note 6)	2,066.8	1,164.0
Accounts receivable, net (Note 1)	2,649.8	2,883.9
Inventories (Notes 1 and 2)	2,040.8	2,357.0
Deferred income taxes (Note 9)	248.8	272.4
Prepaid expenses and other current assets	873.9	765.6
Total current assets	10,959.2	9,734.0
Property, plant and equipment, net (Note 3)	1,931.9	1,957.7
Identifiable intangible assets, net (Note 4)	467.0	467.4
Goodwill (Note 4)	187.6	193.5
Deferred income taxes and other assets (Notes 9 and 18)	873.6	897.0
Total assets	$ 14,419.3	$ 13,249.6
LIABILITIES AND SHAREHOLDERS' EQUITY		
Current liabilities:		
Current portion of long–term debt (Note 8)	$ 7.4	$ 32.0
Notes payable (Note 7)	138.6	342.9
Accounts payable (Note 7)	1,254.5	1,031.9
Accrued liabilities (Notes 5 and 18)	1,904.4	1,783.9
Income taxes payable (Note 9)	59.3	86.3
Total current liabilities	3,364.2	3,277.0
Long–term debt (Note 8)	445.8	437.2
Deferred income taxes and other liabilities (Notes 9 and 18)	855.3	842.0
Commitments and contingencies (Note 15)	—	—
Redeemable Preferred Stock (Note 10)	0.3	0.3
Shareholders' equity:		
Common stock at stated value (Note 11):		
Class A convertible — 90.0 and 95.3 shares outstanding	0.1	0.1
Class B — 394.0 and 390.2 shares outstanding	2.7	2.7
Capital in excess of stated value	3,440.6	2,871.4
Accumulated other comprehensive income (Note 14)	214.8	367.5
Retained earnings	6,095.5	5,451.4
Total shareholders' equity	9,753.7	8,693.1
Total liabilities and shareholders' equity	$ 14,419.3	$ 13,249.6

The accompanying notes to consolidated financial statements are an integral part of this statement.

Table of Contents

NIKE, INC.
CONSOLIDATED STATEMENTS OF CASH FLOWS

	Year Ended May 31,		
	2010	2009	2008
		(In millions)	
Cash provided by operations:			
Net income	$ 1,906.7	$ 1,486.7	$ 1,883.4
Income charges (credits) not affecting cash:			
Depreciation	323.7	335.0	303.6
Deferred income taxes	8.3	(294.1)	(300.6)
Stock–based compensation (Note 11)	159.0	170.6	141.0
Impairment of goodwill, intangibles and other assets (Note 4)	—	401.3	—
Gain on divestitures (Note 17)	—	—	(60.6)
Amortization and other	71.8	48.3	17.9
Changes in certain working capital components and other assets and liabilities excluding the impact of acquisition and divestitures:			
Decrease (increase) in accounts receivable	181.7	(238.0)	(118.3)
Decrease (increase) in inventories	284.6	32.2	(249.8)
(Increase) decrease in prepaid expenses and other current assets	(69.6)	14.1	(11.2)
Increase (decrease) in accounts payable, accrued liabilities and income taxes payable	298.0	(220.0)	330.9
Cash provided by operations	3,164.2	1,736.1	1,936.3
Cash used by investing activities:			
Purchases of short–term investments	(3,724.4)	(2,908.7)	(1,865.6)
Maturities and sales of short–term investments	2,787.6	2,390.0	2,246.0
Additions to property, plant and equipment	(335.1)	(455.7)	(449.2)
Disposals of property, plant and equipment	10.1	32.0	1.9
Increase in other assets, net of other liabilities	(11.2)	(47.0)	(21.8)
Settlement of net investment hedges	5.5	191.3	(76.0)
Acquisition of subsidiary, net of cash acquired (Note 4)	—	—	(571.1)
Proceeds from divestitures (Note 17)	—	—	246.0
Cash used by investing activities	(1,267.5)	(798.1)	(489.8)
Cash used by financing activities:			
Reductions in long–term debt, including current portion	(32.2)	(6.8)	(35.2)
(Decrease) increase in notes payable	(205.4)	177.1	63.7
Proceeds from exercise of stock options and other stock issuances	364.5	186.6	343.3
Excess tax benefits from share–based payment arrangements	58.5	25.1	63.0
Repurchase of common stock	(741.2)	(649.2)	(1,248.0)
Dividends — common and preferred	(505.4)	(466.7)	(412.9)
Cash used by financing activities	(1,061.2)	(733.9)	(1,226.1)
Effect of exchange rate changes	(47.5)	(46.9)	56.8
Net increase in cash and equivalents	788.0	157.2	277.2
Cash and equivalents, beginning of year	2,291.1	2,133.9	1,856.7
Cash and equivalents, end of year	$ 3,079.1	$ 2,291.1	$ 2,133.9
Supplemental disclosure of cash flow information:			
Cash paid during the year for:			
Interest, net of capitalized interest	$ 48.4	$ 46.7	$ 44.1
Income taxes	537.2	765.2	717.5
Dividends declared and not paid	130.7	121.4	112.9

The accompanying notes to consolidated financial statements are an integral part of this statement.

Table of Contents

NIKE, INC.
CONSOLIDATED STATEMENTS OF SHAREHOLDERS' EQUITY

	Common Stock				Capital in Excess of Stated Value	Accumulated Other Comprehensive Income	Retained Earnings	Total
	Class A		Class B					
	Shares	Amount	Shares	Amount				
	(In millions, except per share data)							
Balance at May 31, 2007	117.6	$ 0.1	384.1	$ 2.7	$ 1,960.0	$ 177.4	$ 4,885.2	$ 7,025.4
Stock options exercised			9.1		372.2			372.2
Conversion to Class B Common Stock	(20.8)		20.8					—
Repurchase of Class B Common Stock			(20.6)		(12.3)		(1,235.7)	(1,248.0)
Dividends on Common stock ($0.875 per share)							(432.8)	(432.8)
Issuance of shares to employees			1.0		39.2			39.2
Stock-based compensation (Note 11):					141.0			141.0
Forfeiture of shares from employees			(0.1)		(2.3)		(1.1)	(3.4)
Comprehensive income (Note 14):								
Net income							1,883.4	1,883.4
Other comprehensive income:								
Foreign currency translation and other (net of tax expense of $101.6)						211.9		211.9
Realized foreign currency translation gain due to divestiture (Note 17)						(46.3)		(46.3)
Net loss on cash flow hedges (net of tax benefit of $67.7)						(175.8)		(175.8)
Net loss on net investment hedges (net of tax benefit of $25.1)						(43.5)		(43.5)
Reclassification to net income of previously deferred losses related to hedge derivatives (net of tax benefit of $49.6)						127.7		127.7
Total Comprehensive income						74.0	1,883.4	1,957.4
Adoption of FIN 48 (Note 1 and 9)							(15.6)	(15.6)
Adoption of EITF 06-2 Sabbaticals (net of tax benefit of $6.2)							(10.1)	(10.1)
Balance at May 31, 2008	96.8	$ 0.1	394.3	$ 2.7	$ 2,497.8	$ 251.4	$ 5,073.3	$ 7,825.3
Stock options exercised			4.0		167.2			167.2
Conversion to Class B Common Stock	(1.5)		1.5					—
Repurchase of Class B Common Stock			(10.6)		(6.3)		(632.7)	(639.0)
Dividends on Common stock ($0.98 per share)							(475.2)	(475.2)
Issuance of shares to employees			1.1		45.4			45.4
Stock-based compensation (Note 11):					170.6			170.6
Forfeiture of shares from employees			(0.1)		(3.3)		(0.7)	(4.0)
Comprehensive income (Note 14):								
Net income							1,486.7	1,486.7
Other comprehensive income:								
Foreign currency translation and other (net of tax benefit of $177.5)						(335.3)		(335.3)
Net gain on cash flow hedges (net of tax expense of $167.5)						453.6		453.6
Net gain on net investment hedges (net of tax expense of $55.4)						106.0		106.0
Reclassification to net income of previously deferred net gains related to hedge derivatives (net of tax expense of $39.6)						(108.2)		(108.2)
Total Comprehensive income						116.1	1,486.7	1,602.8
Balance at May 31, 2009	95.3	$ 0.1	390.2	$ 2.7	$ 2,871.4	$ 367.5	$ 5,451.4	$ 8,693.1
Stock options exercised			8.6		379.6			379.6
Conversion to Class B Common Stock	(5.3)		5.3					—
Repurchase of Class B Common Stock			(11.3)		(6.8)		(747.5)	(754.3)
Dividends on Common stock ($1.06 per share)							(514.8)	(514.8)
Issuance of shares to employees			1.3		40.0			40.0
Stock-based compensation (Note 11):					159.0			159.0
Forfeiture of shares from employees			(0.1)		(2.6)		(0.3)	(2.9)
Comprehensive income (Note 14):								
Net income							1,906.7	1,906.7
Other comprehensive income:								
Foreign currency translation and other (net of tax benefit of $71.8)						(159.2)		(159.2)
Net gain on cash flow hedges (net of tax expense of $27.8)						87.1		87.1
Net gain on net investment hedges (net of tax expense of $21.2)						44.8		44.8
Reclassification to net income of previously deferred net gains related to hedge derivatives (net of tax expense of $41.7)						(121.6)		(121.6)
Reclassification of ineffective hedge gains to net income (net of tax expense of $1.4)						(3.8)		(3.8)
Total Comprehensive income						(152.7)	1,906.7	1,754.0
Balance at May 31, 2010	90.0	$ 0.1	394.0	$ 2.7	$ 3,440.6	$ 214.8	$ 6,095.5	$ 9,753.7

The accompanying notes to consolidated financial statements are an integral part of this statement.

Table of Contents

NIKE, INC.

NOTES TO CONSOLIDATED FINANCIAL STATEMENTS

Note 1 — Summary of Significant Accounting Policies

Description of Business

NIKE, Inc. is a worldwide leader in the design, marketing and distribution of athletic and sports–inspired footwear, apparel, equipment and accessories. Wholly–owned NIKE subsidiaries include Cole Haan, which designs, markets and distributes dress and casual shoes, handbags, accessories and coats; Converse Inc., which designs, markets and distributes athletic and causal footwear, apparel and accessories; Hurley International LLC, which designs, markets and distributes action sports and youth lifestyle footwear, apparel and accessories; and Umbro Ltd., which designs, distributes and licenses athletic and casual footwear, apparel and equipment, primarily for the sport of soccer.

Basis of Consolidation

The consolidated financial statements include the accounts of NIKE, Inc. and its subsidiaries (the "Company"). All significant intercompany transactions and balances have been eliminated.

Recognition of Revenues

Wholesale revenues are recognized when title passes and the risks and rewards of ownership have passed to the customer, based on the terms of sale. This occurs upon shipment or upon receipt by the customer depending on the country of the sale and the agreement with the customer. Retail store revenues are recorded at the time of sale. Provisions for sales discounts, returns and miscellaneous claims from customers are made at the time of sale. As of May 31, 2010 and 2009, the Company's reserve balances for sales discounts, returns and miscellaneous claims were $370.6 million and $363.6 million, respectively.

Shipping and Handling Costs

Shipping and handling costs are expensed as incurred and included in cost of sales.

Advertising and Promotion

Advertising production costs are expensed the first time the advertisement is run. Media (TV and print) placement costs are expensed in the month the advertising appears.

A significant amount of the Company's promotional expenses result from payments under endorsement contracts. Accounting for endorsement payments is based upon specific contract provisions. Generally, endorsement payments are expensed on a straight–line basis over the term of the contract after giving recognition to periodic performance compliance provisions of the contracts. Prepayments made under contracts are included in prepaid expenses or other assets depending on the period to which the prepayment applies.

Through cooperative advertising programs, the Company reimburses retail customers for certain costs of advertising the Company's products. The Company records these costs in selling and administrative expense at the point in time when it is obligated to its customers for the costs, which is when the related revenues are recognized. This obligation may arise prior to the related advertisement being run.

Total advertising and promotion expenses were $2,356.4 million, $2,351.3 million, and $2,308.3 million for the years ended May 31, 2010, 2009 and 2008, respectively. Prepaid advertising and promotion expenses recorded in prepaid expenses and other assets totaled $260.7 million and $280.0 million at May 31, 2010 and 2009, respectively.

Table of Contents

NIKE, INC.

NOTES TO CONSOLIDATED FINANCIAL STATEMENTS — (Continued)

Cash and Equivalents

Cash and equivalents represent cash and short–term, highly liquid investments with maturities of three months or less at date of purchase. The carrying amounts reflected in the consolidated balance sheet for cash and equivalents approximate fair value.

Short–term Investments

Short–term investments consist of highly liquid investments, primarily commercial paper, U.S. treasury, U.S. agency, and corporate debt securities, with maturities over three months from the date of purchase. Debt securities that the Company has the ability and positive intent to hold to maturity are carried at amortized cost. At May 31, 2010 and 2009, the Company did not hold any short–term investments that were classified as held–to–maturity.

At May 31, 2010 and 2009, short–term investments consisted of available–for–sale securities. Available–for–sale securities are recorded at fair value with unrealized gains and losses reported, net of tax, in other comprehensive income, unless unrealized losses are determined to be other than temporary. The Company considers all available–for–sale securities, including those with maturity dates beyond 12 months, as available to support current operational liquidity needs and therefore classifies all securities with maturity dates beyond three months as current assets within short–term investments on the consolidated balance sheet.

See Note 6 — Fair Value Measurements for more information on the Company's short term investments.

Allowance for Uncollectible Accounts Receivable

Accounts receivable consists primarily of amounts receivable from customers. We make ongoing estimates relating to the collectability of our accounts receivable and maintain an allowance for estimated losses resulting from the inability of our customers to make required payments. In determining the amount of the allowance, we consider our historical level of credit losses and make judgments about the creditworthiness of significant customers based on ongoing credit evaluations. Accounts receivable with anticipated collection dates greater than 12 months from the balance sheet date and related allowances are considered non–current and recorded in other assets. The allowance for uncollectible accounts receivable was $116.7 million and $110.8 million at May 31, 2010 and 2009, respectively, of which $43.1 million and $36.9 million was classified as long–term and recorded in other assets.

Inventory Valuation

Inventories are stated at lower of cost or market and valued on a first–in, first–out ("FIFO") or moving average cost basis.

Property, Plant and Equipment and Depreciation

Property, plant and equipment are recorded at cost. Depreciation for financial reporting purposes is determined on a straight–line basis for buildings and leasehold improvements over 2 to 40 years and for machinery and equipment over 2 to 15 years. Computer software (including, in some cases, the cost of internal labor) is depreciated on a straight–line basis over 3 to 10 years.

Impairment of Long–Lived Assets

The Company reviews the carrying value of long–lived assets or asset groups to be used in operations whenever events or changes in circumstances indicate that the carrying amount of the assets might not be

Table of Contents

NIKE, INC.

NOTES TO CONSOLIDATED FINANCIAL STATEMENTS — (Continued)

recoverable. Factors that would necessitate an impairment assessment include a significant adverse change in the extent or manner in which an asset is used, a significant adverse change in legal factors or the business climate that could affect the value of the asset, or a significant decline in the observable market value of an asset, among others. If such facts indicate a potential impairment, the Company would assess the recoverability of an asset group by determining if the carrying value of the asset group exceeds the sum of the projected undiscounted cash flows expected to result from the use and eventual disposition of the assets over the remaining economic life of the primary asset in the asset group. If the recoverability test indicates that the carrying value of the asset group is not recoverable, the Company will estimate the fair value of the asset group using appropriate valuation methodologies which would typically include an estimate of discounted cash flows. Any impairment would be measured as the difference between the asset groups carrying amount and its estimated fair value.

Identifiable Intangible Assets and Goodwill

The Company performs annual impairment tests on goodwill and intangible assets with indefinite lives in the fourth quarter of each fiscal year, or when events occur or circumstances change that would, more likely than not, reduce the fair value of a reporting unit or an intangible asset with an indefinite life below its carrying value. Events or changes in circumstances that may trigger interim impairment reviews include significant changes in business climate, operating results, planned investments in the reporting unit, or an expectation that the carrying amount may not be recoverable, among other factors. The impairment test requires the Company to estimate the fair value of its reporting units. If the carrying value of a reporting unit exceeds its fair value, the goodwill of that reporting unit is potentially impaired and the Company proceeds to step two of the impairment analysis. In step two of the analysis, the Company measures and records an impairment loss equal to the excess of the carrying value of the reporting unit's goodwill over its implied fair value should such a circumstance arise.

The Company generally bases its measurement of fair value of a reporting unit on a blended analysis of the present value of future discounted cash flows and the market valuation approach. The discounted cash flows model indicates the fair value of the reporting unit based on the present value of the cash flows that the Company expects the reporting unit to generate in the future. The Company's significant estimates in the discounted cash flows model include: its weighted average cost of capital; long–term rate of growth and profitability of the reporting unit's business; and working capital effects. The market valuation approach indicates the fair value of the business based on a comparison of the reporting unit to comparable publicly traded companies in similar lines of business. Significant estimates in the market valuation approach model include identifying similar companies with comparable business factors such as size, growth, profitability, risk and return on investment, and assessing comparable revenue and operating income multiples in estimating the fair value of the reporting unit.

The Company believes the weighted use of discounted cash flows and the market valuation approach is the best method for determining the fair value of its reporting units because these are the most common valuation methodologies used within its industry; and the blended use of both models compensates for the inherent risks associated with either model if used on a stand–alone basis.

Indefinite–lived intangible assets primarily consist of acquired trade names and trademarks. In measuring the fair value for these intangible assets, the Company utilizes the relief–from–royalty method. This method assumes that trade names and trademarks have value to the extent that their owner is relieved of the obligation to pay royalties for the benefits received from them. This method requires the Company to estimate the future revenue for the related brands, the appropriate royalty rate and the weighted average cost of capital.

Table of Contents

NIKE, INC.

NOTES TO CONSOLIDATED FINANCIAL STATEMENTS — (Continued)

Foreign Currency Translation and Foreign Currency Transactions

Adjustments resulting from translating foreign functional currency financial statements into U.S. dollars are included in the foreign currency translation adjustment, a component of accumulated other comprehensive income in shareholders' equity.

The Company's global subsidiaries have various assets and liabilities, primarily receivables and payables, that are denominated in currencies other than their functional currency. These balance sheet items are subject to remeasurement, the impact of which is recorded in other (income) expense, net, within our consolidated statement of income.

Accounting for Derivatives and Hedging Activities

The Company uses derivative financial instruments to limit exposure to changes in foreign currency exchange rates and interest rates. All derivatives are recorded at fair value on the balance sheet and changes in the fair value of derivative financial instruments are either recognized in other comprehensive income (a component of shareholders' equity), debt or net income depending on the nature of the underlying exposure, whether the derivative is formally designated as a hedge, and, if designated, the extent to which the hedge is effective. The Company classifies the cash flows at settlement from derivatives in the same category as the cash flows from the related hedged items. For undesignated hedges and designated cash flow hedges, this is within the cash provided by operations component of the consolidated statement of cash flows. For designated net investment hedges, this is generally within the cash used by investing activities component of the cash flow statement. As our fair value hedges are receive–fixed, pay–variable interest rate swaps, the cash flows associated with these derivative instruments are periodic interest payments while the swaps are outstanding, which are reflected in net income within the cash provided by operations component of the cash flow statement.

See Note 18 — Risk Management and Derivatives for more information on the Company's risk management program and derivatives.

Stock–Based Compensation

The Company estimates the fair value of options granted under the NIKE, Inc. 1990 Stock Incentive Plan (the "1990 Plan") and employees' purchase rights under the Employee Stock Purchase Plans ("ESPPs") using the Black–Scholes option pricing model. The Company recognizes this fair value, net of estimated forfeitures, as selling and administrative expense in the consolidated statements of income over the vesting period using the straight–line method.

See Note 11 — Common Stock and Stock–Based Compensation for more information on the Company's stock programs.

Income Taxes

The Company accounts for income taxes using the asset and liability method. This approach requires the recognition of deferred tax assets and liabilities for the expected future tax consequences of temporary differences between the carrying amounts and the tax basis of assets and liabilities. United States income taxes are provided currently on financial statement earnings of non–U.S. subsidiaries that are expected to be repatriated. The Company determines annually the amount of undistributed non–U.S. earnings to invest indefinitely in its non–U.S. operations. The Company recognizes interest and penalties related to income tax matters in income tax expense.

NIKE, INC.

NOTES TO CONSOLIDATED FINANCIAL STATEMENTS — (Continued)

See Note 9 — Income Taxes for further discussion.

Earnings Per Share

Basic earnings per common share is calculated by dividing net income by the weighted average number of common shares outstanding during the year. Diluted earnings per common share is calculated by adjusting weighted average outstanding shares, assuming conversion of all potentially dilutive stock options and awards.

See Note 12 — Earnings Per Share for further discussion.

Management Estimates

The preparation of financial statements in conformity with generally accepted accounting principles requires management to make estimates, including estimates relating to assumptions that affect the reported amounts of assets and liabilities and disclosure of contingent assets and liabilities at the date of financial statements and the reported amounts of revenues and expenses during the reporting period. Actual results could differ from these estimates.

Reclassifications

Certain prior year amounts have been reclassified to conform to fiscal year 2010 presentation, including a reclassification to investing activities for the settlement of net investment hedges in the consolidated statement of cash flows for the year ended May 31, 2008. These reclassifications had no impact on previously reported results of operations or shareholders' equity and do not affect previously reported cash flows from operations, financing activities or net change in cash and equivalents.

Recently Adopted Accounting Standards:

In January 2010, the Financial Accounting Standards Board ("FASB") issued guidance to amend the disclosure requirements related to recurring and nonrecurring fair value measurements. The guidance requires additional disclosures about the different classes of assets and liabilities measured at fair value, the valuation techniques and inputs used, the activity in Level 3 fair value measurements, and the transfers between Levels 1, 2, and 3 of the fair value measurement hierarchy. This guidance became effective for the Company beginning March 1, 2010, except for disclosures relating to purchases, sales, issuances and settlements of Level 3 assets and liabilities, which will be effective for the Company beginning June 1, 2011. As this guidance only requires expanded disclosures, the adoption did not and will not impact the Company's consolidated financial position or results of operations. See Note 6 — Fair Value Measurements for disclosure required under this guidance.

In February 2010, the FASB issued amended guidance on subsequent events. Under this amended guidance, SEC filers are no longer required to disclose the date through which subsequent events have been evaluated in originally issued and revised financial statements. This guidance was effective immediately and the Company adopted these new requirements since the third quarter of fiscal 2010.

In June 2009, the FASB established the FASB Accounting Standards Codification (the "Codification") as the single source of authoritative U.S. GAAP for all non–governmental entities. The Codification, which launched July 1, 2009, changes the referencing and organization of accounting guidance. The Codification became effective for the Company beginning September 1, 2009. The issuance of the FASB Codification did not change GAAP and therefore the adoption has only affected how specific references to GAAP literature are disclosed in the notes to the Company's consolidated financial statements.

NIKE, INC.

NOTES TO CONSOLIDATED FINANCIAL STATEMENTS — (Continued)

In April 2009, the FASB updated guidance related to fair value measurements to clarify the guidance related to measuring fair value in inactive markets, to modify the recognition and measurement of other–than–temporary impairments of debt securities, and to require public companies to disclose the fair values of financial instruments in interim periods. This updated guidance became effective for the Company beginning June 1, 2009. The adoption of this guidance did not have an impact on the Company's consolidated financial position or results of operations. See Note 6 — Fair Value Measurements for disclosure required under the updated guidance.

In June 2008, the FASB issued new accounting guidance applicable when determining whether instruments granted in share–based payment transactions are participating securities. This guidance clarifies that share–based payment awards that entitle their holders to receive non–forfeitable dividends before vesting should be considered participating securities and included in the computation of earnings per share pursuant to the two–class method. This guidance became effective for the Company beginning June 1, 2009. The adoption of this guidance did not have a material impact on the Company's consolidated financial position or results of operations.

In April 2008, the FASB issued amended guidance regarding the determination of the useful life of intangible assets. This guidance amends the factors that should be considered in developing renewal or extension assumptions used to determine the useful life of a recognized intangible asset. The intent of the position is to improve the consistency between the useful life of a recognized intangible asset and the period of expected cash flows used to measure the fair value of the asset. This guidance became effective for the Company beginning June 1, 2009. The adoption of this guidance did not have a material impact on the Company's consolidated financial position or results of operations.

In December 2007, the FASB issued amended guidance regarding business combinations, establishing principles and requirements for how an acquirer recognizes and measures identifiable assets acquired, liabilities assumed, any resulting goodwill, and any non–controlling interest in an acquiree in its financial statements. This guidance also provides for disclosures to enable users of the financial statements to evaluate the nature and financial effects of a business combination. This amended guidance became effective for the Company beginning June 1, 2009. The adoption of this amended guidance did not have an impact on the Company's consolidated financial statements, but could impact the accounting for future business combinations.

In December 2007, the FASB issued new guidance regarding the accounting and reporting for non–controlling interests in subsidiaries. This guidance clarifies that non–controlling interests in subsidiaries should be accounted for as a component of equity separate from the parent's equity. This guidance became effective for the Company beginning June 1, 2009. The adoption of this guidance did not have an impact on the Company's consolidated financial position or results of operations.

Recently Issued Accounting Standards:

In October 2009, the FASB issued new standards that revised the guidance for revenue recognition with multiple deliverables. These new standards impact the determination of when the individual deliverables included in a multiple–element arrangement may be treated as separate units of accounting. Additionally, these new standards modify the manner in which the transaction consideration is allocated across the separately identified deliverables by no longer permitting the residual method of allocating arrangement consideration. These new standards are effective for the Company beginning June 1, 2011. The Company does not expect the adoption will have a material impact on its consolidated financial positions or results of operations.

In June 2009, the FASB issued a new accounting standard that revised the guidance for the consolidation of variable interest entities ("VIE"). This new guidance requires a qualitative approach to identifying a controlling financial interest in a VIE, and requires an ongoing assessment of whether an entity is a VIE and whether an

Table of Contents

NIKE, INC.

NOTES TO CONSOLIDATED FINANCIAL STATEMENTS — (Continued)

interest in a VIE makes the holder the primary beneficiary of the VIE. This guidance is effective for the Company beginning June 1, 2010. The Company is currently evaluating the impact of the provisions of this new standard.

Note 2 — Inventories

Inventory balances of $2,040.8 million and $2,357.0 million at May 31, 2010 and 2009, respectively, were substantially all finished goods.

Note 3 — Property, Plant and Equipment

Property, plant and equipment included the following:

	As of May 31,	
	2010	2009
	(In millions)	
Land	$ 222.8	$ 221.6
Buildings	951.9	974.0
Machinery and equipment	2,217.5	2,094.3
Leasehold improvements	820.6	802.0
Construction in process	177.0	163.8
	4,389.8	4,255.7
Less accumulated depreciation	2,457.9	2,298.0
	$ 1,931.9	$ 1,957.7

Capitalized interest was not material for the years ended May 31, 2010, 2009 and 2008.

Note 4 — Acquisition, Identifiable Intangible Assets, Goodwill and Umbro Impairment

Acquisition

On March 3, 2008, the Company completed its acquisition of 100% of the outstanding shares of Umbro, a leading United Kingdom–based global soccer brand, for a purchase price of 290.5 million British Pounds Sterling in cash (approximately $576.4 million), inclusive of direct transaction costs. This acquisition is intended to strengthen the Company's market position in the United Kingdom and expand NIKE's global leadership in soccer, a key area of growth for the Company. This acquisition also provides positions in emerging soccer markets such as China, Russia and Brazil. The results of Umbro's operations have been included in the Company's consolidated financial statements since the date of acquisition as part of the Company's "Other" operating segment.

The acquisition of Umbro was accounted for as a purchase business combination. The purchase price was allocated to tangible and identifiable intangible assets acquired and liabilities assumed based on their respective estimated fair values on the date of acquisition, with the remaining purchase price recorded as goodwill.

Based on our preliminary purchase price allocation at May 31, 2008, identifiable intangible assets and goodwill relating to the purchase approximated $419.5 million and $319.2 million, respectively. Goodwill recognized in this transaction is deductible for tax purposes. Identifiable intangible assets include $378.4 million for trademarks that have an indefinite life, and $41.1 million for other intangible assets consisting of Umbro's

Table of Contents

NIKE, INC.

NOTES TO CONSOLIDATED FINANCIAL STATEMENTS — (Continued)

sourcing network, established customer relationships, and the United Soccer League Franchise. These intangible assets are amortized on a straight–line basis over estimated lives of 12 to 20 years.

During fiscal 2009, the Company finalized the purchase–price accounting for Umbro and made revisions to preliminary estimates, including valuations of tangible and intangible assets and certain contingencies, as further evaluations were completed and information was received from third parties subsequent to the acquisition date. These revisions to preliminary estimates resulted in a $12.4 million decrease in the value of identified intangible assets, primarily Umbro's sourcing network, and an $11.2 million increase in non–current liabilities, primarily related to liabilities assumed for certain contingencies and adjustments made to deferred taxes related to the fair value of assets acquired. These changes in assets acquired and liabilities assumed affected the amount of goodwill recorded.

The following table summarizes the allocation of the purchase price, including transaction costs of the acquisition, to the assets acquired and liabilities assumed at the date of acquisition based on their estimated fair values, including final purchase accounting adjustments (in millions):

	May 31, 2008 Preliminary	Adjustments	May 31, 2009 Final
Current assets	$ 87.2	$ —	$ 87.2
Non–current assets	90.2	—	90.2
Identified intangible assets	419.5	(12.4)	407.1
Goodwill	319.2	23.6	342.8
Current liabilities	(60.3)	—	(60.3)
Non–current liabilities	(279.4)	(11.2)	(290.6)
Net assets acquired	$ 576.4	$ —	$ 576.4

The pro forma effect of the acquisition on the combined results of operations for fiscal 2008 was not material.

Umbro Impairment in Fiscal 2009

The Company performs annual impairment tests on goodwill and intangible assets with indefinite lives in the fourth quarter of each fiscal year, or when events occur or circumstances change that would, more likely than not, reduce the fair value of a reporting unit or intangible assets with an indefinite life below its carrying value. As a result of a significant decline in global consumer demand and continued weakness in the macroeconomic environment, as well as decisions by Company management to adjust planned investment in the Umbro brand, the Company concluded sufficient indicators of impairment existed to require the performance of an interim assessment of Umbro's goodwill and indefinite lived intangible assets as of February 1, 2009. Accordingly, the Company performed the first step of the goodwill impairment assessment for Umbro by comparing the estimated fair value of Umbro to its carrying amount, and determined there was a potential impairment of goodwill as the carrying amount exceeded the estimated fair value. Therefore, the Company performed the second step of the assessment which compared the implied fair value of Umbro's goodwill to the book value of goodwill. The implied fair value of goodwill is determined by allocating the estimated fair value of Umbro to all of its assets and liabilities, including both recognized and unrecognized intangibles, in the same manner as goodwill was determined in the original business combination.

The Company measured the fair value of Umbro by using an equal weighting of the fair value implied by a discounted cash flow analysis and by comparisons with the market values of similar publicly traded companies. The Company believes the blended use of both models compensates for the inherent risk associated with either

NIKE, INC.

NOTES TO CONSOLIDATED FINANCIAL STATEMENTS — (Continued)

model if used on a stand–alone basis, and this combination is indicative of the factors a market participant would consider when performing a similar valuation. The fair value of Umbro's indefinite–lived trademark was estimated using the relief from royalty method, which assumes that the trademark has value to the extent that Umbro is relieved of the obligation to pay royalties for the benefits received from the trademark. The assessments of the Company resulted in the recognition of impairment charges of $199.3 million and $181.3 million related to Umbro's goodwill and trademark, respectively, for the year ended May 31, 2009. A tax benefit of $54.5 million was recognized as a result of the trademark impairment charge. In addition to the above impairment analysis, the Company determined an equity investment held by Umbro was impaired, and recognized a charge of $20.7 million related to the impairment of this investment. These charges are included in the Company's "Other" category for segment reporting purposes.

The discounted cash flow analysis calculated the fair value of Umbro using management's business plans and projections as the basis for expected cash flows for the next 12 years and a 3% residual growth rate thereafter. The Company used a weighted average discount rate of 14% in its analysis, which was derived primarily from published sources as well as our adjustment for increased market risk given current market conditions. Other significant estimates used in the discounted cash flow analysis include the rates of projected growth and profitability of Umbro's business and working capital effects. The market valuation approach indicates the fair value of Umbro based on a comparison of Umbro to publicly traded companies in similar lines of business. Significant estimates in the market valuation approach include identifying similar companies with comparable business factors such as size, growth, profitability, mix of revenue generated from licensed and direct distribution, and risk of return on investment.

Holding all other assumptions constant at the test date, a 100 basis point increase in the discount rate would reduce the adjusted carrying value of Umbro's net assets by an additional 12%.

Identified Intangible Assets and Goodwill

All goodwill balances are included in the Company's "Other" category for segment reporting purposes. The following table summarizes the Company's goodwill balance as of May 31, 2010 and 2009 (in millions):

	Goodwill	Accumulated Impairment	Goodwill, net
May 31, 2008	$ 448.8	$ —	$ 448.8
Purchase price adjustments	23.6	—	23.6
Impairment charge	—	(199.3)	(199.3)
Other[1]	(79.6)	—	(79.6)
May 31, 2009	392.8	(199.3)	193.5
Other[1]	(5.9)	—	(5.9)
May 31, 2010	$ 386.9	$ (199.3)	$ 187.6

(1) Other consists of foreign currency translation adjustments on Umbro goodwill.

Table of Contents

NIKE, INC.

NOTES TO CONSOLIDATED FINANCIAL STATEMENTS — (Continued)

The following table summarizes the Company's identifiable intangible asset balances as of May 31, 2010 and 2009.

	May 31, 2010			May 31, 2009		
	Gross Carrying Amount	Accumulated Amortization	Net Carrying Amount	Gross Carrying Amount	Accumulated Amortization	Net Carrying Amount
	(In millions)					
Amortized intangible assets:						
Patents	$ 68.5	$ (20.8)	$ 47.7	$ 56.6	$ (17.2)	$ 39.4
Trademarks	40.2	(17.8)	22.4	37.5	(10.9)	26.6
Other	32.7	(18.8)	13.9	40.0	(19.6)	20.4
Total	$ 141.4	$ (57.4)	$ 84.0	$ 134.1	$ (47.7)	$ 86.4
Unamortized intangible assets — Trademarks			$ 383.0			$ 381.0
Identifiable intangible assets, net			$ 467.0			$ 467.4

The effect of foreign exchange fluctuations for the year ended May 31, 2010 increased unamortized intangible assets by approximately $2 million.

Amortization expense, which is included in selling and administrative expense, was $13.5 million, $11.9 million and $9.2 million for the years ended May 31, 2010, 2009 and 2008, respectively. The estimated amortization expense for intangible assets subject to amortization for each of the years ending May 31, 2011 through May 31, 2015 are as follows: 2011: $13.4 million; 2012: $12.7 million; 2013: $10.8 million; 2014: $8.7 million; 2015: $5.1 million.

Note 5 — Accrued Liabilities

Accrued liabilities included the following:

	May 31,	
	2010	2009
	(In millions)	
Compensation and benefits, excluding taxes	$ 598.8	$ 491.9
Endorser compensation	266.9	237.1
Fair value of derivatives	163.6	68.9
Taxes other than income taxes	157.9	161.9
Dividends payable	130.7	121.4
Advertising and marketing	124.9	97.6
Import and logistics costs	80.0	59.4
Restructuring charges[1]	8.2	149.6
Other[2]	373.4	396.1
	$ 1,904.4	$ 1,783.9

(1) Accrued restructuring charges primarily consist of severance costs relating to the Company's restructuring activities that took place during the year ended May 31, 2009. See Note 16 — Restructuring Charges for more information.

(2) Other consists of various accrued expenses and no individual item accounted for more than 5% of the balance at May 31, 2010 and 2009.

Table of Contents

NIKE, INC.

NOTES TO CONSOLIDATED FINANCIAL STATEMENTS — (Continued)

Note 6 — Fair Value Measurements

The Company measures certain financial assets and liabilities at fair value on a recurring basis, including derivatives and available–for–sale securities. Fair value is a market–based measurement that should be determined based on the assumptions that market participants would use in pricing an asset or liability. As a basis for considering such assumptions, the Company uses a three–level hierarchy established by the FASB which prioritizes fair value measurements based on the types of inputs used for the various valuation techniques (market approach, income approach, and cost approach).

The levels of hierarchy are described below:

- Level 1: Observable inputs such as quoted prices in active markets for identical assets or liabilities.
- Level 2: Inputs other than quoted prices that are observable for the asset or liability, either directly or indirectly; these include quoted prices for similar assets or liabilities in active markets and quoted prices for identical or similar assets or liabilities in markets that are not active.
- Level 3: Unobservable inputs in which there is little or no market data available, which require the reporting entity to develop its own assumptions.

The Company's assessment of the significance of a particular input to the fair value measurement in its entirety requires judgment and considers factors specific to the asset or liability. Financial assets and liabilities are classified in their entirety based on the most stringent level of input that is significant to the fair value measurement.

Table of Contents

NIKE, INC.

NOTES TO CONSOLIDATED FINANCIAL STATEMENTS — (Continued)

The following table presents information about the Company's financial assets and liabilities measured at fair value on a recurring basis as of May 31, 2010 and 2009 and indicates the fair value hierarchy of the valuation techniques utilized by the Company to determine such fair value.

	May 31, 2010				
	Fair Value Measurements Using			Assets / Liabilities at Fair Value	Balance Sheet Classification
	Level 1	Level 2	Level 3		
	(In millions)				
Assets					
Derivatives:					
Foreign exchange forwards and options	$ —	$ 420.2	$ —	$ 420.2	Other current assets and other long–term assets
Interest rate swap contracts	—	14.6		14.6	Other current assets and other long–term assets
Total derivatives	—	434.8	—	434.8	
Available–for–sale securities:					
U.S. Treasury securities	1,231.7	—	—	1,231.7	Cash and equivalents
Commercial paper and bonds	—	461.9	—	461.9	Cash and equivalents
Money market funds	—	684.5	—	684.5	Cash and equivalents
U.S. Treasury securities	1,084.0	—	—	1,084.0	Short–term investments
U.S. Agency securities	—	298.5	—	298.5	Short–term investments
Commercial paper and bonds	—	684.3	—	684.3	Short–term investments
Total available–for–sale securities	2,315.7	2,129.2	—	4,444.9	
Total Assets	$ 2,315.7	$ 2,564.0	$ —	$ 4,879.7	
Liabilities					
Derivatives:					
Foreign exchange forwards and options	$ —	$ 165.1	$ —	$ 165.1	Accrued liabilities and other long–term liabilities
Total Liabilities	$ —	$ 165.1	$ —	$ 165.1	

Table of Contents

NIKE, INC.

NOTES TO CONSOLIDATED FINANCIAL STATEMENTS — (Continued)

	May 31, 2009				
	Fair Value Measurements Using			Assets / Liabilities at Fair Value	Balance Sheet Classification
	Level 1	Level 2	Level 3		
	(In millions)				
Assets					
Derivatives:					
Foreign exchange forwards and options	$ —	$ 364.9	$ —	$ 364.9	Other current assets and other long–term assets
Interest rate swap contracts	—	13.8	—	13.8	Other current assets and other long–term assets
Total derivatives	—	378.7	—	378.7	
Available–for–sale securities:					
U.S. Treasury securities	240.0	—	—	240.0	Cash and equivalents
Commercial paper and bonds	—	235.3	—	235.3	Cash and equivalents
Money market funds	—	1,079.5	—	1,079.5	Cash and equivalents
U.S. Treasury securities	467.9	—	—	467.9	Short–term investments
U.S. Agency securities	—	304.9	—	304.9	Short–term investments
Commercial paper and bonds	—	391.2	—	391.2	Short–term investments
Total available–for–sale securities	707.9	2,010.9	—	2,718.8	
Total Assets	$ 707.9	$ 2,389.6	$ —	$ 3,097.5	
Liabilities					
Derivatives:					
Foreign exchange forwards and options	$ —	$ 68.9	$ —	$ 68.9	Accrued liabilities and other long–term liabilities
Total Liabilities	$ —	$ 68.9	$ —	$ 68.9	

Derivative financial instruments include foreign currency forwards, option contracts and interest rate swaps. The fair value of these derivatives contracts is determined using observable market inputs such as the forward pricing curve, currency volatilities, currency correlations and interest rates, and considers nonperformance risk of the Company and that of its counterparties. Adjustments relating to these risks were not material for the years ended May 31, 2010 and 2009.

Available–for–sale securities are primarily comprised of investments in U.S. Treasury and agency securities, commercial paper, bonds and money market funds. These securities are valued using market prices on both active markets (level 1) and less active markets (level 2). Level 1 instrument valuations are obtained from real–time quotes for transactions in active exchange markets involving identical assets. Level 2 instrument valuations are obtained from readily–available pricing sources for comparable instruments.

As of May 31, 2010 and 2009, the Company had no material Level 3 measurements and no assets or liabilities measured at fair value on a non–recurring basis.

Table of Contents

NIKE, INC.

NOTES TO CONSOLIDATED FINANCIAL STATEMENTS — (Continued)

Short–term Investments

As of May 31, 2010 and 2009, short–term investments consisted of available–for–sale securities. As of May 31, 2010, the Company held $1,900.4 million of available–for–sale securities with maturity dates within one year and $166.4 million with maturity dates over one year and less than five years within short–term investments. As of May 31, 2009, the Company held $1,005.0 million of available–for–sale securities with maturity dates within one year and $159.0 million with maturity dates over one year and less than five years within short–term investments.

Short–term investments classified as available–for–sale consist of the following at fair value:

	As of May 31,	
	2010	2009
	(In millions)	
Available–for–sale investments:		
U.S. treasury and agencies	$ 1,382.5	$ 772.8
Commercial paper and bonds	684.3	391.2
Total available–for–sale investments	$ 2,066.8	$ 1,164.0

Included in interest expense (income), net for the years ended May 31, 2010, 2009 and 2008 was interest income of $30.1 million, $49.7 million, and $115.8 million, respectively, related to cash and equivalents and short–term investments.

For fair value information regarding notes payable and long–term debt, refer to Note 7 — Short–Term Borrowings and Credit Lines and Note 8 — Long–Term Debt.

Note 7 — Short–Term Borrowings and Credit Lines

Notes payable to banks and interest–bearing accounts payable to Sojitz Corporation of America ("Sojitz America") as of May 31, 2010 and 2009, are summarized below:

	May 31,			
	2010		2009	
	Borrowings	Interest Rate	Borrowings	Interest Rate
	(In millions)			
Notes payable:				
Commercial paper	$ —	—	$ 100.0	0.40%
U.S. operations	18.0	—(1)	31.2	1.81%(1)
Non–U.S. operations	120.6	6.35%(1)	211.7	4.15%(1)
	$ 138.6		$ 342.9	
Sojitz America	$ 88.2	1.07%	$ 78.5	1.57%

(1) Weighted average interest rate includes non–interest bearing overdrafts.

The carrying amounts reflected in the consolidated balance sheet for notes payable approximate fair value.

The Company purchases through Sojitz America certain athletic footwear, apparel and equipment it acquires from non–U.S. suppliers. These purchases are for the Company's operations outside of the United States, Europe and Japan. Accounts payable to Sojitz America are generally due up to 60 days after shipment of goods from the foreign port. The interest rate on such accounts payable is the 60–day London Interbank Offered Rate ("LIBOR") as of the beginning of the month of the invoice date, plus 0.75%.

Table of Contents

NIKE, INC.

NOTES TO CONSOLIDATED FINANCIAL STATEMENTS — (Continued)

As of May 31, 2010, the Company had no amounts outstanding under its commercial paper program. As of May 31, 2009, the Company had $100.0 million outstanding at a weighted average interest rate of 0.40%.

In December 2006, the Company entered into a $1 billion revolving credit facility with a group of banks. The facility matures in December 2012. Based on the Company's current long–term senior unsecured debt ratings of A+ and A1 from Standard and Poor's Corporation and Moody's Investor Services, respectively, the interest rate charged on any outstanding borrowings would be the prevailing LIBOR plus 0.15%. The facility fee is 0.05% of the total commitment. Under this agreement, the Company must maintain, among other things, certain minimum specified financial ratios with which the Company was in compliance at May 31, 2010. No amounts were outstanding under this facility as of May 31, 2010 and 2009.

Note 8 — Long–Term Debt

Long–term debt, net of unamortized premiums and discounts and swap fair value adjustments, is comprised of the following:

	May 31, 2010	May 31, 2009
	(In millions)	
5.375% Corporate bond, payable July 8, 2009	$ —	$ 25.1
5.66% Corporate bond, payable July 23, 2012	27.0	27.4
5.4% Corporate bond, payable August 7, 2012	16.1	16.2
4.7% Corporate bond, payable October 1, 2013	50.0	50.0
5.15% Corporate bond, payable October 15, 2015	112.4	111.1
4.3% Japanese Yen note, payable June 26, 2011	115.7	108.5
1.52125% Japanese Yen note, payable February 14, 2012	55.1	51.7
2.6% Japanese Yen note, maturing August 20, 2001 through November 20, 2020	53.1	54.7
2.0% Japanese Yen note, maturing August 20, 2001 through November 20, 2020	23.8	24.5
Total	453.2	469.2
Less current maturities	7.4	32.0
	$445.8	$437.2

The scheduled maturity of long–term debt in each of the years ending May 31, 2011 through 2015 are $7.4 million, $178.1 million, $47.4 million, $57.4 million and $7.4 million, at face value, respectively.

The Company's long–term debt is recorded at adjusted cost, net of amortized premiums and discounts and interest rate swap fair value adjustments. The fair value of long–term debt is estimated based upon quoted prices for similar instruments. The fair value of the Company's long–term debt, including the current portion, was approximately $453 million at May 31, 2010 and $456 million at May 31, 2009.

In fiscal years 2003 and 2004, the Company issued a total of $240 million in medium–term notes of which $190 million, at face value, were outstanding at May 31, 2010. The outstanding notes have coupon rates that range from 4.70% to 5.66% and maturity dates ranging from July 2012 to October 2015. For each of these notes, except the $50 million note maturing in October 2013, the Company has entered into interest rate swap agreements whereby the Company receives fixed interest payments at the same rate as the notes and pays variable interest payments based on the six–month LIBOR plus a spread. Each swap has the same notional amount and maturity date as the corresponding note. At May 31, 2010, the interest rates payable on these swap agreements ranged from approximately 0.3% to 1.1%.

Table of Contents

NIKE, INC.

NOTES TO CONSOLIDATED FINANCIAL STATEMENTS — (Continued)

In June 1996, one of the Company's Japanese subsidiaries, NIKE Logistics YK, borrowed ¥10.5 billion (approximately $115.7 million as of May 31, 2010) in a private placement with a maturity of June 26, 2011. Interest is paid semi–annually. The agreement provides for early retirement of the borrowing.

In July 1999, NIKE Logistics YK assumed a total of ¥13.0 billion in loans as part of its agreement to purchase a distribution center in Japan, which serves as collateral for the loans. These loans mature in equal quarterly installments during the period August 20, 2001 through November 20, 2020. Interest is also paid quarterly. As of May 31, 2010, ¥7.0 billion (approximately $76.9 million) in loans remain outstanding.

In February 2007, NIKE Logistics YK entered into a ¥5.0 billion (approximately $55.1 million as of May 31, 2010) term loan that replaced certain intercompany borrowings and matures on February 14, 2012. The interest rate on the loan is approximately 1.5% and interest is paid semi–annually.

Note 9 — Income Taxes

Income before income taxes is as follows:

	Year Ended May 31,		
	2010	2009	2008
		(In millions)	
Income before income taxes:			
United States	$ 698.6	$ 845.7	$ 713.0
Foreign	1,818.3	1,110.8	1,789.9
	$ 2,516.9	$ 1,956.5	$ 2,502.9

The provision for income taxes is as follows:

	Year Ended May 31,		
	2010	2009	2008
		(In millions)	
Current:			
United States			
Federal	$200.2	$ 410.1	$ 469.9
State	50.0	46.1	58.4
Foreign	348.5	307.7	391.8
	598.7	763.9	920.1
Deferred:			
United States			
Federal	17.7	(251.4)	(273.0)
State	(1.1)	(7.9)	(5.0)
Foreign	(5.1)	(34.8)	(22.6)
	11.5	(294.1)	(300.6)
	$610.2	$ 469.8	$ 619.5

Table of Contents

NIKE, INC.

NOTES TO CONSOLIDATED FINANCIAL STATEMENTS — (Continued)

A reconciliation from the U.S. statutory federal income tax rate to the effective income tax rate follows:

	Year Ended May 31,		
	2010	2009	2008
Federal income tax rate	35.0%	35.0%	35.0%
State taxes, net of federal benefit	1.3%	1.2%	1.4%
Foreign earnings	−13.6%	−14.9%	−12.9%
Other, net	1.5%	2.7%	1.3%
Effective income tax rate	24.2%	24.0%	24.8%

The effective tax rate for the year ended May 31, 2010 of 24.2% increased from the fiscal 2009 effective rate of 24.0%. The effective tax rate for the year ended May 31, 2009 was favorably impacted by a tax benefit associated with the impairment of goodwill, intangible, and other assets of Umbro (See Note 4 — Acquisition, Identifiable Intangible Assets, Goodwill and Umbro Impairment), and the retroactive reinstatement of the research and development tax credit. The Tax Extenders and Alternative Minimum Tax Relief Act of 2008, which was signed into law during the second quarter of fiscal 2009, reinstated the U.S. federal research and development tax credit retroactive to January 1, 2008. Also reflected in the effective tax rate for the years ended May 31, 2010, 2009 and 2008 is a reduction in our on–going effective tax rate resulting from our operations outside of the United States, as our tax rates on those operations are generally lower than the U.S. statutory rate.

Deferred tax assets and (liabilities) are comprised of the following:

	May 31,	
	2010	2009
	(In millions)	
Deferred tax assets:		
Allowance for doubtful accounts	$ 16.7	$ 17.9
Inventories	47.3	52.8
Sales return reserves	52.0	52.8
Deferred compensation	143.7	127.3
Stock–based compensation	145.0	127.3
Reserves and accrued liabilities	85.8	66.7
Foreign loss carry–forwards	26.2	31.9
Foreign tax credit carry–forwards	148.3	32.7
Hedges	0.4	1.1
Undistributed earnings of foreign subsidiaries	128.4	272.9
Other	37.0	46.2
Total deferred tax assets	830.8	829.6
Valuation allowance	(36.2)	(26.0)
Total deferred tax assets after valuation allowance	794.6	803.6
Deferred tax liabilities:		
Property, plant and equipment	(99.3)	(92.2)
Intangibles	(98.6)	(100.7)
Hedges	(71.5)	(86.6)
Other	(8.1)	(4.2)
Total deferred tax liability	(277.5)	(283.7)
Net deferred tax asset	$ 517.1	$ 519.9

Table of Contents

NIKE, INC.

NOTES TO CONSOLIDATED FINANCIAL STATEMENTS — (Continued)

The following is a reconciliation of the changes in the gross balance of unrecognized tax benefits:

	May 31,		
	2010	2009	2008
		(In millions)	
Unrecognized tax benefits, as of the beginning of the period	$ 273.9	$251.1	$122.5
Gross increases related to prior period tax positions	86.7	53.2	71.6
Gross decreases related to prior period tax positions	(121.6)	(61.7)	(23.1)
Gross increases related to current period tax positions	52.5	71.5	87.7
Settlements	(3.3)	(29.3)	(13.4)
Lapse of statute of limitations	(9.3)	(4.1)	(0.7)
Changes due to currency translation	3.2	(6.8)	6.5
Unrecognized tax benefits, as of the end of the period	$ 282.1	$273.9	$251.1

As of May 31, 2010, the total gross unrecognized tax benefits, excluding related interest and penalties, were $282.1 million, $158.4 million of which would affect the Company's effective tax rate if recognized in future periods. Total gross unrecognized tax benefits, excluding interest and penalties, as of May 31, 2009 was $273.9 million, $110.6 million of which would affect the Company's effective tax rate if recognized in future periods.

The Company recognizes interest and penalties related to income tax matters in income tax expense. The liability for payment of interest and penalties increased $6.0 million, $2.2 million and $41.2 million during the years ended May 31, 2010, 2009 and 2008, respectively. As of May 31, 2010 and 2009, accrued interest and penalties related to uncertain tax positions was $81.4 million and $75.4 million, respectively (excluding federal benefit).

The Company is subject to taxation primarily in the U.S., China and the Netherlands as well as various state and other foreign jurisdictions. The Company has concluded substantially all U.S. federal income tax matters through fiscal year 2006. The Company is currently under audit by the Internal Revenue Service for the 2007, 2008, 2009 and 2010 tax years. The Company's major foreign jurisdictions, China and the Netherlands, have concluded substantially all income tax matters through calendar 1999 and fiscal 2003, respectively. It is reasonably possible that the Internal Revenue Service audits for the 2007, 2008 and 2009 tax years will be completed during the next 12 months, which could result in a decrease in our balance of unrecognized tax benefits. An estimate of the range cannot be made at this time; however, we do not anticipate that total gross unrecognized tax benefits will change significantly as a result of full or partial settlement of audits within the next 12 months.

The Company has indefinitely reinvested approximately $3.6 billion of the cumulative undistributed earnings of certain foreign subsidiaries. Such earnings would be subject to U.S. taxation if repatriated to the U.S. Determination of the amount of unrecognized deferred tax liability associated with the permanently reinvested cumulative undistributed earnings is not practicable.

During the year ended May 31, 2009, a portion of the Company's foreign operations was granted a tax holiday that will phase out in 2019. The decrease in income tax expense for the year ended May 31, 2010 as a result of this arrangement was approximately $30.1 million ($0.06 per diluted share). The effect on income tax expense for the year ended May 31, 2009 was not material.

Deferred tax assets at May 31, 2010 and 2009 were reduced by a valuation allowance relating to tax benefits of certain subsidiaries with operating losses where it is more likely than not that the deferred tax assets will not be realized. The net change in the valuation allowance was an increase of $10.2 million for the year ended May 31, 2010 and a decrease of $14.7 million and $1.6 million for the years ended May 31, 2009 and 2008, respectively.

Table of Contents

NIKE, INC.

NOTES TO CONSOLIDATED FINANCIAL STATEMENTS — (Continued)

The Company does not anticipate that any foreign tax credit carry–forwards will expire. The Company has available domestic and foreign loss carry–forwards of $89.8 million at May 31, 2010. Such losses will expire as follows:

	Year Ending May 31,							
	2011	2012	2013	2014	2015	2016–2028	Indefinite	Total
	(In millions)							
Net Operating Losses	$2.0	$1.9	$3.6	$8.9	$11.1	$25.7	$ 36.6	$89.8

During the years ended May 31, 2010, 2009, and 2008, income tax benefits attributable to employee stock–based compensation transactions of $56.8 million, $25.4 million, and $68.9 million, respectively, were allocated to shareholders' equity.

Note 10 — Redeemable Preferred Stock

Sojitz America is the sole owner of the Company's authorized Redeemable Preferred Stock, $1 par value, which is redeemable at the option of Sojitz America or the Company at par value aggregating $0.3 million. A cumulative dividend of $0.10 per share is payable annually on May 31 and no dividends may be declared or paid on the common stock of the Company unless dividends on the Redeemable Preferred Stock have been declared and paid in full. There have been no changes in the Redeemable Preferred Stock in the three years ended May 31, 2010, 2009 and 2008. As the holder of the Redeemable Preferred Stock, Sojitz America does not have general voting rights but does have the right to vote as a separate class on the sale of all or substantially all of the assets of the Company and its subsidiaries, on merger, consolidation, liquidation or dissolution of the Company or on the sale or assignment of the NIKE trademark for athletic footwear sold in the United States.

Note 11 — Common Stock and Stock–Based Compensation

The authorized number of shares of Class A Common Stock, no par value, and Class B Common Stock, no par value, are 175 million and 750 million, respectively. Each share of Class A Common Stock is convertible into one share of Class B Common Stock. Voting rights of Class B Common Stock are limited in certain circumstances with respect to the election of directors.

In 1990, the Board of Directors adopted, and the shareholders approved, the NIKE, Inc. 1990 Stock Incentive Plan (the "1990 Plan"). The 1990 Plan provides for the issuance of up to 132 million previously unissued shares of Class B Common Stock in connection with stock options and other awards granted under the plan. The 1990 Plan authorizes the grant of non–statutory stock options, incentive stock options, stock appreciation rights, stock bonuses, and the issuance and sale of restricted stock. The exercise price for non–statutory stock options, stock appreciation rights and the grant price of restricted stock may not be less than 75% of the fair market value of the underlying shares on the date of grant. The exercise price for incentive stock options may not be less than the fair market value of the underlying shares on the date of grant. A committee of the Board of Directors administers the 1990 Plan. The committee has the authority to determine the employees to whom awards will be made, the amount of the awards, and the other terms and conditions of the awards. The committee has granted substantially all stock options at 100% of the market price on the date of grant. Substantially all stock option grants outstanding under the 1990 Plan were granted in the first quarter of each fiscal year, vest ratably over four years, and expire 10 years from the date of grant. In June 2010, the Board of Directors amended the 1990 Plan to require, among other things, that the exercise price for non–statutory stock options and stock appreciation rights may not be less than 100% of the fair market value of the underlying shares on the date of grant.

Table of Contents

NIKE, INC.

NOTES TO CONSOLIDATED FINANCIAL STATEMENTS — (Continued)

The following table summarizes the Company's total stock–based compensation expense recognized in selling and administrative expense:

	Year Ended May 31,		
	2010	2009	2008
		(In millions)	
Stock options[(1)]	$134.6	$128.8	$127.0
ESPPs	13.7	14.4	7.2
Restricted stock	10.7	7.9	6.8
Subtotal	159.0	151.1	141.0
Stock options and restricted stock expense — restructuring[(2)]	—	19.5	—
Total stock–based compensation expense	$159.0	$170.6	$141.0

(1) Accelerated stock option expense is recorded for employees eligible for accelerated stock option vesting upon retirement. Accelerated stock option expense reported during the years ended May 31, 2010, 2009 and 2008 was $74.4 million, $58.7 million and $40.7 million, respectively.

(2) In connection with the restructuring activities that took place during fiscal 2009, the Company recognized stock–based compensation expense relating to the modification of stock option agreements, allowing for an extended post–termination exercise period, and accelerated vesting of restricted stock as part of severance packages. See Note 16 — Restructuring Charges for further details.

As of May 31, 2010, the Company had $86.8 million of unrecognized compensation costs from stock options, net of estimated forfeitures, to be recognized as selling and administrative expense over a weighted average period of 2.2 years.

The weighted average fair value per share of the options granted during the years ended May 31, 2010, 2009 and 2008, as computed using the Black–Scholes pricing model, was $23.43, $17.13 and $13.87, respectively. The weighted average assumptions used to estimate these fair values are as follows:

	Year Ended May 31,		
	2010	2009	2008
Dividend yield	1.9%	1.5%	1.4%
Expected volatility	57.6%	32.5%	20.0%
Weighted average expected life (in years)	5.0	5.0	5.0
Risk–free interest rate	2.5%	3.4%	4.8%

The Company estimates the expected volatility based on the implied volatility in market traded options on the Company's common stock with a term greater than one year, along with other factors. The weighted average expected life of options is based on an analysis of historical and expected future exercise patterns. The interest rate is based on the U.S. Treasury (constant maturity) risk–free rate in effect at the date of grant for periods corresponding with the expected term of the options.

Table of Contents

NIKE, INC.

NOTES TO CONSOLIDATED FINANCIAL STATEMENTS — (Continued)

The following summarizes the stock option transactions under the plan discussed above:

	Shares (In millions)	Weighted Average Option Price
Options outstanding May 31, 2007	39.7	$ 35.50
Exercised	(9.1)	33.45
Forfeited	(0.9)	44.44
Granted	6.9	58.50
Options outstanding May 31, 2008	36.6	$ 40.14
Exercised	(4.0)	35.70
Forfeited	(1.3)	51.19
Granted	7.5	58.17
Options outstanding May 31, 2009	38.8	$ 43.69
Exercised	(8.6)	37.64
Forfeited	(0.6)	51.92
Granted	6.4	52.79
Options outstanding May 31, 2010	36.0	$ 46.60
Options exercisable at May 31,		
2008	16.2	$ 32.35
2009	21.4	36.91
2010	20.4	41.16

The weighted average contractual life remaining for options outstanding and options exercisable at May 31, 2010 was 6.2 years and 4.8 years, respectively. The aggregate intrinsic value for options outstanding and exercisable at May 31, 2010 was $926.8 million and $636.0 million, respectively. The aggregate intrinsic value was the amount by which the market value of the underlying stock exceeded the exercise price of the options. The total intrinsic value of the options exercised during the years ended May 31, 2010, 2009 and 2008 was $239.3 million, $108.4 million and $259.4 million, respectively.

In addition to the 1990 Plan, the Company gives employees the right to purchase shares at a discount to the market price under employee stock purchase plans ("ESPPs"). Employees are eligible to participate through payroll deductions up to 10% of their compensation. At the end of each six–month offering period, shares are purchased by the participants at 85% of the lower of the fair market value at the beginning or the end of the offering period. Employees purchased 0.8 million shares, 1.0 million shares and 0.8 million shares during the years ended May 31, 2010, 2009 and 2008, respectively.

From time to time, the Company grants restricted stock and unrestricted stock to key employees under the 1990 Plan. The number of shares granted to employees during the years ended May 31, 2010, 2009 and 2008 were 499,000, 75,000 and 110,000 with weighted average values per share of $53.16, $56.97 and $59.50, respectively. Recipients of restricted shares are entitled to cash dividends and to vote their respective shares throughout the period of restriction. The value of all of the granted shares was established by the market price on the date of grant. During the years ended May 31, 2010, 2009 and 2008, the fair value of restricted shares vested was $8.0 million, $9.9 million and $9.0 million, respectively, determined as of the date of vesting.

Table of Contents

NIKE, INC.

NOTES TO CONSOLIDATED FINANCIAL STATEMENTS — (Continued)

Note 12 — Earnings Per Share

The following is a reconciliation from basic earnings per share to diluted earnings per share. Options to purchase an additional 0.2 million, 13.2 million and 6.6 million shares of common stock were outstanding at May 31, 2010, 2009 and 2008, respectively, but were not included in the computation of diluted earnings per share because the options were anti–dilutive.

	Year Ended May 31,		
	2010	2009	2008
	(In millions, except per share data)		
Determination of shares:			
Weighted average common shares outstanding	485.5	484.9	495.6
Assumed conversion of dilutive stock options and awards	8.4	5.8	8.5
Diluted weighted average common shares outstanding	493.9	490.7	504.1
Basic earnings per common share	$ 3.93	$ 3.07	$ 3.80
Diluted earnings per common share	$ 3.86	$ 3.03	$ 3.74

Note 13 — Benefit Plans

The Company has a profit sharing plan available to most U.S.–based employees. The terms of the plan call for annual contributions by the Company as determined by the Board of Directors. A subsidiary of the Company also has a profit sharing plan available to its U.S.–based employees. The terms of the plan call for annual contributions as determined by the subsidiary's executive management. Contributions of $34.9 million, $27.6 million and $37.3 million were made to the plans and are included in selling and administrative expense for the years ended May 31, 2010, 2009 and 2008, respectively. The Company has various 401(k) employee savings plans available to U.S.–based employees. The Company matches a portion of employee contributions with common stock or cash. Company contributions to the savings plans were $34.2 million, $37.6 million and $33.9 million for the years ended May 31, 2010, 2009 and 2008, respectively, and are included in selling and administrative expense.

The Company also has a Long–Term Incentive Plan ("LTIP") that was adopted by the Board of Directors and approved by shareholders in September 1997 and later amended in fiscal 2007. The Company recognized $24.1 million, $17.6 million and $35.9 million of selling and administrative expense related to cash awards under the LTIP during the years ended May 31, 2010, 2009 and 2008, respectively.

The Company has pension plans in various countries worldwide. The pension plans are only available to local employees and are generally government mandated. The liability related to the unfunded pension liabilities of the plans was $113.0 million and $82.8 million at May 31, 2010 and 2009, respectively.

Table of Contents

NIKE, INC.

NOTES TO CONSOLIDATED FINANCIAL STATEMENTS — (Continued)

Note 14 — Accumulated Other Comprehensive Income

The components of accumulated other comprehensive income, net of tax, are as follows:

	May 31,	
	2010	2009
	(In millions)	
Cumulative translation adjustment and other	$ (94.6)	$ 64.6
Net deferred gain on net investment hedge derivatives	107.3	62.5
Net deferred gain on cash flow hedge derivatives	202.1	240.4
	$214.8	$367.5

Note 15 — Commitments and Contingencies

The Company leases space for certain of its offices, warehouses and retail stores under leases expiring from 1 to 25 years after May 31, 2010. Rent expense was $416.1 million, $397.0 million and $344.2 million for the years ended May 31, 2010, 2009 and 2008, respectively. Amounts of minimum future annual rental commitments under non–cancelable operating leases in each of the five years ending May 31, 2011 through 2015 are $334.4 million, $264.0 million, $219.9 million, $177.2 million, $148.0 million, respectively, and $465.8 million in later years.

As of May 31, 2010 and 2009, the Company had letters of credit outstanding totaling $101.1 million and $154.8 million, respectively. These letters of credit were generally issued for the purchase of inventory.

In connection with various contracts and agreements, the Company provides routine indemnifications relating to the enforceability of intellectual property rights, coverage for legal issues that arise and other items where the Company is acting as the guarantor. Currently, the Company has several such agreements in place. However, based on the Company's historical experience and the estimated probability of future loss, the Company has determined that the fair value of such indemnifications is not material to the Company's financial position or results of operations.

In the ordinary course of its business, the Company is involved in various legal proceedings involving contractual and employment relationships, product liability claims, trademark rights, and a variety of other matters. The Company does not believe there are any pending legal proceedings that will have a material impact on the Company's financial position or results of operations.

Note 16 — Restructuring Charges

During fiscal 2009, the Company took necessary steps to streamline its management structure, enhance consumer focus, drive innovation more quickly to market and establish a more scalable, long–term cost structure. As a result, the Company reduced its global workforce by approximately 5% and incurred pre–tax restructuring charges of $195 million, primarily consisting of severance costs related to the workforce reduction. As nearly all of the restructuring activities were completed in fiscal 2009, the Company does not expect to recognize additional costs in future periods relating to these actions. The restructuring charge is reflected in the corporate expense line in the segment presentation of earnings before interest and taxes in Note 19 — Operating Segments and Related Information.

Table of Contents

NIKE, INC.

NOTES TO CONSOLIDATED FINANCIAL STATEMENTS — (Continued)

The activity in the restructuring accrual for the years ended May 31, 2010 and 2009 is as follows (in millions):

Restructuring accrual — June 1, 2008	$ —
Severance and related costs	195.0
Cash payments	(29.4)
Non–cash stock option and restricted stock expense	(19.5)
Foreign currency translation and other	3.5
Restructuring accrual — May 31, 2009	149.6
Cash payments	(142.6)
Foreign currency translation and other	1.2
Restructuring accrual — May 31, 2010	$ 8.2

The accrual balance as of May 31, 2010 will be relieved throughout the first half of fiscal year 2011, as final severance payments are completed. The restructuring accrual is included in Accrued liabilities in the Consolidated Balance Sheet.

Note 17 — Divestitures

On December 17, 2007, the Company completed the sale of the Starter brand business to Iconix Brand Group, Inc. for $60.0 million in cash. This transaction resulted in a gain of $28.6 million during the year ended May 31, 2008.

On April 17, 2008, the Company completed the sale of NIKE Bauer Hockey for $189.2 million in cash to a group of private investors ("the Buyer"). The sale resulted in a net gain of $32.0 million recorded in the fourth quarter of the year ended May 31, 2008. This gain included the recognition of a $46.3 million cumulative foreign currency translation adjustment previously included in accumulated other comprehensive income. As part of the terms of the sale agreement, the Company granted the Buyer a royalty free limited license for the use of certain NIKE trademarks for a transitional period of approximately two years. The Company deferred $41.0 million of the sale proceeds related to this license agreement, to be recognized over the license period.

The gains resulting from these divestitures are reflected in other (income) expense, net and in the corporate expense line in the segment presentation of earnings before interest and taxes in Note 19 — Operating Segments and Related Information.

Note 18 — Risk Management and Derivatives

The Company is exposed to global market risks, including the effect of changes in foreign currency exchange rates and interest rates, and uses derivatives to manage financial exposures that occur in the normal course of business. The Company does not hold or issue derivatives for speculative trading purposes.

The Company formally documents all relationships between hedging instruments and hedged items, as well as its risk management objective and strategy for undertaking hedge transactions. This process includes linking all derivatives to either specific firm commitments or forecasted transactions. The Company also enters into foreign exchange forwards to mitigate the change in fair value of specific assets and liabilities on the balance sheet, which are not designated as hedging instruments under the accounting standards for derivatives and hedging. Accordingly, changes in the fair value of hedges of recorded balance sheet positions are recognized

Table of Contents

NIKE, INC.

NOTES TO CONSOLIDATED FINANCIAL STATEMENTS — (Continued)

immediately in other (income) expense, net, on the income statement together with the transaction gain or loss from the hedged balance sheet position. The Company classifies the cash flows at settlement from these undesignated hedges in the same category as the cash flows from the related hedged items, generally within the cash provided by operations component of the cash flow statement.

The majority of derivatives outstanding as of May 31, 2010 are designated as either cash flow, fair value or net investment hedges under the accounting standards for derivatives and hedging. All derivatives are recognized on the balance sheet at their fair value and classified based on the instrument's maturity date. The total notional amount of outstanding derivatives as of May 31, 2010 was $6.2 billion, which was primarily comprised of cash flow hedges denominated in Euros, Japanese Yen and British Pounds.

The following table presents the fair values of derivative instruments included within the consolidated balance sheet as of May 31, 2010 and 2009:

	Asset Derivatives			Liability Derivatives		
	Balance Sheet Classification	May 31, 2010	May 31, 2009	Balance Sheet Classification	May 31, 2010	May 31, 2009
			(In millions)			
Derivatives formally designated as hedging instruments:						
Foreign exchange forwards and options	Prepaid expenses and other current assets	$ 315.9	$ 270.4	Accrued liabilities	$ 24.7	$ 34.6
Interest rate swap contracts	Prepaid expenses and other current assets	—	0.1	Accrued liabilities	—	—
Foreign exchange forwards and options	Deferred income taxes and other assets	0.4	81.3	Deferred income taxes and other liabilities	0.1	—
Interest rate swap contracts	Deferred income taxes and other assets	14.6	13.7	Deferred income taxes and other liabilities	—	—
Total derivatives formally designated as hedging instruments		330.9	365.5		24.8	34.6
Derivatives not designated as hedging instruments:						
Foreign exchange forwards and options	Prepaid expenses and other current assets	$ 103.9	$ 12.8	Accrued liabilities	$ 138.9	$ 34.3
Foreign exchange forwards and options	Deferred income taxes and other assets	—	0.4	Deferred income taxes and other liabilities	1.4	—
Total derivatives not designated as hedging instruments		103.9	13.2		140.3	34.3
Total derivatives		$ 434.8	$ 378.7		$ 165.1	$ 68.9

Table of Contents

NIKE, INC.

NOTES TO CONSOLIDATED FINANCIAL STATEMENTS — (Continued)

The following tables present the amounts affecting the consolidated statements of income for years ended May 31, 2010 and 2009:

Derivatives formally designated	Amount of Gain (Loss) Recognized in Other Comprehensive Income on Derivatives(1) Year Ended May 31, 2010	Amount of Gain (Loss) Recognized in Other Comprehensive Income on Derivatives(1) Year Ended May 31, 2009	Location of Gain (Loss) Reclassified From Accumulated Other Comprehensive Income Into Income(1)	Amount of Gain (Loss) Reclassified From Accumulated Other Comprehensive Income into Income(1) Year Ended May 31, 2010	Amount of Gain (Loss) Reclassified From Accumulated Other Comprehensive Income into Income(1) Year Ended May 31, 2009
			(In millions)		
Derivatives designated as cash flow hedges:					
Foreign exchange forwards and options	$ (29.9)	$ 106.3	Revenue	$ 51.4	$ 92.7
Foreign exchange forwards and options	89.0	350.1	Cost of sales	60.0	(13.5)
Foreign exchange forwards and options	4.7	(0.4)	Selling and administrative expense	1.0	0.8
Foreign exchange forwards and options	51.1	165.1	Other (income) expense, net	56.1	67.8
Total designated cash flow hedges	$ 114.9	$ 621.1		$ 168.5	$ 147.8
Derivatives designated as net investment hedges:					
Foreign exchange forwards and options	$ 66.0	$ 161.4	Other (income) expense, net	$ —	$ —

(1) For the year ended May 31, 2010, $5.2 million of income was recorded to other (income) expense, net as a result of cash flow hedge ineffectiveness. For the year ended May 31, 2009, an immaterial amount of ineffectiveness from cash flow hedges was recorded in other (income) expense, net.

	Amount of Gain (Loss) recognized in Income on Derivatives Year Ended May 31, 2010	Amount of Gain (Loss) recognized in Income on Derivatives Year Ended May 31, 2009	Location of Gain (Loss) Recognized in Income on Derivatives
	(In millions)		
Derivatives designated as fair value hedges:			
Interest rate swaps(1)	$ 7.4	$ 1.5	Interest expense (income), net
Derivatives not designated as hedging instruments:			
Foreign exchange forwards and options	$ (91.1)	$ (83.0)	Other (income) expense, net

(1) All interest rate swap agreements meet the shortcut method requirements under the accounting standards for derivatives and hedging. Accordingly, changes in the fair values of the interest rate swap agreements are exactly offset by changes in the fair value of the underlying long–term debt. Refer to section "Fair Value Hedges" for additional detail.

Refer to Note 5 — Accrued Liabilities for derivative instruments recorded in accrued liabilities, Note 6 —Fair Value Measurements for a description of how the above financial instruments are valued, Note 14 — Accumulated Other Comprehensive Income and the Consolidated Statement of Shareholders' Equity for additional information on changes in other comprehensive income for the years ended May 31, 2010 and 2009.

Table of Contents

NIKE, INC.

NOTES TO CONSOLIDATED FINANCIAL STATEMENTS — (Continued)

Cash Flow Hedges

The purpose of the Company's foreign currency hedging activities is to protect the Company from the risk that the eventual cash flows resulting from transactions in foreign currencies, including revenues, product costs, selling and administrative expenses, investments in U.S. dollar–denominated available–for–sale debt securities and intercompany transactions, including intercompany borrowings, will be adversely affected by changes in exchange rates. It is the Company's policy to utilize derivatives to reduce foreign exchange risks where internal netting strategies cannot be effectively employed. Hedged transactions are denominated primarily in Euros, British Pounds and Japanese Yen. The Company hedges up to 100% of anticipated exposures typically 12 months in advance, but has hedged as much as 34 months in advance.

All changes in fair values of outstanding cash flow hedge derivatives, except the ineffective portion, are recorded in other comprehensive income until net income is affected by the variability of cash flows of the hedged transaction. In most cases, amounts recorded in other comprehensive income will be released to net income some time after the maturity of the related derivative. The consolidated statement of income classification of effective hedge results is the same as that of the underlying exposure. Results of hedges of revenue and product costs are recorded in revenue and cost of sales, respectively, when the underlying hedged transaction affects net income. Results of hedges of selling and administrative expense are recorded together with those costs when the related expense is recorded. Results of hedges of anticipated purchases and sales of U.S. dollar–denominated available–for–sale securities are recorded in other (income) expense, net when the securities are sold. Results of hedges of anticipated intercompany transactions are recorded in other (income) expense, net when the transaction occurs. The Company classifies the cash flows at settlement from these designated cash flow hedge derivatives in the same category as the cash flows from the related hedged items, generally within the cash provided by operations component of the cash flow statement.

Premiums paid on options are initially recorded as deferred charges. The Company assesses the effectiveness of options based on the total cash flows method and records total changes in the options' fair value to other comprehensive income to the degree they are effective.

As of May 31, 2010, $187.2 million of deferred net gains (net of tax) on both outstanding and matured derivatives accumulated in other comprehensive income are expected to be reclassified to net income during the next 12 months as a result of underlying hedged transactions also being recorded in net income. Actual amounts ultimately reclassified to net income are dependent on the exchange rates in effect when derivative contracts that are currently outstanding mature. As of May 31, 2010, the maximum term over which the Company is hedging exposures to the variability of cash flows for its forecasted and recorded transactions is 18 months.

The Company formally assesses both at a hedge's inception and on an ongoing basis, whether the derivatives that are used in the hedging transaction have been highly effective in offsetting changes in the cash flows of hedged items and whether those derivatives may be expected to remain highly effective in future periods. Effectiveness for cash flow hedges is assessed based on forward rates. When it is determined that a derivative is not, or has ceased to be, highly effective as a hedge, the Company discontinues hedge accounting prospectively.

The Company discontinues hedge accounting prospectively when (1) it determines that the derivative is no longer highly effective in offsetting changes in the cash flows of a hedged item (including hedged items such as firm commitments or forecasted transactions); (2) the derivative expires or is sold, terminated, or exercised; (3) it is no longer probable that the forecasted transaction will occur; or (4) management determines that designating the derivative as a hedging instrument is no longer appropriate.

NIKE, INC.

NOTES TO CONSOLIDATED FINANCIAL STATEMENTS — (Continued)

When the Company discontinues hedge accounting because it is no longer probable that the forecasted transaction will occur in the originally expected period, or within an additional two–month period of time thereafter, the gain or loss on the derivative remains in accumulated other comprehensive income and is reclassified to net income when the forecasted transaction affects net income. However, if it is probable that a forecasted transaction will not occur by the end of the originally specified time period or within an additional two–month period of time thereafter, the gains and losses that were accumulated in other comprehensive income will be recognized immediately in net income. In all situations in which hedge accounting is discontinued and the derivative remains outstanding, the Company will carry the derivative at its fair value on the balance sheet, recognizing future changes in the fair value in other (income) expense, net. For the year ended May 31, 2010, $5.2 million of income was recorded to other (income) expense, net as a result of cash flow hedge ineffectiveness. For the years ended 2009 and 2008, the Company recorded in other (income) expense an immaterial amount of ineffectiveness from cash flow hedges.

Fair Value Hedges

The Company is also exposed to the risk of changes in the fair value of certain fixed–rate debt attributable to changes in interest rates. Derivatives currently used by the Company to hedge this risk are receive–fixed, pay–variable interest rate swaps. As of May 31, 2010, all interest rate swap agreements are designated as fair value hedges of the related long–term debt and meet the shortcut method requirements under the accounting standards for derivatives and hedging. Accordingly, changes in the fair values of the interest rate swap agreements are exactly offset by changes in the fair value of the underlying long–term debt. The cash flows associated with the Company's fair value hedges are periodic interest payments while the swaps are outstanding, which are reflected in net income within the cash provided by operations component of the cash flow statement. No ineffectiveness has been recorded to net income related to interest rate swaps designated as fair value hedges for the years ended May 31, 2010, 2009 and 2008.

In fiscal 2003, the Company entered into a receive–floating, pay–fixed interest rate swap agreement related to a Japanese Yen denominated intercompany loan with one of the Company's Japanese subsidiaries. This interest rate swap was not designated as a hedge under the accounting standards for derivatives and hedging. Accordingly, changes in the fair value of the swap were recorded to net income each period through maturity as a component of interest expense (income), net. Both the intercompany loan and the related interest rate swap matured during the year ended May 31, 2009.

Net Investment Hedges

The Company also hedges the risk of variability in foreign–currency–denominated net investments in wholly–owned international operations. All changes in fair value of the derivatives designated as net investment hedges, except ineffective portions, are reported in the cumulative translation adjustment component of other comprehensive income along with the foreign currency translation adjustments on those investments. The Company classifies the cash flows at settlement of its net investment hedges within the cash used by investing component of the cash flow statement. The Company assesses hedge effectiveness based on changes in forward rates. The Company recorded no ineffectiveness from its net investment hedges for the years ended May 31, 2010, 2009, and 2008.

Credit Risk

The Company is exposed to credit–related losses in the event of non–performance by counterparties to hedging instruments. The counterparties to all derivative transactions are major financial institutions with investment grade credit ratings. However, this does not eliminate the Company's exposure to credit risk with

Table of Contents

NIKE, INC.

NOTES TO CONSOLIDATED FINANCIAL STATEMENTS — (Continued)

these institutions. This credit risk is limited to the unrealized gains in such contracts should any of these counterparties fail to perform as contracted. To manage this risk, the Company has established strict counterparty credit guidelines that are continually monitored and reported to senior management according to prescribed guidelines. The Company utilizes a portfolio of financial institutions either headquartered or operating in the same countries the Company conducts its business. As a result of the above considerations, the Company considers the impact of the risk of counterparty default to be immaterial.

Certain of the Company's derivative instruments contain credit risk related contingent features. As of May 31, 2010, the Company was in compliance with all such credit risk related contingent features. The aggregate fair value of derivative instruments with credit risk related contingent features that are in a net liability position at May 31, 2010 was $18.3 million. The Company was not required to post any collateral as a result of these contingent features.

Note 19 — Operating Segments and Related Information

Operating Segments. The Company's operating segments are evidence of the structure of the Company's internal organization. The major segments are defined by geographic regions for operations participating in NIKE Brand sales activity excluding NIKE Golf. Each NIKE Brand geographic segment operates predominantly in one industry: the design, production, marketing and selling of sports and fitness footwear, apparel, and equipment. In fiscal 2009, the Company initiated a reorganization of the NIKE Brand into a new model consisting of six geographies. Effective June 1, 2009, the Company's new reportable operating segments for the NIKE Brand are: North America, Western Europe, Central and Eastern Europe, Greater China, Japan, and Emerging Markets. Previously, NIKE Brand operations were organized into the following four geographic regions: U.S., Europe, Middle East and Africa (collectively, "EMEA"), Asia Pacific, and Americas.

The Company's "Other" category is broken into two components for presentation purposes to align with the way management views the Company. The "Global Brand Divisions" category primarily represents NIKE Brand licensing businesses that are not part of a geographic operating segment, selling, general and administrative expenses that are centrally managed for the NIKE Brand and costs associated with product development and supply chain operations. The "Other Businesses" category primarily consists of the activities of Cole Haan, Converse Inc., Hurley International LLC, NIKE Golf and Umbro Ltd. Activities represented in the "Other" category are considered immaterial for individual disclosure. Prior period amounts have been reclassified to conform to the Company's new operating structure described above.

Revenues as shown below represent sales to external customers for each segment. Intercompany revenues have been eliminated and are immaterial for separate disclosure.

Corporate consists of unallocated general and administrative expenses, which includes expenses associated with centrally managed departments, depreciation and amortization related to the Company's headquarters, unallocated insurance and benefit programs, including stock–based compensation, certain foreign currency gains and losses, including hedge gains and losses, certain corporate eliminations and other items.

Effective June 1, 2009, the primary financial measure used by the Company to evaluate performance of individual operating segments is Earnings Before Interest and Taxes (commonly referred to as "EBIT") which represents net income before interest expense (income), net and income taxes in the Consolidated Statements of Income. Reconciling items for EBIT represent corporate expense items that are not allocated to the operating segments for management reporting. Previously, the Company evaluated performance of individual operating segments based on pre–tax income or income before income taxes.

Table of Contents

NIKE, INC.

NOTES TO CONSOLIDATED FINANCIAL STATEMENTS — (Continued)

As part of the Company's centrally managed foreign exchange risk management program, standard foreign currency rates are assigned to each NIKE Brand entity in our geographic operating segments and are used to record any non–functional currency revenues or product purchases into the entity's functional currency. Geographic operating segment revenues and cost of sales reflect use of these standard rates. For all NIKE Brand operating segments, differences between assigned standard foreign currency rates and actual market rates are included in Corporate together with foreign currency hedge gains and losses generated from the centrally managed foreign exchange risk management program and other conversion gains and losses. For the years ended May 31, 2009 and 2008, foreign currency hedge results along with other conversion gains and losses generated by the Western Europe and Central and Eastern Europe geographies were recorded in their respective results.

Additions to long–lived assets as presented in the following table represent capital expenditures.

Accounts receivable, inventories and property, plant and equipment for operating segments are regularly reviewed by management and are therefore provided below.

Certain prior year amounts have been reclassified to conform to fiscal 2010 presentation.

Table of Contents

NIKE, INC.

NOTES TO CONSOLIDATED FINANCIAL STATEMENTS — (Continued)

	Year Ended May 31,		
	2010	2009	2008
		(In millions)	
Revenue			
North America	$ 6,696.0	$ 6,778.3	$ 6,660.5
Western Europe	3,892.0	4,139.1	4,320.0
Central and Eastern Europe	1,149.9	1,373.2	1,309.2
Greater China	1,741.8	1,743.3	1,353.6
Japan	882.0	925.9	822.4
Emerging Markets	2,041.6	1,702.0	1,630.3
Global Brand Divisions	105.3	95.3	117.9
Total NIKE Brand	16,508.6	16,757.1	16,213.9
Other Businesses	2,529.5	2,419.0	2,413.1
Corporate	(24.1)	—	—
Total NIKE Consolidated Revenues	$19,014.0	$19,176.1	$18,627.0
Earnings Before Interest and Taxes			
North America	$ 1,538.1	$ 1,429.3	$ 1,460.4
Western Europe	855.7	939.1	922.5
Central and Eastern Europe	281.2	415.1	358.4
Greater China	637.1	575.2	430.7
Japan	180.3	205.4	178.9
Emerging Markets	492.6	342.6	306.6
Global Brand Divisions	(866.8)	(811.5)	(736.8)
Total NIKE Brand	3,118.2	3,095.2	2,920.7
Other Businesses[1]	299.4	(192.6)	358.6
Corporate	(894.4)	(955.6)	(853.5)
Total NIKE Consolidated Earnings Before Interest and Taxes	2,523.2	1,947.0	2,425.8
Interest expense (income), net	6.3	(9.5)	(77.1)
Total NIKE Consolidated Earnings Before Taxes	$ 2,516.9	$ 1,956.5	$ 2,502.9
Additions to Long–lived Assets			
North America	$ 45.3	$ 99.2	$ 141.9
Western Europe	58.9	69.6	63.5
Central and Eastern Europe	4.3	8.1	5.5
Greater China	80.4	58.5	13.1
Japan	11.6	10.0	21.9
Emerging Markets	10.5	10.9	12.4
Global Brand Divisions	29.9	37.8	22.6
Total NIKE Brand	240.9	294.1	280.9
Other Businesses	52.1	89.6	61.5
Corporate	42.1	72.0	106.8
Total Additions to Long–lived Assets	$ 335.1	$ 455.7	$ 449.2
Depreciation			
North America	$ 64.7	$ 64.3	$ 52.4
Western Europe	57.1	51.4	61.1
Central and Eastern Europe	4.6	4.0	3.7
Greater China	11.0	7.2	3.8
Japan	26.2	29.9	20.4
Emerging Markets	11.0	10.2	10.8
Global Brand Divisions	33.8	42.3	34.3
Total NIKE Brand	208.4	209.3	186.5
Other Businesses	45.7	37.5	28.1
Corporate	69.6	88.2	89.0
Total Depreciation	$ 323.7	$ 335.0	$ 303.6

Table of Contents

NIKE, INC.

NOTES TO CONSOLIDATED FINANCIAL STATEMENTS — (Continued)

(1) During the year ended May 31, 2009, the Other category included a pre–tax charge of $401.3 million for the impairment of goodwill, intangible and other assets of Umbro, which was recorded in the third quarter of fiscal 2009. See Note 4 — Acquisition, Identifiable Intangible Assets, Goodwill and Umbro Impairment for more information.

(2) During the year ended May 31, 2009, Corporate expense included pre–tax charges of $195.0 million for the Company's restructuring activities, which were completed in the fourth quarter of fiscal 2009. See Note 16 — Restructuring Charges for more information.

	Year Ended May 31, 2010	2009
	(In millions)	
Accounts Receivable, net		
North America	$ 848.0	$ 897.7
Western Europe	401.8	508.8
Central and Eastern Europe	293.6	368.3
Greater China	128.9	122.3
Japan	166.8	207.2
Emerging Markets	327.2	268.2
Global Brand Divisions	22.8	53.3
Total NIKE Brand	2,189.1	2,425.8
Other Businesses	442.1	439.7
Corporate	18.6	18.4
Total Accounts Receivable, net	$ 2,649.8	$ 2,883.9
Inventories		
North America	$ 767.5	$ 868.8
Western Europe	347.2	341.6
Central and Eastern Europe	124.8	278.1
Greater China	103.5	110.4
Japan	68.3	95.7
Emerging Markets	262.2	258.2
Global Brand Divisions	20.6	32.4
Total NIKE Brand	1,694.1	1,985.2
Other Businesses	346.7	371.8
Corporate	—	—
Total Inventories	$ 2,040.8	$ 2,357.0
Property, Plant and Equipment, net		
North America	$ 324.7	$ 354.3
Western Europe	282.1	326.5
Central and Eastern Europe	12.3	15.0
Greater China	145.5	78.2
Japan	332.6	318.5
Emerging Markets	47.0	47.3
Global Brand Divisions	99.6	103.1
Total NIKE Brand	1,243.8	1,242.9
Other Businesses	167.4	163.7
Corporate	520.7	551.1
Total Property, Plant and Equipment, net	$ 1,931.9	$ 1,957.7

Table of Contents

NIKE, INC.

NOTES TO CONSOLIDATED FINANCIAL STATEMENTS — (Continued)

Revenues by Major Product Lines. Revenues to external customers for NIKE Brand products are attributable to sales of footwear, apparel and equipment. Other revenues to external customers primarily include external sales by Cole Haan, Converse, Exeter (whose primary business was the Starter brand business which was sold December 17, 2007), Hurley, NIKE Bauer Hockey (through April 16, 2008), NIKE Golf, and Umbro (beginning March 3, 2008).

	Year Ended May 31,		
	2010	2009	2008
	(In millions)		
Footwear	$ 10,333.1	$ 10,306.7	$ 9,731.6
Apparel	5,036.6	5,244.7	5,234.0
Equipment	1,033.6	1,110.4	1,130.4
Other	2,610.7	2,514.3	2,531.0
	$ 19,014.0	$ 19,176.1	$ 18,627.0

Revenues and Long–Lived Assets by Geographic Area. Geographical area information is similar to what was shown previously under operating segments with the exception of the Other activity, which has been allocated to the geographical areas based on the location where the sales originated. Revenues derived in the United States were $7,913.9 million, $8,019.8 million and $7,938.5 million, for the years ended May 31, 2010, 2009 and 2008, respectively. The Company's largest concentrations of long–lived assets primarily consist of the Company's world headquarters and distribution facilities in the United States and distribution facilities in Japan and Belgium. Long–lived assets attributable to operations in the United States, which are comprised of net property, plant & equipment, were $1,070.1 million, $1,142.6 million and $1,109.9 million at May 31, 2010, 2009 and 2008, respectively. Long–lived assets attributable to operations in Japan were $335.6 million, $322.3 million and $303.8 million at May 31, 2010, 2009 and 2008, respectively. Long–lived assets attributable to operations in Belgium were $163.7 million, $191.0 million and $219.1 million at May 31, 2010, 2009 and 2008, respectively.

Major Customers. Revenues derived from Foot Locker, Inc. represented 8% of the Company's consolidated revenues for the year ended May 31, 2010 and 9% for the years ended May 31, 2009 and 2008. Sales to this customer are included in all segments of the Company.

Appendix D

International Financial Reporting Standards (IFRS)

The Need for Global Accounting Standards

As discussed in Chapter 1, the Financial Accounting Standards Board (FASB) establishes generally accepted accounting principles (GAAP) for public companies in the United States. Of course, there is a world beyond the borders of the United States. In recent years, the removal of trade barriers and the growth in cross-border equity and debt issuances have led to a dramatic increase in international commerce. As a result, companies are often reporting financial results to users outside of the United States.

Historically, accounting standards have varied considerably across countries. These variances have been driven by cultural, legal, and political differences, and resulted in financial statements that were not easily comparable and difficult to interpret. These differences caused problems for companies in Europe and Asia, where local economies have become increasingly tied to international commerce.

During the last decade, however, a common set of International Financial Reporting Standards (IFRS) has emerged to reduce cross-country differences in accounting standards, primarily in countries outside of North America. While much of the world has migrated to IFRS, the United States has not. Because of the size of the United States and its significant role in world commerce, however, U.S. GAAP still has a global impact. As a result, there are currently two major accounting standard-setting efforts in the world, U.S. GAAP and IFRS. These two sets of accounting standards add cost and complexity for companies doing business and obtaining financing internationally.

Overview of IFRS

International Financial Reporting Standards (IFRS) have emerged during the last 10 years to meet the financial reporting needs of an increasingly global business environment.

What Is IFRS? International Financial Reporting Standards are a set of global accounting standards developed by an international standard-setting body called the International Accounting Standards Board (IASB). Like the Financial Accounting Standards Board (FASB), the IASB is an independent entity that establishes accounting rules. Unlike the FASB, the IASB does not establish accounting rules for any specific country. Rather, it develops accounting rules that can be used by a variety of countries, with the goal of developing a single set of global accounting standards.

Who Uses IFRS? IFRS applies to companies that issue publicly traded debt or equity securities, called **public companies**, in countries that have adopted IFRS as their accounting standards. Since 2005, all 27 countries in the European Union (EU) have been required to prepare financial statements using IFRS. In addition, over

100 other countries have adopted or are planning to adopt IFRS for public companies (see Exhibit 1). Canada will adopt IFRS by 2011, with Mexico following in 2012. Japan will consider mandatory use of IFRS in 2012. In addition, the G20 (Group of 20) leadership has called for uniform global accounting standards by June 2011.

EXHIBIT 1

IFRS Adopters

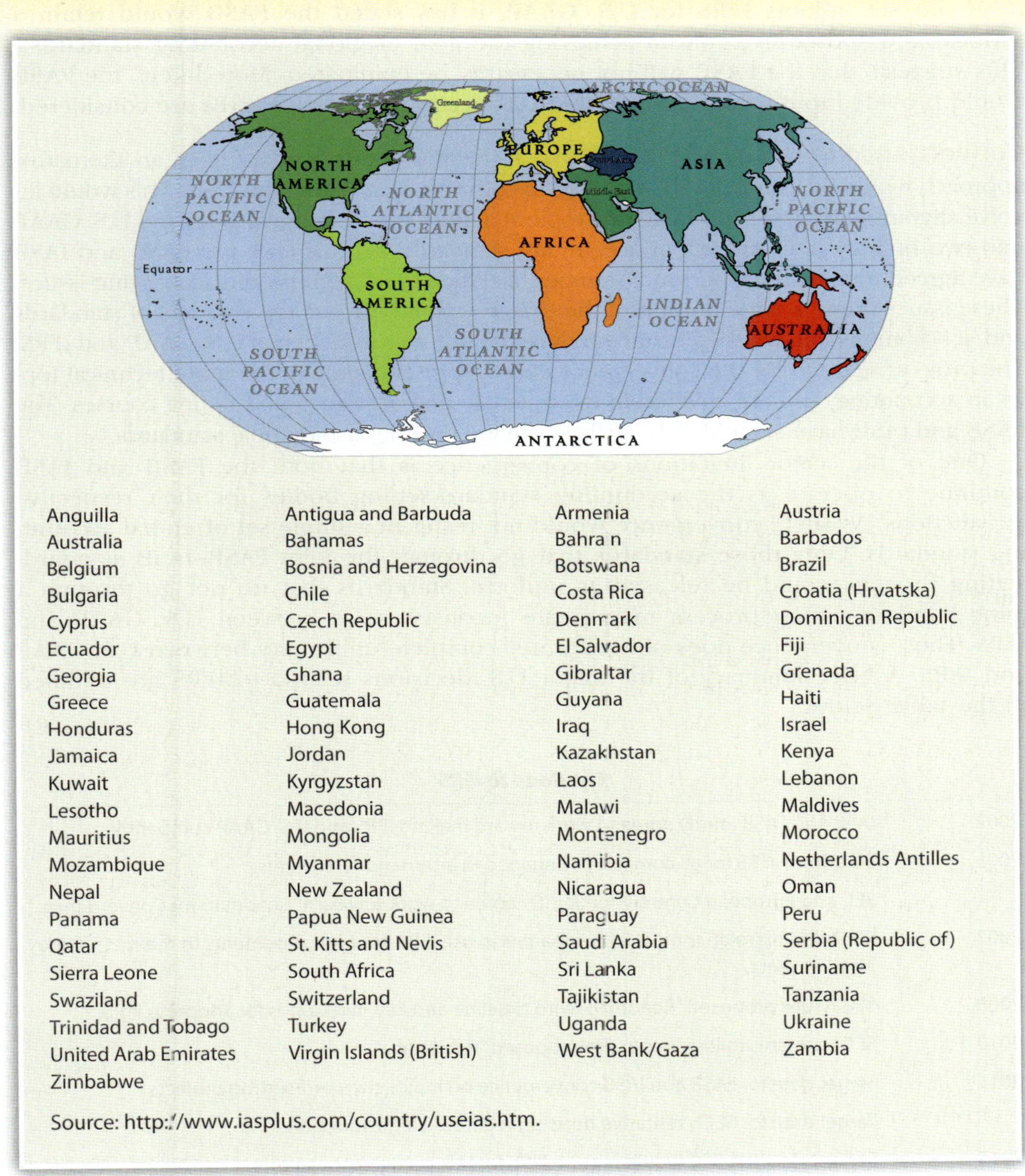

Anguilla	Antigua and Barbuda	Armenia	Austria
Australia	Bahamas	Bahrain	Barbados
Belgium	Bosnia and Herzegovina	Botswana	Brazil
Bulgaria	Chile	Costa Rica	Croatia (Hrvatska)
Cyprus	Czech Republic	Denmark	Dominican Republic
Ecuador	Egypt	El Salvador	Fiji
Georgia	Ghana	Gibraltar	Grenada
Greece	Guatemala	Guyana	Haiti
Honduras	Hong Kong	Iraq	Israel
Jamaica	Jordan	Kazakhstan	Kenya
Kuwait	Kyrgyzstan	Laos	Lebanon
Lesotho	Macedonia	Malawi	Maldives
Mauritius	Mongolia	Montenegro	Morocco
Mozambique	Myanmar	Namibia	Netherlands Antilles
Nepal	New Zealand	Nicaragua	Oman
Panama	Papua New Guinea	Paraguay	Peru
Qatar	St. Kitts and Nevis	Saudi Arabia	Serbia (Republic of)
Sierra Leone	South Africa	Sri Lanka	Suriname
Swaziland	Switzerland	Tajikistan	Tanzania
Trinidad and Tobago	Turkey	Uganda	Ukraine
United Arab Emirates	Virgin Islands (British)	West Bank/Gaza	Zambia
Zimbabwe			

Source: http://www.iasplus.com/country/useias.htm.

U.S. GAAP and IFRS: The Road Forward

The United States has not formally adopted IFRS for U.S. companies. The wide acceptance being gained by IFRS around the world, however, has placed considerable pressure on the United States to align U.S. GAAP with IFRS. There are two possible paths that the United States could take to achieve this: (1) adoption of IFRS by the U.S. Securities and Exchange Commission and (2) convergence of U.S. GAAP and IFRS. These two options are briefly discussed below.

Adoption of IFRS by the SEC The U.S. Securities and Exchange Commission (SEC) is the U.S. governmental agency that has authority over the accounting and financial disclosures for U.S. public companies. Only the SEC has the authority to adopt IFRS for U.S. public companies. In 2008, the SEC presented a "roadmap" to adopting IFRS, which outlined a timetable along with a set of "milestones" that needed to be met before the SEC would be willing to adopt IFRS. In 2010, the SEC reiterated the milestones outlined in the roadmap. According to the work plan, the SEC plans on deciding whether to incorporate IFRS into U.S. GAAP for public companies by 2011. If adopted, companies could begin reporting under IFRS as early as 2015.

If the SEC adopts IFRS for U.S. GAAP, it has stated the FASB would retain a "critical and substantive role in achieving the goal of global accounting standards." This suggests that the FASB will not necessarily be eliminated. More likely, the FASB would provide input to the IASB so that U.S. accounting perspectives are considered.

Convergence of U.S. GAAP and IFRS If the SEC does not adopt IFRS, an alternative approach would be for the FASB and IASB to converge U.S. GAAP and IFRS. This would involve aligning IFRS and U.S. GAAP one topic at a time, slowly merging IFRS and U.S. GAAP into two broadly uniform sets of accounting standards. To this end, the FASB and IASB have agreed to work together on a number of difficult and high-profile accounting issues. These issues frame a large portion of the disagreement between the two sets of standards and, if accomplished, will significantly reduce the differences between U.S. GAAP and IFRS. The projects selected for the convergence effort represent some of the more technical topics in accounting, and are covered in intermediate and advanced accounting courses. The FASB and IASB have set mid-2011 as the deadline for establishing final standards.

One of the major limitations of convergence is that both the FASB and IASB continue to operate as the accounting standard-setting bodies for their respective jurisdictions. As such, convergence would not result in a single set of global accounting standards. Only those standards that go through the joint FASB–IASB standard-setting process would be released as uniform. Standards that do not go through a joint standard-setting process may create inconsistencies between U.S. GAAP and IFRS. Thus, convergence does not guarantee complete uniformity between U.S. GAAP and IFRS. A brief summary of the major U.S. decisions related to IFRS are outlined in the table below.

The Road to IFRS

2002	IASB and FASB jointly agree to work toward making IFRS and U.S. GAAP compatible.
2005	EU adopts IFRS for all companies engaged in international markets.
	SEC and European Commission jointly agree to work toward a "Roadmap for Convergence."
2007	SEC allows foreign (non-U.S.) companies to use IFRS financial statements to meet U.S. filing requirements.
2008	SEC issues proposed "Roadmap" with timeline and key milestones for adopting IFRS.
2010	SEC reiterates milestones in the proposed "Roadmap."
2011	Target date for FASB and IASB convergence on major standard-setting projects.
	Target date for SEC's tentative decision regarding IFRS adoption.
2015	Earliest date the SEC would require IFRS for U.S. public companies.

Differences Between U.S. GAAP and IFRS

U.S. GAAP and IFRS differ both in their approach to standard setting, as well as their financial statement presentation and recording of transactions.

Rules-Based vs. Principles Approach to Standard Setting U.S. GAAP is considered to be a "rules-based" approach to accounting standard setting. The accounting standards provide detailed and specific rules on the accounting for business transactions. There are few exceptions or varying interpretations of the accounting for a business event. This structure is consistent with the U.S. legal and regulatory system, reflecting the social and economic values of the United States.

In contrast, IFRS is designed to meet the needs of many countries. Differences in legal, political, and economic systems create different needs for and uses of financial information in different countries. For example, Germany needs a financial reporting system that reflects the central role of banks in its financial system, while the Netherlands needs a financial reporting system that reflects the significant role of outside equity in its financial system.

To accommodate economic, legal, and social diversity, IFRS must be broad enough to capture these differences, while still presenting comparable financial statements. Under IFRS, there is greater opportunity for different interpretations of the accounting treatment of a business event across different business entities. To support this, IFRS often has more extensive disclosures that support alternative assumptions. Thus, IFRS provides more latitude for professional judgment than typically found in comparable U.S. GAAP. Many countries find this feature attractive in reducing regulatory costs associated with using and auditing financial reports. This "principles-based" approach presents one of the most significant challenges to adopting IFRS in the United States.

Technical Differences Between IFRS and U.S. GAAP Although U.S. GAAP is similar to IFRS, differences arise in the presentation format, balance sheet valuations, and technical accounting procedures. The Mornin' Joe International financial statements presented on pages 716–716G highlight the financial statement format, presentation, and recording differences between U.S. GAAP and IFRS. In addition, the International Connection boxes in Chapters 1, 4, 7, 10, 13, and 16 discuss some of the significant differences between U.S. GAAP and IFRS. A more comprehensive summary of the key differences between U.S. GAAP and IFRS that are relevant to an introductory accounting course is summarized in the table on the following pages.

Discussion Questions

1. Briefly discuss why global accounting standards are needed in today's business environment.
2. What are International Financial Reporting Standards? Who uses these accounting standards?
3. What body is responsible for setting International Financial Reporting Standards?
4. Briefly discuss the differences between (a) convergence of U.S. GAAP with IFRS and (b) adoption of IFRS by the U.S. Securities and Exchange Commission.
5. Briefly discuss the difference between (a) a "rules-based" approach to accounting standard setting and (b) a "principles-based" approach to accounting standard setting.
6. How is property, plant, and equipment measured on the balance sheet under IFRS? How does this differ from the way property, plant, and equipment is measured on the balance sheet under U.S. GAAP?
7. What inventory costing methods are allowed under IFRS? How does this differ from the treatment under U.S. GAAP?

Comparison of Accounting for Selected Items Under U.S. GAAP and IFRS *(Concluded)*

	U.S. GAAP	IFRS	Text Reference
Statement of Cash Flows:	***Statement of Cash Flows***	***Statement of Cash Flows***	
Classification of interest paid or received	Treated as an operating activity	Interest paid may be treated as either an operating or a financing activity, interest received may be treated as an operating or investing activity	Ch 16; LO 3
Classification of dividend paid or received	Dividend paid treated as a financing activity, Dividend received treated as an operating activity	Dividend paid may be treated as either an operating or a financing activity, dividend received may be treated as an operating or investing activity	Ch 16; LO 3

Glossary

A

absorption costing The reporting of the costs of manufactured products, normally direct materials, direct labor, and factory overhead, as product costs. (980)

accelerated depreciation method A depreciation method that provides for a higher depreciation amount in the first year of the asset's use, followed by a gradually declining amount of depreciation. (455)

account An accounting form that is used to record the increases and decreases in each financial statement item. (52)

account form The form of balance sheet that resembles the basic format of the accounting equation, with assets on the left side and Liabilities and Owner's Equity sections on the right side. (18, 258)

account payable The liability created by a purchase on account. (11)

account receivable A claim against the customer created by selling merchandise or services on credit. (12, 65, 402)

accounting An information system that provides reports to stakeholders about the economic activities and condition of a business. (3)

accounting cycle The process that begins with analyzing and journalizing transactions and ends with the post-closing trial balance. (162)

accounting equation Assets = Liabilities + Owner's Equity. (9)

accounting period concept The accounting concept that assumes that the economic life of the business can be divided into time periods. (104)

accounting system The methods and procedures used by a business to collect, classify, summarize, and report financial data for use by management and external users. (206)

accounts payable subsidiary ledger The subsidiary ledger containing the individual accounts with suppliers (creditors). (207)

accounts receivable analysis A company's ability to collect its accounts receivable. (782)

accounts receivable subsidiary ledger The subsidiary ledger containing the individual accounts with customers. (207)

accounts receivable turnover The relationship between net sales and accounts receivable, computed by dividing the net sales by the average net accounts receivable; measures how frequently during the year the accounts receivable are being converted to cash. (417, 782)

accrual basis of accounting Under this basis of accounting, revenues and expenses are reported in the income statement in the period in which they are earned or incurred. (104)

accrued expenses Expenses that have been incurred but not recorded in the accounts. (108)

accrued revenues Revenues that have been earned but not recorded in the accounts. (107)

accumulated depreciation The contra asset account credited when recording the depreciation of a fixed asset. (117)

accumulated other comprehensive income The cumulative effects of other comprehensive income items reported separately in the Stockholders' Equity section of the balance sheet. (687)

activities The types of work, or actions, involved in a manufacturing process or service activity. (1164)

activity base (driver) A measure of activity that is related to changes in cost. Used in analyzing and classifying cost behavior. Activity bases are also used in the denominator in calculating the predetermined factory overhead rate to assign overhead costs to cost objects. (872, 958, 1165)

activity rate The estimated activity cost divided by estimated activity-base usage. (1165).

activity-based costing (ABC) A cost allocation method that identifies activities causing the incurrence of costs and allocates these costs to products (or other cost objects), based on activity drivers (bases). (873, 1164)

adjusted trial balance The trial balance prepared after all the adjusting entries have been posted. (123)

adjusting entries The journal entries that bring the accounts up to date at the end of the accounting period. (105)

adjusting process An analysis and updating of the accounts when financial statements are prepared. (105)

administrative expenses (general expenses) Expenses incurred in the administration or general operations of the business. (257)

aging the receivables The process of analyzing the accounts receivable and classifying them according to various age groupings, with the due date being the base point for determining age. (409)

Allowance for Doubtful Accounts The contra asset account for accounts receivable. (405)

allowance method The method of accounting for uncollectible accounts that provides an expense for uncollectible receivables in advance of their write-off. (403)

amortization The periodic transfer of the cost of an intangible asset to expense. (462)

annuity A series of equal cash flows at fixed intervals. (1203)

assets The resources owned by a business. (9, 54)

available-for-sale securities Securities that management expects to sell in the future but which are not actively traded for profit. (679)

average inventory cost flow method The method of inventory costing that is based on the assumption that costs should be charged against revenue by using the weighted average unit cost of the items sold. (314)

average rate of return A method of evaluating capital investment proposals that focuses on the expected profitability of the investment. (1199)

B

Bad Debt Expense The operating expense incurred because of the failure to collect receivables. (403)

balance of the account The amount of the difference between the debits and the credits that have been entered into an account. (53)

balance sheet A list of the assets, liabilities, and owner's equity as of a specific date, usually at the close of the last day of a month or a year. (15)

balanced scorecard A performance evaluation approach that incorporates multiple performance dimensions by combining financial and nonfinancial measures. (1114)

bank reconciliation The analysis that details the items responsible for the difference between the cash balance reported in the bank statement and the balance of the cash account in the ledger. (369)

bank statement A summary of all transactions mailed to the depositor or made available online by the bank each month. (366)

bond A form of an interest-bearing note used by corporations to borrow on a long-term basis. (626)

bond indenture The contract between a corporation issuing bonds and the bondholders. (628)

book value The cost of a fixed asset minus accumulated depreciation on the asset. (455)

book value of the asset (or net book value) The difference between the cost of a fixed asset and its accumulated depreciation. (118)

boot The amount a buyer owes a seller when a fixed asset is traded in on a similar asset. (468)

break-even point The level of business operations at which revenues and expired costs are equal. (966)

budget An accounting device used to plan and control resources of operational departments and divisions. (1008)

budget performance report A report comparing actual results with budget figures. (1059)

budgetary slack Excess resources set within a budget to provide for uncertain events. (1010)

budgeted variable factory overhead The standard variable overhead for the actual units produced. (1068)

business An organization in which basic resources (inputs), such as materials and labor, are assembled and processed to provide goods or services (outputs) to customers. (2)

business combination A business making an investment in another business by acquiring a controlling share, often greater than 50%, of the outstanding voting stock of another corporation by paying cash or exchanging stock. (676)

business entity concept A concept of accounting that limits the economic data in the accounting system to data related directly to the activities of the business. (7)

business transaction An economic event or condition that directly changes an entity's financial condition or directly affects its results of operations. (9)

C

capital account An account used for a proprietorship that represents the owner's equity. (54)

capital expenditures The costs of acquiring fixed assets, adding to a fixed asset, improving a fixed asset, or extending a fixed asset's useful life. (449)

capital expenditures budget The budget summarizing future plans for acquiring plant facilities and equipment. (1027)

capital investment analysis The process by which management plans, evaluates, and controls long-term capital investments involving property, plant, and equipment. (1198)

capital leases Leases that include one or more provisions that result in treating the leased assets as purchased assets in the accounts. (450)

capital rationing The process by which management plans, evaluates, and controls long-term capital investments involving fixed assets. (1213)

carrying amount The balance of the bonds payable account (face amount of the bonds) less any unamortized discount or plus any unamortized premium. (635)

cash Coins, currency (paper money), checks, money orders, and money on deposit that is available for unrestricted withdrawal from banks and other financial institutions. (363)

cash basis of accounting Under this basis of accounting, revenues and expenses are reported in the income statement in the period in which cash is received or paid. (104)

cash budget A budget of estimated cash receipts and payments. (1024)

cash dividend A cash distribution of earnings by a corporation to its shareholders. (590)

cash equivalents Highly liquid investments that are usually reported with cash on the balance sheet. (374)

cash flow per share Normally computed as cash flow from operations per share. (721)

cash flows from financing activities The section of the statement of cash flows that reports cash flows from transactions affecting the equity and debt of the business. (719)

cash flows from investing activities The section of the statement of cash flows that reports cash flows from transactions affecting investments in noncurrent assets. (718)

cash flows from operating activities The section of the statement of cash flows that reports the cash transactions affecting the determination of net income. (718)

cash payback period The expected period of time that will elapse between the date of a capital expenditure and the complete recovery in cash (or equivalent) of the amount invested. (1200)

cash payments journal The special journal in which all cash payments are recorded. (217)

cash receipts journal The special journal in which all cash receipts are recorded. (212)

cash short and over account An account which has recorded errors in cash sales or errors in making change causing the amount of actual cash on hand to differ from the beginning amount of cash plus the cash sales for the day. (364)

Certified Public Accountant (CPA) Public accountants who have met a state's education, experience, and examination requirements. (6)

chart of accounts A list of the accounts in the ledger. (54)

clearing account Another name for the income summary account because it has the effect of clearing the revenue and expense accounts of their balances. (157)

closing entries The entries that transfer the balances of the revenue, expense, and drawing accounts to the owner's capital account. (156)

closing process The transfer process of converting temporary account balances to zero by transferring the revenue and expense account balances to Income Summary, transferring the income summary account balance to the owner's capital account, and transferring the owner's drawing account to the owner's capital account. (156)

closing the books The process of transferring temporary accounts balances to permanent accounts at the end of the accounting period. (156)

common stock The stock outstanding when a corporation has issued only one class of stock. (585)

common-sized statement A financial statement in which all items are expressed only in relative terms. (778)

compensating balance A requirement by some banks requiring depositors to maintain minimum cash balances in their bank accounts. (375)

comprehensive income All changes in stockholders' equity during a period, except those resulting from dividends and stockholders' investments. (686)

consigned inventory Merchandise that is shipped by manufacturers to retailers who act as the manufacturer's selling agent. (327)

consignee The name for the retailer in a consigned inventory arrangement. (327)

consignor The name for the manufacturer in a consigned inventory arrangement. (327)

consolidated financial statements Financial statements resulting from combining parent and subsidiary statements. (676)

contingent liabilities Liabilities that may arise from past transactions if certain events occur in the future. (507)

continuous budgeting A method of budgeting that provides for maintaining a 12-month projection into the future. (1010)

continuous process improvement A management approach that is part of the overall total quality management philosophy. The approach requires all employees to constantly improve processes of which they are a part or for which they have managerial responsibility. (831)

contra account (or contra asset account) An account offset against another account. (117)

contract rate The periodic interest to be paid on the bonds that is identified in the bond indenture; expressed as a percentage of the face amount of the bond. (629)

contribution margin Sales less variable costs and variable selling and administrative expenses. (964)

contribution margin ratio The percentage of each sales dollar that is available to cover the fixed costs and provide an operating income. (964)

control environment The overall attitude of management and employees about the importance of controls. (359)

controllable expenses Costs that can be influenced by the decisions of a manager. (1106)

controllable revenues Revenues earned by the profit center. (1106)

controllable variance The difference between the actual amount of variable factory overhead cost incurred and the amount of variable factory overhead budgeted for the standard product. (1068)

controller The chief management accountant of a division or other segment of a business. (830)

controlling A phase in the management process that consists of monitoring the operating results of implemented plans and comparing the actual results with the expected results. (831)

controlling account The account in the general ledger that summarizes the balances of the accounts in a subsidiary ledger. (207)

conversion costs The combination of direct labor and factory overhead costs. (836)

copyright An exclusive right to publish and sell a literary, artistic, or musical composition. (463)

corporation A business organized under state or federal statutes as a separate legal entity. (8)

correcting journal entry An entry that is prepared when an error has already been journalized and posted. (72)

cost A payment of cash (or a commitment to pay cash in the future) for the purpose of generating revenues. (833)

cost accounting system A branch of managerial accounting concerned with accumulating manufacturing costs for financial reporting and decision-making purposes. (866)

cost allocation The process of assigning indirect cost to a cost object, such as a job. (872)

cost behavior The manner in which a cost changes in relation to its activity base (driver). (958)

cost center A decentralized unit in which the department or division manager has responsibility for the control of costs incurred and the authority to make decisions that affect these costs. (1104)

cost concept A concept of accounting that determines the amount initially entered into the accounting records for purchases. (8)

cost method A method of accounting for equity investments representing less than 20% of the outstanding shares of the investee. The purchase is at original cost, and any gains or losses upon sale are recognized by the difference between the sale proceeds and the original cost. (673)

cost object The object or segment of operations to which costs are related for management's use, such as a product or department. (833)

cost of finished goods available The beginning finished goods inventory added to the cost of goods manufactured during the period. (840)

cost of goods manufactured The total cost of making and finishing a product. (840)

cost of goods sold The cost of finished goods available for sale minus the ending finished goods inventory. (840)

cost of goods sold budget A budget of the estimated direct materials, direct labor, and factory overhead consumed by sold products. (1021)

engineering change order The document that initiates changing a product or process. (1164)

fiscal year The annual accounting period adopted by a business. (173)

mortgage notes An installment note that may be secured by a pledge of the borrower's assets. (636)

multiple-step income statement A form of income statement that contains several sections, subsections, and subtotals. (255)

N

natural business year A fiscal year that ends when business activities have reached the lowest point in an annual operating cycle. (174)

negotiated price approach An approach to transfer pricing that allows managers of decentralized units to agree (negotiate) among themselves as to the transfer price. (1117)

net income or net profit The amount by which revenues exceed expenses. (15)

net loss The amount by which expenses exceed revenues. (15)

net pay Gross pay less payroll deductions; the amount the employer is obligated to pay the employee. (494)

net present value method A method of analysis of proposed capital investments that focuses on the present value of the cash flows expected from the investments. (1204)

net realizable value The estimated selling price of an item of inventory less any direct costs of disposal, such as sales commissions. (325, 405)

net sales Revenue received for merchandise sold to customers less any sales returns and allowances and sales discounts. (257)

nonfinancial performance measure A performance measure expressed in units rather than dollars. (1076)

normal balance of an account The normal balance of an account can be either a debit or a credit depending on whether increases in the account are recorded as debits or credits. (56)

notes receivable A customer's written promise to pay an amount and possibly interest at an agreed-upon rate. (155, 402)

number of days' sales in inventory The relationship between the volume of sales and inventory, computed by dividing the inventory at the end of the year by the average daily cost of goods sold. (330, 784)

number of days' sales in receivables The relationship between sales and accounts receivable, computed by dividing the net accounts receivable at the end of the year by the average daily sales. (417, 783)

number of times interest charges are earned A ratio that measures creditor margin of safety for interest payments, calculated as income before interest and taxes divided by interest expense. (639, 786)

O

objectives (goals) Developed in the planning stage, these reflect the direction and desired outcomes of certain courses of action. (831)

objectivity concept A concept of accounting that requires accounting records and the data reported in financial statements to be based on objective evidence. (8)

operating leases Leases that do not meet the criteria for capital leases and thus are accounted for as operating expenses. (451)

operating leverage A measure of the relative mix of a business's variable costs and fixed costs, computed as contribution margin divided by operating income. (977)

operational planning The development of short-term plans to achieve goals identified in a business's strategic plan. Sometimes called tactical planning. (831)

opportunity cost The amount of income forgone from an alternative to a proposed use of cash or its equivalent. (1154)

other comprehensive income Specified items that are reported separately from net income, including foreign currency items, pension liability adjustments, and unrealized gains and losses on investments. (686)

other expense Expenses that cannot be traced directly to operations. (258)

other income Revenue from sources other than the primary operating activity of a business. (258)

outstanding stock The stock in the hands of stockholders. (585)

overapplied factory overhead The amount of factory overhead applied in excess of the actual factory overhead costs incurred for production during a period. (874)

owner's equity The owner's right to the assets of the business. (9, 54)

P

paid-in capital Capital contributed to a corporation by the stockholders and others. (584)

par The monetary amount printed on a stock certificate. (585)

parent company The corporation owning all or a majority of the voting stock of the other corporation. (676)

partnership An unincorporated business form consisting of two or more persons conducting business as co-owners for profit. (7, 539)

partnership agreement The formal written contract creating a partnership. (539)

patents Exclusive rights to produce and sell goods with one or more unique features. (462)

payroll The total amount paid to employees for a certain period. (493)

payroll register A multicolumn report used to assemble and summarize payroll data at the end of each payroll period. (498)

pension A cash payment to retired employees. (505)

period costs Those costs that are used up in generating revenue during the current period and that are not involved in manufacturing a product, such as selling, general, and administratvie expenses. (836)

periodic inventory system The inventory system in which the inventory records do not show the amount available for sale or sold during the period. (257)

perpetual inventory system The inventory system in which each purchase and sale of merchandise is recorded in an inventory account. (257)

petty cash fund A special cash fund to pay relatively small amounts. (373)

physical inventory A detailed listing of merchandise on hand. (313)

planning A phase of the management process whereby objectives are outlined and courses of action determined. (831)

posting The process of transferring the debits and credits from the journal entries to the accounts. (61)

predetermined factory overhead rate The rate used to apply factory overhead costs to the goods manufactured. The rate is determined by dividing the budgeted overhead cost by the estimated activity usage at the beginning of the fiscal period. (872)

preferred stock A class of stock with preferential rights over common stock. (586)

premium The excess of the issue price of a stock over its par value or the excess of the issue price of bonds over their face amount. (587, 629)

prepaid expenses Items such as supplies that will be used in the business in the future. (11, 105)

present value concept Cash to be received (or paid) in the future is not the equivalent of the same amount of money received at an earlier date. (1202)

present value index An index computed by dividing the total present value of the net cash flow to be received from a proposed capital investment by the amount to be invested. (1205)

present value of an annuity The sum of the present values of a series of equal cash flows to be received at fixed intervals. (1203)

price-earnings (P/E) ratio The ratio of the market price per share of common stock, at a specific date, to the annual earnings per share. (792)

prime costs The combination of direct materials and direct labor costs. (836)

prior period adjustments Corrections of material errors related to a prior period or periods, excluded from the determination of net income. (597)

private accounting The field of accounting whereby accountants are employed by a business firm or a not-for-profit organization. (3)

process A sequence of activities linked together for performing a particular task. (1076)

process cost system A type of cost system that accumulates costs for each of the various departments within a manufacturing facility. (866, 908)

process manufacturers Manufacturers that use large machines to process a continuous flow of raw materials through various stages of completion into a finished state. (908)

product cost concept A concept used in applying the cost-plus approach to product pricing in which only the costs of manufacturing the product, termed the product cost, are included in the cost amount to which the markup is added. (1159)

product costs The three components of manufacturing cost: direct materials, direct labor, and factory overhead costs. (836)

production bottleneck A condition that occurs when product demand exceeds production capacity. (1161)

production budget A budget of estimated unit production. (1017)

profit The difference between the amounts received from customers for goods or services provided and the amounts paid for the inputs used to provide the goods or services. (2)

profit center A decentralized unit in which the manager has the responsibility and the authority to make decisions that affect both costs and revenues (and thus profits). (1106)

profit margin A component of the rate of return on investment, computed as the ratio of income from operations to sales. (1110)

profit-volume chart A chart used to assist management in understanding the relationship between profit and volume. (973)

profitability The ability of a firm to earn income. (779)

proprietorship A business owned by one individual. (7)

public accounting The field of accounting where accountants and their staff provide services on a fee basis. (6)

public companies Companies that issue publicly traded debt or equity securities. (D-1)

purchase order The purchase order authorizes the purchase of the inventory from an approved vendor. (312)

purchase return or allowance From the buyer's perspective, returned merchandise or an adjustment for defective merchandise. (267)

purchases discounts Discounts taken by the buyer for early payment of an invoice. (266)

purchases journal The journal in which all items purchased on account are recorded. (214)

quick assets Cash and other current assets that can be quickly converted to cash, such as marketable securities and receivables. (510, 781)

quick ratio A financial ratio that measures the ability to pay current liabilities with quick assets (cash, marketable securities, accounts receivable). (510, 781)

R

rate earned on common stockholders' equity A measure of profitability computed by dividing net income, reduced by preferred dividend requirements, by common stockholders' equity. (789)

rate earned on stockholders' equity A measure of profitability computed by dividing net income by total stockholders' equity. (789)

rate earned on total assets A measure of the profitability of assets, without regard to the equity of creditors and stockholders in the assets. (788)

rate of return on investment (ROI) A measure of managerial efficiency in the use of investments in assets, computed as income from operations divided by invested assets. (1110)

ratio of cash to monthly cash expenses Ratio that helps assess how long a company can continue to operate without additional financing or generating positive cash flows from operations. (375)

ratio of fixed assets to long-term liabilities A leverage ratio that measures the margin of safety of long-term creditors, calculated as the net fixed assets divided by the long-term liabilities. (785)

ratio of liabilities to stockholders' equity A comprehensive leverage ratio that measures the relationship of the claims of creditors to stockholders' equity. (21, 785)

ratio of net sales to assets Ratio that measures how effectively a company uses its assets, computed as net sales divided by average total assets. (276, 787)

real (permanent) accounts Term for balance sheet accounts because they are relatively permanent and carried forward from year to year. (156)

realization The sale of assets when a partnership is being liquidated. (550)

receivables All money claims against other entities, including people, business firms, and other organizations. (402)

receiving report The form or electronic transmission used by the receiving personnel to indicate that materials have been received and inspected. (312, 869)

Subject Index

A

B

Company Index

GASB	Go...
GNP	Gross National Product
IMA	Institute of Management Accountants
IRC	Internal Revenue Code
IRS	Internal Revenue Service
JIT	Just-in-time
LIFO	Last-in, first-out
Lower of C or M	Lower of cost or market
MACRS	Modified Accelerated Cost Recovery System
n/30	Net 30
n/eom	Net, end-of-month
P/E Ratio	Price-earnings ratio
POS	Point of sale
ROI	Return on investment
SEC	Securities and Exchange Commission
TQC	Total quality control

For a 240V, single-phase feeder combined with branch circuits, the maximum voltage drop calculated at 5% is determined as follows:

$$240V \times 0.05 = 12V$$

In commercial applications, if the feeder load is not concentrated at the end of the feeder but instead is spread out along the feeder due to multiple taps, the load center length of the feeder should be calculated and used in the voltage drop formulas. This is because the total current does not flow the complete length of the feeder. If the full length is used in computing the voltage drop, the drop determined will be greater than reality. The *load center length* of a feeder is that point in the feeder where, if the load were concentrated at that point, the voltage drop would be the same as the voltage drop to the farthest load in the actual feeder.

To determine the load center length of a feeder with multiple taps, as shown in *Figure 1*, multiply each tap load by its actual routing distance from the supply end of the feeder. Add these products for all loads fed from the feeder then divide this sum by the sum of the individual loads. The resulting distance is the load center length (*L*) for the total load (*I*) of the feeder.

Example 1:

The length of a 240V, three-wire panel feeder is 145'. The total panel load consists of 180A of noncontinuous duty loads. No. 3/0 THHN copper conductors would normally be selected to supply this load. If they are used, will the voltage drop for this panel feeder exceed 2%?

Solution:

Use the first voltage drop formula to determine the voltage drop for the feeder. Look up the resistance for No. 3/0 AWG copper in *NEC Chapter 9, Table 8*. The DC resistance is 0.0766Ω per 1,000'. Using the voltage drop formula as follows:

$$VD = \frac{2 \times L \times R \times I}{1{,}000'}$$

$$VD = \frac{2 \times 145' \times 0.0766\Omega \times 180A}{1{,}000'}$$

$$VD = 3.99V\text{, rounded to }4V$$

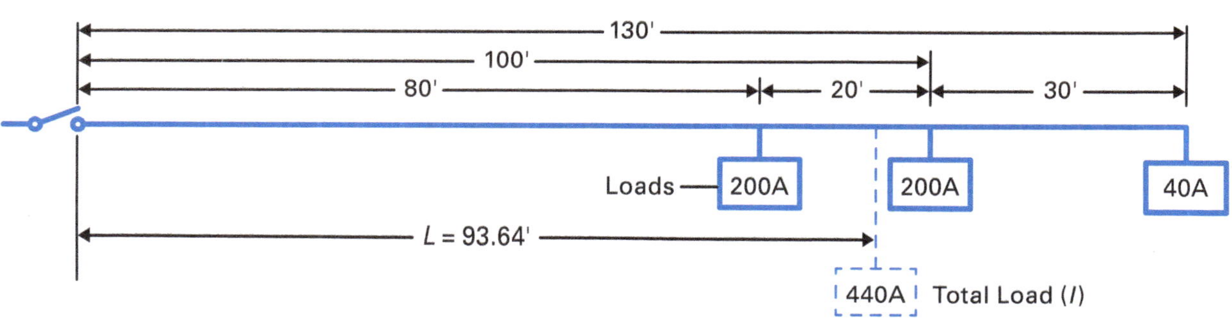

Calculation

Load 1	80'	×	200A =	16,000
Load 2	100'	×	200A =	20,000
Load 3	130'	×	40A =	5,200
Totals			440A	)41,200 = 93.64'

Total Load (*I*) = 440A
Load Center Length (*L*) = 93.64'

Figure 1 Load center length calculation.

Divide by applied voltage to find the percentage of voltage drop:

$$4V \div 240V = 0.0167$$
$$0.0167 \times 100 = 1.67\%$$
$$1.67\% < 2\%$$

Since the voltage drop does not exceed 2%, the No. 3/0 AWG conductors are acceptable. Note that the second formula could have been used, if desired. The two formulas provide similar results.

Example 2:

What size THHN copper conductors would be required for a continuous single-phase feeder load of 180A at 208V for fixed utilization equipment? The total length of the feeder is 318'.

Solution:

Since this is a continuous load, the load is first multiplied by 125% to determine the feeder ampacity:

$$180A \times 1.25 = 225A$$

This feeder will require a No. 4/0 THHN copper conductor to supply the continuous load. The connected load, however, is 180A, and this is the current value that will be used in the voltage drop calculations.

Use the second voltage drop formula to determine the voltage drop for this feeder. Look up the area in cmil for a No. 4/0 THHN copper conductor in *NEC Chapter 9, Table 8*. Use the voltage drop formula results as follows:

Know the Code

Conductor Properties
NEC Chapter 9, Table 8

$$VD = \frac{2 \times L \times K \times I}{\text{wire size in cmil}}$$

$$VD = \frac{2 \times 318' \times 12.9 \times 180A}{211{,}600\ \text{cmil}}$$

$$VD = 6.98V$$

Divide by the applied voltage to find the voltage drop as a percentage:

$$6.98V \div 208V = 0.0336$$
$$0.0336 \times 100 = 3.36\%$$
$$3.36\% > 3\%$$

Since the voltage drop exceeds 3%, the No. 4/0 AWG copper would not meet the recommendations. Using the area in cmil for 250 kcmil copper, the next larger conductor size, provides the following result:

$$VD = \frac{2 \times L \times K \times I}{\text{wire size in cmil}}$$

$$VD = \frac{2 \times 318' \times 12.9 \times 180A}{250{,}000\ \text{cmil}}$$

$$VD = 5.91V$$

Divide by the applied voltage to find the voltage drop as a percentage:

$$5.91V \div 208V = 0.0284$$
$$0.0284 \times 100 = 2.84\%$$
$$2.84\% < 3\%$$

No. 250 kcmil conductors would meet the *NEC®* voltage drop recommendations for this feeder, but the voltage drop is also not insignificant.

Example 3:

What size THHN copper conductors would be required for a tapped 240V, single-phase, three-wire feeder consisting of continuous fixed 240V utilization equipment loads of 180A at 30' and, at the end, a noncontinuous fixed load of 100A at 450'?

Solution:

First, calculate the total load of the feeder by finding 125% of the continuous load and 100% of the noncontinuous load, and then summing the results. This is calculated as follows:

Tap 1 = 180A × 1.25 = 225A

Tap 2 = 100A × 1 = 100A

Total load = Tap 1 + Tap 2

Total load = 225A + 100A = 325A

Know the Code

Ampacities of Insulated Conductors with Not More Than Three Current-Carrying Conductors in Raceway, Cable, or Earth (Directly Buried)
NEC Table 310.16

The total calculated load of the feeder is 325A. Per *NEC Table 310.16*, the minimum conductor size required for this feeder would be 400 kcmil copper.

To determine the conductor size that will prevent excessive voltage drop, use the load center length calculation. Multiply the loads by the distance from the feeder source, and then divide the sum of the two products by the sum of the two loads.

Multiply the loads by the distance from the feeder source:

Tap 1 = 30' × 180A = 5,400

Tap 2 = 450' × 100A = 45,000

Add the products of the continuous and noncontinuous loads:

5,400 + 45,000 = 50,400

Now divide by the sum of the loads:

$$\frac{50{,}400}{180\text{A} + 100\text{A}} = \frac{50{,}400}{280\text{A}} = 180' \text{ for load center}$$

Using the second single-phase voltage drop formula, substitute values using the load center length, 280A, and 400 kcmil to check the voltage drop as follows:

$$\frac{2 \times 180' \times 12.9 \times 280\text{A}}{400{,}000 \text{ cmil}} = 3.25\text{V}$$

The maximum recommended voltage drop is 240V × 3%, or 7.2V. Therefore, 400 kcmil conductors are acceptable. Note that if the full length of the feeder (450') had been used in this example instead of the load center length, the voltage drop would be 8.1V and 500 kcmil conductors would have to be selected. That size and cost would be excessive for this application.

Voltage drop for balanced three-phase circuits with negligible reactance and a power factor of 1 can be calculated using the two voltage drop formulas by substituting the square root of 3 (1.732) for the value of 2 in the first two formulas, which results in the following formulas.

Formula 3:

$$VD = \frac{1.732 \times L \times R \times I}{1{,}000'}$$

Formula 4:

$$VD = \frac{1.732 \times L \times K \times I}{\text{wire size in cmil}}$$

Example 4:

What is the voltage drop in a 208V, three-phase feeder with a noncontinuous load of 230A, a distance from the circuit breaker to the load of 315', and using No. 4/0 copper conductors?

Solution:

Use the third voltage drop formula to determine the voltage drop for this three-phase feeder. Look up the resistance for No. 4/0 copper conductor in *NEC Chapter 9, Table 8*. Use the voltage drop formula as follows:

$$VD = \frac{1.732 \times L \times R \times I}{1{,}000'}$$

$$VD = \frac{1.732 \times 315' \times 0.0608 \times 230\text{A}}{1{,}000'}$$

$$VD = 7.63\text{V}$$

Compare this to the maximum voltage drop permitted for a 208V circuit at 3%:

$$208\text{V} \times 0.03 = 6.24\text{V}$$

In this problem, 7.63V is more than the maximum allowable voltage drop, so this conductor selection will not meet the minimum *NEC*® recommendation. The conductor size should be increased to reduce the voltage drop.

Know the Code

Conductor Properties
NEC Chapter 9, Table 8

Example 5:

What size THHN copper conductors would be required for a panelboard used to supply continuous nonlinear loads of 100A for a 208V, three-phase, four-wire feeder circuit with a length of 150' from the source to the panelboard?

Solution:

Since the feeder is supplying nonlinear loads, the neutral wire becomes a current-carrying conductor per *NEC Section 310.15(E)(3)*. Thus, there are four current-carrying conductors. This will require the ampacity of the wire to be adjusted to 80% per *NEC Table 310.15(C)(1)*:

$$100\text{A} \div 0.8 = 125\text{A}$$

At an ampacity of 125A, the minimum size for the THHN copper conductor per the 90°C (194°F) column of *NEC Table 310.16* is No. 2 AWG. Because this is a feeder conductor, it must also meet the requirements of *NEC Section 215.2(A)(1)*. This requires a minimum ampacity of 125% for continuous loads before the application of any adjustment factors. Multiply the actual load of 100A by 125% to obtain 125A for the required conductor ampacity.

Since the actual load is 100A, you are limited to ampacity values of 60°C (140°F) per *NEC Section 110.14(C)*. Refer to *NEC Table 310.16* and select No. 1/0 copper based on the ampacity requirements of 125A.

Apply the fourth formula, substituting values using the actual connected load in amperes to ensure the voltage drop does not exceed the recommended 3% of 208V, which is 6.24V. Use the voltage drop formula as follows:

$$VD = \frac{1.732 \times L \times K \times I}{\text{wire size in cmil}}$$

$$VD = \frac{1.732 \times 150' \times 12.9 \times 100\text{A}}{105{,}600 \text{ cmil}}$$

$$VD = 3.17\text{V}$$

The No. 1/0 AWG conductors will be adequate for this application since the voltage drop is well below the suggested maximum.

Know the Code

Neutral Conductor
NEC Table 310.15(E)

Know the Code

Adjustment Factors for More Than Three Current-Carrying Conductors
NEC Table 310.15(C)(1)

Know the Code

Minimum Rating and Size
NEC Section 215.2

Know the Code

Temperature Limitations
NEC Section 110.14(C)

1.1.3 Temperature Limitations for Terminating Conductors

NEC Section 110.14(C) includes temperature limitations for terminating conductors. The ampacity rating of conductors must be selected to ensure the temperature rating of any component in the feeder circuit is not exceeded. If the feeder size is less than or equal to 100A, the 60°C (140°F) rating for the feeder conductor must be used unless all feeder components are rated and listed for use at a higher temperature. If the feeder size is larger than 100A, the 75°C (167°F) rating for the feeder conductor is used unless all feeder components are rated and listed for use at a higher temperature.

For example, if the termination rating on a 125A fuse or circuit breaker is 75°C (167°F), type THHN conductors may be used for the feeder. However, the 75°C (167°F) rating for the conductor must be used. Conductors with higher temperature ratings may be used for ampacity adjustment, correction, or both. As you work through this module, keep in mind that, although type THHN conductors are often used in example problems, the limitations of *NEC Section 110.14(C)* still apply.

Know the Code

Temperature Limitations
NEC Section 110.14(C)

Example:

A 200A feeder is required to serve a new panelboard. The terminals in the panelboard are rated at 75°C (167°F), and the terminals in the fusible switch protecting the feeder are rated at 60°C (140°F). What is the minimum size THHN copper conductor required to supply the panelboard?

Solution:

Per *NEC Table 310.16*, No. 2/0 THHN is rated at 195A, and *NEC Section 240.4(B)* would permit connection to the 200A fuse. Because the fuse terminals are rated at 60°C (140°F), the rating must be taken from the 60°C (140°F) column. The minimum allowable size taken from the 60°C (140°F) column for the 200A load is No. 4/0. Thus, the minimum size is a No. 4/0 THHN copper conductor.

Know the Code

Overcurrent Devices Rated 800 Amperes or Less
NEC Section 240.4(B)

1.2.0 Calculating Feeder Ampacity

Feeder ampacity for single-phase circuits with negligible reactance and a power factor of 1 is calculated by dividing VA by the circuit voltage:

$$I = \frac{VA}{V}$$

For example, the ampacity of a 240V, single-phase load rated at 21,600VA is determined by dividing 21,600VA by 240V.

$$I = \frac{21{,}600\text{VA}}{240\text{V}} = 90\text{A}$$

Feeder ampacity for balanced three-phase circuits (wye or delta with negligible reactance and a power factor of 1) is calculated by dividing VA by the product of the line-to-line circuit voltage and the square root of three (1.732), as follows:

$$I = \frac{VA}{V \times 1.732}$$

For example, the ampacity of a 208V, three-phase load rated at 15,200VA is determined by dividing 15,200VA by the product of 208V and 1.732 as follows:

$$I = \frac{VA}{V \times 1.732}$$

$$I = \frac{15{,}200\text{VA}}{208\text{V} \times 1.732}$$

$$I = 42.19\text{A}$$

The ampacity of a 144 kVA, three-phase load at 480V is determined as follows:

$$I = \frac{VA}{V \times 1.732}$$

$$I = \frac{144{,}000\text{VA}}{480\text{V} \times 1.732}$$

$$I = 173.21\text{A}$$

Example 1:

What is the ampacity of a single-phase resistive load with a nameplate rating of 42.5 kW at 240V?

Solution:

Multiply 42.5 kW by 1,000 to determine VA, since watts and volt-amperes are the same value, and then divide the result by 240V.

First, convert nameplate power rating to VA:

$$42.5 \text{ kW} \times 1{,}000 = 42{,}500\text{VA}$$

Divide by voltage to find the ampacity:

$$I = \frac{VA}{V}$$

$$I = \frac{42{,}500\text{VA}}{240\text{V}}$$

$$I = 177.08\text{A}$$

Example 2:

What is the ampacity of a three-phase panel feeder with a calculated load of 135 kVA at 208V?

Solution:

Multiply 135 kW by 1,000 to determine VA. Then, since this is a three-phase circuit, divide the result by the product of the voltage and the square root of three (1.732).

Convert nameplate power rating to VA:

$$135 \text{ kVA} \times 1{,}000 = 135{,}000\text{VA}$$

Find the ampacity for the feeder:

$$I = \frac{VA}{V \times 1.732}$$

$$I = \frac{135{,}000\text{VA}}{208\text{V} \times 1.732}$$

$$I = 374.73\text{A}$$

Example 3:

What size THWN copper conductors are required to supply the primary of a 75 kVA, three-phase transformer? The primary line-to-line voltage is 480V.

Solution:

Multiply 75 kVA by 1,000 to determine total VA and divide the result by the product of 480V and 1.732 to determine the transformer primary current. Then using *NEC Table 310.16*, determine the conductor size.

Convert nameplate power rating to VA:

$$75 \text{ kVA} \times 1{,}000 = 75{,}000\text{VA}$$

Know the Code

Ampacities of Insulated Conductors with Not More Than Three Current-Carrying Conductors in Raceway, Cable, or Earth (Directly Buried)
NEC Table 310.16

1.3.4 The 100' (30 m) Tap Rule

The 100' (30 m) tap rule is limited to installations in a high-bay manufacturing facility with wall heights over 35' (11 m). *NEC Section 240.21(B)(4)* lists specific conditions for the application of the 100' tap rule. This tap rule may be used in buildings where only qualified persons will service and maintain the systems.

The length of this tap is limited to 25' (7.5 m) horizontally, while the total length of the tap cannot exceed 100'. In addition, the *NEC*® requires that the following conditions be met:

- The ampacity of the tap conductors must be at least one-third the ampacity of the feeder overcurrent protective device.
- The tap conductors must terminate in a single circuit breaker or set of fuses that will limit the load to the conductor ratings.
- The tap conductors must be protected from physical damage and cannot be spliced.
- The minimum size of the tap conductors is No. 6 copper or No. 4 aluminum.
- The tap conductors must not penetrate walls, floors, or ceilings.
- The tap to the feeder must be made at least 30' (9 m) above the floor.

Know the Code

Taps over 7.5 m (25 ft) Long
NEC Section 240.21(B)(4)

1.3.5 Outside Taps of Unlimited Length

NEC Section 240.21(B)(5) states that where the tap conductors are located outside of a building, excluding the point of load termination, there is no limit to their length if all the following conditions are met:

- The conductors are suitably protected from physical damage.
- The conductors terminate in a single circuit breaker or set of fuses that limit the load to the ampacity of the conductors. Additional loads may be supplied from the breaker or set of fuses.
- The overcurrent protective device for the conductors is an integral part of the disconnecting means or is located immediately adjacent to the disconnect.
- The disconnecting means is readily accessible and in one of the following locations:
  - Outside of the structure
  - Inside, nearest the point of entrance of the conductors
  - Where installed in accordance with *NEC Section 230.6*, nearest the point of entrance of the conductors

Know the Code

Outside Taps of Unlimited Length
NEC Section 240.21(B)(5)

Know the Code

Conductors Considered Outside the Building
NEC Section 230.6

1.3.6 Transformer Secondary Conductors

NEC Section 240.21(C) provides the installation and length requirements for the secondary conductors of transformers. Although there are many similarities in these tap rules, there are a few differences.

The 10' (3 m) tap rule for a transformer secondary requires that the ampacity of the secondary conductors be at least 10% of the rating of the overcurrent protective device on the primary side, multiplied by the primary to secondary transformer voltage ratio. To install secondary conductors longer than 10' (3 m) inside buildings, the requirements in *NEC Section 240.21(C)(3)* or *NEC Section 240.21(C)(6)* must be met. The outside taps of unlimited length for transformers are similar to the tap rules discussed in the previous section.

NEC Section 240.21(C)(3) allows secondary conductors from a transformer in lengths up to 25' (7.5 m) in industrial installations only, when the following conditions are met:

- Conditions of maintenance and supervision ensure that only qualified workers service the system.
- The ampacity of the secondary conductors is not less than the secondary current rating of the transformer, and the sum of the ratings of the overcurrent protective devices does not exceed the ampacity of the secondary conductors.

Know the Code

Transformer Secondary Conductors
NEC Section 240.21(C)

- All overcurrent protective devices are grouped.
- The secondary conductors are properly protected from physical damage.

NEC Section 240.21(C)(6) allows secondary conductors from a transformer in lengths up to 25' (7.5 m) when the following conditions are met:

- The ratio of the primary to the secondary voltage is multiplied by one-third the size of the overcurrent protective device protecting the feeder conductors.
- The secondary conductors terminate in a single circuit breaker or set of fuses that limit the load to not more than the conductor ampacity permitted by *NEC Section 310.15*.
- The conductors are properly protected from physical damage.

Know the Code

Ampacity Tables
NEC Section 310.15

1.3.7 Tap Calculations

Example 1:

Using the 10' (3 m) tap rule, what size THWN copper conductors are required for a 40 hp, 460V, three-phase motor load tapped from a 400A feeder when all terminations are marked as suitable for 75°C (167°F) connections?

Solution:

According to *NEC Table 430.250*, the FLA for that motor is 52A. All motor loads are calculated at 125%, so 52A × 1.25 = 65A.

Using *NEC Table 310.16*, determine the THWN copper conductor size needed to supply 65A. No. 6 THWN copper is rated for exactly 65A. Assuming all conditions are met for application of the 10' (3 m) tap rule, No. 6 THWN copper conductors are appropriate.

Know the Code

Full-Load Current, Three-Phase Alternating-Current Motors
NEC Table 430.250

Know the Code

Ampacities of Insulated Conductors with Not More Than Three Current-Carrying Conductors in Raceway, Cable, or Earth (Directly Buried)
NEC Table 310.16

Example 2:

What size THWN copper conductors are required for a 25' (7.5 m) tap supplying a load of 100A from a feeder protected by a 600A overcurrent protective device?

Solution:

To apply the 25' (7.5 m) tap rule, the tap conductors must be rated at least one-third the capacity of the feeder overcurrent protective device.

$$600A \div 3 = 200A$$

The conductors must be rated for at least 200A, even though the load is substantially less. Using *NEC Table 310.16*, determine the THWN copper conductor size. No. 3/0 THWN copper is rated for 200A.

1.4.0 Demand Factors

The total load placed upon certain feeders may be reduced by applying *demand factors*. The *NEC®* permits the reduction of these loads by using the demand factors listed in the following *NEC®* tables and sections for a **dwelling unit** and a non-dwelling unit.

Dwelling unit: A single unit providing complete and independent living facilities for one or more persons, including permanent provisions for living, sleeping, cooking, and sanitation. A *multifamily dwelling* is a building containing three or more dwelling units.

- *NEC Table 220.42(A), General Lighting Loads by Non-Dwelling Occupancy*
- *NEC Table 220.47, Demand Factors for Non-Dwelling Receptacle Loads*
- *NEC Table 220.54, Demand Factors for Household Electric Clothes Dryers*
- *NEC Table 220.55, Demand Factors and Loads for Household Electric Ranges, Wall-Mounted Ovens, Counter-Mounted Cooking Units, and Other Household Cooking Appliances over $1\frac{3}{4}$ kW Rating*
- *NEC Table 220.56, Demand Factors for Kitchen Equipment — Other Than Dwelling Unit(s)*
- *NEC Section 220.82, Dwelling Unit*
- *NEC Section 220.83, Existing Dwelling Unit*
- *NEC Table 220.84(B), Optional Calculations — Demand Factors for Three or More Multifamily Dwelling Units*

*Lighting not used for general illumination. Typical applications are task or display accent lighting.

Figure 2 Basic steps in load calculation.

- *NEC Table 220.86, Optional Method — Demand Factors for Feeders and Service Conductors for Schools*
- *NEC Section 220.87, Determining Existing Loads*

Know the Code

General Loads
NEC Section 220.82(B)

Step 2 Apply the demand factor in *NEC Section 220.82(B).*

First 10 kVA at 100%:

10,000VA × 1 = 10,000VA

Remainder at 40%:

Remainder = 31,818VA – 10,000VA = 21,818VA

21,818VA × 0.4 = 8,727.2VA

Subtotal for general loads:

10,000VA + 8,727.2VA = 18,727.2VA, rounded to 18,728VA

Know the Code

Heating and Air-Conditioning Load
NEC Section 220.82(C)

Step 3 Calculate the demands permitted for electric heating and air conditioning per *NEC Section 220.82(C)*. Use the largest of the calculated demand loads.

Air conditioner at 100%:

6,000VA × 1 = 6,000VA

Central electric heating at 65%:

14,400VA × 0.65 = 9,360VA

9,360VA > 6,000VA

Step 4 Add together the demand for general loads and the largest of the heating or air conditioning loads.

Subtotal general loads = 18,727VA

Largest of heating and AC loads = 9,360VA

Total load = 28,087VA

The minimum size service required for this dwelling is determined by dividing the total VA by the line-to-line service voltage:

28,087VA ÷ 240V = 117.03A, rounded to 118A

The minimum service required for this dwelling would be 125A since it is the next largest standard size.

2.3.0 Calculations for Multifamily Dwellings

The service load for multifamily dwellings is not simply the sum of the individual dwelling unit loads. This is because demand factors may be applied when either the standard calculation or the optional calculation is used, which affect the results.

When the standard calculation method is used to calculate the service load, the total lighting, small appliance, and laundry loads as well as the total load from all electric ranges and clothes dryers are subject to the application of demand factors. Additional demand factors may be applied to the portion of the neutral load contributed by electric ranges and the portion of the total neutral load greater than 200A.

When the optional calculation is used, the total connected load is subject to the application of a demand factor that varies according to the number of individual dwelling units in the structure.

A summary of these two calculation methods for multifamily dwellings and the applicable *NEC*® references are shown in *Figure 7*. The selection of a calculation method is not affected by the method used to select the feeders for the individual dwelling units.

The rules for computing the service load are also used for computing a main feeder load when the wiring system has a service that supplies main feeders that, in turn, supply a number of sub-feeders to the individual dwelling units.

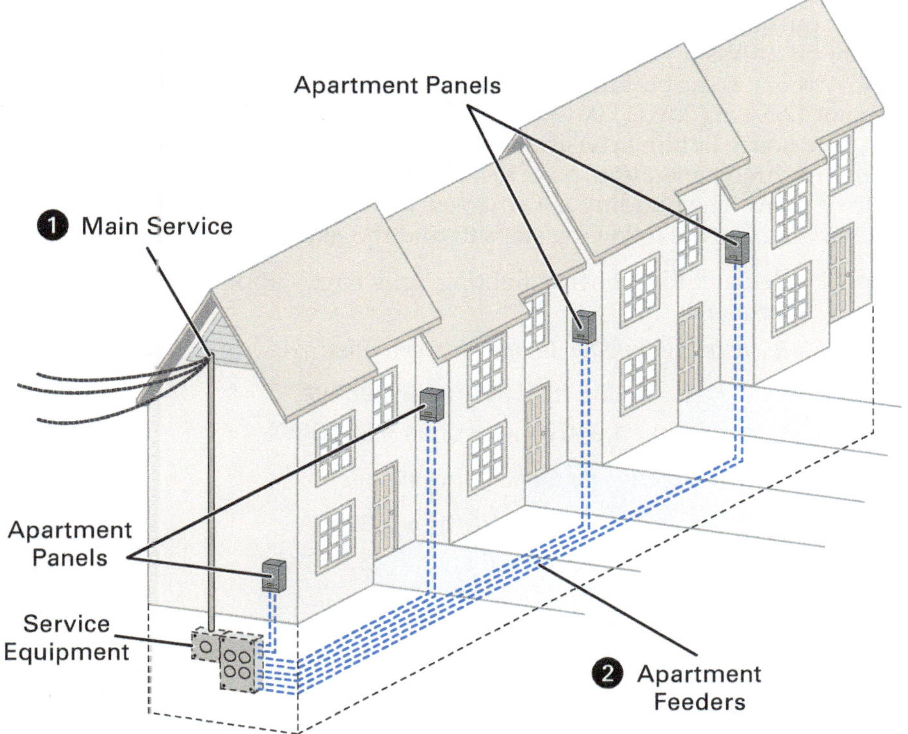

Standard Calculation: Feeder sized per ***NEC Article 220, Part III***

Optional Calculation: Per ***NEC Section 220.84***, if each dwelling unit has:
1. Single feeder
2. Electric cooking equipment
3. Electric space heating

Standard Calculation: Feeder sized per ***NEC Article 220, Part III***

Optional Calculation: Use ***NEC Section 220.84*** if each dwelling unit has a single feeder.

Figure 7 *NEC*® requirements for multifamily dwellings.

2.3.1 Multifamily Dwelling Sample Calculation

A 30-unit apartment building consists of 18 one-bedroom units at 650 ft^2 each, 6 two-bedroom units at 775 ft^2 each, and 6 three-bedroom units at 950 ft^2 each. The kitchen in each unit contains the following:

- 7.5 kW electric range
- 1,250VA dishwasher
- ⅓ hp, 120V garbage disposal at 864VA
- Air conditioning unit rated at 3,600VA

1,500VA × 4 = 6,000VA

Dryers (NEC Table 220.54):

5,000VA (***NEC Section 220.54***) × 4 × 1 = 20,000VA

House lighting:

60W × 40 = 2,400VA

General-purpose receptacles:

180VA × 3 = 540VA

Find the sum of these loads for the total house load.

Total house load = **34,172VA**

Step 7 Determine the largest motor load and multiply the FLA or VA by 25% (*NEC Section 430.24*).

Boiler motor load = 2,880VA × 0.25
Boiler motor load = 720VA

Step 8 Determine the total calculated load.

Net general lighting and small appliance load = 52,988VA
Dishwasher load = 28,125VA
Disposal load = 19,440VA
Range load = 45,000VA
Air conditioning load = 108,000VA
House load = 34,172VA
25% of largest motor load = 720VA

Find the sum of these loads.

Total load = **288,445VA**

Add 25% of continuous loads:

2,400VA (house lighting) × 0.25 = 600VA
Total adjusted load = **289,045VA**

Step 9 Determine the total load current to select service conductors, equipment, and overcurrent protective devices.

289,045VA ÷ 240V = 1,204A

Step 10 Select the service-entrance conductors, **service equipment**, and overcurrent protection. Since the exact calculated load is not a standard size, the rating of the service for this apartment building would be a minimum of 1,600A. This is the next largest standard size and is per-

Know the Code

Demand Factors for Household Electric Clothes Dryers
NEC Table 220.54

Know the Code

Several Motors or a Motor(s) and Other Load(s)
NEC Section 430.24

Service equipment: The necessary equipment, usually consisting of a circuit breaker or switch and fuses and their accessories, connected to the local utility or power provider. The service equipment serves as the primary means of disconnect.

The entire building is heated by a boiler that uses three electric pump motors: a 2 hp squirrel-cage motor and two ½ hp squirrel-cage induction motors. All operate on 240V single-phase, two-wire power supplies. There is a community laundry room in the building with four washers, each of which has a nameplate rating of 12.5A at 120V (1,500VA). There are four clothes dryers rated at 4,500VA each. The house lighting consists of 40 incandescent fixtures rated at 60W each. There are three general-purpose receptacle outlets to support the boilers and laundry room. The building is furnished with a 120/240V, single-phase, three-wire service. Use the following steps to find the required service size:

Step 1 Calculate the general lighting and small appliance loads in each apartment.

General lighting for 18 one-bedroom units:

$$650 \text{ ft}^2 \times 3\text{VA/ft}^2 = 1{,}950\text{VA}$$
$$1{,}950\text{VA} \times 18 \text{ units} = 35{,}100\text{VA}$$

General lighting for 6 two-bedroom units:

$$775 \text{ ft}^2 \times 3\text{VA/ft}^2 = 2{,}325\text{VA}$$
$$2{,}325\text{VA} \times 6 \text{ units} = 13{,}950\text{VA}$$

General lighting for 6 three-bedroom units:

$$950 \text{ ft}^2 \times 3\text{VA/ft}^2 = 2{,}850\text{VA}$$
$$2{,}850\text{VA} \times 6 \text{ units} = 17{,}100\text{VA}$$

Small appliance circuits:

$$1{,}500\text{VA} \times 2 \times 30 \text{ units} = 90{,}000\text{VA}$$

Find the sum of these loads.

$$\text{Total} = 156{,}150\text{VA}$$

Know the Code

Lighting Load Demand Factors
NEC Table 220.45

Step 2 Apply the demand factors using *NEC Table 220.45*. The first 3,000VA is added at 100%. The next 117,000VA is added at 35%, and anything remaining over 120,000VA is added at 25%.

First 3,000VA at 100%:

$$3{,}000\text{VA} \times 1 = 3{,}000\text{VA}$$

Next 117,000VA at 35%:

$$117{,}000\text{VA} \times 0.35 = 40{,}950\text{VA}$$

Remaining 36,150VA at 25%:

$$36{,}150\text{VA} \times 0.25 = 9{,}037.5\text{VA, rounded to } 9{,}038\text{VA}$$

Net general lighting and small appliance load:

$$3{,}000\text{VA} + 40{,}950\text{VA} + 9{,}038\text{VA} = 52{,}988\text{VA}$$

Know the Code

Appliance Load — Dwelling Unit(s)
NEC Section 220.53

Step 3 Calculate the appliance loads using *NEC Section 220.53*.

Dishwashers:

$$30 \times 1{,}250\text{VA} \times 0.75 = 28{,}125\text{VA}$$

Know the Code

General Lighting Loads by Non-Dwelling Occupancy
NEC Table 220.42(A)

Know the Code

General Lighting
NEC Section 220.45

Know the Code

Lighting Load Demand Factors
NEC Table 220.45

The minimum load for general lighting must be compared to the actual installed lighting used within a building, and the larger of the two computations must be used. In most cases, due to energy codes, the installed lighting will generally be lower than that required by *NEC Table 220.42(A)*.

Any loads that are continuous duty are multiplied by 125% to determine the overcurrent protective device and conductor size. All others are calculated at 100%. Noncontinuous loads may have a demand factor applied in accordance with *NEC Section 220.45* and *NEC Table 220.46*.

Example:

Suppose a warehouse building has 57,600 ft² of floor area.

Step 1 From *NEC Table 220.42(A)*:

$$57{,}600 \text{ ft}^2 \times 1.2\text{VA/ft}^2 = 69{,}120\text{VA}$$

Step 2 Apply demand factors per *NEC Table 220.45*.

First 12,500VA at 100%:

$$12{,}500\text{VA} \times 1 = 12{,}500\text{VA}$$

Remaining 56,620VA at 50%:

$$56{,}620\text{VA} \times 0.5 = 28{,}310\text{VA}$$

Find the sum of these loads.

$$\text{Net lighting load} = 40{,}810\text{VA}$$

Know the Code

Show-Window and Track Lighting
NEC Section 220.46

3.1.3 Show Window Loads

NEC Section 220.46(A) requires the lighting load for show window feeders to be calculated at 200VA per linear foot of show window (660VA per linear meter).

Example:

Suppose a show window is 55' in length. What is the feeder load?

Solution:

$$\text{Load} = 55' \times 200\text{VA/linear foot} = 11{,}000\text{VA}$$

NOTE

Remember that any loads that are continuous duty are multiplied by 125% to determine the overcurrent protective device and conductor size. All others are calculated at 100%. Show windows are often considered continuous loads since many remain in use more than three hours at a time.

3.1.4 Track Lighting Loads

Track lighting loads are calculated by allowing 150VA for every 2' (600 mm) of track or fraction thereof. Refer to *NEC Section 220.46(B)*.

Example 1:

The lighting load for 140' of track lighting is determined as follows:

$$140' \div 2' = 70'$$
$$70' \times 150\text{VA} = 10{,}500\text{VA}$$

NOTE

Remember that any loads that are continuous duty are multiplied by 125% to determine the overcurrent protective device and conductor size.

Example 2:

The lighting load of 21' of track lighting is determined as follows:

$$21' \div 2' = 10.5'\text{, rounded to } 11'$$
$$11' \times 150\text{VA} = 1{,}650\text{VA}$$

3.1.5 Outside Lighting Loads

3.1.6 Sign and Outline Lighting Loads

NEC Section 600.5(A) requires that occupancies with a ground floor entry accessible to pedestrians have a 20A outlet installed for each tenant space in an accessible location. This must be a 20A branch circuit that supplies no other load.

NEC Section 220.14(F) states that the load for the branch circuit installed for the supply of exterior signs or outline lighting must be calculated at a minimum of 1,200VA. However, if the actual rating of the sign lighting is greater than 1,200VA, the actual load of the sign must be used.

Know the Code

Required Branch Circuit
NEC Section 600.5(A)

3.2.0 Loads for Retail Stores

Figure 8 shows a small retail store with a show window in front. Note that the storage area has 4 general-purpose duplex receptacles, while the retail area has 14 wall-mounted duplex receptacles and 2 floor-mounted receptacles for a total of 16 in this area. These, combined with the storage area receptacles, bring the total to 20 general-purpose duplex receptacles that do not supply a continuous load. What are the conductor sizes for the service entrance if a 120/240V single-phase service will be used?

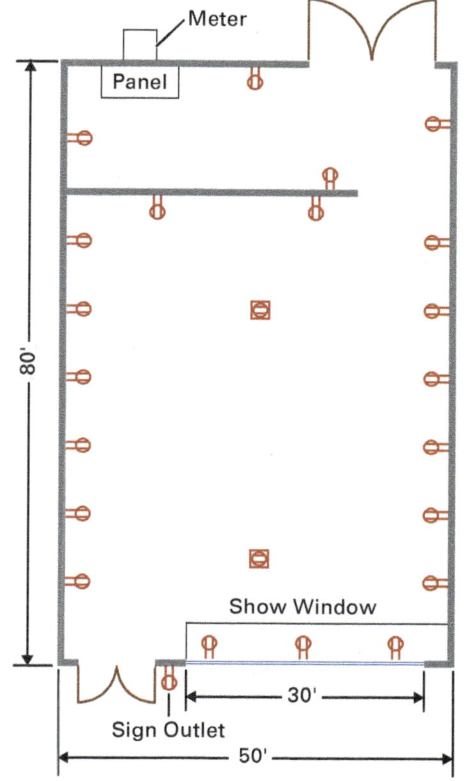

Figure 8 Floor plan of a retail store.

Step 1 Determine the total area of the building by multiplying length by width.

$$50' \times 80' = 4{,}000\ \text{ft}^2$$

Step 2 Calculate the lighting load using *NEC Table 220.42(A)*. According to this table, the load is 1.9VA/ft^2.

$$4{,}000\ \text{ft}^2 \times 1.9\text{VA/ft}^2 = 7{,}600\text{VA}$$

Step 3 Determine the total VA for the 20 general-purpose duplex receptacles.

$$20 \times 180\text{VA} = 3{,}600\text{VA}$$

Step 4 Calculate the load for the 30' of show window based on 200VA per linear foot.

$$30' \times 200\text{VA} = 6{,}000\text{VA}$$

Step 5 Allow one 20A outlet for sign or outline lighting if the store is on the ground floor, per *NEC Section 600.5(A)*. If the actual load of the sign is not known, a minimum load of 1,200VA is used in the calculation per *NEC Section 220.14(F)*.

Step 6 Calculate the total load in VA.

Noncontinuous load:

Receptacle load = 3,600VA

Continuous loads:

Lighting load = 7,600VA
Show window = 6,000VA
Sign = 1,200VA
Total continuous load = **14,800VA**

Calculate at 125% for a continuous load:

14,800VA × 1.25 = 18,500VA

Total load:

Total VA = continuous loads + noncontinuous loads
Total VA = 3,600VA + 18,500VA = **22,100VA**

Know the Code

Ampacities of Insulated Conductors with Not More Than Three Current-Carrying Conductors in Raceway, Cable, or Earth (Directly Buried)
NEC Table 310.16

Step 7 Calculate the current in amperes, which is then used to determine the service size.

22,100VA ÷ 240V = 92A

Consequently, the service-entrance conductors must be rated for no less than 100A. The conductors would be No. 1 AWG copper or No. 1/0 AWG using the 60°C (140°F) column of *NEC Table 310.16* per *NEC Section 110.14(C)(1)(a)* for circuits under 100A.

3.3.0 Loads for Office Buildings

NOTE

The ratings of the service equipment, transformers, and feeders are to be determined, along with the required size of the service grounding conductor. Circuit breakers are used to protect each circuit, and THWN copper conductors are used throughout the electrical system.

A 20,000 ft^2 office building is served by a 480Y/277V, three-phase service. The building includes the following information:

- 10,000VA, 208V, three-phase sign
- 100 duplex receptacles supplying continuous loads rated at 180VA each
- 30' long show window
- 12 kVA, 208Y/120V, three-phase electric range
- 10 kVA, 208Y/120V, three-phase electric oven
- 20 kVA, 480V, three-phase water heater
- Seventy-five incandescent outdoor lighting fixtures at 150W, 120V each
- Two hundred LED lighting fixtures at 125VA input, 277V each
- 7.5 hp, 480V, three-phase motor for fan coil unit
- 40 kVA, 480V, three-phase electric heating unit
- 60A, 480V, three-phase air conditioning unit

A one-line diagram of the electrical system is shown in *Figure 9*. Note that the incoming three-phase, four-wire, 480Y/277V main service terminates into a main distribution panel containing six overcurrent protective devices. Because there are only six circuit breakers in this enclosure, no main circuit breaker or disconnect is required per *NEC Section 230.71(B)*. Five of these circuit breakers protect feeders and branch circuits to 480/277V equipment. The sixth circuit breaker protects the feeder to a 480V to 208Y/120V transformer. The secondary side of this transformer feeds a 208/120V lighting panel with balanced 120V loads.

Start at the loads connected to the 208Y/120V panel and perform the following required steps for calculation:

Know the Code

Two to Six Service Disconnecting Means
NEC Section 230.71(B)

Step 1 Calculate the load for the 100 receptacles.

100 × 180VA = 18,000VA

Apply the demand factor from *NEC Table 220.47*.

First 10,000VA at 100%:

10,000 × 1 = 10,000VA

Remaining 8,000VA at 50%:

8,000VA × 0.5 = 4,000VA

Find the sum of these loads.

Total = **14,000VA**

Know the Code

Demand Factors for Non-Dwelling Receptacle Loads
NEC Table 220.47

Step 2 Calculate the load for the show window using 200VA per linear foot.

200VA/linear foot × 30' = 6,000VA

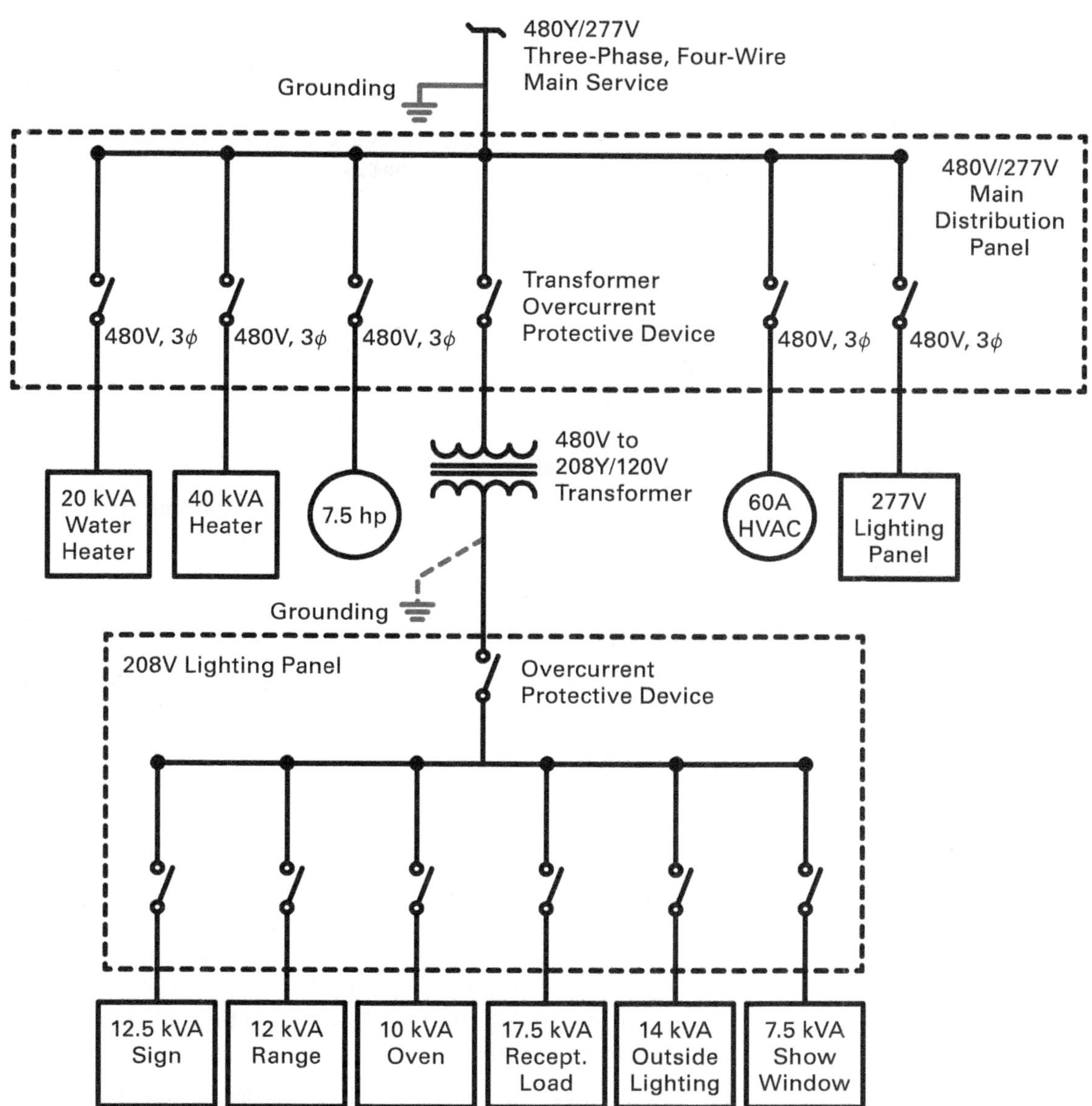

Figure 9 One-line electrical diagram of an office building.

Step 3 Calculate the load for the incandescent outside lighting.

75 × 150VA = 11,250VA

Step 4 Calculate the load for the 10 kVA sign.

10 kVA × 1,000 = 10,000VA

Step 5 Calculate the load for the 12 kVA range (*NEC Section 220.56*).

12 kVA × 1,000 = 12,000VA

Step 6 Calculate the load for the 10 kVA oven (*NEC Section 220.56*).

10 kVA × 1,000 = 10,000VA

Know the Code

Kitchen Equipment — Other Than Dwelling Unit(s)
NEC Section 220.56

Step 7 Determine the sum of the loads on the 208/120V lighting panel.

Noncontinuous loads:

Range = 12,000VA
Oven = 10,000VA
Total noncontinuous load = **22,000VA**

Continuous loads:

Receptacles = 14,000VA
Show window = 6,000VA
Outside lighting = 11,250VA
Sign = 10,000VA
Total continuous load = **41,250VA**

Calculate continuous loads at 125%:

41,250VA × 1.25 = 51,562.5VA, rounded to 51,563VA

Total load:

Total feeder load = continuous loads + noncontinuous loads
Total feeder load = 22,000VA + 51,563VA = **73,563VA**

Step 8 Determine the feeder current rating for the subpanel. Remember that it is a three-phase panel, so the voltage is multiplied by the square root of 3 (1.732).

$$\frac{73{,}563\text{VA}}{208\text{VA} \times 1.732} = 204.19\text{A, rounded to } 204.2\text{A}$$

Step 9 Refer to *NEC Table 310.16* and find that a 4/0 THWN conductor (rated at 230A) is the closest conductor size that will handle the load. A 225A breaker can protect this feeder.

The 208Y/120V feeder is a **separately derived system** from the 480V transformer and is grounded by means of a grounding electrode conductor (*NEC Table 250.66*) that must be at least a No. 2 copper conductor based on the No. 4/0 copper feeder conductors.

Step 10 The transformer is sized to accommodate the calculated load of 73,563VA. Select the overcurrent protective device for the transformer.

$$I = \frac{VA}{V \times 1.732}$$

$$I = \frac{73{,}563\text{VA}}{480\text{V} \times 1.732} = 88.5\text{A}$$

Per *NEC Table 450.3(B)* and because a secondary protective device is used, the maximum setting of the transformer primary overcurrent protective device can be set up to 250% over the current, but no more than that. Thus, its maximum size is calculated as follows with the result rounded down to the nearest whole number:

Maximum OCP = 88.5A × 2.5 = 221A

The secondary protective device maximum setting is 125% of the 208V load. Start by determining the 208V load current:

$$I = \frac{VA}{V \times 1.732}$$

$$I = \frac{73{,}563\text{VA}}{208\text{V} \times 1.732} = 204.19\text{A}$$

Know the Code

Ampacities of Insulated Conductors with Not More Than Three Current-Carrying Conductors in Raceway, Cable, or Earth (Directly Buried)
NEC Table 310.16

Separately derived system: An electrical source, other than a service, having no direct connection(s) to circuit conductors of any other electrical source other than those established by grounding and bonding connections.

Know the Code

Grounding Electrode Conductor for Alternating-Current Systems
NEC Table 250.66

Know the Code

Maximum Rating or Setting of Overcurrent Protection for Transformers 1000 Volts and Less (as a Percentage of Transformer-Rated Current)
NEC Table 450.3(B)

Calculate the secondary protective device at 125% of the 208V load:

$$204.19A \times 1.25 = 255.2375A\text{, rounded down to } 255A$$

The largest permissible standard overcurrent protective device for this current is 250A. If this is used, the feeder conductors would need to be sized for this rating as well, instead of the size determined in *Step 9*.

3.3.1 Calculations for the Primary Feeder

For the feeder calculations, begin with the lighting load. *NEC Table 220.42(A)* requires a minimum general lighting load for office buildings to be based on 1.3VA/ft^2 (14VA/m^2). Since the building has already been sized at 20,000 ft^2, the minimum VA for lighting may be determined as follows:

$$20{,}000 \text{ ft}^2 \times 1.3\text{VA/ft}^2 = 26{,}000\text{VA}$$

The actual connected LED lighting fixture load, however, is as follows:

$$200 \times 125\text{VA} = 25{,}000\text{VA}$$

Since this connected load is less than the *NEC®* requirement, it is neglected in the calculation, and the 1.3VA/ft^2 (14VA/m^2) load value is used instead. Therefore, the total load on the 277V lighting panel can be determined as follows:

$$I = \frac{VA}{V \times 1.732}$$

$$I = \frac{26{,}000\text{VA}}{480\text{V} \times 1.732} = 31.27\text{A}$$

The overcurrent protective device protecting the feeder panel will be sized in accordance with *NEC Section 215.2(A)(1)*.

$$1.25 \times 31.27\text{A} = 39.09\text{A}$$

It would be rated for 40A, the closest standard fuse or circuit breaker size, per *NEC Table 240.6(A)*. However, the smallest main lugs-only panelboard is 125A. A 100A feeder was chosen by the engineer. No. 3 AWG copper or No. 1 AWG aluminum will be used for this feeder.

The feeder load for the water heater in this example is calculated as follows:

$$20 \text{ kVA} \times 1{,}000 = 20{,}000\text{VA}$$

NEC Section 220.51 directs the load on feeders and services for electric space heating to be calculated at 100%. Therefore, the load on the feeder for the heating is calculated at 40 kVA as follows:

$$40 \text{ kVA} \times 1{,}000 = 40{,}000\text{VA}$$

NEC Section 220.50 requires that motor loads be calculated in accordance with *NEC Sections 430.24, 430.25, and 430.26*. Therefore, the FLA of the fan coil motor (11A) taken from *NEC Table 430.250* must be multiplied by 1.25 since this is the largest (and only) motor.

$$11\text{A} \times (480\text{V} \times 1.732) \times 1.25 = 11{,}431.2\text{VA}$$

NEC Section 220.50 requires that hermetic air conditioning compressor motors be sized in accordance with *NEC Article 440, Part IV* and *NEC Section 440.6*. Therefore, the load for the air conditioning unit is calculated and rounded up to the nearest whole number as follows:

$$60\text{A} \times (480\text{V} \times 1.732) = 49{,}882\text{VA}$$

Know the Code

General Lighting Loads by Non-Dwelling Occupancy
NEC Table 220.42(A)

Know the Code

Continuous and Noncontinuous Loads
NEC Section 215.2(A)(1)

Know the Code

Standard Ampere Ratings for Fuses and Inverse Time Circuit Breakers
NEC Table 240.6(A)

Know the Code

Fixed Electric Space Heating
NEC Section 220.51

Know the Code

Motors, Motor Circuits, and Controllers
NEC Article 430

Receptacles

When the number of general-purpose receptacles is unknown, use 1VA/ft^2 (11VA/m^2) for office buildings.

3.3.2 Main Service Calculations

When performing the calculations for the main service, assume that all three-phase loads are balanced and may be calculated in terms of VA or current. Calculation of the load current in amperes simplifies the selection of the main overcurrent protective device and service conductors. A summary of this calculation is shown in *Table 1*.

TABLE 1 Main Service Calculation Example

Type of Load	Calculated Load	Neutral
208/120V system	88.5A	0
277V lighting panel	31.27A	31.27A
Water heater	24A	0
Electric heater (neglected)	0	0
7.5 hp motor	11A	0
Air conditioner	60A	0
25% of largest motor	2.75A	0
Service load	217.52A	31.27A

3.4.0 Loads for Restaurants

The combined load of three or more cooking appliances and other equipment found in a commercial kitchen may be reduced in accordance with *NEC®* demand factors. This provision applies to restaurants, bakeries, and similar locations.

For example, a small restaurant is supplied by a 120/208V, four-wire, three-phase service. The electrical loads include the following:

- 1,000 ft^2 area illuminated by 120V lamps
- Ten duplex receptacles
- 20A, 208V, three-phase motor compressor
- 5 hp, 208V, three-phase roof ventilation fan, running continuously, protected by an inverse time circuit breaker
- More than six units of kitchen equipment with a total connected load of 80 kVA (all units are 208V, three phase)
- Two 20A sign circuits

The main service uses type THHN copper conductors and is calculated as shown in *Figure 10*. Lighting and receptacle loads contribute 30.6A to either phase A or C and 30.6A to the neutral. The 80 kVA kitchen equipment load is subject to the application of a 65% demand factor (per *NEC Table 220.56*), which reduces it to a demand load of 52 kVA. This load requires a minimum ampacity of 144.3A per phase at 208V. The load of the three-phase motors and 25% of the largest motor load bring the service load total to 241.6A for phase A or C and 186A for phase B.

If the phase conductors are three 250 kcmil THHN copper conductors, the grounding electrode conductor and the neutral conductor must each be at least a No. 2 copper conductor.

The fuses are selected in accordance with the *NEC®* rules for motor feeder protection. The ungrounded conductors, therefore, are protected at 300A each.

NEC Section 220.88 allows an optional method for the service calculation of a new or completely rewired restaurant instead of the standard method.

According to *NEC Table 220.88*, add all electrical loads, including heating and cooling loads, to calculate the total connected load. Then select a single demand factor from the column that applies to the total calculated load. Multiply the load by that factor to obtain the total demand load used for sizing the primary feeder or service-entrance conductors.

Know the Code

Demand Factors for Kitchen Equipment — Other Than Dwelling Unit(s)
NEC Table 220.56

Know the Code

New Restaurants
NEC Section 220.88

Know the Code

Optional Method — Permitted Load Calculations for Service and Feeder Conductors for New Restaurants
NEC Table 220.88

Service Loads	Line A, C	Neutral	Line B
Note: Unbalanced loads are calculated entirely on either phase A or C for a worst-case neutral (and conductor) load (*NEC Section 220.61*).			
A. 208/120V loads	15.6	15.6	0
Lighting = $\frac{1.25 \times 1.5\text{VA/ft}^2 \times 1{,}000\text{ ft}^2}{120\text{V}} = 15.6\text{A}$			
Receptacles = $\frac{180\text{VA} \times 10}{120\text{V}} = 15\text{A}$	15	15	0
B. Three-phase loads Kitchen equipment (6 or more units) = $\frac{80{,}000\text{W} \times 0.65}{\sqrt{3} \times 208\text{V}} = 144.3\text{A}$	144.3	0	144.3
C. 20A three-phase motor compressor Dual-element fuse rating = 1.75 × 20A = 35A Use 35A [*NEC Table 430.52(C)(1)*]	20	0	20
D. Three-phase 5 hp fan (16.7A) (*NEC Table 530.250*) Breaker rating = 2.5 × 16.7A = 41.75A Use 45A inverse-trip breaker [*NEC Table 430.52(C)(1)*]	16.7	0	16.7
E. 25% of largest motor load = 0.25 × 20A = 5A	5	0	5
F. Sign circuit = $\frac{1{,}200\text{VA}}{120\text{V}}$ = 10A each × 2 = 20A × 125% = 25A	25	25	0
	241.6A	55.6A	186A

Service Load *NEC Table 310.16* *NEC Table 250.66* *NEC Section 310.15(E)(1)*	1. Conductors: Use No. 250 kcmil THHN copper at 75°C for ungrounded conductors; use No 2. THHN copper conductor for neutral (neutral based on size of grounding electrode conductor).
NEC Section 230.90	2. Overcurrent protective device: Phases A and C = 45A (largest motor device) + 15.6A + 15A + 144.3A + 20A + 25A = 264.9A Use standard size 300A fuses.
NEC Section 240.6(A)	3. Grounding electrode conductor required to be No. 2 copper.

Figure 10 Restaurant service specifications.

3.5.0 Loads for Hotels and Motels

The portion of the feeder or service load contributed by general lighting in hotels and motels without provisions for cooking by tenants is subject to demand factors. In addition, the receptacle load in the guest rooms is included in the general lighting load at 1.7VA/ft^2 (18VA/m^2). However, the demand factor, which represents a load reduction, does not apply to any area where the entire lighting system is likely to be used at the same time, such as the dining room or a ballroom (see the footnote at the bottom of *NEC Table 220.45*).

Example:

Determine the 120/240V feeder load contributed by general lighting in a 100-unit motel. Each guest room is 240 ft^2 in area.

Solution:

The general lighting load is:

$$1.7VA/ft^2 \times 240\ ft^2 \times 100\ units = 40,800VA$$

The demand lighting load per *NEC Table 220.45* is calculated as follows:

First 20,000VA at 60% = 12,000VA

40,800VA – 20,000VA = 20,800VA at 50% = 10,400VA

Total demand lighting = **22,400VA**

This load would be added to any other loads on the feeder or service to calculate the total capacity required.

Know the Code

Lighting Load Demand Factors
NEC Table 220.45

3.6.0 Optional Calculations for Schools

Know the Code

Schools
NEC Section 220.86

Know the Code

Optional Method — Demand Factors for Feeders and Service Conductors for Schools
NEC Table 220.86

NEC Section 220.86 provides an optional method for determining the feeder or service load of a school equipped with electric space heating, air conditioning, or both. This optional method applies to the building load, not to feeders within the building.

The optional method for schools basically involves determining the total connected load in VA, converting the load to VA per square foot or square meter, and then applying the demand factors from *NEC Table 220.86*. If both air conditioning and electric space heating loads are present, only the larger of the loads is to be included in the calculation.

A school building has 200,000 ft^2 of floor area and a 480Y/277V service. The electrical loads are as follows:

- Interior lighting at 1.5VA/ft^2 = 300,000VA
- 300 kVA power load
- 100 kVA water heating load
- 100 kVA cooking load
- 100 kVA miscellaneous loads
- 200 kVA air conditioning load
- 300 kVA heating load

The service load in VA is to be determined by the optional calculation method for schools.

The combined connected load is 1,200,000VA. Note that this excludes the 200 kVA air conditioning load since the heating load is larger. Based on the 200,000 ft^2 of floor area, the load per square foot is determined as follows:

$$\frac{1,200,000VA}{200,000\ ft^2} = 6.0VA/ft^2$$

The demand factor for the portion of the load up to and including 3VA/ft^2 is 100%. The remaining 4.5VA/ft^2 in the example is added at a 75% demand factor for a total load of 1,275,000VA.

$$200,000\ ft^2 \times 1.5VA/ft^2 = 300,000VA$$

$$200,000\ ft^2 \times 3VA/ft^2 \times 0.75 = 450,000VA$$

$$600,000VA + 450,000VA = 1,050,000VA$$

To size the service-entrance conductors, *NEC Section 230.42(A)(1)* must be applied to this demand.

$$1,050,000VA \times 1.25 = 1,312,500VA$$

Know the Code

Continuous and Noncontinuous Loads
NEC Section 230.42(A)(1)

Assuming a relatively short, rigid-conduit overhead service where voltage drop will be negligible, calculate the size of THHW service-entrance conductors as follows for the 480Y/277V, four-wire, three-phase load:

$$\text{Load current} = \frac{1{,}312{,}500\text{VA}}{480\text{V} \times 1.732} = 1{,}578.70\text{A, rounded to } 1{,}579\text{A}$$

NEC Section 240.4(C) requires the conductors to have an ampacity greater than or equal to the rating of the overcurrent protective device when it is rated at more than 800A. The nearest standard rating of a nonadjustable trip overcurrent protective device needed for a 1,579A load is 1,600A, per NEC Table 240.6(A). Therefore, the conductors for this service must have an ampacity of at least 1,600A.

Know the Code

Overcurrent Devices Rated over 800 Amperes

NEC Section 240.4(C)

Because no standard size copper conductor can carry this load, the service will be accomplished by multiple parallel, four-wire runs in separate conduit between the service equipment and the service drop. The desired result is to establish the minimum number of runs with the minimum size of conductors needed to accommodate the load.

To accomplish this, divide the load by a number of different runs and select a wire size from *NEC Table 310.16* that is very close to or exceeds the resulting current load:

$$\text{Option 1} = \frac{1{,}600\text{A}}{3\text{ runs}} = 534\text{A, 1,000 kcmil conductor}$$

$$\text{Option 2} = \frac{1{,}600\text{A}}{4\text{ runs}} = 400\text{A, 600 kcmil conductor}$$

$$\text{Option 3} = \frac{1{,}600\text{A}}{5\text{ runs}} = 320\text{A, 400 kcmil conductor}$$

$$\text{Option 4} = \frac{1{,}600\text{A}}{6\text{ runs}} = 267\text{A, 300 kcmil conductor}$$

Now evaluate the options:

- *Option 1* — Discard it because the large size of the conductors makes them difficult to install and because they provide more capacity than needed.
- *Option 2* — Discard it because of the difficulty of installing this conductor size.
- *Option 3* — This option is a reasonable selection because it meets the load capacity desired with the minimum number of runs.
- *Option 4* — Although this option meets the load requirements, discard it because Option 3 meets the requirement with fewer runs.

The overhead service entrance is therefore minimally sized as five paralleled four-wire runs of 400 kcmil XHHW-2 copper conductor. Type XHHW-2 is selected because it can be used in either wet or dry locations per *NEC Table 310.4(1)*. At this point, if the length of the run had been known, the voltage drop could be checked using the appropriate formula to see if the drop exceeded 2%. If so, the next larger standard wire could be selected instead.

Note that Option 4 with 300 kcmil conductors could be chosen to allow for future needs. Such options may be presented to the client, who can decide if the cost justifies the additional future capacity.

Also note that an alternate solution is to bring a higher line voltage to a small high-voltage substation inside or adjacent to the building. There it could be stepped down to an intermediate voltage and/or then stepped down to 480V and connected directly to switchboard equipment using busbars. This is a fairly common practice, especially in medium-to-large industrial applications.

3.7.0 Shore Power Circuits for Marinas and Boatyards

Know the Code

Marinas, Boatyards, Floating Buildings, and Commercial and Noncommercial Docking Facilities
NEC Article 555

Know the Code

Shore Power Receptacles
NEC Section 555.33(A)

Know the Code

Demand Factors for Shore Power Receptacle Loads
NEC Table 220.120

The wiring systems for marinas and boatyards are designed using the same *NEC*® rules as for other commercial occupancies, except for the application of several special rules dealing primarily with the design of circuits supplying power to boats. They are outlined in *NEC Article 555*.

The smallest sized locking and grounding-type receptacle that may be used to provide shore power for boats is 30A. Each single receptacle that supplies power to boats must be supplied by an individual branch circuit with a rating corresponding to the rating of the receptacle, per *NEC Sections 555.33(A)(3) and 555.33(A)(4)*.

The feeder or service ampacity required to supply the receptacles depends on the number of receptacles and their rating, but demand factors may be applied that will reduce the load of five or more receptacles, per *NEC Table 220.120*.

For example, a feeder supplying ten 30A shore power receptacles in a marina requires a minimum ampacity calculated as follows:

$$10 \times 30A \times 120V = 36{,}000VA$$
$$36{,}000VA \times 0.8 = 28{,}800VA$$
$$28{,}800VA \div 240V = 120A$$

This is the minimum ampacity for the feeder required by the *NEC*® unless individual watt-hour meters are provided for each shore power outlet. These are often added to support billing to individual boat owners for shore power.

3.8.0 Farm Load Calculations

Know the Code

Farm Load Calculations
NEC Article 220, Part V

Know the Code

Agricultural Buildings
NEC Article 547

NEC Article 220, Part V provides a separate method for computing non-dwelling farm loads. Tables of demand factors are provided for use in computing the feeder loads for individual buildings as well as the service load for the entire farm (see *NEC Sections 220.102 and 220.103*). See *NEC Article 547* for specific code requirements for agricultural buildings.

The demand factors may be applied to the 120/240V feeders for any non-dwelling building or load that is supplied by two or more branch circuits. All loads that operate without diversity—that is, the entire load is active at one time—must be included in the calculation at 100% of the connected load. All other loads may be included at reduced demands. The load included at a 100% demand, however, cannot be less than 125% of the largest motor and no less than the first 60A of the total load. In other words, if the nondiverse and largest motor load is less than 60A, a portion of the other loads will have to be included at 100% to reach the 60A minimum.

After the loads from individual buildings are calculated, it may be possible to reduce the total farm load further by applying additional demand factors.

For example, a farm has a dwelling and two other buildings supplied by the same 120/240V service. The electrical loads are as follows:

- *Dwelling* — 100A load per the standard calculation method for dwellings
- *Building No. 1* — 5 kVA continuous lighting load operated by a single switch; a 10 hp, 240V motor; and 21 kVA of other loads
- *Building No. 2* — 2 kVA continuous load operated by a single switch and 15 kVA of other loads

Determine the individual building loads and the total farm load, as illustrated in *Figure 11*. The nondiverse load for Building No. 1 consists of the 5 kVA lighting load and the 10 hp motor for a total of 83.3A. This value is included in the calculation at the 100% demand factor. Since the requirement for adding at least the first 60A of load at the 100% demand factor has been satisfied, the next 60A of the 87.5A from all other loads are added at a 50% demand factor. The remainder of 27.5A is added at a 25% demand factor.

Building No. 1 Feeder Load	**240V Load**	**Neutral**
Lighting (5 kVA nondiverse load) = 5,000VA/240V	20.8	20.8
10 hp motor = 1.25 × 50A	62.5	-0-
Total motor and nondiverse load	83.3	20.8
Other loads = 21,000VA/240V	87.5	87.5
Application of demand factors		
Motor and nondiverse loads @ 100%	83.3	20.8
Next 60A of other loads @ 50%	30.0	30.0
Remainder of other loads (87.5 – 60) @ 25%	6.9	6.9
Feeder Load	**120.2A**	**57.7A**
Building No. 2 Feeder Load		
Lighting (2 kVA nondiverse load) = 2,000VA/240V	8.3	8.3
Other loads = 15,000VA/240V	62.5	62.5
Application of demand factors		
Nondiverse load @ 100%	8.3	8.3
Remainder of first 60 (60 – 8.3) @ 100%	51.7	51.7
Remainder of other loads (62.5 – 51.7) @ 50%	5.4	5.4
Total Farm Load	**65.4A**	**65.4A**
Application of demand factors		
Largest load (Building No. 1) @ 100%	120.2	57.7
Next largest load (Building No. 2) @ 75%	49.1	49.1
Farm load (less dwelling)	169.3	106.8
Farm dwelling load	100.0	100.0
Total Farm Load	**269.3A**	**206.8A**

Figure 11 Summary of farm calculations.

In the case of Building No. 2, the nondiverse load is only 8.3A. Therefore, 51.7A of other loads must be added at the 100% demand factor to meet the 60A minimum.

Using the method given for computing the total farm load, the service load is determined as follows:

Largest load at 100% (Building No. 1) = 120.2A

Second largest at 75% (Building No. 2) = 49.1A

Total for both buildings = **169.3A**

Dwelling = 100A

Total service load = **269.3A**

The total service load of 269.3A requires the ungrounded service-entrance conductors to be at least 300 kcmil THHW copper conductors. The neutral load of the dwelling is assumed to be 100A, which brings the total farm neutral load to 207A.

3.9.0 Motor Circuits

Know the Code

Several Motors or a Motor(s) and Other Load(s)
NEC Section 430.24

Two or more motors may be connected to the same feeder circuit instead of routing an individual circuit to each motor. This saves money and is just as efficient if properly designed. *NEC Section 430.24* covers this type of installation. For two or more motors connected to the same feeder conductors, the rule is to calculate the sum of all motors plus 25% of the largest motor. Note the exceptions in *NEC Section 430.24* regarding motors with duty cycle ratings.

Care must be taken when designing multimotor circuits to prevent several motors from starting at the same time. This would result in a severe voltage drop due to the excessive current that could affect the operation of other equipment or prevent one or more of the motors from starting.

Example:

A 20 hp, 10 hp, and 5 hp motor are connected to the same 208V, three-phase circuit. Determine the total load and minimum size conductors needed to supply these motors.

Know the Code

Full-Load Current, Three-Phase Alternating-Current Motors
NEC Table 430.250

Step 1 Determine the FLA of each motor. Refer to *NEC Table 430.250.*

- 20 hp = 59.4A
- 10 hp = 30.8A
- 5 hp = 16.7A

Step 2 Take 125% of the largest motor FLA.

$$59.4A \times 1.25 = 74.25A$$

Know the Code

Ampacities of Insulated Conductors with Not More Than Three Current-Carrying Conductors in Raceway, Cable, or Earth (Directly Buried)
NEC Table 310.16

Step 3 Add all the loads.

$$74.25A + 30.8A + 16.7A = 121.75A$$

Step 4 Find the minimum size THWN copper conductor from *NEC Table 310.16.* A No. 1 AWG, type THWN copper conductor is rated at 130A and will be suitable for this feeder circuit.

3.0.0 Section Review

1. The feeder load for a show window that is 35' in length is _____.
   a. 3,500VA
   b. 7,000VA
   c. 8,400VA
   d. 10,500VA

2. The general lighting load of a retail store per *NEC Table 220.42(A)* is _____.
   a. 1.2VA/ft^2
   b. 1.9VA/ft^2
   c. 2.2VA/ft^2
   d. 2.6VA/ft^2

3. A 15,000 ft^2 office building has a *minimum* lighting load of _____.
   a. 10,200VA
   b. 19,500VA
   c. 25,000VA
   d. 32,500VA

4. Per *NEC Table 220.56,* the demand factor for eight pieces of commercial kitchen equipment is _____.
   a. 90%
   b. 80%
   c. 70%
   d. 65%

5. The demand lighting load for a 10,000 ft^2 motel with no dining room or ballroom is _____.
   a. 10,200VA
   b. 20,700VA
   c. 26,400VA
   d. 30,200VA

6. A school has a 150 kVA air conditioning load and a 200 kVA heating load. The value to be used when sizing the combined connected load is _____.
   a. the smaller of the two loads
   b. the larger of the two loads
   c. 125% of the larger load
   d. the sum of both loads

7. A feeder supplying six 30A shore power receptacles must have a *minimum* ampacity of _____.
   a. 43,200VA
   b. 34,560VA
   c. 21,600VA
   d. 19,440VA

8. Which of the following is *true* when calculating farm loads?
   a. Only the motor loads are counted.
   b. Only the nonmotor loads are counted.
   c. At least the first 60A must be counted at 100%.
   d. All loads are counted at 75% demand.

9. A 10 hp (30.8A) motor and a 15 hp (46.2A) motor are connected to a three-phase, 208V feeder circuit. The total load is _____.
   a. 77A
   b. 84.7A
   c. 88.55A
   d. 96.25A

Module 26401-23 Review Questions

1. A feeder supplying a lighting and appliance panelboard is sized by adding _____.
   a. 80% of the noncontinuous load and 100% of the continuous load
   b. 100% of the noncontinuous load and 100% of the continuous load
   c. 100% of the noncontinuous load and 110% of the continuous load
   d. 100% of the noncontinuous load and 125% of the continuous load

2. What is the ampacity for each of eight No. 2 THWN copper current-carrying conductors installed in a single conduit?
   a. 57.5A
   b. 80.5A
   c. 91A
   d. 92A

3. What is the rating for a No. 250 kcmil THHN copper conductor in an ambient temperature of 101°F?
   a. 232.05A
   b. 263.9A
   c. 278.4A
   d. 290A

4. What is the rated ampacity per phase for six No. 3/0 THHN copper current-carrying conductors with two conductors per phase (parallel) and all conductors installed in the same conduit?
   a. 280A
   b. 315A
   c. 320A
   d. 360A

5. The voltage drop percentage for a panel feeder with a noncontinuous load of 180A, using 3/0 THWN copper conductors at 480V, three phase, and a length of 248' is _____.
   a. 1.25%
   b. 1.28%
   c. 1.42%
   d. 2.03%

6. What is the required size of THHN copper conductors for a feeder serving two 208Y/120V, four-wire, three-phase, 75°C (167°F) branch circuit panelboards, one with a continuous load of 150A and the other with a noncontinuous load of 180A?
   a. 250 kcmil
   b. 400 kcmil
   c. 500 kcmil
   d. 600 kcmil

7. What is the percentage of voltage drop in a 208V, three-phase feeder serving a 200A load that is 290' away and served by 4/0 THWN copper conductors?
   a. 1.7%
   b. 2.94%
   c. 3.39%
   d. 4.83%

8. For a THHN feeder rated at 225A, which column from *NEC Table 310.16* must be used unless all components in the feeder circuit are rated for a higher temperature?
   a. 60°F
   b. 75°C
   c. 90°C
   d. 140°C

9. What size THWN copper conductors are required to supply a 120/208V, three-phase panelboard with 20.5 kVA of noncontinuous load and 25 kVA of continuous load?
   a. 250 kcmil
   b. No. 1
   c. No. 1/0
   d. No. 4/0

10. What is the load, in amperes, for a single-phase, 240V feeder supplying a load calculated at 23,800VA?
    a. 57.25A
    b. 66.06A
    c. 99.17A
    d. 114.42A

11. What is the load, in amperes, for a three-phase, 208V feeder supplying a load calculated at 96.75 kVA?
    a. 116.37A
    b. 268.56A
    c. 403.13A
    d. 465.14A

12. What is the load, in amperes, for a three-phase, 480V feeder supplying a load calculated at 112.5 kVA?
    a. 135.32A
    b. 312.27A
    c. 468.75A
    d. 540.87A

13. Using the 10' (3 m) tap rule, what size copper THWN conductor is required for a tap from a 400A, 480V, three-phase feeder to serve a 150A load?
    a. No. 1
    b. No. 2
    c. No. 1/0
    d. No. 2/0

14. Using the 25' (7.5 m) tap rule, what is the *minimum* size copper THWN conductor required for a tap from a 400A, 480V, three-phase feeder?
    a. No. 1
    b. No. 2
    c. No. 1/0
    d. No. 2/0

15. What is the *minimum* general lighting load required by the *NEC®* for a single-family dwelling?
    a. $1VA/ft^2$
    b. $2VA/ft^2$
    c. $3VA/ft^2$
    d. $3.5VA/ft^2$

16. The lighting load for dwellings and other *NEC®*-listed occupancies is generally determined by _____.
    a. volt-amperes per square foot
    b. total connected load for the entire building
    c. volt-amperes per linear foot
    d. anticipated connected load for the building

17. Using *NEC Table 220.42(A)*, what is the *minimum* general lighting load required by the *NEC®* for an office building?
    a. $1.2VA/ft^2$
    b. $1.3VA/ft^2$
    c. $1.5VA/ft^2$
    d. $1.6VA/ft^2$

18. When determining the building area for load calculations, building measurements are taken using the _____.
    a. outside dimensions of the building
    b. inside wall dimensions of the building
    c. width and length of each individual room
    d. property line perimeters

19. When both heating and cooling systems are used in a building, which of the following statements is *true*?
    a. The total load for both systems must be combined and then multiplied by a factor of 125%.
    b. The larger of the two loads is used in the calculation.
    c. The smaller of the two loads is used in the calculation.
    d. The total load for both systems must be multiplied by a factor of 150%.

20. When calculating the service size for a single-family dwelling using the standard calculation, what part of the total general lighting and small appliance loads must be calculated at 100%?
    a. First 3,000VA
    b. First 10,000VA
    c. First 15,000VA
    d. First 30,000VA

Answers to odd-numbered Module Review Questions are found in *Appendix A*.

Module 26401-23 Supplemental Exercises

1. Services are frequently sized larger than the required minimum size to account for ________.

2. List four situations in which feeder conductor size is adjusted.

   ____

   ____

3. A continuous load must be multiplied by ________ to determine feeder ampacity.

4. What five conditions must be met for the 10' (3 m) tap rule to be applied?

   ____

   ____

5. What four conditions must be met for the 25' (7.5 m) tap rule to be applied?

   ____

   ____

6. Name two of the applications in which you would not be able to apply a demand factor for a neutral conductor.

   ____

   ____

7. Where in the *NEC®* would you find VA values for determining lighting loads for various occupancies?

   ____

   ____

8. True or False? When calculating the load for the main service, you must include both the heating and air conditioning loads.

9. *NEC Section 230.79(C)* requires a minimum service of ________ for a single-family dwelling.

10. *NEC Section 220.46(A)* requires that the lighting load for show window feeders be calculated at __________ per linear foot of show window.

11. When calculating the lighting load for an office building, you must use 1.3VA/ft^2 (14VA/m^2) or the actual connected load, whichever is the __________.

12. *NEC Section 220.51* permits the load on feeders and services for electric space heating to be calculated at __________.

13. Per *NEC Table 220.56*, a restaurant kitchen with more than six pieces of equipment has a demand factor of __________.

14. The general lighting load in hotel guest rooms is __________.

15. For two or more motors connected to the same feeder conductors, the rule is to calculate the sum of all motors plus __________.

Answers to odd-numbered Supplemental Exercises are found in *Appendix B*.

Answers to Section Review Questions

Answer	Section Reference	Objective
Section 1.0.0		
1. c	1.1.1	1a
2. a	1.2.0	1b
3. b	1.3.4	1c
4. c	1.4.0	1d
Section 2.0.0		
1. c	2.1.1	2a
2. a	2.2.0	2b
3. d	2.3.1	2c
Section 3.0.0		
1. b	3.1.3	3a
2. b	3.2.0	3b
3. b	3.3.1	3c
4. d	3.4.0	3d
5. a	3.5.0	3e
6. b	3.6.0	3f
7. d	3.7.0	3g
8. c	3.8.0	3h
9. c	3.9.0	3i

Section Review Calculations

Section 1.0.0

Question 2

Since this is a single-phase circuit, divide the nameplate power rating by the circuit voltage to find the feeder ampacity.

Convert nameplate power rating to VA:

38.4 kVA × 1,000 = 38,400VA

Divide by voltage to find current:

$I = VA \div V$

I = 38,400VA ÷ 240V = 160A

The ampacity is **160A**.

Question 4

Per ***NEC Table 220.44***:

First 10 kVA at 100% = 10,000VA

Remainder at 50% = 6,400VA × 0.5 = 3,200VA

Net demand load = 13,200VA

The demand load is **13,200VA**.

Section 2.0.0

Question 3

Apply the demand factors using ***NEC Table 220.42***:

First 3,000VA at 100% = 3,000VA

Next 117,000VA at 35% = 40,950VA

Remaining 50,000VA at 25% = 12,500VA

Net general lighting and small appliance load = 56,450VA

The net load is **56,450VA**.

Section 3.0.0

Question 1

Multiply the length of the show window by 200VA:

Load = 35' × 200VA/ft = 7,000VA

The feeder load is **7,000VA**.

Question 3

Since the minimum general lighting load for an office building is 1.3VA/ft^2, multiply the square footage by 1.3VA/ft^2:

Minimum lighting load = 1.3VA/ft^2 × 15,000 ft^2 = 19,500VA

The minimum lighting load is **19,500VA**.

Question 5

Multiply the square footage by 1.7VA/ft^2. Take 60% of the first 20,000VA and 50% of any remainder (no remainder to consider in this example):

1.7VA/ft^2 × 10,000 ft^2 = 17,000VA

Demand lighting load = 17,000VA × 60% = 10,200VA

The demand lighting load is **10,200VA**.

Question 7

Calculate the feeder load and apply the demand factor per ***NEC Table 220.120***:

Gross feeder load = 6 × 30A × 120V = 21,600VA

Net feeder load = 21,600VA × 0.9 (per ***NEC Table 220.120***) = 19,440VA

The minimum ampacity is **19,440VA**.

Question 9

Calculate the total load as follows:

Total load = (largest motor FLA × 1.25) + FLA of all other motor(s)

Total load = (46.2A × 1.25) + 30.8A = 88.55A

The total load is **88.55A**.

User Update

Did you find an error? Submit a correction by visiting **https://www.nccer.org/olf** or by scanning the QR code using your mobile device.

Health Care Facilities

Source: iStock@hxdbzxy

Objectives

Successful completion of this module prepares you to do the following:

1. List the types of health care facilities and their power requirements.
   a. Identify types of essential electrical systems used in health care facilities.
   b. Identify types of distribution systems used in health care facilities.
2. Describe the categories and branch portions of the distribution circuits.
   a. Describe the operation and applications of hospital-grade receptacles.
   b. Identify the receptacle requirements for general care (Category 2) spaces.
   c. Identify the receptacle requirements for critical care (Category 1) spaces.
   d. Identify the grounding requirements for receptacles and fixed electrical equipment.
3. List the required wiring methods in health care facilities.
   a. Identify the wiring requirements for inhalation anesthetizing locations.
   b. Identify the wiring requirements for low-voltage equipment and instruments.
   c. Identify the wiring requirements for diagnostic imaging and treatment equipment installations.
   d. Identify the requirements for communication, signaling, data, and fire alarm systems installed in patient care areas.
   e. Identify the requirements for isolated power systems.

Performance Tasks

This is a knowledge-based module. There are no Performance Tasks.

Overview

In health care facilities, reliable electrical systems and adequate backup power are vital for the safety of patients. For this reason, these systems are strictly regulated in the *NEC*®, as well as in state and local codes. This module covers the installation, alarm system, and backup system requirements of electrical systems in health care facilities, including the requirements for life safety and critical circuits.

NOTE

NFPA 70®, *National Electrical Code*®, and *NEC*® are registered trademarks of the National Fire Protection Association, Quincy, MA.

Digital Resources for Electrical

Scan this code using the camera on your phone or mobile device to view the digital resources related to this craft.

NCCER Industry-Recognized Credentials

If you are training through an NCCER-accredited sponsor, you may be eligible for credentials from NCCER. The ID number for this module is 26402-23. Note that this module may have been used in other NCCER curricula and may apply to other level completions. Contact NCCER at 1.888.622.3720 or go to **www.nccer.org** for more information.

You can also show off your industry-recognized credentials online with NCCER's digital badges. Transform your knowledge, skills, and achievements into badges that you can share across social media platforms, send to your network, and add to your resume. For more information, visit **www.nccer.org**.

1.0.0 Types of Health Care Facilities

Performance Tasks

There are no Performance Tasks in this section.

Objective

List the types of health care facilities and their power requirements.

a. Identify types of essential electrical systems used in health care facilities.
b. Identify types of distribution systems used in health care facilities.

NOTE

This is based on NFPA 70®, *National Electrical Code®* (*NEC®*), and NFPA 99, *Standard for Health Care Facilities*. However, state and local codes vary and may use different standards than those listed here.

Like homes, health care facilities run on electrical power. However, a loss of power at a hospital can result in lost lives. Imagine the impact of an unexpected power failure during a delicate surgery—the loss of electrical service to a health care facility can be devastating.

Severe weather conditions, such as hurricanes, floods, tornados, and earthquakes, can interrupt electrical service. Fires, explosions, and electrical failures in the facility due to shorts or overloads can also prevent the successful transfer of power. A well-planned electrical system is required to prevent or limit the internal disruption of power in these facilities. Loss of power can be corrected in seconds depending on the system employed. Systems should be designed to cope with the longest probable power outage. Safeguards are needed to ensure the proper operation and maintenance of electrical circuitry and mechanical components in vital areas.

In addition to NFPA 70®, *National Electrical Code® (NEC®)*, and NFPA 99, The Joint Commission (TJC) accredits and certifies health care organizations in the United States. The standards for health care facilities are much more rigidly enforced than those for other facilities. This is especially true for fireproofing wall or floor penetrations because patients cannot be evacuated quickly in case of a fire.

TJC inspects each health care facility at the time of occupancy, and then performs an extensive on-site inspection at least once every three years.

Like the NFPA, TJC creates and maintains standards related to emergency electrical power systems in health care facilities. Some of the key TJC standards that apply to these types of power systems include:

- *EC.01.01.01* — Requires health care facilities to have written plans in place that minimize risks in different areas, including utility systems.
- *EC.02.05.01* — Requires health care facilities to manage risks associated with its utility systems.
- *EC.02.05.03* — Requires hospitals to have a reliable emergency electrical power source.
- *EC.02.05.05* — Requires hospitals to inspect, test, and maintain its utility systems.

Always check the most recent national, state, and local codes as well as TJC requirements before beginning any installation.

The installation of electrical systems in health care facilities is governed by *NEC Article 517* and NFPA 99. (*OSHA Standard 29 CFR 1910.307* also applies, but this standard supports the *NEC®*.) *Heath care facilities* are defined as places where medical, dental, or nursing care is provided. These include hospitals, nursing homes, limited care facilities, ambulatory facilities, psychiatric hospitals, dental and medical clinics, and stand-alone day surgery centers. These types of facilities may be permanent construction, such as multilevel hospitals, or movable, such as mobile medical clinics.

To understand the electrical code requirements for health care facilities, it is important to be clear about the definitions for these facilities. The *NEC®* definitions for various facilities are as follows:

- *Ambulatory health care occupancy* — An occupancy used to provide services or treatment simultaneously to four or more patients that provides, on an **outpatient** basis, one or more of the following:
  - Treatment for patients that renders a patient incapable of taking action for self-preservation under emergency conditions without the assistance of others.
  - Anesthesia that renders a patient incapable of taking action for self-preservation under emergency conditions without the assistance of others.
  - Treatment for patients who, due to the nature of their injury or illness, are incapable of taking action for self-preservation under emergency conditions without the assistance of others.
- *Hospital* — A building or portion thereof used on a 24-hour basis for the medical, psychiatric, obstetrical, or surgical care of four or more patients.
- *Limited care facility* — A building or portion thereof used on a 24-hour basis for the housing of four or more persons who are incapable of self-preservation because of age; physical limitation due to accident or illness; or limitations such as intellectual disability, mental illness, or chemical dependency.
- *Nursing home* — A building or portion of a building used on a 24-hour basis for the housing and nursing care of four or more persons who, because of mental or physical incapacity, might be unable to provide for their own needs and safety without the assistance of another person.

Within a health care facility, there are various categories for patient care spaces. A *patient care space* is defined as any portion of a health care facility where patients undergo examination or treatment. Normally, business offices, corridors, lounges, day rooms, dining rooms, and similar areas are not classified as patient care spaces. Patient care spaces include the following:

- *Category 1: Critical care space* — Space in which failure of equipment or a system is likely to cause major injury or death of patients, staff, or visitors.
- *Category 2: General care space* — Space in which failure of equipment or a system is likely to cause minor injury to patients, staff, or visitors.
- *Category 3: Basic care space* — Space in which failure of equipment or a system is not likely to cause injury to patients, staff, or visitors but can cause patients discomfort.
- *Category 4: Support space* — Space in which failure of equipment or a system is not likely to have a physical impact on patient care.

Know the Code

Health Care Facilities
NEC Article 517

Outpatient: A patient who receives services at a hospital but is not admitted for an overnight stay.

NOTE

To qualify as any of the facilities defined here, they must be used simultaneously for four or more patients.

NOTE

In addition to the *NEC®* and NFPA 99, some parts of a health care facility may fall under *IEEE Standard 241, Recommended Practice for Electric Power Systems in Commercial Buildings*.

Hurricane Katrina

After Hurricane Katrina devastated New Orleans, patients and staff in hospitals and other health care facilities suffered through days without electrical power before they were rescued. As a result, The Joint Commission has revised a number of their standards related to electrical power.

Always check the applicable standards for your type of facility before beginning work on a project.

1.1.0 Essential Electrical Systems

In a health care facility, power is divided into two categories: the *nonessential loads* and the *essential electrical system (EES)*. The relationship between these categories is illustrated in *Figure 1*. Nonessential loads are those that are not necessary for the safety of building occupants or for safe and effective patient care. Examples include decorative lighting and televisions. The EES consists of systems or devices that are needed for the safety of all occupants, such as fire alarms, exit lighting, and hallway lighting, and for patient care, such as respirators, cardiac bypass equipment, and suction devices. When the normal electrical source is lost, the facility's alternate source, shown in *Figure 1*, must be able to supply the needs of the EES.

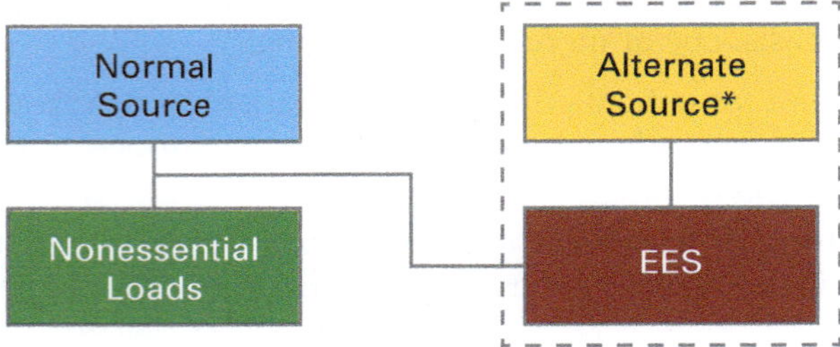

Figure 1 Nonessential and essential loads.

The EES is divided into the equipment branch, the life safety branch, and the critical branch (*Figure 2*). The equipment branch consists of those items that are needed to operate the facility but are not directly related to patient care, such as the facility's telephone system. The life safety branch and critical branch consists of those items that are essential to patient care. The life safety branch supplies power to those items needed to ensure the safety of building occupants as well as patients. These items include exit signs, stairway lighting, alarm system, and communication systems. The critical branch supplies power to areas that are directly related to patient care. These include pharmacies, emergency rooms, intensive care units, and so on.

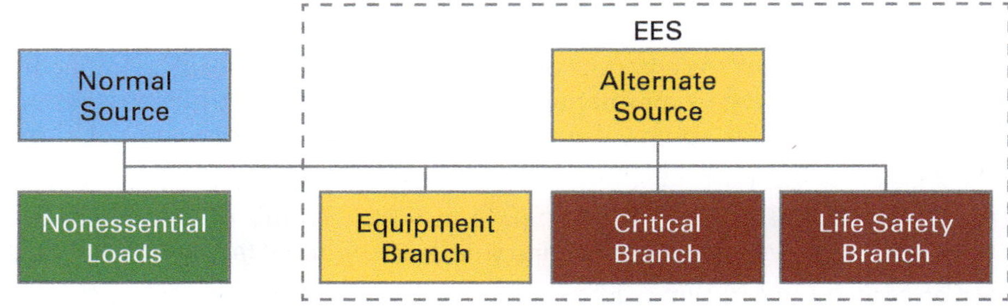

Figure 2 Essential electrical system branches.

The requirements for the EES are based on the care provided at the facility. The levels of EES are Type 1 and Type 2. Type 1 is the most stringent.

Typically, normal power for a system is supplied by electric companies, while an on-site power source (battery system or generators) is used as an alternate power source. Naturally, this depends on the specifics of the health care facility. However, when normal power is from on-site power generators, the alternate power source can be either the utility or other generators. In hospitals, when the normal power for a system is supplied by the utility, a generator is required as the alternate power source. Some facilities that do not admit patients on life support equipment may be able to use battery systems as their alternate power source.

In hospitals and similar facilities, the equipment branch consists of electrical equipment and circuits for three-phase distribution including manual transfer or delayed automatic devices to feed essential equipment loads as described in NFPA 99 and *NEC Section 517.35*. The life safety branch and critical branch includes distribution equipment and circuitry, and the automatic transfer devices needed to transfer from normal power to emergency power. To improve system reliability, each circuit must be installed separately from all other electrical circuits.

The *NEC*® and NFPA 99 both require that the emergency system automatically restore power within 10 seconds of power interruption or loss. These standards also define the electrical loads to be served by the life safety branch and critical branch. In addition, *NEC Section 517.34(A)(10)* allows the installation of additional task illumination, receptacles, and selected power circuits needed for the effective operation of the hospital on the critical branch of the emergency system. This permits some flexibility in customizing the system to fit the needs of the hospital.

Know the Code

Equipment Branch Connection to Alternate Power Source
NEC Section 517.35

Know the Code

Critical Branch
NEC Section 517.34

1.1.1 Type 1 EES

Type 1 EES is required in any facility with a critical care unit or that admits patients requiring electrical life support equipment. Type 1 must automatically restore operation within 10 seconds.

Type 1 EESs for hospitals are made up of three separate branches to supply lighting and power service that has been designated as essential for life safety and effective hospital operation during the time the normal electrical service is interrupted. See *NEC Section 517.31(A)*. These three branches are life safety, critical, and equipment. They are categorized as follows:

- The life safety and critical branches are limited to circuits essential to life safety and critical patient care.
- The equipment branch must supply major electric equipment necessary for patient care and basic hospital operation.

Know the Code

Requirements for the Essential Electrical System
NEC Section 517.31

The number of transfer switches used to transfer power from the normal source to the alternate source is selected based on reliability, design, and load considerations. Each branch of the Type 1 EES must be served by one or more transfer switches, as shown in *NEC Informational Note Figure 517.31(B)(1)*. One transfer switch may serve one or more branches or systems in a facility with a maximum demand on the Type 1 EES of 150 kVA, as shown in *NEC Informational Note Figure 517.31(B)(2)*.

Naturally, this is assuming that the transfer switch has sufficient capacity to serve the combined additional loads and that the alternate source of power is large enough to support the simultaneous transfer of all three branches when normal power is lost.

The life safety branch of a Type 1 EES supplies power for the following equipment, lighting, and receptacles per *NEC Section 517.33*:

- Illumination means of egress
- Exit signs
- Alarm and alerting systems
- Communication systems
- Generator set locations
- Elevators
- Automatic doors

Know the Code

Life Safety Branch
NEC Section 517.33

The critical branch of a Type 1 EES may consist of one or more branches that are designed to serve a limited number of receptacles and locations to reduce the load demand and the chances of a fault condition. Receptacles in general patient care corridors are allowed on the critical branch. However, they must be identified as part of the critical branch (either labeled or color coded) and indicate panelboard and circuit number in compliance with NFPA 99 and *NEC Section 517.18(A)*.

Per *NEC Section 517.34(A)*, the critical branch of the EES supplies power for task illumination, fixed equipment, selected receptacles, and special power circuits feeding the following locations and functions related to patient care:

- Critical care (Category 1) spaces that use anesthetizing gases: task illumination, selected receptacles, and fixed equipment
- Task illumination and selected receptacles in patient care areas, medication preparation areas, pharmacy dispensing areas, and nurses' stations (unless adequately lighted by corridor luminaires). Examples of patient care areas include infant nurseries, selected acute nursing areas, psychiatric bed areas (omit receptacles), ward treatment rooms
- Additional specialized patient care task illumination and receptacles, where needed
- Nurse call systems
- Blood, bone, and tissue banks
- Telecommunications equipment rooms and closets
- Task illumination, selected receptacles, and selected power circuits for general care beds (at least one duplex receptacle per patient bedroom), angiographic labs, cardiac catheterization labs, coronary care units, hemodialysis rooms or areas, emergency room treatment areas (selected), human physiology labs, intensive care, and postoperative recovery rooms (selected)
- Clinical IT-network equipment
- Wireless phone and paging equipment for clinical staff communication
- Additional task illumination, receptacles, and selected power circuits needed for effective hospital operation

Know the Code

Category 2 Spaces
NEC Section 517.18

CAUTION

Equipment to transfer patient corridor lighting from general illumination circuits to night illumination circuits is allowed as long as only one of two circuits can be selected, and both circuits cannot be off at the same time.

NOTE

Single-phase fractional horsepower exhaust fan motors that are interlocked with three-phase motors on the equipment may be connected to the critical branch, per ***NEC Section 517.34(A)(10)***.

Inpatient: A patient admitted into the hospital for an overnight stay.

1.1.2 Type 2 EES

Many nursing homes and limited care facilities require Type 2 EESs. These facilities do not have critical care and intensive care units, but they do provide patient care that is equivalent to hospital **inpatient** care. Therefore, the branches of the emergency system in Type 2 EES are similar to Type 1.

NFPA 99 requires an alternate source of power for any health care facilities where patients are treated in primarily the same manner as in hospitals, even though the facility may not be designated a hospital. Nursing homes and limited care facilities that are adjoining a hospital may use the EESs supplied by the hospital, but both facilities must have their own transfer devices.

EESs for limited care facilities and nursing homes must have two separate branches that are able to supply the lighting and power required for the protection of life safety and the effective operation of the facility during the interruption of normal electrical service. These two branches are the life safety branch and the equipment branch. The number of transfer switches used is based on reliability, design, and load considerations. Every branch of the Type 2 EES must be served by one or more transfer switches as shown in *NEC Informational Note Figure 517.42(B)(1)*. A single transfer switch will serve one or more branches or systems in a facility with a maximum demand on the Type 2 EES of 150 kVA, as shown in *NEC Informational Note Figure 517.42(B)(2)*.

The life safety and equipment branches must be completely independent of all other equipment and wiring. These circuits cannot enter the same cabinets, boxes, or raceways with other wiring except in transfer switches or in exit or emergency lighting fixtures (or their attached junction boxes), as long as the fixtures are supplied from two sources. See *NEC Section 517.42(D)*.

Know the Code

Essential Electrical Systems for Nursing Homes and Limited Care Facilities
NEC Section 517.42

The life safety branch must be installed and connected to the alternate power source so that designated functions are automatically restored to operation within 10 seconds after interruption of the normal source. The life safety branch supplies power for the following equipment, lighting, and receptacles:

- Communication systems, where used for dissemination of instructions during emergencies
- Task illumination battery chargers for emergency battery-powered lighting units and selected receptacles at the generator set location
- Illumination of exits, such as lighting required for corridors, passageways, stairways, landings at exit doors, and all approaches to exits
- Exit direction and exit signs
- Alarm and alerting systems, including fire alarms and alarms required for systems used for the piping of nonflammable medical gases
- Elevator cab communication, control, lighting, and signal systems
- Lighting in recreation and dining areas must be sufficient to illuminate exits

CAUTION

No function other than those listed above may be connected to the life safety branch.

The equipment branch must be installed and connected to the alternate power source so that the equipment listed in *NEC Section 517.44(A)* is automatically restored to operation at appropriate time lag intervals following the restoration of the life safety branch to operation. Its arrangement must also provide for the additional connection of equipment listed in *NEC Section 517.44(B)* by either delayed automatic or manual operation.

Know the Code

Connection to Equipment Branch
NEC Section 517.44

The following equipment may be connected to the equipment branch and arranged for delayed automatic connection to the alternate power source:

- Task illumination and selected receptacles in patient care spaces, medication preparation areas, pharmacy dispensing areas, and nurses' stations unless adequately lighted by corridor luminaires
- Sump pumps and other equipment required to operate for the safety of major apparatus and associated control systems and alarms
- Smoke control and stair pressurization systems
- Kitchen hood supply and/or exhaust systems, if required to operate during a fire in or under the hood
- Supply, return, and exhaust ventilating systems for airborne infectious isolation rooms
- Nurse call systems

Know the Code

Automatic Connection to Life Safety and Equipment Branch
NEC Section 517.43

According to *NEC Section 517.44(B)*, the following equipment may be connected to the equipment branch and arranged for *either* delayed automatic *or* manual connection to the alternate power source:

- Equipment to provide heating for patient rooms, except where:
  - The outside design temperature is higher than 20°F (–6.7°C).
  - The outside design temperature is lower than 20°F (–6.7°C), but selected areas are heated for the comfort of all confined patients.
  - The facility is served by a dual source of normal power.
- In instances in which disruption of power would result in elevators stopping between floors, **throwover** (transfer) switches must be provided to allow temporary operation of any elevator for the release of passengers. For elevator cab lighting, control, and signal system requirements, see *NEC Section 517.43(F)*.
- Additional illumination, receptacles, and equipment may be connected only to the equipment branch.

Throwover: A transfer switch used for supplying temporary power.

Where one switch serves multiple systems as permitted in *NEC Section 517.43*, transfer for all loads must be nondelayed and automatic. Limited care facilities and nursing homes that furnish inpatient critical care must comply with the requirements of *NEC Sections 517.29 and 517.30*. Regardless of how the facility is classified, the category of electrical system will depend on the type of patient care. Where the care type is evidently inpatient hospital care, a hospital-type electrical system must be installed.

Know the Code

Type 1 Essential Electrical Systems
NEC Section 517.29

Nursing homes and limited care facilities that are contiguous with or located on the same site as a hospital may have their EESs supplied by that of the hospital. Where a limited care facility or nursing home is in the same building with a hospital, the nursing home is not required to have its own EES if it gets its power from the hospital. This rule does not allow sharing of transfer devices.

1.1.3 Other Health Care Facilities

In facilities that do not require a Type 1 or Type 2 EES, emergency power may be provided by batteries in accordance with *NEC Section 700.12(C)(4)*. Batteries are required to maintain the emergency load for $1\frac{1}{2}$ hours without the voltage falling below 87.5% of normal.

Know the Code

Storage Batteries and UPS
NEC Section 700.12(C)(4)

1.2.0 Electrical Distribution Systems

Providing a health care facility with reliable electrical power begins with careful system design followed by proper installation. To ensure continuous electrical service from the utility provider, hospitals and certain other health care facilities are placed on a spot network. Spot networks are considered the most reliable and flexible arrangement. Ideally, the feeders used in a spot network are installed in parallel so that a fault in one feeder will not affect or produce faults in another. Each **feeder** must be sized to carry the full load of the system. This type of installation helps to ensure an adequate amount of power during high use periods.

Feeder: A conductor that is not a service or branch circuit conductor and is located after the main disconnect switch but before the final branch circuit overcurrent device.

1.2.1 Double-Ended System

A double-ended substation is typically used when transformation over 750 kVA is needed. The substation shown in *Figure 3* uses a normally open (NO) tie circuit breaker interlocked with the mains circuit breakers so that not all three can be closed simultaneously. When a single mains feeder has loss, the tie circuit breaker may be closed, manually or automatically, placing additional load on the remaining feeder. The substation feeders and equipment can be medium-voltage or low-voltage equipment to reduce current rating requirements. In either case, each of the utility feeders and circuit breakers used must be rated to carry the full load of the facility in the event that one of the mains sources is lost. Double-ended substations have additional benefits, such as lower fault current and the ability to differentiate between motor loads that require specific voltage regulation.

If the double-ended substation design uses an NO, electrically operated tie circuit breaker that automatically closes upon loss of either of the incoming mains feeders, then control and protective relaying must be added to prevent the bus tie circuit breaker from closing when a mains circuit breaker has tripped due to overload or short circuit conditions.

Utility companies may allow double-ended substations to operate with a closed tie and mains circuit breakers. Double-ended substations with mains and normally closed (NC) ties have distinct advantages such as better voltage regulation, transfer capabilities when power loss occurs, immediate switching when a power source is lost, and greater reliability of system operation. However, the disadvantages are greater fault current, greater cost, and a more complex design. The decision to use a closed tie is made by the designer of the system.

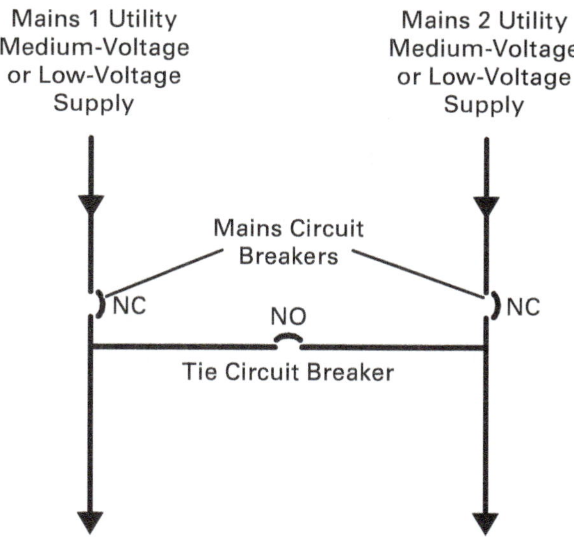

Figure 3 Double-ended substation.

1.2.2 Alternate Power Source

For a Type 1 or Type 2 EES, one or more diesel engine generators are normally used (*Figure 4*). In cases in which multiple generators are used, one is a designated backup generator. Generators may be housed internally or externally to the health facility. If housed in a nonheated environment where temperatures fall below about 30°F (–1.1°C), the starting batteries must be heated and cold-weather diesel engine starting equipment must be used in order to meet the 10-second startup requirement for restoration of power. *Figure 5* is a schematic diagram showing the arrangement of an alternate power source with transfer switching for an EES. As noted in the figure, delayed switching of the EES equipment system may be used if the alternate power source cannot tolerate the total EES load at startup.

Figure 4 Typical diesel engine generator.
Source: Tri-City Electrical Contractors Inc

Code Blue

Sometimes communication systems are used to call a code blue alarm. When a code blue is called, trained staff responds with a crash cart, which contains special equipment and medication used to revive a patient whose heart has stopped beating. Some hospitals use a wall-mounted alarm device such as the one shown here. It is included in the life safety branch of a Type 1 EES.

Source: Tektone

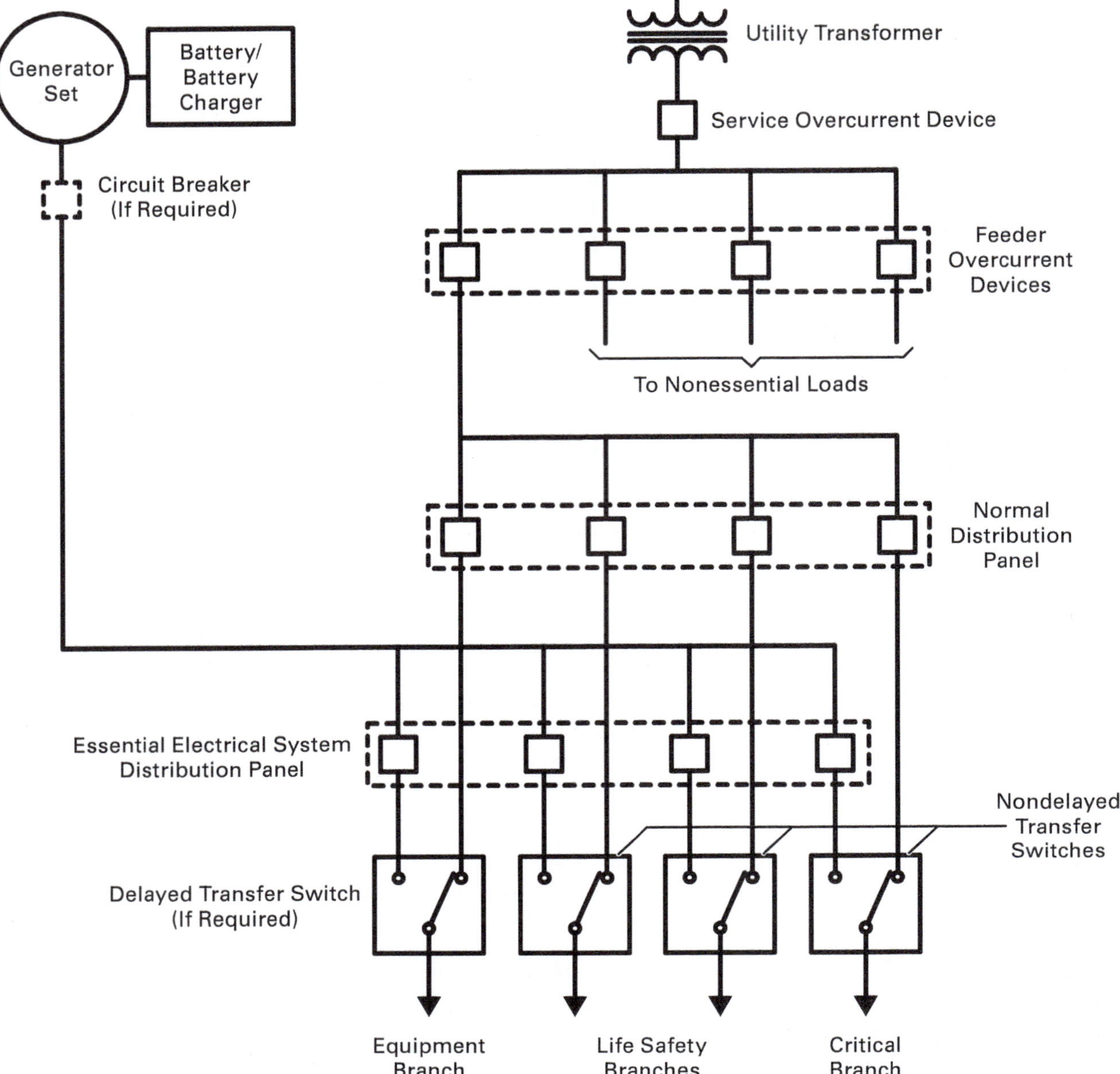

Figure 5 Schematic diagram of an alternate power source with transfer switching for an EES.

1.2.3 Ground Fault Protection

Phase overcurrent device settings are primarily established by the load requirements. They are set to be insensitive to full-load and inrush current and to provide selectivity between downstream and upstream devices. However, phase overcurrent devices cannot distinguish between normal load current and a low-magnitude ground fault short circuit current of the same magnitude. For this reason, ground fault detection is used in addition to the phase overcurrent devices to provide protection.

NEC Sections 215.10 and 230.95 describe requirements for ground fault protection at the feeder. In health care facilities, additional ground fault protection may be required downstream. *NEC Section 517.17(B)* requires two levels of ground fault protection in health care facilities to improve the selectivity between the feeder and building devices. The wiring configuration and estimated ground currents must be carefully analyzed before selecting appropriate ground fault protective devices.

Know the Code

Ground-Fault Protection of Equipment
NEC Section 215.10

Know the Code

Ground-Fault Protection of Equipment
NEC Section 230.95

Know the Code

Ground-Fault Protection of Equipment
NEC Section 517.17

1.2.4 Additional Grounding and Bonding Requirements

Besides the usual grounding and bonding required by *NEC Article 250*, health care facilities require additional precautions for patient care spaces. As specified in *NEC Section 517.14*, where branch circuit panelboards for normal and essential power serve the same patient care vicinity, they must be connected with an insulated continuous copper conductor no smaller than No. 10 AWG. In addition, where two or more panelboards that serve the same patient care vicinity are served from two different transfer switches, their equipment grounding terminals must be connected with an insulated continuous conductor no smaller than No. 10 AWG.

When feeder metal raceway or Type MC or MI cable that qualifies as an equipment grounding conductor, per *NEC Section 250.118*, is installed in a grounded electrical distribution system as specified in *NEC Section 517.19(E)*, the grounding of a panelboard or switchboard must be ensured by one of the following:

- A grounding bushing and continuous copper bonding jumper properly sized, with the jumper connected to either the junction enclosure or ground bus of the panel
- Feeder raceways or Type MC or MI cable connected to threaded hubs or bosses on the terminating enclosures
- Other approved devices

Know the Code

Grounding and Bonding
NEC Article 250

Know the Code

Panelboard Bonding
NEC Section 517.14

Know the Code

Types of Equipment Grounding Conductors
NEC Section 250.118

Know the Code

Category 1 Spaces
NEC Section 517.19

1.0.0 Section Review

1. The essential electrical system used in a limited care facility is a Type _____.
   a. 0 EES
   b. 1 EES
   c. 2 EES
   d. 3 EES

2. Ground fault detection is used in addition to the phase overcurrent devices to provide protection against _____.
   a. inrush current
   b. full-load current
   c. low-magnitude ground fault short circuit current
   d. high-magnitude ground fault short circuit current

2.0.0 Devices Used in Health Care Facilities

Objective

Describe the categories and branch portions of the distribution circuits.

a. Describe the operation and applications of hospital-grade receptacles.
b. Identify the receptacle requirements for general care (Category 2) spaces.
c. Identify the receptacle requirements for critical care (Category 1) spaces.
d. Identify the grounding requirements for receptacles and fixed electrical equipment.

Performance Tasks

There are no Performance Tasks in this section.

Generally, hospitals have two sources of available power: normal and emergency. Devices on emergency power must be easy to identify. This reduces the time wasted in locating receptacles during a power outage. These devices may be identified with a distinctive color such as red, or by labeling. (When color coding is used, it must be the same throughout the facility.) Color coding is easier and less expensive than labeling, and it may prevent later confusion.

For example, if painters remove the labeled cover plates, there is no longer a distinction between devices. In addition, since receptacles in critical care spaces must have panelboard and circuit number labels, the device cover plates tend to become cluttered. *Figure 6* shows an example of color coding used to identify various circuits in a patient headwall. Lighted emergency power receptacles are useful in patient areas that do not have emergency lighting because they make the receptacle easier to locate in the near-darkness of a power outage.

Devices in a hospital should be mounted so they are easy to use. Because a large number of hospital patients spend time in wheelchairs, particular attention should be given to these requirements. All receptacles should be mounted approximately 24" (600 mm) above the floor for the convenience of patients and staff. Always refer to the job plans and specifications.

Figure 6 Example of circuit color coding for a headwall.
Source: Tri-City Electrical Contractors Inc

2.1.0 Hospital-Grade Receptacles

Know the Code

Health Care Facilities
NEC Article 517

Hospital-grade receptacles (*Figure 7*) are listed as suitable for use in health care facilities. Per *NEC Article 517*, health care facilities include (but are not limited to) hospitals, nursing homes, limited care facilities, clinics, medical and dental offices, and ambulatory care centers, whether permanent or movable. Hospital-grade receptacles are often marked with a green dot on the outer face.

Hospital-grade receptacles meet nationally recognized testing laboratory criteria for superior electrical characteristics and mechanical strength. This is needed in a medical environment to ensure that equipment plugs fit tightly into the receptacles and the receptacles are durable.

2.1.1 Isolated Ground Receptacles

Isolated ground receptacles are used where separation of the device ground and the building ground is desired. They are normally used with digital electronic equipment, including computer cash registers, computer peripherals, and digital processing equipment. They prevent transient voltages on the ground system from causing malfunctions in digital circuits. Isolated ground receptacles must not be installed in a patient care vicinity according to *NEC Section 517.16(A)*.

Know the Code

Use of Isolated Ground Receptacles
NEC Section 517.16

Figure 7 Hospital-grade receptacles.
Source: Legrand

2.1.2 Tamper-Resistant Receptacles

Tamper-resistant receptacles prevent foreign objects from coming into contact with energized components inside the receptacle by only operating when both the hot and neutral blades of a plug are simultaneously inserted. These receptacles must be used throughout psychiatric and designated general care pediatric locations. When choosing tamper-resistant receptacles, be careful not to use the type that makes and breaks contacts where life support apparatus may be required.

2.2.0 General Care (Category 2) Spaces

It is difficult to prevent a conductive path from a grounded object to a patient's body in a health care facility. The path may be created accidentally or through instruments directly connected to the patient that act as a source of electric current. This hazard worsens as more equipment is used near a patient, such as in surgical suites and intensive care units. Methods of reducing the likelihood of electric shock to a patient include the following:

- Increasing the resistance of the conductive circuit that includes the patient
- Insulation of exposed surfaces that may become energized
- Lowering the potential difference between exposed conductive surfaces in the patient's vicinity
- Using a combination of the above methods

NEC Section 517.18(A) requires that every patient bed location be supplied with at least two branch circuits, one from the normal system and the other from the critical system. Additionally, any branch circuits from the normal system must originate in the same panelboard. The branch circuit serving patient bed locations cannot be part of a multiwire branch circuit. The *NEC*® lists four exceptions to this requirement:

- Branch circuits that serve only special-purpose outlets or receptacles are not required to be served from the same panels.
- Patient beds located in clinics; medical and dental offices; outpatient facilities; psychiatric, substance abuse, and rehabilitation hospitals; nursing homes; and limited care facilities meeting the requirements of *NEC Section 517.10(B)(2)*, are exempt from this requirement.
- A general care (Category 2) patient bed location served from two separate transfer switches on the emergency system is not required to have circuits from the normal system.
- Circuits served by Type 2 EESs can be fed by the equipment branch of the EES.

Know the Code

Category 2 Spaces
NEC Section 517.18

Know the Code

Applicability
NEC Section 517.10

In addition to two branch circuits, each patient bed location must have a minimum of eight receptacles, per *NEC Section 517.18(B)(1)*. Receptacles may be of the single, duplex, or quadruplex types, or any combination of the three. Some receptacles are supplied as part of a prefabricated patient headwall unit, as shown in *Figure 8*. All receptacles must be hospital grade and grounded by means of an insulated copper equipment grounding conductor sized in accordance with *NEC Table 250.122*.

NEC Section 517.18(C) requires that all receptacles meant to supply designated general care (Category 2) pediatric locations or spaces (bathrooms, playrooms, activity rooms, and patient care spaces) must be tamper-resistant or use a tamper-resistant cover.

Know the Code

Minimum Size Equipment Grounding Conductors for Grounding Raceway and Equipment
NEC Table 250.122

NOTE

This does not apply to psychiatric, substance abuse, and rehabilitation hospitals meeting the requirements of *NEC Section 517.10(B)(2)*. In addition, psychiatric security rooms are not required to have receptacle outlets. *NEC Section 517.19(D)* requires that an equipment bonding jumper no smaller than No. 10 AWG be used to connect the grounding terminal of all grounding-type receptacles of a patient headwall to the patient grounding point, if provided.

(A) Receptacles above Bed

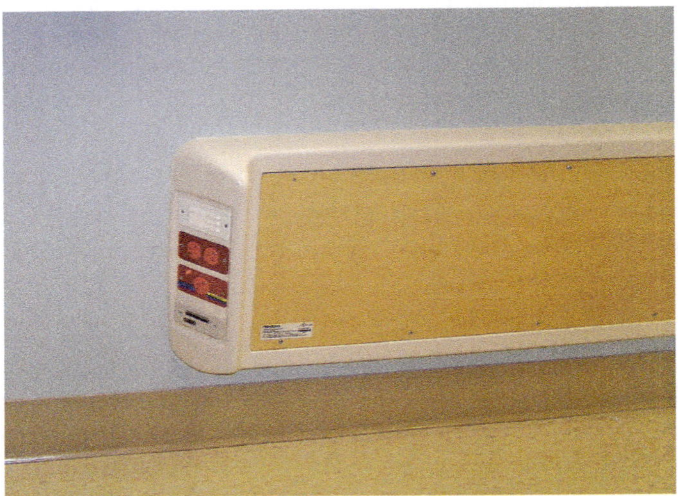

(B) Receptacles behind Bed

Figure 8 Patient bed location receptacles.
Source: Tri-City Electrical Contractors Inc

Patient Headwall Column

This patient headwall column supplies both an oxygen line and electrical power. This combination requires the use of a protective bollard to guard it against damage. When devices are combined in an assembly such as the one shown in the image, a nationally recognized testing laboratory may be required to come in and label the entire assembly. Check with the Authority Having Jurisdiction (AHJ) in your area.

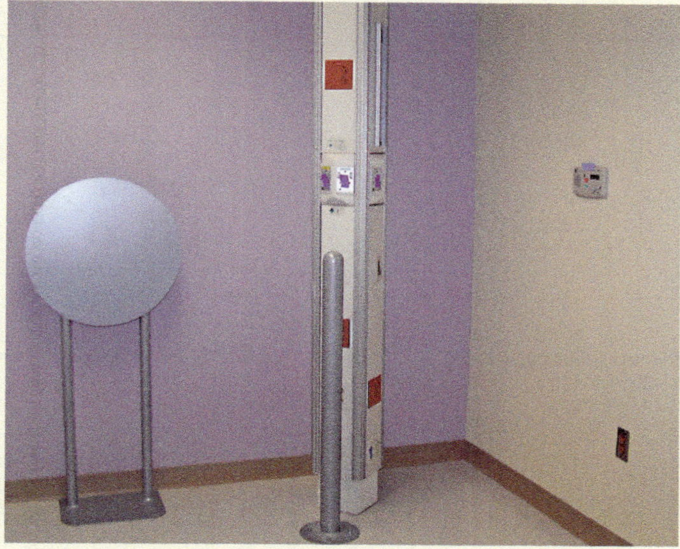

Source: Tri-City Electrical Contractors Inc

2.3.0 Critical Care (Category 1) Spaces

NEC Section 517.19(A) requires that every patient bed location in critical care spaces be supplied by at least two branch circuits, one or more from the normal system and one or more from the critical branch so that patients will have access to electrical power even when there is a fault. At least one branch circuit from the critical branch must supply an outlet only at that bed location. All branch circuits from the normal system must be from a single panelboard. Critical branch receptacles must be identified as such and labeled with the supply panelboard and circuit number. The branch circuit serving patient bed locations shall not be part of a multiwire branch circuit.

NEC Section 517.19(B)(1) requires that each patient bed location in a critical care space be provided with a minimum of 14 receptacles, with at least one of them connected to the normal system branch circuit required in *NEC Section 517.19(A)* or a critical branch circuit supplied by a different transfer switch than the other receptacles at the same location. According to *NEC Section 517.19(C)*, every operating room must have 36 receptacles with at least 12 (but not more than 24) connected to the normal or critical branch. They may be of the single, duplex, or quadruplex types, or any combination. All receptacles must be listed as hospital grade and connected to the reference grounding point by means of an insulated copper equipment grounding conductor.

A typical receptacle configuration in a critical care space is shown in the diagram in *Figure 9*. The normal circuits must be supplied from the same panel (L-1). The critical branch circuits may be supplied from different panels (EML-1 and EML-2). However, the critical branch circuit to patient bed location A cannot supply critical branch receptacles for patient bed location B.

Know the Code

Category 1 Spaces
NEC Section 517.19

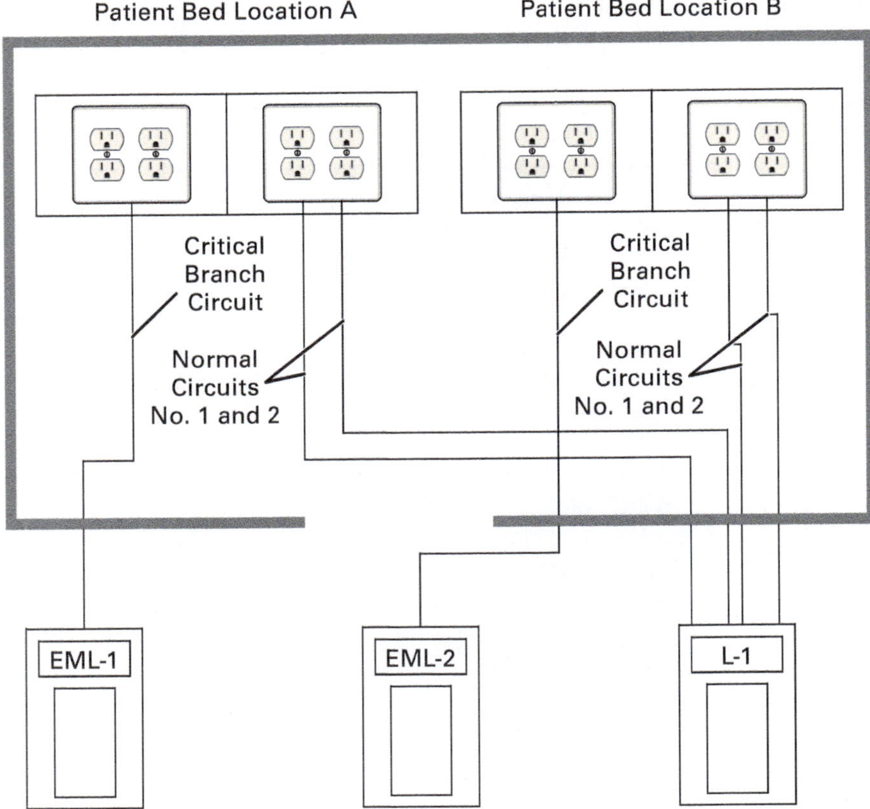

Figure 9 Typical receptacle configuration in a critical care space.

The required power level for each bedside is typically 90VA for single-outlet receptacles and 180VA for duplex receptacles. The following recommendations are for bedside stations:

- Use only hospital-grade permissible power connectors.
- Use no less than two duplex outlets on each side of the patient's bed. The outlets must be protected by overcurrent protective devices in accordance with the *NEC*®.
- Furnish power outlets within a few feet of the junction boxes and equipment support locations.
- Allocate a grounding system in accordance with NFPA 99 and the *NEC*®.
- Plan and design the system to keep power cables to a minimum length. This contributes both to physical and electrical safety.
- Ensure adequate ventilation in all areas where patient monitoring equipment is to be installed.

NOTE

Branch circuits serving only special-purpose receptacles or equipment in critical care spaces may be served by other panelboards. Also, when the location is served by two individual transfer switches on the emergency system, it does not require a branch on the normal system. See Exceptions No. 1 and No. 2 under ***NEC Section 517.19(A)***.

2.4.0 Grounding Receptacles and Fixed Equipment

NEC Section 517.13 pertains to equipment grounding conductors for receptacles and fixed electrical equipment in patient care spaces. These areas require redundant grounding. All branch circuits serving patient care spaces must have an effective ground fault current path by installation in a grounded metal raceway or a cable having a metallic armor or sheath assembly. The metal raceway, metallic armor, or sheath assembly must itself qualify as an equipment grounding conductor, per *NEC Section 250.118*. Type MI and MC cable must have a health care facility rating and be clearly marked as such and terminated using listed fittings.

Know the Code

Equipment Grounding Conductor for Receptacles and Fixed Electrical Equipment in Patient Care Spaces
NEC Section 517.13

Know the Code

Types of Equipment Grounding Conductors
NEC Section 250.118

NEC Section 517.13 contains an exception for luminaires higher than 7½' (2.3 m) above the floor and switches located outside the vicinity of patient care. They are permitted to be connected to an equipment grounding return path that complies with *NEC Section 517.13(A) or (B)*. (Both are unlikely to contact the patient or any equipment connected to the patient.)

According to *Section 517.13(B)*, an insulated copper equipment grounding conductor must be connected to the grounding terminals of receptacles, the metal boxes and enclosures containing receptacles, and all noncurrent-carrying conductive surfaces of fixed electric equipment likely to become energized that are subject to personal contact and operating at over 100V. Metal faceplates may be connected to the equipment grounding conductor by means of metal mounting screws securing the faceplate to a grounded outlet box or grounded wiring device. This permits metal faceplates to be grounded without having to run a separate equipment grounding conductor to the faceplate. The grounding conductor must be sized in accordance with *NEC Table 250.122* and installed in a metal raceway with the branch circuit conductors supplying these receptacles or fixed electric equipment.

The insulated copper conductor is installed either with the branch circuit conductors or as part of listed cable with a metallic armor or sheath assembly. The reason for redundant grounding using an insulated ground wire within a grounded raceway or grounded sheathed cable is so that an effective ground fault current path exists if an insulated grounding conductor or device fails. *NEC Section 517.13(B)(1)* includes the following exceptions:

- For other than isolated ground receptacles, an insulated equipment bonding jumper that directly connects to the equipment grounding conductor is permitted to connect the box and receptacle(s) to the equipment grounding conductor.
- Metal faceplates shall be connected to an effective ground fault current path by means of a metal mounting screw(s) securing the faceplate to a metal yoke or strap of a receptacle or to a metal outlet box.
- To ensure an effective ground fault current path, metal faceplates must be connected through metal mounting screw(s) to either a metal yoke or strap of a receptacle, or a metal outlet box.

Metal-sheathed cable assemblies are not typically authorized for essential electrical circuits because *NEC Section 517.31(C)(3)* requires such wiring to be protected by installation in a nonflexible metal raceway or encased in concrete. Type MC cable is allowed where it is placed in listed prefabricated medical headwalls, fished into existing walls or ceilings where it is not likely to be damaged or casually accessed, located in listed office furniture, or where the equipment requires a flexible connection.

Equipotential grounding is one method of grounding used for sensitive equipment. An **equipotential ground plane** provides a low impedance to current flow over a wide range of frequencies.

Equipotential ground planes shield adjacent sensitive circuits or equipment, contain electromagnetic (EM) noise fields between their source (cable, for example) and the plane, increase filtering effectiveness of contained EM fields, and provide a low-impedance return path for radio frequency (RF) noise current.

Hospital-Grade AC Cable

This AC cable has an internal insulated ground wire that is acceptable for use in patient care spaces. It's identified by a green metal sheath.

Source: Southwire

Electrical Risks to Patients

One of the most dangerous situations is when a patient has an external direct conductive path to the heart, such as a cardiac catheter. In this situation, the patient may be electrocuted at current levels so low that additional protection in the design of equipment, catheter insulation, and control of operational practices is necessary. Patients are at increased risk of electric shock when their body resistance is compromised either accidentally or by needed medical procedures. Situations such as catheter insertion or incontinence may make a patient much more susceptible to the effects of an electric current.

Know the Code

Requirements for the Essential Electrical System
NEC Section 517.31

Equipotential ground plane: A mass of conducting material that, when bonded together, provides a low impedance to current flow over a wide range of frequencies.

Equipotential plane structures include metallic screens or sheet metal under floor tile, the supporting grids of raised access flooring (such as in computer rooms), conductive grids rooted in or attached to a concrete floor, and ceiling grids above sensitive equipment.

An equipotential reference plane can be used within a section of a single sensitive equipment enclosure, among various pieces of interconnected equipment, or over an entire facility. In all cases, the equipotential plane is bonded to both the local building ground and the grounding electrode conductor.

Within sensitive equipment cabinets, all signal return leads, backplanes, and other significant components must be connected via short (less than 5% to 10% of the wavelength of the highest frequency) conductors to the equipment chassis that forms the equipotential plane. All similar equipment-level equipotential planes should be coupled to the grounding electrode conductor as well as the room-level equipotential plane by way of multiple short conductors. The room-level equipotential plane must in turn be linked to one or more building-level equipotential planes via multiple short conductors. This process is continued until the total sensitive electronic equipment system is interconnected to one large continuous equipotential plane. It is best to interlink conductors with single thin-wire cross sections to minimize their impedance at higher frequencies.

NOTE

Special grounding requirements are applied in wet procedure locations. See ***NEC Section 517.20***. These locations are designated by the facility governing body. Patient bathrooms are not considered wet procedure locations. However, they may be wet locations under *NEC*® definition.

2.0.0 Section Review

1. Hospital-grade receptacles are often marked with a(n) _____.
   a. purple dot
   b. orange dot
   c. green dot
   d. blue dot

2. Which of the following is *true* about electrical safety in patient care spaces?
   a. The possibility of electric shock can be reduced by reducing the resistance of the conductive circuit that includes the patient.
   b. All branch circuits from the normal system must originate in different panelboards.
   c. Every circuit supplying a patient bed location must be supplied from the emergency system.
   d. The hazard worsens as more equipment is used near a patient, such as in surgical suites and intensive care units.

3. Every patient bed location in a critical care space must be supplied with at *least* _____.
   a. 8 receptacles
   b. 10 receptacles
   c. 12 receptacles
   d. 14 receptacles

4. Sensitive equipment in health care facilities can be shielded using _____.
   a. equipotential grounding
   b. metallic paint
   c. nonmetallic spacers
   d. white noise

3.0.0 Wiring in Health Care Facilities

Objective

List the required wiring methods in health care facilities.

a. Identify the wiring requirements for inhalation anesthetizing locations.
b. Identify the wiring requirements for low-voltage equipment and instruments.
c. Identify the wiring requirements for diagnostic imaging and treatment equipment installations.
d. Identify the requirements for communication, signaling, data, and fire alarm systems installed in patient care areas.
e. Identify the requirements for isolated power systems.

Performance Tasks

There are no Performance Tasks in this section.

Health care facilities can include hazardous (classified) locations and unclassified locations. Each of these locations has specific wiring requirements.

3.1.0 Inhalation Anesthetizing Locations

Anesthetizing locations are divided into hazardous (classified) locations, where flammable or nonflammable anesthetics may be interchangeably used, and unclassified locations, where only nonflammable anesthetics are used. Although flammable anesthetics are virtually obsolete in the United States, *NEC Section 517.60* and NFPA 99 still cover them because they are in use in other countries that use these codes. In areas where flammable anesthetics are used, the entire location is considered a Class I, Division 1 location up to a level 5' (1.5 m) above the floor. The area remaining up to the structural ceiling is considered to be above a hazardous (classified) location.

Any location or room in which flammable anesthetics or volatile flammable disinfecting agents are stored is considered a Class I, Division 1 location from floor to ceiling. Any inhalation anesthetizing location assigned for the exclusive use of nonflammable anesthetizing agents is considered an other-than-hazardous (classified) location.

Know the Code

Anesthetizing Location Classification
NEC Section 517.60

3.1.1 Wiring and Equipment within Hazardous Anesthetizing Locations

Per *NEC Section 517.61(A)*, wiring and equipment *within* hazardous (classified) anesthetizing locations must comply with the following:

- Except as permitted by *NEC Section 517.160*, each power circuit within, or partially within, a flammable anesthetizing location as referred to in *NEC Section 517.60* must be isolated from any distribution system using an isolated power system.
- Isolated power system equipment must be listed for the purpose, and the system must be designed and installed in accordance with *NEC Section 517.160*.
- In hazardous locations referred to in *NEC Section 517.60*, all fixed wiring and equipment and all portable equipment, including lamps and other utilization equipment operating at more than 10V between conductors, must comply with *NEC Sections 501.1 through 501.25*, *NEC Sections 501.100 through 501.150*, and *NEC Sections 501.30(A) and (B)* for Class I, Division 1 locations. All such equipment must be specifically approved for the hazardous atmospheres involved.
- Where a box, fitting, or enclosure is partially, but not entirely, within a hazardous (classified) location, the entire box, fitting, or enclosure is considered within the hazardous (classified) location.

Know the Code

Wiring and Equipment
NEC Section 517.61

Know the Code

Isolated Power Systems
NEC Section 517.160

Know the Code

Class 1 Locations
NEC Article 501

- Attachment plugs and receptacles in hazardous locations must be listed for use in Class I, Group C hazardous locations and have provision for the connection of a grounding conductor.
- Flexible cords used in hazardous locations for connection to portable utilization equipment, including lamps operating at more than 8V between conductors, must be approved for extra-hard usage in accordance with *NEC Table 400.4* and include an additional grounding conductor.
- Storage devices must be provided for flexible cords. These storage devices must not subject the cord to a bend radius of less than 3" (75 mm).

Know the Code

Flexible Cords and Flexible Cables
NEC Table 400.4

3.1.2 Wiring and Equipment above Hazardous Anesthetizing Locations

Per *NEC Section 517.61(B)*, wiring and equipment installed *above* hazardous (classified) anesthetizing locations must comply with the following:

- Wiring above a hazardous location referred to in *NEC Section 517.60* must be installed in rigid metal conduit, electrical metallic tubing, intermediate metal conduit, Type MI cable, or Type MC cable that employs a continuous gastight/vapor-tight metal sheath.
- Equipment that may produce sparks, arcs, or particles of hot metal, such as lamps and lamp holders for fixed lighting, switches, generators, motors, cutouts, or other equipment having sliding contacts, must be of the totally enclosed type or constructed in such a manner as to prevent the escape of sparks or hot metal particles. (This does not apply to wall-mounted receptacles installed above the hazardous location.)
- Surgical and other luminaires must conform to *NEC Section 501.130(B)*. See also Exceptions No. 1 and No. 2 under *NEC Section 517.61(B)(3)*, which respectively state that the surface temperature limitations set forth for fixed lighting in *NEC Section 501.130(B)(1)* do not apply; and integral or pendant switches that are located above and cannot be lowered into the hazardous (classified) location(s) are not required to be explosion proof.
- Only listed seals may be used, per *NEC Section 501.15*. *NEC Section 501.15(A)(4)* applies to both the horizontal and vertical boundaries of the defined hazardous (classified) locations.
- Attachment plugs and receptacles positioned over hazardous (classified) anesthetizing locations must be listed as hospital grade for services of prescribed voltage, frequency, rating, and number of conductors with provision for the connection of the grounding conductor. This requirement applies to attachment plugs and receptacles of the two-pole, three-wire grounding type for single-phase, 120V, nominal AC service.
- Plugs and receptacles rated at 250V, for connection of 50A and 60A AC medical equipment for use above hazardous (classified) locations, must be arranged so that the 60A receptacle will accept either the 50A or the 60A plug. The 50A receptacles must be designed so as not to accept a 60A attachment plug. The plugs must be of the two-pole, three-wire design with a third contact connecting to the insulated (green or green with yellow stripe) equipment grounding conductor of the electrical system.

Know the Code

Luminaires
NEC Section 501.130

Know the Code

Sealing and Drainage
NEC Section 501.15

3.1.3 Wiring in Unclassified Anesthetizing Locations

Per *NEC Section 517.61(C)*, wiring in unclassified anesthetizing locations must comply with the following:

- Wiring serving unclassified locations, as defined in *NEC Section 517.60*, must be installed in a metal raceway system or cable assembly. The metal raceway system, cable armor, or sheath assembly must qualify as an equipment grounding conductor in accordance with *NEC Section 250.118*.

Know the Code

Types of Equipment Grounding Conductors
NEC Section 250.118

Type MC and MI cable must have an outer metal armor or sheath that is identified as an acceptable equipment grounding conductor. Per Exception under *NEC Section 517.61(C)(1)*, pendant receptacle installations employing at least Type SJO or equivalent hard or extra-hard usage, flexible cords suspended not less than 6' (1.8 m) from the floor are not required to be installed in a metal raceway or cable assembly.

- Receptacles and attachment plugs installed and used in unclassified locations must be listed as hospital grade for services of prescribed voltage, frequency, rating, and number of conductors with provision for connection of the grounding conductor. This requirement applies to the two-pole, three-wire grounding type for single-phase 120V, 208V, or 240V nominal AC service.
- Plugs and receptacles rated at 250V, for connection of 50A and 60A AC medical equipment for use in unclassified locations, must be arranged so that the 60A receptacle will accept either the 50A or the 60A plug. The 50A receptacles must be designed so as not to accept a 60A attachment plug. The plugs must be of the two-pole, three-wire design with a third contact connecting to the insulated (green or green with a yellow stripe) equipment grounding conductor of the electrical system.

3.1.4 Grounding in Anesthetizing Locations

In any anesthetizing location, all metal raceways and metal-sheathed cable and all normally noncurrent-carrying conductive portions of fixed electric equipment must be connected to an equipment grounding conductor, per *NEC Section 517.62*. Grounding in Class I locations must comply with *NEC Section 501.30*.

Grounding specifications and requirements for anesthetizing areas apply only to metal-sheathed cable, metal raceways, and electric equipment. It is not a requirement to ground tables, carts, or any other nonelectrical items. However, in anesthetizing locations where flammables are present, portable carts and tables usually have an acceptable resistance to ground through conductive tires and wheels and conductive flooring to avoid the buildup of static electrical charges. See NFPA 99 for information on static grounding.

3.1.5 Grounded Power Systems in Anesthetizing Locations

As a secondary backup, at least one battery-powered emergency lighting unit must be installed in every anesthetizing location, per *NEC Section 517.63(A)*. This light may be wired ahead of the switch and connected to a critical lighting circuit. Without this backup, failure of the emergency circuit feeder that supplies the operating room with power would likely place the room in complete darkness, which could have fatal results.

Per *NEC Section 517.63(B)*, branch circuits may be fed from a normal grounded service (single- or three-phase system) when they are permanently installed above the hazardous (classified) area or in unclassified locations and supply only listed, stationary, diagnostic and therapeutic equipment, provided that:

- Wiring for isolated and grounded circuits does not occupy the same cable or raceway.
- All conductive surfaces of the equipment are connected to an equipment grounding conductor.
- Equipment (except enclosed X-ray tubes and the leads to the tubes) is located at least 8' (2.5 m) above the floor or outside the anesthetizing location, and switches for the grounded branch circuit are located outside the hazardous (classified) location. (This does not apply to unclassified locations.)

Know the Code

Grounding
NEC Section 517.62

Know the Code

Grounding and Bonding
NEC Section 501.30

NOTE

Equipment operating at not more than 10V between conductors is not required to be grounded.

Know the Code

Battery-Powered Lighting Units
NEC Section 517.63(A)

Know the Code

Branch-Circuit Wiring
NEC Section 517.63(B)

Know the Code

Fixed Lighting Branch Circuits
NEC Section 517.63(C)

Per *NEC Section 517.63(C)*, fixed lighting branch circuits feeding only fixed lighting may be supplied by a normal grounded service, provided that:

- The fixtures are located at least 8' (2.5 m) above the floor and switches are wall-mounted and located above hazardous (classified) locations. (This does not apply to unclassified locations.)
- All conductive surfaces of fixtures are connected to an equipment grounding conductor.
- Wiring for circuits supplying power to fixtures does not occupy the same raceway or cable as circuits supplying isolated power.
- Switches are wall-mounted and located above hazardous (classified) locations.

Know the Code

Remote-Control Stations
NEC Section 517.63(D)

Wall-mounted remote control stations may be installed in any anesthetizing location for the operation of remote control switching operating at 24V or less, per *NEC Section 517.63(D)*.

Know the Code

Location of Isolated Power Systems
NEC Section 517.63(E)

An isolated power system and its grounded supply circuit may be located in an anesthetizing location, providing it is installed above a hazardous (classified) location or in an unclassified location and is listed for the purpose. See *NEC Section 517.63(E)*.

Except as permitted above, each power circuit within, or partially within, a flammable anesthetizing location as referred to in *NEC Section 517.60* must be isolated from any distribution system supplying other-than-anesthetizing locations.

3.2.0 Low-Voltage Equipment and Instruments

Know the Code

Low-Voltage Equipment and Instruments
NEC Section 517.64

Low-voltage equipment that is typically in contact with patients or has exposed current-carrying elements must be moisture-resistant and operate at 10V or less; or they must be approved as intrinsically safe or double-insulated equipment. Refer to *NEC Section 517.64*.

Electrical power to low-voltage equipment must be supplied from an individual portable isolation transformer (autotransformers cannot be used). This equipment must be connected to an isolated power circuit receptacle by means of an appropriate cord and attachment plug, a standard low-voltage isolation transformer installed in an unclassified location, individual dry-cell batteries, or common batteries made up of storage cells located in an unclassified location.

Isolating-type transformers for supplying low-voltage circuits must have an approved means of insulating the secondary circuit from the primary circuit. In addition, the case and core must be connected to an equipment grounding conductor.

Impedance and resistance devices are allowed to control low-voltage equipment. However, they cannot be used to limit the maximum available voltage supplied to the equipment.

Battery-supplied appliances must not be capable of being charged during operation unless the charging circuitry uses an integral isolating-type transformer. In addition, receptacles and attachment plugs placed on low-voltage circuits must be of a type that does not permit interchangeable connection with circuits of higher voltage.

Box Shielding

If an outlet or switch box must be installed in an X-ray area, lead shielding must be molded around the box. This ensures the integrity of the overall X-ray shield in the area. Some electricians peel the lead backing from scrap pieces of lead-shielded gypsum wallboard panels and save it for shielding the boxes in the area.

WARNING!

Any circuit interruptions (even in circuits as low as 10V) caused by a switch or loose or defective connections anywhere in the circuit may produce a spark sufficient to ignite flammable anesthetic gases.

3.3.0 Diagnostic Imaging and Treatment Equipment Installation

The installation of diagnostic imaging and treatment equipment requires specialized training in order for the equipment both to operate as intended and to protect patients and personnel from unintended exposure to radiation. Any equipment for new installations, as well as all used or reconditioned equipment transported to and reinstalled in a new location, must be of an approved type. *NEC Article 517, Part V* covers this type of equipment.

CAUTION

Nothing in this section should be construed as an indication of safeguards against the useful beam or stray X-ray radiation. Radiation safety and performance requirements of several classes of diagnostic imaging and treatment equipment are regulated under Public Law 90-602 and are enforced by the Department of Health and Human Services. In addition, information on radiation protection is available from the National Council on Radiation Protection and Measurements (**www.ncrponline.org/publications**).

3.3.1 Connection to Supply Circuit

Diagnostic imaging and treatment equipment, whether fixed or stationary, must be connected to the power supply in such a way that the wiring methods meet the requirements of the *NEC*®. Equipment supplied by a branch circuit rated at no more than 30A may be supplied through a suitable attachment plug and hard-service cable or cord.

Individual branch circuits are not required for portable, mobile, and transportable medical X-ray equipment requiring a capacity of no more than 60A, per *NEC Section 517.71(B)*. Circuits and equipment functioning on a supply circuit over 1,000V must comply with the requirements of *NEC Article 495*.

3.3.2 Disconnecting Means

Per *NEC Section 517.72(A)*, a disconnecting means rated for at least 50% of the input required for the momentary rating, or 100% of the input required for the long-term rating of the diagnostic imaging and treatment equipment, whichever is greater, must be provided in the supply circuit.

The disconnecting means must be in a location readily accessible from the diagnostic imaging and treatment control. A grounding-type attachment plug and receptacle of proper rating may serve as a disconnecting means for equipment supplied by a 120V branch circuit of 30A or less.

Know the Code

Diagnostic Imaging and Treatment Equipment
NEC Article 517, Part V

3.3.3 Rating of Supply Conductors and Overcurrent Protection

For diagnostic equipment, the amperage of supply branch circuit conductors and the current rating of overcurrent protective devices must be no less than 50% of the momentary rating or 100% of the long-term rating, whichever is greater. See *NEC Section 517.73(A)*.

When feeding two or more branch circuits that supply diagnostic imaging units, the amperage rating of supply feeders and the current rating of overcurrent protective devices must be no less than 50% of the momentary demand rating of the largest unit, plus 25% of the momentary demand rating of the next largest unit, plus 10% of the momentary demand rating of each additional unit.

The minimum conductor sizes for branch and feeder circuits are governed by voltage regulation requirements. In specific installations, manufacturers typically specify the minimum distribution transformer and conductor sizes required, the disconnect rating, and overcurrent protection requirements.

Know the Code

Rating of Supply Conductors and Overcurrent Protection
NEC Section 517.73

3.3.4 Control Circuit Conductors

The number of control circuit conductors installed in a raceway must be determined in accordance with *NEC Section 300.17*. Where protected by overcurrent devices of no more than 20A, No. 18 AWG or No. 16 AWG fixture wires specified in *NEC Section 724.49* and flexible cords are permitted for the control and operating circuits of diagnostic imaging and treatment equipment, as well as auxiliary equipment. See *NEC Section 517.74(B)*.

Know the Code

Number and Size of Conductors and Cables in Raceway
NEC Section 300.17

3.3.5 Transformers and Capacitors

Transformers and capacitors that are a part of diagnostic imaging and treatment equipment are not required to comply with *NEC Articles 450 and 460*. However, capacitors must be mounted within enclosures of insulating material or grounded metal. See *NEC Section 517.76*.

Know the Code

Transformers and Capacitors
NEC Section 517.76

Know the Code

Installation of Cables and Grounded Shields
NEC Section 517.77

Know the Code

Guarding and Grounding
NEC Section 517.78

3.3.6 High-Tension X-Ray Cable

Cable with a grounded shield connecting X-ray tubes and image intensifiers may be installed in cable trays or troughs along with X-ray equipment control and power supply conductors without the necessity of barriers to separate the wiring. See *NEC Section 517.77.*

3.3.7 Guarding and Grounding

All high-voltage parts, including X-ray tubes, must be mounted within grounded enclosures, per *NEC Section 517.78(A)*. The link from high-voltage equipment to the X-ray tubes and other high-voltage devices must be made using high-voltage shielded cable. Air, oil, gas, or other suitable insulating material must be used to insulate the high voltage from the grounded enclosure.

All cable providing low voltages and connecting to oil-filled units that is not completely sealed (such as transformers, condensers, oil coolers, and high-voltage switches) must have oil-resistant insulation. See *NEC Section 517.78(B)*.

3.4.0 Communication, Signaling, Data, and Fire Alarm Systems

Communication, signaling, data, and fire alarm systems, as well as systems operating at less than 120V in patient care spaces, must conform to the same insulation and isolation requirements as electrical distribution systems. Those systems not located in patient care spaces must adhere to requirements in *NEC Articles 640, 725, 760, and 800*, as applicable. Audio visual nurse call systems like the one shown in *Figure 10* may use patient control emergency pull cords as an alternative isolation method.

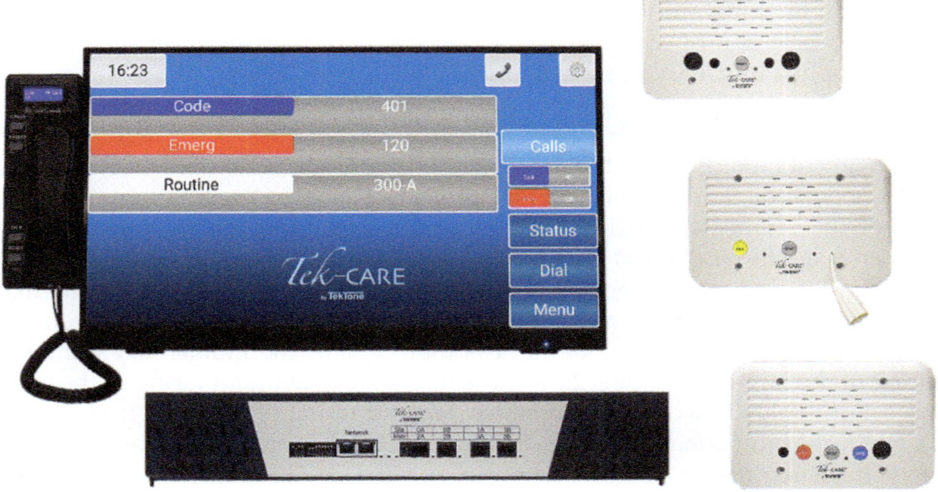

Figure 10 Common signaling devices for nurse call systems.
Source: Tektone

3.5.0 Isolated Power Systems

Isolated power systems are used to prevent power interruption caused by a single line-to-ground fault and to isolate power from any electrical ground in certain critical spaces. *Figure 11* shows an isolated power panel that may be installed in a corridor outside an operating room or other locations where power interruption cannot be tolerated. These panels are also available with various types of receptacles and up to seven ground jacks on the panel face for use in intensive care and coronary care units, cardiac catheterization labs, neonatal units, emergency rooms, critical care spaces, and recovery rooms.

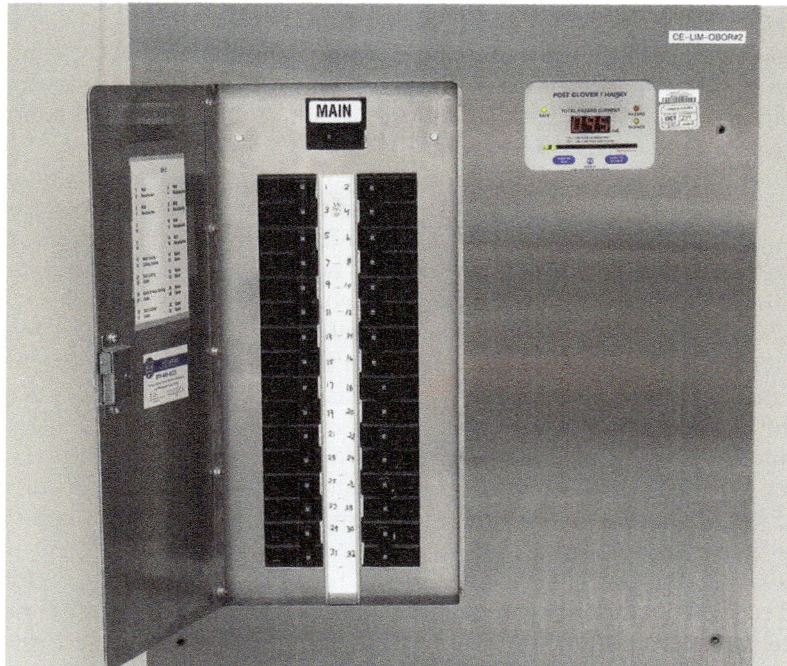

Figure 11 Isolated power panel.
Source: John Lupacchino, Gaylor Electric Inc.

3.5.1 Installation

Per *NEC Section 517.160(A)*, each isolated power circuit must be controlled by a switch or a circuit breaker having a disconnecting pole in each isolated circuit conductor to simultaneously disconnect all power. Isolation is achieved by using one or more isolation transformers, motor generator sets, or electrically isolated batteries. Conductors of isolated power circuits shall not be installed in cables, raceways, or other enclosures containing conductors of another system.

Circuits feeding the primaries of isolation transformers must not exceed 600V between conductors and must be furnished with proper overcurrent protection. The secondary voltage of isolation transformers must not exceed 600V between conductors of each circuit. All circuits fed from these secondaries must be ungrounded and have an approved overcurrent device of proper rating in each conductor. If an electrostatic shield is present, it must be connected to the reference grounding point.

An isolated branch circuit supplying an anesthetizing location must not supply any other location except as noted in *NEC Sections 517.160(A)(4)(a) and (b)*.

Per *NEC Section 517.160(A)(5)*, the isolated circuit conductors must be identified as follows:

- *Isolated Conductor No. 1* — Orange with at least one distinctive colored stripe other than white, green, or gray along the entire length of the conductor
- *Isolated Conductor No. 2* — Brown with at least one distinctive colored stripe other than white, green, or gray along the entire length of the conductor
- *Isolated Conductor No. 3 (for three-phase conductors)* — Yellow with at least one distinctive colored stripe other than white, green, or gray along the entire length of the conductor

No wire-pulling compounds that increase the dielectric constant of a conductor may be used on the secondary conductors of the isolated power supply. Special lubricants are available for this application.

To meet impedance requirements, it may be desirable to limit the size of the isolation transformer to 10 kVA and to use conductor insulation with low leakage. To reduce leakage from line to ground, steps should be taken to minimize the length of branch circuit conductors and use conductor insulation that meets the requirements of Informational Note No. 2 under *NEC Section 517.160(A)(6)*.

Visibility

Many nurse call master stations have video touch screens that allow staff to quickly access information. This screen shows pending calls from patients and indicates that the responsible staff member for each call has been notified. The lower left portion of the screen shows that the staff members will be reminded if the call signal has not been turned off within a set time. At the bottom right of the screen, the staff locator system shows the location of selected staff members.

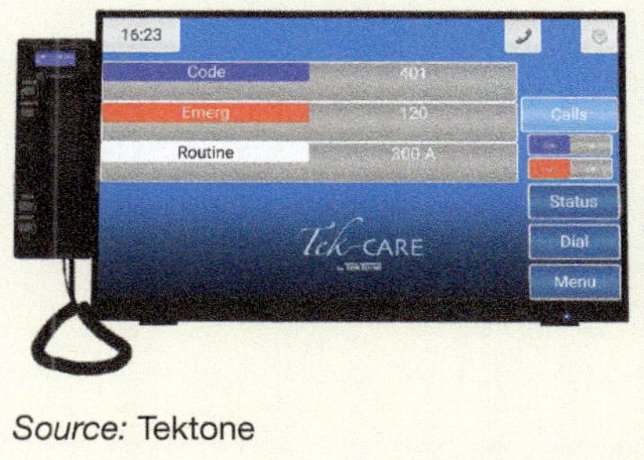

Source: Tektone

Know the Code

Installations
NEC Section 517.160(A)

3.5.2 Line Isolation Monitors

Every isolated power system must be provided with an approved, continually functioning line isolation monitor that indicates possible leakage or fault current from either isolated conductor to ground, in addition to the usual control and protective devices. See *NEC Section 517.160(B)(1)*.

Know the Code

Line Isolation Monitor
NEC Section 517.160(B)

Grounding systems are the primary protective devices for patients. The ungrounded secondary of an isolation transformer reduces the maximum current between either of the isolated power conductors and ground in the grounding system in the event of a single fault. The line isolation monitor provides a warning when a single fault occurs, or when excessively low impedance to ground develops, which might expose the patient to an unsafe condition should an additional fault occur. Excessive current in the grounding conductors will not result from an initial fault. A hazard exists if a second fault occurs before the first fault is cleared.

Monitors must include a green signal lamp, visible to individuals in the anesthetizing area, which remains illuminated when the system is sufficiently isolated from ground. An adjacent red signal lamp must illuminate with an audible warning siren when the total hazard current (consisting of possible capacitive and resistive leakage current) from either isolated conductor to ground reaches a threshold value of 5 mA under normal line voltage conditions. The line isolation monitor should not alarm for any hazard fault current of 3.7 mA or less or a total hazard current of less than 5 mA. The audible siren may sound in another area if desired.

A line isolation monitor must have enough internal impedance. This way, when it is properly connected to the isolated system and any point of the system is grounded, the maximum internal current that will flow through the line isolation monitor is 1 mA.

An ammeter connected in series to verify the total hazard current of the system (the fault hazard current and monitor hazard current) must be mounted in a visible place on the line isolation monitor with the Alarm On zone being approximately at the center of the scale. Locate the ammeter where it is visible to persons in the anesthetizing location.

Like all major electrical installations, health care facilities require extensive testing and performance verification. Typical testing forms are included in *Appendix 26402-23A*.

3.0.0 Section Review

1. Any location or room in which flammable anesthetics or volatile flammable disinfecting agents are stored is considered a Class I, Division 1 location _____.
   a. up to a level 3' (900 mm) above the floor
   b. up to a level 5' (1.5 m) above the floor
   c. up to a level $7^1/_2$' (2.3 m) above the floor
   d. from floor to ceiling

2. *NEC Section 517.64* applies to _____.
   a. low-voltage equipment and instruments
   b. control circuit conductors
   c. isolated power systems
   d. EESs

3. *NEC Article 495* applies to diagnostic imaging and treatment equipment circuits and equipment *over* _____.
   a. 60V
   b. 120V
   c. 480V
   d. 1,000V

4. A type of nonelectrified patient control device is a(n) _____.
   a. bed speaker
   b. call button
   c. emergency pull cord
   d. pillow speaker

5. The secondary voltage of isolation transformers in health care facilities must *not* exceed _____.
   a. 120V between conductors of each circuit
   b. 240V between conductors of each circuit
   c. 480V between conductors of each circuit
   d. 600V between conductors of each circuit

Module 26402-23 Review Questions

1. The installation of electrical systems in health care facilities is governed by _____.
   a. *NEC Article 511*
   b. *NEC Article 517*
   c. *NEC Article 550*
   d. *NEC Article 820*

2. Which of the following facilities provide around-the-clock services to patients?
   a. Hospitals, nursing homes, ambulatory health care facilities, and limited care facilities
   b. Nursing homes, ambulatory health care facilities, and limited care facilities
   c. Ambulatory health care facilities, hospitals, and limited care facilities
   d. Limited care facilities, hospitals, and nursing homes

3. The life safety branch of the EES includes _____.
   a. intensive care units
   b. patient care spaces
   c. pharmacies
   d. exit signs

4. The *maximum* time allowed for transfer switches to return to operation with an emergency power system is _____.
   a. 5 seconds
   b. 10 seconds
   c. 2 minutes
   d. 10 minutes

5. The *maximum* demand of a facility with only one transfer switch in a Type 2 EES is _____.
   a. 10 kVA
   b. 50 kVA
   c. 100 kVA
   d. 150 kVA

6. Which type of facility *must* have a Type 2 EES?
   a. Doctor's office
   b. Nursing home
   c. Dialysis center
   d. Surgical center

7. Throwover switches are often used to allow temporary operation of _____.
   a. elevators
   b. suction devices
   c. heating systems
   d. pharmacies

8. In a Type 2 EES, which of the following *must* have alternate power replaced within 10 seconds of a power failure?
   a. Storage areas
   b. Medication preparation areas
   c. Exit signs
   d. Heating equipment

9. Where branch circuit panelboards for normal and essential power serve the same patient care vicinity, they must be connected together with an insulated continuous copper conductor *no* smaller than _____.
   a. No. 10 AWG
   b. No. 12 AWG
   c. No. 14 AWG
   d. No. 16 AWG

10. Outlets on emergency power are often identified by _____.
   a. color
   b. stripes
   c. flags
   d. arrows

11. Hospital-grade tamper-resistant receptacles _____.
   a. provide power only when the hot and neutral blades of a plug are simultaneously inserted
   b. can be used when an isolated ground is needed
   c. are used in wet areas only
   d. are obsolete

12. Hospital-grade tamper-resistant receptacles *must* be used in _____.
   a. psychiatric locations
   b. critical care units
   c. wet areas
   d. laboratories

13. Each patient bed in the Category 2 patient care space must have a *minimum* of _____.
   a. two receptacles
   b. four receptacles
   c. six receptacles
   d. eight receptacles

14. In an area where flammables are employed, a Class I, Division 1 location extends upward to a level of _____.
   a. 2' (600 mm) above the floor
   b. 5' (1.5 m) above the floor
   c. 10' (3 m) above the floor
   d. 15' (4.5 m) above the floor

15. In order to use a suitable attachment plug and hard-service cable, diagnostic imaging and treatment equipment supplied by a branch circuit must be rated at *no* more than _____.
   a. 15A
   b. 30A
   c. 45A
   d. 60A

Answers to odd-numbered Module Review Questions are found in *Appendix A*.

Module 26402-23 Supplemental Exercises

1. Areas in which failure of equipment or a system is likely to cause major injury or death to patients or caregivers are known as _________.
2. A facility for the treatment of chemical dependency is most likely to be defined as a(n) _________.
3. Patients on life support must be in an area served by a Type _________.
4. In a Type 2 EES, the life safety branch must have power restored within _________ second(s) after normal source interruption.
5. Name some typical applications of isolated ground receptacles.

   ____

   ____
6. *NEC Section 517.19(D)* requires that an equipment bonding jumper no smaller than _________ AWG be used to connect the grounding terminal of all grounding-type receptacles of a patient headwall to the patient grounding point.
7. True or False? In Category 1 spaces, each bed location requires at least one dedicated branch circuit from the critical branch, in addition to a branch from the normal system.
8. All branch circuits serving patient care vicinity spaces must have an effective ground fault current path by installation in a(n) _________.
9. True or False? Nurse call systems may use nonelectrified patient control as an alternative isolation method.
10. Isolated power systems are used to prevent power interruption due to a single line-to-ground fault and to _________.

Answers to odd-numbered Supplemental Exercises are found in *Appendix B*.

Answers to Section Review Questions

Answer	Section Reference	Objective
Section 1.0.0		
1. c	1.1.2	1a
2. c	1.2.3	1b
Section 2.0.0		
1. c	2.1.0	2a
2. d	2.2.0	2b
3. d	2.3.0	2c
4. a	2.4.0	2d
Section 3.0.0		
1. b	3.1.0	3a
2. a	3.2.0	3b
3. d	3.3.1	3c
4. c	3.4.0	3d
5. d	3.5.1	3e

Standby and Emergency Systems

Source: iStock@jaypetersen

Objectives

Successful completion of this module prepares you to do the following:

1. Differentiate between emergency and standby systems and identify their primary components.
   a. Identify emergency and standby power system components.
   b. Explain the principles of transfer switch operation and their configuration/sizing considerations.
2. Describe battery and uninterruptible power supply (UPS) system types and explain their maintenance requirements.
   a. Describe the different types of batteries used.
   b. Explain the maintenance requirements of batteries and their charging considerations.
   c. Identify single- and double-conversion UPS systems.
3. Describe the *NEC*® requirements for emergency/standby power and lighting systems.
   a. Describe legally required standby systems.
   b. Describe the alternate power requirements for health care facilities.
   c. Describe the alternate power requirements for places of assembly.
   d. Describe emergency lighting requirements and devices for public buildings.

Performance Tasks

This is a knowledge-based module. There are no Performance Tasks.

Overview

In places of assembly, power systems provide important functions such as lighting, evacuation routes and others during emergency situations. This module explains the *NEC*® installation requirements for electric generators and storage batteries used during such emergency situations.

NOTE

NFPA 70®, *National Electrical Code*®, and *NEC*® are registered trademarks of the National Fire Protection Association, Quincy, MA.

NCCER Industry-Recognized Credentials

If you are training through an NCCER-accredited sponsor, you may be eligible for credentials from NCCER. The ID number for this module is 26403-23. Note that this module may have been used in other NCCER curricula and may apply to other level completions. Contact NCCER at 1.888.622.3720 or go to **www.nccer.org** for more information.

You can also show off your industry-recognized credentials online with NCCER's digital badges. Transform your knowledge, skills, and achievements into badges that you can share across social media platforms, send to your network, and add to your resume. For more information, visit **www.nccer.org**.

Digital Resources for Electrical

Scan this code using the camera on your phone or mobile device to view the digital resources related to this craft.

1.0.0 Standby and Emergency Systems

Performance Tasks

There are no Performance Tasks in this section.

Objective

Differentiate between emergency and standby systems and identify their primary components.

a. Identify emergency and standby power system components.
b. Explain the principles of transfer switch operation and their configuration/sizing considerations.

Emergency systems are legally required by municipal, state, federal, and other codes, or by the government agency having jurisdiction. When the normal power supply fails, these systems automatically supply illumination and/or power to designated areas and equipment in order to ensure the safety of human life, per *NEC Section 700.1*.

Emergency systems are typically installed in places of assembly that require illumination to allow safe exiting of crowds. Such buildings include theaters, hotels, sports arenas, and health care facilities. They may also be used to provide power for such functions as:

- Ventilation where essential to maintain life
- Fire detection and alarm system operation
- Elevator operation
- Fire pump operation
- Public safety communication system operation
- Industrial processes where current interruption would produce serious life safety or health hazards
- Other similar functions

In the event of failure of the normal power supply, at least either one of emergency lighting or emergency power must be available within the time required for the application without exceeding 10 seconds.

Legally required standby systems are required by municipal, state, federal, and other codes, or by the government agency having jurisdiction. When the normal power supply fails, these systems automatically supply power to selected loads other than those classified as emergency systems, according to *NEC Article 701*.

Legally required standby systems serve loads such as lighting systems, HVACR systems, communication systems, smoke removal systems, sewage disposal, and industrial processes that, upon interruption of the normal electrical supply, could create hazards or hamper rescue or firefighting operations.

The requirements for legally required standby systems are similar to those for emergency systems except for the time required to supply standby power. Upon loss of normal power, legally required systems must be able to supply standby power in 60 seconds or less, instead of 10 seconds or less as required for emergency systems.

Optional standby systems are intended to protect public facilities or private property where performance of the system does not impact life safety. Optional standby systems supply site-generated power to selected loads either automatically or manually. Optional standby systems provide an alternate source of electric power for heating and refrigeration systems, data processing and communication systems, and industrial processes in such facilities as industrial and commercial buildings, farms, and residences. This helps to prevent discomfort, serious interruption of the process, or damage to the product or process during power outage, per *NEC Article 702*.

Know the Code

Scope
NEC Section 700.1

Know the Code

Legally Required Standby Systems
NEC Article 701

Know the Code

Optional Standby Systems
NEC Article 702

1.1.0 System Components

Figure 1 shows a one-line diagram of a typical electrical distribution system that incorporates a basic emergency power system (shown as heavy lines). The components that form an emergency or standby power system are basically the same. They include the following:

- An engine-driven AC generator set
- Automatic transfer switches

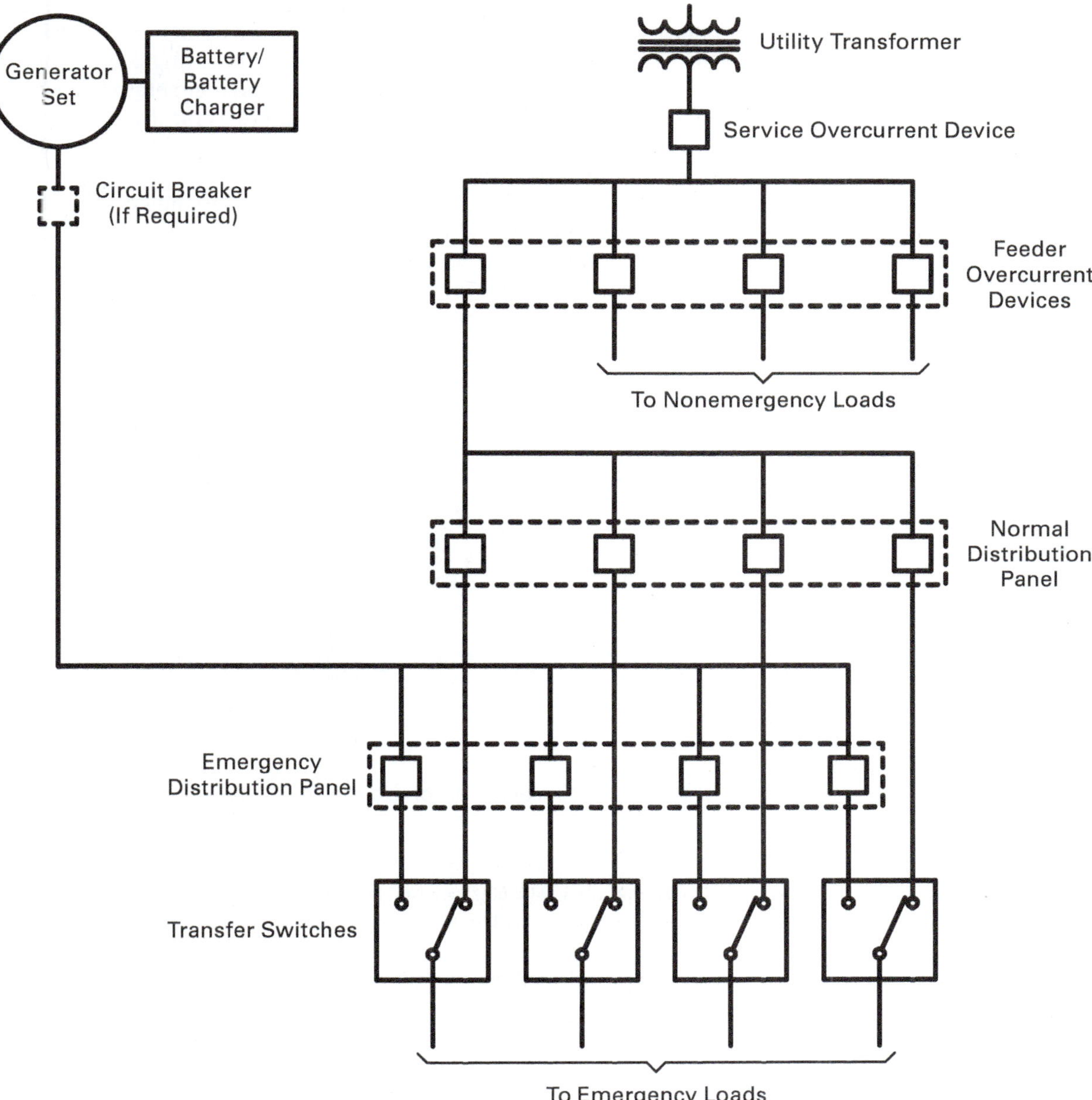

Figure 1 One-line diagram of an electrical distribution system incorporating emergency power system components.

Synchronous generator: An AC generator having a DC exciter. Synchronous generators are used as stand-alone generators for emergency and standby power systems and can also be paralleled with other synchronous generators and the utility system.

Armature: The assembly of windings and metal-core laminations in which the output voltage is induced. It is the rotating part in a revolving field generator.

Exciter: A device that supplies direct current (DC) to the field coils of a synchronous generator, producing the magnetic flux required for inducing output voltage in the stator coils.

1.1.1 Engine-Driven Generator Sets

Many designs and sizes of engine-driven **synchronous generator** sets are used as power sources for emergency and standby systems.

An AC generator (alternator) converts rotating mechanical energy, typically supplied by an air- or water-cooled diesel or gas engine, into electrical energy. The AC generator (*Figure* 2) consists of a rotor, also called the **armature**, and stator, with the shaft of the rotor being driven by the engine. When the engine is running, it turns the rotor that carries the generator field windings. These field windings are energized (or excited) by a DC source called the **exciter**, which is connected to the positive (+) and negative (–) ends of the field windings. The generator is constructed such that the magnetic field's lines of force cut perpendicularly across the stator windings when the engine turns the rotor, causing a voltage to be induced into the stator windings. This voltage reverses each time the polarity changes. For the four-pole generator shown in *Figure* 2, this would occur twice during each revolution. Typically, a generator has four times as many winding slots as shown and is wound to obtain a sinusoidally alternating single- or three-phase output.

The voltage induced in each stator winding depends on the strength of the magnetic field and the velocity with which the lines of force cut across the windings. Therefore, in order to vary the output voltage of a generator of a given diameter and operating speed, it is necessary to vary the strength of the magnetic field. This is controlled by the voltage regulator, which adjusts the output of the exciter.

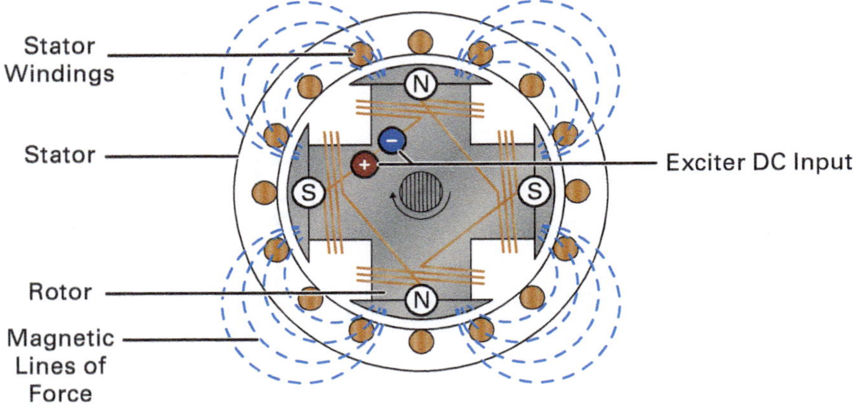

Figure 2 Cross-sectional view of a four-pole AC generator.

Engine-Driven Generator Sets

Many facilities are adding engine-driven generator sets to assist them through brownout situations, rather than just for emergency purposes.

The excitation system for a typical generator is controlled via a voltage regulator (*Figure* 3). The voltage regulator senses the generator output, compares it to a reference value, and then supplies a regulated DC output to the exciter field windings. The exciter produces an AC output in the exciter rotor located on the rotating engine-driven generator shaft. This exciter output is rectified by diodes, also on the generator shaft, to supply DC for the main rotor (generator field). The voltage regulator increases or decreases the exciter voltage as it senses changes in the output generator voltage caused by changes in load, thus increasing or decreasing the generator field strength. The resultant generator output is directly proportional to the field strength.

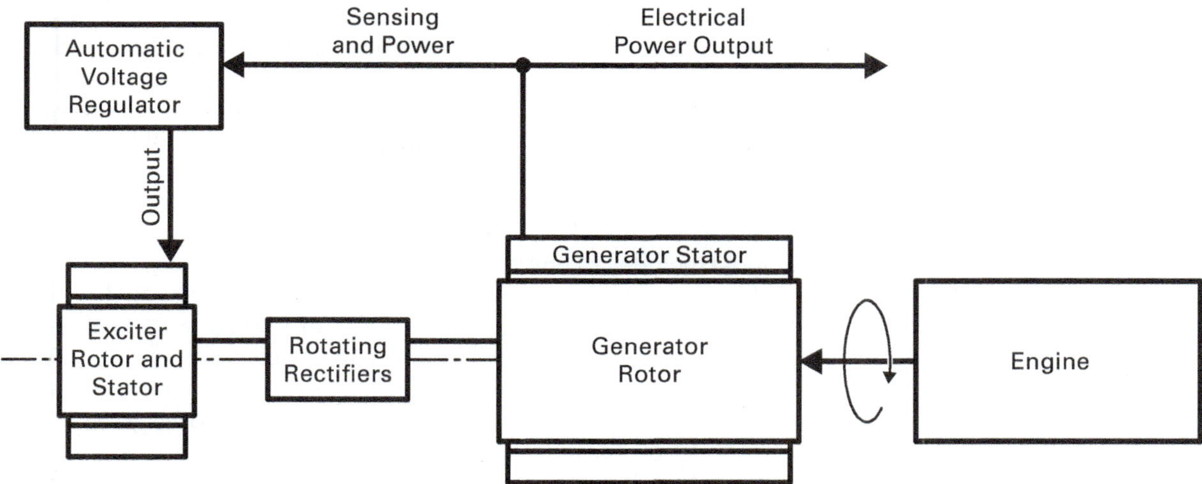

Figure 3 Self-exciter generator schematic.

1.1.2 Generator Selection Considerations and Sizing

A wide variety of generator sets are available. A generator set selected for a specific emergency or standby power application must have the same voltage output and frequency as the normal power supply system. Generator engines are generally four-cycle units with one to six cylinders, depending on size and capacity. In larger units, ignition current is generally supplied by starting batteries. The type of fuel the engine uses to drive the generator is an important consideration in selecting a generator set. Fuels that may be used include LP gas, natural gas, gasoline, and diesel fuel. Factors that affect the selection of fuel include its availability and local regulations governing its storage. Problems of fuel storage can be a deciding factor in the selection and types of generators used. If natural gas is used, its heating content measured in British thermal unit (Btu) must be greater than 1,000 Btus per cubic foot (37 megajoules per cubic meter). Diesel-powered generators are widely used because they require less maintenance and have a longer life.

Typical Engine-Generator Set

A large, water-cooled engine-generator set is shown in the image. This unit is diesel powered and is designed for long periods of operation. Critical applications may require one or more additional units as backup(s). These are commonly referred to as $N + 1$, $N + 2$, or $N + X$ designs. Codes normally require that generators installed in habitable buildings be located inside a separate fire-rated room protected by a fire suppression system.

Source: iStock@anutr tosirikul

Smaller generator sets are available with either air or liquid cooling systems. Larger units typically use liquid-cooled engines. Liquid-cooled engines used with generator sets operate in basically the same way as a liquid-cooled automobile engine. An engine-driven pump forces a mixture of water and antifreeze through passages in the engine cylinder block and head(s). The engine, pump, and radiator form a closed-loop pressurized cooling system. The most common generator set arrangement has a mounted radiator and engine-driven fan to cool the coolant and ventilate the generator room. Alternative methods include a remotely located radiator, or a local or remotely located liquid-to-liquid heat exchanger instead of a forced air-cooled radiator.

Depending on the generator size, compressed air starting systems and battery starting systems can be used to start generator engines. Compressed air starting systems can be used on larger generator sets. Battery starting systems are generally preferred for most applications involving generator sets smaller than 2,000 kW because they are much less expensive than compressed air systems while considered equally reliable. Battery starting systems used with generator sets are usually 12V or 24V. The batteries must have enough capacity to provide the cranking motor current indicated on the generator set specification sheet. The batteries are normally lead-acid, nickel-cadmium, or lithium-ion type. They must be designated for this use or may have to be approved by the Authority Having Jurisdiction (AHJ). For emergency power systems, a float-type battery charger, powered by the normal power source, must be provided to keep the batteries fully charged during standby without damage. As the battery approaches full charge, the charging current automatically tapers off to zero amperes or to a steady-state load on the battery. A high-output engine-driven alternator and automatic voltage regulator (part of the generator set) are provided to recharge the batteries during generator set operation. Batteries and battery charging systems are described in more detail later in *Section 2.0.0.*

The sizing of a generator set for a particular application is typically done using computer software developed specifically for that purpose, or using procedures outlined in the product literature from most generator set manufacturers. As a minimum, the generator set must be sized to supply the maximum starting (surge) demands and steady-state running loads of the connected equipment. Once the starting and running loads have been determined, it is common to add a margin factor of up to 25% for future expansion or to select a generator set of the next largest standard rating. A large connected load that does not run during usual power outages, such as a fire pump, can serve as part of the margin factor. For fuel efficiency, the running load should stay within approximately 50% to 80% of the generator set kW rating.

In applications where the voltage and frequency dip performance specifications are stringent, it is often necessary to oversize a generator set. Applications with the following types of loads and similar devices may also require oversizing the generator:

- Static uninterruptible power supplies (UPSs)
- Variable frequency drives
- Battery-charging rectifiers
- Medical diagnostic imaging equipment
- Fire pump(s)

Cogeneration

If an application requires an around-the-clock electric demand and has a substantial heat requirement, combined heat and power generation using turbine- or engine-generators, referred to as *cogeneration,* may offer substantial energy savings. In other cases, some electric utilities/suppliers offer peak-sharing rate arrangements by using distributed generation facilities. Under distributed generation (electric cogeneration), intermittently operated generators located at a customer site are automatically started and paralleled with the utility supplier on their demand. Either natural gas or diesel engine-powered generators may be furnished by the utility supplier and/or the customer, but they are usually operated and maintained by the customer. In many cases, idle standby power systems can be converted to revenue-producing assets. With peak sharing, the utility/supplier pays monthly credits or grants special interruptible pricing that effectively caps the customer's energy price and provides profit from the sale of excess power. Return on investment on the generating equipment is often three years or less.

Source: U.S. Department of Defense

1.1.3 Generator Set Maintenance and Service

The failure of an emergency or standby generator to start and run could lead to loss of life, personal injury, or property damage. For this reason, a comprehensive maintenance and service program carried out on a scheduled basis is absolutely necessary. Maintenance and service should be performed as scheduled and as recommended by the generator set manufacturer.

1.2.0 Transfer Switches

Transfer switches are a primary part of a building's emergency or standby power system. They are made in both automatic and nonautomatic/remote types.

1.2.1 Transfer Switch Operation

An automatic transfer switch automatically transfers electrical loads from a normal source (utility power) to an emergency source (generator set) when the normal source fails or its voltage is substantially reduced. The transfer switch automatically retransfers the load back to the normal power source when it is restored.

WARNING!

Always follow lockout procedures even if the circuit is de-energized.

The typical automatic transfer switch consists of two major component areas, an electrically operated double-throw transfer switch and related control panel circuits. *Figure 4* shows a basic application of an automatic transfer switch.

As shown in *Figure 4*, voltage inputs from the normal power source and the generator set (when running) are respectively applied to the voltage monitor and voltage/frequency monitor circuits, both located in the control panel. The transfer switch operates to perform the following functions:

- It initiates starting the emergency generator engine via contacts in the transfer switch control panel when the utility voltage drops to an unacceptable level.
- It maintains connection of the load circuits to the normal power source during the starting period to provide use of any existing service on the normal source.
- It measures the output voltage and frequency of the voltage being generated by the generator set with a voltage/frequency-sensitive monitor. Note that combined frequency and voltage monitoring protects against transferring loads to a generator set with an unacceptable output.
- It automatically switches the load circuits to the generator set when both its voltage and frequency are about normal.
- It provides a visual indication and auxiliary contact for remote indication when the generator set is supplying the loads.
- It automatically switches back to the utility power source when it is deemed stable and normal.

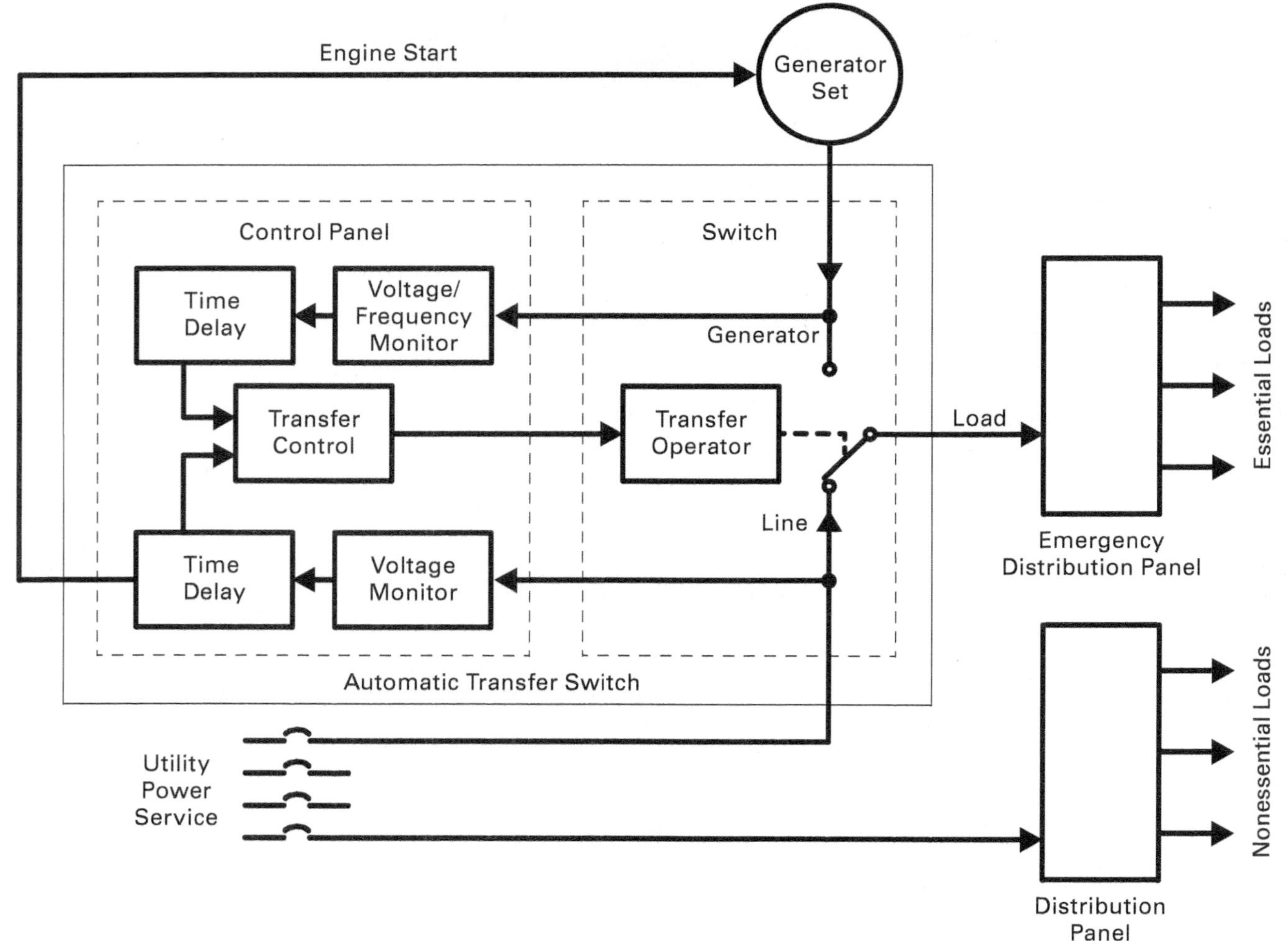

Figure 4 Simplified emergency/standby power distribution with automatic transfer switch.

Time delays are provided in the transfer switch control circuits to program the operation of the switch. One such delay, typically adjustable between 0 and 15 seconds in duration, is provided to avoid unnecessary starting and transfer of the generator set power source for power interruptions of short duration. If the interruption duration exceeds the time delay, the transfer switch will initiate startup of the generator set engine.

Once the load has been transferred to the generator set, another timer delays switching back (retransfer) to the normal source for an adjustable delay period, typically up to 30 minutes, until the source has had time to stabilize. This timer also allows the generator set to operate under load for a preselected minimum time, thus ensuring continued good performance of the engine and its starting system. If the generator set stops inadvertently during this delay, the transfer time delay is automatically bypassed.

A third time delay, usually adjustable from 0 to 10 minutes, is provided to allow generator set engine to cool down. During cooldown, the generator set runs unloaded after the load has been switched back to the utility power. Note that running an unloaded engine for more than 10 minutes is not recommended because it can cause deterioration in engine performance.

The operation of a nonautomatic/remote transfer switch is initiated either by an operator at the transfer switch or by an external signal from a remote control. The nonautomatic/remote transfer switch does not include an automatic controller, but it can be controlled by an automatic transfer switch with field wiring interconnections.

Microprocessor-Controlled Automatic Transfer Switches

Microprocessor-controlled automatic transfer switches are commonly available for voltages up to 600VAC and thousands of amperes of load-switching capability. A typical unit can be programmed to start an engine-generator when the voltage drops to a predetermined level (usually 80% of nominal). When the emergency source reaches 90% of rated voltage and 95% of rated frequency, the unit switches and locks the load to the emergency source. When the outside line voltage is restored to a predetermined point (usually 90%) as sensed by the unit, the unit switches and locks the load to the outside source. The microprocessor control allows programming the unit to switch when the outside line and emergency source are in phase and at or near zero phase difference. Optional programming allows momentary disconnection of a large motor load during switching, along with staged motor restarts after switching. The unit also allows a delayed transition on transfer to ensure decay of rotating motor or transformer fields for UPS system sequencing. The unit can be programmed to activate load-shedding functions prior to switching.

1.2.2 Transfer Switch Configurations and Sizing

Common transfer switch configurations are three pole with a solid neutral for single- and three-phase three-wire or four-wire circuits, or four pole with a switched neutral for use with separately derived three-phase four-wire systems. Because of their location in the electrical distribution system, transfer switches carry load current continuously, whether fed by the normal or the alternate power source. By design, transfer switches must be highly reliable because failure to operate as intended could leave critical load equipment without power, even though power may be available from at least one source.

The sizing of transfer switches is based on the calculated continuous current, in a manner similar to the sizing of circuit conductors. Remember to use transfer equipment continuous current ratings that equal the calculated continuous current for the load equipment or the next higher rating. If future load expansion is a consideration, refer to the maximum rating of the circuit overcurrent protective device when selecting a transfer switch rating. The available fault current and upstream overcurrent device may also affect sizing of the transfer equipment.

1.2.3 Automatic Sequential Paralleling

When two or more electric generating sets perform as a single power source, automatic sequential paralleling offers important advantages to the user. Some of the advantages include increased power capability, greater versatility in installation and operation, and, most importantly, greater reliability of a multiunit system. A typical automatic sequential paralleling emergency system for hospitals is illustrated in *Figure 5*. This system consists of engine-generator sets, paralleling switchboards, a totalizing board, and automatic transfer switches that monitor the total system and control the operation of each individual generating set.

If utility power is interrupted, an automatic transfer switch initiates starting of all three generator sets (A, B, and C) simultaneously. When one of the three generating sets first reaches operating voltage, a special emergency bus directs the power to the top-prioritized areas, such as operating rooms and life safety and support systems.

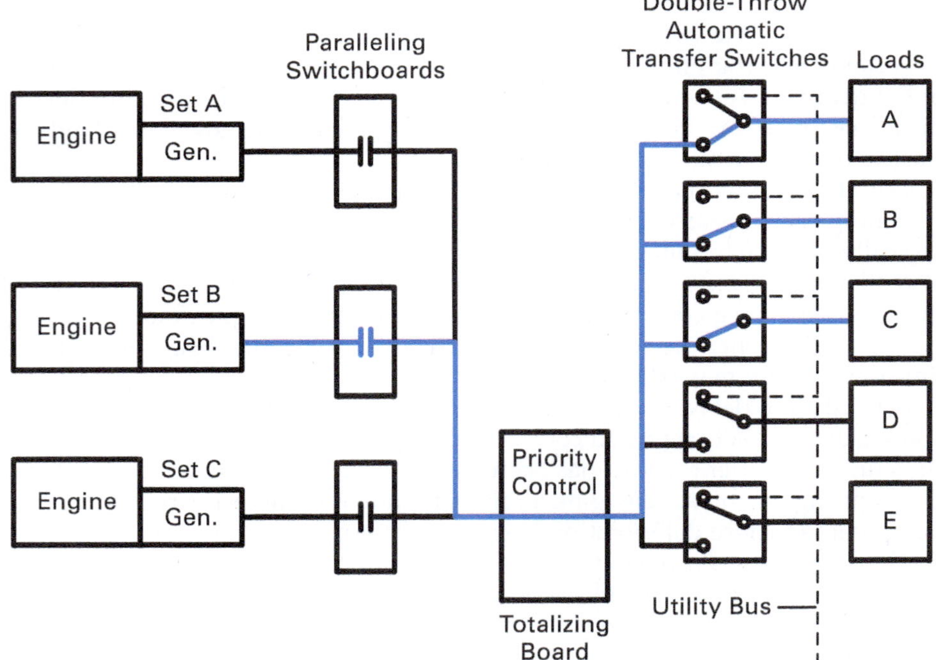

Figure 5 Typical automatic sequential paralleling emergency system.

With automatic sequential paralleling, each set generates power as soon as it starts, and any one can be the lead unit or the first on the bus. Fast speed in assuming the critical load is a major advantage of this system. With all sets in the system answering a request for power, most likely at least one of them will be able to assume the emergency load sooner than a single-set system.

Each generating set has its own synchronizer and electronically governed load sensor designed to automatically disconnect, shed, or add loads on a programmed-priority basis. In the event of an engine-generator failure, a reverse power relay in that set senses the reverse power condition, opens its circuit breaker, and disconnects that load from the bus. Noncritical equipment loads are usually shed first, ensuring continuous power to the critical life safety and support loads.

Other advantages offered by sequential paralleling systems include automatic operation and system expansion. If an addition is built or power needs increase, the system can be expanded. A component can be serviced with only a limited loss of power rather than total power loss, as is the case with a single-unit source. Furthermore, a sequentially paralleled system usually operates at higher overall efficiencies than individual generators.

WARNING!

The failure of an emergency or standby system may result in loss of life or other hazards. For this reason, ***NEC Sections 700.3(C) and 701.3(C)*** require maintenance in accordance with the manufacturer's instructions and industry standards.

Know the Code

Tests and Maintenance
NEC Section 700.3

Know the Code

Commissioning and Maintenance
NEC Section 701.3

Automatic Paralleling and Transfer Switchgear

The automatic paralleling and transfer switchgear shown in the image was designed for two large engine-generator sets. It serves as a standby system for the large data processing center of an insurance company.

1.0.0 Section Review

1. If natural gas is used to supply a generator, its Btu content must be *greater than* _____.
   a. 750 Btus/cubic foot
   b. 1,000 Btus/cubic foot
   c. 1,100 Btus/cubic foot
   d. 1,200 Btus/cubic foot

2. The third and final time delay used in an automatic transfer switch is used to provide for _____.
   a. source power stabilization
   b. temporary power failures
   c. engine cooldown
   d. brownouts

2.0.0 Storage Batteries and UPS Systems

Performance Tasks

There are no Performance Tasks in this section.

Objective

Describe battery and uninterruptible power supply (UPS) system types and explain their maintenance requirements.

a. Describe the different types of batteries used.
b. Explain the maintenance requirements of batteries and their charging considerations.
c. Identify single- and double-conversion UPS systems.

Storage batteries are widely used in starting systems for generator sets, emergency lighting, and many other applications. The demand for reliable battery backup is a priority in any standby and/or emergency system. No matter what type of equipment the battery backs up, the cost of failure is unacceptable. It is therefore a top priority to apply, operate, and maintain batteries correctly.

2.1.0 Storage Batteries

Know the Code

Storage Batteries and UPS
NEC Section 701.12(C)(4)

For the total load of circuits supplying legally required standby power, *NEC Section 701.12(C)(4)* specifies that a storage battery of suitable rating and capacity is required to supply and maintain at least 87.5% of the system voltage for a period of at least $1\frac{1}{2}$ hours. Batteries, whether acid, alkali, or lithium types, must be designed and constructed to meet the emergency service requirements and must be compatible with the charger for the particular installation. Some *NEC®* regulations governing storage batteries used in legally required standby systems are shown in *Figure 6*.

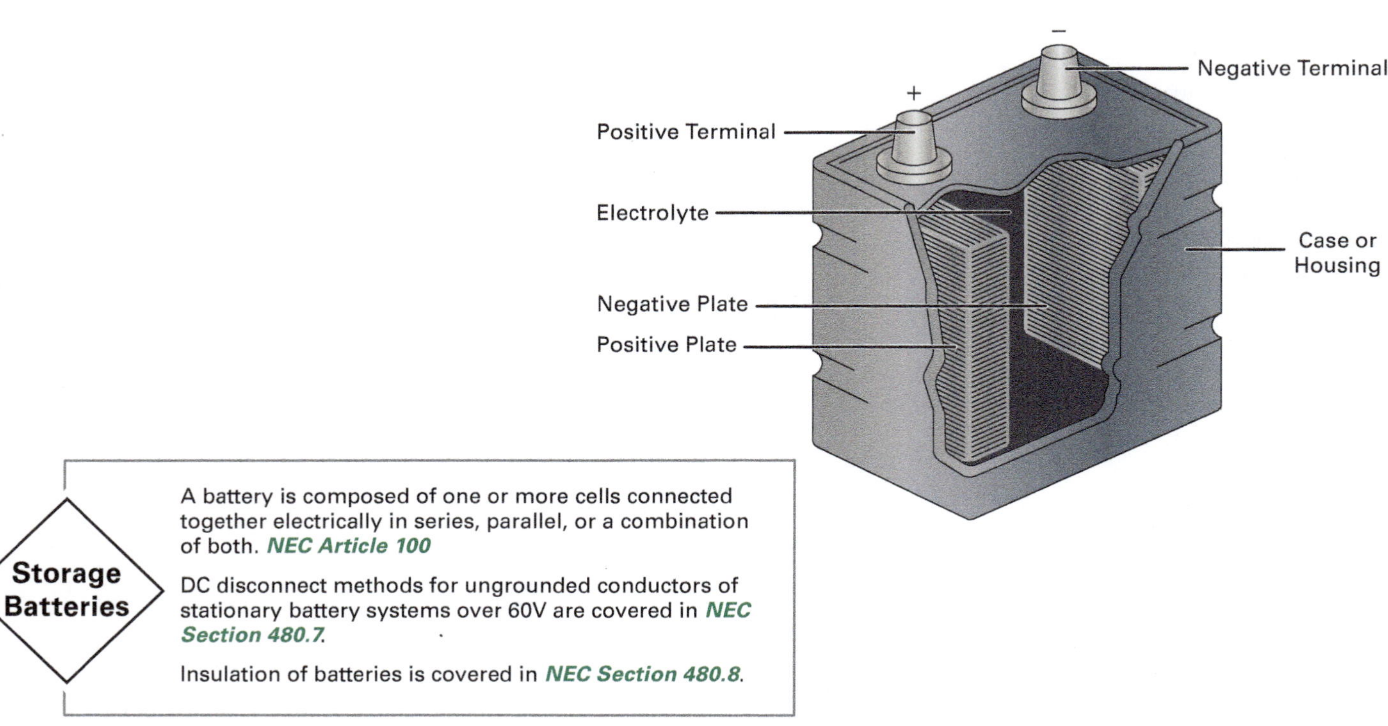

Figure 6 *NEC®* requirements governing storage batteries for legally required standby systems.

Lead-acid, nickel-cadmium, and lithium-ion batteries are rechargeable or *secondary* types of batteries. Batteries use chemical potential to store energy. When the battery is being charged, energy is stored chemically in the electrodes and **electrolyte** of the battery. When the battery is called upon to provide power to its load, the chemical reaction is reversed and the battery discharges. Electrons in the external conductors or posts of the battery flow from the negative electrode through the load, and back to the positive electrode. Battery voltage is computed on the basis of 2.0V per cell for lead-acid types, 1.2V per cell for alkali types, and 2.4V to 3.8V per cell for lithium-ion types. The nominal voltage in a lithium-ion battery varies based on the chemistry of the cell.

Electrolyte: A substance in which the conduction of electricity is accompanied by chemical action, such as the paste that forms the conducting medium between the electrodes of a dry cell or storage cell.

2.1.1 Lead-Acid Batteries

Lead-acid batteries are the original rechargeable battery chemistry. They are well suited to large-scale battery banks and applications that demand high discharge current. While lead-acid batteries are inexpensive, their low energy density, slow charging, and heavy weight make them a less favorable option than newer battery chemistries.

Lead-Acid Battery Construction

The internal construction of a typical standard lead-acid battery is shown in the image. Note the anti-flame propagation vent caps and the built-in lifting brackets.

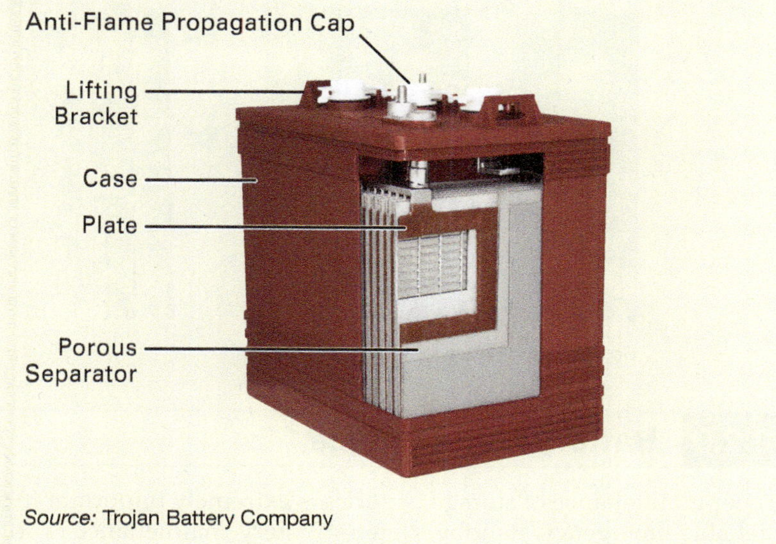

Source: Trojan Battery Company

2.1.2 Nickel-Cadmium Batteries

Nickel-cadmium batteries have been widely used for years. These batteries are inexpensive, perform well in extremely low temperatures and are easy to ship and store. They are still used for critical industrial backup applications. Drawbacks of nickel-cadmium batteries include low energy density, short storage life, and susceptibility to overcharge.

2.1.3 Lithium-Ion Batteries

Lithium-ion batteries are now the most common battery type used in standby and emergency power storage systems. They can be made with several different chemistries, and each type best serves different applications. Lithium iron phosphate is the most common type used for medical devices, UPS systems, and emergency standby applications where batteries are in a permanently charged state and only occasionally discharged. Lithium titanate batteries are used for grid stabilization, starter applications, and energy storage systems.

Lithium-Ion Batteries and Fire Risk

Overcharging can increase pressure within a lithium-ion cell, resulting in rapid and uncontrolled heating known as *thermal runaway*. The cell may catch fire or explode and may in turn cause neighboring batteries to ignite. Lithium-ion batteries require a protection circuit that monitors the battery voltage and cuts off the current to prevent overcharging when a certain voltage is reached. Storing lithium-ion batteries at cooler temperatures and thermal monitoring help to minimize the risk of fire.

Lithium-ion batteries are the most expensive type of battery but offer several advantages over lead-acid and nickel-cadmium chemistries. Of all secondary battery types, lithium-ion cells have the highest energy density, best thermal stability, and longest service life while requiring the least maintenance and recharging fastest. Lithium-ion battery systems can also be expanded easily. Unlike lead-acid and nickel-cadmium cells, lithium-ion cells do not off-gas. The disadvantage of lithium-ion batteries is that they are susceptible to overheating and may catch fire or explode if the cell cannot effectively dissipate this heat. The battery management system (BMS) is recommended to monitor the current, voltage, and temperature of lithium-ion batteries.

Sealed Valve-Regulated Lead-Acid (VRLA) Batteries

High-amperage modular battery units are available that incorporate absorbed glass mat (AGM) battery technology and have a 20-year design life when used in float service. The units can be connected in parallel and in series to obtain the desired voltage and amperage. The units use sealed valve-regulated lead-acid (VRLA) batteries that usually require no special venting under normal operating conditions. However, explosive gases may be vented during use if the batteries are overcharged, damaged, or subjected to a high-temperature environment.

Source: iStock@LeeTorrens

2.2.0 Battery Maintenance

Proper maintenance of storage batteries is extremely important in order to have a reliable emergency/standby system. Battery maintenance is for the cells as well as charging systems and ventilation systems.

2.2.1 Battery Maintenance Overview

It is essential to note the differences in the charging or float voltage for each type of battery. Setting and maintaining proper float voltage is critical to battery life. Overcharging a lead-acid battery will destroy the positive plate, evident by a characteristic dark sediment at the bottom of the cell jar. Undercharging a lead-acid battery will destroy the negative plate, producing a light gray sediment and a crystal-like sparkle on the plates. Overcharging lithium-ion batteries will overheat the cells and may result in fire or explosion.

The nominal open circuit voltage is 2.0V for a lead-acid cell, 1.2V for a nickel-cadmium cell, and 2.4V to 3.8V for a lithium-ion cell. But the charging voltage is higher. An equalizing charge is even higher than a charging float voltage, and it is applied to a battery when any individual cell voltage falls below a maintenance-specified minimum voltage. The equalizing overcharge tends to bring all cells back to float voltage when complete.

When a lead-acid battery is being discharged, the sulfuric acid of the battery is consumed and water is produced. During maintenance, this is observed and noted to determine the battery's state of charge, which is done by using a hydrometer to read the specific gravity of the sulfuric acid. The specific gravity of water is 1.0, whereas the specific gravity of sulfuric acid is near 1.15 and 1.28 respectively when a battery is discharged and near full charge. Note that measuring the specific gravity on nickel-cadmium batteries and lithium-ion batteries is not required.

Adverse temperature environments affect the life and performance of lead-acid batteries. High temperatures will reduce their life significantly. For every 15°F (8.3°C) above 77°F (25°C), the battery life will generally be reduced by 50%. At low temperatures, the performance of discharge quickly falls off. At extremely low temperatures, the battery can freeze once it goes into discharge.

The nickel-cadmium battery provides better durability in temperature extremes. Nickel-cadmium batteries can operate in temperatures as low as −40°F (−40°C) without damage or the threat of freezing. They have some degradation in life expectancy at high temperatures, but not to the extent of lead-acid batteries. For nickel-cadmium batteries, every 15°F (8.3°C) above 77°F (25°C) generally results in a 20% reduction in expected life.

Lithium-ion batteries can be charged from 32°F (0°C) to 113°F (45°C) and discharged from −4°F (−20°C) to 140°F (60°C). Higher temperatures allow increased storage capacity and, however, increase the risk of thermal runaway. Lithium-ion batteries can operate at temperatures of up to 104°F (40°C) with no performance issues.

Corrosion of the intercell connections in a bank of battery cells causes high resistance and even open circuits when the battery is being discharged under load. These problems have the potential to cause major system failures and battery fires. An intercell resistance test using a digital low-resistance ohmmeter during maintenance helps detect these high-resistance connections. It is common practice to use a reading of greater than 20% deviation from the average reading to initiate corrective action. Upon detection, retorque or replace the weak connections to prevent conduction path failures in the battery bank.

A battery bank can be effectively maintained with routine checks and inspections. As part of any successful battery maintenance program, it is necessary to visually inspect the bank's physical condition for damage or corrosion as well as electrolyte level, along with keeping a monitored record of specific gravity, voltage, and temperature readings. These readings will provide a measure of the battery's state of charge. The state of charge, however, is not a complete indication of battery life or capacity. Battery capacity is the most important criterion for replacing a battery.

The method of determining battery capacity is to perform a load test to measure the amount of power a fully charged battery is capable of delivering over a specific time period. Batteries are rated in *amp-hours*. A load test simply measures the percentage by comparing the time that the battery actually carries the load versus the time the battery is supposed to carry the load based on its amp-hour rating. The test is carried out down to a minimum operating voltage, typically 1.75V per cell. Any battery that exhibits less than 80% time capacity is considered failed and should be replaced. Various types of load boxes and monitors are used to perform load tests.

WARNING!

Batteries are hazardous and must be disposed of properly.

Standard UPS Batteries

A UPS battery bank with vented standard lead-acid batteries is shown in the image. Codes normally require that these types of batteries and battery banks be located in a dedicated fire-rated room that is vented to the outdoor air and protected by a fire suppression system. Some codes may require a special explosion-resistant room with reinforced walls, ceilings, floors, and steel doors. Continuous outdoor air exchange for the room is monitored, and all battery charging must be shut down automatically if the ventilation fails. UPS units using sealed batteries do not normally require this type of facility.

Source: Tim Ely

NOTE

There are specific manufacturer procedures to be followed for receiving, handling, and installing battery systems and chargers. They include receiving, inspection, storage, filling of lead-acid batteries, interconnection, and initial charge. Manufacturer services are often used to oversee these steps.

2.2.2 Battery Maintenance Guidelines

Much of the maintenance performed on batteries is done with the batteries in service. Therefore, the methods used should follow the protective procedures outlined in the appropriate standards and the battery manufacturer's instructions. In addition, these methods should preclude circuit interruption or arcing in the vicinity of the battery. One of the reasons is that hydrogen is liberated from all vented cell batteries while they are on float or equalize charge, as well as when they are nearing completion of a recharge. Valve-regulated lead-acid cells will also liberate hydrogen whenever their vents open. Therefore, adequate ventilation by natural or mechanical means must be available to minimize hydrogen accumulation. In addition, the battery area should be a mandated nonsmoking area.

All work performed on a battery shall be done only with the proper and safe tools and with the appropriate protective equipment, including:

- Chemical-resistant goggles and face shields
- Acid-resistant or alkali-resistant gloves
- Chemical-resistant protective aprons and overshoes
- Portable or stationary water facilities for rinsing eyes and skin in case of contact with electrolyte
- Acid- or alkali-neutralizing solution
- Insulated tools
- Class C fire extinguisher or other type as recommended by the battery manufacturer
- Respirator, if required

WARNING!

Some battery manufacturers do not recommend the use of CO_2 (Class C) fire extinguishers due to the possibility of thermal shock and battery container cracking. Always refer to the manufacturer's instructions for safety and maintenance procedures.

Guidelines for maintenance inspections and tests are introduced in the following paragraphs. For more detailed information on battery maintenance scheduling, refer to *IEEE Standard 446*. Anyone performing maintenance should be familiar with the appropriate standards and the battery manufacturer's instructions. This is particularly true for valve-regulated lead-acid cells since some testing is recommended to determine if the cell is drying out. Dry-out can be caused by a number of factors, such as high float voltage and high temperature.

As applicable to the types of batteries involved, the following visual inspections should be performed in accordance with the battery manufacturer's recommendations and/or the facility schedule. A typical maintenance interval for each task is shown here.

Monthly checks include:

- General appearance of the battery/rack area
- Dirt or electrolyte on jars, covers, etc.
- Charger voltage and current output
- Electrolyte level (vented lead-acid, vented nickel-cadmium, and vented lithium-ion cells)
- Jar or cover for cracks or leaks
- Jar or post seals (valve-regulated lead-acid cells)
- Excessive jar or cover distortion (valve-regulated lead-acid cells)
- Evidence of corrosion

Annual checks include:

- Flame arrester clogged (vented lead-acid, vented nickel-cadmium, and vented lithium-ion cells)
- Detailed rack inspection
- Insulating covers on racks
- Seismic rack part and spacers
- Detailed cell inspection (vented lead-acid cells)
- Plates for cracks, sulfate, and hydration (vented lead-acid cells)
- Abnormal sediment accumulation (vented lead-acid cells)
- Jar and post seals (other than valve-regulated lead-acid cells)
- Excessive jar or cover distortion (other than valve-regulated lead-acid cells)
- Excessive gassing (vented lead-acid cells)
- Signs of vibration

As applicable to the types of batteries involved, the following measurements should be performed in accordance with the battery manufacturer's recommendations and/or the user facility schedule. A typical maintenance interval for each task is shown here.

Monthly checks include:

- Battery float voltage
- Pilot cell voltage (vented lead-acid cells)
- Pilot cell electrolyte temperature (vented lead-acid cells)
- Pilot cell electrolyte specific gravity (vented lead-acid cells)
- Ventilation equipment adequacy

Quarterly checks include:

- Individual cell voltage
- Individual cell electrolyte specific gravity (vented lead-acid cells)
- Pilot cell electrolyte temperature (vented lithium-ion, vented nickel-cadmium, vented lead-acid, and valve-regulated lead-acid cells)
- Intercell connection resistance (valve-regulated lead-acid cells)
- Cell impedance, conductance, and resistance (valve-regulated lead-acid cells)
- Ambient temperature (vented lithium-ion, vented lead-acid, and valve-regulated lead-acid cells)

Annual checks include:

- AC ripple current and voltage (valve-regulated lead-acid cells)
- Intercell connection torque (vented nickel-cadmium cells)
- Intercell connection resistance (vented lead-acid cells)
- Battery rack torque
- Ground connections

2.2.3 Battery and Battery Charger Operation

In addition to providing voltage to start generator sets as previously described, standby batteries are widely used in many other emergency power applications, particularly to power emergency lighting systems. Standby batteries used in these applications are normally operated in the float mode where the battery, battery charger, and load are connected in parallel (*Figure 7*). The charging equipment should be of a size that provides all the power normally required by the loads plus enough additional power to keep the battery at full charge. Relatively large intermittent loads will draw power from the battery. This power is restored to the battery by the charger when the intermittent load ceases. If AC input power to the system is lost, the battery instantly carries the full load. If the battery and charger are properly matched to the load and to each other, there is no discernible voltage dip when the system goes to full-battery operation.

When AC charging power is restored, a constant-potential charger will deliver more current than would be necessary if the battery were fully charged. Some constant-potential chargers will automatically increase their output voltage to the equalizer setting after power to the charger is restored. Similarly, a constant current charger may automatically increase its output to the high rate. The battery charger must be sized such that it can supply the load and restore the battery to full charge within an acceptable time. The increased current delivered by a constant-potential charger during this restoration period will decrease as the battery approaches full charge.

The battery charger is an important part of the emergency power system, and consideration must be given to redundant chargers on critical systems. The charger should be operated only with the battery connected to the DC bus. Without this connection, excessive ripple on the system could occur, which could affect the connected equipment and cause improper operation or failure of the equipment. If a system must be able to operate without the battery connected, then a device called a *battery eliminator* should be used. Also, note that a battery charger's output must be derated for altitude when it is installed at locations above 3,300' and for temperature when the ambient temperature exceeds 122°F (50°C). The battery charger manufacturer can provide these derating factors.

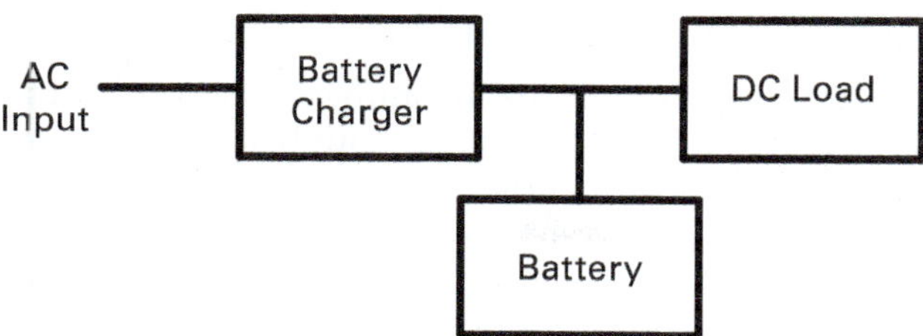

Figure 7 Stationary battery in float operation.

2.3.0 Uninterruptible Power Supply Systems

A static uninterruptible power supply (UPS) system is an electronically controlled, solid-state power control system designed as an alternate source to provide regulated AC power to critical loads in the event of a partial or total failure of the normal source of power, typically power supplied by the electric utility. Today, the term *UPS* commonly refers to a system consisting of a dedicated stationary-type battery, rectifier/battery charger, static inverter, and accessories such as a transfer switch. Note that in the past, UPS was commonly used to describe a type of static inverter often used in large DC systems.

There is a wide diversity in UPS configurations that provide for voltage regulation, line conditioning, lightning protection, redundancy, electromagnetic interference (EMI) management, extended run time, load transfer to other units, and other such features required to protect the critical loads against normal AC source failure and other power system disturbances. UPS systems are available in various designs and sizes, ranging from less than 100W to several megawatts. They may provide single-phase or three-phase power at frequencies of 50 Hz, 60 Hz, or 400 Hz. In addition, static UPS systems may provide power of which the output purity may vary from a near-perfect sine wave with less than 1% total harmonic distortion to a power wave that is essentially a square wave. There are two basic types of UPS systems used in a variety of configurations: double-conversion UPS systems and single-conversion UPS systems.

Typical UPS Unit

The UPS unit shown in the image is a double-conversion 800 kVA unit with a 12-pulse rectifier and an insulated gate bipolar transistor, pulse-width modulation (IGBT-PWM) inverter. It provides computer-grade power with excellent generator compatibility. High efficiency is maintained under light loading by the control system that optimizes the switching frequency for the load level and profile.

Source: Schneider Electric

2.3.1 Double-Conversion UPS Systems

In double-conversion UPS systems, the incoming AC power is first rectified and converted to DC (*Figure 8*). The DC is then supplied as input power to a DC-to-AC converter (inverter). The inverter output is AC, which is used to power the critical loads. This type of system is the static electrical equivalent to the motor-generator set. A battery is connected in parallel with the DC input to the inverter and provides continuous power to it any time the incoming line is outside of its specification or fails. Switching to the battery is automatic with no break in either the input to, or the output from the inverter.

The double-conversion system has several advantages:

- Excellent frequency stability
- High degree of isolation from variations in incoming line voltage and frequency
- Possible zero transfer time
- Quiet operation
- Can provide a sinusoidal output waveform with low distortion

In lower-power UPS applications (0.1 kVA to 20 kVA), the double-conversion system can have some of the following disadvantages:

- Lower efficiency
- Large DC power supply required (typically 1.5 times the full-load rating of the UPS)
- Poor noise isolation from line to load
- Possible shortened service life due to greater heat dissipation

2.3.2 Single-Conversion UPS Systems

In the single-conversion system (*Figure 9*), the incoming line to the UPS is not rectified to produce DC power to provide input to the inverter. The normal AC power is supplied directly to the critical loads through a series inductor or transformer. The normal AC power also supplies a small battery charger used to keep the UPS batteries fully charged. Thus, the battery is only used when the inverter requires its output to supplement or replace the normal power source.

Think About It

Sizing a UPS System

What other factors besides the direct load should be considered when sizing a UPS system?

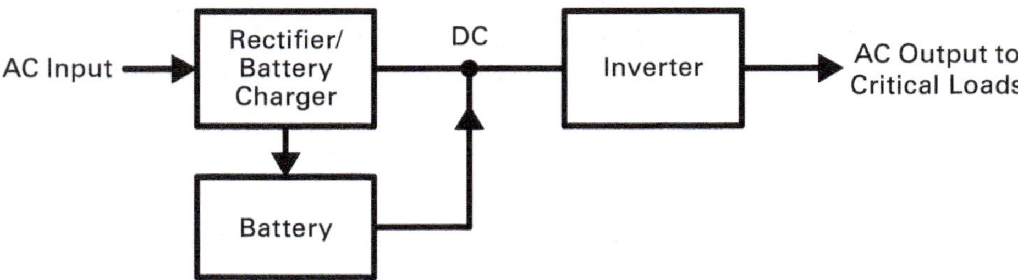

Figure 8 Simplified block diagram of a double-conversion UPS system.

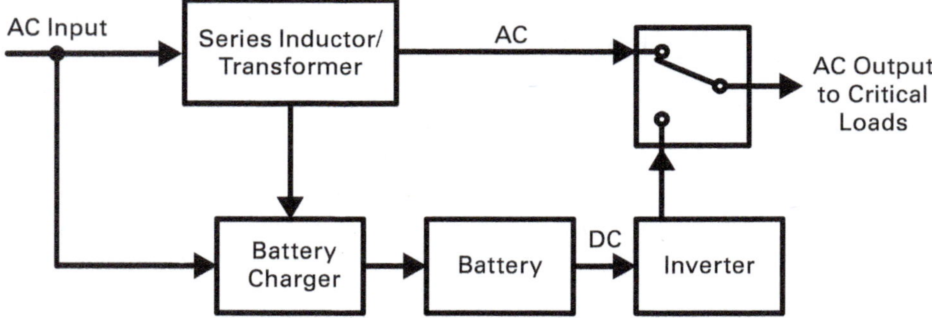

Figure 9 Simplified block diagram of a single-conversion UPS system.

Sealed VRLA Battery UPS Systems

The UPS system shown in the image has operating characteristics similar to the 800 kVA unit. The difference is that this particular unit is equipped with sealed VRLA batteries in a battery cabinet attached to the UPS cabinet. Sealed battery UPS systems can be located in most areas without special ventilation requirements.

Source: Tim Ely

Stored-Energy Flywheel UPS Systems

Battery-free, double-conversion UPS systems use a type of motor-generator and flywheel technology to provide 15 seconds of power at 100% rated load during power outages. These types of systems are sometimes referred to as *ride-through UPS systems*. In most cases, 15 seconds is sufficient to start and stabilize emergency engine-generators, including backup generators, and bring them online for the load, as well as to reestablish the UPS capability. Within the 15-second time frame, there is enough time to wait a few seconds to avoid unnecessary engine-generator starts resulting from momentary outages. The startup time for an engine-generator is normally five to six seconds, with another five or six seconds required to stabilize the output. If the primary engine-generators start, any backup units will be shut down after a predetermined delay. The engine-generator starting voltage and current are normally furnished directly from the UPS so that engine-starting batteries can be eliminated.

This type of UPS system is highly reliable and economical because it is free of all batteries that deteriorate over time and it is a simple rotating electrical device that requires little maintenance. The motor-generator also provides power conditioning by isolating the facility power from the utility power, thus eliminating power line transients and noise.

2.0.0 Section Review

1. For the total load of circuits supplying legally required standby power, a storage battery is required to supply and maintain at least 87.5% of the system voltage for a period of at *least* _____.
   a. 30 minutes
   b. 45 minutes
   c. 1 hour
   d. $1\frac{1}{2}$ hours

2. A battery charger's output must be derated for temperature when the ambient temperature *exceeds* _____.
   a. 86°F
   b. 100°F
   c. 122°F
   d. 140°F

3. One disadvantage of a low-power, double-conversion UPS system is _____.
   a. increased distortion
   b. increased transfer time
   c. poor frequency stability
   d. lower efficiency

3.0.0 *NEC*® Requirements for Emergency Systems

Objective

Describe the *NEC*® requirements for emergency/standby power and lighting systems.

a. Describe legally required standby systems.
b. Describe the alternate power requirements for health care facilities.
c. Describe the alternate power requirements for places of assembly.
d. Describe emergency lighting requirements and devices for public buildings.

Performance Tasks

There are no Performance Tasks in this section.

Several areas of the *NEC*® deal with emergency standby systems along with the means of generating or producing electricity for them. In general, *NEC Article 700* deals with emergency systems. However, there are other *NEC*® requirements that are directly related to the sources of power used for emergency systems. Branch circuits for emergency power are covered to some extent in *NEC Chapters 2 and 3*. Transfer switches are dealt with in *NEC Section 700.5*. Storage batteries used for emergency electrical systems are covered in *NEC Section 701.12(C)(4)* and *NEC Article 480*. Consequently, several areas of the *NEC*® will have to be referred to when designing, installing, or maintaining these systems.

Know the Code

Emergency System
NEC Article 700

Know the Code

Transfer Equipment
NEC Section 700.5

3.1.0 Legally Required Standby Systems

NEC Article 701 covers installation requirements of legally required standby electrical systems. The article's intent is to provide a system when the normal electrical supply is interrupted. The system should be electrically safe and cover circuits and equipment intended to supply, distribute, and control electricity to required facilities for illumination or power (or both).

This article covers only those systems that are permanently installed in their entirety, including the power source.

In general, legally required standby systems serve loads such as lighting systems, HVACR systems, communication systems, smoke removal systems, sewage disposal, and industrial processes that, upon interruption of the normal electrical supply, could create hazards or hamper rescue or firefighting operations.

A legally required standby system must have adequate capacity and rating for the supply of all equipment intended to be operated at one time. Furthermore, it must be suitable for the maximum available fault current at its terminals.

Automatic selective load pickup and load shedding are provided as needed to ensure adequate power to the legally required standby circuits. In this case, the alternate power source is permitted to supply legally required standby and optional standby system loads.

Transfer equipment, including automatic transfer switches, must be identified for standby use and approved by the AHJ. In any operation of the transfer equipment, they must also be designed and installed to prevent the inadvertent interconnection of normal and alternate sources of supply. Consequently, transfer equipment, including transfer switches, must operate in such a manner that all ungrounded conductors of one supply source are completely disconnected before any of the second source are connected.

A means may be provided to bypass and isolate the transfer switch equipment. However, where bypass isolation switches are used, inadvertent parallel operation must be avoided (*Figure 10*).

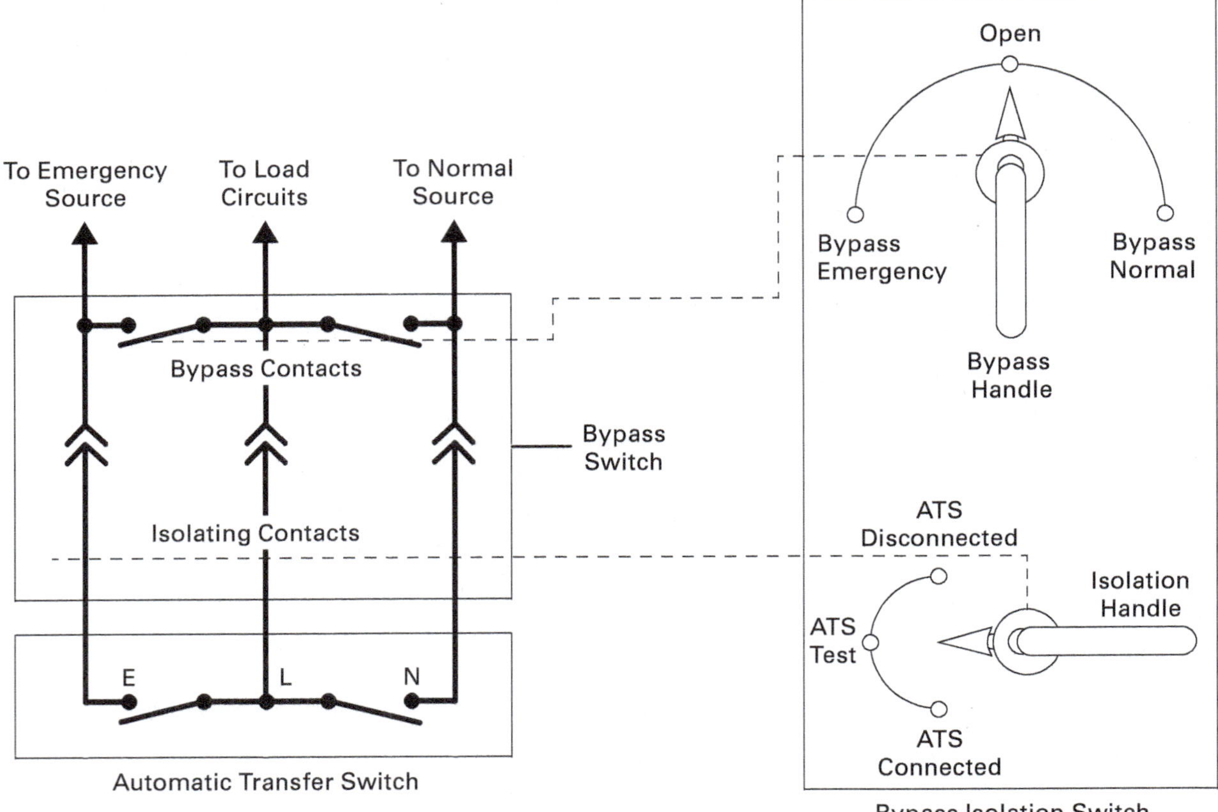

Figure 10 Two-way bypass isolation system.

Know the Code

Mandated Standby
NEC Section 701.7(A)

Know the Code

Grounding
NEC Section 701.7(B)

Think About It

Emergency Systems

Why can't other loads also be connected to an emergency system?

Know the Code

Capacity and Rating
NEC Section 701.4

Where possible, audible and visual signal devices are usually provided to indicate the following:

- Derangement of the standby source
- A load on the standby source
- A malfunctioning battery charger

A sign indicating the type and location of on-site legally required standby power sources must be placed at the service entrance, per *NEC Section 701.7(A)*. Furthermore, when the grounded conductor connected to the emergency source is connected to a grounding electrode conductor remote from the emergency source, *NEC Section 701.7(B)* requires a sign at the grounding location to identify all emergency and normal sources connected there.

In the event of a normal power supply failure, current must be supplied to legally required standby systems so that power will be available within the time required for the application without exceeding 60 seconds. As described in *Section 2.1.0*, *NEC Section 701.12(C)(4)* specifies that for the total load of the circuits supplying legally required standby power, a storage battery of suitable rating and capacity is required to supply and maintain at least 87.5% of system voltage for a period of at least $1\frac{1}{2}$ hours. Generator sets suitable as a power supply for legally required standby systems were covered in *Section 1.1.1*. It is also important to ensure that the prime mover (usually an engine) is acceptable to the AHJ and sized in accordance with *NEC Section 701.4*. It must have adequate capacity and rating for the supply of all equipment intended to be operated at one time.

A means must be provided for automatic starting when the normal service fails. Furthermore, the system must be controlled so that the standby power is automatically transferred to all required electrical circuits. A short-time feature permitting a 15-minute setting must be provided to avoid retransfer in case of short-time reestablishment of the normal service.

Refer to *Figure 11* for a summary of other *NEC*® requirements governing legally required standby systems. See the listed *NEC*® sections for greater detail. Also be aware to adhere to other *NEC*® sections if applicable.

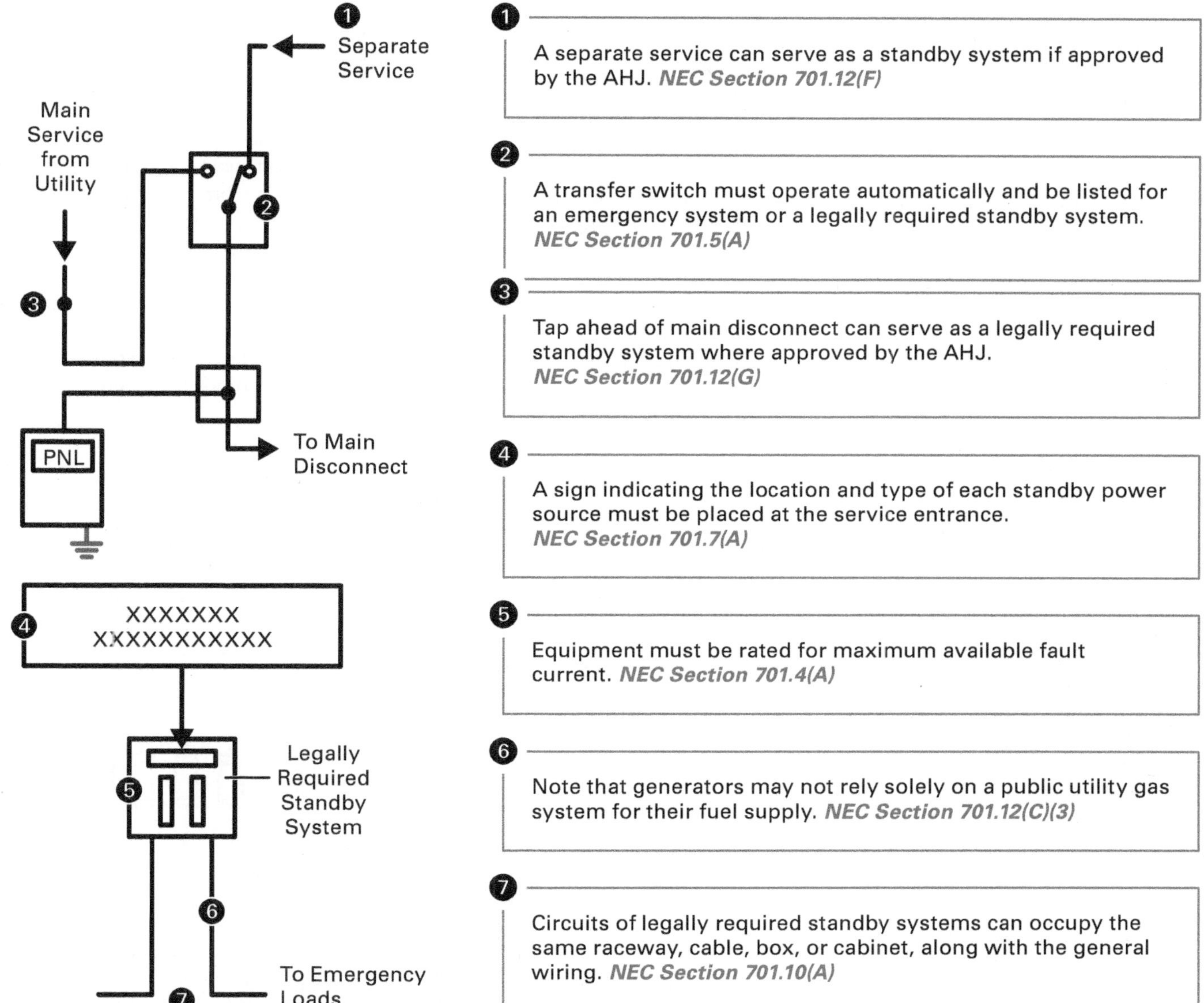

Figure 11 Summary of *NEC*® installation requirements governing legally required standby systems.

3.2.0 Health Care Facilities

Know the Code

Health Care Facilities
NEC Article 517

In order to serve the essential electrical system, *NEC Article 517* requires installing an alternate power source consisting of one or more generator sets or battery systems (where permitted) in health care facilities. Essential electrical systems for hospitals must include three separate branches—the life safety branch, the critical branch, and the equipment branch. During the time the normal electrical service is interrupted, the branches are capable of supplying a limited amount of lighting and power service considered essential for life safety and effective hospital operation. The equipment branch must supply the major electrical equipment necessary for patient care and basic hospital operation.

Each patient bed location must be supplied by at least two branch circuits, one or more from the critical branch and one or more from the normal electrical system. The receptacles supplied from the critical branch must be identified and indicate the panelboard and circuit number supplying them. All receptacles used in patient bed locations must be listed as hospital grade.

The number of transfer switches to be used must be based upon reliability, design, and load considerations. Each branch of the essential electrical system must be served by one or more transfer switches (*Figure 12*). One transfer switch may serve one or more branches in a facility with a maximum demand on the essential electrical system of 150 kVA.

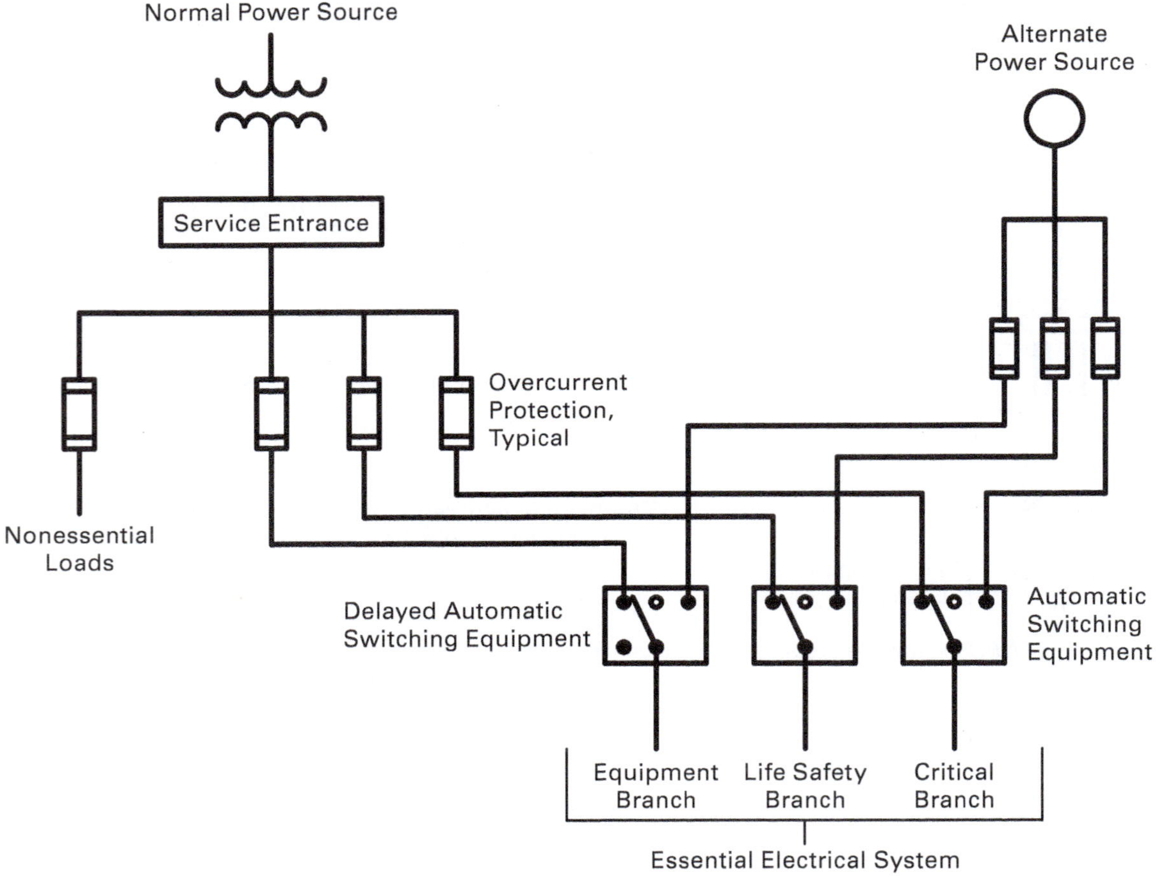

Figure 12 Essential electrical systems must be served by one or more transfer switches.

The life safety and critical branches of the essential electrical system must be kept entirely independent of all other wiring and equipment. Also, they must not enter the same raceways, boxes, or cabinets with each other or other wiring, except as follows:

- In transfer switches
- In exit or emergency lighting fixtures supplied from two sources
- In a common junction box attached to exit or emergency lighting fixtures supplied from two sources

Testing of the system is required upon installation and periodically thereafter. A written record must be kept of all testing and maintenance.

The wiring of the equipment branch is permitted to occupy the same raceways, boxes, or cabinets of other circuits that are not part of the essential electrical system.

The essential electrical system must have adequate capacity to meet the demand for the operation of all functions and equipment to be served by each branch.

The life safety branch must supply power for the following:

- Lighting required for corridors, passageways, stairways, and landings at all exit doors
- Exit signs
- Alarm and alerting systems
- Communication systems
- Generator set accessories
- Elevators
- Automatic doors

The critical branch must supply power for task illumination, fixed equipment, selected receptacles, and special power circuits serving the following areas and functions related to patient care:

- Anesthetizing locations
- Isolated power systems in special environments
- Patient care spaces
- Nurse call system
- Blood, bone, and tissue banks
- Telephone equipment room and closets
- Task illumination, receptacles, and selected power circuits needed for effective hospital operation

Per *NEC Sections 517.35(A) and (B)*, the equipment branch must supply power for the following with a delayed connection:

- Central suction systems
- Sump pumps
- Compressed air systems
- Smoke control and stair pressurization systems
- Kitchen hood supply and exhaust systems
- Supply, return, and exhaust ventilating systems
- Heating equipment
- Pressure maintenance for fire protection systems

Know the Code

Equipment Branch Connection to Alternate Power Source
NEC Section 517.35

Know the Code

Identification
NEC Section 700.10(A)

NEC Section 700.10(A) also requires labels, signs, or some other permanent marking to be used on all enclosures containing emergency circuits to readily identify them as components of an emergency system (*Figure 13*).

All boxes and enclosures for emergency circuits must be painted red, marked with red labels that read "Emergency Circuits," or in some other manner clearly identifiable to electricians and maintenance personnel.

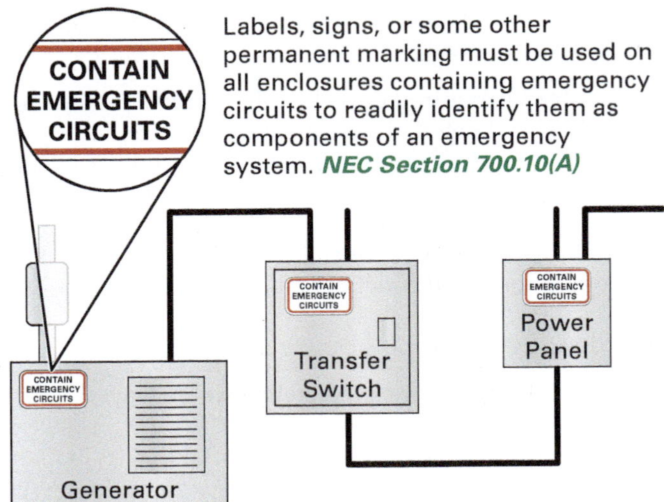

Figure 13 Summary of *NEC*® requirements for emergency circuit identification.

3.3.0 Places of Assembly

Know the Code

Assembly Occupancies
NEC Article 518

Know the Code

Emergency Systems
NEC Article 700

NEC Article 518 covers assembly occupancies—that is, all buildings or portions of buildings or structures designed or intended for assembly of 100 or more persons. Such facilities include assembly halls, restaurants, dance halls, courtrooms, auditoriums, churches, and similar locations. The installation and control of emergency electrical systems in these facilities must comply with *NEC Article 700*. All equipment must be approved for use on emergency systems.

The AHJ must conduct or witness a test on the complete system upon installation and periodically afterward. A written record of such tests and maintenance must be kept.

All boxes and enclosures including transfer switches, generators, and power panels for emergency circuits must be permanently marked so they can be readily identified as a component of an emergency circuit or system. These boxes and enclosures for emergency circuits must be painted red, marked with red labels that read "Emergency Circuits" or in some other manner clearly identifiable to electricians and maintenance personnel.

3.4.0 Emergency Lighting

The loads on emergency circuits for light and power will vary with the building type. However, in almost all areas throughout the US, all public buildings must have exit lights and emergency white lights connected to an emergency electric system for occupants to see while exiting. In general, the following items must be fed from an emergency circuit in public buildings:

- All exit lights
- Sufficient emergency white lights
- Fire alarm systems
- Life safety systems
- Sprinkler system water pumps

3.4.1 Battery-Powered Emergency Lighting

Emergency lighting systems are used to provide the required lighting to a facility for egress or other purposes, such as security when the normal electrical supply is interrupted. In the event of a fire or other emergency, the illumination in an area could be lost or reduced to a level where evacuation may be difficult or impossible. The purpose for emergency lighting is to illuminate evacuation routes and exits so that the chance of personal injury or loss of life can be minimized. Batteries are used in self-contained emergency lighting units and central emergency lighting systems. They may be DC batteries only or UPSs.

Specific requirements for emergency lighting are defined in *NEC Sections 700.15 through 700.27.* The required backup time for emergency lighting batteries is $1\frac{1}{2}$ hours (90 minutes), although some systems may be designed to have a longer backup time. Also, if emergency lighting depends upon the changing of sources (for instance, from AC to DC), the change must occur automatically with no appreciable interruption (less than 10 seconds). In areas that are normally lighted solely by high-intensity discharge (HID) systems, any battery-powered emergency lighting must continue to function once power is restored until the HID fixtures provide illumination. The system design must also consider a single failure of any individual lighting element, such as a lamp, so that any space requiring emergency lighting won't be left in total darkness.

The emergency lighting fixtures may be incandescent, fluorescent, or LED. They vary in style from the industrial type suitable for use in classified areas to decorator types used in offices, convention centers, etc. Emergency lighting fixtures also include exit signs. The lamps illuminate stairs, stairway landings, aisles, corridors, ramps, passageways, exit doors, and any other areas requiring emergency lighting.

Know the Code

Emergency System Circuits for Lighting and Power
NEC Article 700, Part IV

Know the Code

Control — Emergency Lighting Circuits
NEC Article 700, Part V

3.4.2 Emergency Lighting Units

Emergency lighting units, also called *unit equipment*, are the most popular type of emergency lighting equipment in use today (*Figure 14*). These units consist of a rechargeable battery, a battery charger, and one or more lamps, provisions for remote lamps, or both. The unit has the necessary controls to maintain the battery fully charged while the normal source of power is available and to automatically energize the lamps upon the loss of the normal power supply. Most units have the capability for automatic testing and self-diagnostics. The controls will de-energize the lamps immediately or after a time delay (for HID lamps) upon restoration of the normal power supply. If the unit is used with a fluorescent fixture, it will also have a high-frequency inverter and controls intended for that type of fixture.

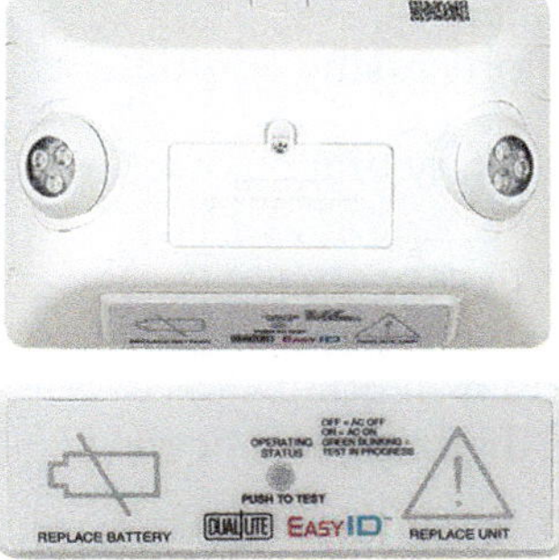

Figure 14 Typical emergency lighting units.
Source: Hubbell Incorporated

Emergency lighting units must be installed in accordance with *NEC Section 701.12(I)* which refers to *NEC Section 700.12(H)*. Install emergency lighting units according to the following standards:

- Ensure that the emergency lighting unit is listed.
- Install the unit so that it is permanently fixed in place.

Know the Code

Battery-Equipped Emergency Luminaires, Used for Legally Required Standby Systems
NEC Section 701.12(I)

Know the Code

Battery-Equipped Emergency Luminaires
NEC Section 700.12(H)

NOTE

Early printings of the 2023 *NEC*® contained an error in ***Section 701.12(I)*** that incorrectly referred to ***701.12(H)***—instead of ***700.12(H)***. See Errata number 70-23-4, available on NFPA's website, for further information.

- If using a flexible cord and plug to connect the unit to the branch circuit, use a cord that does not exceed 3' (900 mm) in length.
- If the same branch circuit serving normal lighting in the area is used, connect the emergency lighting unit ahead of local switches.
- If the same branch circuit or a separate branch circuit serving normal lighting in the area is used, ensure that the branch circuit has a means to monitor the status of the normal-lighting branch circuit and the means is connected ahead of local switches.
- If a separate branch circuit is used that originates from the same panelboard as a normal-lighting circuit, ensure that the branch circuit's disconnecting means has a lock-in feature.
- At the distribution panel, clearly identify the branch circuit that feeds battery-equipped emergency luminaires.
- Follow *NEC Article 700, Part II, IV, or V* when wiring emergency luminaires that obtain power from a battery-equipped emergency luminaire.
- Battery-equipped emergency luminaires serving the area immediately inside an exit door may supply remote luminaires to provide lighting to the exterior of that exit door.

Know the Code

Circuit Wiring
NEC Article 700, Part II

Know the Code

Emergency System Circuits for Lighting and Power
NEC Article 700, Part IV

Know the Code

Control — Emergency Lighting Circuits
NEC Article 700, Part V

These units can be supplied with any of the lead-acid, pocket-plate nickel-cadmium, or lithium-ion batteries described in *Section 2.0.0*. In addition, the units may be supplied with chargers that have an automatic temperature compensation of float/charge voltage. This feature is a must when a valve-regulated lead-acid battery is supplied with the unit. The selection of the battery type depends on the installation itself. For example, pocket-plate nickel-cadmium batteries may be used in high-temperature areas such as near an industrial boiler. On the other hand, valve-regulated lead-acid or sealed sintered-plate batteries may be used in an office area. All of these batteries require periodic maintenance and testing.

The batteries used in emergency lighting units are normally either 6VDC or 12VDC. For the lead-acid cells, the electrolyte specific gravity is normally 1.225 or greater, and the cell capacity is often expressed in ampere-hours at the 10-hour or 20-hour discharge rate of 1.75V per cell at 77°F (25°C).

3.0.0 Section Review

1. A legally required standby system is likely to include loads such as _____.
   a. lighting systems
   b. commercial kitchen equipment
   c. fire alarms
   d. data processing equipment

2. The life safety branch of a hospital's essential electrical system supplies power to _____.
   a. patient care areas
   b. nurse call systems
   c. corridor lighting
   d. anesthetizing locations

3. Wiring considerations for a church are covered in _____.
   a. *NEC Article 430*
   b. *NEC Article 480*
   c. *NEC Article 500*
   d. *NEC Article 518*

4. The required backup time for emergency lighting is _____.
   a. 15 minutes
   b. 30 minutes
   c. 60 minutes
   d. 90 minutes

Module 26403-23 Review Questions

1. In the event of a normal power supply failure, standby power for an emergency system must be available *within* _____.
   a. 10 seconds of the failure
   b. 30 seconds of the failure
   c. 60 seconds of the failure
   d. 5 minutes of the failure

2. Legally required standby systems are covered in _____.
   a. *NEC Article 700*
   b. *NEC Article 701*
   c. *NEC Article 702*
   d. *NEC Article 705*

3. The field windings of an AC generator are located on the _____.
   a. rotor
   b. stator
   c. transfer switch
   d. exciter

4. A stator is _____.
   a. the rotating element of a motor or generator
   b. the stationary part of a motor or generator
   c. a device that supplies direct current
   d. not a part of a motor or generator

5. All of the following are parts of an AC generator, *except* a(n) _____.
   a. stator
   b. rotor
   c. transfer switch
   d. exciter

6. When sizing a generator set, once the starting and running loads have been determined, it is common to add a margin factor for future expansion of *up to* _____.
   a. 10%
   b. 15%
   c. 25%
   d. 33%

7. To prevent engine deterioration, avoid running an unloaded engine for *longer* than _____.
   a. 1 minute
   b. 10 minutes
   c. 30 minutes
   d. 60 minutes

8. The specific gravity of sulfuric acid when a battery is discharged is near _____.
   a. 1.10
   b. 1.15
   c. 1.20
   d. 1.28

9. How often should the intercell connection resistance of a vented lead-acid battery bank be tested with a digital low-resistance ohmmeter?
   a. Monthly
   b. Quarterly
   c. Annually
   d. Biannually

10. Each of the following is an advantage of a double-conversion UPS system, *except* _____.
    a. possible zero transfer time
    b. quiet operation
    c. excellent efficiency in all applications
    d. excellent frequency stability

11. In a single-conversion UPS system, the incoming AC utility power is *first* applied to the _____.
    a. battery charger
    b. inverter
    c. critical load
    d. battery charger and transformer

12. Which of the following covers the installation of emergency systems?
    a. *NEC Article 518*
    b. *NEC Article 700*
    c. *NEC Article 703*
    d. *NEC Section 250.34*

13. In the event of a power failure, the *maximum* time allowed for a legally required standby generator system to be started and switched online is _____.
    a. 20 seconds
    b. 40 seconds
    c. 60 seconds
    d. 80 seconds

14. What is the minimum number of essential electrical system branches that *must* be provided in hospitals?
    a. One
    b. Two
    c. Three
    d. Four

15. All of the following may contain both the life safety branch and critical branch wiring of the essential electrical system used in hospitals, *except* _____.
    a. raceways
    b. transfer switches
    c. exit lighting fixtures supplied from two sources
    d. emergency lighting fixtures supplied from two sources

Answers to odd-numbered Module Review Questions are found in *Appendix A*.

Module 26403-23 Supplemental Exercises

1. In the event of a normal power supply failure, standby power for a legally required standby system must be available within __________ of the failure.

2. In an AC generator, the voltage induced into each stator winding depends on the strength of the __________ and the __________ with which the lines of force cut across the windings.

3. The excitation system for a typical generator is controlled via a(n) __________.

4. Which of the following time delays are *not* incorporated in an automatic transfer switch control circuit?
   a. Time delay to avoid unnecessary starting and transfer of generator power
   b. Time delay for switching (retransfer) back to the normal power source
   c. Time delay for generator engine cooldown
   d. Time delay for engine cooling fan operation

5. The __________ battery has the highest energy density and requires the least maintenance.

6. The nominal open circuit voltage is __________ for a lead-acid cell, __________ for a nickel-cadmium cell, and __________ for a lithium-ion cell.

7. An equalizing charge is __________ than a charging float voltage.

8. Any battery that exhibits less than __________ percent time capacity is considered to have failed a load test.

9. For lead-acid batteries, a general rule of thumb is that for every 15°F above 77°F, the life of the battery will be reduced by __________ percent.

10. When AC charging power is restored, a constant-potential charger will deliver __________ current than is necessary if the battery were fully charged.

11. Uninterruptible power supplies may provide __________ and __________ power at 60 Hz.

12. Where in the *NEC*® would you find information on emergency systems?
    ____
    ____

13. In order to meet the requirements of *NEC Section 701.12(C)(4)*, storage batteries are required to supply and maintain at least __________ percent of the system voltage for the total load of the circuits for a period of at least __________ hour(s).

14. What is the minimum number of people required under *NEC Article 518* for a space to be considered a place of assembly?
    a. 50
    b. 75
    c. 100
    d. 150

15. Which of the following is an approved method of marking boxes and enclosures for emergency circuits?
    a. Painted yellow and white
    b. Painted green with yellow stripes
    c. Painted red
    d. Painted blue and white

Answers to odd-numbered Supplemental Exercises are found in *Appendix B*.

Answers to Section Review Questions

Answer	Section Reference	Objective
Section 1.0.0		
1. b	1.1.2	1a
2. c	1.2.1	1b
Section 2.0.0		
1. d	2.1.0	2a
2. c	2.2.3	2b
3. d	2.3.1	2c
Section 3.0.0		
1. a	3.1.0	3a
2. c	3.2.0	3b
3. d	3.3.0	3c
4. d	3.4.1	3d

Basic Electronic Theory

Source: iStock@Krasyuk

Objectives

Successful completion of this module prepares you to do the following:

1. Describe electronic fundamentals.
   a. Explain basic electronic theory.
   b. Explain semiconductor fundamentals.
2. Identify and describe semiconductor devices.
   a. Describe the operation and uses of diodes.
   b. Describe the operation and uses of transistors.
   c. Describe the operation and uses of semiconductor switching devices.

Performance Tasks

Under supervision, you should be able to do the following:

1. Test a transistor to determine whether it is an NPN or PNP.
2. Identify the cathode on three different styles of SCRs, using the shape or markings for identification.

Overview

Electronics is a science dealing with the behavior and effect of electron flow in specific substances used to create electronic devices. Electronics can be distinguished from electricity in terms of the voltages and currents used. This module explains the function and operation of basic electronic devices, including semiconductors, diodes, rectifiers, and transistors.

NOTE

Digital Resources for Electrical

Scan this code using the camera on your phone or mobile device to view the digital resources related to this craft.

1.0.0 Electronic Fundamentals

Performance Tasks

There are no Performance Tasks in this section.

Objective

Describe electronic fundamentals.

a. Explain basic electronic theory.

b. Explain semiconductor fundamentals.

Semiconductors: Materials that are neither good insulators nor good conductors. Such materials contain four valence electrons and are used in the production of solid-state devices.

Electronics is a science that deals with the behavior and effect of electron flow in specific substances, such as **semiconductors**. Electronics can be distinguished from electricity in terms of the voltages and currents used. Electrical circuit AC voltages are measured in hundreds of volts, and currents are measured in tens of amps. In electronic circuits, low-level DC voltages such as 5V, 10V, 15V, and 24V are common. Current is measured in milliamps (mA) and even microamps (μA).

1.1.0 Basic Electronic Theory

Figure 1 Structure of an atom.

The atom consists of a central nucleus composed of protons and neutrons, surrounded by orbiting electrons (*Figure 1*). The nucleus is relatively large when compared to the orbiting electrons, just as the sun is larger than its orbiting planets.

In an atom, the orbiting electrons are held in place by the electric force between the negative electrons and positive protons, together with the centrifugal force that results from the motion of the electrons rotating around the nucleus. It is similar to how the Earth's gravity keeps its satellite (the moon) from drifting off into space. The law of charges states that opposite charges attract and like charges repel. The positively charged protons in the nucleus, therefore, attract the negatively charged electrons. If this force of attraction were the only one in effect, the electrons would be pulled closer and closer to the nucleus and eventually be absorbed into the nucleus. However, this force of attraction is balanced by the centrifugal force that results from the motion of the electrons around the nucleus (*Figure 2*). The law of centrifugal force states that a spinning object will pull away from its center point. The faster an object spins, the greater the centrifugal force becomes.

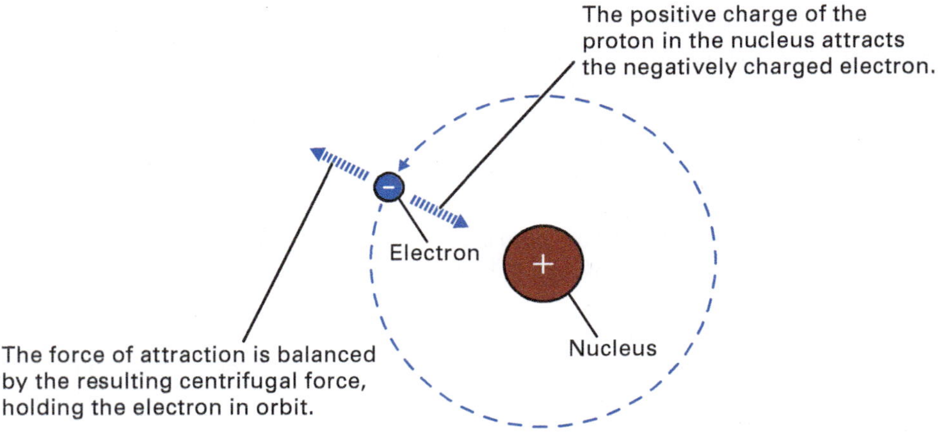

Figure 2 Electron in orbit around the nucleus.

Because the protons and orbital electrons of an atom are equal in number along with equal and opposite in charge, they neutralize each other electrically. Normally, each atom is electrically neutral—that is, it exhibits neither a positive nor a negative charge. However, under certain conditions, an atom can become unbalanced by losing or gaining electrons. If an atom loses a negatively charged electron, the atom will exhibit a positive charge and is then referred to as a *positive ion*. Similarly, an atom that gains an additional negatively charged electron becomes negatively charged itself and is then called a *negative ion*. In either case, an unbalanced condition is created in the atom, causing the formerly neutral atom to become charged. When one atom is charged and there is an unlike charge in another nearby atom, electrons can flow between the two. This flow of electrons is an *electrical current*.

Electron Orbits or Shells

Diagrams of atoms usually depict fixed orbits for electrons. However, this is a classical and convenient method used for notation only and is inaccurate. Modern quantum mechanics indicates that electrons occupy specific areas of space around an atom, depending on their energy level, rather than fixed orbits. The specific areas are called *orbitals*, and the electrons in a particular orbital space may be passing around the nucleus in any number of random circular or elliptical paths within that space. Each electron at a particular energy level is defined in a wave function called an *atomic orbital*. The wave function is obtained by solving a quantum mechanics equation known as the *Schrödinger equation*. As shown in the image, the combined areas of the theoretical orbitals for all atoms appear as a cloud around the nucleus of an atom, with the cloud being denser toward the center.

The sizes and proportions of atomic particles, as well as the distances between them, are also portrayed inaccurately in most diagrams for easier notation and visibility. However, just like a road map that doesn't depict the actual surface of roadways, these crude schematics suffice in showing general information.

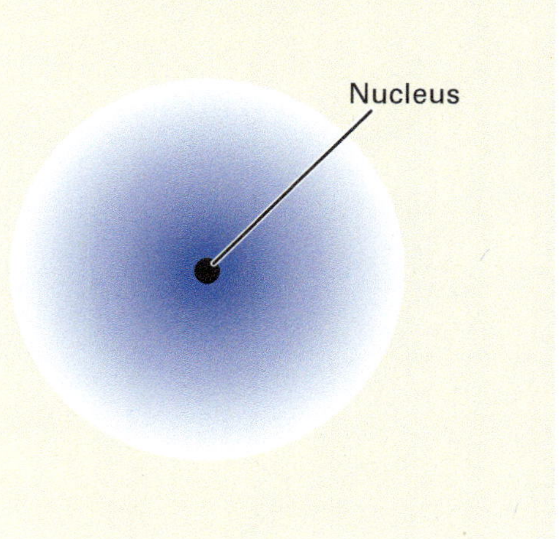

1.2.0 Semiconductor Fundamentals

Semiconductors are the basis for what is known as *solid-state electronics*. Solid-state electronics is the basis for all modern microminiature electronics, such as the tiny integrated circuits and microprocessor chips used in computers. The ability to control the amount of conductivity in semiconductors makes them ideal for use in integrated circuits. In order to understand how semiconductors work, it is first necessary to review the principles of conductors and insulators.

1.2.1 Conductors

Conductors are so-called because they readily carry electrical current. Good electrical conductors are usually also good heat conductors. In each atom, there is a specific number of electrons that can be contained in each orbit or shell. The outer shell of an atom is the valence shell, and the electrons contained in the valence shell are known as *valence electrons*. If the valence shell is not full, these electrons can be easily knocked out of their orbits and become free electrons.

Conductors are materials that have three or fewer valence electrons in their atoms (*Figure 3*). An atom that has only one valence electron makes the best conductor because the electron is loosely held in orbit and is easily released to create current flow.

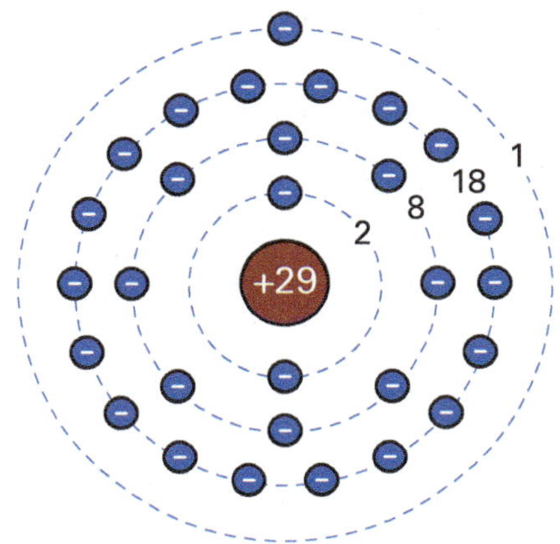

Figure 3 Atom of copper (a conductor).

Gold and silver are excellent conductors, but they are too expensive to use on a large scale. However, in special applications requiring high conductivity, contacts may be plated with gold or silver. You would most likely find such conductors in precision devices where small currents are common and a high degree of accuracy is essential.

Copper is the most widely used conductor because it has excellent conductivity, while being much less expensive than precious metals such as gold and silver. Copper is used as the conductor in most types of wire and provides the current path on printed circuit boards. Aluminum is also used as a conductor, but it is not as good as copper.

1.2.2 Insulators

As you already know, insulators are materials that resist (and sometimes totally prevent) the passage of electrical current. Rubber, glass, and some plastics are common insulators. The atoms of insulating materials are characterized by having more than four valence electrons in their atomic structures. *Figure 4* shows the structure of an insulator atom. Note that it has eight valence electrons; this is the maximum number of electrons for the outer shell of an atom. Therefore, this atom has no free electrons and will not easily pass electric current.

1.2.3 Semiconductors

Semiconductors are materials that are neither good conductors nor good insulators. Semiconductors, such as germanium and silicon, have less free electrons in their outer shell than an insulator, but more than a conductor. Silicon (*Figure 5*) is a commonly used semiconductor because of its ability to withstand heat.

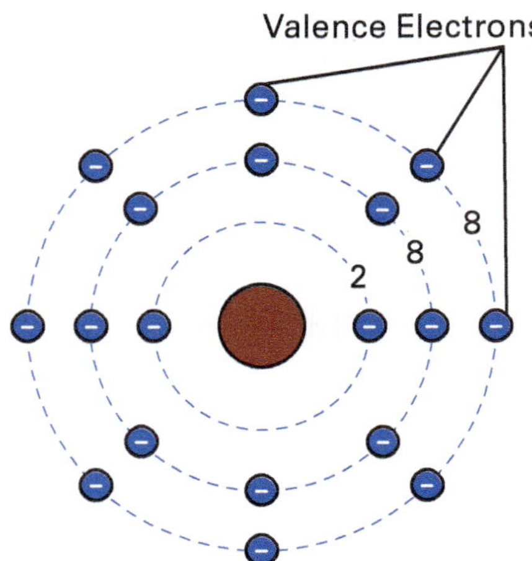

Figure 4 Atom of an insulator.

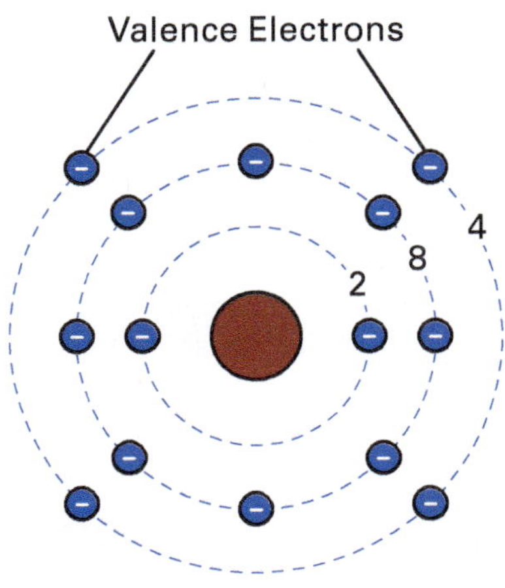

Figure 5 Atom of silicon (a semiconductor).

Semiconductors are valuable in electronic circuits because their conductivity can be readily controlled. Since they are electrically neutral, semiconductors can be made to have positive or negative characteristics by adding certain impurities. This process is known as *doping*.

For example, when a substance with five valence electrons (such as arsenic or antimony) is added to the semiconductor, the semiconductor material will no longer be electrically neutral. Instead, it will take on a negative charge. This is known as an **N-type material**.

When substances with three valence electrons (such as indium or gallium) are added to the semiconductor material, the material takes on a positive charge due to the missing electrons, called *holes*, in the crystalline structure. This is known as a **P-type material**.

N-type material: A material created by doping a region of a crystal with atoms from an element that has more electrons in its outer shell than the crystal.

P-type material: A material created when a crystal is doped with atoms from an element that has fewer electrons in its outer shell than the natural crystal. This combination creates empty spaces in the crystalline structure.

The Number of Electrons in Each Classical Shell of an Atom

The first (innermost) shell of an atom has a maximum of 2 electrons, and the second shell has a maximum of 8 electrons. Unless it is the outermost shell, the third shell can have up to 18 electrons and the fourth and fifth shells can have up to 32 electrons. The maximum number of electrons in the outermost shell cannot exceed 8 electrons.

1.0.0 Section Review

1. In an atom, the orbiting electrons are held in place by _____.
   a. the Earth's gravity
   b. an electric force
   c. the law of charges
   d. an electrical current

2. Which of the following is *not* a good conductor?
   a. Gold
   b. Silver
   c. Copper
   d. Glass

2.0.0 Semiconductor Devices

Objective

Identify and describe semiconductor devices.

a. Describe the operation and uses of diodes.
b. Describe the operation and uses of transistors.
c. Describe the operation and uses of semiconductor switching devices.

Performance Tasks

1. Test a transistor to determine whether it is an NPN or PNP.
2. Identify the cathode on three different styles of SCRs, using the shape or markings for identification.

Diodes and transistors are among the most common types of semiconductor components. Semiconductor diodes are formed by joining two layers of semiconductor material to form a PN junction, while transistors are formed using three layers.

2.1.0 Diodes

A diode is made by joining a piece of P-type material with a piece of N-type material (*Figure 6*). The contacting surface is called the *PN junction*. Other semiconductor devices are used to perform switching functions.

Diodes allow current to flow in one direction but not in the other. This unidirectional current capability is the distinguishing feature of the diode. The activity occurring at the PN junction of the materials is responsible for the unidirectional characteristic of the diode.

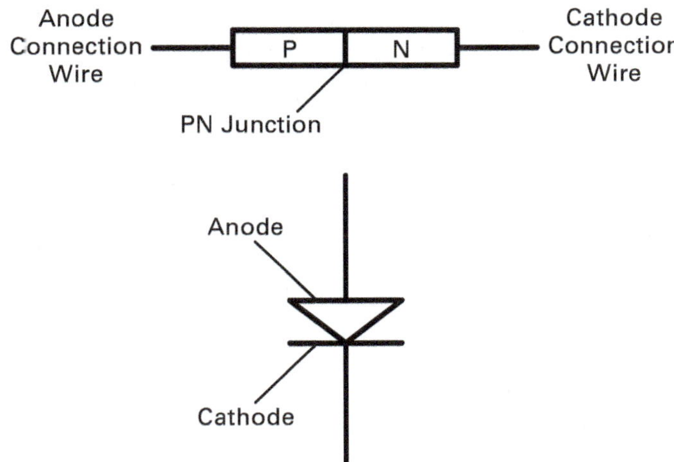

Figure 6 Material structure of a diode.

Forward bias: A condition that exists when voltage is applied to a solid-state device in such a way as to allow the device to conduct easily.

Reverse bias: A condition that exists when voltage is applied to a device in such a way that it causes the device to act as an insulator.

Rectifier: A device or circuit commonly used to change AC voltage into DC voltage, or as a solid-state switch.

Current does not normally flow across a PN junction. However, if a voltage of the correct polarity is applied, current will flow. This is known as **forward bias**, shown in *Figure 7*. Note that the positive side of the voltage source is connected to the P material (the anode) and the negative side to the N material (the cathode). If the polarity of the voltage applied to the PN junction were opposite of the forward-biased junction, the result would be **reverse bias**. No current will flow in the reverse-biased arrangement unless the reverse-bias voltage exceeds the breakover voltage of the junction. This approach is used to create solid-state switching devices.

Modern systems rely heavily on electronic controls, which use low-level DC voltages. Some systems also use special controls powered by DC motors when very precise control is required. The electricity furnished by the power company is AC; it must be converted to DC to be suitable for most electronic circuits. The process of converting AC to DC is known as *rectification* (or *rectifying*) and is accomplished by using **rectifier** diodes.

A diode conducts current only when the voltage at its anode is positive with respect to the voltage at its cathode (forward bias). When the voltage at the anode is negative with respect to the cathode (reverse bias), current will not flow unless the voltage is so high that it overwhelms the diode. Most circuits using diodes are designed so that the diode will not conduct current unless the anode is positive with respect to the cathode.

Periodic Table of the Elements

Some versions of the periodic table, such as the portion of one table shown in the image, contain a vertical list of numbers beside each element. The list represents the numbers of electrons in each of the classical shells of the atom for the element. The total of the electrons for an element equals the atomic number above the element symbol. The period number for each row corresponds to the number of classical shells that exist for the elements in the row. The group numbers across the top with an A or B are an older method of notation for each column of elements.

The group number A elements are the representative elements that have a corresponding number of electrons in the outer shell with a corresponding valence even though an inner shell may be incomplete (except helium [He]). These representative elements become more stable from left to right as the number of electrons in the outer shell increases.

The group number B elements are the transition elements. These elements sometimes have incomplete inner shells as well as incomplete outer shells. For these elements, the common valence is generally represented by the group number.

Be aware that in quantum mechanics theory, the classical main shells shown in the table are made up of various energy-level subshells and the electrons that are allocated to the main shell are assigned to the various subshells.

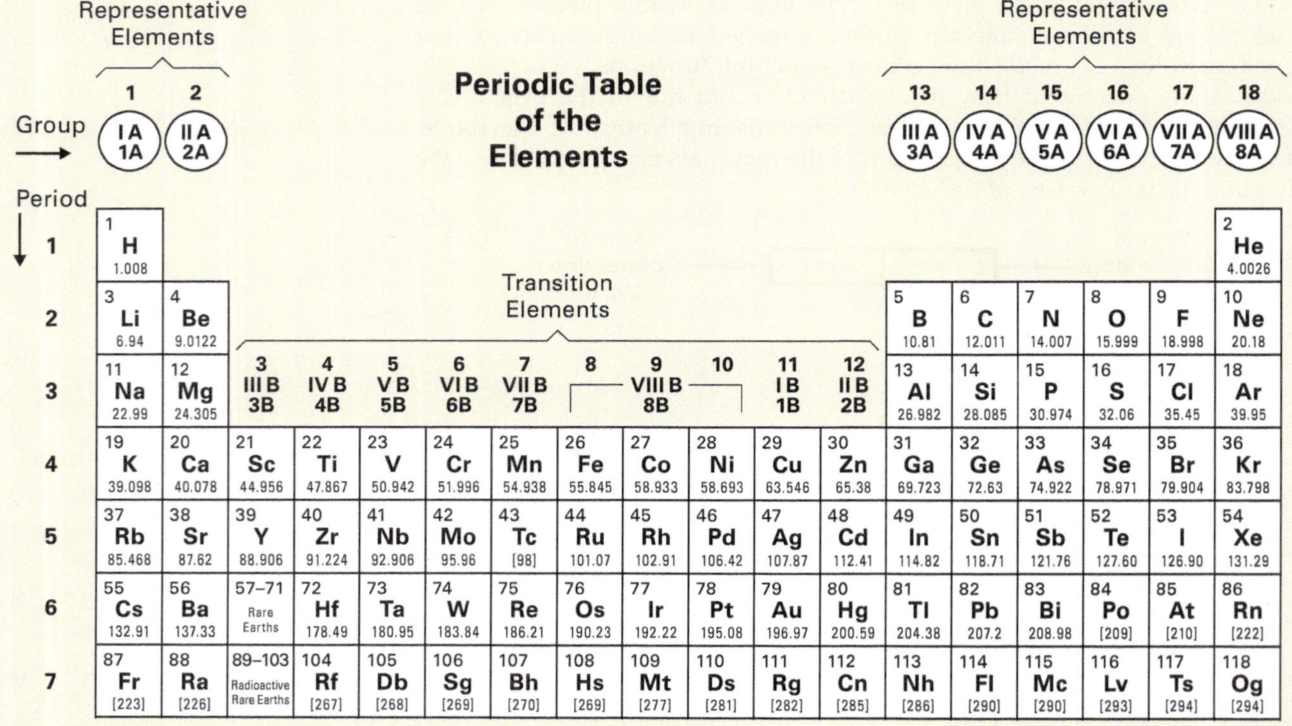

Period	1 (IA 1A)	2 (IIA 2A)	3 (IIIB 3B)	4 (IVB 4B)	5 (VB 5B)	6 (VIB 6B)	7 (VIIB 7B)	8 (VIIIB 8B)	9 (VIIIB 8B)	10 (VIIIB 8B)	11 (IB 1B)	12 (IIB 2B)	13 (IIIA 3A)	14 (IVA 4A)	15 (VA 5A)	16 (VIA 6A)	17 (VIIA 7A)	18 (VIIIA 8A)
1	1 H 1.008																	2 He 4.0026
2	3 Li 6.94	4 Be 9.0122											5 B 10.81	6 C 12.011	7 N 14.007	8 O 15.999	9 F 18.998	10 Ne 20.18
3	11 Na 22.99	12 Mg 24.305											13 Al 26.982	14 Si 28.085	15 P 30.974	16 S 32.06	17 Cl 35.45	18 Ar 39.95
4	19 K 39.098	20 Ca 40.078	21 Sc 44.956	22 Ti 47.867	23 V 50.942	24 Cr 51.996	25 Mn 54.938	26 Fe 55.845	27 Co 58.933	28 Ni 58.693	29 Cu 63.546	30 Zn 65.38	31 Ga 69.723	32 Ge 72.63	33 As 74.922	34 Se 78.971	35 Br 79.904	36 Kr 83.798
5	37 Rb 85.468	38 Sr 87.62	39 Y 88.906	40 Zr 91.224	41 Nb 92.906	42 Mo 95.96	43 Tc [98]	44 Ru 101.07	45 Rh 102.91	46 Pd 106.42	47 Ag 107.87	48 Cd 112.41	49 In 114.82	50 Sn 118.71	51 Sb 121.76	52 Te 127.60	53 I 126.90	54 Xe 131.29
6	55 Cs 132.91	56 Ba 137.33	57–71 Rare Earths	72 Hf 178.49	73 Ta 180.95	74 W 183.84	75 Re 186.21	76 Os 190.23	77 Ir 192.22	78 Pt 195.08	79 Au 196.97	80 Hg 200.59	81 Tl 204.38	82 Pb 207.2	83 Bi 208.98	84 Po [209]	85 At [210]	86 Rn [222]
7	87 Fr [223]	88 Ra [226]	89–103 Radioactive Rare Earths	104 Rf [267]	105 Db [268]	106 Sg [269]	107 Bh [270]	108 Hs [269]	109 Mt [277]	110 Ds [281]	111 Rg [282]	112 Cn [285]	113 Nh [286]	114 Fl [290]	115 Mc [290]	116 Lv [293]	117 Ts [294]	118 Og [294]

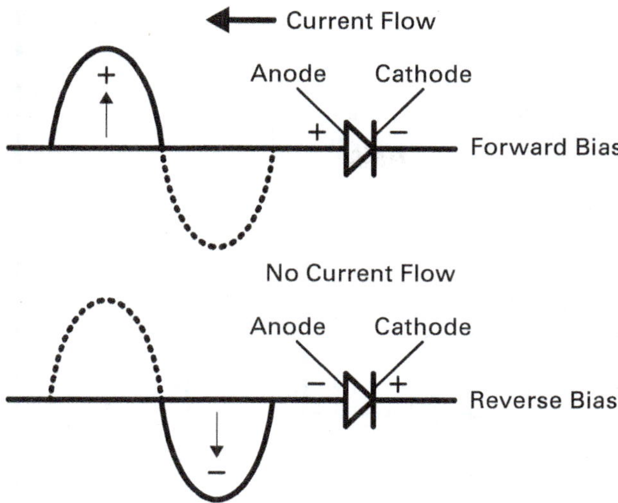

Figure 7 Forward and reverse bias.

2.1.1 Rectifiers

Diodes are commonly used to form rectifiers, which convert AC to DC. In a half-wave rectifier (*Figure 8*), the single diode conducts current only when the AC applied to its anode is on its positive half-cycle. The result is a pulsating DC voltage.

A full-wave rectifier with a special center-tapped transformer is shown in *Figure 9*. In this circuit, one of the diodes conducts on each half-cycle of the AC input. This produces a smoother pulsating DC voltage. Filter capacitors can be used to eliminate most of the ripple.

A bridge rectifier (*Figure 10*) contains four diodes, two of which conduct on each half-cycle. The bridge rectifier provides a smoother DC output and is the most common type used in electronic circuits. An advantage of the bridge rectifier is that it does not need a center-tapped transformer. A filter and voltage regulator added to the output of the rectifier provide the precise, stable DC voltage needed for electronic devices.

In a three-phase power system, a three-phase rectifier (*Figure 11*) is used. It contains six diodes to produce high-efficiency DC power.

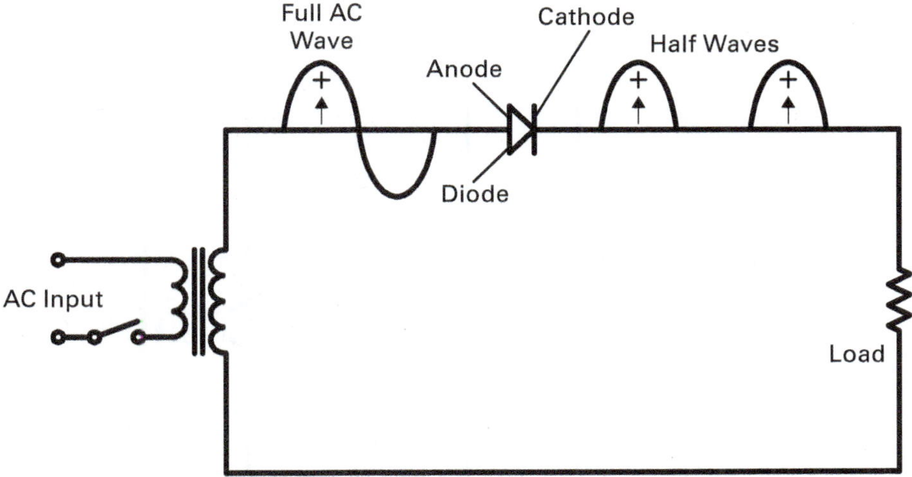

Figure 8 Half-wave rectifier.

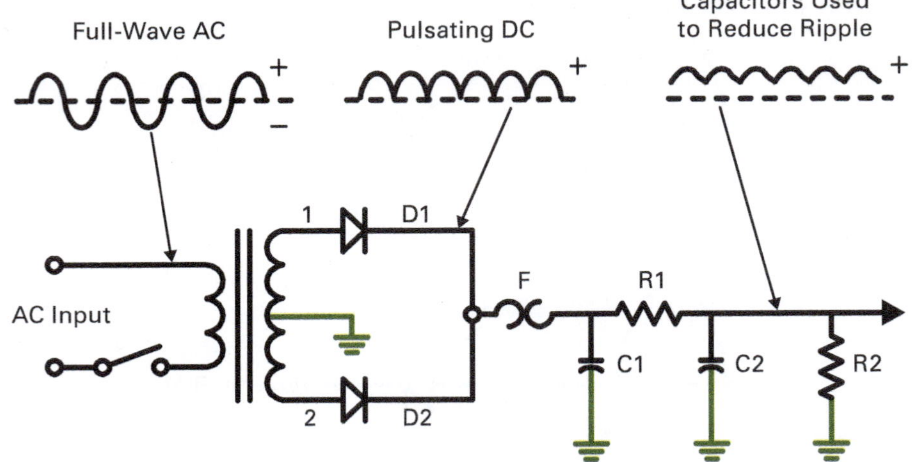

Figure 9 Full-wave rectifier with center-tapped transformer.

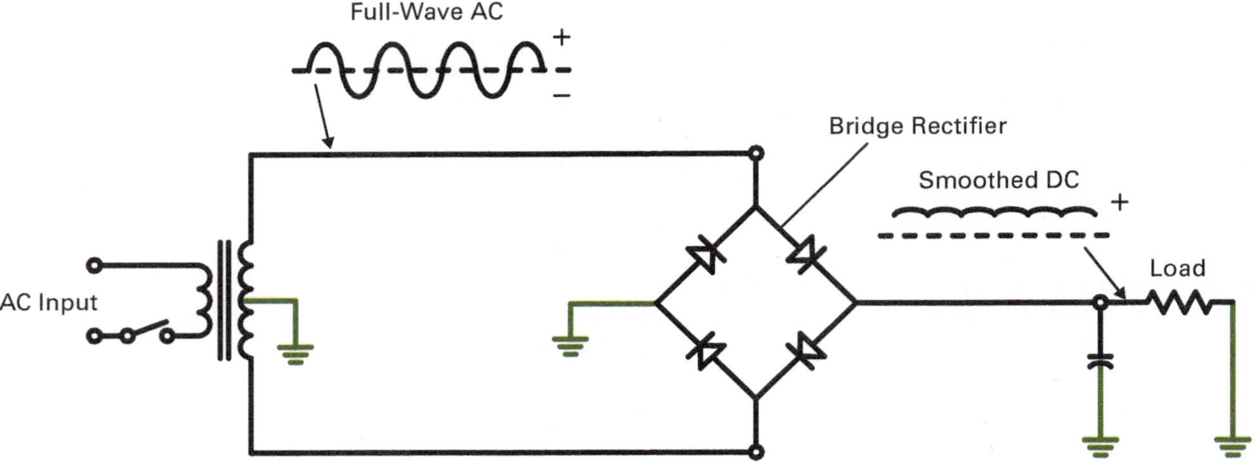

Figure 10 Bridge rectifier.

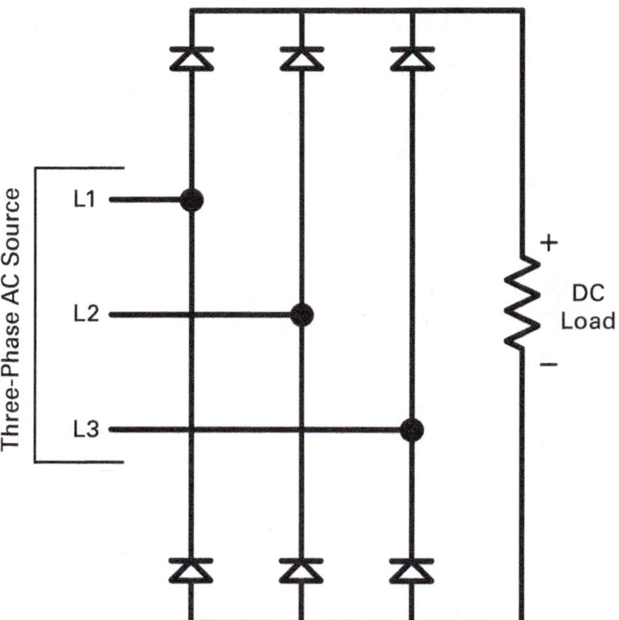

Figure 11 Three-phase rectifier.

TABLE 1 Diode Characteristics

Type	Peak Inverse Voltage (PIV)	Ambient Temperature Range (°C)	Forward Peak (mA)	Current Average (mA)	Capacitance (µF)
1N34A	60	–50 to +75	150	50	150
1N58A	100	–50 to +75	150	50	150

2.1.2 Diode Identification

Most manufacturers' **solid-state device** catalogs list hundreds of semiconductor diodes, along with the specifications of each. *Table 1* shows the specifications for two sample diodes. Note that the diodes are designated 1N34A and 1N58A. Manufacturers have agreed upon certain standard designations for diodes having the same characteristics—the same as for wire sizes and types of insulation.

In *Table 1*, the peak inverse voltage (PIV) is the reverse bias at which **avalanche breakover** occurs. The ambient temperature rating is the range of temperatures over which the diode will operate and still maintain its basic characteristics. Forward current values are given for both the average current (that current at which the diode is usually operated) and the peak current (that current which, if exceeded, will damage the diode). The only difference between these two diodes is in the peak inverse voltage. Therefore, the 1N34A could be substituted for the 1N58A in applications involving signals of less than 60V peak to peak.

In general, there are two basic types of diodes: the silicon diode and the germanium diode. In most cases, silicon diodes have higher PIV and current ratings along with wider temperature ranges than germanium diodes. This is why silicon diodes are the most commonly encountered type in motor and HVAC solid-state controls and power supplies.

PIV ratings for silicon can be around 1,000V, whereas the maximum value for germanium is closer to 400V. Silicon can be used for applications in which the temperature may rise to about 392°F (200°C), whereas germanium has a much lower maximum rating of 212°F (100°C). The disadvantage of silicon, however, is that higher forward bias voltage is required to reach operational conditions.

Diodes have many functions in solid-state devices. For example, silicon diodes are commonly used for constructing rectifiers, and germanium diodes are mainly used in signal and control circuits.

There are several ways in which diodes are marked to indicate the cathode and anode (*Figure 12*). Note that in some cases diodes are marked with the schematic symbol, or there may be a band at one end to indicate the cathode. Other types of diodes use the shape of the diode housing to indicate the cathode end; the cathode end is either beveled or enlarged to ensure proper identification. When in doubt, the polarity of a diode may be checked with an ohmmeter (*Figure 13*). A forward bias will show a low resistance; a reverse bias will show a high resistance.

Solid-state device: An electronic component constructed from semiconductor material. Such devices have all but replaced the vacuum tube in electronic circuits.

Avalanche breakover: A form of electrical current multiplication that can occur in insulating and semiconductor materials. It could be considered a "jailbreak" of electron flow, leading to large currents in materials that otherwise would allow little or no current flow.

CAUTION

The battery voltage of certain ohmmeters may exceed the PIV of the diode being tested. This may result in the destruction of the diode.

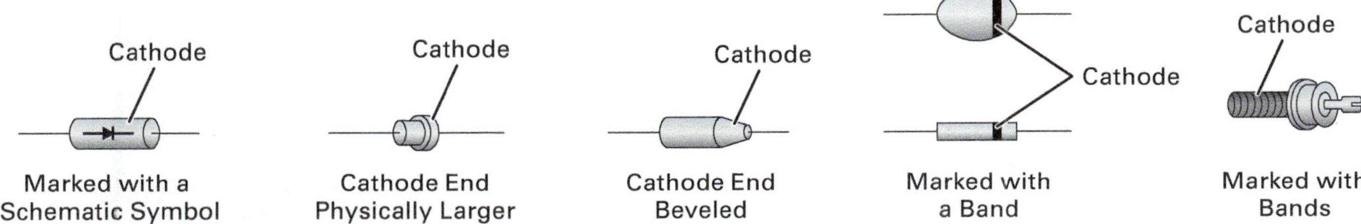

Figure 12 Methods used to identify diodes.

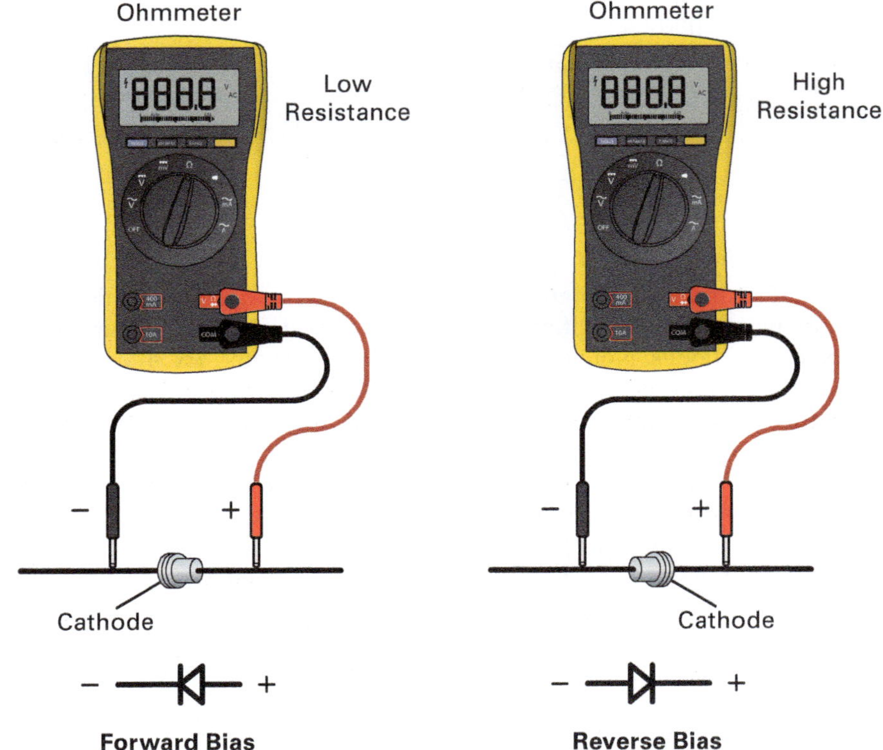

Figure 13 Testing a diode with an ohmmeter.

Silicon Power Rectifier Diodes

Silicon power rectifier diodes are used in high-current DC applications including uninterruptible power supplies, welders, and battery chargers, such as those used for electric forklifts. The stud-mounted silicon power rectifier diode shown in the image is rated for 300A and a PIV of 600V. The cathode is the threaded section, and it is screwed into or secured with a nut to an insulated heat sink that is at the DC potential. The flexible anode lead is connected to the AC power source. These diodes are also made with the anode as the threaded portion and the cathode as the flexible lead.

Source: International Rectifier Corp.

2.1.3 Light-Emitting Diodes

Diodes that give off visible light when energized are called *light-emitting diodes (LEDs)*. All energized forward bias diodes emit some amount of light by giving off energy in the form of photons, but it is not always enough to be visible. In LEDs, however, the number of photons of light energy emitted is sufficient to create a visible light source.

The process of giving off light by applying an electrical source of energy is called *electroluminescence*. *Figure 14* shows that the conducting surface connected to the P-type material is much smaller to allow the emergence of the maximum number of photons of light energy in an LED. Note also in *Figure 15* that the symbol for an LED is similar to that of a conventional diode except that the arrow is pointing away from the diode.

Another solid-state device activated by light is known as a *photo diode*. The schematic symbol for the photo diode is exactly like that of a standard LED except that the arrow is reversed (*Figure 15*). A photo diode must have light in order to operate. It acts similarly to a conventional switch—light turns on the circuit, and the absence of light opens the circuit.

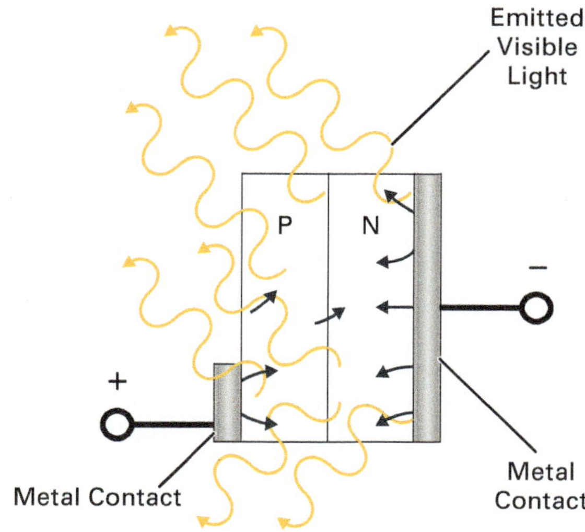

Figure 14 Process of electroluminescence in an LED.

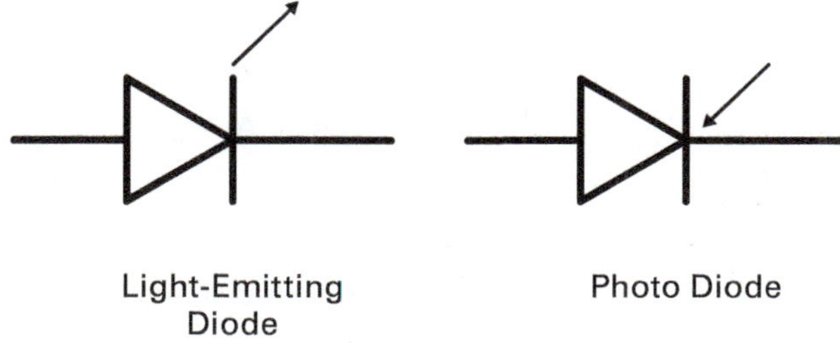

Figure 15 Schematic symbols for an LED and photo diode.

Axial-Lead Silicon Diodes

One of the most common diodes used is the tubular, axial-lead silicon diode. It is used in many low-voltage rectifiers for electronic circuits. The diode shown in the image is rated at 1A with a PIV of 1,400V.

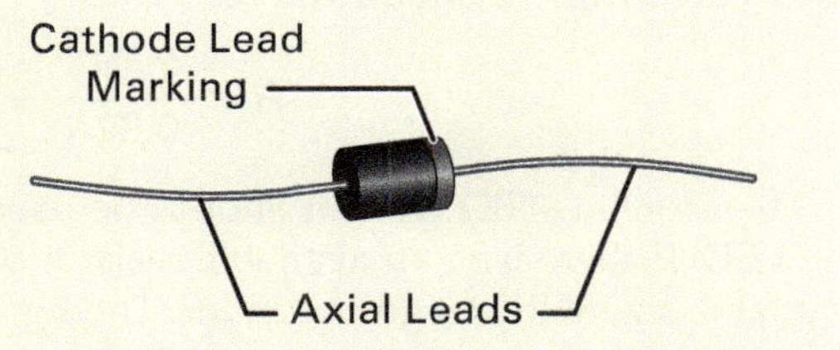

Typical Low-Voltage Bridge Rectifiers

The low-voltage bridge rectifiers shown in the image are rated for 4A and 25A with a PIV of 50V. The metallic heat sink mating surface of the 25A rectifier must be coated with a heat sink compound and then bolted to a grounded heat sink. The heat sink compound helps rapidly transmit heat from the rectifier to the heat sink. In these rectifiers, the cases and heat sink are insulated from the AC and DC voltages.

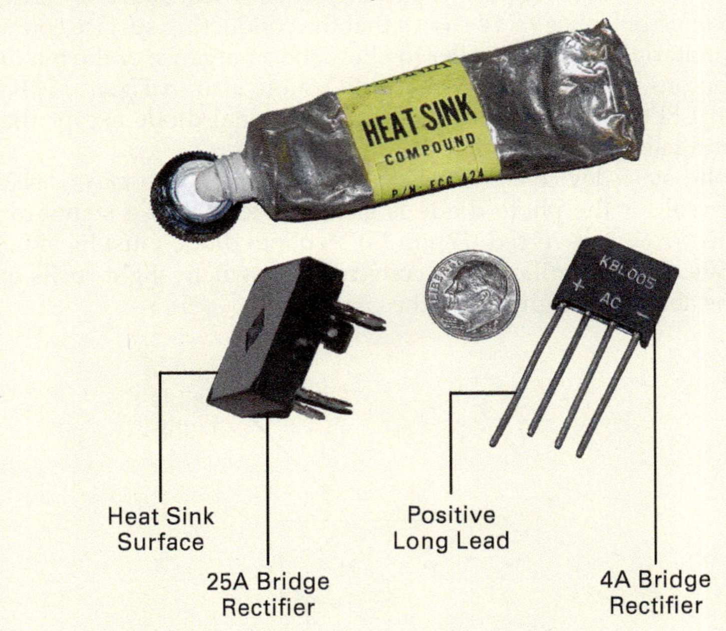

When used in a circuit, an LED is generally operated at about 20 mA or less. So, to limit the amount of current that flows through the LED, a current-limiting resistor must be connected in series with the LED. The amount of resistance needed can be calculated using the voltage of the power supply, along with the following form of Ohm's law:

$$R = \frac{E}{I}$$

Where:

R = resistance (ohms or Ω)

E = voltage or emf (volts or V)

I = current (amps or A)

Example:

An LED is to be connected to a 9VDC circuit. To ensure the LED is operated at about 20 mA, what size resistor must be connected in series with it?

Solution:

To calculate the required resistance, you must first convert the 20 mA current to amps. Since 1A = 1,000 mA, divide the milliamps by 1,000 to convert to amps (20 mA ÷ 1,000 = 0.02A). Then, use the current and source voltage with Ohm's law to determine the required resistance:

$$R = \frac{9\text{VDC}}{0.02\text{A}} = 450\Omega$$

Therefore, a 450Ω resistor should be used to limit the current flow through the LED. If there isn't an available resistor of the calculated size, use the closest available size without going under. The higher the resistance, the more current is limited. Thus, connecting a resistor slightly larger than the calculated value will ensure the current does not exceed 20 mA.

LEDs are used as pilot lights on electronic equipment and as numerical displays. Many programmable HVAC controls use LEDs to indicate when a process is in operation. LEDs are also used in the opto-isolation circuit of solid-state relays for both motor controls and HVAC control systems.

LED Lead Identification

Like conventional diodes, LEDs have identification methods. Most manufacturers use a flat surface in the LED case near one of the leads. The lead closest to this flat surface is the cathode. In other cases, the short lead is designated as the cathode lead. The LED shown in the image uses both methods.

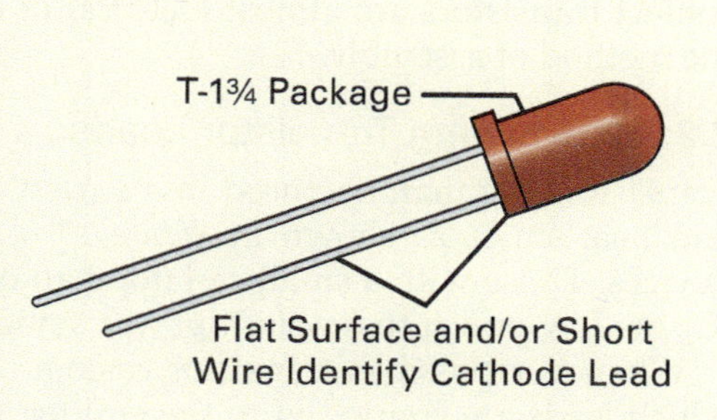

2.2.0 Transistors

A transistor is made by joining three layers of semiconductor material. Regardless of the type of solid-state device being used, it is made by the joining of P-type and N-type materials to form either a negative-positive-negative (NPN) or positive-negative-positive (PNP) transistor. Each type has two PN junctions. A diagram of an NPN transistor is shown in *Figure 16*.

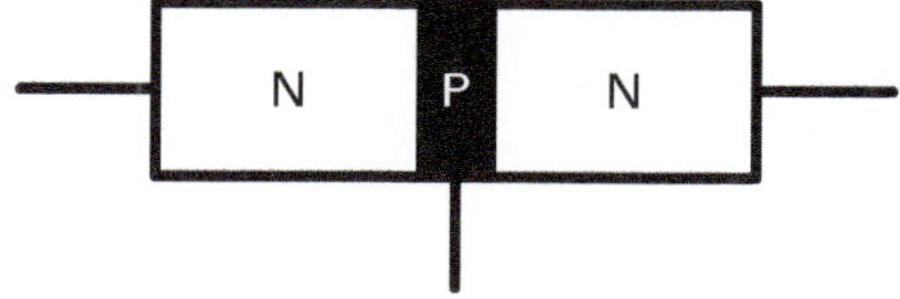

Figure 16 Material arrangement in an NPN transistor.

Control voltages are applied to the center layer, which is known as the *base*. These voltages control when and how much the transistor conducts. You will not encounter many transistors as discrete components. In today's self-contained electronic integrated circuit devices and microprocessors, there may be thousands of transistors. They are so tiny that they can only be seen with a high-powered microscope.

Years ago, when computers were first invented, they required a roomful of electronic equipment. With the evolution of microminiature circuits, it became possible to perform the same work with a single tiny microprocessor chip containing thousands of microscopic electronic devices such as amplifiers and switches.

2.2.1 NPN Transistors

By sandwiching a very thin piece of P-type germanium between two slices of N-type germanium, an NPN transistor is formed. A transistor made in this way is called a *junction transistor*. The symbol for this type of transistor showing the three elements (emitter, base, and collector) is illustrated in *Figure 17*.

The current flow is in the opposite direction of the arrow. Because the arrow points away from the base, current flows from the emitter to the base or from the N-type material to the P-type material.

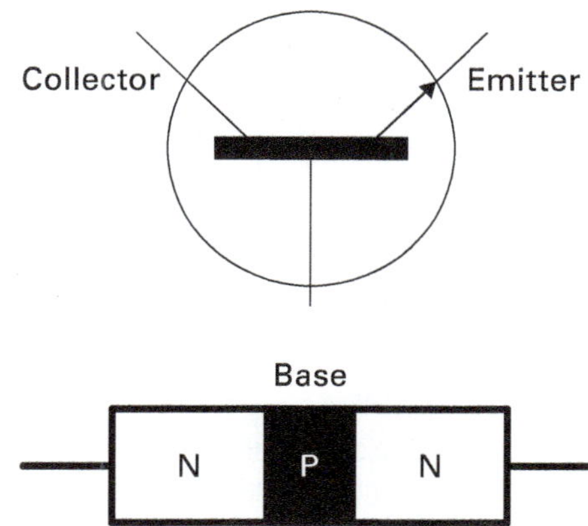

Figure 17 NPN transistor characteristics and schematic symbol.

2.2.2 PNP Transistors

A PNP transistor is formed by placing N-type germanium between two slices of P-type germanium. The schematic symbol for the PNP transistor is almost identical to that of the NPN transistor. The only difference is the direction of the emitter arrow. In the NPN transistor, it points away from the base and in the PNP transistor, it points toward the base.

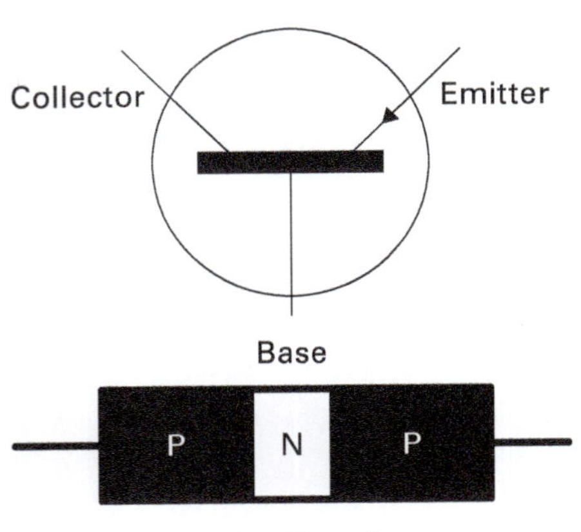

Junction Transistor

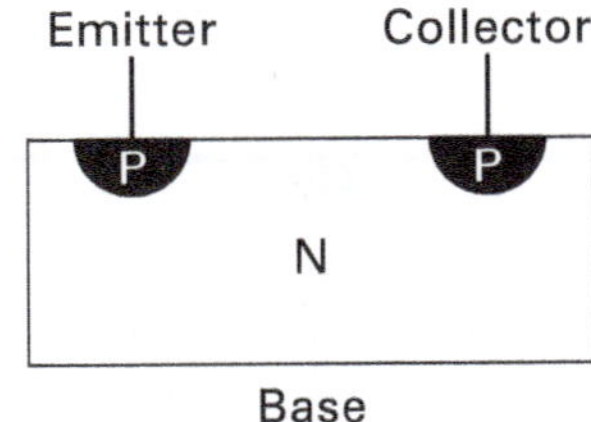

Point-Contact Transistor

Figure 18 PNP transistor characteristics and schematic symbol.

Electron flow in a PNP transistor is from the N-type germanium to the P-type germanium. Since the arrow in *Figure 18* points toward the base, the electron flow is in the opposite direction of the arrow—from base to emitter. This is the reverse of the NPN transistor.

Note also the point-contact transistor shown in *Figure 18*. Junction and point-contact transistors are almost identical in operation. The main difference is in the method of assembly.

2.2.3 Identifying Transistor Leads

Transistors are manufactured in a variety of configurations. Those with studs and heat sinks, as shown in *Figure 19* (A) and *Figure 19* (B), are high-power devices. Those with a small can (top hat) or plastic body, as shown in *Figure 19* (C), are low-power to medium-power devices.

Whenever possible, transistor casings will have some marking to indicate which leads are connected to the emitter, collector, or base of the transistor. A few of the methods commonly used are indicated in *Figure 20*.

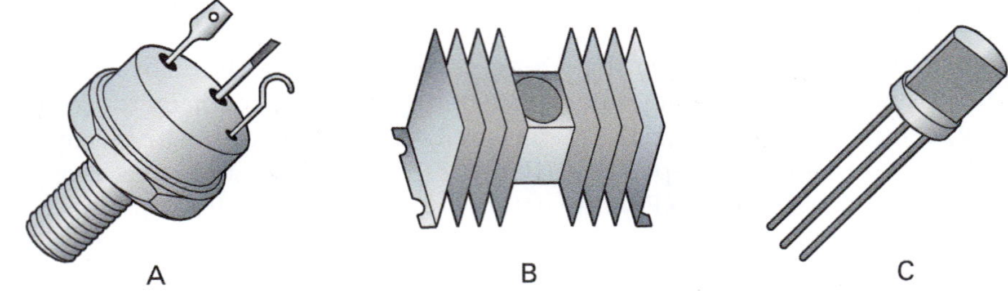

Figure 19 Various transistors.

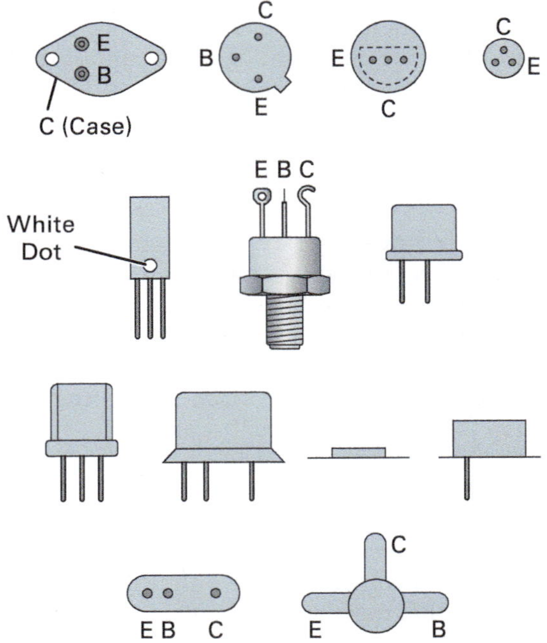

Figure 20 Lead identification of transistors.

Transistor Electron Flow and Current Flow

In a transistor, electrons always flow against the direction of the arrow and current flows in the direction of the arrow.

2.2.4 Field-Effect Transistors

A **field-effect transistor (FET)** controls the flow of current with an electric field. There are two basic types of FETs: the **junction field-effect transistor (JFET)**, and the metal-oxide semiconductor field-effect transistor (MOSFET). A MOSFET is also referred to as an *insulated gate field-effect transistor (IGFET)*.

Field-effect transistor (FET): A transistor that controls the flow of current through it with an electric field.

Junction field-effect transistor (JFET): A field-effect transistor formed by combining layers of semiconductor material.

2.2.5 Junction Field-Effect Transistors

There are two types of JFETs: an N-channel and a P-channel. *Figure 21* shows the schematic symbols for these two types and denotes the terms for each JFET lead.

The difference between these two devices is in the polarity of the voltage to which the transistor is connected. In an N-channel device, the drain is connected to the more positive voltage, and the source and gate are connected to a more negative voltage. A P-channel device has the drain connected to a more negative voltage, and the source and gate are connected to a more positive voltage.

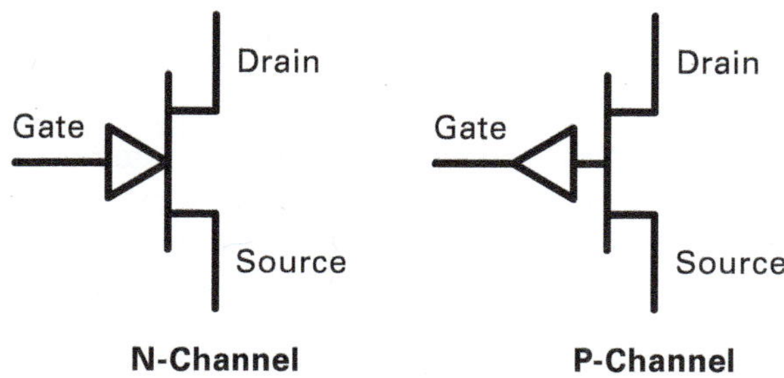

Figure 21 Junction field-effect transistor symbols.

Common Transistors

Transistors are available in a variety of shapes and sizes, as shown in the image.

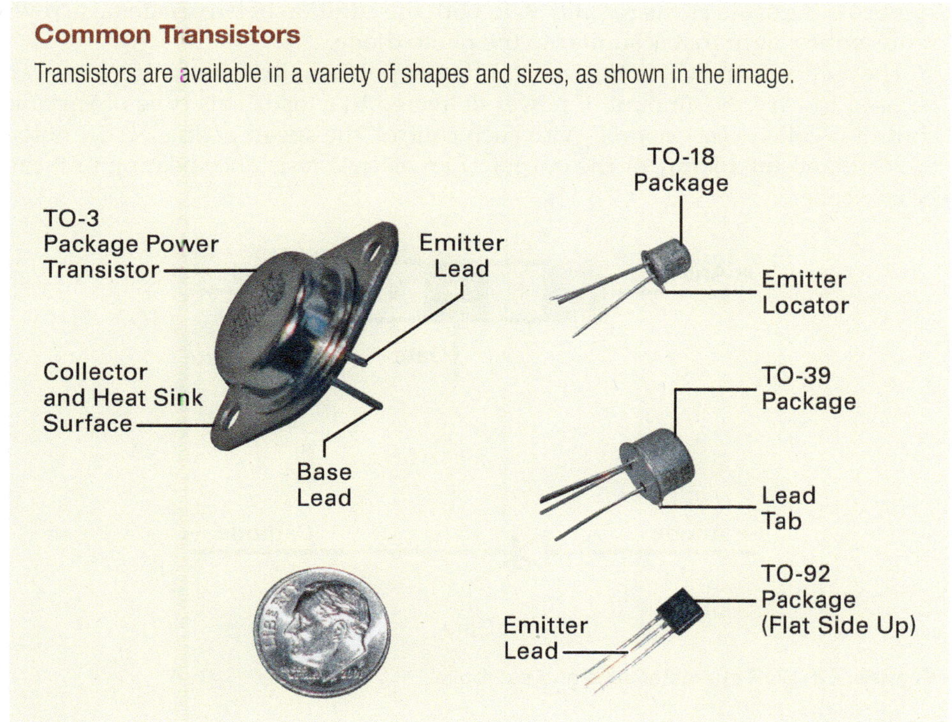

Silicon-controlled rectifier (SCR): A device that is mainly used to convert AC voltage into DC voltage. To do so, however, the gate of the SCR must be triggered before the device will conduct current.

Diac: A three-layer diode designed for use as a trigger in AC power control circuits, such as those using triacs.

Triac: A bidirectional triode thyristor that functions as an electrically controlled switch for AC loads.

2.3.0 Semiconductor Switching Devices

The **silicon-controlled rectifier (SCR)**, along with the **diac** and the **triac**, belongs to a class of semiconductors known as *thyristors*. One common characteristic of all thyristors is that they act as an open circuit until a triggering current is applied. When that happens, the thyristor acts as a low-resistance current path from anode to cathode. It will continue to conduct, even if the gate signal is removed, until either the current is reduced below a certain level or the thyristor is turned off. These devices are used for a variety of purposes, including:

- Emergency lighting circuits
- Lamp dimmers
- Motor speed controls
- Ignition systems

2.3.1 Silicon-Controlled Rectifiers

The SCR is similar to a diode, except it has three terminals instead of one. Like a common diode, current will flow through the SCR in only one direction. However, in addition to needing the correct voltage polarity at the anode and cathode, the SCR also requires a gate voltage of the same polarity as the voltage applied to the anode. When fired, the SCR will remain on until the cathode-to-anode current falls below a value known as the *holding current*. When the SCR is off, another positive gate voltage must be applied before it will start conducting again.

The SCR is made from four adjoining layers of semiconductor material in a PNPN arrangement (*Figure 22*). The SCR symbol is also shown. Note that it is the same as the diode symbol, except for the addition of a gating lead.

There is also a light-activated version of the SCR known as an *LASCR*. Its symbol is the same as the regular SCR, with the addition of two diagonal arrows representing light that is similar to the photo diode.

The ability of an SCR to turn on at different points in the conducting cycle can be used to vary the amount of power delivered to a load. This type of variable control is called *phase control*. With such control, the speed of an electric motor, the brilliance of a lamp, or the output of an electric resistance heating unit can be controlled.

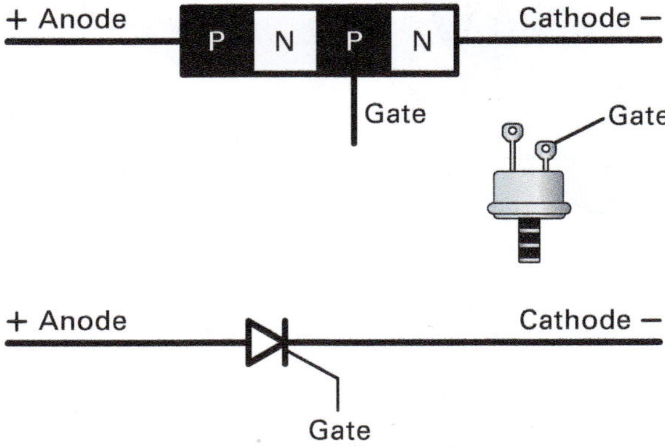

Figure 22 SCR characteristics and symbol.

2.3.2 Diacs

A diac can be thought of as an AC switch. Because the diac is bidirectional, current will flow through it on either half of the AC waveform. One major use of the diac is as a control for a triac. Although the diac is not gated, it will not conduct until the applied voltage exceeds its breakover voltage.

The basic construction and symbols for a diac are shown in *Figure 23*. Note that the diac has two symbols, either of which may be found on schematic diagrams.

2.3.3 Triacs

The triac can be viewed as two SCRs turned in opposite directions with a common gate (*Figure 24*). It could also be viewed as a diac with a gate terminal added. One important distinction, however, is that the voltage applied across the triac does not have to exceed a breakover voltage for conduction to begin.

Like SCRs, triacs are used in phase control applications to control the average power applied to loads. Examples include light dimmers and photocell light switches.

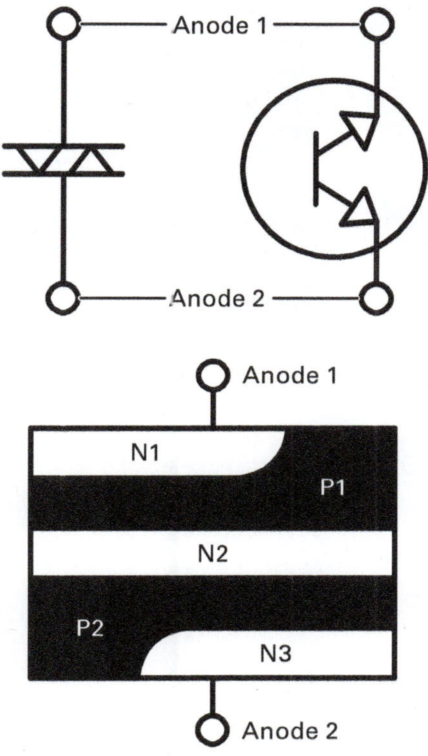

Figure 23 Basic diac construction and symbols.

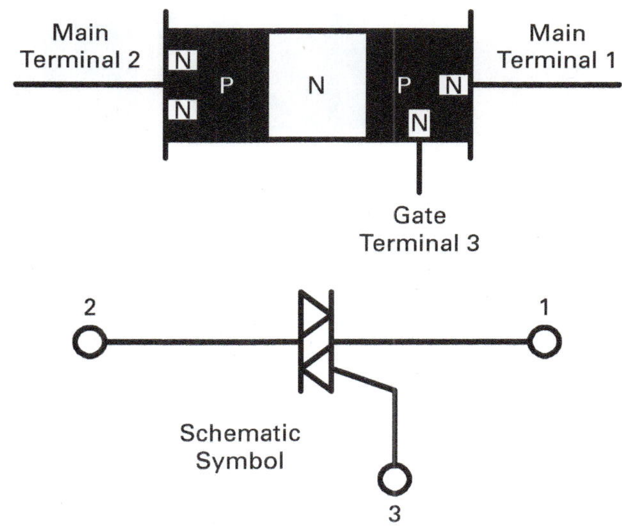

Figure 24 Basic triac construction and symbol.

Typical Triac

A typical triac and its associated heat sink are shown in the image. This version has no visual method of determining lead identification other than the emitter lead locator dot. The manufacturer's literature supplied with the device must be used to identify the lead numbers.

Going Green

Photovoltaic Systems

This photovoltaic array is part of a large power system designed to provide 15 megawatts of power. Constructed at Nellis Air Force Base in Nevada, this solar farm covers 140 acres of land and consists of about 70,000 solar panels. Because the panels track the sun throughout the day, they produce about 30% more power than fixed systems.

Source: US Air Force photo by Airman 1st Class Nadine Y. Barclay

2.0.0 Section Review

1. How many diodes are used in a bridge rectifier?
   a. Two
   b. Three
   c. Four
   d. Five

2. The elements of a transistor are _____.
   a. emitter, base, and collector
   b. emitter, base, and LED
   c. collector, emitter, and LED
   d. collector, base, and rectifier

3. SCRs, diacs, and triacs belong to a class of devices known as _____.
   a. thermistors
   b. transistors
   c. rectifiers
   d. thyristors

Module 26404-23 Review Questions

1. An electron has a _____.
   a. positive charge
   b. negative charge
   c. neutral charge
   d. variable charge

2. The conductor commonly used to print circuits on a printed circuit board is _____.
   a. aluminum
   b. silver
   c. ceramic
   d. copper

3. An atom with five or more valence electrons is _____.
   a. an insulator
   b. easily combined with water
   c. a semiconductor
   d. a conductor

4. Which of the following can be added as an impurity to a semiconductor material to create an N-type semiconductor?
   a. Arsenic
   b. Germanium
   c. Gallium
   d. Indium

5. Which of the following is made by joining a piece of P-type material with a piece of N-type materia?
   a. Transistor
   b. Diode
   c. Half-wave rectifier
   d. Full-wave rectifier

6. What bias has been applied to a PN junction if the cathode is positive with respect to the anode?
   a. Negative bias
   b. Positive bias
   c. Forward bias
   d. Reverse bias

7. A common purpose of a rectifier is to _____.
   a. convert DC into AC
   b. step down voltage
   c. convert AC into DC
   d. step up voltage

8. A half-wave rectifier is constructed of _____.
   a. one diode
   b. two diodes
   c. three diodes
   d. seven diodes

9. What is the *total* number of PN junctions in a transistor?
   a. One
   b. Two
   c. Three
   d. Four

10. What are the two basic types of transistors?
    a. AND and OR
    b. ASCII and SCICA
    c. Digital and analog
    d. NPN and PNP

11. What are the two materials normally used to construct transistors?
    a. L and O materials
    b. P and N materials
    c. A and D materials
    d. Silver and aluminum

12. The term *thyristor* includes which of the following groups of components?
    a. Transistors, FETs, and SCRs
    b. Diacs, triacs, and SCRs
    c. Diodes, diacs, and SCRs
    d. Diacs, triacs, and op-amps

13. How many layers of semiconductor material are used to construct an SCR?
    a. One
    b. Two
    c. Three
    d. Four

14. Which of the following is a characteristic of a diac?
    a. It will conduct on either half of the AC waveform.
    b. The voltage applied to the anode and the gate junction must be of the same polarity.
    c. It will continue conducting after the gating voltage is removed.
    d. It has no breakover voltage rating.

15. A triac is equivalent to _____.
    a. two SCRs
    b. three diacs
    c. three diodes
    d. six SCRs

Answers to odd-numbered Module Review Questions are found in *Appendix A*.

Module 26404-23 Supplemental Exercises

1. The outer shell of an atom is called a(n) __________.
2. Conductor atoms only have __________ or __________ valence electrons.
3. Insulator atoms normally have __________ valence electrons.
4. Two semiconductor materials used in solid-state devices are __________ and __________.
5. A(n) __________ material is a semiconductor that has taken on a negative charge with the addition of other substances.
6. A(n) __________ is made by joining a piece of P-type material with a piece of N-type material.
7. A diode allows flow in __________ direction(s).
8. Diodes are commonly used to convert AC to DC in a process known as __________.
9. A(n) __________ bias has been applied to a PN junction if the cathode is negative with respect to the anode.
10. The beveled or enlarged end of a diode marks the __________ end.
11. The two basic types of transistors are __________ and __________.
12. The three elements of an NPN transistor are the __________, __________, and __________.
13. The semiconductor material comprising the base of a PNP transistor is __________.
14. Thyristors are a class of __________.
15. An SCR is made of __________ adjoining layers of semiconductor material.

Answers to odd-numbered Supplemental Exercises are found in *Appendix B*.

Answers to Section Review Questions

Answer	Section Reference	Objective
Section 1.0.0		
1. b	1.1.0	1a
2. d	1.2.1; 1.2.2	1b
Section 2.0.0		
1. c	2.1.1	2a
2. a	2.2.1	2b
3. d	2.3.0	2c

User Update

Did you find an error? Submit a correction by visiting **https://www.nccer.org/olf** or by scanning the QR code using your mobile device.

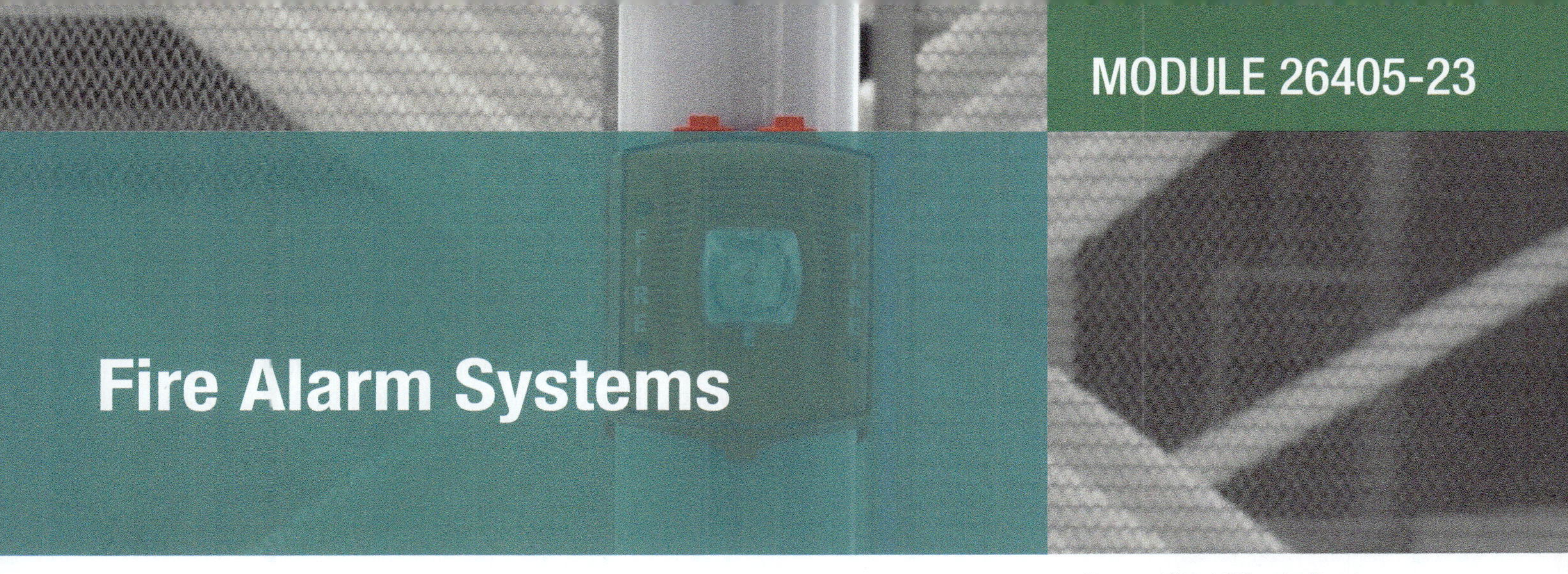

Fire Alarm Systems

Source: iStock@SandroBassi

Objectives

Successful completion of this module prepares you to do the following:

1. Describe the various codes and standards that relate to fire alarm systems.
   a. Explain how codes and standards are implemented and list the organizations responsible for their creation and maintenance.
   b. List the various NFPA codes and standards that apply to fire alarm systems.
2. Describe the basic types of fire alarm systems and their primary components.
   a. Describe the basic types of fire alarm communication systems.
   b. Describe the primary components of fire alarm systems.
3. Describe fire alarm control units and their primary features.
   a. Describe fire alarm control units and their power source requirements.
   b. Explain how users interface with the control unit.
   c. Define and describe initiating circuits and unit outputs.
4. Identify and describe approaches to fire alarm notification and communication/monitoring.
   a. Describe visual and audible notification devices and systems.
   b. Describe important considerations in the use of fire alarm notification signals.
   c. Describe communication and monitoring options for fire alarm systems.
5. Describe fire alarm system installation guidelines and requirements.
   a. Describe the general wiring requirements.
   b. Describe the general installation requirements for wiring and various components.
   c. Describe the installation guidelines for totally protected premises.
   d. Describe the installation guidelines for systems and devices related to fire alarms.
   e. Describe how to troubleshoot fire alarm systems.

Performance Task

Under supervision you should be able to do the following:

1. Connect selected fire alarm system(s).

Overview

Fire alarms provide an essential service that protects both human life and property from the effects of fire. Fire alarms can be complex systems made up of many different technologies. Numerous codes govern fire alarms to ensure that they operate in useful and predictable ways. This module explores the technologies, codes, and wiring approaches used to assemble a fire alarm system. Installation and troubleshooting techniques are also examined.

NOTE

NFPA 70®, *National Electrical Code*®, *NEC*®, NFPA 72®, *National Fire Alarm and Signaling Code*®, and NFPA 101®, *Life Safety Code*®, are registered trademarks of the National Fire Protection Association, Quincy, MA.

Digital Resources for Electrical

Scan this code using the camera on your phone or mobile device to view the digital resources related to this craft.

NCCER Industry-Recognized Credentials

If you are training through an NCCER-accredited sponsor, you may be eligible for credentials from NCCER. The ID number for this module is 26405-23. Note that this module may have been used in other NCCER curricula and may apply to other level completions. Contact NCCER at 1.888.622.3720 or go to **www.nccer.org** for more information.

You can also show off your industry-recognized credentials online with NCCER's digital badges. Transform your knowledge, skills, and achievements into badges that you can share across social media platforms, send to your network, and add to your resume. For more information, visit **www.nccer.org**.

1.0.0 Codes and Standards

Performance Tasks

There are no Performance Tasks in this section.

Objective

Describe the various codes and standards that relate to fire alarm systems.

a. Explain how codes and standards are implemented and list the organizations responsible for their creation and maintenance.
b. List the various NFPA codes and standards that apply to fire alarm systems.

Alarm: In fire systems, a warning of fire danger.

National Fire Protection Association (NFPA): The NFPA administers the development and publishing of codes, standards, and other materials concerning all phases of fire and life safety.

Automatic fire alarm system: A system in which all or some of the circuits are actuated by automatic devices, such as fire, smoke, heat, and flame detectors.

Fire **alarm** systems can make the difference between life and death. In a fire emergency, a quick and accurate response by a fire alarm system can drastically reduce the possibility of deaths and injuries. However, practical field experience is necessary to master this trade. Remember to focus on doing the job properly at all times. Failure to do so could have tragic consequences.

Always seek out and abide by any **National Fire Protection Association (NFPA)**, federal, state, and local codes that apply to each and every fire alarm system installation.

Different types of buildings and applications will have different fire safety goals. Therefore, each building will have a different fire alarm system to meet those specific goals. An **automatic fire alarm system** can be configured to provide fire protection for life safety, property protection, or mission protection.

Life safety fire protection is concerned with protecting and preserving human life. In a fire alarm system, life safety can be defined as warning of a fire situation. This warning occurs early enough to allow notification of building occupants, ensuring sufficient time for their safe evacuation.

Fire alarm systems are generally taken for granted. People go about their everyday business with little or no thought of the safety devices that monitor for abnormal conditions. After all, no one expects a fire to happen. When it does, every component of the life safety fire alarm system must be working properly to minimize the threat to life.

1.1.0 Standards Organizations

Installing and Servicing Fire Alarm Systems

In certain jurisdictions, the person who installs and/or services fire alarm systems must be a licensed fire alarm specialist.

Fire alarm system equipment and its installation are regulated and controlled by various national, state, and local codes. Industry standards have also been developed as a means of establishing a common level of competency. These codes and standards are set by a variety of different associations, agencies, and laboratories that consist of fire alarm professionals across the country. Depending on the application and installation, you will need to follow the standards established by one or more of these organizations.

In the United States, local and state jurisdictions will select a model code and supporting documents that detail applicable standards. If necessary, they will amend the codes and standards as they see fit. Some amendments may be substantial changes to the code, and in certain situations, jurisdictions will author their own sets of codes. Once a jurisdiction adopts a set of codes and standards, it becomes an enforceable legal document within that jurisdiction.

Property and Mission Protection

The design goal of most fire alarm systems is life safety. However, some systems are designed with a secondary purpose of protecting either property or the activities (mission) within a building. The goal of both property and mission protection is the early detection of a fire so that firefighting efforts can begin while the fire is still small and manageable. Fire alarm systems with a secondary goal of property protection are commonly used in museums, libraries, storage facilities, and historic buildings in order to minimize damage to the buildings or their contents. Systems with a secondary goal of mission protection are commonly used where it is essential to avoid business interruptions, such as in hospitals, financial businesses, security control rooms, and telecommunication centers.

The following list details some of the many national organizations responsible for setting the industry standards:

- *UL Solutions* — Establishes standards for fire equipment and systems
- *The NFPA* — Establishes standards for fire suppression and detection systems. The association publishes the **National Fire Alarm and Signaling Code®** (NFPA 72®), the *Life Safety Code®* (NFPA 101®), and the *Fire Code* (NFPA 1). These codes are the primary reference documents used by fire alarm system professionals.
- *Factory Mutual (FM)* — Establishes standards for fire systems
- *National Electrical Manufacturers' Association (NEMA)* — Establishes standards for equipment
- *The Federal Bank Protection Act* — Establishes fire alarm equipment and system standards for banks
- *The Defense Intelligence Agency (DIAM-50-3)* — Establishes standards for military and intelligence installations
- *The National Institute for Certification in Engineering Technologies (NICET)* — Establishes standardized testing of fire alarm designers and installers

National Fire Alarm and Signaling Code®: This is the update of the NFPA standards book that contains the former NFPA 71, NFPA 72®, NFPA 74, and NFPA 1221 standards. NFPA 72® is revised every three years.

1.2.0 The National Fire Protection Association

The NFPA is responsible for setting the national standards and codes for the fire alarm industry. Consisting of fire protection representatives from all areas of business and fire protection services, the NFPA responds to the ever-changing needs of society by using a democratic process to form consensus standards that are acceptable to all members. The NFPA reviews equipment and system performance criteria and input from experienced industry professionals to set an acceptable level of protection for both life and property.

NFPA Codes

The three NFPA code books, NFPA 70®, NFPA 72®, and NFPA 101®, are required for installing alarm systems. Nearly every requirement of NFPA 101®, *Life Safety Code®*, has resulted from the analysis of past fires in which human lives have been lost. Code books are revised and changed periodically, typically every three or four years. For this reason, you should always ensure you are using the latest edition of any code book.

Know the Code

Fire Alarm Systems
NEC Article 760

Circuit: The conductors or radio channel as well as the associated equipment used to perform a definite function in connection with an alarm system.

Initiating device: A manually or automatically operated device with a normal intended operation resulting in a fire alarm or supervisory signal indication from the control unit. Examples of alarm signal initiating devices are thermostats, manual boxes (stations), smoke detectors, and waterflow devices. Examples of supervisory signal initiating devices are water level indicators, sprinkler system valve position switches, pressure supervisory switches, and water temperature switches.

Notification appliance (device): Any audible or visible signal employed to indicate a fire, supervisory, or trouble condition. Examples of audible signal appliances are bells, sirens, electronic/manual horns, buzzers, and chimes. A visible indicator consists of an incandescent lamp, strobe lamp, mechanical target or flag, meter deflection, or the equivalent. Also called an *indicating device*.

Maintenance: Repair service, including periodic inspections and tests, required to keep the protective signaling system and its component parts in an operative condition at all times. This is used in conjunction with the replacement of the system and its components when they become undependable or inoperative for any reason.

1.2.1 NFPA Codes

The following four widely adopted national codes are specified by the NFPA as follows:

- *National Electrical Code®* (NFPA 70®) — The *National Electrical Code®* (*NEC®*) covers all the necessary requirements for all electrical work performed in a building. ***NEC Article 760****, Fire Alarm Systems*, details the specific requirements for wiring and equipment installation for fire protective signaling systems. Specifications include installation methods, connection types, **circuit** identification, and wire types (including gauges and insulation). The *NEC®* places restrictions on the number and types of circuit combinations that can be installed in the same enclosure.
- *National Fire Alarm and Signaling Code®* (NFPA 72®) — The recommended requirements for the installation of fire alarm systems and equipment in residential and commercial facilities are covered in this code. These installation requirements include the **initiating device** (sensor) and visual or audible **notification appliance (device)** of a system. Inspection, testing, and **maintenance** requirements for fire alarm systems and equipment are also covered.
- *Life Safety Code®* (NFPA 101®) — This document is focused on the preservation and protection of human life as opposed to property. Life safety requirements are detailed for both new construction and existing structures. Specifically, necessary protection for unique building features and construction is detailed. In addition, chapters are organized to explain when, where, and for what applications fire alarm systems are required, the necessary means of initiation and occupant notification, and the means by which to notify the fire department. This code also details any equipment exceptions to these requirements.
- *Fire Code* (NFPA 1) — This code was established to help fire authorities continually develop safeguards against fire hazards. A chapter of this code is dedicated to fire protection systems. Information and requirements for testing, operation, installation, and periodic preventive maintenance of fire alarm systems are included in this portion of the code.

1.2.2 NFPA Standards

The NFPA also publishes specific standards that are used by fire alarm system professionals. These include:

- NFPA 75, *Standard for the Fire Protection of Information Technology Equipment*
- NFPA 80, *Standard for Fire Doors and Other Opening Protectives*
- NFPA 90A, *Standard for the Installation of Air-Conditioning and Ventilating Systems*
- NFPA 90B, *Standard for the Installation of Warm Air Heating and Air-Conditioning Systems*
- NFPA 92, *Standard for Smoke Control Systems*

1.0.0 Section Review

1. Which organization establishes standards for equipment?
   a. NFPA
   b. DIAM-50-3
   c. NEMA
   d. NICET

2. NFPA 101® is also known as the _____.
   a. *NEC®*
   b. *Life Safety Code®*
   c. *Fire Code*
   d. *NFAC*

2.0.0 Fire Alarm Systems Overview

Objective

Describe the basic types of fire alarm systems and their primary components.

a. Describe the basic types of fire alarm communication systems.

b. Describe the primary components of fire alarm systems.

Performance Tasks

There are no Performance Tasks in this section.

Fire alarm systems are primarily designed to detect and warn of abnormal conditions, alert the appropriate authorities, and operate the necessary facility safety devices to minimize fire danger. Through a variety of manual and automatic system devices, a fire alarm system links the sensing of a fire condition with people inside and outside the building. The system also communicates to fire professionals that action needs to be taken.

2.1.0 Fire Alarm Communication Systems

Although specific codes and standards must always be followed when designing and installing a fire alarm system, many different types of systems that employ different types of technology can be used. Most of these types of fire alarm systems are categorized by the means of communication between the detectors and the fire alarm **control unit** (FACU). Two major types of fire alarm systems are:

- Conventional hardwired
- Addressable intelligent

2.1.1 Conventional Hardwired Systems

The simplest of all fire alarm systems is a hardwired system using a conventional initiation device, such as a **heat detector**, **smoke detector**, or pull station, and a notification appliance, such as a bell, **horn**, or light. Large buildings or areas that are being protected are usually divided into **zones** to identify the specific area where a fire is detected. A conventional hardwired system is limited to zone detection only, with no means of identifying the specific detector that initiated the alarm. A typical hardwired system might look like *Figure 1* with either two- or four-wire initiating or notification device circuits. In two-wire circuits, the **power supply** for the devices is superimposed on the alarm circuits. In four-wire circuits, the operating power is supplied to the devices separately from the **signal** or alarm circuits. In either two- or four-wire systems, the **end-of-line (EOL) device** is used by the FACU to monitor circuit integrity.

2.1.2 Addressable Intelligent Systems

Two different versions of addressable intelligent systems are available: addressable and analog addressable. Analog addressable systems are more sophisticated than addressable systems.

An addressable system uses advanced technology and detection equipment for discrete identification of an **alarm signal** at the detector level. An addressable system can pinpoint an alarm location to the precise physical location of the initiating detector. The basic idea of an addressable system is to provide identification or control of individual initiation, control, or notification devices on a common circuit. Each component on a **signaling line circuit (SLC)** has an identification number or address. The addresses are usually assigned using switches or other similar means. *Figure 2* is a simplified representation of an addressable or analog addressable fire alarm system.

Control unit: A device with the control circuits necessary to furnish power to a fire alarm system, receive signals from alarm initiating devices (and transmit them to audible alarm indicating appliances and accessory equipment), and electrically supervise the system installation wiring and primary power. The control unit can be contained in one or more cabinets in adjacent or remote locations.

Heat detector: A device that detects abnormally high temperatures or high rates of temperature rise.

Smoke detector: A device that detects visible or invisible particles of combustion.

Horn: An audible signal appliance in which energy produces a sound by imparting motion to a flexible component that vibrates at some nominal frequency.

Zones: Defined areas within a protected premises. A zone can define an area from which a signal can be received, an area to which a signal can be sent, or an area in which a form of control can be executed.

Power supply: A source of electrical operating power, including the circuits and terminations connecting it to the dependent system components.

Signal: A status indication communicated by electrical or other means.

End-of-line (EOL) device: A device used to terminate a supervised circuit. An EOL is normally a resistor or diode placed at the end of a two-wire circuit to maintain supervision.

Alarm signal: A signal indicating an emergency requiring immediate action, such as an alarm for fire from a manual station, waterflow device, or automatic fire alarm system.

Signaling line circuit (SLC): A circuit or path between any combination of circuit interfaces, control units, or transmitters over which multiple system input signals, output signals, or both are carried.

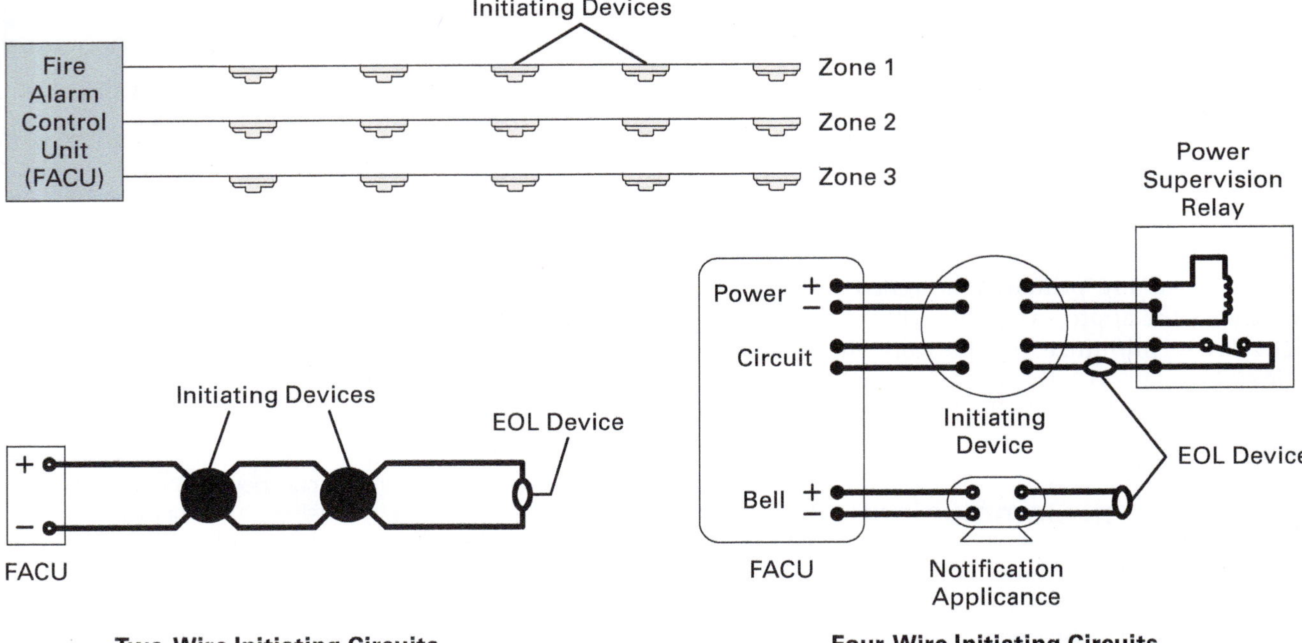

Figure 1 Typical conventional hardwired system.

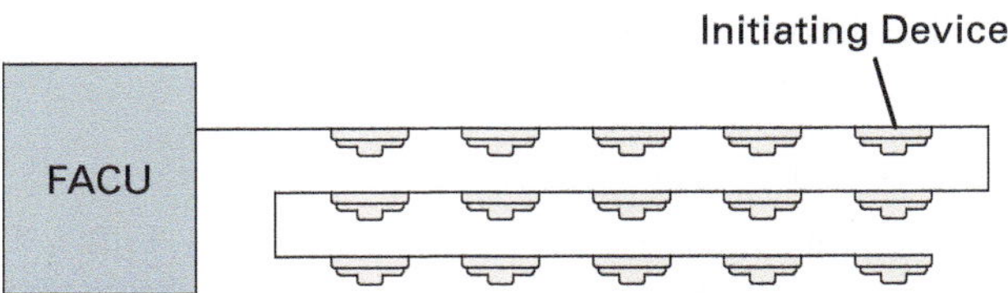

Figure 2 Typical addressable or analog addressable system.

Path (pathway): Any conductor, optic fiber, radio carrier, or other means for transmitting fire alarm system information between two or more locations.

Addressable device: A fire alarm system component with discrete identification that can have its status individually identified or that is used to individually control other functions.

Transmitter: A system component that provides an interface between the transmission channel and signaling line circuits, initiating device circuits, or control units.

The FACU constantly polls each device using an SLC. The response from the device being polled verifies the wiring **path (pathway)** is intact (wiring supervision) and the **addressable device** is in place and operational. Most addressable systems use at least three states to describe the status of the device: normal, trouble, and alarm. Smoke detection devices make the decision internally regarding their alarm state just like conventional smoke detectors. Output devices, like relays, are also checked for their presence and, in some cases, for their output status. Notification output modules also supervise the wiring to the horns, strobes, and other devices, as well as the availability of the power needed to run the devices in case of an alarm. When the FACU polls each device, it also compares the information from the device to the system program. For example, if the program indicates device 12 should be a contact **transmitter**, but the device reports it is a relay, a problem exists that must be corrected. Addressable fire alarm systems have been made with two-, three-, and four-wire conductors, but most are two-wire conductors. Generally, additional conductors are in place for additional current. Some systems may also contain multiple SLCs comparable to multiple zones in a conventional hardwired system.

Analog systems take the addressable system capabilities much further and change the way the information is processed. When a device is polled, it returns much more information than a device in a standard addressable system would. For example, instead of a smoke detector transmitting it is in alarm status, the device actually transmits the level of smoke or contamination present to the FACU. The FACU then compares the information to the levels detected in previous polls. A slow change in levels (over days, weeks, or months) indicates that a device is dirty or malfunctioning. A rapid change, however, indicates a fire condition. Most systems have the capability to compensate for dirt buildup in the detectors. The system will adjust the detector sensitivity to the desired range. Once the dirt buildup exceeds the compensation range, the system reports a trouble condition. The system can also administer self-checks on the detectors to test their ability to respond to smoke. If the airflow around a device is too great to allow proper detection, some systems will generate a trouble report.

The information in some systems is transmitted and received in a totally digital format. Others transmit the polling information digitally but receive the responses in an analog current-level format.

The unit, not the device, performs the actual determination of the alarm state. In many systems, the light-emitting diode (LED) on the detector is turned on by the unit, not by the detector. This decision-making ability of the unit also allows the detector sensitivity to be adjusted at the unit. For instance, an increase in the ambient temperature can cause a smoke detector to become more sensitive, and the alarm sensitivity level at the unit can be adjusted to compensate. Sensitivities can even be adjusted based on the time of day or day of the week. Other detection devices can also be programmed to adjust their own sensitivity.

Compared with the three elementary alarm states found in simpler systems, the ability of an analog addressable system to process more information allows it to provide pre-alarm signals and other information. In many devices, five or more different signals can be received.

Most analog addressable systems operate on a two-conductor circuit. Most systems limit the number of devices to about 100. Because of the high data rates on these SLCs, capacitance also limits the conductor lengths. Always follow the manufacturer's installation instructions to ensure proper operation of the system.

In addressable or analog addressable systems, there are seven basic pathway classes:

- *Class A pathways* — Class A pathways for an addressable system require that the conductors loop in and out of each device. At the last device, the signaling line pathway is returned to the control unit by a different route. The control unit normally communicates with the devices via the outbound circuit but can communicate to the back side of a break via the return pathway. The unit detects the fact that a complete loop no longer exists and provides a trouble indication. All devices remain in operation. Some systems even have the ability to identify which conductor is broken and how many devices are on each side of the break.
- *Class B pathways* — Class B pathways for an addressable system essentially require that two conductors reach each device on the pathway by any means as long as the wire type and physical installation rules are followed. It does not require wiring to pass in and out of each device in a series arrangement. With a pathway capable of 100 devices, it is permissible to go in 100 different directions from the unit. Supervision occurs because the FACU polls and receives information from each device. The route taken is not important. A break in the wiring will result in the loss of communication with one or more devices depending on where the fault is located. This will provide a trouble indication at the control panel.
- *Class C pathways* — Class C pathways provide one or more pathways where operation is verified via end-to-end communication, but the integrity of the pathways is not monitored. The pathway for signals from **protected premises** to the supervising station is unsupervised and the signal may end up taking different routes to the final destination.
- *Class D pathways* — Class D pathways are fail-safe, meaning the intended function of the pathways is performed even if the pathways fail.
- *Class E pathways* — Class E signaling line pathways are not monitored for integrity and are used in situations where supervision is not required.

Protected premises: Physical locations protected by a fire alarm system.

- *Class N pathways* — Class N signaling line pathways are essentially Ethernet (or another network) or IP infrastructure. These pathways are confirmed through end-to-end communication, and loss of communication between endpoints on any path produces a signal indicating the system's minimal operational requirements cannot be met. Because primary and redundant pathways are not permitted to share traffic, problems with one pathway will not affect another pathway.
- *Class X pathways* — Class X signaling line pathways add to the requirements from Class A by requiring that life safety systems continue operating even though multiple issues may be occurring at one time. The overall circuit continues to operate by isolating the affected segment of the circuit. A trouble indication will be indicated if there is a fault.
- *Hybrid circuits* — Hybrid systems may consist of a Class A main trunk with Class B spur circuits in each area. A good example would be a Class A circuit leaving the control unit, entering a junction box on each floor of a multistory building, and then returning to the control unit by a different route. The SLCs on the floors are wired as Class B from the junction box. This provides good system reliability and keeps costs down.

2.2.0 Fire Alarm System Equipment

The equipment used in fire alarm systems is generally held to higher standards than typical electrical equipment. The main components of a fire alarm system include:

- Alarm initiating devices
- Control units
- Primary (main) and secondary (standby) power supplies
- Notification appliances
- Communications and monitoring

2.2.1 Fire Alarm Initiating Devices

Fire alarm systems use initiating devices to report a fire and provide supervisory or trouble reports. Some of the initiating devices used to trigger a fire alarm are designed to sense the signs of fire automatically with automatic sensors. Some report level-of-fire conditions only. Others rely on people to see the signs of fire and activate a manual device. Automatic sensors, also known as *detectors*, sense smoke, heat, and flames. Manual initiating devices typically use some form of pull station.

Figure 3 is a graphic representation of the application of various detectors for each stage of a fire. However, detection may not occur at any specific point in time within each stage, nor will the indicated sensors always provide detection in the stages represented. For example, alcohol fires can produce flame followed by heat while producing few or no visible particles.

Besides triggering an alarm, some fire alarm systems use the input from one or more detectors or pull stations to trigger fire suppression equipment such as a carbon dioxide (CO_2), dry chemical, or water deluge systems.

It is mandatory that devices used for fire detection be **listed** for the purpose they will be used. Common UL Listings for fire detection devices are as follows:

- *UL 38* — Manually actuated signaling box
- *UL 217* — Single- or multiple-station smoke detector
- *UL 268* — System-type smoke detector
- *UL 268A* — Duct smoke detector
- *UL 521* — Heat detector

Listed: Equipment or materials included in a list published by an organization acceptable to the Authority Having Jurisdiction (AHJ) that is concerned with product evaluation, whose listing states either that the equipment or materials meets appropriate standards or has been tested and found suitable for use in a specified manner.

NOTE

The means for identifying listed equipment may vary for each organization concerned with product evaluation—UL, FM, IRI (Industrial Risk Insurers), and so on. Some organizations do not recognize listed equipment unless it is also labeled. The Authority Having Jurisdiction (AHJ) should use the system employed by the listed organization to identify a listed product.

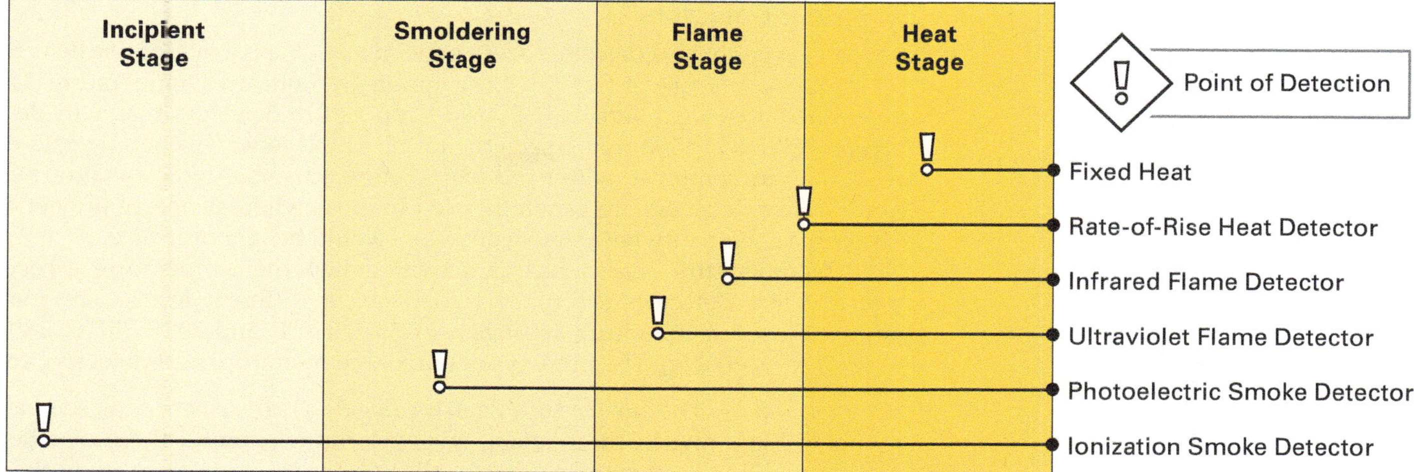

Figure 3 Detection versus stages of a fire.

2.2.2 Conventional versus Addressable Commercial Detectors

Commercial detectors differ from stand-alone residential detectors in that a number of commercial detectors are usually wired in parallel and connected to a FACU. In a typical conventional commercial fire alarm installation, a number of separate zones with multiple automatic sensors are used to partition the installation into fire zones.

As described previously, newer commercial fire systems use addressable automatic detectors and pull stations to supply a coded identification signal. The systems also provide an individual supervisory or **trouble signal** to the FACU, as well as any fire alarm signal, when periodically polled by the FACU. This provides the fire control system with specific device location information to pinpoint the fire, along with detector, pull station, or notification appliance status information. In many new commercial fire systems, analog addressable detectors are used. Along with providing information supplied by an addressable device, these devices communicate information about the fire condition (level of smoke, temperature, etc.) in addition to their identification, supervisory, or trouble signals. In the case of these detectors, the control unit's internal programming analyzes the fire condition data from one or more sensors using recent and historical information from the sensors to determine if a fire alarm should be issued.

Trouble signal: A signal initiated by the fire alarm system or device that indicates a fault in a monitored circuit or component.

2.2.3 Automatic Detectors

Automatic detectors can be divided into the following types:

- *Line detector* — Detection is continuous along the entire length of the detector in this type of detection device. Typical examples may include certain older pneumatic rate-of-rise tubing detectors, the **projected beam smoke detector**, and heat-sensitive cable.
- *Spot detector* — This type of device has a detecting element that is concentrated at a particular location. Typical examples include bimetallic detectors, fusible alloy detectors, some types of **rate-of-rise detectors**, most smoke detectors, and thermoelectric detectors.
- **Air sampling detector** — This device consists of piping or tubing distributed from the detector unit to the area(s) to be protected. An air pump draws air from the protected area back to the detector through air sampling ports and piping or tubing. At the detector, the air is analyzed for fire products.
- *Addressable or analog addressable detector* — As mentioned previously, each of these detectors provides alarms and individual point identification, along with supervisory/trouble information, to the control unit.

Projected beam smoke detector: A type of photoelectric light obscuration smoke detector in which the beam spans the protected area.

Rate-of-rise detectors: Devices that respond when the temperature rises at a rate exceeding a predetermined value.

Air sampling detector: A detector consisting of piping or tubing distribution from the detector unit to the area or areas to be protected. Using air sampling ports and piping or tubing, an air pump draws air from the protected area back to the detector. At the detector, the air is analyzed for fire products.

2.2.4 Heat Detectors

Two major types of heat detectors are in general use. One is a rate-of-rise detector that senses an increase of 15°F (8°C) per minute in room/area temperature. The other is one of several versions of fixed-temperature detectors that activate if the room/area temperature exceeds the rating of the sensor. Generally, rate-of-rise sensors are combined with fixed-temperature sensors in a combination heat detector. Heat detectors are generally used in areas where property protection is the only concern or where smoke detectors would be inappropriate.

Fixed-temperature heat detectors activate when the temperature exceeds a preset level. Detectors are made to activate at different levels. The most commonly used temperature settings are 135°F, 190°F, and 200°F (57°C, 88°C, and 93°C respectively). The three types of fixed-temperature heat detectors are:

Reset: A control function that attempts to return a system or device to its normal, non-alarm state.

- *Fusible link* — The fusible link detector (*Figure* 4) consists of a plastic base containing a switch mechanism, wiring terminals, and a three-disc heat collector. Two sections of the heat collector are soldered together with an alloy that will cause the lower disc to drop away when the rated temperature is reached. This moves a plunger that shorts across the wiring contacts, causing a constant alarm signal. After the detector is activated, a new heat collector must be installed to **reset** the detector to an operating condition.
- *Quick metal* — The operation of the quick metal detector (*Figure* 5) is very simple. When the surrounding air reaches the prescribed temperature—usually 135°F or 190°F (57°C or 88°C)—the quick metal begins to soften and give way. This allows spring pressure within the device to push the top portion of the thermal element out of the way, causing the alarm contacts to close. After the detector has been activated, either the detector or the heat collector must be replaced to reset the detector to an operating condition.
- *Bimetallic* — In a bimetallic detector (*Figure* 6), two metals with different rates of thermal expansion are bonded together. Heat causes the two metals to expand at different rates, causing the bonded strip to bend. This action closes a normally open circuit, which signals an alarm. Detectors with bi-metallic elements automatically self-restore when the temperature returns to normal.

Combination heat detectors contain two types of heat detectors in a single housing. A fixed-temperature detector reacts to a preset temperature, and a rate-of-rise detector reacts to a rapid change in temperature even if the temperature reached does not exceed the preset level.

Rate-of-rise operation (*Figure* 7) occurs when air in the chamber expands more rapidly than it can escape from the vent. The increasing pressure moves the diaphragm and causes the alarm contact and contact screw to close, which results in an alarm signal. This portion of the detector automatically resets when the temperature stabilizes. A fixed-temperature trip occurs when the heat causes the fusible alloy to melt, releasing the spring. The spring depresses the diaphragm, which closes the alarm contact and contact screw. If the fusible alloy is melted, the center section of the detector must be replaced.

Addressable and Analog Addressable Smoke Detectors

Shown in the image is a typical addressable smoke detector. Addressable detectors send the FACU alarm status, detector location, and supervisory/trouble information. An analog addressable smoke detector performs the same functions; however, it has the additional capability of reporting information to the FACU about the level of smoke that it is detecting.

Source: System Sensor

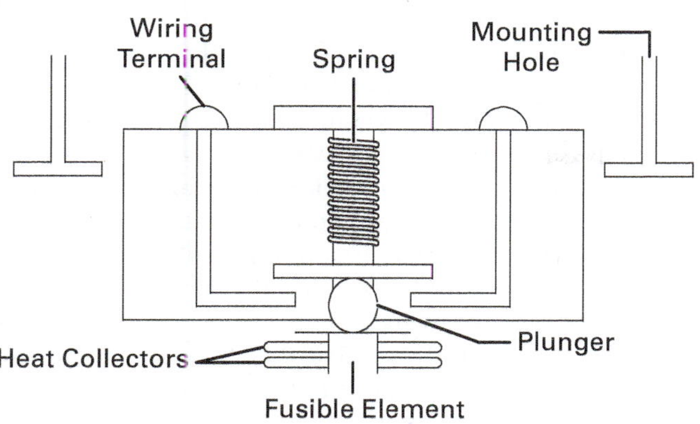

Figure 4 Fusible link detector.

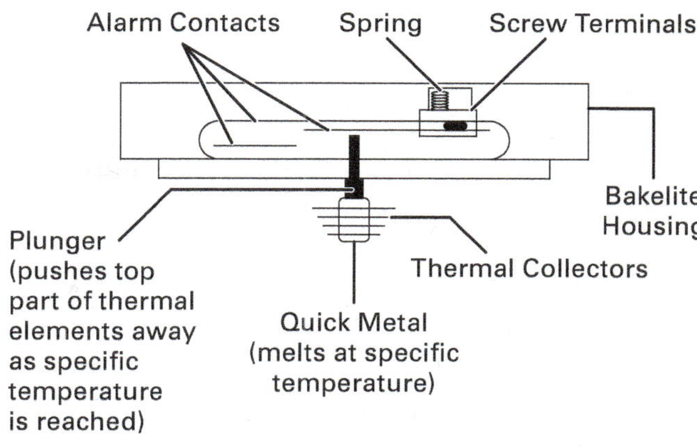

Figure 5 Quick metal detector.

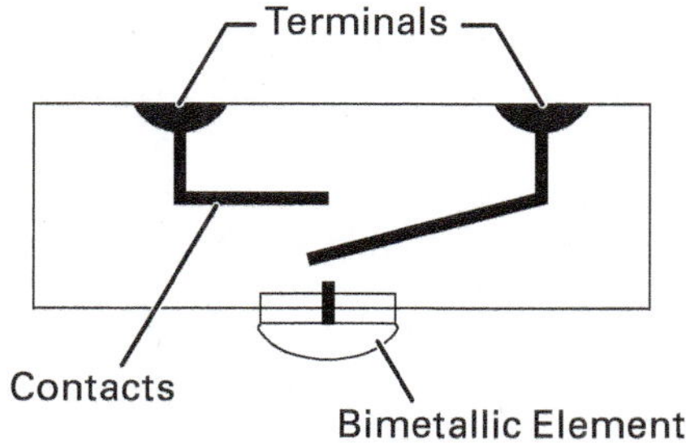

Figure 6 Bimetallic detector.

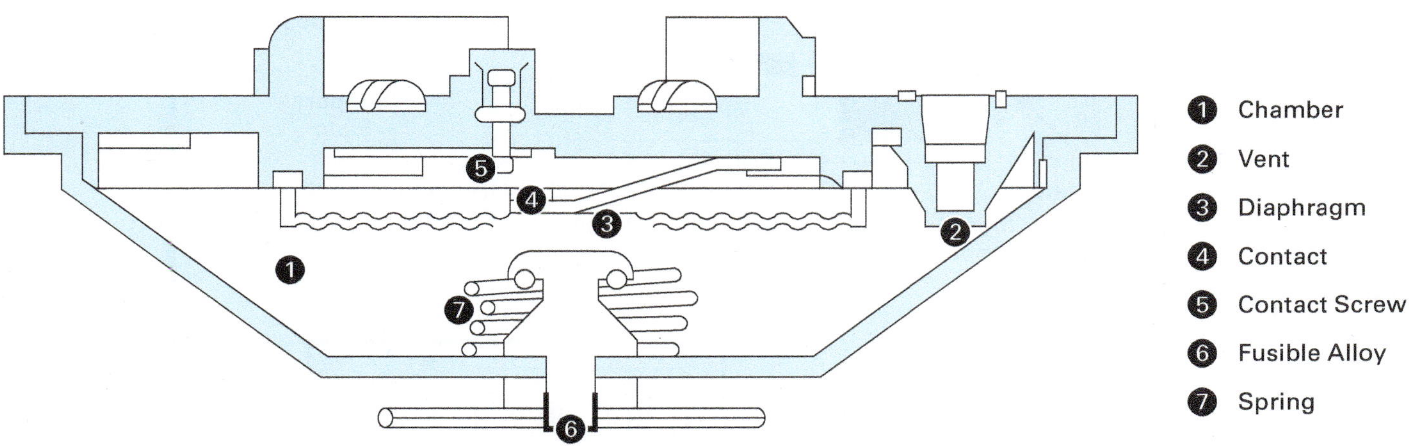

Figure 7 Rate-of-rise with fusible link detector.

As with all automatic detectors, heat sensors are also rated for a listed **spacing** and temperature, as shown in *Table 17.6.2.1* in NFPA 72®. The listed spacing is typically 50' × 50' (15 m × 15 m). The applicable rules and formulas for proper spacing (from NFPA 72® and other applicable standards) are then applied to the listed spacing. Caution is advised because it is difficult or impossible to distinguish the difference in the listed spacing for two different types of heat sensors based on their appearances.

Spacing: A horizontally measured dimension related to the allowable coverage of fire detectors.

The maximum **ceiling** temperature must be 20°F (11°C) or more below the detector's rated temperature. The difference between the rated temperature and the maximum ambient temperature for the space should be as small as possible to minimize response time.

Ceiling: The upper surface of a space, regardless of height. Areas with a suspended ceiling would have two ceilings: one visible from the floor and one above the suspended ceiling.

Heat sensors are not considered life safety devices. They should be used in areas that are unoccupied or in areas that are environmentally unsuitable for the application of smoke detectors. To every extent possible, heat sensors should be limited to use as property protection devices.

Figure 8 Typical photoelectric smoke detector.

2.2.5 Smoke Detectors

There are two basic types of smoke detectors: photoelectric detectors (*Figure 8*), which sense the presence of large smoke particles from smoldering fires, and ionization detectors (*Figure 9*), which sense the smaller smoke particles from fast-burning fires. For residential use, both types are available combined in one detector housing for maximum coverage. For commercial use, either type is also available combined with a heat detector. As mentioned previously, the newer commercial fire systems use smoke detectors that are analog addressable units, which do not signal an alarm. Instead, they return a signal that represents the level of detection to the FACU for further analysis.

An ionization detector uses the change in the electrical conductivity of air to detect smoke. An alarm is indicated when the amount of smoke in the detector rises above a certain level. The detector has a very small amount of radioactive material in the sensing chambers. As shown in *Figure 10* (A), the radioactive material ionizes the air in the measuring and reference chambers, allowing the air to conduct current through the space between two charged electrodes. When smoke particles enter the measuring chamber, they prevent the air from conducting as much current, as shown in *Figure 10* (B). The detector activates an alarm when the conductivity decreases to a set level. The detector compares the current drop in the main chamber against the drop in the reference chamber. This allows it to avoid alarming when the current drops due to surges, radio frequency interference (RFI), or other factors.

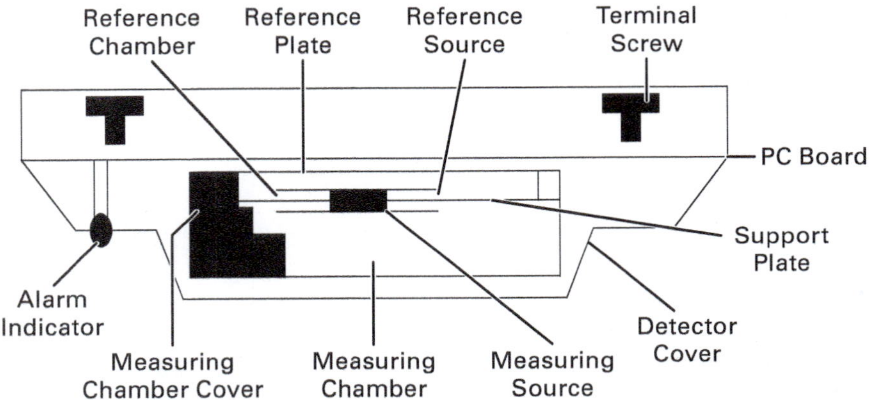

Figure 9 Typical ionization smoke detector.

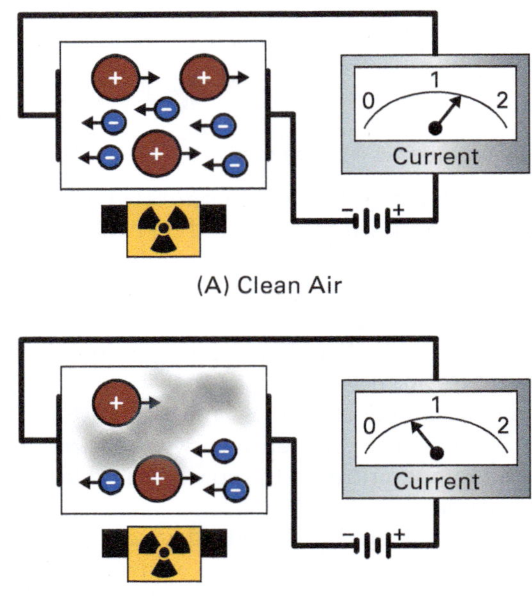

Figure 10 Ionization action.

There are two basic types of **photoelectric smoke detectors**: light-scattering detectors and beam detectors. Light-scattering detectors use the reflective properties of smoke to detect the smoke. The principle of **light scattering** is used for the most common single-housing detectors. Beam detectors rely upon smoke to block enough light to cause an alarm. Early smoke detectors operated on the light **obscuration** principle. Today, photoelectric smoke detectors are used primarily to sense smoke in large open areas with high ceilings. In some cases, prisms are used to direct the beam in a desired path, which allows for increased detection distances. Additionally, using prisms cuts installation costs, and power does not need to be provided.

Light-scattering detectors are usually spot detectors that contain a light source and a photosensitive device arranged so that light rays do not normally fall on the device (*Figure 11*). When smoke particles enter the light path, the light collides with the particles and scatters, hitting the photosensor, which signals the alarm.

Projected beam smoke detectors that operate on the light obscuration principle (*Figure 12*) consist of a light source, a light beam focusing device, and a photosensitive device. Smoke obscures or blocks part of the light beam, which reduces the amount of light that reaches the photosensor, signaling an alarm. The prime use of the light obscuration principle is with projected beam-type smoke detectors that are employed in the protection of large, open high-bay warehouses, high-ceiling churches, and other large areas. A version of this beam detector was used in older style duct detectors.

After a number of fires where smoke spread through building duct systems and contributed to numerous deaths, building codes began to require the installation of duct detectors. Two versions of duct detectors are shown in *Figure 13*. The projected beam detector is an older style duct detector that may be encountered in existing installations.

Duct detectors enable a system to control the spread of smoke within a building by turning off the HVAC system, operating exhaust fans, closing doors and fire/smoke dampers, or pressurizing smoke compartments in the event of a fire. This prevents smoke, fumes, and fire by-products from circulating through the ductwork. Because the air in the duct is either at rest or moving at high speed, the detector must be able to sense smoke in either situation. A typical duct detector has a listed airflow range within which it will function properly. It is not required to function when the duct fans are stopped.

Photoelectric smoke detectors: Detectors employing the photoelectric principle of operation using either the obscuration effect or the light-scattering effect for detecting smoke in its compartment.

Light scattering: The action of light being reflected or refracted off particles of combustion. Used for detection in a modern-day photoelectric smoke detector. This is called the *Tyndall effect*.

Obscuration: A reduction in the atmospheric transparency caused by smoke, usually expressed in percent per foot.

Photoelectric and Ionization Detectors

Photoelectric detectors are often faster than ionization detectors at sensing smoke from slow, smoldering fires. Ionization detectors are often better than photoelectric detectors at sensing fast, flaming fires.

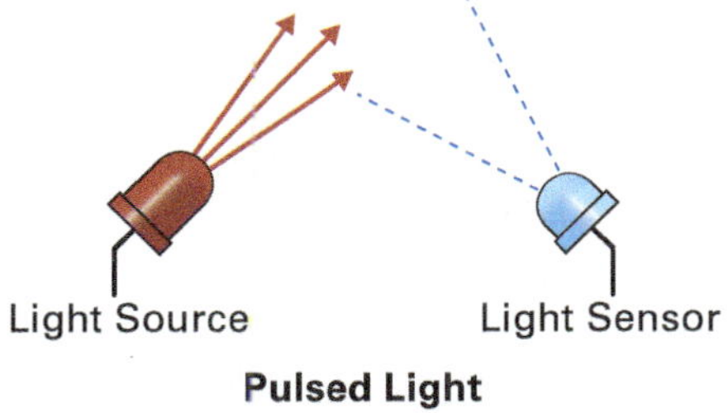

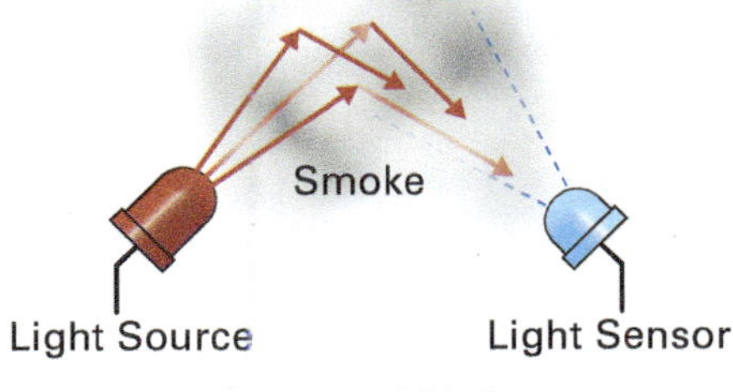

Figure 11 Light-scattering detector operation.

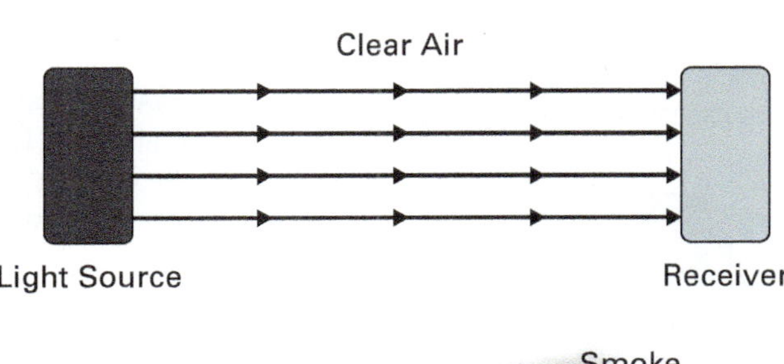

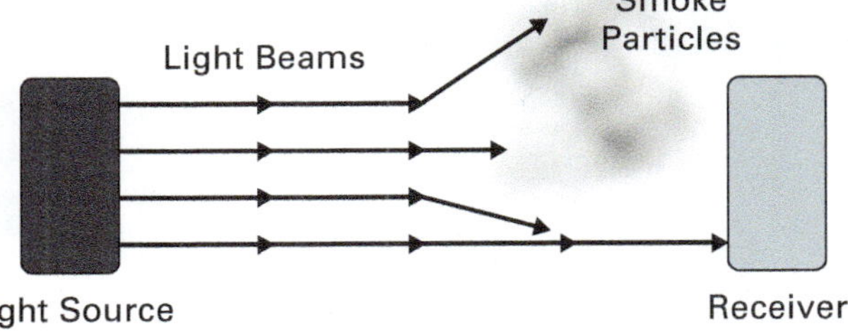

Figure 12 Light obscuration principle.

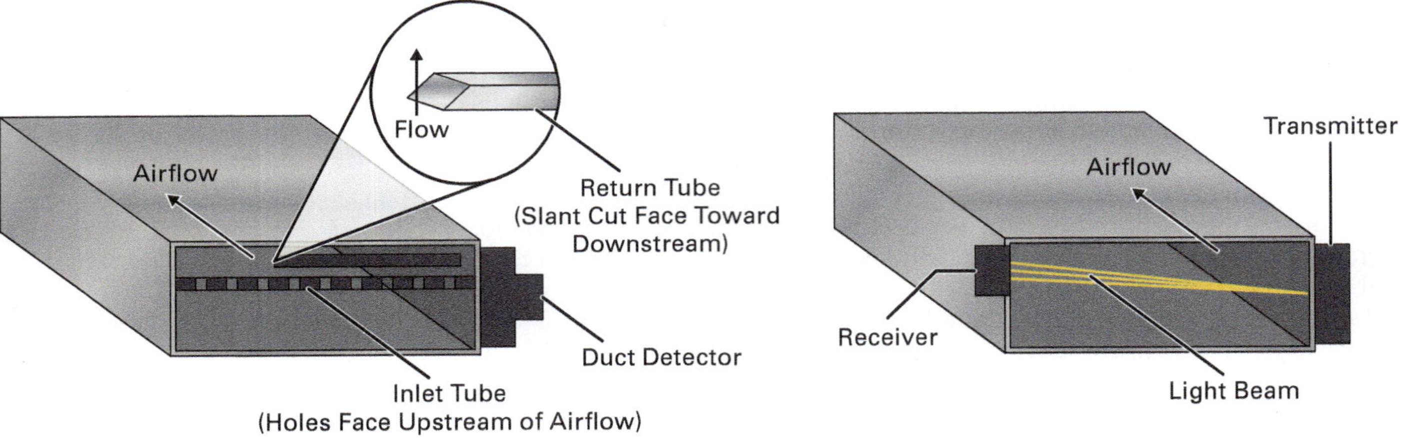

Figure 13 Typical duct detector installations.

At least one duct detector is available with a small blower for use in very low-airflow applications. Duct detectors must not be used as a substitute for open area protection because smoke may not be drawn from open areas of the building when the HVAC system is shut down. Duct detectors can be mounted inside the duct with an access panel or outside the duct with sampling tubes protruding into the duct.

As mentioned previously, the primary function of a duct detector is to turn off the HVAC system to prevent smoke from being circulated. However, NFPA 90A and NFPA 90B require that duct detectors be tied into a general fire alarm system if the building contains one. If no separate fire alarm system exists, then remote audio/visual indicators, triggered by the duct detectors, must be provided in normally occupied areas of the building. Duct detectors that perform functions other than the shutdown of HVAC equipment must be supplied with backup power.

Aspirating smoke detectors (*Figure 14*) use sampling tubes to draw air from several areas (zones). The air is passed through several chambers where humidity is added, and pressure is reduced with a vacuum pump. Reducing the pressure causes water droplets to form around the sub-micron smoke particles and allows them to become visible. A light beam is passed through the droplets and measured by a photoelectric detector. As the number of droplets increases, the light reaching the detector is reduced, which initiates an alarm signal.

Projected Beam Smoke Detectors

The transmitter and receiver for a projected beam smoke detector are shown in the image. These units are designed for use in atriums, ballrooms, churches, warehouses, museums, factories, and other large, high-ceiling areas where conventional smoke detectors cannot be easily installed.

Source: Honeywell Security and Fire

Duct Smoke Detectors

Shown in the image is a typical duct smoke detector with the cover removed. It is designed for HVAC applications. The manufacturer of this unit makes duct detectors based on either photoelectric or ionization technology. Up to 10 of these units can be networked together. When one detector goes into alarm, all the other detectors on the network activate to control the connected fans, blowers, and dampers. However, only the duct detector that initiated the alarm shows an alarm indication to identify it as the source of the alarm.

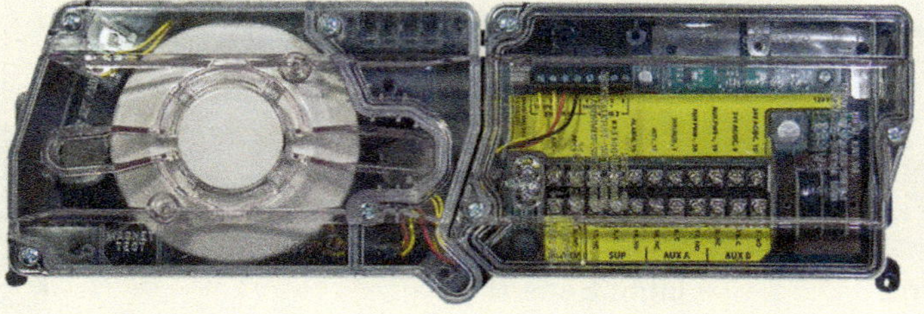

Source: System Sensor

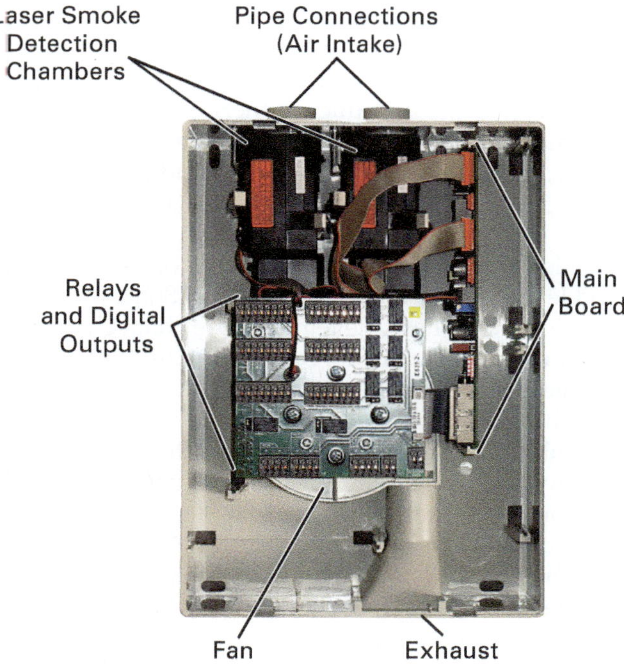

Figure 14 Aspirating smoke detector.
Source: © User:Nabifly / Wikimedia Commons / CC-BY-SA-3.0

2.2.6 Other Types of Detectors

This section describes special-application detectors. These include devices such as the **rate compensation detector**, semiconductor line-type heat detector, fusible line-type heat detector, ultraviolet (UV) **flame detector**, and infrared (IR) flame detector.

A rate compensation detector (*Figure 15*) is a device that responds when the temperature of the surrounding air reaches a predetermined level, regardless of the rate of temperature rise. The detector also responds if the temperature rises quickly over a short period. This type of detector has a tubular casing of metal that expands lengthwise as it is heated. A contact closes as it reaches a certain stage of elongation. These detectors are self-restoring. Rate compensation detectors are more complex than either fixed or rate-of-rise detectors. They combine the principles of both to compensate for thermal lag. When the air temperature is rising rapidly, the unit is designed to respond almost exactly at the point when the air temperature reaches the unit's rated temperature. It does not lag while it absorbs the heat and rises to that temperature. Because of the precision associated with their operation, rate compensation detectors are well suited for use in areas where thermal lag must be minimized.

Rate compensation detector: A device that responds when the temperature of the air surrounding the device reaches a predetermined level, regardless of the rate of temperature rise.

Flame detector: A device that detects the infrared, ultraviolet, or visible radiation produced by a fire. Some devices are also capable of detecting the flicker rate (frequency) of the flame.

Figure 15 Rate compensation detector.

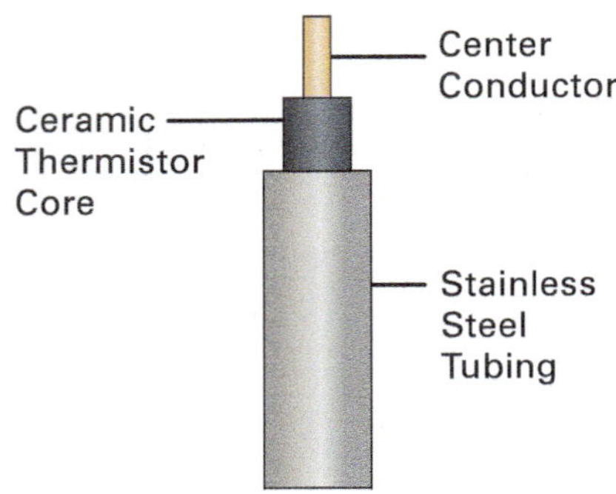

Figure 16 Restorable semiconductor line-type heat detector.

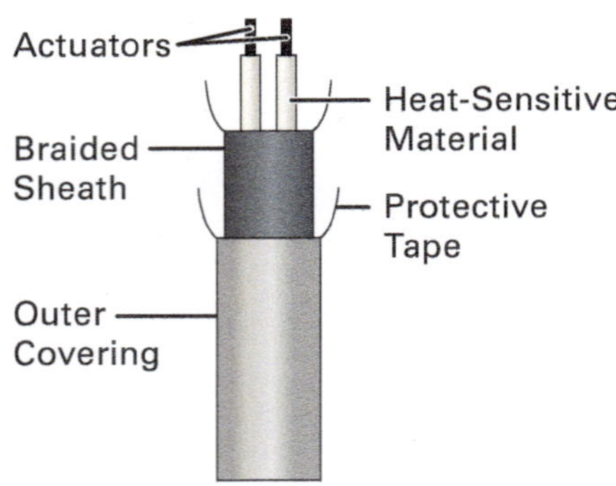

Figure 17 Non-restorable fusible line-type heat detector.

Wavelength: The distance between peaks of a sinusoidal wave. All radiant energy can be described as a wave having a wavelength. Wavelengths serve as the unit of measure for distinguishing between different parts of the spectrum. Wavelengths are measured in microns, nanometers, or angstroms.

A restorable semiconductor line-type heat detector (*Figure 16*) uses a semiconductor material and a stainless steel capillary tube. The capillary tube contains a coaxial center conductor separated from the tube wall by a temperature-sensitive semiconductor thermistor material. Under normal conditions, a small current (below the alarm threshold) flows. As the temperature rises, the resistance of the semiconductor thermistor decreases. This allows more current to flow and initiates the alarm. When the temperature falls, the current flow decreases below the alarm threshold level, stopping the alarm. The wire is connected to special controls or modules that establish the alarm threshold level and sense the current flow. Some of these control devices can pinpoint the location where the temperature change occurs in the length of the wire. Line-type heat detectors are commonly used in cable trays, conveyors, electrical switchgear, warehouse rack storage, mines, pipelines, hangars, and other similar applications.

A non-restorable fusible line-type heat detector (*Figure 17*) uses a pair of steel wires in a normally open circuit. The conductors are held apart by heat-sensitive insulation. The wires, under tension, are enclosed in a braided sheath to make a single cable. When the temperature limit is reached, the insulation melts, the two wires contact, and an alarm is initiated. The melted and fused section of the cable must be replaced following an alarm to restore the system. The wire is available with different melting temperatures for the insulation. The temperature rating should be approximately 20°F (11°C) above the ambient temperature. Special controls or modules are available that can be connected to the wires to pinpoint the fire location where the wires are shorted together.

A UV flame detector (*Figure 18*) uses a solid-state sensing element of silicon carbide, aluminum nitrate, or a gas-filled tube. The UV radiation of a flame causes gas in the element or tube to ionize and become conductive. When sufficient current flow is detected, an alarm is initiated.

An IR flame detector consists of a filter and lens system that screens out any unwanted radiant energy **wavelength** and focuses the incoming energy on light-sensitive components. These flame detectors can respond to the total IR content of the flame alone or to a combination of IR with flame flicker of a specific frequency. They are used indoors and have filtering systems or solar-sensing circuits to minimize unwanted alarms from sunlight.

Most flame detectors installed today are combination UV/IR devices. This helps reduce the chances of a false activation. Additionally, these flame detectors would be cross-zone to provide extra protection from a false trip.

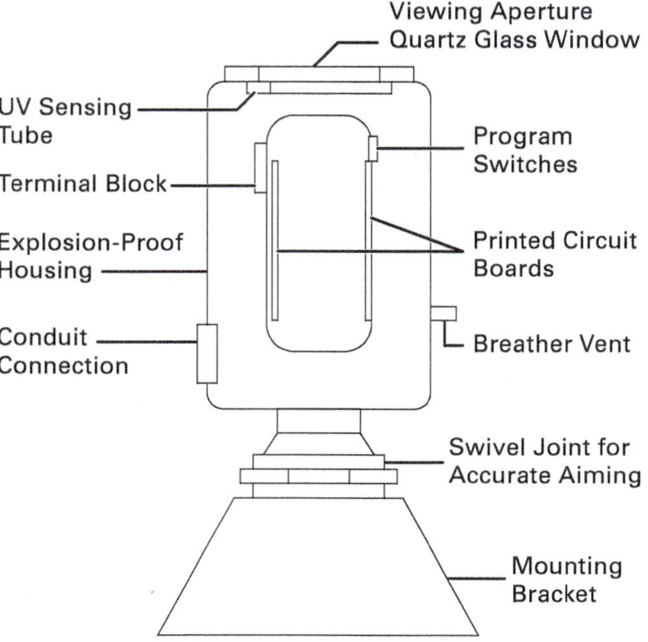

Figure 18 UV flame detector.

2.2.7 Manual (Pull Station) Fire Detection Devices

When required by code, manual pull stations are distributed throughout a monitored commercial area so that they are unobstructed, readily accessible, and in the normal path of exit from the area. Examples of typical pull stations are shown in *Figure 19* and described in the following list:

- *Single-action pull stations* — A single action/motion operates these devices. They are activated by pulling a handle that closes one or more sets of contacts and generates the alarm.
- *Glass-break pull stations* — In these devices, a glass or plastic rod, plate, or special element must be broken to activate the alarm. This is accomplished by using a handle or hammer that is an integral part of the station. When the alarm is activated, one or more sets of contacts are closed, and an alarm is actuated. Usually, the plate, rod, or element must be replaced to return the unit to service, although some stations will operate without the rod or plate.
- *Double-action pull stations* — Double-action pull stations require the user to lift a cover or open a door before operating the pull station. Two discretely independent actions are required to operate the station and activate the alarm. Using a stopper-type cover that allows the alarm to be tripped after a cover is lifted may turn a single-action pull station into a double-action pull station. According to UL, the stopper-type device is listed as an accessory to manual stations and is permissible for use as a double-action pull station device. With certain types of double-action stations, there have been instances when people have confused the sound of a tamper alarm that sounds when the cover is lifted with the sound of fire alarm activation. The sounding of this tamper alarm sometimes causes failure to activate the pull station.
- *Key-operated pull stations* — Applications for key-operated pull stations (*Figure 20*) are restricted. Key-operated stations are permitted in certain occupancies where facility staff members may be in the immediate area and where use by other occupants of the area is not desirable. Typical situations would include certain detention and correctional facilities and some health care facilities, particularly those that provide mental health treatment.

Single-Action Pull Station

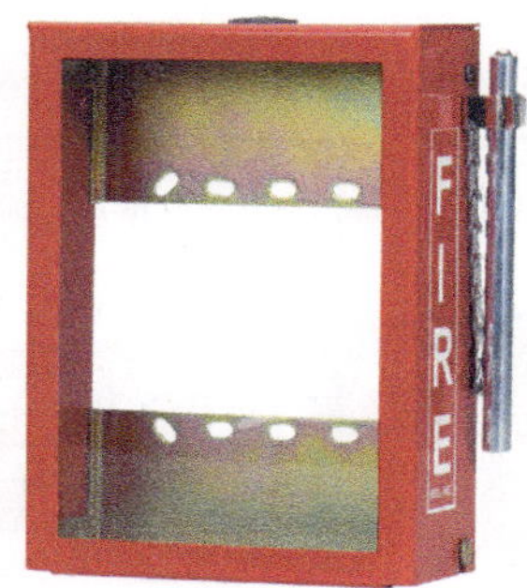

Glass-Break Cover for Pull Station

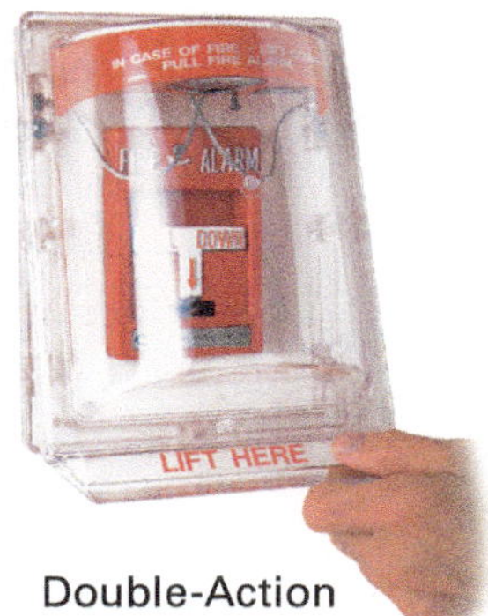

Double-Action Pull Station

Figure 19 Typical pull stations.
Source: Brooks Equipment Company, LLC

Figure 20 Key-operated pull station.

2.2.8 Auto-Mechanical Fire Detection Equipment

This section describes various types of auto-mechanical fire detection equipment. It covers wet and dry sprinkler systems and waterflow alarms.

A wet sprinkler system (*Figure 21*) consists of a permanently piped water system under pressure using heat-actuated sprinklers. When a fire occurs, the sprinklers exposed to high heat open and discharge water individually in an attempt to control or extinguish the fire. They are designed to automatically detect and control a fire, as well as protect a structure. Once a sprinkler is activated, some type of waterflow sensor signals a fire alarm. When activated, a sprinkler system may cause water damage. Wet systems should not be used in spaces subject to freezing.

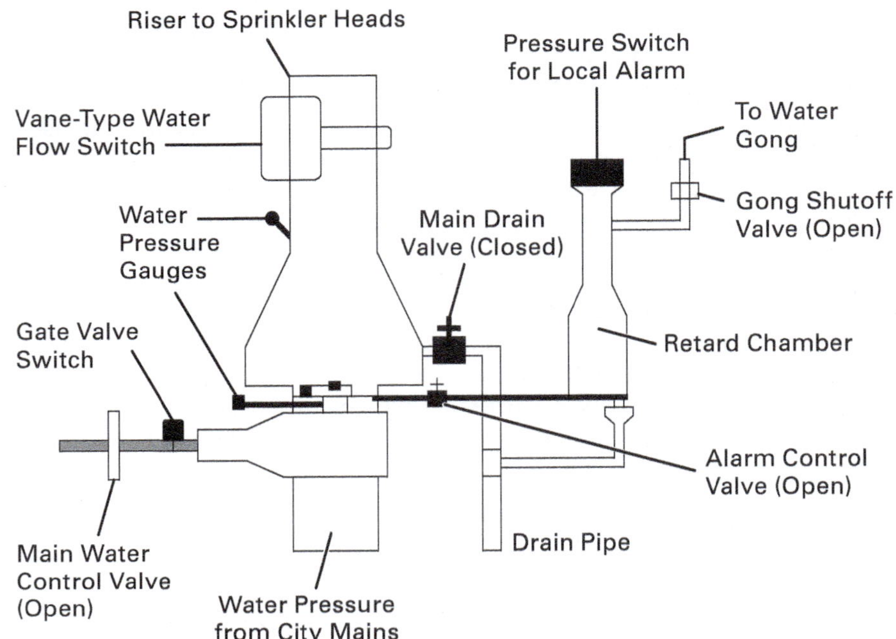

Figure 21 Wet sprinkler system.

Manual Fire Alarm Station Reset

The manual fire alarm shown is operated by pulling on the pull cover. This engages a latching mechanism that prevents the pull cover from being returned to the closed position. The only way the station cover can be reset to the closed position is by using the appropriate reset key.

A dry sprinkler system (*Figure 22*) consists of heat-operated sprinklers that are attached to a piping system containing air under pressure. Normally, air pressure in the pipes holds a water valve closed, which keeps water out of the piping system. When heat activates a sprinkler, the open sprinkler causes the air pressure to be released. This allows the water valve to open, and water to flow through the pipes and out to the activated sprinkler. Once a sprinkler is activated and water starts to flow, a waterflow sensor signals a fire alarm. Because the pipes are dry until a fire occurs, these systems may be used in spaces subject to freezing.

WARNING!

If the air pressure drops and the system fills with water, the system must be drained. Consult a qualified specialist to restore the system to normal operation.

When a building sprinkler is activated by the heat generated by a fire, the sprinkler allows water to flow. As shown in *Figure 21* and *Figure 22*, pressure-type or vane-type waterflow switches are installed in the sprinkler system along with local alarm devices. The waterflow switches detect the movement of water in the system. Activation of these switches by the movement of water causes an initiation signal to be sent to a FACU that signals a fire alarm.

In addition to devices that signal sprinkler system activation, other devices may be used to monitor the status of the system using a FACU. For instance, the position of a control valve may be monitored so that a **supervisory signal** is sent whenever the control valve is turned to shut off the water to the sprinkler system. If this valve is turned off, no water can flow through the sprinkler system, meaning the system is inactive. In some systems, water pressure from the municipal water supply may not be strong enough to push enough water to all parts of a building. In these cases, a fire pump is usually required. When the fire pump runs, a supervisory signal is sent, indicating that the fire pump is activated. If the pump runs to maintain system pressure and does not shut down within a reasonable time, a site visit may be required. When water is scarce or unavailable, an on-site water tank may be required. Supervisory signals may be generated when the temperature of the water drops below the freezing point. Additionally, a signal may be activated if the water level or pressure drops below a safe level. In a dry system, a supervisory signal is generated if the air pressure drops below a usable level. If fire pump power is monitored, lack of power or power phase reversal will cause a trouble signal.

Supervisory signal: A signal indicating the need for action in connection with the supervision of guard tours, the fire suppression systems or equipment, or the maintenance features of related systems.

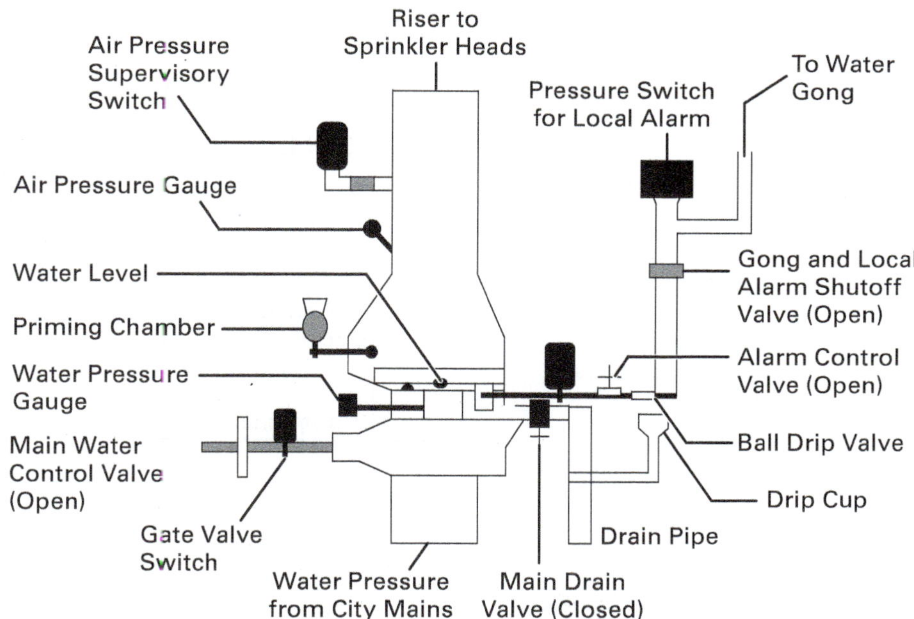

Figure 22 Dry sprinkler system.

Waterflow Detectors

The waterflow detector shown is typical of those used with wet-pipe sprinkler systems. Water flow through the associated pipe deflects the detector's vane. This activates the internal switch contacts, initiating an alarm or auxiliary indication. Water flow in the pipe can be caused by the opening of one or more sprinklers because of a fire, the opening of a test valve, or a leaking or ruptured pipe.

Source: System Sensor

2.0.0 Section Review

1. Which fire alarm system is the *simplest* of all systems?
   a. Proprietary
   b. Conventional hardwired
   c. Class B
   d. Addressable intelligent

2. Which kind of detector can sense along its entire length?
   a. An AHJ detector
   b. An IR/UV detector
   c. A spot detector
   d. A line detector

3.0.0 Control Units

Performance Tasks

There are no Performance Tasks in this section.

Objective

Describe fire alarm control units and their primary features.

a. Describe fire alarm control units and their power source requirements.
b. Explain how users interface with the control unit.
c. Define and describe initiating circuits and unit outputs.

Today, many different companies are manufacturing hundreds of different control units, and more are developed each year. *Figure 23* shows a typical intelligent, addressable control unit. This control unit has a voice command center added for use in high-rise buildings. It provides for automatic evacuation messages, firefighter paging, and two-way communication to a fire command center through a telephone network. Although many control units may have unique features, all control units perform some specific basic functions. As shown in *Figure 24*, they detect problems through their connected sensor devices, and they sound alerts or report the problems to a central location.

Figure 23 Typical intelligent, addressable control unit.
Source: Honeywell Security and Fire

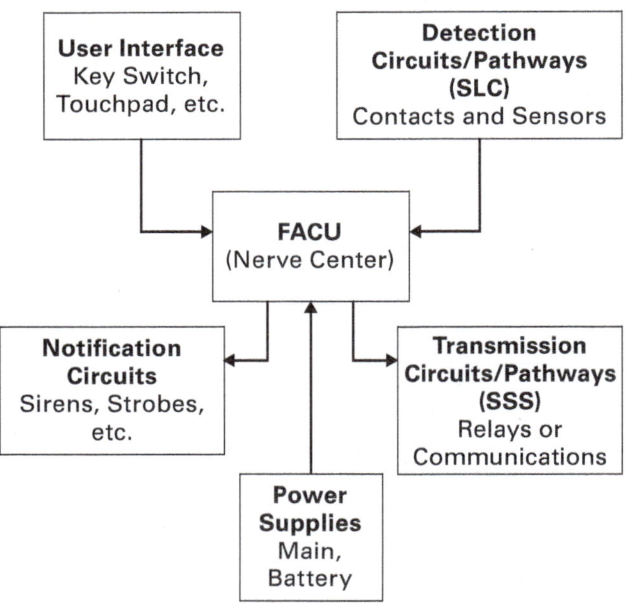

Figure 24 FACU inputs and outputs.

3.1.0 Control Unit Overview

A control unit can allow the user to reprogram the system and, in some cases, activate or deactivate the system or zones. The user may also change the sensitivity of detectors in certain zones of the system. On units that can be used for both intrusion and fire alarms, controls are provided to allow the user to enter or leave the monitored area without setting off the system. In addition, controls allow some portions of the system (fire, panic, holdup, etc.) to remain armed 24 hours a day, 365 days a year. Control units also provide the alarm user, responding authority, or inspector with a way to silence bells or control other system features.

Control units are usually equipped with LED, alphanumeric, or graphic displays to communicate information such as active zones or detectors to an alarm user or monitor. These displays are usually included on the FACU but can also be located remotely if required.

The control unit organizes all the components into a working and functional system and is often called the "brain" of the system. The control unit coordinates the actions that the system takes in response to messages it gets from initiating devices or, in some cases, notification devices that are connected to it. Depending on the inputs from the devices, it may activate the notification devices and transmit data to a remote location via transmission circuits. In most cases, the control unit also conditions the power it receives from the building power system or from a backup battery so that it can be used by the fire alarm system.

3.1.1 FACU Primary and Secondary Power

Primary power for a fire alarm system and the FACU is normally a source of power provided by a utility company. However, primary power for systems and units can also be supplied from emergency uninterruptible backup primary power systems. To avoid service interruption, a fire alarm system may be connected on the line side of the electrical main service disconnect switch. The circuit must be protected with a circuit breaker or fuse no larger than 20 amperes (A).

Secondary power for a fire alarm system can be provided by a battery or an **approved** backup generator. Secondary power must be immediately supplied to the fire alarm system in the event of a primary power failure. As defined by NFPA 72®, standby time for operation of the system on secondary power must be no less than 24 hours for central, local, proprietary, and voice communications. The battery standby time may be reduced if a properly configured battery-backup generator is available. During an alarm condition, the secondary power must operate the system under load for a minimum of 4 minutes, 5 minutes, or 15 minutes after expiration of the standby period, depending on the type of system. Any batteries used for secondary power must be able to be recharged within 48 hours.

Approved: Acceptable to the Authority Having Jurisdiction (AHJ).

3.1.2 FACU Listings

It is mandatory that FACUs be listed for the purpose they will be used. Common UL Listings include UL 864 for the FACU and UL 985 for the household fire warning **system unit**.

In combination fire/burglary units, fire circuits must be on or active at all times, even if the burglary control is disarmed or turned off. Some codes prohibit using combination intrusion and FACUs in commercial applications.

System unit: The active subassemblies at the supervising station used for signal receiving, processing, display, or recording of status change signals. The failure of one of these subassemblies causes the loss of a number of alarm signals by that unit.

A FACU listed for household use by the UL may never be installed in any commercial application unless it also has the appropriate commercial listing, has been granted equivalency by the **Authority Having Jurisdiction (AHJ)** in writing, or is specifically permitted by a document that supersedes the reference standards. The NFPA defines a *household* as a single- or two-family residential unit and applies this term to systems wholly within the confines of the unit. No initiation from, or notification to, locations outside the residence is permitted, except for monitoring. Although an apartment building or condominium is considered commercial, a household system may be installed within an individual living unit. However, any devices that are outside the confines of the individual living unit, such as manual pull stations, must be connected to a FACU listed as commercial.

NOTE

The NFPA does not approve, inspect, or certify any installations, procedures, equipment, or materials, nor does it approve or evaluate testing laboratories. In determining the acceptability of installations, procedures, equipment, or materials, the AHJ may base acceptance on compliance with NFPA or other appropriate standards. In the absence of such standards, said authority may require evidence of proper installation, procedure, or use. The AHJ may also refer to the listings or labeling practices of an organization concerned with product evaluations that is in a position to determine compliance with appropriate standards for the current production of listed items.

NOTE

UL requires that any system controls that affect system operation be protected behind a locked door or locked out by a key.

Authority Having Jurisdiction (AHJ): The organization, office, or individual responsible for approving equipment, installations, or procedures in a particular locality.

3.2.0 User Control Points

User controls allow the alarm user to turn all or portions of the system on or off. User controls also allow the alarm user to monitor the system status, including the sensors or zones that are active, indicating trouble reports, and other system parameters. They also allow the user to reset indicators of system events such as alarms or indications of trouble with phone lines, equipment, or circuits. In today's systems, many devices can be used to control the system, including keypads, key switches, touch screens, telephones (including wireless phones), and computers.

3.2.1 Keypads

Two general types of keypads are in use today: alphanumeric (*Figure 25*) and LED. Either type can be mounted at the control or at a separate location. Both allow the entry of a numerical code to program various system functions. An alphanumeric keypad combines a keypad that is similar to a pushbutton telephone dial with an alphanumeric display that is capable of showing letters and numbers. LED keypads use a similar keypad but display information by lighting small LEDs.

3.2.2 Touch Screens

Touch screens allow the user to access multiple customized displays in graphic or menu formats. This enables rapid and easy interaction with the system.

3.2.3 Telephone/Computer Control

In the past, fire alarm systems were often connected to telephones, so many control unit manufacturers incorporated ways for the telephone to function as a user interface. However, NFPA 72® now places restrictions on systems still using POTS as a means for signal transport. Today, the primary means is through cellular transmission, including 5G. Using a smartphone to operate a fire alarm system is possible if it is used only to receive information, not to reset a fire alarm. Resetting the alarm can only be done on-site. Requiring this action prevents a fire alarm from being reset by someone who is not on-site and may not be aware that there is an actual fire or other event occurring.

NOTE

The NFPA does not permit remote resetting of fire alarm systems that have signaled an alarm.

Figure 25 Alphanumeric keypad and display.
Source: Honeywell Security and Fire

Intelligent Systems

An intelligent system uses analog devices to communicate with a typical intelligent, addressable control unit, as shown in *Figure 23*. The control unit individually monitors the value or status reported by the analog sensors and makes normal, alarm, or trouble decisions. The specific control unit in *Figure 23* is a software-controlled unit capable of monitoring 1,980 individually identifiable and controllable detection/control points. It is also field programmable from the front unit keyboard.

3.3.0 FACU Initiating Circuits and Outputs

An initiating circuit monitors the various types of initiating devices. A typical initiating circuit can monitor for three states: normal, trouble, and alarm. Initiating circuits can be used for monitoring fire devices, non-fire devices (supervisory), or devices for watch patrol or security. The signals from the initiating devices can be separately indicated at the premises and remotely monitored at a supervising station.

3.3.1 Initiating Circuit Zones

The term *zone* as it relates to modern fire alarm systems can have several definitions. Building codes restrict the location and size of a zone to enable emergency response personnel to quickly locate the source of an alarm. The traditional use of a zone in a conventional system was that each initiating circuit was a zone. Today, a single device or multiple initiating circuits or devices may occupy a zone. Generally, a zone may not cover more than one floor, exceed a certain number of square feet, or exceed a certain number of feet in length or width. In addition, some codes require different types of initiating devices to be on different initiating circuits within a physical area or zone. With modern addressable systems, each device is like a zone because each is displayed at the unit. It is common in addressable systems to group devices of several types into a zone. This is usually accomplished by programming the unit rather than by hardwiring the devices. Ultimately, the purpose of a zone is to provide the system monitor with information as to the location of a system alarm or problem. Local codes provide the specific guidelines.

3.3.2 Alarm Verification

To reduce unwanted alarms, most FACUs allow for a delay in activating notification devices upon receiving an alarm signal from an initiating device. In some conventional systems using a **positive alarm sequence** feature, alarm delay is usually adjustable for a period not exceeding three minutes. This allows on-site monitoring personnel to investigate the alarm. If a second detector activates during the investigation period, a fire alarm is immediately sounded. In other conventional systems, verification can be of the reset-and-resample type—the unit resets the detector and waits 10 seconds to 20 seconds for the sensor to retransmit the alarm. If there is an actual fire, the sensor should detect it both times, and an alarm is then activated. In addressable systems, **alarm verification** can be of the wait-and-check type—the unit notes the initiation signal and then waits for about 10 seconds to 20 seconds to see if the initiation signal remains constant before activating an alarm.

Another verification method for large areas with multiple sensors is to wait until two or more sensors are activated before an alarm is initiated. In this method, known as *cross-zoning*, a single detector activation may set a one-minute or less pre-alarm condition warning signal at a manned monitoring location. If the pre-alarm signal is not canceled within the allowed time or a second detector activates, a fire alarm is sounded. The pre-alarm signals are not required by the NFPA. In cross-zoning, two detectors must occupy each space regardless of the space size, and each detector may cover only half of the normal detection area. Cross-zoning, along with other methods of alarm verification, cannot be used on the same devices. Some building codes require alarm verification or some equivalent on all smoke detection devices.

Verification is commonly used in hotels, motels, hospitals, and other institutions with large numbers of detectors. It may also be used in monitored fire alarm systems for households to reduce unwanted alarms.

Positive alarm sequence: An automatic sequence that results in an alarm signal, even when manually delayed for investigation, unless the system is reset. A positive alarm sequence must not be longer than three minutes (180 seconds) but can be adjustable to allow on-site personnel to check the alarm.

Alarm verification: A feature of a fire control unit that allows for a delay in activating alarms upon receiving an initiating signal from one of its circuits. If approved by the Authority Having Jurisdiction (AHJ), the supervising station has up to 90 seconds to verify that the signal is an unwanted alarm. Alarm verification is commonly used in hotels, motels, hospitals, and institutions with large numbers of smoke detectors.

3.3.3 FACU Labeling

Labeled: In the context of fire alarm control units (FACUs), tags that identify various zones and sensors by descriptive names. Units may include dual identifiers, one of which is meaningful to the occupants and the other to firefighting personnel.

Effective system design and installation requires that zones (or sensors) be **labeled** in a way that makes sense to all who will use or respond to the system. In some cases, this may require two sets of labels: one for the alarm user and another for the police and fire authorities. A supervising station operator who will talk to both the police and the alarm user should be aware of both sets of labels. Labeling for the alarm user is done using names familiar to the user (such as Johnny's room, kitchen, and master bedroom). Labeling for the police and fire authorities is done from the perspective of looking at the building from the outside (such as first floor east, basement rear, and second floor west).

3.3.4 Types of FACU Alarm Outputs

Most units provide one or more of the following types of outputs:

- *Relay or dry contacts* — Relay contacts or other dry contacts are electrically isolated from the circuit controlling them, which provides some protection from external spikes and surges. Additional protection is sometimes needed. Always check the contact ratings to determine how much voltage and current the contacts can handle. Check with the manufacturer to determine if this provides adequate protection.
- *Built-in siren drivers* — Built-in siren drivers use a transistor amplifier circuit to drive a siren speaker. Impedance must be maintained within the manufacturer's specifications. Voltage drops caused by long wire runs of small conductors can greatly reduce the output level of the siren. Most AHJs no longer allow a combination system to be used in commercial applications.
- *Voltage outputs* — Voltage outputs are not isolated from the control, and some protection may be required. Spikes and surges, such as those generated by solenoid bells or the back EMF generated when a relay is de-energized, can be a problem.
- *Open collector outputs* — Open collector outputs are outputs directly from a transistor and have limited current output. They are often used to drive a very low-current device or relay. Filtering may be required. Great caution should be used not to overload these outputs, as the circuit board normally has to be returned to the manufacturer if an overload for even a very short duration occurs.

3.0.0 Section Review

1. What part of a fire alarm system coordinates the actions that the system *must* take in response to its other components?
   a. The AHU
   b. The AHJ
   c. The FACU
   d. The NFPA

2. Many fire alarm systems provide graphical control through a(n) _____.
   a. voice interface
   b. touch screen
   c. local uplink
   d. alphanumeric keypad

3. An alarm delay can be up to _____.
   a. one minute
   b. two minutes
   c. three minutes
   d. five minutes

4.0.0 Notification, Communication, and Monitoring

Objective

Identify and describe approaches to fire alarm notification and communication/monitoring.

a. Describe visual and audible notification devices and systems.
b. Describe important considerations in the use of fire alarm notification signals.
c. Describe communication and monitoring options for fire alarm systems.

Performance Tasks

There are no Performance Tasks in this section.

Fire alarms are all about communication. Obviously, their first priority is to notify people in the protected facility. The system performs this task through devices designed to get people's attention. Using various kinds of signals, these devices communicate the nature of the emergency. Fire alarms must also communicate with outside facilities, such as external monitoring services. They accomplish this task through other technology, much of it digital.

4.1.0 Notification Appliances

Notification to building occupants of a fire is the most important life safety function of a fire alarm system. There are two primary types of notification: audible and visible. Concerns resulting from the **Americans with Disabilities Act (ADA)** have prompted the introduction of olfactory (sense of smell) and tactile (sense of touch) types of notification as well.

Americans with Disabilities Act (ADA): An act of Congress intended to ensure civil rights for physically challenged people.

4.1.1 Visual Notification Devices

Strobes are high-intensity lights that flash when activated. Strobe devices can be wall-mounted or ceiling-mounted. They can be separate devices or mounted on or near the audible device. Strobe lights are more effective in residential, industrial, and office areas where they don't compete with other bright objects. Because ADA requirements dictate clear or white xenon (or equivalent) strobe lights, most interior visual notification devices are furnished with clear strobe lights (*Figure 26*). When more than two strobes are visible from any location, they must be synchronized to avoid random flashing, which can be disorienting and may cause seizures in certain individuals. Some strobes are brighter than others to accommodate different applications. These units are always rated in candelas (cd).

Ceiling-Mounted

Wall-Mounted

Figure 26 Typical ceiling-mounted and wall-mounted strobe devices.
Source: System Sensor

4.1.2 Audible Notification Devices

Audible alarm devices are noise-making devices, such as sirens, bells, or horns, that are used as part of a local alarm system to indicate an alarm condition. In some cases, a low-current **chime** or buzzer is also used. An **audible signal** used for fire alarms in a facility that contains other sound-producing devices must produce a unique sound pattern so that a fire alarm can be recognized. If more than one audible signal is used in a facility, they must be synchronized to maintain any sound pattern. NFPA 72® specifies that a standard signal known as *Temporal-Three* is required by most fire alarm systems, including household systems. This signal has three half-second tones, a pause, and then a repeat of the pattern until the alarm is manually reset. Only a fire alarm may use this signal.

Chime: A single-stroke or vibrating audible signal appliance that has a xylophone-type striking bar.

Audible signal: An audible signal is the sound made by one or more audible indicating appliances, such as bells, chimes, horns, or speakers, in response to the operation of an initiating device.

Some bells use an electrically vibrated clapper to repeatedly strike a gong. These types of solenoid-operated bells can also produce electrical **noise**, which will interfere with controls unless proper filters are used. Solenoid-operated bells draw relatively high current, typically 750 milliamps (mA) to 1,500 mA. Another type of bell is a motor-driven bell. In this type of bell, a motor drives the clapper and produces louder sounds than a solenoid-operated bell. Electrical interference is eliminated and less current is required.

Noise: A term used in electronics to cover all types of unwanted electrical signals. Noise signals originate from numerous sources, such as fluorescent lamps, walkie-talkies, amateur and CB radios, machines being switched on and off, and power surges. Today, equipment must tolerate increasing amounts of electrical interference, and the quality of equipment depends on how much noise it can ignore and withstand.

Self-contained sirens are combinations of speakers and sound equipment. They produce siren sounds and can be used for voice announcements. Self-contained siren packaging saves installation time. If more than one siren is required, they must be synchronized.

A horn (*Figure 27*) usually consists of a continuously vibrating membrane or a piezoelectric element. In a supervised notification circuit, all devices are polarized, allowing current to flow in one direction only. A buzzer uses less power and consists of a continuously vibrating membrane like a horn. Chimes are electronic devices, like self-contained sirens, and have a very low current draw.

Figure 27 Typical horn with a strobe light.

Audible Alarms

Audible alarms must have an intensity and frequency that attracts the attention of those with partial hearing loss. Such alarms shall produce a sound that exceeds the prevailing sound level in the space by 15 audible decibels (dBA) or exceeds the maximum sound level for a duration of 60 seconds by 5 dBA, whichever is louder. Sound levels shall not exceed 110 dBA.

Some jurisdictions prohibit bell notification devices in schools as they can be confused with classroom bells.

Strobe Lights

Strobe lights may draw a relatively high current compared to other types of notification devices. For this reason, they may require a separate circuit.

4.1.3 Voice Evacuation Systems

With a voice evacuation system (*Figure 28*), building occupants can be given instructions in the event of an emergency. A voice evacuation system can be used in conjunction with a FACU or as a stand-alone unit with a built-in power supply and battery charger. Voice announcements (*Figure 29*) can be made to inform occupants of what the problem is or how to evacuate. In many cases, the voice announcements are prerecorded and selected as required by the system. The announcements can also be made from a microphone located at the FACU or at a remote unit. *Figure 30* shows several types of speakers used for voice evacuation systems. Temporal-Three signaling is not used with zoned voice evacuation systems.

Digital Voice Messages

Digital voice messages used with various voice evacuation systems are stored in nonvolatile read-only memory integrated circuit chips. These stored messages are used in applications where clear and defined messages of evacuation are required. One major fire alarm manufacturer of voice evacuation systems has more than 100 prestored evacuation messages available.

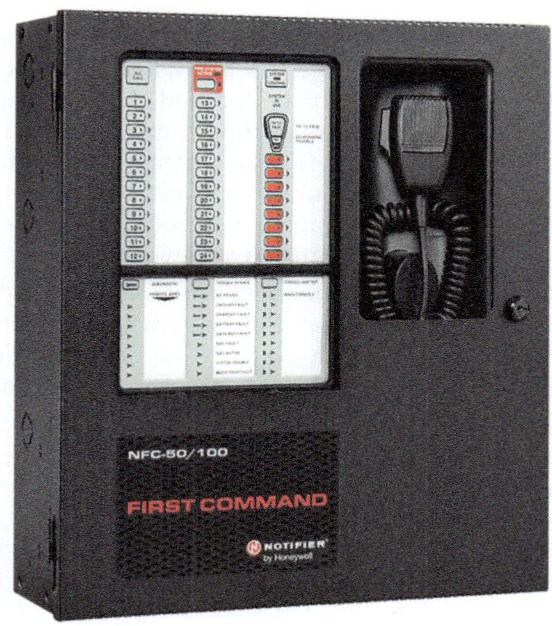

Figure 28 Voice evacuation system.
Source: Honeywell Security and Fire

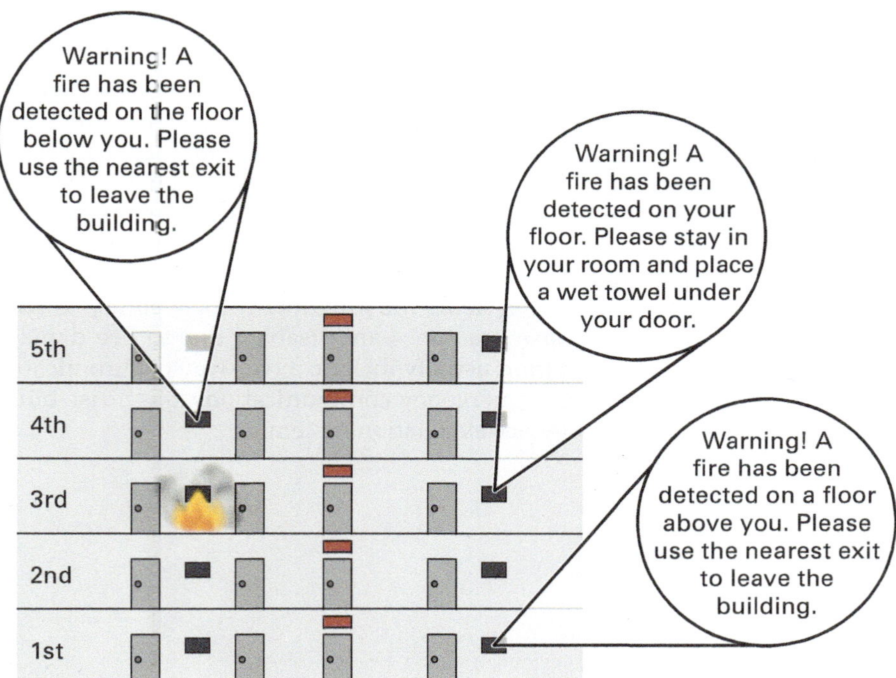

Figure 29 Typical voice evacuation messages.

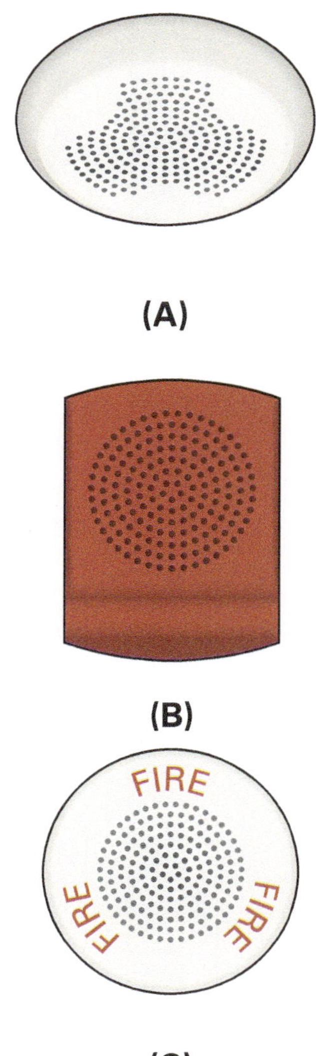

Figure 30 Typical speakers.

4.2.0 Signal Considerations

General alarm: A term usually applied to the simultaneous operation of all audible alarm signals on a system to indicate the need for evacuation of a building.

The following are descriptions of the types of code-authorized signals supplied to various notification devices from a typical fire control unit:

- *General signal* — General signals operate throughout the entire building. Evacuation signals require a distinctive signal. The code requires that a Temporal-Three signal pattern be used in accordance with *ANSI/ASA Standard S3.41* (and *ISO 8201*), NFPA 101®, and NFPA 72®. Temporal-Three signals consist of three short half-second tones with half-second pauses between the tones. This is followed by a one-second silent period, and then the process is repeated.
- *Attendant signal* — Attendant signaling is used where assisted evacuation is required due to factors such as age, disability, and restraint. These systems are commonly used in conjunction with coded chimes throughout the area or a coded voice message to advise staff personnel of the alarm source location. For example, a coded message announcement might state, "Mr. Green, please report to the third-floor nurses' station." No **general alarm** needs to be sounded, and no indicating appliances need to be activated throughout the area. The attendant signal feature requires the approval of the AHJ.
- *Pre-signal* — A pre-signal is an attendant signal with the addition of human action to activate a general signal. It is used when the control delays the general alarm by more than one minute. The pre-signal feature requires the approval of the AHJ. A signal to remote locations must activate upon an initial alarm signal.
- *Positive alarm sequence* — When an alarm is initiated, the general alarm is not activated for 15 seconds. If a staff person acknowledges the alarm within the 15-second window, the general alarm is delayed for 180 seconds so that the staff can investigate. Failure to manually acknowledge the initial attendant signal will automatically cause a general alarm. Failure to abort the acknowledged signal within 180 seconds will also automatically cause a general alarm. If any second selected automatic detector is activated during the delay window, the system will immediately cause a general alarm. An activation of a manual station will also automatically cause a general alarm. This is an excellent technique for the prevention of unwanted general alarms; however, trained personnel are an integral part of these systems. The positive alarm sequence feature requires the approval of the AHJ.
- *Voice evacuation* — Voice evacuation may be either live or prerecorded and automatically or manually initiated. Voice evacuation systems are a permitted form of a general alarm and are required in certain occupancies, as specified in the applicable chapter of NFPA 101®. Voice evacuation systems are often zoned so that only the floors threatened by the fire or smoke are immediately evacuated. Zoned evacuation is used where total evacuation is physically impractical. Temporal-Three signaling is not used with zoned evacuation. Voice evacuation systems must maintain their ability to communicate even when one or more zones are disabled due to fire damage. Buildings with voice evacuation usually include a two-way communication system (fireman's phone) for emergency communications. High-rise buildings are required to have a voice evacuation system.

- *Alarm sound levels* — Where a general alarm is required throughout the premises, audible signals must be clearly heard above maximum ambient noise under normal occupancy conditions. Public area audible alarms should be 75 dBA at 10' (3 m) and a maximum of 110 dBA at minimum hearing distance. Public area audible alarms must also be at least 15 dBA above ambient sound level or at the maximum sound level for over 60 seconds measured at 5' (1.5 m) above finished floor (AFF) level. Audible alarms to alert persons responsible for implementing emergency plans (guards, monitors, supervisory personnel, or others) must be between 45 dBA and 120 dBA at minimum hearing distance. If an average sound level greater than 105 dBA exists, the use of a visible signal is required. Refer to *Chapter 18* in NFPA 72® for more information about average ambient sound levels.

Closed doors may drop the dB levels below those required to wake children or the hearing-impaired. Air conditioners, humidifiers, and similar equipment may cause the noise levels to increase (55 dBA typical). A siren, horn, bell, or other **indicating device** may fail or be disabled by a fire. To ensure the effectiveness of a system, multiple fire sounders should be considered. This may also help in providing ample dB levels to wake sleeping occupants throughout the structure (70 dBA at the pillow is commonly accepted as sufficient to wake a sleeping person).

Indicating device: See notification appliance (device).

All residential alarm sounding devices must have a minimum dB rating of 85 dBA at 10' (3 m). An exception to this rule is when more than one sounding device exists in the same room. A sounding device in the room must be 85 dBA at 10' (3 m), with all additional sounding devices in that room as low as 75 dBA at 10' (3 m). Sound intensity doubles with each 3 dB gain and is reduced by $\frac{1}{2}$ with each 3 dB loss. Doubling the distance to the sound source will cause a 6 dB loss. Please note that sounders located in sleeping rooms within dwelling units must be rated for 520 Hz and must be listed for producing low-frequency waveforms.

- *Coded and non-coded signals* — A **coded signal** is a signal that is pulsed in a prescribed code for each round of transmission. For example, four pulses would indicate an alarm on the fourth floor. Coded systems are no longer installed but are still addressed in NFPA 72® since some are still in place. A **non-coded signal** is a signal that is energized continuously by the control. It may pulse, but the pulsing will not be designed to indicate any code or message.
  - Clockwork transmitters can be prewound or can be wound by pulling the alarm lever. Usually, the box is designed to repeat its code four times before automatically coming to rest. Prewound transmitters must sound a trouble signal when they require rewinding. Solid-state electronic coding devices are also used in conjunction with the FACU to produce coded sounding of the system's audible signaling appliances.

Coded signal: A signal pulsed in a prescribed code for each round of transmission.

Non-coded signal: A signal from any indicating appliance that is continuously energized.

- *Visual appliance signals* — Notification signals for occupants to evacuate must be located by audible and visible signals in accordance with NFPA 72® and *ANSI A117.1*. However, exceptions to this rule are possible. Under the existing NFPA 101® building chapter, only audible signals are required in premises where:
  - No hearing-impaired occupant is ever present under normal operation
  - In hotels and apartments where special rooms are made available to the hearing-impaired
  - Where the AHJ approves alternatives to visual signals (ADA codes may or may not allow these exceptions)

4.3.0 Communication and Monitoring

Communication is a means of sending information to personnel who are too far away to directly see or hear a fire alarm system's notification device. It is the transmission and reception of information from one location, point, person, or piece of equipment to another. Understanding the information that a fire alarm system communicates makes it easier to determine what is happening at the alarm site. Knowing how that information gets from the alarm site to the monitoring site is helpful if a problem occurs somewhere in between.

4.3.1 Monitoring Options

There are several options for monitoring the signals of an alarm system. They include the following:

- *Supervising station* — A location, normally run by private individuals or companies, where operators monitor receiving equipment for incoming fire alarm system signals. The supervising station may be a part of the same company that sold and installed the fire alarm system. It is also common for the installation company to contract with another company to do the monitoring on its behalf.
- *Proprietary station* — A facility similar to a supervising station except that the notification devices are located in a constantly staffed room maintained by the property owner for internal safety operations. The personnel may respond to alarms, alert local fire departments when alarms are activated, or both.
- *Certified supervising station* — Monitoring facilities that are constructed and operated according to a standard and are inspected by a listing agency to verify compliance. Several organizations, including the UL, publish criteria and list the supervising stations that conform to those criteria.

4.3.2 Digital Alarm Communicator Transmitters

Digital alarm communicator transmitter (DACT): A system component at a protected premises to which initiating devices or groups of devices are connected. The DACT will seize the connected telephone line, dial a preselected number to connect to a digital alarm communicator receiver (DACR), and transmit signals indicating a status change of the initiating devices.

Public switched telephone network (PSTN): An assembly of communications facilities and central office equipment, operated jointly by authorized common carriers, that provides the public with the ability to establish communications channels via discrete dialing codes.

A **digital alarm communicator transmitter (DACT)** uses standard **public switched telephone network (PSTN)** lines to send and receive data. While this approach to signal transmission is rarely installed today, there may be instances when you encounter existing legacy systems. Therefore, it is necessary to have a basic understanding of DACTs.

DACTs are connected to a standard voice-grade telephone line through a special connecting device such as an RJ-31X (*Figure 31*). The RJ-31X is a modular telephone jack into which a cord from the digital communicator is plugged. The RJ-31X separates the telephone company's equipment from the fire alarm system equipment and is approved by the Federal Communications Commission (FCC).

In the event of an alarm, a technique known as *line seizure* gives the fire alarm system priority. The DACT is connected to the phones and can control or seize the line whenever it needs to send a signal. If a customer is using the telephone when the alarm system needs to send a signal, the DACT will disconnect the customer until the alarm signal has been sent. Once the signal is sent, the customer's phone is reconnected.

The typical sequence that occurs when the digital communicator for an alarm system is activated is shown in *Figure 32*. When an alarm is to be sent, the digital communicator energizes the seizure relay. The activated relay disconnects the house phones and connects the communicator to the Telco line. After the communicator detects a signal called the *kiss-off tone*, it de-energizes the seizure relay. This disconnects the communicator and reconnects the house phones.

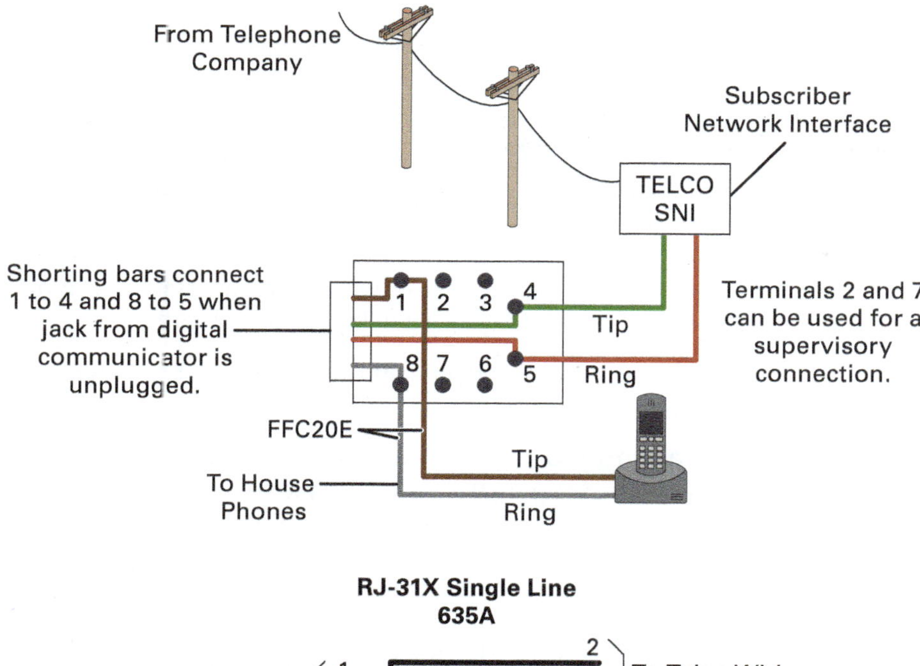

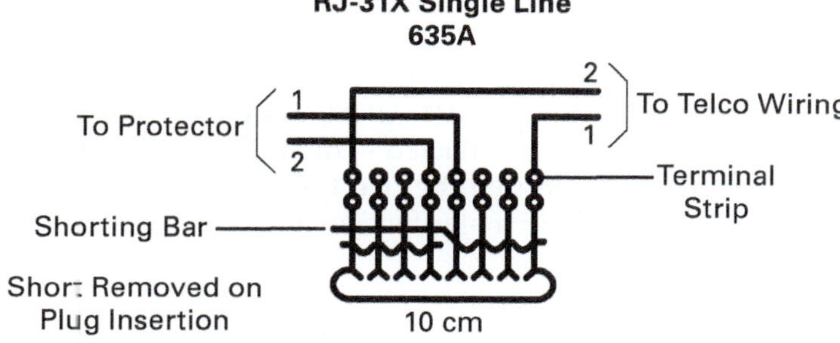

Figure 31 RJ-31X connection device.

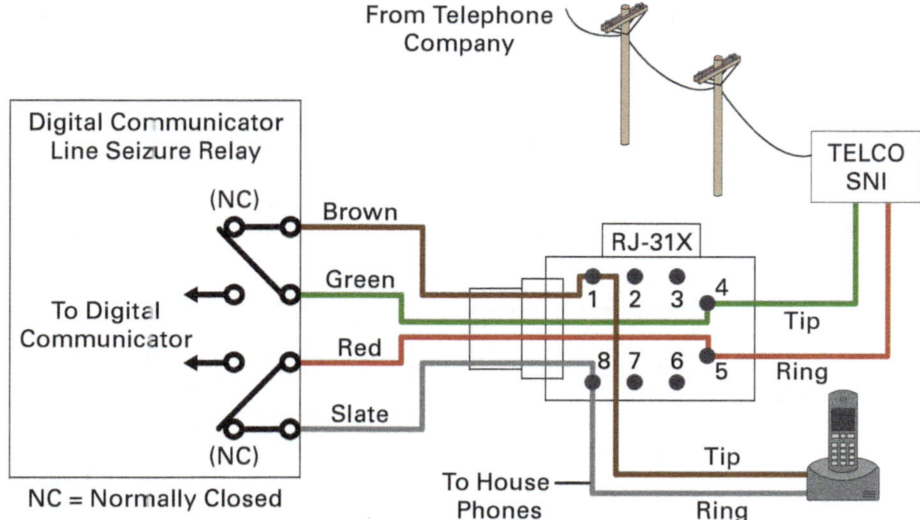

Figure 32 Line seizure.

In combination fire and security systems, the fire alarm supersedes the security alert. The RJ-31X will send the fire alarm signal before sending the security alert signal. The following conditions have been established by NFPA 72® with regard to digital alarm communicators:

- Only loop start lines can be used (ground start lines cannot).
- The communicator must have line seizure capability.
- A failure-to-communicate signal must be shown if 10 attempts are made without getting through.

- They must connect to two separate phone lines at the protected premises. An exception to this condition is that the secondary line may be a radio system (does not apply to household systems).
- Failure of either phone line must be annunciated at the premises within four minutes of the failure.
- If long-distance telephone service, including **wide area telephone service (WATS)**, is used, the second telephone number shall be provided by a different long-distance provider, where available.
- Each communicator shall initiate a test call to the supervising station at least every 24 hours (this does not apply to household systems).

Wide area telephone service (WATS): Telephone company service that provides reduced costs for certain telephone call arrangements. In-WATS or 800-number service calls can be placed anywhere in the continental United States to the called party at no cost to the calling party. Out-WATS is a service whereby, for a flat-rate charge, dependent on the total duration of all such calls, a subscriber can make an unlimited number of calls within a prescribed area from a particular telephone terminal without the registration of individual call charges.

Remote supervising station fire alarm system: A system installed in accordance with the applicable code to transmit alarm, supervisory, and trouble signals from one or more protected premises to a remote location where appropriate action is taken.

A DACT can be used as a **remote supervising station fire alarm system** when acceptable to the AHJ.

4.3.3 Cellular, IP, and Radio Signal Transmission

The primary method of signal transmission today is cellular technology, followed by IP and radio. NFPA 72® allows all these methods to be used alone, based on their reliability. Installed systems cannot use POTS or PSTN by itself. Using either of these requires one of the others to serve as a backup. It would be rare to find a circuit that uses a copper circuit from the protected premises, through the central office, then on to the supervising station. At some point, the circuit would become VoIP. While NFPA 72® allows the use of a managed VoIP, it does not allow the use of an unmanaged system. Therefore, you must be able to recognize the difference between the two types when in the field. Refer to *Chapter 26* in NFPA 72® for additional information.

4.3.4 Cellular Backup

Some fire alarm systems that rely on phone lines for communications have a cellular backup system that utilizes wireless phone technology to restore communications in the event of a disruption in normal telephone line service (*Figure 33*).

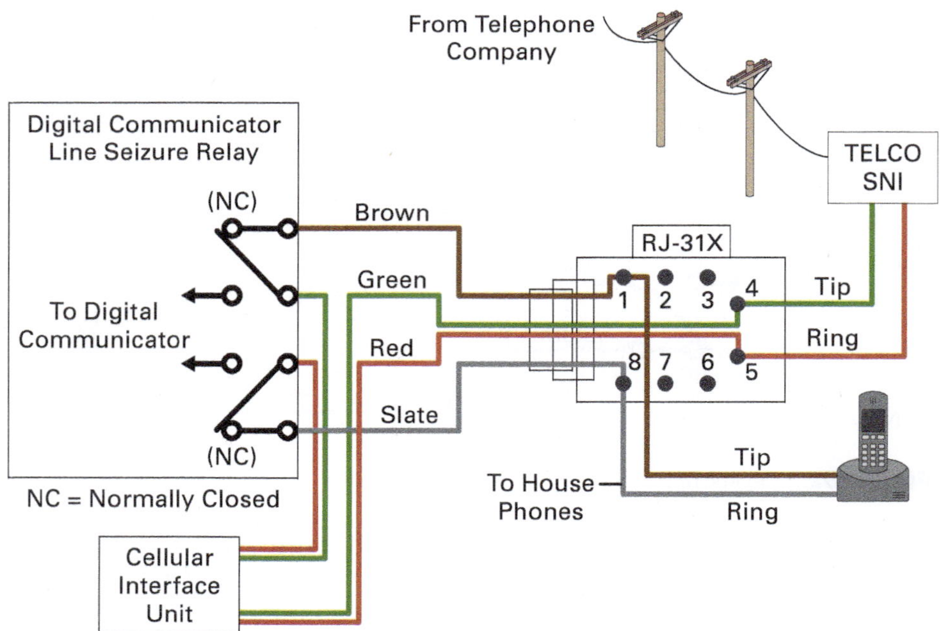

Figure 33 Cellular backup system.

4.0.0 Section Review

1. The ADA specifies that fire alarm strobe lights *must* be clear or _____.
   a. red
   b. white
   c. blue
   d. yellow

2. At minimum hearing distance, a public area audible alarm should be *no* louder than _____.
   a. 10 dBA
   b. 50 dBA
   c. 110 dBA
   d. 120 dBA

3. Digital communicators connect to telephone lines with a(n) _____.
   a. RJ-31X
   b. RJ-11
   c. RJ-45
   d. TIA-568B

5.0.0 Installation Guidelines

Objective

Describe fire alarm system installation guidelines and requirements.

a. Describe the general wiring requirements.
b. Describe the general installation requirements for wiring and various components.
c. Describe the installation guidelines for totally protected premises.
d. Describe the installation guidelines for systems and devices related to fire alarms.
e. Describe how to troubleshoot fire alarm systems.

Performance Task

1. Connect selected fire alarm system(s).

This section contains general installation information applicable to all types of fire alarm systems. For specific information, always refer to the manufacturer's instructions, the building drawings, and all applicable local and national codes.

5.1.0 General Wiring Requirements

NEC Article 760 specifies the wiring methods and special cables required for fire protective signaling systems. The following special cable types are used in protective signaling systems:

- Power-limited fire alarm (FPL) cable
- Power-limited fire alarm riser (FPLR) cable
- Power-limited fire alarm plenum (FPLP) cable
- Nonpower-limited fire alarm (NPLF) circuit cable
- Nonpower-limited fire alarm riser (NPLFR) circuit riser cable
- Nonpower-limited fire alarm plenum (NPLFP) circuit cable

In addition to *NEC Article 760*, the following *NEC®* articles cover other items of concern for fire alarm system installations:

- *NEC Sections 110.11 and 300.6(A), (B), (C), and (D)* cover corrosive, damp, or wet locations.
- *NEC Section 300.21* covers the spread of fire or products of combustion.

Know the Code

Fire Alarm Systems
NEC Article 760

Know the Code

General Requirements for Electrical Installations
NEC Article 110

Know the Code

Wiring Methods and Materials
NEC Chapter 3

Know the Code

Special Occupancies
NEC Chapter 5

Know the Code

Special Equipment
NEC Chapter 6

Know the Code

Special Conditions
NEC Chapter 7

Know the Code

Communications Systems
NEC Chapter 8

- *NEC Section 300.22* covers ducts, plenums, and other air handling spaces.
- *NEC Articles 500 through 516 and 517, Part IV* covers hazardous locations.
- *NEC Article 695* covers fire pumps.
- *NEC Article 722* covers cables for power-limited circuits and fault-managed power circuits.
- *NEC Article 724* covers Class 1 power-limited circuits and Class 1 power-limited remote-control and signaling circuits.
- *NEC Article 725* covers Class 1, Class 2, and Class 3 remote-control, signaling, and power-limited circuits.
- *NEC Article 770* covers optical fiber cables.
- *NEC Article 800* covers general requirements for communications systems.
- *NEC Article 805* covers communications circuits.
- *NEC Article 810* covers antenna systems.

In addition to the *NEC*®, some AHJs may specify requirements that modify or add to the *NEC*®. It is essential that a person or firm engaged in fire alarm work be thoroughly familiar with the *NEC*® requirements, as well as any local requirements for fire alarm systems.

Fire alarm circuits must be installed in a neat and workmanlike manner. Cables must be supported by the building structure in such a manner that the cables will not be damaged by normal building use. One way to determine accepted industry practice is to refer to nationally recognized standards such as ANSI/TIA 568, *Commercial Building Telecommunications Cabling Standard;* ANSI/TIA 569, *Telecommunications Pathways and Spaces;* and ANSI/TIA 570, *Residential Telecommunications Infrastructure Standard.*

5.2.0 Installation Requirements

Fire alarm devices will function as the manufacturer intended only when they are properly installed. Mounting, wiring, spacing, and circuit connections must all be correct, otherwise the system may not alarm reliably or at all. Fire alarm codes as well as the manufacturer's instructions provide the specific details that govern installation. The following sections also summarize many of the key ideas behind a good installation.

5.2.1 Access to Equipment

Access to equipment must not be blocked by an accumulation of wires and cables that prevents the removal of panels, including suspended ceiling panels.

5.2.2 Fire Alarm Circuit Identification

Fire alarm circuits must be identified at the control and at all junctions as fire alarm circuits. Junction boxes must be clearly marked as fire junction boxes to prevent confusion with commercial light and power boxes. AHJs differ on what constitutes clear marking. Check the requirements before starting work. The following are examples of some AHJ-acceptable markings:

- Red painted cover
- The words "Fire Alarm" on the cover
- Red painted box
- The word "Fire" on the cover
- Red stripe on the cover

5.2.3 Power-Limited Circuits in Raceways

Power-limited fire circuits must not be run in the same cable, raceway, or conduit as high-voltage circuits. Examples of high-voltage circuits are electric light, power, and nonpower-limited fire (NPLF) circuits. When NPLF cables must be run in the same junction box, they must be run in accordance with the *NEC*®, including maintaining a $^1/_4$" (6.35 mm) spacing from Class 1, power, and lighting circuits.

5.2.4 Mounting of Detectors

Observe the following precautions when mounting detectors:

- Circuit conductors are not supports and must not be used to support the detector.
- Plastic masonry anchors should not be used for mounting detectors to gypsum drywall, plaster, or drop ceilings.
- Toggle or winged expansion anchors should be the minimum used for gypsum drywall.
- The best choice for mounting is an electrical box. Most equipment is designed to be fastened to a standard electrical box.

All fire alarm devices should be mounted to the appropriate electrical box as specified by the manufacturer. If not mounted to an electrical box, fire alarm devices must be mounted by other means as specified by the manufacturer. The precaution against using plastic masonry anchors does not mean that a plastic anchor designed for use in drywall cannot be used in drywall. Masonry plastic anchors do not open as far on the end as drywall plastic anchors. Always read and follow the manufacturer's instructions, which is necessary to meet the UL Listing requirements.

Firestopping Materials

Shown here are a few examples of the wide variety of firestopping materials on the market. Firestopping and fireproofing are not the same thing. Firestopping is intended to prevent the spread of fire and smoke from room to room through openings in walls and floors. Fireproofing is a thermal barrier that causes a fire to burn more slowly and retards the spread of fire.

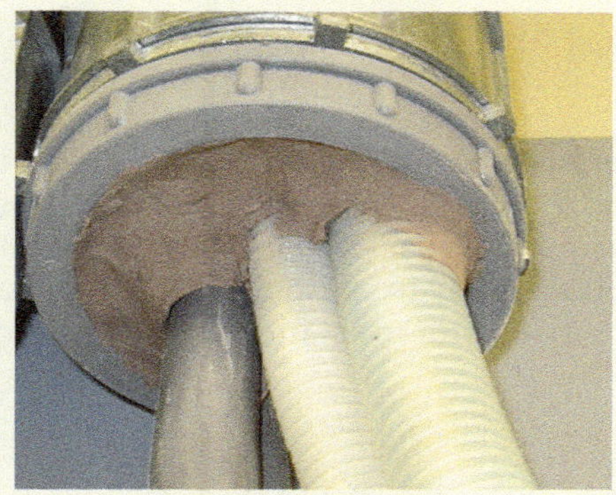

(A) Firestopping Putty

(B) Firestopping Sleeves

(C) Firestopping Bricks and Foam

Sources: Tim Dean (6A); Hilti North America (6B–6C)

5.2.5 Outdoor Wiring

Fire alarm circuits extending beyond one building are governed by the *NEC*®. The *NEC*® sets the standards on the size of cable and methods of fastening required for cabling. Some manufacturers prohibit any aerial wiring. The *NEC*® also specifies clearance requirements for cable from the ground. Overhead spans of open conductors and multiconductor cables of not over 1,000V nominal must be at least 10' (3 m) above finished grade and sidewalks. They must also be 10' (3 m) from any platform or projection from which they might be reached, and where the supply conductors are limited to 150V to ground and accessible to pedestrians only. Other requirements apply to areas with vehicular traffic. In addition, the *NEC*® states that exposed fire alarm wiring can be attached to the building, but it must be protected against physical damage as provided by baseboards, door frames, ledges, etc., according to *NEC Section 760.130(B)(1)*.

Know the Code

Wiring Methods and Materials on Load Side of PLFA Power Source
NEC Section 760.130

5.2.6 Fire Seals

Electrical equipment and cables must not be installed in a way that might help the spread of fire. The integrity of all fire-rated walls, floors, partitions, and ceilings must be maintained. An approved sealant or sealing device must be used to fill all penetrations. Any wall that extends from the floor to the roof or from floor to floor should be considered a firewall. In addition, raceways and cables that go from one room to another through a fire barrier must be sealed.

5.2.7 Wiring in Air Handling Spaces

Wiring in air handling spaces requires the use of approved wiring methods, including:

- Special plenum-rated cable
- Flexible metal tubing (Greenfield)
- Electrical metallic tubing (EMT)
- Intermediate metallic conduit (IMC)
- Rigid metallic conduit (hard wall or Schedule 80 conduit)

Standard cable tie straps are not permissible in plenums and other air handling spaces. Ties must be plenum rated. Bare solid copper wire used in short sections as tie wraps may be permitted by most AHJs. Fire alarm equipment is permitted to be installed in ducts and plenums only to sense the air. All splices and equipment must be contained in approved fire-resistant and low smoke-producing boxes.

5.2.8 Wiring in Hazardous Locations

The *NEC*® includes requirements for wiring in hazardous locations. Some areas that are considered hazardous are listed below:

Know the Code

Special Occupancies
NEC Chapter 5

- *NEC Article 511*, *Commercial Garages, Repair and Storage*
- *NEC Article 512*, *Cannabis Oil Equipment and Cannabis Oil Systems Using Flammable Materials*
- *NEC Article 513*, *Aircraft Hangars*
- *NEC Article 514*, *Motor Fuel Dispensing Facilities*
- *NEC Article 515*, *Bulk Storage Plants*
- *NEC Article 516*, *Spray Application, Dipping, Coating, and Printing Processes Using Flammable or Combustible Materials*
- *NEC Article 517*, *Health Care Facilities*
- *NEC Article 518*, *Assembly Occupancies*
- *NEC Article 520*, *Theaters, Audience Areas of Motion Picture and Television Studios, Performance Areas, and Similar Locations*
- *NEC Article 545*, *Manufactured Buildings and Relocatable Structures*
- *NEC Article 547*, *Agricultural Buildings*

5.2.9 Remote-Control Signaling Circuits

Building control circuits (*Figure 34*) are normally governed by *NEC Articles 724 and 725*. However, circuit wiring that is both powered and controlled by the fire alarm system is governed by *NEC Article 760*. A common residential problem occurs when using a system-type fire alarm that is a combination burglar and fire alarm. Many believe that the keypad is only a burglar alarm device. If the keypad is also used to control the fire alarm, it is a fire alarm device, and the cable used to connect it to the control unit must comply with *NEC Article 760*.

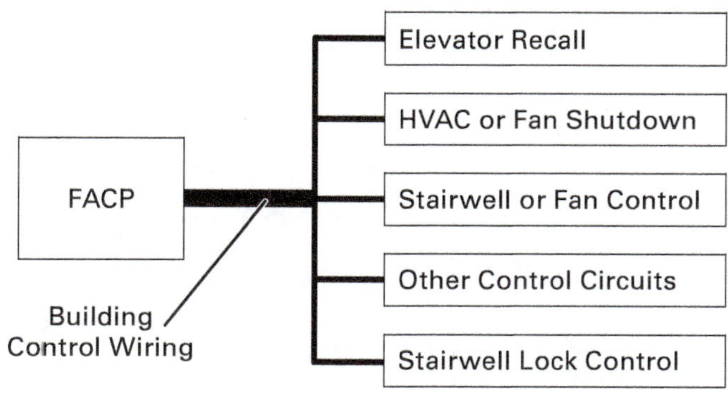

Figure 34 Building control circuits.

5.2.10 Floor-to-Floor Cables

Riser cable, such as FPLR, is required when wiring runs from floor to floor. The cable must be listed as capable of preventing fire from spreading from floor to floor. This requirement does not apply to one- and two-family residential dwellings.

5.2.11 Cables in Raceways

All cables in a raceway must have insulation rated for the highest voltage used in the raceway. Power-limited wiring may be installed in raceways or conduit, exposed on the surface of a ceiling or wall, or fished in concealed spaces. Cable splices or terminations must be made in listed fittings, boxes, enclosures, fire alarm devices, or utilization equipment. All wiring must enter boxes through approved fittings and be protected against physical damage.

5.2.12 Cable Spacing

Power-limited fire alarm circuit conductors must be separated at least 2" (50 mm) from any electric light, power, Class 1, or nonpower-limited fire alarm circuit conductors. This is to prevent damage to the power-limited fire alarm circuits from induced currents caused by the electric light, power, Class 1, or nonpower-limited fire alarm circuits.

5.2.13 Elevator Shafts

Wiring in elevator shafts must directly relate to the elevator and be installed in rigid metallic conduit, rigid nonmetallic conduit, EMT, IMC, or up to 6' (1.8 m) of flexible conduit.

Know the Code

Class 1 Power-Limited Circuits and Class 1 Power-Limited Remote-Control and Signaling Circuits
NEC Article 724

Know the Code

Class 2 and Class 3 Power-Limited Circuits
NEC Article 725

Know the Code

Fire Alarm Systems
NEC Article 760

5.2.14 Terminal Wiring Methods

The wiring for circuits using EOL terminations must be done so that removing the device causes a trouble signal (*Figure 35*).

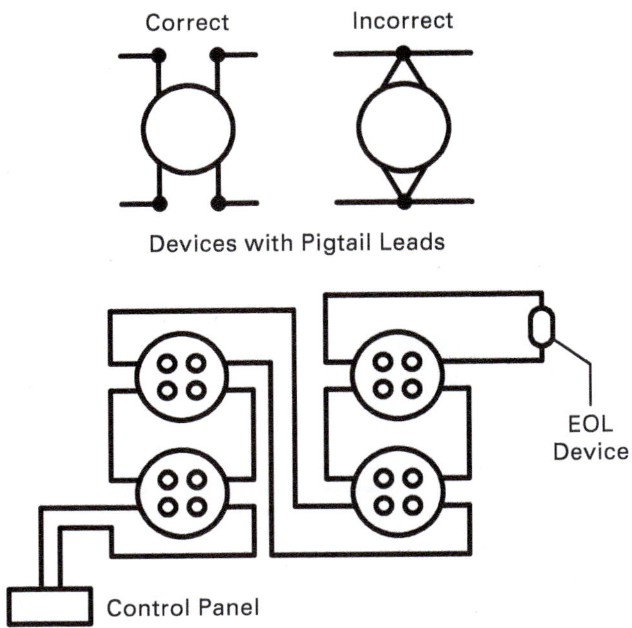

Figure 35 Correct wiring for devices with EOL terminations.

Network Command Center

The PC-based network command center shown is used to display event information from local or wide area network devices in a text or graphic format. When a device initiates an alarm,, the appropriate graphic floor plan is displayed along with operator instructions. Other capabilities of this command center include event history tracking and fire unit programming/control.

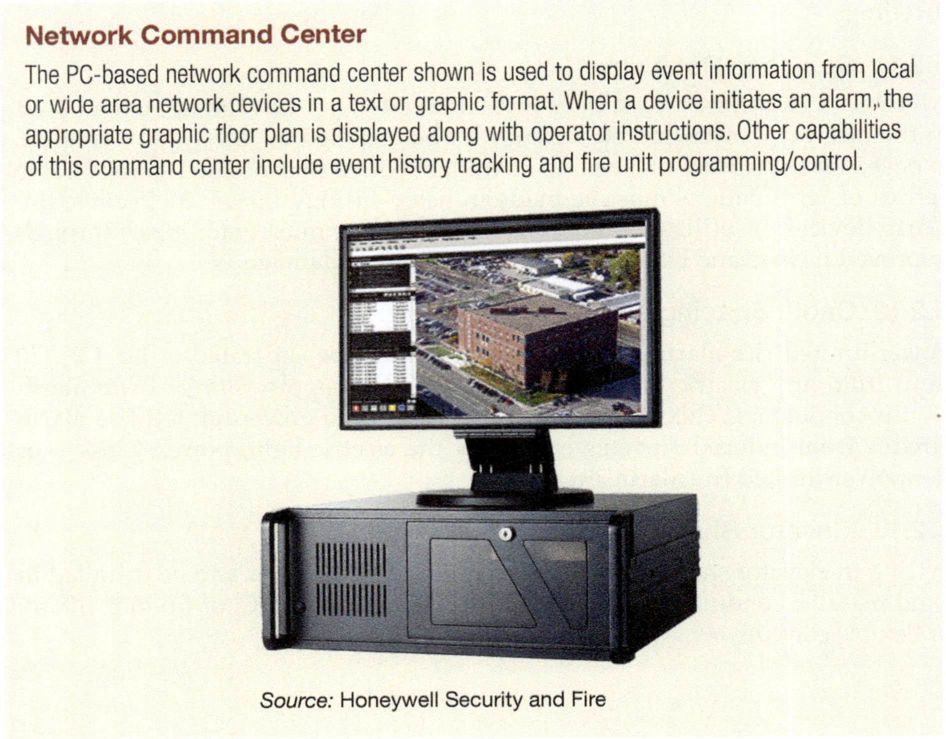

Source: Honeywell Security and Fire

5.2.15 Initiation Device Circuits

In accordance with NFPA 72®, these circuits are based on their performance capabilities under abnormal—or **fault**—conditions in accordance with Class A and Class B pathways.

Fault: An open, ground, or short condition on any line(s) extending from a control unit, which could prevent normal operation.

5.2.16 Notification Appliance Circuits

In accordance with NFPA 72®, these circuits are based on their performance capabilities under abnormal—or fault—conditions in accordance with Class A, Class B, or Class X pathways.

5.2.17 Primary Power Requirements

If more power is needed than can be supplied by one 20A circuit, additional circuits may be used, but none may exceed 20A. To help prevent system damage or unwanted alarms caused by electrical surges or spikes, surge protection devices should be installed in the primary power circuits, unless the fire alarm equipment has self-contained surge protection. In addition, some jurisdictions may require breaker locks and/or other means of identifying circuit breakers for FACUs.

5.2.18 Secondary Power Requirements

An approved generator supply or backup batteries must be used to supply the secondary power of a fire alarm system. The secondary power system must, upon loss of primary power, immediately keep the fire alarm functioning. Refer to NFPA 72® for the minimum length of time the fire alarm must keep functioning under secondary power.

5.3.0 Total Premises Fire Alarm System Installation

This section covers the requirements for the proper installation, testing, and **certification** of fire alarm and related systems for totally protected premises.

Certification: A systematic program that uses randomly selected follow-up inspections of a certified system installed under the program to verify for the listing organization that a fire alarm system complies with all the requirements of the NFPA 72® code. A system installed under such a program is identified by the issuance of a certificate and is designated as a certificated system.

5.3.1 Manual Fire Alarm Box (Pull Station) Installation

The following guidelines apply to the installation of a manual fire alarm box (pull station):

- Manual pull stations must be UL 38-listed or the equivalent. Multipurpose keypads cannot be used as fire alarm manual pull stations unless UL 38-listed for that purpose.
- Manual pull stations must be installed in the natural path of escape (near each required exit from an area) in occupancies that require manual initiation. Ideally, they should be located near the doorknob edge of the exit door. In any case, they must be no more than 5' (1.5 m) from the exit (*Figure 36*). In most cases, manual pull stations are installed with the actuators at the heights of 42" to 54" (1.1 m to 1.4 m) to conform to local ADA requirements. Most new pull stations are supplied with Grade II Braille on them for the visually impaired.

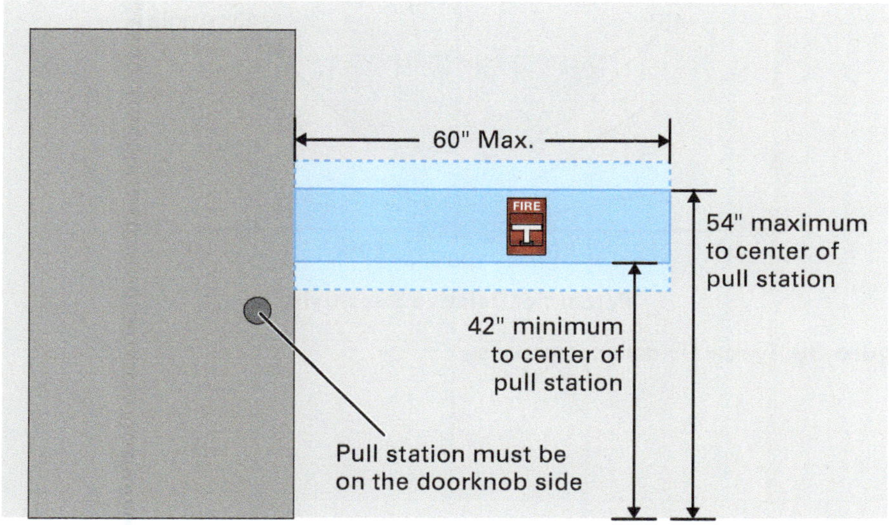

Figure 36 Pull station location and mounting height.

- The force required to operate manual pull stations must be no more than 5 foot-pounds (6.8 newton-meters).
- A manual pull station must be within 200' (61 m) of horizontal travel on the same floor from any part of the building (*Figure 37*). If this distance is exceeded, additional pull stations must be installed on the floor.

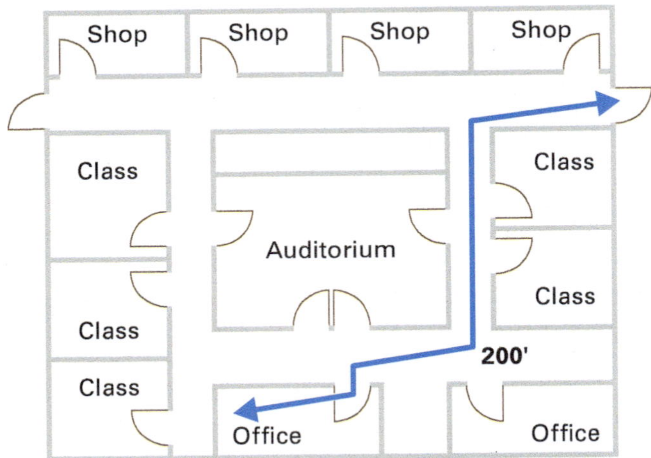

Figure 37 Placement of a pull station.

5.3.2 Flame Detector Installation

When installing UV or IR flame detectors, the manufacturer's instructions and NFPA 72® should be consulted. Most detectors are a combination of UV and IR sensors.

The following should be observed when installing UV flame detectors:

- Response is based on the distance from the fire, angle of view, and fire size.
- While some units have a 180° field of view, sensitivity drops substantially with angles of more than 45° to 50°. Normally, the field of view is limited to less than 90° (*Figure 38*).
- If used outdoors, the unit must be listed for outdoor use.
- A UV detector is considered solar blind, but to prevent unwanted alarms, it should never be aimed near or directly at any path the sun can take.
- The unit must never be aimed into areas where electric arc welding or cutting may be performed.

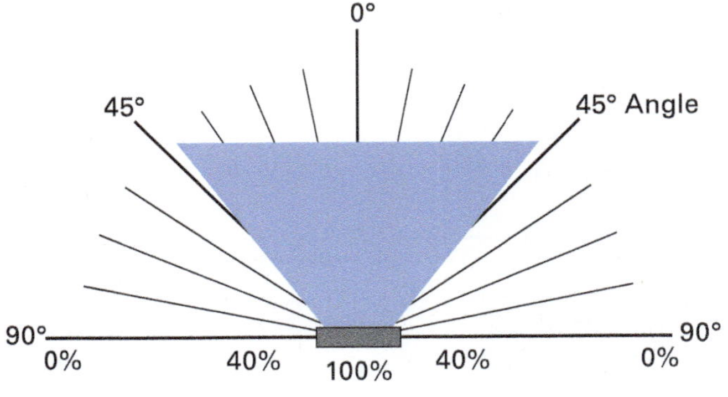

Figure 38 Typical UV detector response.

The following should be observed when installing IR flame detectors:

- Response varies depending on the angle of view. At 45°, the sensitivity drops to 60% of the 0° sensitivity (*Figure 39*).
- IR detectors cannot be used to detect alcohol, liquefied natural gas, hydrogen, or magnesium fires.
- IR detectors work best in low light level installations. High light levels desensitize the units. Discriminating units can tolerate up to 10 footcandles (108 lux) of ambient light. Nondiscriminating units can tolerate up to 2 footcandles (22 lux) of ambient light.
- The units must never be used outdoors.

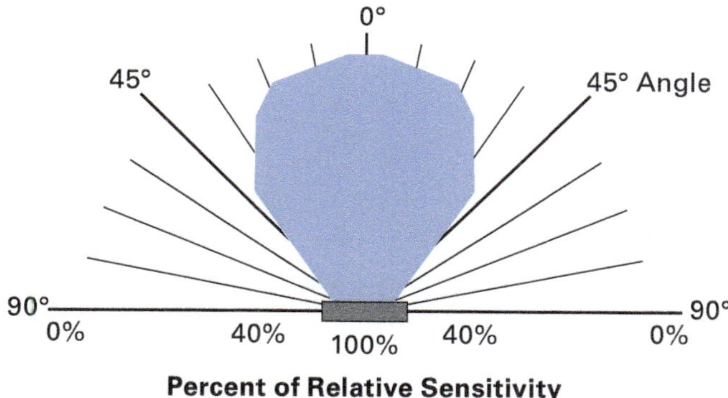

Figure 39 Typical IR detector response.

5.3.3 Smoke Compartment, Smoke Spread, and Stratification

This section defines the term smoke compartment and describes the smoke spread and **stratification** phenomena.

Stratification: The phenomenon in which the upward movement of smoke and gases ceases due to a loss of buoyancy.

Before automatic smoke detectors can be installed, the area of coverage known as the *smoke compartment* must be defined. The smoke compartment is the continuous, smoke-resistant perimeter boundary of a room, space, or area to be protected by one or more automatic smoke detectors between the upper surface of the floor and the lower surface of the ceiling. For the purposes of determining the area to be protected by smoke detectors, the smoke compartment is not the same as a smoke-tight compartment. It should be noted that some rooms with a raised floor and a false ceiling actually have three smoke compartments:

- The compartment beneath the raised floor
- The compartment between the raised floor and the visible ceiling above
- The compartment between the room's visible ceiling and the floor above (or the lower portion of the roof)

Few cases require detection in all these areas. However, some computer equipment rooms with a great deal of electrical power and communications cable under the raised floor may require detection in the compartment under the floor in addition to the compartment above the floor.

The simplest example of a smoke compartment would be a room with the door closed. If no intervening closed door exists between this and adjoining (communicating) rooms, the line denoting the barrier becomes less clear. The determining factor would be the depth of the wall section above the open archway or doorway as follows:

- An archway or doorway that extends more than 18" (450 mm) down from the ceiling greatly delays smoke travel and is considered a boundary, just like a regular wall from floor to ceiling. A doorway that extends more than 4" (100 mm) but less than 18" (450 mm) must be considered a smoke barrier, and the detector spacing must be reduced to $^2/_3$ of the listed spacing distance on either side of the opening (*Figure 40*).

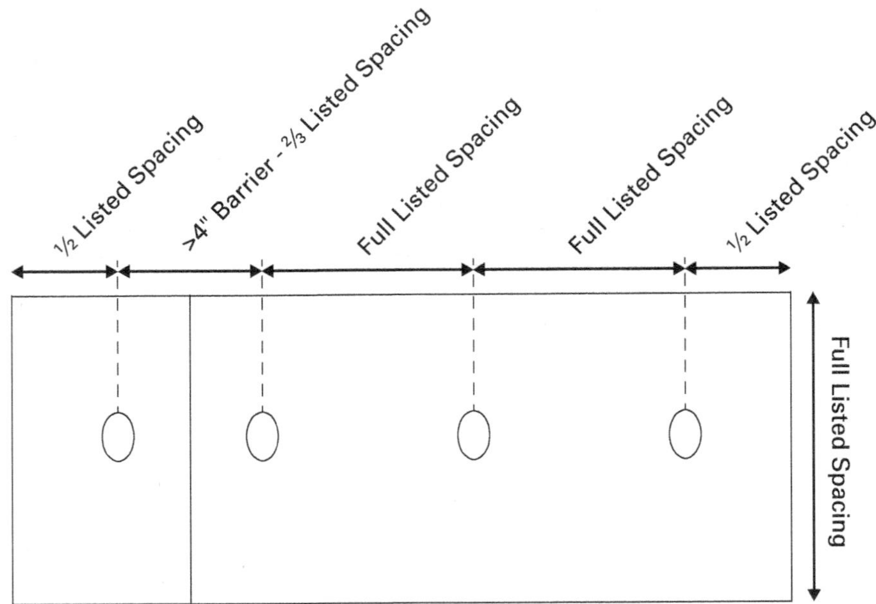

Figure 40 Reduced spacing required for a barrier.

- Open grids above doors or walls that allow free flow of air and smoke are not considered barriers. To be considered an open grid, the opening must meet all the requirements defined and demonstrated in *Figure 41*.
- Smoke doors, kept open by hold-and-release devices and meet all the standards applicable thereto, may also be considered boundaries of a smoke compartment.
- If the space between the top of a low wall and the ceiling is less than 18" (450 mm), the wall is treated as if it extends to the ceiling and is a barrier. Smoke will still be able to travel to the other side of the wall, but it may be substantially delayed. This will delay notification. In this case, detector spacing must be reduced to $^2/_3$ of the listed spacing on either side of the wall. If the space between the top of a low wall and the ceiling is 18" (450 mm) or more, the wall is not considered to substantially affect smoke travel.

In a fire, smoke and heat rise in a plume toward the ceiling because that air is lighter than the surrounding denser, cooler air. In an area with a relatively low, flat, smooth ceiling, the smoke and heat quickly spread across the entire ceiling, triggering smoke or heat detectors. When the ceiling is irregular, smoke and heated air will tend to collect, perhaps stratifying near a peak or collecting in the bays of a beamed or joist ceiling.

In the case of a beamed or joist ceiling, the smoke and heated air will fill the nearest bays and begin to overflow to adjacent bays (*Figure 42*). The process continues until smoke and heat reach either a smoke or heat detector in sufficient quantity to cause activation. Because each bay must fill before it overflows, a substantial amount of time may pass before a detector placed at its maximum listed spacing activates. To reduce this time, the detector spacing is reduced.

When smoke must rise a long distance, it tends to cool and become denser. As the density of the smoke becomes equal to that of the air around it, it stratifies, or stops rising (*Figure 43*). As a fire grows, heat is added, and the smoke will eventually rise to the ceiling. However, a great deal of time may be lost, causing a larger fire and a large number of toxic gases to be present at the floor level. Due to this delay, alternating detectors are lowered at least 3' (0.9 m) (*Figure 44*). The science of stratification is very complex and requires a fire protection engineer's evaluation to determine if stratification is a factor and, if so, to determine how much to lower the detectors to compensate for this condition.

Some conditions that cause stratification include:

- Uninsulated roofs that are heated by the sun, creating a heated air thermal block
- Roofs that are cooled by low outside temperatures, cooling the gases before they reach a detector
- HVAC systems that produce a hot layer of ceiling air
- Ambient air that is at the same temperature as the fire gases and smoke

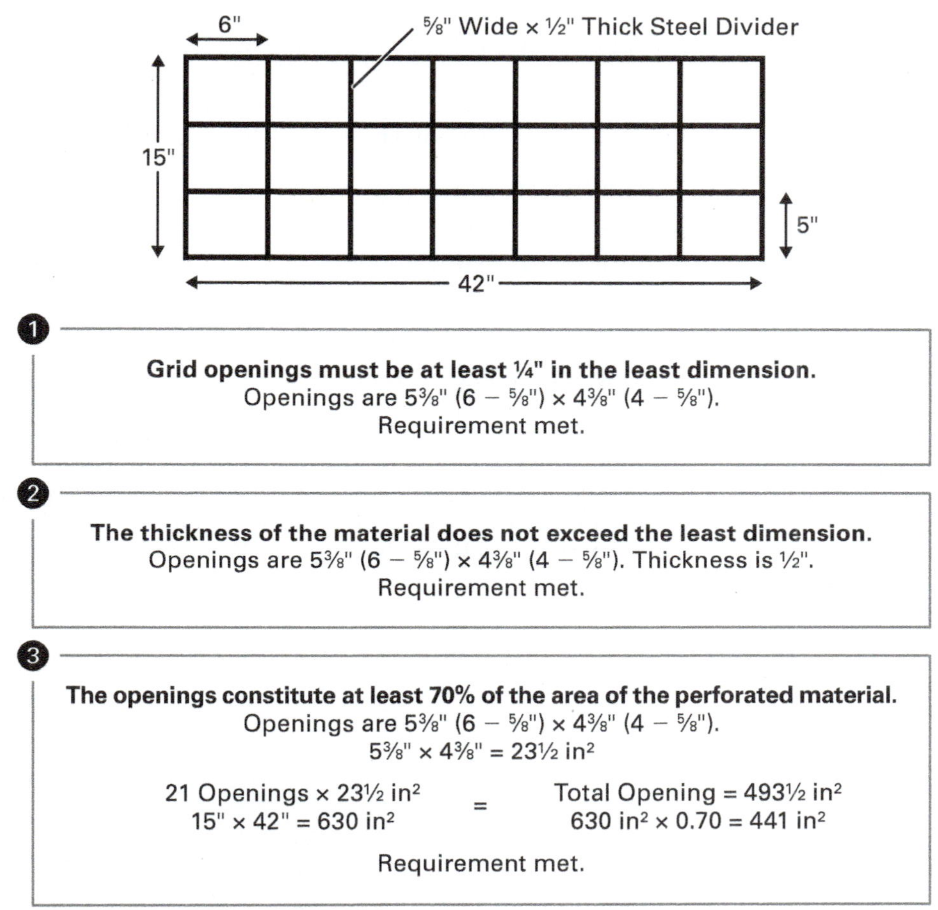

Figure 41 Detailed grid definition.

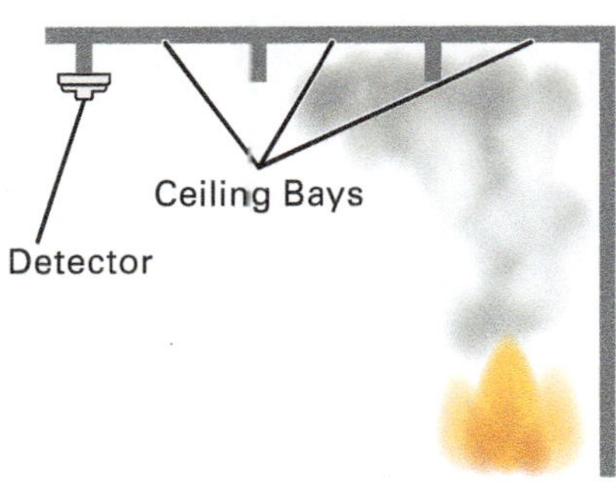

Figure 42 Smoke spread across a beamed or joist ceiling.

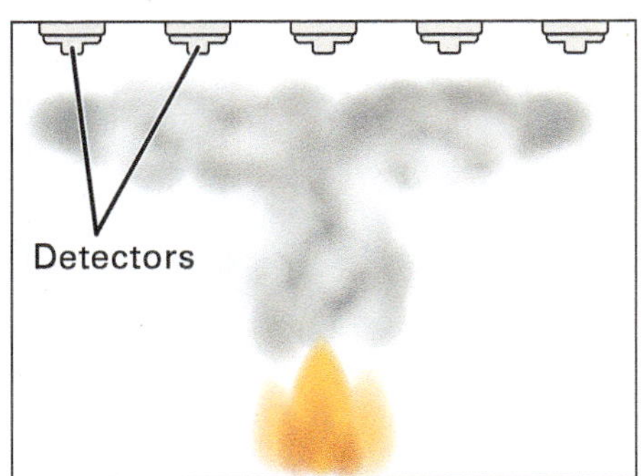

Figure 43 Smoke stratification.

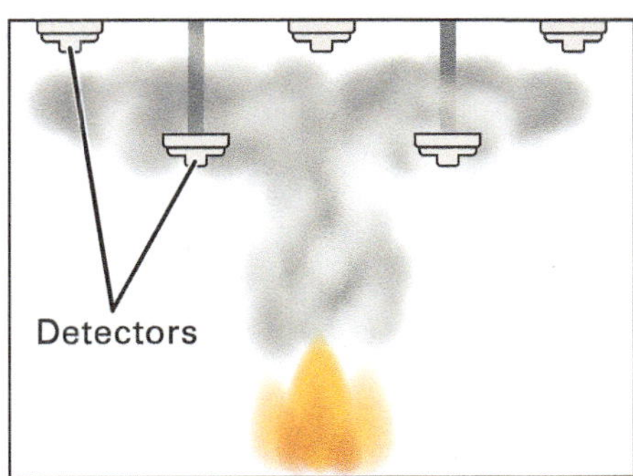

Figure 44 Smoke stratification countermeasure.

There are no clear, set rules regarding which environments will and will not be susceptible to stratification. The factors and variables involved are beyond the scope of this course. For further reading on the subject, contact the NFPA reference department for a bibliography. Note that only alternating detectors are suspended for stratification. Some fires can result in stratification caused by superheated air and gases reaching the ceiling prior to the smoke, causing a barrier that holds the smoke below the detectors. Smoke detectors with integral heat detectors should be effective in such cases without the need to suspend alternating detectors below the ceiling.

Stratification can also occur in high-rise buildings because of the stack effect principle. This occurs when smoke rises until it reaches a neutral pressure level, where it begins to stratify (*Figure 45*). The stack effect can move smoke from the source to distant parts of the building. Penetrations left unsealed can be a major contributor in such smoke migration. Stack effect factors include:

- Building height
- Air tightness
- Air leakage between floors
- Interior/exterior temperature differential
- Vertical openings
- Wind force and direction

Some factors that influence stack effect are variable, such as the weather conditions and which interior and exterior doors might be open. For this reason, the neutral pressure level may not be the same in a given building at different times. One item is very clear concerning stratification: penetrations made in smoke barriers, particularly those in vertical openings such as shafts, must be sealed.

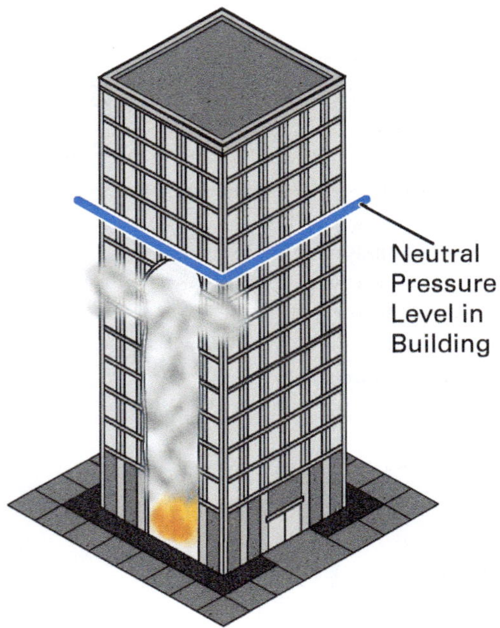

Figure 45 Stack effect in a high-rise building.

Wireless Smoke Detection System

The components that form a wireless smoke detection system are shown. This particular system can be used in situations where the building design or installation costs make hardwiring of the detectors impractical or too expensive. The heart of this system is the translation unit, called a *gateway*. It can communicate with up to four remote receiver units. The receivers can monitor radio frequency signals from up to 80 wireless smoke detectors. Each receiver unit transmits the status of the related wireless detectors via communication wiring to the translator. The translator then communicates this status to an intelligent FACU via a signaling line circuit loop. Note that some jurisdictions do not permit the use of these systems.

Source: Honeywell Security and Fire

5.3.4 General Precautions for Detector Installation

The following are general precautions for detector installation:

- *Recessed mounting* — Detectors must not be recess-mounted unless specially listed for recessed mounting.
- *Air diffusers* — Air movement can have a number of undesirable effects on detectors. The introduction of air from outside the fire area can dilute the smoke, delaying activation. The air movement may create a barrier, which delays or prevents smoke from reaching the detector chamber. Smoke detectors are listed for a specific range of air velocity. This means that they are expected to function with air (and smoke) moving through the detection chamber at any speed within the listed range. Detectors may not function properly if air movement is above or below the listed velocity. Air movement can be measured with an instrument called a *velocimeter*. Unless the airflow exceeds the listed velocity, spot-type smoke detectors should be a minimum of 3' (0.9 m) from air diffusers.
- *Problem locations and sources of unwanted alarms* — Detectors, especially smoke detectors, can register unwanted alarms as a result of the factors outlined in the following paragraphs.

  Electrical interference. Keep detector locations away from fluorescent lights and radio transmitters, including cellular phones. Electrical noise or radio frequencies radiated from these devices can cause unwanted alarms.

  Heating equipment. High temperatures, dust accumulation, improper exhaust, and incomplete combustion from heating equipment are problems for detectors.

Engine exhaust. Exhaust from engine-powered forklifts, vehicles, and generators is a potential problem for ionization-type smoke detectors.

Solvent and chemical fumes. Cleaning solvents and adhesives are a problem for ionization detectors.

Other gases and fumes. Fumes from machining operations, paint spraying, industrial or battery gases, curing ovens/dryers, cooking equipment, sawing/drilling/grinding operations, and welding/cutting operations cause problems for smoke detectors.

Extreme temperatures. Avoid very hot or cold environments for smoke detector locations. Temperatures below 32°F (0°C) can cause unwanted alarms, and temperatures above 120°F (49°C) can prevent proper smoke detector operation. Extreme temperatures affect beam, ionization, and photoelectric detectors.

Dampness or humidity. Smoke detectors must be located in areas where the humidity is less than 93%. In ionization detectors, dampness and high humidity can cause tiny water droplets to condense inside the sensing chamber, making it overly sensitive and causing unwanted alarms. In photoelectric detectors, humidity can cause light refraction and loss of current flow, either of which can lead to unwanted alarms. Common sources of moisture to avoid include slop sinks, steam tables, showers, water spray operations, humidifiers, and live steam sources.

Lightning. Nearby lightning can cause electrical damage to a fire alarm system. It may also cause electrical noise or spikes to be induced in the alarm system wiring or detectors, resulting in unwanted alarms. Surge arrestors installed in the system's primary power supply to protect the system, in conjunction with alarm verification, can reduce the chance of system damage and unwanted alarms.

Dusty or dirty environments. Dust and dirt can accumulate on a smoke detector's sensing chamber, making it overly sensitive. Avoid areas where fumigants, fog, dust, or mist-producing materials are consistently used.

Outdoor locations. Dust, air currents, and humidity typically affect outdoor structures, including sheds, barns, stables, and other open structures. This makes outdoor structures unsuitable for smoke detectors.

Insect-infested areas. Insects in smoke detectors can cause unwanted alarms. Good bug screens on a detector can prevent most adult insects from entering the detector. However, newly hatched insects may still be able to enter. An insecticide strip next to the detector may help solve the problem, but it may also cause unwanted alarms because of fumes. Check with the manufacturer for the use of an approved strip. Ionization detectors are less prone to unwanted alarms from insects.

Construction. Smoke detectors must not be installed until after construction cleanup unless required by the AHJ for protection during construction. Detectors that are installed prior to construction cleanup must be cleaned or replaced. Prior to 1993, the code permitted covering smoke detectors to protect them from dirt, dust, or paint mist. However, the covers did not work very well and resulted in clogged, oversensitive, and damaged detectors.

Installation

When installing fire alarm systems, install the last initiating/notification device in the circuit first, followed by the next-to-last device, and so on, while working toward the FACU. After installing each circuit device, immediately check the wiring for continuity, grounds, and/or shorts. This recommended method helps find wiring problems so that they can be corrected as the work progresses, thereby eliminating potentially time-consuming troubleshooting after the system installation is completed.

Troubleshooting

Troubleshooting older systems requires that you trace and check each detector to isolate the source of an alarm. The fire alarm units of newer systems, such as the one shown, have fault isolation messages and LCD display panels to help pinpoint which detector has alarmed or has a problem.

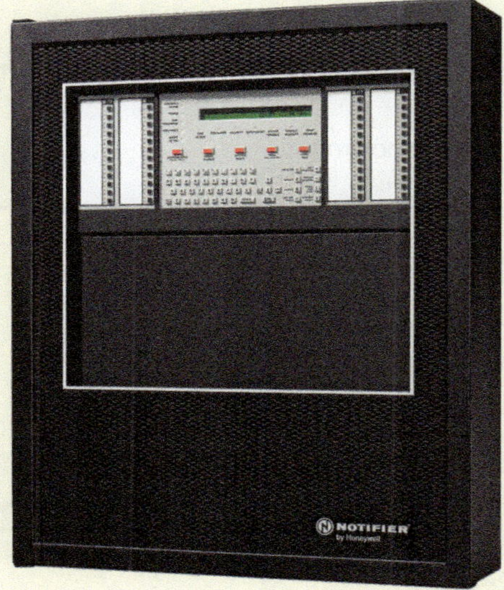

Source: Honeywell Security and Fire

5.3.5 Spot Detector Installations on Flat, Smooth Ceilings

Flat, smooth ceilings are defined as ceilings with a slope equal to or less than 1.5" per foot (or with a pitch of less than 1.5°) and do not have open joists or beams.

The following applies to conventional spot detector installation on flat, smooth ceilings:

- When a smoke detector manufacturer's specifications do not specify a particular spacing, a 30' (9 m) spacing guide may be applied.
- The distance between heat detectors must not exceed their listed spacing.
- There must be detectors located within ½ the listed spacing measured at right angles from all sidewalls.

NOTE

This section assumes the listed spacing for detectors mounted on a smooth and flat ceiling of less than 10' (3 m) in height is 30' (9 m), where 15' (4.6 m) is ½ the listed spacing. Spacing is reduced, as indicated in later sections, when the ceiling height exceeds 10' (3 m) or the ceiling is not smooth and flat as defined by the code.

In the following example, the detector locations for a simple 30' × 60' (9 m × 18 m) long room will be determined. The locations are determined by the intersection of columns and rows marked on a sketch of the ceiling:

- The first column is located by a line that is parallel to the end wall and not more than ½ the listed spacing from the end wall (*Figure 46*).
- The first row is located by a line parallel to the sidewall that is not more than ½ the listed spacing from that sidewall (*Figure 47*).
- The first detector is located at the intersection of the row and column lines.
- The second column is located by a line that is parallel to the opposite end wall and not more than ½ the listed spacing from the end wall.
- The second detector is located at the intersection of the first row and second column lines, provided that the distance between the first and second detectors does not exceed the listed spacing (*Figure 48*). The only time the full listed spacing of any detector is used is when measuring from one detector to the next.

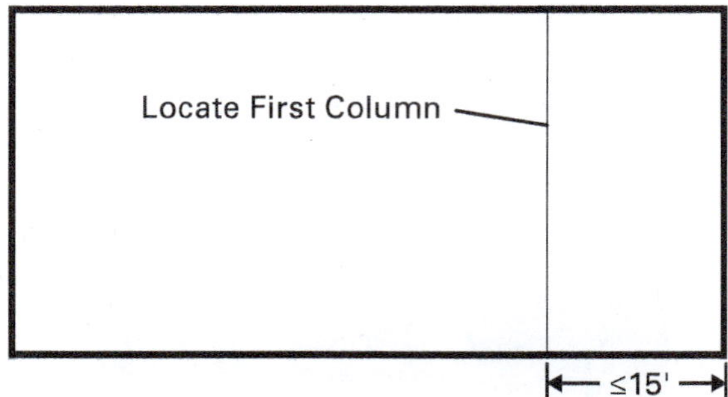

Figure 46 Locating the first column.

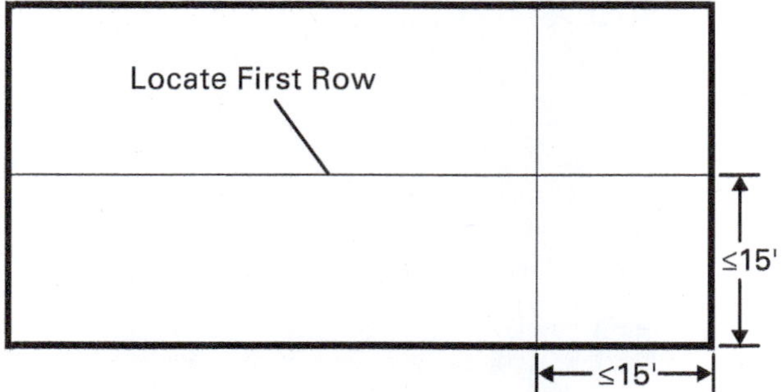

Figure 47 Locating the first row.

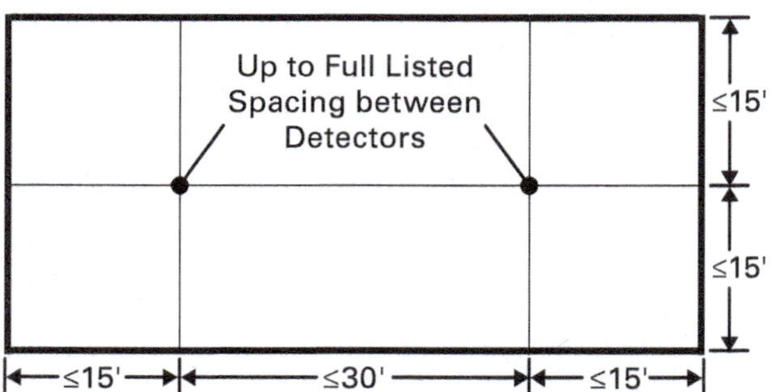

Figure 48 First and second detector locations.

5.3.6 Photoelectric Beam Smoke Detector Installations on Flat, Smooth Ceilings

Two configurations of beam detectors are used for open area installations. Beam smoke detectors can be installed as straight-line devices or as angled-beam devices that employ mirrors or prisms. When used as angled-beam devices, the beam length is reduced for the number of mirrors used, as specified in NFPA 72®. When installing either type of beam smoke detector, always follow the manufacturer's instructions.

Photoelectric beam smoke detectors have two listings: one for width of coverage and one for the minimum/maximum length of coverage (beam length), as shown in *Figure 49*. The beam length is listed by the manufacturer and, in most cases, so is the width coverage/listed spacing (S). When a manufacturer does not list the width coverage, the beam length must not exceed the maximum permitted by the equipment listing. The distance of the beam from the ceiling should normally be between 4" and 12" (100 mm and 300 mm). However, NFPA allows a greater distance to compensate for stratification. Always make sure the beam does not cross any expansion joint or other point of slippage that could eventually cause misalignment of the beam. In large areas, parallel beam detectors may be installed, separated by no more than their listed spacing.

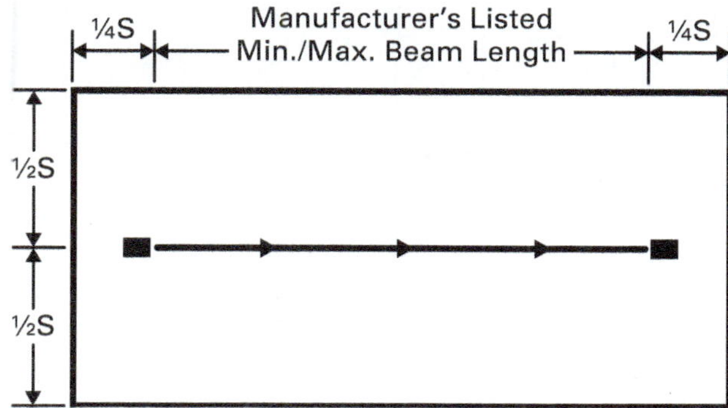

Figure 49 Maximum straight-line single-beam smoke detector coverage (ceiling view).

Using mirrors to direct the light beam from a transmitter in a path other than a single straight line is permitted if the manufacturer's directions are followed and the mirror used is listed for the beam detector model being installed. The use of a mirror will require a reduction in the listed beam length of the detector. When using a mirror, the beam length is the distance between the transmitter and receiver (measured from the transmitter to the mirror, plus the distance from the mirror to the receiver). This distance is reduced to 66% of the manufacturer's listed beam length for a single mirror, and to 44% of the manufacturer's listed beam length for two mirrors. Width spacing (S) is defined, as previously stated, for single- and double-beam installations. The planner should also allow for additional installation and service time when mirrors are used. As with beam detectors without mirrors, make sure the light beam does not cross a building expansion joint.

Beam-Type Detectors

Objects other than smoke can interfere with beam-type detectors. For example, balloons released by children in malls have been known to activate the fire protection system.

5.3.7 Spot Detector Installations on Irregular Ceilings

Any ceiling that is not flat and smooth is considered irregular. For heat detectors, ceilings of any description over 10' (3 m) AFF are considered irregular and require the heat detectors' spacing to be reduced below their listed spacing per NFPA 72®. This is because hot air is diluted by the surrounding cooler air as it rises, reducing its temperature.

Irregular ceilings include:

- *Sloped ceilings* — For sloped ceilings, refer to the special requirements listed in NFPA 72®. Sloped ceilings are usually shed or peaked types.
  - A *shed* ceiling is defined as having the high point at one side with the slope extending toward the opposite side.
  - A *peaked* ceiling is defined as sloping in two directions from its highest point. Peaked ceilings include domed or curved ceilings.
- *Solid joist or beam ceilings* — For solid joist or beam ceilings, refer to the special requirements listed in NFPA 72®.

While heat detectors must have their spacing reduced in areas with high ceilings (over 10'/3 m), smoke detector spacing is not adjusted due to the **ceiling height**.

Ceiling height: The height from the continuous floor of a room to the continuous ceiling of a room or space.

For a roof slope less than 30°, determined as shown in *Figure 50*, all heat detector spacing must be reduced based on the height at the peak. For a roof slope greater than 30°, the average ceiling height must be used for all heat detectors other than those located in the peak. The average ceiling height can be determined by adding the high sidewall and low sidewall heights together and dividing the sum by two. In the case of slopes greater than 30°, the spacing to the second row is measured from the first row and not the sidewall for shed ceilings. See the most recent version of NFPA 72® for heat detector spacing reduction based on peak or average ceiling heights.

Determining If a Slope Is Greater than 30°

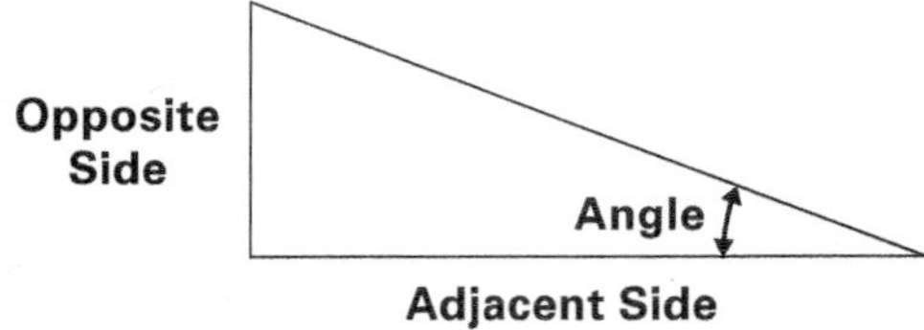

If the opposite side divided by the adjacent side is >0.5774, the angle is >30°.

The tangent of the smallest angle of a right triangle equals the opposite side divided by the adjacent side.

The sum of all the angles of a triangle equals 180°.

The tangent of a 30° angle is 0.5774.

Figure 50 Determining degree of slope.

Once you have determined the ceiling you are working with is a shed ceiling, use the following guidelines for determining detector placement:

- Place the first row of detectors within 3' (0.9 m) of the high sidewall (measured horizontally).
- Use the listed spacing for each additional row of detectors (measured from the detector location, not the sidewall).
- For heat detectors on ceilings over 10' (3 m) high, adjust the spacing per NFPA 72®.
- If the slope is less than 30°, all heat detector spacing is based on the peak height. If the slope is more than 30°, peak heat detectors are based on the peak height, and all other detectors are based on the average height.
- Additional columns of detectors that run at right angles to the slope of the ceiling do not need to be within 3' (0.9 m) of the end walls.
- Smoke detector spacing is not adjusted for ceiling height.

To calculate the average ceiling height, use one of the following methods.

Method 1:

Step 1 Subtract the height of the low ceiling from the height of the high ceiling.

Step 2 Divide the result from *Step 1* by 2.

Step 3 Subtract the result from *Step 2* from the height of the high ceiling.

Method 2:

Step 1 Add the height of the low ceiling to the height of the high ceiling.

Step 2 Divide the result from *Step 1* by 2.

A ceiling must be sloped as defined by the code to be considered a peaked ceiling. It must slope in more than one direction from its highest point. Because domed and curved ceilings do not have clean 90° lines to clearly show that the ceiling slopes in more than one direction, they should be viewed from an imaginary vertical center line. From this perspective, it can be seen if the ceiling slopes in more than one direction.

Heat detectors should be located on a peaked ceiling as follows:

- The first row of detectors on a peaked ceiling should be located within 3' (0.9 m) of the peak, measured horizontally. The detectors may be located alternately on either side of the peak, if desired.

- Regardless of where the first row of detectors is in the 3' (0.9 m) space on either side of the peak, the measurement for the next row of heat detectors is taken from the peak (measured horizontally, not from the heat detector located near the peak). This is different from the way detector location is determined for shed ceilings.
- Heat detectors must have their spacing reduced in areas with ceilings over 10' (3 m).
- As with sloped ceilings, using the peak height for just the row of heat detectors at the peak or all the ceiling heat detectors depends on whether the ceiling is sloped more than 30°. Use the peak height to adjust the heat detector spacing of all the heat detectors in the room when the slope of the ceiling is less than 30°. When the slope is greater than 30°, use the peak height for only the heat detectors located within 3' (0.9 m) of the peak and use the average height for all other heat detectors in the room.

Smoke detectors should be located on a peaked ceiling as follows:

- A row of detectors is located within 3' (0.9 m) of the peak, measured horizontally, on either side or alternated from side to side of the peak.
- The next row of detectors should be placed within the listed spacing of the peak measured horizontally. Do not measure from the detectors located within 3' (0.9 m) of the peak. Regardless of where the first row of detectors is within the 3' (0.9 m) space of the peak, the next row on each side of the peak is installed within the listed spacing of the detector from the peak.
- Additional rows of detectors are installed using the full listed spacing of the detector.
- The sidewall must be within ½ the listed spacing of the last row of detectors.
- Columns of detectors are installed in the depth dimension of the above diagrams (*Figure 46*, *Figure 47*, *Figure 48*, *Figure 49*) using the full listed spacing (same as on a smooth, flat ceiling).
- There is no need to reduce smoke detector spacing for ceilings over 10' (3 m).

Solid joists are defined for heat detectors and smoke detectors based on criteria listed in NFPA 72®.

Heat detector spacing at right angles to the solid joist is reduced by 50%. In the direction running parallel to the joists, standard spacing principles are applied. If the ceiling height exceeds 10' (3 m), spacing is adjusted for the high ceiling in addition to the solid joist, as defined in NFPA 72®.

For spacing requirements of smoke detectors at right angles to the solid joists, refer to special requirements listed in NFPA 72®. In the direction running parallel to the joists, standard spacing principles are applied.

Refer to NFPA 72® to determine **spot-type detector** placement requirements based on a ceiling's height and joist depth. Additional reductions for sloped joist ceilings also apply, as defined in NFPA 72®.

Beamed ceilings consist of solid structural or solid nonstructural members projecting down from the ceiling surface more than 4" (100 mm) and spaced more than 3' (0.9 m) apart center to center as defined by NFPA 72®.

Heat detectors should be located on a beamed ceiling as follows:

- If the beams project more than 4" (100 mm) below the ceiling, the spacing of spot-type heat detectors at right angles to the direction of beam travel must not be more than ⅔ the smooth ceiling spacing.
- If the beams project more than 12" (300 mm) below the ceiling and are more than 8' (2.4 m) on center, each bay formed by the beams must be treated as a separate area.
- Reductions of heat detector spacing in accordance with NFPA 72® are also required for ceilings over 10' (3 m) in height.

NOTE

Always refer to the most current version of NFPA 72® to verify installation requirements for heat or smoke detectors.

Spot-type detector: A device in which the detecting element is concentrated at a particular location. Typical examples are bimetallic detectors, fusible alloy detectors, certain pneumatic rate-of-rise detectors, certain smoke detectors, and thermoelectric detectors.

Smoke detectors should be located on a beamed ceiling as follows:

- If beams are 4" to 12" (100 mm to 300 mm) in depth with an AFF level of 12' (3.7 m) or less, the spacing of spot-type smoke detectors in the direction perpendicular to the beams must be reduced by 50% and may be mounted on the bottoms of the beams.
- If beams are greater than 12" (300 mm) in depth with an AFF level of more than 12' (3.7 m), each beam bay must contain its own detectors. There are additional rules for sloped beam ceilings as defined in NFPA 72®.
- The spacing of projected light beam detectors that run perpendicular to the ceiling beams need not be reduced. However, if the projected light beams are run parallel to the ceiling beams, the spacing must be reduced per NFPA 72®.

NOTE

Always refer to the most current version of NFPA 72® to verify installation requirements for heat or smoke detectors.

Beam construction is a ceiling surface referred to in conjunction with the locations of initiating devices. Beam construction includes ceilings with solid structural or solid nonstructural members projecting down from the ceiling surface more than 4" (100 mm) and spaced more than 3' (0.9 m) center to center.

5.3.8 Notification Appliance Installation

There are several types of notification appliances:

- Audible devices such as bells, horns, chimes, speakers, sirens, and mini sounders
- Visual devices such as strobe lights
- Tactile (sense of touch) devices such as bed shakers and special sprinkling devices
- Olfactory (sense of smell) devices, which are also accepted by the code

The appropriate devices for the occupancy must be determined and listed for the purposes they are used. For example, UL 1480 speakers are used for fire protective signaling systems, and UL 1638 visual signaling appliances are used for private mode emergency and general utility signaling. While NFPA 72® recognizes tactile and olfactory devices, it does not specify installation requirements. If an occupant requires one of these notification types, use equipment listed for the purpose and follow the manufacturer's instructions. As always, consult the local AHJ.

The following guidelines apply to the installation of notification devices:

- Ensure that notification devices are wired using the applicable circuit class.
- In Class B circuits, the unit supervises the wire using an EOL device. Electrically, the EOL device must be at the end of the indicating circuit. Examples of EOL devices are resistors to limit current, diodes for polarity, and capacitors for filtering.
- It is extremely important that any polarized devices be installed correctly. The polarization of the leads or terminals of these devices are marked on the device or noted in the manufacturer's installation data. If the leads of a polarized notification device are reversed, the unit will not detect the problem, and the device will not activate. Moreover, the device will act as an EOL device, preventing the unit from detecting breaks between the device and the actual EOL device. Because it is very easy to accidentally wire a device backwards, testing every device is extremely important. The general alarm should be activated, and every notification device should be checked for proper operation.
- Sidewall-mounted audible notification devices must be mounted at least 90" (2.3 m) AFF level or at least 6" (150 mm) below the finished ceiling. Ceiling-mounting and recessed appliances are permitted.

- A **visible notification appliance** must be mounted at the minimum height of 80" to 96" (2 m to 2.4 m) AFF (NFPA 72®) or, for ADA requirements, either 80" (2 m) AFF or 6" (150 mm) below the ceiling. In any case, the device must be within 16' (4.9 m) of the pillows in a sleeping area. Combination audible/visible appliances must follow the requirements for visible appliances. Non-coded visible appliances should be installed in all areas where required by NFPA 101® or by the local AHJ. Consult ADA codes for the required illumination levels in sleeping areas.
- *Visual notification appliance spacing in corridors* — Visual notification appliances must be located no more than 15' (4.6 m) from the end of the corridor with a separation of no more than 100' (30.5 m) between appliances. Where there is an interruption of the concentrated viewing path, such as a fire door or elevation change, the area is to be considered as a separate corridor. Spacing in corridors may also be based on room size.
- *Visual notification appliance spacing in other applications* — The light source color for visual appliances must be clear or nominal white and must not exceed 1,000 cd (NFPA 72®). In addition, special considerations apply when more than one visual appliance is installed in a room or corridor. NFPA 72® specifies that the separation between appliances must not exceed 100' (30.5 m). Visible notification appliances must be installed in accordance with *Chapter 18* of NFPA 72®.

Visible notification appliance: A notification appliance that alerts by the sense of sight.

5.3.9 FACU Installation Guidelines

The guidelines for installing a FACU are as follows:

- When not located in an area that is continuously occupied, all fire alarm control equipment must be protected by a smoke detector, as shown in *Figure 51*. If the smoke detector is not designed to work properly in that environment, a heat detector must be used. It is not necessary to protect the entire space or room.
- Detector spacing must be adjusted if the ceiling over the control equipment is irregular in one or more respects. This is considered protection against a specific hazard under NFPA 72® and does not require the entire compartment (room) containing the control equipment to be protected under the *0.7 rule*.
- A means of silencing audible notification appliances from a FACU must be protected against unauthorized use. Most FACUs are located inside locked metal cabinets as shipped from the manufacturer. If the silencing switch is key-actuated or is locked within the cabinet, this provision should be considered satisfied. If the silencing means is within a room that is restricted to authorized use only, no additional measures should be required. The NFPA codes do not clearly define nor specify unauthorized or authorized use.

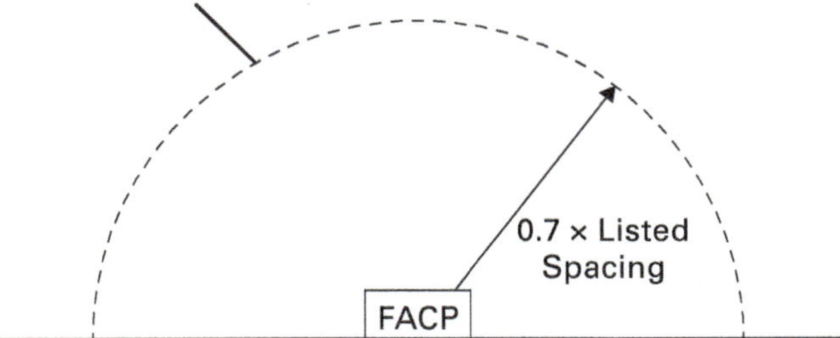

Figure 51 Protection of an FACU.

- FACU connections to the primary light and power circuits must be on a dedicated branch circuit with overcurrent protection rated at 20A or less. Any connections after the distribution panel (circuit breaker box) to the primary power circuit on the premises must be directly related to the fire alarm system. No other use is permitted. This requirement does not necessitate a direct tap into the power circuit ahead of the distribution panel, though connecting ahead of the main disconnect is acceptable with listed service equipment.
- The power disconnection means (circuit breaker) must be clearly identified as a fire alarm circuit control.

NFPA 72® 0.7 Rule

The 0.7 rule, as defined by NFPA 72®, says that all points on the ceiling shall have a detector within a distance equal to or less than 0.7 times the listed spacing (0.7S). The illustration shown demonstrates this rule for a heat detector that has a listed spacing of 28'. No space on the ceiling is more than 0.7 times the detector's listed spacing. In this case, 0.7(28) = 19.6'.

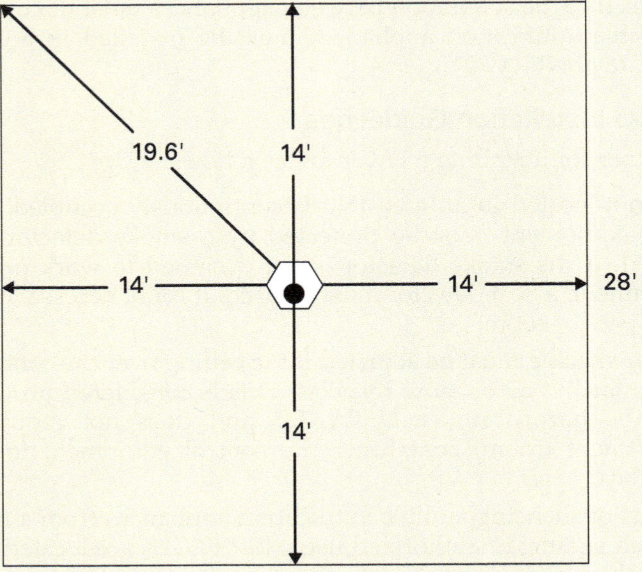

UL 1971 Listing

A UL 1971 listing for a visual notification appliance indicates that it meets the ADA hearing-impaired requirements.

5.4.0 Systems Related to Fire Alarms

This section discusses various systems related to fire alarms, as well as the installation guidelines for each.

5.4.1 Ancillary Control Relay

Ancillary functions, commonly called *auxiliary functions*, include such controls as elevator capture (recall), elevator shaft pressurization, HVAC system shutdown, stairwell pressurization, smoke management systems, emergency lighting, door unlocking, door hold-open device control, and building music system shutoff. For example, sound systems are commonly powered down by the fire alarm system so that the evacuation signal may be heard. In the normal state (*Figure 52*), an energized relay completes the power circuit to the device being controlled.

> **NOTE**
>
> The circuit from the relay to the background music system is a remote-control signaling circuit (see ***NEC Article 724***). If this circuit is both powered and controlled by the fire alarm, then it is a fire alarm circuit (see ***NEC Article 760***).

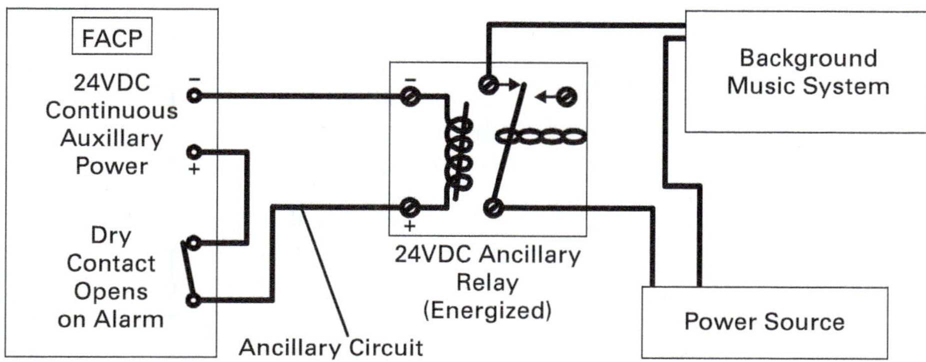

Figure 52 Music system control in normal state.

5.4.2 Duct Smoke Detectors

Duct smoke detectors are not simply conventional detectors applied to HVAC systems. Conventional smoke detectors are listed for open area protection (OAP) under UL 268. Duct smoke detectors are normally listed for a slightly higher velocity of air movement and are tested under UL 268A. The primary function of a duct smoke detector is for the control of smoke movement. This prevents the system from spreading smoke rapidly throughout the building and from providing a forced supply of oxygen to the fire. Duct smoke detectors are not intended primarily for early warning and notification. Relevant fire alarm-related provisions pertaining to HVAC systems can be found in NFPA 90A and NFPA 90B.

NFPA 90A covers the following types of buildings and systems:

- HVAC systems serving spaces over 25,000 ft^3 in volume (708 m^3)
- Buildings of Type III, IV, or V construction that are over three stories in height (NFPA 220)
- Buildings that are not covered by other applicable standards
- Buildings that serve occupants or processes not covered by other applicable standards

NFPA 90B covers the following types of systems:

- HVAC systems that service one- or two-family dwellings
- HVAC systems that service spaces not exceeding 25,000 ft^3 in volume (708 m^3)

> **NOTE**
>
> No duct smoke detector requirements are found under NFPA 90B.

When determining the location of duct detectors prior to installation, use the following guidelines:

- In HVAC units over 2,000 cubic feet per minute (cfm), or 57 cubic meters per minute, duct detectors must be installed on the supply side.
- Duct detectors must be located downstream of any air filters and upstream of any branch connection in the air supply.
- Duct detectors should be located upstream of any in-duct heating element.
- Duct detectors must be installed at each story prior to the common return connection and any recirculation of fresh air inlet in the air return of systems over 15,000 cfm (425 cubic meters per minute) serving more than one story.
- Return air system smoke detectors are not required when the entire space served by the HVAC system is protected by an automatic smoke detector system and when the HVAC is shut down upon activation of any of the smoke detectors.

TABLE 1 Conversions

Capacity Rating	CFM
1 ton / 12,000 Btu	400 cfm
5 tons / 60,000 Btu	2,000 cfm
37.5 tons / 450,000 Btu	15,000 cfm

The approximations given in *Table 1* are useful when the protected-premises personnel do not know the cfm rating of an air handling unit (AHU) but do know either the tonnage (ton) or British thermal unit (Btu) rating. Additionally, the cfm rating may not always appear on AHU nameplates or in building specifications.

When more than one AHU is used to supply air to a common space, and the return air is drawn from this common space, the total capacity of all units must be used in determining the size of the HVAC system (*Figure 53*). This interpretation makes clear the fact that interconnected AHUs should be viewed as a system, as opposed to treating each AHU individually. When multiple AHUs serve a common space, the physical location of each AHU, relative to others interconnected to the same space, is irrelevant to the application of the formal interpretation.

The common space being served by multiple AHUs need not be contiguous (connected) for the interpretation to apply. In *Figure 54*, AHUs #3 and #4 serve a common space and must be added together for consideration (1,100 cfm + 1,100 cfm = 2,200 cfm). Because 2,200 cfm is greater than 2,000 cfm, duct smoke detectors are required on both. The same is true for AHUs #1 and #2.

Duct smoke detectors may not be used as substitutes where open area detectors are required. This is because the HVAC unit may not be running when a fire occurs. Even if the fan is always on, the HVAC is not a listed fire alarm device.

Duct smoke detectors must automatically stop their respective fans upon detecting smoke. It is also acceptable for the FACU to stop the fan(s) upon activation of the duct detector. However, fans that are part of an engineered smoke control or management system are an exception and are not always shut down when smoke is detected.

Remote Duct Smoke Indicator

Duct smoke indicators include a horn, as well as a test and reset function. LEDs on the device provide a visual indication of system conditions. This unit is also equipped with an optional strobe and smoke lens that provides an enhanced visual indication of an alarm.

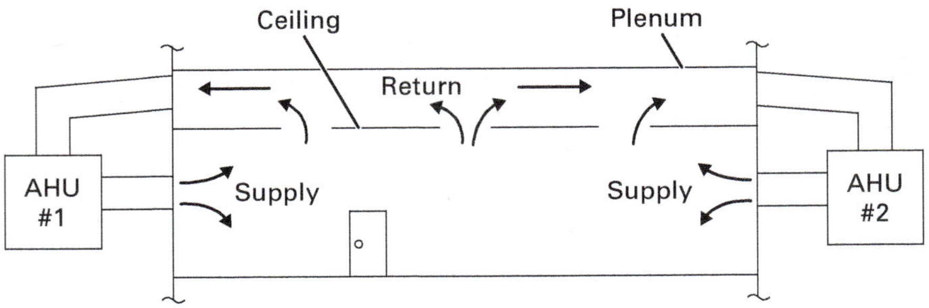

Figure 53 Non-ducted multiple AHU system.

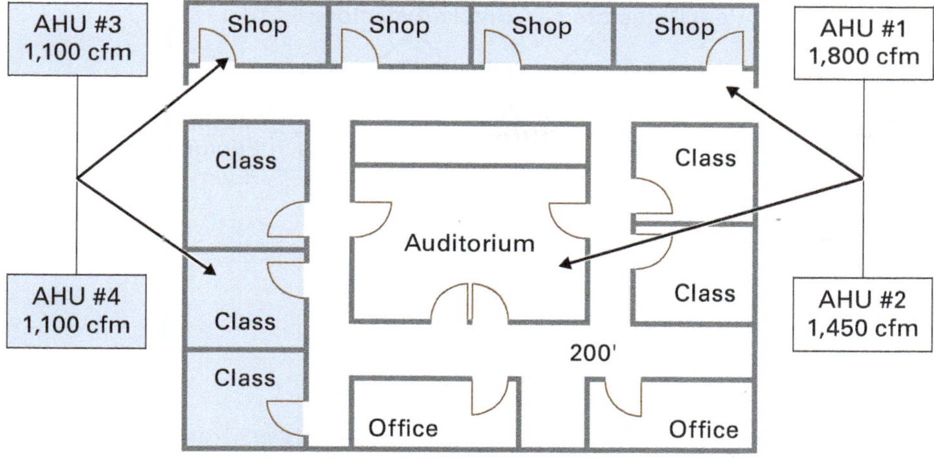

Figure 54 Example in which all AHUs require detectors on the supply side.

When a fire alarm system is installed in a building, all duct smoke detectors in that building must be connected to the fire alarm system as either initiating devices or supervisory devices. However, the code does not require the installation of a building fire alarm system. It does require that the duct smoke detectors be connected to the building fire alarm, if one exists. Duct smoke detectors, properly listed and installed, will accomplish their intended function when connected as initiating or supervisory devices.

When the building is not equipped with a fire alarm system, visual and audible alarm and trouble signal indicators (*Figure 55*) must be installed in a normally occupied area. Smoke detectors whose sole function is stopping fans do not require standby power.

AHUs often come with factory-installed duct detectors. If installed in a building with a fire alarm system, they must be connected to the fire alarm system, and the detector may require standby power. Consult with the AHJ concerning how many duct detectors can be placed in a zone. If it cannot be determined which detector activated after the power failure, the alarm indicator on the detector may be considered an additional function by the local AHJ.

Duct detectors for fresh air or return air ducts should be located 6–10 duct widths from any openings, deflectors, sharp bends, or branch connections. This is necessary to obtain a representative air sample and reduce the effects of stratification and dead air space.

Figure 55 Typical remote duct indicator.
Source: System Sensor

5.4.3 Elevator Recall

Elevator recall is intended to route an elevator car to a non-fire floor, open its doors, and put the car out of normal service until reset (Phase 1 recall). It is usually assumed that the recall floor will be the level of primary exit discharge or a grade level exit. In the event that the primary level of exit discharge is the floor where the fire has been detected, the system should route the car to a predetermined alternate floor, open its doors, and go out of normal service (Phase 2 recall). The operation of the elevators must be in accordance with *ANSI A17.1*.

Phase 1 recall (*Figure 56*) is the method of recalling the elevator to the floor that provides the highest probability of safe evacuation in the event of a fire emergency, as determined by the AHJ.

Phase 2 recall (*Figure 57*) is the method of recalling the elevator to the floor that provides the next highest probability of safe evacuation, after Phase 1, in the event of a fire emergency, as determined by the AHJ. Phase 2 recall is typically activated by the smoke detector in the lobby where the elevator would normally report during a Phase 1 recall.

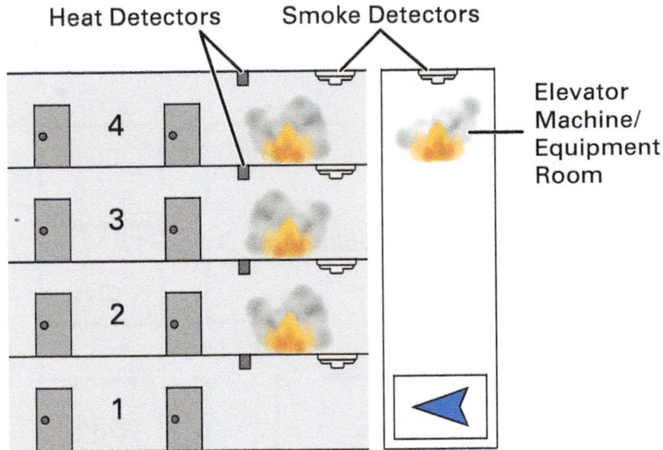

Figure 56 Phase 1 recall.

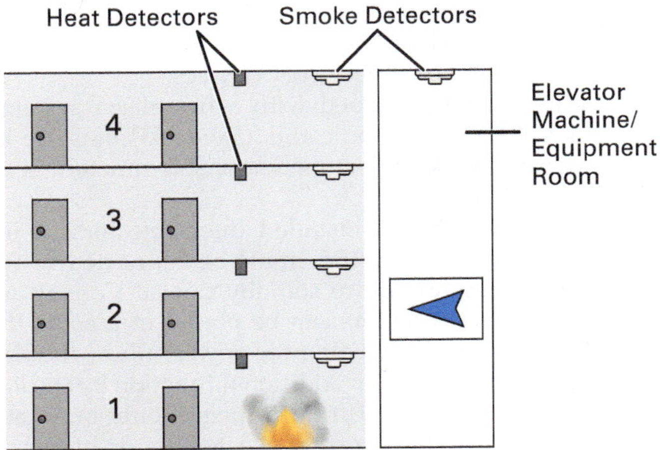

Figure 57 Phase 2 recall.

Hoistway and elevator machine room smoke detectors must report an alarm condition to a building FACU, as well as an indicator light in the elevator car itself. However, notification devices may not be required to be activated if the control unit is in a constantly attended location. In facilities without a building fire alarm system, these smoke detectors must be connected to a dedicated FACU that must be designated as an Elevator Recall Control and Supervisory Panel.

Elevator recall must be initiated only by elevator lobby, elevator hoistway, and elevator machine room smoke detectors. Activation of manual pull stations, heat detectors, duct detectors, and any smoke detector not mentioned previously must not initiate elevator recall. In many systems, it would be inappropriate for the FACU to initiate elevator recall. An exception is any system where the control function is selectable or programmable and the configuration limits the recall function to the specified detector activation only.

Caution should be used when using two-wire smoke detectors to recall elevators. Each elevator lobby, elevator hoistway, and elevator machine room smoke detector must be capable of initiating elevator recall when all other devices on the same **initiating device circuit (IDC)** have been manually or automatically placed in the alarm condition.

Initiating device circuit (IDC): A circuit to which automatic or manual signal initiating devices are connected, such as fire alarm manual boxes (pull stations), heat and smoke detectors, and waterflow alarm devices.

Unless the area encompassing the elevator lobby is a part of a compartment being protected by smoke detectors, such as the continuation of a corridor, the smoke detectors serving the elevator lobby (*Figure 58*) may be applied to protect against a specific hazard per NFPA 72®. The elevator lobby, elevator hoistway, or associated elevator machine room detectors may also be used to activate emergency control functions as permitted by NFPA 101®.

Where ambient conditions prohibit installation of automatic smoke detection, other appropriate automatic fire detection must be permitted. For example, a heat detector may protect an elevator door that opens to a high-dust or low-temperature area. Always refer to local codes.

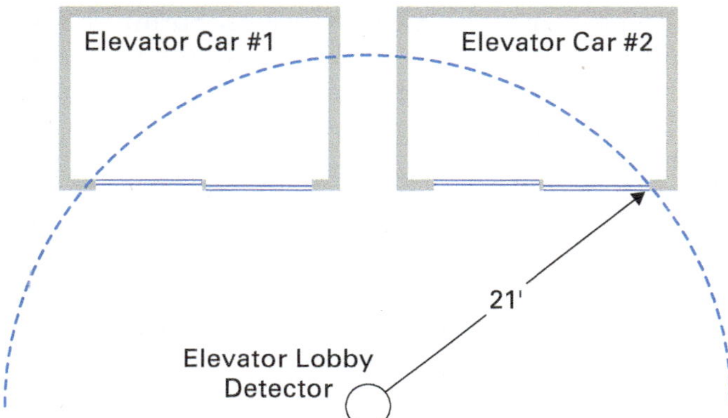

Assumes a 30' listed detector on a smooth and flat ceiling. Target protection should be the extreme edges of the elevator door opening.

Figure 58 Elevator lobby detector.

5.4.4 Special Door Locking Arrangements

No lock, padlock, hasp, bar, chain, or other device intended to prevent free exiting may be used at any door on which panic or fire exit hardware is required (NFPA 101®). Note that these requirements apply only to exiting from the building. There is no restriction on locking doors against unrestricted entry from the exterior.

Upon activation of the fire alarm, stair enclosure doors must unlock to permit exiting. They must also unlock to permit reentry into the building floors. This provision applies to buildings four stories and taller. The purpose of this requirement is to provide for an escape from fire and smoke entering a lower level of the stair enclosure and blocking safe departure. See NFPA 101® for additional details and exceptions.

5.4.5 Suppression Systems

There are dry and wet chemical extinguishing systems, and this section discusses both.

Dry chemical extinguishing systems must be connected to the building fire alarm system if a fire alarm system exists in the structure. The extinguishing system must be connected as an initiating device. The standard (NFPA 17, *Standard for Dry Chemical Extinguishing Systems*) does not require the installation of a building fire alarm system if one was not required elsewhere. Also see NFPA 12 (*Standard onCarbon Dioxide Extinguishing Systems*), NFPA 12A (*Standard on Halon 1301 Fire Extinguishing Systems*), and NFPA 2001 (*Standard on Clean Agent Fire Extinguishing Systems*).

Wet chemical extinguishing systems must be connected to the building fire alarm system if a fire alarm system exists in the structure. As with dry chemical extinguishing systems, the standard (NFPA 17A, *Standard for Wet Chemical Extinguishing Systems*) does not require the installation of a building fire alarm system. Also, see NFPA 16 (*Standard for the Installation of Foam-Water Sprinkler and Foam-Water Spray Systems*).

5.4.6 Supervision of Suppression Systems

Each of the occupancy chapters of NFPA 101® will specify the extinguishing requirements for that occupancy. The code will specify either an approved automatic sprinkler or an approved supervised automatic sprinkler system if a sprinkler system is required.

Where a supervised automatic sprinkler is required, various sections of NFPA 101® are applicable. These code sections begin with the phrase, "Where required by another section of this code." Use of the word *supervised* in the extinguishing requirement section of each occupancy chapter is the method used to implement these two provisions. Sprinkler systems do not automatically require electronic supervision. Supervised automatic sprinkler systems require a distinct supervisory signal. This signal indicates a condition that would impair the proper operation of the sprinkler system and is received at a location constantly attended by qualified personnel or at an approved remote monitoring facility However, when the supervisory signal terminates on a protected premises in areas that are constantly attended by trained personnel, the supervisory signal is not required to be transmitted to a monitoring facility. In such cases, only alarm and trouble signals need to be transmitted. Further, waterflow alarms from a supervised automatic sprinkler system must be transmitted to an approved monitoring station.

The following are some of the sprinkler elements that are required to be supervised where applicable:

- Water supply control valves
- Fire pump power (including phase monitoring)
- Fire pump running
- Water tank levels
- Water tank temperatures
- Water tank pressures
- Air pressure of dry-pipe systems

A sprinkler flow alarm must be initiated within 90 seconds of water flow equal to or greater than the flow from the sprinkler or the smallest orifice (opening) size in the system. The smallest orifice is the size of the opening at the smallest sprinkler. In actual field verification activities, the 90 seconds is measured from the time water begins to flow into the inspector's test drain, *not* from the time the inspector's test valve is opened.

Sprinkler systems that initiate a fire alarm system by a waterflow switch must include at least one manual station that is located where required by the AHJ. Manual stations required elsewhere in the codes or standards can be considered to meet this requirement. Some occupancy chapters of NFPA 101® will allow sprinkler flow switches to substitute for manual stations at all the required exits. If such an option is utilized, this provision requires that at least one manual station be installed where acceptable to the AHJ.

Each shutoff valve, also called an *outside screw and yoke (OS&Y) control valve, post indicator valve (PIV)*, or *butterfly valve*, must be supervised by a tamper switch. A distinctive signal must sound when the valve is moved from a fully open position to the off-normal position. This change must be detected within two revolutions of the hand wheel, or when the stem has moved $\frac{1}{5}$ from its normal open position. A common verification practice is to mark the 12 o'clock position on the valve in its normal (open) position, rotate the hand wheel twice, and stop at the 12 o'clock position on the second pass. The supervisory signal must be initiated by the time the wheel reaches the end of the second pass.

Waterflow and supervisory devices, in addition to their circuits, must be installed such that no unauthorized person may tamper with, open, remove, or disconnect them without initiating a signal. Publicly accessible junction boxes must have tamper-resistant screws or tamper-alarm switches. Most waterflow and valve tamper switch housings come from the manufacturer with tamper-resistant screws (hex or Allen head) and may be configured to signal when the housing cover is removed. If the device, circuit, or junction box requiring protection is in an area that is not accessible to unauthorized personnel, no additional protective measures should be required. Simply sealing, locking, or removing the handle from the valve is not sufficient to meet the supervision requirement.

Waterflow devices that are alarm initiating devices cannot be connected on the same initiating circuit as valve supervisory devices. This is commonly done in violation of the code by connecting the valve tamper switch in series with the initiating circuit's EOL device, resulting in a trouble signal when activated. This method of wiring does not provide for a distinctive visual or audible signal. This statement is true for most conventional systems. It should be noted that at least one known addressable system has a listed module capable of distinctly separating the two types of signals. These devices must be wired on the same circuit to meet the standard.

NOTE

Addressable devices are not connected to initiating circuits. They are connected to signaling line circuits.

A supervisory signal must be visually and audibly distinctive from both alarm and trouble signals. It must be possible to tell the difference between a fire alarm signal, a valve being off-normal (closed), and an open (broken wire) in the circuit.

Where a high-rise building is protected throughout by an approved, supervised automatic sprinkler system, valve supervision and waterflow devices must be provided on each floor (NFPA 101®). In such buildings, a fire command center (central control system) is also required (NFPA 101®). Fire-resistive cable systems may be required (*NEC Article 728*).

Fire Pumps

A fire pump system is necessary when the available water supply is not adequate, in pressure or volume, to supply the fire suppression water needs of a sprinkler or standpipe system. The fire pump system comprises several components, including the pump, a driver (typically electric or diesel), and a controller. A typical fire pump system is shown.

Source: John Viola

5.5.0 Troubleshooting

The troubleshooting approach to any fire alarm system is basically the same. Regardless of the situation or equipment, some basic steps can be followed to isolate problems:

Step 1 Know the equipment. For easy reference, keep specification sheets and instructions for commonly used and serviced equipment. Become familiar with the features of the equipment.

Step 2 Determine the symptoms. Try to make the system perform or fail to perform as it did when the problem was discovered.

Step 3 List possible causes. Write down everything that could possibly have caused the problem.

Step 4 Check the system systematically. Plan activities so that problem areas are not overlooked to eliminate wasted time.

Step 5 Correct the problem. Once the problem has been located, repair it. If it is a component that cannot be repaired easily, replace it.

Step 6 Test the system. After the initial problem has been corrected, thoroughly check all the functions and features of the system to ensure other problems that could have been masked by the initial problem are not present.

5.5.1 Alarm System Troubleshooting Guidelines

A system troubleshooting chart is shown in *Figure 59*. In *Figure 60*, an alarm output troubleshooting chart is shown. Finally, in *Figure 61* an auxiliary power troubleshooting chart is shown.

The following guidelines provide information for resolving potential problems for specific conditions:

- *Sensors* — Always check sensor power, connections, environment, and settings. Lack of detection can be caused by a loose connection, obstacles in the sensor area, or a faulty unit. If unwanted alarms occur, recheck the installation for changing environmental factors. If none are present, cover or seal the sensor to confirm that the alarm originated with the sensor. If alarms still occur, wiring problems, power problems, or electromagnetic interference (EMI) could be the cause. If the alarm stops when the sensor is covered or sealed, the environment monitored by the sensor is the source of the problem. Replacing the unit should be the last resort after performing the above checks.
- *Open circuit problems* — Open circuits will cause trouble signals and account for the largest percentage of faults. Major causes of open circuits are loose connections, wire breaks (ripped or cut), staple cuts, bad splices, cold-solder joints, wire fatigue due to flexing, and defective wire.
- *Short circuit or* **ground fault** *problems* — Short circuits or ground faults will cause alarms or trouble signals. Events occurring past a short will not be seen by the system. Some of the common causes of shorts or ground faults are staple cuts, sharp edge cuts, improper splices, moisture, and cold flow of wiring insulation.

Ground fault: A condition in which the resistance between a conductor and ground reaches an unacceptably low level.

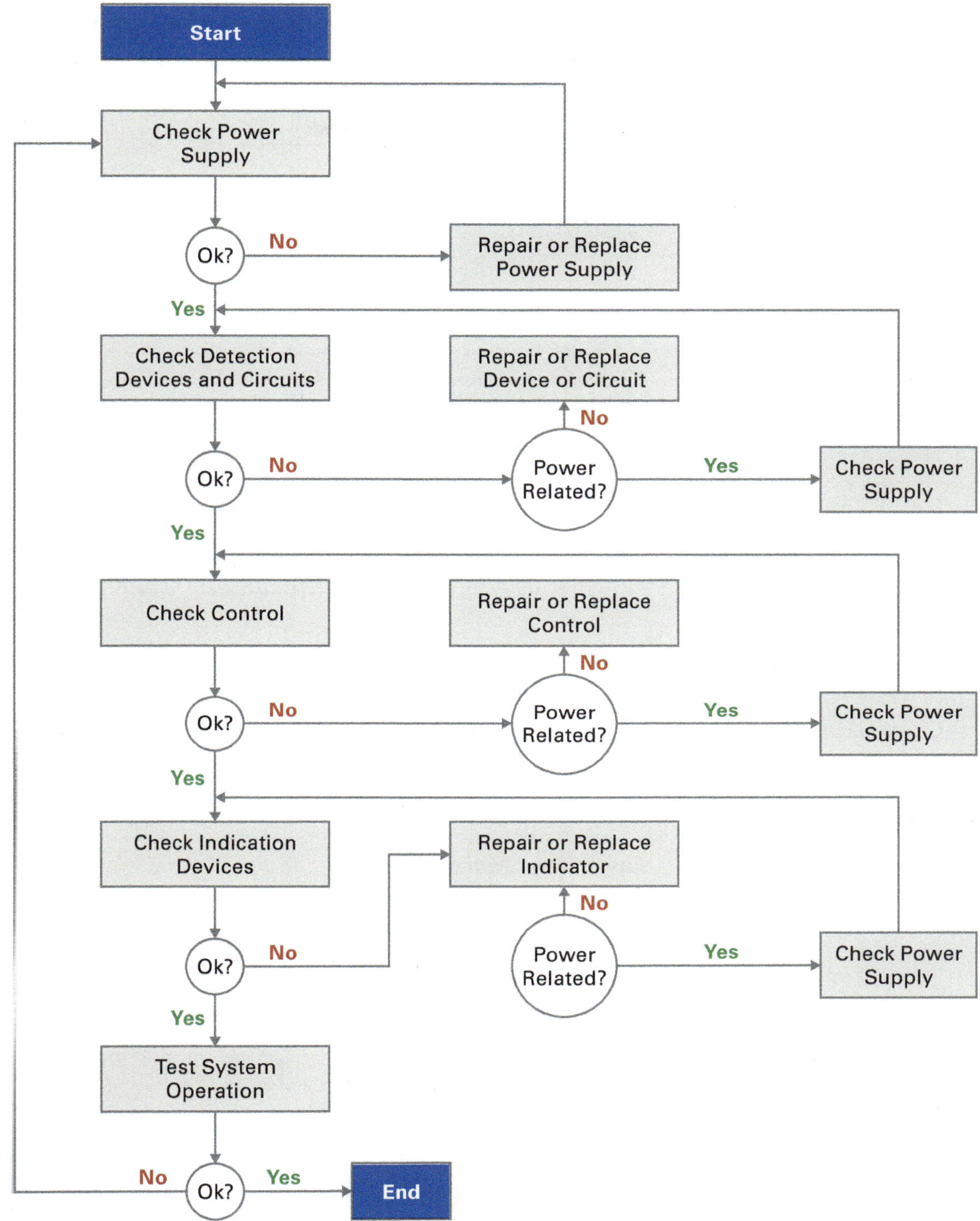

Figure 59 System troubleshooting chart.

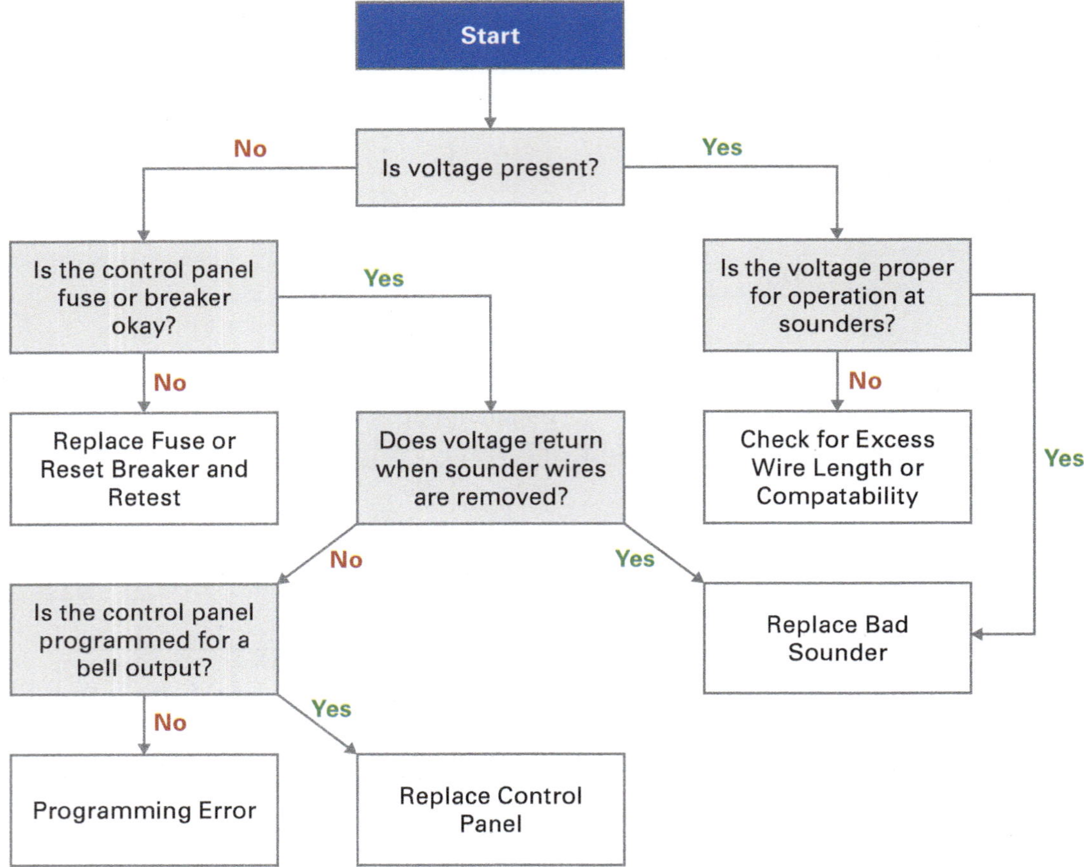

Figure 60 Alarm output troubleshooting chart.

Supervisory Switches

This supervisory switch is typical of those used with sprinkler systems to provide a tamper indication of valve movement. The switch is mounted on a valve with the actuator arm normally resting against the movable target indicator assembly. If the normal position of the valve is altered, the valve stem moves, forcing the actuator arm to operate the switch. The switch activates between the first and second revolutions of the control valve wheel.

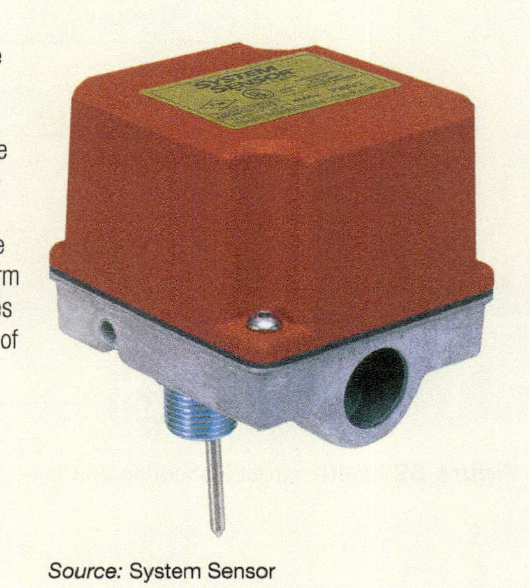

Source: System Sensor

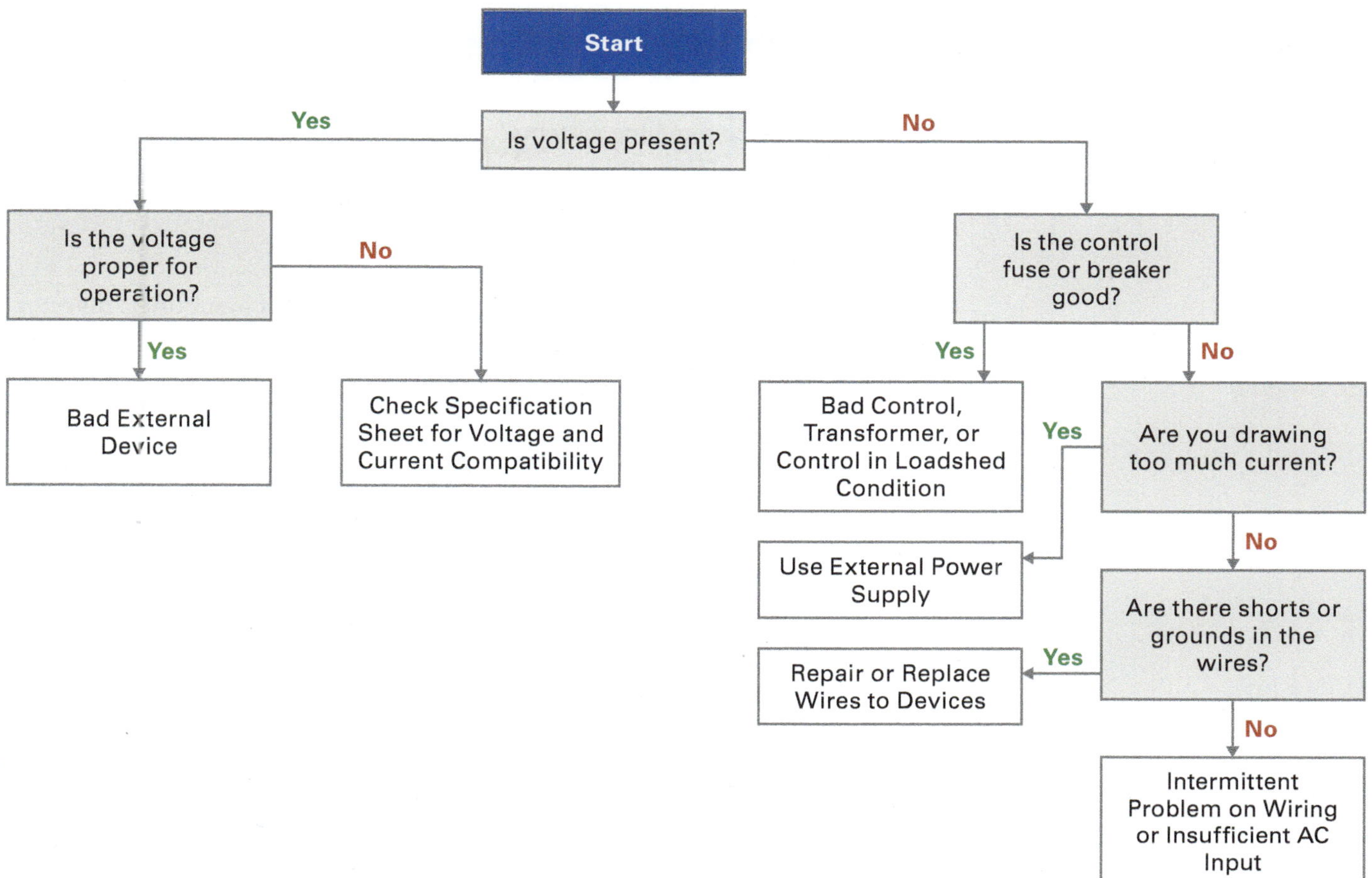

Figure 61 Auxiliary power troubleshooting chart.

5.5.2 Addressable System Troubleshooting Guidelines

There is a wide variety of designs, equipment, and configurations of addressable fire alarm systems. For this reason, some manufacturers of addressable systems provide troubleshooting data in their service literature, but other manufacturers do not. Most of the general guidelines for troubleshooting discussed earlier also apply to troubleshooting addressable systems. In the event general troubleshooting methods fail to find the problem and no troubleshooting information is provided by the manufacturer in the service literature for the equipment, the best thing to do is to contact the manufacturer and ask for technical assistance. This will prevent needless loss of time.

5.0.0 Section Review

1. Which electrical code specifies wiring methods and cables for fire protective signaling systems?
   a. *NEC Article 760*
   b. *NEC Article 770*
   c. *NEC Article 800*
   d. *NEC Article 810*

2. Which of the following is an *unacceptable* means of mounting a detector on gypsum drywall?
   a. Winged expansion anchors
   b. Toggle expansion anchors
   c. An electrical box
   d. Plastic masonry anchors

3. Which of the following fires will an IR detector *not* be able to sense?
   a. Wood
   b. Alcohol
   c. Gasoline
   d. Paper

4. Duct smoke detectors are governed by _____.
   a. UL 268A
   b. UL 1971
   c. NFPA 75
   d. NFPA 80

5. What is the *first* step in troubleshooting fire alarm equipment?
   a. Perform systematic tests.
   b. List the symptoms.
   c. Know the equipment.
   d. Make the system fail.

Module 26405-23 Review Questions

1. The specific requirements for wiring and wiring equipment installation for fire protective signaling systems are covered in _____.
   a. NFPA 1
   b. NFPA 70®
   c. NFPA 72®
   d. NFPA 101®

2. A code that was established to help fire authorities continually develop safeguards against fire hazards is _____.
   a. NFPA 1
   b. NFPA 70®
   c. NFPA 72®
   d. NFPA 101®

3. A defined area within the boundaries of a fire alarm system is known as a(n) _____.
   a. section
   b. signal destination
   c. alarm unit area
   d. zone

4. Most analog addressable systems operate on circuits consisting of _____.
   a. one conductor
   b. two conductors
   c. three conductors
   d. four conductors

5. An SLC that consists of a Class A main trunk with a Class B spur circuit is known as an SLC _____.
   a. dual circuit
   b. combined circuit
   c. twin circuit
   d. hybrid circuit

6. An automatic detector that draws air from the protected area back to the detector is called a(n) _____.
   a. line detector
   b. spot detector
   c. air sampling detector
   d. addressable detector

7. A heat detector that is *not* a fixed-temperature device is a _____.
   a. fusible link detector
   b. rate-of-rise detector
   c. quick metal detector
   d. bimetallic detector

8. Older type duct detectors used the _____.
   a. ionization principle
   b. light scattering principle
   c. light obscuration principle
   d. smoke rate compensation principle

9. The type of pull station that is restricted for use in special applications is the _____.
   a. single-action type
   b. glass-break type
   c. double-action type
   d. key-operated type

10. Primary power circuits supplying fire alarm systems must be protected by circuit breakers *not* larger than _____.
    a. 15A
    b. 20A
    c. 25A
    d. 30A

11. Fire warning system units for residential use must be listed in accordance with UL Standard _____.
    a. 780
    b. 864
    c. 985
    d. 995

12. Addressable systems commonly use a verification method called _____.
    a. positive alarm sequence
    b. wait and check
    c. reset and resample
    d. cross-zoning

13. The specified NFPA 72® Temporal-Three sound pattern for a fire alarm signal is _____.
    a. three short (half-second) tones, three long (1 second) tones, three short tones, a pause, then a repeat
    b. three long (1 second) tones, a pause, then a repeat
    c. three short (half-second) tones, a pause, then a repeat
    d. three short (half-second) tones, three long (1 second) tones, three short tones, three long tones, a pause, then a repeat

14. Public area audible notification devices must have a *minimum* dBA rating of _____.
    a. 65 at 10' (3 m)
    b. 75 at 10' (3 m)
    c. 85 at 10' (3 m)
    d. 95 at 10' (3 m)

15. The use of an attendant signal requires the approval of the _____.
    a. NFPA
    b. manufacturer
    c. UL
    d. AHJ

16. Commercial fire alarm cables that run from floor to floor must be rated at *least* as _____.
    a. general-purpose cable
    b. water-resistant cable
    c. riser cable
    d. plenum cable

17. Power-limited fire alarm circuit conductors must be separated from nonpower-limited fire alarm circuit conductors by at *least* _____.
    a. 2" (50 mm)
    b. 6" (150 mm)
    c. 12" (300 mm)
    d. 24" (600 mm)

18. For smoke compartment definition purposes, an archway that extends down 18" (450 mm) or more from the ceiling is considered the same as a(n) _____.
    a. barrier
    b. boundary
    c. open grid
    d. beam pocket

19. The primary function of a commercial duct smoke detector is to _____.
    a. sound an alarm for duct smoke
    b. shut down an associated HVAC system
    c. detect external open-area fires
    d. disable a music system for voice evacuation purposes

20. In a supervised automatic sprinkler system, a visual or audible supervisory signal *must* be _____.
    a. different from an alarm signal
    b. the same as an alarm signal
    c. different from a trouble signal
    d. different from both the alarm and trouble signals

Answers to odd-numbered Module Review Questions are found in *Appendix A*.

Module 26405-23 Supplemental Exercises

1. Provide the names of the NFPA codes listed below.
   - NFPA 1: __________
   - NFPA 70®: __________
   - NFPA 72®: __________
   - NFPA 101®: __________
2. True or False? Smoke detection devices in an analog addressable fire alarm system make the decision internally regarding their alarm state.
3. __________ is generally used as the actuating medium in a rate-of-rise with fusible link detector.
4. The two basic types of smoke detectors are the __________ and __________ types.
5. The melted and fused cable section in a(n) __________ detector must be replaced once it has been activated.
6. True or False? Primary power for a fire alarm system may be connected on the line side of the electrical main service disconnect switch.
7. A digital alarm communicator receiver (DACR) accepts and displays signals from a digital alarm communicator __________ sent over a PSTN.
8. True or False? Cables installed in plenums and other air handling spaces may be secured using standard cable tie wraps.
9. A manual fire alarm box (pull box) installed at an exit door should be installed near the __________.
10. True or False? Under normal conditions, smoke detectors should be installed after construction cleanup is completed.

Answers to odd-numbered Supplemental Exercises are found in *Appendix B*.

Answers to Section Review Questions

Answer	Section Reference	Objective
Section 1.0.0		
1. c	1.1.0	1a
2. b	1.2.1	1b
Section 2.0.0		
1. b	2.1.1	2a
2. d	2.2.3	2b
Section 3.0.0		
1. c	3.1.0	3a
2. b	3.2.2	3b
3. c	3.3.2	3c
Section 4.0.0		
1. b	4.1.1	4a
2. c	4.2.0	4b
3. a	4.3.2	4c
Section 5.0.0		
1. a	5.1.0	5a
2. d	5.2.4	5b
3. b	5.3.2	5c
4. a	5.4.2	5d
5. c	5.5.0	5e

User Update

Did you find an error? Submit a correction by visiting **https://www.nccer.org/olf** or by scanning the QR code using your mobile device.

Source: iStock@pelucco

Objectives

Successful completion of this module prepares you to do the following:

1. Identify and describe various types of transformers.
   a. Identify common transformer types.
   b. Explain how three-phase transformers can be wired internally.
   c. Identify types of specialty transformers.
2. Identify instrument transformers.
   a. Identify and describe the use of current transformers.
   b. Identify and describe the use of potential transformers.
3. Define harmonics and explain how harmonic issues are identified and resolved.
   a. Describe the common sources of harmonics in office buildings and industrial plants.
   b. Explain how to survey a system to identify the source of harmonics.
   c. Explain how to resolve harmonics.

Performance Tasks

Under supervision, you should be able to do the following:

1. Connect a buck-and-boost transformer to a single-phase circuit so that it will first be in the boost mode and then in the buck mode. Record the voltage increase and decrease for each configuration.
2. Using a clamp-on ammeter, demonstrate the principles of a current transformer, identify the primary winding, and then calculate and measure the effects of increasing the number of turns (loops) in the secondary winding.

Overview

Transformers are used to increase or decrease voltage coming from a power source. They can be constructed in a variety of configurations for different applications. This module covers various types of transformers, and provides information on selecting, sizing, and installing them.

NOTE

Digital Resources for Electrical

Scan this code using the camera on your phone or mobile device to view the digital resources related to this craft.

1.0.0 Identifying Transformers

Objective

Identify and describe various types of transformers.

a. Identify common transformer types.
b. Explain how three-phase transformers can be wired internally.
c. Identify types of specialty transformers.

Performance Task

1. Connect a buck-and-boost transformer to a single-phase circuit so that it will first be in the boost mode and then in the buck mode. Record the voltage increase and decrease for each configuration.

When the AC voltage needed for an application is lower or higher than the voltage available from the source, a transformer is used. The essential parts of a transformer are the primary winding (which is connected to the source) and the secondary winding (which is connected to the load), both wound on an iron core. The two windings are not physically connected.

The alternating voltage in the primary winding induces an alternating voltage in the secondary winding. The ratio of the primary and secondary voltages is equal to the ratio of the number of turns in the primary and secondary windings.

Transformers may step up the voltage applied to the primary winding and have a higher voltage at the secondary terminals, or they may step down the voltage applied to the primary winding and have a lower voltage at the secondary terminals.

A transformer can be constructed as a single-phase or three-phase apparatus. A three-phase transformer (*Figure 1*) has three primary and three secondary windings, which may be connected in either a delta (Δ) or wye (Y) configuration. Combinations such as Δ-Δ, Δ-Y, Y-Δ, and Y-Y are possible. The first letter indicates the connection of the primary winding, and the second letter indicates that of the secondary winding.

A **bank** of three single-phase transformers can serve the same purpose as one three-phase transformer. The connections between the three primary windings and the three secondary windings are delta or wye and are available in all combinations.

NOTE

Transformers are applied in AC systems only and would not work in DC systems because the induction of voltage depends on the rate of change in the current.

Bank: An installed grouping of several units of the same electrical equipment type, such as a bank of transformers, a bank of capacitors, or a meter bank.

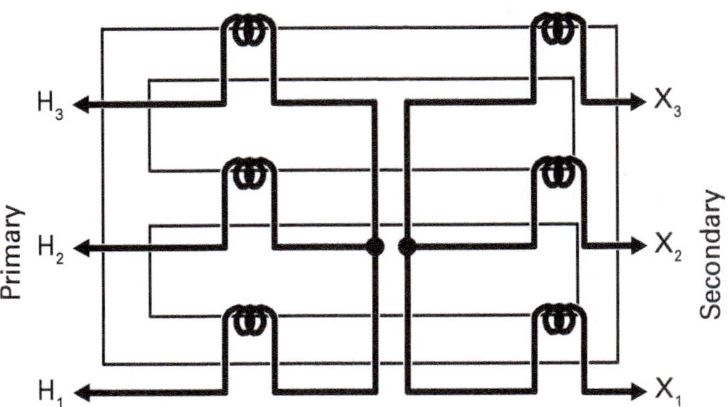

Figure 1 Typical three-phase transformer.

1.1.0 Common Transformers

The principle of operation is the same for all transformers, but the forms, connections, and auxiliary devices differ widely.

Large transformers used in transmission systems are called *power transformers*. They may step up the voltage produced in the generator to make it suitable for commercial transmission, or they may step down the voltage in a transmission line to make it practical for distribution. Power transformers are usually installed outdoors in generating stations and substations. The transformer shown in *Figure 2* is a liquid-cooled power transformer with radiators that disperse the heat from the transformer.

Figure 2 Typical liquid-cooled, three-phase power transformer.
Source: iStock@danielsbfoto

An **autotransformer** is a transformer with only one winding, which serves as both a primary and a secondary. Autotransformers are economical, space-efficient, and especially practical if the difference between the primary and secondary voltages is relatively small. The application of an autotransformer is a good choice when a 480Y/277V or 208Y/120V, three-phase, four-wire distribution system is used.

Autotransformer: Any transformer in which the primary and secondary connections are made to a single winding.

Three-winding transformers have two secondary windings so that they can deliver two different secondary voltages.

In many applications of electrical measuring instruments, the voltage or current in the circuit to be measured is too high for the instruments. In such situations, instrument transformers are used to ensure safe operation of the instruments. An instrument transformer is either a *current transformer* (*Figure 3*) or a *potential transformer* (*Figure 4*).

For example, if the current in a line is approximately 100A and the ammeter is rated at 5A, a bar-type current transformer with a current ratio of 100:5 can be connected in series with the line. The secondary winding is then connected to the ammeter. The current in the secondary is proportional to the current in the line. With a toroid current transformer, an insulated line passes through the center, and proportional current is induced in the toroid winding for application to the meter.

Similarly, the potential transformer reduces the voltage in a high-voltage line to 120V, for which the voltmeter is normally rated. The potential transformer is always connected across the line to be measured. Sometimes it is important to indicate the polarity of the current in both the instrument and the transformer. The polarity is the instantaneous direction of current at a specific moment. Wires with the same polarity usually contain a small black block or cross in electrical diagrams (*Figure 4*).

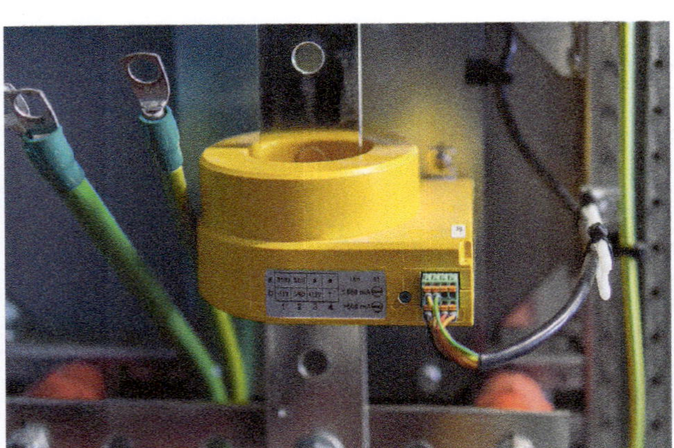

Figure 3 Current transformer monitoring current on a busbar.
Source: ShutterStock@SB7

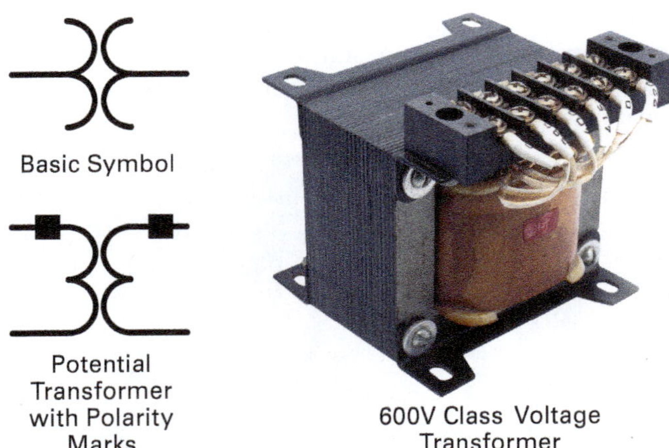

Figure 4 Potential transformer.
Source: Shutterstock@Ph.wittaya (Right)

Transformer Management Systems

Some manufacturers provide monitoring and diagnostic systems for large liquid-cooled power transformers used in substations or in large industrial applications. These systems are used to obtain warnings of impending faults and as a predictor for scheduling maintenance shutdowns. The systems use data from sensors incorporated in the transformers. The sensors monitor the following conditions:

- Dissolved gas in oil
- Top and bottom oil temperature
- Gas pressure
- Ambient temperature
- Oil level
- Winding temperature
- Load and meter values
- Bushing activity

This data is transmitted via a network to a computer and used with IEEE or IEC analytical modeling software offline to access the condition of the equipment and diagnose impending failures. This includes moisture-in-insulation modeling, predictive insulation aging rate, cumulative aging, partial discharge activity, overflux (overvoltage), fault event recording, harmonic monitoring, cooling system efficiency, and other trending information.

1.2.0 Connections in Three-Phase Transformers

Various combinations of primary and secondary three-phase voltages are possible with the proper combination of delta and wye internal connections of three-phase transformers or with banks of single-phase transformers.

Some common power transformer connections are shown in *Figure 5*. In all examples, it is assumed that the primary line voltages between lines A, B, and C are all 1,000V and that the transformation ratio is 10:1. The primary connections are shown by the upper three windings, and the Δ or Y next to the winding indicates how the winding is connected.

In the delta connections, as in *Figure 5* (A) and *Figure 5* (D), the phase voltages of the primaries are the same as the line voltage or 1,000V. In the Y connections of the primaries, as in *Figure 5* (B) and *Figure 5* (C), the phase voltages are 0.577 times the line voltages or 577V. The wye point (N) is indicated as a common point if the windings are wye connected.

The secondaries are shown in the lower row of windings. Each secondary phase winding has only $^1/_{10}$ of the turns used in the corresponding primary phase winding. Therefore, the secondary phase winding supplies a phase voltage that is $^1/_{10}$ of the primary phase voltage. In *Figure 5* (A) and *Figure 5* (D), the secondary phase voltages are 1,000 ÷ 10 = 100V, and in *Figure 5* (B) and *Figure 5* (C), they are 577 ÷ 10 = 57.7V. The secondaries are delta connected in *Figure 5* (A) and *Figure 5* (C), and their line voltages or the voltages between the secondary line wires (a, b, and c) are the same as the secondary phase windings. When the secondaries are wye connected, as in *Figure 5* (B) and *Figure 5* (D), they have a common wye point (N) and the secondary line voltages are 1.732 times the phase voltage. In *Figure 5* (B), the voltages between lines a, b, and c are 1.732 × 57.7 = 100V, and in *Figure 5* (D), they are 1.732 × 100 = 173V. In addition, a fourth secondary wire (n) is brought out from the wye point (N) in *Figure 5* (D), and the secondary voltage between any of the lines (a, b, or c and n) is equal to the secondary phase voltage or 100V.

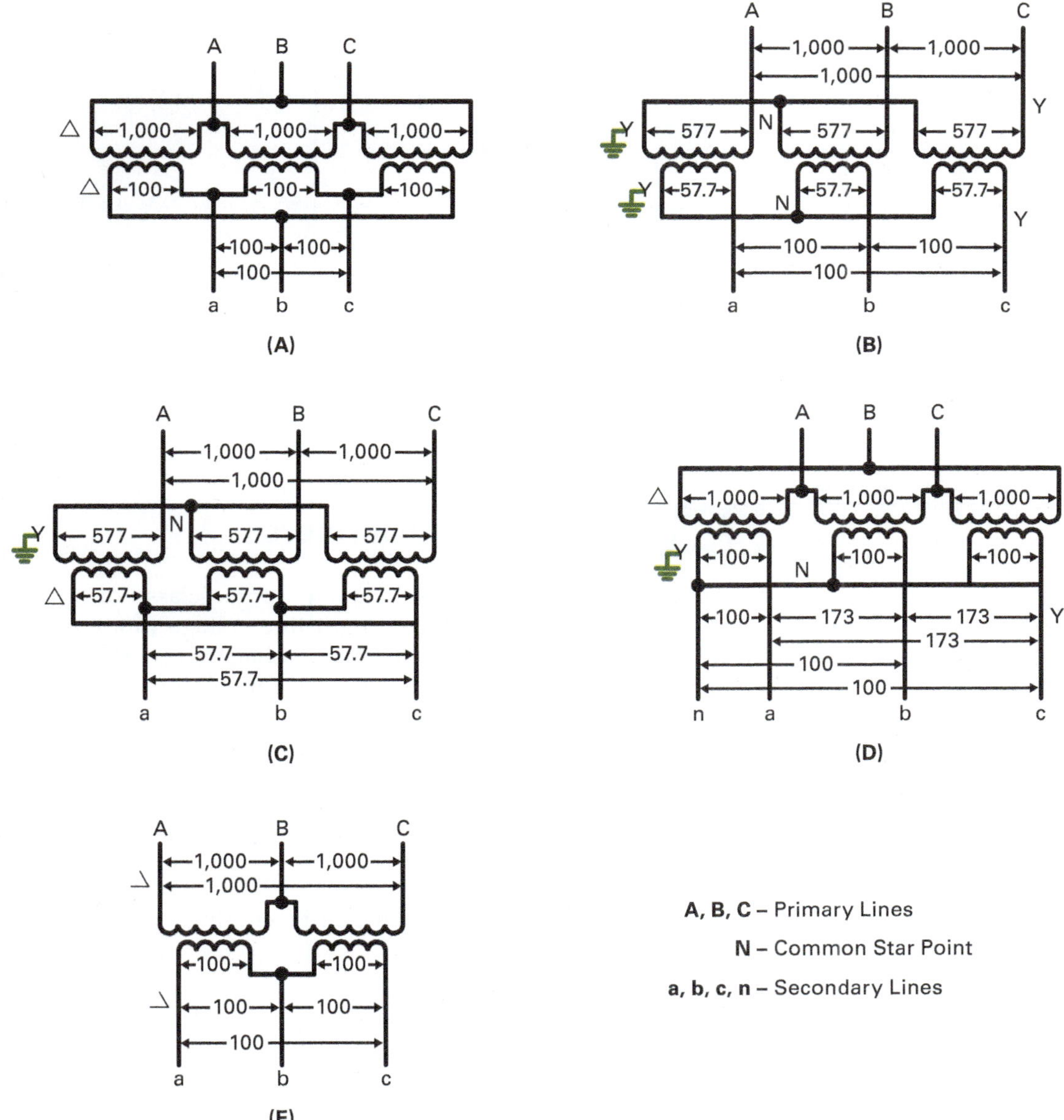

Figure 5 Common power transformer connections.

As you become more experienced in reading electrical diagrams, you should be able to immediately recognize the differences between delta and wye connections in any three-phase system. If the three windings have a common point, it is a wye connection, and the line voltages are 1.732 times higher than the individual phase voltages. If the three windings build a closed path, it is a delta connection, and the line voltages are the same as the phase voltages.

A connection using two single-phase transformers for a three-phase system is shown in *Figure 5* (E). This is an open delta connection that provides a three-phase secondary with only two transformers.

Maintenance Testing of Transformers

In commercial or industrial applications involving large liquid-cooled or dry transformers that are not automatically monitored, manual periodic preventive maintenance testing and performance trending is normally instituted in a manner like that for large motors. These tests include liquid dielectric tests to measure the breakdown voltage of samples of insulating fluids from transformers and DC hi-pot tests of transformer winding insulation.

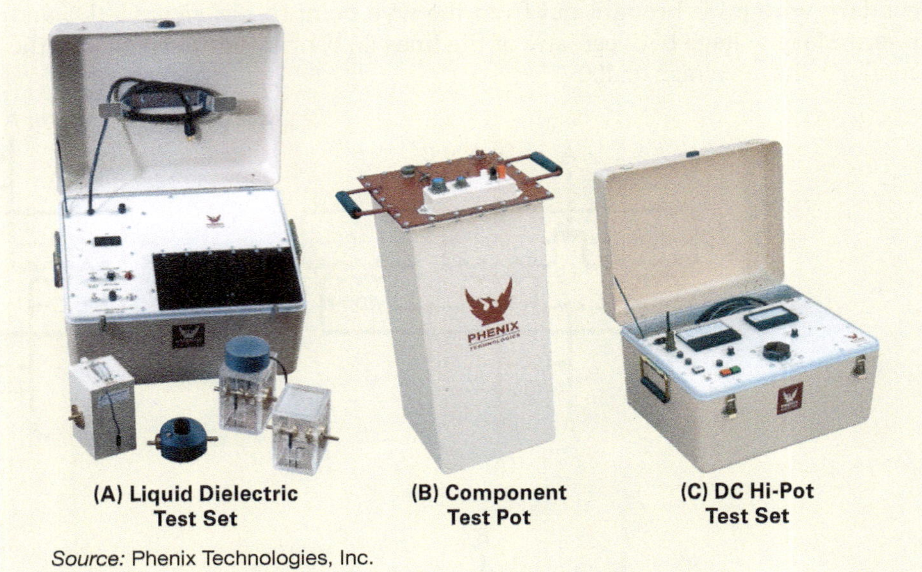

(A) Liquid Dielectric Test Set **(B) Component Test Pot** **(C) DC Hi-Pot Test Set**

Source: Phenix Technologies, Inc.

1.3.0 Specialty Transformers

Specialty transformers make up a large class of transformers and autotransformers used for changing a line voltage to a particular value best adapted to the load device. The primary voltage is generally 600V or less. Many special step-down transformers are used for small work, such as doorbells or other signaling systems, battery-charging rectifiers, and individual low-voltage lamps. Most specialty transformers are self-cooled and air-insulated. Sometimes the cases are filled with a special compound to prevent moisture absorption and to conduct heat to the enclosing structure.

The following transformers are designed for a specific purpose:

- Single-phase transformers with two secondaries
- Single-phase transformers with three windings
- Autotransformers
- Constant-current transformers
- Series transformers
- Rectifier transformers
- Network transformers
- Step-voltage regulators

The following are examples of applications for specialty transformers:

- Sign-lighting transformers in which 120V is stepped down to 25V for low-voltage tungsten sign lamps
- Arc-lamp autotransformers in which 240V is stepped down to the voltage required for best operation of the arc
- Transformers used to change 240V power to 120V for operating portable tools, fans, and welders
- Transformers that step 120V up between 2,000V and 15,000V for the operation of neon signs

1.3.1 Transformers with Multiple Secondaries

One common type of transformer is a single-phase transformer with two secondaries (*Figure 6*). The first secondary has terminals X_1 and X_2 and is connected internally in series with the other secondary, which has terminals X_3 and X_4. Terminals X_1 and X_4 are connected to outside leads, and terminals X_2 and X_3 are connected together, with the junction point connected to a third outside lead. Such transformers are commonly used as distribution transformers where three-wire service is needed from a two-wire, single-phase supply.

The rated secondary voltage (120V in *Figure 6*) is obtained between either outside lead and the middle lead or neutral. In addition, double voltage (240V in *Figure 6*) is available between the two outside leads. This higher voltage is usually needed for HVAC equipment, electric ranges, and dryers, while lamps and small appliances are operated on 120V.

Figure 6 Single-phase transformer with two secondaries.

1.3.2 Three-Winding Transformers

Another widely used type of transformer is a three-winding transformer. A third winding can be added to a transformer, and voltages are induced in this winding proportional to the number of turns, the same as in the other windings. Theoretically, there is no limit to the number of windings that may be provided in a transformer. Practically, however, there is a limit because of the greater complexity, and transformers are rarely provided with more than four windings.

Three-winding transformers are used when transmission voltage is stepped down to produce two secondary voltages. For example, a transformation may be desired from 230 kV down to 69 kV and 34.5 kV to feed separate distribution networks.

Three-winding transformers are built in the same way as two-winding transformers, and they may be either the core or shell types. In the core construction, the additional winding is usually arranged so that it is concentric with the other two. In a shell transformer, the third winding is interleaved with the other two, which makes it more flexible than the core form.

Multiple-Secondary Transformers

The two multiple-secondary transformers in the image are liquid-filled for cooling and insulation purposes and have internal, manually switched voltage taps. They are used for single-phase residential 120V/240V service.

(A) Pad-Mounted Transformer

(B) Pole-Mounted Transformer

Source: Tim Dean (B)

Three-Winding Control Transformers

Small three-winding transformers may be used in control systems. The one in the image has separate 24V and 26V secondary windings and a 120V primary winding.

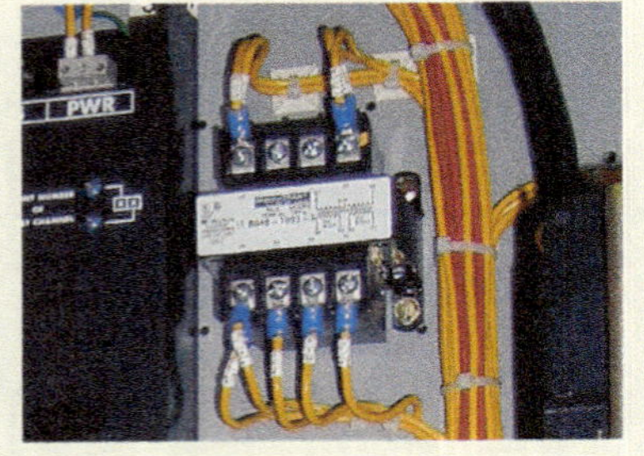

1.3.3 Autotransformers

The usual transformer has two windings that are not physically connected. In an autotransformer, one of the windings is connected in series with the other, thereby forming the equivalent of a single winding (*Figure 7*). This illustration represents a step-up autotransformer, so called because the secondary voltage is higher than the voltage supplied to the primary.

The primary voltage (E_P) is applied to the primary or common winding. The secondary or series winding is connected in series with the primary at the junction terminal. This point may be obtained by a tap, which will divide a single winding into a primary and a secondary.

A voltage induced in the secondary winding adds to the voltage in the primary winding, and the secondary voltage (E_S) is higher than the applied voltage. The ratio of transformation depends on the turns ratio, as in a two-winding transformer.

The primary current (I_P) branches into current I_C through the common winding and the current I_S through the series winding, as indicated by the arrows in *Figure 7*. The values of currents I_C and I_S are inversely proportional to the ratio of turns in the two windings and the primary current ($I_P = I_S + I_C$). Because the currents I_S and I_C oppose each other, the secondary current is lower than the primary current.

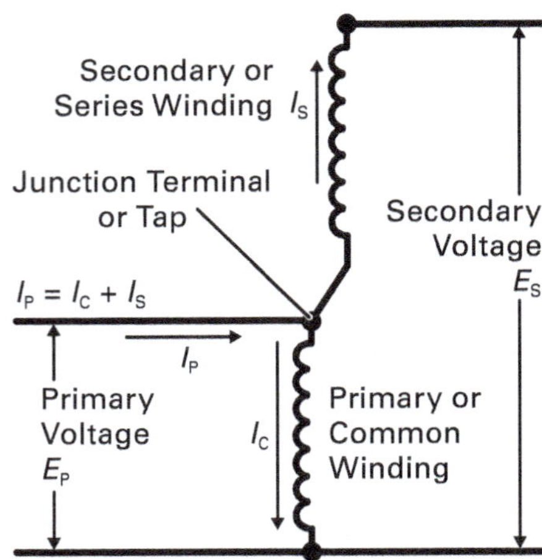

Figure 7 Wiring diagram of a typical autotransformer.

Autotransformers may be used economically to connect individual loads requiring voltages other than those available in the distribution system. An example would be increasing the voltage on a branch circuit from a 120V/208V panel to 240V for more effective use of a motor or resistive load.

An autotransformer, however, cannot be used on a 240V or 480V, three-phase, three-wire delta system. A grounded neutral phase conductor must be available in accordance with *NEC Section 210.9*, which states that branch circuits shall not be supplied by autotransformers unless the system supplied has a grounded conductor that is electrically connected to a grounded conductor of the system supplying the autotransformer.

In general, the *NEC®* requires that separately derived alternating current systems be grounded. The secondary of an **isolation transformer** is a separately derived system. Therefore, it must be grounded in accordance with *NEC Section 250.30*. See *Figure 8*. In the case of an autotransformer, the grounded conductor of the supply is brought into the transformer to the common terminal and the ground is established to satisfy the *NEC®*.

Know the Code

Circuits Derived from Autotransformers
NEC Section 210.9

Know the Code

Grounding Separately Derived Alternating-Current Systems
NEC Section 250.30

Isolation transformer: A transformer that has no electrical metallic connection between the primary and secondary windings.

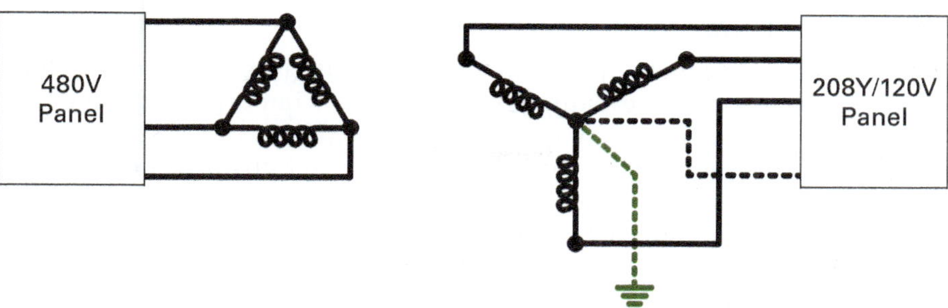

The *NEC*® requires that separately derived AC systems be grounded. The secondary of an isolation transformer is a separately derived system and must be grounded as shown above to comply with ***NEC Section 250.30***.

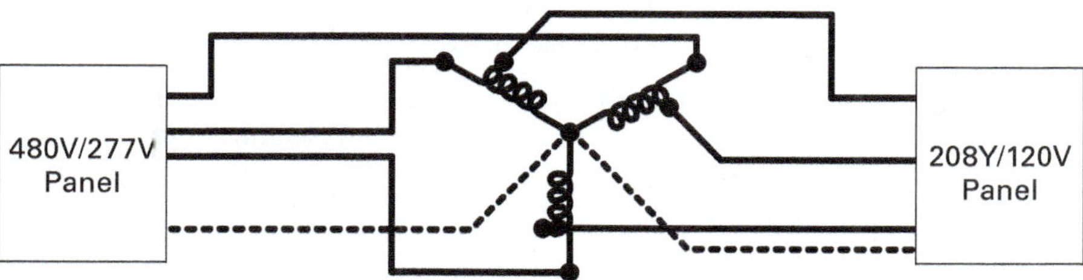

In the case of autotransformers, the grounded conductor of the supply is connected to the transformer common terminal and the ground is established to satisfy ***NEC Section 210.9***.

Figure 8 *NEC*® grounding requirements for isolation and autotransformers.

1.3.4 Constant-Current Transformers

Constant-current transformers are used to supply series airport lighting and street lighting circuits in which the current must remain constant while the number of lamps in series varies because of burnout or bypass switching. This type of transformer has a stationary primary coil connected to a source of alternating voltage and a movable secondary coil connected to the lamp circuit. To allow it to move freely, the secondary coil is suspended from a shaft and rod attached to a rocker arm on which hinges are attached. The tendency of the secondary coil to move downward due to gravity is opposed by both the counterweight and the magnetic repulsion between the coils caused by the current in them.

The constant secondary current is usually between 4A and 7.5A, depending on the current rating of the lamps. In order to maintain a constant secondary current, the voltage of the secondary must vary directly with the number of lamps in series. If the resistance of the secondary is reduced by decreasing the number of lamps in series because of burnout or bypass switching, the current in the transformer will momentarily increase. This will increase the force of repulsion between the coils, which will move apart. The increase in distance between the coils increases the leakage **reactance** of the transformer and causes a greater voltage drop in the transformer, with a consequent decrease in the secondary voltage. The coil will continue to move until the current in the secondary winding reaches its original value, at which position the mechanical forces acting on the secondary coil are again balanced.

Reactance: The imaginary part of impedance; also, the opposition to alternating current due to capacitance (X_C) and/or inductance (X_L).

Incandescent lamps used in series lighting circuits have a film cutout in the socket. When a lamp burns out, the full transformer secondary voltage appears between two spring contacts separated by a thin insulation film in the socket. The voltage punctures the film, causing the series circuit to be re-established.

Advantages of Autotransformers

Autotransformers are less costly than conventional two-winding transformers and have better voltage regulation and a higher ratio of energy output to input (efficiency). They are used in motor starters so that a voltage lower than the line voltage may be applied during the starting period.

1.3.5 Control Transformers

A number of control transformers are used in industrial establishments, both in new construction and in existing installations. It is important to know how to size these transformers for any given application.

In general, the selection of a proper control circuit transformer must be made based on the maximum inrush VA and the maximum continuous VA load to which it is subjected. This data can be determined as follows:

Step 1 Determine the inrush and sealed VA of all coils to be used.

Step 2 Determine the maximum sealed VA load on the transformer.

Step 3 Determine the maximum inrush VA load on the transformer at 100% of the secondary voltage. Add this value to any sealed VA present at the time inrush occurs.

Step 4 Calculate the power factor of the VA load obtained in *Step 3*. The actual coil power factor should be used. If this value is unknown, an inrush power factor of 35% may be assumed.

Step 5 Select a transformer with a continuous VA rating equal to or greater than the value obtained in *Step 2* and whose maximum inrush VA from *Step 3* at the calculated load power factor falls on or below the corresponding curve in *Figure 9*.

The regulation curves in *Figure 9* indicate the maximum permissible inrush loads (volt-amperes at 100% of the secondary voltage), which, if applied to the transformer secondary, will not cause the secondary voltage to drop below 85% of the rated voltage when the primary voltage has been reduced to 90% of the rated voltage.

1.3.6 Series Transformers

A power or distribution transformer is normally used with each of its primary terminals connected across the line. When a transformer is used in series with the main line, the term *series transformer* is applied.

A common application of a series transformer is in an airport system that has runway lamps connected in series. A small transformer is used with one or more lamp(s). The primary is connected in series with the line, and the secondary is connected across the lamp(s). The secondary winding is automatically short-circuited if a lamp burns out. The short circuit is obtained by a film cutout. When the circuit opens and the voltage across the secondary rises, it punctures the film, thereby short-circuiting the transformer secondary.

Series transformers are used in load tap changing circuits and with step-voltage regulators. This reduces the operating voltage to ground when it is too high for the tap changes or reduces the current in the tap changer contacts when the current exceeds the tap changer rating. These series transformers usually serve the purpose of an auxiliary transformer mounted in the main transformer tank.

1.3.7 Step-Voltage Regulators

Regulators of the step-voltage type are transformers provided with load tap changers. They are used to raise or lower the voltage of a circuit in response to a voltage-regulating relay or another control device. Regulators are usually designed to provide secondary voltages ranging from 10% below the supply voltage to 10% above it, or a total change of 20% in 32 steps of $^5/_8$% each.

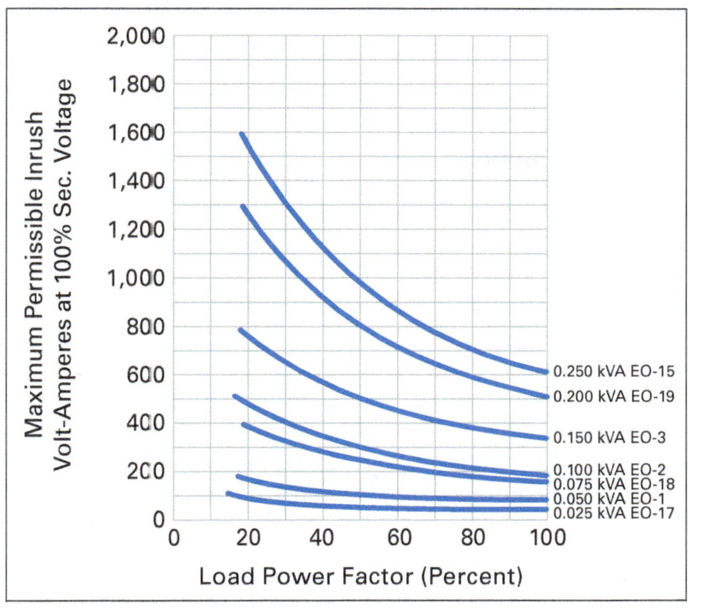

(A) 60/50 Hertz

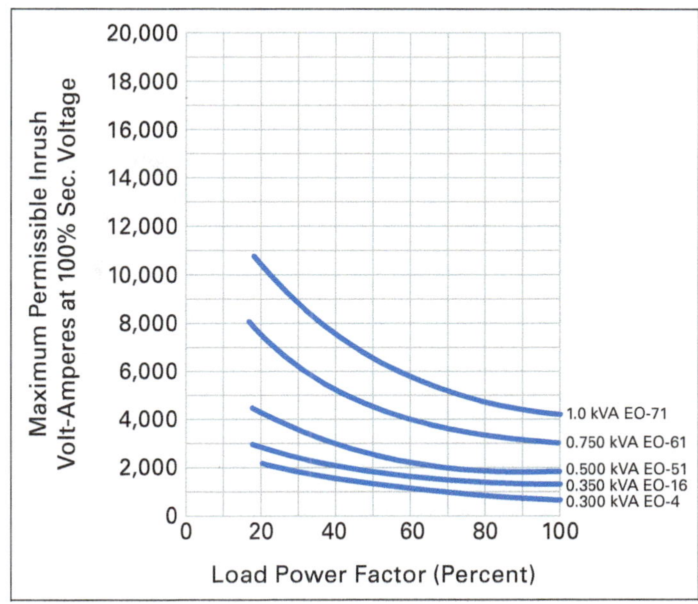

(B) 60/50 Hertz

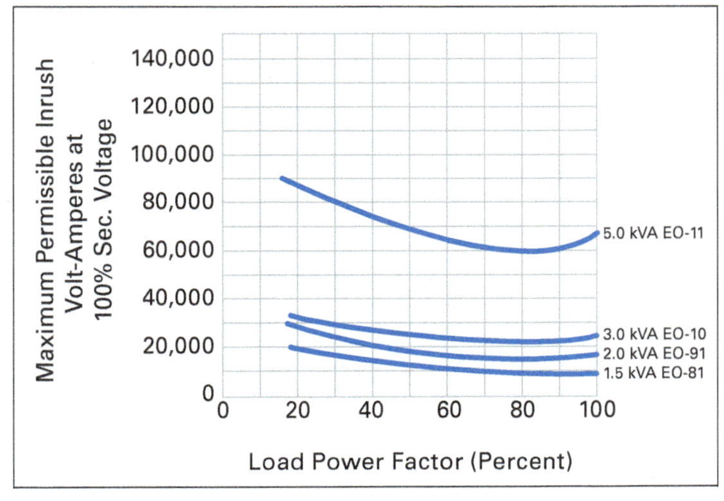

(C) 60/50 Hertz

Figure 9 Regulation curves.

Voltage Regulators

Depending on size, individual single-phase step-voltage regulators can be pole- or pad-mounted and are available in sizes up to 830 kVA at voltages from 2,500V to 19,920V. The step-voltage regulator in the image is liquid-cooled and has both remote and local digital switching control for tap changing. It uses a switching reactor with equalizer windings to balance reactor voltage. An internal voltage supply furnishes power to the switching motor and control devices. Another type of voltage-adjusting transformer is the automatic voltage regulator. It continuously senses and self-adjusts to maintain a selected output voltage level at ±1% for critical loads including computer, medical, communications, and industrial-process equipment. These are dry-type units with a variable-ratio autotransformer consisting of a rotor and stator. The rotor turns only 180° to add to or subtract from the supply voltage and is driven by a reversible motor. Because these units regulate by transformer action instead of impedance change, no waveform distortion occurs. The regulators are available in single- and three-phase versions in sizes up to 1,000 kVA at voltages from 120V to 480V.

1.3.8 Buck-and-Boost Transformers

A buck-and-boost transformer is used to control the voltage applied to low-voltage (12V–48V) equipment. Buck-and-boost transformers can be used to power uninterruptible power supply (UPS) systems for data processing equipment, control circuits, and lighting circuits.

Manufacturers of buck-and-boost transformers usually offer easy-to-use selector charts that allow you to quickly select a buck-and-boost transformer for practically any application. These charts may be obtained from electrical equipment suppliers or ordered directly from the manufacturer—often at no charge. Instructions accompanying these charts will enable anyone familiar with transformers and electrical circuits to use them.

When reviewing the selector charts, it may surprise you to discover that these transformers can handle loads that are much greater than their nameplate ratings. For example, a typical 1 kVA buck-and-boost transformer can easily handle an 11 kVA load when the voltage boost is only 10%. In this case, an isolation transformer will be incorporated as part of an autotransformer to form a buck-and-boost transformer.

An overview of the principles involved in using buck-and-boost transformers is given here:

Assume that you have a 1 kVA (1,000VA) isolation transformer that is designed to transform 208V to 20.8V (*Figure 10*). This results in a transformer winding ratio of 10:1. The primary current may be found using the following equation:

$$\text{Primary current} = 1{,}000\text{VA} \div 208\text{VA} = 4.8\text{A}$$

Because the transformation ratio is 10:1, the secondary amperes will be 48A (4.8A × 10 = 48A), or the amperage may be determined using the following equation:

$$\text{Secondary current} = 1{,}000\text{VA} \div 20.8\text{VA} = 48\text{A}$$

X_1
X_2
48A
20.8V
1 kVA
208V
4.8A
H_2
H_1

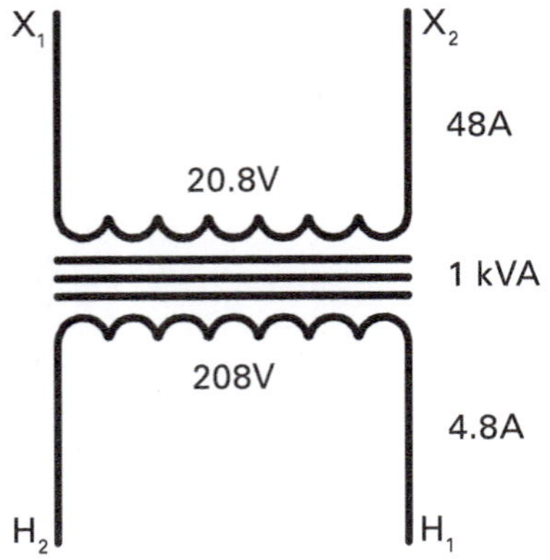

Figure 10 Isolation transformer.

Figure 11 shows how the windings are connected in series to form an autotransformer.

Because you started with 208V at the source and now add 20.8V to it, the load is now 208V + 20.8V = 228.8V. To find the kVA rating of the system at the load, use the following equation:

$$\text{kVA} = (\text{volts} \div 1{,}000) \times \text{amps}$$
$$\text{kVA} = (228\text{V} \div 1{,}000) \times 48\text{A}$$
$$\text{kVA} = 0.228\text{V} \times 48\text{A}$$
$$\text{kVA} = 11\ \text{kVA}$$

The source conducts 10 kVA, and 1 kVA is transformed from the source. The total kVA rating is 10 kVA + 1 kVA = 11 kVA.

The H_1H_2 winding is rated at 4.8A, and the X_1X_2 winding is rated at 48A. Therefore, the line current at 208V would be 4.8A + 48A = 52.8A. The input kVA rating is as follows:

$$\text{kVA} = (\text{volts} \div 1{,}000) \times \text{amps}$$
$$\text{kVA} = (208\text{V} \div 1{,}000) \times 52.8\text{A}$$
$$\text{kVA} = 0.208\text{V} \times 52.8\text{A}$$
$$\text{kVA} = 11\ \text{kVA}$$

The diagrams shown in *Figure 10* and *Figure 11* are usually simplified even more in a line diagram, as shown in *Figure 12*. All three wiring diagrams indicate the same thing, and following the connections on any of these drawings will produce the same results at the load. *Figure 12* shows the calculations for a 240V source.

It should now be evident how a 1 kVA buck-and-boost transformer, when connected in the circuit as described previously, can actually carry 11 kVA in its secondary winding.

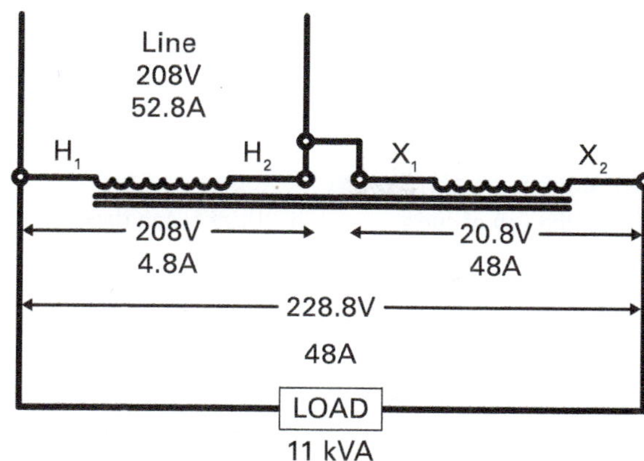

Figure 11 Boost transformer connection.

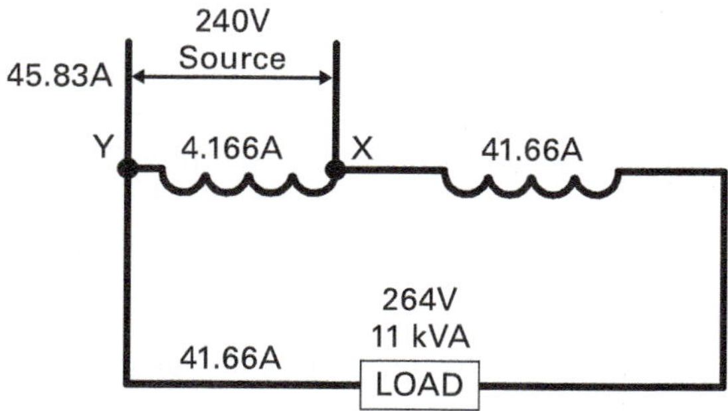

Figure 12 Typical line diagram of a transformer circuit.

Buck-and-Boost Transformers

A small buck-and-boost transformer is shown in the image. It is a single-phase compound-filled unit rated at 0.05 kVA. However, depending on the percentage of voltage buck or boost required, it can be used in circuits with much higher loads.

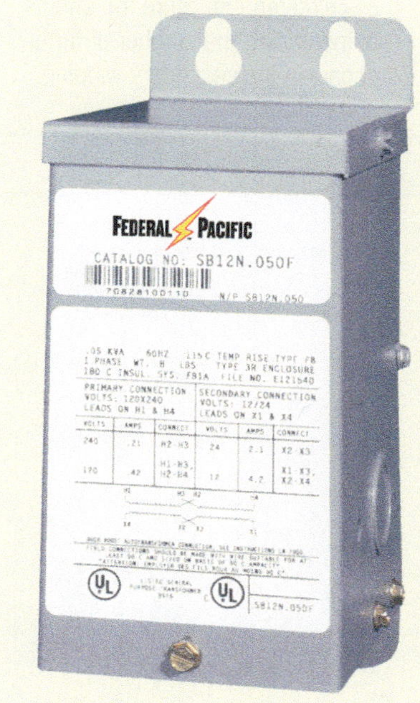

Source: Electro-Mechanical Corp./ Line Power/Federal Pacific

1.0.0 Section Review

1. A transformer with a single winding that serves as both the primary and the secondary is known as a(n) ______.
   a. control transformer
   b. autotransformer
   c. instrument transformer
   d. potential transformer

2. If the three windings in a three-phase transformer have a common point, it is a(n) _____.
   a. delta transformer
   b. delta-delta transformer
   c. wye transformer
   d. autotransformer

3. An arc-lamp is *most* likely to be supplied by a(n) _____.
   a. oil-insulated transformer
   b. autotransformer
   c. rectifier transformer
   d. power transformer

2.0.0 Identifying Instrument Transformers

Performance Task

2. Using a clamp-on ammeter, demonstrate the principles of a current transformer, identify the primary winding, and then calculate and measure the effects of increasing the number of turns (loops) in the secondary winding.

Objective

Identify instrument transformers.

a. Identify and describe the use of current transformers.

b. Identify and describe the use of potential transformers.

Instrument transformers are so named because they are usually connected to an electrical instrument, such as an ammeter, voltmeter, wattmeter, or relay. As mentioned earlier, there are two types of instrument transformers: current and potential.

2.1.0 Current Transformers

The primary winding of a current transformer is connected in series with the power source and the load, and it carries the full-load current. The turns ratio is designed to produce a rated current, such as 5A, in the secondary winding when the rated current flows in the primary winding. The current transformer provides a small current suitable for the current coil of standard instruments and proportional to the load current. The low-voltage, low-current secondary winding providing the current is grounded for safety and economy in the secondary wiring and instruments.

When connecting instrument transformers to wattmeters, watt-hour meters, power factor meters, or other instruments, it is necessary to know the polarity of the leads. One primary lead and one secondary lead of the same polarity are clearly marked on all instrument transformers, usually by a white spot or white marker on the leads.

The direction of current in the two leads of the same polarity is such that, if it is toward the transformer in the marked primary lead, it is away from the transformer in the marked secondary lead. This is done to maintain the same phase sequence in the receiving device as is present on the power lines. In diagrams, the polarity mark is usually indicated in one of three ways (*Figure 13*).

Figure 13 Polarity marks on transformers.

Instrument Transformers

Instrument transformers are classified according to the following factors:

- *Service* — Instrument transformers are designated for either metering or relaying service.
- *Burden* — The burden represents the size and characteristics of the load connected to the transformer secondary. For potential transformers, the burden is expressed in VA at a specified power factor and voltage. For current transformers, the burden is expressed in total impedance at specified values of resistance and inductance. Generally, a transformer must perform as rated within the limits of its burden.
- *Accuracy* — For a metering transformer, an accuracy rating representing the amount of uncertainty (inaccuracy) is assigned for each rated burden of the transformer. For example, a transformer may have an accuracy rating of 0.3 at burden X and 0.6 at burden Y. Standard accuracy classes for instrument transformers are 0.3, 0.6, 1.2, and 2.4.

A current transformer is always a single-phase transformer. If current transformers are used in a three-phase system, one current transformer is inserted into each phase line between the power supply and the instrument. A current transformer is considered a low kVA device. The connection of a current transformer into a single-phase, two-wire line is shown in *Figure 14*.

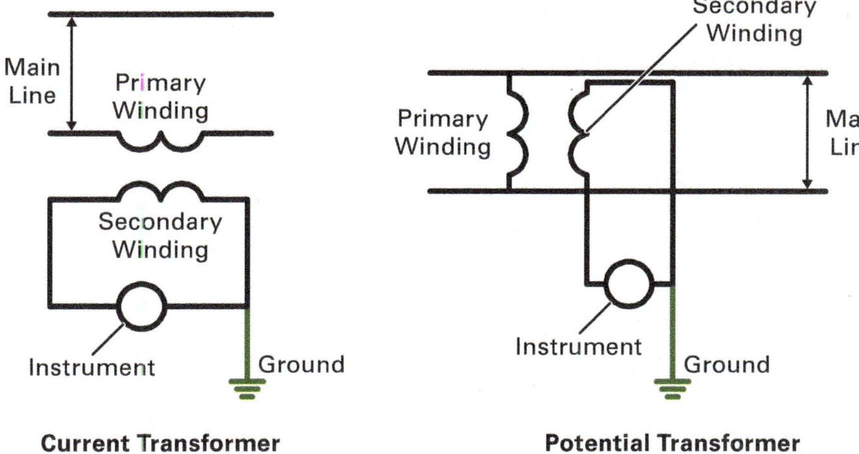

Figure 14 Connection of instrument transformers.

The primary winding of a current transformer must be connected in series with one of the main power lines; thus, the main line load current flows through the primary winding. The secondary winding at the current transformer is connected to a current-responsive instrument. The secondary circuit is grounded for safety. Instruments that use a current transformer may include ammeters, wattmeters, watt-hour meters, power factor meters, some forms of relays, and trip coils of circuit breakers. One current transformer may feed through several devices in series.

Current transformers are built to standard IEEE burden ratings. *Burden* refers to the total load seen by the CT secondary. This load is the total **impedance** of conductors and instruments connected. For example, a CT with a B-1 designation is intended to work properly with no more than 1V impedance in the secondary circuit. This B-1 CT is rated to deliver 25VA at a secondary current of 5A. A CT with a B-8 designation is rated at 200VA at 5A. It is designed to work with an 8V impedance. When current flow is interrupted in the CT secondary, the secondary voltage can rise to dangerously high levels as the CT tries to deliver VA. Therefore, a shorting jumper should be placed across the secondary terminals when no device is connected.

CAUTION

CTs shipped as part of equipment usually come with a shorting jumper installed. Be sure to remove the shorting jumper after the connection to the relaying or metering circuit is verified.

Impedance: The opposition to current flow in an AC circuit. Impedance includes resistance (*R*), capacitive reactance (X_C), and inductive reactance (X_L). It is measured in ohms (Ω).

Three-Phase Current Transformers

A three-phase toroidal current transformer unit with the leads to a motor contactor passing through the center holes is shown in the image. The ground fault sensor is a similar type of transformer.

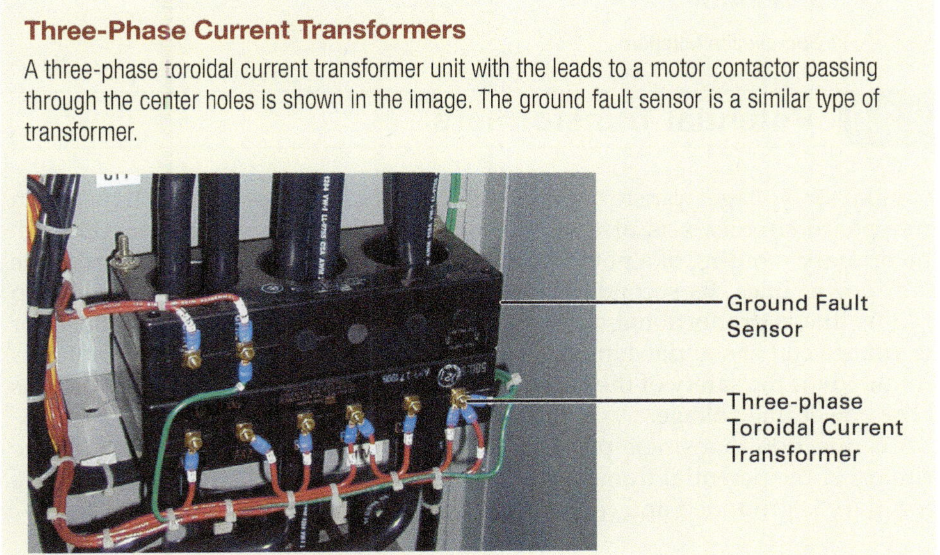

Ampere turns: The product of amperes times the number of turns in a coil.

Before disconnecting an instrument, the secondary of the current transformer must be short-circuited. If the secondary circuit is opened while the primary winding is carrying current, there will be no secondary **ampere turns** to balance the primary ampere turns. Therefore, the total primary current will become exciting current and magnetize the core to a high flux density, which will produce a high voltage across both the primary and secondary windings.

WARNING!

The secondary circuit of a current transformer should never be opened while the primary is carrying current.

Because current transformers are designed for accuracy, the normal exciting current is only a small percentage of the full-load current. The voltage produced with the secondary open circuited is high enough to endanger the life of anyone touching the meters or leads. The high secondary voltage may also overstress the secondary insulation and cause a breakdown. Still other damage may be caused by operation with the secondary open circuited—the transformer core may become permanently magnetized, impairing the accuracy of the transformer. If this occurs, the core may be demagnetized by passing about 50% excess current through the primary, with the secondary connected to an adjustable high resistance that is gradually reduced to zero.

Single-Phase Current Transformers

This is an assembly of three wound-type single-phase current transformers serving a three-phase feeder.

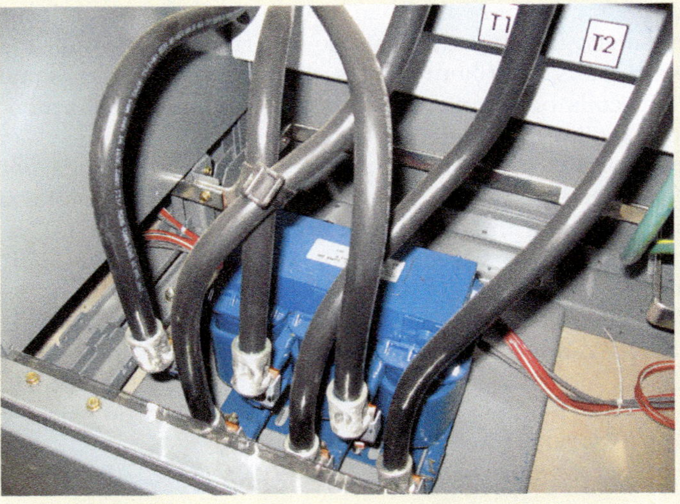

Source: Jim Mitchem

2.2.0 Potential Transformers

Potential or voltage transformers are single-phase transformers. If used on three-phase circuits, sets of two or three potential transformers are applied. The primary winding of a potential transformer is always connected across the main power lines. Its secondary winding provides a low voltage, usually up to 120V, that is proportional to the line voltage. This low voltage is suitable for the voltage coil of standard instruments. The low-voltage secondary winding is grounded for the safety of the secondary wiring and the instrument, regardless of the power line voltage.

A connection to a single-phase, two-wire circuit is shown in *Figure 14*. The primary of the potential transformer is connected across the main line, and the secondary is grounded and connected to an instrument.

The main circuit voltage exists across the primary winding. The secondary of the potential transformer is connected to one or more voltage-responsive devices, such as voltmeters, wattmeters, watt-hour meters, power factor meters, or some forms of relays or trip coils. The voltage across the secondary terminals of the potential transformer is always lower than the primary voltage and is rated at 120V. For example, if a potential transformer with a turns ratio of 12:1 is connected to a 1,440V main line, the voltage in the instrument connected across the secondary terminals will be about 1,440V divided by 12, or 120V.

All potential transformers have a wound primary and a wound secondary. Mechanically, their construction is similar to that of wound current transformers. Their secondary thermal kVA rating rarely exceeds 1.5 kVA.

Potential transformers are available in both oil-filled and dry types. In both types, the primary high-voltage leads are terminated at bushings and the housing contains the secondary low-voltage terminations. When supplied as part of a switchgear assembly, they occupy dedicated spaces.

In certain small services, both current and potential transformers are packaged into a metering unit that is a single enclosure. This reduces the assembly time in field installations.

2.0.0 Section Review

1. Current transformers are built to standard _____.
   a. NEMA enclosure sizes
   b. NFPA ratings
   c. ASTM frame sizes
   d. IEEE burden ratings

2. The voltage across the secondary of a potential transformer is rated at _____.
   a. 24V
   b. 60V
   c. 120V
   d. 240V

3.0.0 Identifying and Resolving Harmonics

Objective

Define harmonics and explain how harmonic issues are identified and resolved.

a. Describe the common sources of harmonics in office buildings and industrial plants.
b. Explain how to survey a system to identify the source of harmonics.
c. Explain how to resolve harmonics.

Performance Tasks

There are no Performance Tasks in this section.

Harmonics are the byproducts of modern electronics. They are especially prevalent wherever there are large numbers of personal computers (PCs), adjustable-speed drives, and other types of equipment that draw current in short pulses.

Harmonics: Oscillations at frequencies that are integral multiples of the fundamental frequency.

This equipment is designed to draw current only during a controlled portion of the incoming voltage waveform. Although this dramatically improves efficiency, it causes harmonics in the load current. This results in overheated transformers and neutrals, as well as tripped circuit breakers.

The problem is evident when you look at a waveform. A normal 60-cycle power line voltage appears on the oscilloscope as a near sine wave, as shown in *Figure 15* (A). When harmonics are present, the waveform is distorted, as shown in *Figure 15* (B) and *Figure 15* (C). These waves are described as nonsinusoidal. The voltage and current waveforms are no longer simply related—hence the term *nonlinear.*

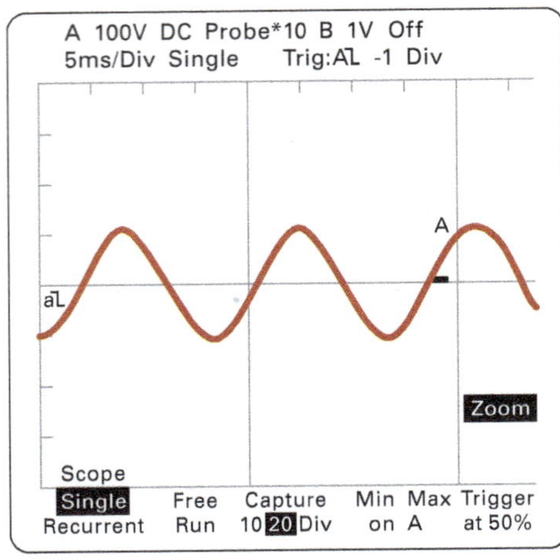

(A) Near Sinewave

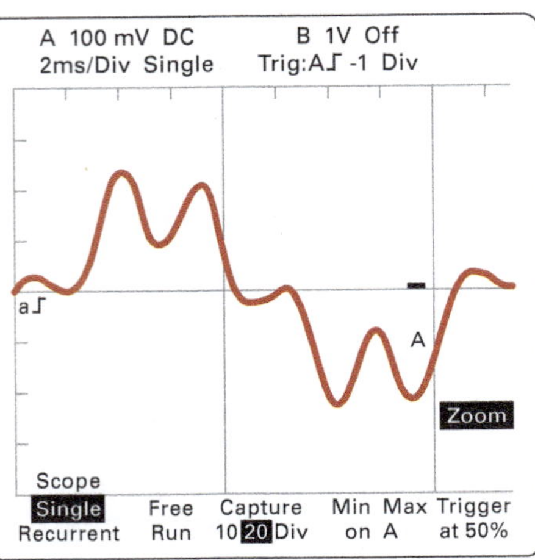

(B) Distorted Waveform

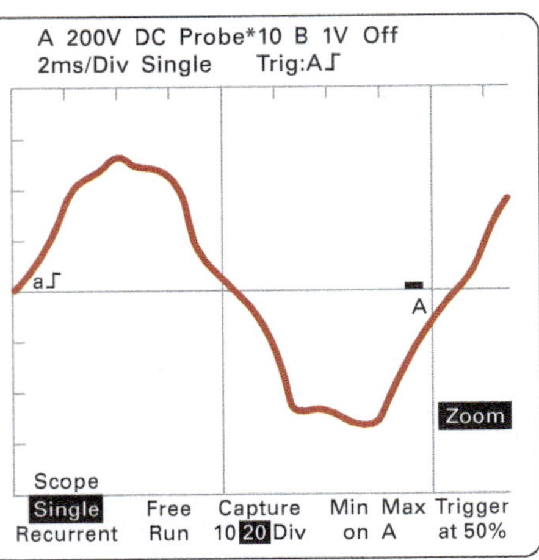

(C) Distorted Waveform

Figure 15 Voltage waveforms.

CAUTION

As part of a regular maintenance program, pay careful attention to overheating of the neutral conductors in distribution systems. Harmonics may cause deterioration of the insulation.

Harmonics

If you were to listen to an ordinary 60-cycle power line, you would hear a monotone hum or buzz. When harmonics are present, you hear a different tune, rich with high notes.

Finding the problem is relatively easy when you know what to look for and where to look. Harmonics are usually anything but subtle. This section gives you some basic pointers on how to find harmonics and some suggested ways to address the problem. However, in many cases, consultants must be called in to analyze the operation and design a plan for correcting the problem.

Harmonics are currents or voltages with frequencies that are integer multiples of the fundamental power frequency. For example, if the fundamental frequency is 60 Hz, then the second harmonic is 120 Hz, the third is 180 Hz, and so on.

Harmonics are created by nonlinear loads that draw current in abrupt pulses rather than in a smooth sinusoidal manner. These pulses cause distorted current waveshapes, which in turn cause harmonic currents to flow back into other parts of the power system. This phenomenon is especially prevalent with equipment that contains diode/capacitor input or solid-state switched power supplies, such as personal computers, printers, and medical test equipment.

In a diode/capacitor, the incoming AC voltage is diode rectified and is then used to charge a large capacitor. After a few cycles, the capacitor is charged to the peak voltage of the sine wave (for example, 168V for a 120V line). The electronic equipment then draws current from this high DC voltage to power the rest of the circuit.

The equipment can draw the current down to a regulated lower limit. Typically, before reaching that limit, the capacitor is recharged to the peak in the next half cycle of the sine wave. This process is repeated over and over. The capacitor basically draws a pulse of current only during the peak of the wave. During the rest of the wave, when the voltage is below the capacitor residual, the capacitor draws no current.

The power line itself can be an indirect source of voltage harmonics. The harmonic current drawn by nonlinear loads acts in an Ohm's law relationship with the source impedance of the supplying transformer to produce the voltage harmonics. The source impedance includes both the supplying transformer and the branch circuit components. For example, a 10A harmonic current being drawn for a source impedance of 0.1Ω will generate a harmonic voltage of 1.0V. Any loads sharing a transformer or branch circuit with a heavy harmonic load can be affected by the voltage harmonics generated.

Many types of devices are very susceptible to voltage harmonics. The performance of the diode/ capacitor power supply is critically dependent on the magnitude of the peak voltage. Voltage harmonics can cause flat-topping of the voltage waveform, lowering the peak voltage. In severe cases, the computer may reset due to insufficient peak voltage.

In an industrial environment, the induction motor and power factor correction capacitors can also be seriously affected by voltage harmonics.

Power correction capacitors can form a resonant circuit with the inductive parts of a power distribution system. If the resonant frequency is near that of the harmonic voltage, the resultant harmonic current can increase substantially, overloading the capacitors and blowing the capacitor fuses. Fortunately, the capacitor failure detunes the circuit and the resonance disappears.

Each harmonic has a name, frequency, and sequence. The sequence refers to phasor rotation with respect to the fundamental (F); that is, in an induction motor, a positive sequence harmonic would generate a magnetic field that rotates in the same direction as the fundamental. A negative sequence harmonic would rotate in the reverse direction. The first nine harmonics, along with their effects, are shown in *Table 1*.

TABLE 1 Harmonic Rates and Effects

Name	F	2nd	3rd	4th	5th	6th	7th	8th	9th
Frequency	60	120	180	240	300	360	420	480	540
Sequence	+	–	0	+	–	0	+	–	0

Sequence	Rotation	Effects (skin effect, eddy currents, etc.)
Positive	Forward	Heating of conductors and circuit breakers
Negative	Reverse	Heating as above, plus motor problems
Zero	None	Heating plus add-in neutral of three-phase, four-wire system

3.1.0 Common Sources of Harmonics

Harmonics have a significant effect in office buildings and industrial establishments. Symptoms of harmonics usually show up in the power distribution equipment that supports the nonlinear loads. There are two types of nonlinear loads: single phase and three phase. Single-phase loads are prevalent in offices; three-phase loads are widespread in industrial plants.

Each component of the power distribution system manifests the effects of harmonics a little differently, but they are all subject to damage and inefficient performance.

3.1.1 Neutral Conductors

In a three-phase, four-wire system, the neutral conductor can be severely affected by nonlinear loads connected to the 120V branch circuits. Under normal conditions for a balanced linear load, the fundamental 60 Hz portions of the phase currents cancel in the neutral conductor.

In a four-wire system with single-phase, nonlinear loads, certain odd-numbered harmonics called *triplens*—odd multiples of the third harmonic: 3rd, 9th, 15th, and so on—do not cancel, but rather add together in the neutral conductor. In systems with many single-phase, nonlinear loads, the neutral current can actually exceed the phase current. The danger here is excessive overheating because there is no circuit breaker in the neutral conductor to limit the current as there are in the phase conductors.

Excessive current in the neutral conductor can also cause higher voltage drops between the neutral conductor and ground at the 120V outlet.

3.1.2 Circuit Breakers

Common thermal-magnetic circuit breakers use a bimetallic trip mechanism that responds to the heating effect of the circuit current. They are designed to respond to the true root-mean-square (rms) value of the current waveform and therefore will trip when they get too hot. This type of breaker has a better chance of protecting against harmonic current overloads.

A peak-sensing electronic trip circuit breaker responds to the peak of the current waveform. As a result, it does not always respond properly to harmonic currents. Since the peak of the harmonic current is usually higher than normal, this type of circuit breaker may trip prematurely at a low current. If the peak is lower than normal, the breaker may fail to trip when it should.

Nonlinear Loads

The diode/capacitor or solid-state switched power supplies found in office equipment typically consist of single-phase, nonlinear loads. In industrial plants, the most common causes of harmonic currents are three-phase, nonlinear loads. These include electronic motor drives, uninterruptible power supplies (UPSs), HID lighting, and welding machines.

3.1.3 Busbars and Connecting Lugs

Neutral busbars and connecting lugs are sized to carry the full value of the rated phase current. They can become overloaded when the neutral conductors are overloaded with the additional sum of the triplen harmonics.

3.1.4 Electrical Panels

Harmonics in electrical panels can be quite noisy. Panels that are designed to carry 60 Hz current can become mechanically resonant to the magnetic fields generated by high-frequency harmonic currents. When this happens, the panel vibrates and emits a buzzing sound at the harmonic frequencies.

3.1.5 Telecommunications

Telecommunications cable is commonly run right next to power cables. To minimize the inductive interference from phase current, telecommunications cables are run closer to the neutral wire. Triplens in the neutral conductor commonly cause inductive interference that can be heard on a phone line. This is often the first indication of a harmonics problem and gives you a head start in detecting the problem before it causes major damage.

3.1.6 Transformers

Commercial buildings commonly have a 120V/208V transformer in a delta-wye configuration (*Figure 16*). These transformers commonly feed receptacles in a commercial building. Single-phase, nonlinear loads connected to the receptacles produce triplen harmonics that algebraically add up in the neutral. When this neutral current reaches the transformer, it is reflected into the delta primary winding, where it circulates and causes overheating and transformer failures.

Another transformer problem results from **core loss** and copper loss. Transformers are normally rated for a 60 Hz phase-current load only.

High-frequency harmonic currents cause increased core loss due to **eddy currents** and **hysteresis**, resulting in more heating than would occur at the same 60 Hz current. These heating effects demand that transformers be derated for harmonic loads or replaced with specially designed transformers.

Core loss: The electric loss that occurs in the core of an armature or transformer due to conditions such as the presence of eddy currents or hysteresis.

Eddy currents: The circulating currents that are induced in conductive materials by varying magnetic fields; they are usually considered undesirable because they represent a loss of energy and produce excess heat.

Hysteresis: The time lag exhibited by a body in reacting to changes in the forces affecting it; hysteresis is an internal friction.

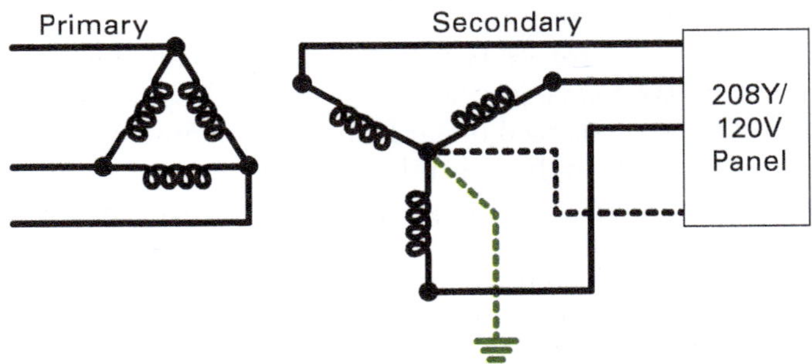

Figure 16 Three-phase, delta-wye transformer configuration.

K-Rated and Zig-Zag Transformers

Specially designed transformers that reduce or compensate for harmonic current include K-rated and zig-zag transformers. To prevent overheating, K-rated three-phase transformers for delta-to-wye connections are sized to handle 100% of the normal 60 Hz load plus a specified nonlinear load defined by a K number. Manufacturers' specifications define the K numbers for various types of loads. If the various harmonics are known, a specific transformer can be custom built. The inherent phase shift of a K-rated transformer will cancel 5th and 7th harmonics but not the triplens. Because triplens are not cancelled, the neutral of the secondary is normally oversized at 200% of the maximum current rating of one of the phase connections.

A zig-zag phase shift transformer cancels triplens and other harmonics at the load side of the transformer by using six windings in the secondary. An extra winding for each phase is connected in series with another phase to produce a phase shift. This type of transformer works well if the loads are balanced. A drawback is that zig-zag transformers use more material in the windings and are heavy. Other techniques such as active filters or ferroresonant transformers are also used for harmonic current suppression in certain applications.

3.1.7 Generators

Standby generators are subject to the same types of overheating problems as transformers. Because they provide emergency backup for harmonics-producing loads such as data processing equipment, they are often even more vulnerable. In addition to overheating, certain types of harmonics produce distortion at the zero crossing of the current waveform, which causes interference and instability in the generator control circuits.

3.2.0 Surveying for Harmonics

A quick survey will help to determine whether you have a harmonics problem and where it is located. Follow these steps to complete the survey:

Step 1 Take a walking tour of the facility and look at the types of equipment in use. If there are many personal computers and printers, adjustable-speed motors, solid-state heater controls, and certain types of fluorescent lighting, there is a good chance that harmonics are present.

Step 2 Locate the transformers feeding the nonlinear loads and check for excess heating. Also, make sure that the cooling vents are unobstructed.

Step 3 Use a true rms meter to check transformer currents.

- Verify that the voltage ratings for the test equipment are adequate for the transformer being tested.
- Measure and record the transformer secondary currents in each phase and in the neutral (if used).
- Calculate the kVA delivered to the load and compare it to the nameplate rating. If harmonic currents are present, the transformer can overheat even if the kVA delivered is less than the nameplate rating.
- If the transformer secondary is a four-wire system, compare the measured neutral current to the value predicted from the imbalance in the phase currents. (The neutral current is the vector sum of the phase currents and is normally zero if the phase currents are balanced in both amplitude and phase.) If the neutral current is unexpectedly high, triple harmonics are likely and the transformer may need to be derated.
- Measure the frequency of the neutral current. 180 Hz would be a typical reading for a neutral current consisting of mostly third harmonics.

Step 4 Survey the subpanels that feed harmonic loads. Measure the current in each branch neutral and compare the measured value to the rated capacity for the wire size used. Check the neutral busbar and feeder connections for heating or discoloration.

Step 5 Neutral overloading in receptacle branch circuits can sometimes be detected by measuring the neutral-to-ground voltage at the receptacle. Measure the voltage when the loads are on. A reading of 2V or less is normal. Higher voltages can indicate trouble, depending on the length of the run, quality of the connections, and other factors.

Step 6 Measure the frequency. A result of 180 Hz would suggest a strong presence of harmonics; 60 Hz would suggest that the phases are out of balance. Pay special attention to undercarpet wiring and modular office panels with integrated wiring that use a neutral shared by three-phase conductors. Because the typical loads in these two areas are computers and office machines, they are often trouble spots for overloaded neutrals.

3.2.1 Meters

Having the proper equipment is crucial to diagnosing harmonics problems. The type of equipment used varies with the complexity of measurements required.

To determine whether you have a harmonics problem, you need to measure the true rms value and the instantaneous peak value of the waveshape. For this test, you need a true rms clamp-on multimeter or a handheld digital multimeter that makes true rms measurements and has a high-speed peak hold circuit.

The term *true rms* refers to the root-mean-square or equivalent heating value of a current or voltage waveshape. True distinguishes the measurement from those taken by average responding meters.

Most low-cost, portable clamp-on ammeters are average responding. These instruments give correct readings for pure sine waves only and typically read low when confronted with a distorted current waveform. The result is a reading that can be as much as 50% low.

True rms meters give correct readings for any waveshape within the instrument's crest factor and bandwidth specifications.

3.2.2 Crest Factor

The crest factor of a waveform is the ratio of the peak value to the rms value. For a sine wave, the crest factor is 1.414. A true rms meter has a crest factor specification. This specification relates to the level of peaking that can be measured without errors.

A quality true rms handheld digital multimeter has a crest factor of 3.0 at full scale. This is more than adequate for most power distribution measurements. At half scale, the crest factor is double. For example, a meter may have a crest factor specification of 3.0 when measuring 400VAC and a crest factor of 6.0 when measuring 200VAC.

The crest factor can be easily calculated using a true rms meter with a peak function or a crest function. A crest factor other than 1.414 indicates the presence of harmonics. In typical single-phase cases, the greater the difference from 1.414, the greater the harmonics. For voltage harmonics, the typical crest factor is below 1.414—a flat-top waveform. For single-phase current harmonics, the typical crest factor is well above 1.414. Three-phase current waveforms often exhibit the double-hump waveform. Therefore, the crest factor comparison method should not be applied to three-phase load currents.

After you have determined that harmonics are present, you can make a more in-depth analysis of the situation using a harmonics analyzer.

NOTE

Most true rms meters cannot be used for signals below 5% of scale because of the measurement noise problem. Use a lower range if it is available.

Think About It

Four-Wire Systems

What condition might cause some conductors of a four-wire system to feel hot to the touch?

3.3.0 Resolving Harmonics

The following are some suggested ways of addressing some typical harmonics problems. Before taking any measures, you should consult a power quality expert to analyze the problem and design a plan tailored to your specific situation.

3.3.1 Harmonics in Overloaded Neutrals

In a three-phase, four-wire wye system, the 60 Hz portion of the neutral current can be minimized by balancing the loads in each phase. *NEC Section 220.61(C)* prohibits reduced sizing of neutral conductors serving nonlinear loads. The triplen harmonics neutral current can be reduced by adding harmonic filters at the load. If neither of these solutions is practical, you can pull in extra neutrals (ideally one neutral for each phase) or you can install an oversized neutral to be shared by the three conductors.

In new construction, undercarpet wiring and modular office partition wiring should be specified with individual neutrals and possibly an isolated ground separate from the safety ground.

Know the Code

Prohibited Reductions
NEC Section 220.61(C)

Think About It

True RMS Meters

Why is it important to use a true rms meter?

Power Quality Analyzers

Portable power quality analyzers like the one in the image can be used to determine harmonics, as well as to make power measurements (kW, VA, and VAR), power factor and displaced power factor measurements, voltage and current readouts and waveforms, inrush current and duration recording, transient measurements, and sag and swell recording. Extensive power quality measurements can be made continuously using the software provided with most energy management systems.

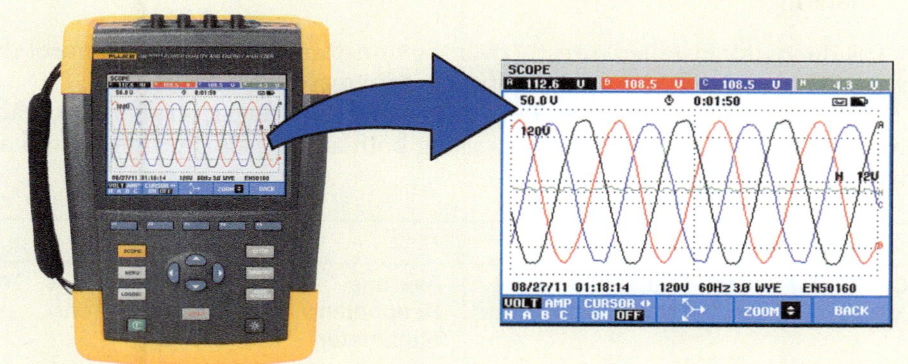

Source: Fluke Corporation, reproduced with permission

3.3.2 Derating Transformers

One way to protect a transformer from harmonics is to limit the amount of load placed on it. This is called *derating* the transformer. The most rigorous derating method is described in *ANSI/IEEE Standard C57.110-2018*. This method is somewhat impractical because it requires extensive loss data from the transformer manufacturer, plus a complete harmonics spectrum of the load current.

The Computer and Business Equipment Manufacturers' Association (CBEMA) recommends a second method that involves several straightforward measurements using common test equipment. It appears to give reasonable results for 208V/120Y receptacle transformers that supply the low-frequency odd harmonics (3rd, 5th, and 7th) commonly generated by computers and office machines.

The test equipment must be capable of taking both the true rms phase current and the instantaneous peak phase current for each phase of the secondary.

To determine the transformer harmonics derating factor (THDF), take the peak and true rms current measurements for the three-phase conductors. If the phases are not balanced, average the three measurements and plug that value into the following equation:

$$\text{THDF} = \frac{1.414 \times \text{true rms phase current}}{\text{instantaneous peak phase current}}$$

This equation generates a value between 0 and 1.0 (typically between 0.5 and 0.9). If the phase currents are purely sinusoidal (undistorted), the instantaneous current peaks at 1.414 times the true rms value and the derating factor is 1.0. If that is the case, no derating is required.

However, with harmonics present, the transformer rating is the product of the nameplate kVA rating times the THDF:

$$\text{derated kVA} = \text{THDF} \times \text{nameplate kVA}$$

For example, a modern office building dedicated primarily to computer software development contains a large number of PCs and other electronic office equipment. These electronic loads are fed by a 120V/208V transformer configured with a delta primary and a wye secondary. The PCs are well distributed throughout the building, except for one large room that contains several machines. The PCs in this room, used exclusively for testing, are served by several branch circuits.

The transformer and main switchgear are located in a ground floor electrical room. An inspection of this room immediately reveals two symptoms of high-harmonic currents:

- The transformer is generating a substantial amount of heat.
- The main panel emits an audible buzzing sound. The sound is not the chatter commonly associated with a faulty circuit breaker, but rather a deep, resonant buzz that indicates the mechanical parts of the panel itself are vibrating.

The ductwork installed directly over the transformer to carry off some of the excess heat keeps the room temperature within reasonable limits.

Current measurements (see *Table 2*) are taken on the neutral and on each phase of the transformer secondary using both a true rms multimeter and an average responding unit.

TABLE 2 Current Measurements

Conductor Name	Multimeter (true rms)	Average Responding Multimeter	Instantaneous Peak Current
Phase 1	410A	328A	804A
Phase 2	445A	346A	892A
Phase 3	435A	355A	828A
Neutral	548A	537A	762A

A 600A, clamp-on current transformer accessory is connected to each meter to allow the meters to make high-current readings.

The presence of harmonics is obvious by a comparison of the phase-current and neutral-current measurements. As *Table 2* shows, the neutral current is substantially higher than any of the phase currents, even though the phase currents are relatively well balanced. The average responding meter consistently shows readings that are approximately 20% low on all phases. Its neutral current readings are only 2% low.

The waveforms explain the discrepancy. The phase currents are badly distorted by large amounts of triplen harmonics, while the neutral current is not affected. The phase current readings listed in *Table 2* clearly demonstrate why true rms measurement capability is required to accurately determine the value of harmonic currents.

The next step is to calculate the transformer harmonic derating factor, or THDF, using the formula shown in this section. The results indicate that, with the level of harmonics present, the transformer should be derated to 72.3% of its nameplate rating to prevent overheating. In this case, the transformer should be derated to 72.3% of its 225 kVA rating, or 162.7 kVA.

The actual load is calculated to be 151.3 kVA. Although this figure is far less than the nameplate rating, the transformer is operating close to its derated capacity.

Next, a subpanel that supplies branch circuits for the 120V receptacles is also examined. The current in each neutral is measured and shown in *Table 3*.

TABLE 3 Neutral Loads

Neutral Conductor Number	Current (Amps)
01	5.0
02	11.3
03	5.0
04	13.1
05	12.4
06	15.0
07	1.8
08	11.7
09	4.5
10	11.8
11	9.6
12	11.5
13	11.3
14	6.7
15	7.0
16	2.3
17	2.6

When a marginal or overloaded conductor is identified, the associated phase currents and the neutral-to-ground voltage at the receptacle are also measured. When a check of neutral No. 6 reveals 15A in a conductor rated for 16A, the phase currents of the circuits (No. 25, No. 27, and No. 29) that share that neutral are also measured (*Table 4*).

Note that each of the phase currents of these three branch circuits is substantially less than 15A and the same phase conductors have significant neutral-to-ground voltage drops.

TABLE 4 Phase Currents and Neutral-to-Ground Voltages

Circuit Number	Phase Current	Neutral-to-Ground Voltage Drop at Receptacle
25	7.8A	3.75V
27	9.7A	4.00V
29	13.5A	8.05V

In the branch circuits that have high neutral currents, the relationship between the neutral and the phase currents is like that of the transformer secondary. The neutral current is higher than any of the associated phase currents. The danger here is that the neutral conductors could become overloaded and not offer the warning signs of tripped circuit breakers.

The recommendations are as follows:

- Refrain from adding additional loads to the receptacle transformer unless steps are taken to reduce the level of harmonics.
- Pull extra neutrals into the branch circuits that are heavily loaded.
- Monitor the load currents on a regular basis using true rms test equipment.

3.0.0 Section Review

1. In a three-phase, four-wire system, overheating in the neutral can be caused by odd multiples of the _____.
   a. F harmonic
   b. second harmonic
   c. third harmonic
   d. seventh harmonic

2. When surveying an installation, the presence of harmonics may be indicated by a _____.
   a. frequency of 180 Hz
   b. receptacle neutral-to-ground voltage of 2V or less
   c. frequency of 120 Hz
   d. neutral current of 0V

3. When calculating the THDF, a purely sinusoidal waveform has a derating factor of _____.
   a. 0
   b. 1
   c. 3
   d. 9

Module 26406-23 Review Questions

1. What is the name given to the large transformers used in transmission systems to step voltage up and down?
   a. Control transformers
   b. Power transformers
   c. Instrument transformers
   d. Potential transformers

2. The purpose of the two secondary windings in a three-winding transformer is _____.
   a. so the transformer may be used on systems with different primary voltages
   b. to produce a nonmagnetic field
   c. to produce a high-impedance field
   d. to produce two secondary voltages

3. How many windings are normally found in an autotransformer?
   a. One
   b. Two
   c. Three
   d. Four

4. What is a transformer called when it is connected in series with the main line?
   a. Reactance transformer
   b. Series transformer
   c. High-voltage transformer
   d. Low-ampere transformer

5. Regulators are usually designed to provide a secondary voltage range of _____.
   a. ±10% of the supply voltage
   b. ±15% of the supply voltage
   c. ±25% of the supply voltage
   d. ±35% of the supply voltage

6. What type of transformer is normally able to handle a load that is much greater than its nameplate rating?
   a. Potential transformer
   b. Reactance transformer
   c. Current transformer
   d. Buck-and-boost transformer

7. Which of the following is always a single-phase transformer?
   a. Power transformer
   b. Reactance transformer
   c. Current transformer
   d. Autotransformer

8. What type of transformer is normally used with metering equipment when the current is too high for the metering equipment?
   a. Potential transformer
   b. Reactance transformer
   c. Current transformer
   d. Autotransformer

9. Which type of transformer is normally used with metering equipment when the line voltage is too high for the metering equipment?
   a. Potential transformer
   b. Reactance transformer
   c. Series transformer
   d. Autotransformer

10. The secondary thermal kVA rating of a conventional potential transformer rarely exceeds _____.
    a. 1 kVA
    b. 1.5 kVA
    c. 1,500 kVA
    d. 15,000 kVA

11. Potential transformers are available in _____.
    a. oil-filled and hydraulic types
    b. oil-filled and dry types
    c. dry and chemical types
    d. dry and coiled types

12. Each harmonic has a _____.
    a. name only
    b. name and frequency only
    c. name, frequency, and sequence
    d. name, frequency, and rotation

13. Neutral busbars and connecting lugs are sized to carry _____.
    a. 75% of the rated phase current
    b. 80% of the rated phase current
    c. 90% of the rated phase current
    d. 100% of the rated phase current

14. The problem of harmonics is often first detected by the presence of inductive interference in _____.
    a. lighting systems
    b. heating systems
    c. telecommunications systems
    d. emergency power systems

15. For a sine wave, the crest factor is _____.
    a. 1.000
    b. 1.414
    c. 2.212
    d. 2.414

Answers to odd-numbered Module Review Questions are found in *Appendix A*.

Module 26406-23 Supplemental Exercises

1. The four different connections possible in a three-phase transformer are ________.

2. True or False? A typical transformer has two windings that are physically connected.

3. Power transformers are usually installed outdoors in ________.

4. True or False? Autotransformers are especially practical if the difference between the primary and secondary voltages is relatively small.

5. In a three-phase, delta-connected transformer, how does the line voltage compare to the phase voltage?

   ____

   ____

6. A constant-current transformer has a(n) ________ primary coil and a(n) ________ secondary coil.

7. In general, the selection of a proper control circuit transformer must be made from a determination of the ________ to which it is subjected.

8. True or False? Buck-and-boost transformers can handle loads that are much greater than their nameplate ratings.

9. The two types of instrument transformers are ________.

10. The polarity in an instrument transformer identifies ________.

11. The primary winding of a potential transformer is always connected across the ________.

12. Symptoms of harmonics in an office building or industrial establishment usually show up in the ________ equipment that supports the nonlinear loads.

13. In a three-phase, four-wire system, the ________ is most likely to be severely affected by nonlinear loads.

14. What trip device is designed to respond to the true rms value of the current waveform?

    ____

    ____

15. A buzzing sound and/or vibration of an electrical panel can be caused by ________.

Answers to odd-numbered Supplemental Exercises are found in *Appendix B*.

Answers to Section Review Questions

Answer	Section Reference	Objective
Section 1.0.0		
1. b	1.1.0	1a
2. c	1.2.0	1b
3. b	1.3.0	1c
Section 2.0.0		
1. d	2.1.0	2a
2. c	2.2.0	2b
Section 3.0.0		
1. c	3.1.1	3a
2. a	3.2.0	3b
3. b	3.3.2	3c

Source: Ridge Tool Company

Objectives

Successful completion of this module prepares you to do the following:

1. Describe the various types of relays used in motor control circuits.
   a. Identify and describe solid-state relays and their uses.
   b. Identify timing relays and explain their uses.
2. Explain how reduced-voltage starting is accomplished.
   a. Describe the use and selection of conventional reduced-voltage motor starting methods.
   b. Describe solid-state, reduced-voltage motor starting methods.
3. Specify an AFD for a given application.
   a. Describe the types of AFDs, along with their operation and components.
   b. Compare the uses, benefits, and problems when selecting an AFD.
4. Compare motor braking methods.
   a. Describe DC injection braking.
   b. Identify dynamic and regenerative braking methods.
   c. Describe friction braking.
5. Describe how to maintain motor controls for peak operation.
   a. Apply the precautions associated with solid-state controls.
   b. Implement the preventive maintenance procedures associated with solid-state controls.
6. Describe how to troubleshoot motor controls.
   a. Explain basic troubleshooting methods.
   b. Describe the electrical troubleshooting methods used to check control circuits and devices.

Performance Task

Under supervision, you should be able to do the following:

1. Identify and connect various control devices.

Overview

Control systems regulate and direct the behavior of devices within an electrical system. They vary in complexity and consist of a variety of components that provide different types of control. This module discusses applications and operating principles of various control system components, such as solid-state relays, reduced-voltage starters, and adjustable frequency drives. It also covers basic troubleshooting procedures.

NOTE

Digital Resources for Electrical

Scan this code using the camera on your phone or mobile device to view the digital resources related to this craft.

1.0.0 Identifying Relays

Performance Tasks

There are no Performance Tasks in this section.

Objective

Describe the various types of relays used in motor control circuits.

a. Identify and describe solid-state relays and their uses.

b. Identify timing relays and explain their uses.

Relays are a type of switching device that starts and stops the flow of current to an electrical device or appliance. This essential functionality makes relays key components of all electrical control systems. Electromechanical relays and contactors are still in use, but they are gradually being replaced by solid-state devices.

1.1.0 Solid-State Relays

Solid-state relay (SSR): A switching device that has no contacts and switches entirely by electronic means.

The **solid-state relay (SSR)** has many advantages over the electromechanical relay (EMR). It has longer life, higher reliability, higher speed switching, and high resistance to shock and vibration. The absence of mechanical contacts eliminates contact bounce, arcing when the contacts open, and hazards from explosives and flammable gases. For this reason, SSRs (*Figure 1*) have replaced EMRs in many applications.

1.1.1 SSR Operation

SSRs can be used in many of the same control applications as EMRs and in many new applications involving electronic control circuit devices. An SSR is activated by the control circuit voltage applied to its input terminals. Depending on the SSR design, this input control voltage can be alternating current (AC) or direct current (DC). AC voltages typically range between 90VAC and 280VAC; DC voltages range between 3VDC and 32VDC. DC voltage inputs are normally applied from digitally controlled motor control circuits. Application of the AC or DC input control voltage to the relay can be done by the closure of a mechanical switch or from the activation of a solid-state device, such as a transistor or integrated circuit.

Internally, an SSR consists of an input control circuit and an output circuit (*Figure 2*). The function of the input control circuit can be compared to that of the coil in an EMR in that it senses the input control signal and provides coupling between the input and output circuits. In most SSRs, the coupling of the switching command to the output circuit is done optically using a light-emitting diode (LED) and photo detector. This type of SSR is called an *optically isolated SSR*. The optical isolation keeps voltage spikes or electrical noise generated on the load side of the SSR from being coupled into the input control circuit side of the SSR.

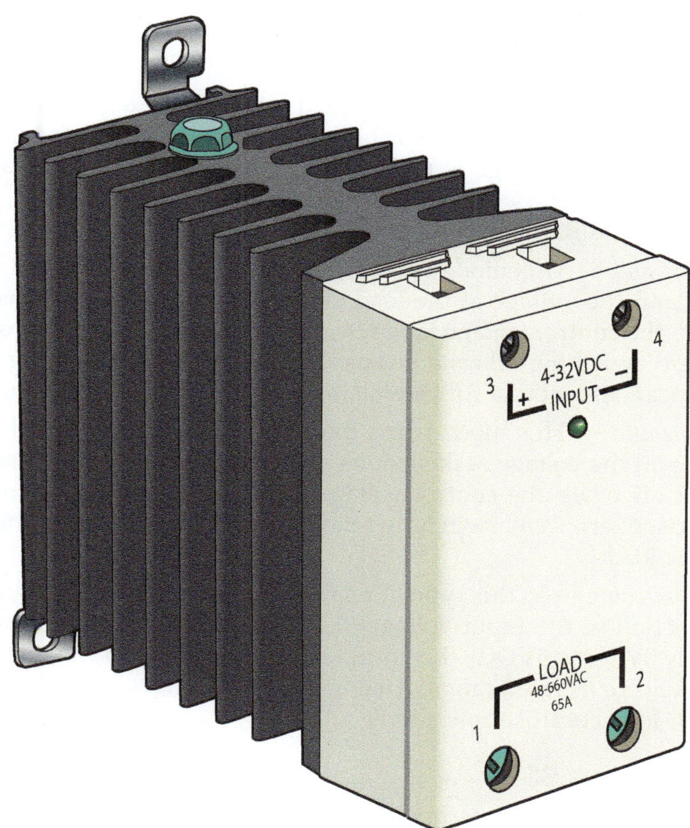

Figure 1 SSR with heat sink.

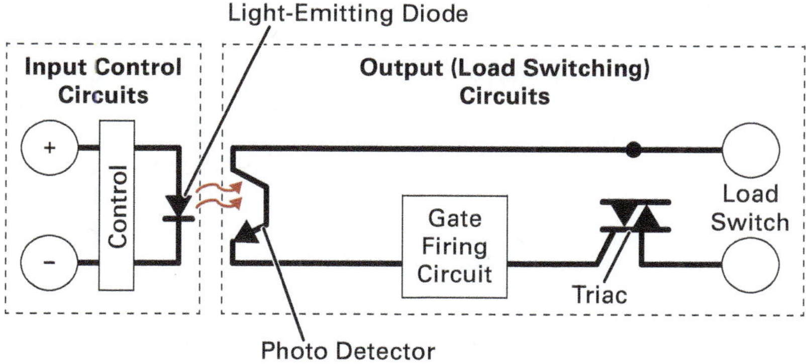

Figure 2 Block diagram of an optically isolated SSR.

When the applied input control voltage level exceeds a predetermined threshold known as the *pickup voltage*, a light beam is generated by the LED and transmitted to the photo detector. This light is used to electronically activate the SSR output switch. The output switch will remain activated until the input control voltage level drops below the relay's minimum dropout voltage level, at which time the LED stops emitting light, which deactivates the output switch.

The output switching circuit electronically performs the same function as the mechanical contacts of an EMR. Depending on the design of the SSR and the type of load to be controlled, the output switching can be performed by power transistors, silicon-controlled rectifiers (SCRs), triacs, or **thyristors**.

Thyristors: Bi-stable semiconductor devices that can be switched off and on. Thyristors turn on with a quick pulse of control current. They turn off only when the working current is interrupted elsewhere in the circuit. SCRs and triacs are forms of thyristors.

Power transistor outputs are typically used to control low-current loads while SCR-switched outputs are typically used to control high-current DC loads. Triac-switched outputs are typically used to control high-current AC loads, while thyristor-switched outputs are used to control either low- or high-current

AC loads, depending on their circuit configuration. The switching circuit can operate in one of these four switching modes, depending on the SSR design:

- *Instant-on* — This mode turns the load on immediately at any point on the AC sine wave when the control voltage is present. It turns the load off when the control voltage is removed and the current in the load crosses zero. Instant-on relays are commonly used to control contactors, magnetic starters, and similar loads.
- *Zero switching* — This mode turns the load on when the control voltage is applied and the voltage at the load crosses zero. The relay turns the load off when the control voltage is removed and the current in the load crosses zero. Zero-switching relays are typically used to control heating elements, ovens, incandescent and tungsten lamps, and programmable controllers.
- *Peak switching* — This mode turns the load on when the control voltage is applied and the voltage at the load is at its peak amplitude. The relay turns the load off when the control voltage is removed and the current in the load crosses zero. Peak switching relays are typically used to control heavy inductive loads.
- *Analog switching* — In this type of relay, the amount of output voltage varies as a function of the input voltage. For any voltage within its input range (typically 0VDC to 5VDC), the output is a percentage of the available output voltage within its rated range. Analog switching relays are commonly used in closed-loop control applications.

1.1.2 EMRs versus SSRs

Differences exist both in the terminology used to describe EMRs and SSRs and in their overall ability to perform certain functions. *Table 1* shows the equivalent or comparable terminology between an EMR and an SSR; *Table 2* indicates the ability of each device to perform certain functions. When making a choice between solid-state and electromechanical devices, compare the electrical and mechanical operating characteristics of each device with the application in which it is to be used.

Each device has its limitations on current and voltage, so the manufacturer's data sheets must be used to select the proper device for the intended load.

The electronic nature of the SSR and its input circuit lends itself for use in digitally controlled logic circuits. Another advantage of the SSR over the EMR is its ability to turn on and off very quickly because it has no moving mechanical parts.

1.1.3 Two-Wire and Three-Wire SSR Control

Two-wire control of an SSR is very similar to that of an EMR, as shown in *Figure 3* (A). For three-wire control there is no auxiliary contact in an SSR to seal in the relay until the Stop button is activated. However, addition of an SCR and a current-limiting resistor will achieve the same results, as shown in *Figure 3* (B). Pressing the Start button turns power on to the gate input of the SCR, causing its state to flip to the On position. It will stay on until pressing the Stop button returns it to the Off position.

1.1.4 Connecting SSRs to Switch Multiple Outputs

SSRs are made with one to four switched outputs. If an application needs a higher current rating than a multipole output SSR can provide, higher-rated single-pole SSRs can have their input signal wired either in series or parallel. *Figure 4* shows both series and parallel connections for the control of a three-phase load such as a motor. When the inputs are wired in series, the voltage used must be higher than the sum of each input's minimum control voltage. Similarly, when the inputs are wired in parallel, the available input current must be higher than the sum of each SSR control current.

TABLE 1 Comparison Chart for EMR and SSR Technology

Comparable or Equivalent Terminology for Electromechanical and Solid-State Relays	
Electromechanical Relays (EMRs)	**Solid-State Relays (SSRs)**
Coil voltage — The minimum voltage necessary to energize or operate the relay. Also referred to as the *pickup voltage*.	*Control voltage* — The minimum voltage required to gate or activate the control circuit of an SSR. Generally, a maximum value is also specified.
Inrush VA — The amount of power necessary to energize or operate the relay coil.	*Control current* — The minimum current required to activate a solid-state control circuit. Generally, a maximum value is also specified.
Sealed VA — The power required to keep the relay energized or operating.	See *control current*.
Dropout voltage — The minimum voltage required to keep the relay energized.	See *control voltage*.
Pull-in time — The amount of time required to operate (open or close) the relay contacts after the coil voltage is applied.	*Turn-on time* — The elapsed time between the application of the control voltage and the application of the voltage to the load circuit.
Dropout time — The amount of time required for the relay contacts to return to their normal (unoperated) position after the coil voltage is removed.	*Turn-off time* — The elapsed time between the removal of the control voltage and the removal of the voltage from the load circuit.
Contact voltage rating — The maximum voltage rating that the contacts can switch safely.	*Load voltage* — The maximum output voltage handling capability of an SSR.
Contact current rating — The maximum current rating that the contacts can switch safely.	*Load current* — The maximum output current handling capability of an SSR.
Surge current — The maximum peak current that the contacts can withstand for short periods of time without damage.	*Surge current* — The maximum peak current that an SSR can withstand for short periods of time without damage.
Contact voltage drop — The voltage drop across the relay contacts when the relay is operating (usually quite low).	*Switch-on voltage drop* — The voltage drop across an SSR when the relay is operating (usually quite low).
Insulation resistance — The amount of resistance measured across relay contacts in the open position.	*Switch-off resistance* — The amount of resistance measured across an SSR when turned off.
—	*Off-state current leakage* — The amount of current leakage through an SSR when turned off but still connected to the load voltage.
—	*Zero-current turn-off* — Turn-off at essentially the zero crossing of the load current that flows through an SSR. A thyristor will turn off only when the current falls below the minimum holding current. If input control is removed when the current is at a higher value, turn-off will be delayed until the next zero current crossing.
—	*Zero-voltage turn-on* — Initial turn-on occurs at a point near the zero crossing of the AC line voltage. If input control is applied when the line voltage is at a higher value, initial turn-on will be delayed until the next zero current crossing.

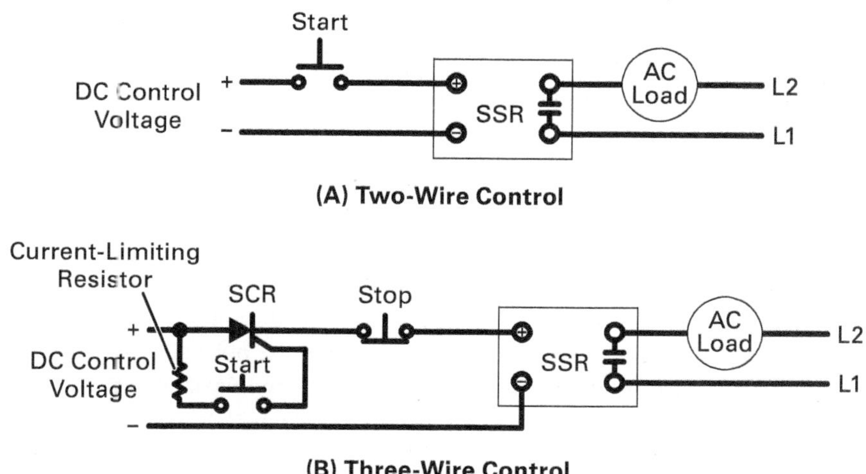

Figure 3 Two-wire and three-wire SSR control.

TABLE 2 EMR and SSR Performance

Advantages and Disadvantages of Electromechanical and Solid-State Relays		
General Characteristics	**EMR**	**SSR**
Arcless switching of the load	-	+
Electronic compatibility for interfacing	-	+
Effects of temperature	+	-
Shock and vibration resistant	-	+
Immunity to improper functioning due to transients	+	-
Radio frequency switching	+	-
Zero-voltage turn-on	-	+
Acoustic noise	-	+
Selection of multipole, multithrow switching capability	+	-
Contact bouncing	-	+
Ability to withstand surge currents	+	-
Response time	-	+
Voltage drop in load circuit	+	-
AC & DC switching with same contacts	+	-
Zero-current turn-off	-	+
Leakage current	+	-
Minimum-current turn-on	+	-
Life expectancy	-	+
Initial cost	+	-
Lifetime (total) cost	-	+
Note: Plus (+) indicates advantage or function; minus (-) indicates disadvantage or lack of function.		

1.1.5 SSR Temperature Considerations

Every solid-state electronic device, including SSRs, will be damaged by excessive temperature. Manufacturers of SSRs specify the maximum permitted environmental temperature, typically 104°F (40°C). As a rule, for every 18°F (10°C) increase above this temperature the life span of the SSR is cut in half. This environmental heat comes from the surrounding area and from various components in the enclosure, such as the voltage drop and current flow through the SSR.

Because the heat created by the SSR is concentrated in a small area, manufacturers add a fan and/or a finned metal mounting base, called a **heat sink**, to carry the heat away. The heat sink is made from a metal with high **thermal conductivity** (or low thermal resistance), typically aluminum.

Heat sink: A metal mounting base that dissipates the heat of solid-state components mounted on it by radiating the heat into the surrounding atmosphere.

Thermal conductivity: The ability of a material or substance to transfer heat away from a given point of contact.

The manufacturer's installation instructions list the type and size of heat sink (if not provided), as well as installation instructions. Following these instructions is required by *NEC Section 110.3(B)*. Installation considerations for heat sinks include the following:

- Use the proper heat sink; if practical, it should have fins for greater heat dissipation.
- Make sure that the mounting surface between the heat sink and the SSR is flat and smooth.
- Ensure that the mounting area meets the manufacturer requirements for free space around the heat sink.
- Use thermal grease or a thermally conductive pad between the SSR and the heat sink to eliminate any air gaps and maximize heat dissipation.
- Make sure all mounting hardware is securely fastened.

Know the Code

Installation and Use
NEC Section 110.3(B)

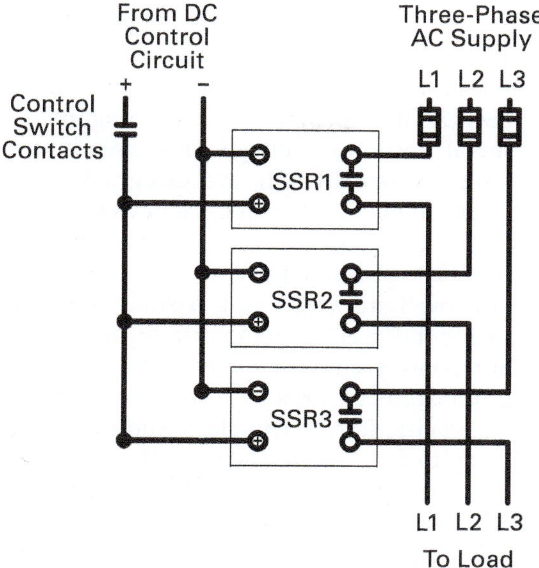

(A) Three SSRs Controlled in Parallel

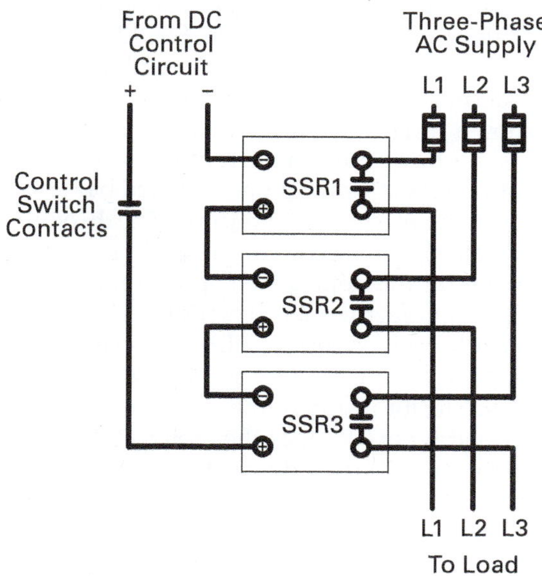

(B) Three SSRs Controlled in Series

Figure 4 Multiple SSRs controlled in parallel or in series to switch a three-phase load.

1.1.6 Overvoltage and Overcurrent Protection

SSR components, such as power transistors, SCRs, and triacs, can be damaged by a shorted load. It is a good practice to install an overcurrent protection fuse to open the output circuit should the load current increase to a higher value than the nominal load current. This fuse should be an ultrafast type designed for use with semiconductor devices.

To protect power transistors, SCRs, triacs, and other devices from overvoltages resulting from transients induced on the load lines, install a peak voltage clamping device in the output circuit, such as a varistor, a Zener diode, or an energy-limiting resistor-capacitor device known as a *snubber.*

1.1.7 SSOLRs

Solid-state overload relay (SSOLR): An electronic device that provides overload protection for electrical equipment.

A solid-state protective relay, commonly called a **solid-state overload relay (SSOLR)**, protects the motor against damage from overheating. Depending on their design, many SSOLRs also provide protection against phase loss, phase imbalance, phase reversal, and undervoltage. They do not protect against short circuits or ground faults. Many SSOLRs are designed to be retrofitted into equipment in which thermal overload protective devices previously were used. Depending on the design, some SSOLRs are self-powered, whereas others must be powered by a separate DC power supply.

Thermal OLRs work mechanically, using a small special-purpose resistor called a *heater* to trip a bimetallic element or spring-loaded melting alloy contact to interrupt the motor control circuit. For each manufacturer, the heater is selected from among hundreds of sizes that are listed within many dozens of tables according to the specific starter, trip class, and motor service factor. With some brands there are up to four different orientations for mounting the heater within the thermal OLR. In comparison, SSOLRs come in a modest number of sizes, with simpler selection and installation. There are two types of SSOLRs: nonprogrammable and programmable.

Nonprogrammable SSOLRs

SSOLRs are made in many sizes and shapes for stand-alone mounting, starter mounting, and DIN-rail mounting. shows an example of one manufacturer's self-powered, stand-alone nonprogrammable SSOLR and a related control diagram. Control power is derived from the three-phase inputs. Regardless of manufacturer and internal circuitry differences, all SSOLRs operate in much the same way. As shown in *Figure 5*, the SSOLR senses the current in each of the three motor leads via three built-in current transformer (CT) windings. In some models, the motor leads attach to a pre-installed bar and terminals within the CT, while other models provide a hole in the CT through which one, two, or three loops of the motor leads can be run. The trip point for the SSOLR is set within the range shown on the adjustable trip current dial on the face of the unit, as directed in the manufacturer's instructions. This setting for the SSOLR is based on the motor full-load amperage (FLA), service factor, and the number of CT loop turns being used. Settings on SSOLRs like the one in the image are for motors with a service factor of 1.15 or more. For motors with a service factor of less than 1.15, use a setting of 0.9 times the motor FLA. If more than one loop of wire is run through the CT, an additional multiplier is the number of CT loops.

CAUTION

If a lightly loaded motor loses one input phase while running, the current flow through the remaining motor leads is usually below the motor FLA, so a standard overload relay will not trip. However, the magnetic fields in the motor will be severely unbalanced and overheating of the motor will occur.

The SSOLR initiates a trip if the phase currents exceed 125% of the trip current dial setting. The time it takes to trip depends on the level of monitored current, the trip class (Class 10, Class 20, and so on), and the length of time since the last trip. A mechanically latched mechanism opens (unlatches) when a trip occurs. This action opens the normally closed (NC) overload trip contact, interrupting current flow in the motor control circuit. The relay's phase loss / phase imbalance circuitry will also initiate a trip if a current imbalance of 25% or greater exists or if one of the phase currents is missing. To provide protection for lightly loaded motors, the phase loss / phase imbalance circuitry remains operational at currents below the trip current. Once tripped, the SSOLR is reset by pressing the RESET button on the face of the unit. Most manufacturers also have a remote reset module that can be installed. Typically, this would be used with cranes, hoists, and similar applications where the controls are mounted in a remote location, making them difficult to access.

An SSOLR can be an instantaneous trip device (instant removal with no time delay) or inverse time, Class 10, 15, 20, 30, or other class device. Some have an adjustment to set the trip class. These models are usually shipped with trip Class 20 selected. Most SSOLRs are also equipped with LED indicators to show when power is applied and when a trip has occurred.

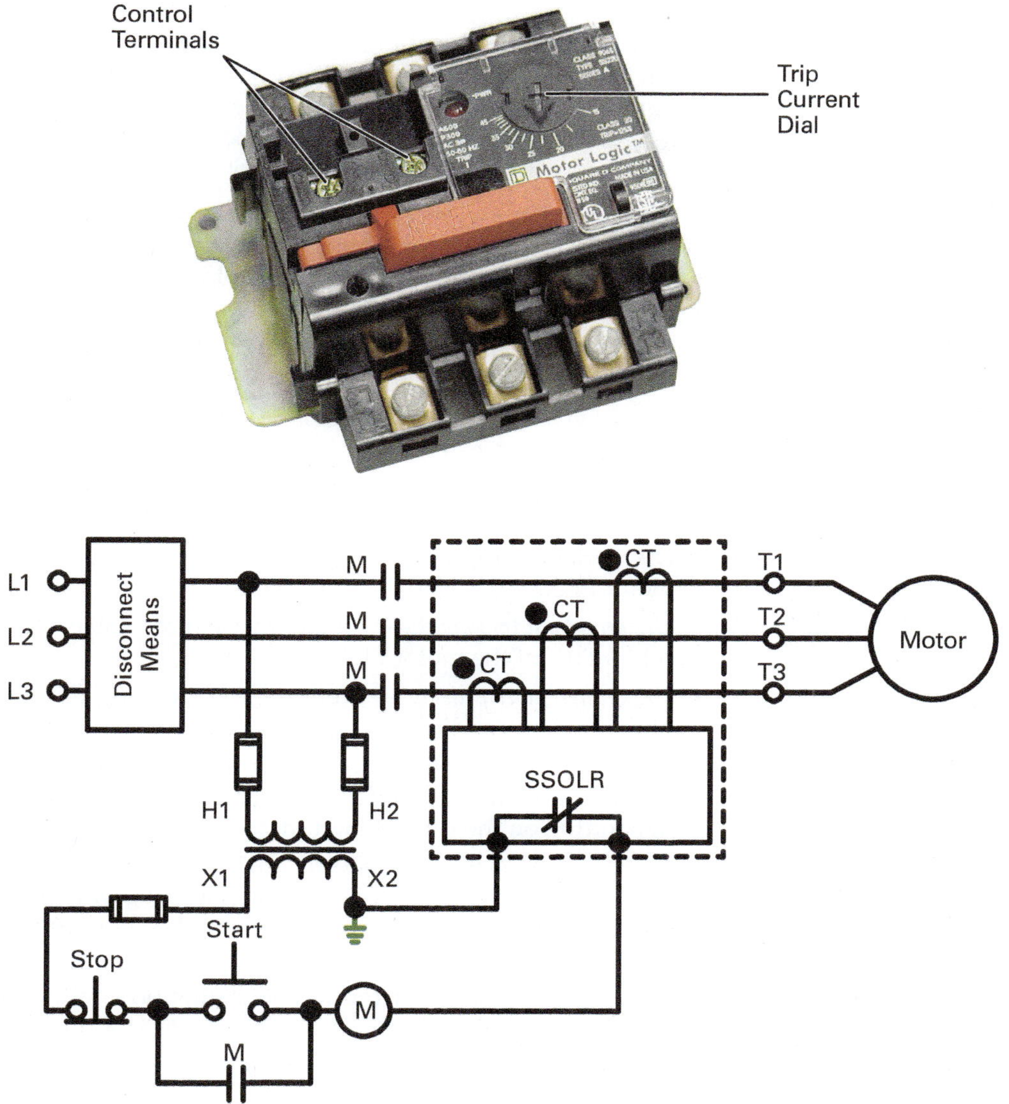

Figure 5 SSOLR.
Source: Schneider Electric (top)

Programmable SSOLRs

Programmable SSOLRs provide the same overload and phase loss / phase imbalance motor protection as nonprogrammable relays. Refer to *NEC Section 430.32(A)(1).* In addition, most have an increased capability to detect several other types of motor-related faults. The programmable SSOLR is connected into the motor circuit in the same way as a nonprogrammable relay. However, most programmable SSOLRs require the use of an external power supply for their solid-state circuitry. Like nonprogrammable SSOLRs, programmable models sense the motor current via CT windings. For some models, these CT windings are internal to the relay. For others, they are mounted externally. External mounting typically occurs in motor circuit applications having high full-load currents (90A and above). Operation of the SSOLR is controlled by a microprocessor that can be programmed so the relay can be used in a wide variety of applications. *Figure 6* shows an example of a programmable SSOLR.

Programming of an SSOLR is done using controls on the front panel of the unit. However, many SSOLR manufacturers also have software programs available that allow an SSOLR to be programmed using a personal computer (PC) connected to the relay via a communications network. Programming procedures for SSOLRs differ among manufacturers and among models from the same manufacturer. For this reason, programming must be done in accordance with the manufacturer's

Know the Code

Separate Overload Device
NEC Section 430.32(A)(1)

Trip Class

When the current flowing through the adjustable overload relay is 600% of the actual dial setting, the trip class is the number of seconds until it will trip.

instructions for the specific relay in use. The number and types of parameters that can be programmed differ from one SSOLR to another depending on their design. For the SSOLR shown in *Figure 6*, setting trip thresholds for the different circuit parameters is done using the Mode Select and Display/Program switches on the front of the unit. The types of functions and trip thresholds that can be programmed with most programmable SSOLRs include the following:

- *Overcurrent trip class* — Selects the trip class (e.g., Class 10, 20, 30). The specific trip class is determined by the motor and application. Class 20 is used for most general-purpose motors rated by the National Electrical Manufacturers Association (NEMA).
- *Effective turns ratio of CTs* — Used by the SSOLR to calculate the true current based on the turns ratio of the internal or externally mounted CTs.
- *Low- and high-voltage trip points* — Typically set to ±10% of the motor nameplate rating.
- *Voltage imbalance trip point* — Sets the percentage of voltage imbalance allowed by the motor. Typically set for 5%.
- *Overcurrent trip point* — Typically set to between 110% and 120% of the motor FLA.
- *Undercurrent trip point* — Sets the level of acceptable undercurrent. Typically set for 80% of the motor FLA.
- *Undercurrent trip delay* — Determines how long the SSOLR will allow an undercurrent condition to exist before it trips.
- *Restart delay time after a trip* — Controls the elapsed time between motor restarts after a trip. Different settings allow for different restart times, depending on the type of fault that has occurred.
- *Number of restarts* — If enabled, this determines the number of automatic restarts that can be initiated. After the programmed number of restarts have been attempted and failed, a manual reset must be performed.
- *Ground fault current trip* — Determines when a Class II ground fault exists because degradation of the motor insulation is allowing current leakage. The threshold is typically set for 10% to 20% of the motor FLA. Class II is for motor protection only; it is not the same as ground fault protection for personnel.

When tripped by an overload, the programmable SSOLR is reset locally by pressing the Reset button on the face of the unit. If it is equipped with a remote reset module, it can be reset from a remote location.

Use of External Current Transformers

When using external current transformers, make sure that all the CT polarity marks face in the same direction and route all the load wires in the same direction through the CT windows.

Figure 6 Typical programmable SSOLR.
Source: Schneider Electric

1.2.0 Timing Relays

Timing relays open or close electric circuits to perform selected operations according to a timed program. Various methods have been used to create timing relays. Adding a bellows chamber and air metering valve to an EMR creates a pneumatic timing relay. Similarly, using silicone oil instead of air creates a **dashpot** timing relay. These are older relay types that may still be found mounted on or alongside other relays in older control cabinets. Using a motor and an adjustable dial pointer creates a motorized timing relay, which is rugged and often found in control enclosure doors because it is easy to set and usually displays the elapsed time. This section will focus on electronic (solid-state) timing relays because of their wide range of capabilities and applications, as well as their increasingly common usage.

Dashpot: A device that uses a gas or fluid to absorb energy from or retard the movement of the moving parts of a relay, circuit breaker, or other electrical or mechanical device.

A simple application involves the use of timing relays to control the sequential energization or de-energization of two or more motors. Most timing relays have adjustable time intervals, and often have more than one selectable timing function, allowing them to be used in more than one application. Before going further, it is first necessary to introduce terms commonly used when describing timing relays, as well as symbols used on schematic and ladder diagrams to identify timed contacts (*Figure 7*). These terms include the following:

- *On-delay relay* — An on-delay relay provides the time delay after the relay is energized.
- *Off-delay relay* — An off-delay relay provides the time delay after the relay is de-energized.
- *Normally open, timed-closed (NOTC) contacts* — NOTC contacts are on-delay, timed-closed contacts. The contacts are normally open. When the relay is energized, timing begins, and the contacts close after the specified delay time has elapsed. The contacts remain closed until the relay is de-energized, at which time the contacts are immediately opened.
- *Normally closed, timed-open (NCTO) contacts* — NCTO contacts are on-delay, timed-open contacts. The contacts are normally closed. When the relay is energized, timing begins, and the contacts are opened after the specified delay time has elapsed. The contacts close immediately when the relay is de-energized.
- *Normally open, timed-open (NOTO) contacts* — NOTO contacts are off-delay, timed-open contacts. When the relay is energized, the NO contacts close immediately and stay closed. When the relay is de-energized, timing begins, and the contacts are opened after the specified delay time has elapsed.
- *Normally closed, timed-closed (NCTC) contacts* — NCTC contacts are off-delay, timed-closed contacts. When the relay is energized, the NC contacts open immediately and remain open. When the relay is de-energized, timing begins, and the contacts are closed after the specified delay time has elapsed.

On-Delay and Off-Delay Relays

On-delay relays and off-delay relays are also commonly called *delay-on-make relays* and *delay-on-break relays*, respectively.

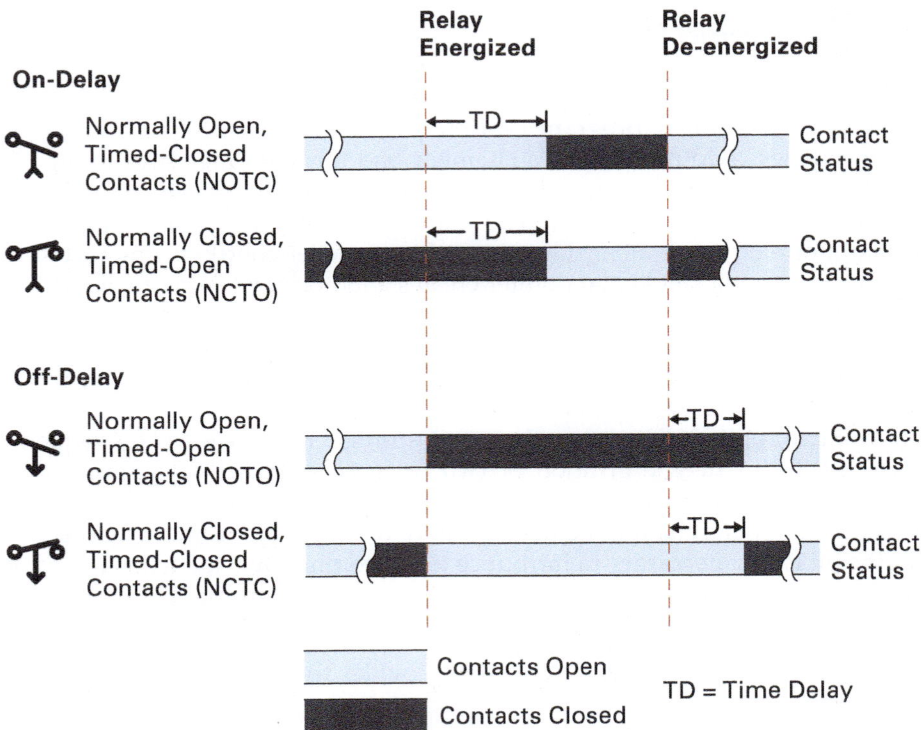

Figure 7 Timed-contact symbols and timing.

1.2.1 Solid-State Timing Relays

The solid-state timing relay (SSTR) gets its name from the fact that its time-delay function is provided by solid-state electronic devices enclosed within the relay body. Early versions of SSTRs only provided a few timing functions and a limited number of timing ranges. Due to the growing trend towards the use of microprocessors, a single relay can be made with as many as 25 or more different selectable timing functions, 6 or more different timing ranges, and a timing accuracy of better than 0.1%. *Figure 8* is an example of a plug-in SSTR with 10 selectable timing functions, 6 timing ranges from 9.99 seconds to 999 hours, and 0.1% accuracy.

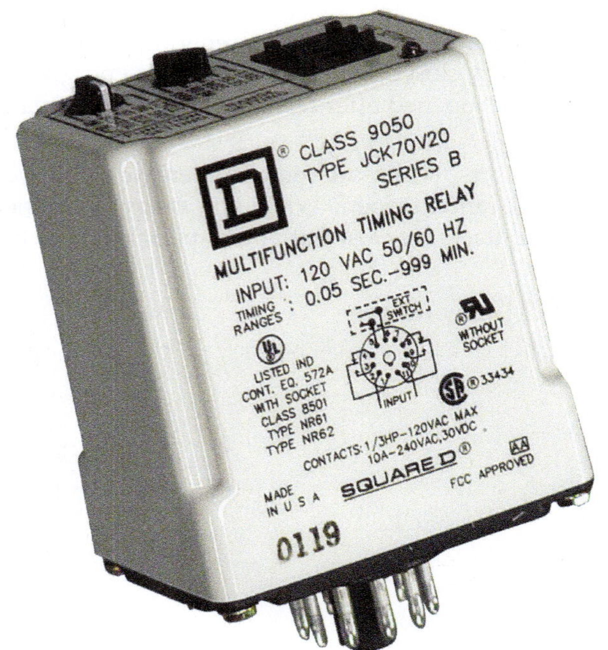

Figure 8 Typical solid-state plug-in timing relay.

SSTR timing functions are provided by two basic forms of control: supply-voltage timing relays and contact-controlled timing relays. These relays provide four common timing functions: on delay, off delay, interval, and single shot. They operate as follows:

- *Supply-voltage timing relay* — A supply-voltage timing relay begins its operation with the application of voltage to its input power terminals or pins. The input power source and pilot devices that control this relay must be suitable for the voltage and current rating of the timing relay in use. The upper half of *Figure 9* shows delay-on-make (on delay) and interval timing modes for a typical supply-voltage timing relay. For the delay-on-make mode, the output contacts switch state after the time delay and remain that way until the input power is turned off. For the interval mode, the output contacts switch state when the input power is turned on and switch back at the end of the interval; it will not repeat until the next time the input power is turned on.
- *Contact-controlled timing relay* — A contact-controlled timing relay normally has continuous power to its input power terminals and begins its operation with the closure of a control switch or pilot device (often called S1) between two terminals. The pilot devices that control this relay must be suitable for the low voltage of the control terminals and be wired only to them. The lower half of *Figure 9* shows delay-on-break (off delay) and single-shot timing modes typical for a contact-controlled timing relay. For the off-delay mode, the output contacts switch state when the control switch is closed and switch back only after the control switch has remained open for the set time delay. For the single-shot mode, the output contacts change state when the control switch is closed and switch back after the time delay has elapsed, regardless of the control switch status.

In addition to the 8-pin and 11-pin plug-in types, SSTRs are made in many other forms, sizes, and mounting methods, with some having a time display or a moving time dial. A wide variety of timing functions are also available, including repeat cycle, unequal repeat cycle, percentage, time totalizer, re-triggerable off delay, or delayed interval.

Transistor-Controlled and Sensor-Controlled Timing Relays

Transistor-controlled and sensor-controlled timing relays are also available. A transistor-controlled timing relay is controlled by a transistor switch located in an external electronic device. A sensor-controlled timing relay is controlled by an external proximity or photoelectric sensor in which the relay itself supplies the power to operate the sensor.

1.2.2 Timing Relay Applications

There are hundreds of applications in which timing relays are used to provide timed control of equipment, operations, or processes. One common application involves the use of a timer to start multiple motors at preset intervals to avoid overloading a feeder circuit with motor inrush current. With large motors, a series of 20-second time delays between each motor startup is common. If the motors are on a conveyor system, the time delay could be as short as 0.5 seconds, with the downstream conveyor starting first. *Figure 10* shows the control wiring for starting three motors with time delays between each one. As shown, the overload relay contacts for all three motors are in series just before L_2, so if any one of them opens from an overload, all motor starters and timing relays will be de-energized.

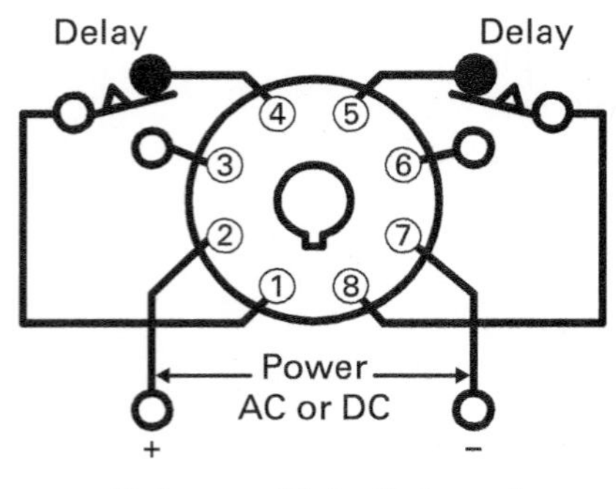

Delay-on-Make/Interval

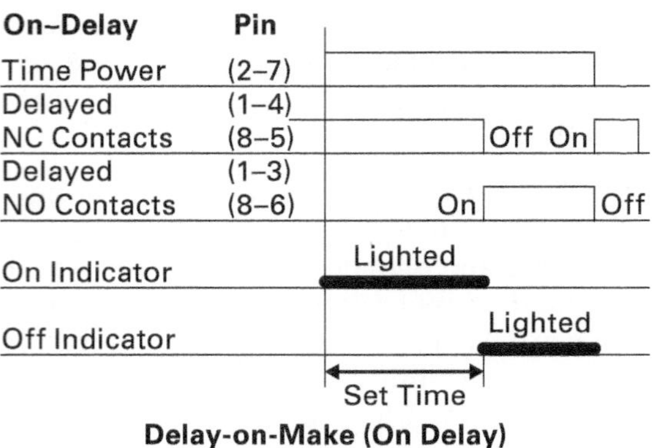

Delay-on-Make (On Delay)

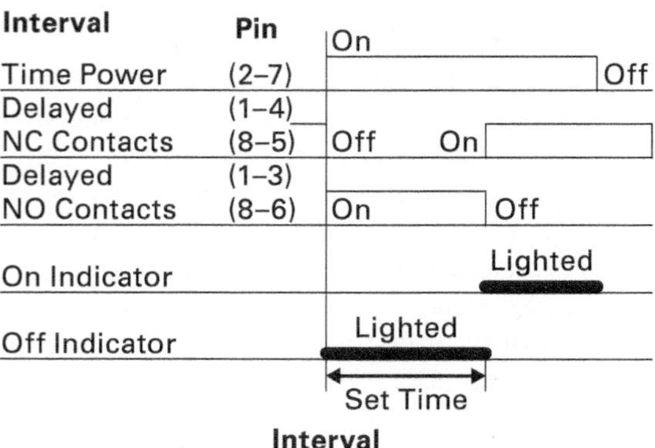

Interval

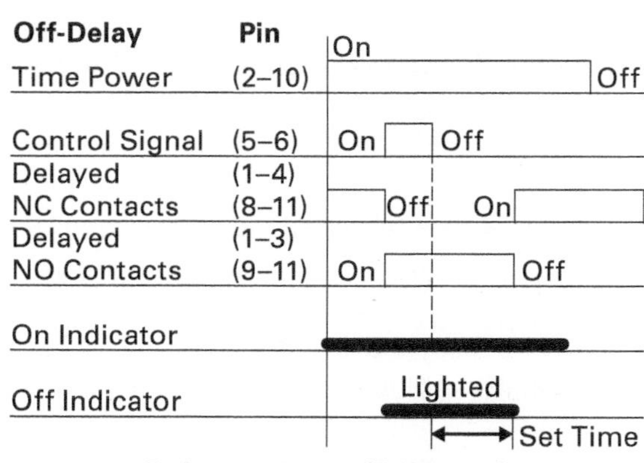

Delay-on-Break (Off Delay)

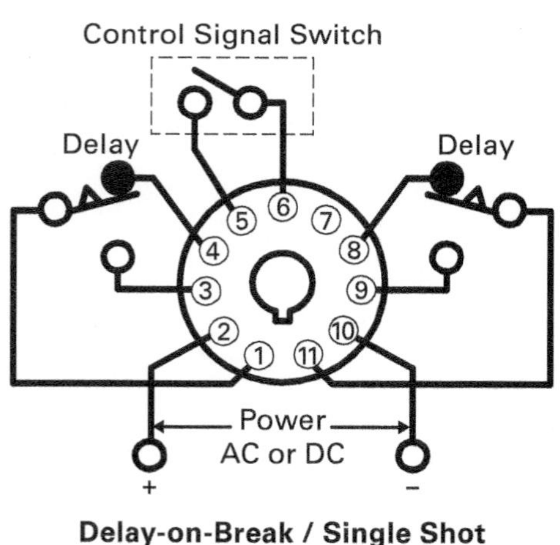

Delay-on-Break / Single Shot

One Shot Pin
On
Time Power (2–10) Off
Control Signal (5–6) On Off
Delayed (1–4)
NC Contacts (8–11) Off On
Delayed (1–3)
NO Contacts (9–11) On Off
On Indicator Lighted
Off Indicator Lighted
Set Time

Single Shot

Figure 9 Plug-in SSR connection diagrams and sequence charts.

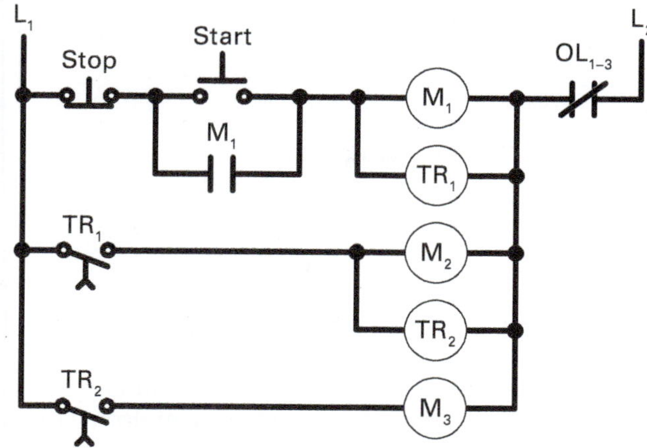

Figure 10 Time-delayed starting for three motors.

When the Start button is pressed, the circuit is completed from L_1 to L_2 through the Stop button, the Start button, the motor starter coil M_1, and the closed overload contacts. The energizing of M_1 closes its NO auxiliary contacts to seal around the Start button. Simultaneously, timing relay TR_1 receives its power and starts its on-delay timing while motor M_1 starts and gets up to speed. When TR_1 finishes its time period, the NO contacts close to energize motor starter M_2 and supply power to TR_2. While TR_2 is timing, motor M_2 is getting up to speed. When TR_2 finishes its time period, the NO contacts close to energize motor starter M_3.

When the Stop button is pressed, M_1 and TR_1 both turn off. The NO contacts on TR_1 open to de-energize M_2 and TR_2. The NO contacts on TR_2 open to de-energize M_3. This process of stopping the motors occurs almost instantaneously.

1.0.0 Section Review

1. In which of these switching modes does the amount of output voltage vary as a function of the input voltage?
   a. Instant-on switching
   b. Analog switching
   c. Peak switching
   d. Zero switching

2. The type of time-delay relay that provides the time delay after the relay is de-energized is a(n) _____.
   a. off-delay relay
   b. on-delay relay
   c. NOTC relay
   d. NCTO relay

2.0.0 Reduced-Voltage Starting Methods

Performance Tasks

There are no Performance Tasks in this section.

Objective

Explain how reduced-voltage starting is accomplished.

a. Describe the use and selection of conventional reduced-voltage motor starting methods.

b. Describe solid-state, reduced-voltage motor starting methods.

Reduced-voltage starting reduces the amount of current an induction motor draws when starting. There are several reasons for using reduced-voltage starting. One common reason is to reduce the large amount of current drawn from utility lines by across-the-line starting of large motors. This occurs because the inrush current drawn by a motor is typically five to six times its nameplate current rating; and for high-efficiency motors, this inrush current can be as high as ten or more times its nameplate rating. The voltage drop caused by this large current demand can stress the upstream service equipment or cause malfunctions in other equipment.

Another common reason for using reduced-voltage starting is to control motor torque at startup so that the torque is applied to a load gradually. This is needed for applications in which a high starting torque can damage gears, belts, and chain drives being driven by the motor or when damage to a product can occur from a sudden forceful start. Reducing the voltage applied to a motor at startup reduces the current drawn by the motor. This reduces the amount of starting torque the motor can deliver because the starting torque is proportional to the current.

Control of inrush current and starting torque is typically accomplished using a reduced-voltage motor starter to supply power to the motor. The driven load and the type of motor generally dictate the type of starter to use. Both conventional and solid-state motors starters are available.

2.1.0 Conventional Methods

Reduced-voltage starting is not the same as speed control. By applying the motor torque to a load gradually, reduced-voltage starting acts as a buffer or shock absorber to the load during initial startup. A speed control operates to control the speed of a motor during its entire operation cycle. Three conventional methods of reduced-voltage starting are:

- Autotransformer
- Part-winding
- Wye-delta

2.1.1 Autotransformer Reduced-Voltage Motor Starting Control

Autotransformer reduced-voltage starters are widely used because of their efficiency and flexibility. See *NEC Section 430.109(D)*. All power taken from the line, except transformer loss, is transmitted to the motor to accelerate the load. Several different taps on the transformer allow for adjustment of the starting torque and inrush current to meet job requirements. Autotransformer reduced-voltage starters are typically used with hard-to-start loads such as reciprocating compressors, grinding mills, pumps, and similar devices. *Figure 11* shows a graph of the starting characteristics for an autotransformer reduced-voltage starting controller.

Know the Code

Autotransformer-Type Controlled Motors
NEC Section 430.109(D)

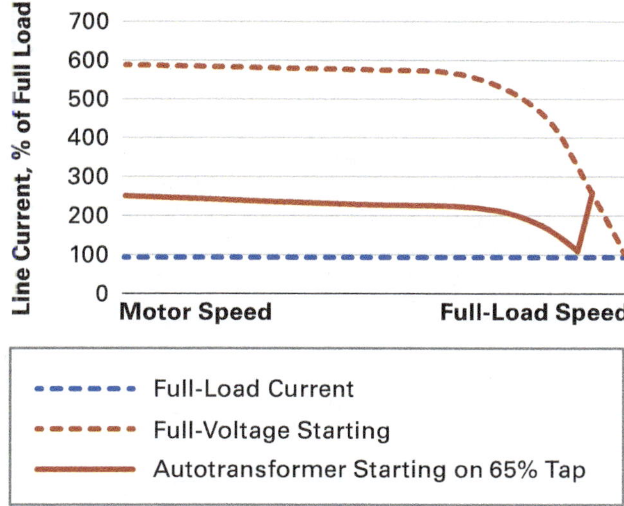

Figure 11 Autotransformer reduced-voltage starting characteristics.

Depending on the manufacturer and model, there are several designs for autotransformer reduced-voltage starting. Some use three-coil autotransformers while others use two-coil autotransformers. Some perform the transition from reduced voltage to full voltage using a **closed-circuit transition** method of motor connection. Others use an **open-circuit transition** method of motor connection. In a closed-circuit transition controller, the motor is never removed from the source of voltage while moving from one voltage level to another. In an open-circuit transition controller, the motor being controlled may be disconnected temporarily from the line while moving from one voltage level to another. Controllers using the closed-circuit transition method are more expensive but are preferred because they cause the least amount of interference to the related electrical distribution system. This is because the motor is never disconnected from the line. Therefore, there is no interruption of line current with a resulting second inrush current during the transition period.

Closed-circuit transition: A method of reduced-voltage starting in which the motor being controlled is never removed from the source of voltage while moving from one voltage level to another.

Open-circuit transition: A method of reduced-voltage starting in which the motor being controlled may be disconnected temporarily from the source of voltage while moving from one voltage level to another.

Figure 12 shows a schematic diagram for an induction motor being controlled by a closed-circuit transition type of autotransformer reducedvoltage controller. As shown, it includes a three-coil autotransformer and two three-pole contactors (1S and 2S) used to connect the autotransformer for reduced-voltage starting. It also includes a three-pole run contactor (R) used to bypass the autotransformer and connect the motor directly across the line for full-voltage running. The size of these three-pole contactors is determined by the maximum horsepower of the motor and its voltage and frequency requirements. The timing of the reduced-voltage interval is controlled by a timing relay (TR) that is adjustable from 1.5 to 15 seconds.

Pressing the Start button energizes timing relay TR. This causes its two sets of normally open instantaneous contacts to close. One set of closed instantaneous contacts provides holding for the timer; the other set completes an electrical path via the NC contacts of contactor R and the timed-open contacts (TR and TO) of the timer relay to energize the coil of contactor 1S. When contactor 1S is energized, its power contacts close, connecting the ends of the autotransformers together. It also causes the auxiliary contacts of contactor 1S to close, thereby energizing contactor 2S. The NC auxiliary contacts of 1S in the control circuit for contactor R open. This provides an electrical interlock to prevent contactors R and 1S from being energized at the same time. When coil 2S is energized, its power contacts close and connect the motor through the autotransformer taps to the power line, starting the motor at reduced inrush current and starting torque. The normally open auxiliary contacts of 2S close to provide a holding circuit for contactor 2S.

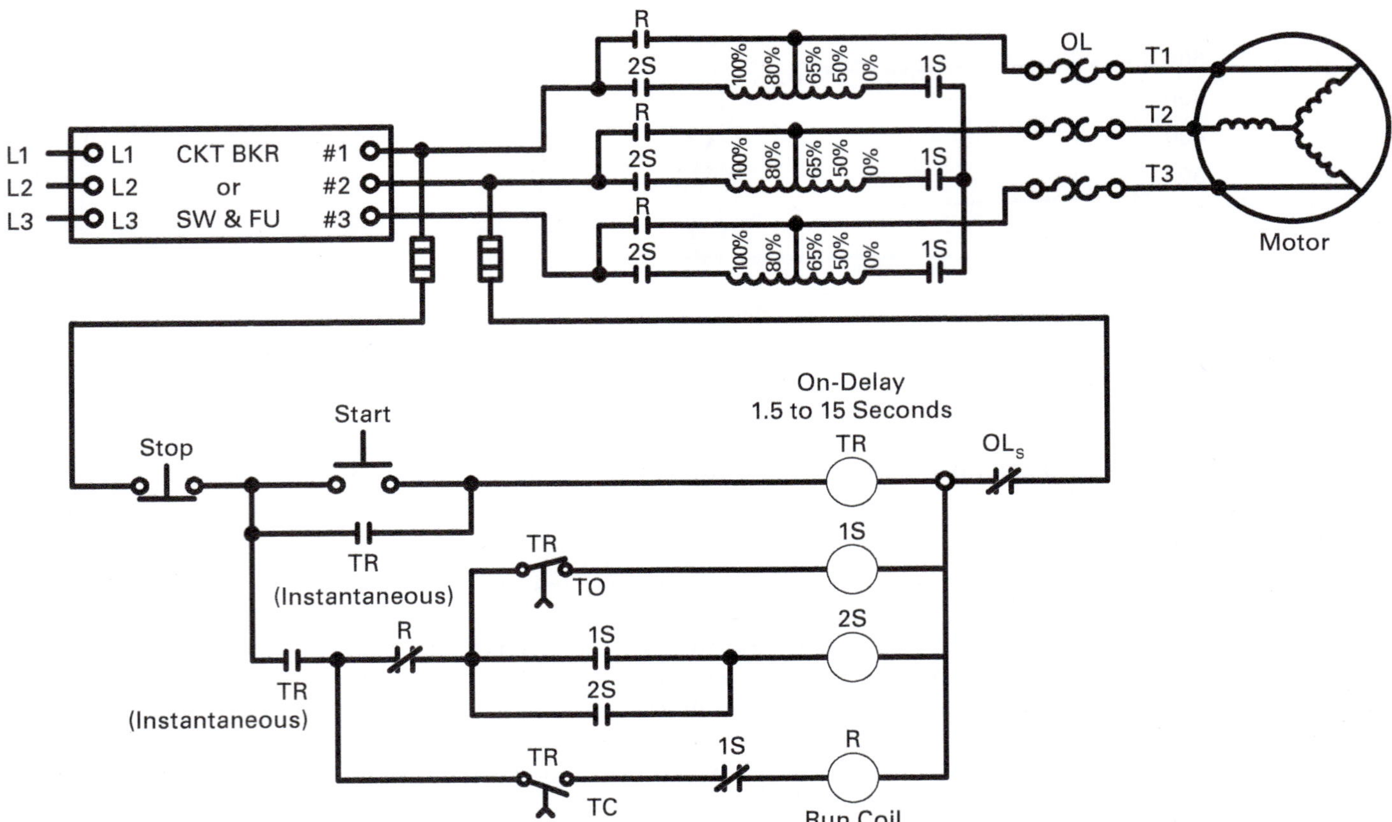

Figure 12 Typical autotransformer reduced-voltage starting circuit.

After a predetermined time (1.5 to 15 seconds), timer relay TR times out and its NCTO contacts open, causing contactor 1S to de-energize. This opens its power contacts and returns its NC auxiliary contacts to the closed position. Simultaneously, the NOTC contacts of timing relay TR close, causing contactor R to energize via the closed auxiliary contacts of contactor 1S. When contactor R energizes, its power contacts close, bypassing the autotransformer and connecting the motor to full-line voltage. Its NC auxiliary contacts also open, causing contactor 2S to de-energize.

Note that during the transition from starting to full-line voltage, the motor was not disconnected from the circuit, indicating a closed-circuit transition method of operation. As long as the motor is running in the full-voltage condition, timing relay TR and contactor R remain energized. Only an overload or pressing the Stop button stops the motor and resets the circuit.

2.1.2 Part-Winding Reduced-Voltage Motor Starting Control

Part-winding reduced-voltage starting is an older method of reduced-voltage starting in which an induction motor is started by first applying power to part of the motor windings for starting, then after a short time delay, applying power to the remaining windings for normal running. Part-winding starters are used with part-winding motors. A part-winding motor is one that has two sets of windings that are connected in parallel during full-voltage operation. Partwinding starters have typically been used with low starting torque loads such as fans, blowers, and motor-generator sets. These starters can be used with nine-lead, dual-voltage motors on the lower voltage and with special part-winding motors designed for any voltage. With half of the windings energized, most motors will produce a starting torque between one-half and two-thirds of NEMA standard values and draw about two-thirds of normal line current inrush. *Figure 13* shows a graph of the typical starting characteristics for a part-winding reduced-voltage starting mode of operation.

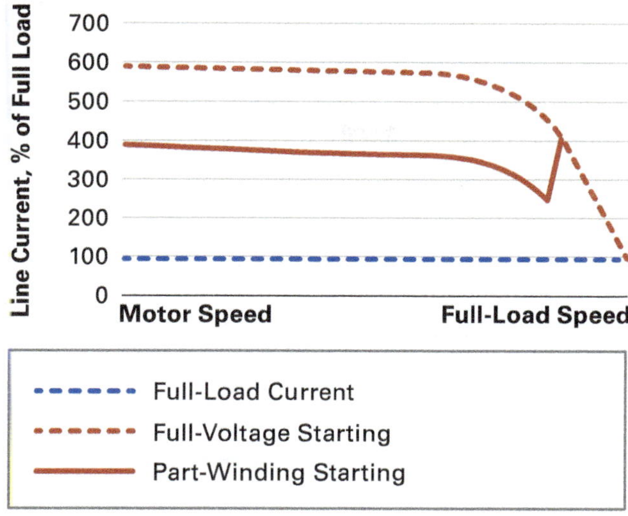

Figure 13 Part-winding reduced-voltage starting characteristics.

2.1.3 Wye-Delta Reduced-Voltage Motor Starting Control

Wye-delta reduced-voltage starting operates by first connecting the leads of the motor being controlled into a wye configuration for starting. Then, after a short time delay, the leads are reconfigured via switched contacts so that the motor is connected into a delta configuration for running. Both closed-circuit transition and open-circuit transition models are available. Wye-delta starters are used for controlling high-inertia loads with long acceleration times, such as with centrifugal compressors, centrifuges, and similar loads. When 6- or 12-lead, delta-connected motors are started wye-connected, approximately 58% of the line voltage is applied to each winding. The motor develops 33% of its full-voltage starting torque and draws 33% of its normal locked-rotor current from the line. When the motor has nearly accelerated, it is reconnected for normal delta operation. *Figure 14* shows a graph of the typical starting characteristics for a wye-delta reduced-voltage starting mode of operation.

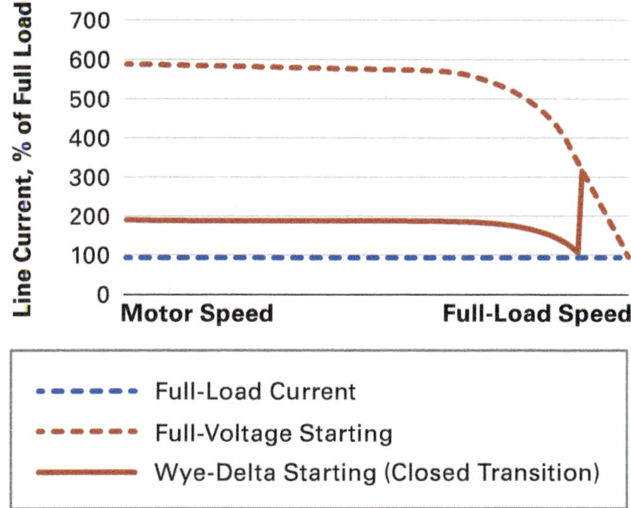

Figure 14 Wye-delta reduced-voltage starting characteristics.

Figure 15 shows a schematic diagram for a wye-delta motor controlled by a closed-circuit transition, wye-delta type of reduced-voltage controller. As shown, it includes a three-pole contactor 1S that is used to short motor leads T4, T5, and T6 during starting to connect the motor in the wye configuration. A three-pole contactor 1M energizes motor leads T1, T2, and T3 for both wye and delta connections. A three-pole contactor 2M energizes motor leads T4, T5, and T6 during running to connect the motor in the delta configuration. It also includes a three-pole contactor 2S that connects resistors in series with the motor windings during the start-to-run transition period. Note that contactor 2S and the resistor bank are unique to the closed-circuit transition starter. An open-circuit transition starter does not have these components.

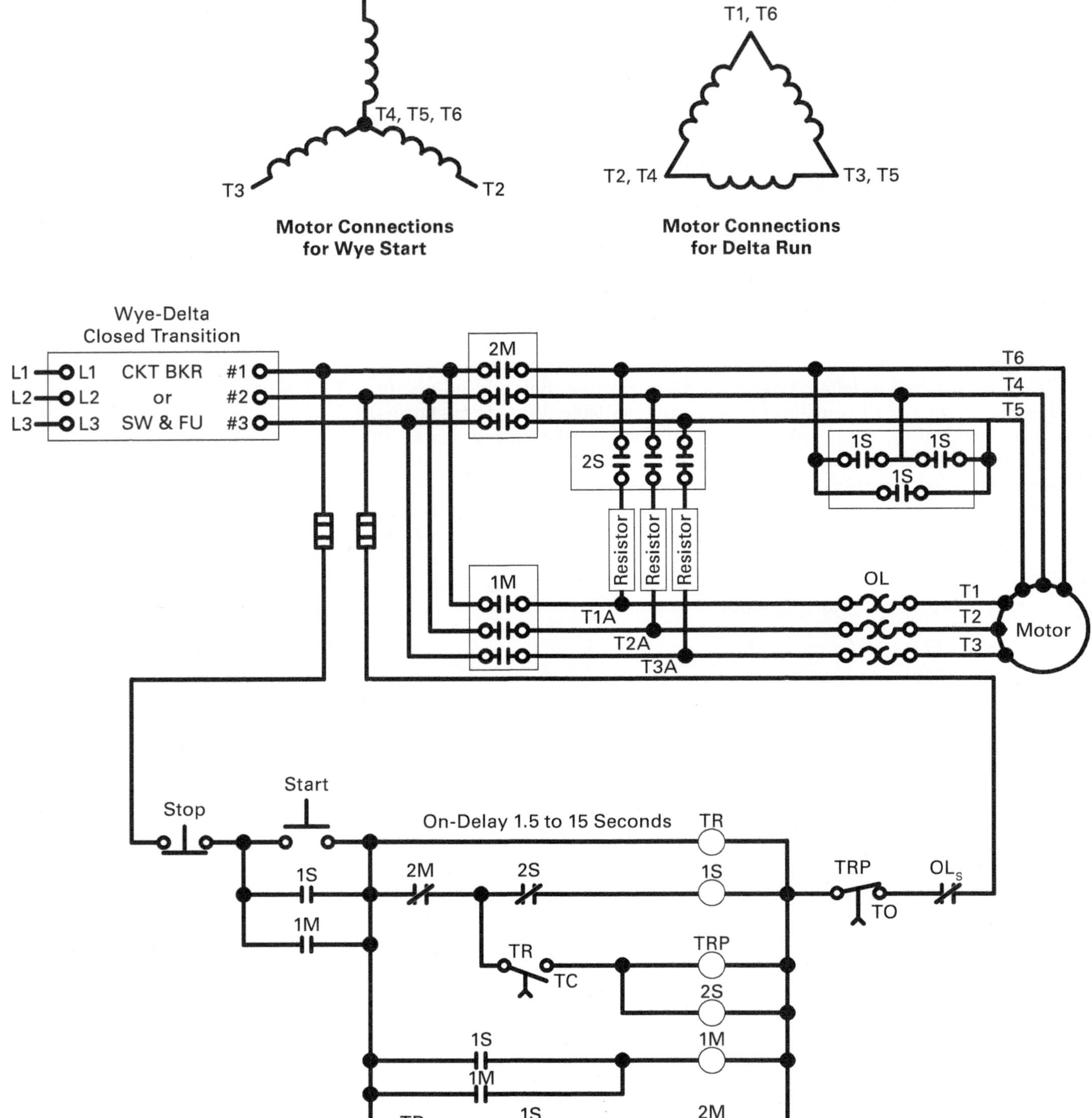

Figure 15 Typical wye-delta reduced-voltage starting circuit.

Pressing the Start button energizes timing relay TR and contactor 1S, whose power contacts connect the motor in a wye configuration. Interlock 1S closes, energizing contactor 1M. The 1M power contacts energize the motor windings in a wye configuration. After a preset time, interval, timer contacts TR and TC close, energizing contactor 2S and timing relay TRP. Interlock 2S opens, dropping out contactor 1S. The motor is now energized in series with the resistors. Interlock 1S closes, energizing contactor 2M, bypassing the resistors, and energizing the delta-connected motor at full voltage. Interlock 2M opens, de-energizing contactor 2S and timing relay TRP. Timing relay TRP opens the control circuit if the duty cycle for the transition resistors is exceeded. As long as the motor remains running in the full-voltage condition, contactors 1M and 2M and timing relay TR all remain energized. If an overload occurs or the Stop button is pressed, it de-energizes contactors 1M and 2M and the timer, removing the motor from the line and resetting the timer.

Wye-Delta Reduced-Voltage Controllers

When using a closed transition type of wye-delta reduced-voltage controller, make sure that there is adequate ventilation to remove the heat dissipated by the resistors.

2.2.0 Solid-State Reduced-Voltage Motor Starting Control

Solid-state reduced-voltage starters perform the same function as electromechanical reduced-voltage starters, but they provide a smoother, stepless start and acceleration. For this reason, they are often referred to as *soft-start controllers*. Because they provide controlled acceleration, they are ideal for use with many loads, including conveyors, compressors, and pumps. Some models can also provide a soft stop when a sudden stop may cause system or product damage. For these reasons, as well as competitive costs, soft-start controllers are becoming the preferred replacement for other methods of reduced-voltage motor starting. *Figure 16* shows a graph of the typical starting characteristics for a solid-state (soft-start) reduced-voltage starting mode of operation.

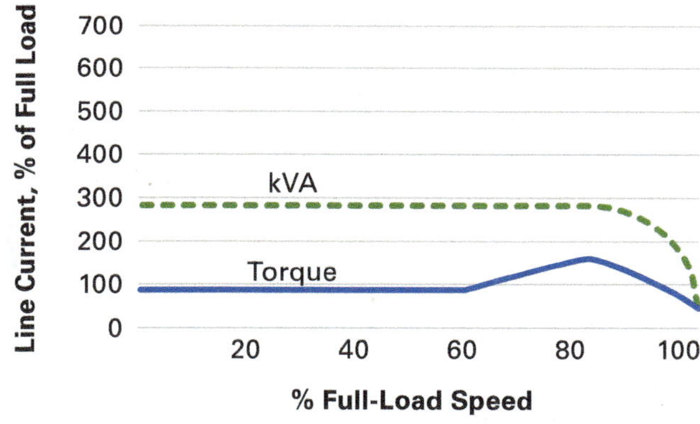

Figure 16 Solid-state reduced-voltage starting characteristics.

There are many designs and models of solid-state reduced-voltage controllers. *Figure 17* shows a simplified schematic diagram for a motor being controlled by a typical solid-state reduced-voltage controller. A similar controller is shown in *Figure 18*. As shown, the controller consists of an electronic circuit board and six SCRs connected back-to-back. The typical circuit board contains a microprocessor and related input/output (I/O) circuitry that function both to control the operation of the SCRs and to protect the motor and starter circuits from damage. The current transformers sense the motor current and feed this information back to the control circuit for comparison and processing throughout the entire motor control process.

The use of six back-to-back SCRs provides control for the full cycle of the AC input voltage to the motor. Each single SCR controls one half cycle of the AC input voltage on one motor lead; the six together provide full-wave control of the input voltage on all the motor leads. When first starting a motor, the gate on each SCR is turned on for a very short time just before the end of its half cycle.

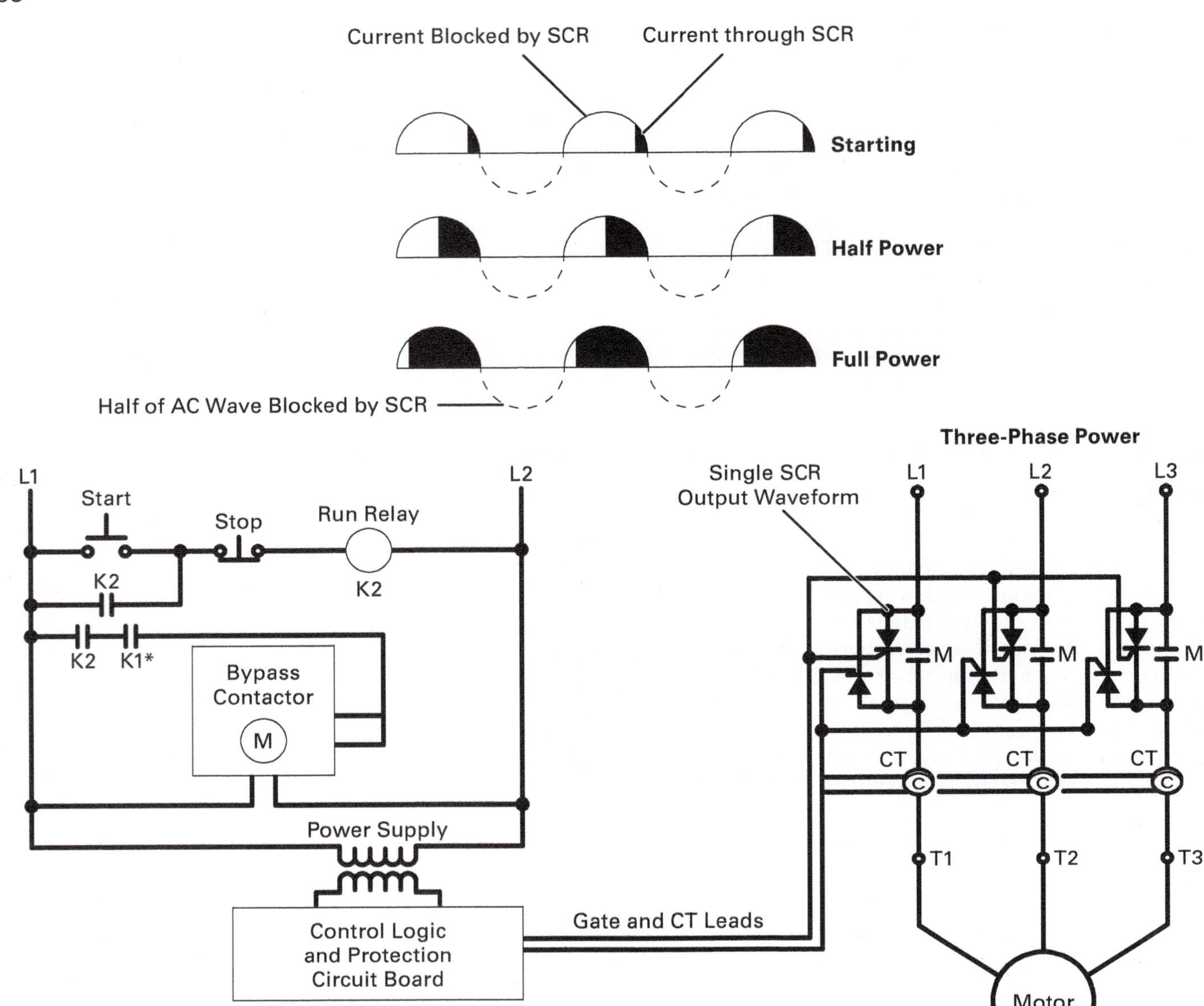

Figure 17 Simplified solid-state reduced-voltage starting circuit.

(The SCR automatically turns off when the voltage supplying it crosses through zero at the end of its half cycle.) By the end of the acceleration time, each SCR is turned on for its entire half cycle, so the motor sees full voltage (less SCR losses). This is shown for a single SCR in the top portion of *Figure 17.*

The circuit shown in *Figure 17* is also equipped with a bypass contactor (M) that is energized when the motor attains full voltage and speed at the end of the voltage ramp-up interval. This is common in some solid-state reduced-voltage controller designs. The contacts of contactor M are connected in parallel with the SCRs. Contactor M is controlled by the closed contacts of the end-of-ramp relay K1 located on the circuit board inside the solid-state controller. When contactor M is energized at the end of the voltage ramp-up interval, its contacts close, causing the SCRs to be bypassed and the motor to be placed directly across the power line.

Settings for torque, time, and other parameters are made in the field to obtain switching of the SCRs as needed to achieve the desired motor performance. Typically, they are manually programmed into the circuit board microprocessor via dipswitches and circuit board controls. Some starting characteristics that normally can be programmed include:

CAUTION

Some solid-state reduced-voltage starters are supplied with the bypass contactor internally connected. However, for others it is separately supplied and connected to the terminals specifically designated for it. These wiring connections must be followed to preserve the overload protection function provided in the solid-state reduced-voltage starter.

Figure 18 Reduced-voltage starting controller.
Source: Wayne Stratton, ABC of Iowa

- *Ramp start* — Ramp start, shown in *Figure 19* (A), is the most common form of soft start. It allows the initial torque value of the ramp to be set and then raises it to full voltage. The starting torque is typically adjusted from 1% to 85% of the locked-rotor torque but must be high enough so the motor begins turning when started and not later. Ramp time adjustment is from 0 to 180 seconds or more.
- *Kick start* — Kick start, shown in *Figure 19* (B), provides an initial boost of current to the motor to help break free the rotor and start the motor. The starting torque is typically adjusted from 1% to 85% of the locked-rotor torque. The duration of the kick start interval is from 0 to 2 seconds.
- *Current limit* — Current limit, shown in *Figure 19* (C), is used when it is necessary to limit the maximum starting current because of long starting times or to protect the motor. The current limit is typically set in the range of 42% to 85% of the locked-rotor current (250% to 500% of the motor full-load current). The ramp time is typically from 0 to 180 seconds or more.
- *Soft stop* — Soft stop, shown in *Figure 19* (D), is used when an extended coast-to-stop period is needed. It is often used with high-friction loads when a sudden stop can cause system or product damage such as in hydraulic pumps. The stop ramp time is typically adjustable from 0 to 60 seconds.

A solid-state reduced-voltage controller typically also contains electronic circuits to protect the motor from overload and the starter from damage. Depending on the design, protection can be provided for shorted SCRs, over-temperature, current imbalance, undervoltage, phase loss, and/or phase reversal.

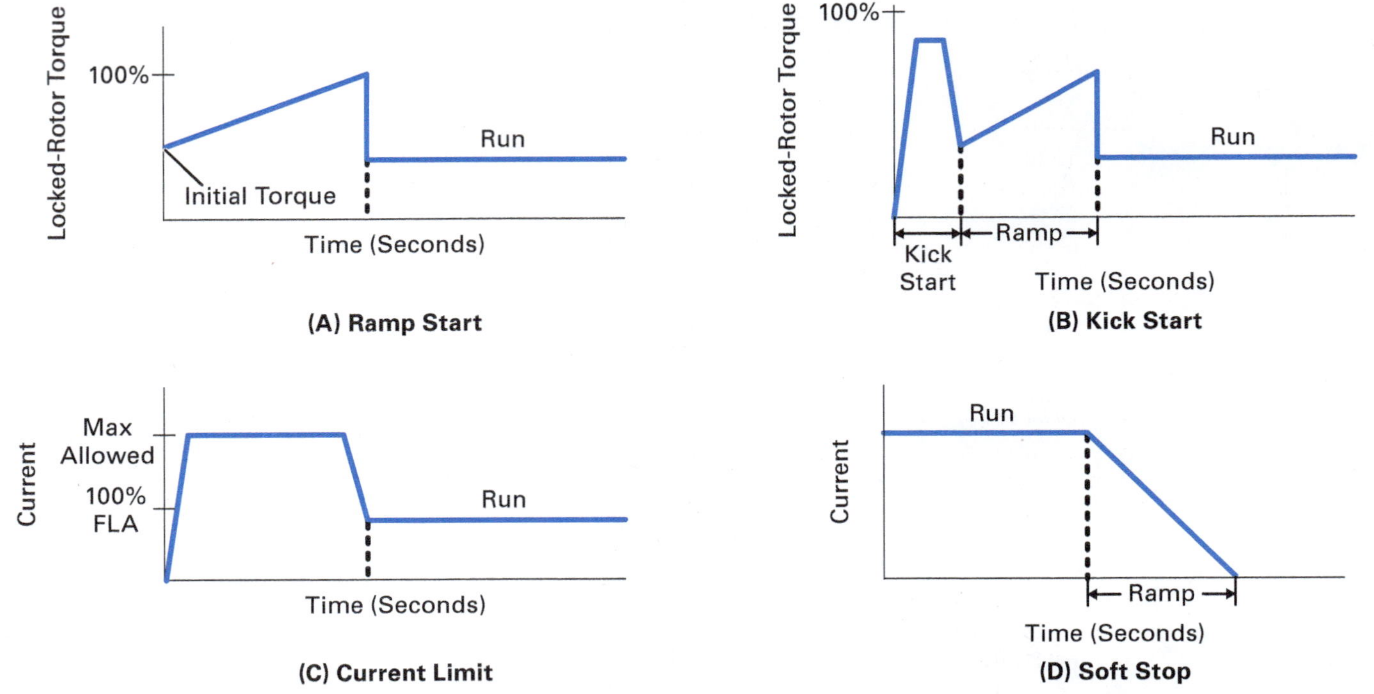

Figure 19 Starting characteristics of solid-state reduced-voltage controllers.

The following characteristics must be considered when selecting a reduced-voltage starter for use with a load driven by a squirrel-cage motor:

- Motor characteristics to satisfy the application starting requirements
- Source of power, including the effect of the motor starting current on the line voltage
- Load characteristics, including the effect of the motor starting torque on driven parts during acceleration
- Motor voltage
- Required startup torque
- Heater selection
- Enclosure type

Table 3 and *Table 4* provide a brief summary of the types of reduced-voltage controllers covered in this module and their characteristics.

TABLE 3 Comparison of Reduced-Voltage Controllers

Type of Reduced-Voltage Controller	Starting Characteristics			Applications
	Voltage at Motor (%)	Line Current (%)	Torque (%)	
Autotransformer	80	64	64	Blowers, pumps, compressors, conveyors
	65	42	42	
	50	25	25	
Part-winding	100	65	48	Reciprocating compressors, pumps, blowers, fans
Wye-delta	100	33	33	Centrifugal compressors, centrifuges
Solid-state	Adjustable	Adjustable	Adjustable	Machine tools, hoists, packaging equipment, conveyor systems

TABLE 4 Advantages and Disadvantages of Reduced-Voltage Controllers

Type of Reduced-Voltage Controller	Advantages	Disadvantages
Autotransformer	• Provides maximum torque per ampere of line current • Starting characteristics easily adjusted • Different starting torques available through autotransformer taps • Suitable for relatively long starting periods • Motor current greater than line current during starting	• Most complex type due to precise sequencing of energization • Large physical size • Low power factor • Expensive in lower hp ratings
Part-winding	• Least expensive • Small physical size • Suitable for low or high voltage • Full acceleration in one step for most standard or special part-winding motors when two-thirds winding connection is used	• Unsuitable for high-inertia loads • Specific motor types required • Motor does not start when required load torque exceeds that developed by the motor when the first half of the motor is energized • Torque efficiency usually poor for high-speed loads
Wye-delta	• Suitable for high-inertia, long-accelerating loads • High torque efficiency • Ideal for stringent inrush current restrictions • Ideal for frequent starts	• Requires special motor • Low starting torque • Momentary inrush occurs during open transition when delta contactor is closed (open-circuit transition modules)
Solid-state	• Voltage gradually applied during start for a soft-start condition • Adjustable acceleration time • Adjustable kick start, current limit, and soft stop	• More expensive than electromechanical types • Requires specialized installation and maintenance • Electrical transients can damage solid-state components • Requires good ventilation

Solid-State Reduced-Voltage Starters

Solid-state reduced-voltage starters are available in a wide variety of sizes to suit various motor applications.

Source: Benshaw

2.0.0 Section Review

1. The type of reduced-voltage starter typically used with hard-to-start loads is _____.
   a. part-winding
   b. wye-delta
   c. thyristor
   d. autotransformer

2. The type of solid-state reduced-voltage starting control that provides an initial boost of current to the motor to help break the rotor free and start the motor is _____.
   a. ramp start
   b. current limit
   c. kick start
   d. soft stop

3.0.0 Adjustable Frequency Drives

Performance Task

1. Identify and connect various control devices.

Objective

Specify an AFD for a given application.

a. Describe the types of AFDs, along with their operation and components.
b. Compare the uses, benefits, and problems when selecting an AFD.

Know the Code

Adjustable-Speed Drive Systems
NEC Section 430, Part X

An adjustable frequency drive (AFD) converts three-phase 50 hertz (Hz) or 60 Hz input power to an adjustable frequency and voltage output to control the speed of an AC motor. AFDs are discussed in *NEC Article 430, Part X*. AFDs are also known as *variable frequency drives, variable speed drives, inverter drives*, or *adjustable speed drives.*

3.1.0 Types of AFDs

Base speed: The shaft speed at which the motor will develop rated horsepower at rated load and voltage, as stated on a motor nameplate.

Slip: The speed difference between the synchronous speed and the base speed. Induction motors develop their torque because of the slip. The amount of slip depends on motor design and motor load.

Insulated gate bipolar transistors (IGBTs): A type of transistor that has low losses and low gate drive requirements. This allows it to be operated at higher switching frequencies.

Squirrel-cage induction motors are only available with **base speeds** determined by the frequency of the incoming power line, **slip**, and number of magnetic poles in the motor. In most cases, these limited choices of base speed do not directly match the needs of the equipment or machinery being driven by the motor. Various methods have been used to match the motor speed to the desired load speed. Mechanical methods change the way the motor is coupled to the load, such as variable pitch pulleys, eddy current drives, sprockets and chains, constantly variable transmissions, hydraulic couplers, etc. Different motor designs that change the motor base speed have also been used, such as wound-rotor motors or Schrage motors. All of these mechanical and motor design methods introduce additional expense and require a lot of maintenance, although some are still in use. None of these methods provide optimum control automation, energy conservation, or ease of use.

Today, the most common method of matching motor speed to the needs of the equipment or machinery is to change the frequency coming to the motor using an AFD. AFDs are easier to use, work well with control automation, and can conserve energy.

The earliest AFDs used SCRs to create the output frequency to the motor in a six-step waveform. This output waveform worked with motors, but required a lot of filtering, with additional expense, weight, and space requirements. With the development of **insulated gate bipolar transistors (IGBTs)** in the early 1980s, a much wider range of applications in AFDs became possible. More recently, with the decreasing cost and greatly expanded capabilities of computer processors, the engineering equations for vector analysis and control of motor power became possible in real time, further increasing the range of possible applications. AFDs that use this are often called *vector drives*. If a feedback sensor on the motor gives the AFD accurate information on drive shaft rotation (via an encoder), known as a *feedback vector drive*, very precise motor control is possible. Today's AFDs can power motors as small as $^1/_2$ hp up through medium voltage motors of 100,000 hp or more.

Going Green

AFDs

AFDs are available for use with a wide range of motors and applications. These drives save energy by eliminating the losses associated with traditional speed control.

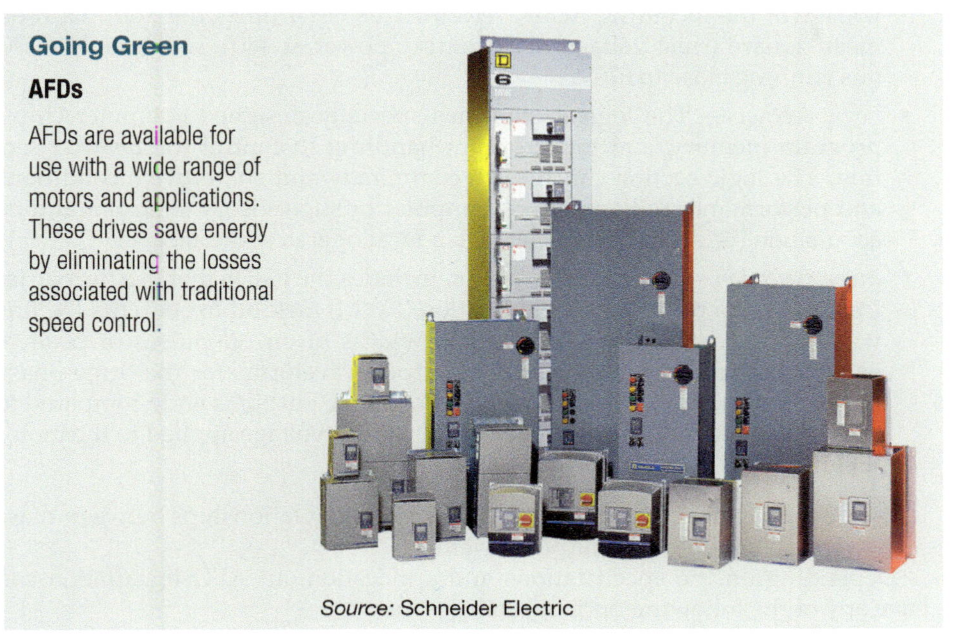

Source: Schneider Electric

3.1.1 AFD Forms and Types

NEMA describes three AFD drive classifications according to the relationship between their input and output.

- *Form FA* — AC input directly to AC output by synthesizing the output waveform from segments of the AC supply without an intermediate DC link. Types include cycloconverters and Matrix converters.
- *Form FB* — DC input to AC output. Uses include electric vehicles and some industrial machines.
- *Form FC* — AC input to DC intermediate bus to AC output. These are the most common and will be the focus of this module.

Although AFDs come in about six different types, three of them (volts/Hz AFDs, sensorless vector AFD, and feedback vector AFDs) are likely to be seen on a regular basis. AFD types are classified by the control method. *Table 5* compares key features of each type. This module will focus on these AFD types and highlight the few places where they differ.

TABLE 5 Key Features of Different AFD Control Methods

Control Methods	Volts/Hz	Sensorless Vector	Feedback Vector
Control criteria	Open loop	Open loop	Closed loop
Typical speed regulation	1%	0.5%	0.01%
Speed range at constant torque	10% to 100%	3% to 100%	0% to 100%
Multiple motor operation	Yes	No	No
Torque at zero speed	Impossible	Poor	Best
Replace existing DC drive	No	Maybe	Yes

3.1.2 AFD Components

An AFD has four main sections:

- *AC input section* — The AC input section includes high-speed overcurrent protection, input voltage spike protection, and SCRs to power the DC bus.
- *DC bus* — The DC bus includes capacitors and inductors (LC filters) as necessary to smooth the DC voltage and provide robust power near the peak voltage of the incoming AC waveform. This is 1.4 times the nominal root-mean-square (rms) voltage, so incoming power at 480V will supply a DC bus running close to 670V.
- *Logic section* — The logic section has specially designed computer chips, program memory, and input/output handling to control the inverter section. The logic section can receive commands and share drive conditions and performance with a remote computer or supervisory control and data acquisition (SCADA) system, or with a local operator interface.
- *Inverter section* — The inverter section includes the IGBTs that use the **carrier frequency** in a pulse-width modulation (PWM) method to chop the DC bus voltage. This is done by varying the widths of on/off pulses of positive or negative voltages to create three output waveforms for the three-phase motor. (For example, when the off portion of the output is wide compared to the on portion, the effective value of the output voltage applied to the motor will be low.)

Carrier frequency: In a pulse-width modulated (PWM) drive, the frequency at which the IGBT can be switched on or off to create an output waveform that mimics a sine wave of desired voltage and frequency. Carrier frequencies typically range from 500 Hz to 20,000 Hz, but need to be at least 10 times the maximum drive output frequency.

See *Figure 20* for a block diagram illustrating the relationships between these sections and a graph of the output waveforms.

Depending on the specifications and application, an AFD installation can have any of the following optional components:

- An input filter section can be provided to keep the AFD from imposing voltage and current harmonics back onto the incoming feeders and utility power line. Filtering methods can include a line reactor, active components, or a drive isolation transformer. *IEEE Standard 519* limits total harmonic distortion at the service to 5%, but without filtering, the AFD can create harmonics of 50% or more on the incoming power line.
- Power line regenerative components or a chopping IGBT and external power resistor can be used to prevent excessive DC bus voltage when the AFD is slowing or stopping the driven load.
- Output filter sections are available in three types: a load reactor, a delta voltage / delta time (dV/dT) filter, or a sine wave filter. These can allow a longer cable from the AFD to the motor and minimize high-frequency noise that can harm the motor or nearby electronics.

3.2.0 AFD Uses and Benefits

Powering a motor with an AFD provides the following benefits:

- *Controlled starting* — AFDs can limit starting current and reduce power line demand/disturbance on startup.
- *Controlled acceleration* — AFDs allow for soft-start, adjustable acceleration based on time or load, and reduced motor size for pure inertial load acceleration.
- *Adjustable operating speed* — Speed control allows a process to be optimized or changed, provides energy savings, and allows process control at reduced speeds set by a programmable controller.
- *Energy savings* — The **Fan Affinity Laws** show that replacement of a damper or throttling valve with a change in motor speed can produce direct energy savings of 25% to 50%. Motors are often oversized to allow for aging, wear, and similar changes. AFDs deliver only the power required and maintain a superior power factor on the incoming power line.

Fan Affinity Laws: The mathematical relationship between fan speed, airflow rate, power used, and torque. Airflow is directly proportional to speed. Torque is proportional to the square of speed. Power used is proportional to the cube of speed. For example, decreasing fan speed by 20% decreases the power used by about 50%.

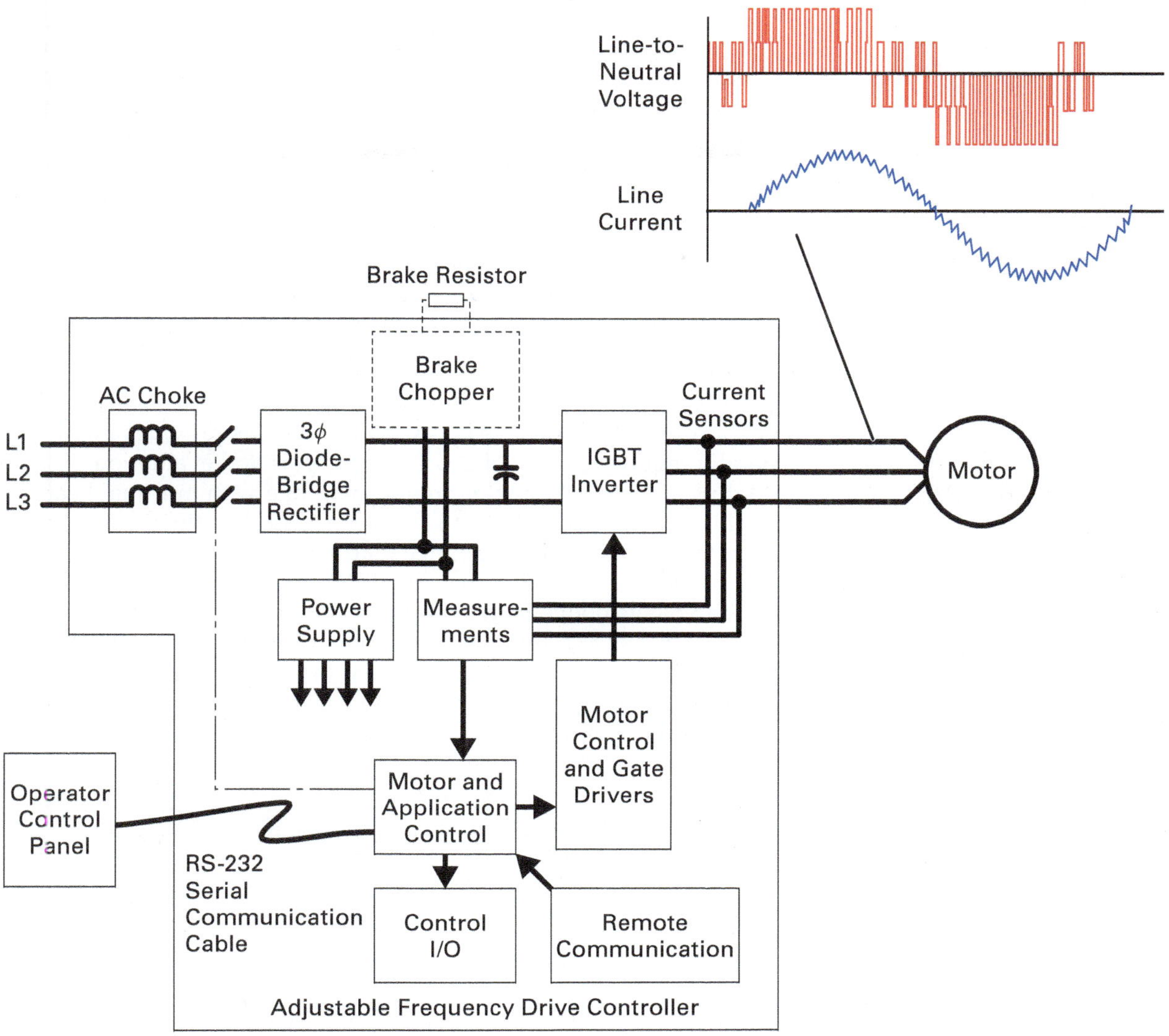

Figure 20 Block diagram of a typical AFD.

- *Adjustable torque limiting* — Current limiting can be used to provide fast, accurate torque control to protect the machinery, product, or process against damage.
- *Controlled stopping* — AFDs provide soft stop, timed stopping, and fast reversal with much less stress on an AC motor compared to plug reverse.
- *Operation above base speed* — Many motors designed to NEMA standards can be operated up to 1.5 times their base speed, with higher limits for 4- or 6-pole motors and lower limits for large motors.

3.2.1 AFD Selection

The first selection consideration is the load characteristics of the machine or equipment being powered. The three common types are variable torque, constant torque, and constant horsepower.

- *Variable-torque loads* — These are typically fans, blowers, pumps, and similar loads where a higher speed requires more power and more torque. These relationships follow the Fan Affinity Laws and are graphed in *Figure 21*. A volt/Hz AFD works very well for variable-torque loads and the installation is cost effective.

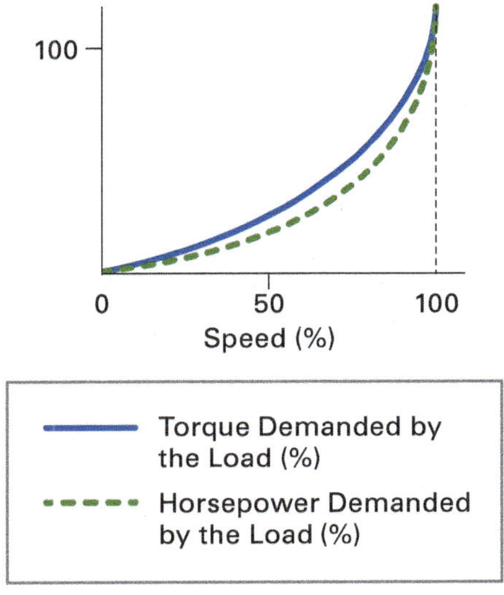

Figure 21 Variable-torque load.

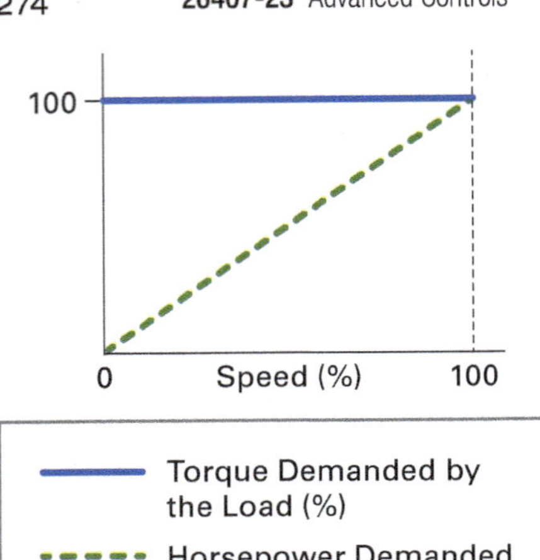

Figure 22 Constant-torque load.

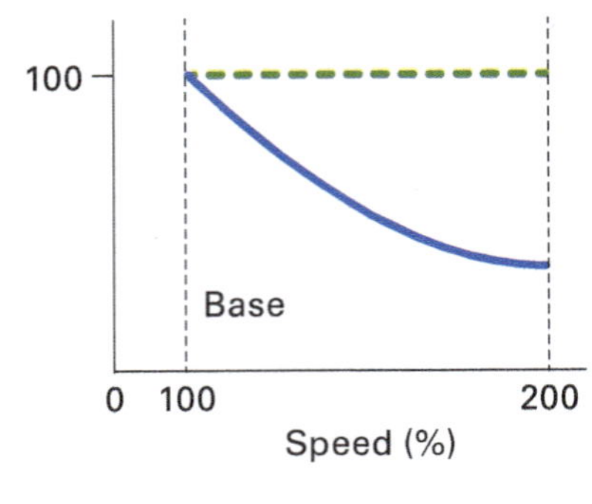

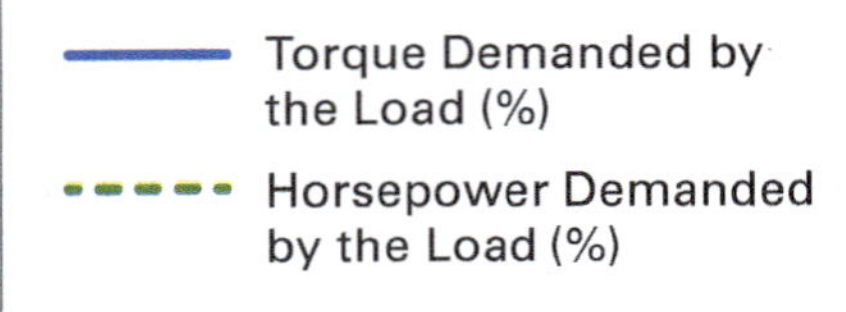

Figure 23 Constant-horsepower load.

- *Constant-torque loads* — These are speed-independent, friction-type loads, such as hoists, conveyors, printing presses, positive displacement pumps, and extruders. A machine with a large flywheel (such as a chipper) will act as a constant-torque load while it is being accelerated up to operating speed. With these loads, the torque remains constant over the speed range, but the horsepower increases as the speed increases. See the graph in *Figure* 22. A vector-type AFD is best for these types of loads.
- *Constant-horsepower loads* — With these loads as the speed increases, the torque decreases, so the horsepower stays the same. Typical machines include lathes, grinders, and many winders. Because the horsepower requirements are constant, an AFD will not provide energy savings, but can provide improved process control. See the graph in *Figure* 23.

Two less common types of loads are constant force (tension control) and wind/unwind. The use of AFDs with these loads provides many benefits, but generally requires careful engineering support and evaluation.

Motors operate over a wide frequency range with minimal heat losses when the ratio of the input voltage to frequency matches the ratio of the nameplate voltage to frequency. This is a range with a constant volts to hertz ratio, as shown in *Figure* 24, and provides constant torque from the motor. The AFD cannot output a voltage above its rated output voltage, so when the motor is operated above its base speed, the motor is producing constant power. Motors without external cooling fans cannot be operated for very long at low speeds, and AFDs (other than vector types) cannot be used at less than about 10% of the incoming line frequency—this is the typical minimum programmed frequency for the AFD output. The red line on the graph in *Figure* 24 shows these relationships.

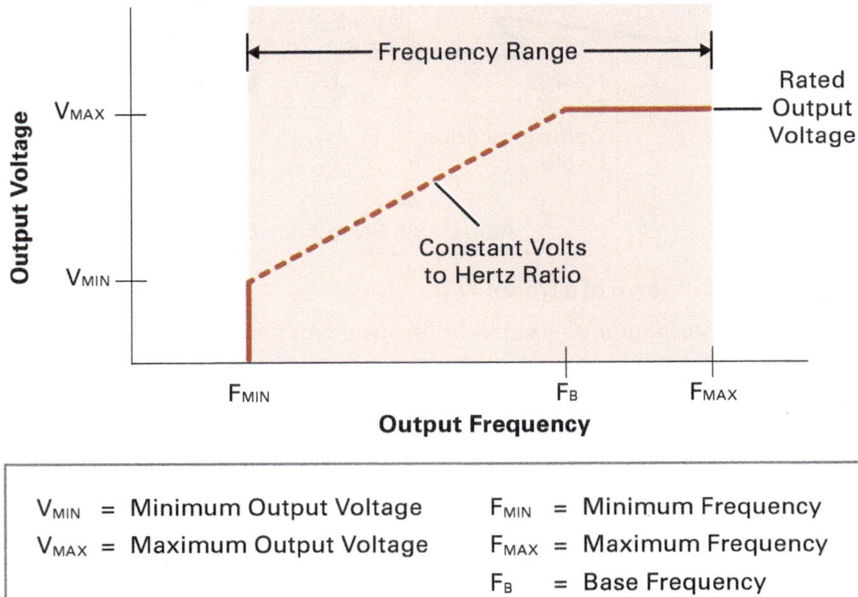

Figure 24 AFD operating frequency range.

The second selection consideration is variations in the load and environment; some of these may require the use of an AFD sized larger than the motor full-load current.

- High-torque loads can require a larger AFD size during starting or running. AFD torque limits usually are 150% for constant-torque applications or 110% for variable-torque applications.

- An impact load can be a punch press with a flywheel or a conveyor that gets a heavy package dropped onto its surface. The AFD must have the capacity to overcome this sudden load change without an overload trip from the sudden change. Often a NEMA Design D motor is used here.
- Breakaway torque is what overcomes the higher friction that a non-moving load has compared to a moving one, such as a cement or slurry mixer. An AFD must be sized to provide the extra current needed to start the load.
- Starting a spinning load can cause an AFD overload fault unless the AFD has been programmed to match the load speed when it starts. Fans and pumps may be turning backward while off, and any load with high inertia may still be spinning while an AFD has suffered a momentary power failure.
- A limited number of AFDs can be powered from single-phase AC to run a three-phase motor. The reduced available single-phase input power requires choosing an AFD to that is larger than the motor rating.
- An AFD can be supplied with just a NEMA-1 terminal cover, but this does not protect it from weather, dust, contamination, or temperature extremes. Oversizing it may be needed if temperatures are likely to be above its rated environmental limit. If in an enclosure, a filtered fan, air conditioner, or other method for cooling may be needed.
- Matching the AFD to the motor design is important. As shown in *Table 6*, NEMA Design A, Design B, and Design E motors are best suited for use with an AFD, although an AFD can be used with the other motor designs.

TABLE 6 AFD Use with Different NEMA Motor Designs

Motor Design Letter	Typical Driven Load Types	Slip	Locked-Rotor Current	Efficiency	Use with AFD
Design A	Fans, blowers, MG sets, centrifugal pumps, and compressors	0.5% to 3%	600% to 700%	High or medium	Good
Design B	Fans, blowers, MG sets, centrifugal pumps, and compressors	0.5% to 5%	600% to 700%	High or medium	Very good
Design C	Conveyors, crushers, stirring, agitating, reciprocal pumps	1% to 5%	600% to 700%	Medium	Poor, risk of overheating
Design D	High-peak loads with or without flywheels	5% to 8+%	600% to 700%	Lower	Can be done, but more difficult
Design E	Fans, blowers, MG sets, centrifugal pumps, and compressors	0.5% to 3%	800% to 1,000%	Highest	Good, but may need a larger drive size

NOTE: Current is % of full-load values. Slip is % below synchronous speed.

AFD Environment

Heat rejection is a major concern with AFDs. The heat produced in the AFD cabinet can be substantial and can cause failure of the AFD SCRs and IGBTs if their operating temperature limits are exceeded. For this reason, operating an AFD at higher altitudes often requires that the unit be derated, because the lower-density air reduces the amount of heat transfer.

3.2.2 AFD Programming

All AFDs are matched to their load by setting adjustable parameters to control the details of the AFD performance. Early models had 50 or more parameters, but today's much more capable AFDs can have up to 600 or more parameters. Follow the manufacturer's installation and/or operation manuals for programming. Common parameters that must be programmed include:

- *Motor nameplate data* — Voltage, frequency, base speed, current, service factor, and power factor.
- *Incoming power data* — Line voltage.
- *AFD input usage* — Input selection for enabling, starting, stopping, reversing, and fault resets.
- *Communications* — Selection of I/O method via wired terminals or communications link and use of an operator interface.
- *Setup* — Minimum and maximum frequency, skip frequencies (to avoid vibration), acceleration and deceleration time(s), short-term current limit, and speed reference source.
- *Output volt/Hz ratio* — For a constant-torque load, the linear volt/Hz ratio provides full output torque at high efficiency over a wide range of frequencies from the AFD. This matches induction motor design. However, for variable-torque loads, the squared volt/Hz ratio will save energy at lower AFD output frequencies by reducing the voltage to match the torque required by the load.
- *Operation above base frequency* — For AFD output frequencies above the base frequency (if permitted by the maximum frequency setting), the voltage output remains constant at the motor nameplate voltage, so motor power is constant, but motor torque is decreased.
- *IR compensation and voltage boost* — These help with starting a high-inertia or high-friction load. Moderate amounts of voltage boost are used for most loads, but the use of IR compensation instead of higher levels of voltage boost is best for more difficult loads.

In many cases, successful programming and startup of an AFD installation may require the skills and knowledge of trained professionals. See *Figure 25A* and *Figure 25B* for a checklist used by one manufacturer to gather the data needed to evaluate the requirements for an AFD system.

3.2.3 AFD Application Precautions

AFDs have a few special application considerations and precautions. These include the following:

- Any fan-cooled motor is at risk of overheating and failure when an AFD operates it at slower speeds (50% of base speed or less) for more than a few minutes. To prevent this, an externally powered fan must be used to maintain the needed cooling airflow. This is particularly true if the motor has a Class F temperature rise or a service factor of 1.
- *NEMA Standard MG-1, Part 30* specifies motor construction requirements for a motor that should withstand the voltage stresses the AFD imposes on its windings. The motor nameplate will be labeled "INVERTER DUTY" or have similar wording. Inverter duty motors are wound using magnet wire with a higher voltage insulation level. This is needed because the high-frequency PWM pulses from the AFD reflect at the first few turns of the motor winding, causing the voltage on these motor windings to be as high as 2.5 times the actual output voltage.
- Non-inverter duty motors operated above 240V are prone to premature failure due to the overvoltage imposed on their windings. The severity of this overvoltage can be reduced with the use of the lowest possible carrier frequency and special AFD power cables. This overvoltage can be reduced or even eliminated with the use of output filtering devices selected by a professional.

AFD APPLICATION CHECKLIST

Motor

New: ________ Existing: ________ Horsepower: __________ Base Speed: _________ Voltage: _________

FLA: ________ LRA: ___________ NEMA Design: ________ Gearbox/Pulley Ratio: _________________

Service Factor: _______________

Lead

Application:

Load Type: Constant Torque______ Variable Torque _______ Constant Horsepower ____________

Load inertia reflected to motor: ____

Required breakaway torque from motor: ___________________________________

Running load on motor: ____

Peak torques (above 100% running): _____________________________________

Shortest/longest required accel. time: _____ /________ secs up to _________ Hz from zero speed

Shortest/longest required decel. time: _____ /________ secs down to _______ Hz from max speed

Operating speed range: ______ Hz to ______ Hz

Time for motor/load to coast to stop: ________ secs

AFD

Source of start/stop commands: ____

Source of speed adjustment: ____

Other operating requirements: ____

Will the motor ever be spinning when the AFD is started? ____________________

Is the load considered to be high intertia? ______________________________

Is the load considered to be hard to start? ______________________________

Distance from AFD to the monitor: __________ feet

Type of AFD (V/Hz, Flux Vector, Closed Loop Vector): _______________________

Options desired: ____

____

____

Other special requirements/conditions: ___________________________________

Figure 25A AFD application checklist (1 of 2).

AFD Application Checklist (Continued)

Power Supply

Supply Transformer________ kVA and ______%Z or short circuit current at drive input: ______ amps

(If the drive does not include a built-in line reactor and the available feeder short circuit current is more than 100 times the drive FLA rating, a 1% line reactor or a drive isolation transformer is required.)

Total horsepower of all drives connected to supply transformer or feeder: ____________________

Is a drive transformer or line reactor desired? ______________

Any harmonic requirements? ______________________

% Voltage THD: ______________ % Current THD: ______________ IEEE 519: ______________

Total non-drive load connected to the same feeder as drive(s): ________________ amps

Service

Start-up Assistance: ____________________ Preventive Maintenance: ____________________

Customer Training: ____________________ Spare Parts: ____________________

Additional Issues

Will the AFD operate more than one motor? ____

Will the power supply source ever be switched with the AFD running? _________________________

Is starting or stopping time critical? _______________

Are there any peak torques or impact loads? _______________

Will user-supplied contactors be used on the input or output of the AFD? ______________________

Will the AFD be in a harsh environment or high altitude? ______________________________________

Does the utility system experience surges, spikes or other fluctuations? ______________________

Figure 25B AFD application checklist (2 of 2).

- AFD manufacturers typically recommend the use of special shielded cables between the AFD and the motor (*Figure 26*). This minimizes the radiation of the high-frequency noise into nearby sensitive equipment or signal cables. Spacing, barriers, cable orientation, and termination restrictions must be followed, particularly in control enclosures.
- Motor grounding wires must be connected from the motor to the ground terminal on the AFD, with that terminal then being connected to the grounding terminals of the grounding electrode system. This reduces the magnitude of electronic noise that can be imposed by the AFD and its attached motor on the facility's grounding electrode system and nearby equipment.
- A motor powered by an AFD often has parasitic or stray voltages coupled onto the motor shaft. If these voltages are discharged through the bearings, they will cause electric discharge machining of the bearing races, typically in the form of parallel grooves (called *fluting*) and premature bearing failure. Certain types of AFD output filtering or the use of shaft grounding brushes will prevent this problem. Other methods sometimes available include the use of electrically insulated bearings or shaft couplings.

AFDs

For retrofit AFD applications, many AFD manufacturers recommend that existing motors be replaced to ensure that the AFD unit is properly sized and is not affected by previous motor misuse or rewinding.

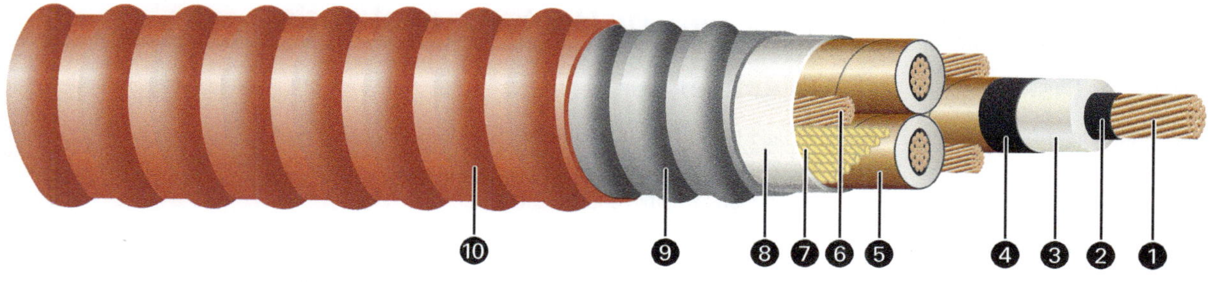

1. **Conductor:** Class B Compressed Stranded Bare Copper per ASTM B3 and ASTM B8
2. **Conductor Shield:** Semiconducting Cross-Linked Copolymer
3. **Insulation:** 220 Mils No Lead Ethylene Propylene Rubber (NL-EPR) 133% Insulation Level
4. **Insulation Shield:** Strippable Semiconducting Cross-Linked Copolymer
5. **Copper Tape Shield:** Helically Wrapped 5 Mil Copper Tape with 25% Overlap
6. **Equipment Grounding Conductor:** Three Separate Ground Wires with a Combined Circular Mil of 50% of the Phase Conductor; Class B Compressed Stranded Bare Copper per ASTM B3 and ASTM B8
7. **Filler:** Wax Paper Filler
8. **Binder:** Polypropylene Tape
9. **Armor:** Continuous Corrugated Welded Aluminum Armor (Armor-X)
10. **Overall Jacket:** Polyvinyl Chloride (PVC)

Figure 26 AFD cable.
Source: Southwire

PWM AFD Outputs to a Motor over Long Cable Runs

When a PWM AFD drive output is connected to a motor over long cable runs, the difference in the motor and cable impedance can cause voltage spikes at the motor terminals. These spikes can greatly exceed 1,000V and have the potential to damage the motor insulation. For small motors, this typically occurs with cable lengths that exceed 33' (10 m) and, for larger motors, with cable lengths that exceed 100' (30 m). For situations involving the use of long cable runs, install a reflective wave trap or similar filter at the motor terminals to prevent overshoots.

3.0.0 Section Review

1. The DC bus includes capacitors and inductors (LC filters) as necessary to _____.
   a. reduce noise coupling from nearby circuits
   b. develop a smooth DC voltage
   c. produce high-speed switching
   d. develop the AC waveform to drive the motor

2. Which of these actions should be taken if an AFD is used at lower speeds on an older motor with a Class F temperature rise or service factor of 1?
   a. Derate the motor load capacity by 18%.
   b. Reduce the input voltage to the motor.
   c. Use a bridge rectifier at the motor input.
   d. Install a separately powered cooling fan on the motor.

4.0.0 Motor Braking Methods

Performance Tasks

There are no Performance Tasks in this section.

Objective

Compare motor braking methods.

a. Describe DC injection braking.
b. Identify dynamic and regenerative braking methods.
c. Describe friction braking.

Braking provides a means of quickly stopping an AC motor when it is necessary to stop it faster than is normally possible by removing the power and letting the motor coast to a stop. Braking can be accomplished in several ways. The method used depends on the application, available power, and circuit requirements. Three common methods of motor braking include the following:

- *DC injection braking of an AC motor* — Braking force is independent of motor speed. Requires a source of DC power. Braking energy is lost as heat within the motor.
- *Dynamic and regenerative braking* — Braking force decreases with decreasing motor speed. Requires connection to the motor controls. Dynamic braking energy is lost to resistors while regenerative braking energy is saved to the incoming power source.
- *Friction braking* — Braking force is independent of motor speed. Does not require any operating power sources. Braking energy is lost as heat within the brake components.

4.1.0 DC Injection Braking

DC injection braking uses a DC voltage applied to (injected into) the motor stator windings for a timed interval (*Figure 27*). The application of direct current to the stator windings creates a stationary magnetic field. This field interacts with the magnetic fields in the rotor to create a braking torque on the rotor, which can bring the motor to a stop and keep it from rotating. The magnitude of the applied DC determines whether the stopping action occurs very quickly (as for an emergency) or more gently (for safety). An advantage of DC injection braking is that motors can be stopped rapidly without wear on brake linings or drums. Since DC injection braking requires the availability and use of incoming power, it cannot be safely used for loads suspended from a crane or hoist—friction braking must be employed instead.

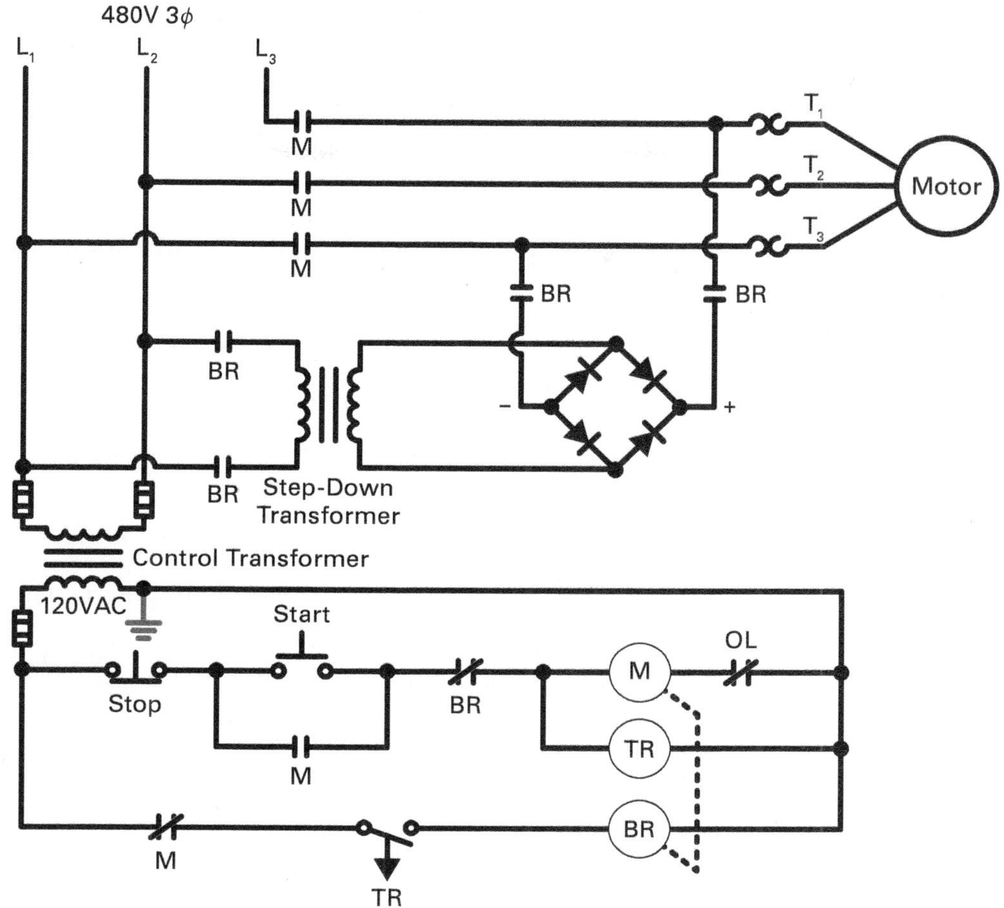

Figure 27 Circuit for DC braking of an AC motor.

In the DC brake circuit of *Figure 27*, a typical motor starter circuit with its magnetic starter (M) and Stop/Start buttons is modified with the addition of an electrically and mechanically interlocked braking relay (BR), an off-delay timing relay (TR), and a DC power supply with a step-down transformer and full-wave bridge rectifier. These operate together as follows:

- Contactor M is de-energized by pressing the Stop button.
- Simultaneously, timing relay TR is de-energized, closing its NOTO contacts.
- Braking relay BR is energized to apply the DC power from the rectifier to the motor.
- When the preset time interval in TR ends, the NOTO contacts open to de-energize braking relay BR.
- This removes the DC braking power from the motor and the Start button can start the motor when pressed.

A transformer with tapped windings is often used to adjust the amount of braking voltage applied to the motor. Current-limiting resistors could be used for the same purpose. The higher the applied DC voltage, the greater the braking torque. This allows for a low or high amount of braking, depending on the application. The time interval set in timing relay TR must be longer than the actual time required for the motor to come to a complete stop—this must be done in the field.

The mechanical and electrical interlocking of starter M and braking relay BR is required because the AC and DC power supplies must never be connected to the motor simultaneously. Total interlocking should always be used on electrical braking circuits.

DC braking can be used with AC motors controlled by any of the reduced-voltage starters discussed earlier. DC braking can also be used with motors controlled by AFDs. In this case, the AFD already has all the components required—the only need is to set the handful of parameters to permit DC injection braking and set both the magnitude and duration of the DC injection.

Three limits exist in the use of DC braking of motors:

- The braking energy is lost as heat in the motor, which can cause overheating and damage to the motor. For applications with frequent use of dynamic braking, an external cooling fan may be required.
- If the braking is very rapid, the torque produced can damage the motor or the connected load, and the heat produced within the motor can damage or destroy the motor windings.
- For safety, the application may include a requirement for a mechanical brake to automatically activate upon loss of power.

4.2.0 Dynamic and Regenerative Braking

In both dynamic and regenerative braking, the power connections to the motor (either AC or DC) are reconfigured so the motor acts as a generator. With dynamic or friction braking, the energy stored in the motor and driven load is converted to external heat and is lost. Regenerative braking offers a more energy-efficient approach. Unlike DC injection braking (in which the braking force is constant regardless of motor speed), dynamic and regenerative braking force is proportional to motor speed and therefore drops to zero when the motor is stopped. In applications requiring a definite stop to a zero speed, dynamic or regenerative braking can be used for most of the speed reduction (minimizing heating within the motor). DC braking is then used to ensure a positive stop.

4.2.1 Dynamic Braking

In addition to use of an AFD for DC injection braking, an AFD can also provide dynamic braking by use of a timed (ramped) stop for the motor and its driven load. When the output frequency from the drive to the motor is less than the speed of the motor, negative torque is developed within the motor. The motor then acts like a generator by converting mechanical power from the shaft into electrical power that is returned to the DC bus within the AFD. AFDs are made with an IGBT switch connected to terminals which, in this application, are connected to an external braking resistor where the excess energy gets dissipated as heat.

Figure 28 shows a simplified diagram of an AFD wired to provide dynamic braking. The drive control logic will turn the IGBT switch on and off as necessary to keep the DC bus voltage from reaching an unsafe level. To function safely and properly, the resistor must be large enough to handle the heat created within it by the braking action. It will be located outside the AFD enclosure and connected using high-temperature wire. The resistor has a high-temperature limit switch wired back to the drive control inputs. If the braking resistor fails, the DC bus voltage in the AFD will exceed its high limit and the AFD will trip offline, with the resulting loss of all motor control. Therefore, the resistors used for dynamic braking must be capable of absorbing at least six times the stored rotational energy of the motor at its operating speed. Dynamic braking is commonly used with traction motors in rail transportation.

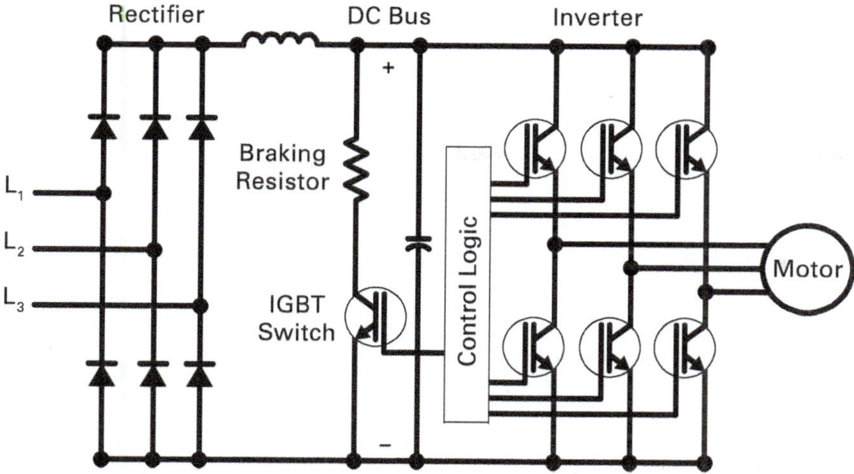

Figure 28 Simplified schematic of an AC drive using dynamic braking.

4.2.2 Regenerative Braking

Due to the growing demand for energy-efficient systems, AFD applications often include regenerative braking. Methods of regenerative braking include the following:

- *Regeneration to the power line* — AFDs that can do this are called *line regenerative.* They are made with active components in their input section instead of diodes. When the DC bus voltage reaches its upper safety limit, the AFDs logic returns the excess energy back to the incoming power line.
- *Sharing the DC bus* — Form FB drives (described earlier) are connected and get their power from a common DC bus with its own rectifier source. When one AFD is braking its load, the excess energy put onto the DC bus can be used by other AFDs on this bus or returned to the incoming power line.
- *Storage in batteries* — The DC bus is directly connected to batteries. When the motor is being operated as a generator, the excess energy from the motor is stored in the batteries. This method is used in electric and hybrid automobiles, resulting in considerable energy savings.

4.3.0 Friction Braking

Motor braking is also done using solenoid-operated friction brakes. Friction brakes are found on printing presses, small cranes, overhead doors, hoisting equipment, machine tool control, incline or decline conveyors, and other applications.

Many friction brakes used with motors are like those used with vehicles. They normally consist of two shoe- or pad-type friction surfaces that contact a wheel mounted on the motor shaft. Brake operation is controlled by a solenoid. The solenoid is energized when the motor is running, causing the brake shoes or pads to be retracted from the wheel. When the motor is turned off, the solenoid is de-energized, and the tension from a return spring in the brake mechanism brings the shoes in contact with the wheel, causing braking to occur as a result of the friction between the shoes and the wheel. The braking torque developed is directly proportional to the braking surface area and spring pressure. The spring pressure is adjustable on nearly all friction brakes.

In the diagram shown in *Figure 29*, the brake solenoid energizes and de-energizes when voltage is applied to and removed from the motor, respectively. To prevent improper brake activation, the brake solenoid is connected directly into the motor power circuit, not its control circuit. Because the brake solenoid in the motor is designed to release the brake when full motor voltage is applied, wiring to the solenoid must be run from a separate contactor when the motor is operated from any of the reduced-voltage starting methods or from an AFD.

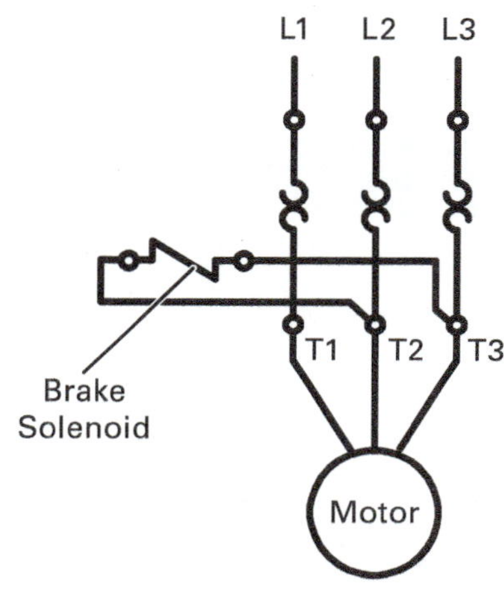

Figure 29 Friction brake solenoid connection.

Rural Applications of AFDs

In rural areas, three-phase power may not be available at an affordable cost. One contractor uses a large DC power supply with a group of form FB AFDs to power an entire grain elevator. This avoids the expense or uncertain application of larger FC-type AFDs.

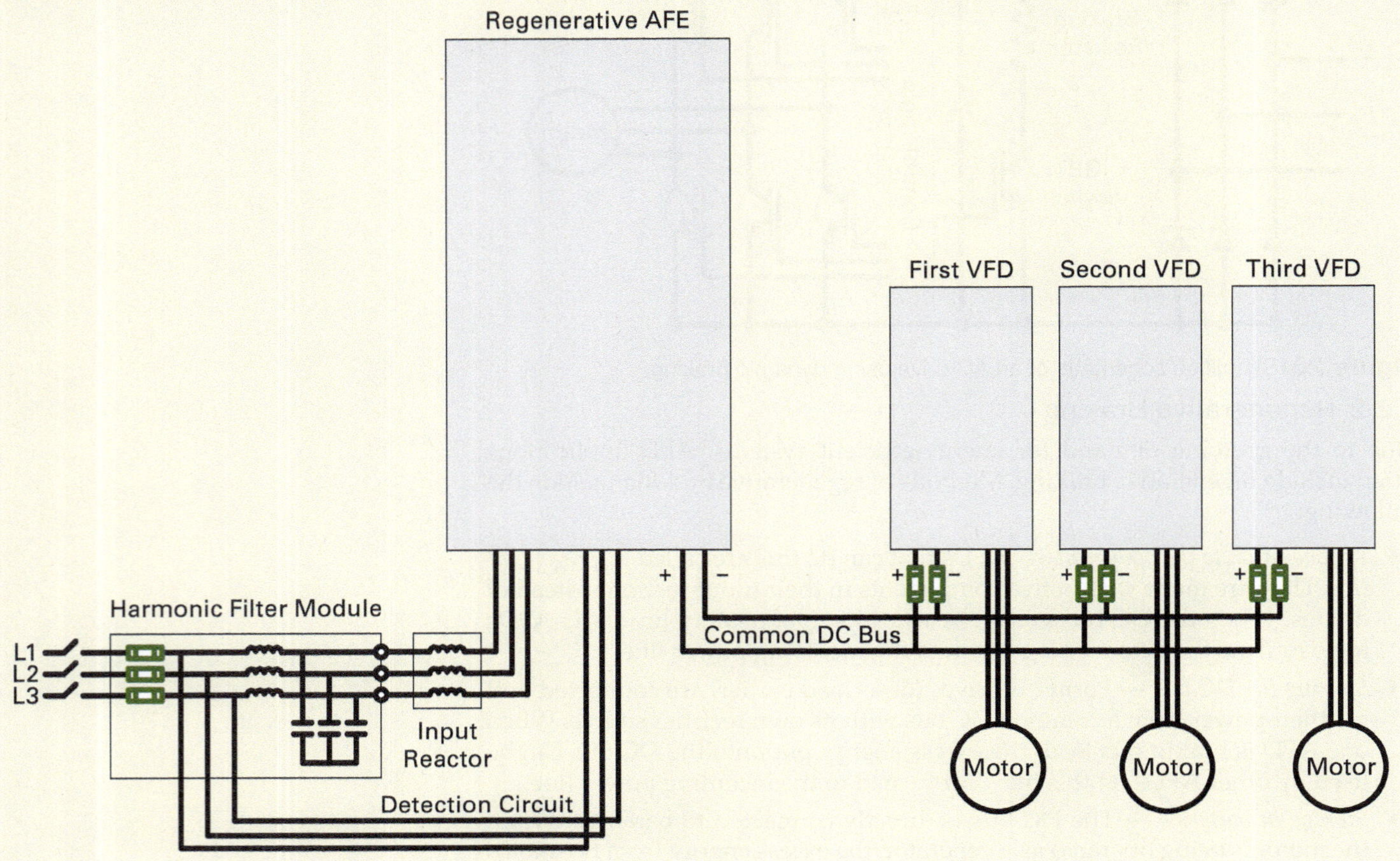

Friction brakes are positive-action, mechanical friction devices. Normal operation is such that when the power is removed from the motor, the brake is set. For this reason, it can be used as a holding brake and is described as *fail-safe*. The advantage of using a friction brake is lower cost. However, friction brakes require more maintenance than other braking methods. Like the brakes used in a vehicle, the shoes or pads must be replaced periodically.

In some applications with very frequent stops and starts, such as a conveyor system brake / spacer belt, a separately controlled clutch/brake assembly is installed on the motor output shaft. The motor will continue to run but the driven load will be disconnected and quickly stopped. This approach allows more frequent stops and starts than is permitted by the motor design.

4.0.0 Section Review

1. The amount of braking torque when using DC braking of an AC motor can be controlled by using a tapped transformer or by _____.
   a. installing an LC filter
   b. adding a current-limiting resistor
   c. adding a switching circuit
   d. replacing the brake pads

2. Line regenerative braking returns braking energy to the power line by _____.
   a. sharing the AFDs DC bus
   b. raising the DC bus voltage
   c. active components in the AFD input section
   d. connection to a battery

3. Friction brakes are controlled by _____.
   a. using a torque converter
   b. adding a current-limiting resistor
   c. a transformer
   d. a solenoid

5.0.0 Working with Motor Controls

Objective

Describe how to maintain motor controls for peak operation.

a. Apply the precautions associated with solid-state controls.

b. Implement the preventive maintenance procedures associated with solid-state controls.

Performance Tasks

There are no Performance Tasks in this section.

Solid-state controls may be damaged by electrical noise, heat, and contaminants. Proper maintenance ensures safe operation of motor controls.

5.1.0 Precautions for Working with Solid-State Controls

WARNING!

Solid-state equipment may contain devices that have potentially hazardous leakage current in the off state. Power should be turned off and the device disconnected from the power source before working on the circuit or load.

CAUTION

Many solid-state devices can be damaged by electrostatic charges. These devices should be handled in the manner specified by the manufacturer. This is particularly true because higher density of the electronic components requires lower operating voltages, thus increasing the possibility of electrostatic damage (ESD).

Solid-state equipment and/or components can be damaged if improperly handled or installed. The following guidelines should be followed when handling, installing, or otherwise working with solid-state equipment or components:

- Microprocessors and other integrated circuit chips are very sensitive to, and can be damaged by, static electricity from sources such as lightning or people. When handling circuit boards, avoid touching the components, printed circuit, and connector pins. Always ground yourself before touching a board. Disposable grounding wrist straps are sometimes supplied with boards containing electrostatic-sensitive components. If a wrist strap is not supplied with the equipment, a wrist strap grounding system should be obtained and used. It allows you to handle static-sensitive components without fear of electrostatic discharge. Store unused boards inside their special metallized shielded storage bags or a conductive tote box (*Figure 30*).
- Solid-state devices can be damaged by the application of reverse polarity or incorrect phase sequence. Input power and control signals must be applied with the polarity and phase sequence specified by the manufacturer.
- The main source of heat in many solid-state systems is the energy dissipated in the output power devices. Ensure the device is operated within the maximum and minimum ambient operating temperatures specified by the manufacturer. Follow the manufacturer's recommendations pertaining to the selection of enclosures and ventilation requirements. For existing equipment, make sure that ventilation passages are kept clean and open.

- Moisture, corrosive gases, dust, and other contaminants can all have adverse effects on a system that is not adequately protected against atmospheric contaminants. If these contaminants collect on printed circuit boards, bridging between the conductors may result in a malfunction of the circuit. This could lead to noisy and erratic control operation or a permanent malfunction. A thick coating of dust could also prevent adequate cooling of the board or heat sink, causing a malfunction.
- Excessive shock or vibration may cause damage to solid-state equipment. Follow all manufacturer instructions for mounting.

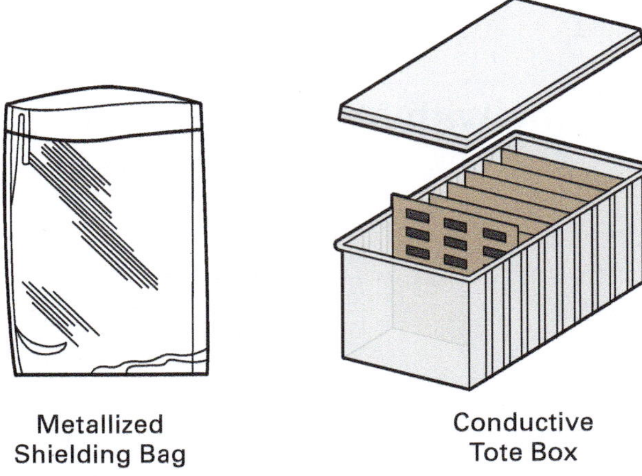

Figure 30 ESD protection bag and tote box.

Electrical noise can also affect the operation of solid-state controls. Sources of electrical noise include machines with large, fast-changing voltages or currents when they are energized or de-energized, such as motor starters, welding equipment, adjustable speed drives, and other inductive devices. The following are basic steps to help minimize electrical noise:

- Maintain enough physical separation between electrical noise sources and sensitive equipment to ensure that the noise will not cause malfunctions or unintended actuation of the control.
- Maintain a physical separation between sensitive signal wires and electrical power and control conductors. This separation can be accomplished by using separate conduits, wiring trays, or methods recommended by the manufacturer.
- Use twisted-pair wiring in critical signal circuits and noise-producing circuits to minimize magnetic interference.
- Use shielded wire to reduce the magnitude of the noise coupled into the low-level signal circuit by electrostatic or magnetic coupling.
- Where signal and power wires or cables must cross, do so at right angles to minimize any magnetically induced voltages (noise) between the cables.
- Follow all requirements of the *National Electrical Code®* with respect to grounding. Additional grounding precautions may be required to minimize electrical noise. These precautions generally deal with ground loop currents arising from multiple ground paths. The manufacturer's grounding recommendations must also be followed.

5.2.0 Motor Control Maintenance

A well-planned and well-executed preventive maintenance program is necessary to achieve satisfactory operation of electrical and electronic motor control equipment. Preventive maintenance keeps the equipment running with little or no downtime. Ideally, routine preventive maintenance for a specific piece of equipment is based on the manufacturer's recommendations, the severity of use, and the surrounding environment.

Before any preventive maintenance work begins that will shut down or otherwise interrupt equipment operation, always notify and/or coordinate with the building manager, shift leader, foreman, or other responsible person.

WARNING!

Before any preventive maintenance tasks are performed, de-energize, lockout, and tagout all circuits and equipment in accordance with the prevailing lockout/tagout policy. If more than one incoming power source exists (such as when there is a separate control circuit, or when other forms of energy are involved) make sure to de-energize all such sources. Note that solid-state electronic equipment may contain devices that have potentially hazardous leakage current in the off state. Such equipment should be isolated from the power source by opening the related disconnect switch, rather than by simply turning off the device.

Preventive maintenance for motor control circuit components normally involves inspection and cleaning of the equipment. Control equipment should be kept clean and dry. Before opening the door or cover of a cabinet or enclosure, clean any foreign material, dirt, or debris from the outside top surfaces to avoid the risk of anything falling onto the equipment. After opening the cabinet or enclosure, inspect the equipment for the presence of any dust, dirt, moisture or evidence of moisture, or other contamination. If any is found, the cause must be determined and eliminated. This could indicate an incorrectly selected, deteriorated, or damaged enclosure; unsealed enclosure openings; internal condensation; condensate from an unsealed conduit; or improper operating procedures, such as operating the enclosure with the door open or the cover removed.

Clean the parts of the control equipment by vacuuming or wiping with a dry cloth or soft brush. Use care not to damage delicate parts. Do not clean the equipment or components using compressed air because it may displace dirt, dust, or other debris into other parts or equipment, and the force may damage delicate components. Liquid cleaners, including spray cleaners, should not be used unless specified by the equipment manufacturer. This is because residues may cause damage or interfere with electrical or mechanical functions. If dust or dirt has accumulated on heat sinks and/or components that generate heat, it should be carefully removed because such accumulation can reduce the heat dissipation capability of these components and lead to premature failures. Ventilation passages should be open and cleaned of any dust and dirt.

Check the mechanical integrity of the equipment. Physical damage or broken parts can usually be found quickly by inspection. A general inspection should be made to look for loose, broken, missing, or badly worn parts. Components and wiring should be inspected for signs of overheating. The movement of mechanical parts, such as the armature and contacts of contactors, disconnect switches, circuit breaker operator mechanisms, and mechanical interlocks, should be checked for functional operation and freedom of motion. Any broken, deformed, or badly worn parts or assemblies should be replaced with manufacturer-recommended components. Any loose terminals or attaching hardware should be retightened securely to the torque specified by the equipment manufacturer.

Ambient Temperature Surrounding Solid-State Devices

Do not overlook any sources of heat that might raise the ambient temperature at an enclosure containing solid-state devices. Consider heat sources such as power supplies, transformers, radiated heat, adjacent furnaces, and even sunlight.

Preventive Maintenance

For programmable overloads, reduced-voltage starters, AFDs, and similar devices, refer to the user's manual / service manual supplied with the equipment for a description and schedule of specific preventive maintenance tasks that apply to the equipment.

The contacts of contactors should be checked for wear caused by arcing. During arcing, a small part of each contact melts, then vaporizes and is blown away. When the contacts are new, they are smooth and have a uniform silver color. As the device is used, the contacts become pitted, and the color may change to blue, brown, or black. These colors result from the normal formation of metal oxide on the contact surfaces and are not detrimental to contact life and performance. Contacts should be replaced under the following conditions:

- *Insufficient contact material* — When less than $\frac{1}{64}$" (0.4 mm) remains, replace the contacts.
- *Irregular surface wear* — This type of wear is normal. However, if a corner of the contact material is worn away and a contact may mate with the opposing contact support member, the contacts should be replaced. This condition can result in contact welding.
- *Pitting* — Under normal wear, contact pitting should be uniform. This condition occurs during arcing, as described above. The contacts should be replaced if the pitting becomes excessive and little contact material remains.
- *Curling of contact surfaces* — This condition results from severe service that produces high contact temperatures and causes separation of the contact material from the contact support member.

Motor control mechanisms should not be lubricated unless recommended by the manufacturer. If lubrication is required, use only the recommended type and amount of lubricant. Remove any surplus lubricant to avoid the risk of establishing a tracking path across insulating surfaces, as well as the risk of excess lubricant migrating into areas that should not be lubricated.

5.0.0 Section Review

1. Shielded wire is used with solid-state devices to _____.
   a. prevent damage from static electricity
   b. reduce the amount of coupled noise
   c. maintain a physical separation between wires
   d. prevent damage to the wiring

2. Which of the following is a recommended method for cleaning solid-state devices?
   a. Compressed air
   b. Soap and water
   c. Dry cloth or soft brush
   d. Liquid spray cleaners

6.0.0 Motor Control Troubleshooting

Objective

Describe how to troubleshoot motor controls.

a. Explain basic troubleshooting methods.

b. Describe the electrical troubleshooting methods used to check control circuits and devices.

Performance Tasks

There are no Performance Tasks in this section.

Troubleshooting motor control systems requires a systematic approach. The process includes:

- Customer interface
- Physical examination of the system
- Basic system analysis with a clear understanding of the sequence of operation, interlocks, and limits
- Use of the equipment manufacturer's troubleshooting resources
- Troubleshooting the motor control circuit and components

6.1.0 Basic Troubleshooting Practices

The process of troubleshooting motor control circuit problems should always begin with obtaining all the information possible about the equipment problem or malfunction.

6.1.1 Customer Interface

Talking to and asking questions of a customer with first-hand knowledge of the problem is always recommended. This can provide valuable information on equipment operation that can aid in the troubleshooting process. Be sure to talk with and listen carefully to the machine or equipment operators and not just to the person who requested the service call because the machine operator often knows the most about the problem. When interviewing the customer about a specific fault or problem, try to determine the following:

- The scope of the problem and when and how it began
- How often the problem occurs
- Whether the equipment has been worked on or tested recently
- Whether the equipment ever operated correctly
- Whether the problem occurred following a specific event, such as the addition of new electrical equipment, relocation of equipment, or new construction work

Before working on the motor control circuit equipment, always explain to the customer the course of action you intend to take and how it might affect the system, such as service interruptions or total system downtime. If the motor circuit with a problem is part of an emergency system (fire or backup), notify the police, fire department, or other off-site monitoring agencies or authorities that you will be working on the system.

6.1.2 Physical Examination

Problems can sometimes be identified by a visual inspection of the motor control circuit equipment, its wiring, and the adjacent area. For newly installed equipment, make sure it has been wired correctly. For nonoperating equipment, look for tripped circuit breakers, motor overloads, and signs of overheating. For operating equipment, check for odors of burning insulation, sounds of arcing, and signs that the unit is abnormally warm. For equipment with adjustable controls or mode selection switches, look for switches and/or controls that may be set to the wrong positions. For programmable equipment, check whether the selected operating and parameter inputs are correct.

6.1.3 Basic System Analysis

A proper diagnosis of a problem requires knowing what the motor control circuit and application equipment being driven by the motor should be doing when they are operating properly. If you are not familiar with how a system or unit should operate, study the manufacturer's service literature to familiarize yourself with the equipment modes and sequence of operation.

The second part of the diagnosis is to find out which symptoms are exhibited by the improperly operating system. This can be done by carefully listening to the customer's complaints and then analyzing the operation of the motor control circuit and application equipment. This usually means making electrical measurements at key points in the motor control circuit. Measured values can be compared with a set of previously recorded values or with values given in the manufacturer's service literature. When troubleshooting, avoid making assumptions about the cause of problems. Always secure as much information as possible before arriving at a diagnosis.

6.1.4 Manufacturer Resources

Today's electronic equipment can be very complex, and no one person is an expert on the wide variety of equipment being used to control motors. For this reason, a good troubleshooter should know how and where to locate information about the specific unit being serviced. This includes making phone calls to manufacturers' technical support centers, using manufacturers' website resources, and using manufacturers' user/service manuals. The user/service manuals supplied with solid-state programmable drive units and similar types of complex equipment contain invaluable operating and troubleshooting information, such as the following:

- Principles of operation
- Functional description of the circuitry
- Illustrations showing the location of each control or indicator and its function
- Illustrations and text describing menu-driven control panel displays
- Step-by-step procedures for the proper use and maintenance of the equipment
- Safety considerations and precautions that should be observed when operating the equipment
- Schematic diagrams, wiring diagrams, mechanical layouts, and parts lists for the specific unit

AFD units and similar microprocessor-controlled devices usually have built-in fault diagnostic circuits to aid in troubleshooting. When a fault occurs that interrupts the operation of the drive, these circuits give a visual indication that a fault trip has occurred. They also generate a fault code that can be selected for display on the unit control panel. When a fault occurs, look up the specific fault code displayed on the panel in a fault troubleshooting table in the user/service manual to help pinpoint the problem area (*Figure 31*).

6.1.5 Troubleshooting Motor Control Circuits and Components

A motor control circuit is a means of supplying power to and removing power from a motor. Most motor circuits consist of a combination of starting mechanisms, both automatic and manual. The simple motor control circuit shown in *Figure 32* is typical of most motor circuits. Troubleshooting electrical problems in motor control circuits may appear complex. However, it can be simplified if the electrical components are divided into smaller functional circuit areas based on the operations they perform. Motor control circuits can be divided into three functional circuit areas: power circuits, control circuits, and the load.

Fault Codes	Fault	Possible Causes	Checking
F1	Overcurrent	Frequency converter has measured too high a current in the motor output: – Sudden heavy load increase – Short circuit in the motor cables – Unsuitable motor	Check the load. Check the motor size. Check the cables.
F2	Overvoltage	The voltage of the internal DC-link of the frequency converter has exceeded the nominal voltage by 35%: – Deceleration time is too fast – High overvoltage spikes at utility	Adjust the deceleration time.
F3	Ground Fault	Current measurement has detected that the sum of the motor phase current is not zero: – Insulation failure in the motor or the cables	Check the motor cables.
F4	Inverter Fault	Frequency converter has detected faulty operation in the gate drivers or IGBT bridge: – Interference fault – Component failure	Reset the fault and restart again; if the fault occurs again, contact your distributor.
F5	Charging Switch	Charging switch is open when the start command is active: – Interference fault – Component failure	Reset the fault and restart again; if the fault occurs again, contact your distributor.
F6	Undervoltage	DC-Bus voltage has gone below 65% of the nominal voltage: t common reason is failure of the	In case of temporary supply voltage break, reset the fault and start

Figure 31 Sample portion of a fault troubleshooting table.

The power circuits, represented by the heavier lines shown in *Figure 32*, provide line power to the motor. Line voltages are usually 240VAC or 480VAC. As shown, the power circuits include the disconnecting means, the overcurrent protective devices (fuses or circuit breakers), the normally open contactor contacts, and the motor overload device. The load circuit is the AC motor.

The thinner lines represent the control circuit used in a magnetic-type starter. The control circuit is used to direct power to a magnetic contactor through the Stop/Start station, thermal overload relay contacts, holding contacts, and the contactor coil. Note that the control circuit can contain several other types of pilot devices used to control the motor. The control circuit can be connected directly to the line, as shown in *Figure 32*, or it can be isolated from the power circuit by a step-down control transformer. Lower voltages, such as 24VAC, 120VAC, and 240VAC, are commonly used with a control transformer. The voltage rating for the coil on the motor starter indicates which control voltage is used.

Isolation to the faulty circuit area (power, control, or load) is based on an analysis of equipment operation and a process of elimination. Troubleshooting can be done in several ways. When troubleshooting a motor circuit when the motor is not working or has a problem, the contactor or motor starter is usually checked first. This is because it is the point where the incoming power, load, and control circuit are connected. Basic voltage readings should be taken at a contactor or motor starter to determine where the problem lies. The same basic procedure used to troubleshoot a motor starter works for contactors because a motor starter is a contactor with added overload protection.

The tightness of all terminals and busbar connections should be checked when troubleshooting control devices. Loose connections in the power circuit of contactors and motor starters cause overheating that can result in equipment malfunction or failure. Loose connections in the control circuit cause control malfunctions. Loose connections of grounding terminals can lead to electrical shock and cause electromagnetic interference.

WARNING!

Although many control circuit components may be tested while de-energized, it is occasionally necessary to test or troubleshoot energized circuits or equipment. To do so, you must be qualified and follow all safety procedures and safe work practices in accordance with the prevailing policies and your safety training.

Consider the following safety practices during troubleshooting and similar work on energized equipment:

- Use barriers or similar means to keep unqualified people safely away.
- Have an escape route.
- Always remain alert. Stop work if you are distracted by unrelated activities.
- Make sure that there is adequate lighting to work safely.
- Remove all conductive apparel (jewelry, metal headgear, etc.).
- Use insulated tools and equipment.
- Use protective shields if there is a possibility of exposure to energized parts.
- Have a definite plan and defined scope of work to perform.

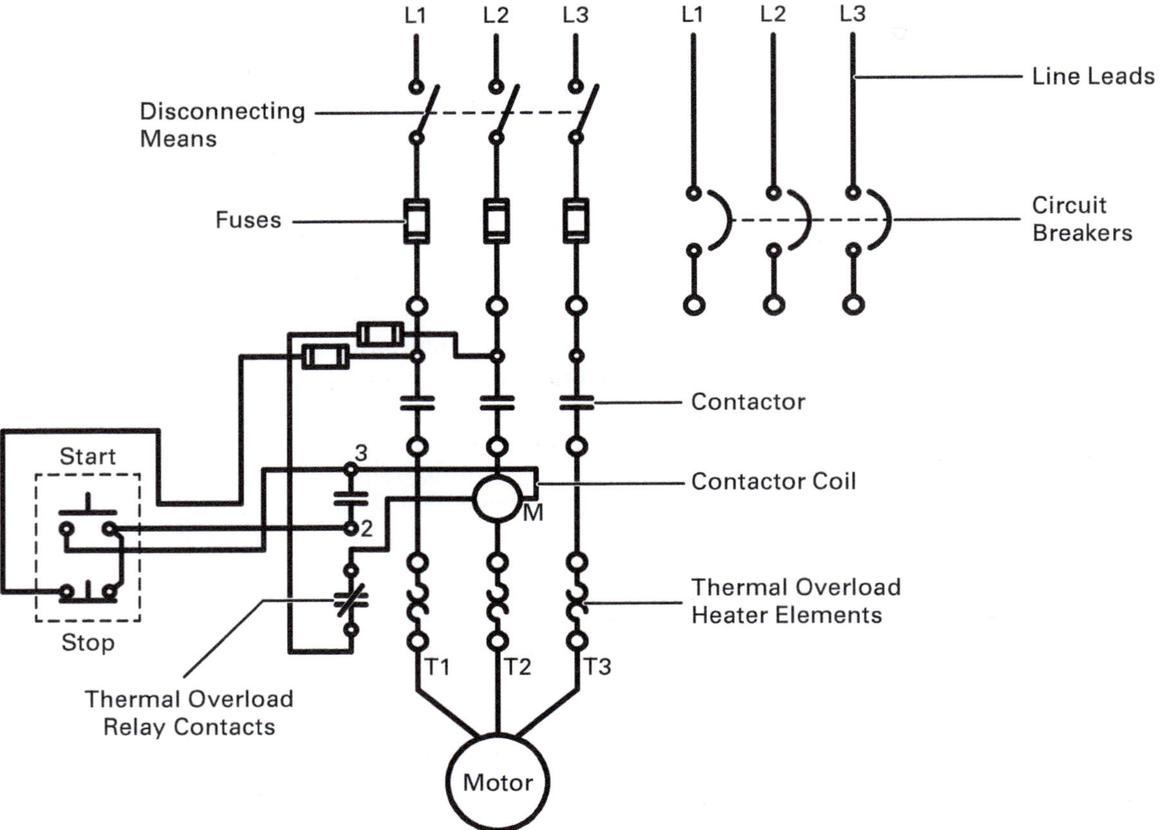

Figure 32 Basic motor control circuit.

Table 7A and *Table 7B* provide additional motor control troubleshooting information. Specific procedures for making electrical measurements and troubleshooting individual components in motor control circuits are provided later in this section. Be sure to consult the manufacturer's information for procedures specific to the application.

TABLE 7A Motor Control Troubleshooting Chart (1 of 2)

Malfunction	Possible Cause	Corrective Action
Constant chatter	Broken pole shader	Replace.
	Poor contact in control circuit	Improve contact or use holding circuit interlock (three-wire control).
	Low voltage	Correct voltage condition; check momentary voltage dip during starting.
Contactor welding or freezing	Abnormal inrush of current	Use larger contactor or check for grounds.
	Rapid jogging	Install larger device for jogging service.
	Insufficient contact pressure	Replace contact springs; check contact carrier for damage.
	Low voltage preventing magnet from sealing	Correct voltage condition; check momentary voltage dip during starting.
	Foreign matter preventing contacts from closing	Clean contacts with approved solvent.
	Short circuit	Remove fault and check to be sure fuse or circuit breaker size is correct.
Short contact life or tip overheating	Filing or dressing	Do not file silver-faced contacts; rough spots or discoloration will not harm contacts.
	Interrupt excessively high	Install larger device or check currents for grounds, shorts, or excessive motor currents; use silver-faced contacts.
	Excessive jogging	Install larger device rated for jogging.
	Weak contact pressure	Adjust or replace contact springs.
	Dirt or foreign matter on contact surfaces	Clean contacts with approved solvent.
	Short circuit	Remove fault and check for proper fuse or circuit breaker size.
	Loose connection	Clean and tighten.
	Sustained overload	Install larger device or check for excessive load current.
Coil overheating	Overvoltage or high ambient temperature	Check application and circuit.
	Incorrect coil	Check rating and if incorrect, replace with proper coil.
	Shorted turns caused by mechanical damage or corrosion	Replace coil.
	Undervoltage; failure of magnet to seal in	Correct system voltage.
	Dirt or rust on pole faces increasing air gap	Clean pole faces.
Overload relays tripping	Sustained overload	Check for grounds, shorts, or excessive currents.
	Loose connection on load wires	Clean and tighten.
	Incorrect heater	Replace relay with correct size heater unit.

TABLE 7B Motor Control Troubleshooting Chart (2 of 2)

Malfunction	Possible Cause	Corrective Action
Failure to trip causing motor burnout	Mechanical binding, dirt, corrosion, etc.	Clean or replace.
	Wrong heater or heaters omitted, and jumper wires used	Check ratings; apply proper heater.
	Motor and relay at different temperatures	Adjust relay rating accordingly.
	Wrong calibration or improper calibration adjustment	Consult factory.
Magnetic and mechanical parts inoperative	Broken shading coil	Replace shading coil.
Noisy magnet humming	Magnet faces not mating	Replace magnet assembly; realign.
	Dirt or rust on magnet faces	Clean and realign.
	Low voltage	Check system voltage and voltage dips during starting.
Failure to pick up and seal	Low voltage	Check system voltage and voltage dips during starting.
	Coil open or shorted	Replace.
	Wrong coil	Check coil number.
	Mechanical obstruction	With power off, check for free movement of contact and armature assembly.
Failure to drop out	Gummy substance on pole faces	Clean with solvent.
	Voltage not removed	Check coil circuit.
	Worn or rusted parts causing binding	Replace parts.
	Residual magnetism due to lack of air gap in magnet path	Replace worn magnet parts.

Some general guidelines for isolating a fault in a motor control circuit are outlined in the following steps:

Step 1 Visually inspect the motor starter contactor and overload relay for signs of heat damage, arcing, or wear. Repair or replace any motor starter components that show visual signs of such damage.

Step 2 If there are no visual signs of damage, reset the overload relay and then press the Start button to energize the motor starter contactor. If the related motor starts, observe the motor starter for several minutes. If the overload relay trips, troubleshoot the motor and related wiring downstream from the motor starter for causes of an overload.

Step 3 If the motor does not start after resetting the overload, check the voltage applied to the line side of the contactor. If the voltage reading is 0V or is not within 10% of the motor voltage rating, check the power wiring and components (fuses, circuit breaker, and disconnect switch) upstream of the motor starter.

Step 4 If voltage is applied to the line side of the contactor and it is at the correct level, press the Start button to energize the contactor. If the contactor coil does not energize, troubleshoot the contactor coil to determine whether it is open. If the coil is not open, troubleshoot the contactor coil control circuit components and wiring for a problem.

Step 5 If the contactor coil energizes, check the voltage at the load side of the contactor. If the voltage reading is acceptable (within 10% of the motor voltage rating), the contacts are good. If there is no voltage reading or the reading is too low, turn the power off and replace the contactor contacts.

Step 6 If voltage is present at the load side of the contactor and it is at the correct level, check the output voltage from the overload relay. If the voltage reading is 0V, turn the power off and replace the overload relay. If the voltage reading is acceptable and the motor is not operating, troubleshoot the motor or power wiring downstream from the motor starter.

6.2.0 Universal Troubleshooting Procedures

There are several troubleshooting procedures that are common to most motor control circuits. These procedures often provide information that leads to detailed troubleshooting specific to the circuit. In many cases though, these common procedures reveal the specific source of the problem directly, leading to its resolution.

6.2.1 Input Voltage / Voltage Imbalance Measurements

All motors and related motor control equipment are designed to operate within a specific range of system voltages, including a safety factor that is typically 10%. This safety factor is added to compensate for temporary supply voltage fluctuations that might occur. Continuous operation of a motor outside the intended range of voltages can damage the motor. Insufficient operating voltage can cause overload/overheating and possible failure of motors and other devices.

For a 230V rated motor, this means the supply voltage should remain in the range of 207V to 253V (230V ±10%). If the motor is rated for 208/230V, the supply voltage must be between 187V (10% below 208V) and 253V (10% above 230V).

Voltage imbalance is very important when working with three-phase equipment. A small imbalance in phase-to-phase voltage can result in a much greater current imbalance. With a current imbalance, more heat is generated in the motor windings. Both current and heat can cause nuisance overload trips and may cause motor failure. For this reason, the imbalance between any two legs of the voltage applied to a three-phase motor or system should not exceed 2%. If a voltage imbalance of more than 2% exists at the input to the equipment, correct the problem in the building or utility power distribution system before operating the equipment. *Figure 33* shows an example of how the amount of voltage imbalance is determined in a three-phase system.

A current imbalance may occur without a voltage imbalance. If the resistance of one leg is higher or lower, Ohm's law will predict a corresponding imbalance in currents. This could be because of a short between adjacent windings within the motor, or if an electrical terminal or contact becomes loose or corroded, resulting in a higher resistance in the leg. Current imbalance in a three-phase system is determined in the same way as voltage imbalance. Current imbalance in any one leg of a three-phase system should not exceed 10%.

6.2.2 Fuse Checks

Fuses or circuit breakers are normally the first components checked when a motor is totally inoperative. One way to test a fuse is by measuring continuity (*Figure 34*). To check the fuses, open the disconnect switch, then remove the fuses using an insulated fuse puller. Test the fuses for continuity using a volt-ohm-milliammeter (VOM) or digital multimeter (DMM) set to measure resistance. If the meter reads 0 ohms (Ω), indicating continuity, the fuse is usually good. If an open circuit (infinite resistance) exists across the fuse, it has failed. A blown fuse is usually caused by some abnormal overload condition, such as a short circuit within the equipment or an overloaded motor. These problems may not always occur when the motor starts, but they may occur after a significant amount of run time generates heat, or only when the load on the motor is increased. Replacing a blown fuse without locating and correcting the cause can result in damage to the motor or control equipment.

Fuses can also be tested with the circuit energized. Set the VOM/DMM to measure AC voltage on a range that is higher than the highest voltage expected. Place one VOM/DMM test lead on the line side of the L_1 fuse. Touch the other test lead to the load side of the L_2 fuse. If voltage is measured, the L_2 fuse is good; if not, the fuse is open. Repeat this procedure so that all fuses are measured with one test lead on the line side and the other test lead on the load side of a different fuse. This method tests one fuse at a time. If the measurement is performed with both test leads on the load side of the fuses, and the VOM/DMM shows no reading, you know that a fuse is blown but not which one.

Electrical Troubleshooting

Most electrical troubleshooting in motor control circuits can be done using a multimeter and an AC clamp-on ammeter. Some types of clamp-on instruments, like the one in the image, incorporate the functions of a clamp-on ammeter and multimeter into one device, allowing it to be used to measure current, voltage, and resistance.

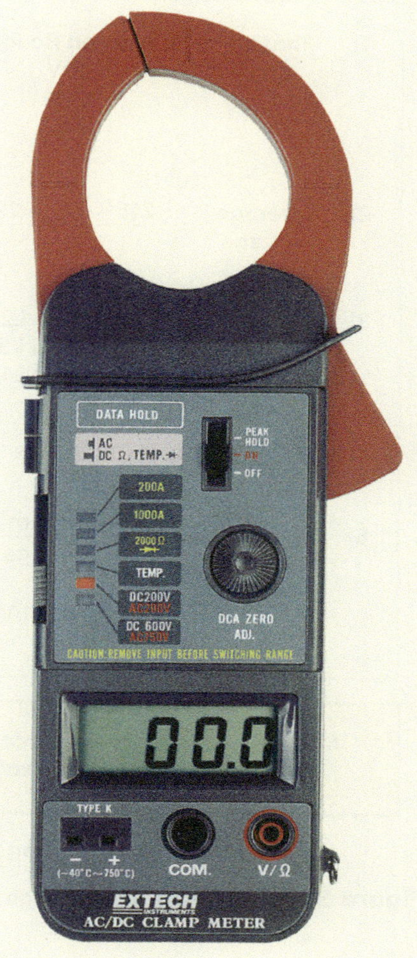

Source: Extech

CAUTION

When checking fuses, false readings may occur if there is another component, such as a control transformer, that may provide a false indication that the fuse is good due to the component's feedback.

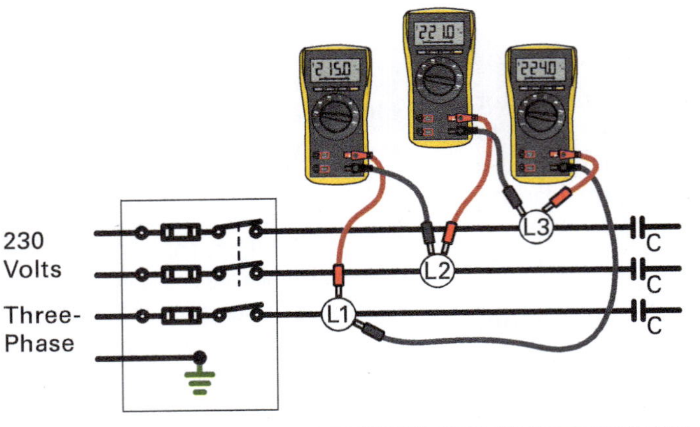

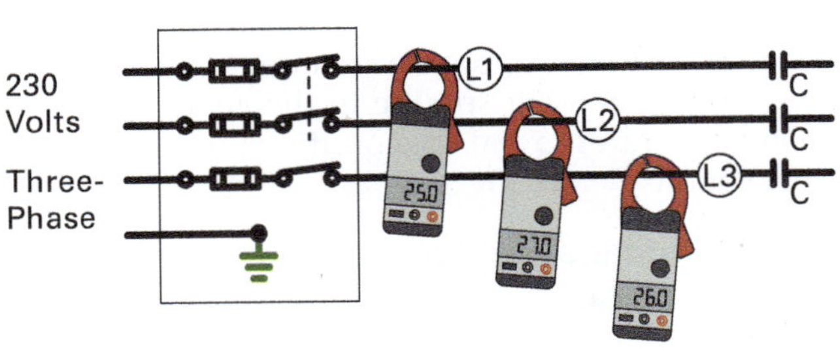

1)

Phase	**Measured Reading**
L1	215V
L2	221V
L3	224V

2) $\text{Average Voltage} = \dfrac{215 + 221 + 224}{3} = 220\text{V}$

3) Individual Phase Imbalance from Average

L1 to L2 = 220 – 215 = 5V
L2 to L3 = 221 – 220 = 1V
L3 to L1 = 224 – 220 = 4V

4) 5V = Maximum Imbalance

5) $\%\ \text{Imbalance} = \dfrac{\text{Maximum Imbalance}}{\text{Average Voltage}} \times 100$

$\%\ \text{Imbalance} = \dfrac{5\text{V}}{220\text{V}} \times 100 = 2.27\%$ **(Out of Balance)**

Maximum voltage imbalance between any two legs must not exceed 2%.

(A) Calculating Voltage Imbalance

1)

Phase	**Measured Reading**
L1	25A
L2	27A
L3	26A

2) $\text{Average Current} = \dfrac{25 + 27 + 26}{3} = 26\text{A}$

3) Individual Phase Imbalance from Average

L1 to L2 = 26 – 25= 1A
L2 to L3 = 27 – 26= 1A
L3 to L1 = 26 – 26= 0A

4) 1A = Maximum Imbalance

5) $\%\ \text{Imbalance} = \dfrac{\text{Maximum Imbalance}}{\text{Average Current}} \times 100$

$\%\ \text{Imbalance} = \dfrac{1\text{A}}{26\text{A}} \times 100 = 3.8\%$ **(In Balance)**

Maximum current imbalance between any two legs must not exceed 10%.

(B) Calculating Current Imbalance

Figure 33 Three-phase input voltage checks.

Troubleshooting

When troubleshooting, observe the following list of guidelines:

- Practice safe testing procedures.
- Change only one component at a time.
- Have a complete understanding of the machine's function.
- Make sure that test equipment is operational and calibrated before using it for troubleshooting.
- Use the correct test equipment with the proper rating for the circuit being tested.
- Do not change wiring connections in circuits that have worked in the past.

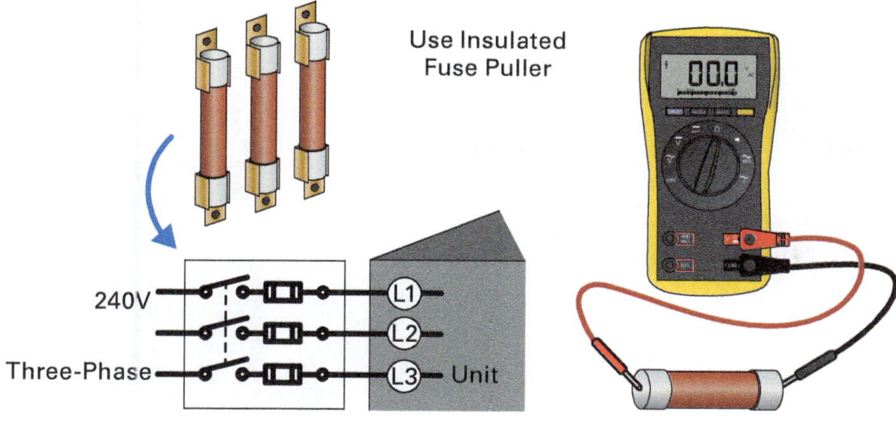

Zero Ω Reading = Good Fuse
Measurable or Infinite Resistance Reading = Bad Fuse

Continuity Check

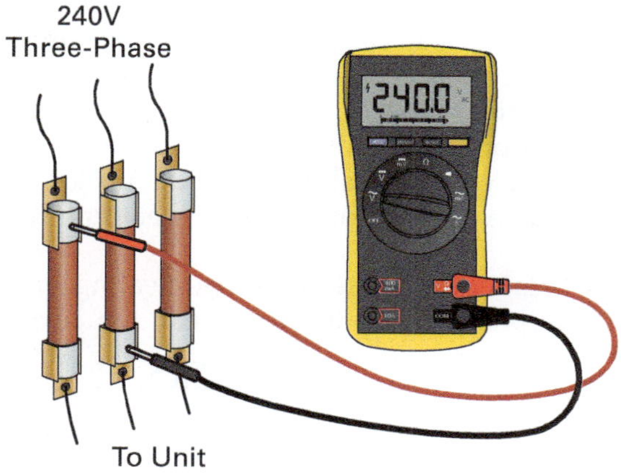

Voltage Check

Figure 34 Fuse checks.

6.2.3 Circuit Breaker Checks

Circuit breaker checks will also be necessary at times. To check a circuit breaker, set the circuit breaker to the Off position. If required, and with proper arc flash protection, remove any panel that covers the circuit breaker to expose the body of the breaker and the wires connected to its terminals. Set up a VOM/DMM to measure AC voltage on a range that is higher than the highest voltage expected. Measure the voltage applied to the circuit breaker line terminals in the following manner (*Figure 35*):

- A to neutral or ground (single-pole breaker)
- A to B (two-pole breaker)
- A to B, B to C, and C to A (three-pole breaker)

After making these measurements, verify that the breaker is closed by first setting it to the Off position, then setting it to the On position. Measure the voltage at the circuit breaker load terminals:

- A1 to neutral or ground (single-pole breaker)
- A1 to B1 (two-pole breaker)
- A1 to B1, B1 to C1, and C1 to A1 (three-pole breaker)

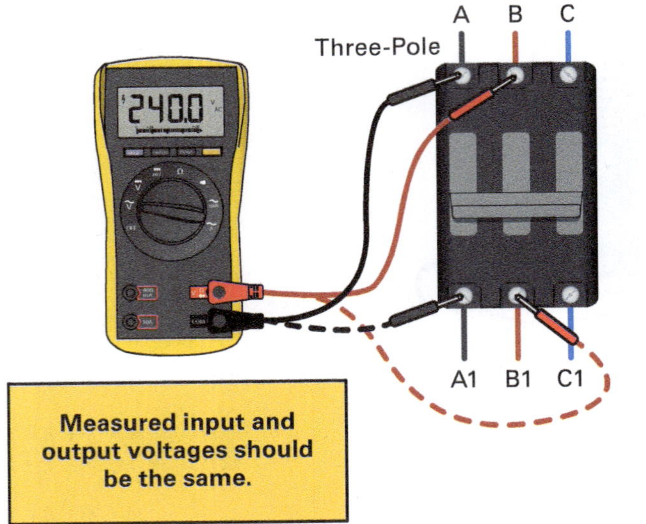

Circuit Breaker Voltage Check

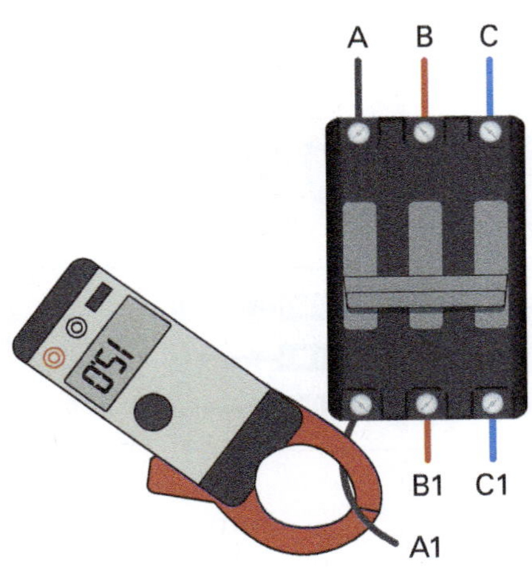

Circuit Breaker Current Check

Figure 35 Circuit breaker checks.

The measured line and load voltages should be the same if the breaker contacts are closed. If the load side voltage is significantly lower than that measured at the line side of the circuit breaker, visually inspect the circuit breaker for loose wires and terminals or signs of overheating that might cause voltage drop. If no cause is found, the circuit breaker should be replaced. Remember, however, that significant voltage drop is not always evident until a load is placed on the circuit breaker.

If the circuit breaker shows signs of overheating or trips when power is applied to the equipment, reset it, then check the current flow through the breaker using an AC clamp-on ammeter. Set up the AC clamp-on ammeter to measure AC current on a range that is higher than the highest current expected. Check the ampere rating marked on the breaker. It is usually stamped on the breaker lever or body. One wire at a time, measure the current flow in the wires connected to the circuit breaker output terminals:

- A1 (single-pole breaker)
- A1 and B1 (two-pole breaker)
- A1, B1, and C1 (three-pole breaker)

If the circuit breaker trips at a current below its rating or is not tripping at a higher current, the circuit breaker should be replaced. Be sure that the breaker is not being tripped because of high ambient temperature or other causes at the load or in the feeder.

Power Monitoring

Power monitoring can be accomplished using either internal relays or external metering devices. Phase loss relays, such as those in the image, are used to monitor three-phase power and help prevent damage to motors caused by undervoltage, phase imbalance, phase loss, and phase reversal.

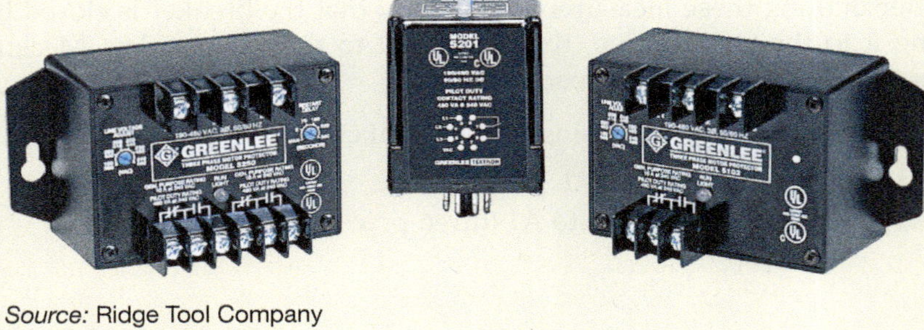

Source: Ridge Tool Company

Digital Logging Meters

Digital logging meters measure various values including voltage, current, resistance, frequency, and temperature. The logging meter in the image can be connected to a PC using special software for extended system monitoring and data storage. These devices provide valuable information when a problem occurs sporadically and is thus difficult to diagnose.

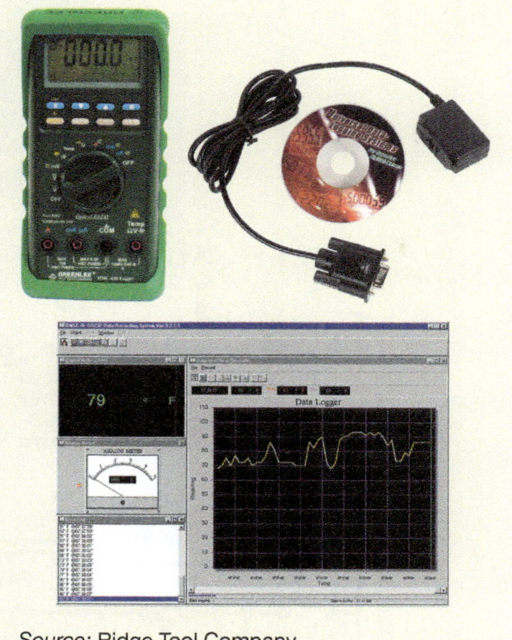

Source: Ridge Tool Company

6.2.4 Troubleshooting Control Circuits

After the source of an electrical problem has been isolated to a control circuit and the control circuit voltage is known to be good, a series of voltage measurements can be made across the electrical devices in the control circuit to find the faulty device. As shown in *Figure 36*, the measurements can start from the line or control voltage side of the circuit and move toward the load device, typically a contactor coil or relay coil. Measurements are made until either no voltage is observed or until the voltage has been measured across all the devices in the circuit. Note that when there are many devices in the circuit being tested, the measurements can be made by starting at the midpoint in the circuit (divide-in-half method) and then working toward either the source of control voltage or the load device, depending on whether the expected voltage was measured at the midpoint. As a result of making the voltage measurements, one of the two situations described below should exist:

- *Zero voltage* — At some point within the circuit, no voltage will be indicated on the VOM/DMM. This pinpoints an open set of switch or relay contacts between the present measurement point and the previous measurement point. *Figure 36* (A) shows an example of this situation, in which the contacts of the low-pressure switch are open, preventing the contactor coil from energizing. If the open is caused by a set of contactor or relay contacts, find out if the related contactor or relay coil is not being energized or is defective. *Figure 36* (B) shows an example of this situation, in which the CR contacts in the control circuit are open, preventing the contactor from energizing. These contacts close when the control relay coil CR is energized. Before assuming that the problem is caused by the open CR contacts, first troubleshoot the control circuit containing the CR relay coil to find out if the coil is energized or de-energized. If it is de-energized, further troubleshoot its control circuit to find out why. For example, if the contacts of the thermostat Cool switch are open, the CR relay coil will not be energized.
- *Voltage present at coil* — If voltage is measured at the contactor coil, and the contactor is not energized, the contactor coil is most likely defective. Turn off the power to the circuit, then disconnect the coil from the circuit and test it as described later in this section. *Figure 36* (C) shows an example of a situation in which 24V is applied to the contactor coil, but it is not energized. In this case, the contactor coil is probably open.

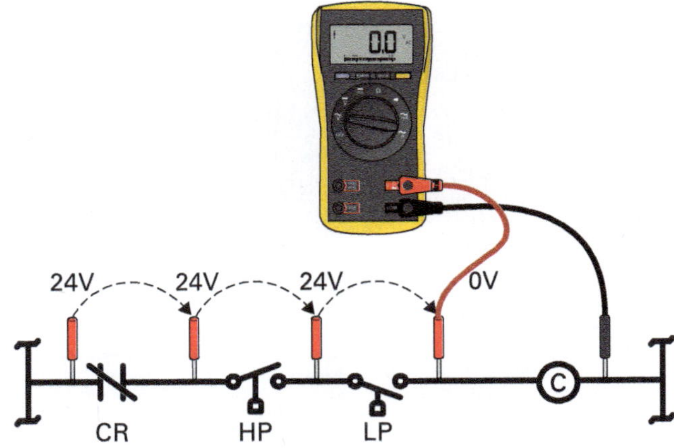

(A) Open Low-Pressure Switch Contacts

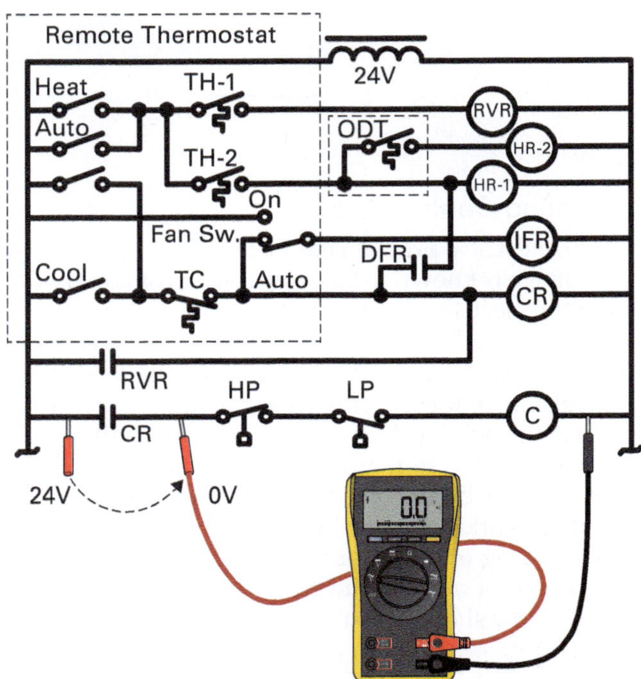

(B) Open CR Relay Contacts – Check Related Coil Control Circuit

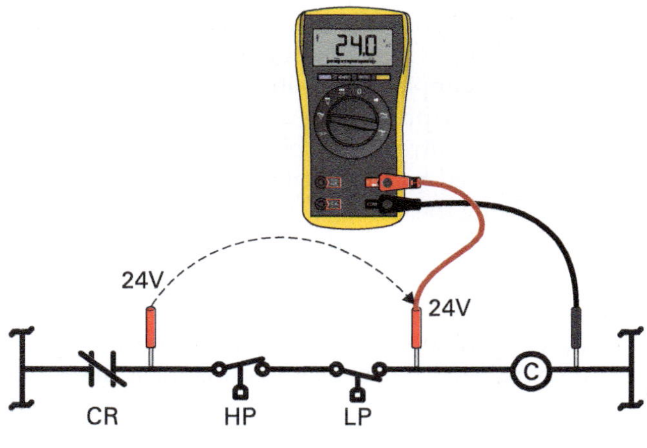

(C) Load Device (Contactor Coil) Is Open

Figure 36 Isolating to a faulty control circuit component.

6.2.5 Control Transformer Checks

Control transformers are checked by measuring the voltages across the secondary and primary windings (*Figure 37*). Typically, the secondary winding is measured first. The VOM/DMM should be set up to measure AC voltage on a range that is higher than the control voltage expected. If the voltage measured across the secondary winding is within 10% of the required voltage, the transformer is good. If no voltage is measured at the secondary winding, the voltage across the primary winding must be measured. Also check the secondary fuse (if provided) to see if it is blown.

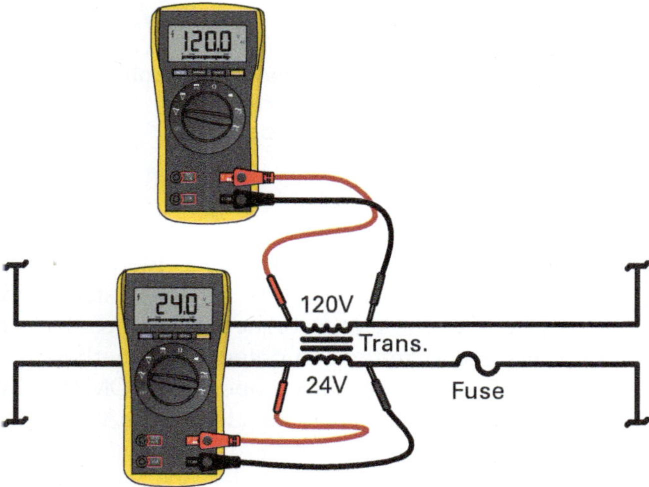

Figure 37 Control transformer checks.

If the voltage measured at the primary winding is within ±10% of the required voltage, the transformer is probably defective. This can be confirmed by performing a continuity check of the transformer primary and secondary windings with power off. If no voltage or low voltage is measured across the primary winding, the power supply voltage to the equipment should be checked. If the power supply voltage is okay, troubleshoot the circuit wiring between the power supply and control transformer primary winding.

6.2.6 Contactor/Relay Coil Resistance Checks

When the correct voltage is being applied to the coil of a contactor or relay and it is not energized, the device is probably faulty. After the coil of a contactor or relay has been identified as the probable cause of an electrical problem, it should be tested. The best way to test a coil is by measuring the resistance across the terminals of the coil. Before measuring resistance, make sure to electrically isolate the coil from the remainder of the circuit by removing all power to the circuit and disconnecting at least one lead of the coil. This is important to get an accurate resistance reading. Otherwise, the meter may read the resistance of other components that are connected in parallel with the coil being measured. *Figure 38* shows a reading of zero ohms indicates a shorted coil and a reading of infinite resistance indicates an open coil. In either case, replace the contactor or relay (or the coil, if replaceable). When the VOM/DMM indicates a measurable resistance, it usually indicates that the coil is good. If a low resistance is measured, connect one of the meter probes to ground or to the unit frame. Touch the other probe to each coil terminal. If a resistance is measured from either terminal to ground, replace the contactor or relay.

Troubleshooting Safety

Safe work practices dictate that troubleshooting should always be performed in de-energized circuits or equipment to the maximum extent possible. Typically, this is done using a continuity tester or by making resistance measurements with a VOM/DMM. Troubleshooting in energized circuits or equipment should be performed only when the cause of a problem cannot be found by troubleshooting the de-energized circuit or equipment.

Measuring Coil Resistance

The actual resistance measured for a contactor or relay coil can vary widely depending on the device. Ideally, the exact resistance value for the device can be found in the manufacturer's service literature. Another way to judge whether the resistance reading is good is by comparing the resistance of the coil being tested with that of a similar coil that is known to be good.

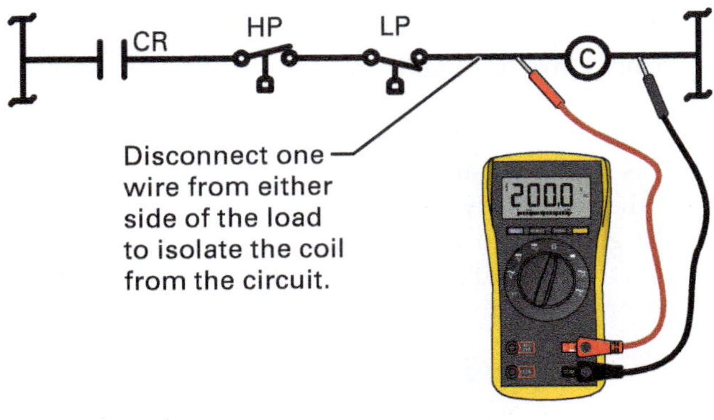

Figure 38 Coil resistance checks.

6.2.7 Relay/Contactor Contact Checks

After a set of contactor or relay contacts has been identified as the probable cause of an electrical problem, the contacts can be tested to confirm their condition. With the power to the circuit turned off, the contacts can be tested by making a continuity measurement to determine whether the contacts are open or closed (*Figure 39*). If the contacts are open, the VOM/DMM indicates an infinite resistance reading. If the contacts are closed, the VOM/DMM indicates a short (0Ω).

When testing relay contacts with the power off, remember that only the normally open or normally closed position of the contacts is being tested. It may have no bearing on the status of the contacts when the system is powered up.

When working with contactor/relay contacts, remember the following:

- Contacts that open when the contactor/relay is energized are called *normally closed* contacts.
- Contacts that close when the contactor/relay is energized are called *normally open* contacts.

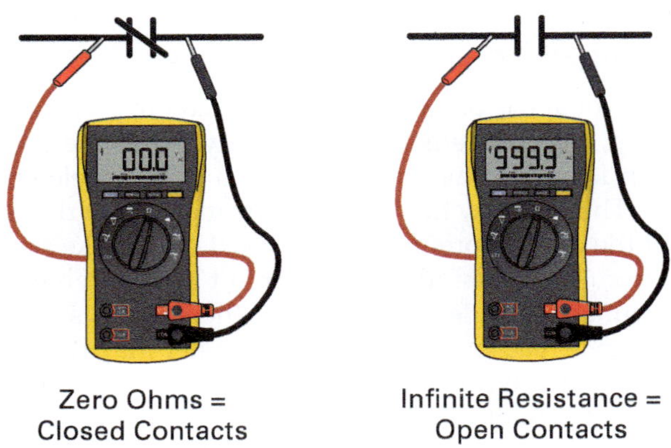

Figure 39 Checking the continuity of contactor/relay contacts.

6.2.8 Troubleshooting Circuit Boards

Solid-state motor control devices, such as AFDs, reduced-voltage starters, and similar equipment, contain printed circuit boards. When a board is installed and operating, it is unlikely to fail unless the failure is caused by some outside influence. Because of their complexity, many boards are difficult to troubleshoot and repair in the field. It often takes special automated test equipment at the manufacturer's plant to accomplish this task. For this reason, if a board fails, it is usually replaced with a new one. If the board is still under warranty, the manufacturer will generally replace the board at no cost. Do not try troubleshooting components on a board unless instructed to do so. After a board has been worked on, the manufacturer has no way of knowing whether the board was damaged through a manufacturing error or because it has been altered. In these cases, many manufacturers will not replace the board without payment.

Most boards are expensive, so be certain that the board is defective before replacing it. A board should be replaced only when all the input signals to the board are known to be good, but the board fails to generate the proper output signal(s). Many boards contain a microprocessor that controls all sequences of operation for the drive control system. To determine the condition (functional or defective) of the board, it is necessary to check for the presence of the proper input signals. It is also necessary to verify that the board generates the proper output signal(s) in response to the input signal(s). Some boards have test points where measurements of key input and output signals can be made. The schematic or wiring diagram will identify the signal that should be available at each point.

To diagnose a board's condition correctly, you must understand the sequence of operation. If you are not familiar with the operation of the board used in the system, study the schematic and sequence of operation described in the manufacturer's service literature. When you understand what the system and/or board should be doing, you must find out what the board is actually doing, or which symptoms are present in the unit. To aid in this analysis, many microprocessor-controlled boards have built-in diagnostic circuits that can run a check of motor functions and parameters and report their status. When troubleshooting, always use any available built-in diagnostic features and follow the manufacturer's related troubleshooting instructions.

Before replacing a board that appears to have failed, try to determine whether an external cause might account for the problem. There are a variety of possibilities:

- Electrical noise (EMI/RFI) from communications equipment, switching power supplies, and other sources will cause microprocessors to fail or operate erratically. The source of interference should be removed or the board should be shielded.
- As explained earlier, microprocessors and other integrated circuit chips can be damaged by static electricity from sources such as lightning or people. When handling circuit boards, avoid touching the components, printed circuits, and connector pins. Always ground yourself before touching a board. Store unused boards properly in electrostatically protected packaging.
- Voltage surges and excessive voltage can also cause board failures. Make sure that the applied voltage is within allowable limits and that the unit (and therefore the board) is properly grounded.
- Excessive heat can damage the board. The enclosure in which the board is installed should not be altered in any way that will restrict airflow to the board.

Many boards have dipswitch-selectable options or operating modes used to select site-specific parameters. When replacing a board with dipswitch-selectable options, make sure to set any dipswitches to the correct position for the application. For each dipswitch, determine its position on the failed board, then set the same dipswitch on the replacement board to the same position. The manufacturer's literature will show the default settings for the dipswitches. Do not use a graphite pencil to set a dipswitch—it can deposit particles that may short the switch or cause unpredictable action.

Checking for Proper Contact Closure

The contacts of an energized contactor can be checked for proper closure under loaded conditions by measuring for a voltage drop across the related line and load terminals of the contactor with a multimeter. The multimeter should indicate 0V across each set of power contacts if they are closing properly. If the meter indicates a voltage, this means a voltage drop is occurring across the contacts being measured because of a poor or high-resistance connection.

6.0.0 Section Review

1. The difference between motor starters and contactors is _____.
   a. motor starters have ventilating fans to prevent overheating
   b. motor starters provide additional overload protection
   c. contactors have built-in rectifier circuits
   d. the contacts on motor starters have gold-plated contacts

2. The voltage imbalance between any two legs of a three-phase voltage source should *not* exceed _____.
   a. 2%
   b. 5%
   c. 7%
   d. 10%

Module 26407-23 Review Questions

1. Which of the following statements is *true* of solid-state relays?
   a. They have a shorter life than electromechanical relays.
   b. They have higher reliability than electromechanical relays.
   c. They have slower switching speeds than electromechanical relays.
   d. They can be operated at higher temperatures than electromechanical relays.

2. Which of the following is a characteristic of SSRs, but *not* of EMRs?
   a. Zero current turn-off
   b. Surge current
   c. Coil voltage
   d. Dropout time

3. When connecting a solid-state relay for three-wire control of a load, what is typically used to seal in or provide holding for the Start button after it has been pressed?
   a. A triac
   b. An auxiliary solid-state relay contact
   c. An SCR
   d. An IGBT

4. The trip current setting for a solid-state overload relay is based on the _____.
   a. number of loops on the current transformer
   b. motor FLA, service factor, and number of current loops
   c. motor FLA
   d. motor service factor

5. The programmable threshold that determines how long a solid-state overload relay will allow an undercurrent condition to exist before it trips is known as the _____.
   a. undercurrent trip delay
   b. undervoltage trip point
   c. ground fault current trip
   d. undercurrent trip point

6. A timing relay that provides the timed delay after the relay is energized is called a(n) _____.
   a. delay-on-break relay
   b. on-delay relay
   c. timed-closed relay
   d. off-delay relay

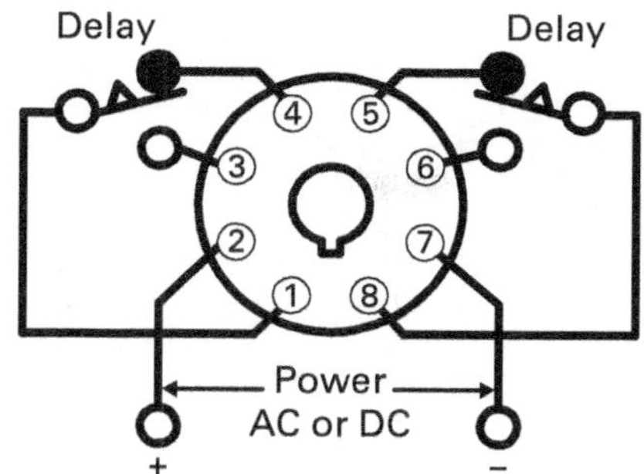

Delay-on-Make/Interval

On-Delay	Pin	
Time Power	(2–7)	
Delayed NC Contacts	(1–4) (8–5)	Off On
Delayed NO Contacts	(1–3) (8–6)	On Off
On Indicator		Lighted
Off Indicator		Lighted
		Set Time

Delay-on-Make (On Delay)

Interval	Pin	
Time Power	(2–7)	On Off
Delayed NC Contacts	(1–4) (8–5)	Off On
Delayed NO Contacts	(1–3) (8–6)	On Off
On Indicator		Lighted
Off Indicator		Lighted
		Set Time

Interval

Figure RQ01

7. For the 8-pin timing relay shown in *Figure RQ01*, the delayed NC contacts are _____.
   a. pins 1–3 and 8–6
   b. pins 1–4 and 8–5
   c. pins 2–7
   d. pins 1–3 and 8–5

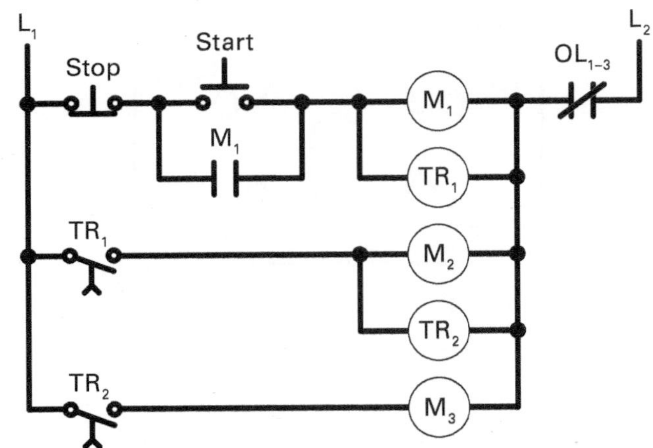

Figure RQ02

8. In *Figure RQ02*, the contacts of timing relays TR_1 and TR_2 are _____.
   a. NOTC contacts
   b. NCTO contacts
   c. NOTO contacts
   d. NCTC contacts

9. Which method of reduced-voltage starting provides for adjustment of the motor starting torque and current using taps?
   a. Solid state
   b. Wye-delta
   c. Resistive
   d. Autotransformer

10. The *most* common form of reduced-voltage soft starting used with solid-state reduced-voltage controllers is _____.
    a. kick start
    b. current limit
    c. ramp start
    d. quick start

11. The NEMA classification for the form of adjustable frequency drive with an AC input and an AC output that uses an intermediate DC conversion is _____.
    a. FA
    b. FB
    c. FC
    d. FD

12. Which of the following *best* describes the motor torque when the horsepower output of the motor varies directly with the speed of the motor?
    a. Constant torque
    b. Variable torque
    c. Constant horsepower
    d. Variable horsepower

13. In *most* applications, the motors used with AFDs are standard NEMA _____.
    a. Design A, Design B, or Design C
    b. Design A, Design B, or Design E
    c. Design B, Design D, or Design F
    d. Design C, Design D, or Design E

14. Parasitic voltage damage in motors powered by AFDs can be prevented using _____.
    a. nonmetallic shims
    b. AFD output filtering
    c. insulated motor housings
    d. electrically continuous shaft couplings

15. A method of braking in which a DC voltage is applied to the stator winding of an AC motor for a timed interval is called _____.
    a. regenerative braking
    b. friction braking
    c. dynamic braking
    d. DC injection braking

16. A method of braking an AC motor that involves the use of braking resistors is called _____.
    a. regenerative braking
    b. friction braking
    c. dynamic braking
    d. DC injection braking

17. To clean electronic circuit components, use _____.
    a. compressed air
    b. a vacuum
    c. a damp cloth
    d. spray cleaners

18. In any motor control circuit, the load circuit is the _____.
    a. motor
    b. relay contacts
    c. AFD
    d. control panel

19. Current imbalance in any leg of a three-phase power source must be within _____.
    a. 2%
    b. 5%
    c. 10%
    d. 25%

20. When testing a circuit breaker, the voltage readings on the line and load terminals with the breaker contacts closed should _____.
    a. double the line side
    b. read 120VAC
    c. be the same
    d. have an imbalance of less than 2%

Answers to odd-numbered Module Review Questions are found in *Appendix A*.

Module 26407-23 Supplemental Exercises

1. List four reasons for using solid-state relays (SSRs) instead of electromechanical relays.

   ____

   ____

2. An SSR that uses a light-emitting diode and photo detector to couple the switching command to the output circuit is called a(n) __________.
3. The inputs of two or more single-output SSRs can be connected __________ or __________ to obtain multiple-switched outputs.
4. True or False? SSOLRs are designed to protect the motor and control devices against short circuits.
5. True or False? One reason for using reduced-voltage starting motor control is to reduce the current drawn from utility lines by the across-the-line starting of large motors.
6. The autotransformer reduced-voltage starter motor control that will cause the least amount of electrical interference to the associated electrical distribution system uses the __________ method of voltage transition.
7. True or False? An open-circuit transition type of wye-delta reduced-voltage starting motor control uses a contactor to connect a resistor bank into the motor winding circuit during the start-to-run period.
8. Solid-state reduced-voltage starting motor controllers are commonly called __________.
9. In a solid-state reduced-voltage motor control, the effective voltage delivered to the motor is varied from zero to full voltage by controlling the precise time that the __________.
10. A metallized shielded storage bag should be used to protect microprocessors and other integrated circuit chips from __________.
11. True or False? Never clean motor control circuit components using compressed air.
12. An AFD controller converts three-phase input power to an adjustable __________ output for application in an AC motor.
13. List three common types of adjustable speed loads.

    ____

    ____

14. Name four different methods for motor braking.

    ____

    ____

15. True or False? AFD units and other microprocessor-controlled devices normally have built-in fault diagnostic circuits used to aid in troubleshooting.

Answers to odd-numbered Supplemental Exercises are found in *Appendix B*.

Answers to Section Review Questions

Answer	Section Reference	Objective
Section 1.0.0		
1. b	1.1.1	1a
2. a	1.2.0	1b
Section 2.0.0		
1. d	2.1.1	2a
2. c	2.2.0	2b
Section 3.0.0		
1. b	3.1.2	3a
2. d	3.2.3	3b
Section 4.0.0		
1. b	4.1.0	4a
2. c	4.2.2	4b
3. d	4.3.0	4c
Section 5.0.0		
1. b	5.1.0	5a
2. c	5.2.0	5b
Section 6.0.0		
1. b	6.1.5	6a
2. a	6.2.1	6b

User Update

Did you find an error? Submit a correction by visiting **https://www.nccer.org/olf** or by scanning the QR code using your mobile device.

Source: iStock@geotrac

Objectives

Successful completion of this module prepares you to do the following:

1. State the operating principles of HVAC systems and identify major components.
   a. State the operating principles of HVAC systems.
   b. Describe the major components of HVAC systems.
2. Identify various thermostats and describe their installation requirements.
   a. Explain the operating principles of various thermostats.
   b. Explain how thermostats are installed.
3. Identify and describe HVAC controls and devices.
   a. Identify and describe basic comfort cooling system controls.
   b. Identify and describe common furnace controls.
   c. Identify and describe common heat pump controls.
   d. Describe digital and analog controls used in HVAC systems.
   e. Describe the basic HVAC system sequence of operation.
   f. Describe how to troubleshoot HVAC systems.
4. Identify the *NEC*® requirements that apply to HVAC systems.
   a. Identify the *NEC*® requirements for HVAC control circuits.
   b. Identify the *NEC*® requirements for HVAC equipment.

Performance Tasks

Under supervision, you should be able to do the following:

1. Install a thermostat and hook it up using the standard color coding system.
2. Configure and test the operation of an HVAC system thermostat.

Overview

Heating, ventilation, and air conditioning (HVAC) systems are electrically powered and controlled systems that electricians encounter regularly, especially in residential and commercial construction. Electricians provide the power supply, and in some cases, they install and terminate the control wiring and assist in troubleshooting. It is important for electricians to develop a basic understanding of HVAC systems and their common components.

NOTE

Digital Resources for Electrical

Scan this code using the camera on your phone or mobile device to view the digital resources related to this craft.

NCCER Industry-Recognized Credentials

If you are training through an NCCER-accredited sponsor, you may be eligible for credentials from NCCER. The ID number for this module is 26408-23. Note that this module may have been used in other NCCER curricula and may apply to other level completions. Contact NCCER at 1.888.622.3720 or go to **www.nccer.org** for more information.

You can also show off your industry-recognized credentials online with NCCER's digital badges. Transform your knowledge, skills, and achievements into badges that you can share across social media platforms, send to your network, and add to your resume. For more information, visit **www.nccer.org**.

1.0.0 HVAC Operating Principles and Major Components

Performance Tasks

There are no Performance Tasks in this section.

Objective

State the operating principles of HVAC systems and identify major components.

a. State the operating principles of HVAC systems.
b. Describe the major components of HVAC systems.

Heating, ventilating, and air conditioning (HVAC) systems are essential to provide comfort in homes and businesses across the world. Electricians are often involved in their installation, providing the necessary power and control wiring. Before presenting the details related to the control of these systems, it is important to understand how they work and what aspects of their operation require control.

1.1.0 Heating and Ventilation Systems

Heat transfer: The movement of heat energy from a warmer substance to a cooler substance.

Condensing furnace: A gas furnace with two heat exchangers to extract the maximum amount of heat from the combustion process. It was named after its process, where the combustion byproducts are cooled to the point where water vapor condenses into a liquid.

Early humans burned fuel as a source of heat. Today, a central heating source, such as a furnace or boiler, does the job using the principle of **heat transfer**. To warm or cool a space, heat must be transferred from one place to another.

For example, in a common household furnace, fuel oil, natural gas, or propane gas is burned to create heat, which warms metal plates called *heat exchangers* (*Figure 1*). Air drawn from living spaces is circulated over the heat exchangers, where the heat is transferred to the air. The heated air is then returned to the living spaces. This type of system is known as a *forced-air system* and is the most common type of central heating system in the United States.

Figure 2 shows the interior of a high-efficiency gas furnace. This design has two heat exchangers to extract the maximum amount of heat from the burning fuel. The heat transfer process is extremely effective in a **condensing furnace** like the one pictured in *Figure 2*; PVC pipe is used to vent the byproducts of combustion.

Water is also used as a heat exchange medium. Water is heated in a boiler, then pumped through pipes to heat exchangers scattered throughout the structure, where the heat is transferred to the surrounding air. The heat exchangers are often baseboard heating units located in the conditioned space. This type of system is known as a *hydronic heating system*. They are more common in the northern parts of the United States.

Natural gas and fuel oil are the most widely used fossil fuels. Of these two, natural gas is the most common. Oil heat is more prevalent in the Northeast and rural areas. Propane gas is used in many parts of the country in place of oil and natural gas, primarily in rural areas where natural gas pipelines are unavailable.

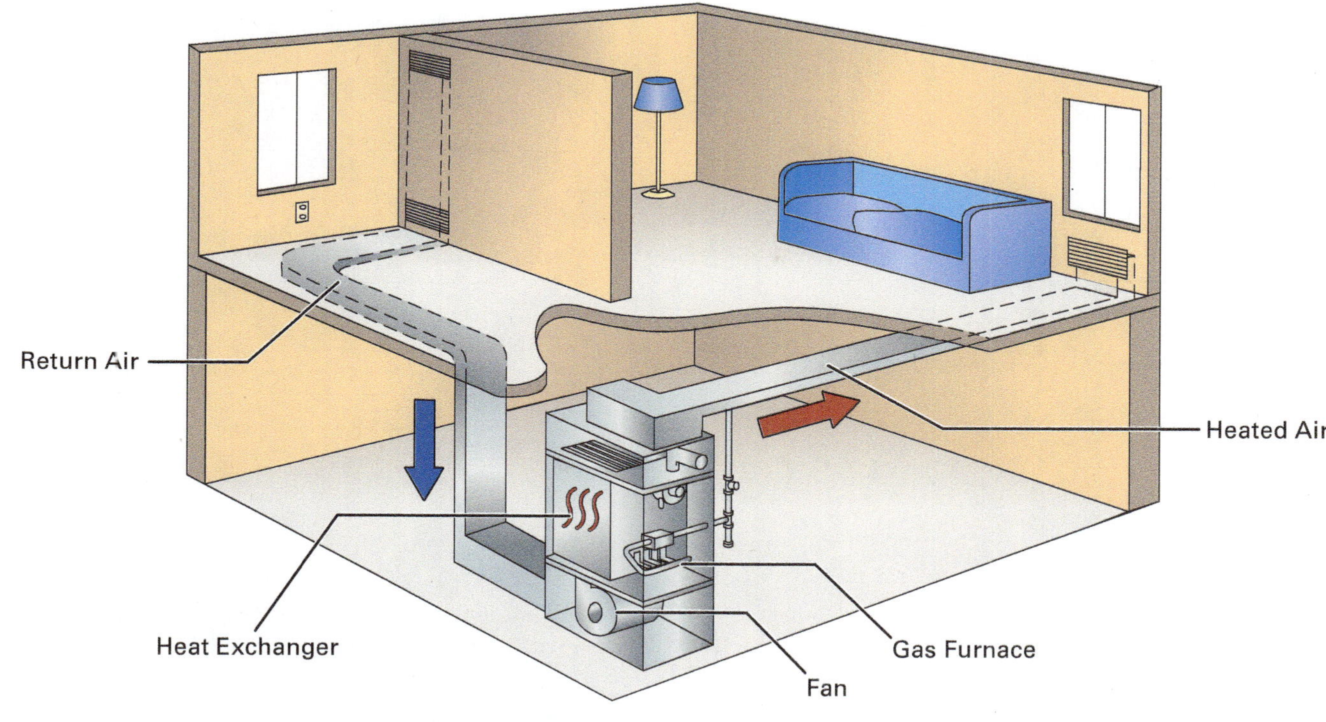

Figure 1 Typical forced-air heating system.

Electricity is another common heat source. It is needed for all other centralized heating and cooling systems to operate. In an electric-resistance heating system, electricity flows through coils of resistive wire, causing the coils to become hot. Air from the conditioned space is passed over the coils, where the heat is transferred to the air. Electric-resistance heating alone is no longer common, although it is often used as a supplemental heat source for **heat pumps**.

Heat pumps: Refrigerant-based heating and cooling units that can reverse the direction of the refrigeration cycle to absorb heat from outdoor air or water and transfer it indoors.

In some areas of the country, a heating system may be fueled by wood or coal. Due to increases in the cost of fossil fuel over the years and because wood is a relatively inexpensive and renewable resource in some places, wood-burning stoves, and furnaces remain popular in rural areas.

Ventilation generally refers to the introduction of fresh air into a closed space to improve air quality. Fresh air provides the oxygen we breathe. In addition to fresh air, we also need clean air. The air in our homes, schools, and offices can contain dust, pollen, and mold, as well as vapors and odors from various sources. Relatively simple air circulation and filtration methods, including natural ventilation, help keep indoor air clean and fresh. Common methods of improving indoor air quality (IAQ) also include the addition of humidifiers (*Figure 3*) and high-efficiency filtration products.

Many industrial environments require special ventilation and air management systems. Such systems are needed to eliminate noxious or toxic fumes and airborne particles that may be created by the processes and materials used at the facility.

The US Government has strict regulations governing IAQ in industrial environments and the release of toxic materials into the atmosphere. Where noxious or toxic fumes may be present, indoor air must be consistently replaced with fresh air. Fans and blowers are normally used for this purpose. Special filtration systems may also be required.

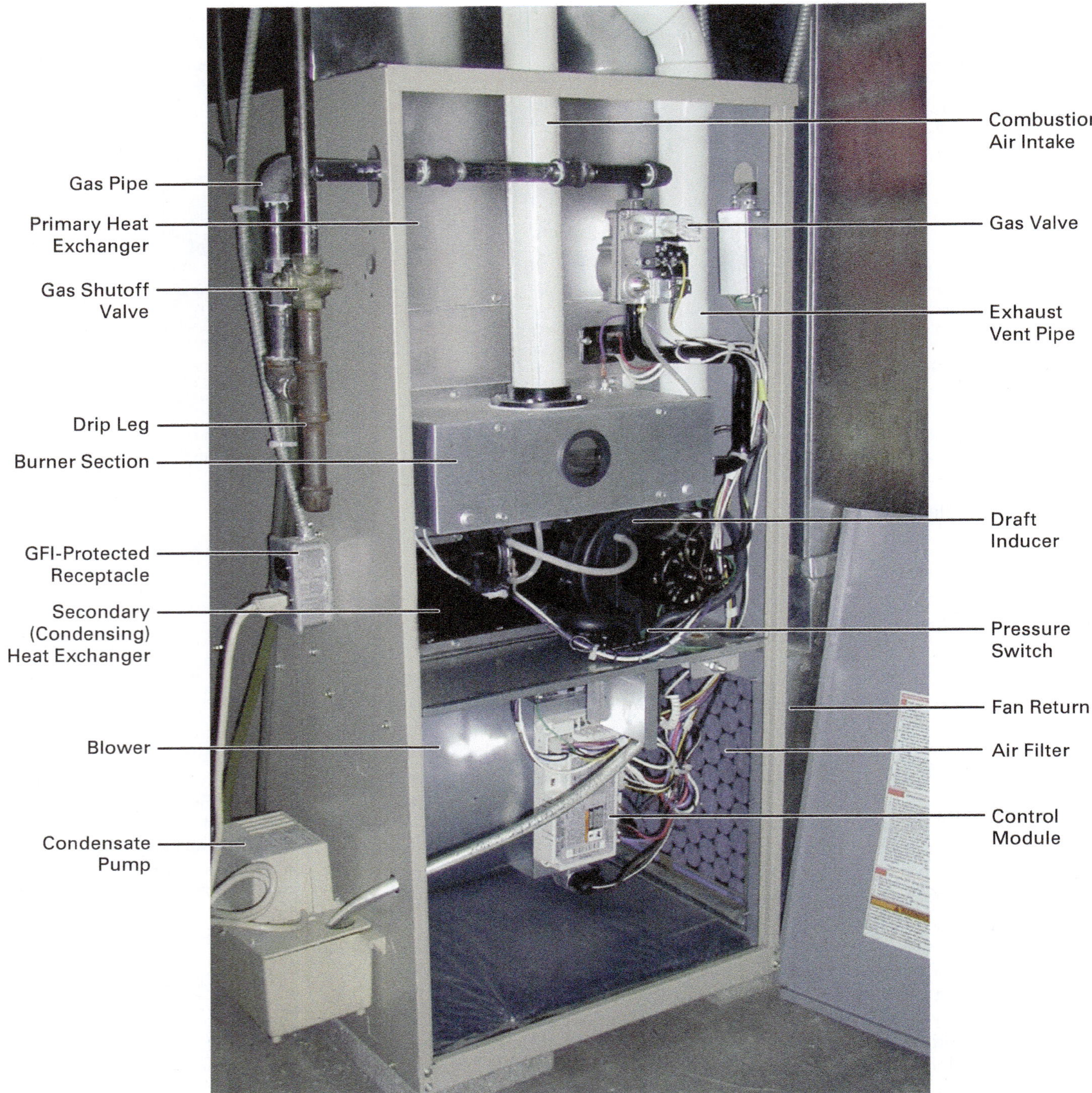

Figure 2 High-efficiency condensing gas furnace.

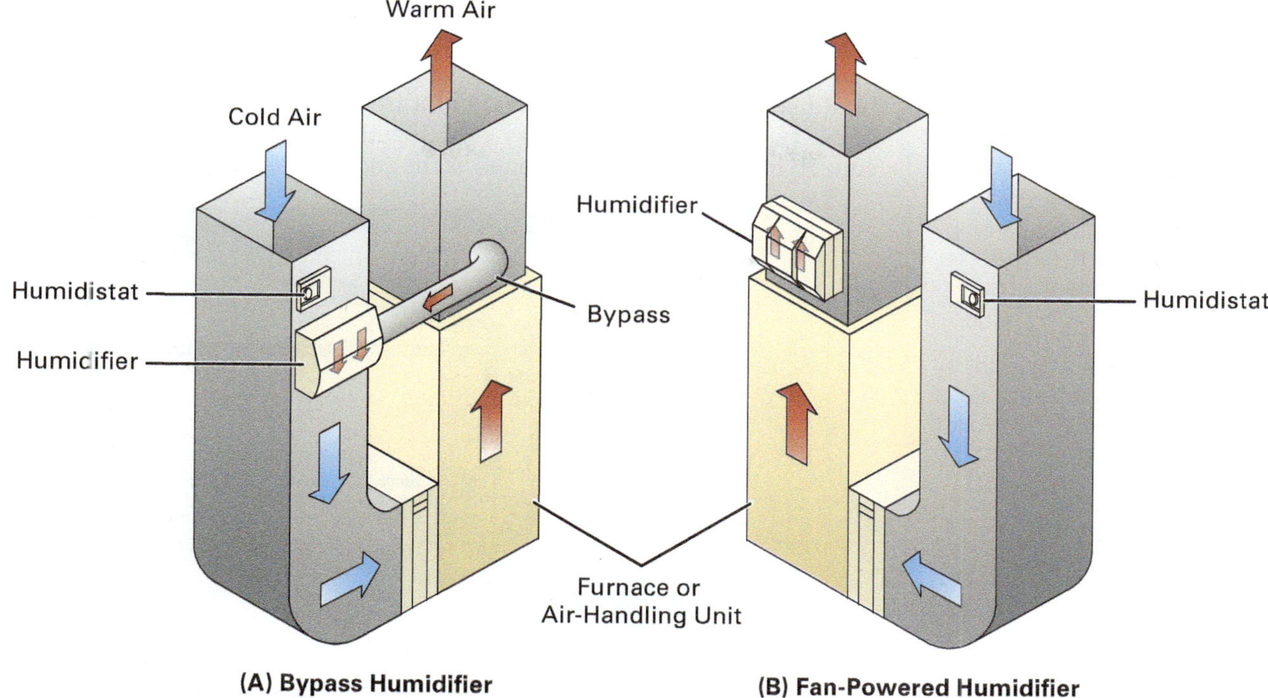

Figure 3 Bypass and fan-powered humidifiers in a forced-air heating system.

1.2.0 Air Conditioning

All cooling systems contain components that function together in a process known as the **refrigeration cycle**. Understanding the basic refrigeration cycle will help you better understand how various HVAC controls interact to keep the system operating properly.

There are many types of systems used to provide cooling for personal comfort, food preservation, and industrial processes. Each of these systems uses a **mechanical refrigeration** system to transfer heat. The operation of the various mechanical refrigeration systems is basically the same. However, the **refrigerant** used, the size and design of the components, and the installation locations of their basic components can vary significantly.

Did You Know?

The Refrigeration Cycle

Simply stated, the refrigeration cycle relies on the ability of refrigerants to absorb and transfer heat. If a cold refrigerant is brought into contact with warmer air, it will absorb heat from the air. Having given up heat to the refrigerant, the air occupying the space becomes cooler. The greater the difference in temperature between the air and the refrigerant, the more rapidly heat will be transferred and the cooler the space will become. When the hot refrigerant is then exposed to cooler outdoor air, the refrigerant will release the heat it absorbed indoors.

Refrigeration cycle: The thermodynamic cycle through which a circulating refrigerant transfers heat from one location to another.

CAUTION

It is unlawful to release today's common refrigerants into the atmosphere. Refrigerants must be recovered, recycled, and/or reclaimed by qualified technicians certified through testing developed by the US Environmental Protection Agency (EPA). Only technicians certified in accordance with Section 608 of the Clean Air Act may purchase and handle refrigerants or connect to systems containing refrigerants.

Mechanical refrigeration: The use of machinery to provide a cooling effect or, in the case of a heat pump, a heating effect.

Refrigerant: A fluid that assists in the transfer of heat through the manipulation of its pressure, temperature, and physical state in various parts of an HVAC or refrigeration circuit.

A mechanical refrigeration system (*Figure 4*) is a sealed system operating at various pressures and temperatures. The relationship between temperature and pressure is critical to system operation. The same refrigerant can be in its liquid state and very cold at one point in the system and very hot at another. These two points are often very close together. This is possible because of pressure changes caused by the **compressor** and **expansion device**.

Compressor: The component of a refrigeration system that converts low-pressure, low-temperature refrigerant gas into high-temperature, high-pressure refrigerant gas through compression.

Expansion device: A device that provides the pressure drop needed to reduce the pressure and temperature of a refrigerant as it enters the evaporator; also known as a *metering device*.

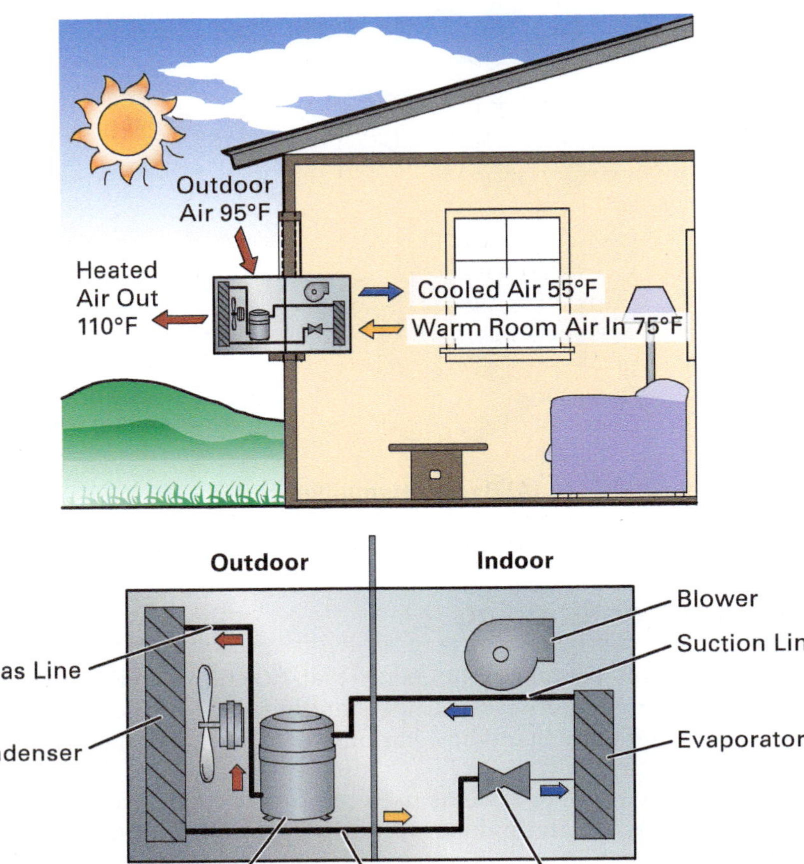

Figure 4 Basic refrigeration cycle.

1.2.1 System Components

The four components common to most HVAC systems include the following:

- **Evaporator** — A heat exchanger where the heat from the area or item being cooled is transferred to the refrigerant.
- *Compressor* — A device that creates the pressure differences in the system needed to make the refrigerant flow and the refrigeration cycle work.
- **Condenser** — A heat exchanger where the heat absorbed by the refrigerant is transferred to the cooler outdoor air or to another substance, such as water.
- *Expansion device* — A device that provides a pressure drop that lowers the boiling point of the refrigerant just before it enters the evaporator. It is also known as a *metering device*.

Evaporator: A heat exchanger that transfers heat from air or water to the refrigerant vapor/liquid mixture flowing through, causing the refrigerant to vaporize.

Condenser: A heat exchanger that transfers heat from refrigerant vapor to air or water, causing the vapor to condense to its liquid state.

Also shown in *Figure 4* is the refrigerant piping used to connect the basic components and provide the path for refrigerant flow. The arrows show the direction of flow through the system. Together, the components and lines form a closed refrigeration system. The refrigeration lines are designated as follows:

- *Suction line* — The tubing that carries heat-laden refrigerant vapor from the evaporator to the compressor.
- *Hot gas line* (also called the *discharge line*) — The tubing that carries hot refrigerant vapor from the compressor to the condenser.
- *Liquid line* — The tubing that carries liquid refrigerant from the condenser to the expansion device located at the entrance to the evaporator.

The refrigerant is the medium through which heat can be moved into or from a space or substance. A refrigerant can be any substance that picks up heat by evaporating at a low temperature and pressure and gives up heat by condensing at a higher temperature and pressure. The events that take place within the system happen again and again in the same order.

Remember that the operation is basically the same for all mechanical refrigeration systems. The components listed in this section are present in nearly every system, although they vary in design and appearance. Various accessories are also used in some systems to perform special functions.

1.2.2 Refrigeration Cycle

Although it is not necessary for you to understand everything about HVAC system operation, you need a basic understanding of their operation to perform your duties as an electrician. It is true that many of the problems in HVAC systems are electrical in nature, but it can be very difficult to diagnose failures unless you understand the symptoms of electrical problems.

The refrigeration cycle is based on two principles:

- As a liquid changes to vapor, it absorbs large quantities of heat. The reverse is also true: as a vapor condenses into a liquid, a great deal of heat must be rejected.
- A substance's boiling and condensing temperatures can be changed by altering the pressure.

The evaporator receives a mixture of low-temperature, low-pressure refrigerant liquid and vapor from the expansion device. A typical evaporator is a series of tubing coils that expose the cool liquid refrigerant to the warmer air passing over the coils. Heat from the air is transferred through the tubing to the cooler refrigerant, causing the refrigerant to boil and vaporize. It is important to realize that even though it is boiling, it is still not considered "hot" because refrigerants boil at very low temperatures when the pressure is low. So, it is a low-temperature, low-pressure refrigerant vapor that travels through the suction line to the compressor.

The evaporator is designed so that, ideally, the refrigerant is completely vaporized before it reaches the end of the evaporator. It is during the change of state from a liquid to a vapor that most of the heat is transferred. What may surprise you is that until all the liquid has changed to its vapor state, its measurable or *sensible* temperature does not change. Once the change of state is complete and only vapor remains, the refrigerant can absorb a bit more heat, but heat transfer slows down significantly. However, as it absorbs additional heat, the temperature of the vapor begins to increase. This additional, measurable heat is referred to as **superheat**.

Superheat: The measurable heat absorbed by a refrigerant after it has been converted to its vapor state (vaporized) and continues to absorb heat.

Hermetic and Semi-Hermetic Compressors

Hermetic compressors are typically used in residential and light commercial air conditioners and heat pumps. The term *hermetic* means to be sealed airtight. Thus, hermetic compressors are sealed and cannot be opened or repaired in the field.

Semi-hermetic compressors, also known as *serviceable compressors*, are used in large-capacity air conditioning, refrigeration, and chilled-water units. Semi-hermetic compressors can be partially disassembled for field repair.

(A) Hermetic Compressors

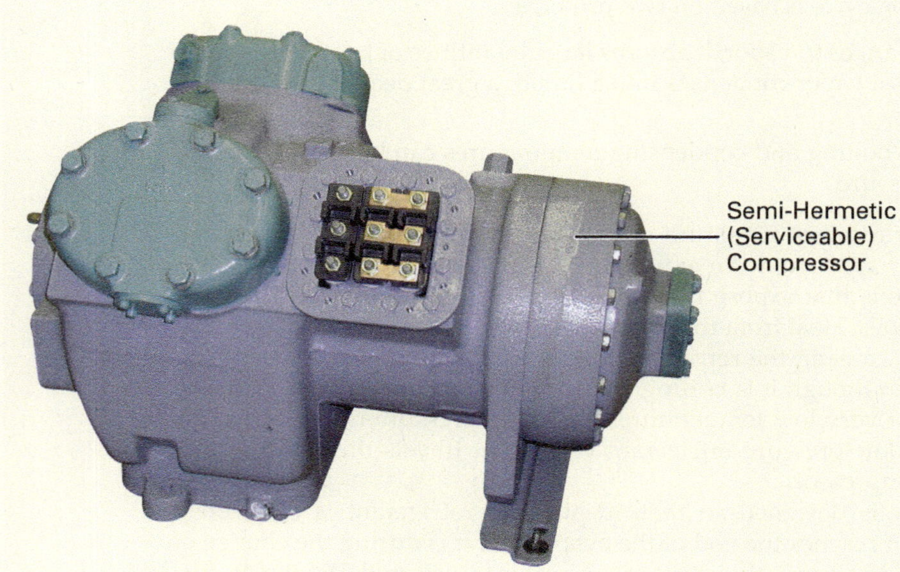

(B) Semi-Hermetic Compressor

The compressor receives the low-temperature, low-pressure vapor and compresses it. You may recall from previous studies that liquids cannot be compressed. Thus, it is important that little or no liquid refrigerant leaves the evaporator.

The compressed refrigerant vapor leaves the compressor as a high-temperature, high-pressure vapor. The vapor then travels to the condenser through the hot gas, or discharge, line.

Like the evaporator, the condenser is a series of tubing coils through which the refrigerant flows. As cooler air moves across the tubing, the hot refrigerant vapor gives up heat. As it continues to give up heat to the outside air, it cools to its condensing temperature, and the change from a vapor to a liquid begins. As more cooling takes place, all the refrigerant eventually condenses to a liquid. Once all the vapor has condensed to its liquid state, the measurable temperature begins to increase as more heat is rejected. This additional cooling of the liquid, known as **subcooling**, ideally takes place before the refrigerant leaves the condenser. The high-pressure liquid travels through the liquid line to the inlet of the expansion device.

Subcooling: The measurable heat removed from a refrigerant after it has been converted to its liquid state (condensed) and continues to reject heat.

The expansion device regulates the flow of refrigerant into the evaporator. It also decreases its pressure and, indirectly, its temperature. It restricts the refrigerant flow by forcing it through a tiny hole or *orifice*, converting the high-temperature, high-pressure liquid refrigerant into the low-temperature, low-pressure liquid/vapor mixture needed to absorb heat in the evaporator.

Modern Air Conditioning

Dr. Willis Carrier, founder of Carrier Corporation, is credited with the invention of modern air conditioning. In 1902, he developed a system that could control humidity and temperature using a nontoxic, nonflammable refrigerant.

Air conditioning started as a means of solving a problem in a printing facility where heat and humidity were causing paper shrinkage. Later systems served similar purposes in textile plants.

The concept was not applied to comfort air conditioning until about 20 years later when Carrier's centrifugal chillers began to be installed in department stores and movie theaters.

Source: The file "Willis Carrier 1915.jpg" is marked with CC PDM 1.0

1.2.3 Heat Pumps

A special type of air conditioner known as a *heat pump* is widely used in the warmer regions of the country to provide both cooling and heating. Heat pumps are far more efficient at producing heat than simple electric-resistant heat.

In most applications, heat pumps must be combined with supplemental electric, geothermal, or fossil fuel heat sources to ensure adequate heating capacity on the coldest days. In dual-fuel arrangements, a furnace takes over for the heat pump completely when the outdoor temperature falls below a predetermined temperature. Electric heat can supplement the heat pump's heating capacity by operating simultaneously.

Heat pumps (*Figure 5*) produce heat by reversing the cooling cycle. For this reason, heat pumps are sometimes referred to as *reverse-cycle air conditioners*. They operate on the principle that there is always some extractable heat in the air, even though the air may seem very cold. In fact, the temperature would have to be −460°F (−273.15°C), referred to as *absolute zero*, for there to be a total absence of heat.

In the heating mode, a special valve known as a *reversing valve* switches the compressor input and output so that the condenser operates as the evaporator and the evaporator becomes the condenser. Because of this role reversal, the coils in a heat pump are referred to as the *outdoor coil* and *indoor coil* instead of the condenser and evaporator. Each coil can perform either function, depending on the operating mode.

NOTE

Although this presentation of cooling system operation revolves around the heating or cooling of air, it is important to remember that water is also an effective heat transfer medium.

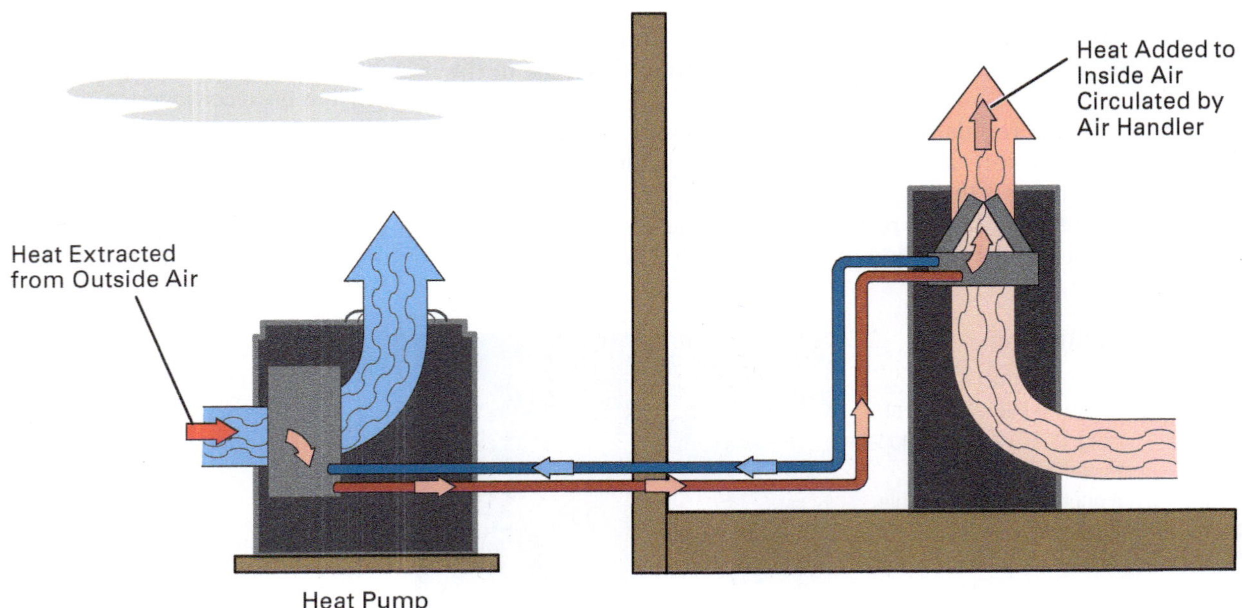

Figure 5 Heat pump—heating mode operation.

1.0.0 Section Review

1. In a hydronic heating system, the heat transfer medium is _____.
   a. air
   b. water
   c. natural gas
   d. ammonia

2. In a mechanical refrigeration circuit, the purpose of the evaporator is to _____.
   a. convert refrigerant from high pressure to low pressure
   b. transfer heat from the refrigerant to the outdoor air
   c. transfer heat from the indoor air to the refrigerant
   d. provide the pressure difference needed to circulate the refrigerant

2.0.0 Thermostats

Objective

Identify various thermostats and describe their installation requirements.

a. Explain the operating principles of various thermostats.

b. Explain how thermostats are installed.

Performance Tasks

1. Install a thermostat and hook it up using the standard color coding system.
2. Configure and test the operation of an HVAC system thermostat.

The room thermostat (*Figure 6*) is the primary control in an HVAC system. It can be as simple as a single temperature-sensitive switch or as complex as a collection of sensing elements and switching devices that provide various control functions. In this module, the term *thermostat* generally refers to control devices that are wall mounted in a conditioned space.

Many residences and small commercial businesses, such as retail stores and shops, have a single thermostat. Large office buildings, shopping malls, and factories are divided into cooling and heating zones and may have many thermostats. Because each zone often needs to operate independently of the others, each thermostat must control either a separate system or the airflow from a common system.

Figure 6 Room thermostat.
Source: iStock@koinseb

2.1.0 Thermostat Operating Principles

Programmable electronic thermostats are now very common. However, thermostats with **bimetal** sensing elements are still manufactured and used in some applications. Although not quite as precise as the electronic thermostat, bimetal devices are considerably less expensive and have proven effective and reliable over the years. Most bimetal thermostats will maintain the space temperature within ±2° of the setpoint. A calibrated electronic thermostat can maintain the temperature within ±1°.

A bimetal element (*Figure 7*) is composed of two different metals bonded together. One metal is usually copper or brass; the other is often a metal called **Invar®**, which contains 36% nickel. When heated, the copper or brass has a more rapid expansion rate than the Invar®, which causes the element's shape to change. The movement that occurs when the bimetal changes shape is used to open or close switch contacts in the thermostat.

Bimetal: An assembly made of two dissimilar metals that changes shape in response to temperature change due to the expansion and contraction properties of the two metals, creating movement that can open or close a switch.

Invar®: An alloy of steel containing 36% nickel and one of the two metals in most bimetal control devices.

WARNING!

Older thermostats contain mercury. Mercury is a toxic metal. Even short-term exposure may result in damage to the lungs and central nervous system. Mercury is also an environmental hazard. Do not dispose of thermostats containing mercury bulbs with regular trash and garbage. Contact your local waste management or environmental authority for disposal/recycling instructions. Thermostats containing mercury are no longer manufactured due to the related hazards.

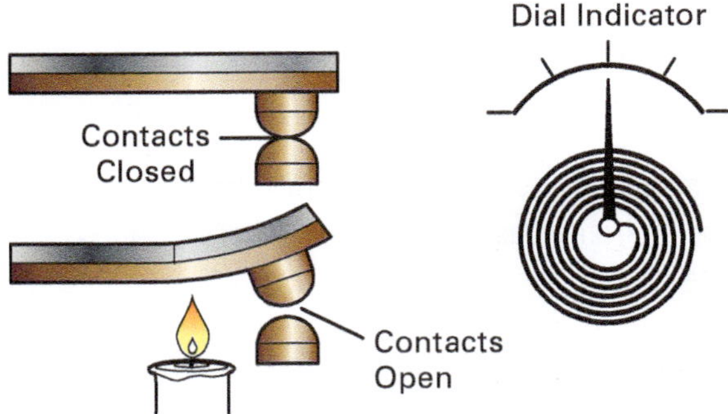

Figure 7 Bimetal sensing elements.

Most residential and small commercial thermostats operate on a low-voltage power supply (24VAC). With low-voltage control circuits, there is little risk of electrical shock. Low-voltage components are also less expensive and less likely to produce arcing and damage contact surfaces.

2.1.1 Heating-Only Thermostats

A mechanical heating-only thermostat typically contains a temperature-sensitive bimetal element, as shown in *Figure 8*. In this arrangement, the heating unit, such as a furnace, will not start unless the thermostatic switch closes a circuit to call for heat.

When the temperature in the conditioned space reaches the thermostat setpoint, the switch will open. Because of the residual heat in the heat exchangers and the continued rotation of the fan as it cools the heat exchanger before coming to a stop, the room temperature may overshoot the setpoint. To avoid occupant discomfort, an adjustable *heat anticipator* adds a small amount of heat, causing the thermostat to open before the temperature in the space reaches the setpoint. The heat anticipator is a tiny resistance heater in series with the switch contacts. The anticipator increases the thermostat's responsiveness and accuracy.

2.1.2 Cooling-Only Thermostats

The cooling thermostat (*Figure 9*) works in reverse compared to a heating thermostat. When the bimetal coil warms, the switch closes and starts the cooling system compressor. When the temperature falls, the bimetal element returns to its original position to turn the cooling system off.

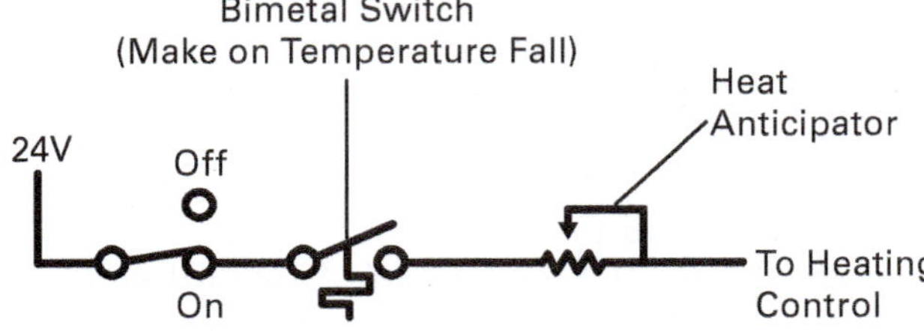

Figure 8 Heating-only thermostat.

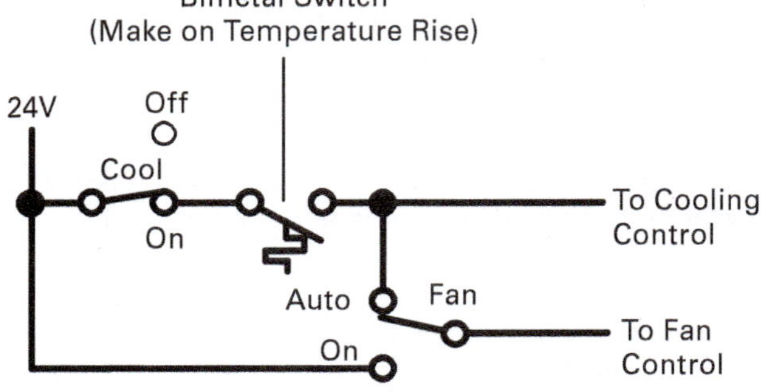

Figure 9 Cooling-only thermostat.

Mechanical cooling thermostats contain a device called a **cooling compensator** to help improve indoor comfort. The cooling compensator (*Figure 10*) is a fixed resistor in parallel with the thermostatic switch. Heating anticipators are normally adjustable while cooling compensators are not.

Cooling compensator: A fixed resistor installed in a thermostat to act as a cooling anticipator by creating a slight warming effect.

No current flows through the compensator when cooling is on because it has a much higher resistance than the switch contacts. When the thermostat contacts are open, however, a very small current can flow through the compensator and the contactor coil, creating a tiny amount of heat.

Because of the compensator resistance, the current is not enough to energize the contactor. The heat created by the current flowing through the compensator warms the thermostat, making the thermostatic switch contacts close sooner than they would otherwise. In this way, the cooling compensator accounts for the lag that would normally occur between the thermostat temperature and space temperature.

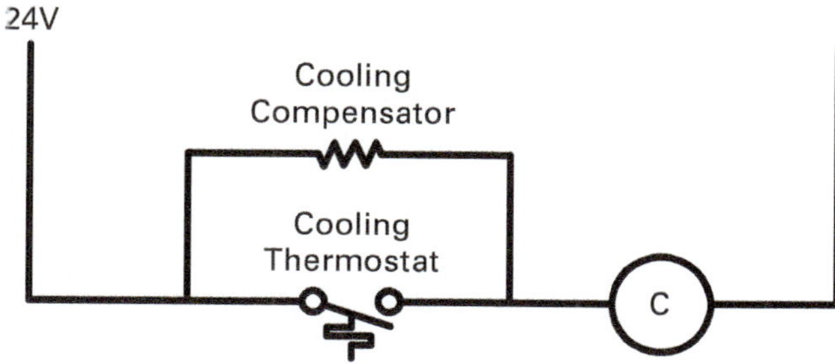

Figure 10 Cooling compensator.

Going Green

Large Water-Cooled Chillers

As the name implies, chillers cool water to be used as a heat transfer medium. The chilled water is then circulated through the building in piping systems to a number of fan-coil or air-handling units. Many chillers are air-cooled, but many are also water-cooled.

Water-cooled chillers are generally combined with a cooling tower that serves as an additional heat exchanger. Water flowing through the chiller condenser is routed to the cooling tower, where the heat is then transferred to air before returning to the condenser.

Water-cooled systems are more energy efficient than most air-cooled systems. A large water-cooled centrifugal chiller used for training is shown here.

2.1.3 Heating-Cooling Thermostats

When heating and cooling are combined for year-round comfort, it is impractical to use a separate thermostat for each mode. Therefore, the two are combined into one heating-cooling thermostat (*Figure 11*).

A switch is usually provided on heating-cooling thermostats to switch between heating and cooling. However, many thermostats can change from one mode to the other automatically.

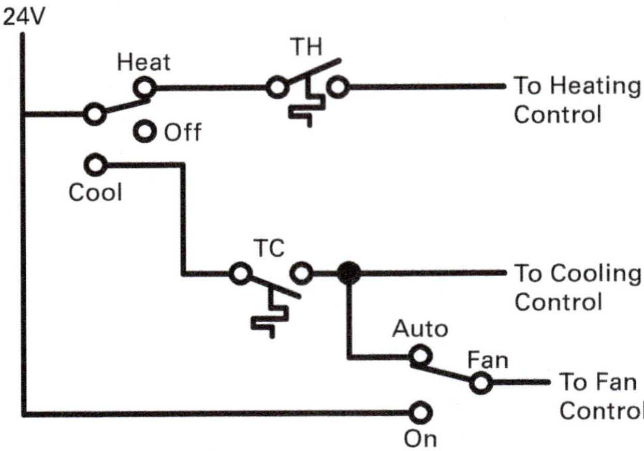

Figure 11 Heating-cooling thermostat.

2.1.4 Automatic-Changeover Thermostats

The disadvantage of a common heating-cooling thermostat is that the building occupant must determine whether heating or cooling is needed at a particular time and set the thermostat switch accordingly. That is often impractical, especially during the change of seasons.

Automatic-changeover thermostat: A thermostat that automatically switches between heating or cooling as needed.

Subbase: The mounting base of a thermostat that houses the wiring terminals.

The **automatic-changeover thermostat** can select either mode. The thermostat shown in *Figure 12* is essentially the same as the thermostat in *Figure 11*, with the addition of an Auto position on the **subbase**. The occupant can still select heating or cooling independently if preferred. When the switch is in the Auto position, however, the thermostat makes the selection. All that is necessary is for one of the two thermostatic switches to close, indicating the conditioned space is too warm or too cold.

Differential: The difference between the cut-in and cut-out points of a thermostat or pressure switch.

The thermostat is constructed to maintain a minimum **differential** between energizing and de-energizing the system. The differential is normally 2°F (1.11°C) or less. For example, if the heating setpoint is 70°F (21°C), the furnace will turn on at 69°F to 70°F (~21°C) and run until the temperature is 70°F to 71°F (~22°C).

Deadband: A temperature range that separates the heating and cooling modes in an automatic-changeover thermostat, within which there is no system activity.

Automatic-changeover thermostats also have a minimum interlock setting, commonly known as the **deadband**. The deadband is a built-in feature that prevents the heating and cooling setpoints from being too close. Within the deadband, there is no system activity. A typical deadband setting is 3°F (1.67°C). The deadband keeps the system from cycling back and forth between heating and cooling.

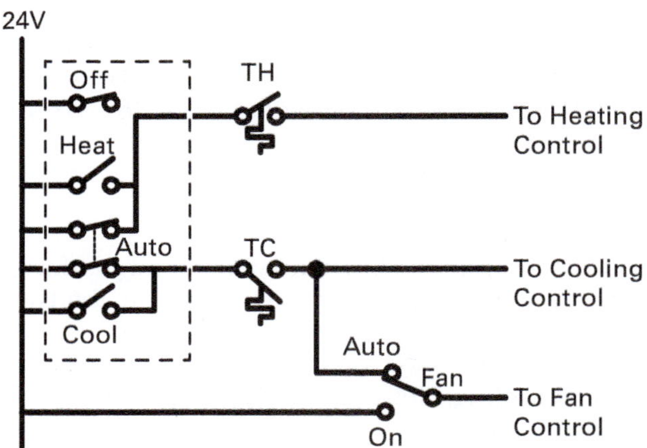

Figure 12 Automatic-changeover thermostat.

2.1.5 Multistage Thermostats

Multistage systems provide energy savings by using only a portion of the system capacity when the heating or cooling load is less than the maximum. A multistage thermostat (*Figure 13*) is needed to control these systems.

For example, a cooling system may have two compressors or perhaps a single compressor with multiple speeds. If the demand for cooling is low, the first-stage cooling circuit of the thermostat starts one of two compressors or a multispeed compressor at low speed. If the demand for cooling is high, the second-stage cooling circuit of the thermostat energizes the second compressor or operates a multispeed compressor at its highest speed.

Furnaces can also have multiple stages of operation. A two-stage heating thermostat can control a multistage gas furnace or groups of electric heating elements in an air-handling unit.

Multistage room thermostats are commonly used with heat pumps since they typically require supplemental heat in the coldest weather. The supplemental heat source represents a second stage of heat. Thermostats designed for heat pumps usually have an emergency heat switch as well. If the heat pump becomes inoperative, the switch locks out the compressor and heats the area with auxiliary electric heat (or other connected heat sources) until the problem is corrected. An indicator light or message on the thermostat typically comes on when the selector switch is in the emergency heat position to remind the user of the operating mode. Once the unit has been repaired, the switch is returned to the normal operating position.

NOTE

Figure 13 shows two control transformers. Although this was common in the past, it is rare in today's systems. When only one transformer is provided, a jumper is installed across the R and RC terminals of the thermostat.

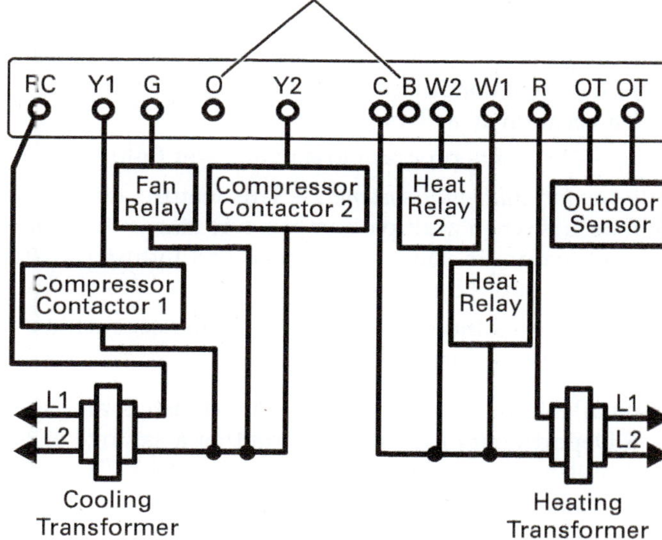

Figure 13 Multistage thermostat hookup.

2.1.6 Programmable Thermostats

Today's programmable thermostats are electronic and extremely versatile. Early programmable thermostats looked very much like conventional thermostats. They used a motor-driven time clock driving a wheel with cams set to raise and lower the temperature settings at timed intervals. Programmable mechanical thermostats are now obsolete.

Modern electronic programmable thermostats (*Figure 14*) use microprocessors and integrated circuits to provide various control and energy-saving features. Most can handle all types of common HVAC equipment, including heat pumps, through settings made by the installer.

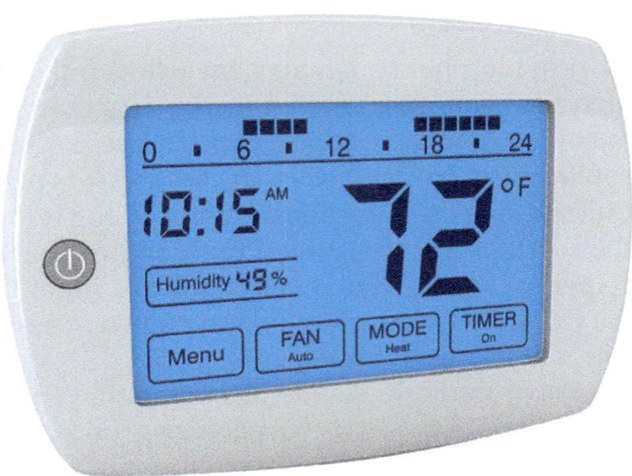

Figure 14 Electronic programmable thermostat.
Source: iStock@lucadp

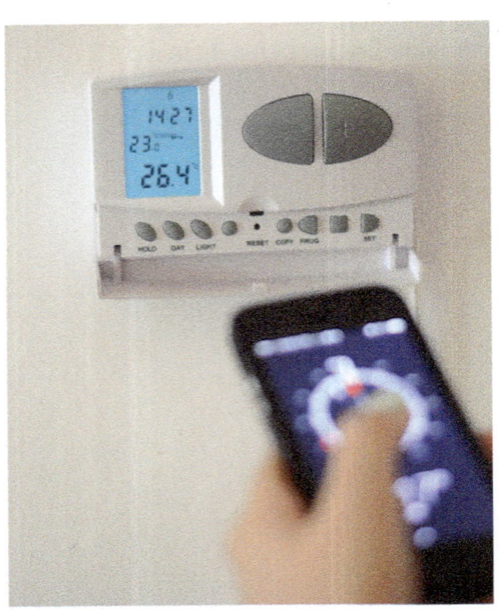

Figure 15 Wi-Fi® enabled thermostat controlled through a smartphone app.
Source: iStock@adrian825

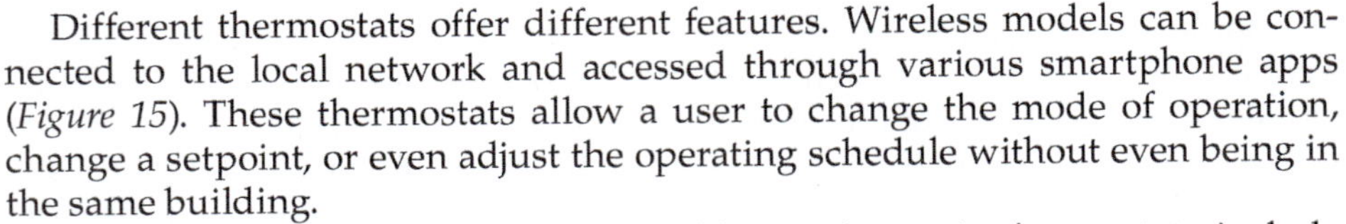

Different thermostats offer different features. Wireless models can be connected to the local network and accessed through various smartphone apps (*Figure 15*). These thermostats allow a user to change the mode of operation, change a setpoint, or even adjust the operating schedule without even being in the same building.

Additional features commonly available on electronic thermostats include the following:

- *Override control* — Allows the occupant to override the program when desired. For example, you might override the night setback on Monday so the setpoint doesn't change at the normal time and is delayed until a football game is over.
- *Multiple programs* — Allows the occupant to design and select different schedules for different conditions. For example, you can program a special schedule for a vacation away from home.
- *Battery backup* — Prevents program loss in a power failure.
- *Staggered startup for multi-unit systems* — This feature avoids excessive current use that occurs when multiple compressors start at the same time. This is an important feature in some commercial and industrial settings where billing for power is based on peak use.
- *Maintenance tracking* — Indicates when maintenance, such as air filter replacement, should be performed.

The savings available from programmable thermostats are significant. For example, the US Department of Energy reports that a savings of 10% per year can be expected by simply turning your thermostat back 7°F to 10°F (3.9°C to 5.6°C) from its normal setting for 8 hours a day.

2.1.7 Line-Voltage Thermostats

Most of the thermostats you encounter will operate at low voltages. However, a few heating systems are controlled via line voltage. Line-voltage thermostats, as their name implies, directly control the power supply to the heating elements.

Line-voltage thermostats are commonly used to control baseboard electric heaters and electric floor or ceiling heating cables. Conventional line-voltage thermostats use a bimetal sensing element that does not provide precise temperature control. This is because the bimetal elements and switch contacts must be heavier to carry the larger current. Because they are heavier, they do not respond as quickly or easily as the smaller, lighter contacts in 24VAC room thermostats.

Digital line-voltage thermostats provide much more precise temperature control. However, most line-voltage thermostats, regardless of type, are heating-only models.

2.2.0 Thermostat Installation

Even the best thermostat cannot perform correctly if it is improperly installed. Selecting the proper location for the thermostat is the first step in the installation procedure.

2.2.1 Installation Guidelines

The thermostat should be installed in the space in which it controls the temperature. Avoid the following areas when selecting a location:

- Drafty areas or areas where the air is stagnant
- Areas where hot or cold air from the system would blow directly on the thermostat
- Areas where radiant heat from direct sunlight or heat from appliances will affect accuracy
- Areas adjacent to outside doors
- Walls that shake or vibrate, such as when a door closes
- Outside walls and walls where an unconditioned space lies on the opposite side

NOTE

Some thermostats can accommodate one or more remote temperature sensors that allow the thermostat itself to be located outside the conditioned space.

Before installing a thermostat, carefully study the manufacturer's instructions and recommendations before beginning. Ensure the thermostat is compatible with the type of heating and cooling system installed. Digital thermostats often have a long menu of advanced options that need to be set before the system is started. It is best to determine those answers before beginning the installation. When the installation is complete, the thermostat must be operationally checked as directed in the installation instructions.

Locate the thermostat and subbase 5' (1.52 m) above the finished floor in an area with good air circulation at room temperature. Locating the thermostat near the return air duct inlet is usually a good idea, as it can sense the temperature in the airstream returning to the system blower.

When unpacking the new thermostat and subbase, handle it with care. Rough handling can damage the thermostat. Save all the instructional information and literature for future reference.

CAUTION

Thermostats containing solid-state devices are sensitive to static electricity. To avoid damage, discharge any static electricity from your body before handling a digital thermostat. This can be accomplished by touching a grounded metal pipe or conduit. Also, avoid touching the electronic devices on the board.

NOTE

The Americans with Disabilities Act (ADA) requires different mounting heights for thermostats in designated environments. If the installation location is subject to ADA requirements, ensure the mounting height is in accordance with current ADA standards.

2.2.2 Thermostat Wiring

The thermostat wiring is connected to a terminal strip or junction box in the furnace and air conditioning unit. Standard color coding is used in the HVAC industry to identify the wires and their function. *Figure 16* shows the color code and how the terminals are typically designated.

It is important to understand one concept of thermostat control wiring. The Common wire from the transformer carries one leg of the 24VAC control power to all devices. It typically remains intact from point to point, without switches. The R wire, which also originates at the transformer and represents the other control power leg, is switched by many devices, including the thermostat. For example, R at the thermostat is switched to control the indoor blower and departs the thermostat as G. Together, G and C provide 24VAC to energize an indoor blower relay or blower control circuit.

The terminal designation arrangement is fairly standardized among thermostat and equipment manufacturers. It is not safe to assume, however, that the person who installed an existing system followed the color scheme! When replacing an existing thermostat, check and record any deviations from the standard color code to avoid mistakes.

There are additional codes for more complex thermostats. For example, the letter O designates orange and is often used to control the reversing valve in a heat pump. When there are multiple stages of heating or cooling, those terminals are designated with the appropriate letter plus a number, such as Y2 or W2.

Thermostat Wiring

Thermostat cables come in a variety of conductor configurations. Simple two-conductor cables can be used in a heating-only installation. Thermostat cable with three, four, five, and eight conductors are readily available for use in more complex installations.

Normally, 18-gauge thermostat wire is adequate. However, long runs of thermostat cable can produce a voltage drop that affects equipment operation. If you have a run of thermostat cable that seems excessively long, use 16-gauge wire to reduce the voltage drop.

Terminal Designation	Wire Color	Function
C	Blue or Black	Common Wire from 24VAC Transformer (Not Always Required at Thermostat)
R	Red	Switched Leg of 24VAC Control Circuit
G	Green	Fan Control
Y	Yellow	Cooling Control Y1 = Stage 1 Y2 = Stage 2
W	White	Heating Control W1 = Stage 1 W2 = Stage 2
O	Orange	Heat Pump Reversing Valve Control

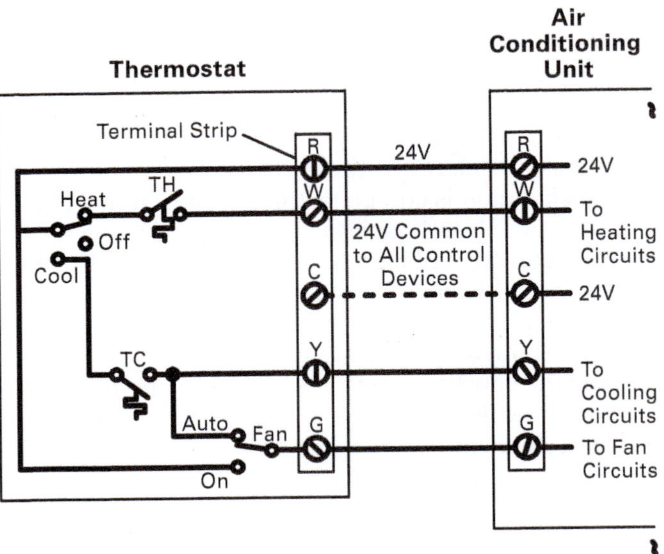

Figure 16 Thermostat wiring and color codes.

Thermostat wiring should be done in accordance with national and local electrical codes. See *NEC Section 424.20* for limitations on using a thermostat as a disconnect device. All wiring connections should be secure. To avoid damaging the control wire conductor, always use a stripping tool designed to strip small-gauge wire. Color coded wiring should be used where possible for easy reference should system troubleshooting be required later.

Thermostat wires should not be spliced. If splicing cannot be avoided, soldered splices are recommended. If wires are stapled to prevent movement, ensure the staple does not go through the wire insulation. Seal the wire opening in the wall space behind the thermostat to block drafts within the wall stud space.

Know the Code

Thermostatically Controlled Switching Devices
NEC Section 424.20

2.2.3 Checking Heating Circuit Current Draw

The next step in the thermostat installation process is to determine the heating circuit current draw. This information is needed to set the heat anticipator on electromechanical thermostats controlling fossil fuel systems. Digital thermostats use a different method of compensating for temperature lag. The cooling anticipator in electromechanical thermostats is not adjustable.

Locate the current demand for the gas valve in a gas furnace or the primary control of an oil furnace. The current is usually printed on the gas valve (*Figure 17*) or the primary control label. It may also be found in the manufacturer's installation and service literature.

Alternatively, and for greater accuracy, measure the actual current of the heating control circuit. Energize the heating system from the thermostat after the wiring is complete. Then measure the current draw on the W control wire while the heating system is running.

CAUTION

To prevent equipment damage, make sure the power is off before handling and connecting thermostat wiring.

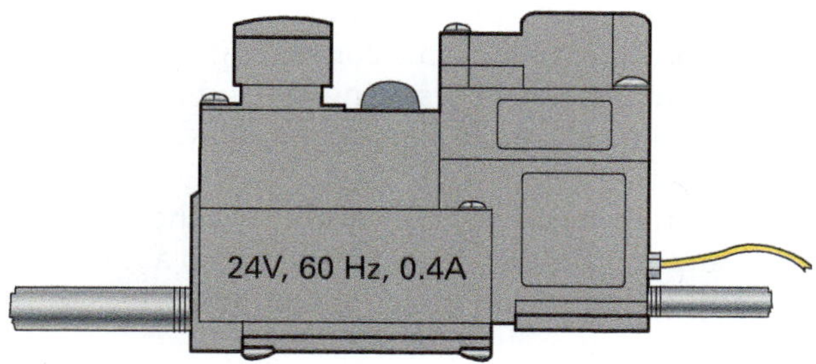

Figure 17 Gas valve current demand.

2.2.4 Adjusting Heat Anticipators

The heat anticipator (*Figure 18*) on an electromechanical thermostat is adjustable. It should initially be set at the current rating on the gas valve or oil burner primary control. As noted in the previous section, the current in the heating control circuit (W terminal) can be measured while the heating system is in operation.

An adjustable heat anticipator has a slide wire adjustment with the pointer scale marked in tenths of an ampere. This is used to set the anticipator to match the current draw of the furnace heating circuit.

For example, if the current draw of a gas valve is shown as 0.45A, the installer should adjust the anticipator setting to 0.45A on the scale. The heat anticipator adjustment determines the cycle length by artificially heating the bimetal coil. As more heat is directed at the bimetal coil, a shorter heating cycle will occur. Conversely, as less heat is directed at the bimetal coil, a longer heating cycle will result.

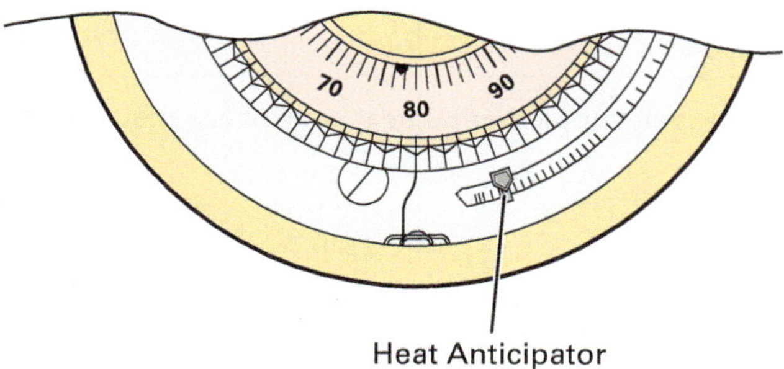

Figure 18 Thermostat heat anticipator.

After the heat anticipator is initially set, small adjustments in the setting can be made to improve performance if necessary. Changing the setting of the anticipator shortens or lengthens the heating cycle. If the system cycles too rapidly or remains on too long and overshoots the thermostat setting, adjust the heat anticipator accordingly. Most anticipators have an arrow and the word "LONGER" stamped on the scale, indicating the direction to move the setting to increase the length of the heating cycle.

2.2.5 Cycle Rate Settings

Electronic thermostats do not contain a traditional heat anticipator. Instead, many have an adjustable *cycle rate*. The cycle rate refers to the number of times per hour the heating or cooling system can be energized. The heating and cooling cycle rates are set separately. The thermostat literature will have directions for changing the cycle rate.

2.2.6 Final Testing

The final step in the installation process is to check the heating and/or cooling system. Turn on the power to the unit containing the control transformer to energize the control circuit. Start by setting the fan switch to On. The system blower should start and run without significant delay. If it works, return the fan switch to the Auto position.

Next, set the operating mode to Heat and leave the fan switch in the Auto position. Turn the setpoint dial to at least 5°F (~2.8°C) above room temperature. The burner typically starts within 15 to 30 seconds. The fan will start after a short delay to allow the heat exchanger to warm up.

If the heating system operates as expected, adjust the setpoint to 5°F below the room temperature. The main burner should shut off within 15 seconds while the blower continues to run for up to 3 minutes.

Next, set the operating mode to cooling and leave the fan switch set to Auto. Adjust the cooling setpoint to 5°F (2.8°C) below the room temperature. The cooling system may come on immediately, but a delay of up to 5 minutes may occur. The indoor fan should start with the air conditioning unit or soon thereafter.

After the cooling system has started, set the thermostat to at least 5°F (2.8°C) above the room temperature. The cooling equipment should turn off within 15 seconds. Ensure that all the equipment remains off when the thermostat is turned to Off, and the fan is set to the Auto position.

CAUTION

To avoid compressor damage, do not check cooling operation unless the outside temperature is at least 50°F (10°C) and the crankcase heater (if so equipped) has been on for at least 24 hours. Otherwise, condensed liquid refrigerant inside the compressor shell can cause serious damage to the compressor as it starts.

Compressor Short-Cycle Time Delay

Many thermostats are equipped with a compressor short-cycle time-delay function to protect the compressor from rapid restarts. The delay allows the refrigerant pressures on the suction and discharge sides of the compressor to reach equilibrium.

2.0.0 Section Review

1. A second stage of supplemental heat control is a required characteristic for most _____.
   a. cooling systems
   b. heat pumps
   c. oil burners
   d. boilers

2. The thermostat terminal normally assigned to cooling control is _____.
   a. Y
   b. G
   c. C
   d. R

3.0.0 HVAC Controls

Objective

Identify and describe HVAC controls and devices.

a. Identify and describe basic comfort cooling system controls.
b. Identify and describe common furnace controls.
c. Identify and describe common heat pump controls.
d. Describe digital and analog controls used in HVAC systems.
e. Describe the basic HVAC control system sequence of operation.
f. Describe how to troubleshoot HVAC systems.

Performance Tasks

1. Install a thermostat and hook it up using the standard color coding system.
2. Configure and test the operation of an HVAC system thermostat.

HVAC control systems are designed to manage most aspects of system operation. The controls for a small system, such as a window air conditioner, are very simple—a couple of control switches and a thermostat. As the system gets larger and provides more features, the controls become more complicated.

3.1.0 Comfort Cooling Controls

Large commercial systems may use pneumatic or electronic controls with conventional electrical controls. These systems may have 30 or 40 control devices, while a window air conditioner has just a few.

The good news is that only a few control devices are in the average residential cooling system. When you learn to recognize them and understand the role each plays, it won't matter how many are used to control a particular system.

3.1.1 Motor Speed Control

Greater efficiency can be achieved by varying the speed of compressors and fan motors to adapt to changing heating and cooling loads. For example, HVAC equipment commonly uses multispeed or variable-speed blowers. In addition, two-speed compressors are used in small systems.

For multispeed motors, the speed is selected for each mode by connecting to the various motor leads identified for each speed (*Figure 19*). Indoor blowers commonly operate at different speeds in the heating and cooling modes. The blower speed used for heating is typically lower than that for cooling.

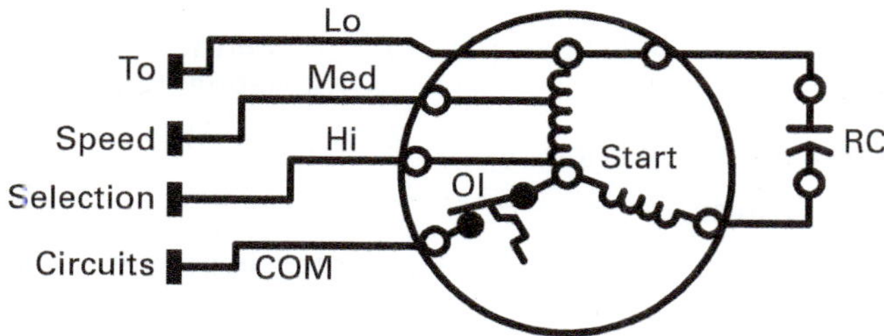

Figure 19 Permanent split capacitor (PSC) multispeed motor.

Modern electronic furnace controls use microprocessor chips to achieve continuous control. The furnace control system shown in the simplified diagram in *Figure 20* controls the combustion system as well as the blower speed. It may also be able to sense any changes within the system, such as a dirty air filter or closed zone valve, or perhaps vary the blower speed based on the demand for heating or cooling.

Many of today's systems use electronically commutated motors (ECMs) on the indoor blower (*Figure 21*). ECMs are true variable-speed motors. Although they are powered by AC, the voltage is rectified at the motor, feeding DC to the motor windings. The speed of the blower is then determined by field programming of the microprocessor on the control board.

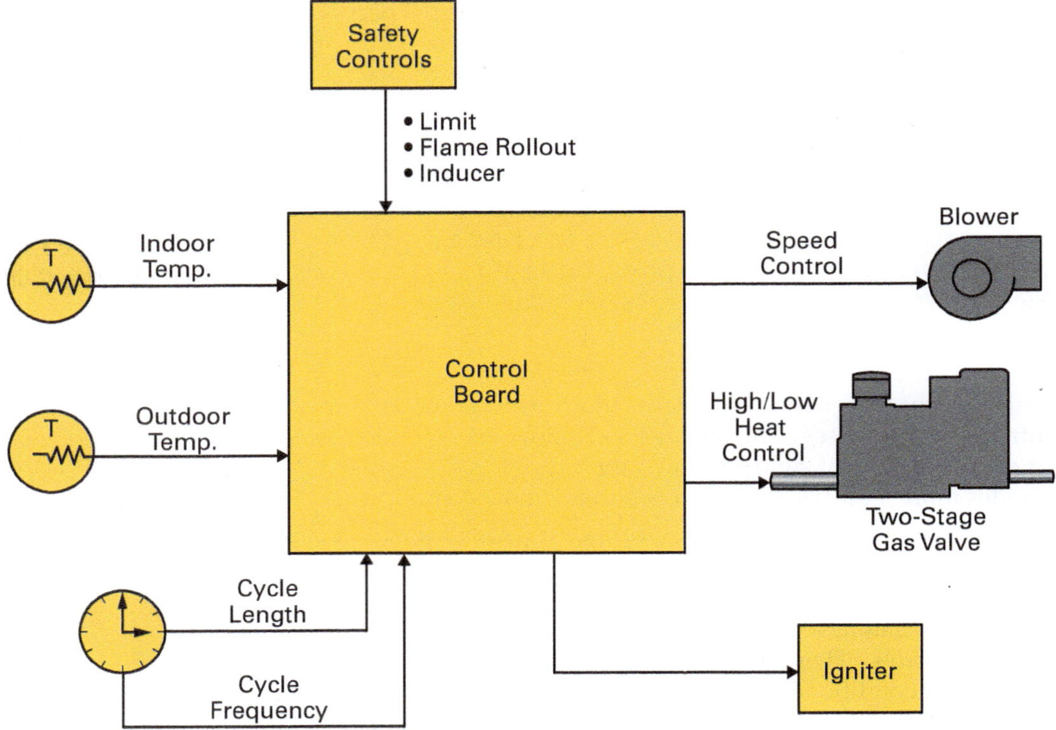

Figure 20 Electronic furnace control.

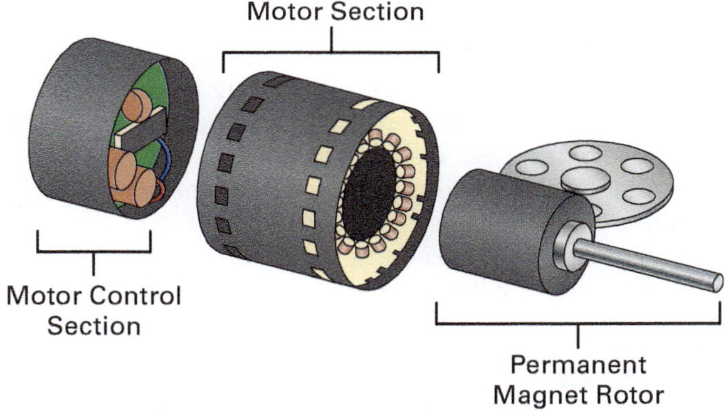

Figure 21 ECM motor construction.

3.1.2 Lockout Circuits

The purpose of a lockout relay in a control circuit is to prevent the automatic restart of the HVAC equipment after a safety device has shut it down. If the lockout relay has been activated, the system may be reset only by first interrupting the control power supply to the system. This allows the holding contacts to return to their normal position, assuming the fault has been resolved.

In *Figure 22*, the lockout relay coil, because of its high resistance, is not energized during normal operation. However, when any one of the safety controls opens the circuit to the compressor contactor coil, then full current flows through the lockout relay coil, energizing it and opening the contacts. These contacts remain open, keeping the compressor contactor circuit open until the safety control resets (manually or automatically, depending on the device) and the control power is interrupted.

Performance of the lockout relay depends on the resistance of its coil being much greater than the resistance of the compressor contactor coil. If the lockout relay fails, it should be replaced with an exact duplicate to maintain the proper resistance balance. This type of relay is sometimes called an *impedance relay*.

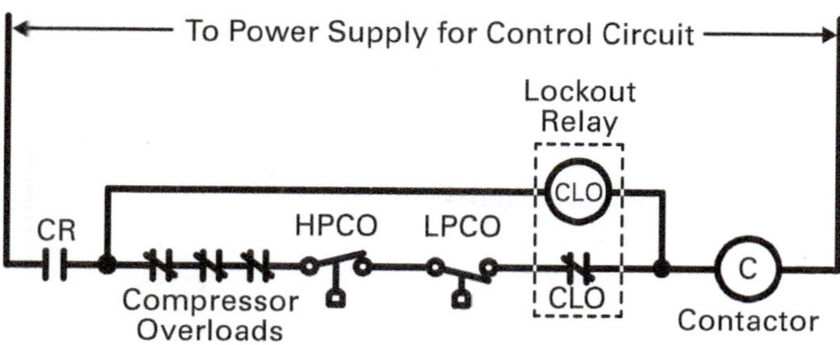

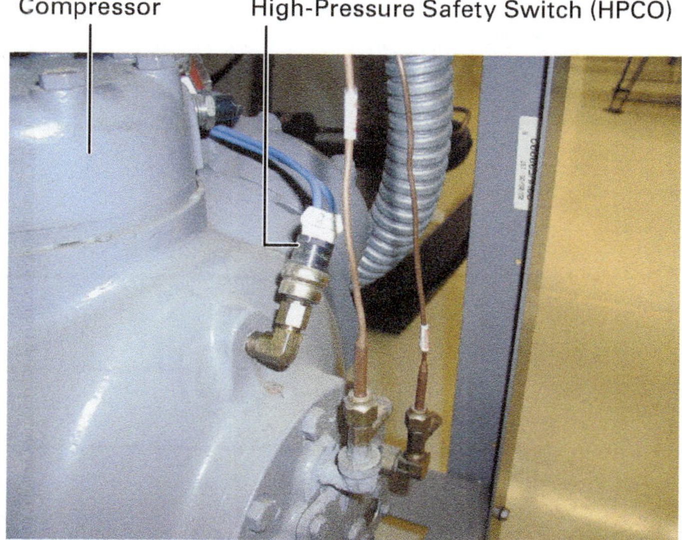

Figure 22 Lockout relay used in an HVAC control circuit.

It is permissible to add a control relay coil in parallel with the contactor coil when a system demands another control. The resistance of the contactor coil and the relay coil in parallel decreases the total resistance and does not affect the operation of the lockout relay.

CAUTION

Never place additional lockout relays, lights, or other load devices in parallel with the lockout relay coil. Doing so might prevent the lockout relay from operating, defeating its purpose.

3.1.3 Time-Delay Relays

The time-delay relay's purpose is to delay or extend another process for a predetermined length of time. The length of the delay or extension depends on the time built into the relay coil and may vary from a fraction of a second to several minutes. A common use for a time-delay relay is to delay the startup and shutdown of a furnace blower (*Figure 23*), but there are many possible applications for them.

Time-delay relays used to stage compressors in multiple-compressor systems have been replaced, for the most part, with electronic timers. The electronic timers can control conventional relays or may have relay contacts as an integral part of the timer. Advantages of the electronic timer include more accurate and versatile timing sequences and greater reliability.

A *heat sequencer* is a special type of time-delay relay used to energize multiple resistance heaters in a heat pump air handler or electric furnace. A sequencer is basically multiple time-delay relays housed in a single enclosure, with contacts heavy enough to carry the current of an electric-resistance heater. It is common for electric furnaces to be equipped with several banks of heaters, each controlled by its own sequencer. To avoid the current surge when all heaters are energized at once, the timing of the sequencers is selected to bring the various heaters on in stages.

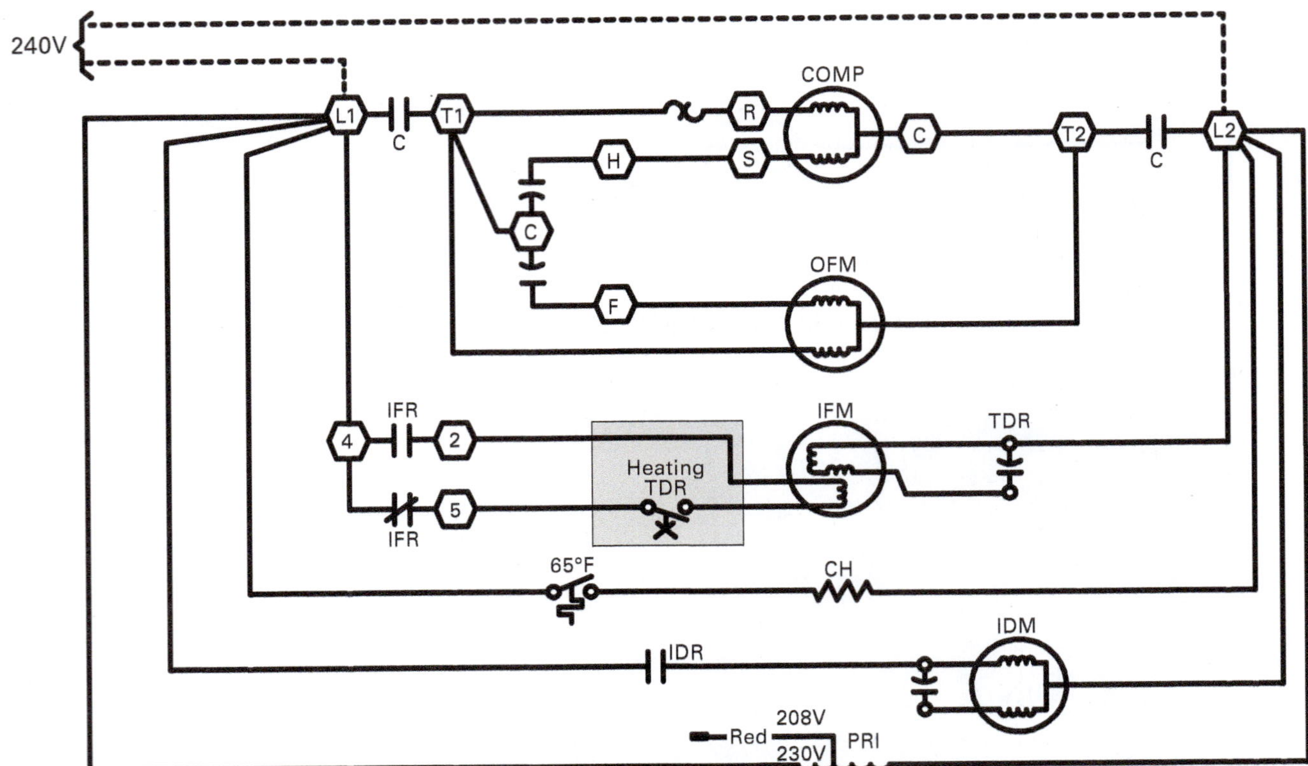

Figure 23 Time-delay relay used to control a blower.

3.1.4 Compressor Short-Cycle Timer

An existing large differential pressure across a compressor can prevent it from starting and possibly damage the compressor. When a refrigerant circuit shuts down, it should not be restarted until the pressures in the high-pressure and low-pressure sides of the system have had time to equalize. Short cycling can be caused by a momentary power interruption or someone changing the thermostat setting back and forth rapidly.

A compressor short-cycle protection circuit prevents the compressor contactor from re-energizing for a specified period after it is de-energized. Lockout periods typically range from 30 seconds to five minutes.

Short-cycle timers are available as self-contained modules, often sold as optional accessories. The two most common types are delay-on-make and delay-on-break. The first begins the delay period when it is energized. While this is practical for some applications, it doesn't work well for air conditioning compressors. A delay-on-break timer is best used for compressor protection. The delay period for this type begins as soon as it is de-energized. It will not close again until the programmed time has elapsed.

Figure 24 Non-adjustable high- and low-pressure switches.

3.1.5 Control Circuit Safety Switches

Compressor control circuits normally include several different types of safety switches. These include pressure switches, freezestats, and outdoor thermostats.

Many systems use one or more pressure safety switches in the compressor control circuit (*Figure 24*). These are safety devices designed to protect the system from excessively high or low pressures. A pressure safety switch is normally closed and wired in series with the compressor contactor. The schematic diagram in *Figure 22* shows both a low-pressure cutout (LPCO) and a high-pressure cutout (HPCO) in the control circuit. Note that the switches shown in *Figure 24* are not adjustable. Pressure switches generally have a fixed setpoint when used as a safety device in refrigeration applications.

High-pressure safety switches are designed to open if the compressor discharge pressure is too high. Low-pressure switches are designed to open if the suction pressure is too low. When the system pressure begins to rise above or drop below the normal range, the related high-pressure or low-pressure switch will open, de-energizing the compressor contactor.

Some manufacturers use a type of low-pressure switch called a *loss-of-charge switch* that opens if the refrigerant charge is too low. They are typically set to a much lower value than a low-pressure safety switch.

Another type of safety switch is the freeze-protection thermostat (FPT), commonly called a *freezestat*. Its purpose is to prevent hydronic coil freeze-up. A freezestat is a normally closed temperature safety switch with a long capillary tube laced across the face of a coil. It will open if the temperature passing over a hot water or chilled water coil drops below its setpoint, typically around 40°F (~4°C) or slightly lower. This usually results in an outside air damper closing and/or the blower slowing down.

Heat pumps often use an outdoor thermostat to disable the supplemental electric heat, or a portion thereof, when the ambient temperature drops below a predetermined setpoint. This improves efficiency by minimizing the number of electric heat strips available unless it is very cold.

Pressure Problems

High- and low-pressure safety switches prevent system operation if the system pressures are outside a preset range. Common causes of high head pressure are dirty condenser coils or a failed condenser fan motor. Common causes of low suction pressure include a loss of refrigerant charge and blocked air filters which reduce airflow across the indoor coil.

3.2.0 Furnace Controls

Gas furnaces are equipped with several devices designed to shut off the furnace if a hazardous condition is sensed. Common furnace controls include the high-temperature limit switch, rollout switch, airflow control, and inducer proving switch.

3.2.1 High-Temperature Limit Switch

Figure 25 shows an example of a high-temperature limit switch. This bimetal switch, also called a *snap disc*, is thermally actuated and usually mounted above or beside the heat exchangers. Temperature limit switches must be located where they can sense the monitored temperature accurately. Most have a fixed setting.

Overheating can occur due to a blocked vent or a failed blower motor. If the furnace overheats, the high-temperature limit switch opens, de-energizing the gas valve and shutting off the gas supply. These switches may reset automatically when the temperature drops below the setpoint.

3.2.2 Rollout Switch

Another type of temperature limit switch is called a *rollout switch* (*Figure 26*). It is mounted on or near the heat exchanger to stop the burner if the temperature in the combustion vestibule indicates the burner flame is "rolling out" of the heat exchanger. Beyond its function and temperature setting, it looks the same as the high-temperature limit switch.

3.2.3 Inducer Proving Switch

Modern gas furnaces use an inducer motor to induce a draft through the combustion chamber and heat exchanger. These furnaces have either a centrifugal switch or a pressure-operated switch in the heating control circuit to verify the operation of the inducer motor before the burner can ignite. If the inducer motor fails to operate, the switch remains open, preventing the gas valve from opening.

The centrifugal switch has a set of contacts located near the inducer motor shaft. The centrifugal force created by the spinning shaft throws the contacts outward, closing a switch that allows control power to be applied to the furnace gas valve.

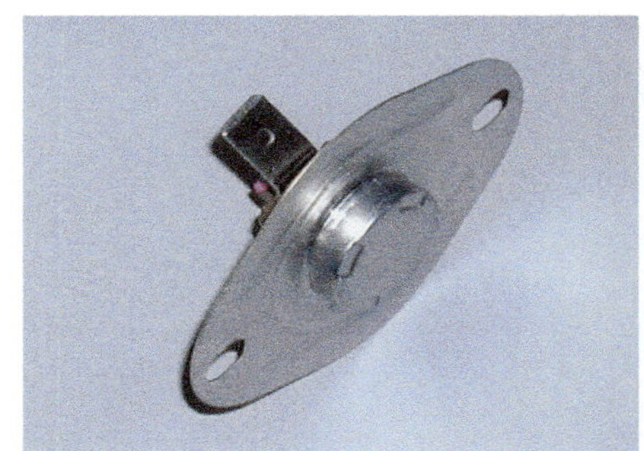

Figure 25 High-temperature limit switch.

Figure 26 Rollout switch.
Source: Schneider Electric

The disadvantage of a centrifugal switch is that it can stick in either the closed or open position. In addition, even when it proves the inducer motor is running, it does not prove that airflow is being produced. It is an indirect safety device; it can only sense whether the inducer motor is spinning.

A pressure switch (*Figure 27*) to prove inducer operation is more common in today's furnaces. It measures the differential pressure between the heat exchanger and the surrounding atmosphere. When the inducer motor is operating properly, a negative pressure is created that causes the pressure switch to close, allowing control power through to the furnace gas valve. This is a direct safety device since it directly monitors the pressure in the heat exchanger.

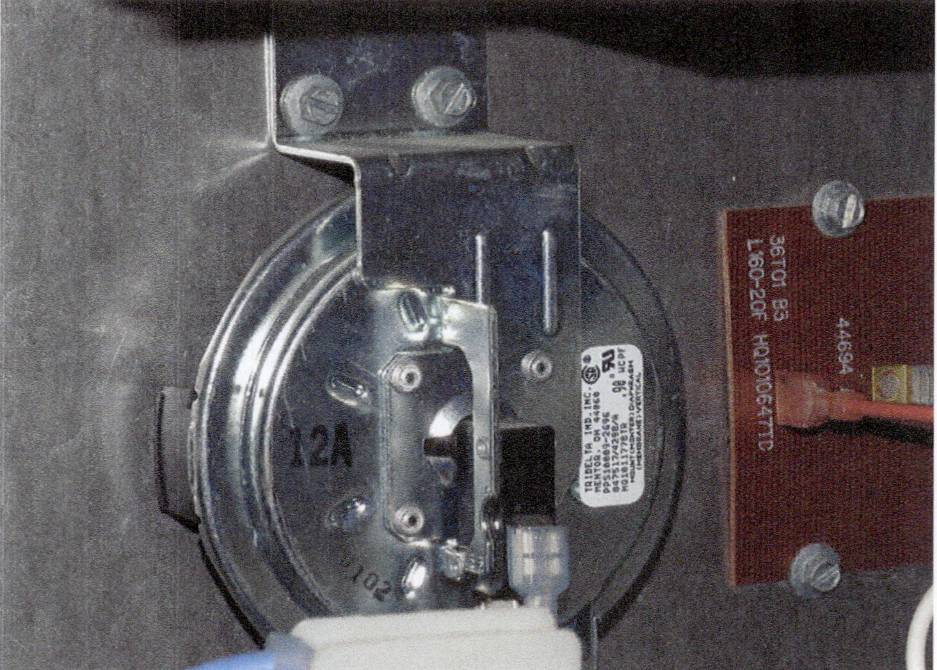

Figure 27 Combustion airflow pressure switch.

3.3.0 Heat Pump Defrost Controls

In the heating mode, when heat is transferred from the outdoor air to the refrigerant in the outdoor coil, moisture condenses on the coil. Because of the refrigerant and outdoor temperatures, moisture tends to condense and freeze on the coil surface. Over time, the frost builds up, blocking airflow and preventing effective heat transfer. This is normal and expected for a heat pump.

To eliminate ice buildup on the outdoor coil, heat pumps require a defrost mode. In air-to-air heat pumps, the defrost cycle is the same as the cooling cycle, with one exception. In the cooling mode, hot refrigerant flows through the outdoor coil to melt the frost. The cycle can last up to 10 minutes. However, in the defrost mode, the outdoor fan remains off to maximize the heat delivered to the coil.

During a defrost cycle, the heat pump is not providing any heat indoors. In fact, cold air is blowing into the conditioned space. To prevent discomfort to building occupants, one or more supplemental electric heaters are energized to reheat and temper the air temperature before it enters the room.

There are many ways to control the defrost cycle. One common method uses a combination of time and temperature. The logic behind this method is that defrost is needed only if the unit has been operating long enough for frost to form on the coil and the temperature is low enough for moisture to freeze on the coil. If both conditions do not exist, a defrost cycle is unnecessary.

Modern heat pumps use electronic defrost controls in which all the circuitry, including the relays, is mounted on a printed circuit board (*Figure 28*). A **thermistor** sends temperature information from the outdoor coil to the board. An electronic clock in the timing logic receives a signal as long as the heating thermostat is closed. If the defrost cycle is interrupted by the opening of the heating thermostat, the timing logic will remember where it left off. If the coil temperature still indicates the presence of frost when the unit cycles on again, the unit will automatically return to defrost mode.

Thermistor: A temperature sensor that exhibits a predictable change in its resistance proportional to the temperature.

Figure 28 Electronic defrost control board.

A jumper or other selection device on the board allows the installer to select the defrost frequency—30, 60, or 90 minutes, for example—based on local conditions.

An important feature of many of these boards is a defrost test cycle. It is activated by placing a jumper across two terminals on the board for just a moment (*Figure 29*). The timer is overridden, and the usual 10-minute running cycle can be reduced to less than a minute. A major advantage of an electronic defrost control is that it is self-contained except for external thermistors, and they are very reliable.

Electronic defrost controls may be programmed for *demand defrost*, which combines time, temperature, and pressure information to determine whether there is enough frost buildup to require a defrost cycle. It also terminates a cycle when it senses the coil is frost-free, regardless of the cycle time. Minimizing the number and length of the defrost cycles results in significant energy savings and greater comfort.

Figure 29 Defrost speed-up jumper.

3.4.0 HVAC Digital Control Systems

Modern buildings use computer technology to control all building functions, including the HVAC, lighting, fire protection, and building security systems. These control systems are known by many names, including *building management systems (BMS)*, *building automation systems*, and *facility management systems*. All are based on some type of *direct digital control (DDC) system*.

Many building management systems are a component of *integrated building design*. Integrated building design is a collaborative process that relies on a project design team from its inception through its design and construction phases. The process generally pursues *green building* concepts as well as energy efficiency. A green building is a sustainable structure that is designed, built, and operated in a manner that efficiently uses resources in an environmentally sound way.

The most common green building certification system is Leadership in Energy and Environmental Design (LEED), administered by the US Green Building Council (USGBC). LEED provides a point system to score green building design and construction. The system is categorized into nine basic areas: Integrative Process, Location and Transportation, Sustainable Sites, Water Efficiency, Energy and Atmosphere, Materials and Resources, Indoor Environmental Quality, Innovation, and Regional Priority.

Buildings are awarded points based on the number of sustainable strategies met in each category, and certifications are earned based on the total score. The certification levels are LEED Certified, Silver, Gold, and Platinum. HVAC systems provide energy management, IAQ, and other opportunities for points toward LEED certification.

To minimize resource consumption in modern green building designs, the BMS must be able to integrate control strategies across multiple building systems. The basic building block of any BMS is a series of digital controllers used to monitor and control various building functions. *Figure 30* shows an example of BMS architecture.

The lower portion of *Figure 30* shows the controllers the BMS will interface with to control the individual pieces of HVAC equipment. The middle portion shows the next level of building control, the interface of the building's other system management functions. Building management systems have features and functions that go far beyond simply maintaining the desired conditions within a space. They include the following:

- Database management
- Alarm management
- Data collection
- Tenant billing
- Load shedding
- Lighting control
- Building access

The top portion of *Figure 30* shows the final level of building control—human interface using local or remote computers and/or the internet. The building's digital controllers are connected via the network communication bus. The communication network links all controllers in the building to a centralized computer for human access and integrated building system control strategies. BMS functions can be applied to installations ranging in size from a residence to a large multibuilding campus.

Figure 31 shows an example of a processor module used to control the interface between a BMS and a specific piece of HVAC equipment.

Electrostatic Discharge

We've all experienced static electricity discharges after walking across a carpeted floor and touching a light switch or doorknob. These startling discharges are strong enough to seriously damage or destroy delicate electronic devices. Before touching, removing, or replacing any electronic device, always ground yourself by touching the equipment chassis, a water pipe, or a metallic electrical conduit. This will release any static charge in your body and prevent damage to the electronic device.

3.4.1 Controlling Devices

The microprocessor can execute instructions and obtain remarkable results, and it can do so at astounding speeds. If it has no way to communicate with other devices, however, it is useless. Communication is done through both digital and analog signals. These signals come from what are referred to as *points* in the HVAC industry.

Digital devices might be relays, switches, lights, and other devices that can be operated in either an on or off (binary) condition. Analog devices include thermistors, photocells, and pressure transducers. Interfacing with an analog device is somewhat more complicated. An analog signal that can have an infinite number of values is converted to a form that can be represented digitally.

Most real-world processes are continuously changing (*Figure 32*). Physical quantities such as pressure, temperature, liquid levels, and fluid flow rates tend to change gradually. Changes of this type produce many discrete values before ever reaching a final steady state. The problem of converting from analog form to digital form requires the use of an **analog-to-digital converter**.

Analog-to-digital converter: A device designed to convert analog signals such as temperature and humidity to a digital form that can be processed by logic circuits.

Analog and digital signals can be further divided into inputs and outputs. Analog-in (AI) signals are obtained from sensors representing characteristics such as temperature, pressure, and humidity. Analog-out (AO) signals are commands, such as changing the position of a modulating chilled-water valve by 5% of its travel. Digital-in (DI) signals are contact closures or openings, showing status or alarm conditions in a two-position mode. Digital-out (DO) signals are two-position commands like start/stop or open/close states.

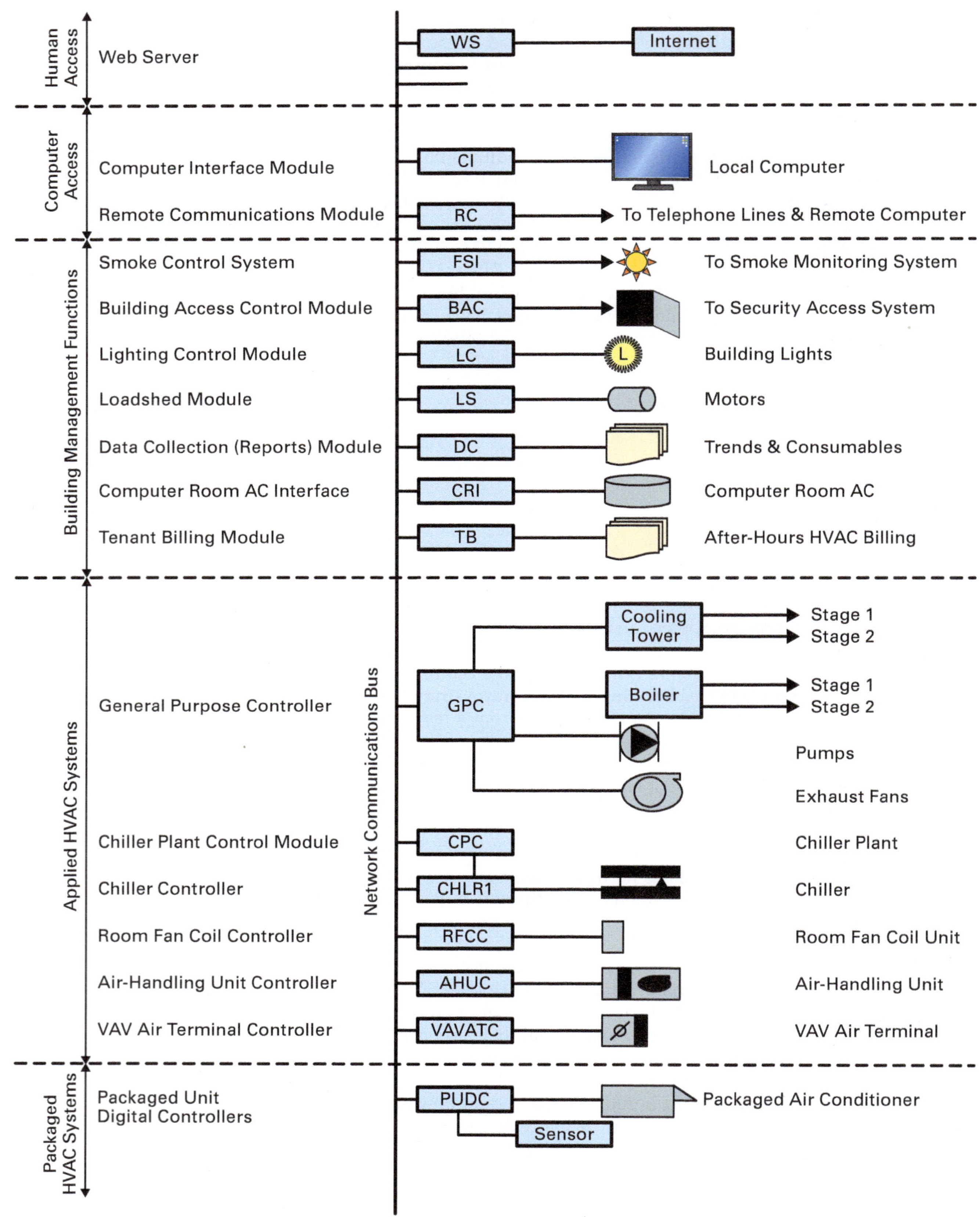

Figure 30 Centralized building management system.

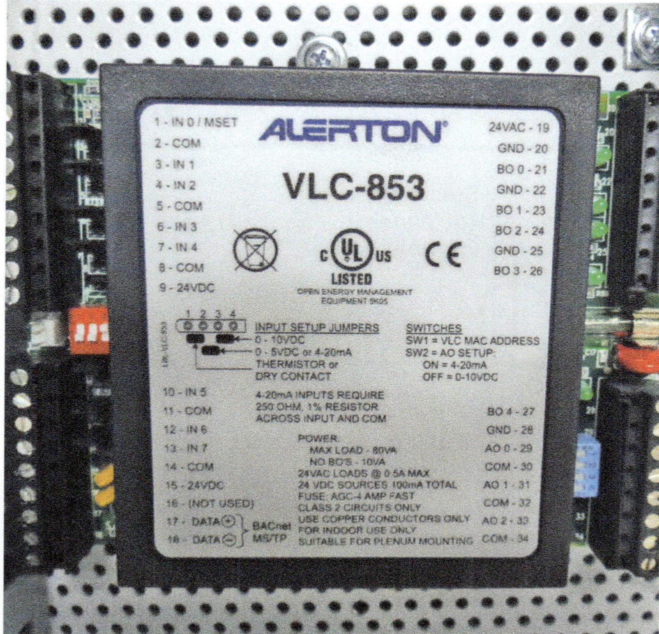

Figure 31 HVAC system control module.

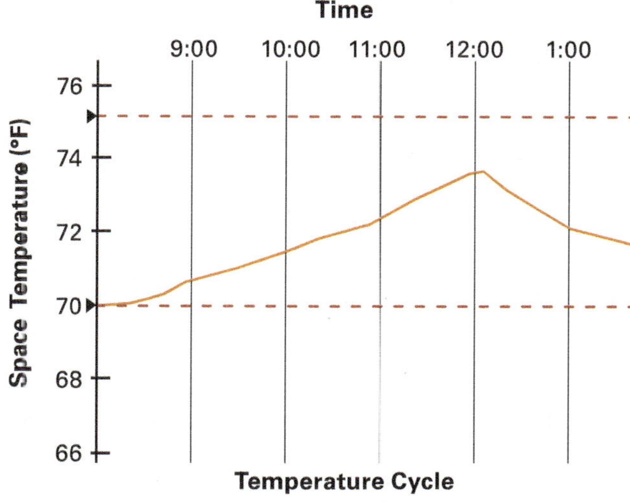

Figure 32 Changes are small and occur gradually.

3.4.2 Digital Control System Example

The key to a successful control system is the integration of all the sensors and unit controllers. We will look at the integration of a typical *constant-volume* HVAC system.

A constant-volume system is one in which the volume of supply airflow remains constant, and the air temperature is controlled to achieve the requested conditions. The constant-volume system contrasts with a *variable air volume (VAV)* system in which the supply air temperature remains constant, and the volume of air changes to meet the demand. In a VAV system, a single unit can serve many individual zones.

A schematic of a constant-volume system is shown in *Figure 33*. The control system is comprised of several control loops: economizer control of mixed air, heating-cooling sequencing, and humidification-dehumidification sequencing.

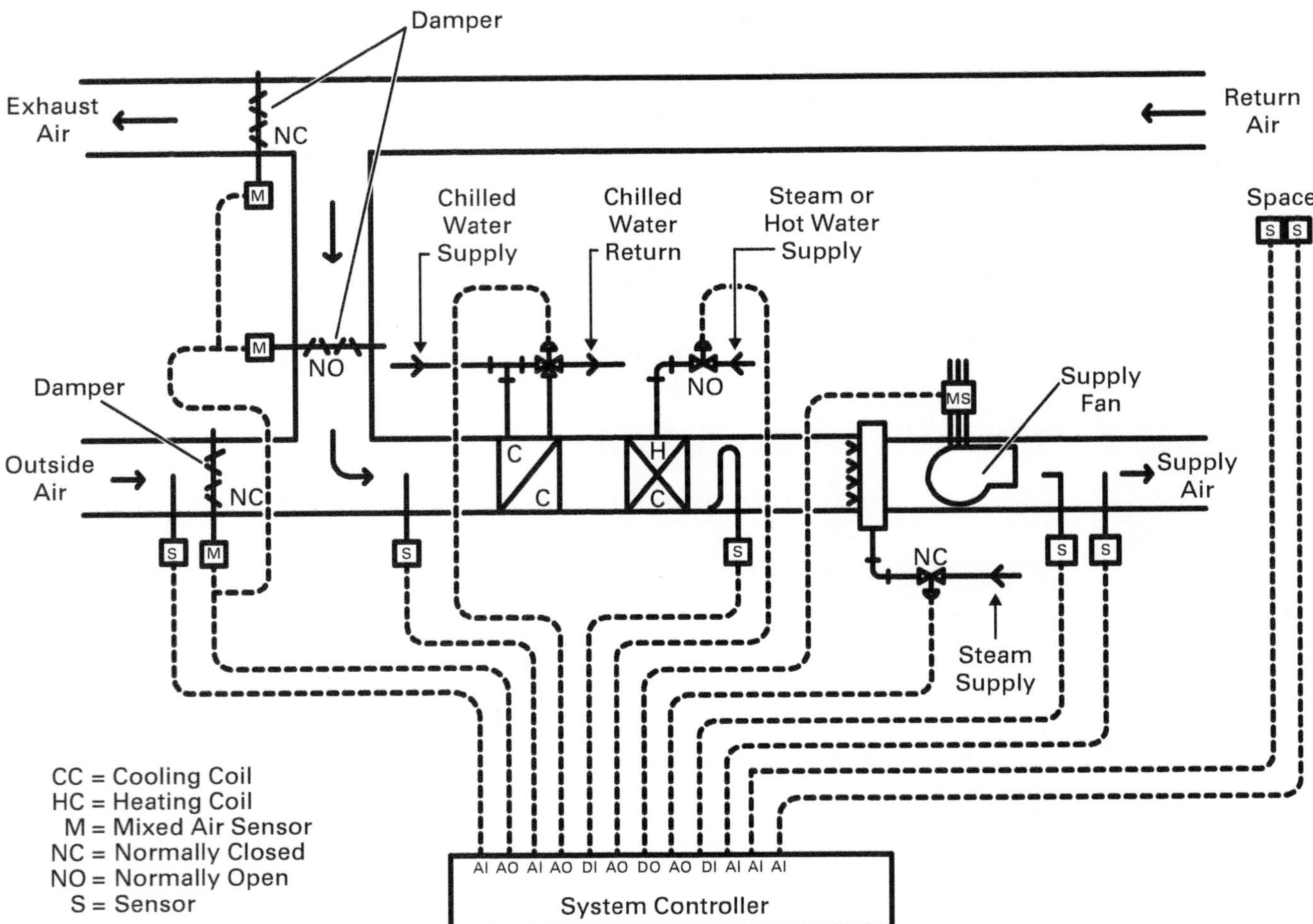

Figure 33 Example commercial hydronic, constant-volume HVAC system.

When the system blower is running, as sensed by a static pressure sensor in the supply duct, the damper control system is activated. A mixed air sensor maintains the supply air temperature by modulating the outdoor air, return air, and exhaust dampers, controlling how much air is admitted from each source. When the outdoor air temperature exceeds the setting of the outdoor air sensor, the outdoor and exhaust air dampers return to their minimum open position, as programmed, to provide the required ventilation only. In commercial buildings, a minimum amount of ventilation air must always be provided.

A space temperature sensor, working through the controller, maintains the space temperature by modulating the heating water valve in sequence with the chilled-water valve. A space humidity sensor monitors the space humidity. When the relative humidity drops below the setpoint, the humidifier steam valve modulates toward the open position. The valve's position is relative to the demand. The heating water and chilled-water valves are also positioned in proportion to the need for heating or cooling. To dehumidify a space, the chilled-water valve opens. With chilled water flowing through the coil, water vapor condenses and drains away. If the space gets too cold during a dehumidification cycle, the heating water valve is opened to reheat the air until the humidity is under control.

A freezestat, with its capillary tube laced along the face of the heating coil, will de-energize the unit fan, close the outdoor and exhaust dampers, and open the return air damper if the coils are exposed to temperatures that could cause them to freeze. Whenever the system blower is de-energized, most of the related components are also disabled.

3.5.0 Control Circuit Operating Sequence

An air conditioner control circuit cannot get much simpler than the one for a room air conditioner (*Figure 34*). It has a main control switch to enable the unit and a thermostat with a sensing bulb that responds to the temperature in the conditioned space. Once the unit is plugged in and turned on, it will cycle on and off by itself based on the temperature at the sensing bulb. Note that there is no transformer; the control circuit operates at line voltage.

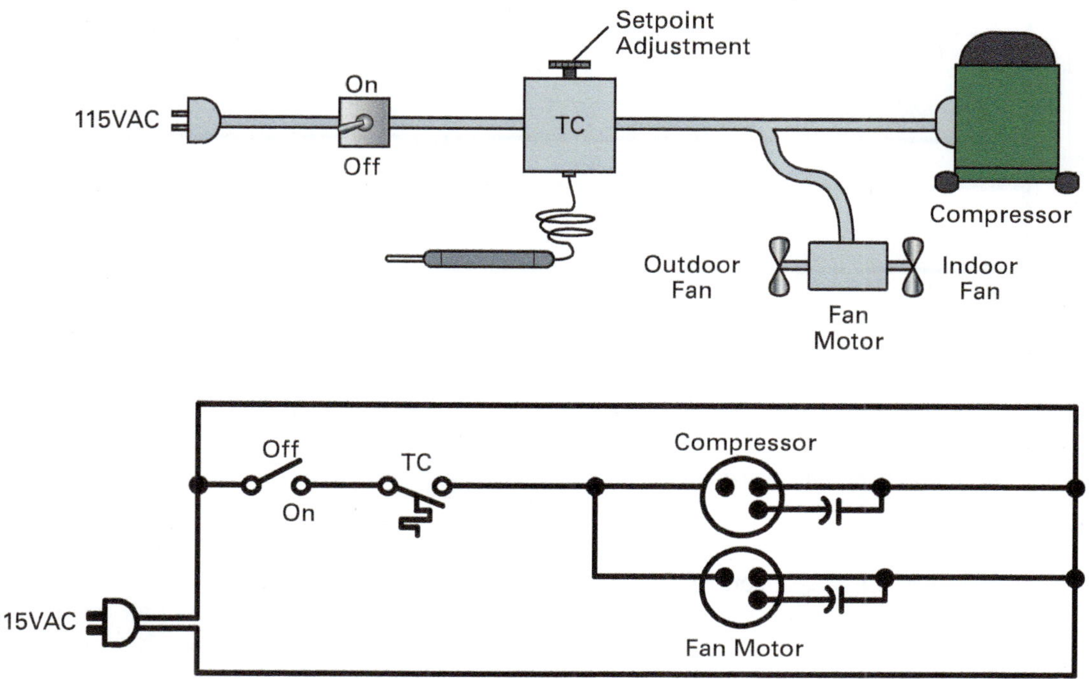

Figure 34 Room air conditioner circuit.

Figure 35 shows a control circuit more typical of a basic cooling system. It has features that are common to most cooling control circuits, such as the following:

- The control circuit operates at 24VAC.
- The indoor fan has a separate control. By setting the fan switch to On, the occupant can use the fan for ventilation without operating the compressor. When the Fan switch is in the Auto position, the fan relay (IFR) will energize whenever the room thermostat (TC) closes.
- The outdoor fan motor (OFM) runs whenever the compressor is on. When the unit is on, and TC closes, it completes the path to the compressor contactor coil (C). The normally open C contacts in the upper part of the circuit close, completing the current path to the compressor and OFM.
- The compressor will usually have some kind of overload protection. In this case, an automatic-reset thermal overload device (OL) is provided. It is embedded in the stator winding of the motor. On small refrigeration compressors, it is often mounted externally.

No matter how complex the control circuit appears, you will find the basic control arrangement shown in *Figure 35*—or something very much like it—at the heart of the circuit. Everything else will be special features to improve equipment safety, convenience, or operating efficiency. This is illustrated in *Figure 36*. This diagram represents a packaged cooling and gas heating unit. The circuit looks different because there are many more components.

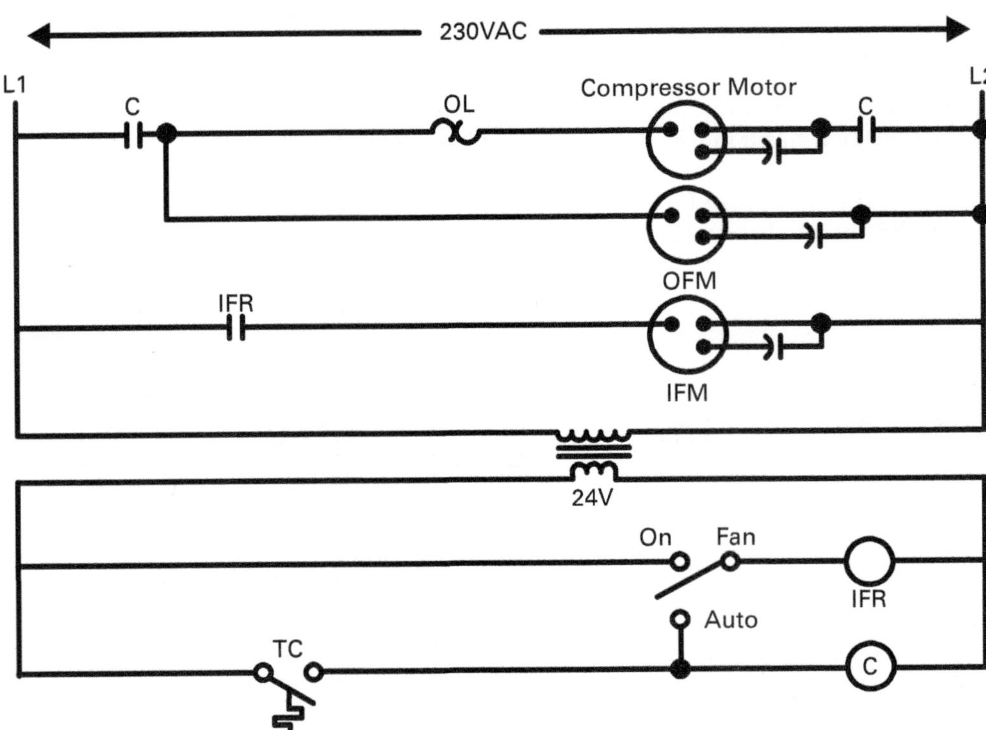

Figure 35 Typical cooling system control circuit.

However, if you trace the cooling control function in *Figure 36*, you will see it is essentially the same as the simple system shown in *Figure 35*. The heating controls have been added near the bottom of the diagram, along with a heating-cooling thermostat. The cooling control circuit has more options, such as compressor short-cycle protection, a crankcase heater, and a current-sensitive overload device. Take away these components, and you have a cooling control circuit nearly identical to the one in *Figure 35*.

Figure 36 shows the line voltage connected to L1 and L2 and the two conductors of the transformer secondary emanating from transformer terminals 1 and 3. Terminal 3 is designated as R, and Terminal 1 represents Common. This diagram reflects how devices are actually connected and is a common approach used by manufacturers. Although it may have some features of a ladder diagram, it is more accurately referred to as a *connection diagram*. Ideally, an HVAC unit is equipped with both a ladder diagram and a connection diagram to facilitate troubleshooting and comprehension.

Other characteristics of the circuit shown in *Figure 36* include the following:

- The unit has a two-speed indoor fan that runs on high speed for cooling and low speed for heating. In heating, the indoor fan is controlled by the time-delay relay.
- Operation of the inducer fan must be proven before the gas valve can be energized. The inducer pressure switch (PS) in the draft hood will close when the induced-draft motor (IDM) provides the needed pressure in the heat exchanger. If the induced-draft fan stops, the pressure will drop, and the switch will open, de-energizing the gas valve. The IDM is energized by the induced-draft relay (IDR) as soon as the heating thermostat closes.
- The heating section has two additional safety devices in series with the gas valve. A flame rollout switch (RS) will open if the burner flame rolls out into the control vestibule. This usually indicates insufficient combustion air or perhaps a leak in the heat exchanger. The limit switch (LS) is a heat-sensitive switch that extends into the air stream. If the heat exchangers overheat, it will de-energize the gas valve. The most common cause of overheating is insufficient airflow. This could be caused by a blower failure or clogged air filter.

Think About It

Circuit Analysis

Use the diagram in *Figure 36* to determine the answers to these questions.

1. Does the induced-draft motor turn off if the rollout switch opens?
2. If you connect a voltmeter from L2 to Terminal 4 of the IFR while the compressor contactor is de-energized, what voltage, if any, would the meter read?
3. Is the IFR energized or de-energized in the heating mode?

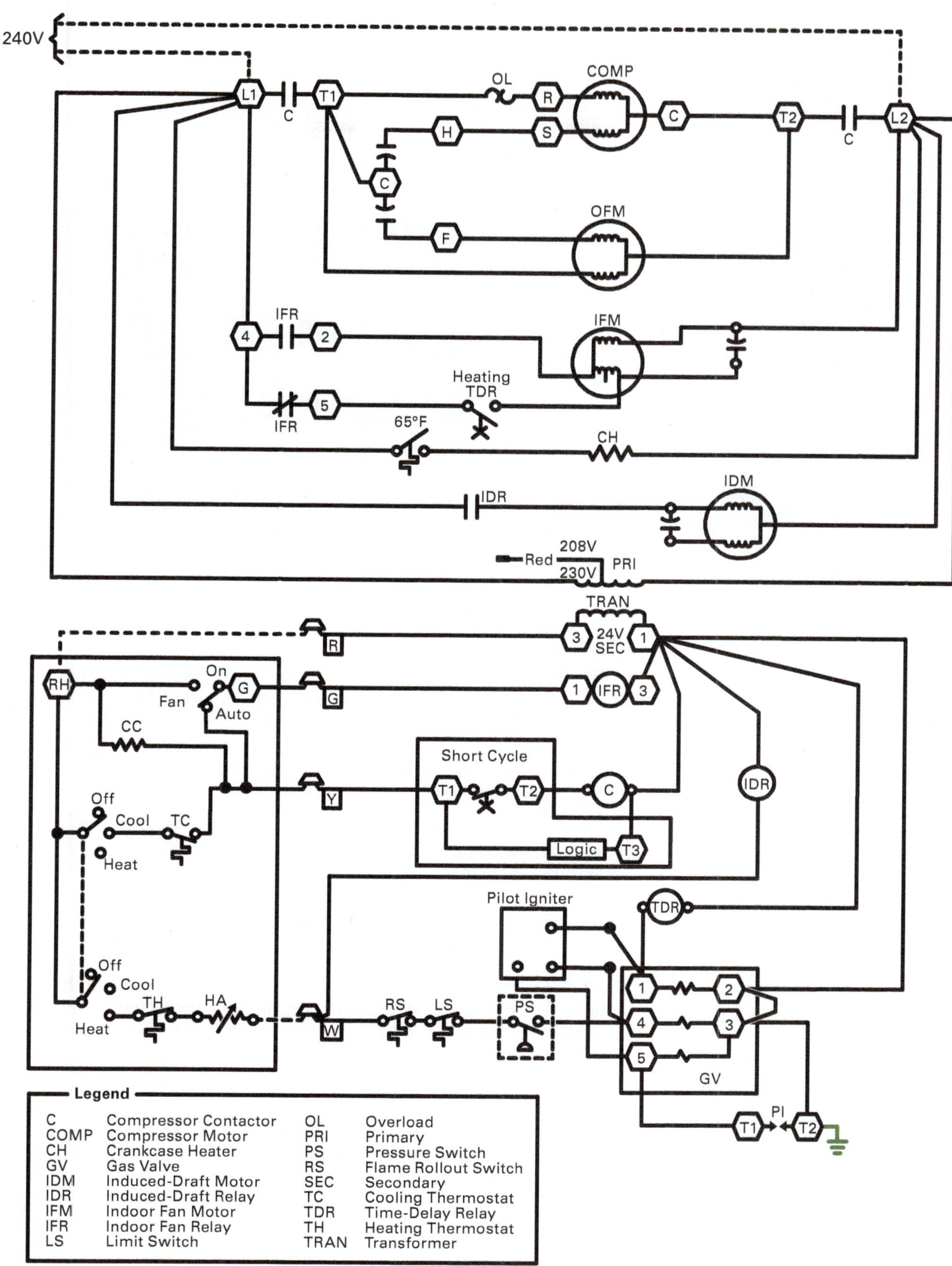

Figure 36 Circuit diagram for a packaged heating and cooling unit.

Thermistors

Thermistors are temperature-sensitive semiconductor devices. Their resistance varies in a predictable way with variations in temperature. This allows them to be used in a variety of control applications.

Thermistors have either a positive or negative coefficient of resistance. If the resistance increases as the temperature rises, it has a positive coefficient. If the resistance increases as the temperature drops, it has a negative coefficient. In HVAC systems, they are used to sense the air temperature in room thermostats, motor winding temperature when embedded in motor windings, the outdoor coil temperature as part of a defrost circuit, and countless other applications.

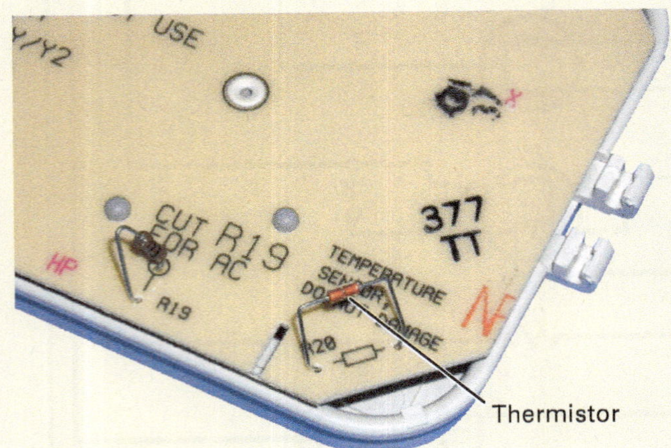

(A) Thermistor Used In a Room Thermostat

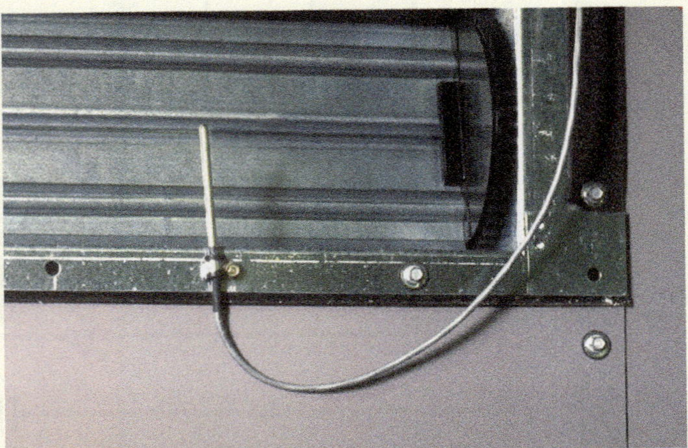

(B) Thermistor Used to Control Outdoor Air Damper

3.6.0 Troubleshooting

Troubleshooting heating and cooling systems requires skill and practice, as there are many possible failure points. However, in nearly all cases, the electrician can determine the cause of the trouble by using a systematic approach, checking one part of the system at a time in the right order.

WARNING!

HVAC systems contain high voltages, rotating components, and hot surfaces. Be careful when troubleshooting HVAC equipment and always wear the appropriate PPE.

Table 1A, *Table 1B*, and *Table 1C* are examples of troubleshooting charts. They are arranged so that the problem is listed first. The possible responses to identify the problem are listed in the order in which they should be checked. Finally, solutions to the various problems are offered, including step-by-step procedures where necessary. *Table 2* shows a more thorough troubleshooting guide for electric heat.

WARNING!

When damaged, the terminals of hermetic and semi-hermetic compressor motors in pressurized systems have been known to blow out. To prevent injury, avoid handling the wiring at the compressor terminals whenever possible. Use test points upstream from the compressor, such as on the load side of the contactor.

NOTE

Troubleshooting guides and their arrangement vary significantly. The guides provided here are examples only and do not offer a comprehensive troubleshooting guide for any specific system or unit. Always acquire the specific troubleshooting guide and wiring diagrams for the equipment being serviced.

CAUTION

It is unlawful to release today's common refrigerants into the atmosphere. Refrigerants must be recovered, recycled, and/or reclaimed by qualified technicians who are certified through testing developed by the US Environmental Protection Agency (EPA). Only technicians certified in accordance with Section 608 of the Clean Air Act may purchase and handle refrigerants or connect to systems containing refrigerants.

TABLE 1A HVAC Troubleshooting Guide (1 of 3)

Malfunction	Responses	Corrective Action
Compressor and condenser motor will not start, but the blower motor operates.	Check the thermostat to ensure it is set to Cool.	Adjust setting.
	Check the thermostat to ensure it is set below room temperature.	Adjust setting.
	Check all low-voltage connections for tightness.	Repair loose connections.
	Check the condensate overflow switch for an open condition.	Clear drain line, adjust switch position, or replace faulty switch.
	Check the pressure safety switches for an open condition.	Resolve refrigerant pressure issue or replace switch if defective. An EPA-certified HVAC technician must check the system charge.
Compressor, condenser fan motor, and indoor blower motor will not start.	Check the thermostat to ensure it is set to Cool.	Adjust setting.
	Check the thermostat to ensure it is set below room temperature.	Adjust setting.
	Check all low-voltage connections for tightness.	Repair loose connections.
	Check for a blown fuse or tripped circuit breaker.	Determine the cause of the open circuit and then replace the fuses or reset the circuit breaker.
	Check control transformer's secondary voltage for 24VAC output.	Replace open control circuit fuse or defective transformer.
	Check the line-voltage power source for correct voltage.	Resolve cause of power loss or low voltage.
Condensing unit cycles too frequently.	Check room thermostat location for drafts and similar factors.	Relocate as necessary.
	Check all low-voltage wiring connections for tightness.	Repair loose connections.
	Check if the thermostat cycle rate is incorrect.	Adjust cycle rate for fewer cycles per hour.
Inadequate cooling with condensing unit and indoor blower running continuously.	Check for refrigerant undercharge.	An EPA-certified HVAC technician must check the system charge.
	Check refrigerant circuit for blockages or failed expansion device.	An EPA-certified HVAC technician must check the system operating pressures.
	Check indoor and outdoor coils for cleanliness.	Clean coils as necessary.

Think About It

Baseboard Heat

What does the *NEC*® require for a disconnecting means when powering baseboard electric heaters?

TABLE 1B HVAC Troubleshooting Guide (2 of 3)

Malfunction	Responses	Corrective Action
Condensing unit runs, but the indoor blower motor does not run.	Check all low-voltage connections for tightness.	Repair loose connections.
	Check for 24VAC at the indoor fan relay coil and closed contacts.	Locate open in control circuit or replace faulty relay.
	Check for correct voltage at motor terminals.	Test motor windings and run capacitor; replace if necessary.
	Check for blower mechanical problems such as seized bearings or a loose/broken drive belt or blower wheel.	Repair or replace defective components.
Thermostat calls for heat (electric), but the blower motor does not operate.	Check all low-voltage and line-voltage connections for tightness.	Repair loose connections.
	Check for blown fuses or a tripped circuit breaker.	Determine the cause of the open circuit and then replace the fuses or reset the circuit breaker.
	Check control transformer's secondary voltage for 24VAC output.	Replace open control circuit fuse or defective transformer.
	Check for 24VAC at the indoor fan relay coil and closed contacts.	Locate open in control circuit or replace faulty relay.
	Check for correct voltage at motor terminals.	Test motor windings and run capacitor; replace if necessary.
	Check for blower mechanical problems such as seized bearings or a loose/broken drive belt or blower wheel.	Repair or replace defective components.
Thermostat calls for heat (electric); blower motor operates but delivers cold air.	Visually check the heating elements for breaks.	Replace broken elements.
	Test the heater LS for an open condition.	If the LS is open while cold, replace it. If it opens after a short operating time, look for cause of low airflow.
	Test the heat sequencer for control power and proper operation.	Replace defective sequencer or determine cause of open control circuit.

TABLE 1C HVAC Troubleshooting Guide (3 of 3)

Malfunction	Responses	Corrective Action
Thermostat calls for heat, and blower motor operates continuously, but system is unable to satisfy thermostat.	Check air distribution system for leaks.	Repair duct as necessary.
	Check for a blocked air filter.	Clean or replace filter.
	Check operation of individual heating elements.	Repair or replace defective elements as necessary.
	Test the heater LS for intermittent cycling.	Look for the cause of low airflow, such as a clogged air filter, dirty air conditioning coil, intermittent blower motor operation, loose drive belt, or loose blower wheel.
Excessive vibration at the indoor unit.	Inspect blower vibration isolators to ensure all are installed and intact.	Replace vibration isolators as necessary.
	Inspect blower to ensure all shipping materials have been removed.	Remove shipping materials as necessary.
	Check the blower motor mount for security.	Tighten mounting hardware as necessary.

TABLE 2 Troubleshooting Guide for Electric Heat

Generally the Cause (Check First)	Occasionally the Cause (Check Second)	Rarely the Cause (Check Last)
Problem: No heat—unit fails to operate		
• Power failure • Blown fuses or tripped circuit breaker • Thermostat switch not in proper position	• Control transformer • Control relay or contactor	• Faulty wiring • Loose terminals
Problem: Not enough heat—unit short cycles		
• Limit controls • Low air volume • Dirty blower wheel • Dirty filters • Heating element fuse(s) • Heat sequencer • Heat relay • Thermostat heat anticipator or cycle rate improperly set	• Control relay or contactor • Fan control • Thermostat level • Thermostat location • Outdoor thermostat • Blower bearings • Blower motor	• Loose wiring connections • Low voltage • Faulty wiring • Loose blower wheel • Ductwork small or restricted
Problem: Too much heat—unit cycle is too long		
• Thermostat heat anticipator or cycle rate incorrectly set • Thermostat out of calibration	• Thermostat location	• Control relay or contactor
Problem: No heat—unit runs continuously		
• Thermostat faulty • Control relay or contactor	• Faulty wiring	• Thermostat not level • Thermostat location
Problem: Cost of operation too high		
• Blower motor • Dirty filters • Outdoor thermostat setting incorrect	• Low air volume • Insufficient building insulation • Excessive building infiltration	• Low voltage • Fan control • Blower belt broken or slipping • Dirty blower wheel • Ductwork small or restricted
Problem: Mechanical noise		
• Blower bearings • Blower out of balance • Blower belt slipping	• Blower motor • Cabinet	• Low voltage • Control transformer
Problem: Air noise		
• Blower • Cabinet • Dirty coil	• Ductwork or grilles restricted	• Blower wheel • Dirty filters
Problem: Odor		
• Foreign substances (dirt or dust) on heating elements	• Low air volume • Humidifier contains stagnant water • Wet duct liner	• Faulty wiring • Loose terminals • Control transformer • Dirty filters • Dirty or plugged heat exchanger

Manufacturers of HVAC equipment provide troubleshooting and maintenance manuals for their equipment. These manuals are helpful tools for troubleshooting specific HVAC equipment. When unpacking new equipment, controls, and other components, always save any manuals or instructions that accompany the items. File them in a safe place so that you and others can readily find them. Many electricians like to secure the documents to the inside of an equipment cabinet door.

Crankcase Heaters

Lubricating oil circulates with the refrigerant throughout a refrigerant circuit. The oil is used to lubricate the compressor, but the refrigerant flows through the crankcase, consistently picking up small amounts of oil and carrying it along. When a compressor sits in cold temperatures and isn't running, refrigerant vapors tend to migrate outdoors to the unit and condense inside the crankcase. If the compressor is started with this condensed liquid refrigerant in the crankcase, the rapid expansion of the refrigerant to its vapor state (a violent boiling action) can carry most or all the oil away, leaving the compressor without lubrication. Liquid refrigerant can also enter the cylinders. Since liquids cannot be compressed, serious mechanical damage can occur.

Crankcase heaters are used to keep the crankcase warm, preventing refrigerant from condensing inside. Crankcase heaters come in a variety of sizes and shapes. One type, called a *bellyband heater*, clamps around the bottom of a welded hermetic compressor shell, as shown in the image here. Other styles are inserted into a well in the base of the compressor shell beneath the crankcase.

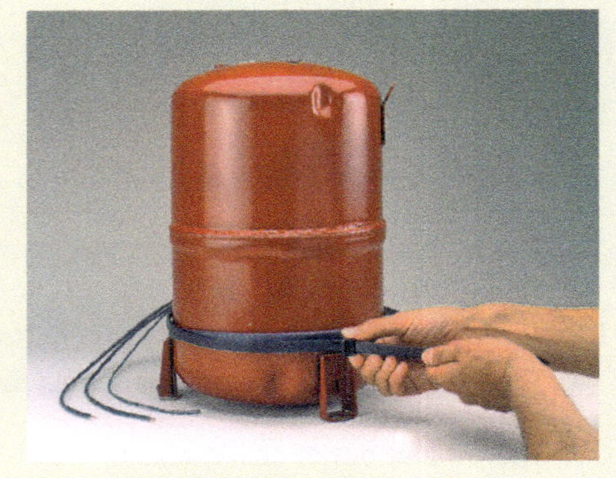

Source: Pentair Thermal Management LLC

The crankcase heater on some systems remains energized all the time. Others are controlled by integral thermostats that apply power to the heater only when the temperature is low and cycle off when the compressor is running. The heater shown in the figure has a positive temperature coefficient (PTC) characteristic; the current and heat production varies based on the temperature. The colder it gets, the more heat it produces. Crankcase heaters are important in heat pumps since they must operate in cold conditions.

3.0.0 Section Review

1. The purpose of a lockout relay in a comfort cooling control circuit is to _____.
   a. prevent the unit from operating on cool days
   b. keep unauthorized personnel from operating the equipment
   c. keep the equipment from operating during maintenance procedures
   d. prevent an automatic restart of the HVAC equipment

2. The purpose of a control to monitor the pressure in a gas furnace heat exchanger is to _____.
   a. verify the inducer motor is running and providing the correct airflow
   b. prevent the blower fan from turning on if the gas valve is not operating
   c. prevent the heat exchanger temperature from exceeding a preset level
   d. make sure the gas valve is operating before ignition begins

3. During a defrost cycle, heat pumps melt ice on the outside coil using _____.
   a. air supplied by another electric heater
   b. the compressor crankcase
   c. the thermostat heat anticipator
   d. hot refrigerant from the compressor

4. Which of the following would be considered a digital device?
   a. Pressure transducer
   b. Relay
   c. Thermistor
   d. Photocell

5. Which of the following would be an optional feature for an air conditioning control system?
   a. Indoor fan motor
   b. Compressor contactor
   c. Compressor short-cycle protection
   d. Outdoor fan motor

6. Which of these causes could be immediately eliminated if a compressor and condenser fan will not start?
   a. Defective indoor fan motor
   b. Thermostat failure
   c. Open pressure switch
   d. Thermostat not set below room temperature

4.0.0 *NEC®* Requirements

Objective

Identify the *NEC®* requirements that apply to HVAC systems.

a. Identify the *NEC®* requirements for HVAC control circuits.

b. Identify the *NEC®* requirements for HVAC equipment.

Performance Tasks

There are no Performance Tasks in this section.

This section summarizes the *NEC®* requirements for HVAC controls, compressors, room air conditioners, baseboard heaters, and electric space-heating cables.

4.1.0 *NEC®* Requirements for HVAC Controls

Several sections of the *NEC®* cover the requirements for HVAC controls. For example, *NEC Article 424, Part III* deals with the control and protection of fixed electric space-heating equipment. *NEC Article 440, Part V* covers the requirements for compressor controls, such as contactors. *NEC Article 440, Part VI* deals with compressor and branch circuit overload protection.

In general, a means must be provided to disconnect heating equipment, including motor controllers and supplementary overcurrent protective devices, from all ungrounded conductors (neutrals). The disconnecting means may be a switch, circuit breaker, unit switch, or thermostatically controlled switching device. Both the selection and use of disconnecting devices are governed by the type of overcurrent protection provided and the rating of any motors that are part of the equipment.

In certain heating units, supplementary overcurrent protective devices other than branch circuit overcurrent protection are required. These supplementary overcurrent protective devices are normally applied when heating elements rated at more than 48A are supplied as a subdivided load.

In this case, the disconnecting means must be on the supply side of the supplementary overcurrent protective device and within sight of it. This disconnecting means may also serve to disconnect the heater and any motor controllers, provided the disconnect is within sight of the controller and heater, or it can be locked in the open position. If the motor is rated over $^1/_8$ hp, a disconnecting means must comply with the rules for motor disconnecting unless a unit switch is used to disconnect all ungrounded conductors.

A heater without supplementary overcurrent protection must have a disconnecting means that complies with rules like those for permanently connected appliances. A unit switch may be the disconnecting means in certain occupancies when another means of disconnect is provided as specified in the *NEC®*.

Figure 37 summarizes some of the *NEC®* requirements for HVAC controls, including thermostats, motor controllers, disconnects, and overcurrent protection. Additional *NEC®* regulations on motor controllers are covered in other modules.

Know the Code

Control and Protection of Fixed Electric Space-Heating Equipment
NEC Article 424, Part III

Know the Code

Controllers for Motor-Compressors
NEC Article 440, Part V

Know the Code

Motor-Compressor and Branch-Circuit Overload Protection
NEC Article 440, Part VI

You are also encouraged to study *NEC Articles 424 and 440*. Although most of this material has been covered in this module, reviewing these *NEC*® regulations is a good training exercise.

4.2.0 *NEC*® Requirements for HVAC Equipment

The *NEC*® has specific requirements for various types of HVAC equipment. These include compressors, room air conditioners, electric baseboard heaters, and energy management systems.

4.2.1 Compressors

NEC Article 440 contains provisions for motor-driven equipment, as well as for the branch circuits and controllers for the equipment. It also accounts for the special considerations related to hermetic compressors that are cooled by the refrigerant as it passes through the crankcase.

It must be noted, however, that the rules of *NEC Article 440* are in addition to, or are amendments to, the rules given in *NEC Article 430*. The basic rules of *NEC Article 430* also apply to air conditioning and refrigerating equipment unless exceptions are indicated in *NEC Article 440*. *NEC Article 440* further clarifies the application of *NEC*® rules to this type of equipment.

Where refrigeration compressors are driven by conventional motors (open-drive applications), the motors and controls are subject to *NEC Article 430*. They are not subject to *NEC Article 440*.

Other *NEC*® articles that will be covered in this module (besides *NEC Articles 430 and 440*) include the following:

- *NEC Article 422*, *Appliances*
- *NEC Article 424*, *Fixed Electric Space-Heating Equipment*

Room air conditioners are covered in *NEC Article 440, Part VII*. However, they must also comply with the rules of *NEC Article 422*.

Household refrigerators and freezers, drinking water coolers, and beverage dispensers are considered appliances by the *NEC*®, and their application must comply with *NEC Article 422* while also satisfying the rules of *NEC Article 440* since such devices contain hermetic compressors.

Hermetic compressors, circuits, controllers, and equipment must also comply with the applicable provisions of the following:

- *NEC Article 460*, *Capacitors*
- *NEC Article 470*, *Resistors and Reactors*
- *NEC Articles 500 through 503*, which cover hazardous (classified) locations and Class I, II, and III locations
- *NEC Articles 511, 513 through 517*, which cover special occupancies

Table 3 summarizes the requirements of *NEC Article 440*. *Figure 38*, *Figure 39*, *Figure 40*, and *Figure 41* elaborate on many of these requirements. *Figure 38* provides detailed *NEC*® information about motor compressors. Compressor branch and control circuit requirements are illustrated in *Figure 39*. *Figure 40* lists the requirements for HVAC-related lighting and switches. The requirements for 125V receptacles relative to HVAC equipment locations are illustrated in *Figure 41*.

Know the Code

Air-Conditioning and Refrigerating Equipment
NEC Article 440

Know the Code

Motors, Motor Circuits, and Controllers
NEC Article 430

Heat Pump Installations

Electric heat pump installations typically require supplemental electric heat to be installed in the indoor air-handling unit. They are needed because the heating capacity of the heat pump declines as the outdoor temperature drops and to temper the supply air during defrost cycles.

The size of the electric heaters depends on several variables. Some codes require the electric heaters be sized to satisfy the building's full heating load if the compressor is inoperative. In some colder climates, that could mean 20 kW or more of electric heating capacity must be provided. If a heat pump is being used to replace a fossil-fueled furnace in an existing structure and a large amount of electric-resistance heat is required, carefully evaluate the existing electrical service to ensure the service can handle the new load. In some cases, a new electrical service is required.

However, heat pumps can also be paired with fossil-fueled systems to create dual-fuel systems. The heat pump provides heat at temperatures down to the point where its capacity matches the structure's heat loss, while the furnace handles the heating load at colder temperatures.

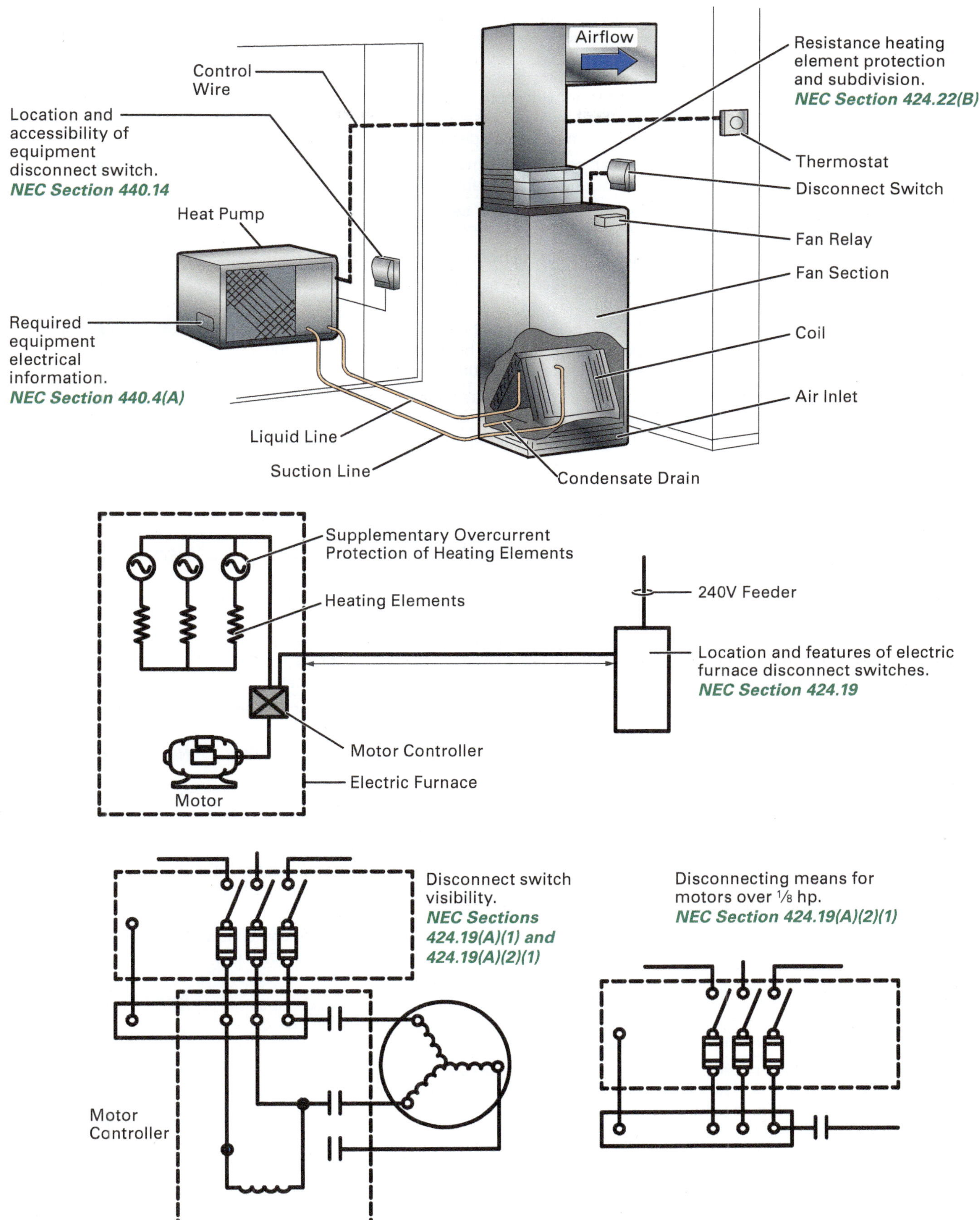

Figure 37 Summary of *NEC®* requirements for HVAC systems.

TABLE 3 Summary of *NEC*® Requirements for Hermetic Compressors

Application	*NEC*® Regulation	*NEC*® Reference
Labeling of hermetic compressors	Hermetic compressors must be provided with a nameplate containing the manufacturer's name, trademark or symbol, and the applicable electrical data. The words *thermally protected* must be present if they apply. The fault current rating and date of calculation must also be displayed.	*NEC Section 440.4(A)* *NEC Section 440.10(B)*
Marking on controllers	A controller serving hermetic compressors must be marked with the maker's name, trademark or symbol, and the applicable electrical data.	*NEC Section 440.5*
Ampacity and rating	Conductors for hermetic compressors must be sized according to *NEC Tables 310.16 through 310.19* or calculated per *NEC Section 310.14*.	*NEC Section 440.6*
Highest-rated motor	The largest motor is the motor with the highest full-load current.	*NEC Section 440.7*
Single machine	The entire HVAC system is considered a single machine, regardless of the number of motors involved.	*NEC Section 440.8*
Rating and interrupting capacity	The disconnecting means for hermetic compressors must be selected based on the nameplate full-load current or branch circuit selection current, whichever is greater, and the locked-rotor current, respectively.	*NEC Section 440.12(A)*
Cord-connected equipment	For cord-connected equipment, a plug and receptacle are permitted to serve as the means of disconnect.	*NEC Section 440.13*
Location	A disconnect must be located within sight of the equipment. It may be mounted on or within the HVAC equipment when practical.	*NEC Section 440.14*
Short circuit and ground fault protection	Amendments to *NEC Article 240* are provided in *NEC Article 440, Part III* for circuits powering hermetic compressors that must be protected from overcurrent due to short circuits and grounds.	*NEC Section 440.21*
Rating of short circuit and ground fault protective device	The rating must not exceed 175% of the compressor full-load current. If necessary, to accommodate starting, the device may be increased to a maximum of 225%. Do not exceed the manufacturer's value per *NEC Section 440.22(C)*.	*NEC Section 440.22(A)*
Compressor branch circuit conductors	Branch circuit conductors supplying a single compressor must have an ampacity greater than or equal to 125% of either the motor compressor full-load current or the branch circuit selection current, whichever is greater.	*NEC Section 440.32*
	Conductors supplying more than one compressor must be sized for the total load plus 25% of the largest motor's full-load current.	*NEC Section 440.33*
Combination load	Conductors must be sufficiently sized for the other loads plus the required ampacity for the compressor per *NEC Sections 440.32 and 440.33*.	*NEC Section 440.34*
Multimotor load equipment	Conductors must be sized to carry the circuit ampacity marked on the equipment per *NEC Section 440.4(B)*.	*NEC Section 440.35*
Controller rating	Controllers must have both a continuous duty full-load current rating and a locked-rotor current rating not less than the nameplate full-load current or branch circuit selection current, whichever is greater, and locked-rotor current, respectively.	*NEC Section 440.41(A)*
Application and selection of controllers	Each motor compressor must be protected against overload and failure to start by one of the approaches specified in *NEC Sections 440.52(A)(1) through (4)*.	*NEC Section 440.52(A)*
Overload relays	Overload relays and other devices for motor overload protection that are not capable of opening short circuits must be protected by a suitable fuse or inverse time circuit breaker.	*NEC Section 440.53*
Equipment on 15A or 20A branch circuit; time delay required	Short circuit and ground fault protective devices protecting 15A or 20A branch circuits must have a sufficient time delay to permit the compressor and other motors to start.	*NEC Section 440.54(B)*

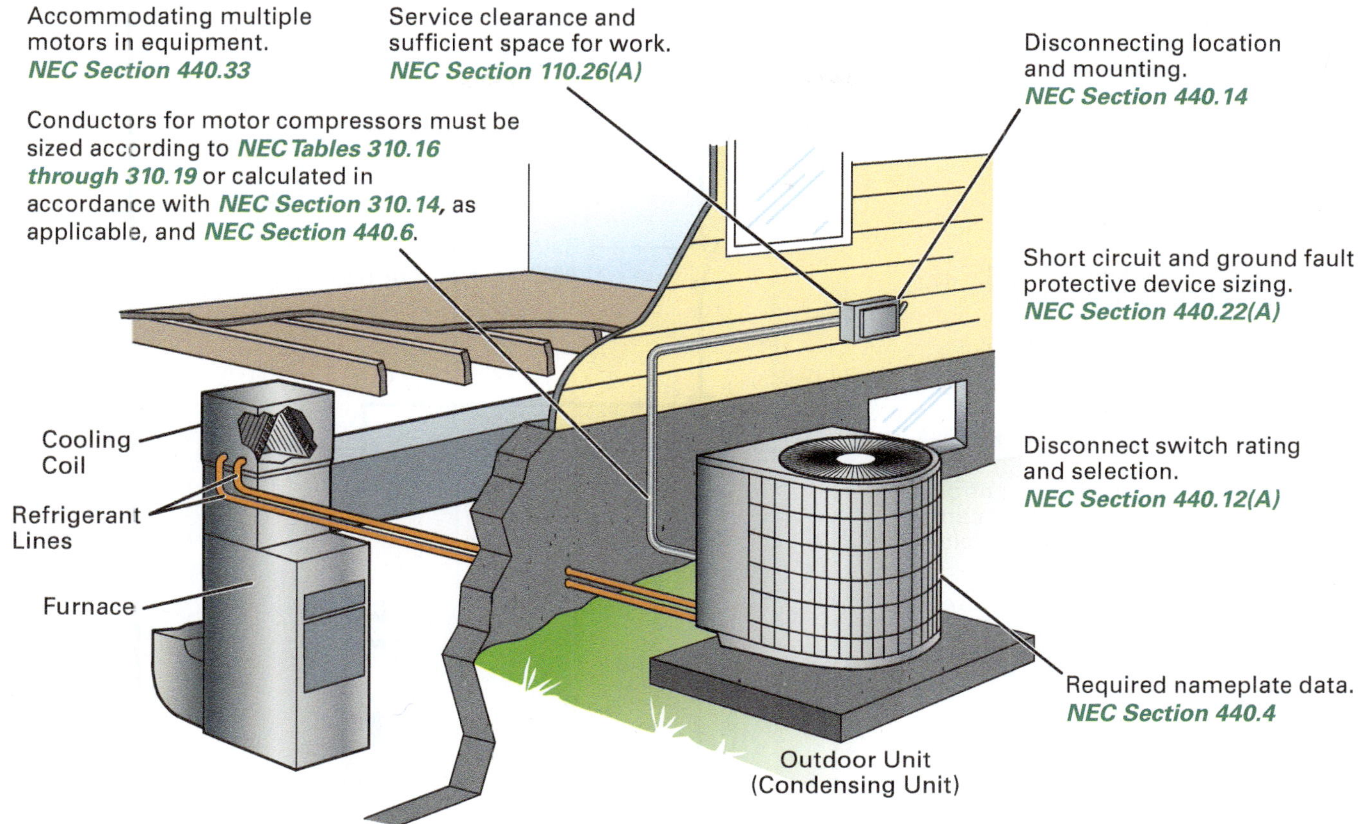

Figure 38 *NEC®* regulations governing motor compressors.

4.2.2 Room Air Conditioners

There are millions of room air conditioners in use throughout the United States. Consequently, the *NEC®* deemed it necessary to provide *NEC Article 440, Part VII* to ensure that such equipment would be installed so as not to present a hazard to life or property. These *NEC®* requirements apply to electrically energized room air conditioners that control temperature and humidity.

In general, this section of the *NEC®* considers a room air conditioner, regardless of any provisions for heating, to be an AC-powered appliance installed in a conditioned room or space that incorporates one or more hermetic compressors. This *NEC®* provision covers only single-phase equipment rated at 250V or less. This type of equipment can be cord- and plug-connected.

Three-phase room air conditioners (rare) and those rated at over 250V are not covered under *NEC Article 440, Part VII*. This type of equipment must be directly connected (hardwired) using a wiring method outlined in *NEC Chapter 3*.

Most room air conditioners covered under *NEC Article 440* are cord- and plug-connected to receptacles on general-purpose branch circuits. The rating of any such unit must not exceed 80% of the branch circuit rating if connected to a 15A, 20A, or 30A general-purpose branch circuit. The rating of cord- and plug-connected room air conditioners must not exceed 50% of the branch circuit rating if lighting units and other appliances are also supplied.

Figure 42 depicts the *NEC®* application rules for room air conditioners on branch circuits that also serve other loads, such as lighting. Note that the cord and plug can serve as the disconnecting means. The required overload protective device may be supplied as an integral part of the appliance and need not be included in the branch circuit calculations. *Figure 43* provides details related to room air conditioners on a dedicated circuit.

Equipment grounding, as required by *NEC Section 440.61*, may be supported by a grounded receptacle.

Know the Code

Provisions for Room Air Conditioners
NEC Article 440, Part VII

Know the Code

Wiring Methods and Materials
NEC Chapter 3

Know the Code

Grounding
NEC Section 440.61

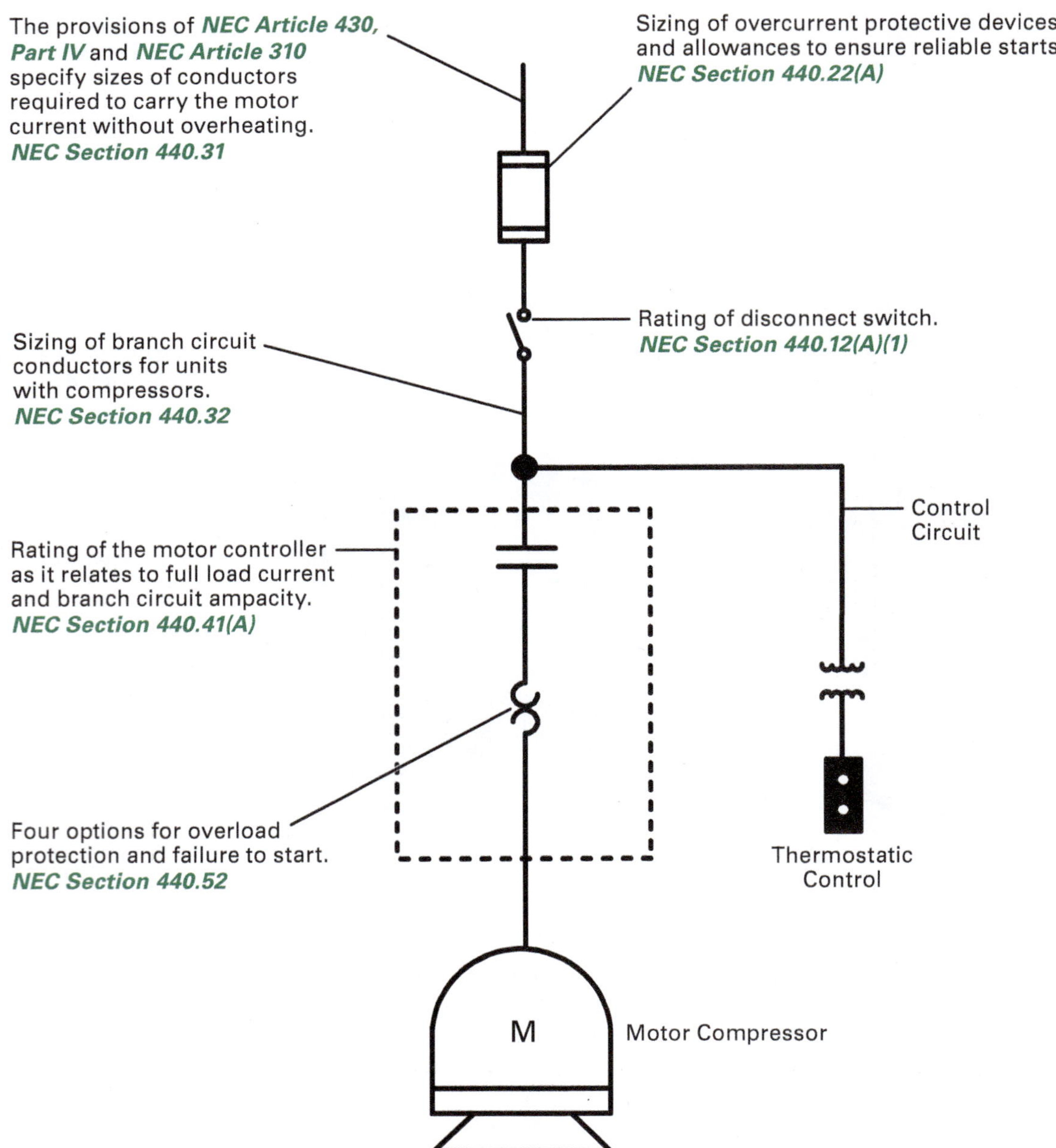

Figure 39 Compressor branch and control circuits.

4.2.3 Electric Baseboard Heaters

All requirements of the *NEC*® apply for the installation of electric baseboard heaters, especially *NEC Article 424, Fixed Electric Space-Heating Equipment*. Electric baseboard heaters must not be used where exposed to physical damage without adequate protection. Heaters and related equipment must be approved for installation in damp or wet locations and must be installed so that water cannot enter wired sections of the heater or the electrical components.

Proper spacing between the heater and combustible materials must be provided. Each unit must be properly grounded per *NEC Article 250*. *Figure 44* presents some of the *NEC*® regulations governing the installation of electric baseboard heaters.

Know the Code

Grounding and Bonding
NEC Article 250

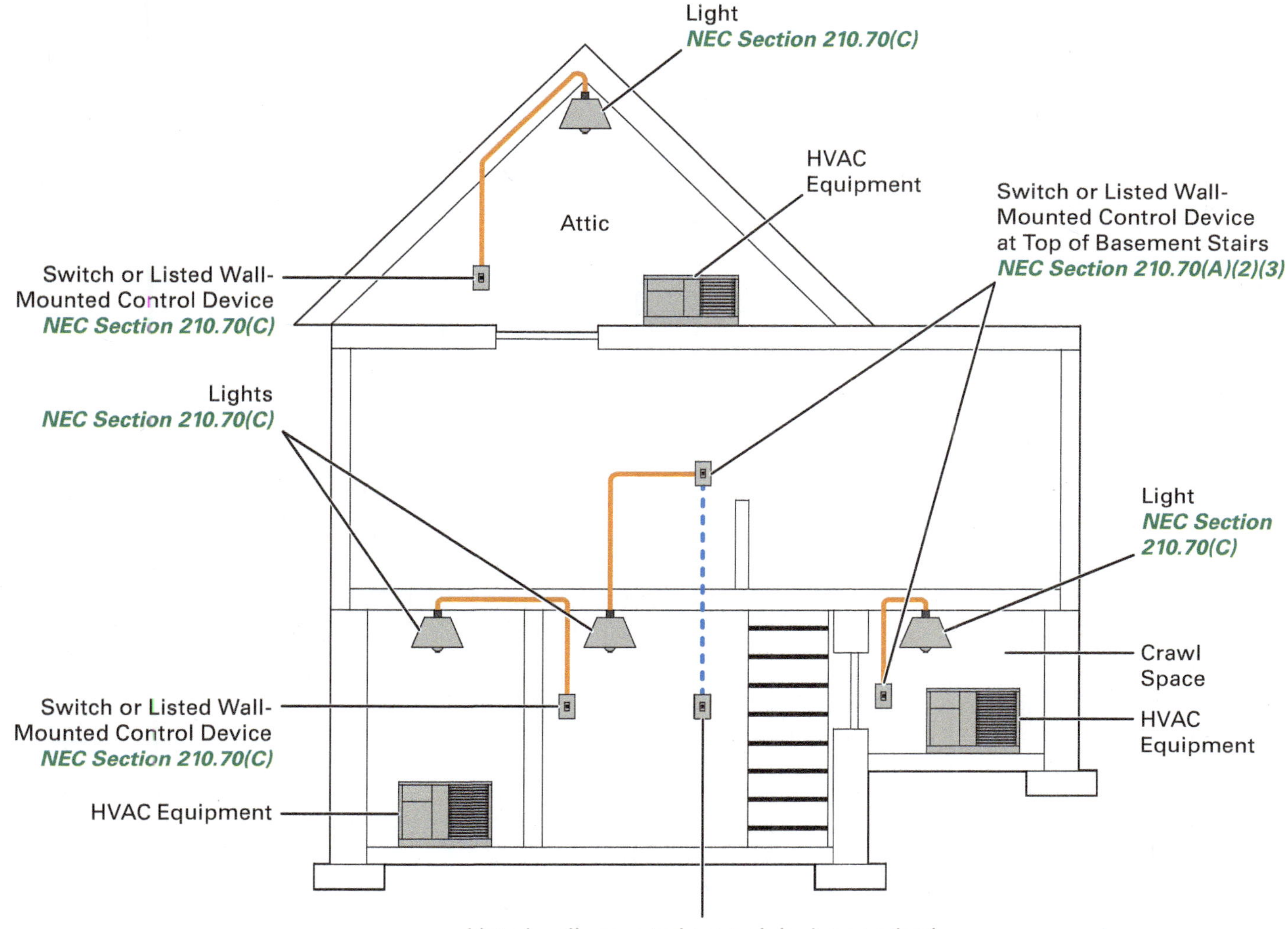

Figure 40 *NEC*® requirements for lighting and switches for HVAC equipment.

4.2.4 Electric Space-Heating Cable

Always ensure that heating cable is connected to the proper voltage. A 120V cable connected to a 240V circuit will result in a melted or damaged cable because the heat output is quadrupled. Likewise, a 240V heating cable connected to a 120V circuit will produce only 25% of its rated wattage. See *Figure 45* for a summary of *NEC*® requirements governing the installation of electric space-heating cable.

4.2.5 Energy Management Systems

An energy management system consists of monitors, communications equipment, controllers, timers, and other devices that monitor or control electrical loads, power production or source selection, or storage sources. *NEC Section 750.20* covers alternate power sources that can be controlled by the energy management system. *NEC Section 750.30(A)* covers the systems connected to load-shedding controls that cannot be controlled by the energy management system. *NEC Article 705* covers interconnected electric power production sources, such as solar photovoltaic (PV) systems. *NEC Article 706* applies to permanently installed energy storage systems.

Know the Code

Alternate Power Systems
NEC Section 750.20

Know the Code

Load Shedding Controls
NEC Section 750.30(A)

Know the Code

Interconnected Electric Power Production Sources
NEC Article 705

Know the Code

Energy Storage Systems
NEC Article 706

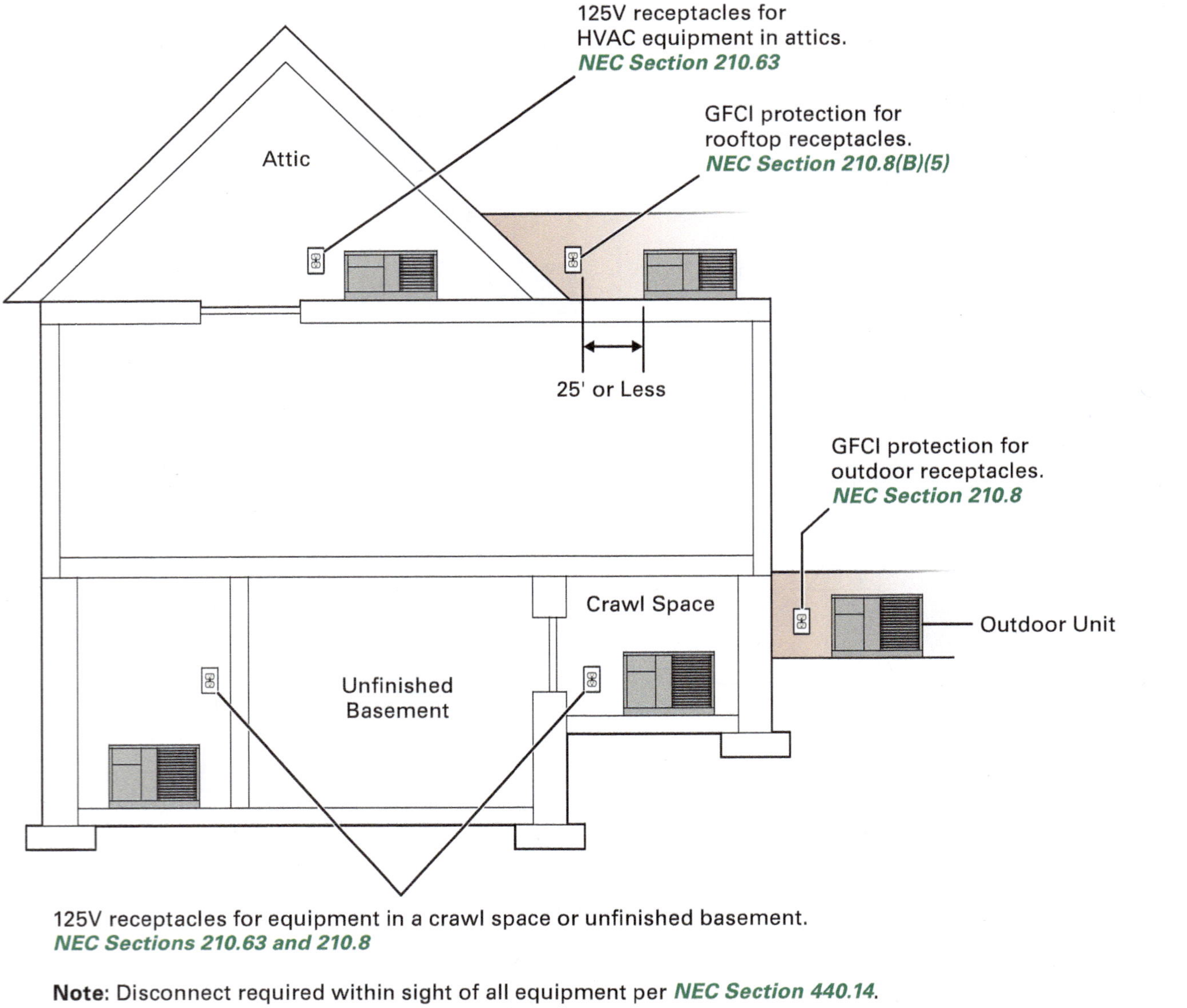

125V receptacles for
HVAC equipment in attics.
NEC Section 210.63
GFCI protection for
rooftop receptacles.
NEC Section 210.8(B)(5)
Attic
25' or Less
GFCI protection for
outdoor receptacles.
NEC Section 210.8
Crawl Space
Outdoor Unit
Unfinished
Basement
125V receptacles for equipment in a crawl space or unfinished basement.
NEC Sections 210.63 and 210.8
Note: Disconnect required within sight of all equipment per NEC Section 440.14.

Figure 41 *NEC*® requirements for locating 125V receptacles near HVAC equipment.

Air conditioning unit maximum rating
when powered by a shared circuit.
NEC Section 440.62(C)
Location and accessibility of
manual controls.
NEC Section 440.63
Maximum cord length of 10' for 120VAC
units and 6' for 208/240VAC units.
NEC Section 440.64
Cord and plug as a disconnect.
NEC Section 440.63
20A
Circuit
Breaker
Lighting
Receptacle
Receptacle
for Room
Air Conditioner

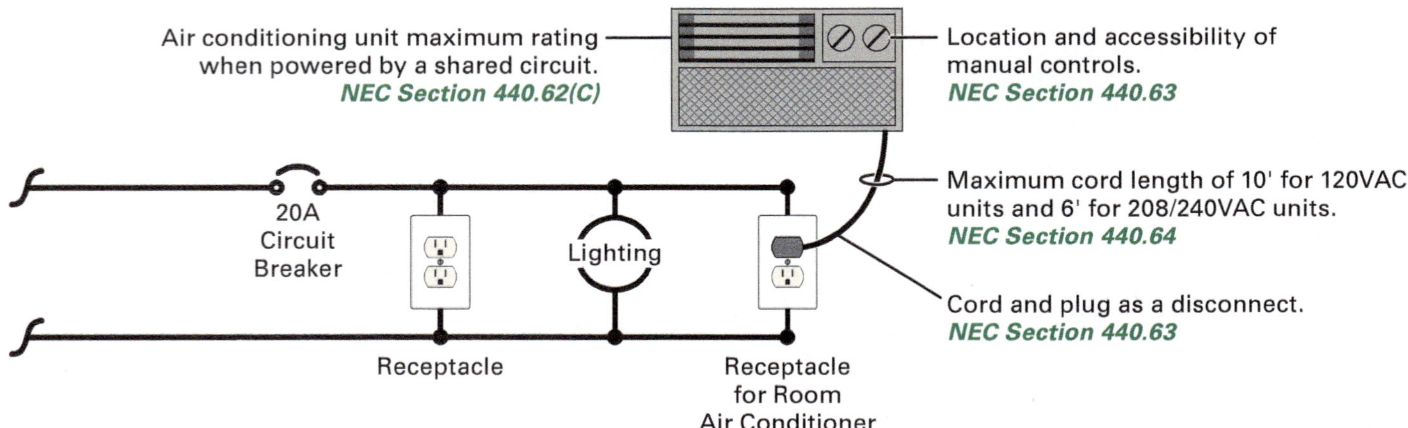

Figure 42 Branch circuits for room air conditioners.

Maximum electrical rating for units on a dedicated circuit.
NEC Section 440.62(B)
Location and accessibility of manual controls.
NEC Section 440.63
Maximum cord length of 10' for 120VAC units and 6' for 208/240VAC units.
NEC Section 440.64
Cord and plug as a disconnect.
NEC Section 440.63
Receptacle for Room Air Conditioner

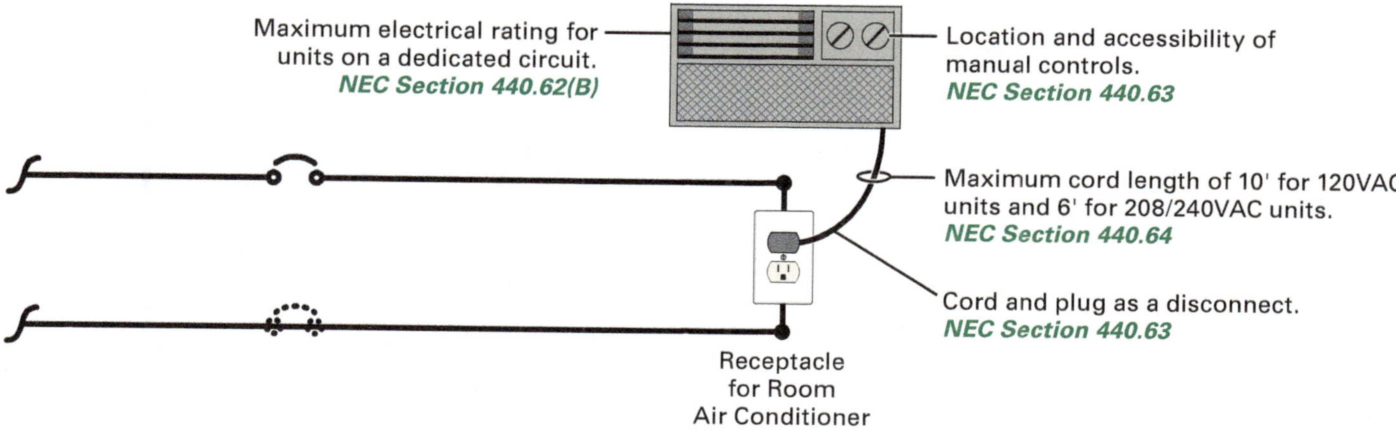

Figure 43 Room air conditioner connected to a dedicated branch circuit.

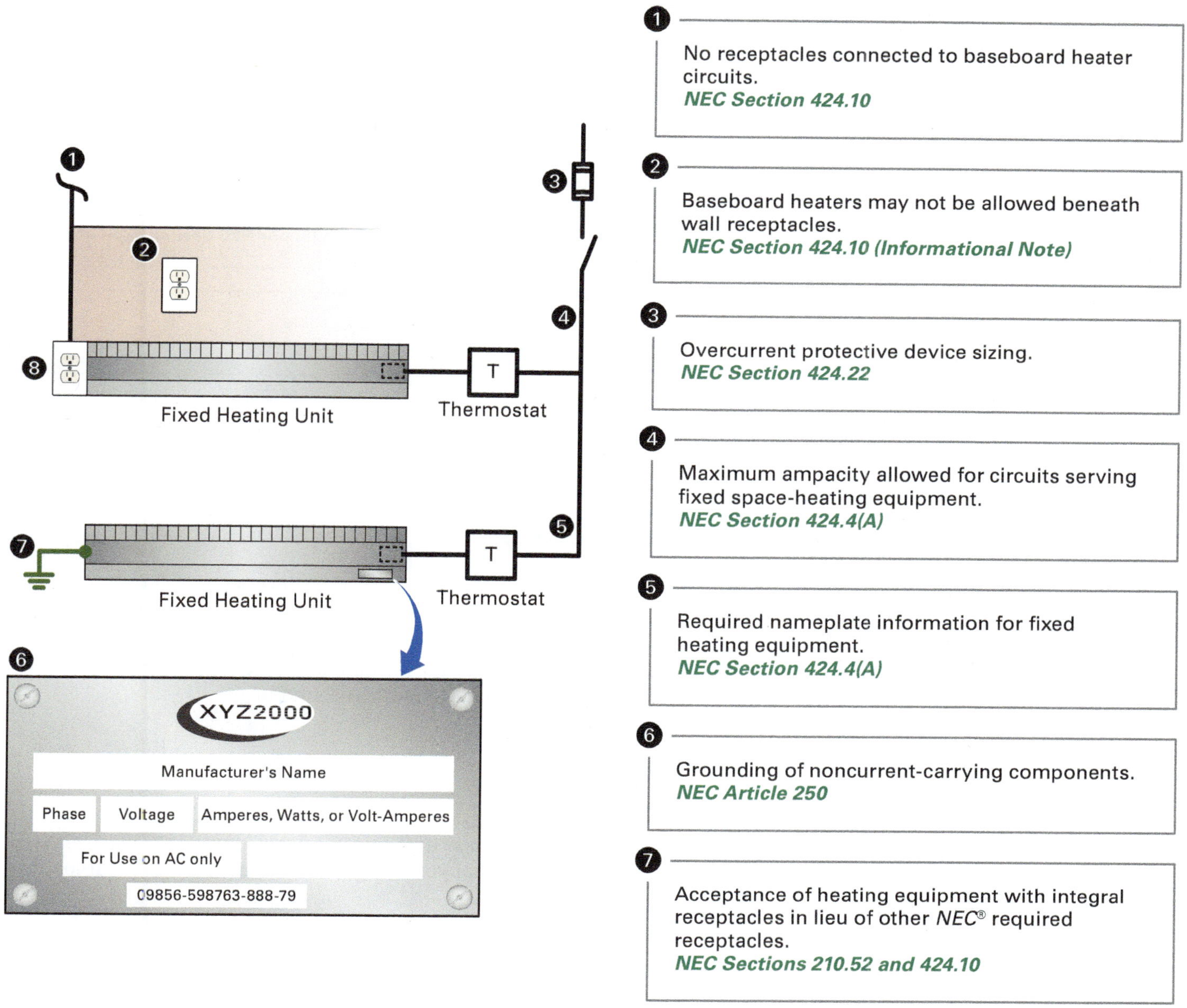

1
2
3
4
5
6
7
8
Fixed Heating Unit
Thermostat
T
Fixed Heating Unit
Thermostat
T
XYZ2000
Manufacturer's Name
Phase
Voltage
Amperes, Watts, or Volt-Amperes
For Use on AC only
09856-598763-888-79
1 No receptacles connected to baseboard heater circuits. NEC Section 424.10
2 Baseboard heaters may not be allowed beneath wall receptacles. NEC Section 424.10 (Informational Note)
3 Overcurrent protective device sizing. NEC Section 424.22
4 Maximum ampacity allowed for circuits serving fixed space-heating equipment. NEC Section 424.4(A)
5 Required nameplate information for fixed heating equipment. NEC Section 424.4(A)
6 Grounding of noncurrent-carrying components. NEC Article 250
7 Acceptance of heating equipment with integral receptacles in lieu of other NEC® required receptacles. NEC Sections 210.52 and 424.10

Note: *NEC Table 240.3* refers to *NEC Article 424*.

Figure 44 *NEC*® installation guidelines for electric baseboard heaters.

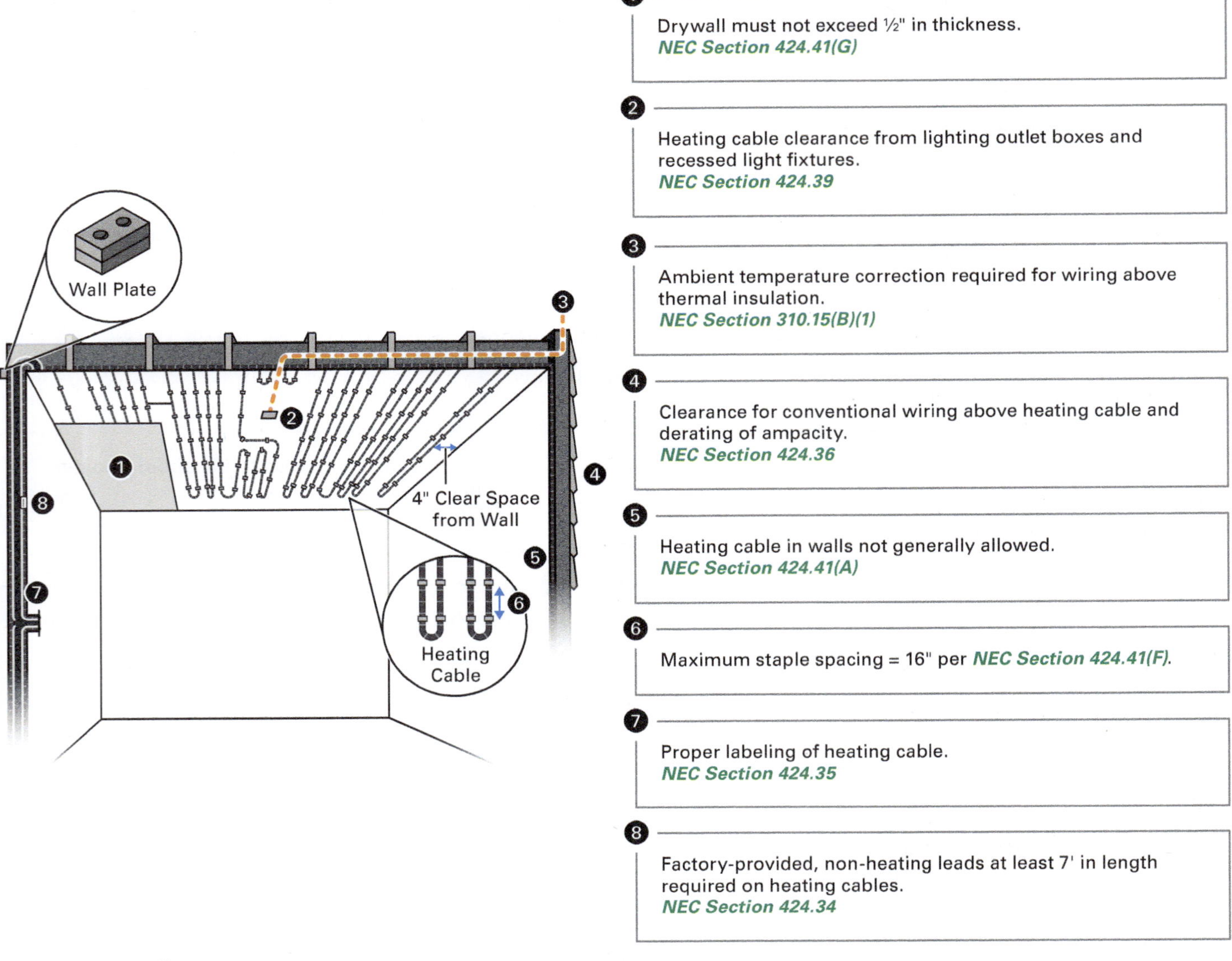

Figure 45 *NEC*® regulations for the installation of electric space-heating cable.

4.0.0 Section Review

1. The *NEC*® requirements for the location and accessibility of air conditioning equipment disconnects is found in _____.
   a. *NEC Section 440.4*
   b. *NEC Section 440.14*
   c. *NEC Section 440.52*
   d. *NEC Section 440.65*

2. Conductors supplying more than one hermetic compressor *must* be sized for the total load plus what percentage of the largest motor's full-load current?
   a. 10
   b. 15
   c. 25
   d. 35

Module 26408-23 Review Questions

1. In a boiler system, the heat exchange medium is _____.
   a. water
   b. refrigerant
   c. air
   d. oxygen

2. The component in an air conditioning or refrigeration system to which the heat from the conditioned space or item being cooled is transferred to the refrigerant is the _____.
   a. compressor
   b. condenser
   c. expansion device
   d. evaporator

3. The device that provides the pressure drop that lowers the boiling point of the refrigerant in a refrigerant circuit is the_____.
   a. compressor
   b. condenser
   c. expansion device
   d. evaporator

4. In the mechanical refrigeration cycle, the refrigerant leaving the evaporator is a _____.
   a. high-pressure, high-temperature liquid
   b. low-pressure, low-temperature vapor
   c. high-pressure, low-temperature vapor
   d. low-pressure, low-temperature liquid

5. Low-voltage (24VAC) control circuits are used in HVAC systems because _____.
   a. step-down transformers can only produce 24V output
   b. 24V power is safer
   c. it is mandated by law
   d. it is the same voltage used to operate the compressor and fan motors

6. A heat anticipator is used in an electromechanical heating thermostat to _____.
   a. start the heat before the temperature falls to the thermostat setpoint
   b. keep the thermostat warm on cold days
   c. turn on a light to let the occupants know when the furnace is starting
   d. shut down the furnace shortly before the thermostat setpoint would otherwise be satisfied

7. The differential in an automatic-changeover thermostat is _____.
   a. the difference between the cut-in and cut-out points of the thermostat
   b. the difference between the cooling and heating setpoints
   c. always at least 5°F (~2.8°C)
   d. the difference between the settings of the heat anticipator and the cooling compensator

8. A good location for a thermostat is _____.
   a. anywhere that it will receive direct sunlight
   b. about 5' (1.52 m) above the floor on an outside wall
   c. about 5' (1.52 m) above the floor on an inside wall
   d. in a corner where there is minimum air circulation

9. In a standard thermostat wiring scheme, the R wire originates from the _____.
   a. fan relay
   b. secondary of the 24V control transformer
   c. reversing valve
   d. heating thermostat

10. In a standard thermostat wiring scheme, the G terminal would be connected to the _____.
    a. primary control
    b. cooling control
    c. indoor blower relay
    d. reversing valve

11. The function of a heat sequencer is to _____.
    a. make sure the condenser fan starts before the compressor
    b. prevent the compressor from restarting before system pressures can equalize
    c. stagger the start of electric heaters to prevent circuit overload
    d. run the compressor every five minutes to make sure it does not seize

12. The purpose of a compressor short-cycle timer is to _____.
    a. prevent the compressor contactor from re-energizing before system pressures can equalize
    b. ensure the compressor runs for at least five minutes when it cycles on
    c. keep track of how often the compressor turns on
    d. run the compressor every five minutes to make sure it does not freeze up

13. When a typical heat pump is operating in defrost mode, what usually happens indoors?
    a. The unit continues to provide compression heat.
    b. The indoor blower turns off.
    c. Frost melts from the indoor coil and drains away.
    d. An electric heater cycles on to temper the cold air.

14. The type of digital control building system designed to serve multiple zones is the _____.
    a. constant-volume system
    b. variable temperature system
    c. variable air-volume system
    d. low-temperature system

15. In the electrical control circuit of a cooling-only system, the outdoor fan motor _____.
    a. runs continuously
    b. runs at a constant low speed
    c. runs whenever the compressor is on
    d. runs whenever the compressor is off

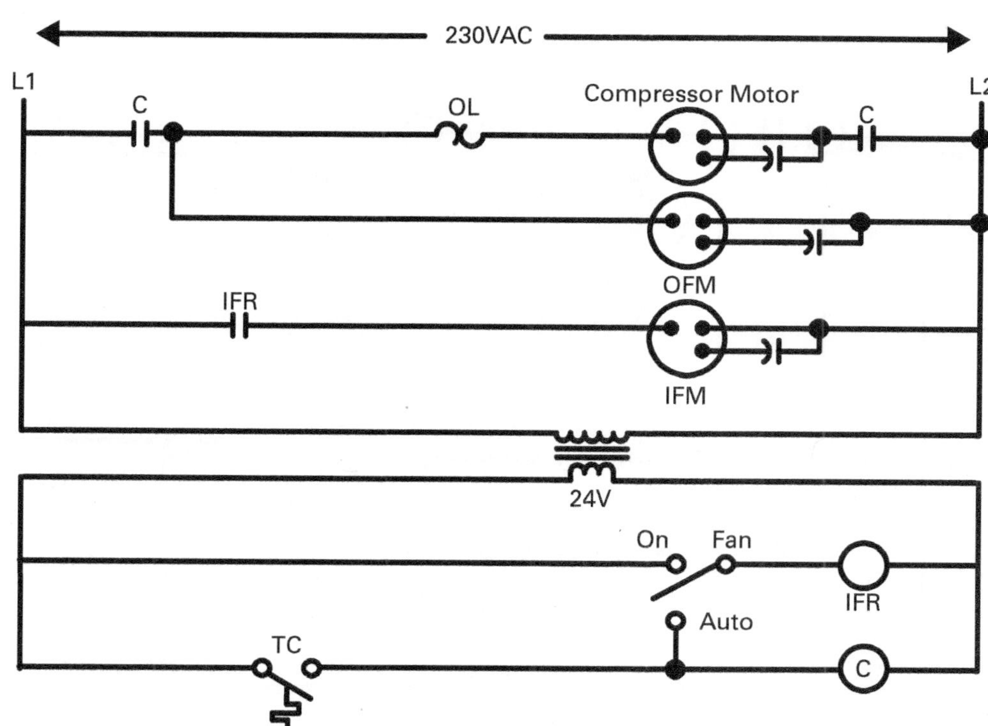

Figure RQ01

16. In *Figure RQ01*, if the compressor motor, OFM, and indoor fan motor (IFM) all fail to operate on a call for cooling from the TC, the *most likely* cause is _____.
    a. outdoor fan motor failure
    b. compressor failure
    c. control transformer failure
    d. compressor contactor failure

17. In *Figure RQ01*, if the IFR operates and the fan starts when the thermostat fan switch is set to On, and the relay operates when the switch is set to Auto, the *most likely* cause is a defective _____.
    a. indoor fan relay
    b. thermostat
    c. indoor fan motor
    d. compressor

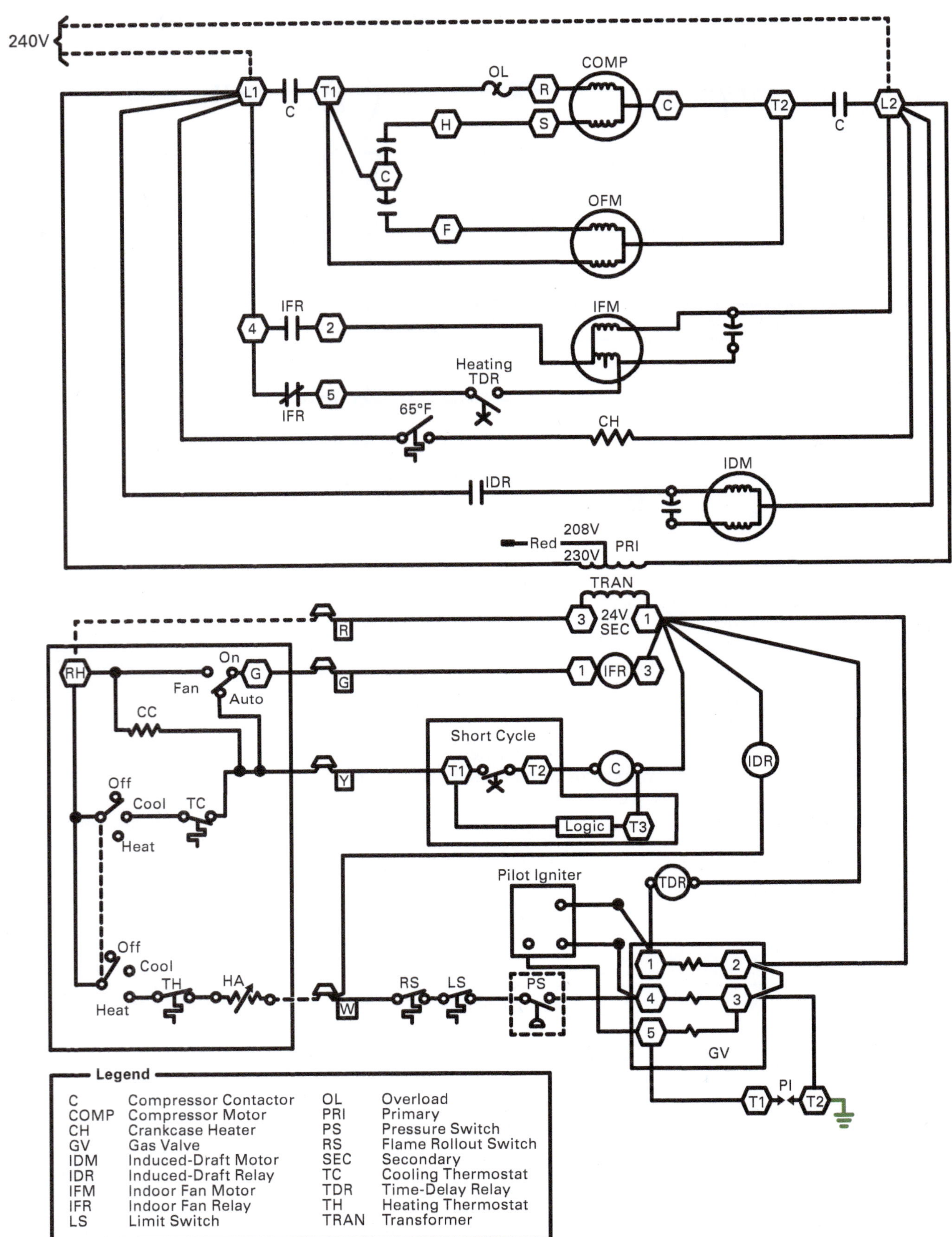
240V
L1
C
T1
OL
R
COMP
C
T2
C
L2
H
S
C
OFM
F
IFR
4
2
IFM
Heating
TDR
5
IFR
65°F
CH
IDM
IDR
Red
208V
230V
PRI
TRAN
R
3
24V
SEC
1
RH
On
G
Fan
Auto
G
1
IFR
3
CC
Short Cycle
Y
T1
T2
C
IDR
Logic
T3
Off
Cool
TC
Heat
Pilot Igniter
TDR
Off
Cool
TH
HA
Heat
W
RS
LS
PS
1
2
4
3
5
GV
T1
PI
T2
Legend
C Compressor Contactor
COMP Compressor Motor
CH Crankcase Heater
GV Gas Valve
IDM Induced-Draft Motor
IDR Induced-Draft Relay
IFM Indoor Fan Motor
IFR Indoor Fan Relay
LS Limit Switch
OL Overload
PRI Primary
PS Pressure Switch
RS Flame Rollout Switch
SEC Secondary
TC Cooling Thermostat
TDR Time-Delay Relay
TH Heating Thermostat
TRAN Transformer

Figure RQ02

18. In *Figure RQ02*, the yellow wire from the thermostat to the short cycle timer is connected to terminal _____.
    a. 1
    b. T3
    c. T2
    d. T1

19. According to *NEC Section 440.7*, the largest motor is considered the one that ____.
    a. weighs the most
    b. has the highest locked-rotor current
    c. has the highest full-load current
    d. has the highest input voltage

20. The provisions for room air conditioners are referenced in _____.
    a. *NEC Article 424, Part V*
    b. *NEC Article 427, Part IV*
    c. *NEC Article 430, Part XIII*
    d. *NEC Article 440, Part VII*

Answers to odd-numbered Module Review Questions are found in *Appendix A*.

Module 26408-23 Supplemental Exercises

1. List the four basic refrigerant circuit components used in a cooling/refrigeration system.

   ____

   ____

2. Heat pumps provide heat by __________.

3. Why does a bimetal strip bend as the temperature changes?

   ____

   ____

4. What is a disadvantage of a bimetal thermostat when compared to an electronic thermostat?

   ____

   ____

5. The heat anticipator in a heating-only thermostat is a(n) __________ in series with __________.

6. What prevents an automatic-changeover thermostat from cycling back and forth between heating and cooling?

   ____

   ____

7. When you are installing a 24V thermostat, to which terminals of the thermostat should you connect the 24VAC power supply, and what color wires would you use?

   ____

   ____

8. Attempting to start a compressor against a(n) _________ in the discharge side can damage the compressor.

9. A limit control is a heat-actuated switch positioned above or beside _________.

10. The *NEC*® requirements for fixed electric space-heating equipment are covered in _________.

11. Which two conditions are typical factors in the initiation of a defrost cycle in a heat pump?

____

____

12. What is the difference between a digital signal and an analog signal?

____

____

13. The key to a successful control system is the integration of the _________ and the _________.

14. True or False? Heating equipment must have a disconnect switch or other means of disconnecting it from all ungrounded conductors.

15. Permanently installed energy storage systems are covered in the *NEC*® in _________.

Answers to odd-numbered Supplemental Exercises are found in *Appendix B*.

Answers to Section Review Questions

Answer	Section Reference	Objective
Section 1.0.0		
1. b	1.1.0	1a
2. c	1.2.1	1b
Section 2.0.0		
1. b	2.1.5	2a
2. a	2.2.2; *Figure 16*	2b
Section 3.0.0		
1. d	3.1.2	3a
2. a	3.2.3	3b
3. d	3.3.0	3c
4. b	3.4.1	3d
5. c	3.5.0	3e
6. a	3.6.0; *Table 1*	3f
Section 4.0.0		
1. b	4.1.0; *Figure 38*; *Table 3*	4a
2. c	4.2.1; *Table 3*	4b

User Update

Did you find an error? Submit a correction by visiting **https://www.nccer.org/olf** or by scanning the QR code using your mobile device.

MODULE 26409-23

Heat Tracing and Freeze Protection

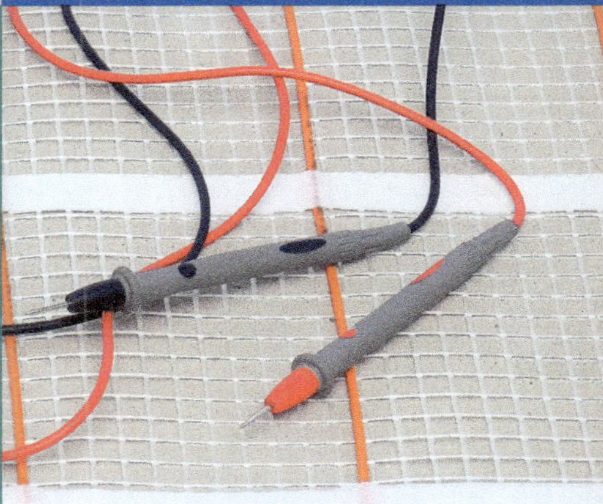

Source: iStock@suravikin

Objectives

Successful completion of this module prepares you to do the following:

1. Describe heat-tracing applications, components, controls, and selection/installation considerations related to piping.
   a. Describe common pipeline heat-tracing applications, cables, and power distribution considerations.
   b. Describe methods of controlling and monitoring heat-tracing systems.
   c. Explain how typical heat-tracing systems operate.
   d. Explain how to select the equipment and components for a typical heat-tracing system.
   e. Explain how heat-tracing system components are installed and the related *NEC*® requirements.
2. Describe roof, gutter, and downspout deicing systems and the relevant selection/installation considerations.
   a. Describe roof, gutter, and downspout deicing systems.
   b. Explain how roof, gutter, and downspout deicing system components are selected and installed.
3. Describe snow-melting and anti-icing systems and the relevant selection/installation considerations.
   a. Describe snow-melting and anti-icing system components.
   b. Explain how snow-melting and anti-icing system components are selected and installed.
4. Describe other electric heat-tracing and warming systems and the relevant selection/installation considerations.
   a. Describe domestic hot-water temperature maintenance systems and the relevant selection/installation considerations.
   b. Describe electric floor-heating systems and the relevant selection/installation considerations.

Performance Task

Under supervision, you should be able to do the following:

1. Prepare and connect heat-tracing cable in a power connection box or splice box.

Overview

Electrical heat-tracing systems keep piping systems at or above a given temperature for the purposes of freeze protection and temperature maintenance. In cold climates, freeze protection is needed because the thermal insulation installed around pipes is not enough to prevent the process fluids from freezing. This module presents heat-tracing and freeze-protection systems along with various applications and installation requirements.

NOTE

Digital Resources for Electrical

Scan this code using the camera on your phone or mobile device to view the digital resources related to this craft.

1.0.0 Introduction to Heat Tracing

Performance Task

1. Prepare and connect heat-tracing cable in a power connection box or splice box.

Objective

Describe heat-tracing applications, components, controls, and selection/installation considerations related to piping.

a. Describe common pipeline heat-tracing applications, cables, and power distribution considerations.
b. Describe methods of controlling and monitoring heat-tracing systems.
c. Explain how typical heat-tracing systems operate.
d. Explain how to select the equipment and components for a typical heat-tracing system.
e. Explain how heat-tracing system components are installed and the related *NEC*® requirements.

This module focuses on the circuitry and components used for electric heat-tracing systems. It also introduces other widely used types of electric heating and heat-tracing systems. The systems covered in this module include:

- Pipe heat-tracing systems
- Roof, gutter, and downspout deicing systems
- Snow-melting and anti-icing systems
- Domestic hot-water temperature maintenance systems
- Floor-heating and warming systems

Applying heat to piping that carries process fluids is a common requirement in many industries including petroleum, plastics, chemicals, pharmaceuticals, power generation, and food processing. Electric-cable heating systems, called *heat-tracing systems*, maintain the piping systems at or above a specified temperature. This is done to prevent the systems from freezing, to maintain fluid temperature and consistent flow, and/or to prevent condensation in the system. Non-electrical steam and hot-liquid heat-tracing systems can also be used for these purposes. However, electric heating is often the most practical and least expensive method of protecting piping, especially when long pipe runs are involved.

1.1.0 Piping Heat-Tracing Applications and Materials

The main reasons for using electric heat tracing on piping are freeze protection and temperature maintenance of the process fluids. In cold climates, the thermal insulation installed around pipes is not enough to prevent the process fluids from freezing. Piping that carries water, fuel, or chemicals usually needs to be heat traced to prevent freezing or thickening of the fluid at low temperatures. Heat tracing may also be applied to a tank or **vessel** to compensate for heat loss through thermal insulation.

Vessel: A container such as a barrel, drum, or tank used for holding fluids or other substances.

Liquids that drop below their freezing point form a solid obstruction in the piping system, thereby stopping fluid flow. As the liquid turns into a solid, it may also expand, causing severe damage to the piping. Pipes installed in the ground below frost level are sometimes an exception and do not require heat tracing. This is because the temperature at this depth remains relatively constant regardless of the outdoor air temperature.

Many industrial processes require temperature maintenance of piping to prevent the loss of heat in process fluids flowing through them or contained in tanks or vessels. Temperature maintenance can be divided into two main categories: *broad temperature control* and *narrow temperature control*. Broad temperature control is used to maintain the viscosity of process fluids to keep them flowing. Typical applications of broad temperature control are on fuel lines, cooking oil lines, and grease disposal lines. Narrow temperature control is used to keep process fluids within a narrow temperature range to maintain fluid viscosity and to prevent degradation of the fluid composition. Typical applications of narrow temperature control are on sulfur, acrylic acid, food syrup, and sugar solution lines.

Temperature maintenance is also used to prevent condensation from forming in piping systems. The **dew point** is the temperature at which a liquid first condenses from a vapor that is cooled. If an object's surface temperature drops below the dew point, condensation will occur. At night for example, humid air cools and often reaches its dew point, which results in the fallout of liquid water to the ground. Under certain conditions, this same event can occur inside some piping systems.

Dew point: The temperature to which a vapor must cool before it begins to condense into its liquid state.

The moisture that results from condensation in piping systems can cause operating difficulties, especially in gas burners where the control valve may become fouled by the liquid. In addition, natural-gas lines that contain condensed moisture may freeze at a variety of locations, stopping the flow. Moisture is especially harmful to compressors (since it cannot be compressed), and in the presence of hydrogen sulfide, it can produce harmfully corrosive sulfuric acid. Hydrogen sulfide is produced in some oil refineries during the crude oil distillation process.

A basic electric heat-tracing system consists of a power distribution system, electric heating cables, and interface components (*Figure 1*). Systems that are more complex may also incorporate a control and monitoring function with controllers, sensors, and alarms.

Several types of cables are used for heat tracing as well as other heating applications. These cables fall into three categories:

- **Self-regulating heating cable**
- **Power-limiting heating cable**
- **Mineral-insulated (MI) heating cable**

Self-regulating heating cable: A type of heating cable that inversely adjusts its heat output in response to an increase or decrease in the ambient temperature.

Power-limiting heating cable: A type of heating cable that shows positive temperature coefficient (PTC) behavior based on the properties of a metallic heating element. The PTC behavior exhibits a much smaller change in resistance in response to a change in temperature than that shown by self-regulating heating cables.

Mineral-insulated (MI) heating cable: A type of constant-wattage, series-resistance heating cable used in long line applications where high temperatures need to be maintained, high-temperature exposure exists, or high power output is required.

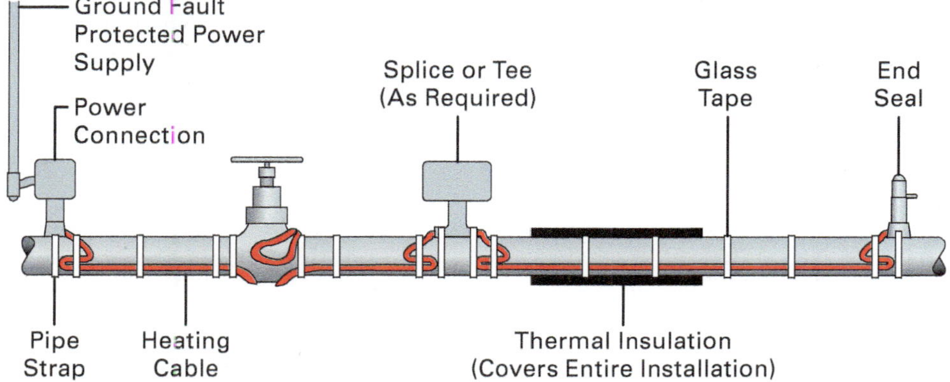

Figure 1 Basic electric heat-tracing system.

1.1.1 Self-Regulating Cables

Self-regulating cables are used for applications that require a heat output that varies with changes in the temperature of the air or other medium surrounding the heating cable. A self-regulating cable increases its heat output with a decrease in the ambient temperature and decreases its heat output with an increase in the ambient temperature. Typically, this type of cable is used for freeze protection and temperature maintenance on metal and plastic pipes. It is also widely used for other applications such as snow melting, anti-icing, and roof and gutter deicing.

One type of self-regulating cable is made in the form of a heater strip consisting of two parallel bus wires in a polymeric self-regulating conductive core heating element (*Figure 2*). The entire element is then surrounded by an insulating jacket, a braided tin-copper shield, and an outer jacket. Another type of self-regulating cable is similar in construction but uses a polymeric self-regulating conductive fiber as the heating element instead of the core-type heating element.

The self-regulating conductive core and conductive fiber heating elements are made of a polymer mixed with conductive carbon. This composition creates multiple electrical paths for conducting current between the parallel bus wires along the entire length of the cable. The core or fiber heating element of a self-regulating heating cable can be visualized as an array of parallel resistors connected between the bus wires, with each resistor having a value related to temperature. For this reason, a self-regulating cable is also referred to as a **parallel-resistance heating cable**.

Parallel-resistance heating cable: An electric heating cable with parallel connections, either continuous or in zones. The watt density per lineal length is approximately equal along the length of the heating cable, allowing for a drop in voltage down the length of the heating cable.

Self-regulating heating cables produce heat from the flow of current through the polymeric core or fibers. In both types of cables, the number of electrical paths between the bus wires changes in response to temperature variations. As the temperature surrounding the heater cable gets colder, the conductive core or fibers contract microscopically. This decreases the electrical resistance and creates numerous parallel electrical paths between the bus wires. Increased current flows across these parallel paths, producing heat that warms the core or fiber along the length of the cable.

As the temperature surrounding the heater cable gets warmer, the conductive core or fibers expand microscopically. This increases the electrical resistance and decreases the number of electrical paths between the bus wires. The current flow is decreased as a result and heat output lessens in response to the rise in the ambient temperature. Through the process of contraction and expansion, the core or fiber heating element acts as a self-regulating thermostat protecting the cable from damage due to high temperatures. This feature allows this type of cable to be overlapped on pipes and valves during installation without causing damage to the cable from overheating. *Figure 3* shows a graph of resistance and power versus temperature for a self-regulating heat-tracing cable.

Because of their parallel construction, self-regulating heating cables can be cut to length and spliced in the field. Self-regulating cables with a core heating element, also called *monolithic cables*, are used on metal and plastic pipes to maintain temperatures up to 225°F (107°C). Those with fiber heating elements are used on metal pipes for process temperature maintenance up to 250°F (121°C).

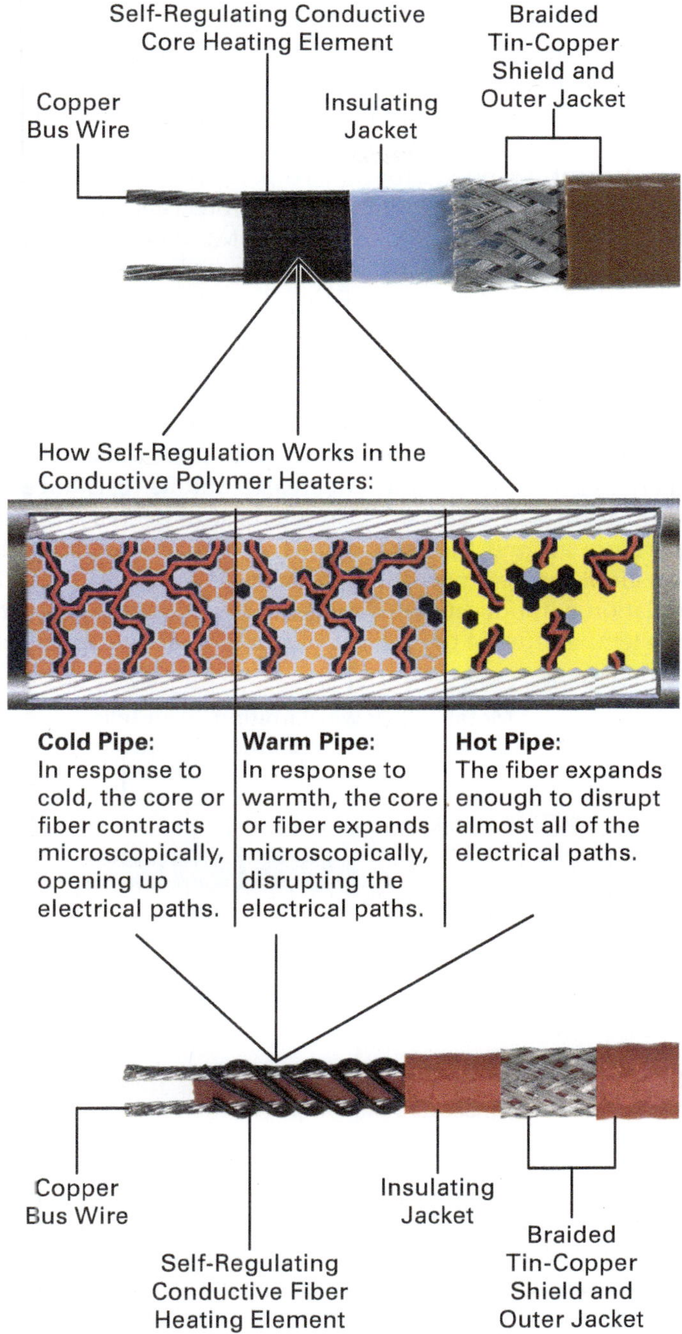

Figure 2 Typ cal construction of self-regulating heat-tracing cables.
Source: Pentair Thermal Management LLC

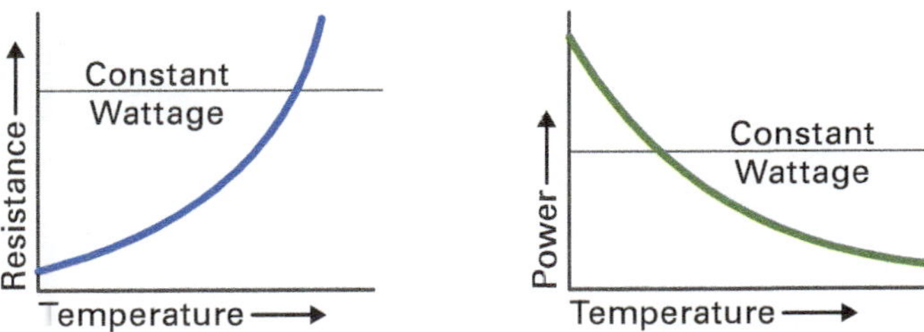

Figure 3 Resistance and power versus temperature for self-regulating heat-tracing cable.

1.1.2 Power-Limiting Cables

Power-limiting heating cables are a type of parallel-resistance, self-regulating heating cable. They are used in process temperature-maintenance applications on metal pipes that require a high power output and/or high-temperature exposure. The power-limiting heater cable (*Figure 4*) consists of a coiled-resistor alloy heating element wrapped around two parallel bus wires. It is connected alternately between the two bus wires at fixed intervals, usually every 2' or 3' (0.6 m to 0.9 m) along the cable length. The distance between the two contact points forms a heating zone. For this reason, power-limiting heating cables are also referred to as *zoned heating cables*. Power-limiting heating cables can be cut to length at the jobsite. However, the portion of cable between the cut and the next connection point of the heating and bus wires will not receive electricity and therefore will not provide any heating.

The resistor alloy heating element used in power-limiting heating cables has a positive temperature coefficient (PTC). This means the heating element's resistance increases as its temperature increases and its resistance decreases as its temperature decreases. The result is an increase or decrease of power output as the temperature around the cable decreases or increases, respectively. PTC allows power-limiting heating cables to be overlapped on pipes and valves during installation without causing damage to the cable from overheating. This is because the temperature of the heating element is reduced at the points where the cable overlaps.

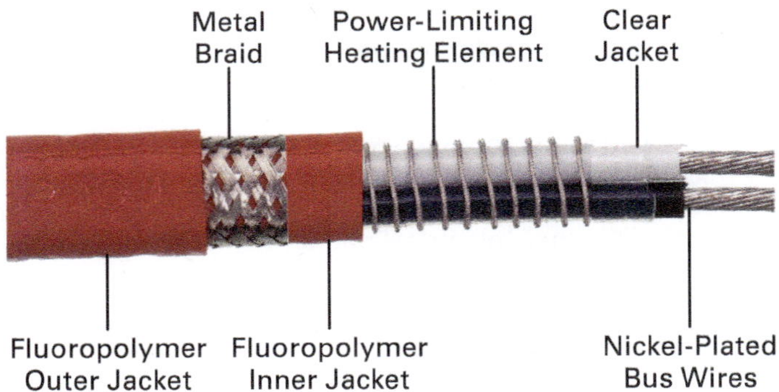

Figure 4 Construction of a power-limiting heating cable.
Source: Pentair Thermal Management LLC

1.1.3 Mineral-Insulated (MI) Cables

Series-resistance heating cable: A type of heating cable in which the resistance of the conductor provides the heat. The wattage output depends on the total circuit length and on the voltage applied.

Nichrome: An alloy based on nickel with chromium added (10% to 20%), and sometimes iron (up to 25%). Nichrome is often used for high-temperature applications such as in the fabrication of electric heating elements.

MI cables are a type of constant-wattage, **series-resistance heating cable**. They are widely used for tracing long pipes in applications where the temperature or power output requirements exceed the capabilities of self-regulating or power-limiting heating cables. MI cables (*Figure 5*) consist of one or two heating conductors made of **nichrome**, copper, or other metals insulated with magnesium oxide and encapsulated by a metal sheath made of copper, stainless steel, nickel (Alloy 825), or another suitable metal. Unlike self-regulating and power-limiting cables, MI cables cannot be cut to length and terminated in the field. They must be ordered from the manufacturer and are cut to specified lengths and assembled with sealed connections at the factory.

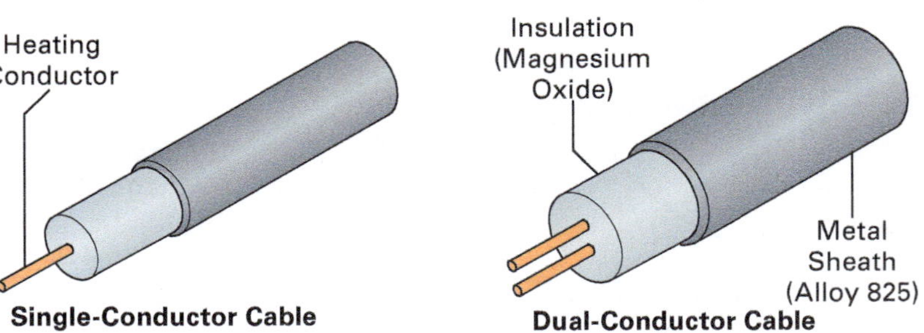

Figure 5 Construction of MI cables.
Source: Pentair Thermal Management LLC

1.1.4 Long Cable Installations

Heat tracing of long pipe runs is required in many applications, such as when transporting fluids to storage or transfer facilities, tank farms, piers for ocean transport vessels, or between different processing stages in petrochemical facilities. Such applications may involve cable lengths ranging between 1,250' and 5,000' (380 m to 1,500 m) that are powered from a single source. For many of these long runs, specially designed self-regulating and mineral-insulated heating cable systems are used.

For some long heat-tracing applications, specially designed series-resistance heating cables are used (*Figure 6*). They are generally used when the circuit length exceeds the ratings of conventional self-regulating heating cables. A series-resistance heating cable is a **constant-wattage heating cable** with one or two resistance conductors designed for use in single- or three-phase systems. Typically, the resistance conductors are electrically insulated and protected by a high-temperature, heavy-wall fluoropolymer jacket, fluoropolymer insulation, a metal grounding braid, and a fluoropolymer outer jacket. Resistance heating of the conductor provides the cable heat. The wattage output depends on the total circuit length and voltage applied. Series-resistance heating cables are commonly used in circuit lengths of 5,000' (1,500 m) or more with a single power supply at voltages up to 600VAC.

Constant-wattage heating cable: A heating cable that has the same power output over a large temperature range. It is used in applications requiring a constant heat output regardless of varying outside temperatures. Zoned parallel-resistance, mineral-insulated, and series-resistance heating cables are examples of constant-wattage heating cables.

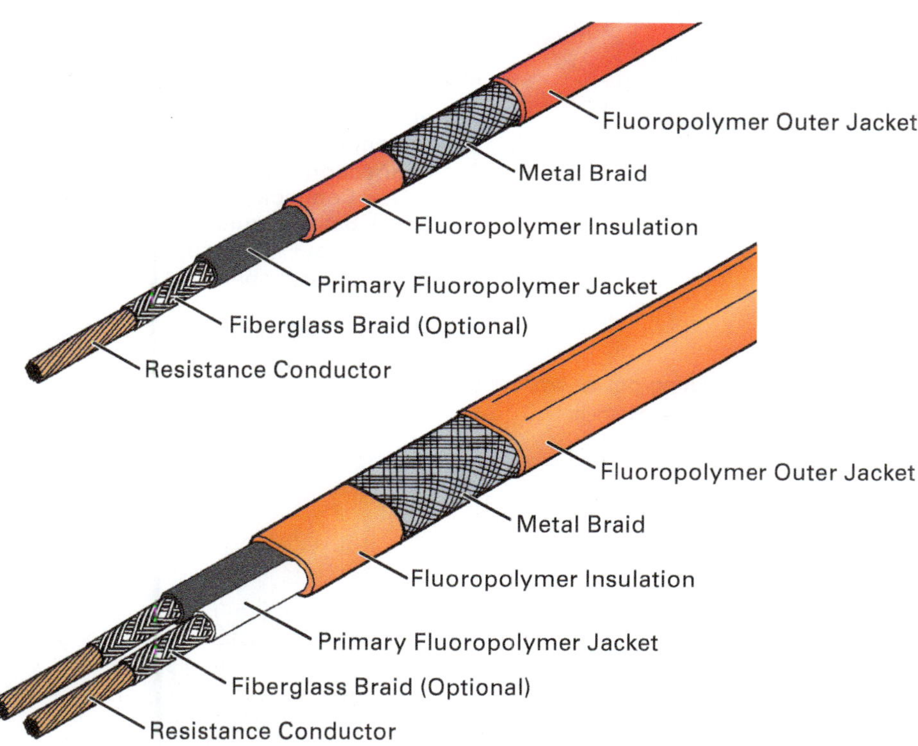

Figure 6 Construction of a series-resistance heating cable.
Source: Pentair Thermal Management LLC

1.1.5 Heating Cable Components and Accessories

Installation of a heat-tracing system requires appropriate components and accessories to interface the cable with the power source, properly support and terminate the cable(s), and make splices in cable runs as needed to achieve a properly functioning system. The specific components and accessories must be designed for use with the type of cable being installed, its application, and its environment. Always refer to the manufacturer's catalogs and installation instructions to determine the proper components and accessories to use.

Selecting Heat-Tracing Cables

Select a self-regulating heat-tracing cable based on the application and the temperature requirements. The temperature produced by a specific type of cable depends on the type of polymeric core or fiber it contains and on the watts per foot it produces. When selecting heat-tracing cables, refer to the manufacturer's cable datasheets and product literature and follow the recommendations pertaining to your application.

Except for specific model numbers, the components and accessories used with self-regulating and power-limiting cable heating systems are similar in design. *Figure 7* shows a typical Class I, Division 2 self-regulating/power-limiting heating cable system. *Figure 8* shows an MI cable system. The names for the various components and accessories also describe the purpose for each item. Systems rated for Class I, Division 1 are available.

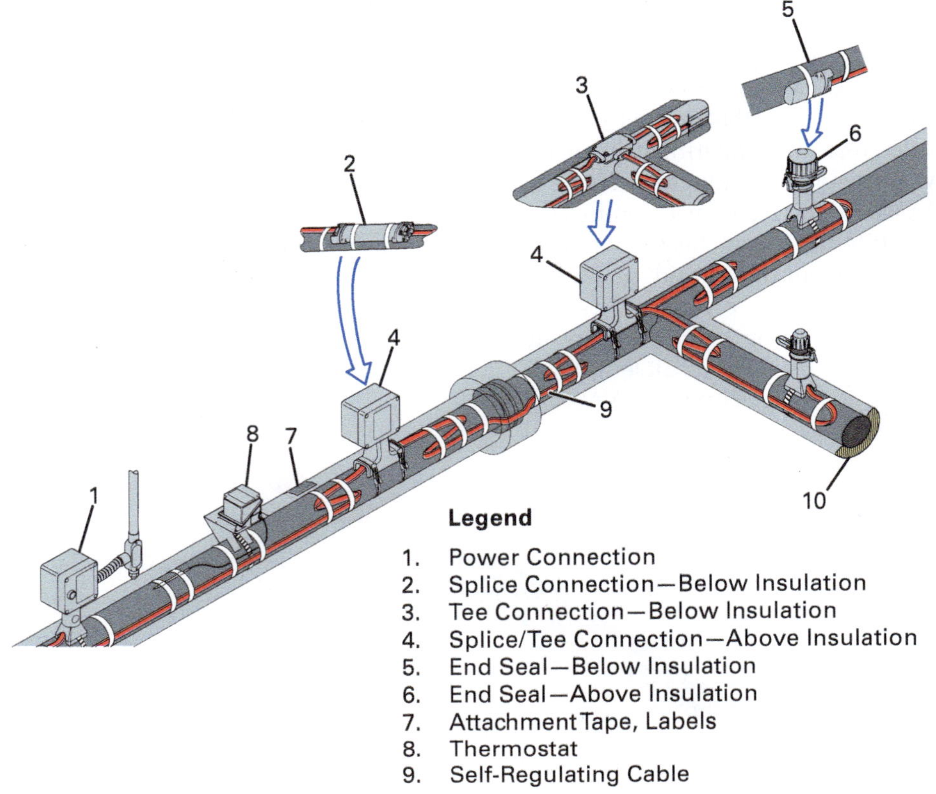

Figure 7 Self-regulating/power-limiting heating system for Class I, Division 2.
Source: Pentair Thermal Management LLC

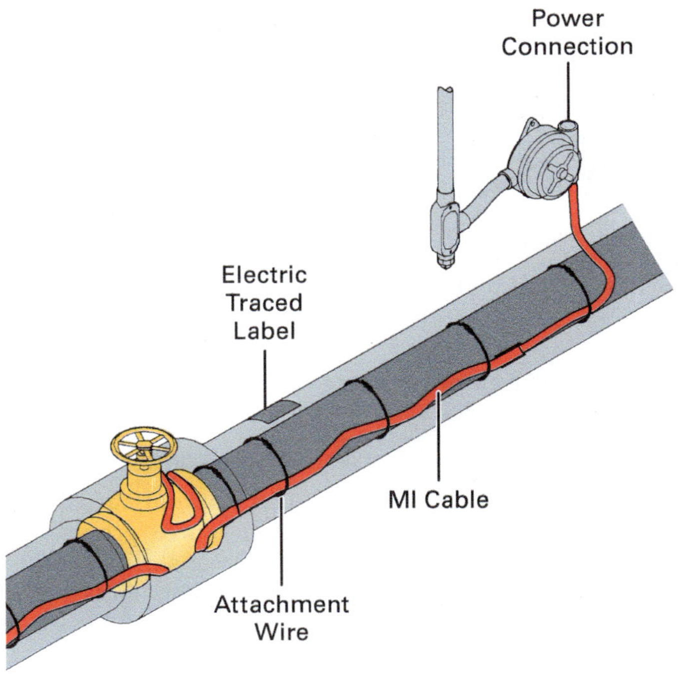

Figure 8 MI cable system.
Source: Pentair Thermal Management LLC

1.1.6 Thermal Insulation Used with Heat-Tracing Systems

Piping systems with heat-tracing cables are insulated in the same way as piping systems without heat tracing. The only difference is that the heat-tracing cables are installed first, under the layer of thermal insulation. It is important to insulate the heat-tracing cables and piping in order to reduce unnecessary heat loss to the surrounding atmosphere. In some cases, the traced line is wrapped with aluminum foil and then covered with insulation. The foil increases the radiation heat transfer.

For proper transfer of heat, it is essential that the space between the pipe and the tracer cable be kept free of particles of insulating material. The transfer of the tracer heat may be improved by putting a layer of heat-conductive cement (graphite mixed with sodium silicate or other binders) between the tracer cable and the pipe.

Figure 9 shows various tracer and insulation configurations. Straight piping may be protected from weather with metal jacketing or a polymeric or mastic system. When metal jacketing is used, it should be sealed with closure bands and a sealant applied to the outer edge where the bands overlap. Some insulating materials commonly used with heat tracing are:

- Rigid cellular urethane
- Polyisocyanurate foam
- Fiberglass
- Calcium silicate
- Cellular glass

Some important factors to consider when selecting an insulation material used with heat tracing are:

- Thermal characteristics
- Mechanical properties
- Chemical compatibility
- Moisture resistance
- Personal safety characteristics
- Fire resistance

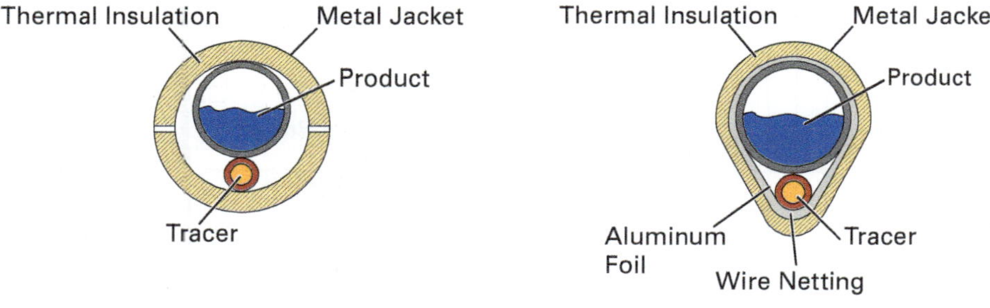

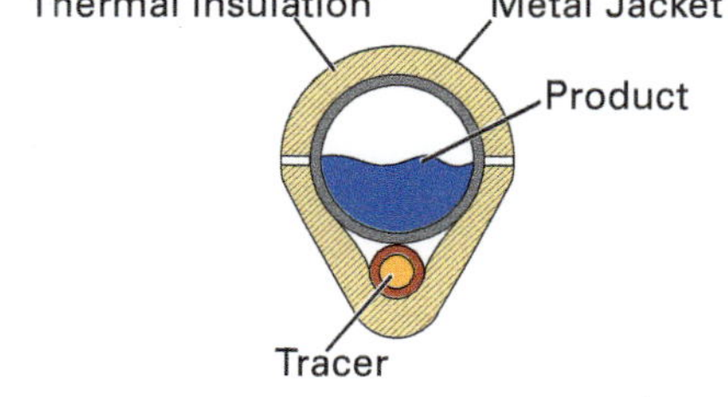

Figure 9 Heat tracer/insulation configurations.
Source: Pentair Thermal Management LLC

1.1.7 Heat-Tracing System Power Distribution

A typical power distribution scheme used with heat-tracing systems is shown in *Figure 10*. Three-phase utility power is applied to a dedicated step-down transformer for the heat-tracing system. The transformer supplies a reduced voltage to a distribution panel that contains the main circuit breaker and branch circuit breakers. The main circuit breaker is used to disconnect power from the panel board and to protect the panel buses, the transformer, and the wiring between the transformer and the distribution panel. The branch circuit breakers are ground fault interrupting circuit breakers used to apply the operating voltages to the power connection boxes of the one or more heat-tracing circuits. Typical cable supply voltages are 120/277VAC and 208/240VAC.

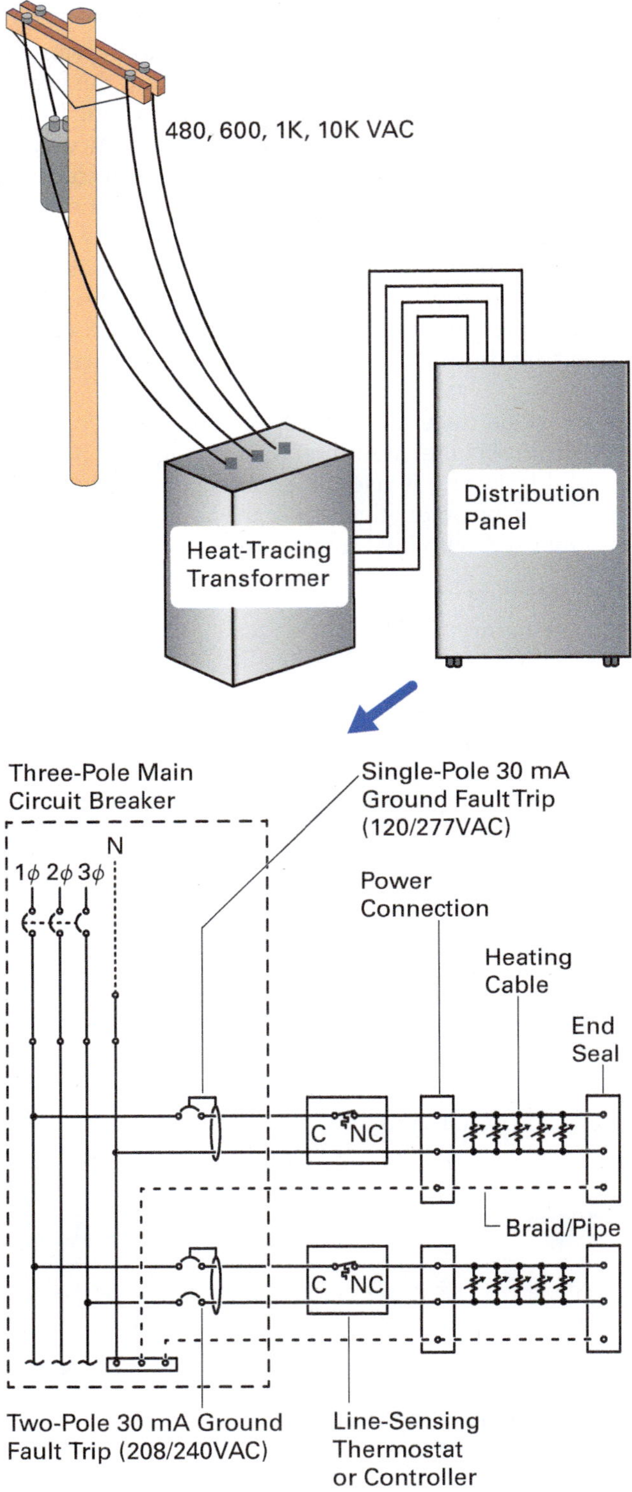

Figure 10 Heat-tracing system power distribution.

1.2.0 Heat-Tracing System Control

Control of heat-tracing systems is used to adjust the output of the heating source to keep the pipes from freezing or to maintain process piping at correct temperatures. Temperature control of a heat-tracing system can be accomplished in several ways. The method selected depends on the application requirements and on how critical temperature maintenance is to the process. The most common control methods are:

- Self-regulating control
- Ambient-sensing control
- Proportional ambient-sensing control
- Line-sensing control
- Dead-leg control

Beyond control, several schemes can be incorporated into heat-tracing systems to monitor their operation and detect any failures. The operating characteristic to be monitored depends on the application requirements and on how critical temperature maintenance is to the process. More than one characteristic can be monitored in a system if the application requires it. The most widely monitored system characteristics are:

- Ground fault
- Continuity
- Current
- Temperature

The temperature control methods and monitored characteristics identified here are described in greater detail in the sections that follow.

Skin-Effect Electric Heat-Tracing Systems

Skin-effect electric heat-tracing systems are used to heat-trace long transfer pipelines up to 12 miles (19 km) in length. These systems must be specifically designed for each application. In skin-effect heat-tracing systems, heat is produced by a combination of a ferromagnetic heat tube and a temperature-resistant, electrically insulated conductor that passes through the tube. At the far end, the two components are connected together; at the near end, the two are connected to an AC supply. Current flows through the insulated conductor and into the heat tube where, by skin and proximity effects, the return current passes through and is concentrated toward the inner surface of the heat tube, causing the outer surface of the heat tube to remain at ground potential. The current flowing in the heat tube is converted to heat that is supplemented by heat generated in the insulated conductor. The heat tube may be directly welded or cemented to the pipeline, allowing the heat to be transferred by conduction through the coupling media from the heat tube to the pipeline.

1.2.1 Self-Regulating Control

A self-regulating control uses the built-in properties of self-regulating heating cables to maintain the desired pipe temperature. It is used for basic freeze protection and broad temperature maintenance applications. Because no moving parts are involved, self-regulating control is the most economical and reliable method of control. However, self-regulating control should not be used for applications that require maintaining a narrow operating temperature range, involve temperature-sensitive fluids, or where energy consumption is a major concern.

Figure 11 Ambient-sensing thermostat used to control heat-tracing circuits.
Source: Pentair Thermal Management LLC

1.2.2 Ambient-Sensing Control

An ambient-sensing control uses a mechanical thermostat or electronic controller to measure the ambient temperature and turn on the heat-tracing system only when the surrounding temperature drops below a predetermined setpoint. For this reason, it is more energy efficient than a self-regulating control and therefore is widely used in freeze protection systems. *Figure 11* shows an ambient-sensing thermostat typical of those used in nonhazardous areas to directly control a single heat-tracing circuit or as a pilot control of a contactor used to turn multiple heat-tracing circuits on and off.

1.2.3 Proportional Ambient-Sensing Control

A proportional ambient-sensing control (PASC) treats all pipes as if they contained stagnant fluid and provides power to the heat-tracing system based on the ambient temperature.

A PASC uses a programmable electronic controller connected to remote temperature-input modules and contactor control modules to regulate one or more heat-tracing cables. The PASC system monitors the ambient temperature and continuously adjusts the heat input to compensate for heat loss that occurs because of changing ambient temperature. To maintain the desired temperature, a programmed algorithm calculates the cycle time during which the heating circuits are energized. The heat-tracing cable is energized more often as the temperature decreases and less often as the temperature increases. On cold days, the heat-tracing cable is turned on more often to maintain correct pipe temperatures. On warm days, it may not be turned on at all. A PASC is used when a self-regulating control is not precise enough. It is suitable for freeze protection, as well as all broad temperature-control and many narrow temperature-control applications. It is also one of the most energy-efficient forms of temperature control.

1.2.4 Line-Sensing Control

A line-sensing control uses a mechanical thermostat or electronic controller to measure the actual pipe temperature, not the ambient temperature surrounding the pipe. With this method of control, each heating circuit must have a separate control. Each heating circuit is turned on and off independently when signaled by its respective control device. Line-sensing controls are used in narrow temperature maintenance situations because they provide the highest degree of temperature control using the least amount of energy. Because this method requires the use of multiple control devices, it has the highest installation cost. *Figure 12* shows a line-sensing thermostat typical of those used in hazardous areas to directly control a single heat-tracing circuit or as a pilot control of a contactor used to turn multiple heat-tracing circuits on and off.

Figure 12 Typical line-sensing thermostat used to control heat-tracing circuits.
Source: Pentair Thermal Management LLC

1.2.5 Dead-Leg Control

The dead-leg method of control uses a segment of inactive pipe, or **dead leg**, in a piping system as a single control point for the larger system. The dead leg contains system fluid in a permanent no-flow condition. A thermostat measures the temperature of the fluid in the dead leg and uses it to represent the rest of the system. Dead-leg control provides much better control than ambient-sensing control at about the same cost. It is more economical than line-sensing control because it uses only one thermostat. However, temperature control is imprecise, especially in high-flow areas of the system. Today, the use of dead-leg control systems is on the decline. They are being replaced by electronic control systems such as PASC that duplicate the dead leg electronically.

Dead leg: A segment of pipe designed to be in a permanent no-flow condition. This pipe section is often used as a control point for a larger system.

Wet Thermal Insulation

Proper operation of heat-tracing systems depends upon the thermal insulation being dry. Electric heat tracing normally does not have sufficient heat output to dry wet insulation, nor is there a clear path for the moisture to leave if a vapor retarder has been applied outside the insulation. Some insulating materials, even if removed from the piping and force-dried, never regain their initial thermal insulation integrity after being wet.

1.2.6 Ground Fault Monitoring

A ground fault monitoring system monitors the current leakage from the system heating cable, power wiring, and components to ground using ground fault (leakage) circuit breakers and/or current-sensing devices that measure current (*Figure 13*). *NEC Section 427.22* requires the use of ground fault equipment with heat-tracing circuits. The function of ground fault circuit breakers is to protect the equipment, not personnel. The ground fault circuit breakers used in heat-tracing circuits are designed to trip at 30 mA, rather than at 5 mA like the GFCIs used for personnel protection. Personnel protection GFCIs are not used in heat-tracing applications because they often experience nuisance trips in this application.

Ground fault trips are usually caused by mechanical damage to the heating cable or power wiring, or by moisture in the junction boxes. When current leakage in the heat-tracing circuit exceeds the trip setting of the ground fault circuit breaker or other protective device, it shuts off the circuit. If the protective device is a ground fault circuit breaker, it may have an auxiliary contact used to trigger a remote trip alarm.

Know the Code

Ground-Fault Protection of Equipment
NEC Section 427.22

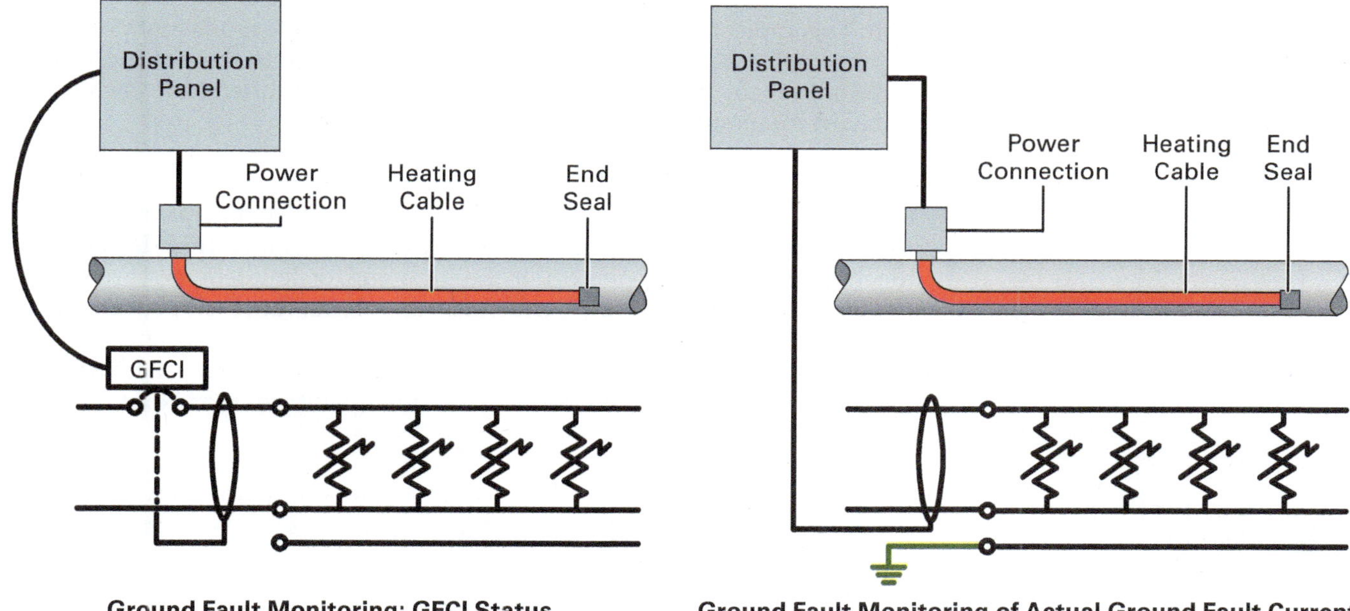

Figure 13 Simplified heat-tracing circuit with ground fault monitoring.
Source: Pentair Thermal Management LLC

Induction and Impedance Electric Heat-Tracing Systems

Induction heat-tracing systems are used in some high-temperature, high-power applications where very rapid heating is needed. Induction heat-tracing systems use the piping as a heating element by placing it in the magnetic field of an AC source. Low-resistance wire is coiled around a conductive pipe, and the alternating current flowing through the coiled wire generates a rapidly changing magnetic field that induces eddy currents and hysteresis losses. These eddy currents and hysteresis losses create a large amount of heat, similar to the way heat is produced in a transformer. A disadvantage of using induction heat tracing is that it does not produce uniform heating.

Impedance heat-tracing systems are used to generate heat in a pipe or vessel wall. This is done by causing current to flow through the pipe or vessel by direct connection to an AC voltage source. A dual-winding isolation transformer isolates the distribution system from the heating system.

1.2.7 Continuity Monitoring

Continuity monitoring verifies that voltage is present at the end termination of a heat-tracing cable run. This can be done by using an end-of-circuit LED that remains on when the circuit is operative and shuts off if the circuit is open (*Figure 14*). In some systems, an end-of-circuit transmitter is used. Installed at the end of the line, it communicates the status of the circuit (continuity or open) to a centralized receiver. This type of system has the capability to send a low-voltage monitoring signal down the heat-tracing circuit even when it is shut down.

1.2.8 Current Monitoring

Current monitoring uses a heat-tracing controller or current-monitoring relay to signal an alarm when the current in the heat-tracing circuit is too low or too high. This type of circuit will generate an alarm if there is a loss of power to the heating cable, the circuit is open, or there is damage to the heating cable bus wires or branch circuit wiring. *Figure 15* shows a simplified heat-tracing circuit with current monitoring.

1.2.9 Temperature Monitoring

Temperature monitoring continuously measures the temperature of the pipe with a digital controller connected to a resistance temperature detector (RTD) attached to the pipe (*Figure 16*). If the high and/or low temperature setpoints are exceeded, the controller generates an alarm. Low-temperature alarms can be generated by low power or loss of power to the heating cable, wet or missing thermal insulation, heating cable damage, or controller failure. High-temperature alarms can be caused by fluid temperatures that exceed the preset threshold or by controller failure.

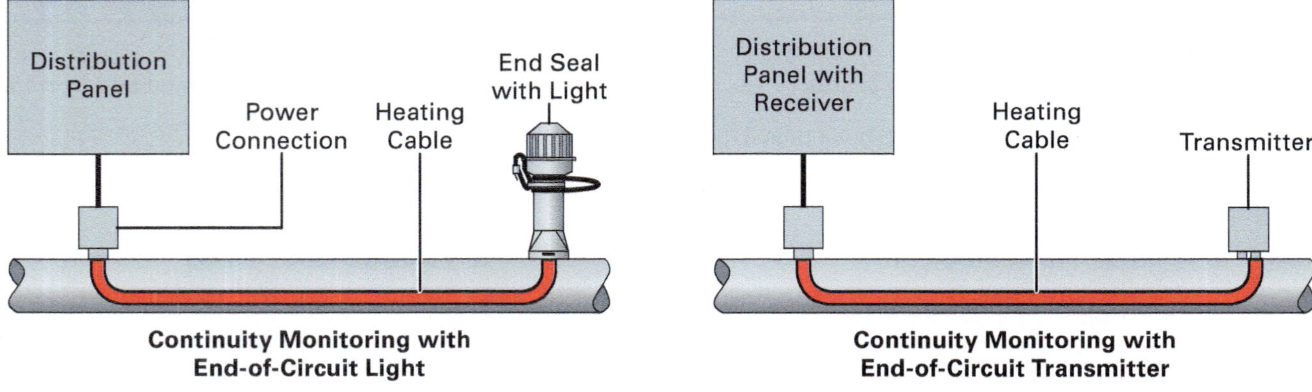

Figure 14 Simplified heat-tracing circuit with end-of-circuit continuity monitoring.
Source: Pentair Thermal Management LLC

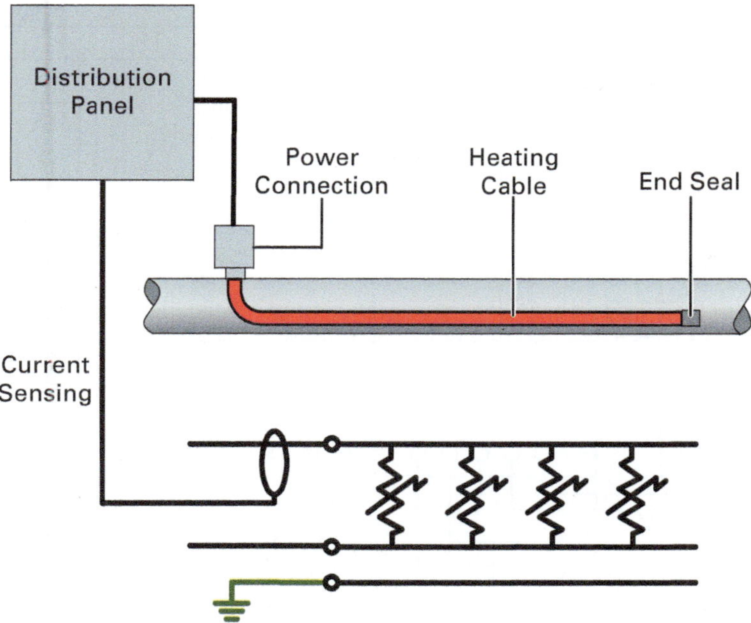

Figure 15 Simplified heat-tracing circuit with current monitoring.
Source: Pentair Thermal Management LLC

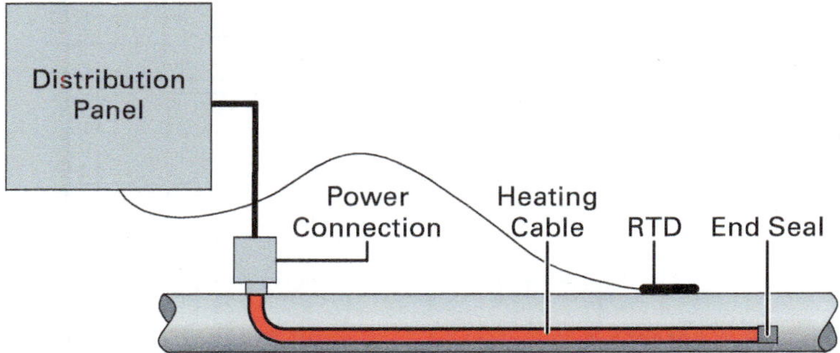

Figure 16 Simplified heat-tracing circuit with temperature monitoring.
Source: Pentair Thermal Management LLC

1.3.0 Heat-Tracing System Operation

A wide variety of schemes can be used to control and monitor electric heat-tracing systems for various applications. This section briefly describes a circuit configuration (*Figure 17*) that controls and monitors a heat-tracing system consisting of multiple circuits. The system uses a microprocessor-based controller that regulates the heating circuits by selecting different modes of control, including ambient control, PASC, or line-sensing control. The controller can operate as a standalone unit, or it can be networked to one or more remote monitoring and control modules (RMCs) and/or remote monitoring modules (RMMs).

In response to signals from the controller, each RMC provides multiple relay-controlled outputs that cause the associated heating cable circuits to switch on or off. Each RMM collects ambient temperature and/or pipe temperature inputs from RTD sensors located in the individual heater circuits. The RMM processes this information and forwards it to the controller. Based on the status inputs, the controller determines which circuits need to be turned on or off. It then signals the RMC to energize or de-energize the circuits, respectively, using the appropriate heating cable power contactors.

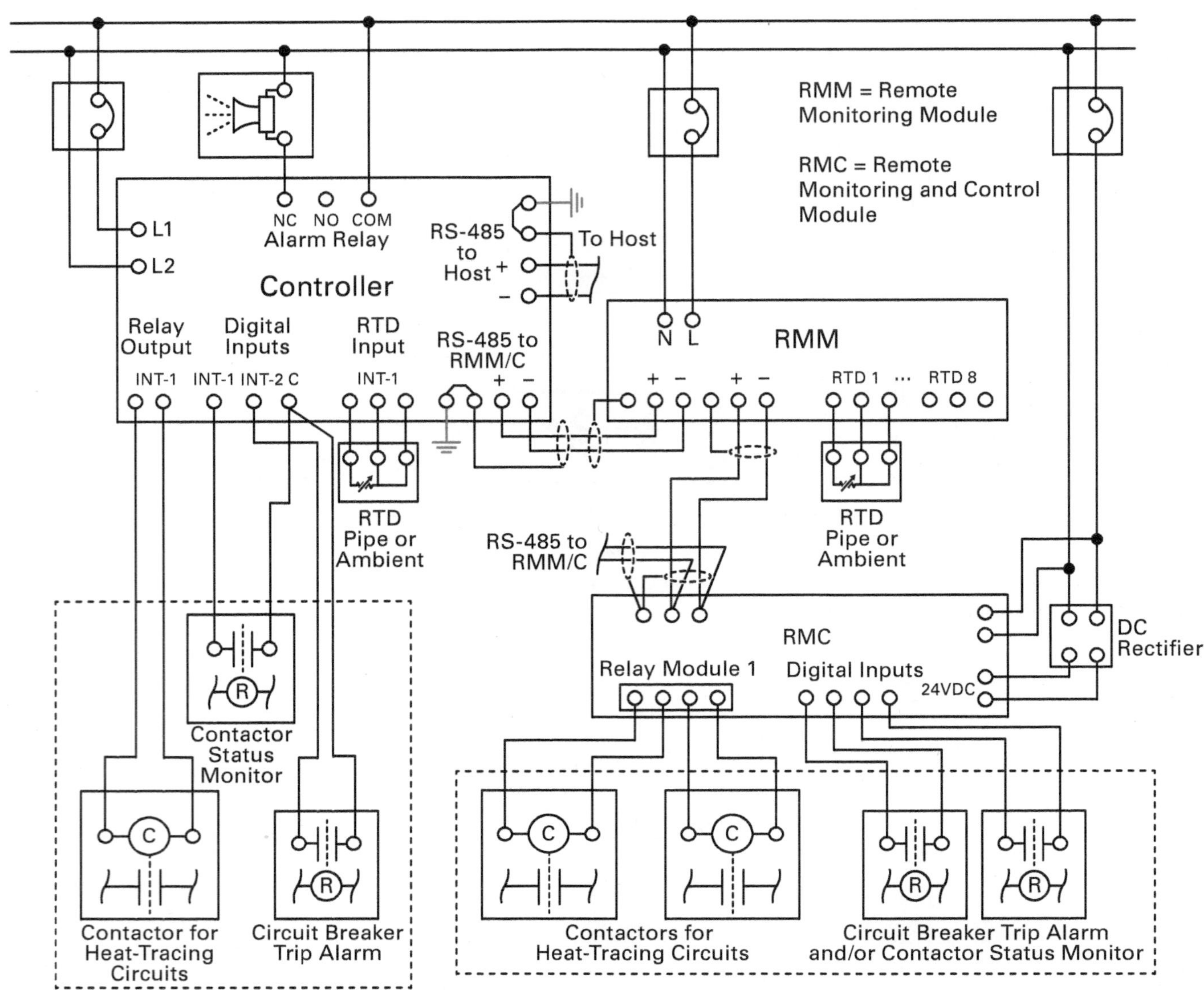

Figure 17 Typical heat-tracing system circuit configuration.
Source: Pentair Thermal Management LLC

Twisted-pair RS-485 cables transfer data between the various devices in the monitoring and control network. This allows each module to be placed in the best location. RMCs are typically located in the heat-tracing system power distribution panel, whereas RMMs are placed at the local sensor location. A system's setup parameters, status, and alarm conditions can be viewed by the system operator at the controller. In some systems, this information is made available at a remote location by an RS-232/RS-485 link to a PC running heat-trace monitoring and control software.

In some systems, temperature-monitoring signals are communicated to the controller using power line carrier technology. In such systems, a power line interface (PLI) unit receives temperature and continuity inputs transmitted over the heat-tracing circuit power wires from special end-of-line heat cable circuit transmitters. Power line carrier technology uses frequency-shift keying to encode digital data on the power line network. Digital ones and zeros are transmitted by coupling high-frequency signals onto the heat-tracing bus wires and the AC power line. The power line carrier technology allows temperature and continuity data to be sent to the controller without running additional wiring to the sensor locations. *Figure 18* shows the wiring for a typical system using power line carrier technology to transmit temperature and continuity status.

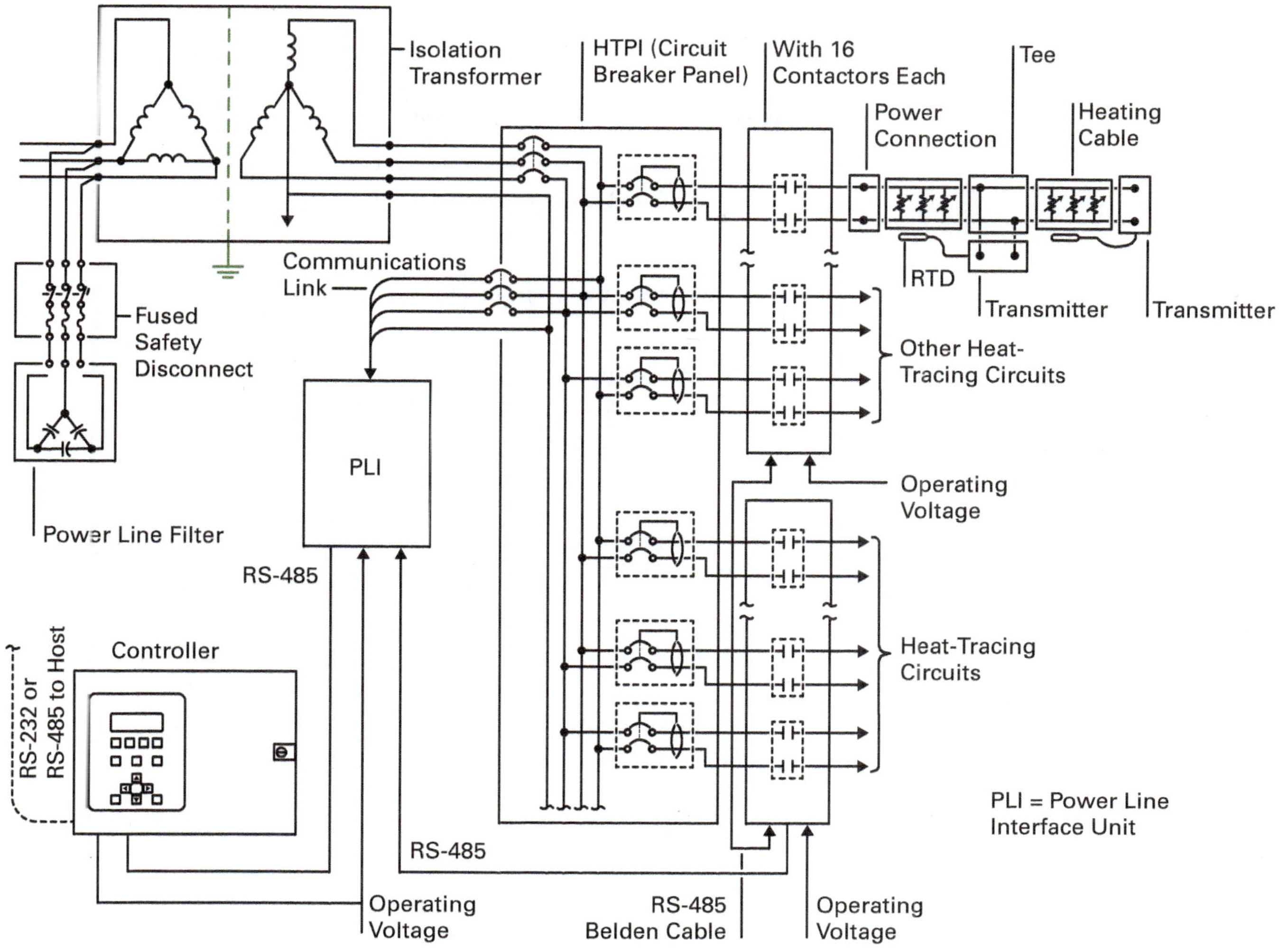

Figure 18 Heat-tracing system using power-line carrier technology.
Source: Pentair Thermal Management LLC

1.4.0 Equipment Selection and Installation for Pipe Heat-Tracing Systems

The design of a complex pipe heat-tracing system and the selection of its components requires extensive knowledge of the industrial processes and process fluids used in numerous industries. For this reason, the design and component selection for a pipe heat-tracing system is usually performed by a qualified master electrician, engineer, and/or the heat-tracing product manufacturer's engineering representative.

The following steps outline the stages and considerations for the component selection process.

Step 1 Determine the application:

- Freeze protection
- Temperature maintenance
- Both freeze protection and temperature maintenance

Step 2 Determine the application requirements based on:

- Pipe size and material (metal or PVC)
- Pipe location (aboveground or belowground)
- Thermal insulation type and thickness
- Type of process fluid (water, fuel, oil, or grease)
- Ambient and maintenance temperatures
- Maximum fluid temperature

Step 3 Determine the appropriate type of heating cable based on:

- Power output
- Maximum exposure temperature
- Available voltages
- Outer protective jacket
- Cable length(s)

Step 4 Determine the type of system temperature-monitoring control based on the application requirements:

- Self-regulating control
- Ambient-sensing control
- Proportional ambient-sensing control
- Line-sensing control
- Dead-leg control

Step 5 Determine the number of electrical circuits and transformer load based on:

- Total heating cable length
- Supply voltage
- Minimum **startup temperature**

Startup temperature: The lowest temperature at which a heat-tracing cable is energized.

Step 6 Select the correct components and accessories.

Heat-Tracing System Application and Design Guides

Most equipment manufacturers have application and design information to aid in the component selection of their various heat-tracing products and systems. This information is often readily available at the manufacturer's website. It is also provided in product publications like the ones in the image. Even if you are not directly involved with the design process, reading these documents will provide you with a better understanding of these systems.

TABLE 1 Example of Data Used to Determine Maximum Circuit Length

Heating Cable	Supply (VAC)	Startup Temperature	Maximum Circuit Length for Circuit Breaker Size			Maximum Amp per Foot
			15A	20A	30A	
5XL1-CR or -CT	120	40°F	165'	220'	250'	0.072
		0°F	110'	145'	220'	0.108
8XL1-CR or -CT	120	40°F	120'	160'	190'	0.100
		0°F	85'	115'	170'	0.139
5XL2-CR or -CT	208/277	40°F	285'	380'	450'	0.042
		0°F	190'	255'	385'	0.0492

The minimum number of circuits required for an installation is determined by dividing the total length of heating cable needed for the job by the maximum circuit length that can be used for that type of cable. The maximum circuit length is determined by the type of cable, supply voltage, startup temperature, and circuit breaker size. Manufacturers provide this information in their design and/or installation literature. *Table 1* shows some examples of data from a manufacturer's design guide used to determine the maximum circuit lengths of different cables.

1.5.0 Installation Guidelines

Always install the heat-tracing system and its components in strict accordance with the system design specifications, the manufacturer's instructions, and all prevailing local codes. *NEC Article 427* covers the requirements for fixed electric heating equipment installed on pipes and vessels in unclassified areas. The *NEC*® requirements are covered later in this section.

Know the Code

Fixed Electric Heating Equipment for Pipelines and Vessels
NEC Article 427

1.5.1 Installation of Heating Cable and Components

WARNING!

To prevent injury from falling when installing heat tracing on overhead piping, use appropriate fall protection equipment and follow all safety procedures.

Some general guidelines for the installation of heat-tracing cable and its components are covered in this section.

Adhere to the following guidelines prior to the installation:

- Inspect all the cables, components, and accessories to make sure they are the ones specified for the job and that they are not damaged. Make sure that the rating of the heating cable is suitable for the service voltage available.
- Verify that the heating cable has not been damaged during shipping by testing it for continuity and electrical insulation resistance. Test the insulation resistance between the cable conductors and the metallic grounding braid in accordance with the cable manufacturer's instructions. When testing insulation, use a 2,500VDC megohmmeter (also known as a *megger*). The minimum insulation resistance should meet the value specified by the cable manufacturer, typically greater than 20 megohms (MΩ), regardless of length.
- Make sure there is enough heating cable available to complete the job. The minimum amount of heating cable required is equal to the total length of pipe plus the additional cable needed to make all the electrical connections and to trace each component such as valves, flanges, and pipe supports. Information on how much additional cable to provide for tracing each of these items can be found in the job specifications and/or in the manufacturer's installation instructions. Generally, 2' (600 mm) of cable is added for each electrical power connection, splice, tee, and end seal. *Table 2* lists some recommendations for the length of additional cable needed to trace valves, flanges, and supports.

NOTE

If the heating cable is spiraled (wrapped) around the pipe instead of being installed in a straight run, additional cable length must be allowed per foot of pipe. The amount of additional cable depends on the pipe size and the distance between the spirals. For a given pipe size, the amount of cable and the distance between the spirals, called the *pitch*, is determined by multiplying the total pipe length by an appropriate spiral factor. Equipment manufacturers normally provide tables in their installation instructions that give the spiral factors and cable lengths to add per foot for the different sizes of pipe.

TABLE 2 Typical Lengths of Additional Cable Required to Heat Trace Piping Components

Pipe Size	Screw Valves	Flange Valves	Butterfly Valves	Pipe Supports	Pipe Elbows	Pipe Flange
1"	6"	6"	6"	6"	3"	3"
2"	6"	1'	6"	1'	6"	6"
3"	1'	2'	1'	1'	6"	6"
4"	2'	3'	1'	1'	9"	6"
6"	3'	4'	1'	2'	9"	1'
8"	4'	5'	2'	2'	9"	1'
10"	5'	7'	2'	3'	1'	1'
12"	7'	8'	2'	3'	1'	1'
14"	8'	10'	3'	4'	1'	2'

- Check and/or test each control device before installation for the correct operating temperature range, proper span, and setpoints.
- Store the heating cable and its components in a clean, dry place where they will be protected from mechanical damage.

Adhere to the following guidelines during installation:

- Do not expose the heating cable to sharp edges. Avoid using excessive pulling force, kinking or crushing the cable, or walking on or driving over the cable.
- Heating cable must be installed on a clean, smooth portion of the pipe, avoiding any sharp bends or jagged edges. It should be positioned to avoid damage due to impact, abrasion, or vibration, while still maintaining proper heat transfer. Always install heat-tracing cable in accordance with the manufacturer's instructions. *Figure 19* shows how to install heating cable on some common piping components.
- Heating cable must be installed in a manner that facilitates the removal of valves, small in-line devices, and instruments without completely removing the cable or excessive thermal insulation or cutting the heating cable.
- Except for self-regulating cable, avoid overlapping heating cable sections. This can cause excessive temperatures at overlap points.
- Heating cable cold leads must be positioned to penetrate the thermal insulation in the lower 180° segment. This helps to minimize water entrance.
- Attach the heating cable to the pipes using fiberglass tape, aluminum tape, or plastic cable ties per the manufacturer's instructions. If using plastic cable ties, make sure they have a temperature rating that matches the system exposure rating.
- Protect the heating cable ends from moisture and mechanical damage if they are to be left exposed before connection.
- After the installation is complete, retest the cables electrically in the same manner as pre-installation testing. This test ensures that the integrity of the cable has not been compromised, and it ensures the integrity of splices and terminations.

CAUTION

Do not use metal attachments, vinyl electrical tape, or duct tape to fasten heating cable to the pipe. Do not twist the bus wires together in a self-regulating cable as this will cause a short circuit.

The following conditions must be satisfied when installing temperature sensors:

- Sensors must be mounted to avoid the direct temperature effects of the heating cable.
- Sensors must be mounted 3' to 5' (0.9 m to 1.5 m) from any junction where two or more sections of cable meet or join.
- Sensors must be located 3' to 5' (0.9 m to 1.5 m) from any **heat source** or heat sink in the system.
- Where piping is routed through areas with different ambient conditions, such as inside and outside a heated building, separate sensors and associated controls are required for each area.

Heat source: Any component that adds heat to an object or system.

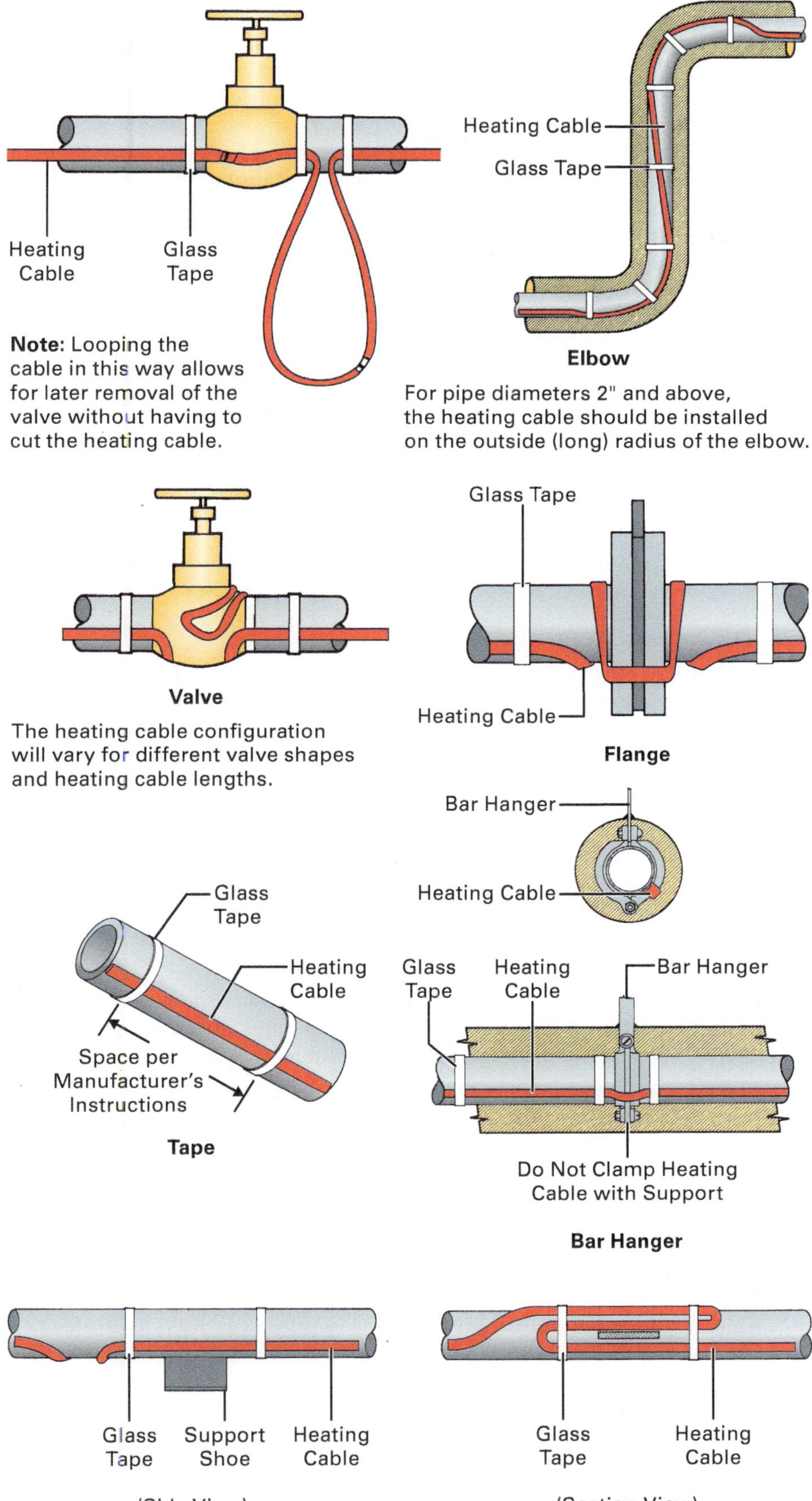

Figure 19 Installing a heating cable on common piping components.
Source: Pentair Thermal Management LLC

Pulling Heating Cable

When pulling heating cable, it helps to use a reel holder that feeds the cable out smoothly with little tension. The heating cable should be strung loosely but close to the pipe being traced to avoid interference with supports and equipment.

1.5.2 Installation of Thermal Insulation

Before installing thermal pipe insulation over the heat-tracing system components, the heat-tracing cable should be visually checked for signs of damage and electrically tested for continuity and electrical insulation resistance integrity. All testing should be done by properly trained personnel. Test the electrical insulation resistance between the cable conductors and the metallic grounding braid in accordance with the cable manufacturer's instructions. When testing insulation resistance, use a 2,500VDC megger. Regardless of the heating cable length, the resistance reading should meet the value specified by the cable manufacturer, usually 20 MΩ or above. Record the original value of each circuit for future reference.

Correct temperature maintenance of a heat-traced pipe system requires that dry thermal insulation be properly installed. To reduce the chance of heating cable damage, install the thermal insulation as soon as possible after the heating cable and related devices have been attached. The insulation material and its thickness should be listed in the job specifications. If not, follow the recommendations of the heat-tracing equipment manufacturer. All pipe work, including fittings, wall penetrations, and other potential heat loss areas, must be completely insulated. The outside of the pipe insulation should be marked "Electric Traced" at appropriate intervals on alternate sides to warn people of the pipe tracing. Mark the location of all heating-cable system components on the outside of the insulation as well.

1.5.3 *NEC*® Requirements

NEC Article 427 covers the requirements for fixed electric heating equipment installed on pipes and vessels in unclassified areas. If the equipment is installed in hazardous (classified) areas, *NEC Articles 500 through 516* also apply.

Some of the *NEC*® requirements for fixed electric heating equipment installed on piping and vessels are summarized below:

- Branch circuits and overcurrent devices supplying the equipment should be sized to at least 125% of the total heater load per *NEC Sections 210.20(A) and 427.4.*
- Ensure equipment is suitable for the chemical, thermal, and physical environment, and install in accordance with the manufacturer's drawings and instructions per *NEC Section 427.10.*
- Physical guards, isolation, or thermal protection are required for the external surfaces of any equipment that operates at temperatures above 140°F (60°C) to prevent contact with personnel per *NEC Section 427.12.*
- Attach the heating elements to the pipe or vessel surface being heated with appropriate fasteners other than the thermal insulation. Where the heating element is not in direct contact with the surface, provide a means to prevent overheating the heating element per *NEC Sections 427.14 and 427.15.*
- Identify the presence of electric heating equipment using permanent caution signs or markings at the intervals specified in *NEC Section 427.13.*
- Do not bridge exposed heating equipment across expansion joints unless provision is made for expansion and contraction per *NEC Section 427.16.*
- Ground fault protection for equipment is required per *NEC Section 427.22,* except where there is a ground fault alarm system that is maintained only by qualified personnel and continuous operation is necessary for safe operation of the equipment or process.
- Provide a readily accessible means of disconnecting equipment, such as indicating switches or circuit breakers. A factory-installed cord and plug that is accessible to the equipment may be used if the equipment is rated at 20A or less and 150V or less per *NEC Section 427.55.*

Know the Code

Fixed Electric Heating Equipment for Pipelines and Vessels
NEC Article 427

Know the Code

Special Occupancies
NEC Chapter 5

Know the Code

Branch Circuits Not Over 1000 Volts ac, 1500 Volts dc, Nominal
NEC Article 210

Overcurrent Protective Devices

The overcurrent protective devices used in a heat-tracing system must be sized in accordance with the design specifications. Guidelines for correct sizing of overcurrent devices are normally given in the equipment manufacturer's design literature or computer selection programs. Ground fault circuit breakers or other ground fault protective devices with a nominal 30 mA trip level (a common trip level for heat-tracing applications) are mandatory in most areas. See *NEC Section 427.22* for an exclusion related to industrial establishments. Because these devices need an effective ground path, the *NEC*® requires that a conductive covering of the heating cable be connected to an electrical ground.

1.0.0 Section Review

1. An MI heating cable is a type of _____.
   a. self-regulating cable
   b. parallel-resistance heating cable
   c. power-limiting cable
   d. constant-wattage, series-resistance heating cable

2. A line-sensing control uses a mechanical thermostat or electrical controller to measure the _____.
   a. actual pipe temperature
   b. ambient temperature around the pipe
   c. estimated pipe temperature
   d. heating cable temperature

3. The use of power line carrier technology allows temperature and continuity data to be sent to the controller _____.
   a. using Bluetooth® technology
   b. without running additional wiring to the sensor locations
   c. as cellular data
   d. through twisted-pair RS-485 cables

4. The design and component selection for a complex pipe heat-tracing system is usually performed by a master electrician, engineer, or the _____.
   a. electrician on-site
   b. piping system designer
   c. heat-tracing product manufacturer's representative
   d. insulating contractor

5. When heating cable is wrapped in a spiral around the pipe instead of in a straight run along its length, the additional cable needed is determined by the _____.
   a. pipe size and the pitch
   b. pipe size and the cable wattage per foot
   c. pitch and the cable wattage per foot
   d. pitch and the cable type

2.0.0 Roof, Gutter, and Downspout Deicing Systems

Objective

Describe roof, gutter, and downspout deicing systems and the relevant selection/installation considerations.

a. Describe roof, gutter, and downspout deicing systems.

b. Explain how roof, gutter, and downspout deicing system components are selected and installed.

Performance Tasks

There are no Performance Tasks in this section.

Roof, gutter, and downspout deicing systems are used to prevent ice dams and icicles from forming on roofs and in gutters and downspouts (*Figure 20*). Ice dams form because melting snow and ice freeze when they reach the colder roof edge. Once ice dams are formed, water tends to collect behind them. The water backs up and seeps under the roofing materials, where it can leak into the building and cause water damage. Another danger is icicles that form when water dripping off the roof flows over ice-filled gutters. When outside temperatures rise, these heavy icicles can become a safety hazard as they break away from the gutters and roof.

Figure 20 Roof and gutter icing.

2.1.0 System Components and Control

Roof, gutter, and downspout deicing systems provide a continuous heated path for melting snow and ice. The heated path keeps the water above freezing temperatures so that it can drain from the roof to a safe discharge area. *Figure 21* shows the components used with a typical roof, gutter, and downspout deicing system. In this system, the continuous heating path is created by self-regulating, low-wattage heating cables specifically designed for roof, gutter, and downspout deicing applications. As current flows through the cable's self-regulating polymeric core, the heat output is adjusted in response to the outside temperature.

The method used to control the roof deicing system determines its capability to operate when needed as well as the amount of power consumed. Control is usually exercised in one of three ways:

- Manual control
- Ambient thermostat control
- Automatic moisture/temperature control

Manual control involves turning a switch on and off to control the system power contactor. Someone must monitor the outside temperature and manually turn on the system whenever it drops below freezing. Less prone to human error is an automatic roof deicing system control that uses an ambient-sensing thermostat. When it senses that the outside temperature is below freezing, it automatically turns on the roof and gutter system, energizing the heating cable(s).

The most energy-efficient method of roof deicing system control is an automatic moisture/temperature controller. It consists of a control panel, one or more aerial-mounted snow sensors, and one or more ice sensors that are located in the gutters and at other critical areas that need to be monitored. This arrangement turns on the roof, gutter, and downspout deicing system when it begins to snow or when ice begins to form. *Figure 22* shows typical wiring for single- and multiple-circuit roof deicing systems.

Electric Panel for Roof Deicing

Some roof deicing systems use mesh-type heating panels or mats instead of self-regulating heating cables to control ice and snow buildup and prevent ice dams from forming. For new roofing installations, the mats can be installed under the roofing material, making them invisible.

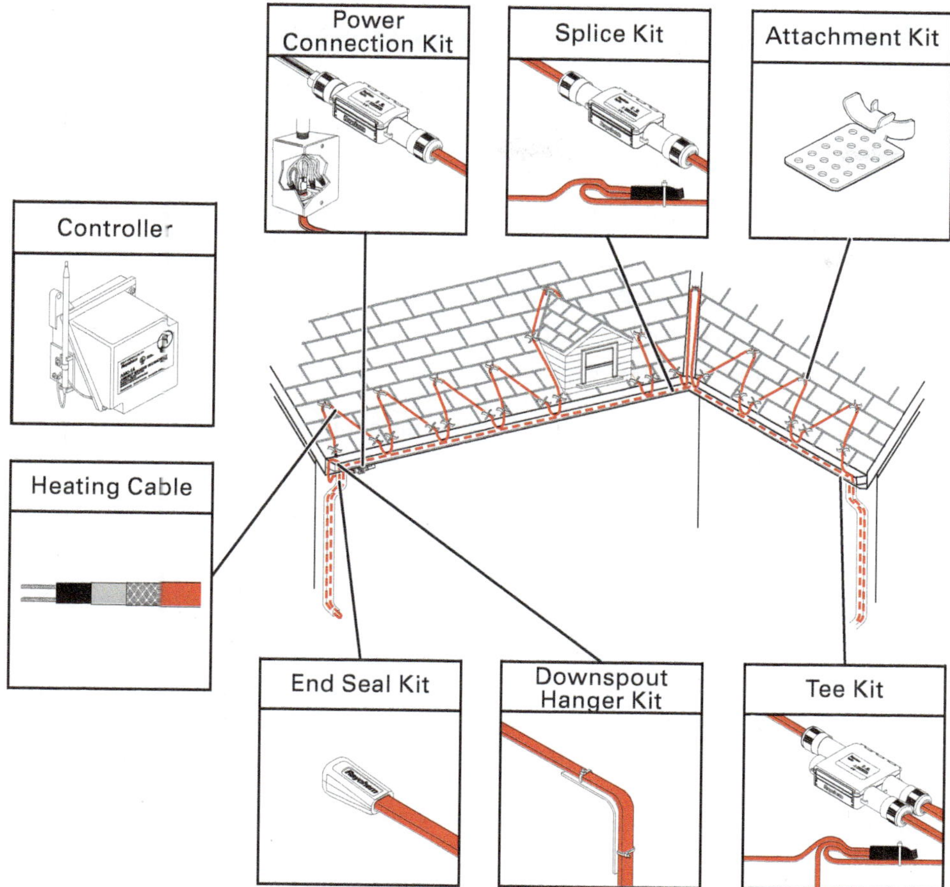

Figure 21 Components of a typical roof, gutter, and downspout deicing system.
Source: Pentair Thermal Management LLC

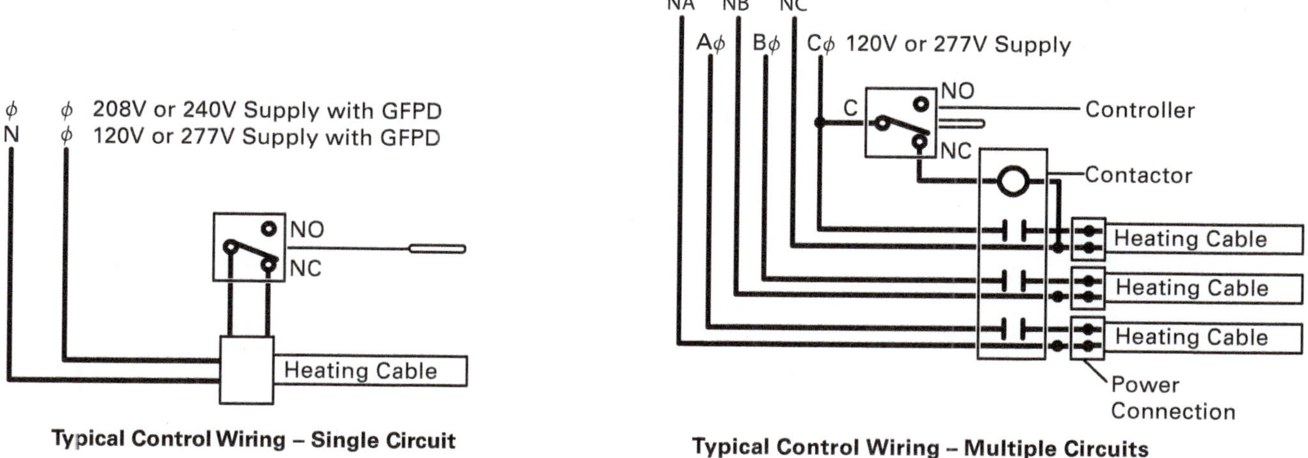

Figure 22 Typical wiring for single- and multiple-circuit roof, gutter, and downspout deicing systems.

2.2.0 Component Selection and Installation

Each equipment manufacturer provides specific guidelines for the component selection and installation of its roof deicing systems. Some general guidelines for the component selection process are described in the following steps.

Step 1 Determine the cable layout based on the roof construction:

- Type of construction (sloped roof, sloped roof with gutters, or flat roof)
- Location of roof/wall intersections
- Location of valleys, gutters, and downspouts

Step 2 Determine the method of cable attachment based on the roof construction materials and surface area:

- Roof, gutters, downspouts, and drip edges
- Mechanical or adhesive attachment clips

Step 3 Determine the method of system temperature control based on dependability, precision, and energy consumption requirements:

- Manual control
- Ambient thermostat control
- Automatic moisture/temperature control

Step 4 Determine the transformer load and number of electrical circuits based on:

- Total heating cable length
- Supply voltage
- Minimum startup temperature

Step 5 Select the correct components and accessories.

Know the Code

Fixed Outdoor Electric Deicing and Snow-Melting Equipment
NEC Article 426

Always install roof, gutter, and downspout deicing systems in strict accordance with the system design specifications, the manufacturer's instructions, and all prevailing local codes. *NEC Article 426* covers the requirements for fixed outdoor electric deicing and snow-melting equipment. The *NEC*® requirements are covered later in this section.

2.2.1 Installation of Heating Cable and Components

Some general guidelines for the installation of roof, gutter, and downspout systems are listed in this section.

WARNING!

To prevent injury from falling off roofs when installing roof, gutter, and downspout systems, use appropriate fall protection equipment and follow all required safety procedures.

Adhere to the following guidelines prior to installation:

- Inspect all cables, components, and accessories to make sure they are the ones specified for the job and that they are not damaged. Make sure that the rating of the heating cable is suitable for the service voltage available.

- To verify that the heating cable has not been damaged during shipping, test it for continuity and electrical insulation resistance. Test the insulation resistance between the heating cable conductors and the metallic grounding braid in accordance with the cable manufacturer's instructions. When testing insulation, use a 2,500VDC megger. The minimum insulation resistance should meet the value specified by the cable manufacturer, typically 1,000 MΩ or more, regardless of length.
- Check and/or test each control device before installation for the correct operating temperature range, proper span, and setpoints.
- Store the heating cable and its components in a clean, dry place where they will be protected from mechanical damage.

Adhere to the following guidelines as the installation progresses:

- Handle heating cable in a way that avoids exposing the cable to sharp edges. Also avoid using excessive pulling force, kinking or crushing the cable, walking or driving over the cable, or covering the heating cable with any roofing material unless it is a mat-type system designed for such use.
- Install the components and attachment accessories first in the locations indicated on the project drawings.
- Install the heating cable. Start at the end seal and work backwards. Make sure the heating cable provides a continuous path for water to flow off the roof (*Figure 23*). Leave drip loops where appropriate. Also, be sure to leave a drip loop at each component so that water will not track down the heating cable and into the component.
- Loop and secure the heating cable at the bottom of the downspouts in accordance with the manufacturer's instructions to prevent any ice buildup from the draining water and to protect the heating cable from mechanical damage.
- Use UV-resistant cable ties wherever you require two heating cables to stay together.
- Verify that the heating cable has not been damaged during installation by testing it for continuity and electrical insulation resistance. Test the insulation resistance between the heating cable conductors and the metallic grounding braid in accordance with the cable manufacturer's instructions. Use a 2,500VDC megger. If the heating cable is installed on a metal gutter, downspout, and/or metal roof, also measure the insulation resistance between the braid and metal surface. The minimum insulation resistance should meet the value specified by the cable manufacturer, typically 1,000 MΩ or more, regardless of length. Record the original value for each circuit for future reference.

Figure 23 Heating cable providing a continuous path for water to flow off the roof.
Source: Braslavets Denys/Shutterstock.com

Know the Code

Fixed Outdoor Electric Deicing and Snow-Melting Equipment
NEC Article 426

Know the Code

Special Occupancies
NEC Chapter 5

Know the Code

Branch Circuits Not Over 1000 Volts ac, 1500 Volts dc, Nominal
NEC Article 210

Know the Code

Disconnecting Means
NEC Section 427.55

2.2.2 *NEC®* Requirements

NEC Article 426 covers the requirements for fixed outdoor electric deicing and snow-melting equipment installed in unclassified areas. If the equipment is installed in hazardous (classified) areas, *NEC Articles 500 through 516* also apply.

Some of the *NEC®* requirements for exposed fixed outdoor electric deicing and snow-melting equipment are summarized below:

- Size branch circuits and overcurrent devices supplying the equipment to at least 125% of the total heater load per *NEC Sections 210.20(A) and 426.4*.
- Ensure equipment is suitable for the environment and install in accordance with the manufacturer's drawings and instructions per *NEC Section 426.10*.
- Physical guards, isolation, or thermal protection are required for the external surfaces of any equipment that operates at temperatures above 140°F (60°C) to prevent contact with personnel per *NEC Section 426.12*.
- Identify the presence of electric heating equipment using clearly visible, permanent caution signs or markings per *NEC Section 426.13*.
- Do not bridge exposed heating equipment across expansion joints unless provision is made for expansion and contraction per *NEC Section 426.21*.
- Ground fault protection with a trip level specified by the manufacturer is required for equipment per the Exceptions in *NEC Section 210.8(A)(3)* and *NEC Section 426.28*.
- Provide a readily accessible means of disconnecting equipment, such as indicating switches or circuit breakers. A factory-installed cord and plug that is accessible to the equipment may be used if the equipment is rated at 20A or less and 150V or less per *NEC Section 427.55*.

2.0.0 Section Review

1. For roof and gutter deicing systems, an automatic moisture/temperature controller is considered the _____.
   a. least expensive approach
   b. most energy-efficient method
   c. least reliable approach
   d. simplest method

2. On outdoor electric deicing installations, prevent water from tracking into components by installing _____.
   a. collection containers
   b. the cable along the top edge of the gutter
   c. the cable in a serpentine pattern
   d. a drip loop at each component

3.0.0 Snow-Melting and Anti-Icing Systems

Performance Tasks

There are no Performance Tasks in this section.

Objective

Describe snow-melting and anti-icing systems and the relevant selection/installation considerations.

a. Describe snow-melting and anti-icing system components.

b. Explain how snow-melting and anti-icing system components are selected and installed.

Snow-melting and anti-icing systems are used to prevent the buildup of snow and ice on concrete surfaces of driveways, walkways, stairways, loading ramps, building entryways, and bridge road surfaces (*Figure 24*), where they can create hazards for people and vehicles.

Figure 24 Bridge road surface protected by a snow-melting and anti-icing system.
Source: Pentair Thermal Management LLC

3.1.0 Snow-Melting and Anti-Icing System Components

Figure 25 shows the components used with one manufacturer's snow-melting and anti-icing system. In this system, heating is provided by one or more self-regulating heating cables specifically designed for snow-melting and anti-icing applications. The cables are cut on the job. They are installed in a serpentine pattern with a 1' (30 cm) spacing between loops, securely fastened to rebar or wire mesh, and then completely encased in concrete. All electrical connections and terminations are made in externally accessible junction boxes. The capability of the heating cable to melt snow is proportional to its wattage rating. As current flows through the cable's self-regulating polymeric core, the heat output is adjusted in response to the ambient temperature of the surrounding concrete.

Some snow-melting and anti-icing systems use one or more factory-made electrical snow-melting mats instead of regular heating cable. The heating mats consist of self-regulating heating cable looped in a serpentine pattern within a screened mesh framework. Like the regular heating cable, the mats are embedded in concrete and electrically connected at externally accessible junction boxes.

The method used to control the snow-melting and anti-icing system determines its ability to operate when needed as well as the amount of power consumed. Control is done in one of three ways:

- Manual control
- Ambient thermostat control
- Automatic snow control

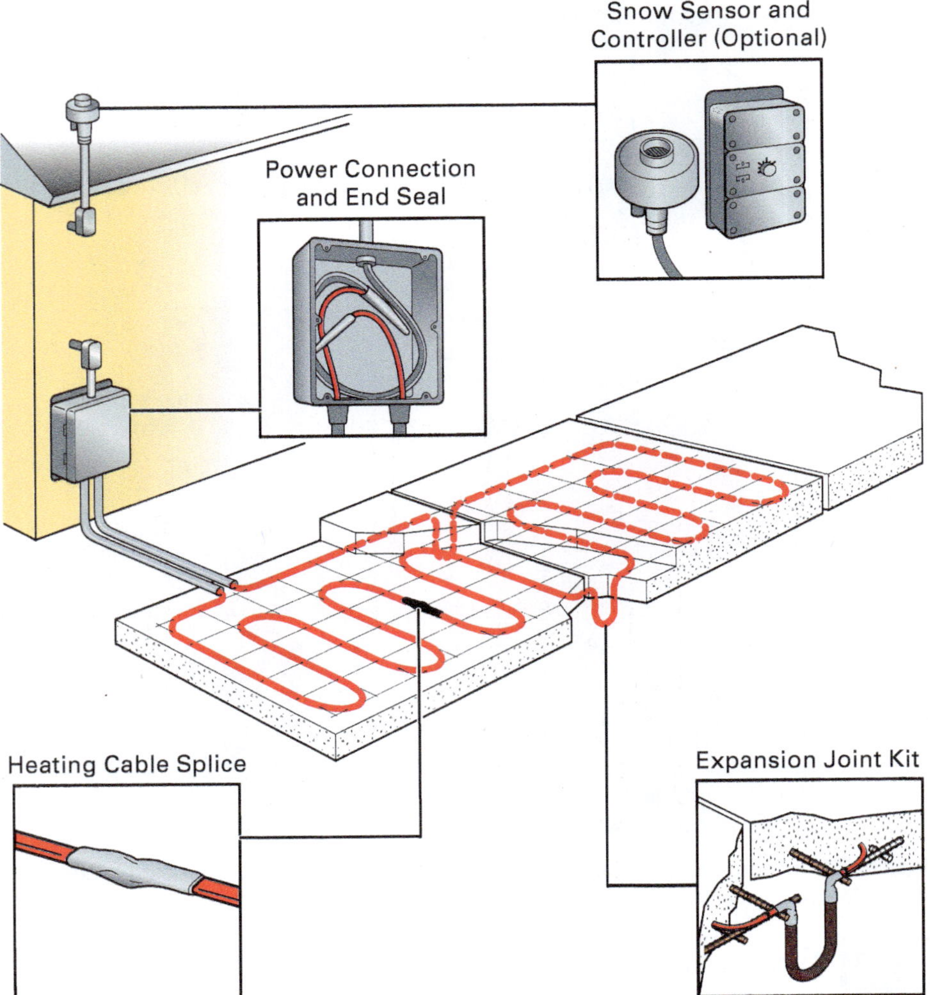

Figure 25 Components of a typical snow-melting and anti-icing system.
Source: Pentair Thermal Management LLC

Except for specific models of equipment, the manual control and ambient thermostat control methods used with snow-melting and anti-icing systems are similar to those described earlier for roof deicing systems. Ambient thermostat control is used to prevent the formation of ice on the pavement surface during all cold weather conditions. This control method keeps all points on the surface above 32°F (0°C) during freezing weather.

The most energy-efficient method of control is an automatic snow controller working in conjunction with a snow sensor. When the snow sensor detects rain or snow in the presence of low temperatures, it signals the snow controller to energize the contactor that supplies power to the snow-melting and anti-icing system. When the precipitation stops or the temperature rises above freezing, the controller de-energizes the system. An off-delay timing function incorporated into the controller can be used to extend the melting time. It keeps the melting equipment in operation for a preset time after the sensor no longer detects precipitation accompanied by below-freezing temperatures. *Figure 26* shows typical wiring for a snow-melting and anti-icing system under the control of an automatic snow controller.

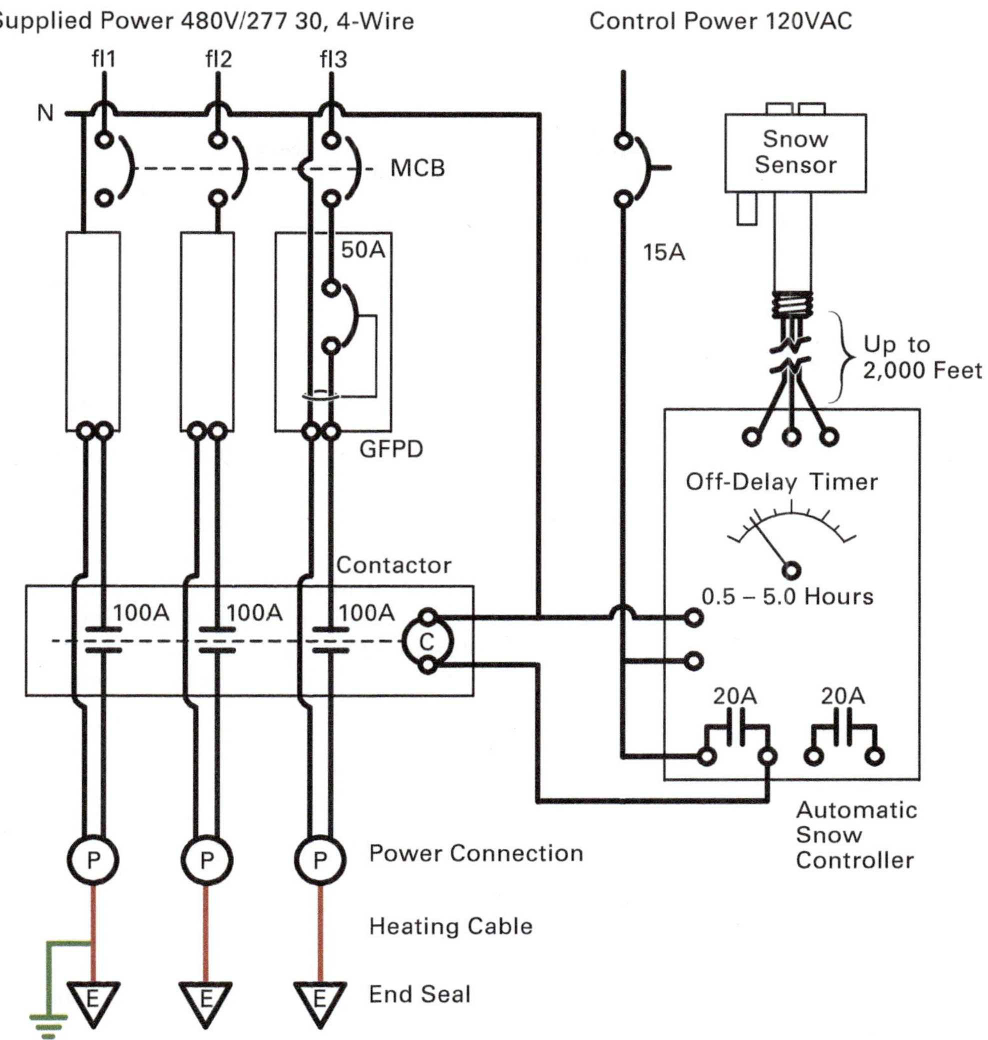

Figure 26 Typical wiring for a snow-melting and anti-icing system controlled by an automatic snow controller.
Source: Pentair Thermal Management LLC

3.2.0 Component Selection and Installation

Each equipment manufacturer provides specific guidelines for the component selection and installation of its snow-melting and anti-icing systems. The stages and considerations for the component selection process for a regular heating cable (non-mat) system are described in the following steps.

Step 1 Determine the spacing between the cables based on the ambient temperature and other weather characteristics of the region.

Step 2 Determine the cable layout and total length of cable based on the application and surface area to be heated.

Step 3 Determine the method of system temperature control based on dependability, precision, and energy consumption requirements:

- Manual control
- Ambient thermostat control
- Automatic snow control

Step 4 Determine the number of electrical circuits and transformer size based on:

- Total heating cable length
- Supply voltage
- Minimum startup temperature

Step 5 Select the correct components and accessories.

Always install snow-melting and anti-icing systems in strict accordance with the system design specifications, the manufacturer's instructions, and all prevailing local codes. *NEC Article 426* covers the requirements for fixed electric deicing and snow-melting equipment installed in unclassified areas. The *NEC*® requirements are covered in the following section.

Know the Code

Fixed Outdoor Electric Deicing and Snow-Melting Equipment
NEC Article 426

NOTE

Refer to the manufacturer's instructions for metric equivalents and equipment-specific spacing requirements.

3.2.1 Installation of Heating Cable and Components

Before starting the installation, the cable and its components should be inventoried, tested, and stored as described earlier for the cable and components used in roof, gutter, and downspout systems. Make sure there is enough heating cable available to complete the job. The minimum amount of heating cable required can be calculated using the following formula. Typically, 3' (0.9 m) of additional cable should be allowed for making power connections, 1' (300 mm) for each splice, and 1½' (450 mm) for each connection made at expansion joint kits.

$$\text{Total heating cable length in feet} = \frac{\text{heated area in feet}^2 \times 12}{\text{heated cable spacing}} + \text{end and component cable allowances}$$

The general guidelines for cable handling and installation described earlier also apply when installing heating cable for snow-melting and anti-icing systems. However, there are some cable and component installation guidelines unique to snow-melting and anti-icing systems installed in concrete. They are described as follows:

Cracks in Concrete

Heating cable should only be embedded in concrete pavement or slabs designed for that purpose. Concrete pavement or slabs with poor structural integrity can develop cracks that extend to the depth of the heating cable, possibly damaging the cable and causing a fire.

- Install the heating cable in a serpentine pattern covering the area to be heated. Space the cable in accordance with the job specifications, typically 1' (30 cm) on center. This distance should be maintained within 1" (25 mm). Some locations require closer spacing to provide more snow-melting or anti-icing capability.
- Do not route heating cable within 4" (100 mm) of the edges of the pavement, drains, anchors, or other objects in the concrete.
- Install the heating cable 1½" to 2" (38 mm to 50 mm) below the finished surface and fasten it to the reinforcing bars or wire mesh (*Figure 27*).

3.2.2 *NEC*® Requirements

NEC Article 426 covers the requirements for all fixed outdoor electric deicing and snow-melting equipment. Except for the requirements that pertain only to exposed equipment, the *NEC Article 426* requirements described earlier for roof, gutter, and downspout deicing systems also apply to snow-melting and anti-icing equipment.

Some of the requirements unique to equipment embedded in concrete or similar material are summarized as follows:

Know the Code

Watt Density
NEC Section 426.20(A)

Know the Code

Spacing
NEC Section 426.20(B)

- Embedded panels or units must not exceed 120 watts per square feet (W/ft^2) or 1,300 watts per square meter (W/m^2) per *NEC Section 426.20(A)*.
- Embedded adjacent cable runs should be spaced according to the cable rating, but no less than 1" (25 mm) on center per *NEC Section 426.20(B)*.

- Place embedded panels, units, or cables a masonry or asphalt base at least 2" (50 mm) thick, with at least $1\frac{1}{2}$" (38 mm) of masonry or asphalt applied over the finished surface per *NEC Section 426.20(C)(1)*.
- Fasten embedded panels, units, or cables in place by approved means while the concrete, masonry, or asphalt finish is applied per *NEC Section 426.20(D)*.

Know the Code

Cover
NEC Section 426.20(C)

Know the Code

Secured
NEC Section 426.20(D)

Figure 27 Heating cables in concrete sidewalk form.
Source: Pentair Thermal Management LLC

3.0.0 Section Review

1. Snow-melting and anti-icing systems rely on cables installed in a serpentine pattern with a(n) _____.
   a. 8" (200 mm) spacing between the loops
   b. 1' (300 mm) spacing between the loops
   c. 18" (450 mm) spacing between the loops
   d. 3' (0.9 m) spacing between the loops

2. Snow-melting cable should *not* be routed within how many inches of the edges of the pavement, drains, anchors, or other objects in the concrete?
   a. 1' (25 mm)
   b. 2" (50 mm)
   c. 4" (100 mm)
   d. 6" (150 mm)

4.0.0 Other Tracing and Warming Systems

Performance Tasks

There are no Performance Tasks in this section.

Objective

Describe other electric heat-tracing and warming systems and the relevant selection/installation considerations.

a. Describe domestic hot-water temperature maintenance systems and the relevant selection/installation considerations.
b. Describe electric floor-heating systems and the relevant selection/installation considerations.

Electric heat-tracing cable and components can be used to maintain the temperature of domestic hot-water circulating loops. In addition, electric heating cable is often used for space heating by embedding or encasing heating cables in the floor. Both applications are presented in the following sections.

4.1.0 Domestic Hot-Water Temperature Maintenance Systems

Electrical heat tracing can be used for temperature maintenance of domestic hot water in lines wherever the hot-water circulating loop is expansive, such as hospitals, schools, prisons, and commercial high-rise office buildings. For these applications, specially designed self-regulating heating cable is installed on all the domestic hot-water pipe branches and risers within the building, underneath the standard pipe insulation (*Figure 28*). The heating cable adjusts its power output to compensate for supply-line heat losses that result from variations in water and ambient temperature. The power output of the cable is increased or decreased only at the points where the heat losses occur. Unlike conventional domestic hot-water systems, heat-traced hot-water systems do not require overheating the supply water to allow for cooling. System design is also simplified and costs are reduced because return water lines, circulating pumps, and balancing valves used in conventional domestic hot-water systems are not needed.

Except for the specific model, the components and accessories used in heat-traced domestic hot-water systems are the same as those used with other heat-tracing systems. These include power connections, heating cable, end seals, cable splices, and tees. The system control and monitoring methods are also similar.

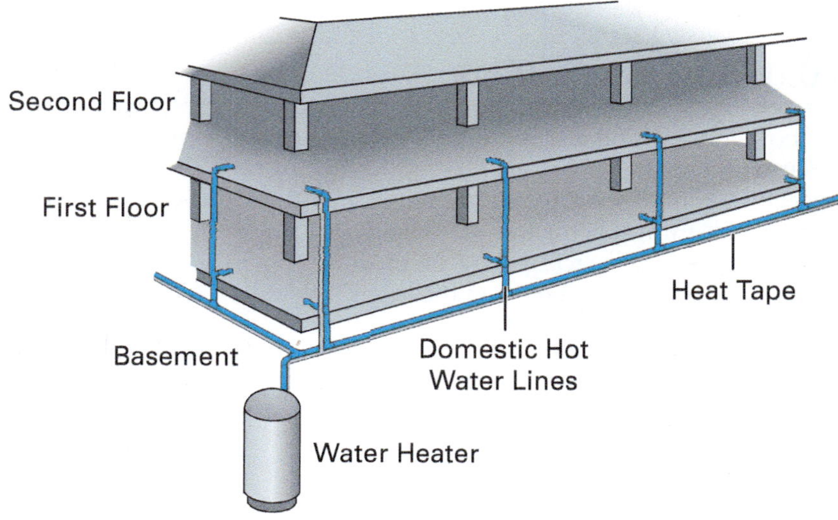

Figure 28 Heat-traced domestic hot-water system.
Source: Pentair Thermal Management LLC

4.1.1 Component Selection and Installation

Each equipment manufacturer provides specific guidelines for the component selection and installation of its domestic hot-water temperature maintenance systems. The stages and considerations for general guidelines for the component selection are outlined in the following steps.

Step 1 Review the plumbing design plan and determine its application.

Step 2 Determine the temperature requirements based on the application.

Step 3 Determine the type of self-regulating heating cable based on the application:

- Ambient temperature
- Nominal pipe temperature requirements

Step 4 Determine the maximum circuit cable length based on:

- Cable type
- Circuit breaker size
- Minimum water temperature at system startup

Step 5 Determine the number of electrical circuits based on:

- Total heating cable length
- Desired circuit layout for floors, risers, zones, and wings

Step 6 Select the correct components and accessories.

Installation and testing of heat-tracing cables used for domestic hot-water temperature maintenance is done in the same way as described earlier for heat tracing other types of pipe systems. The heating cables are typically installed on copper tubing beneath fiberglass insulation. At least 2' (0.6 m) of additional cable should be allowed for making power connections and splices, and 3' (0.9 m) should be allowed for heat tracing at pipe tees. Leave a service loop of extra heating cable at connections or at places in the piping where future service is expected.

Know the Code

Fixed Electric Heating Equipment for Pipelines and Vessels
NEC Article 427

4.1.2 *NEC*® Requirements

NEC Article 427 covers the requirements for fixed electric heating equipment installed on pipes and vessels, including domestic hot-water heat-tracing systems. Refer to the *NEC Article 427* requirements summarized earlier in the section on heat-tracing pipe systems. *NEC Article 517* contains specific requirements for health care facilities.

Know the Code

Health Care Facilities
NEC Article 517

4.2.0 Floor-Heating and Warming Systems

Floor-heating and warming systems, also called *radiant floor-heating systems,* are used to heat or warm a floor mass that, in turn, radiates the heat to the cooler air in the room. Rooms with radiant heat in the floor tend to have a uniform air temperature from the ceiling to the floor, whereas a room heated with warm, forced air from a furnace will often be cold near the floor and hot near the ceiling. Floor heating systems are commonly used as either main or supplemental heating to heat or warm concrete floors, floors over unheated spaces, and tile and marble floors. Some floor heating systems can be used to warm hardwood and carpeted floors. To prevent frost-heave damage, floor systems are sometimes used to warm the soil beneath cold storage and large freezer floors.

Different types of heating elements are made for use in electric radiant floor-heating systems. One type uses continuous self-regulating or series-resistance heating cable specifically designed for floor warming applications (*Figure 29*). This heating cable is installed so that it snakes across the floor area in continuous loops. The closer together the loops, the more heat generated in that area. The heat from the cable is absorbed by the surrounding floor materials from which it is slowly radiated into the room. Heating cable can be incorporated into floors by embedding it in mortar; running it in conduits embedded in concrete, sand, or soil; or mounting it to the exposed bottom surface of concrete floors.

Many floor warming systems use one or more factory-made electrical heating mats instead of a continuous cable. These are typically installed over a wood floor-joist system or concrete-slab floor system. Some heating mats consist of an electric cable fastened to a flexible mesh support structure. The mat is unrolled, cut to size, taped or stapled in place, then embedded in thin-set masonry beneath the finished floor material (*Figure 30*). Some systems use mesh mats that are installed on a plywood subfloor or concrete substrate over which carpet is installed.

Temperature control of a floor warming system is usually managed using an appropriate thermostatic control installed in accordance with the manufacturer's instructions. For systems using continuous cable, the sensing bulb of the thermostatic control is installed in the floor at the same depth as the heating cable, midway between adjacent runs of cable, and away from the room walls. The bulb should be installed inside a PVC conduit so that it can be easily removed for service, if necessary.

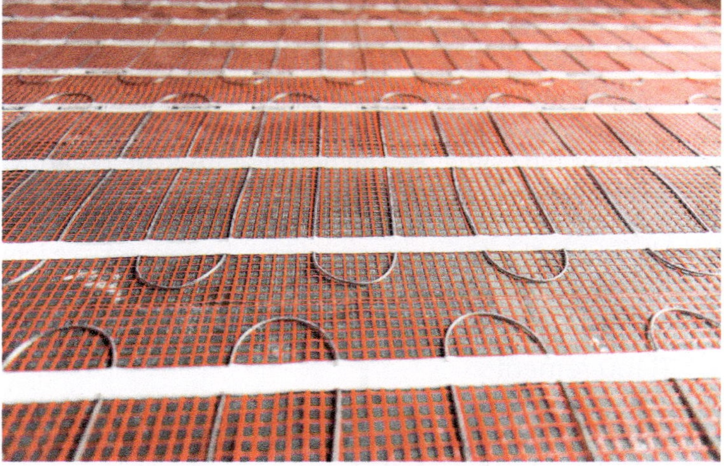

Figure 29 Basic concrete and masonry electric radiant floor-heating system.
Source: iStock@Manuta

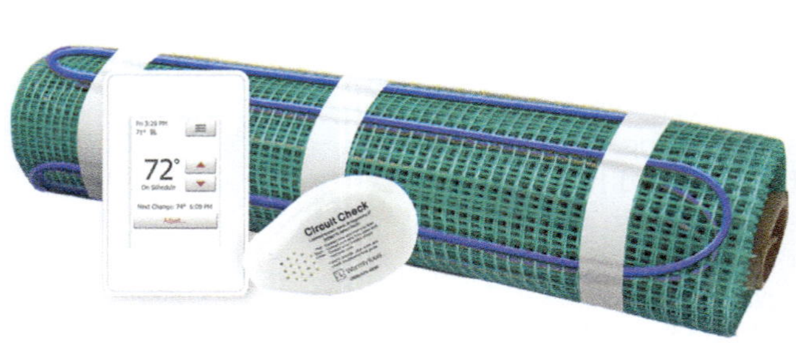

Figure 30 Typical electric floor-heating mat installation.
Source: WarmlyYours Radiant Heating

Radiant Floor-Heating Systems

Radiant floor-heating systems have been used for many centuries. Evidence shows that around 1,300 BC, a radiant floor heating system was used in a Turkish king's palace. Over a period ranging from about 80 BC to AD 324, the Romans used improved versions of these heating systems in upper-class houses and public baths throughout their empire. Those systems consisted of chambers built under the floor or tile flues built into a stone floor. Heated combustion gases, produced by a fire enclosed in a chamber located at one end of the floor, were routed through the floor chambers or flue tiles to exhaust vents placed in the outside walls at the other end of the floor.

Going Green

Electric Floor Heating

Often, the bathroom is the only room requiring additional warmth in the morning. Using a floor warming system in the bathroom allows the homeowner to keep the remainder of the home at a lower temperature, resulting in a significant energy savings over time.

4.2.1 Component Selection and Installation

There is a wide diversity in floor-heating and warming system applications, equipment, and related installation methods. Because of this diversity, it is impractical to give general guidelines for component selection and system installation. Each equipment manufacturer has readily available product literature that gives system design and component selection criteria for specific products and floor heating or warming applications. Floor heating and warming systems must be installed in strict accordance with the system design specifications, the manufacturer's instructions, and all prevailing local codes. When installing floor heating and warming systems, follow the general guidelines given earlier in this module for storing, handling, and testing the heating cable.

4.2.2 *NEC*® Requirements

NEC Article 424 covers the requirements for fixed electric space-heating equipment. If the equipment is installed in hazardous (classified) areas, *NEC Articles 500 through 516* also apply. Refer to *NEC Article 424* for the requirements for heating cables installed in concrete or poured masonry floors. These requirements are summarized as follows:

- Extending heating cable beyond the room or area where it originates is permitted per *NEC Section 424.38(A)*.
- Splice heating cable *only* by using splices identified in the manufacturer's instructions (*NEC Section 424.40*).
- Follow manufacturer's guidelines when installing adjacent runs of heating cable per *NEC Section 424.44(A)*.
- Fasten heating cable in place by approved nonmetallic means while the concrete is applied per *NEC Section 424.44(B)*.
- Protect non-heating cable leads exiting the floor by installing them in conduit per *NEC Section 424.44(C)*.
- Provide ground fault circuit interrupter protection for personnel for heating cables installed in electrically heated floors of bathrooms and kitchens, and in hydromassage bathtub locations per *NEC Section 424.44(E)*.
- Inspect and approve heating cable installations before cables are concealed per *NEC Section 424.46*.
- Do not install heating panels or panel sets where they bridge expansion joints unless provision is made for expansion and contraction per *NEC Sections 424.98(B) and 424.99(B)(1)*.

Know the Code

Fixed Electric Space-Heating Equipment
NEC Article 424

Know the Code

Special Occupancies
NEC Chapter 5

4.0.0 Section Review

1. In hospitals, schools, and prisons, electrical heat-tracing systems are used for _____.
   a. temperature maintenance of domestic hot-water piping systems
   b. viscosity control on chemical piping
   c. adjusting the dew point
   d. moisture control inside air lines

2. On floor heating and warming systems, heating panels and/or panel sets are *not* installed without provisions for expansion and contraction _____.
   a. near conduit
   b. in concrete slabs
   c. where they bridge expansion joints
   d. in concealed areas

Module 26409-23 Review Questions

1. As the ambient temperature surrounding a self-regulating heating cable gets colder, the _____.
   a. cable's heat output decreases
   b. cable's conductive polymeric core expands
   c. resistance of the bus wires decreases
   d. resistance of the polymeric core decreases

2. Which type of heating cable contains a resistor alloy heating element with a positive temperature coefficient?
   a. Power-limiting
   b. Self-regulating
   c. Mineral-insulated
   d. Series-resistance

3. Which of the following methods of heat-tracing system control uses a programmed algorithm to calculate the cycle time during which the heating circuits are energized?
   a. Line-sensing control
   b. Ambient-sensing control
   c. Proportional ambient-sensing control
   d. Dead-leg control

4. Which type of heat-tracing monitoring system measures current leakage from the system cables?
   a. Current monitoring
   b. Ground fault monitoring
   c. Continuity monitoring
   d. Temperature monitoring

5. The *minimum* number of circuits required for a pipe heat-tracing installation is determined by dividing the total length of the heating cable needed _____.
   a. by seven
   b. by nine
   c. into sections with a demand of no more than 20A per section
   d. by the maximum circuit length that can be used for the specific cable in use

6. When determining the *minimum* amount of heating cable needed to heat-trace a run of pipe, add about _____.
   a. 1' (300 mm) of cable for each splice
   b. 2' (600 mm) of cable for each splice
   c. 3' (900 mm) of cable for each splice
   d. 4' (1.2 m) of cable for each splice

7. When installing temperature sensors in a pipe heat-tracing system, the sensors should be located _____.
   a. less than 1' (<300 mm) from any heat source or heat sink
   b. 1' to 3' (300 mm to 900 mm) from any heat source or heat sink
   c. 3' to 5' (0.9 m to 1.5 m) from any heat source or heat sink
   d. 5' to 8' (1.5 m to 2.4 m) from any heat source or heat sink

8. The continuity and electrical insulation resistance of heating cables should be tested _____.
   a. before installation
   b. during installation
   c. during and after installation
   d. before and after installation

9. Which of the following methods of control for a roof deicing system is the *most* energy efficient?
   a. Manual control
   b. Ambient thermostat control
   c. Automatic moisture/temperature control
   d. Automatic snow control

10. What is the operating temperature of equipment above which deicing or snow-melting cable must be guarded to prevent contact with personnel?
    a. 110°F (43°C)
    b. 120°F (49°C)
    c. 130°F (54°C)
    d. 140°F (60°C)

11. The *most* energy-efficient method of snow-melting control is _____.
    a. manual control
    b. ambient thermostat control
    c. automatic snow control with a sensor
    d. end component control

12. The requirements for the installation of electrical snow-melting and deicing systems are defined in _____.
    a. *NEC Article 424*
    b. *NEC Article 425*
    c. *NEC Article 426*
    d. *NEC Article 427*

13. The spacing between embedded adjacent cable runs for a snow-melting and deicing system must *not* be less than _____.
    a. 1" (25 mm) on center
    b. 6" (150 mm) on center
    c. 10" (250 mm) on center
    d. 12' (300 mm) on center

14. Domestic hot-water temperature maintenance cable is typically _____.
    a. cut to the exact length required
    b. used with uninsulated systems
    c. installed on PVC pipe
    d. installed on copper tubing

15. While concrete is applied, floor heating cable shall be fastened in place by _____.
    a. staples
    b. straps
    c. approved nonmetallic means
    d. wire ties

Answers to odd-numbered Module Review Questions are found in *Appendix A*.

Module 26409-23 Supplemental Exercises

1. List five types of electric heat-tracing and freeze-protection systems.

   ____

   ____

2. A self-regulating cable __________ its heat output when there is a decrease in the ambient temperature.

3. Power-limiting cables are a type of __________, __________ heating cable.

4. True or False? MI heating cables can be cut to length in the field as needed.

5. The transfer of heat from a tracer heating cable to a pipe can be improved by putting a layer of __________ between the tracer cable and the pipe.

6. List four operating characteristics that may be monitored to detect failures in heat-tracing systems.

   ____

   ____

7. When determining the amount of heating cable required for a job, you would typically add __________ of cable for each electrical power connection, splice, tee, and end seal.

8. Where in the *NEC*® would you find the requirements for roof, gutter, and downspout deicing systems?

   ____

   ____

9. The *NEC*® requirements for fixed electric heating equipment installed on pipes and vessels also apply when heat tracing _____.
   a. snow-melting and anti-icing systems
   b. domestic hot-water systems
   c. floor-heating and warming systems
   d. roof, gutter, and downspout deicing systems

10. Which of the following statements about the installation of the thermostatic control used to control the temperature in a floor warming system is *false*?
    a. It should be placed in direct contact with the floor mortar or concrete.
    b. It should be placed midway between adjacent cable runs.
    c. It should be installed at the same depth as the heating cable.
    d. It should be installed away from the room walls.

Answers to odd-numbered Supplemental Exercises are found in *Appendix B*.

Answers to Section Review Questions

Answer	Section Reference	Objective
Section 1.0.0		
1. d	1.1.3	1a
2. a	1.2.4	1b
3. b	1.3.0	1c
4. c	1.4.0	1d
5. a	1.5.1	1e
Section 2.0.0		
1. b	2.1.0	2a
2. d	2.2.1	2b
Section 3.0.0		
1. b	3.1.0	3a
2. c	3.2.1	3b
Section 4.0.0		
1. a	4.1.0	4a
2. c	4.2.2	4b

Motor Operation and Maintenance

Source: iStock@Hramovnick

Objectives

Successful completion of this module prepares you to do the following:

1. Identify the factors that affect motor reliability and life span.
   a. Identify the common causes of motor failure.
   b. Identify motor characteristics.
2. Describe maintenance and troubleshooting requirements for electric motors.
   a. Identify the tools, basic care, and maintenance requirements for electric motors.
   b. Explain the requirements for maintaining motor bearings.
   c. Explain how to perform motor insulation testing.
   d. Explain how to troubleshoot an electric motor.
3. Describe the guidelines for installing and commissioning electric motors.
   a. Explain alignment and adjustment requirements.
   b. Describe startup procedures.

Performance Tasks

This is a knowledge-based module. There are no Performance Tasks.

Overview

For motors to operate at optimum levels over a long span of time, proper care and maintenance are required. This module covers motor care procedures, including cleaning, testing, and preventive maintenance. Basic troubleshooting procedures are also presented.

NOTE

NCCER Industry-Recognized Credentials

If you are training through an NCCER-accredited sponsor, you may be eligible for credentials from NCCER. The ID number for this module is 26410-23. Note that this module may have been used in other NCCER curricula and may apply to other level completions. Contact NCCER at 1.888.622.3720 or go to **www.nccer.org** for more information.

You can also show off your industry-recognized credentials online with NCCER's digital badges. Transform your knowledge, skills, and achievements into badges that you can share across social media platforms, send to your network, and add to your resume. For more information, visit **www.nccer.org**.

Digital Resources for Electrical

Scan this code using the camera on your phone or mobile device to view the digital resources related to this craft.

1.0.0 Motor Reliability and Life Span

Performance Tasks

There are no Performance Tasks in this section.

Objective

Identify the factors that affect motor reliability and life span.

a. Identify the common causes of motor failure.

b. Identify motor characteristics.

Three-phase, squirrel-cage induction motors (*Figure 1*) are the most common motors in heavy commercial and industrial use. The life expectancy of a squirrel-cage induction motor depends largely on the condition of its insulation, which should be suitable for the operating requirements, along with the performance of any required maintenance. Electric motors are sometimes called *rotating electrical machinery, electric machinery,* or just *machines*.

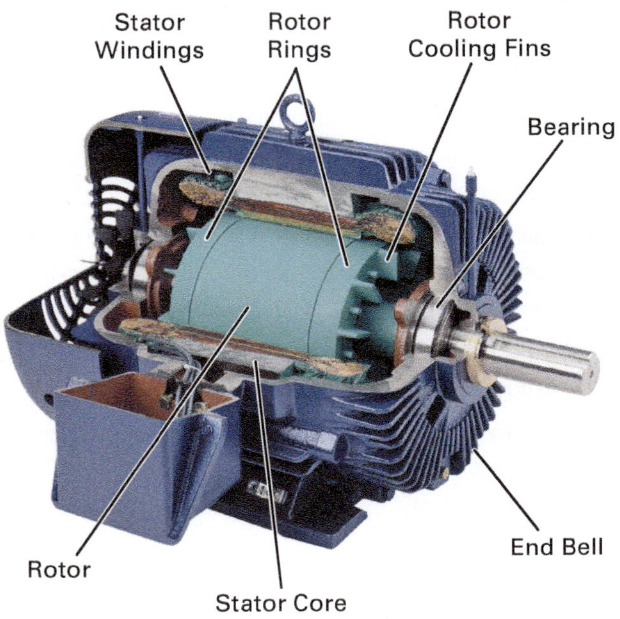

Figure 1 Squirrel-cage motor construction.
Source: Marathon Electric Motors

1.1.0 Causes of Motor Failure

When a motor malfunctions, it is due to either mechanical or electrical causes. These failures can be traced to one or more of the following:

- *Worn or tight bearings* — Worn or tight bearings are usually caused by failing bearing lubrication or improper lubrication. If the bearings have failed or are worn to such an extent that they allow the rotor to drag on the stator, then the rotor, stator, and stator windings can be irreparably damaged. When bearings begin to fail, the condition can be detected by periodically checking the motor for excessive heat, noise, or vibration at the bearings before damage occurs. Heat and vibration can be measured using appropriate testers at the motor bearing housing. Bearing misalignment within the motor can also cause excessive wear or tightness. This is usually caused by a condition called **soft foot**. This occurs when the feet of a motor frame are forced to anchor against an uneven surface, resulting in distortion of the motor frame. Proper mounting surfaces and shimming must be used to prevent soft foot when a motor is installed.

Soft foot: When the feet of a motor frame are forced to anchor against an uneven surface, resulting in distortion of the motor frame. This can cause misalignment of bearings.

- *Vibration* — Motor vibration can be caused by a bent shaft, misalignment of shafts between a motor and a directly coupled load, or loose anchorage. Vibration may result in excessive bearing wear or failure. Dial indicators can be used to check for bent shafts or misalignment.
- *Moisture* — Motor insulation must be kept reasonably dry, although many applications make this practically impossible unless a **totally enclosed (TE) motor** is used. Infrequently used or stored motors must be kept dry to prevent premature insulation failure.
- *Dust and dirt* — Dust and dirt can restrict ventilation and increase a motor's operating temperature. Overheating can cause premature bearing and winding failure. Cleaning is usually accomplished by periodically blowing out ventilation passages or fins with compressed air. The compressed air must be dry and regulated to a safe pressure for use.
- *Insulation deterioration* — Assuming no other mechanical or electrical causes, the winding insulation of all motors will deteriorate over time and will eventually break down, causing arcing and/or burnout of the windings. A **megohmmeter**, commonly called a *megger*, is used to periodically check the insulation resistance of the windings to chart the progress of insulation deterioration in megohms. Megohmmeters are also used as a troubleshooting tool for motors. Some megohmmeters can perform other motor performance and evaluation tests.
- *Overloading* — Overloading a motor can cause overheating and eventual bearing failure or premature insulation failure of the windings. Overloading usually occurs because the driven load has been changed to accommodate a higher capacity, heavier capacity, or an increased duty cycle. When driven loads are altered for these reasons, existing motors must be evaluated to be certain they can withstand the new load.
- *Single-phasing* — The loss of a single phase of a polyphase power source for a running motor can cause the failure of the remaining motor phase windings if the motor is not protected by the proper equipment. This can occur in older installations where failure of one voltage phase due to a partial primary power failure or a failed fuse does not cause removal of all voltage phases from the motor. These types of installations should be updated using proper motor controllers and/or loss-of-phase protection.

Totally enclosed (TE) motor: A motor that is encased to prevent the free exchange of air between the inside and outside of the case.

Megohmmeter: An instrument or meter capable of measuring resistances more than 200 MΩ. It employs much higher test voltages than are used in ohmmeters, which measure up to 200 MΩ. A megohmmeter is also commonly referred to as a *megger*.

Severe electrical, mechanical, or environmental operating conditions can damage the stator winding of a three-phase, squirrel-cage motor. Such winding failures and their causes are shown in *Figure 2A* and *Figure 2B*. Motors that have suffered severe core damage because of overheating or mechanical damage from the rotor are usually discarded. This is because severe core damage generally results in abnormal core losses or the loss of efficiency if the motor is rewound. In an emergency, some motors with severe damage can be rewound after some or most of the damaged core laminations are restacked. However, this will result in a shortened operating life. Therefore, these motors should be replaced as soon as possible. Depending on the type of facility and the number and size of the motors used within the facility, motors below some facility-established horsepower rating may not be salvaged when they fail, nor should they be included in periodic predictive testing programs. However, the cause of failure for any motor should be investigated and corrected to prevent rapid failures of any replacement motors.

Many times, a motor that was originally of adequate capacity for a given load is later found to be inadequate. The following are some reasons for this problem:

- More severe duty imposed on the machine tool, such as a different die job in a punch press
- Heavier material or material of different machining characteristics
- Changed machine operation

Single-Phased Undamaged Winding (Caused by a Missing Voltage Phase in a Wye-Connected Motor)

Single-Phased Damaged Winding (Caused by a Missing Voltage Phase in a Delta-Connected Motor)

Phase-to-Phase Short (Caused by Contamination, Abrasion, Vibration, or Voltage Surge)

Turn-to-Turn Short (Caused by Contamination, Abrasion, Vibration, or Voltage Surge)

Shorted Coil (Caused by Contamination, Abrasion, Vibration, or Voltage Surge)

Winding Grounded at Edge of Slot (Caused by Contamination, Abrasion, Vibration, or Voltage Surge)

Figure 2A Stator winding failures and causes (1 of 2).
Source: Electrical Apparatus Service Association

Winding Grounded in Slot (Caused by Contamination, Abrasion, Vibration, or Voltage Surge)

Shorted Connection (Caused by Contamination, Abrasion, Vibration, or Voltage Surge)

Unbalanced Voltage Damage (Severe for One Phase, Slight for Another Phase, and Caused by Unbalanced Power Source Loads or Poor Connections)

Overload Damage to All Windings
Note: Undervoltage and overvoltage (exceeding NEMA standards) will result in the same type of insulation deterioration.

Locked Rotor Overload Damage to All Windings (May Also Be Caused by Excessive Starts or Reversals)

Voltage Surge Damage (Caused by Lightning, Capacitor Discharges, Voltage Kickbacks Caused by De-Energizing Large Inductive Loads, or Voltage Disturbances Caused by Solid-State Devices)

Figure 2B Stator winding failures and causes (2 of 2).
Source: Electrical Apparatus Service Association

Connecting measuring instruments in the motor circuit may disclose the reason for motor overheating, failure to start the load, or other abnormal symptoms. It is also frequently desirable to connect recording instruments in the motor circuit for other purposes, such as analyzing the output of the machine or gauging processing operations.

Control circuits for many older induction motor installations were not provided with thermal overload relays or loss-of-phase protection. Single phasing of polyphase induction motors on such circuits frequently causes motor winding failure, which often results from blowing a fuse while the motor is up to speed and under load. Under such conditions, the portion of the winding remaining in the circuit will attempt to carry the load until it fails due to overheating.

Increasing the load on the motor beyond its rated capacity increases the operating temperature, which shortens the life of the insulation. Momentary overloads usually do no damage; consequently, there is a tendency to use thermal overload protection in modern control systems for motors rated at 600V or less. Monitoring the actual winding temperature is the ideal method of determining whether a motor is overloaded. Other methods, such as motor protection relays and electrical trip units for medium-voltage and 600V motors, are used to mimic thermal measurement and protect a motor from protracted overload conditions. These devices calculate (model) winding temperature by monitoring current and time using a microcomputer inside the device.

1.2.0 Motor Characteristics

Motors have specific service conditions and starting configurations to ensure optimum performance. In addition, motors are designed to operate within specific temperature ranges known as **insulation classes**.

Insulation classes: Categories of insulation based on the thermal endurance of the insulation system used in a motor. The insulation system is chosen to ensure that the motor will perform at the rated horsepower and service factor load.

1.2.1 Motor Service Conditions

The National Electrical Manufacturers Association (NEMA) has defined standards for usual service conditions for motors. For standard motors to perform in accordance with their ratings, they must be operated within the limits of the following NEMA usual service conditions:

- *Ambient or room temperature not over 40°C (104°F)* — If the ambient temperature is over 40°C due to inadequate airflow in the motor location, the motor service factor must be reduced, or a larger motor or motor with a higher insulation temperature must be used. The larger motor will be loaded below full capacity, so the temperature rise will be lower, and the potential for overheating will be reduced.
- *Altitude does not exceed 3,300' (1,000 m)* — Motors are typically designed to operate at altitudes below 3,300'. Motors with Class A or B insulation systems and lower temperature rises as defined by NEMA will operate satisfactorily at altitudes above 3,300' in locations where the decrease in ambient temperature compensates for the increase in temperature rise. Motors having a service factor of 1.15 or higher will operate satisfactorily at unity service factor and an ambient temperature of 40°C at altitudes above 3,300' up to 9,000' (1,000 m up to 2,743 m).
- *Voltage variation of not more than 10% of nameplate voltage* — Operation outside these limits or a voltage imbalance over 5% can result in overheating or loss of torque and may require the use of a larger motor.
- *Frequency variation of not more than 5% of nameplate frequency* — Operation outside of these limits results in a substantial speed variation and causes both overheating and reduced torque.
- *Plugging, jogging, or multiple starts* — Unless rated for this use, standard motors should not be used.

Motors are often exposed to damaging atmospheres such as excessive moisture, steam, salt air, abrasive or conductive dust, lint, chemical fumes, and combustible or explosive dust or gases. To protect such motors, special enclosures or encapsulated windings and special bearing protection are required. However, the location of supplementary enclosures must not interfere with the ventilation of the motor.

Motors exposed to damaging mechanical or electrical loading such as unbalanced voltage conditions, abnormal shock or vibration, torsional impact loads, plugging, jogging, multiple starts, or excessive thrust or overhang loads may require special mountings or protection designed for the specific installation.

1.2.2 Starting Configurations

Squirrel-cage motors are usually designed for across-the-line starting, meaning they can be connected directly to the power source by means of a suitable contactor. For large motors and in some other types of motors, the starting currents are very high. Usually, the motor is built to withstand starting currents, but because these currents are often six times or more than the rated load current, there may be a large voltage drop in the power system. Some method of reducing the starting current must therefore be used to limit the system voltage drop to a tolerable value.

Reduced-voltage starting significantly reduces the torque and acceleration characteristics of any motor. Therefore, it is necessary to have the motor unloaded or nearly so when the motor is started. Reduction of the starting voltage is the primary method of reducing motor starting current. Reduction of the starting current may be accomplished using a variable-frequency motor controller, soft starter, or any one of the following reduced-voltage starting methods:

- *Primary resistor or reactance* — Primary resistor or reactance starting uses series reactance or resistance to reduce the current on the first step. After a preset time interval, the motor is connected directly across the line. This method can be used with any standard motor.
- *Autotransformer* — Autotransformer starting uses autotransformers to reduce the voltage and current on the first step. After a preset time interval, the motor is connected directly across the line. This method can be used with any standard motor.
- *Wye-delta* — Wye-delta starting impresses the voltage across the Y connection to reduce the current on the first step. After a preset time interval, the motor is connected in delta, permitting full-load operation. The motor must have a winding capable of wye-delta connection.
- *Part-winding* — Part-winding starting involves motors with two separate winding circuits. Upon starting, only one winding circuit is engaged, and current is reduced. After a preset time interval, the full winding of the motor is put directly across the line. The motor must have two separate winding circuits. To avoid possible overheating and subsequent damage to the winding, the time between the connection of the first and second windings is limited to four seconds.

All these starting methods require special starters designed for the particular method and must be controlled between the start and run functions by an adjustable timer or current relay.

1.2.3 Insulation Systems

An insulation system is an assembly of insulating materials associated with conductors and the supporting structural parts of a motor. Insulation systems are divided into classes according to the thermal endurance of the system for temperature rating purposes. Four classes of insulation systems are used in motors: A, B, F, and H. Do not confuse these insulation classes with motor designs, which are also designated by letter. Each insulation class is classified as follows:

- *Class A* — Class A insulation systems have a suitable thermal endurance when operated at the limiting Class A temperature of 105°C (221°F). Typical materials used include cotton, paper, cellulose acetate films, enamel-coated wire, and similar organic materials infused with suitable substances.
- *Class B* — Class B insulation systems have suitable thermal endurance when operated at the limiting Class B temperature of 130°C (266°F). Typical materials include mica, glass fiber, and other materials (organic or inorganic) with compatible bonding substances having suitable thermal stability.
- *Class F* — Class F insulation systems have suitable thermal endurance when operated at the limiting Class F temperature of 155°C (311°F). Typical materials include mica, glass fiber, and other materials (organic or inorganic) with compatible bonding substances having suitable thermal stability.
- *Class H* — Class H insulation systems have suitable thermal endurance when operated at the limiting Class H temperature of 180°C (356°F). Typical materials used include mica, glass fiber, silicone elastomer, and other materials (organic or inorganic) with compatible bonding substances (for example, silicone resins) having suitable thermal stability.

1.0.0 Section Review

1. Excessive heat, noise, or vibration in a motor is an indication of _____.
   a. bad wiring
   b. worn bearings
   c. loose motor mount
   d. low input voltage

2. The NEMA standard for maximum voltage imbalance is _____.
   a. 5%
   b. 10%
   c. 20%
   d. 25%

2.0.0 Motor Maintenance

Performance Tasks

There are no Performance Tasks in this section.

Objective

Describe maintenance and troubleshooting requirements for electric motors.

a. Identify the tools, basic care, and maintenance requirements for electric motors.
b. Explain the requirements for maintaining motor bearings.
c. Explain how to perform motor insulation testing.
d. Explain how to troubleshoot an electric motor.

Motor failures account for a high percentage of industrial and heavy commercial electrical repair work. The care given to an electric motor while it is being stored or operated affects the life and usefulness of the motor. A motor that receives good maintenance will outlast a poorly treated motor many times over. Maintaining a motor in good operating condition requires periodic preventive maintenance actions along with periodic predictive testing. Predictive testing is required to determine if any faults exist or if faults are likely to occur in the near future. When a motor is determined to be in the process of failing, it should be removed and replaced. If a motor has been replaced before its core has been damaged, it can usually be sent to a motor rebuild facility for salvage as a spare.

2.1.0 Motor Maintenance Requirements

The frequency and thoroughness of the maintenance and testing of a motor depend on such factors as:

- Number of hours and days the motor operates
- Importance of the motor
- Nature of service
- Environmental conditions

Most heavy-duty commercial/industrial squirrel-cage motors are TE motors. TE motors are available in the following configurations:

- *TEFC motor* — A TEFC motor is a fan-cooled (FC) motor cooled by a fan attached to the rear shaft of the motor. The fan is covered by a shroud that directs the fan air through cooling passages and/or fins external to the motor. TEFC motors are the most common type of TE motor. They are also available in versions rated for severe service duty in corrosive environments, wash-down duty in food service, and explosion-proof duty in hazardous environments (*Figure 3*).
- *TEBC motor* — A TEBC motor is a blower-cooled (BC) motor cooled by a separately powered blower attached to the motor. TEBC motors are typically used in heavy-duty variable-speed motor applications.
- *TEAO motor* — A TEAO motor is a finned air-over (AO) motor that powers and is cooled by the slipstream from a large fan.
- *TENV motor* — A TENV motor is a nonventilated (NV) motor used in smaller-horsepower variable-speed applications.

Figure 3 TEFC explosion-proof motor.
Source: Courtesy of Baldor Electric Company

NOTE

Variable-speed motors are specified in the United States as inverter-grade motors that can withstand heat and surges up to 2,400V.

WARNING!

TENV motors run at very hot temperatures. Do not touch these motors during or immediately after operation.

2.1.1 Tools for Maintenance and Troubleshooting

In addition to typical equipment such as voltmeters and ammeters, motor maintenance equipment should also include an insulation resistance tester, such as a multivoltage megohmmeter. *Table 1* provides a list of practical tools and test equipment for the electrical maintenance of motors and other electrical apparatus.

Ventilation and Temperature Control

Adequate ventilation and temperature control are essential for proper motor operation. Inspect the fan and auxiliary cooling system as part of the regular maintenance program. Many larger motors include resistance temperature detectors embedded in the windings and bearing housings. This provides continuous monitoring of the winding and bearing temperatures to alert maintenance personnel to abnormal conditions.

TABLE 1 Tools and Test Equipment for Electrical Maintenance

Tools or Equipment	Application
Multimeters, voltmeters, ohmmeters, clamp-on ammeters, wattmeters, and clamp-on power factor meters	These measure circuit voltage, resistance, current, and power. They are useful for circuit tracing and troubleshooting.
Potential and current transformers and meter shunts	These increase the range of test instruments to permit the reading of high-voltage and high-current circuits.
Motor-rotation and phase-rotation testers	These determine the proper three-phase connections for the desired rotation direction of a motor prior to connecting the motor. They also check the phasing of the power source so that the motor can be connected to the desired phases.
Tachometer	This checks rotating machinery speeds.
Recording meters	These provide a permanent record of voltage, current, power, temperature, and other data on charts for analytic study.
Insulation resistance tester, thermometer, and psychrometer	These test and monitor insulation resistance, using a thermometer and psychrometer for temperature and humidity correction.
Vibration testers and transistorized stethoscopes	These detect faulty rotating machinery bearings and leaky valves.
Milli or microhmmeter	These provide a precise measurement of coil resistance.
Dial indicator with mounting devices	This is used to check for bent motor shafts and performing shaft alignment for directly coupled motor loads.

2.1.2 Basic Care and Maintenance

Every motor in operation or storage should be observed regularly as recommended by the motor manufacturer to identify exposure to any adverse condition for which it is not rated. Operating motors should also be checked for excessive dust, debris, or lint on or around the motor. Ensure that airflow is not blocked by objects or room conditions and that the cooling fins are not coated in dust. Low-pressure compressed air may be used to blow clean the motor housing ventilation paths or cooling fins.

WARNING!

Before performing any motor maintenance procedures other than external visual inspection or noise monitoring, always lock out and tag the equipment according to approved procedures. If guards covering rotating components must be removed to gain access to motor bearings, remove the guards in accordance with approved facility procedures and use great care near the rotating components. When using compressed air, exercise caution by wearing the appropriate PPE and using an airflow tip with air pressure limited to 30 psi or less. Excess air pressure can result in injury.

Inspect the motor starter and verify that the motor reaches the proper speed each time it is started. Check other motor parts and accessories such as belts, gears, couplings, chains, and sprockets, for excessive wear or misalignment. Periodically lubricate the motor as recommended by the manufacturer (discussed in detail later in *Section 2.2.1*). Be alert to any unusual noise which may be caused by metal-to-metal contact, such as bad bearings. Note any abnormal odor, which might indicate scorched insulation varnish.

Use an infrared thermometer (*Figure 4*) to check the bearing housings for evidence of excess heat and the motor itself for excess temperature rise, as listed on the motor nameplate. Compare the results to previously logged data. Use a vibration tester (*Figure 5*) to determine if excess vibration is occurring as compared to previously logged data. A stethoscope may be used to detect unusual bearing noise during motor rundown.

Vibration testers indicate the vibration velocity in inches per second (in/sec), millimeters per second (mm/sec), or centimeters per second (cm/sec), depending on the model selected. Other models are also available that display only the total peak value of the velocity amplitude in either in/sec or mm/sec. A printer or a data logger is used with some models to capture data for further analysis.

NOTE

Before using a vibration tester, make sure the equipment being checked is firmly anchored. When using the tester, make sure that its accelerometer is held firmly or secured against a bearing housing directly over the shaft center line of the bearing and as close to the middle of the actual bearing as possible. Magnetically mounted accelerometers can be used only on solid ferrous metal surfaces with no nonferrous metal in between. Make sure the magnet does not rock on the housing surface. For rounded housings, use a V-mount magnet. Place an identifying mark on the equipment where the test was made to ensure that subsequent vibration measurements are made in exactly the same spot.

2.1.3 Periodic Predictive Testing

Periodic predictive testing can be conducted on two levels. Online (dynamic) tests can be conducted with the motor operating. Offline (static) tests are conducted with the motor stopped and the power locked out and tagged. Of the two types of testing, offline testing for insulation resistance and polarization index (PI) is the most common and will be described in detail in *Section 2.3.1* and *Section 2.3.2*. Online motor analysis is a relatively new technology that evaluates a number of motor parameters on a noninterference basis while a motor is running. This type of testing uses computerized portable test equipment like that shown in *Figure 6*.

Online motor analysis is normally done in facilities with many large motors and may be conducted more frequently than offline testing. This test equipment can be used for monitoring power circuit quality, overall motor condition, load conditions, and performance efficiency. It can provide data collection and trending information to aid in periodic maintenance evaluation in addition to the data collected during offline testing. Some of these instruments are equipped with accelerometer probes that can provide sophisticated vibration data in the form of time/amplitude velocity waveforms and/or Fast Fourier Transform (FFT) velocity spectrum waveforms. The waveform data is usually analyzed by specially trained personnel and/or software to determine the probable causes of any abnormal vibration.

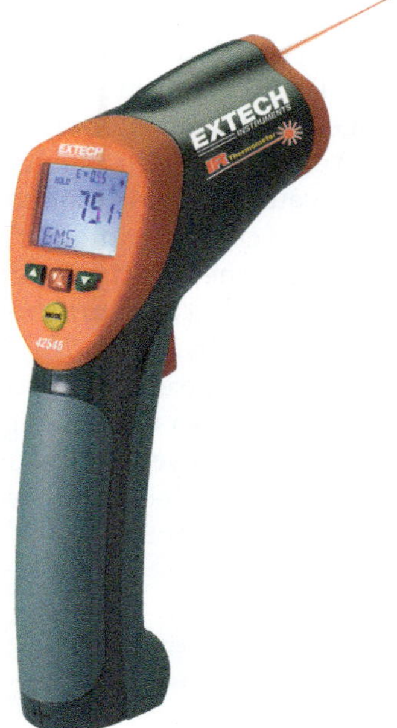

Figure 4 Infrared thermometer.
Source: Courtesy of Extech Instruments, a FLIR Company

Figure 5 Vibration tester.
Source: Reproduced with Permission, Fluke Corporation

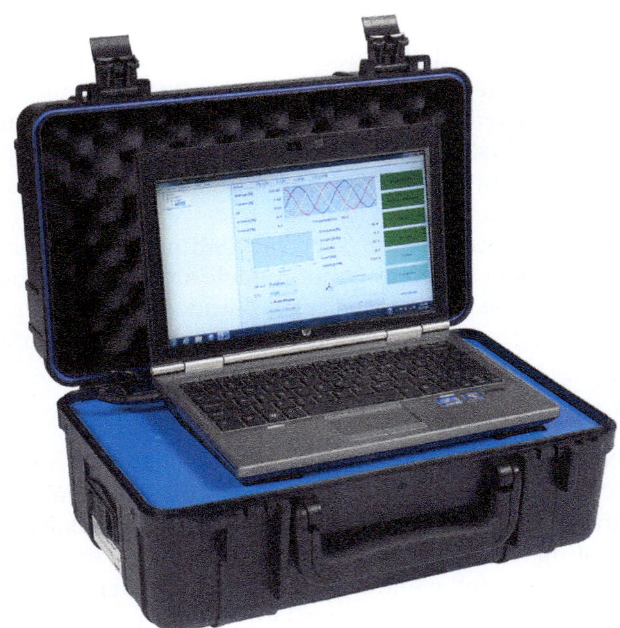

Figure 6 Online motor analysis instrument.
Source: SKF USA, Inc.

2.1.4 Receiving and Storing Motors

When an electric motor is received on a jobsite, always follow the manufacturer's recommendations for unloading, uncrating, and installing the motor. Failure to follow these recommendations can cause injury to personnel and possible damage to the motor. When the motor has been uncrated, check for damage that might have occurred during shipment. Check the motor shaft to verify that it turns freely. Clean the motor of any debris, dust, moisture, or foreign matter that might have accumulated during shipment. Make sure it is dry before putting it into storage or service.

WARNING!

Never attempt to start a wet or damp motor.

Motors may be put into storage when the project on which they are to be used is incomplete or when they will be used as backups. The first consideration when storing motors for any length of time is the storage environment. A clean, dry, and warm location (one that does not undergo severe changes in temperature over 24 hours) is best. Ambient temperature changes cause condensation to form on and in the stored motor. Moisture in motor insulation can cause motors to fail on startup; therefore, guarding against moisture is vital when storing motors of any type. Some motors have internal heaters to protect against moisture buildup during storage. These heaters must be monitored while in use.

A means for transporting the motor from the place of storage is also important. Motors should not be lifted by their rotating shafts. Doing so can damage the alignment of the rotor in relation to the stator. Only the eyebolts on motor frames are intended for lifting the motor. Some factory-mounted accessories or covers also have eyebolts, which must not be used to lift the motor.

WARNING!

Never handle a motor by its shaft. Motor shaft keyways have sharp edges that can cause severe cuts. The motor itself may also become damaged.

The following is a list of recommendations for proper motor storage:

- Keep the motors clean and dry.
- Supply supplemental heating in the storage area, if necessary, or connect and monitor the internal heaters if so equipped.
- Store motors in an orderly fashion (grouped by horsepower or other criteria).
- Rotate motor shafts periodically as specified by the motor manufacturer so that they do not remain in the same position all the time. Maintain a shaft rotation log (*Figure 7*) for each motor.
- Motors should not need additional lubrication while in storage.
- Protect shafts and keyways during storage and while transporting motors from one location to another.
- Test motor winding resistance upon receiving the unit and periodically during storage. Maintain a winding resistance test log for each motor.

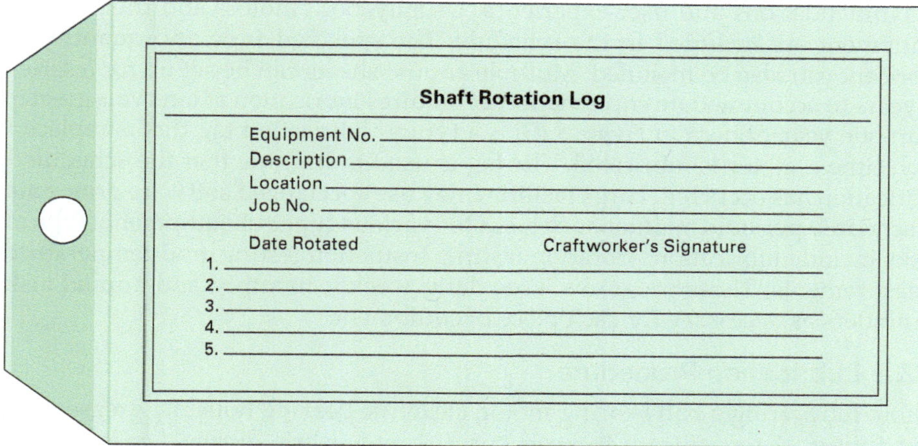
Shaft Rotation Log

Equipment No. ________
Description ________
Location ________
Job No. ________

	Date Rotated	Craftworker's Signature
1.		
2.		
3.		
4.		
5.		

Figure 7 Typical shaft rotation log tag.
Source: Jim Mitchem

Eyebolt Lifting Capacity

The eyebolt l fting capacity is based on a lifting alignment that corresponds to the eyebolt center line. The eyebolt capacity lessens as deviation from this alignment increases.

2.2.0 Motor Bearing Maintenance

AC motors account for a large percentage of industrial and heavy commercial maintenance and repair, with many motor failures caused by faulty bearings. Consequently, most industrial facilities strongly emphasize proper care of motor bearings. Motor reliability is improved when a carefully planned lubrication schedule is followed.

If an AC motor failure does occur, the first step is to find out why. There are various causes of motor failures, including excessive load, binding or misalignment of motor drives, wet or dirty environments, and bearing failures. Motors equipped with sealed bearings are much less prone to bearing failure.

2.2.1 Frequency of Lubrication

The frequency of motor lubrication depends not only on the bearing type but also on the motor application and its service environment. Small- to medium-size motors equipped with ball bearings (except sealed bearings) should be greased every three to six years if the motor duty is normal. For larger motors or severe applications (high temperature, wet or dirty locations, or corrosive atmospheres), lubrication may be required more often. In most cases, the lubrication schedule for a motor is specified in the manufacturer's operation and service literature.

Figure 8 (A) shows a form that can be used to record annual equipment lubrication. The form can be developed based on the equipment manufacturer's recommendations and user experience. Usually, both motors and their driven equipment are included in the schedule. The specified type and quantity of lubricant can also be included. Multiple annual sheets can be set up for a series of years to accommodate equipment that requires lubrication at intervals greater than one year. Shown in *Figure 8* (B) is a typical lubrication tag that is replaced each time a motor is lubricated. The tag is used to indicate that the scheduled lubrication has occurred. Large facilities may use specialized software programs to schedule periodic maintenance tasks for various types of equipment. Typical tasks include lubrication, vibration testing, insulation testing, and temperature measurements. These programs issue daily, weekly, monthly, and annual task reminders as necessary for each piece of equipment.

2.2.2 Lubrication Procedure

Before lubricating a ball bearing motor, clean the bearing housing, grease gun, and fittings. Exercise care to keep out dirt and debris during lubrication. If multiple lubricants are allowed in accordance with the motor manufacturer's operation and service literature, use only one when periodically relubricating a motor. Do not mix lubricants.

To lubricate a motor, remove the relief plug from the bottom of the bearing housing (*Figure 9*). This prevents excessive pressure from building up inside the bearing housing during lubrication. If possible, run the motor and add grease to the grease fitting until it begins to flow from the relief hole. Some manufacturers specify that only a certain amount of lubricant be injected into the bearing housing. A grease meter can be used in conjunction with a grease gun to precisely measure the amount of grease injected (*Figure 10*).

After grease is injected, run the motor for 5 minutes to 10 minutes to expel any excess grease, then reinstall the relief plug and clean the bearing housing. Avoid overlubrication. When excess grease is forced into a bearing, churning of the grease may occur, resulting in high bearing temperatures and eventual bearing failure.

Transistorized Stethoscopes

A transistorized stethoscope is equipped with a transistor-type amplifier and is used to determine the condition of motor bearings. A little practice in interpreting its use may be required, but in general, it is relatively simple. When the stethoscope is applied to a motor bearing housing, a smooth purring sound should be heard if the bearing is operating normally. If a thumping, grinding, or growling sound is detected, it could be an indication of a failing bearing.

Year ________ **Equipment Lubrication Schedule**

Equipment Location and/or Number	Lubricant	Jan	Feb	Mar	Apr	May	Jun	Jul	Aug	Sept	Oct	Nov	Dec

(A)

Lubrication Tag

Equipment No. ________
Description ________
Location ________
Job No. ________
Part Lubricated ________
____
____
____
Lubricant Type ________
Quantity of Lube ________
Signature ________
Date ________

(B)

Figure 8 Typical equipment lubrication schedule and tag.
Source: Jim Mitchem (8B)

Figure 9 Grease fitting and relief plug for a TEFC motor.
Source: Courtesy of Baldor Electric Company

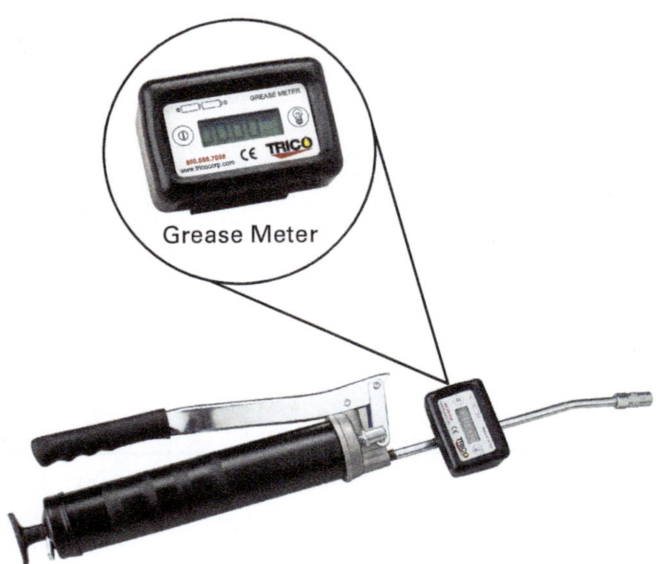

Figure 10 Grease gun and meter.
Source: © Trico Corporation. All rights reserved.

2.2.3 Checking Bearings

WARNING!

In some cases, it may be necessary to remove guards from rotating motor shafts to accomplish bearing checks. The motor must be locked out and tagged before removing the guards and then powered up to perform the checks. Always follow the facility safety procedures when performing checks with guards removed and the equipment operating. Stay clear of any rotating shaft components when performing these checks.

Three simple methods are commonly used to check bearings during motor operation: listening for unusual noises, performing temperature measurements, and performing vibration testing. If the bearing housing is unusually hot, or if a growling or grinding sound is being emitted from the area of the bearings, one of the bearings is probably nearing failure. Special stethoscopes can be used to listen to the bearings while the motor is running or while it runs down after being stopped. A "thunk" sound that occurs just before rotation stops is usually indicative of failure.

As an absolute minimum, bearing temperature and/or vibration testing should be done both before and after the equipment's scheduled lubrication. Enter the temperature and/or vibration data in a log and compare it to previously logged data. Note any increase in temperature and/or vibration. In some cases, it may be necessary to decouple the load to see if a defective load is causing the problem. LOTO procedures must be followed in such cases.

Motors should also be checked for end play, which is the backward and forward movement in the shaft. Ball bearing motors will typically have $^1/_{32}$" to $^1/_{16}$" (0.79 mm to 1.59 mm) of end movement.

NOTE

Keep in mind that some bearings may safely operate in a higher temperature range than other bearings, even in ranges exceeding 85°C (185°F). Check the manufacturer's specifications for the motor under test.

WARNING!

For bent shaft or shaft alignment checks, the motor must be locked out and tagged before any guards are removed and any checks are performed.

Other inspections may include periodically checking for misalignment or bent shafts and excessive belt tension. A magnetic base dial indicator can be used to check for a bent shaft on an uncoupled motor or driven load. The indicator is connected to either the motor or the load, or to a nearby solid ferrous metal surface, with the indicator feeler in contact with the end of the shaft (*Figure 11*). Rotate the shaft back and forth only between the edges of any keyway in the shaft. There should be no shaft misalignment (runout) detected for either the motor or load; otherwise, replace the motor or load, whichever has the bent shaft.

Parallel or angular misalignment (runout) of an uncoupled motor shaft to a directly driven load shaft (*Figure 12*) can be checked using a magnetic V-base holder or clamp base holder with a dial indicator at the rear of one of the shafts (usually the motor shaft). Manually rotate the first shaft while the indicator feeler is in contact with the rear of the other shaft (usually the load shaft), as shown in *Figure 13*. If the coupling halves are on the shafts and the outside diameter of the couplings is accurately machined in relation to the center of the coupling, then they can be used in the measurements; otherwise, the one on the shaft where the dial indicator will be used must be repositioned or removed. When positioning the dial indicator feeler against that shaft, make sure it is first positioned at the rear of the shaft and is depressed enough to cause the indicator needle to rotate 180°. Then rotate the dial markings so the zero reading is at the needle position.

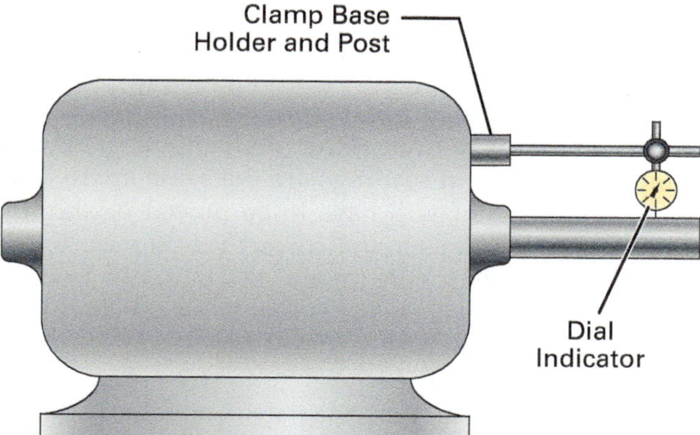

Figure 11 Checking for a bent shaft on a motor.

Figure 12 Typical direct-drive configuration without coupling.
Source: Tim Dean

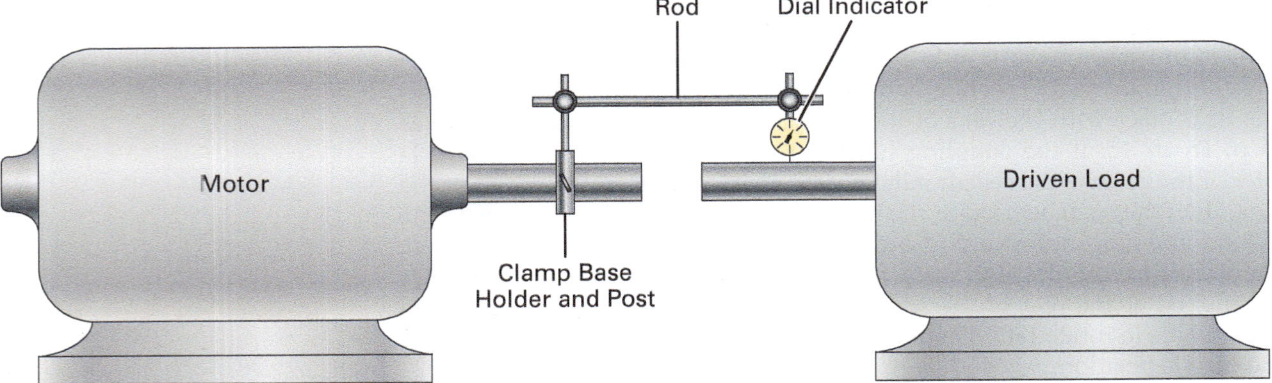

Figure 13 Checking shaft alignment between a motor and its load.

To make the alignment measurements, rotate the shaft with the holder base back and forth so the indicator feeler does not enter any keyway on the other shaft. Note the locations of the minimum and maximum readings on the other shaft. Move the indicator to the front of that shaft and repeat the measurements. If the minimum and maximum readings are the same, there is a parallel shaft runout, and the load or motor will have to be moved or shimmed equally at both ends to retain the parallelism and correct the runout. If the readings are different, there is angular shaft runout, and the motor or load will have to be moved or shimmed unequally at each end to remove the angular runout. Then, any resulting parallel runout will have to be corrected.

By trial and error, loosen the anchoring, as necessary, and move or shim the motor/load in the direction necessary to equalize the maximum and minimum readings at both locations to correct any angular runout. Repeat the alignment measurements for any parallel runout until the difference between the minimum and maximum readings is essentially zero around the shaft at both positions of the dial indicator. Then anchor the motor/load and recheck for any resulting runout. If it is possible to rotate the other shaft, reverse the indicator setup and repeat the measurements to double check. Before anchoring the motor/load, make sure that soft foot was not caused by moving and/or shimming the motor/load.

Figure 14 (C) shows a typical dial indicator with various holders. *Figure 14* (D) shows stainless steel slotted shims. Stainless steel shims are preferred to prevent rust deterioration over time. The shim assortment includes shims of various thicknesses. The thickness is marked on the shim so that records can be kept of the total thickness used under each foot of the equipment. This enables easier reinstallation of the same equipment if it must be removed.

NOTE

Other methods of shaft alignment are sometimes used. These include laser alignment or mechanically accurate adapter frames (bell housings) for some pumps and motors.

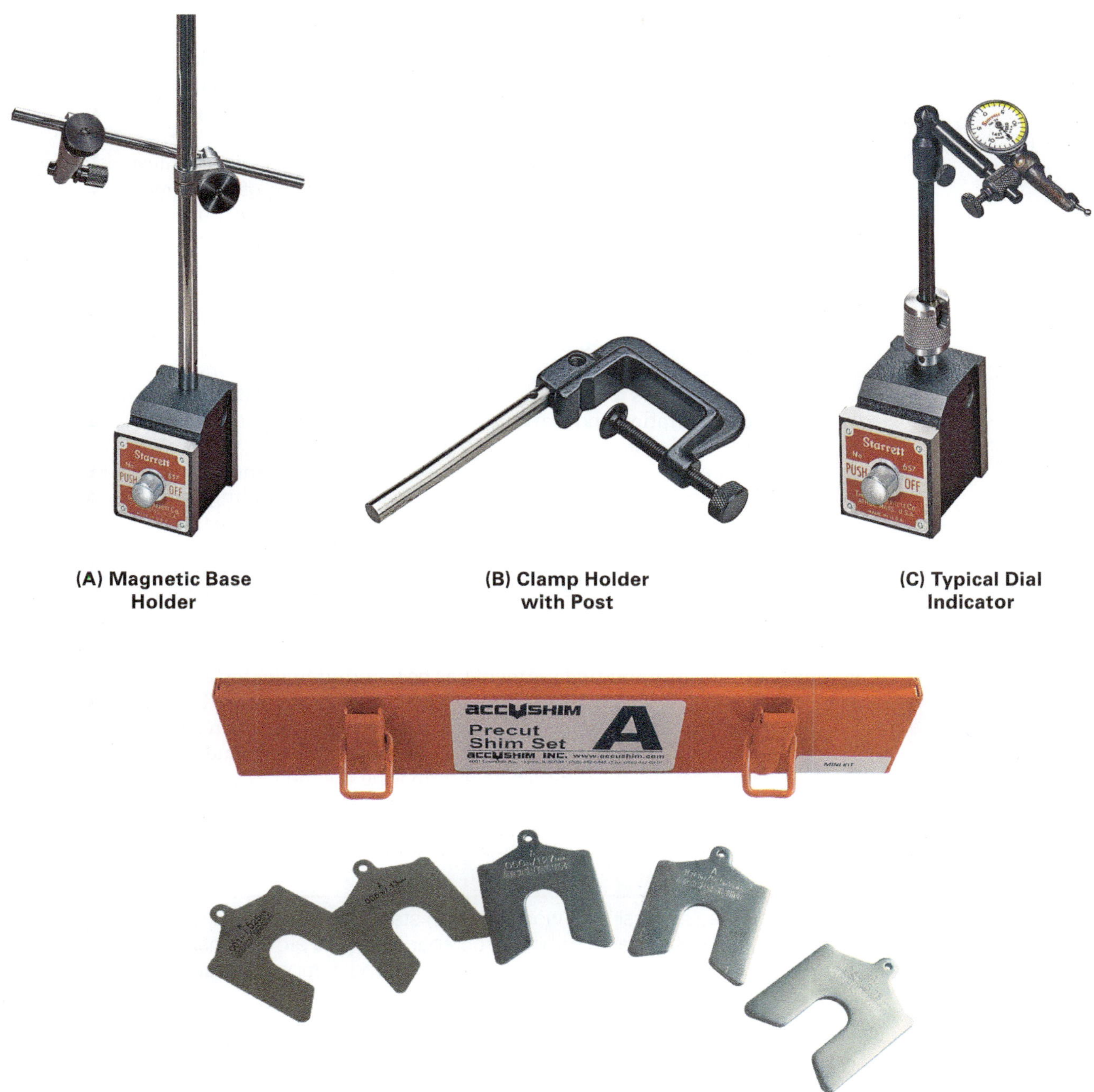

(A) Magnetic Base Holder

(B) Clamp Holder with Post

(C) Typical Dial Indicator

(D) Slotted Shims

Figure 14 Typical dial indicator with various holders and stainless steel slotted shims.
Source: The L.S. Starrett Company (14A, 14B, 14C)

2.3.0 Motor Insulation Testing

Insulation breakdown: The failure of insulation to prevent the flow of current, sometimes evidenced by arcing. If the voltage is gradually raised, breakdown will begin suddenly at a certain voltage level. Current flow is not directly proportional to voltage. When a breakdown current has flowed, especially for a period of time, the next gradual application of voltage will often show breakdown beginning at a lower voltage than initially.

An insulation resistance test indicates the condition of motor insulation and may indicate **insulation breakdown** or the presence of moisture, dirt, or other conductive material. Insulation resistance testing is high-energy testing and must be done in compliance with employer regulations, government regulations, and the tester manufacturer's instruction manuals.

2.3.1 Insulation Resistance Tests

Insulation resistance tests indicate the condition of insulation, particularly with regard to contamination by moisture and dirt. The actual value of the resistance will vary depending on the equipment type, size, voltage rating, and winding configuration.

The principal purpose of periodic insulation resistance tests is to compare, or trend, relative values of insulation resistance of the same apparatus taken under similar conditions throughout its service life. Such tests usually reveal the deterioration of insulation and may indicate approaching failure.

Measuring insulation resistance is straightforward. Identify any two points between which there is insulation, and make a connection across them using a megohmmeter. The measured value represents the equivalent resistance of all the existing insulation between the two points and any component resistance present between the two points. Three-phase motors have three to twelve motor leads present in the motor terminal box, depending on the winding configuration and starting method. Most common are the nine leads present in the dual-voltage squirrel-cage motor.

Before a motor is placed in service, test the insulation resistance of each winding segment to ground and to all other winding segments connected to ground. A look at the connection diagrams on the motor nameplate will indicate point numbers for each test connection. The positive lead is connected to frame and ground along with all other motor leads except for the winding segment under test. The negative lead is connected to one end of the segment under test with the other end(s) isolated or insulated. The insulation resistance is tested from one segment to all other segments and to ground. The test is repeated until each winding segment has been individually tested.

This test is easily performed on a motor in storage or before connection to the electric supply. Some facilities require testing only the resistance of all windings to earth. The motor feeder conductors may be included in the test to avoid de-terminating and then re-terminating the motor connections. In this case, the test is often performed from the motor starter or local disconnect switch, with one test lead connected to ground and the other to any T lead to the motor.

WARNING!

When accessing or working within starter compartments, you may be exposed to shock hazards within the compartment and arc flash hazards from the motor control center (MCC) bus and surrounding compartments. Follow company policies and use all appropriate PPE.

If the insulation resistance test indicates potential problems, isolate the feeders from the motor windings and test between individual phases or winding segments to identify the problem. Typical insulation resistance values used for new equipment installations are shown in *Appendix 26410-23A*. Other contractors may use different values. Specific values may also be obtained from the equipment manufacturer. In all cases in which comparison is used over time for trending data, the same test connections must be used.

WARNING!

When using an insulation tester, the motor frame must be directly connected to the building/earth ground. Only qualified individuals may use this equipment.

Megohmmeters (*Figure 15*) are available in several varieties. Some are powered by a hand-cranked **generator**, others are battery-powered, and some have rechargeable batteries or a line-powered internal power supply. Some supply test voltages as low as 50V or as high as 10,000V or more, but the most common is 500V. In all cases, the test voltage is DC.

Generator: A rotating machine that is used to convert mechanical energy to electrical energy. In a broader sense, it is general apparatus or equipment used to convert or change energy from one form to another.

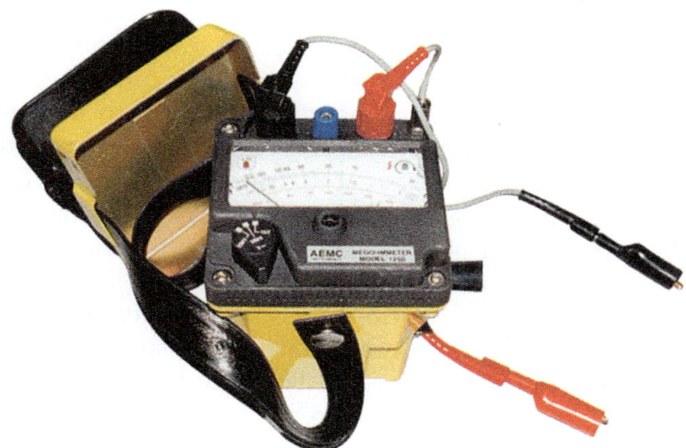

Figure 15 Typical megohmmeter.

Digital Surge / DC Hi-Pot / Resistance Tester

The unit in the image shown combines automated standard temperature-compensated resistance tests and hi-pot/surge tests in one portable field tester. It also provides a completely automated polarization index test and dielectric absorption test. Test results for up to 10 motors in the field can be stored, retrieved, printed, and uploaded to a desktop program for file management and analysis.

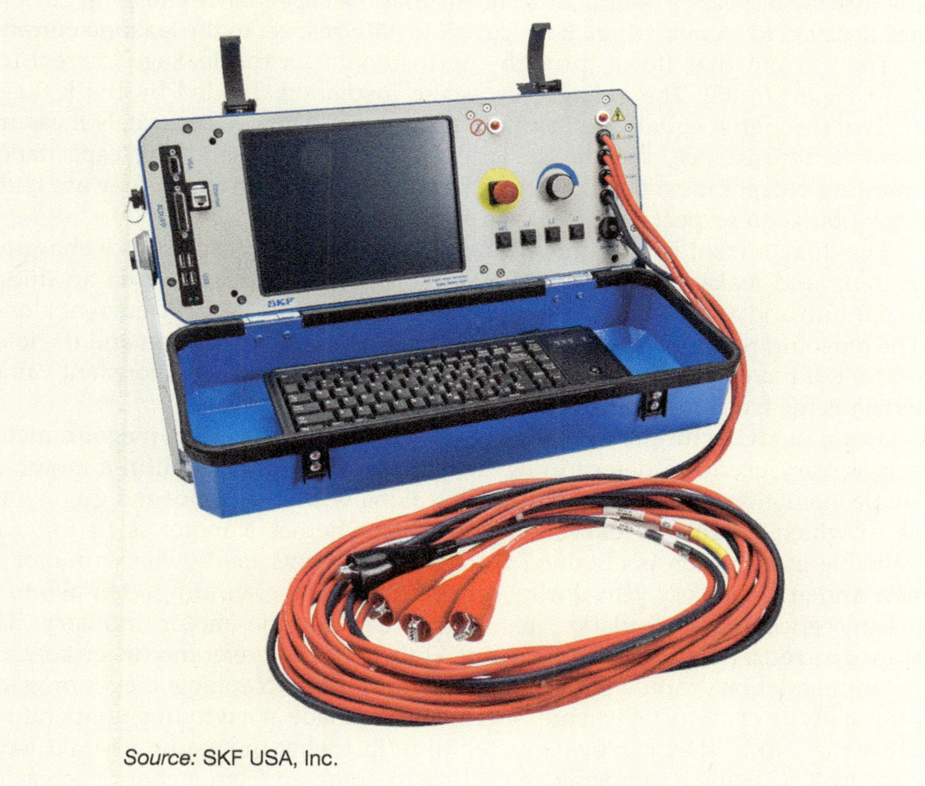

Source: SKF USA, Inc.

Absorption current: The current caused by insulating material becoming polarized by the electricity flowing through the conductor (*polarization current*) and the random and slow movement of electrons when an electric field is applied over electrons (*electron drift*).

Capacitance charging current: Initial high-current flow that quickly decays to zero after the insulation is charged to full voltage. Sometimes referred to simply as *charging current*.

Leakage current: AC or DC current flow through insulation and over its surfaces, and AC current flow through a capacitance. Current flow is directly proportional to voltage. The insulation and/or capacitance are considered a constant impedance unless breakdown occurs.

Before conducting resistance tests, you must first understand the concept of **absorption current**. The insulation between two connection points can be thought of as a dielectric, thus forming a capacitance. A phenomenon known as *dielectric absorption* occurs whereby the dielectric soaks up electrons and releases them when the potential is removed. This is in addition to the current that charges the capacitance, but it occurs much more slowly because it depends on the nature of the dielectric. Two items for which this is of concern are capacitors and wound equipment. Such current is referred to as *absorption current,* or I_A in *Figure 16* (A). Absorption current consists of two components: polarization current and electron drift. Polarization current is due to the reorientation of molecules in the infused insulation materials. It can take several minutes for this to occur and for the polarization current to drop to zero. The second component is the current caused by the gradual drift of electrons through most organic materials. This drift current is minor and occurs until the electrons and ions become trapped by the mica surfaces commonly found in insulation systems. For clean and dry motors, the insulation resistance between about 30 seconds and a few minutes is primarily determined by the absorption current.

This phenomenon may be demonstrated by taking a large capacitor, charging it to its rated voltage, and allowing it to remain at that voltage for some length of time. Then discharge the capacitor quickly and completely until a voltmeter placed across it reads zero. Remove the voltmeter and again allow the capacitor to sit for some length of time with its leads open-circuited. Take another voltmeter reading. Any voltage present is due to the dielectric absorption phenomenon. Some types of capacitors exhibit this phenomenon to a greater degree than other types. The larger the capacitor, the more apparent the effect.

The current required to charge whatever capacitance is present is known as **capacitance charging current**, or I_C in *Figure 16* (B). Like the dielectric absorption current, it decays to zero but more quickly. It is this current that typically determines how long it takes to make an accurate megohm measurement. When the reading appears to stabilize, it means that the capacitance charging current has decayed to a point where it is negligible with respect to the **leakage current**.

The current that flows through the insulation is the leakage current, or I_L in *Figure 16* (C). The voltage across the insulation divided by the leakage current through it equals the insulation resistance. Thus, to accurately measure insulation resistance, the dielectric absorption current and the capacitance charging current must be allowed to decay to the point at which they are truly negligible with respect to the leakage current.

The total current is the sum of the absorption current, capacitance charging current, and leakage current, or I_T in *Figure 16* (D). It decays from an initial maximum and approaches a constant value, which is the leakage current alone. The megohm reading depends on the voltage across the insulation and the total current. It increases from an initial minimum and approaches a constant value, which is the true measured insulation resistance.

Motor manufacturers, installers, users, and repairers find megohmmeter testing very useful in determining the quality of the insulation in a motor. A single insulation resistance measurement, along with experience and guidelines as to which reading to expect, can indicate whether a motor is fit for use. Valuable information is obtained from measurements made when a motor is new and at least every year during service. Because the windings' temperature greatly effects the insulation resistance reading, the motor industry has standardized a winding temperature of 40°C (104°F) as a reference when specific recommendations can be made about the minimum acceptable megohm value for each type of motor. When measurements are made at a winding temperature other than 40°C, they can be corrected to reflect what the reading would have been at 40°C using a temperature coefficient obtained from a chart, such as K_t in *Figure 17*.

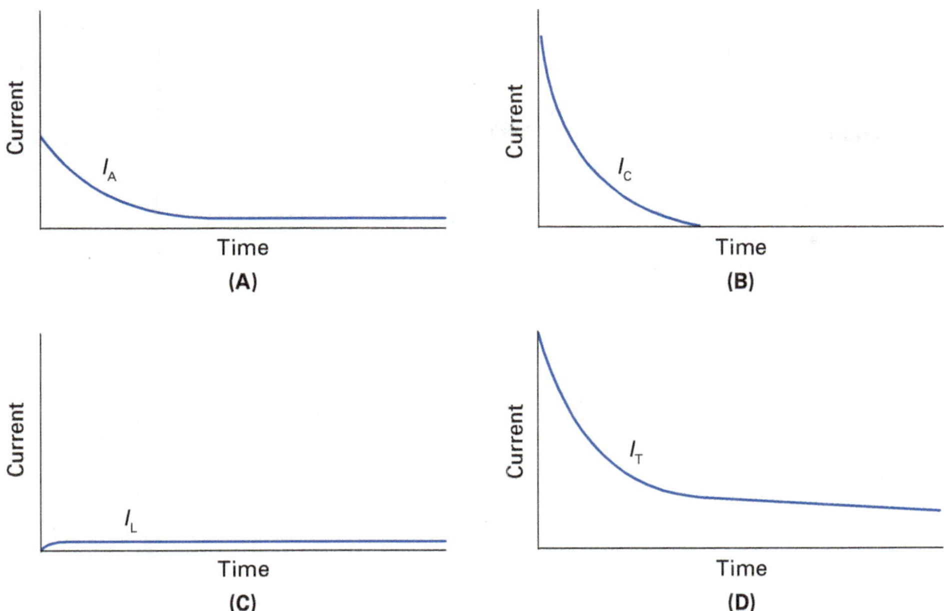

Figure 16 Current curves related to insulation testing.

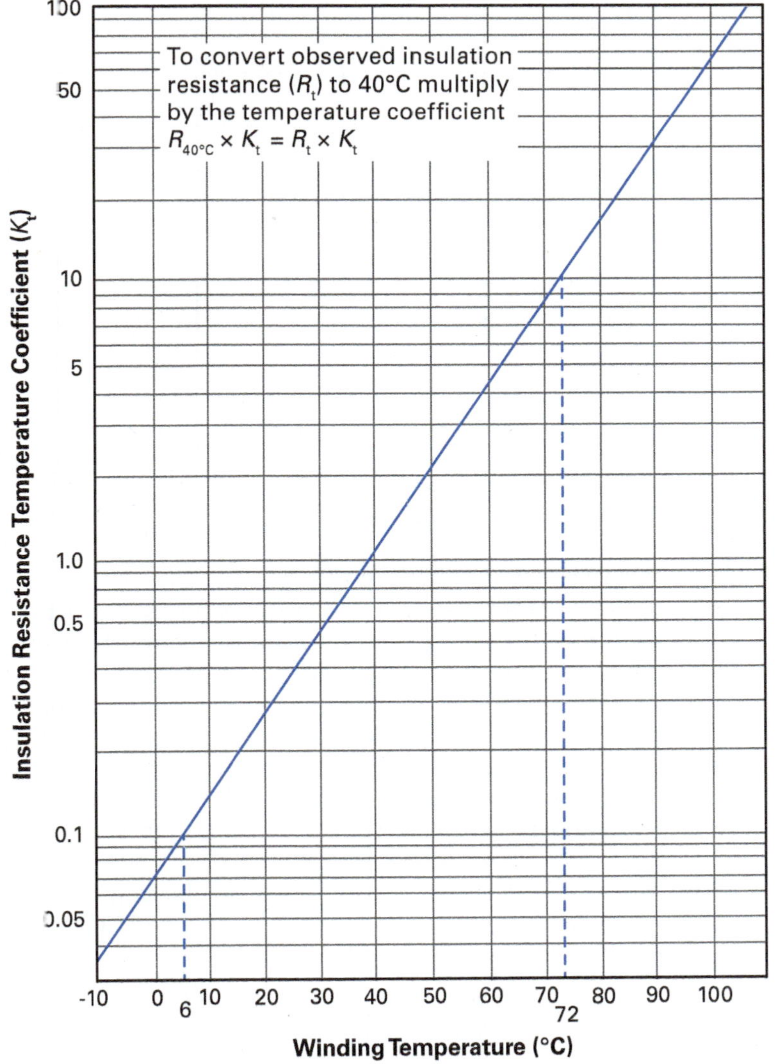

Figure 17 Approximate temperature coefficient for insulation resistance.

Figure 18 shows a dashed line representing the actual readings obtained on a motor over several years and a solid line showing the same readings corrected to a standard reference. The corrected temperature readings show a gradual decline characteristic of the motor's normal aging process until, in 2020, a sharp drop occurred. That drop signaled a problem with the insulation that would probably lead to an insulation failure. Such failure results in either a grounded motor or a short circuit between the motor windings, which would be costly in repair and downtime. Therefore, at the earliest practical opportunity, this motor was sent out for rewinding. The rewinding restored the high megohm readings, and the steady, gradual decline resumed. Today, due to the high cost of shop labor, rewinding a motor of this size (20 hp) might need to be weighed against the cost of replacement. *Figure 19* shows only the corrected temperature readings at 40°C that are normally kept on motors.

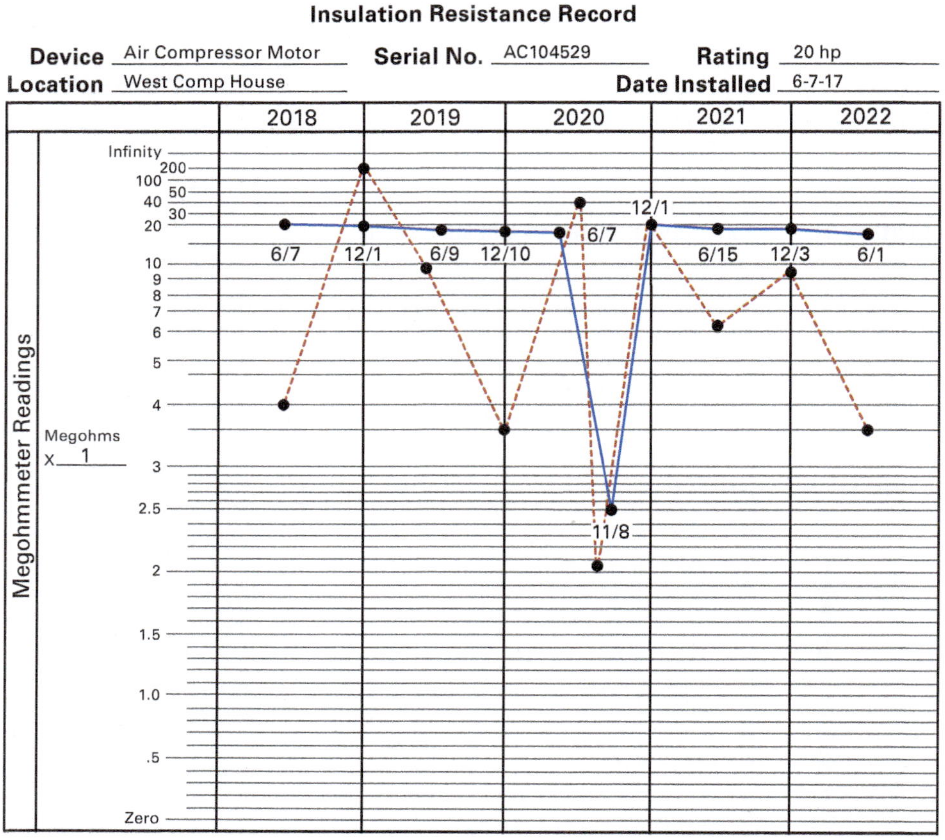

Insulation Resistance Record

Device Air Compressor Motor **Serial No.** AC104529 **Rating** 20 hp

Location West Comp House **Date Installed** 6-7-17

Figure 18 Chart of insulation resistance readings.

Another factor that affects insulation resistance readings is moisture. Motors may have excessive moisture in and around the insulation from either high humidity or having been submerged. This is a temporary effect. By letting the motor dry out naturally or accelerating the process by baking, the readings will increase. It is important not to start the motor until a satisfactory reading is obtained because doing so might cause an insulation failure.

The tests used to evaluate the effect of absorption current on resistance are the dielectric absorption ratio (DAR), typically applied on smaller machines, and the PI tests.

The condition of insulation may be inferred by evaluating the effect of the dielectric absorption current on resistance over time. The DAR, also called a *60/30 test*, is determined by the following formula:

$$\text{DAR} = \frac{\text{resistance after 60 seconds}}{\text{resistance after 30 seconds}}$$

The resistance readings will gradually rise due to a decrease in dielectric absorption.

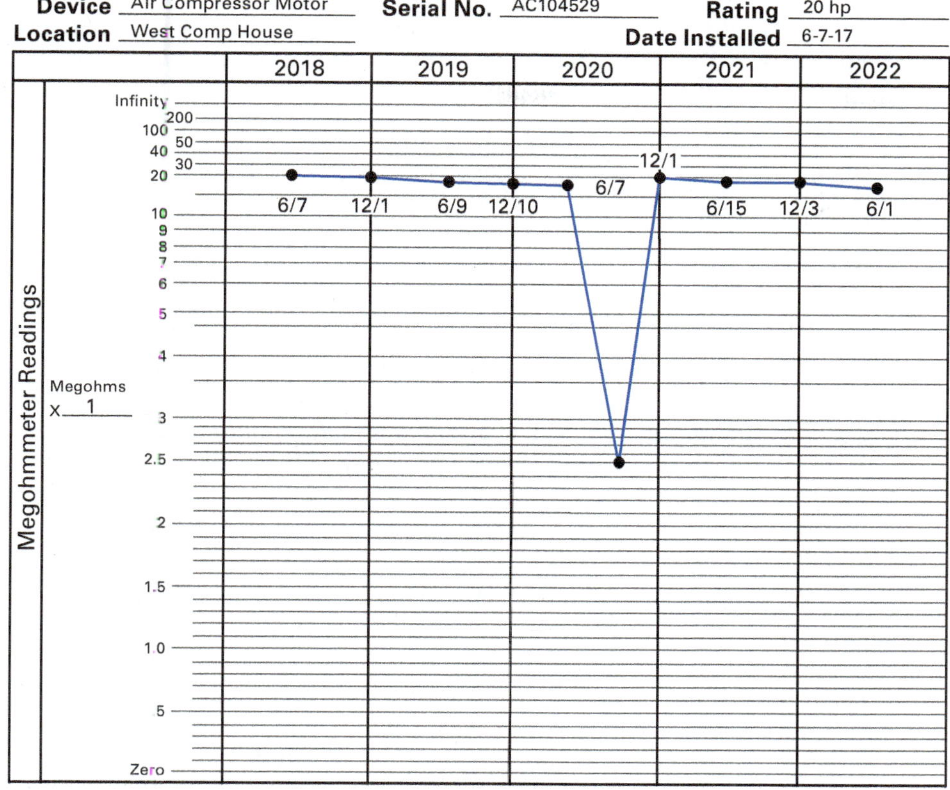

Figure 19 Temperature-corrected resistance readings alone.

2.3.2 Determining the Polarization Index

Knowing the PI of a motor or generator can be useful in appraising the machine's fitness for service. It is commonly used for motors over 200 hp. The index is calculated from measurements of the winding insulation resistance and is intended to evaluate the condition of the insulation.

Before measuring the insulation resistance, remove all external connections to the motor and completely discharge the windings to the grounded frame. Apply either 500VDC or 1,000VDC between the winding and ground using a direct-indicating, power-driven megohmmeter. Use the higher value (1,000VDC) for motors rated 500V and above. Apply the voltage for ten minutes and keep it constant for the duration of the test.

The PI, sometimes called the *polarization index ratio (PIR),* is calculated as the ratio of the ten-minute value to the one-minute value of the insulation resistances measured consecutively:

$$\text{PIR} = \frac{\text{resistance after 10 minutes}}{\text{resistance after 1 minute}}$$

The recommended minimum value of PI for AC and DC motors and generators is 2.0. Machines with a PI under 2.0 are considered suspect. However, a PI over 4.0 may indicate dry, brittle insulation that is also suspect. The PI is useful in evaluating windings for the following:

- Buildup of dirt or moisture
- Gradual deterioration of the insulation (by comparing earlier test results on the same motor)
- Fitness for overpotential tests
- Suitability for operation

Causes of Invalid Test Data

Many times, valid data cannot be obtained for dielectric absorption ratios, PI ratios, and insulation resistance tests. For dielectric absorption ratios and PI ratios for small equipment, such as small motors, the capacitance is very low, and the resistance readings will increase very rapidly. In this case, the test voltage must be reduced to spread the capacitance charging current over a longer period. For insulation resistance data, the insulation resistance of modern equipment is so effective and so high that the range of a megohmmeter may be exceeded when attempting to read valid resistance data. In these cases, insulation test equipment with a gigaohm or teraohm range must obtain valid data for calculating the PI or insulation resistance trend.

2.3.3 Insulation Testing Considerations

The procedures for performing insulation resistance testing and evaluation of the results are found in the test equipment instructions. These procedures and guidelines are based on *IEEE Standard 43-2013, Recommended Practice for Testing Insulation Resistance of Electric Machinery.*

When testing components before they are installed in a system, it is sometimes necessary to verify that the components meet their insulation resistance specifications. Wire and cable, connectors, switches, transformers, resistors, capacitors, and other components are specified to have a certain minimum insulation resistance. The megohmmeter is the proper instrument to use. Remember, the part may have a limitation on the voltage that may be applied, or the insulation resistance may be specified at a particular voltage. Consult the manufacturer's data for any voltage restrictions. Pay careful attention to these restrictions to avoid improper comparisons and/or damage to the part.

Use caution when selecting the test voltage. The voltage rating of the part or motor across the points where the measurement is made should not be exceeded. Many users prefer to use the highest available voltage that does not exceed the rating. In other cases, the customary test voltage is 500V, regardless of a higher rating, because higher voltage can make it harder to obtain proper data.

2.4.0 Troubleshooting Motors

To detect defects in electric motors, the windings are typically tested for ground faults, opens, shorts, and reverses. The methods used in performing these tests may depend on the type of motor being tested. If a defect is found, the motor must be removed and replaced. The possible defects include:

WARNING!

Before testing or troubleshooting a motor beyond a simple visual/auditory inspection, disconnect the power and follow the proper LOTO procedures.

- *Grounded winding* — A winding becomes grounded when it makes electrical contact with the metal frame of the motor. Causes may include end plate bolts contacting conductors or windings, winding wires pressing against the laminations at the corners of slots damaged during rewinding, or conductive parts of the centrifugal switch contacting the end plate.
- *Open circuits* — Loose connections or broken wires represent an open circuit in an electric motor.
- *Shorts* — A short occurs when two or more windings of separate phases contact each other at a point, creating a path other than the one intended. This condition may develop in a relatively new winding if the winding is wound too tight at the factory and excessive force was used to place the wires in position. Shorts may also result from excessive heat from overloads, which can degrade the insulation. Shorted turns are caused by loose or broken turns within a winding that contact each other in a manner that effectively causes the turns within the winding to be reduced. This causes high current in the winding, which results in overheating and insulation damage.
- *Reverses* — Reverses occur when two phases of a three-phase power source are reversed. This causes high current, which results in overheating and insulation damage.

2.4.1 Insulation Testing

Before performing an insulation resistance test, check to ensure that the circuits and equipment to be tested are rated at or above the output voltage of the megohmmeter and that all equipment scheduled for testing is disconnected, locked out, and tagged according to facility or employer procedures.

Check the megohmmeter and other test equipment for proper operation in accordance with the manufacturer's instructions. Before conducting tests, temporarily ground all the leads of the equipment under test. Then conduct the insulation tests as prescribed in the manufacturer's instructions. For winding resistance tests, the test voltage is applied for one minute or until the reading is essentially stable. After testing, discharge the windings by placing a ground on the windings and maintaining it for four times the duration of the test.

Record the temperature and humidity immediately after the test. Also, note the condition of the environment and the running or idle time of the equipment.

After the readings have been recorded, correct them for the winding temperature using a temperature chart (supplied with most megohmmeters). For enclosed motors without internal winding temperature monitoring, the winding temperature must be estimated. The winding temperatures of motors that have not been operating for eight hours or more can assume the same temperature as the outside motor skin temperature as measured with a thermometer (infrared or other). For motors that have been operating, the winding temperature can be estimated by adding the skin temperature to the ambient air temperature.

For new equipment, the corrected insulation resistance readings should be similar to those shown in *Appendix 26410-23A* or as specified by the manufacturer. Elaborate motor insulation tests, such as time resistance and step voltage tests, use various megohmmeter reading ratios and indexes, such as absorption ratio and PI, to determine the effects of temperature and humidity on insulation breakdown (*Figure 20*).

Figure 20 Bench testing motor insulation.
Source: Reproduced with Permission, Fluke Corporation

2.4.2 Grounded Coils

The usual effect of one grounded coil in a winding is the repeated blowing of a fuse or tripping of the circuit breaker when the motor attempts to start, provided that the machine frame is grounded. Two or more grounds will produce the same result and will also short out part of the winding in the phase in which the grounds occur. A simple test to determine whether a ground exists in the winding can be made using a conventional continuity tester. Before testing with this instrument, make certain that the motor disconnect switch is open, locked out, and tagged. Place one test lead on the frame of the motor and the other, in turn, on each of the line wires on the load side of the motor controller. If there is a grounded coil at any point in the winding, the lamp of the continuity tester will light or, in the case of a meter, the reading will show low or zero resistance.

2.4.3 Water-Damaged Motors

Motors that have been water damaged can sometimes be dried out and salvaged if rust is minimal. The NEMA guidelines for handling water damaged equipment recommend that salvage be done only by trained personnel in consultation with the motor manufacturer. This normally requires that these motors be sent to a manufacturer-authorized outside motor repair facility where they are disassembled, cleaned, and dried using ovens, steam heat, forced air, electric heat, or infrared heat in accordance with the motor manufacturer's instructions. When dried, they are subjected to extensive insulation testing and bearing replacement or lubrication and then reassembled.

2.0.0 Section Review

1. A tachometer is used to _____.
   a. check winding resistance
   b. measure shaft rotation speed
   c. measure vibration
   d. record temperature variations

2. The back and forth movement of a motor shaft is known as _____.
   a. rotation
   b. end play
   c. vibration
   d. shaft roll

3. When using an insulation tester on a motor, the motor frame *must* be _____.
   a. at room temperature
   b. properly lubricated
   c. connected to ground
   d. suspended by the shaft

4. The condition in which two or more windings come into contact is a(n) _____.
   a. open circuit
   b. short circuit
   c. motor reversal
   d. grounded winding

3.0.0 Motor Installation and Commissioning Guidelines

Performance Tasks

There are no Performance Tasks in this section.

Objective

Describe the guidelines for installing and commissioning electric motors.

a. Explain alignment and adjustment requirements.
b. Describe startup procedures.

A motor must be securely installed on a flat, rigid foundation or mounting surface to minimize vibration and maintain alignment between the motor and load shafts. Failure to provide a proper mounting surface may cause vibration, misalignment, and bearing damage.

Foundation caps and sole plates are designed to act as spacers for the equipment they support. If these devices are used, be sure they are evenly supported by the foundation or mounting surface.

3.1.0 Alignment and Adjustment

Accurate alignment of the motor with the driven equipment is extremely important. Many different types of flexible couplings are available with a range of torque capabilities, bore sizes, and materials based on horsepower requirements.

3.1.1 Alignment

Two typical types of couplings used to reduce vibration between motors and their loads are shown in *Figure 21*. One is a jaw type that is sometimes called a *Lovejoy® coupling*. This type is secured to the shaft with a square key and setscrew. The flexible insert between the coupling halves is available in various materials with varying degrees of flexibility, depending on the application. They are also available with snap-in flexible inserts that can be externally removed and replaced without disturbing the coupling halves. The coupling halves are available in sintered iron (a magnetic alloy), cast iron, aluminum, or stainless steel. Couplings of this type are fail-safe because they will still work even if the insert fails. Installation of the coupling is easy, and alignment is not as critical as with other kinds of couplings.

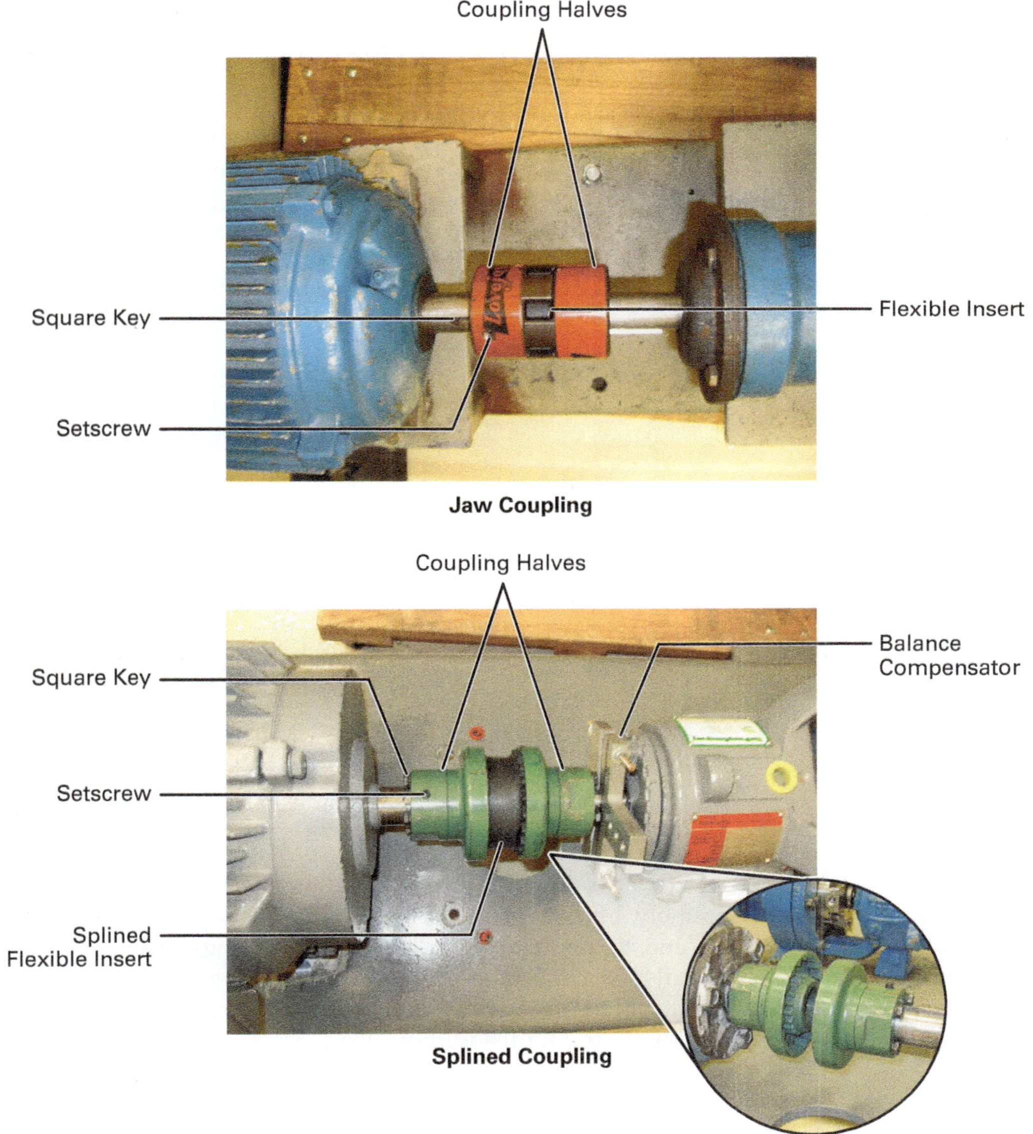

Figure 21 Typical vibration-reducing couplers.
Source: Tim Dean

The other type of coupling shown in *Figure 21* has internal splines in the coupling halves and a flexible insert between them. The coupling halves are secured to the shafts with square keys and setscrews. The couplings are available with different materials for the coupling halves and the flexible insert between them, depending on the application and torque requirements. Normally, precise alignment of these couplings is critical, but depending on the flexibility of the insert material, some types can tolerate a certain amount of angular or parallel runout. Also, note the balance compensator on the load shaft in this application. It is used to reduce vibration caused by the load.

If possible, use flexible couplings for direct-drive motors. Consult the drive or equipment manufacturer for more information. Mechanical vibration and roughness during operation may indicate poor alignment. Use dial indicators to check alignment, as discussed previously. Maintain the manufacturer's recommended spacing between coupling hubs.

CAUTION

Do not over-tension belts. Over-tightening causes excessive bearing and pulley wear, leading to premature failure.

For belt-drive motors, make sure the pulley ratio recommended by the manufacturer is not exceeded. Align the sheaves carefully to minimize belt wear and axial bearing loads. Belt tension should be sufficient to prevent belt slippage at rated speed and load. However, belt slippage may occur during startup.

The One-Megohm Rule of Thumb

The one-megohm rule states that the minimum acceptable rating for equipment rated at 1,000V or less is 1 MΩ. For equipment rated over 1,000V, the minimal acceptable reading is 1 MΩ minimum, plus 1 MΩ per kilovolt rating. The rule only applies to winding temperatures corrected to 40°C (104°F). To correct for the ambient temperature, the reading must be adjusted up for winding temperatures above 40°C and down for winding temperatures below 40°C. The reasoning is that equipment insulation resistance decreases at higher temperatures and increases at lower temperatures. The readings are adjusted as follows:

- For every 10°C above 40°C, double the megohm reading.
- For every 10°C below 40°C, divide the megohm reading in half.

For example, assume a 2,300V, 600 hp motor has a reading of 2.3 MΩ. The motor has been operating, and the winding temperature is 60°C (140°F). The minimum acceptable reading is 3.3 MΩ at 40°C. The temperature-corrected reading is as follows:

$$60°C - 40°C = 20°C$$

$$20°C \div 10°C = 2\ M\Omega$$

Therefore, the insulation resistance reading must be doubled twice because the reading must be doubled once for each 10°C above 40°C. This results in the following:

$$2.3\ M\Omega \times 2 = 4.6\ M\Omega$$

$$4.6\ M\Omega \times 2 = 9.2\ M\Omega$$

The temperature-corrected reading is 9.2 MΩ. This is acceptable because it is greater than the 3.3 MΩ minimum requirement.

3.1.2 End Play Adjustment

NOTE

End play adjustment applies to large motors with adjustable bearings. It is almost never done on motors below 500 hp, except for sleeve bearing direct-coupled motors.

The axial position of a horizontal motor frame with respect to its load is extremely important, except for motors designed for vertical mounting that have end thrust bearings. The motor bearings are not designed for excessive external axial thrust loads. Improper adjustment will cause failure. To establish the motor shaft's electrical center (live center), loosen the bearings (if applicable), and operate the motor with no load. Mark the shaft position in relation to the end bell on the shaft. Shim or reposition and tighten the bearings as necessary. After coupling the motor to the load, ensure the marked position is maintained when the motor is operating.

3.1.3 Doweling

After proper alignment is verified, dowel pins are often inserted through the mounting feet of motors into their foundation. This will allow the motor to be returned to precisely the same position if removal for repairs is required. If doweling is desired or required, drill dowel holes through diagonally opposite motor feet and into the foundation or sole plate. Ream all holes to the proper size for the dowel pin, then install the proper size dowels.

3.2.0 Startup

Before starting a motor, especially one that has been in storage, it is important to perform a prestart inspection and check procedure and make sure the motor is properly lubricated. The initial checks are performed before the motor is connected to the load shaft.

Installation Checklist

Some contractors or facilities may use a motor installation checklist like the one shown.

Description

Equip. #		
Circuit #		
Initial Megger Test @ ______ Volts	A to ⏚ B to ⏚ C to ⏚	A to B B to C C to C
Elect. Complete	Initial Date	
Final Align Complete	Initial Date	
Instrumentation Complete	Initial Date	
Final Megger Test Includes Feed Wires	A to ⏚ B to ⏚ C to ⏚	A to B B to C C to C
Rotation Check	Initial Date	
Coupling Belts Guard	Initial Date	
Test Run	Initial Date	
Operating AMPS	A B C	

NW Graphics Form # EQ-18 6/91

Accepted For Service ______________ Date ________

Alignment Readings

I.D.

O.D.

Piping Complete	Initial Date
Flush	Initial Date
Lube	Initial Date
Level Align Grout	Initial Date
Final Alignment	Initial Date
Mechanical Ok To Run	Initial Date

Accepted For Service ______________ Date ________

Source: Jim Mitchem

NOTE

To check for proper motor rotation, you must know the required rotation direction of the load. Depending upon the equipment being serviced, the proper rotation is often clearly marked on the motor or load housing. If not, a millwright or mechanic will likely be responsible for confirming proper rotation.

3.2.1 First-Time Startup

Before making any prestart checks, make sure all power to the motor and any accessories are locked out and tagged. Make sure the motor shaft is completely free of the load shaft and cannot cause it to rotate as you work with the motor. Then perform the following checks:

- Make sure the motor installation and mounting are secure.
- If the motor has been in storage or idle for some time, check the insulation integrity using an insulation resistance tester.
- Verify the desired direction of the motor and corresponding power source phases using a motor-rotation tester and a phase sequence meter.
- Lubricate the motor in accordance with the manufacturer's instructions.
- Connect the wiring and inspect all electrical connections for proper termination, clearance, mechanical strength, and electrical continuity.
- Perform a final insulation resistance test, including the wiring to the motor.
- Remove any protective covering from the motor shaft.
- Replace all panels and covers that were removed during installation.
- Apply power and momentarily start (bump) the motor to verify correct rotation. If wrong, again lock out and tag the motor and switch two phases. Then bump the motor again to check.
- Start the motor and ensure that operation is smooth without excessive vibration or noise. If so, run the motor for one hour with no load connected.
- After one hour of operation, lock out and tag the motor again. Connect the load to the motor shaft as previously described. For direct-drive couplings, make sure the coupling is aligned and not binding.
- Verify that all coupling guards (*Figure 22*) and protective devices are installed and the motor is properly ventilated.

Figure 22 Typical coupling guard over rotating components.
Source: Tim Dean

Angular or Uneven Mounting Surfaces

For mounting surfaces that are angular or uneven under one or more equipment feet, the feet or mounting surface can be machined, or shims can be used. Shims are often required during the motor alignment process. Special shims, such as those in the image shown, can also be used. These shims have an elastomeric coating that can be compressed to about half its thickness under final anchoring torque to fill an angular or uneven surface under the motor feet. After a short time, the coating hardens to prevent any change due to subsequent equipment operation.

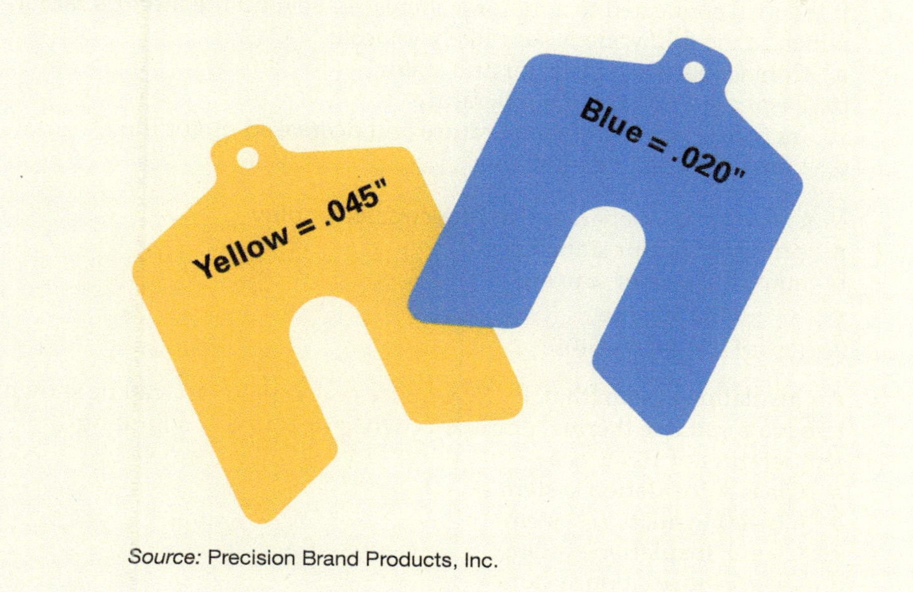

Source: Precision Brand Products, Inc.

3.2.2 Coupled Startup

The first coupled startup should have no load applied to the driven equipment. Apply power and check the operating current on each phase of the motor. Verify that the driven equipment is not transmitting excessive vibration back to the motor through the coupling or foundation. Vibration should be minimal. If not, balancing the load, such as a large blower wheel, may be required. Pumps and similar loads may be suffering from bearing damage or failure, leading to vibration. Run the motor for approximately one hour with the driven equipment in an unloaded condition. The equipment can now be loaded and operated within specified limits. Do not exceed the nameplate ratings for amps or temperature rise for steady, continuous loads.

NOTE

This procedure assumes that the first-time startup procedure was performed and was successful.

3.0.0 Section Review

1. The two types of couplings used to connect motor shafts to loads are _____.
   a. jaw and pulley
   b. spline and jaw
   c. spline and pulley
   d. bearing and jaw

2. Bumping is generally done to check _____.
   a. bearing wear
   b. excessive vibration
   c. shaft couplings
   d. direction of rotation

Module 26410-23 Review Questions

1. Single-phasing means that _____.
   a. a three-phase motor is attached to a single-phase power source
   b. two of the legs of a three-phase power source are lost
   c. one of the legs of a three-phase power source is lost
   d. phase rotation of the input voltage needs to be adjusted

2. If the load connected to a motor is increased beyond the motor's rating, which of the following is *most* likely to occur?
   a. Contact between the rotor and stator
   b. Decreased operating temperature
   c. Increased operating temperature and decreased motor life
   d. Loss of bearing lubrication

3. Motors with two separate winding circuits employ _____.
   a. primary resistor starting
   b. autotransformer starting
   c. wye-delta starting
   d. part-winding starting

4. An insulation system that, by experience or accepted test, can be shown to have a suitable thermal endurance when operated at a limiting temperature of 105°C is a _____.
   a. Class A insulation system
   b. Class B insulation system
   c. Class F insulation system
   d. Class H insulation system

5. Typical materials used in a Class H insulation system include _____.
   a. cotton
   b. paper
   c. cellulose acetate films
   d. silicone elastomer

6. Typical materials used in a Class F insulation system include _____.
   a. cotton
   b. paper
   c. cellulose acetate films
   d. mica

7. An insulation system that, by experience or accepted test, can be shown to have a suitable thermal endurance when operated at a limiting temperature of 130°C is a _____.
   a. Class A insulation system
   b. Class B insulation system
   c. Class F insulation system
   d. Class H insulation system

8. Which of the following may be eliminated as a concern in planning good motor maintenance?
   a. Number of hours and days the motor operates
   b. Environmental conditions
   c. Manufacturer of the motor
   d. Importance of the motor in the production scheme

9. Proper electrical connection of a motor is determined by _____.
   a. checking with a rotation tachometer
   b. using a motor-rotation and phase-rotation tester
   c. using a recording meter
   d. observing the rotation of the motor

10. Which of the following statements concerning motors in storage is *true*?
    a. Shafts should be turned according to manufacturer instructions.
    b. Shafts should not be moved or turned until the motor is put in use.
    c. Shafts should be turned 180° once a year to distribute bearing grease.
    d. Shafts should be turned once every three years to keep them from rusting.

11. Which of these is considered the *best* attachment point for lifting a motor?
    a. Eyebolt
    b. Shaft
    c. Base
    d. End bell

12. A type of motor bearing with a very low rate of failure is a _____.
    a. radial bearing
    b. pin bearing
    c. sealed bearing
    d. ball bearing

13. Which of the following is usually an indication of a bad motor bearing?
    a. Hot bearing housing
    b. Low current draw
    c. Low pull-in torque
    d. Sparking at the brushes

14. PI is the ratio of the resistance after 10 minutes to the resistance after _____.
    a. 60 minutes
    b. 30 minutes
    c. 5 minutes
    d. 1 minute

15. For motors with adjustable bearings, excessive end play in a motor shaft is corrected by _____.
    a. shimming the bearings
    b. adjusting the coupling
    c. inserting dowel pins in the mounting feet
    d. repositioning the load

Answers to odd-numbered Module Review Questions are found in *Appendix A*.

Module 26410-23 Supplemental Exercises

1. The life expectancy of a typical squirrel-cage induction motor depends largely upon the condition of its __________.
2. A(n) __________ is the tool used for an insulation resistance test.
3. The control circuits of many older induction motors were not provided with __________ or loss-of-phase protection.
4. With regard to the NEMA usual service conditions, if the ambient temperature is over 40°C (104°F), the motor service factor must be __________ or a(n) __________ motor must be used.
5. The four classes of insulation systems used in motors are __________, __________, __________, and __________.
6. An electric motor winding that makes contact with the motor frame is described as being __________.
7. To detect defects in electric motors, the windings are normally tested for four conditions: __________, __________, __________, and __________.
8. Open circuits are often the result of __________ or __________.
9. When a motor suffers from shorted turns, it results in __________.
10. If you have a grounded winding on a motor, you would expect the reading on an ohmmeter to read a(n) __________.

Answers to odd-numbered Supplemental Exercises are found in *Appendix B*.

Module 26410-23 Answers to Section Review Questions

Answer	Section Reference	Objective
Section 1.0.0		
1. b	1.1.0	1a
2. a	1.2.1	1b
Section 2.0.0		
1. b	2.1.1; *Table 1*	2a
2. b	2.2.3	2b
3. c	2.3.1	2c
4. b	2.4.0	2d
Section 3.0.0		
1. b	3.1.1; *Figure 21*	3a
2. d	3.2.1	3b

User Update

Did you find an error? Submit a correction by visiting **https://www.nccer.org/olf** or by scanning the QR code using your mobile device.

Medium-Voltage Terminations/Splices

Source: Ridge Tool Company

Objectives

Successful completion of this module prepares you to do the following:

1. Describe how to splice medium-voltage cable.
   a. Identify medium-voltage power cable configurations and components.
   b. Describe a typical procedure for making a straight splice.
   c. Describe a typical procedure for making an inline tape splice.
   d. Identify various manufactured termination and splice kits.
2. Describe termination classes and important considerations when creating terminations.
   a. Identify termination classes.
   b. Identify stress control methods.
3. Define high-potential testing and explain how such testing is conducted.
   a. Identify types of high-potential tests.
   b. Explain how to make various test connections.
   c. Describe typical procedures for conducting high-potential tests.

Performance Task

Under supervision, you should be able to do the following:

1. Prepare a cable and complete a splice or stress cone.

Overview

Both taping systems and manufactured slip-on kits are used to make splices and terminations. This module identifies types of medium-voltage cable and describes how to make various splices and terminations. It also covers high-potential testing.

NOTE

NFPA 70®, *National Electrical Code*®, and *NEC*® are registered trademarks of the National Fire Protection Association, Quincy, MA.

NCCER Industry-Recognized Credentials

If you are training through an NCCER-accredited sponsor, you may be eligible for credentials from NCCER. The ID number for this module is 26411-23. Note that this module may have been used in other NCCER curricula and may apply to other level completions. Contact NCCER at 1.888.622.3720 or go to **www.nccer.org** for more information.

You can also show off your industry-recognized credentials online with NCCER's digital badges. Transform your knowledge, skills, and achievements into badges that you can share across social media platforms, send to your network, and add to your resume. For more information, visit **www.nccer.org**.

Digital Resources for Electrical

Scan this code using the camera on your phone or mobile device to view the digital resources related to this craft.

1.0.0 Splicing Medium-Voltage Power Cable

Performance Tasks

There are no Performance Tasks in this section.

Objective

Describe how to splice medium-voltage cable.

a. Identify medium-voltage power cable configurations and components.
b. Describe a typical procedure for making a straight splice.
c. Describe a typical procedure for making an inline tape splice.
d. Identify various manufactured termination and splice kits.

Know the Code

Medium Voltage Conductors, Cable, Cable Joints, and Cable Terminations
NEC Article 315

Ribbon tape shield: A helical (wound coil) strip under the cable jacket.

Medium-voltage cable, covered in *NEC Article 315*, is defined as a single or multiconductor solid dielectric insulated cable rated at 2,001V to 35,000V. There are many types of medium-voltage power cables in use today. Five of the most common are shown in *Figure 1* and listed as follows:

- **Ribbon tape shield**
- Drain wire shielded
- Cable UniShield®
- Concentric neutral (CN)
- Jacketed concentric neutral (JCN)

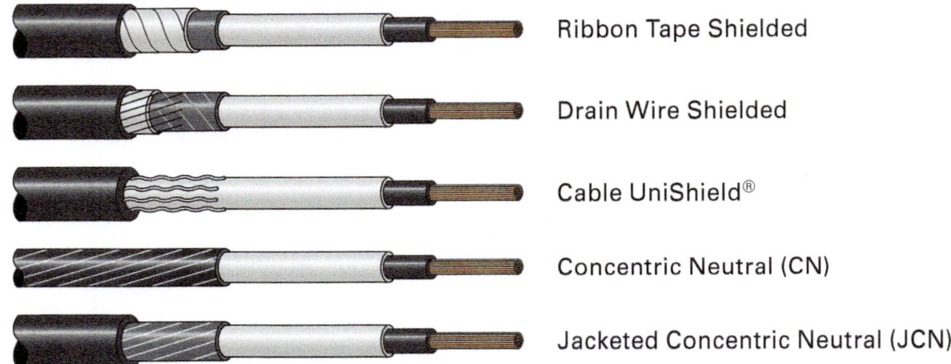

Figure 1 Basic types of medium-voltage cable.

1.1.0 Medium-Voltage Cable Configurations and Components

Know the Code

Medium Voltage Conductors, Cable, Cable Joints, and Cable Terminations
NEC Article 315

Refer to *NEC Article 315* for requirements for medium-voltage cable. Conductors used with dielectric cables are available in four basic configurations (*Figure 2*). These configurations can be described as follows:

- *Concentric stranding (Class B)* — Not commonly used in modern shielded power cables because of the penetration of the extruded **strand shielding** between the conductor strands, making the strand **shield** difficult to remove during field cable preparation.
- *Compressed stranding* — Compressed to 97% of the concentric conductor diameters. This compression of the conductor strands blocks the penetration of an extruded strand shield, thereby making it easily removable in the field. For sizing lugs and connectors, sizes remain the same as with concentric stranding.
- *Compact stranding* — Compacted to 90% of the concentric conductor diameters. Although this conductor has full ampacity ratings, the general rule for sizing is to consider it one conductor size smaller than concentric or compressed cable. This reduced conductor size results in a proportional reduction of all cable layers, a consideration when sizing for molded rubber devices.
- *Solid wire* — This conductor is not commonly used in industrial shielded power cables.

Strand shielding: The semiconductive layer between the conductor and insulation that compensates for air voids that exist between the conductor and insulation.

Shield: A conductive barrier against electromagnetic fields.

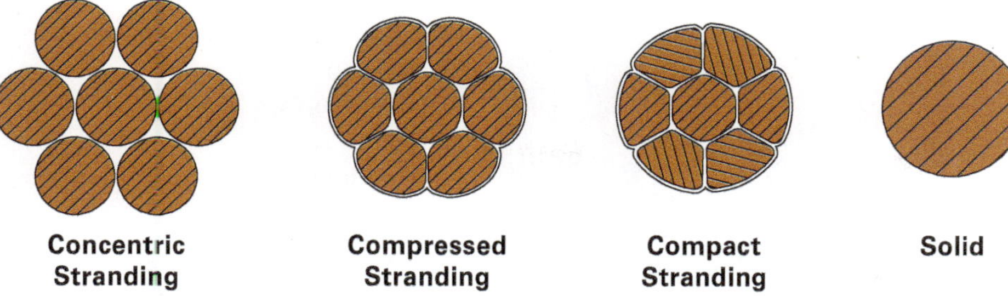

Figure 2 Basic cable configurations.

All medium-voltage power cables are essentially the same, consisting of the following:

- Conductor
- Strand shielding
- Insulation
- **Insulation shielding** system (semiconductive and metallic)
- Jacket

Insulation shielding: An electrically conductive layer that provides a smooth surface in contact with the insulation's outer surface. It is used to eliminate electrostatic charges external to the shield and provide a fixed, known path to ground.

Each component is vital to an optimal power cable performance and must be understood to make a dependable **splice** or termination (*Figure 3*).

Splice: Two or more conductors joined with a suitable connector and reinsulated, reshielded, and rejacketed with compatible materials applied over a properly prepared surface.

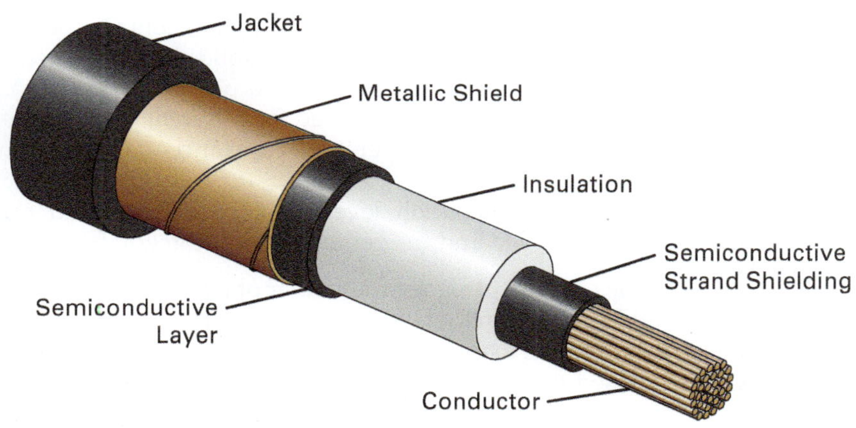

Figure 3 Basic components of medium-voltage cable.

1.1.1 Strand Shielding

Strand shielding is the semiconductive layer between the conductor and insulation that compensates for air voids between the materials.

Air is a poor insulator, having a nominal **dielectric strength** of only 76 V/mil, whereas most cable insulations have dielectric strengths over 700 V/mil. Without strand shielding, an electrical potential exists that will overstress these air voids.

Dielectric strength: The maximum voltage a material can withstand before dielectric breakdown occurs.

As air breaks down or ionizes, it produces corona discharges. This forms ozone, which chemically deteriorates the cable insulation. The semiconductive strand shielding eliminates this potential by simply shorting out the air.

Modern cables are generally constructed with an extruded strand shield (*Figure 4*).

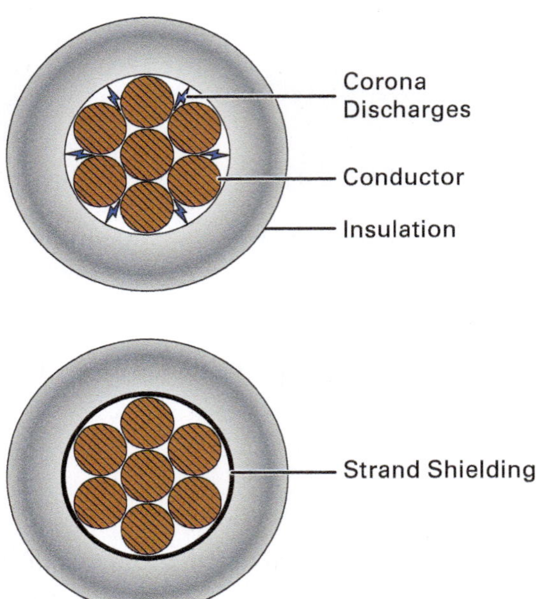

Figure 4 Strand shielding.

1.1.2 Insulation

Insulation consists of many different variations, such as extruded solid dielectric or laminar (oil paper or varnish cambric). Its function is to contain the voltage within the cable system. The most common types of solid dielectric insulation in industrial use today are polyethylene, cross-linked polyethylene (XLP), and ethylene propylene rubber (EPR). Each is preferred for different properties, such as superior strength, flexibility, and temperature resistance, depending upon the cable characteristics required.

The selection of the cable insulation level must be made based on the applicable phase-to-phase voltage and the general system category that follows:

- *100% level* — Cables in this category may be applied where the system is provided with relay protection that clears ground faults within one minute. These cables are applicable to most cable installations on grounded systems and may also be used on other systems for which the application of cable is acceptable, provided the clearing requirement is met in completely de-energizing the faulted section.
- *133% level* — This insulation level corresponds to that formerly designated for ungrounded systems. Cables in this category may be applied where the clearing time requirements of the 100% level category cannot be met, yet there is adequate assurance the faulted section will be de-energized in a period not exceeding one hour. In addition, they may be used when additional insulation strength over the 100% level category is desirable.
- *173% level* — Cables in this category should be applied on systems where the time required to de-energize a grounded section is indefinite. Their use is also recommended for resonant grounded systems. Consult the manufacturer for insulation thickness requirements.

The insulation level is determined by the thickness of the insulation. For example, 15 kV cable at 100% has 175 mils of insulation, while the same type of cable at 133% has 220 mils. This variance holds true up to 1,000 kcmil.

1.1.3 Insulation Shield System

The outer shielding is composed of two conductive components: a semiconductive (semicon) layer under a metallic layer. The principal functions of a shield system (*Figure 5*) include:

- Confining the dielectric field within the cable
- Obtaining a symmetrical radial distribution of voltage **stress** within the dielectric
- Protecting the cable from induced potentials
- Limiting radio interference
- Reducing the hazard of shock
- Providing a ground path for leakage and fault currents

Stress: An internal force set up within a body to resist or hold it in equilibrium.

NOTE

The shield must be grounded for the cable to perform these functions.

The semicon component is available either as a tape or an extruded layer. Some cables have an additional layer painted on between the semicon and the cable insulation. Its function is similar to strand shielding—to eliminate the problem of air voids between the insulation and the metallic component (in this case, the metallic shielding). In effect, it shorts out the air that underlies the metallic shield, preventing corona and its resultant ozone damage.

The metallic shield is the current-carrying component that allows the insulation shield system to perform as intended. The various cable types differ most in this layer. Therefore, most cables are named after their metallic shield (for example, tape shielded, drain wire shielded, or UniShield®). The shield type (cable identification) thus becomes important information to know when selecting devices for splices and terminations.

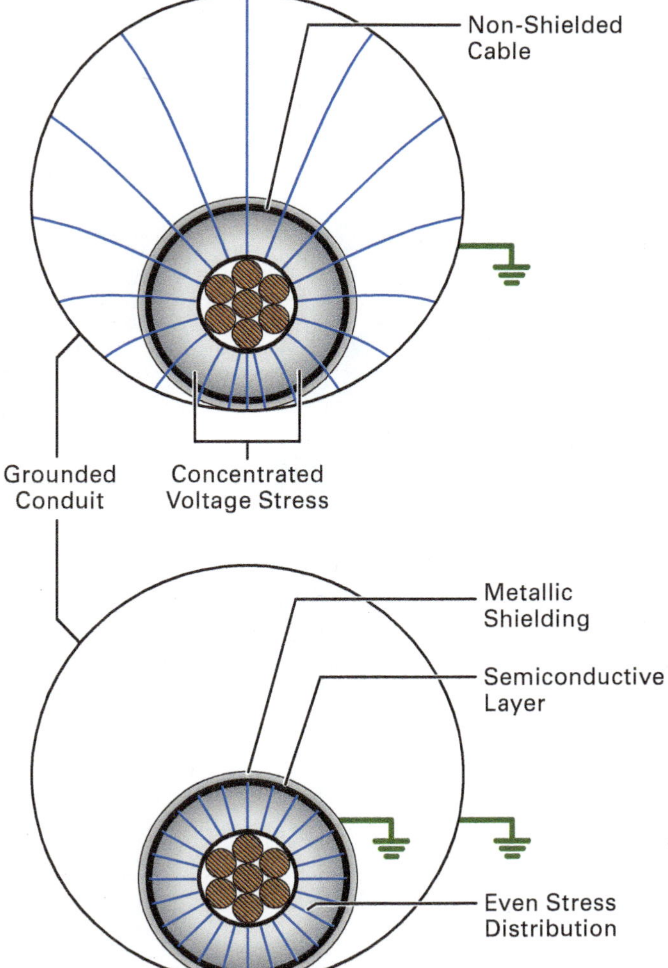

Figure 5 Insulation shield system.

1.1.4 Jacket

The jacket (*Figure 6*) is the tough outer covering that provides mechanical protection as well as a moisture barrier. Often, the jacket serves as both an outer covering and the semicon component of the insulation shield system, combining two cable layers. However, because the jacket is external, it cannot serve as the semicon component of the complete system. Typical materials used for cable jackets are PVC, neoprene, and lead. Frequently, industrial three-conductor cables have additional protection in the form of an **armor** layer.

Armor: A mechanical protector for cables; usually a formed metal tube or helical winding of metal tape formed so that each convolution locks mechanically upon the previous one (interlocked armor).

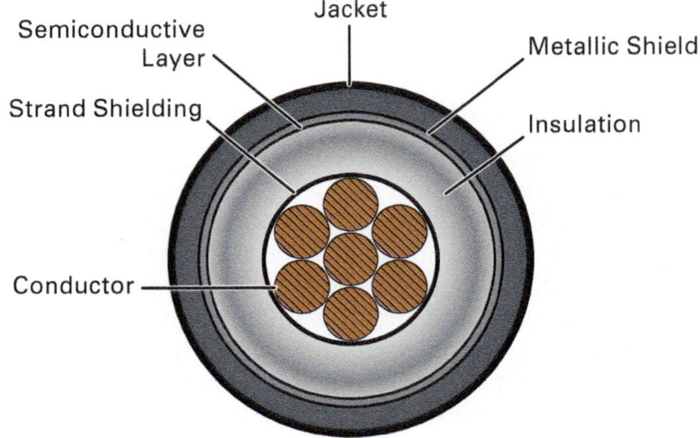

Figure 6 Jacket and insulation.

Medium-Voltage Cables

Shown in the image is an example of a medium-voltage cable. It is typical of the cables you may have to splice and/or terminate using methods described in this module.

Source: General Cable

1.2.0 Making Straight Splices

Whenever possible, splicing should be avoided. However, splicing is often an economic necessity. There can be many reasons for making splices, including:

- Insufficient supplied length of cable due to reel limitations or cumbersome cable length
- Cable failures
- Cable damaged after installation
- Insufficient room for cable training radius
- Excessive twisting of cable would otherwise result
- A tap into an existing cable (tee or wye splices)

For damaged cable and taps, the only solutions are to splice the cable or replace the entire length. In many cases, the economy of modern splicing products makes splicing an optimal choice (*Figure 7*).

Figure 7 Cutaway view of a splice.
Source: TE Connectivity

Whatever the reason for splicing, splices must have the same rating as the cable. In this way, the splice does not derate the cable and become the weak link in the system. Every splice must provide mechanical and electrical integrity at least equal to the original conductor insulation. Furthermore, all terminations and splices must be made under the best environmental conditions possible on the jobsite. The slightest amount of moisture, dirt, or foreign material can render the splice useless.

Splices can be completed by tapering, also called *penciling*, the cable ends and taping with several layers of high-dielectric insulating tape covered with several layers of environmental jacketing tape. An alternative method is to use a stress-control, void-filling material and heat-shrink insulating and environmental tubing to rebuild the cable to its original insulation thickness. With this method, tapering is not required.

A typical straight splice for a single, unshielded conductor (ranging from 601V to 5,000V) is shown in *Figure 8*. In general, the conductor jacket and insulation should be removed for $\frac{1}{2}$ the connector length plus $\frac{1}{4}$" (6 mm). Then, a protective wrap of electrical tape is applied to the jacket ends to protect the jacket and insulation while cleaning the conductor and securing the connector, as shown in *Figure 8* (A).

After performing the preceding operations, remove the tape, additional jacket, and insulation in an amount equal to 25 times the thickness of the overall insulation, as shown in *Figure 8* (B), extending in both directions from the first insulation cut. For example, if the thickness of the insulation is $\frac{1}{4}$" (6 mm), the outside edge of the splice will be:

$$25 \times \frac{1}{4}" = 6\frac{1}{4}" \text{ or } 6.25" \text{ (150 mm)}$$

WARNING!

Although any conductor splice or termination must be done with care, extreme caution must be exercised with higher voltages. In general, the higher the voltage, the more fine-tuning the splice or termination will require. Splicing is a skill that requires special training. Many localities and industries require certification of training and experience to splice, terminate, and test medium- and high-voltage cable systems.

Therefore, the outside edge of the splice will be $6\frac{1}{4}$" (150 mm) beyond the insulation cut. To continue, pencil the insulation with a sharp knife or insulation cutter, taking care not to nick the conductor.

Refer to *Figure 8* (C). Starting from A or B, wrap the splice area with high-voltage insulating rubber splicing tape, stretching the rubber tape about 25%, and, if using lined tape, unwinding the interliner as you wrap. The finished splice should be built up to $1\frac{1}{2}$ times the factory insulation if rubber (two times if thermoplastic), as measured from the top of the connector. For example, if the rubber insulation is $\frac{1}{4}$" (6 mm), the finished splice would be $\frac{3}{8}$" (10 mm) thick when measured from the top of the connector.

To finish off the splice and ensure complete protection, cover the entire splice with four layers of vinyl electrical tape, extending about $1\frac{1}{2}$" (37 mm) beyond the edge of the splicing compound.

The five basic tasks in building a splice are:

- Preparing the surface
- Joining the conductors with connector(s)
- Reinsulating
- Reshielding
- Rejacketing

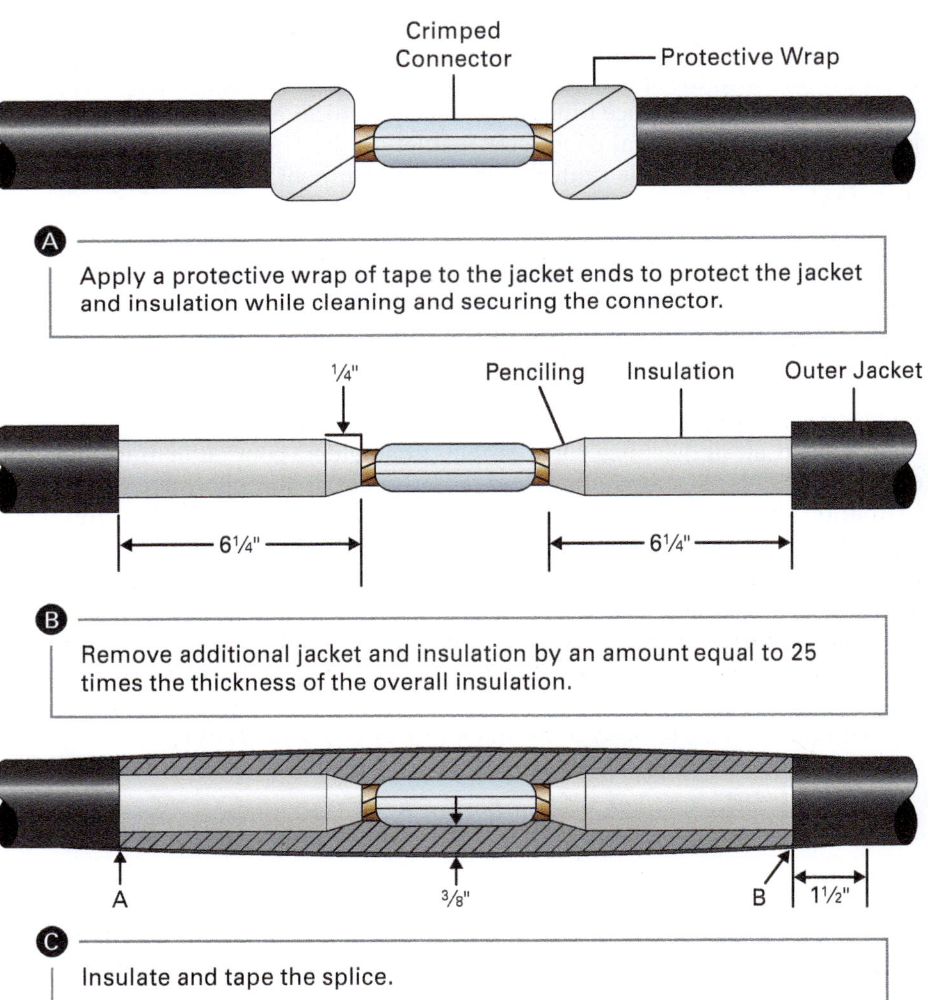

Figure 8 Making a basic splice.

Making Terminations and Splices

Correct cable preparation, proper installation of all components, and good workmanship are all required to make splices and terminations like those in the image shown. Manufacturers have done much in the last few years to develop products that make splicing and terminating cables easier, but the expertise, skills, and care of the installer are still necessary to make dependable splices and terminations.

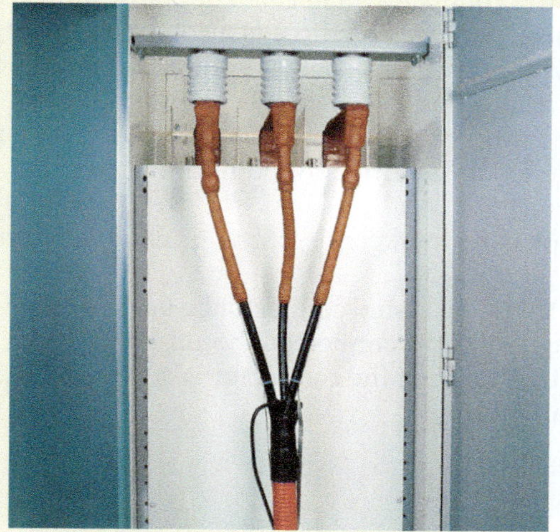

Source: TE Connectivity

1.2.1 Preparing the Surface

Careful surface preparation is essential to making effective cable splices. Begin with good cable ends; it is a common practice to cut off a portion of the cable after pulling to ensure an undamaged end. Always use sharp, high-quality tools. When the various layers are removed, cuts should extend only partially through the layer. For example, when removing cable insulation, be careful not to cut completely through and damage the conductor strands. Specialized tools are available to aid in the removal of the various cable layers. Another good technique for removing polyethylene cable insulation is to use a nylon string as the cutting tool.

When penciling is required (not normally necessary for molded rubber devices), a full, smooth taper is necessary to eliminate the possibility of air voids.

Completely remove the semicon layer(s) and the resulting residue. Two methods are commonly used to remove the residue, including:

- *Abrasives* — A 120-grit abrasive cloth is fine enough to protect the medium-voltage interface and yet coarse enough to remove semicon residue without loading up the abrasive cloth. This abrasive must have nonconductive grit. Do not use emery cloth or any other abrasive containing conductive particles because these could embed into the cable insulation. When using an insulation diameter-dependent device (for example, molded rubber devices), take care not to abrade the insulation below the minimums specified for the device.
- *Solvents* — Use the solvent recommended by the cable manufacturer and the splicing kit manufacturer. Avoid any solvent that leaves a residue. Do not use excessive amounts of solvent because this can saturate the semicon layers and render them nonconductive. Always wipe the cable from the conductor back toward the jacket.

CAUTION

Always read the Safety Data Sheet (SDS) before using any solvent. Avoid solvents that present health hazards, especially with long-term exposure. Choose a nontoxic solvent whenever possible.

Extruded Semiconductors

Some extruded semiconductors peel more easily if they are heated slightly. A heat-shrink blowgun works well.

1.2.2 Joining the Conductors with Connectors

After the cables are completely prepared, the rebuilding process begins. If a premolded or heat-shrink splice is being installed, the appropriate splice components must be slid onto the cable(s) before the connection is made. The first step is reconstructing the conductor with a suitable connector. Connector selection is based on the conductor material (copper or aluminum). A suitable connector for medium-voltage cable splices is a compression or crimp type. Do not use mechanical-type connectors, such as split-bolt connectors.

Aluminum conductors should be connected with an aluminum-bodied connector preloaded with contact aid (antioxide paste) to break down the insulating aluminum oxide coating on both the connector and conductor surfaces.

When the conductor is copper, connect it with either copper or aluminum-bodied connectors.

It is recommended that a UL Listed connector be used that can be applied with any common crimping tool. This connector should be listed for use at medium voltages. In this way, the choice of the connector is at the user's discretion and is not limited by the available tools.

Think About It

Mechanical Connectors

Could you use the connectors shown here to make a high-voltage connection?

1.2.3 Reinsulating

There are several methods used to reinsulate splices:

- *Taping* — This approach is not dependent upon cable types and dimensions. Tape has a history of dependable service and is generally available. However, wrapping tape on a medium-voltage cable can be time-consuming and error-prone since the careful buildup of tape requires accurate half-lapping and constant tension to reduce air voids.
- *Heat-shrink tubing* — Heat-shrinkable products use cross-linked polymer tubing that shrinks when heated to its transition temperature. This provides a tight, even seal around the connection area and the cable components. These products can be installed using a flame torch or an electric hot air gun. Heat-shrink splices are range-taking, meaning they can be used on a wide range of cable types. The only information required to select a heat-shrink splice is the conductor size and the voltage range of the cable. By using shim tubing, heat-shrink splice kits can be used as reducer splices over a very broad range of cable sizes. These products are also available with an adhesive coating on the inside that provides a superior water seal.
- *Molded rubber splices* — These factory-made splices are designed for the installer's convenience. In many cases, these splices are also factory tested and designed to be installed without special installation tools. Most molded rubber splices use EPR as the reinsulation material. The EPR must be cured during the molding process using either a peroxide or sulfur cure.

Cable Preparation Tools

It is essential to use the proper tool when preparing conductors for termination or splicing. Shown is a cable preparation tool used for removing the outer cable jacket. It can also be used for stripping the insulation.

This semiconductor scoring tool has a blade adjustable for both cutting depth and angle. Once set to the proper depth, the blade is set perpendicular to the cable, and a ring cut is made around the cable at the desired point. After the ring cut is made, the blade is angled so each rotation around the cable results in a spiral cut.

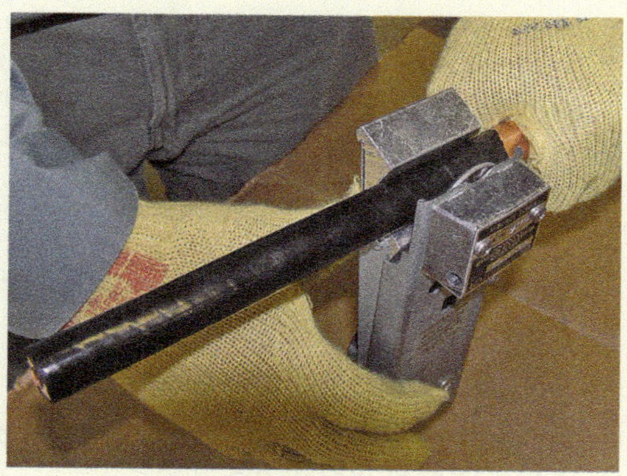

Source: Jim Mitchem

Abrasives

Aluminum oxide (ALO) cloth is nonconductive and suitable for use in preparing cable splices. Most people assume that since it contains aluminum, this cloth is conductive, but the oxide of aluminum is actually an insulator.

Cable Preparation Kits

Cable preparation kits contain solvent-saturated cloths and 120-grit nonconductive abrasive cloth. Using these premoistened cloths saves time during surface preparation and prevents solvent spillage or storage issues on the jobsite.

Linerless Splicing Tapes

Linerless splicing tapes reduce application time because there is no need to stop during taping to tear off the liner. This also allows the splicer to maintain a constant tape tension, thus reducing the possibility of taped-in voids.

1.2.4 Reshielding

The cable's two shielding systems (strand shield and insulation shield) must be rebuilt when constructing a splice. The same methods are used as outlined in the reinsulation process: tape, heat shrink, and molded rubber.

For a tape splice, the cable strand shielding is replaced by semicon tape. This tape is wrapped over the connector area to smooth the crimp indents and connector edges. The insulation shielding system is replaced by a combination of tapes. The semicon layer is replaced with the same semicon tape used to replace the strand shield.

The cable's metallic shield is generally replaced with a flexible woven mesh of tin-plated copper braid. This braid is for electrostatic shielding only and is not designed to carry shield currents. For conducting shield currents, a jumper braid is installed to connect the metallic shields of the two cable ends. This jumper must have an ampacity rating equal to that of the cable shields.

The insulation shielding of a heat-shrink splice contains a layer of conductive material bonded to the outside of the insulation tubing, similar to how the cable is designed. The bonded conductive layer is continuous across the splice, so the tubing placement is not as critical as with a premolded splice. The inner insulation and outer conductive layer are bonded together in one dual-wall tube, which prevents air pockets between the insulation and semicon layers of the splice. The metallic shield is reinstated with ground braids and stainless steel spring clamps to ensure proper fault-carrying capacity of the splice.

For a molded rubber splice, conductive rubber is used to replace the cable strand shielding and the semicon portion of the insulation shield system. Again, the metallic shield portion must be jumpered with a metallic component of equal ampacity.

A desirable design parameter of a molded rubber splice is that it be installable without special tools. To accomplish this, very short electrical interfaces are required. These interfaces are attained through proper design shapes of the conductive rubber electrodes.

1.2.5 Rejacketing

Rejacketing is accomplished in a tape splice using rubber splicing tape overwrapped with vinyl tape.

In a heat-shrink splice, rejacketing is completed using heavy-wall, adhesive-coated tubing or, where space is limited, a wraparound sleeve.

In a molded rubber splice, rejacketing is accomplished by the proper design of the outer semicon rubber, effectively resulting in a semicon jacket.

When a molded rubber splice is used on internally shielded cable such as tape shield, drain wire shield, or UniShield® cables, a shield adapter is used to seal the opening that results between the splice and cable jacket.

Rejacketing

Shown is an example of a heat-shrinkable wraparound jacket repair sleeve used to protect splices in cables subjected to mechanically abusive environments. It can also be used to provide a moisture barrier for repairing and rejacketing lead-covered shields and moisture-impervious cables.

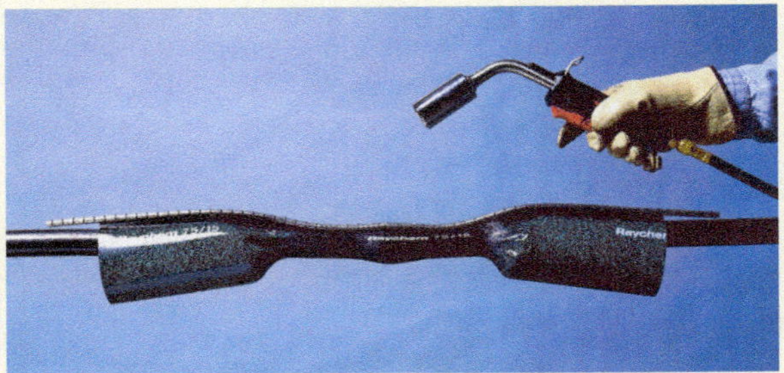

Source: TE Connectivity

Tape Splice Kits

Tape splice kits contain all the necessary tapes, along with detailed instructions. These versatile kits ensure the proper materials are available at the jobsite and make an ideal emergency splice kit.

Reshielding

Shown is an example of a partially completed splice of a shielded single-conductor power cable. The splice is being made using a heat-shrinkable splice kit for use with shielded power cables.

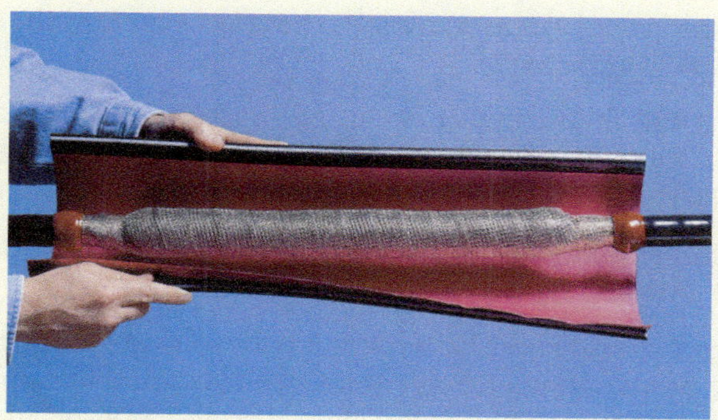

Source: TE Connectivity

1.3.0 Making Inline Tape Splices

This section provides an example of a tape splicing procedure using one manufacturer's splicing kit. The procedure applies to metallic and wire shield cable with voltage ratings from 5 kV to 25 kV, with a normal maximum temperature rating of 90°C and 130°C emergency operation. *Figure 9* shows the various cable sections.

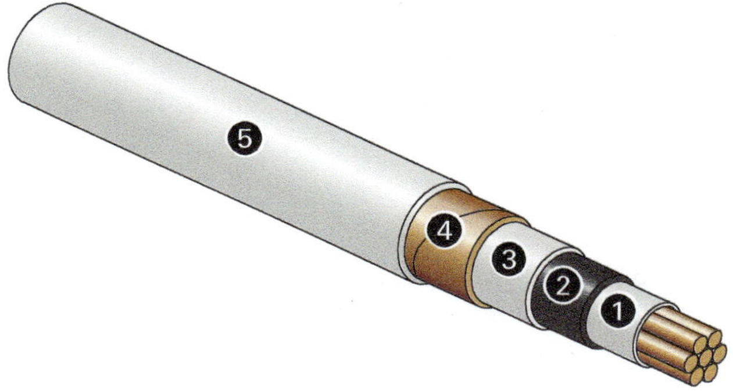

Figure 9 High-voltage cable construction.
Source: 3M

1.3.1 Preparing the Cable

Prepare the cable as follows:

Step 1 Train the cable in position and cut it carefully so the cable ends will butt squarely.

Step 2 Thoroughly scrape the jacket 3" (75 mm) beyond dimension A in *Figure 10* to remove all dirt, wax, and cable-pulling compound so the tape will bond, making a moisture-tight seal.

Step 3 Remove the cable jacket and nonmetallic filler tape from the ends to be spliced for distance A plus ½ the connector length.

Step 4 Remove the cable metallic shielding to expose 1" (25 mm) beyond the cable jacket. If shielded wire cable is used, see *Figure 11*. Be careful not to nick the semicon material.

Step 5 Tack the metallic shielding in place with solder.

CAUTION

Be careful not to cut into the metallic shielding or insulation when removing the jacket.

CAUTION

Do not overheat the thermoplastic insulation.

CAUTION

Do not use emery cloth, as it contains metal particles.

Step 6 Remove the semicon material, leaving $\frac{1}{4}$" (6 mm) exposed beyond the cable metallic shielding. Be sure to remove all traces of this material from the exposed cable insulation by cleaning it with a nonconductive abrasive cloth.

Step 7 Remove the cable insulation from the end of the conductor for a distance of $\frac{1}{2}$" (13 mm) plus $\frac{1}{2}$ the connector length. Be careful not to nick the conductor.

Step 8 Pencil the insulation at each end, using a penciling tool or a sharp knife, for a distance equal to B in *Figure 10*. Buff the tapers with an abrasive cloth so no voids remain after the joint is insulated.

Step 9 Taper the cable jacket smoothly at each end for a distance equal to $\frac{1}{4}$" (6 mm). Buff the tapers with an abrasive cloth.

Step 10 Clean the entire area by wiping it with solvent-saturated cloth from the cable preparation kit. Solvent may be used on thermoplastic insulation, but the area must be completely dry and free of all solvent residue, especially in the conductor strands and underneath the cable shield, before proceeding.

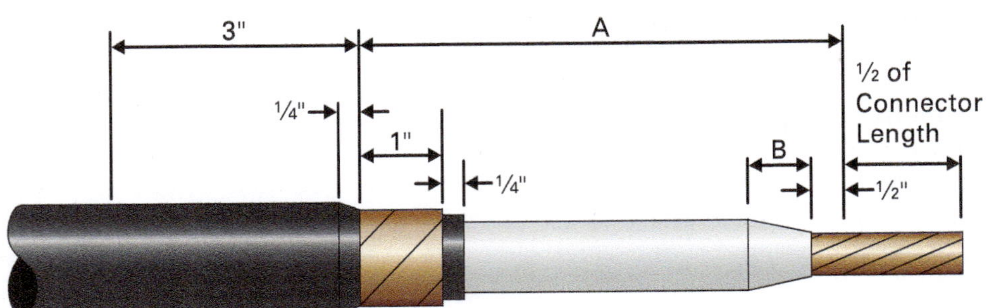

Figure 10 Recommended cable preparation procedures for an inline splice.
Source: 3M

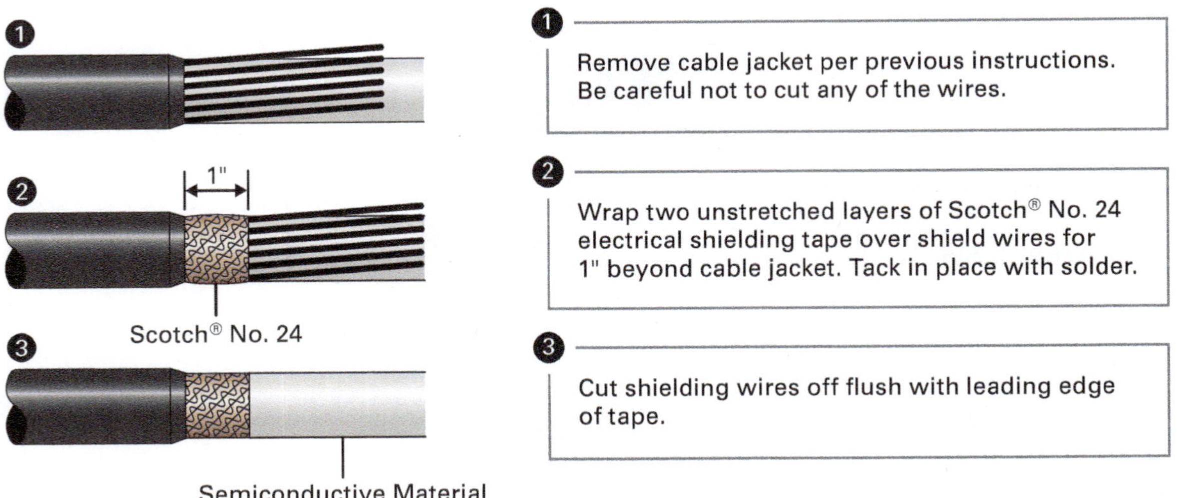

Figure 11 Wire shield procedure.
Source: 3M

Selecting a Splice Method

For the versatility to handle practically any splicing emergency, for situations where only a few splices need to be made, or when little detail is known about the cable, the most effective splice is made with a tape kit or heat-shrink kit.

For those times when cable size, insulation diameter, and shielding type are known and when numerous splices will be made, use heat-shrink or molded rubber splices for dependability and simplicity, as well as quick application.

1.3.2 Connecting the Conductors

Connect the conductors as follows:

Step 1 Join the conductors with an appropriate connector. Use a crimp connector to connect thermoplastic-insulated cables. Follow the connector manufacturer's directions. Use antioxidant paste for aluminum conductors. When using a solder-sweated connector, protect the cable insulation with temporary wraps of cotton tape. Be sure to remove all antioxidant paste from the connector area after crimping the aluminum connector.

CAUTION

Do not use acid core solder or acid flux.

Step 2 Fill the connector indents with Scotch® electrical semiconducting tape No. 13, as shown in *Figure 12*. Smoothly tape two half-lapped layers of highly elongated tape over the exposed conductor and connector area. Cover all threads of the semicon strand shielding and overlap the cable insulation with semicon tape. Stretching the tape increases its conductance and will not harm it in any way.

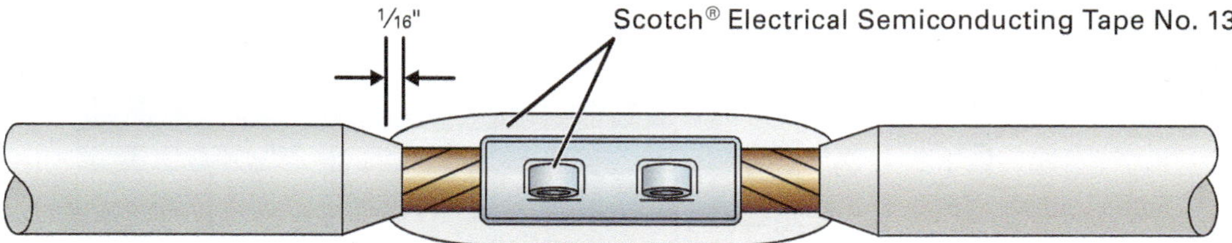

Figure 12 Connecting conductors.
Source: 3M

1.3.3 Applying Primary Insulation

Apply the primary insulation as follows:

Step 1 Apply Scotch® rubber splicing tape No. 23 (*Figure 13*) half-lapped over the hand-applied semicon tape and exposed insulation up to 1/4" (6 mm) from the cable semicon material. Continue to apply the tape half-lapped in successive level wound layers until the thickness is equal to the dimension shown in *Figure 13*. The outside surface should taper gradually along distance C, reaching its maximum diameter over the penciled insulation.

Step 2 Wrap one half-lapped layer of Scotch® No. 13 tape over the splicing tape, extending over the cable semicon material and onto the cable metallic shielding 1/4" (6 mm) at each end. Highly elongate this tape when taping over the edge of the cable metallic shielding.

Step 3 Wrap one half-lapped layer of Scotch® No. 24 electrical shielding tape over the semicontape, overlapping 1/4" (6 mm), onto the cable metallic shielding at each end. Solder the ends to the metallic **shielding braid**.

Step 4 Wrap one half-lapped layer of Scotch® No. 33+ vinyl electrical tape, covering the entire area of the shielding braid. Stretch it tightly to flatten and confine the shielding braid.

NOTE

To eliminate voids in critical areas, highly elongate the splicing tape in the connector area and at the splice ends near the cable semicon material. Stretch the tape just short of its breaking point. Doing so will not alter its physical or electrical properties. Throughout the rest of the splice area, less elongation may be used. Normally, No. 23 tape is stretched to 75% of its original width in these less-critical areas. Always attempt to exactly half-lap to produce a uniform buildup.

CAUTION

Do not lay a solder bead across the shielding braid. Do not use acid core solder or acid flux.

Shielding braid: A shield of small, interwoven wires.

CAUTION

Do not overheat the thermoplastic insulation.

NOTE

Whenever possible, substitute Scotch® No. 130C linerless splicing tape for Scotch® No. 23 tape.

Step 5 Attach Scotch® No. 25 ground braid as shown in *Figure 14*, soldering it to the cable metallic shielding at each end. Use a wire or strap with at least the same ampacity as the shield (No. 6 AWG is usually adequate).

Step 6 If a splice is to be grounded, use the following procedure to construct a moisture seal at the ground braid:

a. If a stranded ground is used, provide solder block to prevent moisture penetration into the splice.

b. Wrap two half-lapped layers of Scotch® No. 23 tape, covering the last 2" (50 mm) of the cable jacket.

c. Wrap two half-lapped layers of Scotch® No. 23 tape for 3" (75 mm) along the ground strap, beginning at a point where the ground is soldered to the shield.

d. Lay the ground strap over the Scotch® No. 23 tape that was applied on the jacket for 1" (25 mm), and then bend the strap away from the cable. Press the strap hard against the cable jacket.

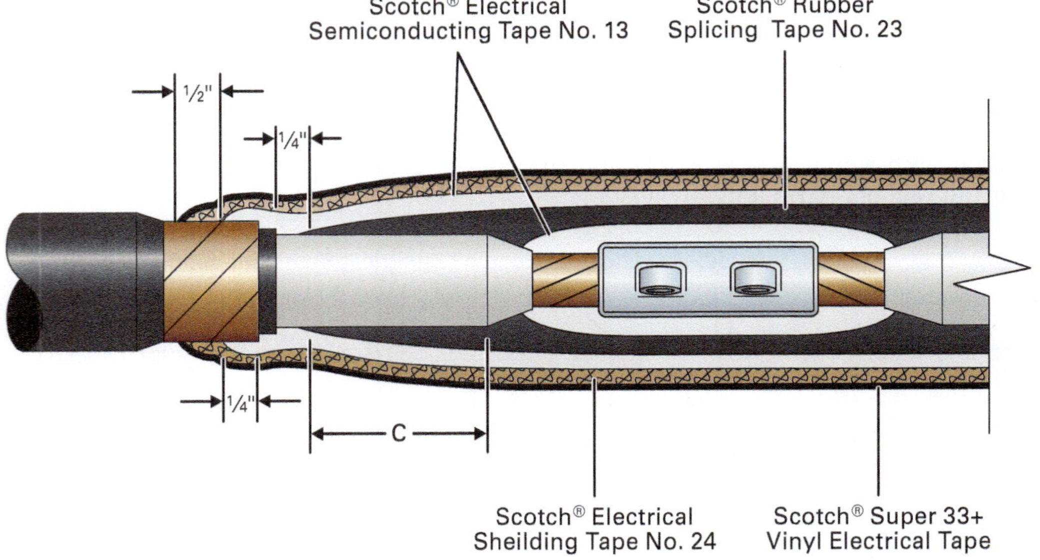

Figure 13 Applying primary insulation.
Source: 3M

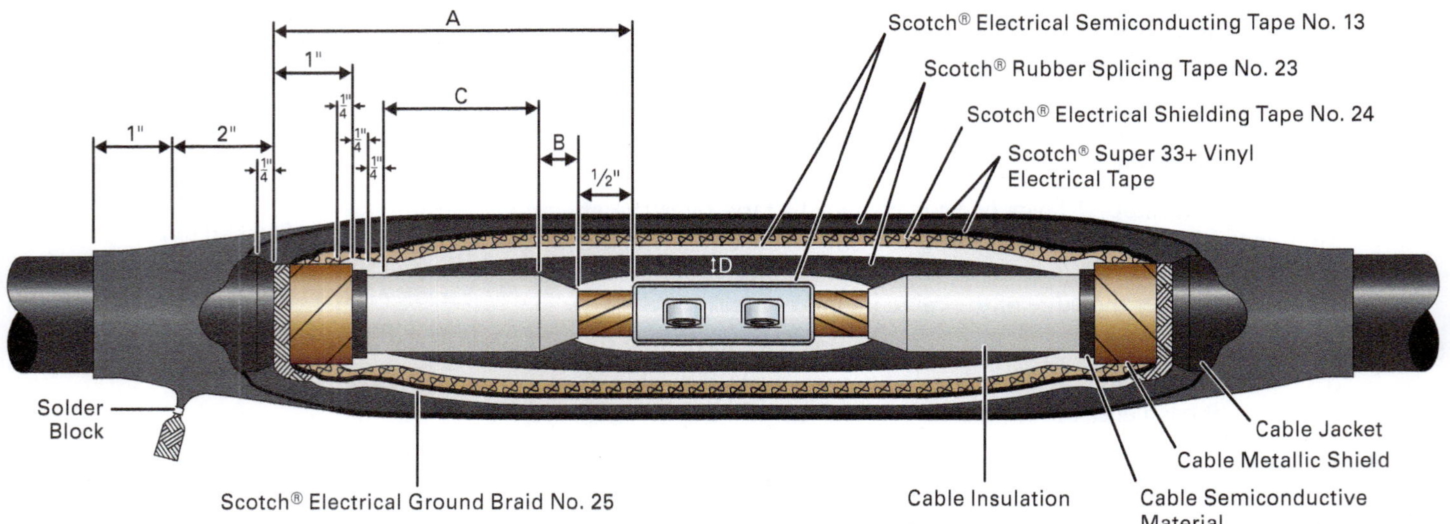

Figure 14 Summary of an inline tape splice.
Source: 3M

1.3.4 Applying the Outer Sheath

Apply the outer sheath as follows:

Step 1 Wrap four half-lapped layers of Scotch® No. 23 tape (or equivalent) over the entire splice 2" (50 mm) beyond the splicing tape. Highly stretch the tape to form a good moisture seal and eliminate voids. Make sure the tape covers the ground braid to complete the moisture seal.

Step 2 Wrap two half-lapped layers of Scotch® No. 33+ over the entire splice 1" (25 mm) beyond the splicing tape and 1" (25 mm) along the grounding braid. A summary of the end preparation and taping is shown in *Figure 14*.

1.3.5 Tee Tape Splice

A tee tape splice (tap) is performed in basically the same way as the inline tape splice, except a third conductor is attached, as shown in *Figure 15*. Tee splices require greater skill to construct because the tape must be highly elongated to prevent voids in the crotch area.

Heat-shrink splices are also available up to 25 kV. These splices provide a reliable and efficient method of making tee splices.

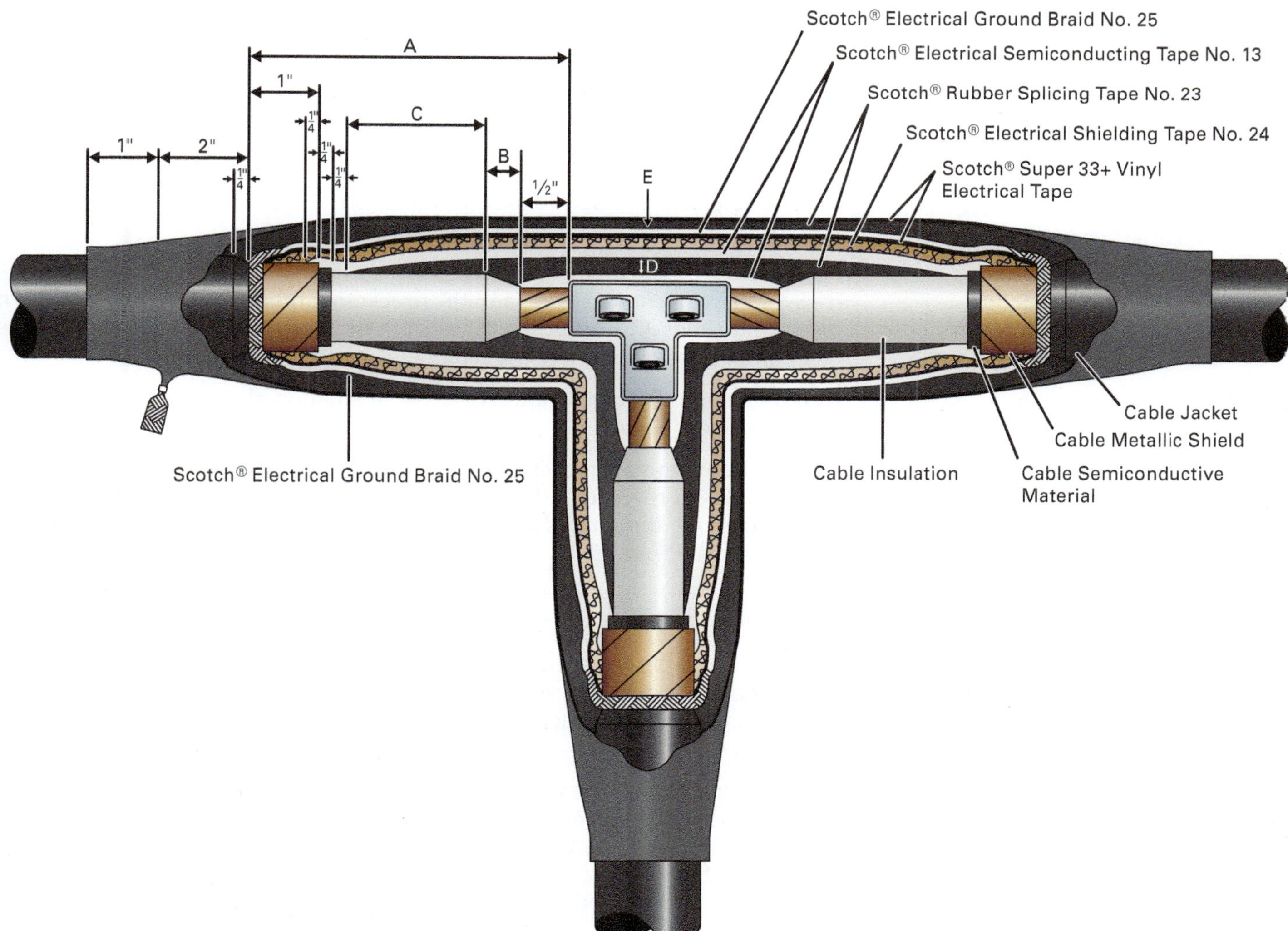

Figure 15 Summary of a tee tape splice.
Source: 3M

1.4.0 Manufactured Termination and Splice Kits

Manufactured termination and splice kits consist of cable preparation materials, semiconductor material, stress control means, and materials for jacketing, sealing, and grounding. The stress control and jacket materials are applied using a shrink-to-fit method. Both heat- and cold-shrink materials are available.

1.4.1 Heat-Shrink Kits

Heat-shrink splice kits have large use ranges and allow the connection of different conductor sizes, different insulation types (for example, paper insulation to polymeric insulation), and different cable constructions (for example, three-conductor cable spliced to single-conductor cable).

The following instructions are for a heat-shrink kit used on copper tape-shielded cable. This same kit will splice UniShield®, wire shield, lead-sheathed cable, or any combination thereof.

To use a quick inline splicing kit, proceed as follows:

Step 1 Select the appropriate kit for the cable diameter using the selection charts provided by the kit manufacturer.

Step 2 Verify the ground braid or bond wire has a cross section equivalent to that of the cable's metallic shield.

Step 3 Cut back the cable to the dimensions specified in the kit manufacturer's instructions for the type of cable being spliced (*Figure 16*). If necessary, abrade the insulation to remove embedded semicon.

Step 4 Clean the cable jackets for the length of the tubes.

NOTE

Some of the newer solvents do not evaporate quickly and need to be removed using a clean, lint-free cloth. Failure to do so could leave a residue on the surface and interfere with the electrical integrity of the cable.

WARNING!

Some solvents are toxic and must be handled with extreme caution. Refer to the solvent manufacturer's SDS for safety precautions associated with the solvent being used.

Step 5 Place the nested tubes and the rejacketing tube over the cable, as shown in *Figure 17*. Protect the tubes from the sharp ends of the conductor as they are placed over the cable.

Step 6 Install the connector. Wipe the insulation down using an oil-free solvent (*Figure 18*).

Step 7 Tightly wrap the exposed conductor with the stress relief material (SRM) provided in the splicing kit. Be sure to fill all gaps and low spots around the connector. Also, install SRM over the semicon cutback areas (*Figure 19*).

NOTE

If the connector diameter is larger than the insulation diameter, apply two overlapped layers of SRM along the length of the entire connector.

WARNING!

To avoid the risk of accidental fire or explosion when using gas torches, always check all connections for leaks before igniting the torch and follow the manufacturer's safety instructions.

Step 8 Center the stress control tube over the splice and shrink it into place using a manufacturer-approved heat source (*Figure 20*). When shrinking the stress control or insulating tube, apply the outer tip of the flame using a smooth brushing motion. Be sure to keep the flame moving to avoid scorching the material. Unless otherwise instructed, start shrinking at the center of the tube, then work the flame outward on all sides to ensure uniform heat.

Figure 16 Preparing the cables.
Source: TE Connectivity

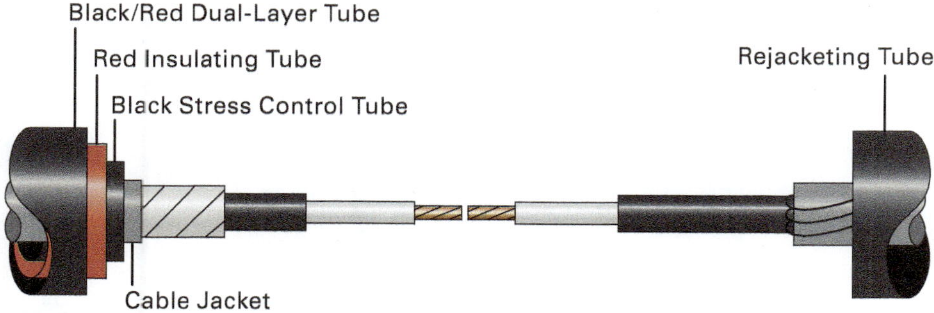

Figure 17 Placing the nested tubes on the cable.
Source: TE Connectivity

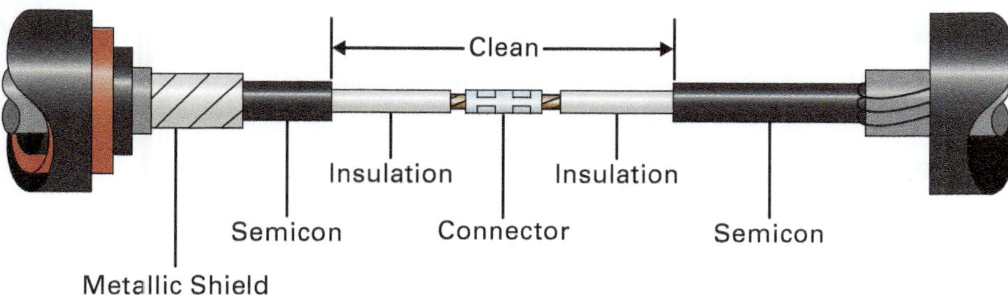

Figure 18 Installing the connector.
Source: TE Connectivity

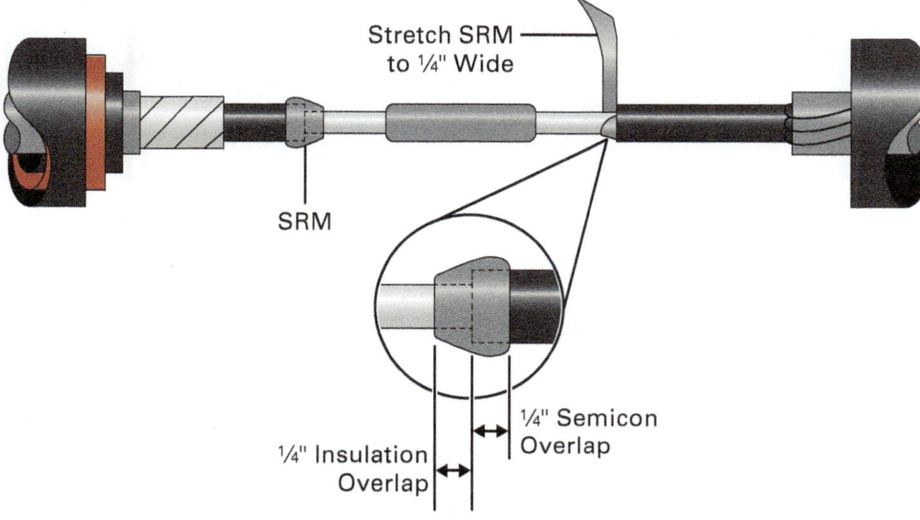

Figure 19 Installing the stress relief material.
Source: TE Connectivity

Step 9 Position the insulating tube over the stress control tube and shrink it into place (*Figure 21*).

Step 10 Apply sealant to the tube ends to provide a positive environmental seal. Build the sealant to the level of the insulating tube (*Figure 22*).

Step 11 Position the insulating/conductive tube over the insulating tube and seal the ends before shrinking it into place (*Figure 23*).

Step 12 Install metallic shielding mesh using manufacturer-supplied constant-tension clamps for metallic tape shielding or crimp connectors for wire shielding (*Figure 24*).

Step 13 Position the rejacketing tube and shrink it into place. Check the ends for correct adhesive flow (*Figure 25*).

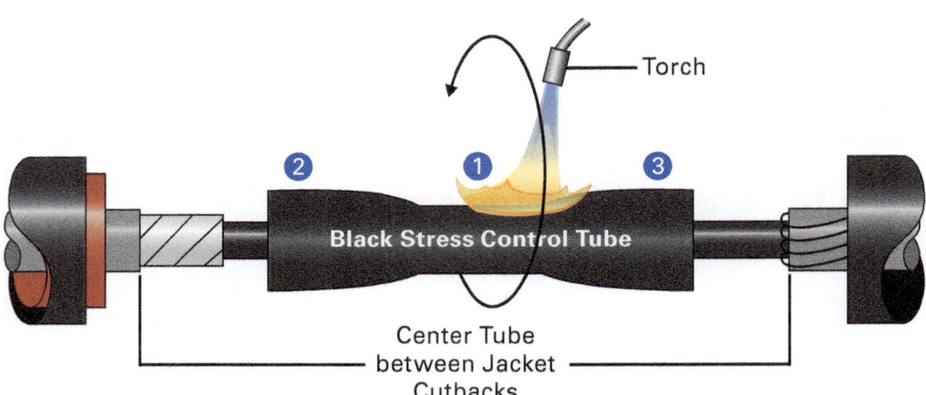

Figure 20 Shrinking the stress control tube.
Source: TE Connectivity

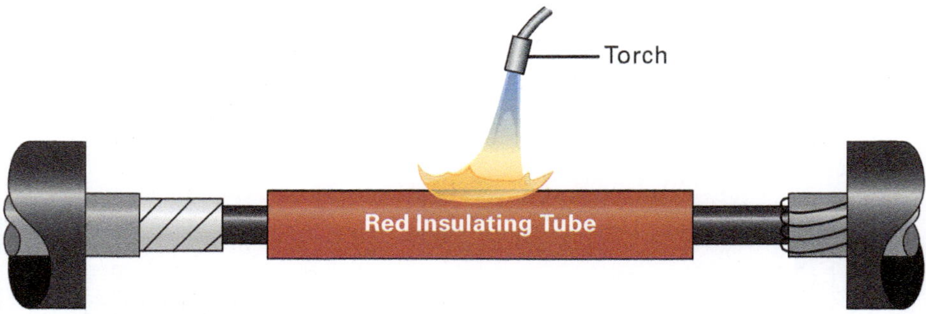

Figure 21 Shrinking the insulating tube.
Source: TE Connectivity

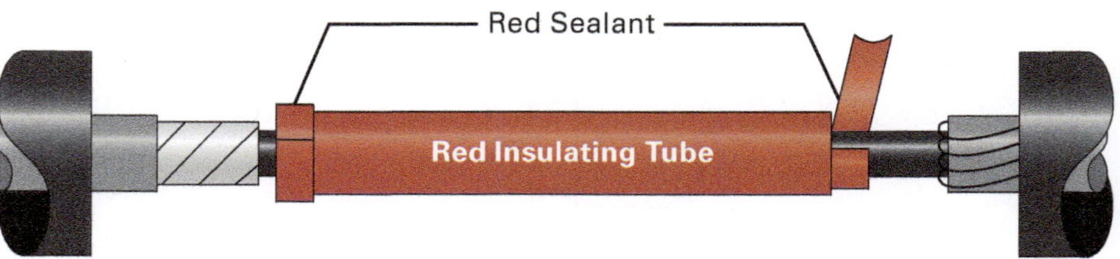

Figure 22 Applying sealant.
Source: TE Connectivity

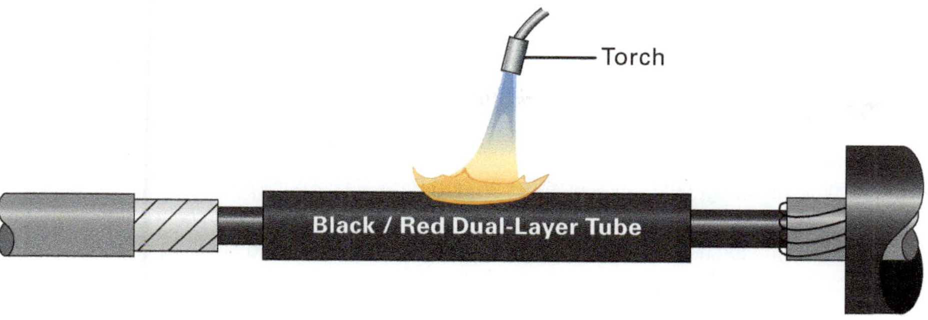

Figure 23 Shrinking the insulating/conductive tube.
Source: TE Connectivity

Figure 24 Installing metallic shielding mesh.
Source: TE Connectivity

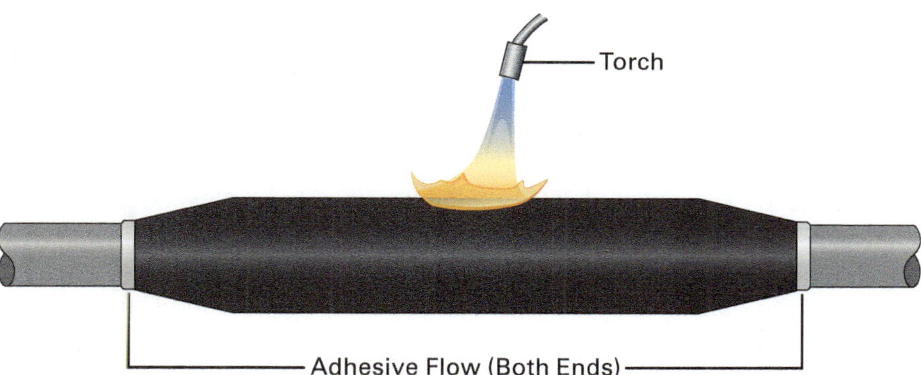

Figure 25 Shrinking the rejacketing tube and checking for adhesive flow.
Source: TE Connectivity

Manufacturer's Instructions

High-quality products usually include detailed installation instructions. Always follow these instructions carefully. A suggested technique is to check off each step as it is completed. Some manufacturers also offer hands-on training programs designed to teach the proper installation of their products. It is highly recommended that inexperienced splice and termination installers take advantage of such programs.

The Use of Propane Torches and Hot-Air Heat Guns

Making proper splices and terminations using heat-shrink tubing and materials requires that the proper heat level be applied to the heat-shrink material. One manufacturer recommends that a clean-burning propane torch, like the one shown, be used for heating the heat-shrink tubing materials when making splices and terminations on high-voltage cables. The torch should have an output heat rating of about 90,000 Btuh. Heat-shrink splices and terminations on low-voltage cables and/or smaller high-voltage cables (up to 15 kV) can be made using either a propane torch or a hot-air heat gun. The propane torch should have a heat output rating of about 20,000 Btuh; the hot-air heat gun should have a heat output rating of about 750°F to 1,000°F.

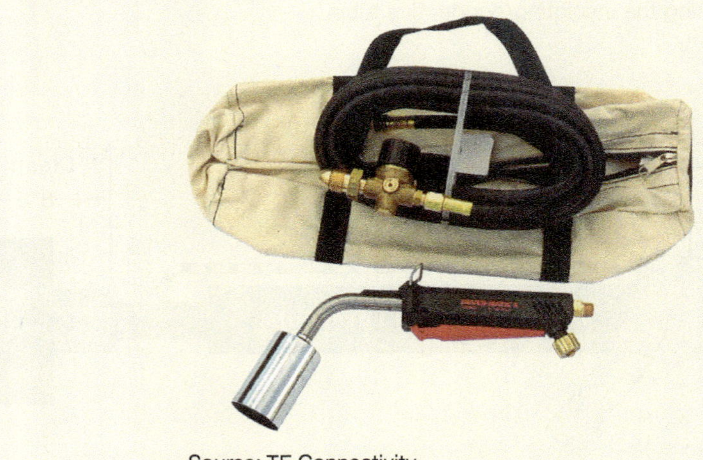

Source: TE Connectivity

1.4.2 Cold-Shrink Kits

The following instructions are for a cold-shrink kit used on ribbon shielding cable. Kits are also available for wire shield and UniShield®. Complete instructions are included in each kit, and once you understand the directions in this module for ribbon shielding cable, the directions for the other types should be readily understood as well. To use a cold-shrink kit, prepare the cables as follows:

Step 1 Clean each cable jacket by wiping it with a dry cloth about 2" (50 mm) from each end.

Step 2 Refer to *Figure 26* (note that the dimensions shown will vary with the type of kit used). Remove the jacket to distances B and C for cables X and Y, respectively.

Step 3 Remove the metallic shielding for distance A.

Step 4 Remove the cable semicon material, allowing it to extend $\frac{1}{4}$" (6 mm) beyond the metallic shielding (dimension A).

Step 5 Remove the insulation for dimension D and taper the edges $\frac{1}{8}$" (3 mm) at approximately 45°.

Step 6 Clean the exposed insulation using the cleaning pads in the kit. Do not use solvent or abrasive on the cable semicon layer. If abrasive must be used on the insulation, do not reduce the diameter below that specified for minimum splice application.

Step 7 Apply two highly elongated, half-lapped layers of Scotch® No. 13 semiconducting tape starting at 1" (25 mm) on the cable metallic shield and extending $\frac{1}{2}$" (13 mm) onto the cable insulation. Leave a smooth leading edge and tape back to the starting position (*Figure 27*).

Step 8 On cable X, apply one half-lapped layer (adhesive side out) of the orange vinyl tape supplied in the kit over the metallic shield, beginning approximately $\frac{1}{4}$" (6 mm) on the previously applied No. 13 tape and ending over the cable jacket.

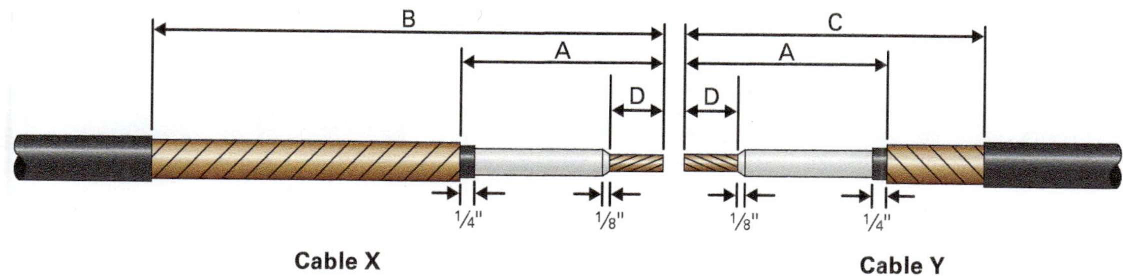

Figure 26 Cable preparation details.
Source: 3M

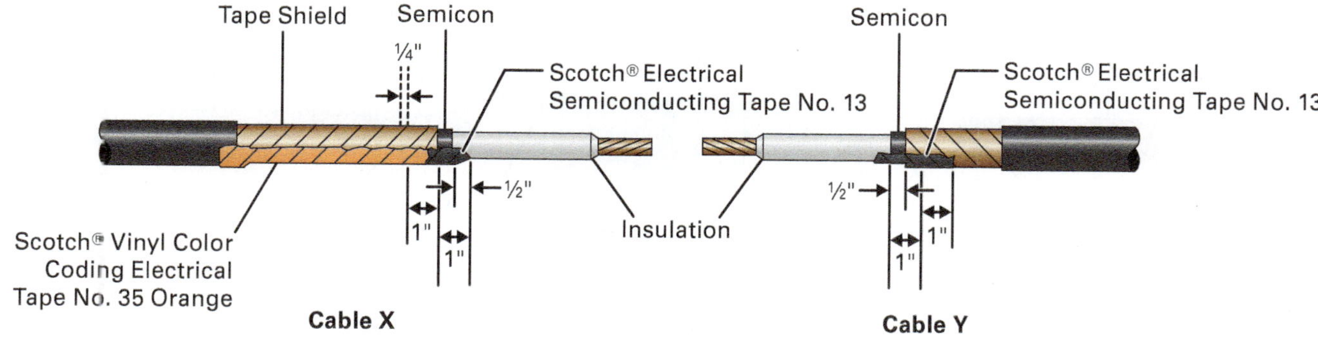

Figure 27 Components of a ribbon shielding cable splice.
Source: 3M

Splice the installation as follows:

Step 1 Slide the longer PST cold-shrink insulator onto the X jacket and the shorter PST onto the Y jacket, directing the pull tabs away from the cable ends, as shown in *Figure 28*.

Step 2 Apply a few wraps of vinyl tape over cable X.

Step 3 Lubricate the exposed insulation, No. 13 tape, and orange vinyl tape of cables X and Y with silicone grease. Do not allow the grease to extend onto the metallic shield of cable Y.

Step 4 Lubricate the splice bore with silicone grease and install it onto cable X, leaving the conductor exposed for the connector, as shown in *Figure 29*.

Step 5 Remove the vinyl tape from the cable X conductor.

Step 6 Install a connector crimped per the manufacturer's instructions.

Step 7 Slide the splice body into its final position over the connector, using the bumps formed on the splice ends as guides for centering (*Figure 30*).

Step 8 Remove the orange vinyl tape and wipe off any remaining silicone grease.

NOTE

Rotating the splice while pulling will ease the installation. Make certain all splicing components (PSTs and splice body) are located properly on their respective cable ends before installing the connector.

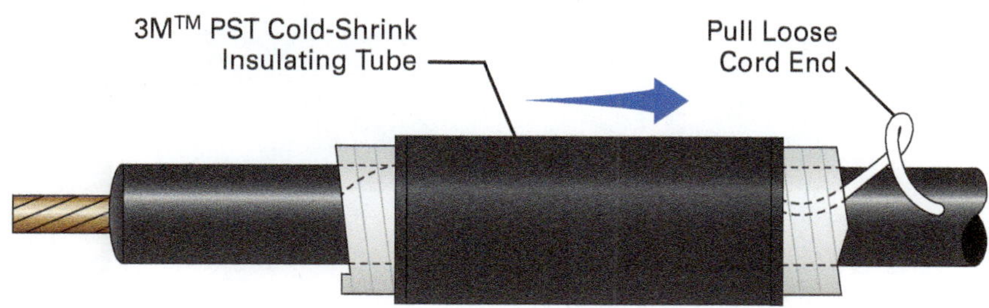

Figure 28 Installing PST cold-shrink insulator.
Source: 3M

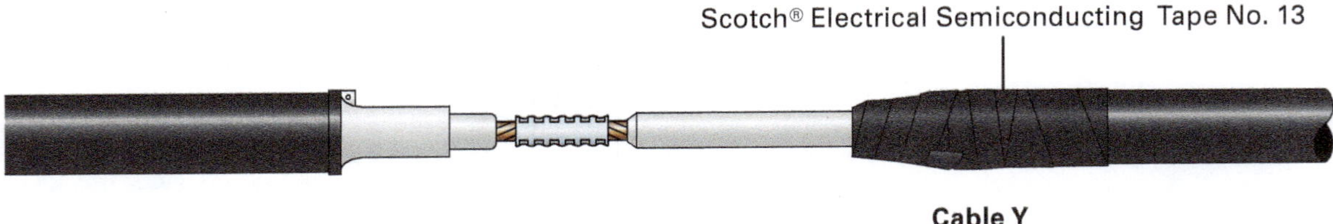

Figure 29 Wrapping No. 13 tape onto the cable.
Source: 3M

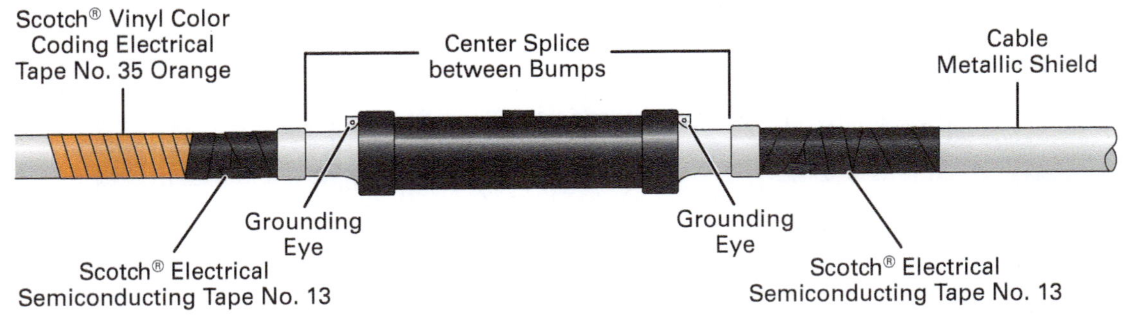

Figure 30 Use bumps formed on splice ends as guides for centering.
Source: 3M

Installing Multiple Tubes

When installing multiple tubes, make sure the surface of the last tube is still warm before positioning and shrinking the next tube. If the installed tube has cooled, reheat the entire surface.

Quick Inline Splicing Kits

Shown is an example of one manufacturer's cold-applied inline cable splice kit. It is used for splicing metallic shielded cables without the need to use a torch. The rejacketing component of the kit is a gel-wrap sleeve that seals the entire splice area, thereby providing mechanical and environmental protection for the splice.

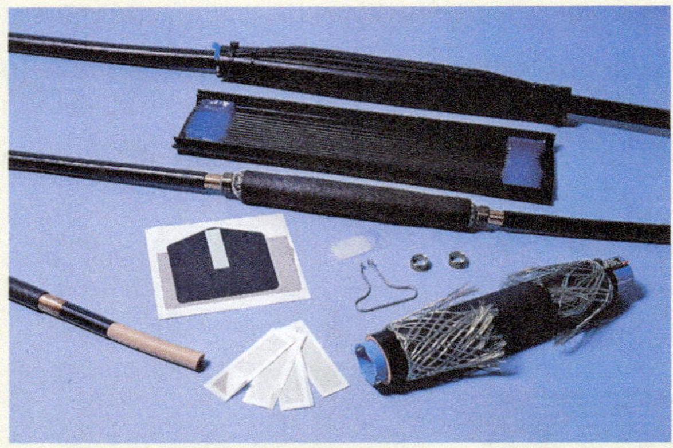

Source: TE Connectivity

Install the shield continuity assembly as follows:

Step 1 Position the shield continuity assembly over the splice body and hold it in place with a strap or two of vinyl tape at each end of the splice body (*Figure 31*). Form the shield continuity strap over the splice shoulder on each side (*Figure 32*).

Step 2 Unwrap the coil and straighten it for 1" to 2" (25 mm to 50 mm), then hold the coil and shield strap in place with your thumb. Pull to unwrap the coil around the cable and rewrap it around the cable metallic shield and itself. Cinch (tighten) the applied coil after the final wrap. Repeat for the other end of the splice.

Step 3 To seal the shield strap, cut the supplied strip of vinyl mastic into four equal lengths. After removing the liner, place one pad under the strap, with the mastic side toward the strap, and located at the end of the splice body (*Figure 32*). Place a second pad over the strap and first pad and press together, mastic to mastic. This will be wrapped with No. 13 tape. Repeat for the other end of the splice body.

Step 4 Beginning just beyond the splice body, wrap No. 13 tape over the vinyl mastic pads extending onto the splice for approximately $\frac{1}{4}$" (6 mm) and returning to the starting point.

NOTE

The assembly coils must be facing the cable and positioned so they will only make contact with the metallic shielding when applied. Avoid positioning the flat strap over the splice grounding eyes.

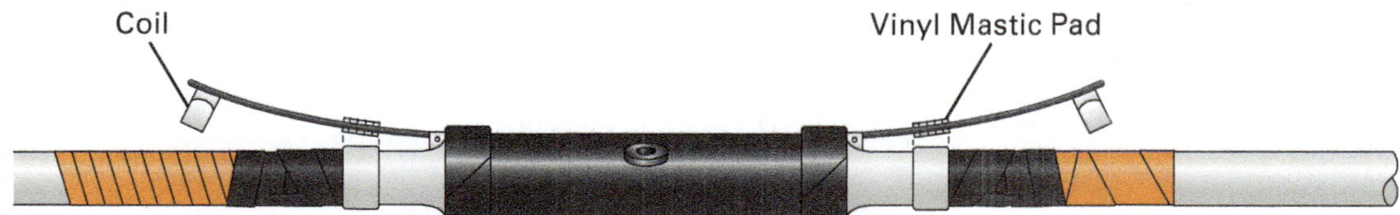

Figure 31 Wrap vinyl tape at each end of the splice body.
Source: 3M

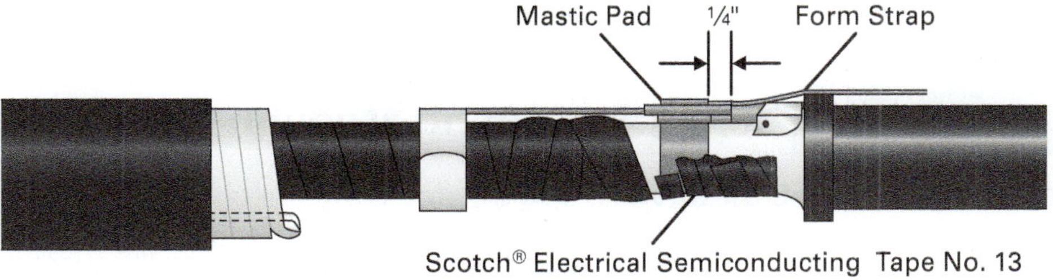

Figure 32 Form the shield continuity strap over the splice shoulder on each side.
Source: 3M

Install the cold-shrink insulators as follows:

Step 1 Position each PST so its leading edge will butt against the splice body grounding eye.

Step 2 Remove the core by unwinding it counterclockwise and tugging (*Figure 33*).

Figure 33 Remove core by unwinding counterclockwise.
Source: 3M

If the installation calls for grounding the splice, fasten the alligator ground clamp (provided with most kits) to the exposed shield continuity strap approximately at the center of the splice. A ground strap conductor can then be fastened to the alligator clamp. Discard the black plastic shoe packaged with the ground clamp.

1.0.0 Section Review

1. It is important to compensate for air voids in cable because air _____.
   a. is likely to contain contaminants
   b. is a poor insulator
   c. is an excellent resistor
   d. has a stronger dielectric value than insulation

2. When making a straight splice for a single, unshielded conductor, the conductor jacket and insulation should be removed for ½ the connector length plus _____.
   a. ⅝" (16 mm)
   b. ½" (13 mm)
   c. ¼" (6 mm)
   d. ⅛" (3 mm)

3. To eliminate air voids in critical areas when making a splice, _____.
   a. loosely apply additional layers of tape
   b. stretch the tape nearly to its breaking point
   c. avoid overlapping the layers of tape
   d. apply the tape sticky side out

4. Before using a cold-shrink kit, clean the cable jacket using _____.
   a. deionized water
   b. a water-based solvent
   c. an oil-based solvent
   d. a dry cloth

2.0.0 Terminating Medium-Voltage Cable

Performance Task

1. Prepare a cable and complete a splice or stress cone.

Objective

Describe termination classes and important considerations when creating terminations.

a. Identify termination classes.
b. Identify stress control methods.

There are three main classes of medium-voltage termination. Each class of termination is described in the sections that follow.

2.1.0 Termination Classes

A Class 1 cable termination provides the following:

- Some form of electric stress control for the cable insulation shield terminus
- Complete external leakage insulation between the conductor(s) and ground
- A seal to prevent the entrance of the external environment into the cable and to maintain the pressure, if any, within the cable system

A Class 2 termination provides only some form of electric stress control for the cable insulation shield terminus and complete external leakage insulation but no seal against external elements. Terminations falling into this classification include stress cones with rain shields, special outdoor insulation added to give complete leakage insulation, and the more recently introduced skip-on terminations for cables with extruded insulation when not providing a seal as in Class 1.

A Class 3 termination provides only some form of electric stress control for the cable insulation shield terminus. This class of termination would be for use primarily indoors. Typically, this would include hand-wrapped stress cones (tapes or pennants) as well as slip-on stress cones.

Some Class 1 and Class 2 terminations have external leakage insulation made of polymeric material. There is some concern about the ability of such insulation to withstand weathering, ultraviolet radiation, contamination, and leakage currents, and that a test capable of evaluating the various materials would be desirable. A number of test procedures are available today for this purpose; however, none of them have been recognized and adopted by the industry as a standard. Consequently, this module does not include such tests.

These IEEE classes make no distinction between indoor and outdoor environments. This is because contamination and moisture can be highly prevalent inside most industrial facilities, such as paper plants, steel mills, and petrochemical plants.

As a general recommendation, if there are airborne contaminants or if fail-safe power requirements are critical, use a Class 1 termination.

Terminations

Shown is an example of the types of high-voltage cable terminations encountered at a power substation.

Source: TE Connectivity

Lead Shield Repair Kits for PILC Cable

Shown is an example of a repair kit available from one manufacturer for the repair of a damaged lead sheath in paper-insulated, lead-covered (PILC) cable. The kit consists of a wraparound sleeve with an oil-resistant sealing mastic.

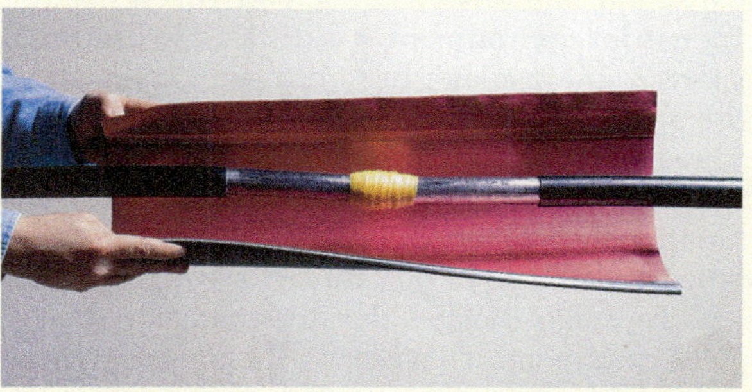

Source: TE Connectivity

2.1.1 Sealing to the External Environment

To qualify as a Class 1 termination, the termination must provide a seal to the external environment. Both the conductor/lug area and the shielding cutback area must be sealed. These seals keep moisture out of the cable to prevent degradation of the cable components. Several methods are used to make these seals, including factory-made seals, mastics used with heat-shrink kits, tape seals (silicone tape must be used for a top seal), and compound seals.

2.1.2 Grounding Shield Ends

All shield ends are normally grounded. However, individual circumstances may exist where the shield is grounded at only one end. The cable shield must be grounded somewhere in the system. When using solid dielectric cables, solderless ground connections are recommended, eliminating the danger of overheating cable insulation when soldering.

2.1.3 External Leakage Insulation

Insulation must serve two functions: protection from flashover damage and protection from tracking damage.

Terminations can be subjected to flashovers such as lightning-induced surges or switching surges. A good termination must be designed to survive these surges. Terminations are assigned a basic lightning impulse insulation level (BIL) according to their insulation class. For example, a 15 kV class termination has a BIL rating of 110 kV crest (*Table 1*).

TABLE 1 Insulation Classes and BIL Ratings

Insulation Class (kV)	BIL (kV Crest)
5.0	75
6.7	95
15.0	110
25.0	150
34.5	200
46.0	250
69.0	350

Terminations are also subject to *tracking*. Tracking can be defined as the process that produces localized deterioration on the surface of the insulator resulting in the loss of insulating function by forming a conductive path on the surface.

A termination can be considered an insulator with a voltage drop between the conductor and the shield. As such, a leakage current develops between these points. The magnitude of this leakage is inversely proportional to the resistance on the insulation surface (*Figure 34*).

Both contamination (dust, salt, and airborne particles) and moisture (humidity, condensation, and mist) will decrease this resistance. This results in tracking. In an industrial environment, it is difficult to prevent these conditions. Therefore, a track-resistant insulator must be used to prevent failures.

A high-performance Class 1 termination contains insulator skirts sized and shaped to form breaks in the moisture/contamination path, thus reducing the probability of tracking problems. In addition, these skirts can reduce the physical length of a termination by geometrically locating the creepage distance over the convolutions of the insulator, an important factor when space is a consideration.

Good termination design dictates that the insulators be efficiently applied under normal field conditions. This means the product should be applied by hand with a minimum of steps, parts, and pieces. Because they are inorganic materials, both porcelain and silicone rubbers provide excellent track resistance. Heat-shrink termination materials are the only non-tracking materials available and have shown superior long-term reliability.

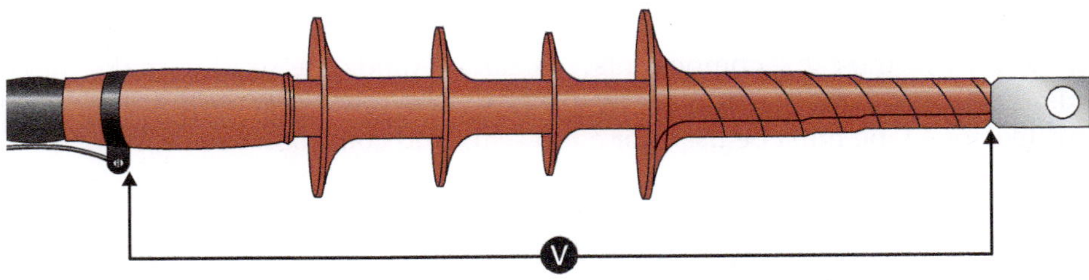

Figure 34 A terminator may be considered an insulator.

2.2.0 Stress Control Methods

In a continuous shielded cable, the electric field is uniform along the cable axis, with variation in the field only in a radial section. *Figure 35* shows the field distribution over a radial section.

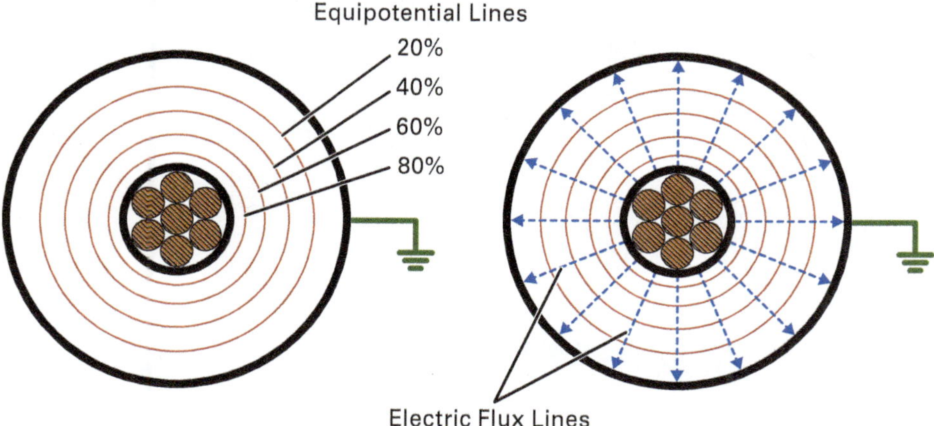

Figure 35 Field distribution over a radial cable section.

The spacing of the electric flux lines and corresponding equipotential lines is closer near the conductor than at the shield, indicating a higher electric stress on the insulation at the conductor. This stress increase or concentration is a direct result of the geometry of the conductor and shield in the cable section and is accommodated in practical cables by insulation thickness sufficient to keep the stress within acceptable values.

When terminating a shielded cable, it is necessary to remove the shield to a point some distance from the exposed conductor, as shown in *Figure 36* (A). This is to secure a sufficient length of insulation surface to prevent breakdown along the interface between the cable insulation and the insulating material to be applied in the termination. The exact length required is determined by the operating voltage and the properties of the insulating materials. This removal of a portion of the shield results in discontinuity of the electrical field. See *Figure 36* (B) and *Figure 36* (C). The electric flux lines originating along the conductor converge on the end of the shield, with the attendant close spacing of the equipotential lines signifying the presence of high electric stresses in this area. This stress concentration is of much greater magnitude than that occurring near the conductor in the continuous cable. As a result, steps must be taken to reduce the stresses occurring near the end of the shield if cable insulation failure is to be avoided.

All terminations must at least provide stress control. This stress control may be accomplished by two commonly used methods:

- Geometric stress control
- Capacitive stress control

2.2.1 Geometric Stress Control

This method involves an extension of the shielding (*Figure 37*), which expands the diameter at which the terminating discontinuity occurs, thereby reducing the stress at the discontinuity. It also reduces stresses by enlarging the radius of the shield end at the discontinuity.

2.2.2 Capacitive Stress Control

This method consists of a material possessing a high **dielectric constant (K)**, generally around K30, and also a high dielectric strength.

Dielectric constant (K): A measurement of a material's ability to store a charge.

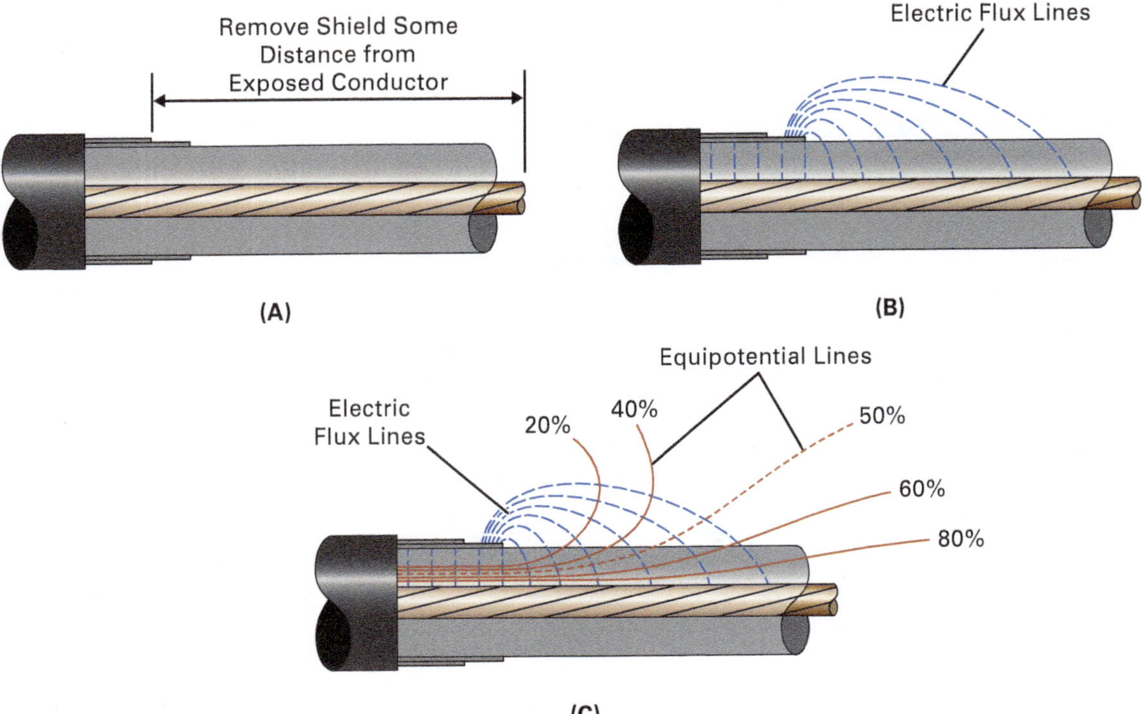

Figure 36 Removing the shield.

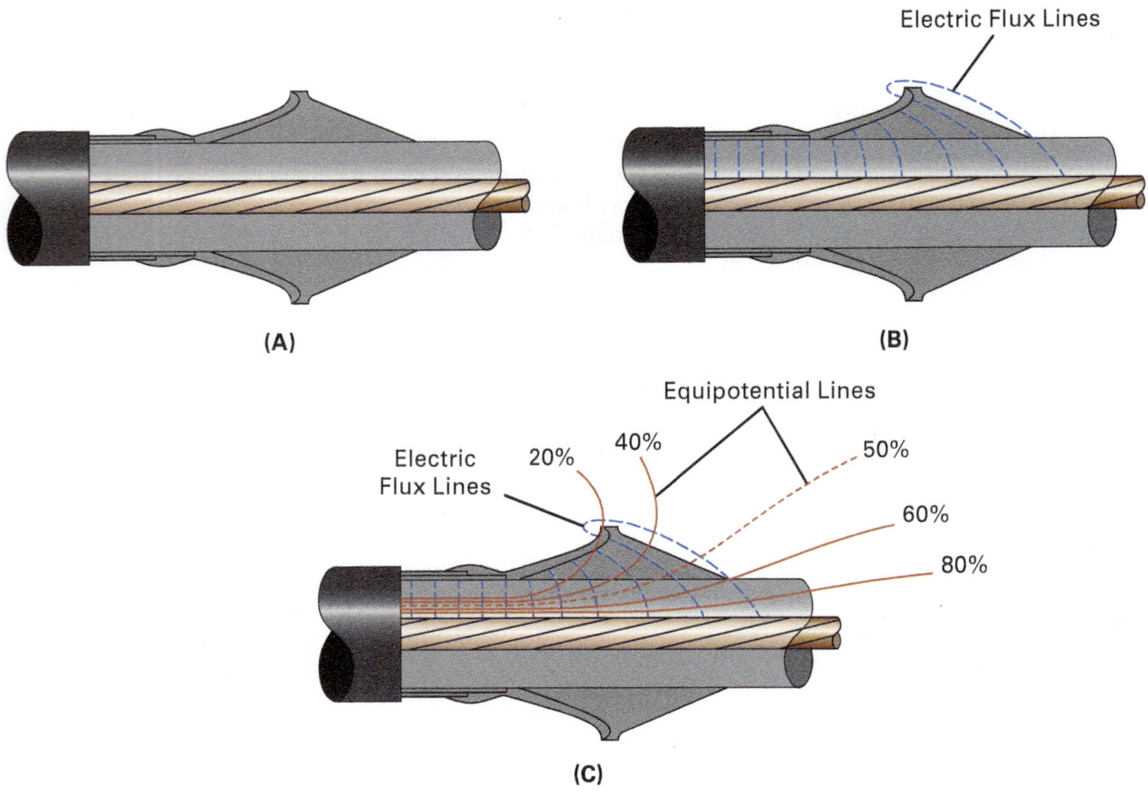

Figure 37 Geometric stress control.

The value of K is generally an order of magnitude higher than the cable insulation. Located at the end of the shield cutback, the material capacitively changes the voltage distribution in the electrical field surrounding the shield terminus. Lines of electrical flux are regulated to equalize the electrical stresses in a controlled manner along the entire area where the shielding has been removed, as shown in *Figure 38* (A) and *Figure 38* (B).

By changing the electrical field surrounding the termination, the stress concentration is reduced from several hundred volts per mil to values found in continuous cable (usually less than 50 V/mil at rated cable voltage).

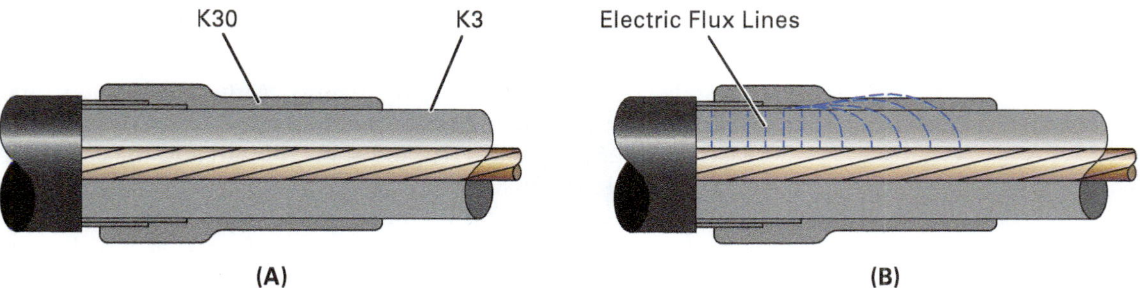

Figure 38 Equalizing electrical stresses.

2.0.0 Section Review

1. The BIL rating of a 15 kV class termination is_____.
   a. 75 kV crest
   b. 95 kV crest
   c. 110 kV crest
   d. 150 kV crest

2. The dielectric strength of the material used for capacitive stress control is typically around _____.
   a. K10
   b. K20
   c. K30
   d. K40

3.0.0 High-Potential (Hi-Pot) Testing

Objective

Define high-potential testing and explain how such testing is conducted.

a. Identify types of high-potential tests.
b. Explain how to make various test connections.
c. Describe typical procedures for conducting high-potential tests.

Performance Tasks

There are no Performance Tasks in this section.

Suitable dielectric tests are commonly applied to determine the condition of insulation in cables, transformers, and rotating machinery. When properly conducted, a **high-potential (hi-pot) test** indicates such faults as cracks, discontinuity, thin spots, or voids in the insulation; excessive moisture or dirt; faulty splices; and faulty terminations. An experienced operator may not only frequently predict the expected breakdown voltage of the item under test but can often make a good estimate of its future operating life.

High-potential (hi-pot) test: A high-potential test in which equipment insulation is subjected to a voltage level higher than that for which it is rated to find any weak spots or deficiencies in the insulation.

The use of direct current (DC) has several important advantages over alternating current (AC). The test equipment itself may be much smaller, lighter in weight, and lower in price. When properly used and interpreted, DC tests give much more information than is obtainable with AC testing. There is far less chance of damage to equipment and less uncertainty in interpreting results. The high-capacitance current frequently associated with AC testing is not present to mask the true leakage current, nor is it necessary to break down the material being tested to obtain information regarding its condition. Although DC testing may not simulate the operating conditions as closely as AC testing, the many advantages of using DC make it worthwhile.

Most medium-voltage cable testing is done with DC, primarily due to the smaller size of machines and the ability to easily provide quantifiable values of charging, leakage, and absorption currents. Although both AC and DC testers may damage a cable during tests, the damage in a DC test only occurs if the increasing current is not interrupted soon enough and the capacitance stored is discharged across the insulation.

Hi-pot testers for medium-voltage cable also have a microammeter and a range dial to allow measurement of up to 5 mA, at which level the circuit breaker trips or the reactor collapses.

WARNING!

Extreme caution must be exercised when conducting hi-pot testing of high-voltage cable. The cable will recharge itself as the absorption current migrates after the test unless grounds are constantly maintained.

Hi-pot testing may be divided into the following broad categories:

- *Design tests* — Tests usually made in the laboratory to determine proper insulation levels prior to manufacturing.
- *Factory tests* — Tests made by the manufacturer to determine compliance with the design or production requirements.
- *Acceptance tests* — Tests made immediately after installation but prior to putting the equipment or cable into service.
- *Proof tests* — Tests made soon after the equipment has been put into service and during the guarantee period.
- *Maintenance tests* — Tests performed during normal maintenance operations or after servicing or repairing equipment or cable.
- *Fault locating tests* — Tests conducted to determine the location of a specific fault in a cable installation.

The maximum test voltage, testing techniques, and interpretation of the test results will vary somewhat, depending on the type of test. Unfortunately, in many cases, the specifications do not spell out the test voltage, nor do they outline the test procedure to be followed. Therefore, it is necessary to apply a considerable amount of common sense and draw strongly upon experience when conducting these tests. There are certain generally accepted procedures, but the specific requirements of the organization requiring the tests are the ones that should govern. It is obvious that an acceptance test must be much more severe than a maintenance test, and a test made on equipment already faulted would be conducted in a manner different from a test being conducted on a piece of equipment in active service.

Special testing instruments are available for all the tests listed prior. However, testing instruments will be used mostly by electricians to perform routine production tests and acceptance tests for newly installed systems.

The general criteria for acceptance of a DC hi-pot test are a consistent leakage for each voltage step (linear) and a decrease in current over time at the final voltage. The level of charging current should also be consistent for each step.

Think About It

Disc Assemblies

What is the purpose of the large circular assemblies shown?

Source: TE Connectivity

Hi-Pot Testing Overview

DC voltage hi-pot tests are made on cables by applying an appropriate, increasing level of DC voltage in steps and measuring the leakage current (microamps) through the cable insulation at each step. The voltage level and measured current values are plotted on graph paper, and the shape of the resultant curve is used for determining the condition of the cable insulation being tested.

3.1.0 Types of Hi-Pot Tests

DC hi-pot tests are performed primarily to determine the condition of the insulation. The extent of the highest breakdown voltage may or may not be of interest, but the relative condition of the insulation near and somewhat above the operating voltage is certainly required. There are many ways of achieving these results. Two of the most popular are the leakage current-versus-voltage and current-versus-time tests. The current-versus-time test is frequently made immediately after the current-versus-voltage test and yields the best results when performed in this manner.

Before performing a test, first, determine what type of test will be performed and the appropriate test voltage. Refer to the cable and termination product supplier literature for test voltage recommendations and limitations. Next, decide on the test configuration. When testing a circuit, the standard test setup is to test each conductor to its own shield and ground with all other conductors and their shields grounded also. Review the physical setup of the test equipment and circuit under test to ensure the safety of test participants and others. Barriers, flagging, or other means must be used to keep others away from the test area, including the other end of the cable under test. Test results will not be dependable when humidity is high or in windy conditions. Determine the method of documenting test results.

After taking all safety precautions, disconnect all accessory equipment, connected loads, and potential transformers from the cable or rotating machine being tested. Make sure the shield, frame, and unused phases are grounded and the hot side of the hi-pot tester is connected to the conductor under test.

Raise the voltage slowly in discrete steps, allowing sufficient time at each step for the leakage current to stabilize. As the voltage is raised, the leakage current will first be relatively high and then decrease with time until a steady minimum value is reached.

The initial high value of current is known as the *charging current*. It depends primarily on the capacitance of the item under test. The lower steady-state current consists of the actual leakage current and the dielectric absorption current (which is relatively minor as far as these tests are concerned). Note the value of the leakage current at each step of voltage, and as the voltage is raised, a curve is plotted of leakage current versus voltage. As long as this curve is relatively flat (that is, equal increments of voltage giving equal increments of current, as shown in point A to point B in *Figure 39*), the item under test is considered to be in good condition. At some point, the current will start rising more rapidly (point C). This will show up on the plot as a knee in the curve. It is very important the voltage increments be small enough so the starting point of this knee can be noted. If the test is carried beyond the start of the knee, the current will increase at a much more rapid rate, and breakdown will soon occur (point D). Unless breakdown is actually desired, it is typical to halt a test as soon as the beginning of the knee is observed.

With a little experience, the operator can extrapolate the curve and estimate the point of breakdown voltage. This procedure enables the operator to anticipate the breakdown point without damaging the insulation because if the test is stopped at the start of the knee, no harm is done.

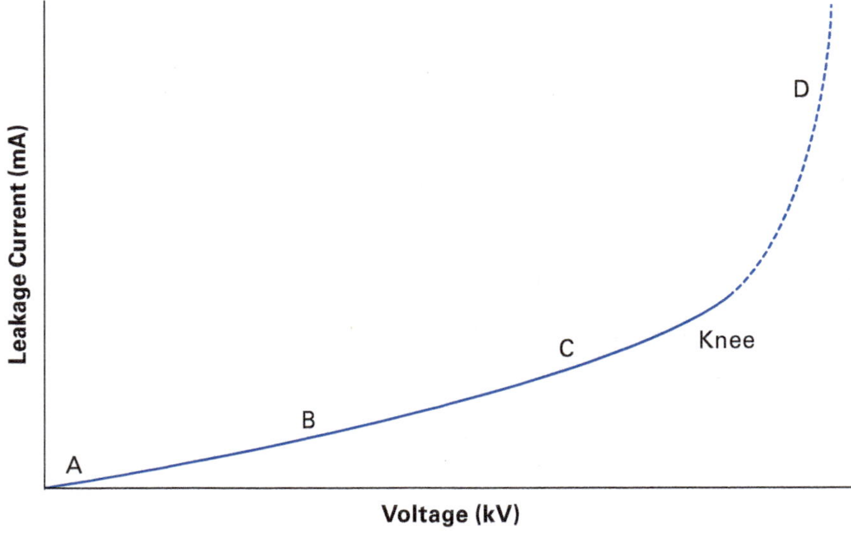

Figure 39 Current-versus-voltage curve.

Although the important thing to watch for is the rate of current change as the voltage is raised, much information may be obtained from the value of the current. A comparison of the leakage current from phase to phase, a comparison of leakage current with values measured in other equipment under similar conditions, or a comparison with the leakage current values obtained on tests made of the same equipment on prior occasions will indicate the condition of the insulation. In general, higher leakage current indicates poorer insulation, but this is difficult to evaluate from a single test. As long as the leakage current-versus-voltage curve is of the general shape shown in *Figure 39* and the knee occurs at a sufficiently high voltage (above the maximum test voltage required), the equipment being tested may be considered satisfactory.

On long cable runs or with rotating machinery with a high capacitance between windings or from winding to frame, the time for stabilization of the leakage current (decrease from E to F in *Figure 40*) may run as high as several minutes, several hours, or more. To minimize the testing time under these conditions, it is common to time the current decay to where it definitely slows and take a reading at each voltage step after the same fixed interval. For example, the voltage would be brought up to the first step, allowed to remain at that point for four minutes, and then the current reading would be taken. The voltage is next raised to the second step, the same four-minute wait is allowed, and the current reading is taken again. This is continued throughout the test. Although this method will not give the true leakage current at any point, it will still produce the proper curve and permit a comparative evaluation.

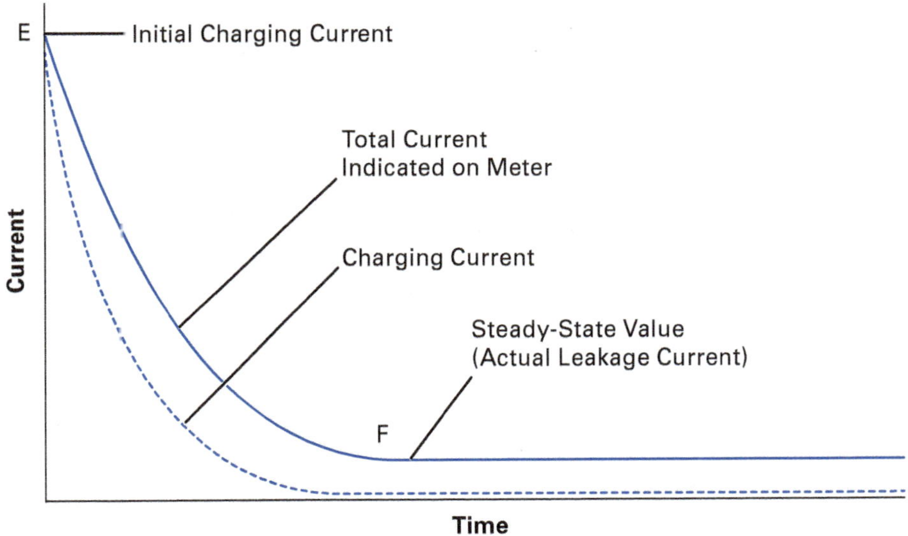

Figure 40 Current-versus-time curve.

When the final test voltage is reached, leave the tester on and plot the current-versus-time curve (*Figure 41*) by recording the current at fixed intervals as it decays from the initial high charging value to the steady-state leakage value. This curve for good cable should indicate a continuous decrease in leakage current with time or a stabilization of the current without any increase during the test.

Any increase in current during this test would indicate a bad cable or machine (*Figure 42*). Stop the test immediately if such an indication occurs. After the current has stabilized and the last reading has been taken, shut off the high voltage. The kilovoltmeter on the tester will indicate the actual voltage present in the equipment under test, as the tester's internal circuitry permits the charge to gradually leak off. After the voltage reaches zero, put an external ground on the cable or machine and disconnect it from the tester. It is important to wear rubber gloves at this point since the effect of absorption currents may cause a buildup of voltage in the item under test until after it has been grounded for some time. Maintain the ground until the cable is terminated and for at least five times the test duration.

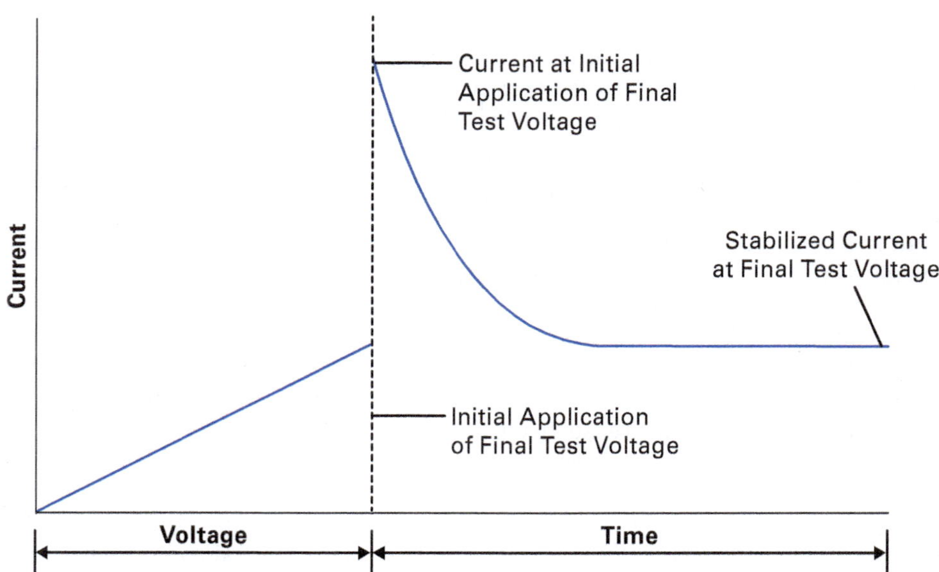

Figure 41 Current-versus-voltage and current-versus-time curves at maximum voltage.

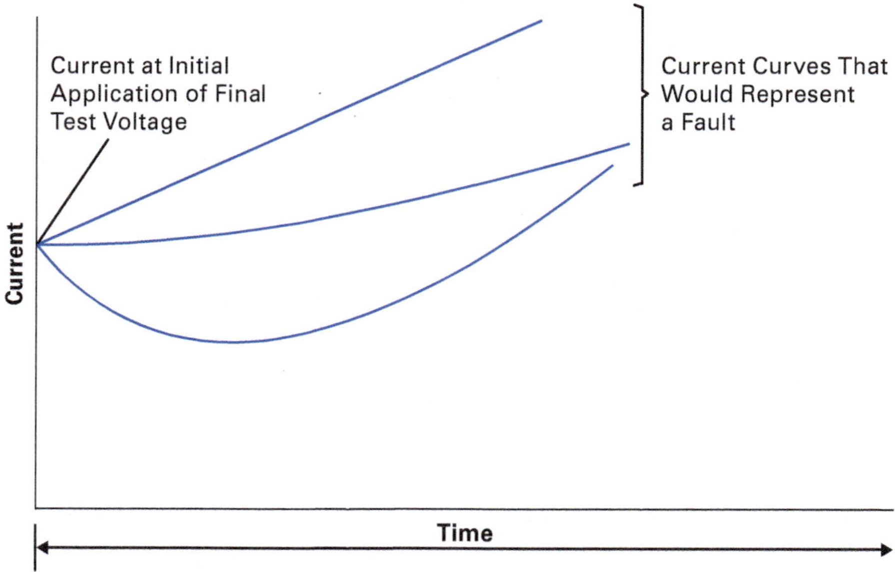

Figure 42 Faulty insulation.

Hi-Pot Testing Safety

All safety precautions must be taken when performing hi-pot testing of equipment or cables. This includes de-energizing and grounding the equipment to be tested to eliminate any charge. All circuit energizing switches must be opened, locked out, and tagged. Disconnect all jumpers running from terminations to feeders, potential transformers, and lightning arresters. Current transformers might be left in the circuit if their insulation level is sufficiently high.

When making the current-versus-voltage test, a rapid climb in current may occur not due to defects in the equipment itself but because of surface leakage or corona at the connections, cable ends, or blades of connected switches. Corona discharge is usually not significant until about 20 kV DC and is worse in windy and humid conditions. Bagging the cable ends in a plastic bag or slipping an empty plastic bottle over the cable end often satisfactorily controls corona. When corona cannot be controlled, all DC testers incorporate internal circuitry (selective guard circuit) to bypass this stray current so that it does not interfere with the leakage measurements. Proper use of the guard circuit and corona ring, when necessary, results in good leakage current readings even below one microamp. This technique consists of providing a separate path for these stray currents, bypassing them around the metering circuit, and only feeding the leakage current to be measured through the metering circuit. To accomplish this, DC testers have two return paths:

- The metered return binding post, which provides a return path through the microammeter circuit
- The bypass return binding post, which provides a return path bypassing the meter

Currents entering the first binding post will be measured, but currents entering the second binding post will not be measured. A panel switch is provided to connect the cabinet ground internally to either of these two binding posts (which enables ground currents to be measured or bypassed, depending on the test being performed).

Hi-Pot Test Voltages

As a rough rule, acceptance tests are made at about 80% of the original factory test voltage. Proof tests are usually made at about 60% of the factory test voltage. The maximum voltage used in maintenance testing depends on the age, previous history, and condition of the equipment, but an acceptable value would be approximately 50% to 60% of the factory test voltage.

3.2.0 Making Connections

Before performing any test, it is important that the test operator carefully plan the test procedure and connections so the required measurements may be taken without misinterpretation or error.

WARNING!

This test may only be performed by qualified individuals operating under the appropriate safe work plan or permit.

After taking all safety precautions, make the hi-pot test connections as follows:

Step 1 On the tester, make sure the main On/Off switch is turned to the Off position, the high-voltage On switch is in the Off position, and the voltage control is turned fully counterclockwise to the zero voltage position.

Step 2 Connect a grounding cable from the safety ground stud of the tester (*Figure 43*) to a good electrical ground and make sure the connection is secure at both ends.

WARNING!

The ground connection is essential to preventing an electric shock hazard. Never operate the tester without it.

Step 3 Connect the return line from the item under test to the metered return or bypass return binding post of the tester and move the grounding switch on the tester panel to the appropriate position. The return lines connected to either the bypass return or metered return binding post should be insulated for about 100V, so ordinary building-grade wire may be used.

Step 4 Plug the shielded cable furnished with the tester into the receptacle at the top of the unit. If the tester has an oil-filled output receptacle, make sure the oil level is at the mark indicated on the oil stick. If the oil level is low, add the proper amount of high-grade transformer or other insulating oil. After the cable is plugged into the receptacle, tighten the clamping nut to hold it securely in place.

Step 5 Connect the shield grounding strap from the cable to the shield ground stud on the tester adjacent to the receptacle.

Step 6 Connect the other end of the output cable to the item under test. This connection should be made mechanically secure, avoiding any sharp edges. It is usually advisable to tape the connection using high-grade electrical tape to minimize corona at this point. If the voltages to be used are high or if, for any other reason, corona is anticipated, its effect may be minimized by using a corona ring or corona shield.

Step 7 Plug the line cord into a 120V, 60 Hz, single-phase outlet and clip the ground wire coming from the line cord to the conduit receptacle mounting screw or another ground source.

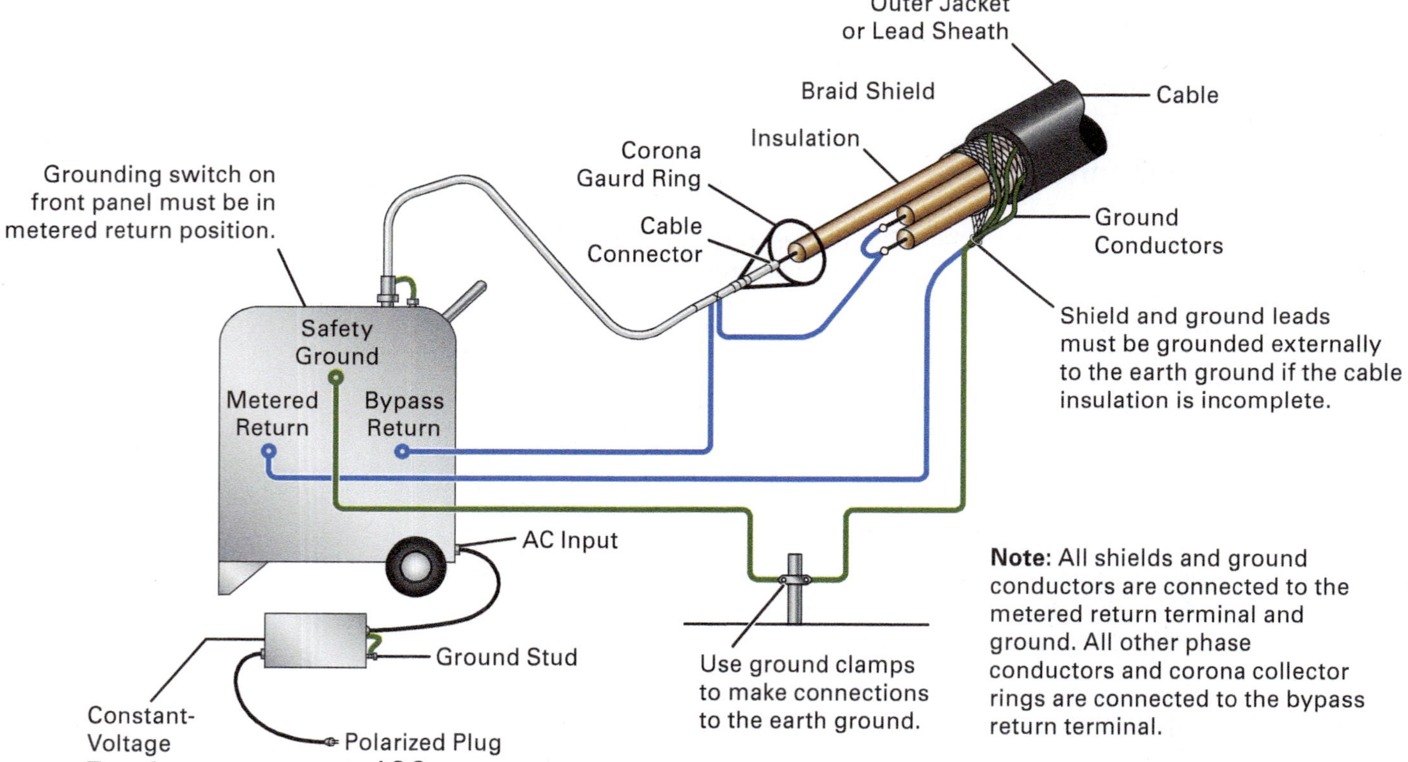

Figure 43 Hi-pot connections for testing multiple-conductor shielded cable.

If a bench-type tester or any other unit with an output bushing rather than a receptacle is used, the same procedure is followed except that the output cable is fastened to the bushing and should be supported along its length, preferably using nylon cord so it stays well away from any grounded or conductive surface. The high-voltage connection between the tester and the item under test should be as short and direct as possible.

When shielded cable is used, it is important the shield be trimmed back from each end for about an inch or more for every 10,000V. The shield at the tester end should be fastened to the ground stud on the tester. The shield at the test end should be taped, and no connection made to it.

If the item under test is beyond the reach of the tester cable supplied, use an extension running between the end of the tester cable and the item under test. If this extension is made of shielded cable, splice the central conductor to the end of the tester cable, and connect the shields of the two cables together with a jumper at the splice. Take care to run the jumper well away from the splice itself to avoid leakage or breakdown.

The splice should be well-taped. If no shielded cable is available, the single wire extension used should be supported well away from all other objects, as described previously. When operating at voltages within the corona levels, bring the tester close enough to the item under test so an extension cable is not needed. Note that extension cable is a frequent cause of erratic readings, especially if the quality degrades at the high voltages used.

When line regulation is poor (because of location, heavy or intermittent equipment loads in the vicinity, or the use of portable generating equipment), it may be necessary to connect a voltage regulator (constant-voltage transformer) between the tester and the 120V supply. A regulator is particularly desirable when using a tester with a sensitive vacuum tube current meter with ranges of less than 10µA full scale or when highly capacitive loads are being tested.

Because the DC output voltage of the tester is dependent on the AC line input voltage, an unstable line voltage causes fluctuation of the tester output voltage with corresponding fluctuation of the current meter. This is especially noticeable when measuring low current of a few microamps or when testing loads with considerable capacitance. When the load is highly capacitive, it charges up to the test potential and tends to maintain that potential because of the high leakage resistance. A sudden drop in line voltage causes the tester output voltage to also drop so that the load capacitance is then charged to a higher value than the tester output. Since the load is at a higher voltage than the tester, the direction of current flow is reversed, and the current meter is driven down the scale. A sudden increase in line voltage causes the opposite effect, with the tester voltage suddenly rising above the voltage to which the load has been charged, causing a rapid increase in the current meter reading. As a result, the current meter fluctuates, so obtaining a meaningful leakage current reading might be difficult.

The use of a line voltage regulator under such conditions greatly increases the usefulness and ease of equipment operation. In general, the power rating of the regulator should be based on the maximum power output capability of the tester multiplied by a factor of about 1.3. For example, a tester rated at 75 kV at 2.5 mA can deliver the following output power:

$$75 \text{ kV} \times 2.5 \text{ mA} = 187.5\text{W}$$

Now, use the multiplier of 1.3 to find the power rating:

$$187.5\text{W} \times 1.3 = 243.75\text{W}$$

Consequently, for this example, a 250W, harmonic-free regulator should be used. This is preferable to the standard type of unit, though either may be used with satisfactory results. If considerable testing at very light loads is done, it might also be desirable to have a smaller regulator to use under those conditions since a small regulator operating at $\frac{1}{2}$ to $\frac{3}{4}$ of its capacity will give better results than a lightly loaded large regulator.

To use the voltage regulator, turn the microamp range switch to the highest range. On multiple voltage range units, turn the kilovolt range switch to the range that will allow testing to the maximum voltage required. The main power switch or circuit breaker may now be turned on, and the test may begin.

Figure 44 and *Figure 45* illustrate typical connection diagrams for testing high-voltage windings. Connections for monitoring the internal leakage at bushings are shown in *Figure 46* and *Figure 47.*

NOTE

Figure 44 and *Figure 45* illustrate typical connection diagrams. The experienced operator will soon develop the technique of making the connections most suitable to the test being performed.

In the connection diagrams in *Figure 44* and *Figure 45,* the guard circuit may be omitted by tying the connections shown going to the bypass return binding post to the metered return binding post instead. This is the difference shown by the connections in *Figure 48* and *Figure 49. Figure 50* shows a typical connection diagram for testing insulation between conductors.

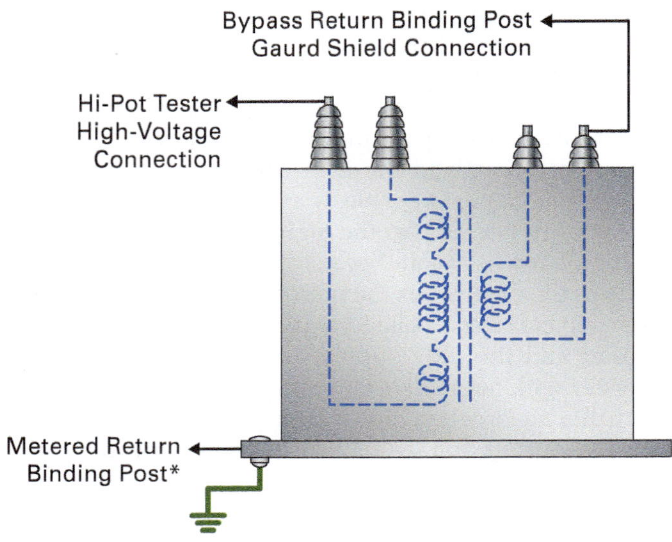

Figure 44 Testing a high-voltage winding to a grounded core or case with a secondary winding to a bypass.

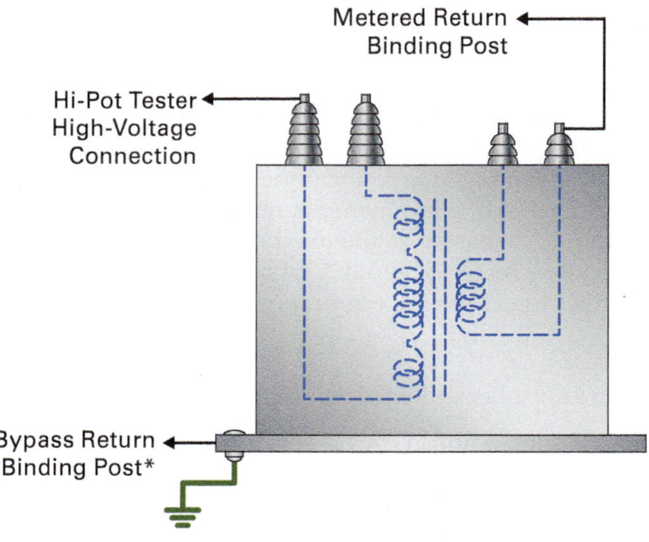

Figure 45 Testing a high-voltage winding to a low-voltage winding with the ground and case to a bypass.

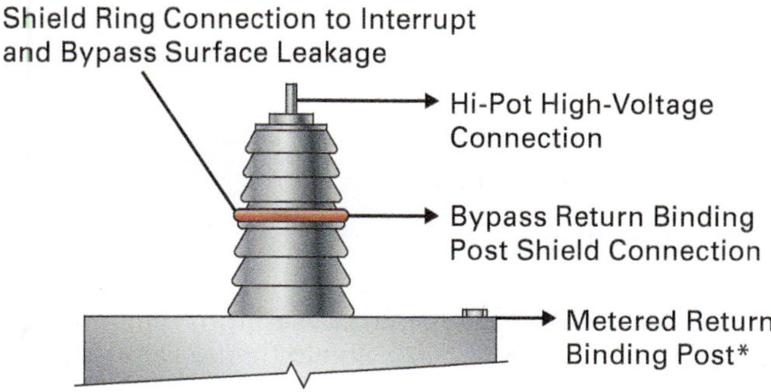

Figure 46 Measuring bushing internal leakage.

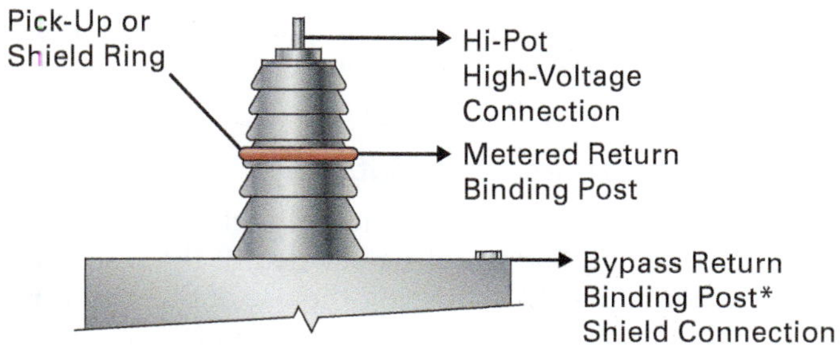

Figure 47 Measuring bushing surface leakage.

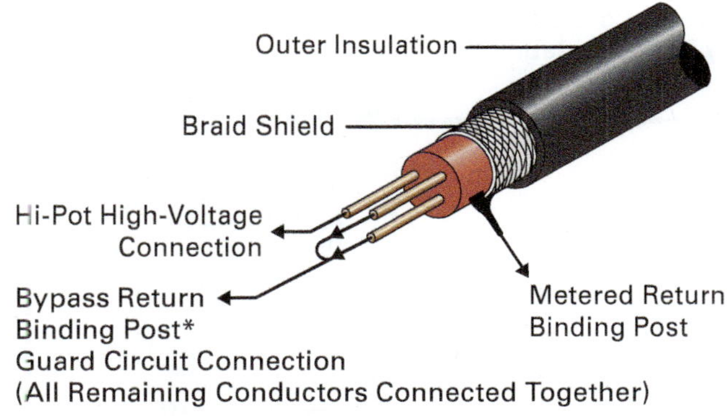

Figure 48 Testing cable insulation between one conductor and the shield.

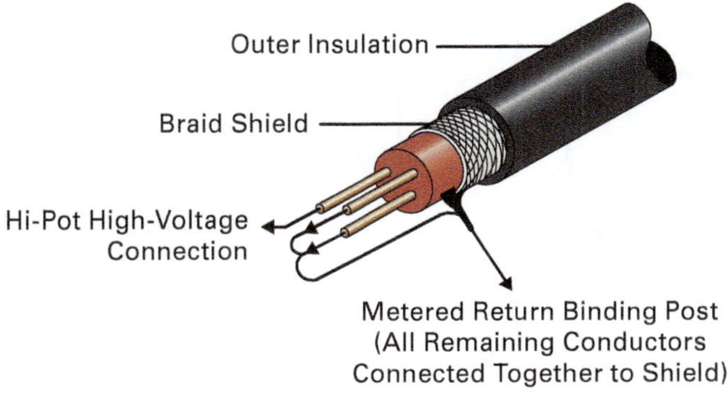

Figure 49 Testing cable insulation between one conductor and all others and the shield.

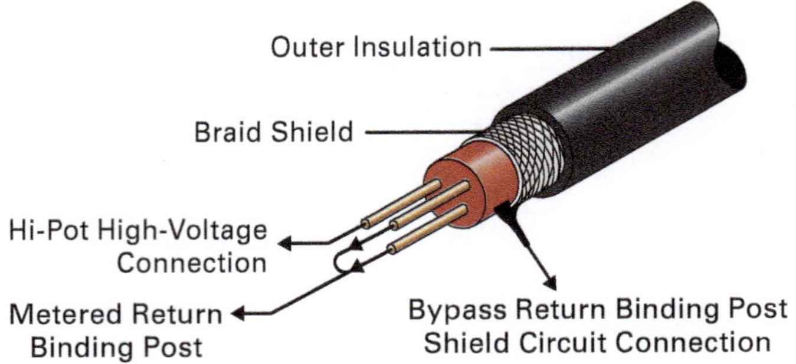

Figure 50 Testing cable insulation between conductors.

If the return path is grounded, set the panel grounding switch to the metered return position. The total load current (leakage/corona) will display on the meter.

If the return path is not grounded, set the panel grounding switch to the bypass return position, and the effect of corona currents on the meter reading will be minimized.

3.2.1 Selective Guard Service Connections

The connection diagrams in *Section 3.2.0* frequently refer to the bypass return or metered return binding post. The simplified sketch of the tester output circuit shown in *Figure 51* will aid in understanding the use of these terminals.

Examination of the diagram shows that any current to be measured must be returned to the tester through the metered return binding post, and any current not to be measured, but is to be bypassed around the meter, should be returned to the bypass return binding post.

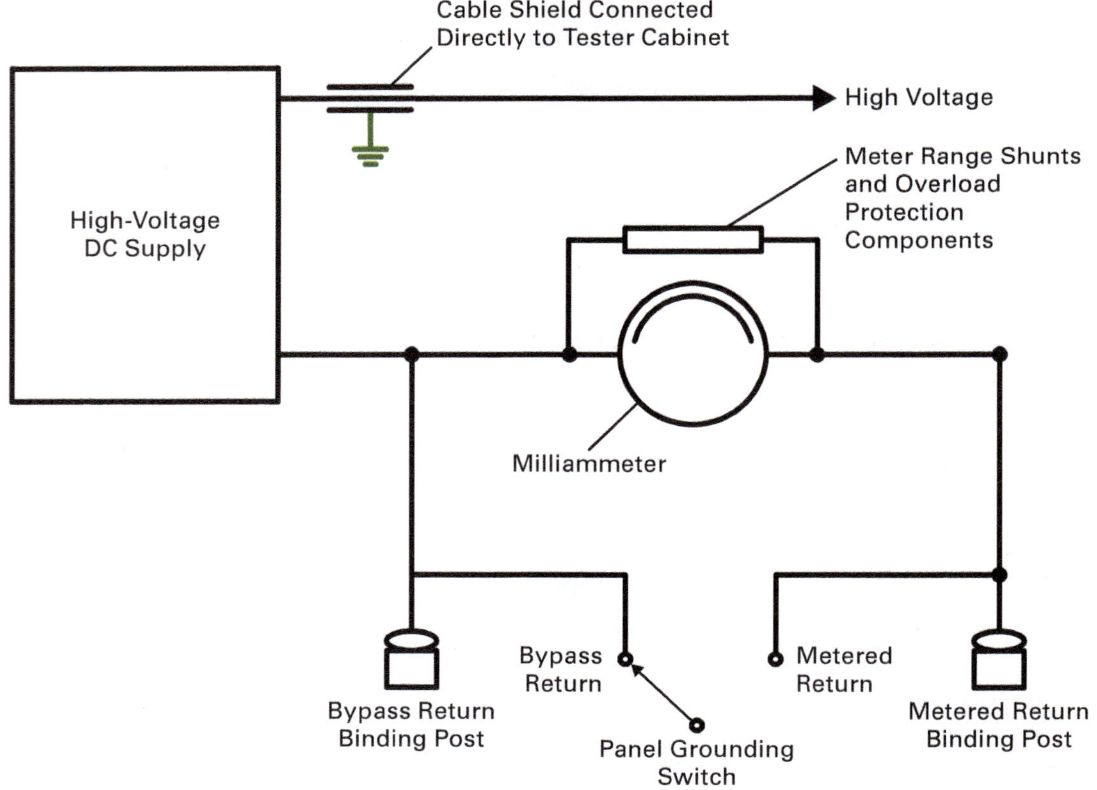

Figure 51 Simplified hi-pot tester output circuit diagram.
Source: Jim Mitchem

As corona currents flow from the high-voltage connection to ground, they may be bypassed around the milliammeter by grounding the bypass return binding post with the grounding switch on the control panel. This gives a direct return path back to the high-voltage supply for corona currents and bypasses them around the meter.

Example:

Assume a three-conductor shielded cable is to be tested for leakage current between one of the conductors and the outer shield. To make the proper tester connection, the test should be analyzed per the following paragraphs.

The current to be measured must return to the low side of the tester through the metered return binding post; therefore, the high-voltage connection should be made to the one conductor in question, and the shield should be connected to the metered return binding post.

Since the measurement of current flow between the high-voltage connection and the other two conductors in the cable is not desirable, these two conductors should be connected together and returned to the bypass return binding post.

To minimize the measurement of the corona current from the high-voltage connection to ground, the bypass return binding post should be grounded by setting the grounding switch on the control panel to the bypass position. This will provide a return path for the corona current around the meter, and the corona current will not affect the meter readings.

To measure the leakage current between one conductor and the other two conductors (which are tied together), the return path for the two conductors should be through the metered return post, and the shield should then be connected to the bypass return post. Again, to minimize the measurement of the corona current, the grounding switch should be in the bypass return position.

The corona current alone may be measured by connecting the shield and the two conductors together and connecting them to the bypass return binding post. If the grounding switch is then placed in the metered return position, the return path for the corona current will be through the microammeter, and the corona current will be the only current measured.

The grounding switch on the control panel will either include or exclude the corona current in the meter reading, depending upon its position.

It was previously assumed there were no restrictions placed on the cable with respect to grounding to illustrate the general case. In many cases, however, the shield is permanently grounded, and therefore certain modifications in the test setup must be made to achieve corona-free stability and accuracy in the leakage current readings.

If the leakage current from one conductor to the shield is being measured, the shield should be connected to the metered return binding post as before. However, since the shield is now permanently grounded, the metered return binding post should also be grounded by placing the panel grounding switch in the metered return position. If the panel grounding switch were placed in the bypass return position, then the metered return post and the bypass return post would both be grounded, shorting out the microammeter. Therefore, the grounding switch must be put in the metered return position when one side of the test item is permanently grounded.

As outlined above, all unwanted currents that flow between the high-voltage point and any ungrounded elements in the cable may be returned through the bypass line and therefore be excluded from the leakage current reading. However, this does not include corona current because corona current always flows between the high-voltage point and ground. Since we cannot shunt the corona current around the microammeter by grounding the bypass return line as we did before, we must use some auxiliary method of intercepting the corona current before it reaches ground. This can be easily accomplished using a corona or guard ring. A corona or guard ring is nothing more than a metal loop that encompasses the high-voltage connection and intercepts the corona current. The ring is connected to the tester through the bypass return binding post and therefore keeps the corona current out of the meter reading.

Adjusting Voltage Regulator Microamp and Kilovolt Range Switches

The microamp range may be changed while the test is underway, but the kilovolt range may not. Safety interlocks within the unit automatically shut off the high voltage as the voltage range switch is turned while the test is in progress.

3.2.2 Corona Guard Ring and Guard Shield

When using a corona ring, the diameter should be made as small as possible without causing an arc to jump between the high-voltage connection and the ring. This will ensure interception of as much corona current as possible. A wire should be connected to the ring, and the other end should be connected to the bypass return binding post. This will bypass the intercepted corona current around the microammeter and allow essentially the same stability and accuracy obtained previously.

Corona may also be minimized by electrically shielding or smoothing the connection. This may be done by smoothly wrapping the connection with metal foil or conductive tape or enclosing it in a round can or cover so that all jagged edges, wire points, and rough surfaces are within the metal enclosure. This corona shield (*Figure 52*) must be electrically connected to the high-voltage point and completely insulated from ground so that both the shield and high-voltage connection are at the same potential.

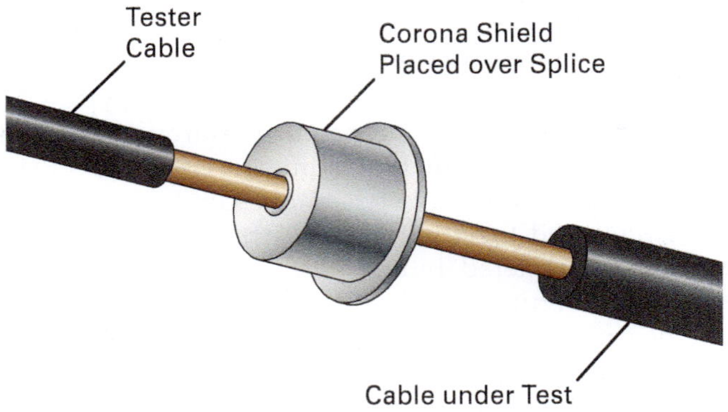

Figure 52 Corona shield.

3.3.0 Detailed Operating Procedure

These instructions are meant to illustrate a typical operating procedure. An actual test must account for special conditions peculiar to the installation, ranges, and operating controls of the tester available, as well as the operator's requirements. To test the system, proceed as follows:

Step 1 Assemble the necessary equipment and supplies at the test site. In addition to the tester, connecting cable, and so forth, bring a clipboard or other writing surface, pencils, colored pencils, scratch paper, graph paper (which is very convenient for plotting the test results while the test is underway), an electronic pocket calculator, and a watch.

Step 2 Determine the type of test to be made. For example, will the voltage be raised to breakdown, or will the voltage be raised to the specific test value only? If the item on the test is found to be defective, should the test stop before breakdown until the repairs can be made later, or should the test be continued to the preselected value regardless of breakdown so that repairs can be made immediately?

WARNING!

This test may only be performed by qualified individuals operating under the appropriate safe work plan or permit.

Step 3 Determine the maximum test voltage to use. Since the value chosen depends not only on the type of test being made but also on the material to be tested, it is necessary that all factors involved be considered. Generally, proof testing is usually conducted at 60% of the factory test voltage. Acceptance testing would call for a maximum value of about 80% of the factory test voltage. For maintenance testing or on older work, the minimum test voltage should be at least 1.7 times the operating voltage, up to a maximum value between 50% and 60% of the factory test voltage. In many cases, the value of the maximum test voltage to be used may be obtained from the cable manufacturer.

Step 4 Choose suitable increments so the voltage may be raised to the final test value in about eight to ten steps (more or less to suit the individual conditions).

Step 5 Once the maximum test voltage and increments have been chosen, prepare the graph paper so the test results can be plotted as the readings are taken. In this way, the condition of the cable is under constant surveillance, and if testing short of breakdown is decided upon, the operator has the necessary control to stop the test at the start of the knee of the current-versus-voltage curve.

To prepare the graph paper, mark the current scale on the shorter side of the paper and the voltage scale on the longer side. Suitable voltage increments should be chosen to produce a convenient plot. The current scale should include values well above the expected maximum leakage current. If the magnitude of leakage current is not known, it may be advisable to either make a low-voltage test run or to hold off plotting the first few points until the magnitude is seen.

Step 6 Connect the tester to the equipment under test, as described previously.

Step 7 Make sure the adjustable voltage control is turned to the Off position (fully counterclockwise), the high-voltage switch is in the center or Off position, and the power switch is in the Off position. Connect the input line cord to the 120V, 60 Hz receptacle, and connect the alligator clip at the end of the line cord to ground.

Step 8 Turn the kilovoltmeter range switch and microammeter range switch to the appropriate positions.

Step 9 Turn the main On/Off switch or circuit breaker to the On position.

Step 10 Operate the high-voltage On switch. Note that the lever-type high-voltage switch has a spring return from the Down position but will remain in the Up position. If it is desired to keep the high voltage under strict manual control, use the Down position of the high-voltage switch. As soon as it is released to the Off position, the high voltage will be turned off, and it will become necessary to return the powerstat control to zero before the high voltage can be reapplied.

If the high-voltage switch is placed in the Up position, the switch may be released and will remain in the Up position, and high voltage will be available until the switch is manually returned to the center Off position. On units with a keyed interlock, it is necessary to turn the key to the right to enable the Up position of the high-voltage lever switch to be operated.

Step 11 Slowly rotate the variable voltage control from the extreme counterclockwise position (zero volts) to raise the voltage to the first increment, as previously determined. The voltage should be raised at a slow enough rate to avoid having the microammeter pointer go off the scale. The slower the voltage is raised, the lower the maximum charging current and microammeter reading will be. If the charging current is allowed to exceed the maximum current rating of the tester, the circuit breaker will trip. The circuit breaker will also trip if the unit under test fails.

Since most testers are equipped with zero return interlocks for operator safety, it is necessary to return the voltage control to the zero position before high voltage can be reapplied once it is shut off, whether due to circuit breaker tripping, kilovolt range selector switch rotation, or operation of the high-voltage On lever switch to the Off position.

Step 12 When the first increment of voltage is reached, watch the microammeter indicate gradually decreasing current as the cable or machine under test becomes charged. As the current drops to lower portions of the scale, switch the microammeter progressively to lower ranges until the current stabilizes. Note the length of time it takes for the current to stabilize before accurate results can be obtained. The same stabilization period is allowed at each voltage step. After the current is stabilized, whether it takes 10 seconds, a minute, or 10 minutes, record the value of the voltage and current.

Step 13 If the microamp scale for plotting the current-versus-voltage curve has been predetermined, the current reading at the first voltage step can now be plotted. If the scale has not yet been determined, record this value, and after a few more increments, determine a scale and plot the current readings.

Step 14 After the current is stabilized and a point is plotted, turn the microammeter range switch back to the higher range and gradually raise the voltage to the next increment. Allow the current to stabilize for the same length of time as for the previous increment. Take a second reading and continue the test, gradually raising the voltage step-by-step and plotting the current versus voltage at each step. It is important that the voltage be raised at the same rate in each step.

Step 15 Closely watch the rate of current change at each voltage increment. The curve should indicate a linear (even) rate of change up to the final test voltage. If this is the case, the material being tested is all right. Upon any indication of a rapid rise in current, stop the test immediately unless, of course, you wish to test to breakdown. Even a slight knee in the curve may be an indication of imminent breakdown.

Step 16 This step-by-step raising of voltage and plotting of current should be continued until the maximum test voltage previously selected is reached. If a current-versus-time plot is also desired, the time should be noted immediately upon reaching the final voltage step. Then, as the current slowly decays, readings of current and time should be taken at suitable increments, and the current-versus-time curve may be plotted. For a safe insulation system, this curve should indicate a continuous decrease in leakage current with time until the current stabilizes. At no time during this part of the test should there be any increase in current.

Step 17 At the end of the test, move the high-voltage lever switch to the Off position. Allow the material being tested to discharge either through the internal discharge circuit of the tester or by using a hot stick and rubber gloves and grounding the output.

Step 18 The kilovoltmeter on the tester will directly indicate the voltage at the output terminal regardless of whether the tester is On or Off. Do not touch the cable or equipment being tested until the kilovoltmeter reads zero.

Step 19 After the kilovoltmeter reads zero, disconnect all test leads, and immediately reconnect all cable conductors or equipment terminals to ground and leave grounded.

WARNING!

Always wear rubber gloves during this portion of the test. The dielectric absorption effect of cable, in particular, and to some extent that of rotating equipment, will tend to restore a dangerous voltage on the disconnected item until it has been adequately grounded for a considerable length of time.

Step 20 The other phases of a multiphase installation may be tested in a similar manner.

In many cases, once the fault occurs, its exact location may be determined without too much difficulty. However, in those cases where a fault occurs in a long run of cable, special fault-finding techniques incorporating special testing equipment could be of great assistance.

3.3.1 Go/No-Go Testing

The tests described previously provide a good indication of the condition of the equipment or cable and, with the proper interpretation, may even allow prediction of the expected life of the device under test. However, to do the job properly takes time and a certain amount of experience and skill, both in conducting and evaluating the operation.

A much shorter and simpler test may be sufficient in those cases where the contractor, purchaser, or operator is only interested in knowing whether the installation meets a specific high-voltage breakdown requirement (that is, whether the equipment or cable will withstand X kilovolts without breakdown).

WARNING!

This test may only be performed by qualified individuals operating under the appropriate safe work plan or permit.

The procedure for conducting a go/no-go test is as follows:

Step 1 Set the microammeter range switch to the highest range.

Step 2 Gradually raise the test voltage at a rate that will keep the charging current below the microammeter's full-scale point. Raise the voltage at this steady rate until the required test value is reached.

Step 3 Maintain the voltage at this value for the length of time required by the specification, or in the absence of any specification, until after the current has stabilized for a minute or more.

Step 4 If the leakage current does not become excessive (remains below the maximum specified value or is low enough to avoid tripping the circuit breaker), the equipment has passed the test.

Step 5 Failure is indicated by a gradual or abrupt increase of current sufficient to trip the circuit breaker. This leakage current should not be confused with the charging current. The charging current may be minimized by raising the voltage at a slower rate.

Step 6 If the current seems to be rising too high, stop raising the voltage at that point and wait. If the current immediately starts decreasing, the indication is that of charging current, and the test may be continued.

Step 7 If the current holds steady or increases, it is due either to leakage current or to corona current. Methods of minimizing the effect of corona current were explained earlier.

Step 8 At the end of the test, reduce the voltage to zero and follow the procedures recommended by the tester manufacturer.

NOTE

This type of test is not by any means a thorough analysis of cable condition. However, it is a sufficient test and is all that is necessary in a great number of cases. For example, the contractor installing the cable must immediately know if the installation is good. If it is defective, this test will reveal it in the shortest possible time. If the installation is faulty, the test cannot harm it any further, and the contractor may proceed to make the necessary repairs. The only information sought in this type of test is that the cable will not fail below a required test voltage level.

3.3.2 Insulation Resistance Measurements

The DC tester is an invaluable tool for making insulation resistance measurements at higher voltages. Using the same connections and following the same precautions given for hi-pot testing, raise the voltage to the desired value and read the microammeter after the current has stabilized (no further decay). The insulation resistance may then be calculated using Ohm's law:

$$R = E \div I$$

Where:

R = insulation resistance (in megohms)

E = voltage (kV meter reading x 1,000)

I = current (in microamps)

The insulation resistance may be calculated at each voltage step as the leakage current-versus-voltage test is made. Curves of insulation resistance versus voltage will yield much information to the experienced operator. It also helps to keep records of the insulation resistance at a specific voltage so that they can be compared from test to test or from year to year. This will give a good basis for comparison for proper insulation evaluation.

Insulation resistance may also be measured with a standard megger. These instruments will give a direct reading of insulation resistance at a 500V (or higher, depending on the model) test potential.

Insulation resistance measurements help determine whether the items under test are suitable for hi-pot testing. If the insulation resistance is abnormally low, the material is defective, and there is no need to make the hi-pot test. If the insulation resistance is high, then the hi-pot test may be made.

Instead of waiting for the current to stabilize before calculating the insulation resistance, readings of voltage and current can be taken at fixed time intervals during the leakage current-versus-time test, and calculations of insulation resistance as a function of time can be made. A plot of the insulation resistance versus time is known as the *absorption curve* and is often used when testing rotating machinery. In a good insulation system, this curve will rise rapidly at first (because of the decaying charging current) and gradually level off (an indication of stabilization of leakage current). The more pronounced the rise, the better the insulation. A relatively flat curve will indicate moist or dirty insulation.

The ratio of the insulation resistance at the end of 10 minutes to the insulation resistance at the end of one minute is called the *polarization index*. If the value of the polarization index is less than two, it usually indicates excessive moisture or contamination. Values of 10 or more are common when testing large motors or generators.

Caution should be exercised in evaluating the importance of insulation resistance measurements. The absolute value is not critical, but the relative order of magnitude or the change in value as the test progresses is significant. Such factors as temperature and humidity can have a very large effect on the reading.

Insulation Resistance Tests

The use of a megger for measuring insulation resistance should not be confused with a hi-pot test, since insulation resistance, in general, has little or no direct relationship to dielectric or breakdown strength. For example, an actual void in the insulation may show an exceedingly high value of insulation resistance even though it would permit breakdown at a relatively low voltage.

3.0.0 Section Review

1. DC hi-pot tests are performed primarily to determine the _____.
   a. highest breakdown voltage
   b. condition of the insulation
   c. lowest breakdown voltage
   d. remaining service life

2. A hi-pot tester operates on a supply voltage of _____.
   a. 24V
   b. 60V
   c. 120V
   d. 240V

3. A simple test that may be used to determine whether an installation meets a specific high-voltage breakdown requirement is a _____.
   a. current-versus-voltage test
   b. current-versus-time test
   c. voltage-versus-time test
   d. go/no-go test

Module 26411-23 Review Questions

1. Medium-voltage cable is rated at _____.
   a. 480V to 1,200V
   b. 600V to 2,400V
   c. 1,000V to 6,000V
   d. 2,001V to 35,000V

2. Which of the following cable configurations has the smallest overall diameter for the same amount of current-carrying ability?
   a. Compact stranding
   b. Compressed stranding
   c. Eccentric stranding
   d. Concentric stranding

3. What are the two materials normally used to construct insulation shielding systems?
   a. Semicon and PVC plastic
   b. Semicon and metallic material
   c. Copper and aluminum
   d. Silver-plated aluminum (silver and aluminum)

4. When air breaks down or ionizes, it produces _____.
   a. moisture
   b. hydrogen sulfate
   c. photoreceptors
   d. corona discharges

5. Which of the following *best* describes the semicon layer between the conductor and insulation that compensates for air voids between the materials?
   a. Metallic shield
   b. Jacket
   c. Polyethylene
   d. Strand shielding

6. Resonant grounded systems typically require an insulation level of _____.
   a. 100%
   b. 133%
   c. 153%
   d. 173%

7. Which of the following can render a high-voltage splice useless?
   a. Movement
   b. Light
   c. Foreign matter
   d. Heat

8. What is normally the final step in a high-voltage cable splice?
   a. Rejacketing
   b. Reinsulating
   c. Reshielding
   d. Cleaning

9. When splicing aluminum conductors, which of the following should be applied to the contact areas of the connector?
   a. Antioxide paste
   b. Abrasives
   c. Solvents
   d. Vinyl insulating tape

10. The main difference between AC and DC current testing is that AC testing _____.
    a. uses smaller, less expensive test equipment
    b. results in less chance of equipment damage
    c. produces quantifiable test results
    d. provides true simulation of operating conditions

Answers to odd-numbered Module Review Questions are found in *Appendix A*.

Module 26411-23 Supplemental Exercises

1. The five main components of a power cable include the __________, __________, __________, __________, and __________.

2. What are the three most common types of solid dielectric insulation?

   ____

   ____

3. What are the six main functions of a shield system?

   ____

   ____

   ____

   ____

   ____

   ____

4. List the five basic steps in building a splice.

____
____
____
____
____

5. When penciling is required, a full, smooth taper is necessary to __________.

6. True or False? Mechanical-type connectors are ideal for use in medium-voltage connections.

7. Contact aid (antioxide paste) is used on aluminum conductors and connectors to __________.

8. Name the two common methods for providing stress control.

____
____

9. True or False? All shield ends are normally grounded.

10. Name the six general categories of hi-pot tests.

____
____
____
____
____
____

Answers to odd-numbered Supplemental Exercises are found in *Appendix B*.

Answers to Section Review Questions

Answer	Section Reference	Objective
Section 1.0.0		
1. b	1.1.1	1a
2. c	1.2.0	1b
3. b	1.3.3	1c
4. d	1.4.2	1d
Section 2.0.0		
1. c	2.1.3; *Table 1*	2a
2. c	2.2.2	2b
Section 3.0.0		
1. b	3.1.0	3a
2. c	3.2.0	3b
3. d	3.3.1	3c

Special Locations

Source: iStock@Photoshopix

Objectives

Successful completion of this module prepares you to do the following:

1. Identify and select equipment, components, and wiring methods for various special locations and applications.
   a. Identify and select equipment, components, and wiring methods for places of assembly.
   b. Identify and select equipment, components, and wiring methods for theaters and similar locations.
   c. Identify and select equipment, components, and wiring methods for carnivals, circuses, and fairs.
   d. Identify and select equipment, components, and wiring methods for agricultural buildings.
   e. Identify and select equipment, components, and wiring methods for temporary installations.
   f. Identify and select equipment, components, and wiring methods for wired office partitions.
2. Identify and select equipment, components, and wiring methods for marinas, boatyards, and bodies of water.
   a. Identify and select equipment, components, and wiring methods for marinas and boatyards.
   b. Identify and select equipment, components, and wiring methods for natural and man-made bodies of water.
3. Identify and select equipment, components, and wiring methods for pools, spas, tubs, and fountains.
   a. Identify general wiring requirements for pools, spas, tubs, and fountains.
   b. Identify and select equipment, components, and wiring methods for permanently installed pools.
   c. Identify and select equipment, components, and wiring methods for storable pools.
   d. Identify and select equipment, components, and wiring methods for spas, hot tubs, and therapeutic tubs.
   e. Identify and select equipment, components, and wiring methods for fountains.

Performance Tasks

This is a knowledge-based module. There are no Performance Tasks.

NOTE

Digital Resources for Electrical

Scan this code using the camera on your phone or mobile device to view the digital resources related to this craft.

Overview

As an electrician, it is your responsibility to familiarize yourself with all the *NEC*® requirements for any electrical installation you undertake, as well as any local or regional codes that may also apply. This module describes the *NEC*® requirements for selecting and installing equipment, enclosures, and devices for special locations that require unique attention. These locations include places of public assembly, theaters, carnivals, agricultural and livestock facilities, marinas, swimming pools, and temporary facilities.

NCCER Industry-Recognized Credentials

If you are training through an NCCER-accredited sponsor, you may be eligible for credentials from NCCER. The ID number for this module is 26412-23. Note that this module may have been used in other NCCER curricula and may apply to other level completions. Contact NCCER at 1.888.622.3720 or go to **www.nccer.org** for more information.

You can also show off your industry-recognized credentials online with NCCER's digital badges. Transform your knowledge, skills, and achievements into badges that you can share across social media platforms, send to your network, and add to your resume. For more information, visit **www.nccer.org**.

1.0.0 Requirements for Special Locations and Applications

Performance Tasks

There are no Performance Tasks in this section.

Objective

Identify and select equipment, components, and wiring methods for various special locations and applications.

a. Identify and select equipment, components, and wiring methods for places of assembly.
b. Identify and select equipment, components, and wiring methods for theaters and similar locations.
c. Identify and select equipment, components, and wiring methods for carnivals, circuses, and fairs.
d. Identify and select equipment, components, and wiring methods for agricultural buildings.
e. Identify and select equipment, components, and wiring methods for temporary installations.
f. Identify and select equipment, components, and wiring methods for wired office partitions.

Places of assembly, theaters, carnivals, agricultural buildings, temporary sites, and other special locations generally require more stringent wiring methods than traditional occupancies. These special wiring methods provide added protection against unique hazards that may exist, such as large crowds (places of assembly or theaters), exposed cable wiring (carnivals, fairs, and other temporary installations), and the presence of livestock (agricultural buildings).

Temporary wiring installations and wired partitions present their own unique electrical hazards. Temporary wiring does not provide long-term conductor or device protection, whereas wired partitions, such as those used in office buildings, are often constructed of sheet metal with sharp edges that create a potential for ground fault conditions resulting from conductor insulation damage.

Electricians who install wiring in these and similar locations must refer to and comply with specific articles in the *NEC*®.

Special Occupancies—Construction Jobsite Trailers

Wiring methods for construction jobsite trailers are regulated by *NEC Section 550.4(A)*.

1.1.0 Places of Assembly

To qualify as an assembly occupancy per *NEC Article 518*, a building or structure must be designed to hold 100 or more people and be used for purposes such as meetings, worship, entertainment, eating and drinking, amusement, or awaiting transportation. Convention centers, churches, arenas, dance halls, auditoriums, cafeterias, public offices (*Figure 1*), and bus or train stations are some examples of places of assembly.

Often, an assembly occupancy is attached to other buildings, structures, or rooms. Only the portion of the building designed to assemble more than 100 people is regulated by *NEC Article 518*. Other portions of the structure, such as offices and kitchens, are governed by different *NEC*® articles.

Figure 1 City Hall, Alachua, Florida.
Source: Moxie Media

Know the Code

Assembly Occupancies
NEC Article 518

NOTE

If the assembly area contains a projection booth, stage platform, or accommodations for the presentation of theatrical or musical performances, it is governed by *NEC Article 520*.

1.1.1 Wiring Methods in Assembly Occupancies

For the most part, the building materials used in assembly occupancies are required to have a specific **fire rating** to retard the spread of fire through adjacent spaces. Approved wiring methods allowed in fire-rated construction include the following:

- Metal raceways
- Flexible metal raceways
- Nonmetallic raceways encased in at least 2" (50 mm) of concrete
- Mineral-insulated, metal-sheathed (MI) cable
- Metal-clad (MC) cable (*Figure* 2) or armored (AC) cable

Raceways or cable assemblies must either qualify as an approved equipment grounding conductor per *NEC Section 250.118* or contain an insulated grounding conductor sized in accordance with *NEC Table 250.122*. In portions of assembly occupancies that are not required to be of fire-rated construction, wiring methods may include nonmetallic-sheathed (NM) cable, AC cable, electrical nonmetallic tubing, and rigid nonmetallic conduit (such as PVC). Wiring methods for assembly occupancies are covered in *NEC Section 518.4*.

Fire rating: Time in hours or minutes that a material or assembly can withstand direct exposure to fire without igniting and spreading the fire.

CAUTION

Local codes may prohibit certain wiring methods. Always check with the Authority Having Jurisdiction (AHJ) before selecting a wiring method.

NOTE

Temporary wiring used to power display booths in trade shows and similar exhibitions commonly held in assembly occupancies is covered by ***NEC Article 590***.

Know the Code

Types of Equipment Grounding Conductors
NEC Section 250.118

Know the Code

Minimum Size Equipment Grounding Conductors for Grounding Raceway and Equipment
NEC Table 250.122

Know the Code

Wiring Methods
NEC Section 518.4

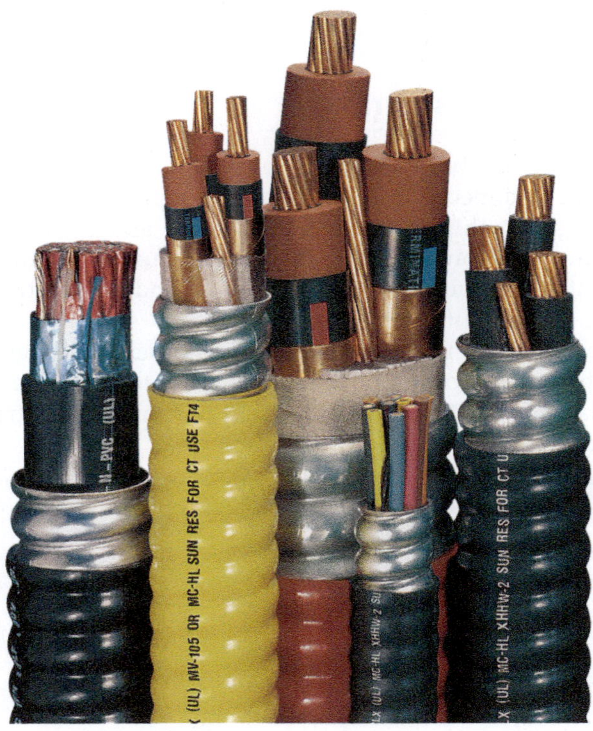

Figure 2 MC cable.
Source: The Okonite Company

Going Green

Electric Vehicle Charging Systems

As energy costs increase, hybrid and electric automobiles have become increasingly common. *NEC Article 625* covers wiring for electric vehicle charging systems. The code contains provisions for using a listed hybrid vehicle charging system as an emergency power backup in the event of a power failure (see *NEC Section 625.48*).

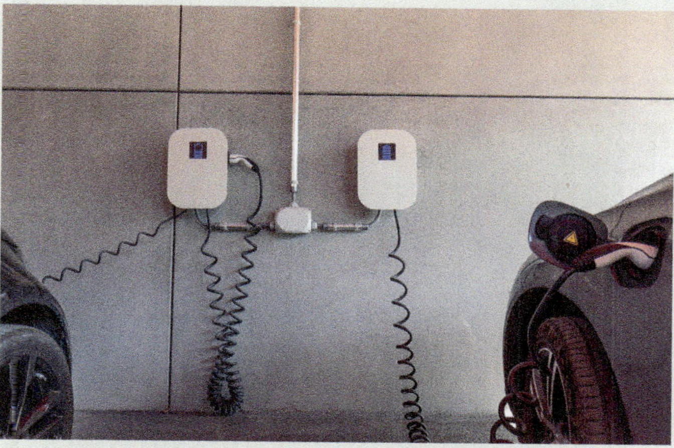

Source: iStock@Canetti

1.1.2 Finish Ratings

In addition to fire ratings, building codes often establish a finish rating for combustible (wood) supports when they are used in the construction of assembly buildings or structures. A finish rating for places of assembly is defined as the length of time it takes for a wood support exposed to fire to reach an average temperature rise of 250°F (121°C) or an individual temperature rise of 325°F (163°C) when the temperature is measured on the plane of the wood nearest the fire.

The use of electrical nonmetallic tubing and rigid nonmetallic conduit in places of assembly containing combustible supports is restricted to certain areas including club rooms, conference and meeting rooms in hotels or motels, courtrooms, dining facilities, restaurants, mortuary chapels, museums, libraries, and places of religious worship. In addition to location restrictions, the raceways must be installed and concealed in walls, floors, and ceilings that provide a thermal barrier of material with a finish rating of at least 15 minutes. See *NEC Section 518.4(D)(1)*.

NOTE

Check with the AHJ to determine the fire and finish rating requirements for each area.

Know the Code

Spaces with Finish Rating
NEC Section 518.4(D)

1.2.0 Theaters, Audience Areas, and Similar Locations

NEC Article 520 covers indoor or outdoor spaces used for dramatic or musical presentations, motion picture projection, or similar purposes. This article also covers specific audience seating areas within motion picture or television studios. A typical seating area is shown in *Figure 3*.

Know the Code

Theaters, Audience Areas of Motion Picture and Television Studios, Performance Areas, and Similar Locations
NEC Article 520

Figure 3 Theater seating area.
Source: iStock@Caiaimage/Robert Daly

1.2.1 Wiring Methods in Theaters, Audience Areas, and Similar Locations

Wiring methods for theaters are covered in *NEC Section 520.5*. Fixed wiring methods include metal raceways, nonmetallic raceways encased in a minimum of 2" (50 mm) of concrete, MI cable, MC cable, or AC cable containing an insulated equipment grounding conductor sized in accordance with *NEC Table 250.122*. Areas in occupancies not required to be of fire-rated construction, as determined by applicable building codes, may contain wiring methods consisting of NM cable, AC cable, electrical nonmetallic tubing, or rigid nonmetallic conduit.

Wiring for portable equipment such as **portable switchboards**, stage set lighting, and stage effects may be in the form of approved flexible cords and cables if the cords or cables are not fastened or secured by uninsulated staples or nails. See *NEC Section 520.5(C)*.

Know the Code

Wiring Methods
NEC Section 520.5

Know the Code

Portable Equipment
NEC Section 520.5(C)

Portable switchboards: Movable lighting switchboards used for road shows and similar presentations, usually supplied by a flexible cord or cable.

Number of Conductors in a Raceway

The maximum number of conductors in metallic or nonmetallic raceways, as permitted by the *NEC®* for theaters or audience areas of motion picture and television studios, follows the requirements of *NEC Chapter 9, Table 1*. It states that for one conductor, the raceway fill is limited to 53% of the raceway's interior cross section; for two conductors, it is 31%; and for more than two conductors, the limit is 40%.

Know the Code

Percent of Cross Section of Conduit and Tubing for Conductors and Cables
NEC Chapter 9, Table 1

When conductors are installed in a gutter or wireway in areas covered by *NEC Article 520*, the total cross-sectional area of all conductors cannot exceed more than 20% of the gutter or wireway cross section in which they are installed. This complies with the *NEC*® cross-section requirements for most conductors installed in an auxiliary gutter (*NEC Section 366.22*) or wireway (*NEC Section 376.22*). However, if the number of current-carrying conductors in an auxiliary gutter or wireway exceeds 30, derating of the conductor ampacity (which is typically required in other locations) is not required in theaters or audience areas per *NEC Section 520.6*.

Know the Code

Number of Conductors
NEC Section 366.22

Know the Code

Number of Conductors in Raceway
NEC Section 520.6

Fire Rating and Building Construction Standards

NFPA 703, *Standard for Fire-Retardant-Treated Wood and Fire-Retardant Coatings*, contains criteria for identifying and defining retardant-impregnated wood and building materials coated with fire retardant. This standard, along with NFPA 5000®, *Building Construction and Safety Code*®, is applied in the design and construction of theaters and similar structures.

Protective Guarding, Branch Circuits, and Portable Equipment

Electrical circuits, switches, and equipment in theaters and similar areas covered by *NEC Article 520* are often operated by people with limited or no electrical safety training. For this reason, any energized part must be enclosed or guarded to prevent electrical shock. In addition, all switches must be designed for external operation only. Every dimmer, **rheostat**, and similar device must be installed in cabinets that enclose all energized parts.

In addition to supplying receptacles, branch circuits in theaters and similar areas may also supply stage set lighting. Receptacles and conductors in these branch circuits must have an ampere rating equal to or greater than the branch circuit overcurrent protective device to which they are connected. As with any branch circuit receptacle, the voltage rating of the receptacle must not be less than the circuit voltage. See *NEC Section 520.9*.

Portable electrical equipment, such as stage or studio lighting, and power distribution equipment may be temporarily used outdoors if the use of such energized equipment is continuously supervised by qualified personnel and the equipment is barricaded to prevent public access.

Rheostat: A slide and contact device that increases or decreases the resistance in a circuit by changing the position of a movable contact on a coil of wire.

Know the Code

Branch Circuits
NEC Section 520.9

1.2.2 Fixed Stage Switchboards

The design and construction of switchboards installed in theaters and similar locations must be of the **dead-front type** and must be listed. Fixed stage switchboards are covered in *NEC Article 520, Part II*.

Per *NEC Section 520.21*, fixed stage switchboards:

- Must be listed
- Must be readily accessible but are not required to be located on or adjacent to the stage (multiple fixed stage switchboards are permitted at different locations)
- Must contain overcurrent protective devices for all branch circuits supplied by that switchboard
- Are permitted to supply both stage and nonstage equipment

Dead-front type: Types of equipment or enclosures covered or protected to prevent exposure of energized parts on the operating side of the equipment.

Know the Code

Fixed Stage Switchboards
NEC Article 520, Part II

Know the Code

General
NEC Section 520.21

Dimmers

As stated in *NEC Section 520.25(A)*, dimmers used for stage and auditorium lighting may be designed to control voltage through either the grounded or ungrounded circuit conductor supplying the controlled lighting (*Figure 4*). In installations where the ungrounded conductor is connected through the dimmer, the dimmer must be protected by an overcurrent protective device with a rating no greater than 125% of the dimmer current rating. In addition, all ungrounded conductors connected to the line side of the dimmer must be opened when either the switch or circuit breaker supplying the dimmer is opened.

Know the Code

Disconnection and Overcurrent Protection
NEC Section 520.25(A)

Figure 4 Digital console with stage-lighting dimmer.
Source: iStock@genkur

Resistance-type dimmer: A manual-type dimmer in which light intensity is controlled by increasing or decreasing the resistance in the lighting circuit.

Reactor-type dimmer: A dimming system that incorporates windings or coils that are linked by a magnetic core, an inductive reactor that functions like a capacitor, and a relay. The reactor stores current from the source and reduces lamp power.

An older **resistance-type dimmer** or **reactor-type dimmer** may be installed in either the grounded or ungrounded lighting circuit conductor. Newer solid-state dimmers may not be supplied with a voltage exceeding 150V between conductors unless the dimmer is rated for the voltage (*Figure 5*). When a grounded conductor is connected to a solid-state dimmer, the conductor must be common to both the input and output circuits. The metal chassis of a solid-state dimmer must be connected to the equipment grounding conductor.

Figure 5 Dimming panel.
Source: iStock@Gennadiy Kravchenko

Types of Switchboard Control

Stage switchboard control may include manual control, remote control, intermediate control, constant power, or any combination of these types. See *NEC Section 520.26*. In a manually controlled stage switchboard, all dimmers and switches are manually operated by handles that are mechanically linked to the control devices.

Know the Code

Type of Switchboard
NEC Section 520.26

In a remotely controlled switchboard, dimmers and switches are electrically controlled from a pilot-type console or panel. These pilot panels may be part of the switchboard itself or located in a separate area.

Intermediate control incorporates a design in which primary and secondary switchboards are used. The secondary switchboard functions as a patch panel or secondary panelboard, containing lighting circuit interconnections and overcurrent protective devices. It is typically in a different location than the main or primary stage switchboard.

Constant-power stage switchboards contain only overcurrent protective devices and no control elements.

Stage Switchboard Feeders

As stated in *NEC Section 520.27(A)(1)*, a manual or remotely operated stage switchboard may be supplied by a single feeder that is disconnected by a single disconnecting device. In intermediate control, multiple feeders may supply the secondary switchboard (patch panel) if all feeders are part of the same electrical system. When neutral conductors are included in the same raceway with multiple feeders to a secondary switchboard, the neutral conductor must be of sufficient ampacity to carry the maximum **unbalanced load** of the secondary switchboard feeders but is not required to be of a greater ampacity than the neutral conductor supplying the primary switchboard.

Installations in which individual feeders supply a single primary switchboard must have a disconnecting means for each feeder and have a labeling system that states the number and location of each disconnecting means. If the disconnecting means are located in more than one distribution panelboard, the primary stage switchboard must be designed so that barriers are installed to separate feeders from different disconnecting means locations, with labels indicating the disconnect locations.

In a three-phase, four-wire, **solid-state phase-control dimmer**, the feeder neutral conductor is considered a current-carrying conductor. However, the feeder neutral conductors in a three-phase, four-wire, **solid-state sine-wave dimmer** is not considered a current-carrying conductor. When a combination of phase control and sine-wave control is used, the neutral conductor is considered a current-carrying conductor.

To calculate feeder sizes supplying stage switchboards, the total controlled load may be used if (1) all feeders supplying the switchboard are protected by an overcurrent protective device that is rated no greater than the feeder ampacity and (2) the opening of the overcurrent protective device does not affect the operation of the exit or emergency lighting systems.

1.2.3 Wiring Methods for Fixed Equipment (Other than Switchboards)

Wiring methods for fixed stage equipment, including the **footlight** units, **border light** units, **proscenium** sidelights, portable strip lights, backstage lamps, stage receptacles, connector strips, curtain machines, and smoke ventilators, are covered in *NEC Article 520, Part III*.

The maximum branch circuit rating for footlights, border lights, and proscenium sidelights is 20A unless heavy-duty lampholders are used. See *NEC Sections 520.41(A) and (B)*.

Conductors that supply footlights, border lights, proscenium sidelights, portable strip lights (*Figure 6*), and connector strips must have a minimum insulation temperature rating of 125°C (257°F). However, when calculating the conductor's ampacity using *NEC Table 310.16*, the 60°C (140°F) column must be used. See *NEC Section 520.42*. Cable or conductor drops from overhead connector strips must have an insulation rating of 90°C (194°F) and must also have their ampacity calculated using the 60°C (140°F) column of *NEC Table 310.16*. No more than 6" (150 mm) of conductor can extend into the connector strip. In any of these cases, the derating factor based on the number of conductors does not apply.

Know the Code

Single Feeder
NEC Section 520.27(A)(1)

Unbalanced load: Three-phase loads in which the loads are not evenly distributed between the phases.

Solid-state phase-control dimmer: A solid-state dimmer in which the wave shape of the steady-state current does not follow the wave shape of the applied voltage (that is, the wave shape is nonlinear).

Solid-state sine-wave dimmer: A solid-state dimmer in which the wave shape of the steady-state current follows the wave shape of the applied voltage (that is, the wave shape is linear).

Footlight: A border light installed on or in a stage.

Border light: A permanently installed overhead strip light.

Proscenium: The wall and arch that separate the stage from the auditorium.

NOTE

NEC Sections 210.23(C) and (D) cover rules associated with circuits supplying heavy-duty lampholders.

Know the Code

Ampacities of Insulated Conductors with Not More Than Three Current-Carrying Conductors in Raceway, Cable, or Earth (Directly Buried)
NEC Table 310.16

Figure 6 Strip lights.
Source: iStock@Dnai Amponndanai

Footlights

As stated in *NEC Section 520.43(A)*, when footlights are enclosed in a metal trough, the trough must be constructed of sheet metal that is at least 0.032" (0.81 mm) thick and treated to prevent rust. All lampholder terminals must be spaced a minimum of ½" (13 mm) from any metal trough surface, and lampholder terminations must be made by a soldered connection.

In nonmetallic troughs, individual outlet boxes for lampholders must be connected by rigid metal conduit, intermediate metal conduit, flexible metal conduit, MC cable, or MI cable. Again, all terminations must be soldered connections.

Know the Code

Metal Trough Construction
NEC Section 520.43(A)

CAUTION

Footlights that are designed to disappear into a storage recess when not in use must be designed so that the power supply is automatically disconnected when the lights are retracted into the storage recess.

Cords and Cables for Border Lights

Because border lights produce extreme heat, certain rules apply to the type of cord or cable that can be used to supply these lights. See *NEC Section 520.44(C)(1)*. The cord or cable must be listed as **extra-hard usage cable**, must be properly supported, and can only be used in applications that require flexible conductors. The ampacity of these cords or cables is governed by *NEC Section 400.5*.

If the cord or cable is not in direct contact with heat-producing lighting or equipment, the cable or cord ampacity may be calculated using *NEC Table 520.44(C)(2)(1)*. The values in the table reflect the ampacity for multiconductor cords and cables with no more than three current-carrying copper conductors and an ambient temperature of 86°F (30°C). The derating factors in *NEC Table 520.44(C)(2)(2)* must be applied when more than three current-carrying conductors are in the cable or cord.

Know the Code

Cords and Cables for Border Lights, Drop Boxes, and Connector Strips
NEC Section 520.44(C)

Extra-hard usage cable: Cable designed with additional mechanical protection for use in areas where it may be subject to physical damage.

Miscellaneous Fixed Equipment, Receptacles, and Outlets

Per *NEC Section 520.45*, any receptacle used to supply onstage electrical equipment must be rated in amperes and the conductors supplying the receptacle must comply with *NEC Articles 310 and 400*. In addition, receptacles that supply portable stage-lighting equipment must be of the pendant type or installed in suitable pockets or enclosures (per *NEC Section 520.46*).

Backstage lighting is usually utilitarian in design because it is out of view of the audience. When bare bulbs are used as backstage lighting, lamp guards must be installed (*Figure 7*) and a minimum space of 2" (50 mm) must be maintained between lamps and any combustible material (per *NEC Section 520.47*). Electrical devices that are used to control the movement of curtains must be listed for that purpose (per *NEC Section 520.48*).

Know the Code

Receptacles
NEC Section 520.45

Smoke Ventilators

Per *NEC Section 520.49*, electrical devices controlling stage smoke ventilators must be supplied by a normally closed circuit, rated for the full voltage of the circuit to which it is connected, located above the scenery in a loft area, and mounted in a metal enclosure having a tightly sealing self-closing door. In addition, the circuit supplying the device must be controlled by at least two externally operated switches, with one switch being located onstage at a readily accessible spot and the other switch location determined by the AHJ for the electrical installation.

Know the Code

Smoke Ventilator Control
NEC Section 520.49

1.2.4 Onstage Portable Switchboards

Portable stage switchboards are typically used for road show presentations and other similar portable activities (per *NEC Section 520.50*). Portable onstage switchboards may be supplied with power from road show connection panels, often referred to as *patch panels*, or from cord or cable power outlets. Portable onstage switchboards are used to supply lighting and receptacles just like fixed onstage switchboards.

Figure 7 Lamp guard.
Source: iStock@PCharnnarong

Road Show Connection Panel (Patch Panel)

A patch panel is often used to connect portable stage switchboards to fixed lighting outlets by way of permanently installed supplementary circuits. In these installations, the panel, supplementary circuits, and outlets must follow certain rules as outlined in *NEC Section 520.50* and summarized here:

- Circuit conductors must terminate in a polarized, grounding-type inlet that is matched to the current and voltage rating of the fixed-load receptacle.
- When transfer switches are used between fixed and portable switchboards, all circuit conductors must transfer at the same time.
- Any exterior device that supplies current to supplementary circuits must be protected by overcurrent protective devices.
- Individual supplementary circuits within the road show patch panel and theater must be protected by overcurrent protective devices installed within the panel.

Know the Code

Road Show Connection Panel (A Type of Patch Panel)
NEC Section 520.50

NOTE

Patch panel construction is regulated by ***NEC Article 408***.

Power Outlets and Supply Conductors

Power outlets that supply onstage portable switchboards must be enclosed fused switches, fused disconnects, or circuit breakers that are externally operated with provisions for an equipment grounding conductor. See *NEC Section 520.51*. These supply devices must be readily accessible from the stage floor, mounted onstage, or at the location of the permanent switchboard.

Extra-hard usage cords or cables must be used to connect the power outlets to the switchboard. See *NEC Section 520.54(A)*. These cables or cords must terminate totally within the enclosed power outlet and switchboard enclosure or in a connector assembly identified for that purpose.

A single-conductor current cable cannot be smaller than No. 2 AWG, and the equipment grounding conductor must be at least No. 6 AWG. See *NEC Section 520.54(C)*. If single conductors are installed in parallel to increase ampacity, the conductors must be the same size and length. Single-conductor supply cables may be grouped together but not bundled together.

Portable onstage switchboard supply conductors may be reduced in size based on the length of conductor required between the voltage supply and switchboard or between the voltage supply and an intermediate overcurrent protective device.

For supply conductors not longer than 10' (3 m), all the conditions in *NEC Section 520.54(D)* must be met for the conductors to be reduced in size, as follows:

- Supply conductors must be at least one-fourth the current rating of the associated overcurrent protective device.

Know the Code

Supply
NEC Section 520.51

Know the Code

Supply Conductors
NEC Section 520.54

CAUTION

As with any electrical system, if more than one nominal voltage exists within the same premises, each ungrounded conductor must be identified according to the system from which it originates.

- Supply conductors must terminate at a single overcurrent protective device that limits the load to no greater than the supply conductor ampacity.
- Supply conductors cannot penetrate floors, walls, or ceilings or pass through doors or other traffic areas.
- Supply conductor terminations must be made using an approved method.
- Supply conductors cannot contain splices or connectors.
- Supply conductors must not be bundled together.
- Supply conductors must be supported above the floor in an approved manner.

If the supply conductors are over 10' (3 m) in length but not longer than 20' (6 m), all the conditions in *NEC Section 520.54(E)* must be met for the conductors to be reduced in size, as follows:

- Supply conductors must have an ampacity that is at least one-half the current rating of the associated overcurrent protective device.
- Supply conductors must terminate at a single overcurrent protective device that limits the load to no greater than the supply conductor ampacity.
- Supply conductors cannot penetrate floors, walls, or ceilings or pass through doors or other traffic areas.
- Supply conductor terminations must be made using an approved method.
- Supply conductors must be supported at least 7' (2.1 m) above the floor except at termination points.
- Supply conductors must not be bundled together.
- Tap conductors must not contain splices or connectors (other than the tap itself).

Know the Code

Spread of Fire or Products of Combustion
NEC Section 300.21

Supply conductors that are not reduced in size based on the listed conditions may pass through holes in walls per *NEC Section 520.54(F)*. If the wall is fire rated, the penetration must be in accordance with the rules of *NEC Section 300.21*.

Supply conductors must be protected against physical damage. See *NEC Section 520.54(G)*. When supply cables pass through enclosures, a protective bushing must be installed to protect the cable. In addition, the arrangement of the cables through and within the enclosure should be such that no tension is applied at the point of termination or connection.

For long lengths of supply conductors that require interconnecting connectors, *NEC Section 520.54(H)* states that no more than three mating connectors may be used where the total length of conductor from supply to switchboard does not exceed 100' (30 m). If the conductor exceeds 100' (30 m) in length, one additional mating connector is permitted for each additional 100' (30 m) of conductor.

Know the Code

Construction
NEC Section 520.53

Single-pole portable cable connectors must be of the locking type and, if installed in parallel as input devices, must be labeled with a warning that parallel connections are present. See *NEC Section 520.53(C)*. At least one of the following conditions must exist to permit the usage of single-pole separable connectors:

- Connectors can be connected or disconnected only if the supply is de-energized and the connectors are interlocked at the source.
- If sequential-interlocking line connectors are used, load connectors must be connected in the following sequence: (1) equipment grounding conductor, (2) grounded conductor, and (3) ungrounded conductor(s). Alternatively, a caution tag must be attached adjacent to the line connectors that lists the sequence of connection. Disconnection is in the reverse order.

The supply neutral terminal and busbar within a portable switchboard designed to operate from a three-phase, four-wire with ground supply must have a rated ampacity that is at least twice the ampacity of the largest ungrounded supply conductor terminal within the switchboard. See *NEC Section 520.53(B)*.

Neutral conductors supplying portable switchboards that incorporate solid-state phase-control dimmers are considered current-carrying conductors and must be sized accordingly. See *NEC Section 520.54(J)(2)*. However, neutral conductors supplying portable switchboards that incorporate solid-state sine-wave dimmers are not considered current-carrying conductors. When single conductors not installed in raceways are used as feeders for multiphase circuits powering portable switchboards containing solid-state phase-control dimmers, the neutral conductor must have a rated ampacity that is at least 130% of the ungrounded conductors. In cases in which the switchboard contains sine-wave dimmers, the neutral ampacity is required to be only at least 100% of the ungrounded conductors.

Only qualified personnel may install portable supply conductors, connect and disconnect connectors, or energize and de-energize supply circuits per *NEC Section 520.54(K)*. Portable switchboards must visibly display a label in a conspicuous place indicating this requirement. An exception to this rule states that a portable switchboard may be connected to a permanently installed supply receptacle by an unqualified person if the receptacle is protected by an overcurrent protective device that is not greater than 150A and if the switchboard complies with all the following requirements:

- Listed multipole connectors are used for each supply interconnection.
- The general public may not have access to supply connections.
- Multiconductor cords and cables are listed for extra-hard usage, with a rated ampacity equal to or greater than the load and not less than the ampacity of the connectors used.

Know the Code

Qualified Persons
NEC Section 520.54(K)

Portable Switchboard Construction, Circuits, Interior Wiring, and Devices

Portable switchboards must be installed within an enclosure that offers protection to the equipment and the general public. See *NEC Sections 520.53(A) through (E)*. There can be no exposed energized parts within the enclosure, and all switches and circuit breakers must be enclosed and externally operated. Each ungrounded conductor in every circuit supplied by the switchboard must have overcurrent protection. Dimmer terminals must not be exposed, and faceplates must be installed to prevent accidental contact. The short circuit current rating must be marked on the switchboard.

Portable onstage switchboards must be equipped with a pilot light that is connected to the supply circuit of the switchboard. The power to the pilot light must not be interrupted by the opening of the master switch, and power must be supplied by an individual branch circuit rated at no more than 15A. Individual portable switchboards must contain overcurrent protection for branch circuits (per *NEC Section 520.52*).

Know the Code

Overcurrent Protection for Branch Circuits
NEC Section 520.52

Conductors within the switchboard enclosure (except busbars) must be stranded. Minimum insulation temperature ratings for dimmer conductors are dependent on the type of dimmer and must be at least equal to the operating temperature of the dimmer. Conductors connected to resistance-type dimmers must have a minimum insulation temperature rating of 392°F (200°C), while conductors connected to reactor-type, autotransformer, and solid-state dimmers must be rated for a minimum of 257°F (125°C).

Dressing Rooms

Pendant-type lampholders are not permitted in dressing or makeup rooms per *NEC Section 520.71*. Incandescent lamps installed less than 8' (2.5 m) from the floor must be equipped with open-ended guards that are riveted to the outlet box cover or locked in place in some other fashion. See *NEC Section 520.72*.

Know the Code

Pendant Lampholders
NEC Section 520.71

Know the Code

Lamp Guards
NEC Section 520.72

Know the Code

Switches Required
NEC Section 520.73

Know the Code

Pilot Lights Required
NEC Section 520.74

Know the Code

Carnivals, Circuses, Fairs, and Similar Events
NEC Article 525

Wall switches must be installed in the dressing rooms to control lights or receptacles adjacent to mirrors and above the dressing table countertops (per *NEC Section 520.73*). These switches must be equipped with a pilot light located adjacent to the door outside the dressing room to indicate when the receptacles are energized. Other general-use receptacles in dressing rooms do not require switch control (per *NEC Section 520.74*).

1.3.0 Carnivals, Circuses, Fairs, and Similar Events

Carnivals, circuses, and fairs present several unique wiring and safety concerns. These concerns include large crowds, high power demands for operating rides and concessions, outdoor installations, unpredictable animal behavior, and a need to rapidly set up and tear down equipment. *NEC Article 525* lists the requirements for portable wiring associated with equipment and portable structures used in carnivals (*Figure 8*), circuses, fairs, and similar functions. The wiring in permanent structures, such as audience areas and assembly halls, located within these activities are covered by *NEC Articles 518 and 520*. The wiring in permanent amusement attractions is covered by *NEC Article 522*.

Figure 8 Carnival.
Source: iStock@Lainey Stelly

1.3.1 Overhead Conductor Clearances

Know the Code

Clearance for Overhead Conductors and Cables
NEC Section 225.18

Tents and concessions must maintain vertical clearances from overhead conductors in accordance with *NEC Section 225.18*. For portable structures such as the one shown in *Figure 9*, a clearance of 15' (4.5 m) must be maintained in any direction from overhead conductors operating at 600V or less, unless the conductors are supplying power to the portable structure per *NEC Section 525.5(B)(1)*. A portable structure may not be located under or within 15' (4.5 m) of conductors that have an energized voltage greater than 600V per *NEC Section 525.5(B)(2)*.

1.3.2 Power Sources

Areas that house service equipment must be lockable or located to prevent access by unqualified persons. The equipment must be mounted on a surface with a solid backing and protected from the weather or constructed with weatherproof enclosures and components. Refer to *NEC Section 525.10(B)*.

Figure 9 Tents.
Source: iStock@Juan Garcia

Portable structures at carnivals, circuses, or fairs often receive their power from separately derived systems or different services. In these situations, if the structures are less than 12' (3.7 m) apart, all equipment grounding conductors must be bonded together at portable structures per *NEC Section 525.11*. The bonding conductor must be sized in accordance with *NEC Table 250.122*, based on the largest overcurrent protective device supplying the portable structures and no smaller than No. 6 AWG.

1.3.3 Wiring: Cords, Cables, and Connectors

As stated in *NEC Section 525.20(A)*, flexible cords and cables exposed to potential physical damage—common for fairs and similar events—must be listed for extra-hard usage. Cords and cables not exposed to possible physical damage may be listed for hard usage. If the cords or cables are to be used outdoors, they must also be listed for wet locations and be sunlight resistant. Permanent wiring for portable amusement rides and other attractions, as opposed to temporary wiring, may be extra-hard usage flexible cords and cables if the cords or cables are not exposed to possible physical damage.

Single-conductor cables must be a minimum of No. 2 AWG in size per *NEC Section 525.20(B)*. *NEC Section 525.20(C)* permits the use of open conductors only in **festoon lighting** (*Figure 10*), which is regulated by *NEC Article 225*. Flexible cords or cables may not contain any splices or taps between boxes or fittings.

Cord and cable connectors may not be laid on the ground unless the connector is rated for wet locations. Even then, connectors must not be located in any audience traffic area or other areas (unless guarded) that are accessible to the general public. Cords or cables may not be draped or hung on rides or similar structures unless designed for the purpose. If the cable or cord presents a tripping hazard, it may be covered with nonconductive matting if the matting does not present an additional tripping hazard. Cables or cords may also be buried to eliminate the tripping hazard.

Know the Code

Minimum Size Equipment Grounding Conductors for Grounding Raceway and Equipment
NEC Table 250.122

Know the Code

Wiring Methods
NEC Section 525.20

Know the Code

Outside Branch Circuits and Feeders
NEC Article 225

Festoon lighting: Outdoor lighting that is strung between supporting points.

Figure 10 Festoon Lighting.
Source: iStock@MAKSYM BOSATSKYI

1.3.4 Wiring: Rides, Tents, and Concessions

Per *NEC Section 525.21(A)*, all rides and similar portable structures must be equipped with a disconnect switch that is within 6' (1.8 m) of the operator and within the operator's sight. The disconnecting means must always be readily available to the operator, even when the ride is running. If the disconnecting means is accessible to the public, it must also be lockable. A **shunt trip** in the operator's console may be used to open the fused disconnect or circuit breaker.

Lamps that are part of portable lighting inside tents and concessions must be guarded per *NEC Section 525.21(B)*. When outlet boxes or other device boxes are installed outdoors, the boxes must be weatherproof and mounted so the bottom of the box is at least 6" (150 mm) above the ground. See *NEC Section 525.22(A)*.

NEC Section 525.23(A) states that ground fault circuit interrupter (GFCI) protection is required on all 125V, single-phase, 15A and 20A nonlocking-type receptacles that are used to assemble or disassemble rides, amusements, or concessions, or when those receptacles are exposed to the public. Any equipment supplied by 125V, single-phase, 15A or 20A circuits and exposed to the public must also be GFCI-protected. The GFCI protection may be an integral part of the attachment plug or installed directly in the power supply cord within 12" (300 mm) of the attachment plug. Locking-type receptacles are not required to be GFCI-protected per *NEC Section 525.23(B)*. Egress lighting must not be GFCI-protected per *NEC Section 525.23(C)*. Listed cord sets incorporating GFCI protection for personnel are permitted per *NEC Section 525.23(D)*.

Know the Code

Rides, Tents, and Concessions
NEC Section 525.21

Shunt trip: A low-voltage device that remotely causes a higher voltage overcurrent protective device to trip or open the circuit.

Know the Code

Ground-Fault Circuit-Interrupter (GFCI) Protection
NEC Section 525.23

1.3.5 Grounding and Bonding

All metal raceways, metal-sheathed cable, metal enclosures of electrical equipment, metal frames and metal parts of portable structures, trailers, trucks, or any other equipment that contains or supports electrical equipment connected to the same electrical source must be bonded together and connected to an equipment grounding conductor. See *NEC Section 525.30*. The equipment grounding conductor may serve as the bonding means.

The equipment grounding conductor must be connected to the system's grounded conductor at the service disconnect. In a separately derived system such as a generator, the equipment grounding conductor must be connected at the generator or in the first disconnecting means supplied by the generator (*Figure 11*). Refer to *NEC Section 525.31*.

Know the Code

Equipment Bonding
NEC Section 525.30

Know the Code

Equipment Grounding
NEC Section 525.31

CAUTION

Never connect the grounded circuit conductor to the equipment grounding conductor anywhere on the load side of the service disconnect or generator disconnect.

Figure 11 First means of disconnect supplied downstream of a carnival generator.
Source: Courtesy of Semcor

1.4.0 Agricultural Buildings

NEC Article 547 covers agricultural buildings in which excessive dust and dust with water may accumulate, including all areas of poultry, livestock, and fish confinement systems. It also contains provisions for agricultural buildings that contain a corrosive atmosphere that may be caused by poultry or animal excrement, corrosive particles mixed with water, and wet or damp corrosive areas caused by cleaning and sanitizing solutions.

Know the Code

Agricultural Buildings
NEC Article 547

1.4.1 Wiring Methods

Wiring systems in agricultural buildings may contain jacketed MC cable, nonmetallic-sheathed, corrosion-resistant (NMC) cable, copper service-entrance (SE) cable, underground feeder (UF) cable, rigid nonmetallic conduit, liquid-tight flexible nonmetallic conduit, and any other cable or raceway approved and suitable for the location, with approved fittings. See *NEC Section 547.20*.

Per *NEC Section 547.21*, cables must be secured within 8" (200 mm) of any box, cabinet, or fitting to which they connect. If nonmetallic boxes are mounted directly to an agricultural building surface, the $\frac{1}{4}$" (6 mm) airspace requirement of *NEC Section 300.6(D)* does not apply.

Know the Code

Indoor Wet Locations
NEC Section 300.6(D)

Enclosures, boxes, conduit bodies, and fittings installed in dusty areas of agricultural buildings must be designed to minimize the entrance of dust, with no screw or mounting holes. In damp or wet locations, these enclosures, boxes, conduit bodies, and fittings must be listed for wet locations or mounted to prevent the entrance of moisture or water (*Figure 12*). Wiring methods used in corrosive atmospheres must provide corrosion resistance. Aluminum and magnetic ferrous (carbon steel) materials are not suitable for corrosive atmospheres.

NOTE

NEC Table 110.28 lists properties for various types of electrical enclosures, including those that offer corrosion resistance.

Where flexible connections are required, such as supplying power to motors and other vibrating or moving equipment, *NEC Section 547.25* requires the use of liquid-tight flexible metal or liquid-tight flexible nonmetallic conduit with dust-tight connectors, or flexible cord listed for hard usage.

Grounding conductors installed underground in agricultural buildings must be insulated. See *NEC Section 547.27*.

Per *NEC Section 547.28*, ground fault protection must be provided for all 125V, single-phase, 15A and 20A receptacles installed in areas having an **equipotential plane**, outdoors, in damp or wet locations, and in dirt confinement areas for livestock.

Equipotential plane: An area in wire mesh or other conductive material embedded in or placed under concrete that may conduct current.

1.4.2 Motors and Luminaires

NEC Section 547.30 requires that all motors and rotating electrical machinery be totally enclosed or designed to reduce the entry of moisture, dust, or corrosive materials (*Figure 13*). Luminaires must also be designed to minimize the entry of dust, moisture, or corrosive particles. If luminaires are exposed to physical damage, guards must be installed. Luminaires exposed to water must be listed as suitable for use in wet locations. Refer to *NEC Sections 547.31(A) through (C)*.

Figure 12 Outdoor box listed for wet location.
Source: iStock@matt_benoit

Figure 13 Totally enclosed motor.
Source: Courtesy of Baldor Electric Company

Electrified Truck Parking Spaces

NEC Article 626 covers the electrical conductors and equipment used to supply commercial power to tractor trailers, such as those with refrigeration units that must remain in operation when the truck is not running.

Fans in Poultry Buildings

Chicken farms have an elaborate system of auxiliary power supplies in the form of generators and transfer switches. Failure of a livestock ventilation system can result in death by asphyxiation from a lack of oxygen and increased carbon dioxide, heat prostration, or poisoning from the buildup of gases such as ammonia and methane. One chicken farmer said that he would lose most of his chickens if the ventilation fans were shut down for as little as 20 minutes.

Source: iStock@matt_benoit

1.4.3 Electrical Supply from a Single Distribution Point

NEC Section 547.40 states that any agricultural buildings or structures located on the same premises must be electrically supplied from a distribution point (*Figure 14*). If two or more buildings are supplied overhead from a distribution point, a **site-isolating device** must be installed and the installation must qualify for exceptions or comply with the requirements listed in *NEC Sections 547.41(A)(1) through (9)*. The requirements are summarized as follows:

- Pole mounted
- Simultaneously open all ungrounded service conductors from the premises wiring
- Mounted in an enclosure bonded to the grounded and grounding conductors
- System grounded conductors bonded to a grounding electrode system by means of a grounding electrode conductor at the site-isolating device
- Rated for the calculated load
- Not required to provide overcurrent protection
- If not readily accessible, capable of being remotely operated by a readily accessible operating handle not more than 6'-7" (2 m) above grade at its highest position
- Permanently marked on or adjacent to the operating handle, identifying it as a site-isolating device

Figure 14 Agricultural building distribution point.

A service disconnect and overcurrent protection for two or more buildings supplied from a distribution point may be located at the buildings or at the distribution point. If located at the buildings, supply conductor sizes must comply with *NEC Article 220, Part V* and conductor installation must follow the requirements of *NEC Article 225, Part II*. Grounding and bonding of the supply conductors must be in accordance with *NEC Section 250.32*. If the equipment grounding conductor and the largest supply conductor are constructed from the same material, they must be the same size. If they are of different materials, the equipment grounding conductor must be adjusted according to *NEC Table 250.122*, as specified in *NEC Section 547.41(B)(3)(1)*.

Know the Code

Electrical Supply to Building(s) or Structure(s) from a Distribution Point
NEC Section 547.40

Know the Code

Site-Isolating Device
NEC Section 547.41(A)

Site-isolating device: A disconnecting means at the point of distribution that is used to isolate the service for the purpose of electrical maintenance, emergency disconnection, or the connection of an optional standby system.

NOTE

If the electric utility provides a site-isolating device as part of their installation, no additional site-isolating device is required.

Know the Code

Farm Load Calculations
NEC Article 220, Part V

Know the Code

Buildings or Other Structures Supplied by a Feeder(s) or Branch Circuit(s)
NEC Article 225, Part II

Know the Code

Minimum Size Equipment Grounding Conductors for Grounding Raceway and Equipment
NEC Table 250.122

When the service disconnect and overcurrent protection for two or more buildings are located at the distribution point, supply conductors to the buildings must meet the requirements of *NEC Section 250.32* and *NEC Article 225, Parts I and II*.

If more than one service supplies an agricultural site, each distribution point must have a permanent plaque or directory installed to indicate the location of each distribution point and the buildings or structures served by each one (per *NEC Section 547.43*).

Know the Code

Identification
NEC Section 547.43

1.4.4 Equipotential Planes

NEC Sections 547.44(A)(1) and (2) require that equipotential planes be installed in indoor and outdoor animal confinement areas having concrete floors or slabs with metallic equipment that may become energized and accessible to animals (per *NEC Section 547.44*). Refer to *Figure 15*. The plane must cover the area in which the animals may stand while accessing the metallic equipment.

Know the Code

Equipotential Planes and Bonding of Equipotential Planes
NEC Section 547.44

Equipotential planes must be bonded to the grounding system with a bare or insulated solid copper conductor no smaller than No. 8 AWG, per *NEC Section 547.44(B)*. Bonding connections to wire mesh or other conductor elements may be made using approved pressure connectors or clamps of brass, copper, or copper alloy.

Figure 15 Concrete area with accessible metal piping and animal contact.
Source: iStock@Joanna Goleniewska

1.5.0 Temporary Installations

Know the Code

Temporary Installations
NEC Article 590

Temporary wiring is covered in *NEC Article 590*. It includes wiring used to supply temporary power and lighting to construction sites and for remodeling, maintenance, repair, demolition, holiday decorative lighting, electrical tests, emergencies, experiments, and developmental work. Temporary wiring, excluding holiday decorative lighting (*Figure 16*), must be removed immediately upon completion of the temporary need. Holiday lighting may remain up no longer than 90 days.

Figure 16 Holiday lighting.
Source: iStock@Joanna Goleniewska

1.5.1 Feeder and Branch Circuit Conductors

Feeder and branch circuit conductors used in temporary wiring may be multiconductor cables that are identified for hard usage or extra-hard usage according to *NEC Table 400.4* and must originate from approved panelboards or power outlets. Per *NEC Sections 590.4(B)(1) and 590.4(C)(1)*, Type NM, Type NMC, and Type SE cable may be used for temporary wiring in any dwelling or other structure without consideration to height limitations or concealment within walls, floors, or ceilings. Single insulated feeder and branch circuit conductors may be used to supply power for temporary testing, emergencies, experiments, and developmental work where accessible to qualified persons only. Holiday decorative lighting may also be supplied by single insulated branch circuit conductors if the voltage to ground does not exceed 150V, the wiring is not subjected to physical damage, and the conductors are supported on insulators no more than 10' (3 m) apart. If the lighting is hung in festoon (swag) fashion, the conductors must be arranged so that no conductor strain is felt at the lampholder.

Know the Code

Flexible Cords and Flexible Cables
NEC Table 400.4

Know the Code

General
NEC Section 590.4

1.5.2 Grounding

Temporary branch circuits must include a separate equipment grounding conductor unless the branch circuit conductors are installed in a continuous metal raceway that meets the requirements of an equipment grounding conductor. Refer to *NEC Section 590.4(D)(1)*. MC cables that qualify as equipment grounding conductors may also be used.

1.5.3 Disconnects

Disconnecting switches or plug connectors must be installed to disconnect all ungrounded conductors supplying temporary circuits. See *NEC Section 590.4(E)*. Multiwire branch circuits must be provided with a disconnecting means that simultaneously disconnects all ungrounded conductors at the power outlet or panel from which they originate. Only identified handle ties may be used.

1.5.4 Protection and Support

All cables and conductors must be protected from pinch points, sharp corners, and other potentially damaging conditions. In addition, proper fittings must be installed where flexible cords and cables enter boxes. See *NEC Sections 590.4(H) and (I)*. Cable assemblies must also be adequately supported with staples, cable ties, straps, or other approved means at intervals to provide protection from physical damage, per *NEC Section 590.4(J)*. Vegetation may not be used to support overhead runs of branch circuit or feeder conductors, except for holiday lighting. In the latter case, the conductors or cables must be arranged and supported with strain relief or other devices to avoid conductor damage from the movement of limbs and branches.

1.5.5 Receptacles

Receptacles in temporary wiring must be of the grounding type and must be electrically connected to the equipment grounding conductor, per *NEC Section 590.4(D)*.

WARNING!

Receptacles that supply temporary power on construction sites may not be installed on any branch circuit that supplies temporary lighting, nor may they be connected to the same ungrounded conductor of multiwire circuits supplying temporary lighting.

NOTE

Per ***NEC Section 590.4(G)***, Exception No. 1, it is not necessary to install a box for splices or connections on construction sites when using nonmetallic multiwire cord or cable assemblies as long as the equipment grounding conductor's continuity is maintained. Boxes are also not required where circuit conductors being spliced are all from metal-sheathed cable assemblies terminated in listed fittings that mechanically secure the cable sheath to maintain effective electrical continuity. All other splices require a box, conduit body, or other enclosure with a cover installed.

1.5.6 Temporary Lighting

General illumination luminaires must be designed to protect the lamp from contact or breakage per *NEC Section 590.4(F)*. All exposed lamps must be equipped with a lamp guard (*Figure 17*). Metal-cased sockets may not be installed unless the lamp shell is grounded. All holiday or other decorative lighting must be listed per *NEC Section 590.5*.

Figure 17 Lamp guard in place on temporary lighting at construction site.
Source: Courtesy Delta Electrical Inc.

1.5.7 Wiring and Equipment Greater than 600V

If any wiring or equipment operates at greater than 600V at any temporary location, it must be guarded by a fence, barrier, or other effective means and be accessible only to authorized and qualified personnel familiar with the equipment or wiring. See *NEC Section 590.7*.

Know the Code

Guarding
NEC Section 590.7

1.5.8 Ground Fault Protection

The *NEC*® applies specific rules to power derived from an electric utility company or from an on-site generator (per *NEC Section 590.6*). Ground fault protection must be provided on all 125V, single-phase, 15A, 20A, or 30A temporary receptacles that are not part of the permanent wiring, unless temporary power is being supplied by the permanent wiring. If a receptacle that is part of the permanent wiring is used for temporary electric power, it also must be GFCI-protected (*Figure 18*). GFCI protection may also be incorporated into a cord set or device to comply with this rule.

The only exception to the GFCI rule is in industrial locations where a greater hazard would be introduced if power were interrupted or the system design is not compatible with GFCI protection (*NEC Section 590.6(A)*, Exception). In these locations, GFCI protection is not required if only qualified personnel are involved and an assured equipment grounding conductor program is in place. However, if GFCI or special-purpose ground fault circuit interrupter (SPGFCI) protection becomes available and is the appropriate voltage and amperage for the application, it must be used.

Know the Code

Ground-Fault Protection for Personnel
NEC Section 590.6

Figure 18 Receptacles on construction sites must be GFCI-protected.
Source: iStock@TammyJerry6465

1.5.9 Assured Equipment Grounding Conductor Program

If GFCI protection is not supplied, there must be a written assured equipment grounding conductor program in place at each site requiring temporary wiring. See *NEC Section 590.6(B)(2)*. At least one designated person must enforce the program to ensure all cord sets, receptacles (temporary), and cord-and-plug equipment are equipped with equipment grounding conductors and maintained in accordance with applicable requirements of the *NEC*®. At a minimum, the assured equipment grounding conductor program must contain the following:

- The equipment grounding conductors must be electrically continuous and tested for continuity.
- Each receptacle and plug must be tested for correct grounding conductor termination. These tests must be performed before first use, when there is evidence of damage, after repairs and before next usage, and at intervals not exceeding three months.
- All test results must be recorded and available for review.

1.6.0 Wired Partitions

Know the Code

Office Furnishings
NEC Article 605

Wired partitions allow for convenient rearrangement of office spaces. *NEC Article 605* provides the requirements for lighting accessories and wired office partitions. When installed in interconnecting office partitions, conductors and connections must be contained within wiring channels identified for such use (per *NEC Section 605.4*). When two or more wired partitions are electrically connected, the electrical connection between the partitions must be made with a flexible assembly specifically designed for such purposes or with a flexible cord if all the following conditions are met (per *NEC Section 605.5*):

- The flexible cord must be rated for extra-hard usage, have No. 12 AWG or larger conductors, and contain an insulated grounding conductor.
- The partitions must be mechanically secured together (contiguous).
- The cord may be no longer than 2' (600 mm).
- The cord must be terminated at an attachment plug-and-cord connector equipped with a strain-relief device.

Know the Code

Wiring Methods and Materials
NEC Chapter 3

Per *NEC Section 605.7*, partitions that are fixed to the building surfaces must be permanently connected to the building's electrical system using the general wiring methods found in *NEC Chapter 3*. As with any multiwire branch circuit, a disconnecting means must be provided that simultaneously disconnects all ungrounded conductors.

Know the Code

Freestanding-Type Office Furnishings, Cord- and Plug-Connected
NEC Section 605.9

Individual freestanding (not fixed) partitions, or groups of freestanding partitions that are mechanically secured together and do not exceed 30' (9 m) in length when connected, may be connected to the building's electrical system using a single flexible cord, provided all the following conditions in *NEC Sections 605.9(A) through (D)* are met:

- The flexible cord is rated for extra-hard usage, has No. 12 AWG or larger conductors, contains an insulated equipment grounding conductor, and is no longer than 2' (600 mm).
- The supply receptacle is on a separate circuit that serves only partitions and no other loads and is located no farther than 12" (300 mm) from the partition connected to it.
- Individual partitions or grouped partitions cannot contain more than thirteen 15A, 125V receptacles.
- Individual partitions or grouped partitions cannot contain multiwire circuits.

1.0.0 Section Review

1. To accommodate fire-rated construction, wiring methods allowed in assembly occupancies include MI cable, MC cable, AC cable, metal raceways, flexible metal raceways, and nonmetallic raceways encased in _____.
   a. at least 18" (450 mm) of sand
   b. a metal cable tray
   c. at least 2" (50 mm) of concrete
   d. at least 6" (150 mm) of concrete

2. Wiring for portable equipment such as portable switchboards and stage effects in theaters and audience areas may be in the form of approved flexible cords and cables if they are _____.
   a. not fastened or secured by uninsulated staples or nails
   b. brightly colored for visibility
   c. contained within a metal or nonmetallic raceway
   d. rated for extra-hard usage

3. The wiring in permanent amusement attractions is covered by _____.
   a. *NEC Article 505*
   b. *NEC Article 511*
   c. *NEC Article 518*
   d. *NEC Article 522*

4. All 125V, single-phase, 15A and 20A receptacles mounted in an agricultural building having an equipotential plane are required to have _____.
   a. twist-load devices
   b. arc fault protection
   c. tamper-resistant covers
   d. ground fault protection

5. In temporary installations, which of the following items or materials *cannot* be used for the support of overhead runs of branch circuit or feeder conductors unless it is holiday lighting?
   a. Vegetation
   b. Wooden structures
   c. Metal structures
   d. Concrete

6. When two or more wired partitions are electrically connected, the connection may be made using a flexible cord if specific conditions are met, including that the cord is *no* longer than _____.
   a. 2' (600 mm) in length
   b. 4' (1.2 m) in length
   c. 6' (1.8 m) in length
   d. 8' (2.4 m) in length

2.0.0 Marinas, Boatyards, and Bodies of Water

Objective

Identify and select equipment, components, and wiring methods for marinas, boatyards, and bodies of water.

a. Identify and select equipment, components, and wiring methods for marinas and boatyards.
b. Identify and select equipment, components, and wiring methods for natural and man-made bodies of water.

Performance Tasks

There are no Performance Tasks in this section.

The permanent presence of water, for obvious reasons, creates additional electrical hazards that must be addressed using specific wiring components and techniques to achieve a safe installation. Marinas and boatyards require significant attention to detail, as they often require power to be provided up to the water's edge and beyond.

2.1.0 Marinas and Boatyards

NEC Article 555 covers all commercial and dwelling unit docking facilities, boatyards, boat basins, boathouses, and yacht clubs used for the purpose of repairing, berthing, launching, storing, or fueling boats and/or the moorage of floating buildings (*Figure 19*).

Know the Code

Marinas, Boatyards, Floating Buildings, and Commercial and Noncommercial Docking Facilities
NEC Article 555

Figure 19 Marina with floating docks.

Figure 20 Electrical distribution system at a marina.

2.1.1 General Requirements for Devices, Equipment, and Enclosures

A marine power outlet is any receptacle, circuit breaker, fused switch, meter, and any other similar device approved for marine use. Electrical distribution systems within boatyards and piers (*Figure 20*) cannot exceed 250V phase to phase per *NEC Section 555.5*. Where qualified personnel service the equipment under engineering supervision, the system voltage is permitted to be up to 600V per *NEC Section 555.5*.

Ground fault protection requirements are listed in *NEC Sections 555.35(A), (B), and (C)*. When mounting transformers in areas covered by *NEC Article 555*, the bottoms of transformers must be above the **electrical datum plane** as defined in *NEC Section 555.3*. Electrical service equipment cannot be installed on or in a floating structure but instead must be mounted adjacent to the structure and elevated at least 12" (300 mm) above the electrical datum plane per *NEC Section 555.4*.

Electrical connections within boxes or enclosures that are not rated for submersion must be located at least 12" (305 mm) above the deck of a floating pier as stated in *NEC Section 555.30*. If the junction box is rated for submersion, it may be located below the electrical datum plane for floating piers but must be above the waterline. Any electrical connection on a fixed pier must be at least 12" (305 mm) above the deck of the pier but never below the electrical datum plane per *NEC Section 555.30(A)* (*Figure 21*).

Conduit may not be the sole support for electrical enclosures installed on piers above deck level. External box ears or lugs must be used to support these enclosures per *NEC Section 555.31(A)*. If internal screws are used to secure boxes or enclosures to the pier structure, the screw heads must be sealed to prevent water from entering through the mounting holes. The location of electrical equipment, boxes, or enclosures must not be in the way of mooring lines per *NEC Section 555.31(B)*.

NEC Section 555.30 states that a person must be able to operate circuit breakers or switches that have been installed in watertight enclosures without removing the enclosure cover. However, watertight enclosures housing such devices must be designed with a weep hole to discharge condensation.

Know the Code

Maximum Voltage
NEC Section 555.5

Know the Code

Ground-Fault Protection of Equipment (GFPE) and Ground-Fault Circuit Interrupter
NEC Section 555.35

Electrical datum plane: Horizontal plane affecting electrical installations based on the rise and fall of water levels in land areas and floating piers and landing stages.

NOTE

Metric conversions in the *NEC*® may vary depending on the type of installation and are often more specific in areas of increased hazard, such as near water.

Know the Code

Electrical Equipment and Connections
NEC Section 555.30

Know the Code

Electrical Equipment Enclosures
NEC Section 555.31

Figure 21 Electrical connections within a box not rated for submersion must be mounted at least 12" (305 mm) above the deck.
Source: iStock@Rupreet Sikand-Mouton

Floating Buildings

Wiring methods for buildings that float on water, are permanently moored, and electrically supplied by a system not located on the premises, are covered by *NEC Article 555, Part III.*

2.1.2 Service and Feeder Conductor Load Calculations

All general lighting and receptacle loads for marinas and boatyards must be calculated using the standard general lighting load calculation procedures of *NEC Article 220, Part III.* When service or feeder circuit conductors are used to supply a number of receptacles for shore power to boats, the demand factors shown in *NEC Table 220.120* may be applied to determine the circuit rating and conductor sizes.

Other rules may apply to shore power installations and are listed in the notes following *NEC Table 220.120.* One such rule is that if two separate receptacles having different voltages and amperage ratings are installed in a single boat slip, only the receptacle with the greater volt-ampere (VA) demand needs to be included in the total load calculation. For example, if one receptacle is rated 30A at 125V (3,750VA) and another is rated 50A at 250V (12,500VA) within the same slip, the total load calculation for these two receptacles would be based on the higher 12,500VA only.

Consideration must be given to ambient temperatures and types of equipment when applying demand factors. Extremely hot or cold temperatures may result in increased demand factors for circuits with loaded heating, air conditioning, or refrigeration equipment.

Know the Code

Feeder and Service Load Calculations
NEC Article 220, Part III

Know the Code

Demand Factors for Shore Power Receptacle Loads
NEC Table 220.120

Know the Code

Wiring Methods and Materials
NEC Chapter 3

Know the Code

Wiring Methods and Installation
NEC Section 555.34

2.1.3 Wiring Methods

The standard wiring methods in *NEC Chapter 3* apply to locations covered by *NEC Article 555* if the methods are rated for wet locations. When portable power cables are used as permanent wiring on the underside of fixed or floating piers, or where flexibility is required on the floating sections of piers (*Figure* 22), the cable must meet the following criteria found in *NEC Sections 555.34(A)(2) and (B)(3)*:

- Rated for extra-hard usage
- Insulation rated for a minimum of 75°C (167°F) and 600V
- Listed for wet locations
- Sunlight-resistant
- Manufactured with an outer jacket resistant to temperature extremes, oil, gasoline, ozone, abrasions, acids, and chemicals
- Properly supported by nonmetallic clips to pier structural members other than deck planking
- Located on the underside of piers where not subject to physical damage
- Protected by nonmetallic sleeves where penetrating structural members

Figure 22 Cable may be used on floating sections of piers.
Source: iStock@John Fuller

In installations where cables are used to supply power to floating sections of a pier, either a listed marine power outlet with terminal blocks/bars or an approved, corrosion-resistant junction box containing terminal blocks must be installed on each pier section for conductor terminations. Any exposed metal boxes, covers, screws, and the like must be corrosion-resistant. See *NEC Section 555.34(B)(3)(b)*.

Overhead wiring in and around boatyards and marinas must be installed in a manner that avoids contact with masts and other boat parts, as well as portable lifts moving about the yard. *NEC Section 555.34(B)(2)* requires a minimum overhead clearance of 18' (5.49 m). In addition, all electrical conductors and cables must maintain a minimum of 20' (6 m) from the outer perimeter or any section of the boatyard that may be used to move vessels or for stepping or unstepping (raising or lowering) boat masts per *NEC Section 555.34(B)(1)*.

Per *NEC Section 555.34(B)(4)*, rigid metal, intermediate metal conduit, reinforced thermosetting resin conduit, or nonmetallic conduit must be installed above the deck of a pier and **landing stage** (*Figure 23*) and below the enclosure that the landing stage serves. Full-thread connections must be used to connect the conduit to the enclosure. When rigid nonmetallic conduit is installed in these locations, nonmetallic fittings that provide a threaded connection must be used to connect the conduit to the enclosure. All installations must be approved for damp or wet locations.

Landing stage: A floating platform used for the loading and unloading of passengers and cargo from boats or ships.

Figure 23 Landing stage where people access or exit boats.
Source: iStock@nobtis

Submeters

If individual kilowatt-hour submeters are installed to measure usage at each boat slip, a factor of 0.9 (90%) may be used instead of applying the factors of *NEC Table 555.6* to determine the total load demand.

2.1.4 Grounding

All metal boxes, metal cabinets, metal enclosures, metal frames of utilization equipment, and grounding terminals of grounding-type receptacles in locations covered by *NEC Article 555* must be connected to an equipment grounding conductor.

NEC Section 555.37(B) requires that the equipment grounding conductor must be copper, insulated, no smaller than No. 12 AWG, and green or green with one or more yellow stripes, unless the equipment grounding conductor is larger than No. 6 AWG. In the latter case, the equipment grounding conductor may be marked by other approved methods as described in *NEC Section 250.119*. For instances in which MI cable is used, the equipment grounding conductor may be identified with an approved means at each termination.

Branch circuit equipment grounding conductors must terminate at a grounding terminal in a remote panelboard or on the grounding terminal in the main service equipment per *NEC Section 555.37(D)*. An insulated equipment grounding conductor must interconnect the grounding terminal in a remote panelboard to the grounding terminal in the service equipment. See *NEC Section 555.37(C)*.

Know the Code

Marinas, Boatyards, Floating Buildings, and Commercial and Noncommercial Docking Facilities
NEC Article 555

Know the Code

Equipment Grounding Conductor
NEC Section 555.37

Know the Code

Identification of Wire-Type Equipment Grounding Conductors
NEC Section 250.119

2.1.5 Disconnecting Means for Shore Power

NEC Section 555.36 requires that a disconnecting means be provided to disconnect each individual shore power receptacle from the electrical supply. The disconnecting means may be a circuit breaker or switch that opens all ungrounded supply circuit conductors, and all disconnecting means must be properly marked to identify which receptacle they control. The disconnecting means must be located within 30" (762 mm) of the receptacle. Receptacles must be mounted at least 12" (305 mm) above the deck surface of the pier and not below the electrical datum plane on a fixed pier (per *NEC Section 555.33*). *Figure 24* shows disconnects for receptacles in the form of circuit breakers.

Know the Code

Disconnecting Means for Shore Power Connection(s)
NEC Section 555.36

Know the Code

Receptacles
NEC Section 555.33

Figure 24 Watertight shore power enclosure with accessible circuit breakers.
Source: iStock@Mauro_Repossini

Figure 25 GFCI-protected nonshore power receptacle.

2.1.6 Receptacles

The two types of receptacles in a marina are shore power receptacles and nonshore power receptacles. *NEC Section 555.33(A)(1)* states that shore power receptacles must be listed as marina power outlets, listed for set locations or installed in enclosures that provide protection from the weather. Strain relief must be provided for the cable when it is plugged into the receptacle. Each shore power receptacle must be protected by an individual branch circuit that corresponds to the rating of the receptacle, which can be rated at no less than 30A. Shore power receptacles rated 30A and 50A must be of the locking and grounding type, while receptacles rated 60A or higher must be of the pin and sleeve type. See *NEC Section 555.33(A)(4).*

GFCI protection for personnel must be provided on single-phase nonshore power receptacles that do not exceed 150V to ground and 60A, and on three-phase nonshore power receptacles that do not exceed 150V to ground and 100A (*Figure 25*). See *NEC Section 555.35(B)(2).*

Know the Code

Outlets for Other than Shore Power
NEC Section 555.35(B)(2)

Any nonshore power receptacle installed in a marine power outlet enclosure must be marked to indicate that the receptacle is not to be used as shore power for boats. See *NEC Section 555.33(B).*

2.1.7 Hazardous Locations in and around Marinas and Boatyards

Marina or boatyard wiring that is located near fuel dispensing areas must comply with *NEC Article 514*. In general, all power and lighting wiring in marinas and boatyards must be located on the opposite side from fueling systems and piping on wharfs, piers, or docks.

Know the Code

Motor Fuel Dispensing Facilities
NEC Article 514

NEC Tables 514.3(B)(1) and 514.3(B)(2) classify areas in and around fuel dispensing locations as either Class I, Division 1 or Class I, Division 2. When applying these tables to marina or boatyard fuel dispensing areas, you must first determine whether the area is considered closed construction or open construction.

Closed-construction-type docks, piers, or wharfs are those areas in which no space exists between the bottom of the dock, pier, or wharf and the waterline. The class and division designations for closed construction are as follows:

- *Class I, Division 1* — Voids, pits, or similar areas below closed-construction-type floating docks, piers, or wharfs that support fuel dispensers in which flammable liquid or vapor can accumulate. *Figure 26* shows a fuel dispenser mounted on a closed-construction pier. Areas directly below the fuel dispenser are voids and are rated Class I, Division 1.

- *Class I, Division 2* — Spaces above the surface of closed-construction floating docks, piers, or wharfs that are within 18" (450 mm) horizontally in all directions extending to grade from the dispenser enclosure. Also, sections of a dock, pier, or wharf that do not support fuel dispensers but directly adjacent and are 20' (6 m) or more from sections that do support fuel dispensers, with air spaces between them to allow for vapor dissipation. Those sections of pier that border the fuel dispensing pier are classified as Class I, Division 2, as illustrated in *Figure 27*.

Open-construction-type docks, piers, or wharfs are built on stringers that are supported by pilings, floats, pontoons, or similar devices in which space exists between the bottom of the dock, pier, or wharf and the waterline. The class and division designations for open construction are as follows:

- *Class I, Division 1* — Voids, pits, and similar areas within 20' (6 m) of the dispenser where flammable liquids or vapors may accumulate.
- *Class I, Division 2* — Areas 18" (450 mm) above the surface of open-construction-type fuel dispensing docks, piers, or wharfs, extending 20' (6 m) horizontally in all directions from the outside edge of the dispenser, and down to the water level.

Figure 26 Class I, Division 1 area below fuel dispenser in the void between the pier and the water.

Figure 27 Docks or sections of pier that border this fuel dispensing pier are classified as Class I, Division 2.
Source: iStock@deyangeorgiev

2.2.0 Natural and Man-Made Bodies of Water

Natural bodies of water include lakes, streams, ponds, and rivers, all of which may naturally vary in depth. *Figure 28* is an example of a natural body of water, while *Figure 29* illustrates a man-made or artificial body of water. Man-made bodies of water refer to aeration ponds, fish-farm ponds, storm retention basins, water treatment ponds, and irrigation channels. Electrical installations in and around natural and man-made bodies of water are covered in *NEC Article 682*.

Know the Code

Natural and Artificially Made Bodies of Water
NEC Article 682

Related Standards

Additional requirements may be found in NFPA 303, *Fire Protection Standard for Marinas and Boatyards* and NFPA 30A, *Code for Motor Fuel Dispensing Facilities and Repair Garages.*

Figure 28 Natural body of water.

Figure 29 Man-made body of water.
Source: iStock@bruev

2.2.1 Electrical Datum Plane

The electrical datum plane is an imaginary horizontal plane based on changing water levels. Electrical datum planes are referred to extensively in *NEC Articles 555 and 682* because both articles deal with changing water levels that can affect electrical installations in and around natural and artificial bodies of water as well as marinas and boatyards. The definition of an electrical datum plane is provided in *NEC Section 682.5* and varies based on the following conditions:

- Where land areas are affected by tidal fluctuations, the electrical datum plane is 2' (600 mm) above the highest high tide for the area.
- Where land areas are not affected by tidal fluctuations, the electrical datum plane is 2' (600 mm) above the highest water level for the area under normal conditions.

Know the Code

Marinas, Boatyards, Floating Buildings, and Commercial and Noncommercial Docking Facilities
NEC Article 555

- In areas subject to flooding, the electrical datum plane is 2' (600 mm) above the prevailing high-water mark determined by the AHJ.
- For floating structures that are installed to rise and fall in response to the water level without lateral movement, the electrical datum plane is 30" (750 mm) above the point at which the floating structure touches the water and a minimum of 12" (300 mm) above the deck level.

2.2.2 Location of Electrical Distribution Equipment and Enclosures

NEC Section 682.10 requires that all electrical equipment and enclosures installed in or near natural and man-made bodies of water be listed and approved for the location. Equipment or enclosures not identified for submersible use must not be located below the applicable electrical datum plane.

Per *NEC Section 682.11*, service equipment and the service disconnect that serve floating structures and submersible equipment must be located on land and meet one of the following conditions:

- Located at least 5' (1.5 m) from the shoreline and installed to allow a minimum of 12" (300 mm) between live parts and the electrical datum plane.
- Located no closer than the shoreline and with live parts installed at least 10' (3 m) above the electrical datum plane.

Electrical connections that are not identified for submersible use must be located at least 12" (300 mm) above the deck of a floating or fixed structure but never below the established electrical datum plane (per *NEC Section 682.12*).

2.2.3 GFCI Protection, Grounding, and Bonding

Outlets supplied by branch circuits not exceeding 150V to ground and 60A, single-phase, must be GFCI-protected per *NEC Section 682.15(A)*. The GFCI protection device must be located at least 12" (300 mm) above the established electrical datum plane.

Equipment grounding conductors must meet the requirements listed in *NEC Sections 682.31(A) through (E)* and summarized as follows:

- Metal boxes, metal cabinets, or other metal enclosures, metal frames of utilization equipment, and grounding terminals of grounding-type receptacles must be connected to an equipment grounding conductor in the same raceway, cable, or trench as circuit conductors.
- Equipment grounding conductors must be insulated copper conductors no smaller than No. 12 AWG.
- Feeders supplying a remote panelboard or other distribution equipment must include an insulated grounding conductor that connects from the service grounding terminal to a grounding terminal or busbar in the remote panelboard.
- Branch circuit equipment grounding conductors must terminate on the grounding bus in the remote panelboard or the grounding terminal in the main service panel.
- Cord-and-plug equipment must be double-insulated or grounded by means of an equipment grounding conductor in the cord and connected to a grounding-type attachment plug at the supply end.

Metal piping, tanks, metal parts in contact with the water, and noncurrent-carrying metal parts that could become energized must be bonded to the grounding terminal in the distribution equipment per *NEC Section 682.32*.

Know the Code

Electrical Equipment Transformers
NEC Section 682.10

Know the Code

Location of Electrical Distribution Equipment
NEC Section 682.11

Know the Code

Electrical Connections
NEC Section 682.12

Know the Code

Outlets
NEC Section 682.15(A)

Know the Code

Equipment Grounding Conductors
NEC Section 682.31

2.2.4 Equipotential Planes

An equipotential plane bonds together the grounding grids, structural steel, conductive equipment enclosures, and all other metal parts to reduce or eliminate any gradient (variable) voltage potential between system components, structures, enclosures, and even the water itself. Per *NEC Section 682.33(A)*, equipotential planes must be installed in areas adjacent to all outdoor service equipment with metal enclosures or disconnecting means that are used to supply or control equipment in or on the water and are accessible to personnel. The plane must encompass the immediate area around and directly below the equipment and must extend outward at least 36" (900 mm) in all directions from which a person would be able to stand and reach the equipment.

Know the Code

Equipotential Planes and Bonding of Equipotential Planes
NEC Section 682.33

Equipotential planes must be bonded to the electrical grounding system using an insulated, covered, or bare solid copper conductor no smaller than No. 8 AWG, per *NEC Section 682.33(C)*. Connections of the bonding conductor to the grounding system must be made by exothermic welding or using listed stainless steel, brass, copper, or copper alloy pressure connectors or clamps.

2.0.0 Section Review

1. What type of shore power receptacles may be used for 50A service?
   a. Only pin and sleeve
   b. Only locking and grounding
   c. Both pin and sleeve and locking and grounding
   d. Neither pin and sleeve nor locking and grounding

2. The equipotential planes around natural and man-made bodies of water must be bonded to the electrical grounding system using a conductor *no* smaller than No. _____.
   a. 4 AWG
   b. 6 AWG
   c. 8 AWG
   d. 10 AWG

3.0.0 Pools, Spas, Tubs, and Fountains

Performance Tasks

There are no Performance Tasks in this section.

Objective

Identify and select equipment, components, and wiring methods for pools, spas, tubs, and fountains.

a. Identify general wiring requirements for pools, spas, tubs, and fountains.
b. Identify and select equipment, components, and wiring methods for permanently installed pools.
c. Identify and select equipment, components, and wiring methods for storable pools.
d. Identify and select equipment, components, and wiring methods for spas, hot tubs, and therapeutic tubs.
e. Identify and select equipment, components, and wiring methods for fountains.

Know the Code

Swimming Pools, Fountains, and Similar Installations
NEC Article 680

NEC Article 680 applies to electrical wiring and equipment associated with the construction and installation of permanently installed swimming pools (*Figure 30*), storable pools, spas and hot tubs, fountains (*Figure 31*), therapeutic tubs and tanks, and hydromassage bathtubs. The sections that follow summarize the requirements for each type of pool and tub, beginning with some general requirements.

Figure 30 Permanently installed pool.
Source: iStock@piovesempre

Figure 31 Fountain.
Source: iStock@LipGhee

3.1.0 General Wiring Requirements

NEC Article 680 applies to pools, spas, tubs, and fountains.

3.1.1 Grounding Requirements

Because of the proximity to water, all electrical equipment in a pool area must be grounded. The following equipment and devices must be grounded per *NEC Section 680.7*:

- Underwater and through-wall luminaires, except low-voltage lighting listed for usage without a grounding conductor
- Electrical equipment located within 5' (1.5 m) of the inside wall of the body of water

- All associated water-circulating equipment
- Junction boxes
- Transformer and power supply enclosures
- Ground fault circuit interrupters
- Panelboards not associated with the service equipment but supplying electrical equipment associated with the body of water

Figure 32 shows a panel located within the equipment room of a permanently installed swimming pool.

Per the definition of a corrosive environment in *NEC Article 100*, areas where pool sanitation chemicals are stored, as well as areas with circulation pumps, automatic chlorinators, filters, open areas under pool decks, and similar locations are considered corrosive environments. All wiring in these areas must be listed and identified for use in these locations.

Know the Code

Definitions
NEC Article 100

Figure 32 Panel in equipment room of swimming pool.

3.1.2 Cord-and-Plug Connections

Flexible cords with a maximum length of 3' (900 mm) may be used to connect fixed or stationary equipment (except underwater luminaires) to their power supply for easy removal or disconnection for maintenance or repair (per *NEC Section 680.8*). The cord must contain a copper equipment grounding conductor no smaller than No. 12 AWG that terminates on the supply end to a grounding-type attachment plug and is connected to a fixed metal part of the equipment on the other end. All components of the removable equipment must be bonded together.

3.1.3 Clearances

Clearances between open overhead electrical conductors and the water's edge are set forth in *NEC Table 680.9(A)*. *Figure 33* shows overhead conductors in the voltage range of over 750V near a community swimming pool.

Know the Code

Overhead Conductor Clearances
NEC Table 680.9(A)

Figure 33 Overhead conductors near a community swimming pool.
Source: iStock@Serhiy Stakhnyk

NEC Table 680.9(A) lists overhead conductor clearances. The values in the table assume a maximum water level. The distances do not apply to communication, radio, and television coaxial cables. These cables must maintain a minimum height of 10' (3 m) above swimming and wading pools, diving boards and towers, or other observation platforms. However, the values in *NEC Table 680.9(A)* do apply to network-powered broadband communications system conductors operating at 0V to 750V to ground.

3.1.4 Electric Pool Heaters

Heater elements on electric pool water heaters must be subdivided into loads not exceeding 48A each and must be protected by overcurrent protective devices not greater than 60A. The ampacity of branch circuit conductors and the overcurrent device rating may not exceed 125% of the total nameplate load. Refer to *NEC Section 680.10(A)*.

3.1.5 Underground Wiring

Wiring may not be installed directly under a pool unless the wiring is needed to supply associated pool equipment, per *NEC Section 680.11(B)*. In these cases, the wiring must be installed in materials suitable for the conditions subject to that location, including rigid metal conduit, intermediate metal conduit, a nonmetallic raceway system, reinforced thermosetting resin conduit, or Type MC cable. Conduit installations must conform to the minimum cover requirements as outlined in *NEC Table 300.5(A)*.

Know the Code

Minimum Cover Requirements, 0 to 1000 Volts ac, 1500 Volts dc, Nominal, Burial in Millimeters (Inches)
NEC Table 300.5(A)

3.1.6 Disconnecting Means

A disconnecting means that simultaneously disconnects all ungrounded conductors must be provided for all utilization equipment other than lighting (per *NEC Section 680.13*). The disconnecting means must be installed in a readily accessible location at least 5' (1.5 m) horizontally from the inside wall of a pool, hot tub, spa, or fountain unless a barrier that requires a reach path of 5' (1.5 m) or more is permanently installed between the disconnect and pool's edge. *Figure 34* shows service panel for the pool, which houses the disconnecting means for all utilization equipment around the pool and in the adjacent equipment room. Note that the service equipment is greater than 5' (1.5 m) from the pool.

NOTE

The horizontal distance is the shortest path from the pool's edge to the disconnecting device.

Know the Code

Maintenance Disconnecting Means
NEC Section 680.13

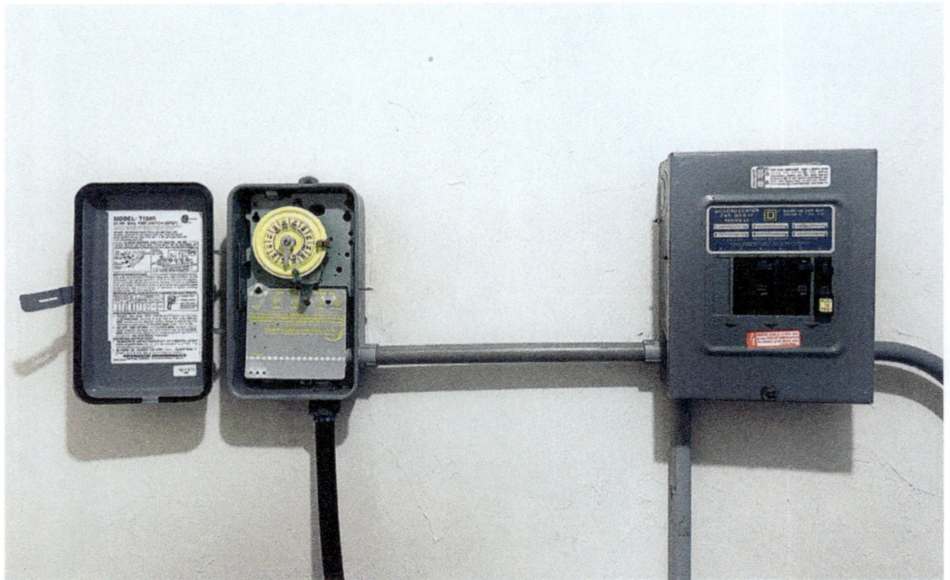

Figure 34 Service and disconnecting means for the pool equipment.

3.2.0 Permanently Installed Pools

Permanently installed pools must follow specific wiring and equipment requirements as specified in *NEC Article 680, Parts I and II*. These include special requirements for motors and auxiliary equipment, receptacles, lighting, junction boxes, feeders, and bonding.

3.2.1 Motors

When installed in corrosive environments, as defined in *NEC Article 100*, wiring methods must comply with *NEC Section 680.14(A)* or be installed in Type MC cable listed for that location. Where installed in noncorrosive environments, branch circuits must comply with the general requirements in *NEC Chapter 3*. All raceways or cables must contain an insulated copper equipment grounding conductor sized in compliance with *NEC Section 250.122*, but no smaller than No. 12 AWG per *NEC Section 680.7(A)*.

When flexibility is necessary due to motor vibration, *NEC Section 680.21(A)(1)* requires that the connection from the motor be made with liquid-tight flexible metal or liquid-tight flexible nonmetallic conduit (*Figure 35*). Cord-and-plug connections are also permitted as long as the cord is no longer than 3' (900 mm) and incorporates a copper equipment grounding conductor sized in accordance with *NEC Section 250.122* but not smaller than a No. 12 AWG. The cord must terminate in a grounding-type attachment plug.

Figure 35 Pool recirculation motor connected with liquid-tight flexible metal conduit.

Know the Code

Swimming Pools, Fountains, and Similar Installations
NEC Article 680

Know the Code

Definitions
NEC Article 100

Know the Code

Wiring Methods and Materials
NEC Chapter 3

Know the Code

Flexible Connections
NEC Section 680.21(A)(1)

Know the Code

Size of Equipment Grounding Conductors
NEC Section 250.122

3.2.2 Receptacle and Area Lighting

General-purpose receptacles must be located at least 6' (1.83 m) from the inside walls of a pool per *NEC Section 680.22(A)(1)*. Receptacles that are used to provide power to pump motors or other loads must be a grounding-type receptacle having GFCI protection per *NEC Section 680.22(A)(2)*. These types of receptacles must also be located at least 6' (1.83 m) from the wall of the pool.

Every pool installed at a dwelling unit must be provided with at least one 125V, 15A or 20A receptacle supplied by a general-purpose branch circuit. The receptacle must be located within 20' (6 m) of the pool's inside wall but no less than 6' (1.83 m) and at a height of no more than 6'-6" (2 m) above the grade or deck level, per *NEC Section 680.22(A)(1)*. These receptacles must be GFCI-protected. All other receptacles rated 125V through 250V 60A or less and located within 20' (6 m) of the inside walls of a pool must also have GFCI protection for personnel, per *NEC Section 680.22(A)(4)*.

Area lighting includes all lighting around or above pool areas except those luminaires installed in or under water. *Figure 36* is an example of pole-mounted area lighting, while *Figure 37* shows area lighting.

Know the Code

Lighting, Receptacles, and Equipment
NEC Section 680.22

Figure 36 Pole-mounted area lighting around a pool.
Source: iStock@ggrexy

Figure 37 Area lighting around a pool.
Source: iStock@ben-bryant

Residential Pools

In single-family dwelling units, pool motors located within the residence or in an accessory building associated with the residence may be connected using any of the approved wiring methods in *NEC Chapter 3*. If the motor branch circuit conductors are run in a cable assembly, the equipment grounding conductor may be uninsulated but must be contained within the outer insulation of the cable.

As stated in *NEC Section 680.22(B)*, the installation of new luminaires, lighting outlets, or paddle fans above outdoor pools or within 5' (1.5 m) horizontally from the inside walls of the pool must maintain a clearance of no less than 12' (3.7 m) above maximum water level of the pool. For new indoor installations, a reduced minimum clearance of 7'-6" (2.3 m) is permitted if the branch circuit has ground fault protection and the luminaires are totally enclosed or, in the case of fans, if the fan is identified for use beneath ceilings such as on porches or patios.

Existing luminaires or lighting outlets (installed before the pool was built) that are located less than 5' (1.5 m) from the inside edge of the pool must also be at least 5' (1.5 m) above the maximum water level, rigidly attached to the existing structure, and GFCI-protected.

Luminaires, lighting outlets, and ceiling fans that are installed 5' to 10' (1.5 m to 3 m) from the inside edge of a pool must be GFCI-protected, unless they are installed 5' (1.5 m) or more above the maximum water level and rigidly attached to the structure adjacent to or enclosing the pool. Luminaires within 16' (4.9 m) of the pool using cord-and-plug connections must comply with *NEC Section 680.22(B)(5)*. An exception is made for certain listed low-voltage luminaires in *NEC Section 680.22(B)(6)*.

Switches must be located at least 5' (1.5 m) from the pool's edge unless separated from the pool by a solid fence, wall, or other permanent barrier, unless the switch is listed for use within 5' (1.5 m) of a pool, per *NEC Section 680.22(C)*. *Figure 38* shows an emergency shutoff switch (red switch) for an attached spa. The switch on the right is an automatic timer switch for the spa that can be set for various time periods, with an automatic shutoff after the time expires. These switches must be readily accessible.

Outlets used for remote control operations, signaling, fire alarm, or communication circuits must be located a minimum of 10' (3 m) from the inside edge of the pool per *NEC Section 680.22(D)*.

Figure 38 Spa emergency shutoff switch and adjacent timer.

3.2.3 Underwater Luminaires

NEC Section 680.23(A)(4) states that the maximum voltage supplying underwater luminaires is limited to 150V between circuit conductors. Underwater luminaires may be directly supplied by a branch circuit or by way of a transformer or power supply and must be listed for swimming pool and spa use, with an ungrounded secondary and a grounded metal barrier between the primary and secondary windings.

To reduce or prevent shock during relamping, *NEC Section 680.23(A)(3)* requires any underwater luminaire that operates at more than the low-voltage contact limit to have a GFCI installed in the branch circuit supplying the luminaire. *Figure 39* shows the GFCI circuit breaker in the panel serving the pool lighting and equipment. The ground fault circuit interrupter must be installed so that any shock hazard is eliminated should contact occur between a person and any ungrounded part of the branch circuit or the luminaire to ground. Underwater luminaires supplied by a transformer and operated at less than the low-voltage contact limit do not require ground fault protection.

Wall-mounted underwater luminaires must be installed so that the top of the lens is at least 18" (450 mm) below the water level. However, if specifically listed for lesser depths, it can be mounted less than 18" below but never less than 4" (100 mm) below the normal water level. If an underwater luminaire is installed at the bottom of the pool facing upward, it must either have the lens guarded to prevent contact with people or be listed for use without a guard. Underwater luminaires that depend on water for cooling must be inherently protected against overheating when not submerged.

Wet-Niche Luminaires

NEC Section 680.23(B) governs wet-niche luminaires. Wet-niche luminaires are becoming less common as dry-niche, no-niche, and through-wall lighting assemblies are gaining popularity. A wet-niche luminaire in a pool or fountain is mounted in a forming shell that is completely surrounded by water, with the forming shell providing a conduit connection. All metal parts of the luminaire and forming shell that come in contact with the water must be made of brass or other approved corrosion-resistant metal.

Forming shells designed with nonmetallic conduit connections (other than low-voltage systems not requiring grounding) must be equipped with a grounding lug that will accept a No. 8 AWG copper conductor. Only rigid metal conduit, intermediate metal conduit, liquid-tight flexible nonmetallic conduit, or rigid nonmetallic conduit may connect to a wet-niche forming shell and must run directly from the shell to a junction box. *Figure 40* shows a nonmetallic forming shell designed for use with a low-voltage LED luminaire.

Conduit to shells may be metal or nonmetallic conduit that is approved for swimming pool installations. Metal conduit must be constructed of brass or other approved corrosion-resistant metal. Nonmetallic conduit must contain a No. 8 AWG insulated solid or stranded copper conductor to function as a bonding jumper between metal parts, unless a low-voltage luminaire not requiring grounding is installed. The bonding jumper must be terminated in the shell, junction box, transformer enclosure, or GFCI enclosure (if installed). After the grounding termination is made in the forming shell, it must be covered with a listed **potting compound** to protect it from deterioration.

Other than listed low-voltage lighting systems not requiring grounding, all wet-niche luminaires that are supplied by a flexible cord or cable must contain an insulated copper equipment grounding conductor no smaller than No. 16 AWG that grounds all exposed noncurrent-carrying metal parts of the luminaire and shell. The grounding conductor must be terminated on a grounding terminal within the supply junction box or transformer enclosure and shell. The ends of the flexible cord jacket and the termination within the luminaire must be sealed with an approved potting compound to prevent water from entering the cable.

Know the Code

Underwater Luminaires
NEC Section 680.23

Figure 39 GFCI circuit breaker supplying the underwater luminaire.

Potting compound: An approved and listed insulating compound, such as epoxy, which is mixed and installed in and around electrical connections to encapsulate and seal the connections to prevent the entry of water or moisture.

Figure 40 Nonmetallic forming shell.
Source: iStock@angsabiru

Positive locking device: A screw, clip, or other mechanical locking device that requires a tool or key to lock or unlock it.

The wet-niche luminaire must be secured and bonded to the forming shell by a **positive locking device** (typically an Allen screw) that provides a low-resistance path, requiring a wrench or other tool to remove the luminaire from the forming shell. Wet-niche luminaires must be supplied with sufficient cable or cord length to allow the luminaire to be removed and placed on the deck or other dry location for servicing, without requiring the servicing technician to enter the water.

Dry-niche Luminaires

Per *NEC Section 680.23(C)*, unless listed as a low-voltage luminaire not requiring grounding, dry-niche luminaires require means for grounding at each conduit entry. Dry-niche luminaries must provide water drainage. A junction box is not required, but if used, follow *NEC Section 680.24(A)(2)* for spacing and flush deck box requirements.

Know the Code

Dry-Niche Luminaires
NEC Section 680.23(C)

No-niche Luminaires

Per *NEC Section 680.23(D)*, follow installation and construction requirements specified in *NEC Section 680.23(B)* and *NEC Section 680.23(B)(3)*. Connect the forming shell to a mounting bracket.

Know the Code

No-Niche Luminaires
NEC Section 680.23(D)

Through-Wall Lighting Assemblies

Per *NEC Section 680.23(E)*, use a threaded entry hub or a nonmetallic hub to accommodate termination of the supply conduit. Follow installation and construction requirements in *NEC Sections 680.23 and 680.23(B)(3)* Connect the forming shell to a conduit termination point.

Know the Code

Through-Wall Lighting Assembly
NEC Section 680.23(E)

Branch Circuit Wiring

Branch circuits supplying enclosures and junction boxes connected to wet-niche and no-niche luminaires and branch circuits supplying field-wiring compartments of dry-niche luminaires in corrosive environments, as defined in *NEC Article 100*, must comply with requirements in *NEC Section 680.14* or must be liquid-tight flexible nonmetallic conduit. Electrical metallic tubing (EMT) may be used if installed on or in a building. Electrical nonmetallic tubing, MC, or AC cable may be used only if installed inside a building.

Know the Code

Corrosive Environments
NEC Section 680.14

Equipment Grounding

Other than listed low-voltage luminaires not requiring grounding, all through-wall lighting assemblies, wet-niche, dry-niche, and no-niche luminaires must all be connected to an insulated copper equipment grounding conductor containing no joints or splices, sized in accordance with *NEC Table 250.122*, and must be no smaller than No. 12 AWG per *NEC Section 680.23(F)(2)*. Two exceptions to an unbroken equipment grounding conductor are as follows:

- Where more than one underwater luminaire is supplied by the same branch circuit, the equipment grounding conductor may be broken at the interconnection between the grounding terminals of junction boxes, transformer enclosures or other supply circuit enclosures to wet-niche luminaires, or between the field-wiring compartments of dry-niche luminaires.
- Underwater luminaires supplied from a transformer, GFCI, clock-operated switch, or manual snap switch installed between the panelboard and a junction box directly connected by conduit to the luminaire may have the circuit equipment grounding conductor terminated on the enclosure holding the transformer, GFCI, clock-operated switch, or manual switch.

Know the Code

Minimum Size Equipment Grounding Conductors for Grounding Raceway and Equipment
NEC Table 250.122

Know the Code

Branch-Circuit Wiring
NEC Section 680.23(F)

Conductors

Per *NEC Section 680.23(F)(3)*, load-side conductors of GFCIs or transformers supplying underwater luminaires operating at no more than the low-voltage contact limit must not be installed in raceways, boxes, or enclosures containing other conductors unless at least one of the following conditions are met:

- The other conductors are GFCI-protected.
- The other conductors are grounding and bonding conductors.
- The other conductors supply a feed-through GFCI.
- A GFCI may be installed in a panelboard containing other circuits protected by non-GFCI devices.

Matching Luminaire and Niche

Underwater luminaires and forming shells must be listed and matched. To ensure proper matching, listed luminaires are marked on the exterior of the luminaire to identify the compatible forming shell in which the luminaire may be installed. Likewise, forming shells are marked on the interior surfaces to identify the luminaires that may be installed inside the shell. This marking system is part of UL 676, *Standard for Underwater Luminaires and Submersible Junction Boxes*.

Pool Electrocutions

The Consumer Product Safety Commission reported 14 electrocutions in addition to other electrical shock incidents involving circuits around swimming pools in the 10-year period between 2004 and 2014. Educating consumers about the hazards of electricity in pool areas and adhering to the electrical standards of the *NEC*® appears to be helping though—a similar number of electrocutions had been reported in the 6-year period between 1997 and 2003, so the average rate of incidence per year has dropped.

3.2.4 Transformer or GFCI Junction Boxes and Enclosures

Junction boxes (*Figure 41*) that are used as terminal points for conduit running to wet-niche luminaire niches or the mounting brackets of no-niche luminaires must comply with the following construction and installation requirements of *NEC Sections 680.24(A)(1) and (2)*:

- The junction box must be listed as a swimming pool junction box.
- It must be equipped with threaded hubs or a nonmetallic hub.
- The box must be made of copper, brass, plastic, or other approved corrosion-resistant material.
- The box must provide electrical continuity between all metal conduit connections and the grounding terminals by means of copper, brass, or other approved corrosion-resistant metal that is integrated into the box construction.
- If the luminaire operates at more than the low-voltage contact limit, the junction box must be mounted at least 4" (100 mm) above ground (measured from the bottom of the box) or at least 8" (200 mm) above the maximum water level of the pool, whichever provides the greater elevation, and at least 4' (1.2 m) from the inside wall of the pool unless separated by a fence or other permanent barrier.
- If the luminaire operates at or below the low-voltage contact limit, the junction box may be mounted as a flush deck box if the box is filled with an approved potting compound to prevent the entry of moisture and the flush box is located at least 4' (1.2 m) from the inside wall of the pool.

Enclosures used to house transformers, GFCIs, or similar devices that directly connect by conduit to a niche or no-niche luminaire mounting bracket must comply with the construction and installation requirements of *NEC Sections 680.24(B)(1) and (2)*. These requirements are the same as for wet-niche luminaires, except the use of a flush deck box is not permitted. Also, *NEC Section 680.24(B)(1)* requires the use of a duct seal or other approved seal at the conduit connection to prevent air circulation between the conduit and enclosure.

Know the Code

Junction Boxes and Electrical Enclosures for Transformers or Ground-Fault Circuit Interrupters
NEC Section 680.24

Figure 41 Junction box for a wet-niche luminaire.
Source: John Lupacchino, Gaylor Electric Inc

Regardless of type, every enclosure must meet the following requirements:

- Enclosures must be protected from physical damage, per *NEC Section 680.24(C)*.
- Enclosures must be provided with at least one grounding terminal more than the number of conduit connections provided by the enclosure, per *NEC Section 680.24(D)*.
- Terminations of flexible cords into enclosures must be provided with a strain relief to protect the cord, per *NEC Section 680.24(E)*.
- Grounding terminals of enclosures must be connected to the panelboard equipment grounding terminal, per *NEC Section 680.24(F)*.

3.2.5 Feeders

Feeders that supply swimming pool branch circuit panelboards, feeders on the load side of the service equipment associated with pools, or the source of a separately derived system supplying pools must follow specific wiring methods and grounding rules. Some of these requirements are as follows:

- Where feeders are installed in corrosive environments, as defined in *NEC Article 100*, the wiring methods of that portion must be as required in *NEC Section 680.14* or must be liquid-tight flexible nonmetallic conduit.
- Aluminum conduit may not be installed in the pool area where it is exposed to corrosion. See *NEC Section 680.14(A)*.
- The grounding conductor must be sized according to *NEC Section 250.122* but never smaller than No. 12 AWG.

Know the Code

Definitions
NEC Article 100

Know the Code

Corrosive Environments
NEC Section 680.14

3.2.6 Equipotential Bonding

Equipotential bonding in pool or fountain systems can be described as the interconnection of all exposed and buried, noncurrent-carrying conductive parts and surfaces (not just metal), with an approved grounded bonding conductor to reduce any **voltage gradients** in the pool or fountain area.

Per *NEC Section 680.26(B)*, the bonding conductor used must be solid copper, insulated or bare, and no smaller than No. 8 AWG. Interconnections between boxes and enclosures made with noncorrosive rigid metal conduit such as brass may also be considered as bonded. However, bonding made with a solid No. 8 AWG copper is not required to be extended to remote panelboards, electrodes, or service equipment. All bonded connections must comply with *NEC Section 250.8*.

Voltage gradients: Fluctuating voltage potentials that can exist between two surfaces or components and may be caused by improper or insufficient bonding or grounding.

The following equipment, surfaces, and pool components must be included in the equipotential bonding system and comply with all rules of *NEC Articles 680 and 250*:

- All conductive pool shells including concrete or concrete block shells (not vinyl liners and fiberglass pools) must be bonded. Pool shells constructed using structural reinforcing steel that is not encapsulated in a nonconductive compound must be bonded together using steel tie wires per *NEC Section 680.26(B)(1)(a)*. Pool shells constructed with encapsulated structural reinforcing steel must have a copper conductive grid installed in accordance with *NEC Section 680.26(B)(1)(b)*.
- Pool perimeter surfaces including any paved, unpaved, poured concrete or other conductive surfaces that extend outward to a maximum of 3' (900 mm) when measured horizontally from the inside walls of the pool require bonding per *NEC Section 680.26(B)(2)*. Refer to *Figure 42*.

Know the Code

Equipotential Bonding
NEC Section 680.26

Know the Code

Connection of Grounding and Bonding Equipment
NEC Section 250.8

- All metal components, metal fittings, and underwater lighting niches and mounting brackets must be included in the equipotential bonding system. Low-voltage luminaires in nonmetallic niches are, however, excepted. See *NEC Sections 680.26(B)(3) through (5)*.
- Any metal part associated with the pool water-circulating system or pool covers must be bonded, including pumps and motors, per *NEC Section 680.26(B)(6)*.
- Follow the specific manufacturer's recommendations regarding grounding and bonding of pool water heaters. *Figure 43* shows the enclosure of a pool heater bonded to the equipotential bonding system.
- Metal raceways, metal-sheathed cables, metal piping, and any fixed metal parts that are within 5' (1.5 m) horizontally from the inside walls of the pool, or 12' (3.7 m) vertically from the maximum water level, tower, stand, platform, or diving structure, must also be bonded unless separated by permanent barrier per *NEC Section 680.26(B)(7)*.
- Per *NEC Section 680.26(C)*, the pool water itself must be bonded using a corrosion-resistant conductive surface with a minimum area of 9 in^2 (5,800 mm^2) contacting the pool water.

NOTE

Even though double-insulated water pump motors are not required to be bonded, a solid No. 8 AWG copper bonding conductor of sufficient length must be provided in the area of the water pump motor in case the motor is replaced with a motor that is not double insulated. See ***NEC Section 680.26(B)(6)(a)***.

Figure 42 Pool perimeter conductive surfaces.
Source: iStock@ucpage

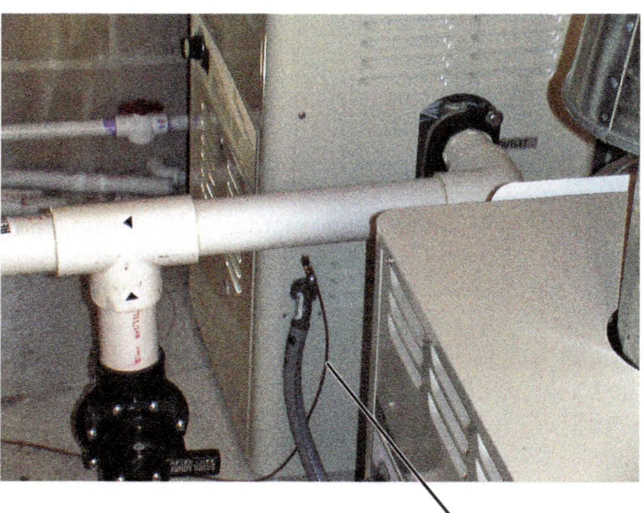

Figure 43 Pool heater bonded to the equipotential bonding system.

3.2.7 Specialized Pool Equipment

Accessory equipment not directly related to the lighting and operation of the pool itself falls into the category of specialized pool equipment. Examples of specialized pool equipment include underwater audio equipment, electrically operated pool covers, and deck area heating.

Underwater Audio Equipment

Underwater speakers must be mounted in an approved metal forming shell that is recessed in the wall or floor of the pool and covered with a metal screen that is bonded to the forming shell, per *NEC Section 680.27(A)(1)*. The screen must be held in place by a positive locking device that requires a tool to open or remove the screen. Both the forming shell and screen must be constructed of brass or other approved corrosion-resistant metal per *NEC Section 680.27(A)(3)*. The forming shell must also be equipped with a bonding terminal that will accommodate a No. 8 AWG copper conductor.

Know the Code

Specialized Pool Equipment
NEC Section 680.27

Electrically Operated Pool Covers

All electrical equipment associated with the operation of an electric pool cover must be located at least 5' (1.5 m) from the inside wall of the pool unless a permanent barrier is in place between the pool and equipment. See *NEC Section 680.27(B)(1)*. Motors that are installed below grade level must be totally enclosed, and the device controlling the pool cover motor must be located so that the operator has a full view of the pool during cover operation. Both the motor and controller must be connected to a GFCI-protected circuit, per *NEC Section 680.27(B)(2)*.

Deck Area Heating

Electrically operated unit heaters or permanently wired radiant heaters installed within 20' (6 m) from the inside wall of a pool must be rigidly mounted in place and guarded to prevent contact with the heating elements, per *NEC Section 680.27(C)(1)*. No type of heater may be installed over the pool or within 5' (1.5 m) from the pool's edge. Permanently wired radiant heaters must be installed at least 12' (3.7 m) above the pool decking per *NEC Section 680.27(C)(2)*.

WARNING!

Electrical heating cables that are designed to be embedded in surfaces to produce heat transfer into the decking surface are not permitted in swimming pool decks.

Accessories Can Complete the Bonding Requirement

The bonding requirement of ***NEC Section 680.26(C)*** can be fulfilled by any of the other parts that are in direct contact with the water and already required to be bonded in other sections of ***NEC Article 680***, such as shells, conduit, ladders, and other parts, if the total water contact area of the bonded metal parts measures a minimum of 9 in^2 (5,800 mm^2).

Location Measurements

Location measurements assume the shortest distance between the receptacle and the inside wall of the pool without encountering walls, hinged doorways, or any other permanent barrier.

3.3.0 Storable Pools

Know the Code

Pumps
NEC Section 680.31

Know the Code

Ground-Fault Circuit-Interrupter (GFCI) and Special Purpose Ground-Fault Circuit-Interrupter (SPGFCI) Protection
NEC Section 680.32

Know the Code

Luminaires
NEC Section 680.33

Cord-connected storable pool filter pumps must be double-insulated and have any internal, nonaccessible, noncurrent-carrying metal parts grounded using an equipment grounding conductor that is part of the supply cord and terminated in a grounding-type attachment plug per *NEC Section 680.31*. The attachment plug must be designed with integral GFCI protection, or the power supply cord must incorporate GFCI protection within 12" (300 mm) of the attachment plug. *Figure 44* shows a type of storable pool.

The pool filter pump, while important, is not the only equipment requiring GFCI protection. *NEC Section 680.32* requires that all electrical equipment associated with storable pools and all 125V through 250V, 60A or less receptacles installed within 20' (6 m) of the inside walls of the pool have GFCI or SPGFCI unless a permanent barrier is installed between the equipment or receptacle and the pool. In no case may a receptacle be installed within 6' (1.83 m) of the inside walls of the pool unless a permanent barrier is installed, per *NEC Section 680.34*.

Underwater luminaires must be installed in or on the wall of a storable pool, spa, or hot tub. Refer to *NEC Section 680.33*. The lens, luminaire body, and transformer enclosure (if used) must be constructed of a polymeric impact-resistant material with no exposed metal parts. If the luminaire operates within the low-voltage contact limit or less, it must be a listed cord-and-plug assembly using a transformer listed for the application, with a primary voltage rating not to exceed 150V. Underwater luminaires operating at voltages greater than the low-voltage contact limit but less than 150V require GFCI protection.

Figure 44 Storable pool.
Source: iStock@Cleardesign1

3.4.0 Spas, Hot Tubs, and Therapeutic Pools and Tubs

Know the Code

Emergency Switch for Spas and Hot Tubs
NEC Section 680.41(A)

Spas and hot tubs may be installed indoors or outdoors. Regardless of their location, all spas and hot tub electrical installations, except in single-family dwellings, must include a clearly labeled emergency shutoff or control switch that controls power to the recirculation and/or jet system motor. This emergency shutoff must be located at a readily accessible point for the user but no less than 5' (1.5 m) away from the spa or hot tub per *NEC Section 680.41(A)*.

3.4.1 Outdoor Installations

Spas and hot tubs installed outdoors must follow the same rules as permanently installed pools installed outdoors, in addition to the requirements listed in *NEC Section 680.42* and summarized as follows:

- Packaged spas or hot tubs that are listed for outdoor installations or self-contained spas or hot tubs equipped with a factory-installed control panel or panelboard may be connected using a GFCI-protected cord and plug with a maximum cord length of 15' (4.6 m).
- Metal-to-metal bonding of common frame or base components is permitted.
- Metal parts used to secure wooden staves are not required to be bonded.
- If a self-contained or packaged outdoor spa / hot tub is supplied by the interior wiring of a single-family dwelling or associated building, the supply wiring method must comply with *NEC Chapter 3* and must include a copper equipment grounding conductor (No. 12 AWG or larger) that is insulated or enclosed within the outer sheath of the wiring method.

Know the Code

Outdoor Installations
NEC Section 680.42

Know the Code

Wiring Methods and Materials
NEC Chapter 3

3.4.2 Indoor Installations

Spas and hot tubs installed indoors must also follow the same rules for permanently installed pools and comply with the wiring methods of *NEC Chapter 3*. One exception is that indoor packaged spas or hot tubs rated 20A or less may be connected by cord and plug to allow for easy removal or disconnection during maintenance or repair. In addition, the rules of *NEC Section 680.43*, summarized below, also apply:

- At least one 125V, 15A, or 20A receptacle must be provided and must be located no less than 6' and no more than 10' (between 1.83 m and 3 m) from the inside wall of the unit. No receptacle may be located closer than 6' (1.83 m) from the inside walls of the spa or hot tub.
- Any 125V through 250V, 60A or less receptacle located within 10' (3 m) of the inside walls of an indoor spa or hot tub must be GFCI- or SPGFCI-protected.

Know the Code

Indoor Installation
NEC Section 680.43

Wall switches must be installed at least 5' (1.5 m) from the inside walls of the spa or hot tub, per *NEC Section 680.43(C)*. Luminaires, lighting outlets, and ceiling fans installed over indoor spas or hot tubs must be a minimum of 12' (3.7 m) above the maximum water level in installations without GFCI protection, per *NEC Section 680.43(B)(1)(a)*. For installations with GFCI protection, the minimum clearance is 7'-6" (2.3 m) as specified in *NEC Section 680.43(B)(1)(b)*.

The following components associated with indoor spas and hot tubs must be bonded together per *NEC Section 680.43(D)*:

- All metal fittings within or attached to the spa or hot tub, including handrails (*Figure 45*)
- Noncurrent-carrying metal parts of electrical equipment, including circulating pump motors unless part of a listed self-contained spa or hot tub
- Any metal raceway, piping, or metal surface within 5' (1.5 m) of the inside walls of the spa or hot tub, unless separated by a permanent barrier
- Any electrical device or control not associated with the spa or hot tub, but located within 5' (1.5 m) of it

Figure 45 Spa handrails must be bonded.
Source: iStock@alexeys

Bonding may be accomplished by the interconnection of threaded metal pipe and fittings, metal-to-metal mounting on a common frame or base, or by an insulated, covered, or bare No. 8 AWG or larger solid copper bonding jumper. See *NEC Section 680.43(E)*. In addition to bonding, any electrical equipment that is located within 5' (1.5 m) of the inside wall of the spa or hot tub, or any electrical equipment associated with the circulating system, must also be grounded per *NEC Section 680.43(F)*. Receptacles that supply self-contained, packaged, or field-assembled spas and hot tubs must be GFCI-protected except as noted in *NEC Section 680.44*.

Know the Code

Ground-Fault Circuit-Interrupter (GFCI) and Special Purpose Ground-Fault Circuit-Interrupter (SPGFCI) Protection
NEC Section 680.44

3.4.3 Therapeutic Pools and Tubs

NEC Article 680, Part VI covers pools and tubs used for therapeutic purposes in health care facilities, gymnasiums, athletic training rooms, and similar areas. Permanently installed therapeutic pools follow the same *NEC*® requirements as permanently installed swimming pools and must also comply with *NEC Article 680, Parts I and VI*.

Know the Code

Swimming Pools, Fountains, and Similar Installations
NEC Article 680

Electrical outlets that supply self-contained, packaged, or field-assembled therapeutic tubs or hydrotherapeutic tanks must be GFCI-protected unless the listed unit includes integral GCFI protection for all electrical parts within the unit or operates from a three-phase system greater than 250V or with a heater load of more than 50A, per *NEC Sections 680.62(A)(1) and (2)*. Bonding requirements for therapeutic tubs or hydrotherapeutic tanks are listed in *NEC Section 680.62(B)* and summarized as follows:

Know the Code

Therapeutic Tubs (Hydrotherapeutic Tanks)
NEC Section 680.62

- All metal fittings within or attached to the tub or tank must be bonded together.
- All noncurrent-carrying metal parts of the water circulation system (including pump motors) must be bonded.
- Any metal-sheathed cables, raceways, metal piping, and metal surfaces within 5' (1.5 m) of the inside walls of the tub or tank must be bonded unless separated by a permanent barrier.
- Any electrical device or control that is not associated with the operation of the tub or tank but is within 5' (1.5 m) of the tub or tank must be bonded.

This bonding requirement may be satisfied by the interconnection of threaded metal pipe and fittings, metal-to-metal mounting on a common frame, connections made using approved metal clamps, or by the installation of an insulated, covered, or bare solid copper bonding jumper no smaller than No. 8 AWG.

All electrical equipment located within 5' (1.5 m) of the inside wall of the tub or tank and all electrical equipment associated with the tub or tank's water circulation system must be grounded to the equipment grounding conductor of the supply circuit as specified in *NEC Section 680.62(D)*. In addition, *NEC Section 680.62(E)* requires that any receptacle located within 6' (1.83 m) of a therapeutic tub or tank be GFCI-protected, and all luminaires installed in the area of therapeutic tubs or tanks must be totally enclosed, per *NEC Section 680.62(F)*.

3.4.4 Hydromassage Bathtubs

Hydromassage bathtubs, also known as *whirlpool tubs*, are commonly installed in the master bathrooms of new residential construction and are often added when older bathrooms are renovated. A hydromassage bathtub is a permanently installed bathtub equipped with a recirculation pump, piping system, and jets. By design, the tub can accept, circulate, and discharge water in each usage. Hydromassage bathtubs must be installed in accordance with *NEC Article 680, Part VII*.

NEC Section 680.71 requires that hydromassage tubs be supplied by an individual branch circuit. This can be an issue when installing these tubs in retrofit installations, especially on the upper floors. In addition, a readily accessible GFCI must be provided between the supply and the tub, and all 125V receptacles located within 6' (1.83 m) of the inside wall of the tub must be GFCI-protected. The tub electrical equipment must be accessible without damaging the building structure or finish per *NEC Section 680.73*, which is often accomplished using a removable panel either on the tub itself or through an adjacent wall. Where the hydromassage tub is cord-and-plug connected with the supply receptacle accessible only through a service access opening, the receptacle must be installed so that its face is within direct view and not more than 12" (300 mm) from the opening. Both metal piping systems and grounded metal parts in contact with the water must be effectively bonded using an insulated, covered, or bare solid copper bonding jumper no smaller than No. 8 AWG (*NEC Section 680.74*). The bonding jumper must be connected to a circulating pump motor terminal intended for this purpose. Double-insulated circulating pump motors do not require bonding. The bonding jumper is not required to be extended or attached to remote panelboards, service equipment, or any electrode.

Hydromassage Bathtubs

When installing a hydromassage bathtub in an installation where the final finish will be a tiled surround, make sure the tub or surround design provides for permanent access to the electrical equipment.

Know the Code

Protection
NEC Section 680.71

Know the Code

Accessibility
NEC Section 680.73

Know the Code

Bonding
NEC Section 680.74

3.5.0 Fountains

Fountains have become increasingly popular in residential and commercial landscapes. Permanently installed fountains (*Figure 46*), ornamental pools, display pools, and reflection pools must comply with *NEC Article 680, Parts I and V*. In addition, fountains that use common water from a swimming pool (*Figure 47*) must also comply with *NEC Article 680, Part II*.

NOTE

Self-contained portable fountains and water drinking fountains are not covered by *NEC Article 680*.

Know the Code

Swimming Pools, Fountains, and Similar Installations
NEC Article 680

Figure 46 Permanently installed fountain.
Source: iStock@possum1961

Figure 47 Fountain using pool water.
Source: iStock@CynthiaAnnF

3.5.1 Luminaires, Submersible Pumps, and Equipment

Luminaires, submersible pumps, and other submersible equipment installed in fountains must have GFCI protection unless they operate at the low-voltage contact limit or less and are supplied by a listed transformer intended for pool and fountain applications. See *NEC Section 680.51(A)*.

Luminaires may not operate at voltages over 150V between conductors, and submersible equipment may not operate at voltages over 300V between conductors. See *NEC Section 680.51(B)*. Luminaires must also be installed so that the top of the luminaire is below the normal water level of the fountain unless the luminaire is listed for out-of-water operation. Luminaires installed with the lens facing upward must have the lens guarded against contact by people or be listed for use without a guard per *NEC Section 680.51(C)*.

Know the Code

Luminaires, Submersible Pumps, and Other Submersible Equipment
NEC Section 680.51

NEC Section 680.51(F) requires that luminaires and other submersible equipment be installed to allow easy removal from the fountain for relamping or other maintenance without having to reduce the water level. Luminaires and other submersible equipment may not be permanently embedded into the fountain's structure.

Electrical submersible equipment that must remain submersed in water for proper operation and safety must be equipped with a low-water shutoff device per *NEC Section 680.51(D)*. Submersible equipment must also be equipped with threaded conduit entries or a factory- or field-installed flexible cord no longer than 10' (3 m), per *NEC Section 680.51(E)*. If the cord extends beyond the perimeter of the fountain, the cord must be enclosed in an approved wiring enclosure. Any metal parts in contact with the water must be constructed of brass or other corrosion-resistant material.

3.5.2 Junction Boxes and Other Enclosures

Junction boxes and other enclosures associated with fountains must comply with *NEC Section 680.24*, which covers junction boxes and enclosures in permanently installed pools. In addition, underwater junction boxes and enclosures installed in fountains must also comply with the requirements listed in *NEC Section 680.52(B)*, summarized as follows:

- Designed with threaded conduit entries or compression-type sealing (grommet) fittings for cord entry
- Listed for submersible use and constructed of copper, brass, or other approved corrosion-resistant material
- Filled with a listed potting compound to prevent water entry
- Firmly supported and bonded
- Supported by conduit only if the conduit is copper, brass, stainless steel, or other approved metal conduit
- If supplied by nonmetallic conduit, provided with additional support using approved corrosion-resistant metal support devices or fasteners

Know the Code

Junction Boxes and Electrical Enclosures for Transformers or Ground-Fault Circuit Interrupters
NEC Section 680.24

Know the Code

Underwater Junction Boxes and Other Underwater Enclosures
NEC Section 680.52(B)

3.5.3 Bonding and Grounding

Any metal piping associated with a fountain must be bonded to the branch circuit equipment grounding conductor that supplies the fountain, per *NEC Section 680.54(B)*. Other than low-voltage luminaires not requiring grounding, all electrical equipment located within 5' (1.5 m) of the inside wall, any electrical equipment associated with the recirculation system, and any panelboards that are not part of the service equipment but supply electrical equipment associated with the fountain must be grounded per *NEC Section 680.54(A)*.

NEC Section 680.55(B) requires that any electrical equipment associated with a fountain that is supplied by a flexible cord have all its exposed noncurrent-carrying metal parts grounded using an insulated copper equipment grounding conductor that is part of the flexible cord. The other end of the equipment grounding conductor must be terminated to an equipment grounding terminal in the supply junction box or other supply enclosure. Any 60A or less, 125V through 250V receptacle installed within 20' (6 m) of a fountain must be GFCI-protected per *NEC Section 680.58*.

Know the Code

Grounding and Bonding
NEC Section 680.54

Know the Code

Supplied by a Flexible Cord
NEC Section 680.55(B)

3.5.4 Cord-and-Plug Equipment

NEC Section 680.56(A) requires that any electrical equipment associated with a fountain and supplied by a cord and plug be GFCI-protected. In addition, the flexible cord must be rated for extra-hard usage and listed for wet usage per *NEC Section 680.56(B)*. Ends and terminations of the flexible cord and the grounding connection within the equipment must be covered with or encapsulated in a suitable potting compound to prevent the entry of water into the cable or deterioration of the terminations, per *NEC Section 680.56(C)*.

Know the Code

Cord-and-Plug-Connected Equipment
NEC Section 680.56

3.5.5 Signs Placed in Fountains

NEC Section 680.57(C)(1) requires that any fixed or stationary electric sign installed within a fountain be at least 5' (1.5 m) from the outside edge of the fountain. This places the sign out of reach of passersby or those sitting on the fountain edge. Fixed signs must also be equipped with a local disconnecting means in accordance with *NEC Sections 600.6 and 680.13* and must be grounded and bonded in accordance with *NEC Section 600.7.* Portable signs may not be installed in fountains or within 5' (1.5 m) from the inside walls of the fountain, per *NEC Section 680.57(C)(2).*

Know the Code

Electric Signs and Outline Lighting
NEC Article 600

Cord and Cable Types

NEC Table 400.4 lists cords and cables according to their trade names (for example, portable power cable or heater cord) and type letter (SE, SEW, SJ, or other designation). Cords or cables used in fountains must have a type letter that ends with W to indicate a cable or cord suitable for a wet location.

3.0.0 Section Review

1. What length and size of flexible cord may be used near a swimming pool to connect fixed stationary equipment to a power supply?
   a. 2' (600 mm), No. 14 AWG
   b. 3' (900 mm), No. 10 AWG
   c. 4' (1.2 m), No. 14 AWG
   d. 5' (1.5 m), No. 12 AWG

2. Raceways and cables serving motors associated with permanently installed pools must contain an insulated copper equipment grounding conductor sized *no* smaller than No. _____.
   a. 6 AWG
   b. 8 AWG
   c. 10 AWG
   d. 12 AWG

3. Underwater luminaires installed in storable pools can be powered through a cord-and-plug arrangement using a transformer listed for the application if the transformer-primary power requirement does *not* exceed _____.
   a. the low-voltage contact limit
   b. 100V
   c. 150V
   d. 250V

4. Which of the following methods of bonding is acceptable for spas and hot tubs?
   a. No. 14 AWG solid copper bonding jumper
   b. No. 10 AWG solid copper bonding jumper
   c. Threaded metal pipe and fittings
   d. Plastic pipe and fittings

5. Junction boxes and other enclosures associated with fountains must comply with *NEC Section 680.24* and *must* be _____.
   a. designed to eliminate threaded conduit entries
   b. filled with an approved potting compound to prevent water entry
   c. supported only by nonmetallic conduit
   d. constructed of plastic

Module 26412-23 Review Questions

1. To qualify as an assembly occupancy, a structure must be designed to hold at *least* _____.
   a. 50 people
   b. 100 people
   c. 200 people
   d. 500 people

2. The use of electrical nonmetallic tubing and rigid nonmetallic conduit in spaces of assembly is restricted to certain areas such as club rooms if the building contains _____.
   a. combustible supports
   b. conduit supports
   c. conductive supports
   d. clamping supports

3. In a manually controlled stage switchboard, all dimmers and switches are operated by handles that are _____.
   a. automatically linked to the control devices
   b. mechanically linked to the control devices
   c. electrically linked to the control devices
   d. manually linked to the control devices

4. For portable structures such as tents at circuses and similar areas, what is the clearance required in any direction from overhead conductors operating at 600V or less?
   a. 10' (3 m)
   b. 15' (4.5 m)
   c. 18' (5.5 m)
   d. 20' (6 m)

5. The size of the bonding conductor for portable buildings at carnivals, circuses, or fairs must be in accordance with NEC Table 250.122, based on the largest overcurrent device supplying the portable structures, but never smaller than No. _____.
   a. 2 AWG
   b. 6 AWG
   c. 8 AWG
   d. 12 AWG

6. When outlet boxes or other device boxes are installed outdoors at circuses, fairs, and similar locations, the boxes must be weatherproof and mounted so the bottom of the box is at *least* _____.
   a. 6" (150 mm) off the ground
   b. 8" (200 mm) off the ground
   c. 12' (300 mm) off the ground
   d. 18' (450 mm) off the ground

7. If two or more agricultural buildings are supplied overhead from a distribution point, a _____.
   a. service-splitter device must be installed
   b. current-monitoring device must be installed
   c. motion-detecting device must be installed
   d. site-isolating device must be installed

8. Holiday lighting must be removed within _____.
   a. 30 days of the date of installation
   b. 60 days of the date of installation
   c. 90 days of the date of installation
   d. 180 days of the date of installation

9. It is *not* necessary to install a box for splices or connections on construction sites in nonmetallic multiwire cord or cable assemblies as long as the equipment grounding conductor's _____.
   a. termination is maintained
   b. insulation is maintained
   c. continuity is maintained
   d. location is maintained

10. Electrical distribution systems within boatyards and piers *cannot* exceed _____.
    a. 250V phase to phase
    b. 480V phase to phase
    c. 600V phase to phase
    d. 1,000V phase to phase

11. Any electrical connection on a fixed pier must be at least 12" (305 mm) above the deck of the fixed pier, but *never* below the _____.
    a. service height
    b. electrical datum plane
    c. seepage point
    d. fuel dispensing system

12. Where land areas are affected by tidal fluctuations, the electrical datum plane is 2' (600 mm) above the *highest* _____.
    a. water level for the area
    b. water mark for the area
    c. flood plane for the area
    d. high tide for the area

13. Which of the following does *not* need to be grounded in a pool area?
    a. Junction boxes
    b. Electrical equipment that is 16' away from the inside wall of the pool
    c. Ground fault circuit interrupters
    d. Transformer and power supply enclosures

14. If a flexible cord or cable supplies a wet-niche luminaire, the cord or cable must contain an insulated copper equipment grounding conductor *no* smaller than No. _____.
    a. 6 AWG
    b. 8 AWG
    c. 12 AWG
    d. 16 AWG

15. For spas and hot tubs, wall switches must be located away from the inside walls of the tub by at *least* _____.
    a. 2' (600 mm)
    b. 4' (1.2 m)
    c. 5' (1.5 m)
    d. 6' (1.8 m)

Answers to odd-numbered Module Review Questions are found in *Appendix A*.

Module 26412-23 Supplemental Exercises

1. True or False? An office cafeteria with a capacity of 20 people qualifies as an assembly occupancy.
2. Raceways or cable assemblies must either qualify as an approved equipment grounding conductor per *NEC Section 250.118* or contain a(n) __________ sized in accordance with *NEC Table 250.122*.
3. Wiring methods for theaters are covered in __________.
4. The type of stage switchboard that contains only overcurrent protective devices and no control elements is known as a(n) __________.
5. A portable structure, such as a carnival tent, may not be located under or within __________ of conductors that have an energized voltage greater than 600V.
6. True or False? Aluminum grounding conductors are permitted in agricultural buildings.
7. Equipotential planes are required in both indoor and outdoor animal confinement areas with concrete floors or slabs where __________.
8. Each individual shore power receptacle must be provided with a disconnecting means located within __________ of the receptacle.
9. In areas subject to flooding, the electrical datum plane is __________ above the prevailing high-water mark as determined by the AHJ.
10. Heater elements on electric pool water heaters must be subdivided into loads not exceeding __________ each.

Answers to odd-numbered Supplemental Exercises are found in *Appendix B*.

Answers to Section Review Questions

Answer	Section Reference	Objective
Section 1.0.0		
1. c	1.1.1	1a
2. a	1.2.1	1b
3. d	1.3.0	1c
4. d	1.4.1	1d
5. a	1.5.4	1e
6. a	1.6.0	1f
Section 2.0.0		
1. b	2.1.6	2a
2. c	2.2.4	2b
Section 3.0.0		
1. b	3.1.2	3a
2. d	3.2.1	3b
3. c	3.3.0	3c
4. c	3.4.1; 3.4.2	3d
5. b	3.5.2	3e

User Update

Did you find an error? Submit a correction by visiting **https://www.nccer.org/olf** or by scanning the QR code using your mobile device.

Objectives

Successful completion of this module prepares you to do the following:

1. Explain business and organizational structures in the construction industry.
   a. Understand organizational charts.
   b. Describe organizational roles and relationships, including job descriptions and responsibility, authority, and accountability.
2. Describe frontline leadership and communication skills.
   a. Describe the qualities and role of a leader, including leadership styles and ethical leadership.
   b. Explain the communication process and distinguish between verbal, nonverbal, written, and visual communication types.
   c. Compare problem-solving and decision-making.
3. Identify key skills for team leadership and motivation.
   a. Choose strategies to motivate individuals and a team.
   b. Describe key approaches to building and leading teams.
   c. Recognize how to approach leadership challenges, such as transitioning from peer to leader, addressing performance issues, and resolving conflict.
4. Identify a frontline leader's safety leadership responsibilities.
   a. Assess the impact of incidents.
   b. Explain the purpose of OSHA and describe the role of OSHA in administering worker safety.
   c. Describe the importance of safety and health programs.
   d. Explain the frontline leader's role in incident preparedness and response.
   e. Recognize the importance of supporting your crew's total health.
5. Demonstrate an understanding of construction project phases, project planning and scheduling, field reporting, and cost and resource management.
   a. Identify construction project phases.
   b. Summarize crew planning and scheduling responsibilities, including creating lookahead schedules.
   c. Describe the frontline leader's role in field reporting.
   d. Explain approaches to managing costs and controlling project resources, such as materials, tools, and equipment.

Performance Tasks

Under supervision, you should be able to do the following:

1. Organize and deliver a safety-related toolbox talk, applying communication skills.
2. Complete a job safety analysis.
3. Develop and present a lookahead schedule.

Digital Resources for Fundamentals of Crew Leadership

Scan this code using the camera on your phone or mobile device to view the digital resources related to this craft.

Overview

As a frontline leader, you must be able to communicate effectively, provide direction to your crew, plan and schedule work, manage costs, and ensure the jobsite is safe for everyone. Whether you are already a frontline leader or want to become one, this module will help you learn more about the requirements and skills needed to succeed.

NCCER Industry-Recognized Credentials

If you are training through an NCCER-accredited sponsor, you may be eligible for credentials from NCCER. The ID number for this module is 46100. Note that this module may have been used in other NCCER curricula and may apply to other level completions. Contact NCCER at 1.888.622.3720 or go to **www.nccer.org** for more information.

You can also show off your industry-recognized credentials online with NCCER's digital badges. Transform your knowledge, skills, and achievements into badges that you can share across social media platforms, send to your network, and add to your resume. For more information, visit **www.nccer.org**.

1.0.0 Business and Organizational Structures

Performance Tasks

There are no Performance Tasks in this section.

Objective

Explain business and organizational structures in the construction industry.

a. Understand organizational charts.

b. Describe organizational roles and relationships, including job descriptions and responsibility, authority, and accountability.

Crew leader: A person appointed leader of a team or crew, usually an experienced craft professional who has demonstrated leadership qualities. Also known as *frontline leader*, *frontline supervisor*, *lead person*, or *foreman*.

Superintendent: An on-site supervisor who is responsible for one or more crew leaders or frontline supervisors.

Project manager: Person responsible for managing one or more projects.

When a crew is assembled to complete a job, one person is appointed the leader. Different companies give this role different titles, such as **crew leader**, *frontline supervisor, lead person*, or *foreman*. In this module, this role is called the *crew leader* or *frontline leader*. A crew leader or frontline leader is often an experienced craft professional who has demonstrated leadership qualities.

A **superintendent** is essentially an on-site field supervisor who is responsible for one or more crew leaders or frontline supervisors. A **project manager** may be responsible for managing one or more projects. This training will concentrate primarily on the supervisory role of the frontline leader. These individuals work with others on projects as part of an organization.

1.1.0 Organizations and Organizational Structures

Organization: A group of people working together.

Organizational chart: A diagram that shows how the various management and operational responsibilities relate to each other within an organization. Named positions are ranked top to bottom, from those functional units with the most and broadest authority to those with the least. Lines connect positions and indicate chains of authority and other relationships.

An **organization** is a group of people working together. Businesses, clubs, and associations are examples of types of organizations. On a jobsite, the relationships among the people within the company or project create a type of organization.

1.1.1 Organizational Charts

A formal organization will have an **organizational chart** that shows all of the positions in the organization and how those positions are related. A detailed organizational chart, or org chart, may also show the name of the person in each position. *Figure 1* shows an example of an organizational chart for a construction company. Each position on that organizational chart represents an opportunity for career advancement for a crew leader.

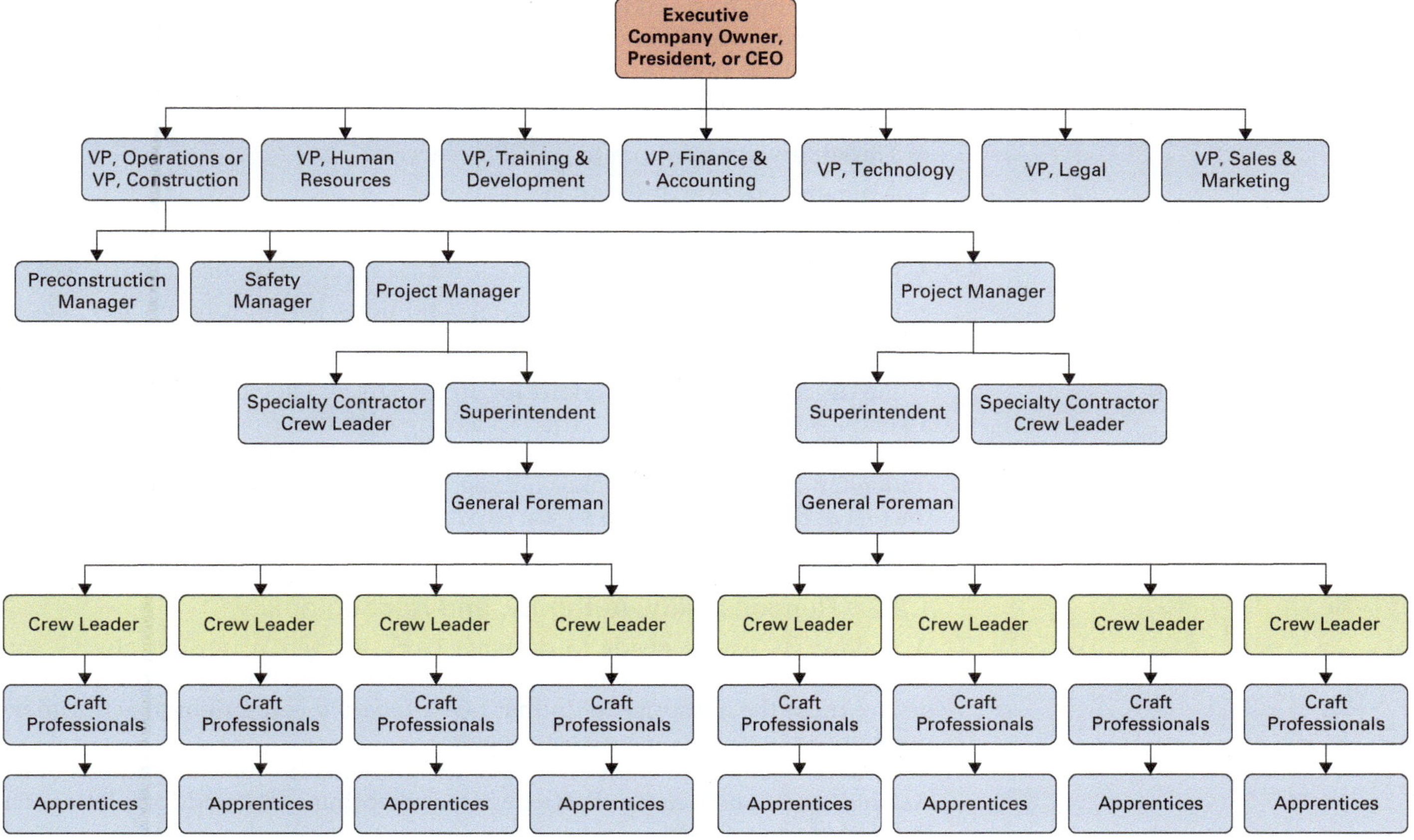

Figure 1 Sample organization chart for a construction company.

As shown in *Figure 1*, most companies have separate groups or departments that focus on running specific functions. Smaller companies may have one or two individuals who perform multiple functions. Larger companies will often create specific roles or departments to handle more complex projects and larger teams.

Companies may have additional roles or teams, such as architectural and engineering design functions. Depending on the size of these groups, they may become separate departments.

NOTE

Organizational charts vary widely based on the size of the company and the specific construction sector in which they operate. For example, an industrial company might have crew leaders who report to a plant manager. Some larger companies will have a superintendent per shift, who will report to a project superintendent, who reports to the project manager. If you are interested in learning more about your company's organizational chart, ask your supervisor or manager.

1.2.0 Organizational Roles and Relationships

As a crew leader, you will assign others the responsibility to perform specific jobs or tasks. Your crew and team members will perform best if the following is true:

- They have a clear job description that explains their job duties.
- They have the required skills and abilities to perform the task.
- They know who has **authority**, **responsibility**, and **accountability**.
- They have a clear understanding of expectations.
- They are trained on policies and procedures.
- They have all needed tools, equipment, and material.

1.2.1 Job Descriptions

As part of the hiring process, most companies give each employee a **job description**. A job description is a statement that describes the duties and responsibilities of a position with a company. A **duty** is a work task an employee is expected to perform. Responsibility involves accepting a task and completing it to the best of one's ability.

Authority: The right to act or make decisions in carrying out an assignment.

Responsibility: The act of accepting a task and completing it to the best of one's ability.

Accountability: In relation to job completion, accepting responsibility and being personally answerable for the results.

Job description: A description of the scope and responsibilities of a worker's job so that the individual and others understand what the job entails.

Duty: A work task an employee is expected to perform.

A job description should include enough detail so that an employee understands their job. It also should have any information needed to evaluate the employee's job performance. A job description should contain at least the following:

- Job title
- The supervisor to whom the position reports
- A general position description
- Specific duties and responsibilities
- Required and desired qualifications, including certifications and licenses
- Other information, such as working conditions, job type, hours, pay ranges, and more

Job descriptions set a standard for an employee. They outline the tasks that an employee should handle. After reviewing a job description, a new employee should understand all of the duties and responsibilities of the job. Having a clear understanding of the job makes it easier for new employees to work well with the rest of the crew while they gain experience. Clear job descriptions help crew leaders to judge performance and identify training needs for new employees.

1.2.2 Responsibility, Authority, and Accountability

A good crew leader needs to delegate work to their team, but always stay accountable for the outcome. When you assign a crew member work, you are giving them the authority to do that task. *Authority* is the right to act or make decisions in carrying out an assignment.

When the employee takes on a job or assignment, they take on responsibility. As noted previously, *responsibility* involves accepting a task and completing it to the best of one's ability.

In relation to job completion, *accountability* is accepting responsibility and being personally answerable for the results.

Each project or company has differences in the type and amount of authority, responsibility, and accountability a supervisor or worker has. As a crew leader, you must give sufficient responsibility and authority to allow employees to be successful at their job activities. You then must hold employees responsible for completing those assigned activities.

As shown in *Figure 2*, even though you may delegate authority and responsibility to crew members, the overall accountability for tasks assigned to a crew always rests with the frontline leader or crew leader.

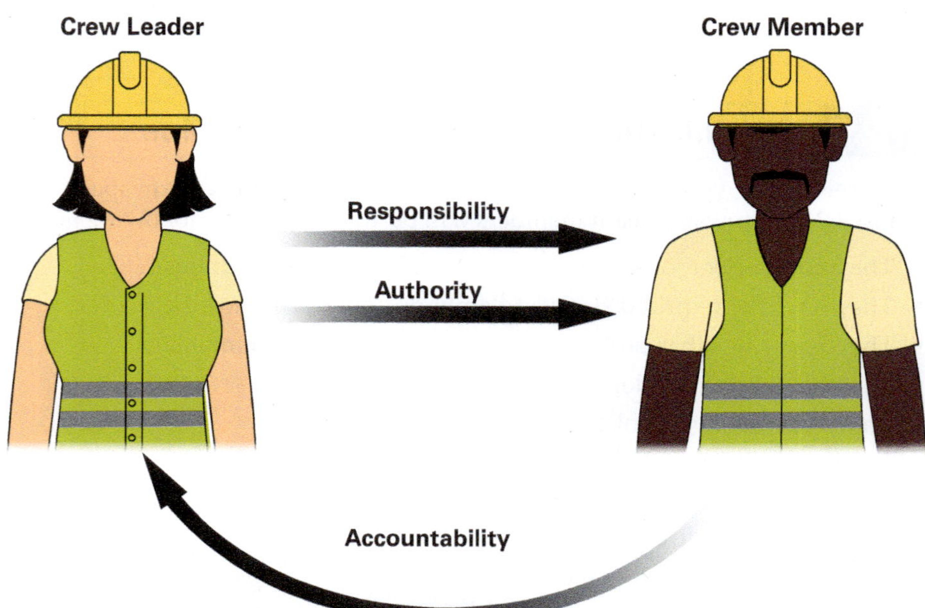

Figure 2 Accountability always rests with the frontline leader.

1.2.3 Policies and Procedures

Most companies have formal policies and procedures established to help crew leaders carry out their duties.

- A **policy** is a general statement establishing guidelines for a specific activity. Examples include policies on vacations, breaks, workplace safety, and checking out tools.
- **Procedures** are formal instructions to carry out and meet policies. For example, a procedure written to implement a policy on workplace safety would include guidelines for reporting incidents and following general safety practices.

Policy: A general statement establishing guidelines for a specific activity.

Procedures: Formal instructions to carry out and meet policies.

A crew leader must understand any company policies and procedures that relate to their work, especially safety practices. The **Occupational Safety and Health Administration (OSHA)** is a national public health agency that is part of the US Department of Labor. To promote a safe and healthy work environment, OSHA issues standards and rules for working conditions, facilities, equipment, tools, and work processes. When OSHA inspectors visit a jobsite, they often question crew leaders and employees about the company safety policies. During incident investigations, the inspector will verify if the responsible crew leader knew and followed the applicable company policy.

Occupational Safety and Health Administration (OSHA): A national public health agency that is part of the US Department of Labor. To promote a safe and healthy work environment, OSHA issues standards and rules for working conditions, facilities, equipment, tools, and work processes.

1.0.0 Section Review

1. Which of the following is shown on an organizational chart?
   a. How to organize materials on a jobsite
   b. How positions in an organization are related
   c. How prevailing wages are determined
   d. How to coordinate work with other crafts

2. Although you may delegate authority and responsibility for tasks to crew members, as a frontline leader, you have the overall _____.
   a. policy
   b. accountability
   c. job description
   d. authority

2.0.0 Leadership and Communication

Objective

Describe frontline leadership and communication skills.

a. Describe the qualities and role of a leader, including leadership styles and ethical leadership.
b. Explain the communication process and distinguish between verbal, nonverbal, written, and visual communication types.
c. Compare problem-solving and decision-making.

Performance Tasks

There are no Performance Tasks in this section.

In addition to being an experienced craft professional, a frontline leader also must demonstrate leadership qualities and strong morals. They must be able to communicate effectively, solve problems, and make good decisions. Frontline leaders are generally promoted up from a work crew. A worker's ability to accomplish tasks, get along with others, meet schedules, and stay within the budget have a significant influence on the selection process. The frontline leader must lead the team to work safely and provide a quality product.

This section explains the importance of developing and improving leadership skills as a frontline leader. It will cover the qualities and roles of a leader, as well as effective ways to communicate with coworkers and employees at all levels, solve problems, and make decisions.

2.1.0 The Qualities and Role of a Leader

There are many ways to define leadership. One simple definition of leadership is the ability of a person to influence others to achieve a common goal. A leader is someone who sees how to accomplish or improve things. A leader then rallies people to move toward that vision. Effective leadership requires communicating ideas effectively to engage others to act accordingly.

Leaders often have power based on a role or title. However, leadership is much more than power. An effective leader inspires others to act, while also directing the way that they act. A leader must have respect, so others follow their directions. A leader also must have the critical thinking skills to know the best way to use available resources.

Motivate: To make someone feel determined or enthusiastic or to make someone behave in a particular way.

Some people develop leadership qualities as part of their upbringing. Others may work hard to develop the qualities that **motivate** others to follow and perform. Leadership is a skill you can learn through experience and training as well as hard work, focus, and practice.

2.1.1 Functions of a Leader

What is the purpose or function of a leader? The answer will vary based on the specific project, the work environment, the team they lead, and the tasks they must perform.

As shown in *Table 1*, a frontline leader has certain functions that apply to almost every work situation.

TABLE 1 Frontline Leadership Functions

Leadership Duties and Responsibilities	Leadership Functions
Planning the Work	Organize, plan, staff, direct, and control work
Safety and Compliance	Ensure that the team understands and follows company policies and procedures
Empathy	Be sensitive to the needs and qualities of a diverse workforce
Motivating and Coaching	Give team members the confidence to make decisions and take responsibility for their work
Conflict Resolution	Maintain a cohesive team by resolving tensions and differences
Professionalism	Represent the team or group and represent the company or organization
Accountability	Accept responsibility for the successes and failures of the team's performance

2.1.2 Leadership Traits and Behavior

Trait: A distinguishing quality of a person.

Behavior: The way a person responds to a specific situation.

As previously noted, leadership is a skill you can learn and develop through experience and training. As you continue to grow your leadership skills, remember that while each leader has some unique approaches, the most effective leaders share some common traits and behaviors. A **trait** is a distinguishing quality of a person. A **behavior** is the way a person responds to a specific situation.

Effective leaders share the following traits and behaviors:

- Follows company policies and procedures
- Has necessary technical knowledge

- Can plan, prioritize, and organize work
- Leads by example
- Is fair and ethical
- Solves problems, makes decisions, and assumes responsibility
- Communicates effectively
- Can promote an idea
- Is enthusiastic and shows strong initiative
- Is able to motivate individuals and teams
- Is loyal to their company and crew
- Extends respect and trust to all team members
- Can teach others and learn from others

First and above all, excellent leaders lead by example. They work and live by the standards that they set for their crew members. A leader will not ask someone to complete a task that they are not willing to do themselves.

Leaders tend to have a high level of drive and determination, as well as a persistent attitude. When faced with obstacles, effective leaders don't get discouraged. Leaders identify the potential problems and make plans to overcome them. They then work toward achieving the intended goal. In the event of failure, effective leaders learn from their mistakes and apply that knowledge to future situations. They also learn from their successes.

Respect is an important aspect of leadership. Leaders earn respect by being fair to employees and by listening to their complaints and suggestions. Using appropriate incentives and **rewards** to motivate a crew helps leaders earn respect. In addition, frontline leaders who have a positive attitude tend to gain the respect of their team and their peers. A **peer** is someone who is in a position or level in an organization equal or similar to yours.

Rewards: Tangible items given to an employee as recognition for good work.

Peer: Someone who is in a position or level in an organization equal or similar to yours.

Trust is an equally important part of being a great frontline leader. Trust is a group's belief that their leader is committed, capable, and will do what's best for all involved. To build trust, effective leaders create interactions and conversations with the team. They treat everyone on the team as an individual.

Leaders are good communicators who lay out the goals of a project to their crew members clearly. To do this, you may need to overcome language barriers, bias, or differences in personalities to ensure that each member of the crew understands the established goals of the project.

Effective leaders can motivate their team to work to their full potential. They will work to develop crew members' skills. They encourage them to improve and learn so they can contribute more to the team effort. Effective leaders strive for excellence from themselves and their team, so they work hard to provide the necessary skills and leadership.

It is important for leaders to have an expert knowledge of the activities they supervise. This is important because the crew members need to know that they have someone to turn to when they have a question or a problem, need some guidance, or must make modifications or changes on the job.

In addition, leaders must possess organizational skills. They know what needs to be accomplished, and they use their resources to make it happen. Because they can't do it alone, leaders require the help of their team members to share in the workload. Effective leaders delegate work to their crew members. They also implement company policies and procedures to complete the work safely, effectively, and efficiently.

Finally, outstanding leaders have the experience, authority, and self-confidence that allow them to make decisions and solve problems. To accomplish their goals, leaders must be able to calculate risks, take in and understand information, set a course of action, make decisions, and assume the responsibility for those decisions.

2.1.3 Leadership Styles

Many terms are used to describe different leadership styles. As a frontline leader, you will never lead the exact same project twice. Having a leadership style that is also adaptable is important for you, the project, and your company's success.

Situational leadership: A leadership style that involves adjusting to the specific situation or task and the leadership needs of the group.

Situational leadership is a leadership approach that involves adjusting the way you lead to reflect the specific situation or task and the needs of the group. The main idea behind situational leadership is that there is no "one size fits all" or best style of leadership. Instead, you must adapt or adjust your leadership style to the situation.

As shown in *Figure 3*, situational leadership provides a model with four primary leadership styles:

- *Directing:* The leader tells a team what to do and how to do it.
- *Coaching:* The leader coaches individuals to improve skills. The leader encourages more back-and-forth between leaders and the team.
- *Supporting:* A leader supports the group, participating to help increase motivation. The leader offers less direction. Instead, the leader has team members take a more active role in coming up with ideas and making decisions.
- *Delegating:* A leader allows other people to own the task, and they facilitate it happening. Team members make most of the decisions and take most of the responsibility for what happens.

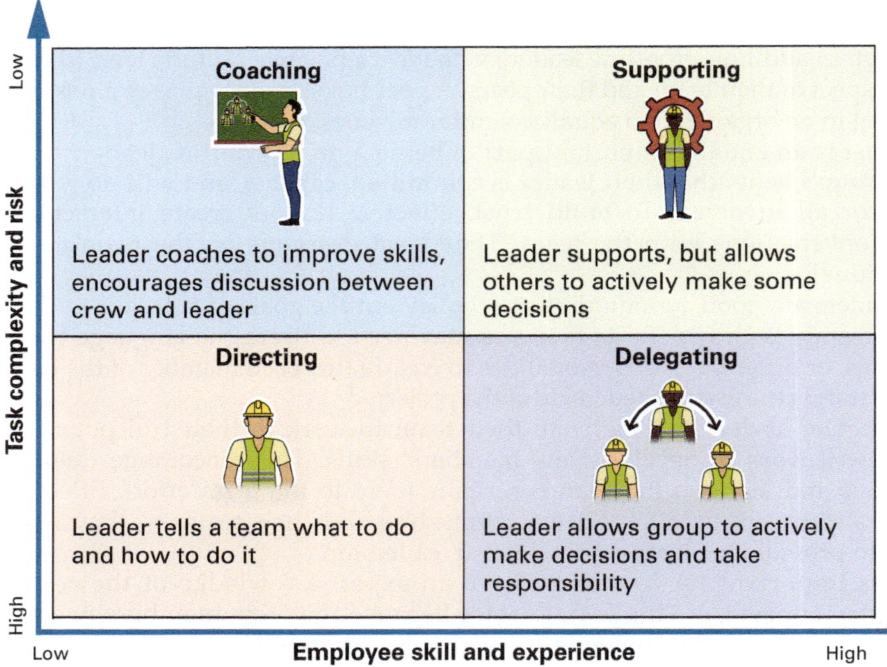

Figure 3 Situational leadership styles.

Knowing which leadership style to apply depends on several key factors:

- *Team relationships:* Consider your team, how well they work together, and how productive they are. A group that is not efficient or productive might benefit from a Directing style. That style emphasizes direction, organization, and clearly defined roles. On the other hand, a highly cohesive group might benefit from a Supporting style, which gives the team more inputs on decisions.
- *Team skills:* Consider the skills and abilities of the individuals completing the task. Giving a task to a team or team member who lacks the skills to complete the task is risky, is dangerous, and may end in failure.

- *Work tasks:* Consider the actual work or tasks at hand. You must have an expert knowledge of the tasks and activities to ensure they are done well, completely, and in the safest way possible. You may need to coach or train workers who do not have experience to help them complete the task.
- *Work situation:* Consider the situation you're facing. In some cases, the situation itself will override all other factors.

For example, if the crew does not have enough experience for the job ahead, you may want to use a *Directing* style. A Directing style works with people and teams who have limited experience or skill performing a task. It also works when team members are insecure or unmotivated to try a task. The Directing style requires your close supervision to spot signs of progress, which you can use to motivate ongoing development. If a job task or situation is very risky, a Directing style can help reduce the risk by providing clear and very specific direction.

If your team is working well and showing strong progress on work tasks, you might use a *Coaching* style. You still direct how and when specific tasks are completed, but you also discuss why the task matters and where it fits into the overall project or job. With this style, you recognize the enthusiasm, interest, and commitment of the team. You also reinforce the importance of learning and gaining task-related experience.

You may want to use a *Supporting* style if the team is reasonably skilled and work tasks are not complex, but commitment and attitude are an issue. The goal of the Supporting style is to create alignment. As a leader, you can discuss a person's commitment by asking open-ended questions. These questions should help you understand what is behind the performance challenges and create possible solutions. The Supporting style of leadership also works well when work is creative, as it is helpful to brainstorm and exchange ideas with crew members.

The *Delegating* style works best with an experienced, strong, committed crew on a well-defined project. The Delegating style of leadership is also effective when jobs have repetitive tasks that require few decisions. To use the Delegating style, however, your company must give you enough authority as the frontline leader to do the job.

Effective leadership takes many forms. The correct style for a particular situation depends on the team and the work you need to accomplish. Knowing the factors to consider can help you decide which type of leadership to apply in which situation. This flexibility allows you to meet each situation with the leadership style that brings out the best in your team and gives them the highest chance of success.

2.1.4 Ethics in Leadership

Ethics are the moral principles that guide a person's actions when dealing with others. *Figure 4* outlines three basic types of ethics. Frontline leaders must maintain strong ethics and the highest standards of honesty and legality. Every day, a leader makes decisions that have fairness and moral implications. When you make an unethical decision, it reflects poorly on you. It also impacts your team, other project team members, and the company as a whole.

As a leader, you will find yourself in situations where you will need to weigh the ethical results of a choice or decision. For example, imagine a crew member shows symptoms of heat exhaustion. Do you keep that employee working just because the superintendent says the project is behind schedule? If you are aware that your crew did not properly erect the reinforcing steel, do you stop the pour and correct the situation? In both cases, you must act ethically as a leader and make the right choice. If supervision ever asks a frontline leader to carry out an unethical decision, that individual must inform the next level of authority of the unethical nature of the issue.

Ethics: The moral principles that guide an individual's or organization's actions when dealing with others.

NOTE

Anyone who is aware of illegal activity can face legal concerns simply by not acting. This is true even if the activities were requested by one's supervisor.

Business or legal ethics	Professional or balanced ethics	Situational ethics
Adheres to all laws and published regulations related to business relationships or activities.	Carries out all activities in such a manner as to be honest and fair to everyone under one's authority.	Relates to specific activities or events that may initially appear to be a gray area. For example, you may ask yourself, "How will I feel about myself if my actions were going to be published in the news or if I need to justify my actions to my family, friends, and colleagues? Would I still do the same thing?"

Figure 4 Types of ethics.

2.2.0 Communication

Communication: The process of exchanging facts, information, and ideas. Communication comes in many forms, including verbal, written, visual, and nonverbal.

Successful crew leaders learn to communicate well with people at all levels of an organization. **Communication** is the act of accurately and effectively sharing facts, feelings, and opinions with another. Simply stated, communication is the process of exchanging information and ideas. Communication comes in many forms, including verbal, written, visual, and nonverbal.

2.2.1 Why Communication Matters

Effective communication on a jobsite or project is critical for many reasons (*Figure 5*). First and foremost, clear communication is a key part of safety. Everyone on a jobsite must receive and understand communications about safety policies and procedures. If this does not happen, it creates safety issues for everyone in the group.

Miscommunication is also expensive (*Figure 5*). One study indicated that over half of all rework is due to poor communication and bad information. If communication on a construction site fails, it can cause delays and quality issues for the project. It can also result in damage to equipment or property. The good news is that communication is a skill that can be taught, practiced, and improved.

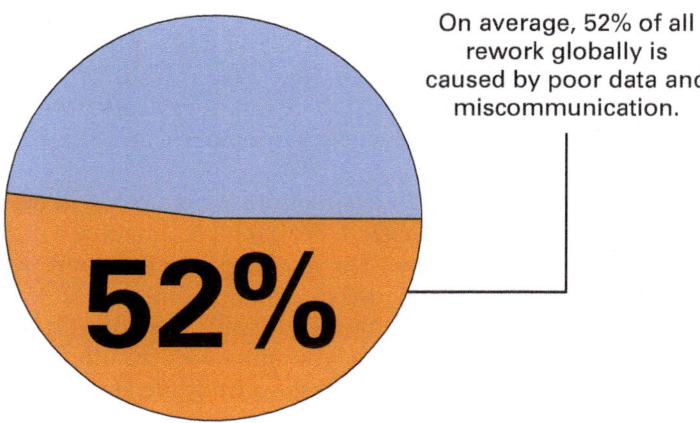

Figure 5 Industry impacts of miscommunication in the construction industry.

2.2.2 The Communication Process

Clear communication has three basic steps, as shown in *Figure 6*.

1. *Sender sends message to receiver.* A sender sends a message to a receiver, as a verbal, written, visual, or nonverbal communication. A message can be a set of directions, an opinion, or a personal message such as praise or a warning. Whatever it is, a message is an idea or fact that the sender wants the receiver to know.
2. *Receiver interprets message and repeats the message to provide feedback.* The receiver is the person who takes in the message. When the receiver gets the message, they figure out what it means by listening, viewing, or reading, and then repeat the message to provide feedback. *Feedback* is the receiver's communication back to the sender in response to the message. Feedback is a very important part of the communication process. It shows the sender how the receiver interpreted the message and if the receiver understood it as intended. In other words, feedback is a checkpoint to make sure the receiver and sender are on the same page.
3. *Sender validates that receiver correctly understood the message.* The sender confirms the receiver heard and understood the message.

This process is called **three-way communication**. Three-way communication is also sometimes called *repeat-back communication*.

Three-way communication is a simple way to make sure that communication is clear. If this process is easy, why is good communication so hard to achieve? When we try to communicate, many things can get in the way. These obstacles or **distractions** are anything that disrupts the communication flow between sender and receiver. Also called *noise*, distractions can include poorly worded messages, emotions, interpretations of a word, or the actual noise from a construction site. Distractions can happen at any point in the communication process.

As noted in *Figure 7*, there are four different types of three-way communication. The following sections review these different types of communication and discuss ways to increase the effectiveness of your communication, regardless of type.

Three-way communication: A form of communication with an initial message from a sender, which is then repeated by the receiver to confirm accuracy, and then validated by the sender. Also called *repeat-back communication*.

Distractions: Anything that disrupts the communication flow between sender and receiver. Also called *noise*.

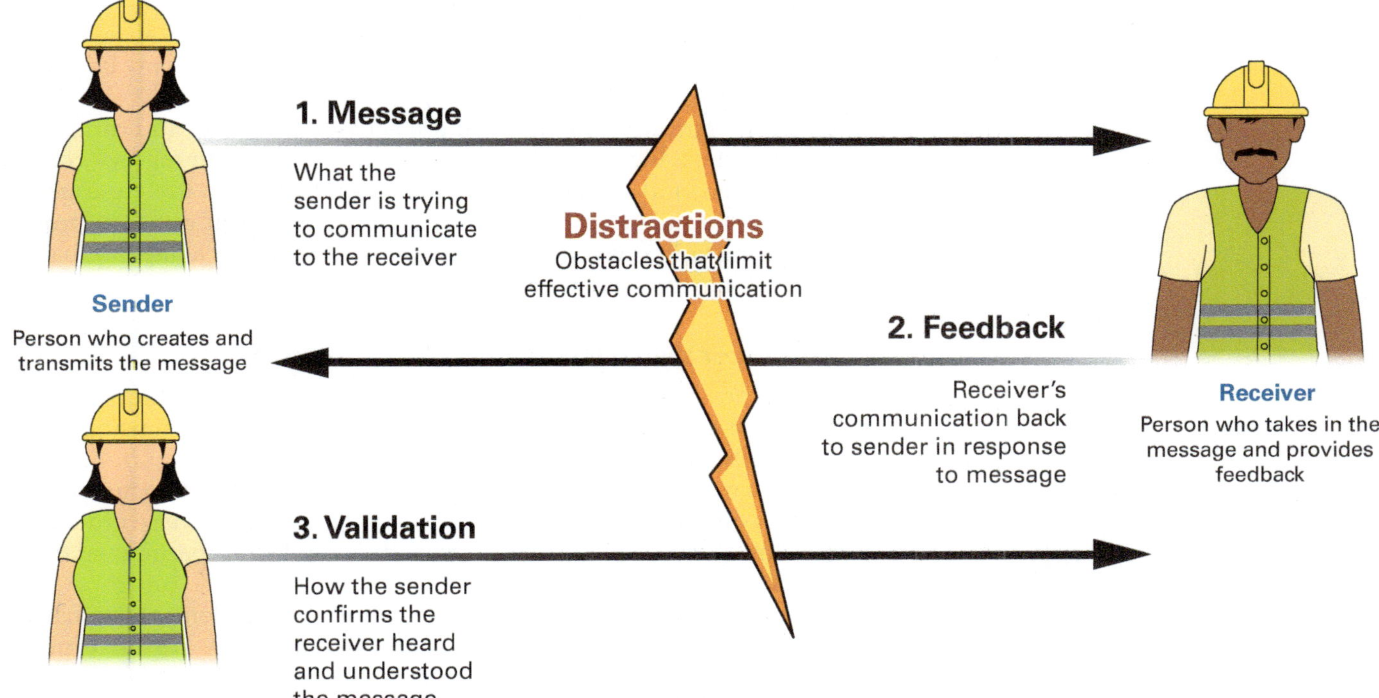

Figure 6 The three-way communication process.

Verbal	Written
• Spoken or oral communication • Examples: face-to-face conversations, telephone call, videoconference, voice chat	• Messages or information sent using words • Can be digital or physical • Examples: text message, email, training guide, weekly report, change request, purchase order
Visual	**Nonverbal**
• Using visual elements, such as photos, graphics, charts, colors, and fonts to convey messages • Examples: sketches, diagrams, graphs, photos, construction drawings, signs	• Things the speaker and the receiver see or hear while communicating • Examples: appearance, personal environment, use of time, facial expressions, body movements, hand gestures, tone of voice, and eye contact

Communication Types

Figure 7 Types of communication.

2.2.3 Verbal Communication

Verbal communication: Messages that are sent using voice or other audible sounds. Also called *spoken communication* or *oral communication*.

Verbal communication includes messages that are sent face-to-face or by telephone, videoconferencing, voice chat, or other methods. Verbal communication is also called also *spoken* or *oral* communication.

With verbal communication, the way you speak is as important as the message itself. As a leader, you should assess your audience before you speak. Even in a meeting as standard as a daily huddle, using clear verbal communication sets your crew up for a successful day. Consider each person's knowledge of the topic and any language, gender, or cultural differences. Do not talk down to anyone in a group. Everyone, whether in a senior or junior position, deserves respect and courtesy.

You should also be sure to use words and phrases that the receiver can understand. For example, avoid technical language, acronyms, or slang if the receiver does not know these terms. In addition, speak at a reasonable pace, which gives the audience time to understand one point at a time.

If you are receiving a message, be sure to listen actively and avoid distractions that interfere with the delivery of the message. There are many barriers to effective listening, particularly on a busy construction jobsite.

As a receiver, you can show that you are actively listening. You can accomplish this without saying a word. Examples include maintaining eye contact, nodding your head, and taking notes. If you are not clear on the message, ask questions to get additional explanation or information. You can also provide feedback by using your own words, or *paraphrasing*, to repeat a message back to the sender. This lets the sender know that you understood the message.

2.2.4 Written or Visual Communication

Written communication: The process of sending messages or information using words, whether digitally or physically.

Visual communication: The process of using visual elements, such as photos, graphics, colors, and fonts, to convey messages.

Much of the information on a job or project is in written or visual form. **Written communication** is the process of sending messages or information using words, whether digitally or physically. Examples include everything from a text message to an email to a printed training guide. A lot of project documentation is written, including weekly reports, requests for changes, purchase orders, and contracts. Many of these items are written so they can form a permanent record for business and historical purposes.

Visual communication is the process of using visual elements to convey messages. Photos, diagrams, graphics, charts, and colors are all types of visual communication. Visual communication is widely used because it is an effective way to convey information quickly. Traffic signs, for example, use standard visual symbols because they are clear and well-understood. Many messages on a job also use visual communication. Examples include the project plans, drawings, or a video of a worksite incident. Visual communication can help workers who speak different languages or have limited language skills.

Written and visual communication used together are even more clear. For example, tags and signs on a project (*Figure 8*) use both written words and visual elements to help make them clear to all workers on a jobsite.

Information Sign

Caution Sign

Warning Sign

Safety Sign

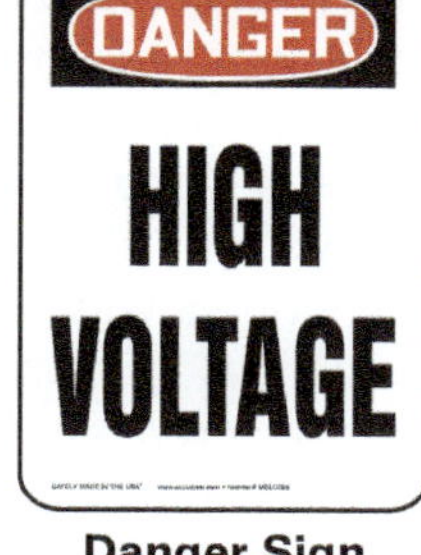

Danger Sign

Figure 8 Communication tags and signs combine written and visual communication.
Source: Courtesy of AccuformNMC.com LLC

When writing or creating a written or visual message, you first should assess the receiver (the reader). The receiver must be able to read the message and understand the content. If they cannot, the communication process will be unsuccessful. Always consider the actual meaning of words or diagrams and how others might interpret them. *Table 2* and *Table 3* provide checklists to help make your written and visual communications effective.

TABLE 2 Checklist for Effective Written Communication

Did You . . .?	Yes/No
Assess your audience. Consider existing knowledge. Consider any language, gender, or cultural differences.	
State the purpose of the message clearly.	
Present the information in a logical manner.	
Provide an adequate level of detail.	
Avoid emotion-packed words or phrases.	
Avoid making judgments, unless asked to do so.	
Avoid using unfamiliar acronyms or abbreviations.	
Avoid using technical language unless you know your audience knows those terms.	
Make sure that the communication is clear and your handwriting is readable.	
Proofread your work. Check for typos, spelling errors, and grammatical errors. Do not assume spell-check or autocorrect got it right.	
Be prepared to provide a verbal or visual explanation if needed.	

TABLE 3 Checklist for Effective Visual Communication

Did You . . .?	Yes/No
Avoid complex graphics. (Simple is better.)	
Use colors and graphical elements to highlight key information.	
Ensure that the visual is large enough to be useful.	
Present the information in a logical order.	
Provide an adequate level of detail and accuracy.	
Provide a legend or written description if you include symbols.	
Be prepared to provide a written or verbal explanation of the diagram if needed.	

2.2.5 Nonverbal Communication

Nonverbal communication: Things the speaker and the receiver see or hear while communicating. Examples include facial expressions, body movements, hand gestures, tone of voice, and eye contact.

Unlike verbal or written communication, **nonverbal communication** does not involve spoken or written words or images. Nonverbal communication refers to things the speaker and the receiver see or hear while communicating. This includes appearance, personal environment, use of time, and body language. Examples include facial expressions, body movements, hand gestures, tone of voice, and eye contact.

Nonverbal communication can provide an external sign of someone's inner emotions. It often occurs at the same time as verbal communication. You can express feelings in many ways without realizing it. You may show you are happy by smiling and giving someone a warm handshake. You may show you are angry by raising your voice.

People observe your physical, nonverbal cues when you are communicating. In fact, nonverbal signals can have more impact than your verbal communication. Be aware of nonverbal cues to avoid miscommunication based on your posture, facial expression, or other signals. For example, if you have your arms crossed in a defensive posture while speaking, the person might assume you are angry, even if you are not.

On a jobsite, nonverbal communication is also a matter of safety. For example, a major aspect of rigging safety is having clear communication between a crane operator and the designated signal person on the ground. This communication relies on common signals, including nonverbal hand signals. The Emergency Stop signal used in rigging operations is a nonverbal communication. Anyone on the ground within sight of the crane operator can use this signal in the event of an emergency (*Figure 9*).

Figure 9 The Emergency Stop signal is an example of nonverbal communication.

Did You Know?

The Major Impact of Nonverbal Communication

Over the years, many studies have tried to measure how much of all communication is nonverbal. The specific numbers vary by study but indicate that between 55 to 93 percent of all communication is nonverbal. This means that your nonverbal signals send an even more powerful message than your verbal communication. Always remember that people might not remember what you say, but they do remember how you make them feel. Nonverbal cues have a major impact on how you make people feel when you communicate.

Did You Know?

Communication Is Number One

Research shows that the most common thing a supervisor does daily is communicate. They may do this as either a sender or receiver of messages. Eighty percent of a typical supervisor's day is spent communicating through writing, speaking, listening, or using body language. Of that time, studies suggest that around 20 percent is written communication, while 80 percent involves verbal communication.

2.2.6 Additional Communication Considerations

As a leader in the field, the way that you communicate has significant impact on the safety, quality, and productivity of your group. Regardless of your communication method, remember that everyone communicates differently. In some cases, you might need to communicate in multiple ways. You might also need to adjust your level of detail to ensure that everyone understands the intended meaning. For instance, a visual learner may need a map to comprehend directions. Another team member might just need a verbal explanation of which turns to take to a destination. *Figure 10* shows an example of ways to tailor the message to your audience.

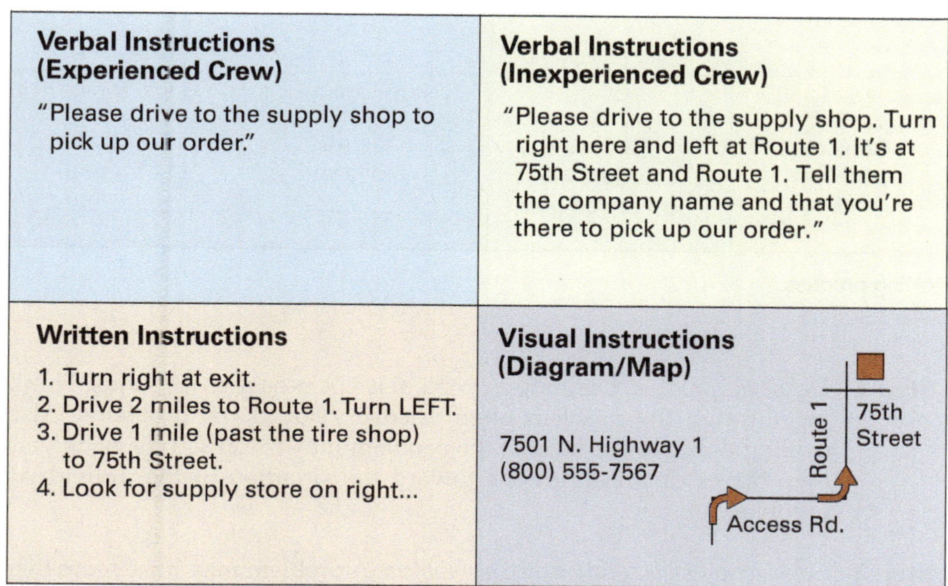

Figure 10 Assess your audience and then tailor your message.

The construction industry is a diverse and multicultural one. It is quite common to have a crew with people from different cultural backgrounds working together. Language and cultural differences can make communication even more challenging. Even if employees speak the same language, different understandings of words or symbols can create confusion or cause offense.

An important part of effective communication is to remember that people are different and to adjust your communication style to meet the needs of the person or people receiving your message. This means field leaders need to invest the time to learn how to communicate well with each individual. This requires you to know each crew member, recognize how each person learns, how each person delivers feedback, how each person works with others, and who they are as individuals, not just coworkers.

2.3.0 Problem-Solving and Decision-Making

Problem-solving and **decision-making** are a large part of every field leader's daily work. They are a part of life for all supervisors, especially in fast-paced, deadline-oriented industries like construction.

What is the difference between problem-solving and decision-making? Problem-solving is a process used to identify possible solutions to a situation. Decision-making refers to the action of making a choice. Decision-making involves starting or stopping a plan or choosing a different plan of action as

Problem-solving: A process used to identify possible solutions to a situation.

Decision-making: The action or process of making a choice. Decision-making involves starting an action, stopping one, or choosing a different plan or action.

appropriate for the situation. A decision may be complicated and involve many steps, but it is simply a choice.

The key difference between problem-solving and decision-making is that solving problems is a process, while making decisions is an action based on experience or information learned during the problem-solving process.

2.3.1 Problem-Solving

The ability to solve problems is an important skill in any workplace. It is especially important for craft professionals, whose workday is often not predictable or routine. Your group will look to you as a leader to solve problems regularly.

Figure 11 shows a five-step process for solving problems, which you can apply to any situation.

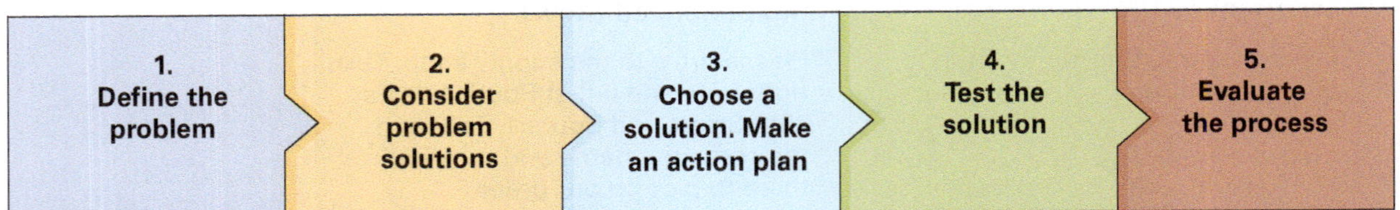

Figure 11 The problem-solving process.

Step 1 *Define the problem.* Defining a problem is not as easy as it sounds. Thinking through the problem often uncovers additional problems. Also, drilling down to the facts of the problem may mean setting aside your own biases or presumptions toward the situation or the individuals involved.

Step 2 *Consider possible solutions to the problem.* A problem may have more than one solution. Think through a number of solution options. As you do this, get inputs from people most affected by the problem, those who must correct the problem, and those who will be most affected by any potential solution.

Step 3 *Choose the solution that seems best and make an action plan.* After you consider several options to solve the problem, you must think through each possible solution and pick the best one. Again, you do not have to do this alone. Ask for feedback from others who have a stake in solving the problem well. Keep an open mind. The best solution might be taking pieces of two different solutions and combining them to create a new solution.

Step 4 *Test the solution to determine whether it actually works.* A solution might sound perfect before you try it but turn out not to be effective when you do. Alternatively, you might discover from trying to apply a solution that it is acceptable with a little change. If a solution doesn't work, think about how you could improve it, and then test your new plan.

Step 5 *Evaluate the process.* After your solution is in place, review the steps you took to discover and implement the solution. Could you have done anything better? The next time you are faced with a similar situation, you can use this experience to help solve the problem more effectively.

This problem-solving process can apply to almost any situation. *Figure 12* walks through a scenario to show how problem-solving works in practice. A

Problem Scenario

You are leading a team assigned to a new shopping mall project. The project will take about 18 months to complete. The only available parking is half a mile from the jobsite. The crew must carry heavy toolboxes and safety equipment from their cars and trucks to the work area at the start of the day, and then carry them back at the end of their shifts.

1. Define the problem	2. Consider problem solutions	3. Choose a solution Make an action plan	4. Test the solution	5. Evaluate the process
1. Problem: Workers are wasting time and energy hauling their tools and equipment to and from the worksite.	**2. Problem solution options:** Think about different ways to solve the problem. Several workers have proposed solutions: • Install lockers for tools and equipment closer to the worksite. • Have workers drive up to the worksite to drop off their tools and equipment before parking. • Bring in another construction trailer.	**3. Solution choice and action plan:** The worksite superintendent doesn't want an additional trailer in your crew's area. You and the team agree the shuttle service is the best option. It solves the time and energy issue *and* workers can keep their tools with them. The project supervisor plans to arrange a large van and driver to provide the shuttle service. **Note that this is a decision point in the problem-solving process.**	**4. Test the solution:** At first, the solution works, but a new problem arises. Everyone starts and leaves at the same time. The van can only hold half of the team and their equipment. To solve this problem, the supervisor schedules shuttle pickups every 15 minutes and adjusts work schedules so workers board the van at two different times. **Note that this is also a decision point in the problem-solving process.**	**5. Evaluate the process:** This process gave management and workers a chance to express an opinion and discuss the various solutions. Everyone feels pleased with the process and the solution.

Figure 12 Applying the problem-solving process, with decision points.

key point to note is that it's important to receive input from anyone in your group affected by the problem or the solution. Each solution will have pros and cons, so it's important to receive input from the workers affected by the problem. For example, workers will probably object to any plan (like the drop-off plan) that leaves their tools vulnerable to theft. Gaining the inputs of others will help you gain the trust and respect of your team.

2.3.2 Decision-Making

Figure 12 also shows where decisions are made as part of the problem-solving process. Decision-making is a choice made by using one's judgment. This judgment might be based on experience or on information learned during a problem-solving process. In general, you will have to make three types of decisions as a field leader, as shown in *Figure 13*.

No matter what the type, some decisions are simple or can be made based on past experiences. Other decisions are more difficult to make. These decisions require more careful thought about how to carry out an activity by using problem-solving techniques.

Note that decisions do have impacts, which you will need to consider. If you choose to use a shuttle to transport workers to a jobsite in shifts, as shown in *Figure 12*, using the shuttle may create a safety liability while workers are transported.

Decision Type	Description	Examples
Yes or no decisions	Decisions in which the answer is yes or no. Also called *whether* decisions, because you have to decide whether to take an action or not.	• Whether to hire a van to use as a shuttle service • Whether or not to promote a team member • Whether to alert a supervisor to an unsafe condition • Whether to proceed with a concrete pour
Options decisions	Decisions that require you to choose from a group of options. Also called *which* decisions, because you have to choose which option to take.	• Which of the three options will best address the problem of workers having to haul tools and equipment to and from the worksite? • Which toolbox talk would be most important to deliver to the team today? • Which team member should I have drive to the supply shop to pick up the order?
Contingent decisions	Decisions already made but on hold, until other specific events happen. These decisions can be very powerful because you can "pre-decide" what you will do in the event those events occur.	• If Carlo is late again two more times, I will set up a performance conversation. • If the materials arrive early, we will store them in the back of the jobsite. • If the team completes this task on time, I will find a clear way to recognize and reward the success.

Figure 13 Types of decisions.

2.0.0 Section Review

1. Which of the following is *not* a trait or behavior of effective frontline leaders?
   a. They lead by example.
   b. They are good communicators who lay out project goals to their crew.
   c. They motivate the team to work to their full potential.
   d. They have limited knowledge of the activities they supervise.
2. Which of the following is *not* a good practice to ensure effective communication?
   a. Speaking clearly at a reasonable pace
   b. Using highly technical language, acronyms, and slang
   c. Using visual cues, such as sketches or diagrams, to clarify instructions
   d. Using three-way communication to validate that a message was clear
3. While problem-solving is a process used to identify one or more possible solutions to a problem, the action of making a choice is called _____.
   a. decision-making
   b. a problem statement
   c. a decision statement
   d. action planning

3.0.0 Team Leadership and Motivation

Performance Tasks

There are no Performance Tasks in this section.

Objective

Identify key skills for team leadership and motivation.

a. Choose strategies to motivate individuals and a team.
b. Describe key approaches to building and leading teams.
c. Recognize how to approach leadership challenges, such as transitioning from peer to leader, addressing performance issues, and resolving conflict.

In your role as a frontline leader, you will have incredible impact on the individuals on your team. Motivating individuals and building successful teams are important and challenging tasks for any leader. You will also face leadership challenges as a new or developing leader, including managing performance issues, handling conflict, and leading team members who were once your peers. In this section, you will learn strategies and approaches to succeed as a team leader.

3.1.0 Motivating Individuals

The ability to motivate others is a key skill that leaders must develop. To motivate is to make someone feel determined or enthusiastic or to make someone behave in a particular way. On a jobsite, a leader uses authority and influence to encourage individuals to put in their best effort to accomplish the project goals. Lack of motivation affects job quality and productivity, reducing profits and growth for companies, businesses, contractors, or organizations that rely on people to complete the work.

As a supervisor or crew leader, it is important to understand what motivates each individual on your team. Different things motivate different people in different ways. This means there is no single best approach to motivating all of your crew members, because what motivates one crew member may not motivate another. In addition, what works to motivate a crew member once may not motivate that same person again in the future.

How can you know what motivates the members of your project team? Effective communication skills, specifically active listening, are a key part of getting to know each person on your team. You can also learn more about what motivates an employee by looking at factors in the employee's performance. Examples of factors that may indicate an individual's motivation include the level or rate of unexcused absenteeism, the number of complaints, and the quality and quantity of work produced.

Generally, the factors that motivate individuals are the same as those that create job satisfaction. These include the following:

- Clear expectations and goals from leaders
- Training to help individuals be successful
- Consistent sense of **accomplishment** and growth
- Recognition and rewards
- A good work environment and culture

Accomplishment: An individual's need to set challenging goals and achieve them.

A crew leader's ability to provide strong support in these areas increases the likelihood of high **morale** within a crew. Morale refers to an individual's emotional outlook toward work and the level of satisfaction gained while performing the jobs assigned. High morale means that employees will be motivated to work hard, and they will have a positive attitude about coming to work and doing their jobs. A motivated team is also generally a more productive and safer team, which can have a positive effect on project success.

Morale: An individual's emotional outlook toward work and the level of satisfaction gained while performing the jobs assigned.

3.1.1 Clear Expectations and Goals

As a leader, it is important for you to clearly communicate your expectations. A lack of clear expectations can leave your team feeling lost and demotivated. To get the best performance from your team and to motivate them, you need

Did You Know?

Money Doesn't Always Buy Motivation

Many leaders consider money to be a good motivator. Money can drive motivation, but it often is only a temporary solution. If you give someone a raise, they tend to work harder for a period of time. However, research shows that this behavioral change does not last. Further, after someone has reached a level of financial security, factors other than money may come into play. Over time, too much reliance on money for motivation can negatively impact a worker's commitment. Remember, employees are individuals who are motivated by different things, including pride in their work, work environment, and more. For those people, a great workplace may mean more to them than better pay.

Figure 14 Examples of unclear and clear expectations.

to set clear goals for completing tasks. You also need to ensure that everyone on the team understands the deadlines for those tasks. *Figure 14* includes an example of clear expectations.

Set achievable short-term and long-term goals, including tasks to be done and expected timeframes. Having short-term goals gives you a chance to provide regular feedback, positive praise, and rewards. However, because short-term goals can change, also setting long-term goals gives the team additional opportunities for success. Do not set workers up for failure, as this leads to frustration, and frustration can lead to reduced productivity.

In addition to setting clear goals and expectations, you must also deliver timely feedback. People want and need feedback and positive reinforcement for their contributions and efforts. However, telling someone they did a good job last year or criticizing them for work from a month ago is meaningless. When sharing timely feedback, always include specifics to help the individual know what they did well or where they could improve.

You always should share negative feedback in private. When delivering negative feedback, approach the problem as a coaching moment, working with the individual to understand their challenges and working with them to correct the problem. Every failure or miss can be an opportunity for you to help that individual grow, if the conversation and feedback are constructive.

Positive feedback can be shared privately or publicly. When you praise a person in front of their team, it may also encourage other members of the team. Praise can be a valuable tool to reinforce behaviors that you want. (Not all people like to be publicly praised, so consider that before you offer public praise.)

3.1.2 Accomplishment and Growth

Accomplishment refers to an individual's need to set challenging goals and achieve them. A sense of accomplishment motivates most people. That is why setting and working toward recognizable goals tends to make employees more productive. A person with a sense of achievement is likely to be better motivated and help to motivate others.

A person who can align a task to their sense of meaning is much more likely to complete it. Frontline leaders can help their team feel a sense of accomplishment by keeping the work challenging and interesting. Workers who are completing the same task every day or performing work above or below their skill level can quickly become demotivated. For many individuals, overcoming the challenge of new or difficult assignments is much more satisfying than performing repetitive, boring tasks.

Remember, however, that too many or significant changes in work may have a negative impact on morale, because people often prefer some consistency and predictability in their work. Crew members react to change in many different ways and reasons. For some individuals, change creates anxiety and uncertainty, which can result in a negative attitude toward the work. To help manage change with your crew, remember to share why the change is occurring and explain what the employees and company will gain.

As a leader, you must ensure the individuals on your team feel that their skills and abilities are valued and make a difference. Employees who do not feel valued tend to have performance and attendance issues. Leaders should work to ensure the following is true for every crew member:

- They feel like an important part of the team with a skill set that contributes to the project success.
- They know that every position helps them build skills and experience that will last throughout a career.
- They have a chance to learn new things and develop their skill sets.
- They see opportunities to grow and progress within the company.

Professional and personal growth are other critical factors in motivation. **Professional growth** refers to gaining new skills and work experience that can help you reach a goal in your career. It is important that employees know that they aren't limited to their current jobs. Let them know that they have a chance to grow with the company and to be promoted as acknowledgment for excelling in their work when such opportunities occur.

Professional growth: Gaining new skills and work experience that can help one to reach a goal in one's career.

Whenever possible, show your team that you value their professional growth by giving them more advanced responsibilities when they are ready to perform them safely. People who are presented with challenging tasks often are motivated to work harder and improve. This approach is a win–win since the construction project benefits from a higher level of productivity, while the worker experiences professional growth.

Effective leaders encourage each of their crew members to work to their full potential. In addition, they share information and skills with their employees to help them advance within the organization.

Personal growth is about improving your talents and potential, both in and out of the workplace. For example, a team member may find it very rewarding to master a new competency on the job. Experiencing this type of personal growth at work helps to motivate, reduce boredom, and spark enthusiasm for additional growth.

Personal growth: Improving one's talents and potential, both in and out of the workplace.

Personal growth also takes place outside the workplace. Crew leaders should encourage their employees to identify goals for themselves both professionally and personally and then support their efforts to accomplish those goals. As an example, training can be a way to improve both professional and personal skills, such as time management, communication, financial management, and more.

3.1.3 Training and Upskilling

Another key factor in motivating individuals—and ensuring productive and safe projects—is providing sufficient training and opportunities for **upskilling**. Upskilling is a type of training that provides someone with more advanced skills through additional education. Upskilling provides employees with the tools and knowledge they need to perform their current job more effectively, more efficiently, or in a more modern way.

Upskilling: A type of training that provides someone with more advanced skills through additional education.

As people enter the construction workforce, many will have completed training programs but may not have the specific practical experience needed to complete a task on a project site. When a new employee joins your crew, you will need to take an active role in confirming their skills and helping with on-the-job training if there are gaps. A frontline supervisor on a construction jobsite only has a short time to evaluate their crew members on what tasks they can do or how much experience the crew member actually has.

In the first week, with any new employee, you should ensure that you train the new employee on any jobsite processes and allow time to do a task verification (*Figure 15*). After you have established the skills the individual has, you can work on a plan to leverage those skills while establishing new ones. If you identify gaps, you can create a training plan for that individual to address those areas.

3.1.4 Recognition and Rewards

Recognition: Acknowledgement of an employee's accomplishments through verbal and nonverbal communications.

Positive feedback is a form of **recognition**. Recognition acknowledges an employee's accomplishments through verbal and nonverbal communications. Individuals want to have good work appreciated, applauded, and acknowledged by others. You can accomplish this by thanking employees, offering an award for Employee of the Month, or giving tangible or monetary awards.

The following are tips to remember for giving recognition and praise:

- Be available on the jobsite so that you see good work as it is happening.
- Provide positive feedback publicly or in private.
- Give recognition and praise only when truly deserved. People quickly recognize insincere praise and will lose respect for the person delivering it.
- Encourage improvement by showing confidence in the ability of the crew members to do above-average work.
- Use goal setting as a tool to build confidence and create opportunities for praise.

Rewards are tangible recognition for good work. Rewards can be monetary, such as opportunities for raises, bonuses, or other incentive pay. Other types of rewards might include company gear, vouchers for new boots, gift cards, a team outing at the end of the week, or the best spot in the parking area for a month.

3.1.5 Good Work Environment and Culture

Having a good work environment and culture is critical for creating strong employee motivation and high morale. As a leader, you can create a good work environment and culture for your team in several ways.

Treat employees well. Be considerate, kind, and respectful. Treat people fairly. Mentor your employees. Coaching and supporting employees boosts their self-esteem, their self-confidence, and their motivation. Remember that small things matter. Having clean lunch areas, good housekeeping, and a comfortable workplace communicates that you respect the group.

Figure 15 When a new employee starts, be sure to evaluate the crew member's skills.
Source: kali9/E+/Getty Images

Communicate actively. As a leader, you should make yourself available for questions, opinions, and ideas. Actively engaging and communicating with workers plays a crucial role in motivating your team, as it shows that you appreciate and value their feedback. Involve employees in discussions so that they feel their opinions are valued. This, in turn, leads to a sense of pride and active participation. Making yourself available also prevents team members from feeling isolated from leadership.

When you communicate, be positive. Approaching your leadership responsibilities by threatening employees with negative consequences can result in higher employee turnover instead of motivation.

As much as possible, maintain a sense of humor, especially toward your own failings as a human being. No one is perfect. Your employees will appreciate that and be more motivated to encourage you.

Help individuals manage stress. In a job that can be demanding, fast-paced, and tiring at times, managers in the construction industry must take measures to ensure that their team is not exposed to undue stress. Work with your supervisors to ensure you have a safe and reasonable work environment. This means not only physical spaces, but also policies and procedures. For example, allowing workers to take time off to deal with personal matters or emergencies shows that the company prioritizes their well-being. Engage with your supervisors to help address resources and to organize shifts in such situations to ensure that project progress and construction costs are not negatively impacted.

Lead by example. Employees will be far more motivated to follow someone who is willing to do the same things they are required to do. Being a good leader and motivator means leading by example. Employees will not be motivated to work if upper management does not display the same level of commitment to the job that they are asked to have. For example, if you ask everyone to work late, but then leave early to go see a movie, this will be noticed and may create feelings of resentment and decrease team morale. As a leader, you can inspire your team by displaying the behaviors you would like to see from them, including working hard, showing personal and professional integrity, and having a can-do attitude.

3.2.0 Leading Teams

As a crew leader, you will need to lead a team of individuals from a range of backgrounds and experiences and create a high-performing team. To do so, you will need to delegate work to that team and implement policies and procedures that support the team. You will also need to address challenges like language barriers and **harassment**.

Harassment: Unwelcome conduct that is based on race, color, religion, sex, national origin, age, disability, or genetic information. Harassment includes verbal or physical conduct that impacts a person's work performance or creates an intimidating, hostile, or offensive work environment.

3.2.1 Delegating to Your Team

Once the various activities that make up the job have been determined, the crew leader must identify the person or persons who will be responsible for completing each activity. This requires that the crew leader be aware of the skills and abilities of the people on the crew. Then you must put this knowledge to work by matching the crew's skills and abilities to specific tasks needed to complete the job.

After matching crew members to specific activities, you must then delegate the assignments to the responsible person(s). Generally, when delegating responsibilities, the crew leader verbally communicates directly with the person who will perform or complete the activity.

When delegating work, remember to do the following:

- *Delegate work to a crew member who can do the job properly.* If it becomes evident that the worker doesn't perform to the desired standard, either teach the crew member to do the work correctly or turn it over to someone else who can (without making a public spectacle of the transfer).
- *Make sure crew members understand what to do and the level of responsibility.* Be clear about the desired results, specify the boundaries and deadlines for accomplishing the results, and note the available resources.

- *Identify the standards and methods of measurement for progress and accomplishment.* Also identify the consequences of not achieving the desired results. Discuss the task with the crew member and check for understanding by asking questions. Allow the crew member to contribute feedback or make suggestions about how to perform the task in a safe and quality manner.
- *Give the crew member the time and freedom to get started.* Don't make them feel pressured by too much supervision. When making the work assignment, be sure to tell the employee how much time there is to complete it and confirm that this time is consistent with the job schedule.
- *Check in on progress.* Be sure to periodically check in on the crew member's progress. This will allow you to see how the task is going and allow the crew member to ask questions. Checking in along the way will also help you clear up any misunderstandings early and avoid rework.
- *Examine and evaluate the result.* After the task is complete, ask the crew member for their comments on how the work went. Provide your own feedback. Having this discussion will help you know what kind of work to assign that crew member in the future. It will also provide a means of measuring your effectiveness in delegating work.

There may be a time when someone else in the company issues written or verbal instructions to a crew member or your crew without going through you as the crew leader. If this happens, work with that individual to understand why they took that approach. Then help that person understand why it is important for them to work through you for this type of instruction, whenever possible, so that you can manage the work of the entire crew safely and productively.

3.2.2 Implementing Policies and Procedures

Every company establishes policies and procedures that crew leaders are expected to implement and employees are expected to follow. Company policies and procedures are essentially guidelines for how the organization does business. They can also reflect organizational philosophies, such as putting safety first or making the customer the top priority. Examples of policies and procedures include safety guidelines, credit standards, and billing processes.

The following tips can help you effectively implement policies and procedures:

- Learn the purpose of each policy. This will help you follow the policy and apply it appropriately and fairly.
- If you're not sure how to apply a company policy or procedure, check the company manual or ask your supervisor.
- Always follow company policies and procedures. Remember that they combine what's best for the customer and the company. In addition, they provide direction on how to handle specific situations and answer questions.

NOTE

Try to obtain a supervisor's policy interpretation in writing or print out their email response so that you can append the decision to your copy of the company manual for future reference.

Crew leaders may need to issue directions to their crew members. A *direction* is a form of communication that initiates, changes, or stops an activity. Directions may be general or specific, written or verbal, formal or informal. It is up to you how you issue directions, but the policies and procedures of the company may govern your choice.

When issuing directions, do the following:

- Make them as specific as possible. Avoid being general or vague unless it is impossible to foresee all the circumstances that could occur in carrying out the directions.
- Recognize that you do not have to write directions for simple tasks unless your company requires this.
- Write directions for more complex tasks, tasks that will take considerable time to complete, or tasks that are permanent (standing) orders.

- Consider what is being said, the audience to whom it applies, and the situation under which it will be implemented to determine the appropriate level of formality for the direction.

3.2.3 Addressing Language Barriers

Leading a diverse team also means addressing language barriers. Millions of US workers speak languages other than English. Jobsites where two or more languages are used are common. In addition, even among English speakers, accents and dialects can present communication barriers.

As you have learned, any barrier in communication keeps people from being able to understand each other clearly. If a person does not fully understand the task a frontline supervisor gives them, the task may be completed incorrectly, which can cause delays, cause additional expenses, or create an unsafe situation. As a supervisor of a crew, you need to know that each crew member understands the work to be done. The following tips will help when communicating across language barriers:

- Be patient. Give workers time to process the information in a way they can comprehend.
- Avoid humor. Humor is easily misunderstood. The worker may misinterpret what you say as a joke at the worker's expense.
- Do not assume an individual is not intelligent simply because they don't understand what you are saying.
- Speak slowly and clearly. Avoid the tendency to raise your voice.
- Use face-to-face communication whenever possible. Other forms of communication can be more difficult when a language barrier is involved.
- Use the plans and drawings or make sketches to ensure people understand clearly.
- For critical written instructions, ensure the individual's literacy level matches the level of difficulty and language of the document. A person may speak clearly in a second language, but struggle with written understanding.
- Communicate in multiple ways or adjust your level of detail or terminology to ensure that everyone understands the meaning as intended.
- Confirm understanding. Ask for feedback with open-ended questions that require more than yes-or-no answers. Use three-way communication and have an individual repeat back what they heard to ensure mutual understanding and prevent miscommunication. If a worker is not fluent in English, ask the person to demonstrate their understanding through other means.

Many organizations offer language classes for supervisors and employees to help create more effective communication on jobsites. Whenever possible, take advantage of these training opportunities and encourage your crew to do so.

3.2.4 Preventing Harassment

As a frontline supervisor of a team, you must be aware of harassment as a potential challenge. As defined by the US Equal Employment Opportunity Commission (EEOC), harassment is unwelcome conduct that is based on race, color, religion, sex, national origin, age, disability, or genetic information. Harassment includes verbal or physical conduct that impacts a person's work performance or creates an intimidating, hostile, or offensive work environment.

The following are examples of activities that might qualify as harassment:

- Telling offensive jokes
- Calling someone offensive names
- Making verbal or physical advances or assaults

- Making threats or intimidating others
- Displaying offensive objects or pictures

Harassment becomes unlawful when a person must endure the offensive conduct to remain employed or the conduct is severe or common enough to create an intimidating, hostile, or abusive work environment. While not all acts of harassing behavior may be serious enough to be considered a violation of the law, all such behavior destroys teamwork and negatively affects jobsite safety and productivity.

Anyone can be a victim of harassment. Historically, many have thought of harassment as an act perpetrated by someone in power over another. However, a harasser can be a supervisor, a supervisor in another area, a coworker, or any other person in the work environment.

The EEOC enforces sexual harassment laws within industries. When investigating allegations of harassment, the EEOC looks at the whole record, including the circumstances and the context in which the alleged incidents occurred. Supervision may hold the crew leader responsible if they were aware of sexual harassment and did nothing to stop it. You should not only take action to stop harassment, but also should serve as a good example for the rest of the crew.

Prevention is the best way to eliminate harassment in the workplace. Your employer will have a harassment policy that clearly communicates zero tolerance for harassment and outlines a complaint or grievance process. This process should include taking immediate and appropriate action when an employee complains. This anti-harassment policy should apply to all employees (including managers, supervisors, and coworkers) and nonemployees (such as suppliers, owners, vendors, and others). Creating an open and inclusive work environment will discourage harassment.

As a leader, you must understand and uphold your employer's policies and procedures on harassment. If you believe that someone has violated the harassment policy, immediately notify your supervisor. If you are not comfortable reporting the incident to your immediate supervisor, you may report the complaint to any employee in a supervisory position or Human Resources. If you are not sure how to proceed in a situation, reach out to your Human Resources partners for guidance.

3.3.0 Leadership Challenges

As the leader of a team, you will need to manage leadership challenges and opportunities every day on the job. While the specific challenges will vary based on your team, the project, and other conditions, you must learn to address these when they arise. Such challenges can include navigating your initial transition from peer to leader, managing performance issues with your crew, or resolving conflicts that arise on the jobsite.

3.3.1 Transitioning from Peer to Leader

Making the transition from crew member to a crew leader can be difficult, especially when the new position involves overseeing a group of former peers. When you move from being a peer to a leader, your relationship with your former team members changes in important ways.

When you become a crew leader, you are no longer responsible for your work alone. You are now accountable for the work of a diverse team of individuals with varying skill levels, personalities, work styles, and cultural and educational backgrounds.

Crew leaders must learn to put personal relationships aside and work for the common goals of the entire crew. The crew leader can overcome these problems by working with the crew to set mutual performance goals and by freely communicating with them within permitted limits. Use their knowledge and strengths along with your own so that they feel like they are key players on the team. *Table 4* lists some additional suggestions on how to make the transition from peer to leader easier.

TABLE 4 Making the Transition from Peer to Leader

Strategy	Tactic
Reset boundaries with existing friends	Expectations and boundaries must be set with existing friends. Having a strong, professional working relationship is important, but you may need to reduce time spent with old peers outside of the project. Be clear and explain that, on the job, business comes before personal relationships.
Demonstrate that you have earned this leadership role	Quickly demonstrate good leadership for your team to earn employees' trust and respect. Be fair and consistent in everything you do. The perception of favoritism will tear a crew apart and negatively impact the outcome of any project.
Make the best decisions for the project and your company	Always make decisions that are best for the business. While it can be hard to make a decision that impacts someone who was a peer and is a friend, don't compromise to make a popular decision.

3.3.2 Managing Performance Issues

At the end of the day, if someone is simply not being accountable and completing their work, it might be time for a difficult conversation. In the workplace, a difficult conversation is one in which you have to manage emotions and information in a sensitive way to deal with a workplace issue. A difficult conversation may involve the following:

- Communicating business decisions
- Discussing poor performance or behavior
- Addressing conflict
- Handling complaints
- Ending employment or other changes in job status

As a leader and manager, you will need to have a difficult conversation at some point in your career. These conversations are never enjoyable, but you can handle them effectively by following some basic steps.

Identify the problem to resolve. Ensure that you have a clear understanding of the problem that you want to resolve. Before you start preparing for the conversation, ask: Why do you want to have the conversation? What do you want to achieve? Is the outcome you're looking for realistic?

Gather the information you need. Make sure you know the facts of the situation before approaching the employee. Bring any documents you will need to the meeting. For example, if you are discussing how an employee is late to work, you will want to have relevant policies and tardiness data at hand. If you are not sure about any internal workplace policies and procedures, you can always seek advice from a supervisor or Human Resources manager.

Think about the employee's point of view. Before you speak, you should think about the matter from your employee's point of view. Engage in the conversation with an open mind and truly seek to understand the situation from the employee's point of view.

Get the timing right. Try to schedule the conversation as soon as possible, but not if emotions are running high. Choose a time and place appropriate for the discussion, where you will not be rushed or interrupted. Generally, avoid having negative discussions at the end of the week and, if an employee needs time to process the conversation, offer to take a break and meet again later that day or the next.

Prepare what you are going to say. Write down the key points you need to cover, so that you can keep your conversation on track and stay in control. While it is important to prepare notes, avoid preparing a rehearsed script, as it may hamper your ability to listen effectively, react accordingly, or find alternative solutions.

Give the employee time to prepare. Make an appointment with the employee and provide some context to give them some time to prepare. Remember that knowing this conversation is coming may be stressful for the employee, so phrase the approach carefully and don't leave it too long. Examples of ways to phrase the appointment might be:

> "I'd like to talk about a series of quality issues I'm noting and get your point of view. Can you come see me tomorrow?"

> "I think we have different perceptions about what it means to have a clean work area. I'd like to hear your thoughts on this. Are you free this afternoon?"

Seek support if you need it. If you're not comfortable having the conversation one-on-one with the employee, enlist help from your manager or Human Resources person.

After the conversation, be sure to take the following steps:

- *Document the discussion.* Write down any agreements that were reached, and indicate the date, time, and who was present. This will be helpful if you need to revisit the discussion at a future date. Your *job diary*, which you will learn about later, is a useful tool here.
- *Follow up with the employee.* Confirm what you had agreed in writing and send these to the employee. Be sure to give the employee time to actually act upon the steps they agreed to.
- *Take some time to reflect on the matter.* Learn from the experience and think about what you could do differently next time. Debrief with your supervisor or Human Resources if you feel you need to discuss the matter.

Also, remember that you should never discuss this matter with other staff members. You must treat the employee the same as you had prior to the conversation and remain completely professional.

If you do need to have this type of difficult conversation, do it as soon as you start to have concerns or see early signals of conflict. The worse a situation becomes, the harder it can be to manage and resolve. In the meantime, your project and the rest of the crew are being affected.

As previously noted, the best communication strategy is to have an open-door policy or informal one-on-one conversations so that issues can be dealt with as naturally as possible. Be approachable and keep in touch with your team, so they are more likely to come to you with problems before they escalate.

3.3.3 Conflict Resolution

Conflicts will happen during a project. When you have many groups, including owners, general contractors, and specialty contractors all working together to complete a project, disagreements are likely to happen. Conflicts can arise within your crew as well. Each person or group might have a different view or opinion on how something should be done. Those differing opinions often lead to conflicts.

As a leader of the team, you will have many opportunities to look for positive and proactive means to resolve conflict. Resolving conflicts can lead to a better understanding or a new way of doing things that improve the overall project. If you handle conflict well, it will further earn the respect and trust of your crew. The following are some strategies to use when addressing conflict:

Recognize that conflict is normal. Not all conflict is bad. Conflicts on the construction site can be good. If the individuals engaged in the conflict are mature, conflict can improve processes and approaches by creating conversation about new ways to do work.

Do not ignore the conflict. Take action early to avoid further complications down the line. Even a small dispute that may appear inconsequential can balloon into a larger problem if it goes unresolved. If you allow the parties involved to work it out on their own, you still need to follow up and make sure that there aren't any lingering issues.

Understand the real issue behind the conflict. You must understand the real issues causing the conflict to determine the best solution. Conflicts are often caused by different interpretations of plans and specifications, change orders, scheduling, and poor communication. Work stress can also be an underlying issue. Conflicts, for example, may happen more often later in the day or in a work shift, due to fatigue. Use your active-listening skills to listen to everyone involved. This shows everyone that their opinions matter and that you are committed to working with them to resolve the issue fairly.

Remain neutral and focus on business, not people. Conflicts can escalate quickly from a simple disagreement to a shouting match. If appropriate, call for a short break before starting the discussion again. Remind everyone that resolving conflicts is about making the best business decision for the project, not personal feelings. Both parties should sit down and stay focused on developing a solution that is in the best interest of the project.

Compromise and work with the team. Conflicts rarely have a clear-cut right and wrong. As you work to resolve the conflict, you will need to encourage others to be willing to compromise and work together to solve the problem. The effort here must stay focused again on the desired business result: "What is the best decision for this situation?" Construction is all about cooperation and collaboration. However, if the conflict involves safety rules and regulations or adhering to building codes, any solution must follow the proper policy, procedure, or regulation.

Avoid conflict through clear communications. Poor communication on the jobsite often leads to conflicts. Make sure that you clearly communicate expectations with everyone on the project. Keeping everyone up to date with any changes to the project or schedule can help avoid conflict.

Communicate the resolution and follow up. Resolving conflicts may not result in a win for everyone. It is important that once resolution is reached, everyone gets an explanation and is clear on what is expected moving forward. They might not always agree with the decision. Having a clear expectation will help others accept the decision. Whenever an agreement is reached, follow up to determine if both sides are working as discussed or if issues still exist. You also will remind everyone that, although the conflict might have been difficult, the resolution produced a good outcome for the project.

If you cannot resolve a conflict on your own, always reach out to your supervisor for guidance. Your supervisor or another senior leader can make a decision and communicate it to the appropriate individuals.

Remember, the goal of any construction project is to see the successful completion of the job on time and within budget. When conflicts arise, it can threaten the goal of on-time and on-budget job completion. As the leader of your crew, you must learn to address and resolve conflicts, so that the project work can proceed. Resolving conflicts can be challenging. It all comes down to making the best business decision to keep the project moving forward.

3.0.0 Section Review

1. Which of the following is *not* a way to motivate a team?
   a. Providing training and helping individuals feel a sense of accomplishment and growth
   b. Setting expectations without clear short-term and long-term goals
   c. Offering recognition and rewards when appropriate
   d. Having a good work environment and culture

2. One sign of a high-performing team is _____.
   a. the leader cannot delegate work to the team
   b. harassment is common on the worksite
   c. everyone on the team follows policies and procedures
   d. language barriers prevent effective communication

3. As a frontline leader, steps to successfully resolving conflict may involve any of the following *except* _____.
   a. remaining neutral and focusing on the business, not on people
   b. compromising and working with the team
   c. ignoring the conflict
   d. understanding the real issues causing the conflict

4.0.0 Safety and Safety Leadership

Performance Tasks

1. Organize and deliver a safety-related toolbox talk, applying communication skills.
2. Complete a job safety analysis.

Objective

Identify a frontline leader's safety leadership responsibilities.

a. Assess the impact of incidents.
b. Explain the purpose of OSHA and describe the role of OSHA in administering worker safety.
c. Describe the importance of safety and health programs.
d. Explain the frontline leader's role in incident preparedness and response.
e. Recognize the importance of supporting your crew's total health.

Hazards: Conditions or activities that, if left uncontrolled, have the potential for harm.

Incidents: Unplanned events that result in property damage, fatalities, injuries, illnesses, or near misses.

Craft professionals routinely face **hazards**. Examples of these hazards include falling from heights, working on scaffolds, using cranes in the presence of power lines, operating heavy machinery, and working on electrically powered or pressurized equipment. Despite these hazards, applying preventive safety measures can significantly reduce the number of **incidents**.

Safety matters because people matter. As a crew leader, some of your most important responsibilities are to enforce the company's safety program, make sure that all workers are performing their tasks safely, and ensure that everyone on the jobsite remains safe and goes home healthy (*Figure 16*). You must recognize safety risks and work to eliminate or reduce them.

To be successful, the crew leader should do the following:

- Be aware of the human and business impacts of incidents.
- Understand all federal, state, and local governmental safety regulations applicable to your work.
- Be the most visible example of the best safe work practices.
- Be involved in training workers in safe work methods.
- Conduct training sessions.
- Get involved in safety inspections and incident investigations.

Crew leaders are in an important position to ensure that their crew members perform all jobs safely. Providing employees with a safe working environment by preventing incidents and enforcing safety standards will go a long way toward maintaining the job schedule, ensuring a timely job completion within budget, and keeping your team healthy.

Figure 16 Committing to safety is a key part of a crew leader's role.
Source: RainStar/E+/Getty Images

4.1.0 The Impact of Incidents

An incident is an unplanned event that results in property damage, a fatality, injury, illness, or a near miss. A near miss is an unplanned event that does not result in personal injury but may result in property damage or is worthy of recording.

Incidents including work-related injuries, sickness, and fatalities cause immense suffering for workers and their families. Resulting project delays and budget overruns can cause huge losses for employers, and worksite incidents damage the overall morale of everyone on a project or jobsite.

Businesses lose billions of dollars every year because of on-the-job incidents. As just one measure of the business impact of incidents, construction companies in the United States pay over $1 billion per week in **workers' compensation** for nonfatal injuries. Workers' compensation, often called *workers' comp*, is insurance that companies have to cover medical expenses, lost wages, and other costs for employees who are injured or become ill while completing work for their job. It also pays death benefits to families of employees who are killed on the job.

Workers' compensation: Insurance that companies have to cover medical expenses, lost wages, and other costs for employees who are injured or become ill while completing work for their job.

Preventing injuries means protecting the lives of workers, while reducing significant costs for their employers. It is estimated that the full impact of workplace injuries and fatalities cost companies approximately $151 billion per year. These costs affect the individual employee, the company, and the construction industry as a whole.

Organizations encounter both direct and indirect costs associated with workplace incidents.

- Direct costs are the money companies must pay out to workers' compensation claims and sick pay.
- Indirect costs are all of the costs a company must account for as the result of a worker's injury or death, such as time off from work.

The direct and indirect costs of incidents are comparable to the visible and hidden portions of an iceberg, as shown in *Figure 17*. The visible part of the iceberg represents direct costs, some of which are covered by insurance. The hidden part of the iceberg represents the indirect costs, which are a greater financial burden than the direct costs.

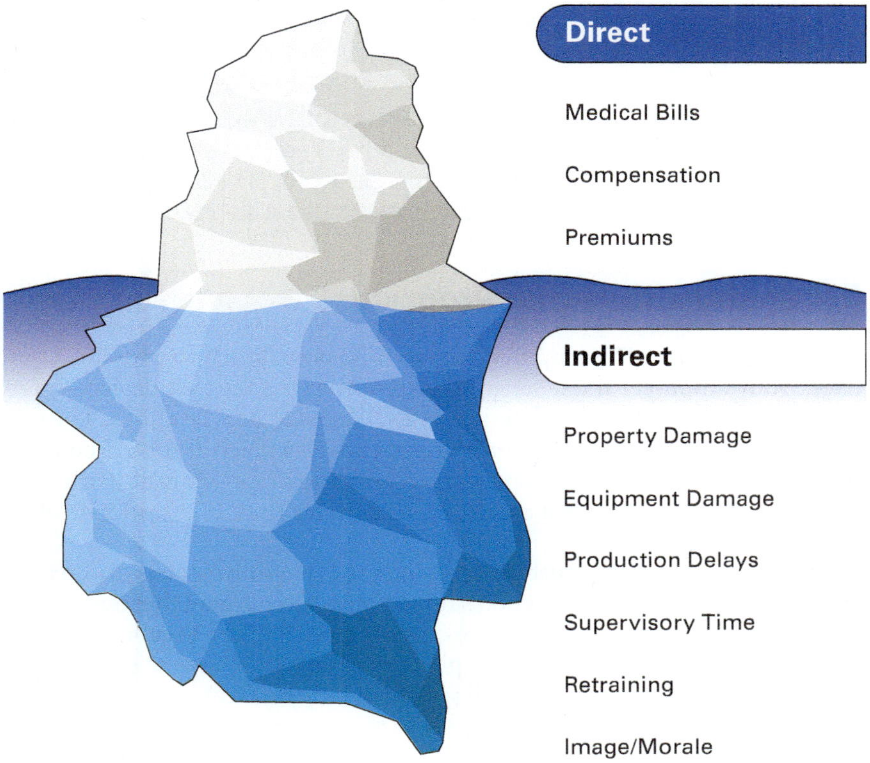

Figure 17 Incidents create both direct and indirect costs.

4.2.0 OSHA

To reduce safety and health risks and the number of injuries and fatalities on the job, the federal government has enacted laws and regulations, including the Occupational Safety and Health Act of 1970 (OSH Act of 1970). This law created the Occupational Safety and Health Administration (OSHA), which is part of the US Department of Labor. OSHA also provides education and training for employers and workers. Through the administration of OSHA, the US Congress seeks to ensure safe and healthful working conditions for workers by setting and enforcing standards and by providing training, outreach, education, and assistance.

OSHA has many functions. OSHA issues standards and rules for working conditions, facilities, equipment, tools, and work processes. It does extensive research into occupational incidents, illnesses, injuries, and deaths to reduce the number of occurrences and adverse effects. In addition, OSHA regulatory agencies conduct workplace inspections to ensure that companies follow the standards and rules. The agencies also have the right to take legal action if companies are not in compliance with OSHA standards and rules.

OSHA has established significant monetary fines for the violation of its regulations. *Table 5* lists the maximum OSHA penalty amounts as of 2022. In addition to the fines, there are possible criminal charges for willful violations resulting in death or serious injury. The attitude of the employer and their safety history can have a significant effect on the outcome of a case.

> **Did You Know?**
> **OSHA 10 and OSHA 30 Authorized Certification**
> OSHA helps to make safety training available through their Outreach Training Program's authorized 10-hour and 30-hour safety courses. The goal of these courses is to promote workplace safety and health and to make workers more knowledgeable about workplace hazards and their rights. As a crew leader, you may already have completed the OSHA-authorized 10-hour training program, which is designed for entry-level workers. The OSHA-authorized 30-hour training program provides more in-depth training and is intended for supervisors or others with some safety responsibility. If you want to take an OSHA-authorized 10-hour or 30-hour training program, work with your supervisor to obtain this training.

TABLE 5 OSHA Maximum Penalty Amounts

Type of Violation	Maximum Penalty
Serious	$14,502 per violation
Other-Than-Serious	
Posting Requirements	
Failure to Abate	$14,502 per day
Willful or Repeated Violation	$145,027 per violation

> **Did You Know?**
> **State OSHA Programs**
> Nearly half the states in the United States and some of its territories have state-run OSHA programs. These programs are set up under federal OSHA guidelines and must establish job health and safety standards that are at least as effective as the federal standards. The states/territories have the option of adopting more stringent standards or setting standards for hazards not addressed in the federal program. Of the 22 states and territories with nonfederal OSHA programs, six of them limit their coverage to state and local government employees.

4.3.0 Safety and Health Programs

Under the OSH Act of 1970, employers have a responsibility to provide a safe workplace. Your employer must set up a program to manage workplace safety and health and to reduce work-related injuries, illnesses, and fatalities. The program must be appropriate for the conditions of the workplace. It should consider the number of workers employed and the hazards they face while at work. On a project site, a hazard usually is a condition or activity that, if left uncontrolled, has the potential for harm.

One way employers help create a safe working environment is to create a **construction safety plan**. A construction safety plan is a document that outlines the procedures, rules, and regulations that are or will be put in place to protect workers during a construction project. The safety plan should include steps to prevent incidents and respond if they occur, including emergency medical services and processes to review and report incidents. For some projects, a **site-specific safety plan (SSSP)** will include a focused set of information that accounts for a jobsite's unique hazards. Safety plans should be created before a construction project is underway, but also should be updated on a regular basis as conditions on the site change.

Construction safety plan: A document that outlines the procedures, rules, and regulations that are or will be put in place to protect workers during a construction project.

Site-specific safety plan (SSSP): A safety plan that includes a focused set of information that accounts for a jobsite's unique hazards.

4.3.1 Education and Training

All employees should receive a safety policies and procedures manual and initial training when they are hired. A company's safety manual should cover the company's safety expectations and the procedures that must be followed to create a safe work environment and meet OSHA requirements. During orientation, appropriate company staff should guide new employees through the safety policies and procedures manual, focusing on the sections most important for their job. An employer must ensure that any barriers to worker understanding, such as language barriers, are removed or addressed.

In addition to formal training, safety is a topic you need to discuss with your crew every day on the jobsite. You need to help employees be aware of and avoid the hazards to which craft professionals are exposed. As a leader, you should plan to conduct frequent safety trainings and meetings with your crew, including holding toolbox talks (*Figure 18*). These meetings are important to building a strong safety culture and reinforcing your company's commitment to protecting your workers.

Toolbox talks are one way to effectively keep all workers aware and informed of safety issues and guidelines. Toolbox talks, sometimes referred to as *tailgate meetings* or *safety briefings*, are short, informal safety meetings held at the start of each day or shift. Toolbox talks are 5- to 10-minute meetings that review specific health and safety topics. *Table 6* provides a checklist for delivering effective safety briefings or toolbox talks.

Toolbox talks: Short, informal safety meetings held at the start of each day or shift. Sometimes referred to as *tailgate meetings* or *safety briefings*.

Always document your toolbox talks or other safety training. Even if certain OSHA standards do not require documentation of safety training, keep a record of each safety session signed by all attendees. In the record, include the date, a summary of the training session, the trainer, and attendees.

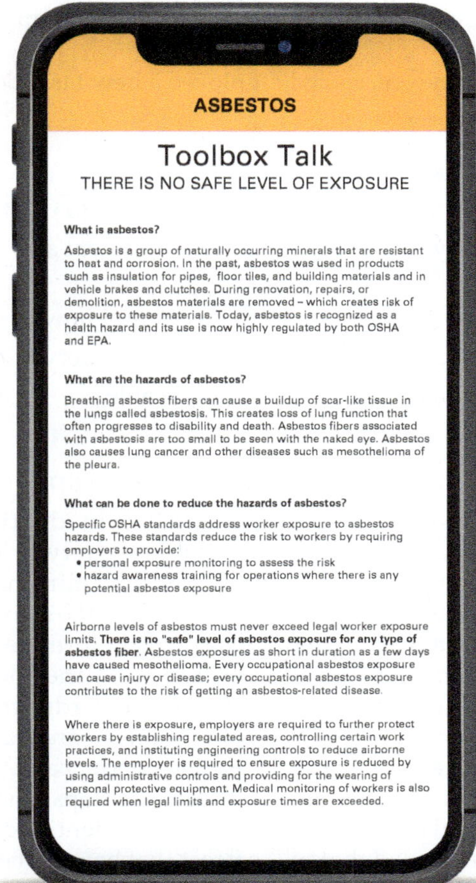

Figure 18 Safety management software can help companies deliver and track worker training. Some of the solutions help you schedule, track, and deliver toolbox talks.

TABLE 6 Delivering Effective Safety Briefings or Toolbox Talks

Did You . . .?	Yes/No
Schedule time in advance and create time to allow workers to participate.	
Speak clearly and directly at a natural pace.	
Try to find a spot free of noise and other distractions. If the workers cannot hear you talking, or are distracted by other activities in the area, they won't be focusing on your talk.	
Use props to help make your point and provide visual communication cues. For example, have a safety harness with you for your talk on fall protection.	
Reinforce safety basics, focus on high-risk scenarios, and inform workers about changes to the jobsite and working conditions that may have occurred since their last shift.	
Discuss any incidents or injuries that have occurred and how they could have been prevented.	
Focus the discussion on active work. For example, do not hold a toolbox talk on sitework when electrical work is the only thing being done that day.	
If appropriate, break out a toolbox talk into smaller groups to focus on individual crafts or work activities for certain individuals.	
Focus on the positive too. Highlight safe working practices. Provide positive reinforcement and applaud workers following safety rules and regulations.	
Always give workers an opportunity to ask questions at the end of the toolbox talk.	

One-on-one or small group training is also a critical part of keeping everyone on the project safe. When you assign an inexperienced employee a new task, you must ensure that the employee can do the work in a safe manner. You can accomplish this by providing safety information or training for groups or individuals.

When assigning an inexperienced employee a new task, do the following:

- Define the task.
- Explain how to do the task safely.
- Explain what tools and equipment to use and how to use them safely.
- Identify the necessary personal protective equipment and train the employee in its use.
- Explain the nature of the hazards in the work and how to recognize them.
- Stress the importance of personal safety and the safety of others.
- Review Safety Data Sheets that may be applicable.

4.3.2 Hazard Identification, Assessment, Prevention, and Control

Crew leaders and workers play an important role in identifying and reporting hazards. Hazards are often identified in job safety or job hazard analyses, which also document how the hazards will be eliminated or mitigated. A **job safety analysis (JSA)**, or *job hazard analysis (JHA)*, is a technique that focuses on job tasks as a way to identify hazards before they occur. It focuses on the relationship between the worker, the task, the tools, and the work environment. After you identify uncontrolled hazards, you will take steps to control them by eliminating or reducing them to an acceptable risk level.

Job safety analysis (JSA): A technique that focuses on job tasks as a way to identify hazards before they occur. It focuses on the relationship between the worker, the task, the tools, and the work environment. Also known as *job hazard analysis (JHA)* or *activity hazard analysis (AHA)*.

Figure 19 shows an example of a form used to conduct a JSA. In a JSA, the task at hand is broken down into its individual parts or steps, and then each step is analyzed for its potential hazards. Once a hazard is identified, certain actions or procedures are recommended that will correct that hazard. For example, during a JSA, it is determined that using a chain hoist to install a pump motor in a tight space would be safer than having a worker do it manually. By using the chain hoist, the chance that the worker's hand would get crushed during installation is reduced. Using the JSA process would help protect the worker from injury.

JOB SAFETY ANALYSIS

TITLE OF JOB OR TASK

TASK	START	END	HAZARDS	CONTROLS
1.				
2.				
3.				
4.				
5.				
6.				
7.				
8.				

Required Training: Required Personal Protective Equipment (PPE):

Job Name: ____________

Job Number: ____________

Supervisor: ____________

Date: ____________

Weekly Vehicle Checklist: ___ Tire Pressure ___ Transmission Fluid ___ Oil ___ Lights ___ Air Filter ___ Wkly Mileage

Name of Employees:

PRINT NAME	SIGN NAME	TOTAL HOURS

Figure 19 Job safety analysis form.

A job safety analysis can also be used during planning to ensure that safety is planned into the job. Taking this approach helps ensure that safety does not get compromised for the sake of schedule and productivity.

Crew leaders must protect workers from existing or potential hazards in their work areas. It is the crew leader's responsibility to determine what working conditions are unsafe and to inform employees of hazards and their locations. In addition, they should encourage their crew members to tell them about hazardous conditions. To accomplish this, crew leaders must be present and available on the jobsite.

4.3.3 Management Leadership and Employee Participation

A culture of commitment to safety and a strong safety and health program require management leadership and employee participation. As a frontline leader, the best way for you to encourage employee participation in safety and health is to lead by example. Your behavior sets standards for your crew members. If you cut corners on safety, you are telling your crew they may do so as well.

You should always be sure to do the following:

- Stay actively involved in your company's safety and health program.
- Exceed expectations when it comes to safety. Help others follow the rules and ask your crew if there are safer ways to do a task.
- Host safety training and meetings. Discuss safety at the start of each shift. Have regular toolbox talks. Include safety in all meetings, even if the primary purpose is schedule, cost, or production related.
- Be a visible participant on safety walks.
- Review and provide feedback on hazard analyses.
- Always follow up on safety concerns raised by the workers.

CAUTION

Team members often "follow the leader" when it comes to unsafe work practices. Sometimes, supervisory personnel engage in unsafe practices and take more risks because they are more experienced. However, inexperienced or careless workers who take the same risks won't be as successful in avoiding injury. As a leader, you must follow all safety practices to encourage your crew to do the same.

Your employer will use their policies and procedures for incident investigation and documentation. Be sure to follow any of these guidelines, when the situation arises.

4.4.0 Incident Preparedness and Response

While the goal is to have zero incidents on a worksite, you and your team must understand how to respond quickly to a safety incident. If an incident occurs, you should follow the safety policies and procedures in the construction safety plan. As a frontline leader, you are responsible for making sure everyone on your team understands the safety plan. You also may have reporting and investigation responsibilities after an incident.

4.4.1 Administering First Aid

First aid: Help given to a sick or injured worker on the worksite immediately after an injury occurs.

When someone is hurt or has a medical event, your first goal is ensuring the best outcome: minimizing the health impact to the person. **First aid** is help given to a sick or injured worker on the worksite immediately after an injury occurs. The primary purpose of first aid is to provide immediate and temporary medical care to employees involved in incidents, as well as employees experiencing non-work-related health emergencies, such as chest pain or breathing difficulty.

Many companies have very specific policies on administering first aid. If you are unsure of these policies, ask your supervisor and your safety team for guidance. You need to know how to handle these situations before an incident occurs. A quick response can be the difference between life and death. The victim of an injury or sudden illness at a jobsite may be at a remote location. The site may be far from a rescue squad, fire department, or hospital, presenting a problem in the rescue and transportation of the victim to a hospital.

AED (automated external defibrillator): A device used to help those experiencing sudden cardiac arrest.

Your employer must ensure prompt first aid treatment for any injured employees. To do this, they will provide access to readily available first aid kits. You and everyone on your team should be aware of the location and contents of first aid kits available on the jobsite. Many jobsites also have an **AED (automated external defibrillator)** that is used to help those experiencing sudden cardiac arrest (*Figure 20*). Many lives have been saved due to a prepared team who knew where the AED device was stored and how to use it.

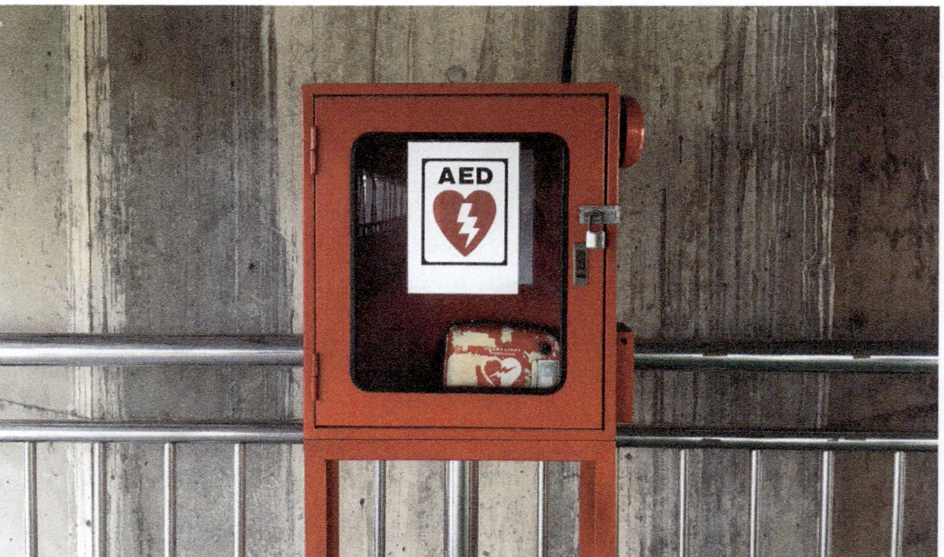

Figure 20 Many jobsites have an AED to help those experiencing sudden cardiac arrest. You should always know where AED devices are stored.
Source: PardiMer/Shutterstock

Your company will have an on-site medical professional or at least one member of the workforce who is trained and certified in first aid, including the use of an AED and CPR. **CPR (cardiopulmonary resuscitation)** is a lifesaving technique that is used when someone's heartbeat or breathing has stopped. The benefits of having personnel trained in first aid at jobsites include the following:

- Immediate and proper treatment of minor injuries. First aid may prevent minor injuries from developing into more serious conditions. OSHA does not require companies to record when simple first aid is used to address the injury or illness.
- Ability to determine if the injured person requires professional medical attention.
- Ability to help stabilize an injured person before professional medical care arrives.
- Help to eliminate or reduce medical expenses, lost work time, and sick pay.

If further medical treatment is needed, preparedness and a rapid communication process will mobilize the right people as soon as possible. Emergency numbers should be posted on the jobsite. As a leader, you should be very familiar with the construction safety plan and work with your Human Resources and safety leaders to ensure it stays updated. You need to locate your local off-site medical provider for emergency or nonemergency care prior to an incident occurring.

CPR (cardiopulmonary resuscitation): A lifesaving technique that is used when someone's heartbeat or breathing has stopped.

NOTE

The American Red Cross, Medic First Aid, and many other local organizations provide basic and advanced first aid courses at nominal costs. These courses include both first aid and CPR. The local area offices of these organizations can provide further details regarding the training available. CPR certifications must be renewed every two years.

4.4.2 Reporting and Investigating Incidents

As a frontline leader, you must know and follow your company's incident reporting processes. You also must ensure your team is following those policies. Your team should know from their training to immediately report any unusual event, incident, or injury. The policies and definitions around reporting should be included in safety manuals and construction safety plans.

If your employer is subject to the recordkeeping requirements of the OSH Act of 1970, it must maintain records of all recordable occupational injuries and illnesses using standard OSHA forms. In the event of an incident, the employer also is required to investigate the cause of the incident and determine how to avoid it in the future. According to OSHA regulations, the employer must investigate each work-related death, serious injury or illness, or incident having the potential to cause death or serious physical harm. The employer should document any findings from the investigation, as well as the action plan to prevent future occurrences. The company should complete these actions immediately, with photos or video if possible.

As a crew leader, you may be involved with an incident investigation. If required by company policy, you also will need to make a formal investigation and submit a report after an incident. An investigation looks for the causes of the incident by examining the circumstances under which it occurred and talking to the people involved. Investigations are perhaps the most useful tool in the prevention of future incidents. As shown in *Figure 21*, an incident investigation has four major parts.

NOTE

Three OSHA forms are used for injury and illness recordkeeping:

- OSHA Form 300, Log of Work-Related Injuries and Illnesses
- OSHA Form 300A, Summary of Work-Related Injuries and Illnesses
- OSHA Form 301, Injury and Illness Incident Report

All of these forms are available online at the OSHA website. OSHA has also launched their Injury Tracking Application (ITA) to allow for direct entry of OSHA Form 300A information. For more information, scan the QR code at the front of the module.

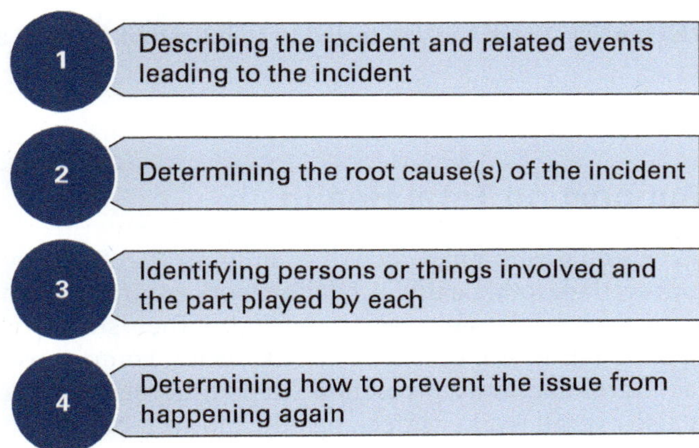

Figure 21 An incident investigation has four major parts.

Root cause: A core issue or fundamental reason for the occurrence of a problem.

Root cause analysis (RCA): A method of problem-solving used for identifying the root causes of faults or problem.

A key step is determining the **root cause** of the incident. A root cause is a core issue or fundamental reason for the occurrence of a problem. Understanding the root cause is critical to avoiding similar incidents in the future. In many cases, the root cause was a flaw in the system that failed to recognize the unsafe condition or the potential for an unsafe act.

Finding a root cause to a problem can be difficult. A **root cause analysis (RCA)** is a method of problem-solving used for identifying the root causes of faults or problems. A *Five Whys Analysis* is one type of root cause analysis that is helpful with incident investigations. The method is simple: When a problem occurs, you start with the broadest explanation for an incident and narrow it down to a more specific problem by asking "why" five times. The technique is even more effective when you include experienced team members who were actively part of the situation or have had similar experiences. It is especially useful when the root cause is not that obvious. *Figure 22* shows an example of how a Five Whys Analysis can apply to an incident investigation.

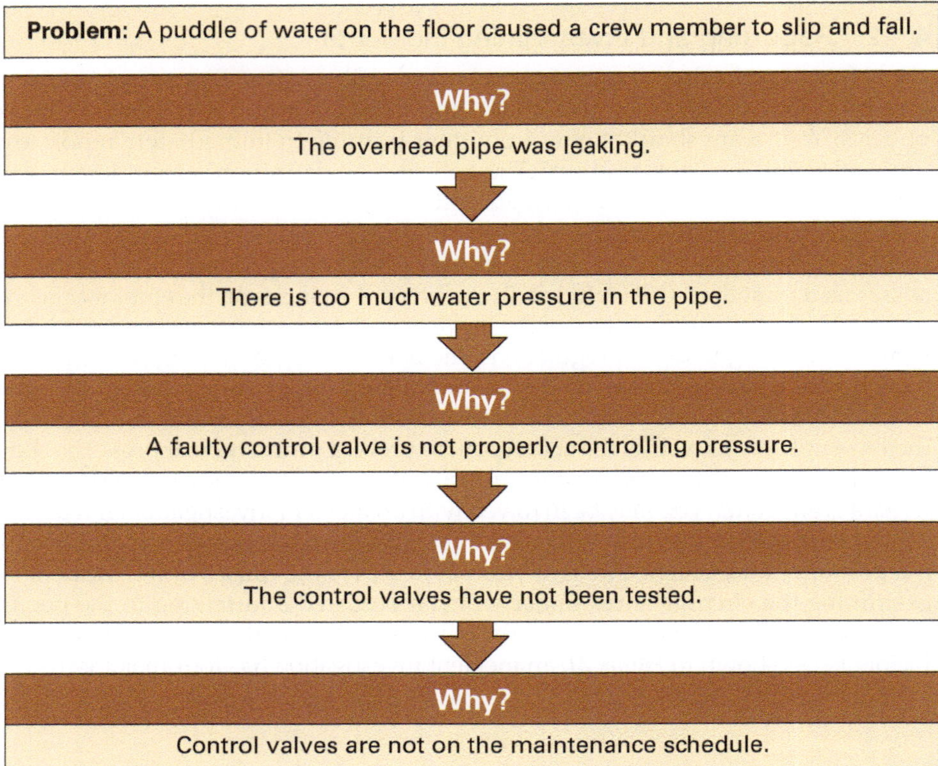

Figure 22 Using a Five Whys Analysis to understand the root cause of an incident.

4.5.0 Supporting Total Health

Substance abuse: The inappropriate overuse of drugs and chemicals, whether they are legal or illegal.

More than ever, employers must focus not only on their employees' physical well-being, but on their total health. A healthy work environment not only helps to ensure workers return home safely at the end of their shift, but also ensures they can have a healthy life outside of work. Many companies are adopting practices that address not only protection from work-related safety and health hazards, but also overall worker safety, health, and well-being.

Two key aspects of total health for your workforce include addressing **substance abuse** and mental health. As a frontline leader, you will not be able to address the root causes of these issues for your workers. You do, however, have the important responsibility to enforce company policies and procedures in these areas and work with your management or Human Resources Department to help employees in these situations.

4.5.1 Substance Abuse

Substance abuse is a serious safety issue in the workplace. Substance abuse is the inappropriate overuse of drugs and chemicals, whether they are legal or illegal. All substance abuse results in some form of mental, sensory, or physical **impairment**. Impairment is the point where someone's intake of substances affects their ability to perform appropriately. Alcohol can be abused by consuming to the point of intoxication. Legal prescription drugs can be abused by using the wrong dosage, using other people's medications, or self-medicating. Illegal drugs, such as cocaine, crystal meth, or marijuana in some states, can cause impairment.

Impairment: The point where someone's intake of substances affects their ability to perform appropriately.

Crew leaders must enforce company policies and procedures regarding substance abuse. There are legal consequences and safety implications associated with substance abuse. Suppose several crew members go out and smoke marijuana or drink during lunch. Then they return to work to erect scaffolding for a concrete pour in the afternoon. If you can smell marijuana on the worker's clothing or alcohol on their breath, you must step in and take action. An impaired worker is more likely to cause an incident that could cause serious injury or death to themselves or others (*Figure 23*).

If you observe an employee showing impaired behavior for any reason, immediately contact your supervisor and/or Human Resources Department for assistance. You should work with management to deal with suspected drug and alcohol abuse and should not deal with these situations yourself. Reporting the concern helps you protect the business and the employee's and other workers' safety.

It is often difficult to detect substance abuse because the effects can be subtle. The best way is to look for physical signs or sudden changes in behavior that are not typical of the employee. *Table 7* lists some examples of potential signs and behavioral changes that might indicate substance abuse.

Figure 23 An impaired worker is a dangerous one.
Source: vejaa/iStock/Getty Images

Did You Know?

Substance Abuse Does Not Pay

An employee who is involved in an incident while under the influence of drugs or alcohol may be denied workers' compensation insurance benefits.

TABLE 7 Potential Signs of Substance Abuse in a Worker

Physical Signs	Behavioral Changes
• Smelling of alcohol or drugs • Slurring of speech or an inability to communicate effectively • Wearing sunglasses indoors or on overcast days to hide dilated or constricted pupils, conditions which impair vision • Significant changes in personal appearance, cleanliness, or health	• Unscheduled absences • Failure to report to work on time • Significant changes in the quality of work • Unusual energy or tiredness • Sudden and irrational temper flare-ups • Sneaky behaviors, such as disappearing to wooded areas, storage areas, or other private locations • Attempting to borrow money from coworkers • Losing tools or company equipment

4.5.2 Mental Health

Mental health is a critically important, but often overlooked, part of overall construction safety and health. Construction workers have more risk factors than employees in other industries. These risk factors make workers more likely to experience mental health challenges, with a specific set of risks around suicide. Construction workers are six times more likely to die by suicide than they are to die from a fall.

With proper treatment, mental health conditions can be managed and overcome so those experiencing them can have full and productive lives. As with substance abuse, however, these conditions can lead to people being distracted, less productive than normal, and possibly unsafe and unable to perform their normal jobs. Because of this, mental health and suicide prevention need to be safety considerations.

As a leader, you cannot solve these challenges for your workers, but you can create a better environment. Use your toolbox talks to discuss mental health as part of overall total worker safety. In your safety huddles, check in on how your teammates are doing. Encourage your crew to talk to supervisors and colleagues when they feel stressed, anxious, or on the brink of burnout. Help ensure they are aware of any available counseling resources and that they are taking time off when they need it.

Even more so than substance abuse, it can be very difficult to identify a worker struggling with a mental health issue. *Table 8* lists some examples of potential signs and behavioral changes that might indicate someone is struggling with mental health issues.

If you observe an employee showing signs of mental health issues or have concerns for any reason, immediately contact your supervisor and/or Human Resources Department for assistance. You should work with management to deal with suspected mental health issues and should not deal with these situations yourself. Reporting the concern helps you protect the business and the employee's and other workers' safety.

Did You Know?

Mental Health Is a Critical Part of Safety

Many organizations in the construction industry are focused on helping normalize conversations around mental health and make it less challenging to have these conversations. The National Institute for Occupational Safety and Health (NIOSH), for example, has a Total Worker Health® program focused on improving workforce well-being by protecting their safety and enhancing their health and productivity. Other focused nonprofits, like the Construction Industry Alliance for Suicide Prevention (CIASP), provide specific resources, like toolbox talks, that you can use to help with these conversations with your crew.

TABLE 8 Signs That May Indicate Someone Is Struggling with Mental Health Issues

Behavioral Changes	Performance Changes	Verbal Cues	Life Events
• Becoming withdrawn • Acting anxious or reckless • Misusing drugs and alcohol	• Missing work • Showing up late • Being less productive • Being unable to think clearly or solve problems • Having increased safety incidents	• Talking about feeling trapped • Talking about wanting to die • Saying they feel like a burden • Saying they feel like it would be better if they were gone	• Dealing with a divorce or breakup • Handling a death in the family • Working through a major illness or injury • Having financial issues

Source: Construction Industry Alliance for Suicide Prevention (ciasp.org)

4.0.0 Section Review

1. One of a crew leader's most important responsibilities to the employer is to ____.
   a. enforce company safety policies
   b. estimate material costs for a project
   c. make recommendations for setting up a crew
   d. provide input for fixed-price contracts
2. Which of these is *not* a function of OSHA?
   a. Issuing standards and rules for working conditions
   b. Researching occupational incidents and injuries
   c. Conducting workplace inspections
   d. Distributing company safety manuals
3. Which of the following should all employees receive upon being hired?
   a. A copy of the company's safety policies and procedures
   b. A new set of tools
   c. A leadership assessment to help map their career path
   d. First-aid and CPR training
4. A problem-solving method that is useful in investigating incidents and identifies the core issue of a problem is _____.
   a. problem-solving
   b. root cause analysis
   c. incident recordkeeping
   d. event playback
5. A focus on overall worker safety, health, and well-being, including mental health, is _____.
   a. home health
   b. complete worker safety
   c. occupational safety
   d. total health

5.0.0 Project Planning, Scheduling, and Cost and Resource Management

Objective

Demonstrate an understanding of construction project phases, project planning and scheduling, field reporting, and cost and resource management.

a. Identify construction project phases.
b. Summarize crew planning and scheduling responsibilities, including creating lookahead schedules.
c. Describe the frontline leader's role in field reporting.
d. Explain approaches to managing costs and controlling project resources, such as materials, tools, and equipment.

Performance Task

3. Develop and present a lookahead schedule.

This section describes the various phases of a construction project. It examines **estimating**, **planning**, **scheduling**, and **cost control** through managing material, people, tools, and other resources. All workers who participate in a job are responsible at some level for their assigned jobs. For example, the contractor's responsibility begins with obtaining the contract and it doesn't end until the client takes ownership of the project. The project manager is generally the person with overall responsibility for coordinating the project. Finally, the superintendent and frontline leadership, like a foreman, supervisor, or crew leader, are responsible for coordinating the work of one or more workers, one or more crews of workers within the company, or one or more crews of subcontractors.

Estimating: The process of calculating the cost of a project.

Planning: The process of laying out all details of a construction project before construction begins.

Scheduling: Involves defining which activities happen in what order and assigning dates and times to those tasks.

Cost control: The process that helps keep expenses under control by managing labor, material, and other costs to ensure that the project finishes on budget.

5.1.0 Construction Project Phases

A simple way to think about a construction project is in three phases: the *design and development phase*, the *preconstruction phase*, and the *construction phase*. *Figure 24* shows the flow of a typical project from beginning to end through these phases.

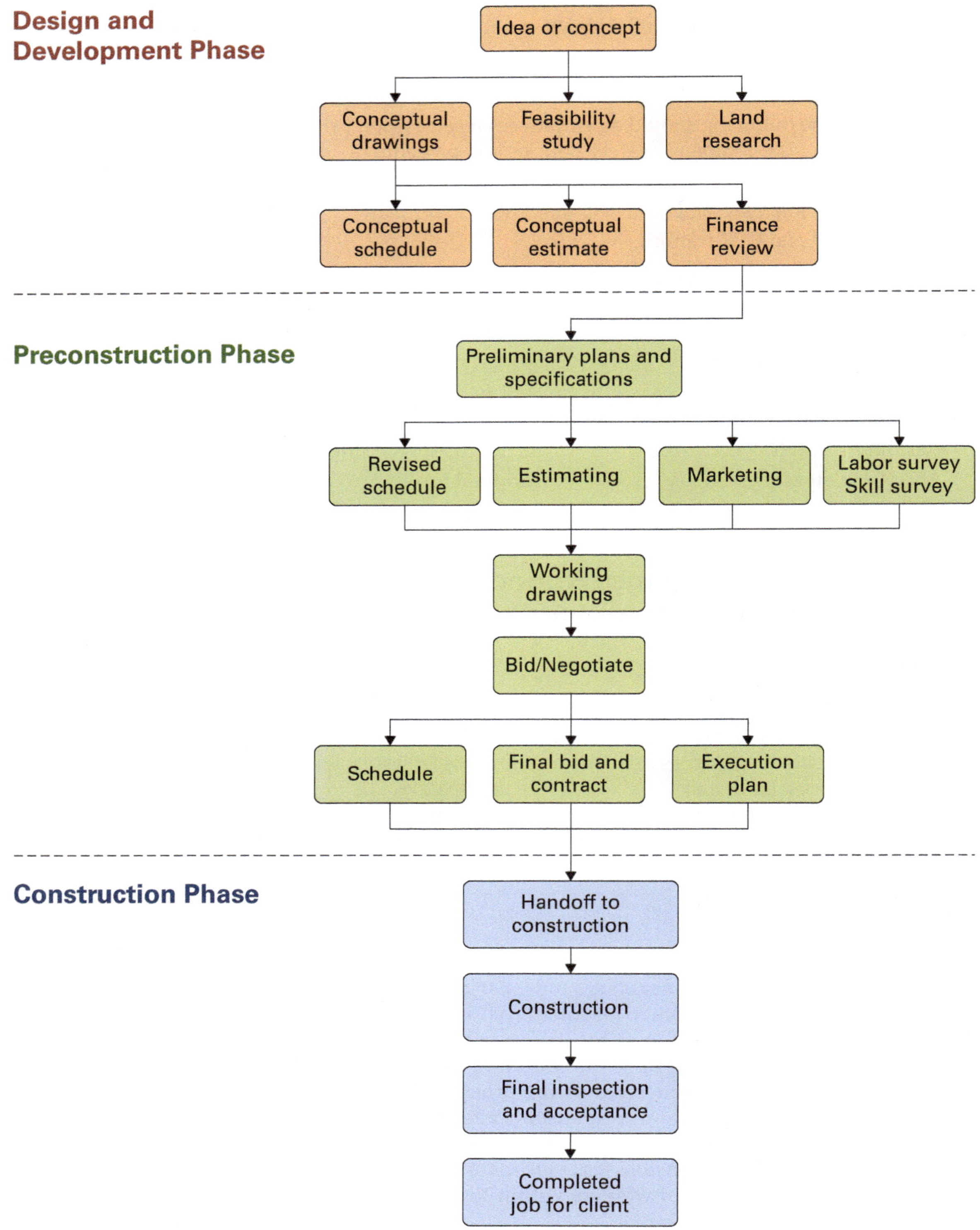

Figure 24 Construction project phases and flow.

5.1.1 Design and Development Phase

The design and development phase is the first stage of a project (*Figure 25*). It starts when an owner decides to build a new facility or add to an existing facility. This process involves land research and feasibility studies to ensure that the project has merit. A **feasibility study** is an analysis that considers all of a project's relevant factors—including budget, technical elements, legal aspects, and scheduling—to determine the likelihood that the project can be completed successfully.

Feasibility study: An analysis that considers all of a project's relevant factors—including budget, technical elements, legal aspects, and scheduling—to determine the likelihood that the project can be completed successfully.

Design and Development Phase

Idea or concept

Conceptual drawings | Feasibility study | Land research

Conceptual schedule | Conceptual estimate | Finance review

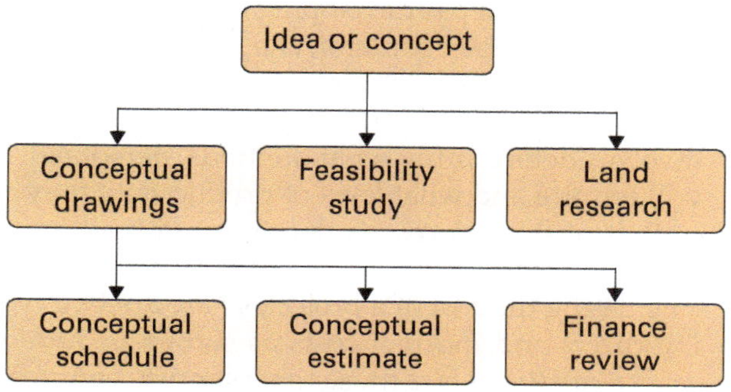

Figure 25 The design and development phase is the first stage of a project.

Architects or engineers develop the conceptual drawings that define the project graphically. They then provide the owner with sketches of room layouts and elevations and make suggestions about what construction materials to use.

During the design and development phase, architects, engineers, and/or the owner develop an estimate for the proposed project and establish a preliminary budget. Once that budget is established, the owner will determine how to pay for, or finance, the project. The owner will also complete a review to determine whether the project costs will exceed its market value and that the project provides a reasonable profit during its existence. If needed, the development team begins preliminary reviews for zoning, building restrictions, landscape requirements, and environmental impact studies.

5.1.2 Preconstruction Phase

If all steps in the design phase are completed successfully, the project moves to the preconstruction phase (*Figure 26*). The preconstruction stage includes planning that occurs before the start of construction. The preconstruction planning process does not always involve you, as a crew leader, but you should understand it to do your job well.

Preconstruction Phase

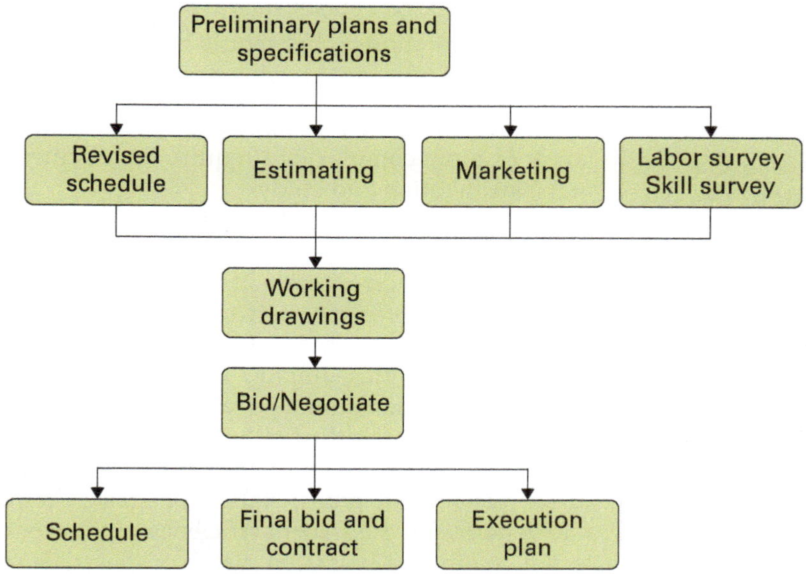

Preliminary plans and specifications

Revised schedule | Estimating | Marketing | Labor survey Skill survey

Working drawings

Bid/Negotiate

Schedule | Final bid and contract | Execution plan

Figure 26 The preconstruction phase is the second stage of a project.

When the architects and engineers begin to develop the project drawings and specifications, they consult with other design professionals such as structural, mechanical, and electrical engineers. They perform the calculations, make a detailed technical analysis, and check details of the project for accuracy.

The design professionals create preliminary drawings and specifications. They use these drawings and specifications to communicate the necessary information to the contractors, subcontractors, suppliers, and workers who will contribute to the project.

A key next step is developing the proposal, bid, or negotiated price for the job. This is when the estimator, the project manager, and the field superintendent develop a preliminary plan for completing the work. They apply their experience and knowledge from previous projects to develop the plan. The process involves determining what methods, personnel, tools, and equipment the work will require and what level of productivity they can achieve.

Part of this process is determining how much the project will cost. Before building a project, an estimate must be prepared. Estimating is the process of calculating the cost of a project. There are two types of costs to consider, including direct and indirect costs as shown in *Table 9*. Direct costs, also known as *general conditions*, are those that planners can clearly assign to a budget. Indirect costs are overhead costs shared by all projects. Planners generally calculate these costs as an overhead percentage to labor and material costs.

TABLE 9 Examples of Direct and Indirect Costs

Direct Costs	Indirect Costs
• Materials	• Office rent
• Labor	• Utilities
• Tools	• Telecommunications
• Equipment	• Accounting
	• Office supplies and signage

Did You Know?

Profit Powers Businesses

Profit is the fuel that powers a business. It allows the business to invest in new equipment and facilities, to provide training, and to maintain a reserve fund for times when business is slow. In large companies, profitability attracts investors who provide the capital necessary for the business to grow. For these reasons, contractors can't afford to consistently lose money on projects. If they can't operate profitably, they are forced out of business. As a frontline leader, you can help your company remain profitable by managing budget, schedule, quality, and safety as outlined in the drawings, specifications, and project schedule.

Profit: The amount of money that the contractor will make after paying all the direct and indirect costs.

Production: The amount of construction materials put in place. It is the quantity of materials installed on a job.

Productivity rate: A measure of how much work gets done over a period of time, also called *output per labor hour*.

Planners must also consider other factors when estimating project costs, including the following:

- Timing of all phases of work
- Types of materials to be installed and their availability
- Equipment and tools required and their availability
- Personnel requirements and availability
- Site and local conditions, such as soil types, accessibility, or available staging areas
- Climate conditions that should be anticipated during the project
- Relationships with the other contractors and their representatives on the job

On a simple job, crews can handle these items almost automatically. However, larger or more complex jobs require the planner to give these factors more formal consideration and study.

The bid price includes the estimated cost of the project as well as the **profit**. Profit refers to the amount of money that the contractor will make after paying all the direct and indirect costs. If the direct and indirect costs exceed the estimate for the job, the difference between the actual and estimated costs must come out of the company's profit. This reduces what the contractor makes on the job.

Many companies employ professional cost estimators to determine the cost of a project. Estimators will focus on **production** and **productivity rate**. Production is a quantity or amount of construction materials or work put in place. It is the quantity of materials that will be installed on a job, such as 1,000 linear feet of waste pipe installed for a task. On the other hand, the productivity rate depends on the level of efficiency of the work. The productivity rate relates to the quantity of work completed or materials put in place by the crew over a certain period of time. For example, productivity could be the amount of waste pipe installed each day by one worker or a crew.

Production levels are set during the estimating stage. The estimator determines the total amount of materials to be placed based on the drawings, plans, and specifications. After the job is complete, supervision can assess the actual amount of materials installed and can compare the actual production to the estimated production.

During the estimating stage, the estimator uses company records of productivity to determine how much time and labor it will take to place a certain quantity of materials. From this information, the estimator calculates the productivity necessary to complete the job on time.

For example, say you need a crew of two people to paint 8,100 ft^2 in nine days. To calculate the required average productivity, divide 8,100 ft^2 by 9 days. The result is 900 ft^2/day. As the work progresses, you can compare the daily production of any crew of two painters doing similar work with this average (*Figure 27*).

NOTE

Many software programs and mobile apps are available to simplify the cost-estimating process. Estimating programs are typically set up to include a takeoff form and a form for estimating labor by category. Most of these programs include a database that contains current prices for labor and materials, so they automatically price the job and produce a bid. The programs can also generate purchase orders for materials on the job. Many of them are tailored to specific industries, such as construction or manufacturing, as well as specific trades within the industries, such as plumbing, electrical, HVACR, and insulating contractors.

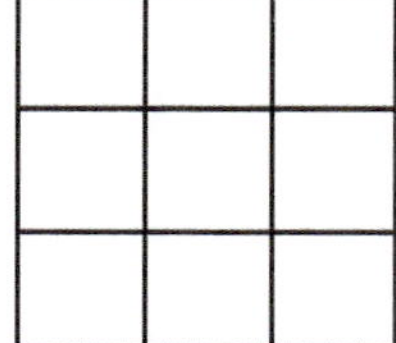

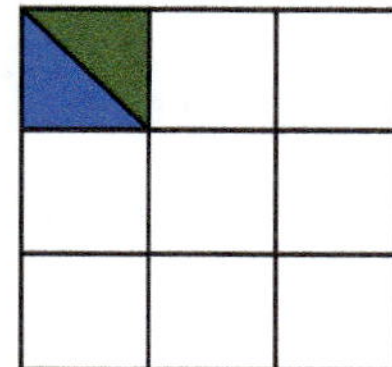

Figure 27 Production and productivity.

During the preconstruction phase, the owners hold many meetings to review and refine estimates, adjust plans to conform to regulations, and secure a construction loan. If the project is one that requires a marketing program, such as a condominium, office building, or shopping center, the marketing may start during preconstruction. In such cases, the selling of the building space often starts before actual construction begins.

Next, the design team produces a complete set of drawings, specifications, and bid documents. After this, the owner will select the method to obtain contractors. The owner may choose to negotiate with several contractors or select one through competitive bidding. Everyone concerned must also consider safety as part of the planning process. A safety crew leader may walk through the site as part of the pre-bid process.

Contracts for construction projects can take many forms. The most common types of contracts are *lump sum* and *time and materials* contracts.

In a *lump sum contract*, also called a *fixed price* or *firm-fixed price contract*, the owner generally provides detailed drawings and specifications, which the contractor uses to calculate the cost of materials and labor. The contractor also adds a percentage to these costs representing company overhead expenses, such as office rent, insurance, and accounting/payroll costs. At the end, the contractor adds a profit factor.

When submitting the bid, the contractor will state very specifically the conditions and assumptions on which the company based the bid. The **scope**, or *scope of work*, is the list of the commitments and activities that all contractors, subcontractors, and suppliers are expected to do during a project.

Scope: The list of the commitments and activities that all contractors, subcontractors, and suppliers are expected to do during a project. Also called *scope of work*.

In a *time and materials contract*, also known as a *T&M contract*, the owner pays back the contractor for labor, materials, and other costs encountered in the performance of the contract. Typically, the contractor and owner agree in advance on hourly or daily labor rates for different categories of worker. These rates include an amount representing the contractor's overhead expense. The owner also reimburses the contractor for the cost of materials and equipment used on the job. Since the buyer reimburses the contractor for the cost of materials and pays an hourly wage, any unexpected delays, roadblocks, and other changes to the scope of work are covered. T&M contracts thus work best for projects in which the scope of work is not well-defined.

On a time and materials contract project, you play an important role by understanding the scope of the work and making sure that everything is tracked so that your company is reimbursed for the work. You must identify changes or problems that increase the scope or amount of planned labor or materials. You also must ensure you and your team are following your company policies and getting proper authorization before starting any work.

After the client awards the contract, planners create a final schedule and an execution plan that defines the actual work methods and resources needed to perform the work.

NOTE

You may also hear about other types of contracts, such as cost-plus and guaranteed maximum price. Some types of contracts, such as unit-rate and hybrid, combine several aspects of these other contract types. Scan the QR code in the front of this module to access additional resources on construction contract types.

5.1.3 Construction Phase

After the contract is signed, the construction phase can start (*Figure 28*). The designated contractor enlists the help of mechanical, electrical, elevator, and other specialty subcontractors to complete the construction phase. The contractor may perform one or more parts of the construction and rely on subcontractors for the remainder of the work. However, the general contractor is responsible for managing all the trades necessary to complete the project.

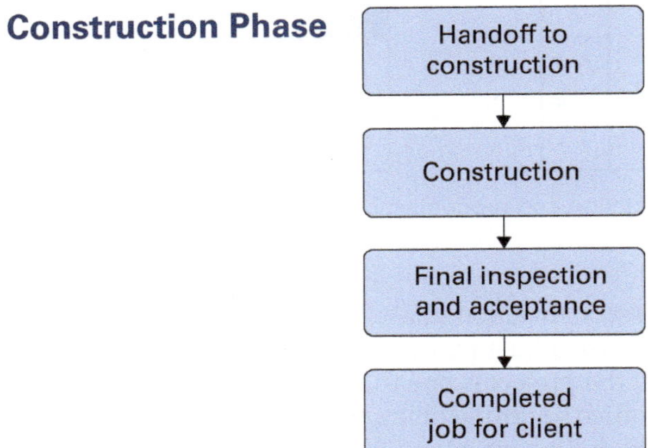

Figure 28 The construction phase is the third stage of a project.

The initial set of drawings for a construction project reflects the completed project as conceived by the architect and engineers. During construction, changes may be necessary because of factors unforeseen during the design phase. For example, when electricians must reroute cabling or conduit, or the installed equipment location is different than shown on the original drawing, such changes must be marked on the drawings. Without this record, technicians called to perform maintenance or modify the equipment later will have trouble locating all the cabling and equipment.

Project supervision must document any changes made during construction or installation on the drawings as the changes occur. Before digital drawings, architects would note changes on hard-copy drawings using a colored pen or pencil. These marked-up versions are commonly called **redline drawings**. With new digital drawings created using building information modeling tools, architects and engineers can revise and share the latest drawing versions almost instantly to mobile phones and tablets. After the drawings have been revised to reflect any redline changes, the final drawings are called **as-built drawings**. As-built drawings are a revised set of drawings submitted by a contractor upon completion of a project or job. These drawings, sometimes called *record drawings*, reflect all changes made during construction and show the exact specifications of the completed work.

Redline drawings: Marked-up versions of construction drawings documenting any changes made during construction or installation.

As-built drawings: A revised set of drawings that reflect all changes made during the construction process and show the exact specifications of the completed work.

The main part of your role as a frontline leader happens during the construction phase, including daily work planning and scheduling, cost control, and resource management, including material delivery and storage, tool control, and equipment control. All of these tasks drive production and productivity, as well as the overall profitability of the project.

As construction nears completion, the architect/engineer, owner, and government agencies start their final inspections and acceptance of the project. If the general contractor has managed the project, the subcontractors have performed their work, and the architects/engineers have regularly inspected the project to ensure it satisfies the local code, then the inspection process can finish up in a timely manner. This results in a satisfied client and a profitable project for all.

On the other hand, if the inspection reveals faulty workmanship, poor design, incorrect use of materials, or violation of codes, then the inspection and acceptance will take longer. It may result in a dissatisfied client or an unprofitable project.

Construction **project delivery methods** provide different ways to organize the services of development, planning, and construction in order to execute a project.

NOTE

Scan the QR code in the front of this module to access additional resources on construction project delivery methods.

Project delivery methods: Different ways to organize the services of development, planning, and construction in order to execute a project.

5.2.0 Planning and Scheduling

In the previous sections, you learned about the phases of a construction project, including the design and development phase, the preconstruction phase, and the construction phase. As noted, the main part of your role as a frontline leader happens during the construction phase.

During construction, you may be directly involved in daily work planning and scheduling. You also may be involved in cost control and resource management, including material delivery and storage, tool control, and equipment control.

5.2.1 Understanding Overall Schedules

Construction planning and scheduling refers to the process through which you map out what will take place during a project, what resources you need, when key activities will take place, which personnel will be involved, and anything else pertinent to the project.

Construction planning refers to the process of laying out all details of a construction project beforehand. Construction scheduling involves defining which activities happen in what order and assigning dates and times to those tasks. Construction schedules are linked to resources such as materials, labor, and equipment to help create the most efficiency in your project. Construction scheduling is deeply connected to planning.

Planning and scheduling are closely related and are both very important to a successful job. Planning identifies the required activities and how and in what order to complete them. Scheduling involves establishing start and finish times/dates for each activity.

A schedule for a project typically shows the following:

- Operations listed in sequential order
- Units of construction
- Duration, or length of time, of an activity
- Estimated dates to start and complete each activity
- Quantity of materials to be installed

Figure 29 shows an example of a high-level project schedule. As noted, the development of a schedule for a project starts as early as the design and development phase. As the project moves through each phase and the work is better defined, the schedule also becomes more clearly defined.

When a crew is close to completing specific work—say, within three weeks of working on Foundation 1—a **Level 4 schedule** is created. A Level 4 schedule offers additional detail to provide working schedules to the crews doing the

NOTE

Scan the QR code in the front of this module to access additional resources on schedule levels.

Level 4 schedule: A schedule that offers additional detail to provide working schedules to the crews doing the work, usually within three to six weeks of completing specific work.

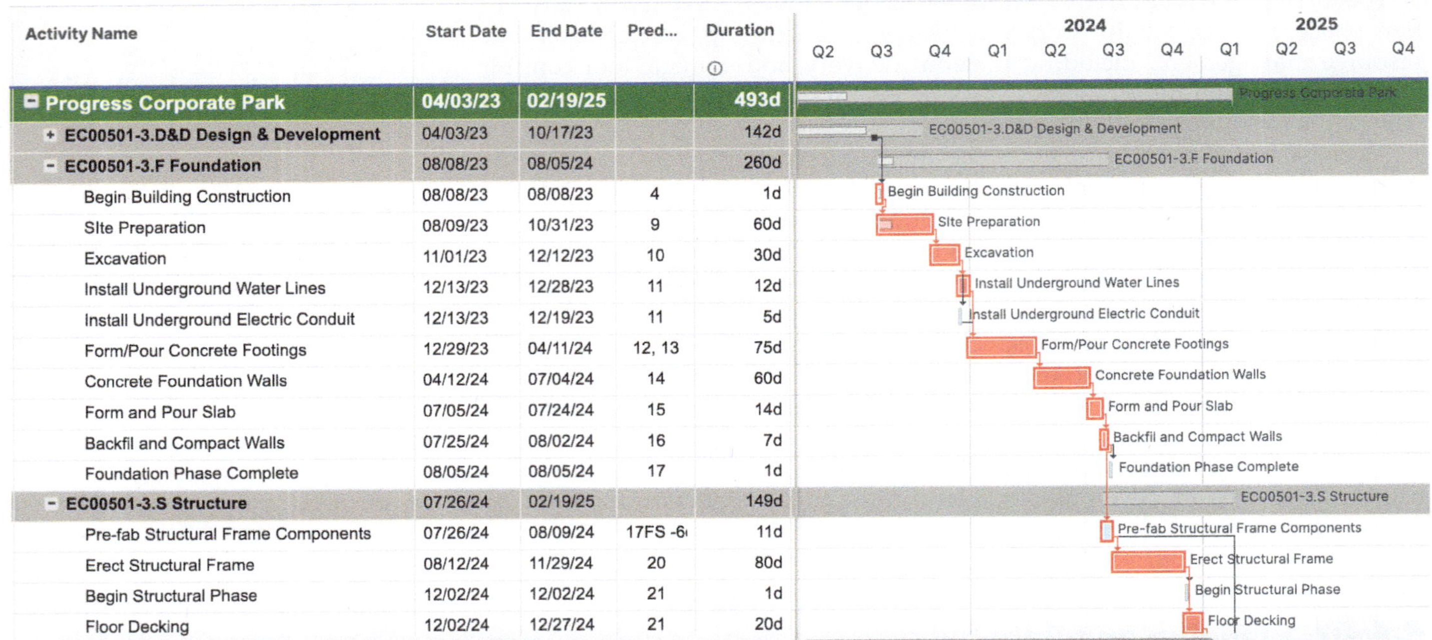

Activity Name	Start Date	End Date	Pred...	Duration
Progress Corporate Park	04/03/23	02/19/25		493d
EC00501-3.D&D Design & Development	04/03/23	10/17/23		142d
EC00501-3.F Foundation	08/08/23	08/05/24		260d
Begin Building Construction	08/08/23	08/08/23	4	1d
SIte Preparation	08/09/23	10/31/23	9	60d
Excavation	11/01/23	12/12/23	10	30d
Install Underground Water Lines	12/13/23	12/28/23	11	12d
Install Underground Electric Conduit	12/13/23	12/19/23	11	5d
Form/Pour Concrete Footings	12/29/23	04/11/24	12, 13	75d
Concrete Foundation Walls	04/12/24	07/04/24	14	60d
Form and Pour Slab	07/05/24	07/24/24	15	14d
Backfil and Compact Walls	07/25/24	08/02/24	16	7d
Foundation Phase Complete	08/05/24	08/05/24	17	1d
EC00501-3.S Structure	07/26/24	02/19/25		149d
Pre-fab Structural Frame Components	07/26/24	08/09/24	17FS -6	11d
Erect Structural Frame	08/12/24	11/29/24	20	80d
Begin Structural Phase	12/02/24	12/02/24	21	1d
Floor Decking	12/02/24	12/27/24	21	20d

Figure 29 Example of a construction project schedule.

work (*Figure 30*). A Level 4 schedule allows a supervisor to create a plan, schedule handoffs from crew to crew, and estimate all of the resources that must be in place for the work to happen.

In the schedule in *Figure 30*, ironworkers must fabricate and set the rebar and carpenters must build the forms before the handoff is made to place the concrete. Each of these activities is a critical path activity. A **critical path** is the sequence of dependent tasks that form the longest duration. In *Figure 29* and *Figure 30*, the critical path in the schedule is shown in red. In other words, until one activity is complete, workers cannot start the other tasks, and the project will likely be delayed by the amount of time the previous activity was delayed.

Critical path: In manufacturing, construction, and other types of creative processes, the required sequence of tasks that directly controls the ultimate completion date of the project.

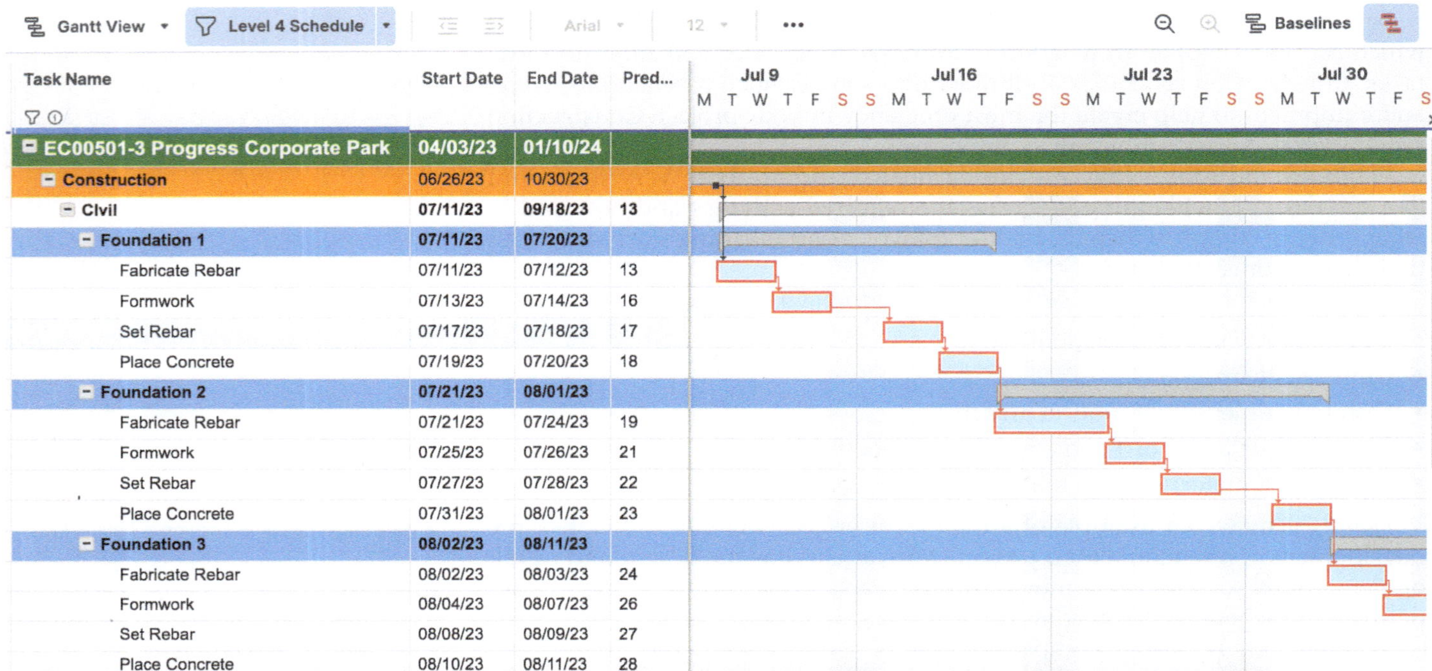

Task Name	Start Date	End Date	Pred...
EC00501-3 Progress Corporate Park	04/03/23	01/10/24	
Construction	06/26/23	10/30/23	
Civil	07/11/23	09/18/23	13
Foundation 1	07/11/23	07/20/23	
Fabricate Rebar	07/11/23	07/12/23	13
Formwork	07/13/23	07/14/23	16
Set Rebar	07/17/23	07/18/23	17
Place Concrete	07/19/23	07/20/23	18
Foundation 2	07/21/23	08/01/23	
Fabricate Rebar	07/21/23	07/24/23	19
Formwork	07/25/23	07/26/23	21
Set Rebar	07/27/23	07/28/23	22
Place Concrete	07/31/23	08/01/23	23
Foundation 3	08/02/23	08/11/23	
Fabricate Rebar	08/02/23	08/03/23	24
Formwork	08/04/23	08/07/23	26
Set Rebar	08/08/23	08/09/23	27
Place Concrete	08/10/23	08/11/23	28

Figure 30 A Level 4 schedule provides enough details for project foremen to forecast handoffs and needed resources.

Task Name	Start Date	End Date	Materials Available	Assigned To	Notes	Status
Civil	**07/11/23**	**09/18/23**				
Foundation 1	**07/11/23**	**07/20/23**				
Fabricate Rebar	07/11/23	07/12/23	Yes	JKR		Not Started
Formwork	07/13/23	07/14/23	Yes	JKR		Not Started
Set Rebar	07/17/23	07/18/23	N/A	JKR	Quality signoff	Not Started
Place Concrete	07/19/23	07/20/23	Yes	JKR		Not Started
Foundation 2	**07/21/23**	**08/01/23**				
Fabricate Rebar	07/21/23	07/24/23	Yes	JKR		Not Started
Formwork	07/25/23	07/26/23	Yes	JKR		Not Started
Set Rebar	07/27/23	07/28/23	N/A	JKR	Quality signoff	Not Started
Place Concrete	07/31/23	08/01/23	Yes	JKR		Not Started
Foundation 3	**08/02/23**	**08/11/23**				
Fabricate Rebar	08/02/23	08/03/23	On Order	JKR		Not Started
Formwork	08/04/23	08/07/23	Yes	JKR		Not Started
Set Rebar	08/08/23	08/09/23	N/A	JKR	Quality signoff	Not Started
Place Concrete	08/10/23	08/11/23	Yes	JKR		Not Started

Figure 31 A step-by-step lookahead in a Level 4 schedule provide details for frontline leaders to plan handoffs.

For work to happen, you will need resources such as materials, available crew, available construction equipment, completed permits, and more. Developing a **lookahead schedule** helps ensure that all resources are available for the project when needed. This is often included in a Level 4 schedule. A lookahead schedule is useful for planning and scheduling work that is happening in the short term, usually within one to three weeks (*Figure 31*).

Lookahead schedule: For planning and scheduling work that is happening in the short term, usually within one to three weeks; used for anticipating material, labor, tool, and other resource requirements, as well as identifying potential schedule conflicts or other problems. Also called *short-term schedule*.

5.2.2 Creating a Short-Term or Lookahead Schedule

As a frontline leader of a crew, you must be able to create, read and interpret a lookahead schedule. You can use this information to plan work more effectively, set realistic goals, and compare the starts and completions of tasks to those on the schedule. As the leader of the team executing the work, you are a key expert to help produce a plan at this level of detail. *Table 10* provides a checklist for planning and scheduling.

TABLE 10 Crew Leader Planning and Scheduling Checklist

Did You...?	Yes/No
Determine the best method for performing the job.	
Identify the responsibilities of each person on the work crew.	
Determine the duration, or length in time, and sequence of each activity.	
Identify the tools and equipment needed to complete the job.	
Ensure that the required materials are at the worksite when needed.	
Make sure that heavy construction and other equipment is available when required.	
Work with other contractors in such a way as to avoid interruptions and delays.	

The following outlines the process you must complete to develop a plan and a schedule and to use the schedule to manage work.

Understand or Establish a Goal

A goal is a specific outcome that one works toward. The goals you must accomplish are often set in the higher-level schedules. For example, the project superintendent of a residential construction project could establish a goal to have a house dried-in or ready for the application of roofing and siding by a certain date. To meet that goal, you and the superintendent would need to agree to a goal to have the framing completed by a given date. You then establish subgoals for your crew to complete each element of the framing (floors, walls, roof) by a set time.

Identify the Required Work Activities and Divide Them into Tasks

To plan effectively, you must be able to break a work activity assignment down into smaller tasks. Large jobs include a greater number of tasks than small ones, but all jobs can be broken down into manageable components.

Make a list of all the activities that the plan requires to complete the job. This includes individual work tasks and special tasks, such as inspections or the delivery of materials. Next, start to divide work activities into tasks. As you do this, remember that almost every work activity has three general parts: preparing for the activity, performing the activity, and cleaning up after the activity.

Figure 32 shows a suitable breakdown for the work activity to install square vinyl floor tiles in a cafeteria. You could create even more detail by breaking down any one of the tasks into subtasks. In this case, however, that much detail is unnecessary and wastes your time and the project's money.

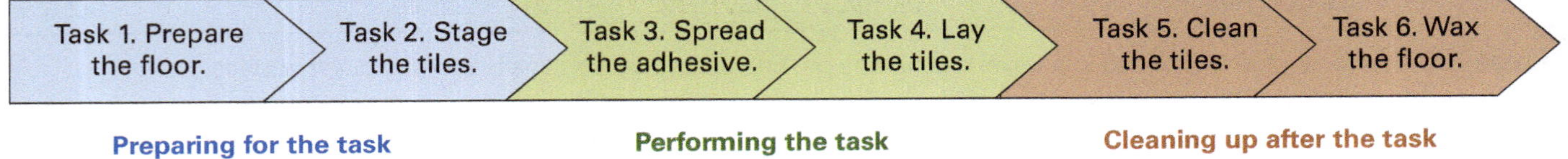

Figure 32 Example task breakdown of the work activity to install square vinyl floor tiles in a cafeteria.

When breaking down an activity into tasks, make each task *identifiable* and *definable*. A task is identifiable when you know exactly the types and amounts of resources it requires. A task is definable if it has a specific duration. The activity breakdown does not need to be overly detailed or complex unless the job has never been done before or must be performed with strictest efficiency.

At this point, you should just be concerned with generating a list, not with determining how to accomplish the activities, who will perform them, how long they will take, or the necessary sequence to complete them.

Plan Resources Needed for Each Task

Once a job has been broken down into activities and tasks, you must identify and account for all of the resources you need to complete them. Resource planning includes considerations for safety, materials, site-specific issues, equipment, tools, and labor (*Table 11*). Each of these is discussed in more detail in the sections that follow.

Organize the Work into a Logical Sequence

The next step in planning is to use the list of activities and resources needed to organize the work activities into a logical sequence. When doing this, keep in mind that certain steps can't happen before the completion of others. For example, concrete placement cannot happen until after rebar is set. Some construction work activities, such as installing 12" footing forms, are done so often that they require little planning. However, other jobs, such as placing a new type of mechanical equipment, require substantial planning.

Assign Responsibility for Each Task

After you have identified the tasks, you must determine who will complete each activity. This requires that you are aware of the experience, skills, and abilities of

TABLE 11 Key Resource Considerations During Planning

Resource Planning Area	Key Responsibilities
Safety Planning	Using the company safety manual as a guide, you must assess the safety issues associated with the job and take necessary measures to minimize any risk to the crew.
Materials Planning	You may be required to estimate quantities of materials during construction. You also have a key role in the receipt, storage, and control of the materials after they reach the jobsite.
Site Planning	Many planning elements are involved in sitework, including access roads, parking, site security, material and equipment staging and storage, sedimentation control, stormwater runoff, and more.
Equipment Planning	You may need to plan the types of equipment needed, the use of the equipment, and the length of time it will be on the site. You must work with the main office to make certain that the equipment reaches the jobsite on time. You must reserve time for equipment maintenance to prevent equipment failure.
Tool Planning	To plan tool usage, you must determine the tools required, tell your crew who will provide the tools, ensure that the crew is qualified to use the tools safely and effectively, and establish proper tool controls.
Labor Planning	In many companies, the project manager or job superintendent determines the size and makeup of the crew. Then supervision expects you to accomplish the goals and objectives with the crew provided. If you are responsible for planning for labor, you must identify the skills needed to perform the work, determine the number of people having the required skills, and decide who will be on the crew.

everyone in your team. You must put this knowledge to work by matching the crew's skills and abilities to specific tasks. Your job is to draw from their expertise to get the job done well and in a safe and timely manner.

Assign a Duration to Each Task

Next, assign a duration or length of time that it will take to complete each activity and determine the start date and time for each. Then place each activity into a schedule format. This step is important because it helps you compare the task time estimates to the scheduled completion date or time.

Make note of any activities that cannot start until previous work has been completed and ensure those do not start before the other work is complete. You also will need to ensure you have not assigned too much work to any one person or team.

Some of the information to support short-term scheduling comes from the estimate or cost breakdown. *Figure 33* shows how you can use estimate or cost breakdown information to set short-term production goals for a team.

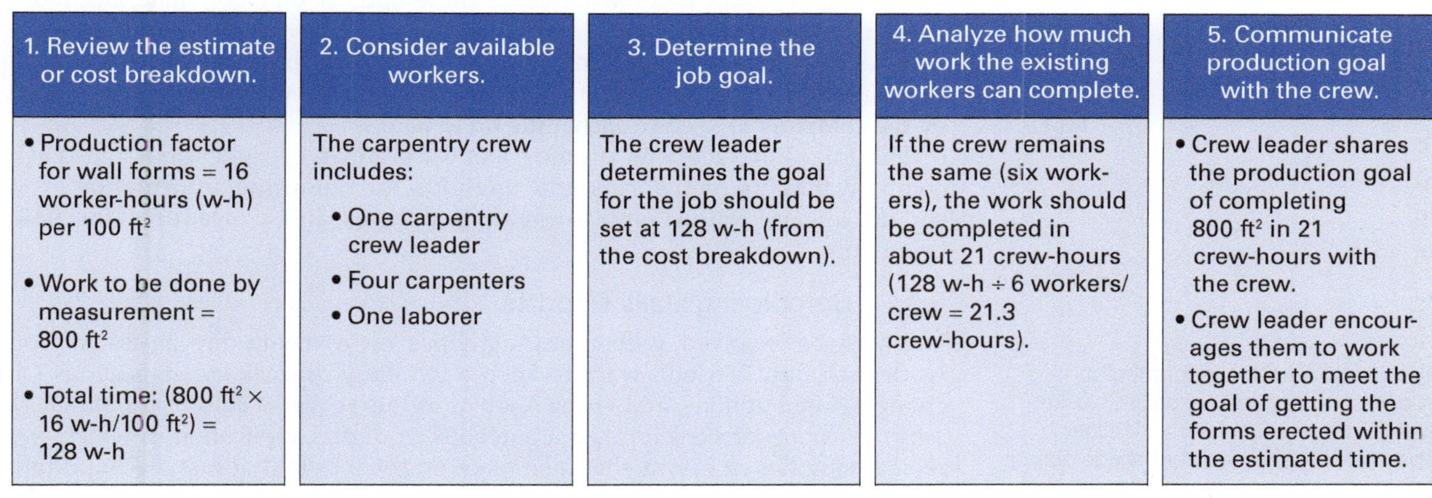

Figure 33 Crew leaders can use lookaheads or short-term scheduling to set production goals.

In this example, the crew leader used the short-term schedule to translate production into work hours and to schedule work so that the crew can accomplish it within the estimate. A crew can improve production when they know the amount of work to accomplish and the time available to complete the work, and can provide input when setting goals. In addition, setting production targets provides the motivation to exceed schedule targets.

Communicate the Schedule and Assigned Responsibilities

After the schedule is complete, you must then assign work responsibilities to the crew. Each person in the crew should know what they are responsible for accomplishing on the job.

Use the Schedule to Monitor and Control Work

NOTE

Most scheduling apps and programs include this feature that automatically helps you focus on the lookahead period for a job.

Schedules only have value if they are actively used as tools to monitor and control work. A lookahead or short-term schedule provides you with the information you need to plan for work and track progress. Before starting a job, actively review the schedule to:

- Determine the materials, tools, equipment, and labor needed to complete the job.
- Determine when the various resources are needed.
- Follow up to ensure that the resources are available on the jobsite when needed.

You should also verify the availability of needed resources three to four working days before the start of the job. This should occur even earlier for larger jobs. Advance preparation will help avoid situations that could potentially delay starting the job or cause it to fall behind schedule. As work continues, use your schedule to monitor whether actual production begins to slip behind estimated production and develop plans to recover the schedule as needed.

Follow Up and Confirm Work Is Completed Well

After you delegate tasks to the appropriate crew members, you must follow up to confirm that the crew completed the tasks correctly and efficiently. To do this effectively, you must be present on the jobsite to make sure all the resources are available to complete the work, to confirm that team members are working on their assigned activities, to answer any questions, and to help to resolve any problems that occur while the work is being done.

5.3.0 Crew Leader Field Reporting Responsibilities

A field-reporting system consists of a series of forms that are completed by you and other leaders on the project to share updates on labor, materials, tools, equipment, and more.

As a frontline leader, you may not be directly involved in updating overall schedules. However, the daily field or progress reports you submit will be used by the company to keep the schedule up to date.

The following sections provide some examples of field reporting. Each company has its own forms and methods for obtaining information. You should always follow your company's policies and procedures for field reporting.

5.3.1 Completing Daily Reports

Job diary: A written record that a supervisor maintains periodically (usually daily) of the events, communications, observations, and decisions made during the course of a project.

You will be involved with many activities on a day-to-day basis. As you work each day, you will want to keep a **job diary** to track events such as job changes, interruptions, and visits. A job diary, also called a *daily report, site diary, construction log,* or *site journal,* is a notebook or digital application in which you record activities or events that take place on the jobsite that may be important later (*Figure 34*).

July 8, 2023

Weather: Hot and Humid

Project: Opal Garage Annex

- The paving contractor crew arrived late (10 am).
- The owner representative inspected the footing foundation at approximately 1 pm.
- The concrete slump test did pass. Two trucks had to be ordered to return to plant, causing a delay.
- David Lopez had an incident on the second floor. I sent him to the on-site medical personnel for medical first aid treatment. The cause of the incident is being investigated.

Figure 34 Sample page from a job diary.

For this comparison process to be of use, the information you and others submit from the field must be accurate. In the event of a legal or contractual conflict with the client over costs, job diaries can be helpful as evidence in legal proceedings or in reaching a settlement. *Table 12* outlines an example scenario where your action of accurate field reporting will help benefit your company.

TABLE 12 Accurate Field Reporting Benefits Your Company

Scenario	Field Reporting Action
You are running a crew of five concrete finishers for a specialty contractor. When you and your crew show up to finish a slab, the general contractor (GC) informs you, "We're a day behind on setting the forms, so I need you and your crew to stand down until tomorrow."	Follow your company's field reporting policy to report the change. For example, you might first call your office to let them know about the delay. Then you would record it in your job diary. A six-man crew for one day represents 48 worker-hours. If your company charges $30 an hour, that's a potential loss of $1,440, which the company would want to recover from the general contractor. If there is a dispute, your entry in the job diary could result in a favorable decision for your employer.

Today, many companies use mobile applications that allow you to complete daily reporting on your mobile phone or tablet while you are on-site. You can quickly enter information throughout the day and attach photos and other documents to add more information. They generally also make it easy to send to your supervisor via email or text message (*Figure 35*). Your supervisor will be notified when the report is complete.

Whether print or digital, when making entries in a job diary, make sure that the information is accurate, factual, complete, consistent, organized, and up to date. Do not include any emotional details; keep the report focused on facts. This is especially true if documenting personnel problems. If the company

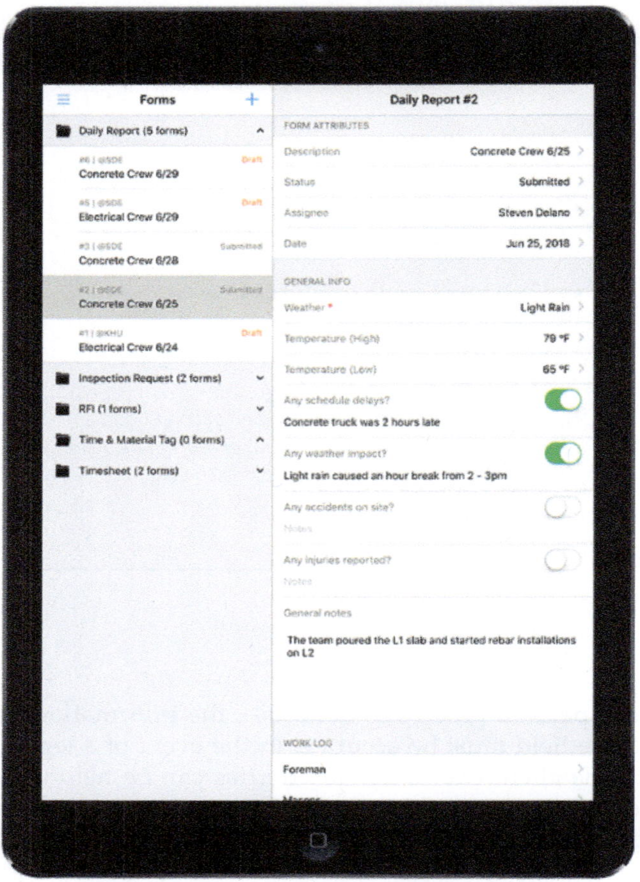

Figure 35 Mobile apps make it easier to complete daily reporting on-site.
Source: Fieldwire, https://www.fieldwire.com/

requires maintaining a job diary, follow company policy in determining which events and what details you should record. The information needs to be detailed enough so that, if needed, you could determine what happened on any day years later. If you are unsure what to include, it is better to have more information than too little. Check in with your supervisor to confirm if your daily reporting is including the right information.

5.3.2 Tracking Employee Costs through Time Sheets

Work breakdown structure (WBS): A method of organizing the entire scope of work in a logical manner based on how the work will be executed.

When the project budget is set up, many companies create a work breakdown for each project. A **work breakdown structure (WBS)** organizes the entire scope of work in a logical manner based on how the work will be executed. Within the WBS, planners assign each major task a unique charge number or code (*Figure 36*). Anyone working on that task charges that number or code on their time sheet so that project managers can readily track cost performance.

As a frontline leader, you not only need to ensure everyone is completing their time sheets, but also that they are coding those time sheets to the proper codes in the WBS. Doing so ensures you and your company are tracking and managing labor costs against specific work.

For example, as shown in *Figure 36*, if all time sheets are correctly coded, you and the company can determine the labor cost to install each of the three types of pipe: carbon steel piping, stainless steel piping, and the high-density polyethylene (HDPE) piping. You can also calculate how much it costs to install the piping for the entire project.

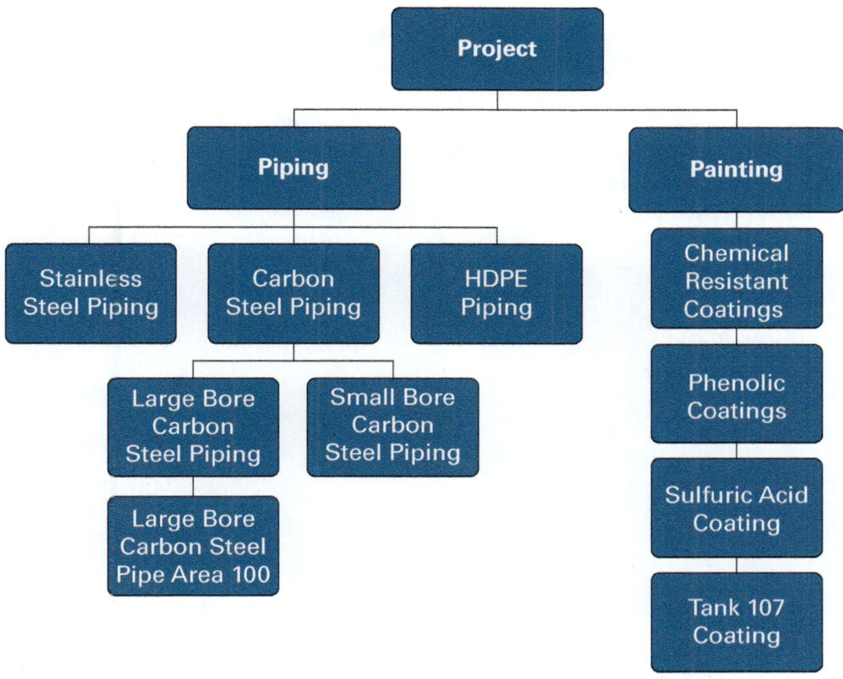

Level	Work	Account Code
Level 0	Piping	B
Level 1	Stainless Steel Piping	B-SS
Level 1	Carbon Steel Piping	B-CS
Level 1	HDPE Piping	B-HP
Level 2	Large Bore Carbon Steel Piping	B-CS-L
Level 2	Small Bore Carbon Steel Piping	B-CS-S
Level 3	Large Bore Carbon Steel Pipe Area 100	B-CS-L-100
Level 0	Painting	L
Level 1	Chemical Resistant Coatings	L-CR
Level 2	Phenolic Coating	L-CR-P
Level 3	Sulfuric Acid Tanks Coating	L-CR-P-ST
Level 4	Tank 107 Coating	L-CR-P-ST-107

Figure 36 An example of a work breakdown structure (WBS) for piping and painting on a project.

5.4.0 Frontline Leader Cost and Resource Management Responsibilities

Being aware of costs and controlling them is the responsibility of every employee on the job. As a frontline leader, it is your job to ensure that employees uphold this responsibility. Cost control is the process by which you keep expenses under control by managing labor, material, and other costs to ensure that the project finishes on budget.

5.4.1 Managing Costs

As you have learned, profit refers to the amount of money that the contractor will make after paying all the direct and indirect costs. If the costs exceed the estimate for the job, the difference between the actual and estimated costs must come out of the company's profit. This reduces what the contractor makes on the job.

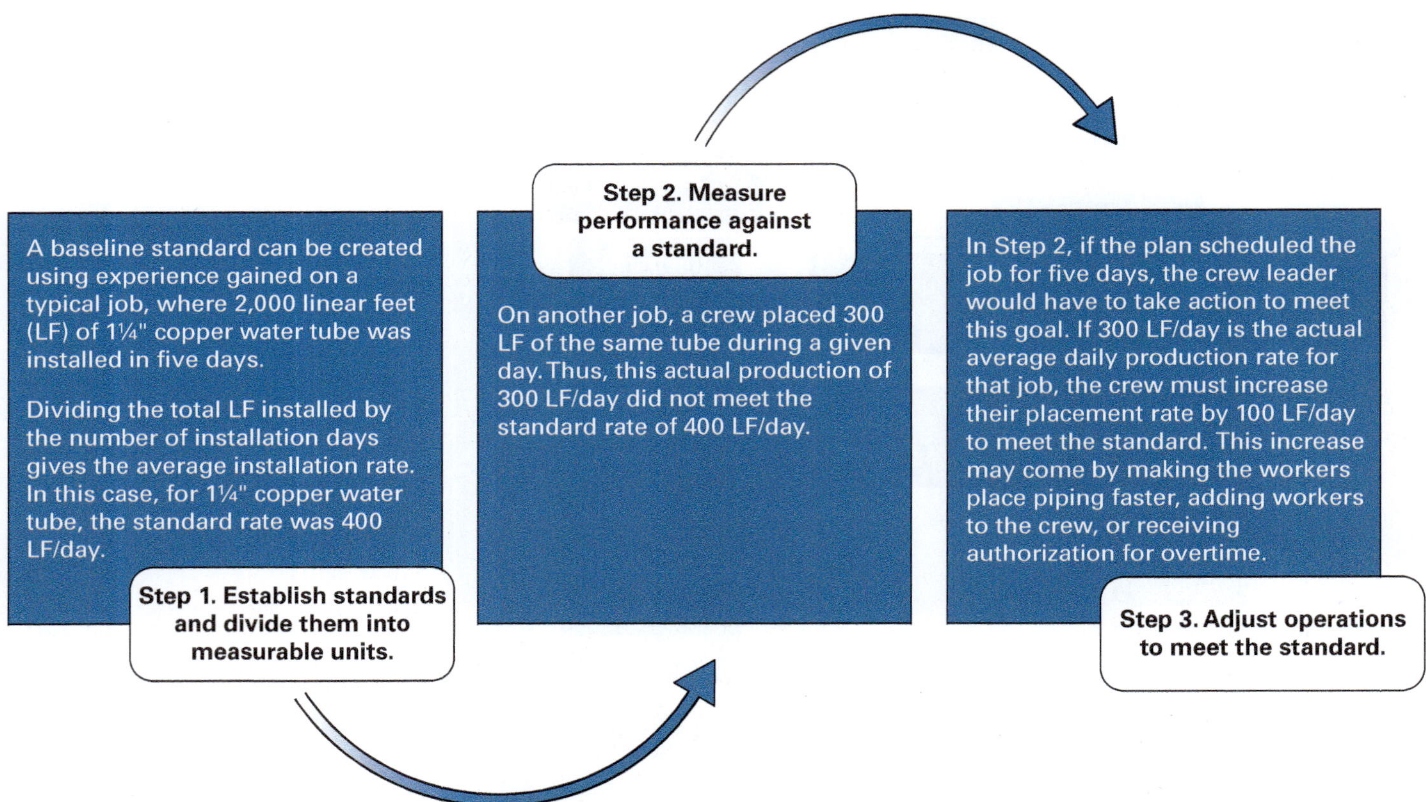

Figure 37 An effective cost control process monitors production and productivity to help manage costs.

NOTE

Before starting any action, you should check with company supervision to see that the action proposed is acceptable and within the company's policies and procedures.

Early identification of cost changes is very important and a key part of your role. As shown in *Figure 37*, an effective cost control process to monitor production and productivity includes several key steps. Identifying changes provides enough notice to correct the causes of overruns and manage those costs. You must learn to anticipate changes from plans and specifications based on experience and take measures to prevent them from occurring. If a situation cannot be fully corrected, early notification allows time for communicating and for managing expectations. No one likes surprises when it comes to increased project costs.

Table 13 lists some of the factors that can make actual costs exceed estimated costs, along with some potential actions you can take to avoid these situations.

A key factor in managing costs is controlling waste. Waste in construction can add up to loss of critical and costly materials and may result in job delays. You need to ensure that every crew member knows how to complete the work assigned and use materials efficiently. One example of waste is a carpenter who saws off a piece of lumber from a full-sized piece, when he could have found the length needed in the lumber scrap pile.

Doing rework is another form of waste (*Figure 38*). For example, less-experienced or less-trained crew members may make mistakes that cause work to have to be done over. You can help avoid these errors by providing on-the-spot training and by checking on newer, less experienced workers more often. Rework also can result from a conflict in craft scheduling that requires removal and reinstallation of finished work. Rework also increases safety risks on a job. Rework often involves demolition, time pressure, and frustration from the team, all of which create a higher likelihood of an incident.

Some issues that cause rework, such as mistakes on drawings, may be outside of your control. However, you can manage this risk by ensuring that you always have the most current set of drawings and examining the drawings carefully before you start work. Finding errors before the work begins increases safety and saves time, labor, materials, and more, which saves costs overall.

TABLE 13 Factors That Drive Cost Changes

Factor	Proactive Action
Client-related changes	Clients may want to change the scope of a project after it has started. You must be able to assess the potential impact of such changes and, if necessary, confer with the employer to determine the course of action. If contractor-related losses are occurring, you and the superintendent will need to work together to get the costs back in line.
Late delivery of materials, tools, and/or equipment	Review and update your lookahead schedules on a regular basis. Plan ahead to ensure that job resources will be available when needed.
Inclement weather	Work with the superintendent and other field leaders to have alternate plans ready.
Higher-than-expected wages or unexpected overtime due to low manpower	Plan ahead to ensure that labor resources will be available when needed. Ensure you are accurately recording daily work using your field reporting systems and job diary. Work with your supervisor or the superintendent to identify other staffing approaches.
Contractor or owner delays due to work availability	Ensure you are accurately recording daily work using your field reporting systems and job diary. Work with the superintendent and other field leaders to have alternate plans ready.
Unmotivated workers	Apply the leadership and team motivation strategies discussed earlier in this course. Remember, different things motivate different people in different ways. This means there is no single best approach to motivating all of your crew members.
Incidents	Continue to lead by example, reinforce the critical nature of safety, and follow the guidelines discussed earlier in the course. Work with the superintendent and other field leaders to help evaluate and improve the safety and health program, if needed.
Owner-related changes	Owners may want to change the scope of a project after it has started. You must be able to assess the potential impact of such changes and, if necessary, confer with the employer to determine the course of action. If contractor-related losses are occurring, you and the superintendent will need to work together to get the costs back in line.
Waste due to rework, material usage, and more	Train less-experienced workers on how to complete work. Review and update your lookahead schedules on a regular basis. Ensure crew members know how to use materials efficiently. Ensure you have the latest drawings and reference them daily.

Figure 38 Rework is another form of waste on a construction site.
Source: Vladimir Cetinski/iStock/Getty Images

5.4.2 Ensuring Crew Productivity

People typically represent more than half the cost of a project and thus have an enormous impact on profitability. For that reason, it is essential for you to manage your crew and their work environment in a way that maximizes their productivity.

One way to manage costs and increase productivity is to make sure you have the right skills on your crew to execute the level of tasks that you have to complete. *Crew mix* is a concept that describes the number of experienced or journey-level workers relative to the number of apprentices or less-experienced workers in a crew. For safety, quality, and productivity reasons, you do not want a worker trying to complete a task for which they are not skilled. However, you also do not want to have higher-wage crew members doing work that can be done by lower-wage crew members. For example, paying a journeyman electrician to pull wire costs more than paying an electrician helper who is skilled enough to do that work under the supervision of a journeyman electrician. As a frontline supervisor, you may not have control of your specific crew mix, but you can work to align their skills levels most appropriate to the specific work. Doing this well can reduce the overall project costs.

Other practices can help to ensure productivity:

- Keeping the crew adequately staffed at all times to avoid job delays
- Ensuring that all workers have the required resources when needed
- Ensuring that everyone knows where to go and what to do after each task is completed
- Making reassignments as needed
- Ensuring that all workers have completed their work properly

The time on the job should be for business, not for taking care of personal problems. Anything not work related should be handled after hours, away from the jobsite, if possible. Even the planning of after-work activities, arranging social functions, or running personal errands should occur after work or during breaks. Limited and necessary exceptions to these rules should be permitted (for example, making or meeting medical appointments), and these should be spelled out in company or crew policies.

Given the nature of construction work, frequent breaks can be needed to ensure worker safety. However, if crew members are often taking unscheduled breaks or goofing off, you will need to confront the behavior and coach these workers. Document any discussions in your job diary. If needed, you should redirect repeated violations to the attention of higher management as guided by company policy.

You can minimize or avoid delays caused by other crews or contractors by carefully tracking the project schedule. In doing so, you can anticipate delays that will affect your work and either take action to prevent the delay or redirect the crew to another task.

The availability and location of materials, equipment, and tools can have a serious effect on a crew's productivity. In the sections that follow, you will learn more about how to manage these resources to minimize such problems.

5.4.3 Handling Material Delivery and Storage

Your specific responsibilities for material delivery and storage will depend on the policies and procedures of the company. In general, you will be responsible for ensuring on-time delivery of materials, verifying the materials were delivered, and storing the materials (*Figure 39*). You also must prevent the waste and theft of materials.

NOTE

Scan the QR code in the front of this module to access additional resources on the steps involved in the development of an estimate, including creating a quantity takeoff sheet.

You will also be involved in planning materials for tasks such as job-built formwork and scaffolding or acquiring materials if you run out. If you run out of a specific material, be sure to consult the appropriate supervisor on how to proceed, because most companies have specific purchasing policies and procedures.

Figure 39 The receipt, storage, and control of materials after they reach the jobsite is an important part of a frontline leader's work.
Source: July Alcantara/E+/Getty Images

Source: metamorworks/Shutterstock

Did You Know?

Just-in-Time (JIT)

Just-in-time (JIT) delivery is a strategy in which materials arrive at the jobsite when needed. This means that a crew may install the materials right off the truck. This method reduces the need for on-site storage and staging areas. It also reduces the risk of loss or damage while moving products about the site. Other modern material management methods include the use of radiofrequency identification (RFID) tags that make it easy to inventory and locate material in crowded staging areas. Using an RFID inventory control system requires special scanners.

It is essential that the materials required for each day's work be on the jobsite when needed. You should confirm in advance the placement of orders for all materials and that they will arrive on schedule. A week or so before the delivery date, follow up to make sure there will be no delayed deliveries or items on backorder. If other people are responsible for providing the materials for a job, you must follow up to make sure that the materials are available when needed. Otherwise, delays can occur as crew members wait for the delivery of materials.

You may be responsible for the receipt of materials delivered to the worksite. When this happens, you should require a copy of the shipping invoice or similar document and check each item on the invoice against the actual materials to verify delivery of the correct amounts.

You should also check the condition of the materials to verify that nothing is defective before signing the invoice. This can be difficult and time-consuming because it requires the crew to open cartons and examine their contents. However, this step cannot be overlooked, because a signed invoice indicates that the recipient accepted all listed materials and in an undamaged state. If the crew leader signs for the materials without checking them, and then finds damage, no one will be able to prove that the materials came to the site in that condition (*Figure 40*).

Figure 40 When receiving materials, check the condition of the materials to verify that nothing is defective before signing the invoice.
Source: kali9/E+/Getty Images

After checking and signing the shipping invoice, you should give the original or a copy to the superintendent or project manager. The company then will file the invoice for future reference because it serves as the only record the company has to check bills received from the supplier company.

Another essential element of materials control is selecting where to store materials on a jobsite. *Table 14* outlines three factors to consider when selecting an appropriate material storage location.

TABLE 14 Considerations When Selecting a Material Storage Location

Factor	Description
Access	If possible, store materials near where the crew will use them, so the crew can access them easily. Not having to carry the materials long distances will greatly reduce time, effort, and installation costs.
Damage Protection	Store materials in a secure area to avoid damage. Be sure that the storage area suits the materials. For instance, temperature-sensitive materials, such as chemicals or paints, should be stored in climate-controlled areas to prevent waste.
Security	Theft or vandalism of construction materials increases direct and indirect costs. These include replacement materials, lost production time while replacing needed materials, and the costs of additional security precautions. In addition, a contractor's insurance costs may increase due to theft and vandalism.

The best way to avoid theft and vandalism is to have a secure jobsite. At the end of each workday, store unused materials and tools in a secure location, such as a locked construction trailer. If the jobsite is fenced or the building has lockable access, the materials can be stored within. Many sites have security cameras and/or intrusion alarms to help minimize theft and vandalism.

5.4.4 Planning and Controlling Tool Usage

Among companies, various policies govern who provides hand and power tools to employees. Some companies provide all the tools, while others furnish only the larger power tools. You should be familiar with and enforce any company policies related to tools.

As a crew leader, you are responsible for planning tool usage for a job. This task includes the following:

- Determining the tools required
- Informing the workers who will provide the tools (company or worker)
- Making sure the workers are qualified to use the tools safely and effectively
- Determining what controls to establish for tools

Tool control involves controlling the issue, use, and maintenance of all tools provided by the company. It also involves storing the tools in a location that provides easy access to your crew (*Figure 41*).

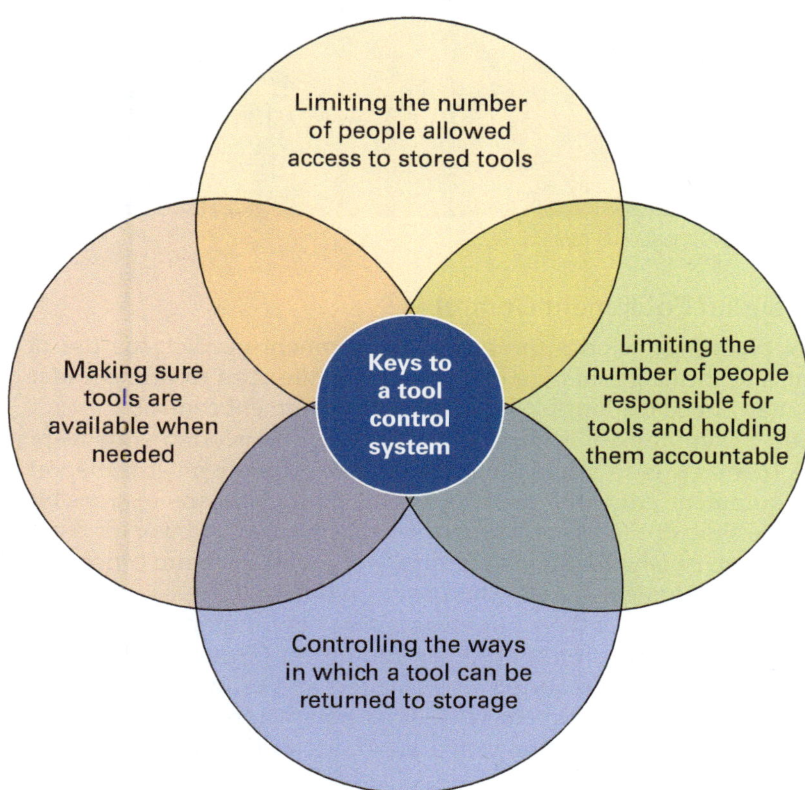

Figure 41 Studies show there are four keys to an effective tool control system.

Using the proper tools correctly saves time and energy. In addition, proper tool use reduces the chance of damage to the tool during use, as well as injury to the user and to nearby workers. This is especially true of edge tools and those with any form of fixed or rotating blade. A dull tool is far more dangerous than a sharp one.

Tools must be adequately maintained and properly stored. Making sure that tools are cleaned, dried, and lubricated prevents rust and ensures that the tools are in the proper working order. This applies to tools supplied by the company as well as tools that belong to the workers.

If a tool is damaged, it is essential to repair or replace it promptly. Otherwise, an incident or injury could result. Users should take care of company-issued tools as if they were their own. Workers should not abuse tools simply because they are not their property.

One of the major sources of low productivity on a job is the time spent searching for a tool. To prevent this from occurring, supervision should establish a storage location for company-issued tools and equipment. You should make sure that crew members return all company-issued tools and equipment to this designated location after use. Similarly, workers should organize their personal toolboxes so that they can readily find the appropriate tools and return their tools to their toolboxes when they are finished using them. If needed, coach less-experienced team members on how to master this important professional skill.

NOTE

Regardless of whether a worker or the company owns a tool, OSHA holds companies responsible for the consequences of using a tool on a jobsite. The company is accountable if an employee receives an injury from a defective tool. Therefore, the crew leader needs to be aware of any defects in the tools the crew members are using.

Did You Know?

Connected Tools Are Controlled Tools

Tool companies are using technology to help you track tools and equipment on a jobsite. These smart tool systems have a software application that allows you to add tools enabled with Bluetooth® technology to the tracking system. You can also attach powered tags to large equipment or materials and add those to the tracking system. As crew members sign out tools, the assignment is tracked in the system, so you can track which tools are in use, by whom, and where they are on the jobsite at any point. You can also track materials and equipment in the same way. By helping to ensure all of your equipment, tools, and materials are accounted for and easy to find, these systems help companies control costs by saving time and replacement costs.

Source: DEWALT Industrial Tool Co.

5.4.5 Ensuring Equipment Control

Equipment planning includes the types of equipment needed, the use of the equipment, and the length of time it will be on the site. As a frontline leader of a crew, you may not be responsible for long-term equipment control.

However, the equipment required for a specific job is often your responsibility. The first step is to schedule when a crew member must transport the required equipment from the shop or rental yard. You are responsible for informing the shop of the location of its use and confirming a worker returns it to the shop when finished with it. You must work with the main office to make certain that the equipment reaches the jobsite on time.

Coordinating the use of the equipment is also very important. Some equipment operates in combination with other equipment (*Figure 42*). For example, dump trucks are generally required when loaders and excavators are used. You should also coordinate equipment with other contractors on the job. Sharing equipment can save time and money and avoid duplication of effort.

Figure 42 Coordinating equipment requires knowing which equipment operates in combination with other equipment.

Source: RyanOverman/iStock/Getty Images

It is common for equipment to lie idle at a jobsite because of a lack of proper planning for the job and the equipment arriving early. For example, if wire-pulling equipment arrives at a jobsite before the conduit is in place, this equipment will be out of service while awaiting the conduit installation. In addition to the wasted rental cost, the equipment could also be damaged, lost, or stolen while awaiting use.

You need to control equipment use, ensure that the crew operates the equipment according to its instructions, and make sure they are adhering to time and cost guidelines. You must also assign or coordinate responsibility for maintaining and repairing equipment as indicated by the applicable preventive maintenance schedule. Delaying maintenance and repairs can lead to costly equipment failures.

You must also ensure that crew equipment operators are properly trained. This includes ensuring that the equipment operators have the necessary credentials to operate the equipment, including applicable licenses.

You are also responsible for the proper operation of all other equipment resources, including cars and trucks. Reckless or unsafe operation of vehicles will likely result in damaged equipment, leading to disciplinary action for the workers, fines and repair costs levied by the vehicle vendors, and a loss of confidence in your ability to control the actions of your crew.

You should also arrange to secure all equipment at the close of each day's work to prevent theft. If continued use of the equipment is necessary for the job, you should make sure to lock it in a safe place. If it is not, return it promptly.

5.0.0 Section Review

1. Which of these activities occurs during the design and development phase of a project?
   a. Architect/engineer sketches are prepared, and a preliminary budget is developed.
   b. Final inspections are completed.
   c. Detailed project drawings and specifications are prepared.
   d. Contracts for the project are awarded.

2. Which of these activities is *not* part of creating a lookahead schedule?
   a. Identifying the required work activities and dividing them into tasks
   b. Planning resources needed for each task
   c. Organizing the work into a logical sequence
   d. Assigning cost estimates to each task

3. A job diary should typically record any of the following *except* _____.
   a. job interruptions and visits
   b. personal details and emotions
   c. changes needed to project drawings
   d. the actual time each job task took to complete

4. Which of the following is a *correct* statement regarding project cost?
   a. Cost is handled by the Accounting Department and isn't a concern of the crew leader.
   b. The difference between the estimated cost and the actual cost affects a company's profit.
   c. Wasted material is factored into the estimate and is never a concern.
   d. The contractor's overhead costs aren't included in the cost estimate.

Module 46100 Review Questions

1. Who is generally the on-site field supervisor who is responsible for one or more crew leaders?
   a. Project Manager
   b. Lead Engineer
   c. Superintendent
   d. Pre-Construction Manager

2. Accepting responsibility for job completion and being personally answerable for the results is known as _____.
   a. responsibility
   b. delegation
   c. authority
   d. accountability

3. Which of the following is *not* true of situational leadership?
   a. It involves adjusting the way you lead to the specific situation and needs of the group.
   b. It assumes all situations do not require the same leadership.
   c. It allows you to adapt your leadership style to the situation.
   d. It has four styles, including directing, coaching, supporting, and delegating.

4. When you communicate with your team verbally, be sure to _____.
   a. assess your audience before you speak
   b. use technical language as much as possible
   c. speak quickly to save time
   d. assume everyone has the same basic understanding of the topic

5. The *first* step in problem solving should be _____.
   a. choosing a solution to the problem
   b. evaluating the solution to the problem
   c. defining the problem
   d. testing the solution to the problem

6. Which of these is a way to lower the motivation and morale of your employees and team?
   a. Focusing on task completion only, not professional growth
   b. Giving recognition and rewards
   c. Setting clear expectations and goals
   d. Providing opportunities for training and upskilling

7. During an employee's first week of work on your crew, you should be sure to set aside time to _____.
   a. eat lunch together
   b. do a task verification
   c. quiz the employee on company policies
   d. evaluate social engagement

8. Which of these steps is important when delegating work to an individual or a team?
   a. Letting individuals set their own standards of measurement
   b. Checking in only after the work is complete
   c. Ensuring crew members understand what to do and have the skill to do it
   d. Allowing the team to set their own deadlines and get their own resources

9. Which common jobsite documents can help a crew leader overcome a language barrier with a worker?
   a. OSHA incident records
   b. Contracts and schedules
   c. Plans and drawings
   d. Permits

10. As a leader, you can help to manage performance issues by _____.
   a. ignoring the problem that needs resolving
   b. gathering information and preparing well for the employee conversation
   c. discussing the performance issues publicly with the rest of the team
   d. having the conversation when the employee is unprepared

11. The negative impact of incidents may include all of the following *except* _____.
   a. lower workers' compensation costs
   b. damage to the overall morale of everyone on a project or jobsite
   c. increased project costs to the company
   d. project delays

12. OSHA was established in 1970 to _____.
   a. collect dues for membership
   b. ensure safe and healthful working conditions for workers
   c. manage workers' compensation claims
   d. conduct medical research

13. Which of the following statements regarding safety training sessions is *correct*?
   a. The project manager usually holds them.
   b. They are held only for new employees.
   c. They should be conducted frequently by a frontline leader.
   d. They are required only after an accident has occurred.

14. A key step in an incident investigation is to determine the incident's _____.
   a. root cause
   b. secondary driver
   c. cost impacts
   d. design flaws

15. If you observe an employee showing impaired behavior or signs of mental health issues, you should work with _____.
   a. OSHA
   b. the safety inspector
   c. the owner or client
   d. your supervisor and/or Human Resources

16. What is completed during the design phase to ensure a project can be delivered successfully?
    a. Feasibility study
    b. As-built drawings
    c. Installation work packages
    d. Project schedule

17. A contract in which the client pays the contractor for their labor, materials, equipment, and other costs they incur during the performance of the contract is known as a _____.
    a. fixed-price contract
    b. time-spent contract
    c. time and materials contract
    d. cost-reimbursable contract

18. Which of the following would be tracked in a job diary?
    a. Job changes, interruptions, and visits
    b. The crew's time off
    c. Training needs and career development
    d. Personal information provided by an employee

19. Which of the following is a source of data in the field-reporting system?
    a. The cost estimate for the project
    b. The daily job diary
    c. The Level 1 schedule
    d. The lookahead schedule

20. To prevent job delays due to late delivery of materials, the crew leader should _____.
    a. demand a discount from the supplier to compensate for the delay
    b. tell a crew member to go look for the delivery truck
    c. refuse the late delivery and reorder the materials from another supplier
    d. check with the supplier in advance of the scheduled delivery

Answers to odd-numbered Module Review Questions are found in *Appendix A*.

Answers to Section Review Questions

Answer	Section Reference	Objective
Section 1.0.0		
1. b	1.1.2	1a
2. b	1.2.2	1b
Section 2.0.0		
1. d	2.1.2	2a
2. b	2.2.3	2b
3. a	2.3.0	2c
Section 3.0.0		
1. b	3.1.1	3a
2. c	3.2.0	3b
3. c	3.3.3	3c
Section 4.0.0		
1. a	4.0.0	4a
2. d	4.2.0	4b
3. a	4.3.1	4c
4. b	4.4.2	4d
5. d	4.5.0	4e
Section 5.0.0		
1. a	5.1.1	5a
2. d	5.2.2	5b
3. b	5.3.1	5c
4. b	5.4.1	5d

APPENDIX A REVIEW QUESTION ANSWER KEYS

MODULE 26401-23

Answer	Section Reference
1. d	1.0.0
3. b	1.1.1
5. a	1.1.2
7. b	1.1.2
9. c	1.2.0
11. b	1.2.0
13. c	1.3.1
15. c	1.4.3
17. b	1.4.3
19. b	2.0.0

MODULE 26401-23 CALCULATIONS

Question 3

Per ***NEC Table 310.16***, the ampacity of No. 250 kcmil THHN copper conductor is 290A. Find 91% of the ampacity for 101°F [***NEC Table 310.15(B)(1)***]:

290A × 0.91 = 263.9A for each conductor

The ampacity for each conductor is **263.9A**.

Question 5

Write down the appropriate formula for calculating voltage drop in a three-phase circuit, and refer to ***NEC Chapter 9, Table 8***, *Conductor Properties*, for the conductor resistance. Then use the formula to find the voltage drop:

$$VD = \frac{1.732 \times L \times R \times I}{1{,}000'}$$

$$VD = \frac{1.732 \times 248' \times 0.0776 \times 180A}{1{,}000'}$$

$VD =$ 5.9998V, rounded to 6V

Divide by applied voltage to find the percentage of voltage drop:

$$\frac{6V}{480V} = 0.0125 \text{ or } 1.25\%$$

The voltage drop is **1.25%**.

Question 7

Write down the appropriate formula for calculating voltage drop in a three-phase circuit, and refer to ***NEC Chapter 9, Table 8*** for the conductor resistance. Then use the formula to find the voltage drop:

$$VD = \frac{1.732 \times L \times R \times I}{1{,}000'}$$

$$VD = \frac{1.732 \times 290' \times 0.0608 \times 200A}{1{,}000'}$$

$VD =$ 6.108V

Divide by applied voltage to find the percentage of voltage drop:

$$\frac{6.108V}{208V} = 0.0294 \text{ or } 2.94\%$$

The voltage drop is **2.94%**.

Question 9

To determine the required conductor size, you must first find the total ampacity of all the loads. Start by finding the continuous load current (I):

$$I \text{ (continuous)} = \frac{VA}{V \times 1.732}$$

$$I \text{ (continuous)} = \frac{25{,}000VA}{208V \times 1.732}$$

I (continuous) = 69.4A

Then, find the noncontinuous load current (I):

$$I \text{ (noncontinuous)} = \frac{VA}{V \times 1.732}$$

$$I \text{ (noncontinuous)} = \frac{20{,}500VA}{208V \times 1.732}$$

I (noncontinuous) = 56.9A

Using the results, calculate the total ampacity as follows:

Total ampacity = noncontinuous load + 125% of continuous load

Total ampacity = 56.9A + (69.4A × 1.25)

Total ampacity = 56.9A + 86.75

Total ampacity = 143.65A

Using ***NEC Table 310.16***, 143.65A corresponds to **1/0**.

Question 11

First, convert the 96.75 kVA load to VA by multiplying by 1,000:

96.75 kVA × 1,000 = 96,750VA

Use the result and the applied voltage with the formula for calculating feeder ampacity:

$$I = \frac{VA}{V \times 1.732}$$

$$I = \frac{96{,}750VA}{208V \times 1.732}$$

$I =$ 268.56A

The load is **268.56A**.

Question 13

The tap must be rated at no less than the calculated load of 150A. Using ***NEC Table 310.16***, 150A corresponds to **1/0**.

MODULE 26402-23

Answer	Section Reference
1. b	1.0.0
3. d	1.1.0
5. d	1.1.2
7. a	1.1.2
9. a	1.2.4
11. a	2.1.2
13. d	2.2.0
15. b	3.3.2

MODULE 26403-23

Answer	Section Reference
1. a	1.0.0
3. a	1.1.1
5. c	1.1.1
7. b	1.2.1
9. c	2.2.2
11. d	2.3.2; *Figure 9*
13. c	3.1.0
15. a	3.2.0

MODULE 26404-23

Answer	Section Reference
1. b	1.1.0
3. a	1.2.2
5. b	2.1.0
7. c	2.1.0
9. b	2.2.0
11. b	2.2.0
13. d	2.3.1
15. a	2.3.3

MODULE 26405-23

Answer	Section Reference
1. b	1.2.1
3. d	2.1.1
5. d	2.1.2
7. b	2.2.4
9. d	2.2.7
11. c	3.1.2
13. c	4.1.2
15. d	4.2.0
17. a	5.2.12
19. b	5.4.2

MODULE 26406-23

Answer	Section Reference
1. b	1.1.0
3. a	1.1.0
5. a	1.3.7
7. c	2.1.0
9. a	2.2.0
11. b	2.2.0
13. d	3.1.3
15. b	3.2.2

MODULE 26407-23

Answer	Section Reference
1. b	1.1.0
3. c	1.1.3
5. a	1.1.7
7. b	1.2.1; *Figure 9*
9. d	2.1.1
11. c	3.1.1
13. b	3.2.1
15. d	4.1.0
17. b	5.2.0
19. c	6.2.1

MODULE 26408-23

Answer	Section Reference
1. a	1.1.0
3. c	1.2.1
5. b	2.1.0
7. a	2.1.4
9. b	2.2.2; *Figure 16*
11. c	3.1.3
13. d	3.3.0
15. c	3.5.0
17. b	3.5.0; *Figure 36*
19. c	4.2.1; *Table 3*

MODULE 26409-23

Answer	Section Reference
1. c	1.1.1
3. c	1.2.3
5. d	1.4.0
7. c	1.5.1
9. c	2.1.0
11. c	3.1.0
13. a	3.2.2
15. c	4.2.2

MODULE 26410-23

Answer	Section Reference
1. c	1.1.0
3. d	1.2.2
5. d	1.2.3
7. b	1.2.3
9. b	2.1.1; *Table 1*
11. a	2.1.4
13. a	2.2.3
15. a	3.1.2

MODULE 26411-23

Answer	Section Reference
1. d	1.0.0
3. b	1.1.0
5. d	1.1.1
7. c	1.2.0
9. a	1.2.2

MODULE 26412-23

Answer	Section Reference
1. b	1.1.0
3. b	1.2.2
5. b	1.3.2
7. d	1.4.3
9. c	1.5.6
11. b	2.1.1
13. b	3.1.1
15. c	3.4.2

MODULE 46100

Answer	Section Reference
1. c	1.1.0
3. d	2.1.3
5. c	2.3.1
7. b	3.1.2
9. c	3.2.3
11. a	4.1.0
13. c	4.3.1
15. d	4.5.2
17. c	5.1.2
19. b	5.3.1

APPENDIX B SUPPLEMENTAL EXERCISE ANSWER KEYS

MODULE 26401-23

Question 1

future expansion

Section Reference 1.0.0

Question 3

125%

Section Reference 1.1.1

Question 5

The total length of the tap conductors must not exceed 25' (7.5 m).

The tap conductors must be rated at no less than one-third the capacity of the overcurrent protective device protecting the feeder.

The tap conductors must terminate in a single circuit breaker or a single set of fuses that will limit the load to the conductor rating.

The tap conductors must be enclosed in a raceway or otherwise suitably protected from damage.

Section Reference 1.3.2

Question 7

NEC Table 220.42(A)

Section Reference 1.4.3

Question 9

100A

Section Reference 2.2.2

Question 11

largest

Section Reference 3.3.1

Question 13

65%

Section Reference 3.4.0

Question 15

25% of the largest motor

Section Reference 3.9.0

MODULE 26402-23

Question 1

critical care spaces

Section Reference 1.0.0

Question 3

1 EES

Section Reference 1.1.1

Question 5

Digital electronic equipment, including computer cash registers, computer peripherals, and digital processing equipment

Section Reference 2.1.1

Question 7

True

Section Reference 2.3.0

Question 9

True

Section Reference 3.4.0

MODULE 26403-23

Question 1

60 seconds

Section Reference 1.0.0

Question 3

voltage regulator

Section Reference 1.1.1

Question 5

lithium-ion

Section Reference 2.1.3

Question 7

higher

Section Reference 2.2.1

Question 9

50

Section Reference 2.2.1

Question 11

single-phase; three-phase

Section Reference 2.3.0

Question 13

87.5; $1\frac{1}{2}$

Section Reference 3.1.0

Question 15

c

Section Reference 3.3.0

MODULE 26404-23

Question 1

valence shell

Section Reference 1.2.1

Question 3

more than four

Section Reference 1.2.2

Question 5

N-type

Section Reference 1.2.3

Question 7

one

Section Reference 2.1.0

Question 9

forward

Section Reference 2.1.0

Question 11

NPN; PNP

Section Reference 2.2.0

Question 13

N-type germanium

Section Reference 2.2.2

Question 15

four

Section Reference 2.3.1

MODULE 26405-23

Question 1

NFPA 1: *Fire Code*

NFPA 70®: *National Electrical Code®*

NFPA 72®: *National Fire Alarm and Signaling Code®*

NFPA 101®: *Life Safety Code®*

Section Reference 1.2.1

Question 3

Air

Section Reference 2.2.4

Question 5

non-restorable fusible line-type heat

Section Reference 2.2.6

Question 7

transmitter

Section Reference 4.3.2

Question 9

doorknob edge of the exit door

Section Reference 5.3.1

MODULE 26406-23

Question 1

Δ-Δ, Δ-Y, Y-Δ, and Y-Y

Section Reference 1.0.0

Question 3

generating stations and substations

Section Reference 1.1.0

Question 5

They are the same.

Section Reference 1.2.0

Question 7

the maximum inrush VA and the maximum continuous VA load

Section Reference 1.3.5

Question 9

Current and potential

Section Reference 2.0.0

Question 11

Main power lines

Section Reference 2.2.0

Question 13

Neutral conductor

Section Reference 3.1.1

Question 15

harmonics

Section Reference 3.1.4

MODULE 26407-23

Question 1

They have longer life.

They are more reliable.

They have faster switching speeds.

They resist shock and vibration better.

Section Reference 1.1.0

Question 3

in series; in parallel

Section Reference 1.1.4

Question 5

removing and rotating the solenoid unit 180°

Section Reference 2.0.0

Question 7

False

Section Reference 2.1.3

Question 9

SCRs are turned on

Section Reference 2.2.0

Question 11

True

Section Reference 5.1.0

Question 13

Variable torque

Constant torque

Constant horsepower

Section Reference 3.2.1

Question 15

True

Section Reference 6.1.4

MODULE 26408-23

Question 1

Evaporator, condenser, compressor, and expansion device

Section Reference 1.2.1

Question 3

The metals from which it is made expand and contract at different rates as the temperature changes

Section Reference 2.1.0

Question 5

tiny resistance heater; the switch contacts

Section Reference 2.1.1

Question 7

The R terminal, using the red wire.

Section Reference 2.2.2; Figure 16

Question 9

the heat exchanger

Section Reference 3.2.1

Question 11

time and temperature

Section Reference 3.3.0

Question 13

sensors; unit controllers

Section Reference 3.4.2

Question 15

NEC Article 706

Section Reference 4.2.5

MODULE 26409-23

Question 1

Pipe heat tracing

Roof, gutter, and downspout deicing

Snow melting and anti-icing

Domestic hot-water temperature maintenance

Floor heating and warming

Section Reference 1.0.0

Question 3

parallel-resistance; self-regulating

Section Reference 1.1.2

Question 5

head-conductive cement

Section Reference 1.1.6

Question 7

2' (600 mm)

Section Reference 1.5.1

Question 9

b

Section Reference 4.1.2

MODULE 26410-23

Question 1

insulation

Section Reference 1.0.0

Question 3

thermal overload relays

Section Reference 1.1.0

Question 5

Class A, B, F, and H

Section Reference 1.2.3

Question 7

grounded windings, open circuits, shorts, and reverses

Section Reference 2.4.0

Question 9

high current in the winding, causing overheating and insulation damage

Section Reference 2.4.0

MODULE 26411-23

Question 1

conductor, strand shielding, insulation, insulation shielding system, and jacket

Section Reference 1.1.0

Question 3

Confine the dielectric field within the cable.

Obtain a symmetrical radial distribution of voltage stress within the dielectric.

Protect the cable from induced potentials.

Limit radio interference.

Reduce the hazard of shock.

Provide a ground path for leakage and fault currents.

Section Reference 1.1.3

Question 5

eliminate the possibility of air voids

Section Reference 1.2.1

Question 7

break down the insulating aluminum oxide coating on both the connector and conductor surfaces

Section Reference 1.2.2

Question 9

True

Section Reference 2.1.2

MODULE 26412-23

Question 1

False

Section Reference 1.1.0

Question 3

NEC Section 520.5

Section Reference 1.2.1

Question 5

15' (4.5 m)

Section Reference 1.3.1

Question 7

metallic equipment may become energized and accessible to animals

Section Reference 1.4.4

Question 9

2' (600 mm)

Section Reference 2.2.1

APPENDIX 26401-23A

Load Calculation Form

General Lighting Load					**Phase**	**Neutral**
Square footage of dwelling	[1]	@ 3VA =	[2]			
Kitchen small appliance circuits	[3]	@ 1500 =	[4]			
Laundry branch circuit	[5]	@ 1500 =	[6]			
Subtotal of general lighting loads per ***NEC Section 220.45***			[7]			
Subtract 1st 3000VA per ***NEC Section 220.45***			[8]		[9]	
Remaining VA times 35% per ***NEC Section 220.45***			[10]		[11]	
Total demand for general lighting loads =					[12]	[13]
Fixed Appliance Loads (Nameplate or *NEC*® FLA of motors) per ***NEC Section 220.14***						
			[14]			
			[15]			
			[16]			
			[17]			
			[18]			
			[19]			
Subtotal of fixed appliances			[20]			
If 3 or less fixed appliances take @ 100% =					[21]	[22]
If 4 or less fixed appliances take @ 75% =					[23]	[24]
Other Loads per ***NEC Section 220.14***						
Electric range per ***NEC Table 220.55*** [neutral @ 70% per ***NEC Section 220.61(B)(1)***]					[25]	[26]
Electric dryer per ***NEC Table 220.54*** [neutral @ 70% per ***NEC Section 220.61(B)(1)***]					[27]	[28]
Electric heat per ***NEC Section 220.51***	omit smaller load per ***NEC Section 220.60***				[29]	[30]
Air conditioning ***NEC Section 220.50(B)***						
Largest Motor =	× 25% per ***NEC Section 430.24*** =				[31]	[32]
Total VA Demand =					[33]	[34]
(VA divided by 240V) **Amps =**					[35]	[36]
Service OCD and minimum size grounding electrode conductor (***NEC Table 250.66)*** =					[37]	[38]
AWG per ***NEC Section 310.12(A)***, ***NEC Section 220.61***, and ***NEC Table 310.16*** for neutral					[39]	[40]

APPENDIX 26402-23A

Typical Testing and Performance Verification Forms

BED TOWER EXPANSION

Part 3 – Bed Tower Expansion & Renovation

SECTION 16020

TESTS AND PERFORMANCE VERIFICATION

PART 1 - GENERAL

1.1 RELATED DOCUMENTS

General: Drawings and general provisions of the Contract, including General and Supplementary Conditions and Division 1 Specification sections, apply to work specified in this section.

1.2 DESCRIPTION

A. Time: Perform verification work as required to show that the System is operating correctly in accordance with contract documents and manufacturer's literature. All verification shall be done after 3-day full operational period.

B. Submission: Submit check out memos and completed testing results of all systems, cable, equipment, devices, etc., for acceptance prior to being energized or utilized.

1.3 QUALITY ASSURANCE

A. Compliance: Testing shall comply to the following standards:

1. NEMA
2. ASTM
3. NETA
4. ANSI C2
5. ICEA
6. NFPA

1.4 QUALIFICATIONS OF TESTING FIRM

A. Qualification: The testing firm shall be an independent testing organization which can function as an unbiased testing authority, professionally independent of the manufacturers, supplier, and installers of equipment or systems evaluated by the testing firm.

B. Experience: The testing firm shall be regularly engaged in the testing of electrical equipment devices, installations, and systems.

C. Accreditation: The testing firm shall meet OSHA criteria for accreditation of testing laboratories, Title 29, Part 1907, or be a Full Member company of the InterNational Electrical Testing Association.

D. Certification: The lead, on-site, technical person shall be currently certified by the InterNational Electrical Testing Association (NETA) or National Institute for Certification in Engineering Technologies (NICET) in electrical power distribution system testing.

16020 - 1

E. Personnel: The testing firm shall utilize engineers and technicians who are regularly employed by the firm for testing services.

F. Proof of Qualifications: The testing firm shall submit proof of the above qualifications when requested.

G. Companies: Must use NETA-certified pre-qualified testing firms.

PART 2 - TEST

2.1 EQUIPMENT

A. Instruments: Supply all instruments required to read and record data. Calibration date shall be submitted on test reports. All instruments shall be certified per NETA standards.

B. Adjustments: Adjust system to operate at the required performance levels and within all tolerances as required by NETA Standards.

2.2 APPLICATIONS

A. Switchboards, Panelboards and Mechanical Equipment Feeders: After feeders are in place, but before being connected to devices and equipment, test for shorts, opens, and intentional and unintentional grounds.

B. Ratings 250V or Less: Cables 250V or less in size #1/0 AWG and larger shall be meggered using an industry-approved "megger" with 500V internal generating voltage. Readings shall be recorded and submitted to the Engineer for acceptance prior to energizing same. Submit 5 copies of tabulated megger test values for all cables.

C. Cables 600V or Less: Cables 600V or less in size #1/0 AWG and larger shall be meggered using an industry-approved "megger" with 1000V internal generating voltage. Readings shall be recorded and submitted to the Engineer for acceptance prior to energizing same. If values are less than recommended NETA values, notify Engineer. Submit 5 copies of tabulated megger test values for all cables.

D. Ratings 600V or Less: Cables 600V or less in size #1/0 AWG and larger shall be meggered using an industry-approved "megger" with 500V internal generating voltage. Readings shall be recorded and submitted to the Engineer for acceptance prior to energizing same. Submit 5 copies of tabulated megger test values for all cables.

E. Ratings Above 600V: Cables above 600V in all sizes shall first be meggered using an industry-approved "megger" having 2500V internal generating voltage. When proper readings are obtained, the cables shall be "hi-potted" using (5) potentials and periods as recommended by NETA, cable manufacturer for the type and voltage class of cables installed. Do not exceed 80% of factory test voltage. Readings ("megger" and "hi-pot") shall be recorded and submitted to the Engineer for acceptance prior to energizing it. Submit 5 copies of tabulated megger test values for all cables.

F. Main circuit breakers and feeder circuit breakers 200A and greater shall be tested using primary injection testing as per NETA Specifications. Reports to include manufacturer's time current curve number and trip time. Submit 5 copies to the Engineer at substantial completion.

G. Transformers 75 kVA and larger. Perform Insulation resistance test and turns ratio test. Submit 5 copies to Engineer at substantial completion.

2.3 MOTORS

A. Procedure: Test run each motor 25 hp and larger. Tabulate and submit 5 copies of the Test Information at substantial completion for final inspection. Refer to form at the end of this Section.

B. Provisions: With the system energized, line-to-line voltage and line current measurements shall be made at the motors under full load conditions. The condition shall be corrected when measured values deviate plus or minus 10% from the nameplate ratings.

C. Insulation: Test the insulation resistances of all motor windings to ground with an appropriate test instrument, as recommended by the motor manufacturer, before applying line voltage to the motors. If these values are less than the manufacturer's recommended values, notify the contractor providing the motor for correction before initial start up.

D. Power Factor: Check power factor of all motors 5 hp and larger while driving its intended load, and at all operating speeds.

2.4 GROUNDS

A. Electrode Ground: The resistance of electrodes (main service, generators, transformer, etc.) shall not exceed 10 ohms and shall be measured before equipment is placed in operation. Testing shall be performed on all grounding electrode installations. Testing of main ground shall be 3-point method in accordance with IEEE Standard 81, Section 9.04; 2-point method for distribution equipment. Testing to be completed before service energized. Submit all ground test readings to the Engineer in tabulated format at substantial completion.

B. Electrode Ground: The resistance of electrodes (main service, generators, transformer, etc.) shall not exceed 10 ohms and shall be measured by The Contractor before equipment is placed in operation. Testing shall be performed on all grounding electrode installations. Testing shall be 3-point method in accordance with IEEE Standard 81. Submit all ground test readings to the Engineer in tabulated format at substantial completion.

C. Electrode Ground: The resistance of electrodes (main service, generators, transformer, etc.) shall not exceed 5 ohms and shall be measured by The Contractor before equipment is placed in operation. Testing shall be performed on all grounding electrode installations. Testing shall be 2-point method in accordance with IEEE Standard 81. Submit all ground test readings to the Engineer in tabulated format at substantial completion.

2.5 EQUIPOTENTIAL GROUND

A. Equipotential Ground: Test all metal conductive surfaces likely to become energized within patient care areas. Test all large conductive surfaces likely to become energized within a volume defined as 6 foot from the patient bed horizontally or 7 foot 6 inches vertically.

1. Large metal surfaces not likely to be energized, which do not require testing:
   a. Window frames
   b. Door frames
   c. Floor drains
   d. Moveable metal cabinets

2. Test Method:
   a. Use impedance and voltage measurements
   b. Utilize established ground bus or ground bar in panel serving area.
   c. Measure voltage from reference point to conductive surfaces and all receptacle ground contacts.
   d. Measure impedance between reference point and receptacle ground contacts.
   e. Check for proper polarity.
   f. Identify the reference ground for each room on the ground test report. Provide a blue dot label with a permanent adhesive backing located on the bottom center of the reference ground outlet cover.

3. Maximum Acceptable Values:
   a. Voltage: 20 mV plus or minus 20 percent
   b. Impedance: 0.1 ohm plus or minus 20 percent
   c. Quiet ground impedance: 0.2 ohm plus or minus 20 percent

4. Equipment:
   a. Millivolt meter with 1 Kohm impedance and proper frequency response, in accordance with NFPA 99.
   b. Polarity tester

5. Ground Test Report: Complete ground test report included at the end of this specification section, and make available copies of such to engineer and inspecting authority at final inspection.

2.6 PRIMARY CABLE

A. Utilize DC proof test: Test new cable from primary circuit utility interface to utilization equipment, after complete installation.

TESTS AND PERFORMANCE VERIFICATION

1. Defer test until all terminations have been completed. Disconnect permanently connected switches and other devices, except for connection to power grid.

2. Apply a DC voltage for 5 minutes from the appropriate test equipment to the conductor of the cable to be tested, and the low potential or grounded terminal connected to the cable shield.

3. Record leakage currents after 15, 20, 30, 45, and 60 seconds and at one-minute intervals. Apply test voltage in accordance with ICEA Standards.

B. Repair or Replacement: Repair or replace, as directed, any cables or terminals not meeting or exceeding minimum standards. Retest replaced cable or repaired splices.

2.7 DRY-TYPE TRANSFORMERS

A. Required Factory Tests: Required factory tests shall be as follows;

1. Ratio
2. Polarity
3. Losses
   a. No load
   b. Full load
4. Resistance Measurements
5. Impedance
6. Temperature
7. Impulse Strength
8. Sound Level
9. Exciting Current
10. Low-frequency Dielectric Strength
11. ANSI Point and Curve

B. Submission: Submit test results with shop drawings.

2.8 EMERGENCY SYSTEM

A. General: Submit emergency system tests in accordance with NFPA 110. Refer to emergency section of the specification for additional information.

PART 3 - EXECUTION

3.1 SUBMITTALS

A. Equipotential Ground Test Report: Complete report form at the end of this specification.

B. Cable Test Report: Submit Cable Test Report in Triplicate.

C. Transformer Test Report: Indicate comparative data of ANSI and NEMA Standards. Indicate all characteristic values as specified herein. Certified copies of tests on electrically duplicate units are acceptable.

D. Check-Out Memos: Complete all information on forms at the end of this specification, project information, and certificate of completed demonstration memo. Submit data for examination and acceptance prior to final inspection request.

E. Tabulated Data: Submit data on 8-1/2 x 11 inch sheets with names of the personnel who performed the test.

F. Final: Submit accepted memos before a request for final inspection.

3.2 QUANTITIES

A. Quantity: Submit 5 copies of the check-out memo on each major item of equipment. Insert accepted memos in each brochure with the performance verification information and submittal data.

END OF SECTION

TESTS AND PERFORMANCE VERIFICATION

Facility Name:__________ Project Name:__________ AHCA Log No.

Date:_________Tested By:

Maximum Test Intervals:
General Care - 12 mos.
Critical Care - 6 mos.
Wet Locations - 12 mos.

Name:

Company:

Ground Test Report

Type Meter Used and External Network If Used:

Note: Maximum Readings Permitted: 20 mV New Construction
0.1 Ohm New Construction

Room No.	Area Type / Description (C) = Critical Care (G) = General Care	Voltage Measurement			Impedance Measurement		Remarks - If Voltage Readings More Than 20 mV in Existing Const. Note Tests & Investigation Required.
		No. of Recepts.	No. of Other	Max. Reading in Millivolts	No. of Recepts.	Max Reading in Ohms	

TESTS AND PERFORMANCE VERIFICATION

Project Name: ____________________

Motor Test Information

Name of Checker: ____________________

Date Checked: ____________________

(a) Name and Identifying Mark of Motor ____________________

(b) Manufacturer ____________________

(c) Model Number ____________________

(d) Serial Number ____________________

(e) RPM ____________________

(f) Frame ____________________

(g) Code Letter ____________________

(h) Horsepower ____________________

(i) Nameplate Voltage and Phase ____________________

(j) Nameplate Amps ____________________

(k) Actual Voltage ____________________

(l) Actual Amps ____________________

(m) Starter Manufacturer ____________________

(n) Starter Size ____________________

(o) Heater Size, Catalog No., and Amp Rating ____________________

(p) Manufacturer of Dual-Element Fuse ____________________

(q) Amp Rating of Fuse ____________________

(r) Power Factor at __________ Speed ____________________
(For variable speed motors, provide recording chart over operating range)

TESTS AND PERFORMANCE VERIFICATION

Tabulated Data

Voltage and Amperage Readings

Switchgear or Panelboard

Full Load Amperage Readings:

Date

Time

Phase
A
B
C
N

Full Load Voltage Readings:

Date

Time

Phase A to N ___________ A to B
B to N ___________ A to C
C to N ___________ B to C

No Load Voltage Readings

Date

Time

Phase A to N ___________ A to B
B to N ___________ A to C
C to N ___________ B to C

______________________ Engineer's Representative

______________________ Contractor's Representative

APPENDIX 26410-23A

Common Test Voltages and Minimum Insulation Resistance Values for Various Devices

Electrical Equipment and Wiring			
Maximum Voltage Rating	Minimum DC Test Voltage	Normal DC Test Voltage for New Installations	Minimum Insulation Resistance at 20°C for New Installations
250V	250	500	25 MΩ
600V	500	1,000	100 MΩ
5,000V	2,500	2,500	1,000 MΩ
8,000V	2,500	2,500	2,000 MΩ
15,000V	2,500	5,000	5,000 MΩ
25,000V	5,000	5,000	20,000 MΩ

Transformer Windings				
Transformer Winding Rating	Minimum DC Test Voltage	Normal DC Test Voltage for New Installations	*Minimum Insulation Resistance at 20°C for New Installations	
			Oil-Filled	Dry-Type
0V to 600V	500	1,000	100 MΩ	500 MΩ
601V to 5,000V	1,500	2,500	1,000 MΩ	5,000 MΩ
>5,000V	2,500	5,000	5,000 MΩ	25,000 MΩ

*Note: Refer to manufacturer's literature for specfic acceptance criteria. Actual insulation resistance of transformer winding is dependent on transformer type, insulation, kVA rating, and winding temperature.

Motor Winding Insulation Resistance Testing			
Motor Winding Rating	Minimum DC Test Voltage	Normal DC Test Voltage for New Installations	*Minimum Insulation Resistance at 20°C for Installations
0V to 600V	500	1,000	15 MΩ
601V to 5,000V	1,500	2,500	30 MΩ
5,001V to 15,000V	2,500	5,000	50 MΩ

*Note: Minimum insulation resistance for rotating equipment in megohms = equipment kV + 1.

Figure A01

ADDITIONAL RESOURCES

26401-23 Load Calculations – Feeders and Services

National Electrical Code® Handbook, Latest Edition. Quincy, MA: National Fire Protection Association.

26402-23 Health Care Facilities

National Electrical Code® Handbook, Latest Edition. Quincy, MA: National Fire Protection Association.

NFPA 99, *Standard for Health Care Facilities*, Latest Edition. Quincy, MA: National Fire Protection Association.

26403-23 Standby and Emergency Systems

Liquid-Cooled Generator Sets Application Manual, Latest Edition. Minneapolis, MN: Cummins Onan.

National Electrical Code® Handbook, Latest Edition. Quincy, MA: National Fire Protection Association.

OT III Transfer Switches Application Manual, Latest Edition. Minneapolis, MN: Cummins Onan.

26404-23 Basic Electronic Theory

Electronics, Allan R. Hambley. 2nd Edition. 2000. New York, NY: Pearson Education, Inc.

National Electrical Code® Handbook, Latest Edition. Quincy, MA: National Fire Protection Association.

26405-23 Fire Alarm Systems

NFPA 72®, *National Fire Alarm and Signaling Code®*, National Fire Protection Association. Available at **www.nfpa.org**.

NFPA 101®, *Life Safety Code®*, National Fire Protection Association. Available at **www.nfpa.org.**

26406-23 Specialty Transformers

C57.110-2018 – IEEE Recommended Practice for Establishing Liquid-Filled and Dry-Type Power and Distribution Transformer Capability When Supplying Nonsinusoidal Load Currents, 2018. Available online at **standards.ieee.org**.

National Electrical Code® Handbook, Latest Edition. Quincy, MA: National Fire Protection Association.

26407-23 Advanced Controls

Motor Control Technology for Industrial Maintenance, Thomas E. Kissell. New York, NY: Pearson Education, Inc.

National Electrical Code® Handbook, Latest Edition. Quincy, MA: National Fire Protection Association.

NFPA 70B, *Recommended Practice for Electrical Equipment Maintenance.* Quincy, MA: National Fire Protection Association.

Application Guide for AC Adjustable Speed Drive Systems (PDF), Arlington, VA: National Electrical Manufacturers Association. Available for download as document NEMA ICS 7.2-2015 (or the most recent edition) from: **www.nema.org**

Softstarter Handbook, publication 1SFC132060M0201. Available for download from ABB at: **https://library.e.abb.com/public/6b4e1a3530814df0c12579bb0030e58b/1SFC132060M0201.pdf**

26408-23 HVAC Controls

NFPA 70®, *National Electrical Code* (*NEC*®), Latest Edition. Quincy, MA: National Fire Protection Association.

Refrigeration and Air Conditioning: An Introduction to HVAC/R. Larry Jeffus and David Fearnow. New York, NY: Pearson Education, Inc.

System Diagnostics and Troubleshooting Procedures. John Tomczyk. Mt. Prospect, IL: Esco Press.

26409-23 Heat Tracing and Freeze Protection

IEEE Standard 515, IEEE Standard for the Testing, Design, Installation, and Maintenance of Electrical Resistance Trace Heating for Industrial Applications, Latest Edition. Piscataway, NJ: IEEE.

Industrial Heat-Tracing Systems Component Selection Guide. Menlo Park, CA: Raychem HTS.

National Electrical Code® Handbook, Latest Edition. Quincy, MA: National Fire Protection Association.

Selection Guide for Self-Regulating Heat-Tracing Systems. Houston, TX: Tyco Thermal Controls.

26410-23 Motor Operation and Maintenance

NCCER Module 15209, *Introduction to Bearings.*

26411-23 Medium-Voltage Terminations/Splices

3M™ Premium MV Outdoor Cold Shrink Termination - Fully Integrated (QTIII) video: **solutions.3m.com**.

Inline Crimp Connector Splice Installation video: **solutions.3m.com.**

National Electrical Code® Handbook, Latest Edition. Quincy, MA: National Fire Protection Association.

26412-23 Special Locations

National Electrical Code® Handbook. Latest Edition. Quincy, MA: National Fire Protection Association.

GLOSSARY

Absorption current: The current caused by insulating material becoming polarized by the electricity flowing through the conductor (*polarization current*) and the random and slow movement of electrons when an electric field is applied over electrons (*electron drift*).

Accomplishment: An individual's need to set challenging goals and achieve them.

Accountability: In relation to job completion, accepting responsibility and being personally answerable for the results.

Addressable device: A fire alarm system component with discrete identification that can have its status individually identified or that is used to individually control other functions.

AED (automated external defibrillator): A device used to help those experiencing sudden cardiac arrest.

Air sampling detector: A detector consisting of piping or tubing distribution from the detector unit to the area or areas to be protected. Using air sampling ports and piping or tubing, an air pump draws air from the protected area back to the detector. At the detector, the air is analyzed for fire products.

Alarm: In fire systems, a warning of fire danger.

Alarm signal: A signal indicating an emergency requiring immediate action, such as an alarm for fire from a manual station, waterflow device, or automatic fire alarm system.

Alarm verification: A feature of a fire control unit that allows for a delay in activating alarms upon receiving an initiating signal from one of its circuits. If approved by the Authority Having Jurisdiction (AHJ), the supervising station has up to 90 seconds to verify that the signal is an unwanted alarm. Alarm verification is commonly used in hotels, motels, hospitals, and institutions with large numbers of smoke detectors.

Americans with Disabilities Act (ADA): An act of Congress intended to ensure civil rights for physically challenged people.

Ampere turns: The product of amperes times the number of turns in a coil.

Analog-to-digital converter: A device designed to convert analog signals such as temperature and humidity to a digital form that can be processed by logic circuits.

Approved: Acceptable to the Authority Having Jurisdiction (AHJ).

Armature: The assembly of windings and metal-core laminations in which the output voltage is induced. It is the rotating part in a revolving field generator.

Armor: A mechanical protector for cables; usually a formed metal tube or helical winding of metal tape formed so that each convolution locks mechanically upon the previous one (interlocked armor).

As-built drawings: A revised set of drawings that reflect all changes made during the construction process and show the exact specifications of the completed work.

Audible signal: An audible signal is the sound made by one or more audible indicating appliances, such as bells, chimes, horns, or speakers, in response to the operation of an initiating device.

Authority: The right to act or make decisions in carrying out an assignment.

Authority Having Jurisdiction (AHJ): The organization, office, or individual responsible for approving equipment, installations, or procedures in a particular locality.

Automatic fire alarm system: A system in which all or some of the circuits are actuated by automatic devices, such as fire, smoke, heat, and flame detectors.

Automatic-changeover thermostat: A thermostat that automatically switches between heating or cooling as needed.

Autotransformer: Any transformer in which the primary and secondary connections are made to a single winding.

Avalanche breakover: A form of electrical current multiplication that can occur in insulating and semiconductor materials. It could be considered a "jailbreak" of electron flow, leading to large currents in materials that otherwise would allow little or no current flow.

Bank: An installed grouping of several units of the same electrical equipment type, such as a bank of transformers, a bank of capacitors, or a meter bank.

Base speed: The shaft speed at which the motor will develop rated horsepower at rated load and voltage, as stated on a motor nameplate.

Behavior: The way a person responds to a specific situation.

Bimetal: An assembly made of two dissimilar metals that changes shape in response to temperature change due to the expansion and contraction properties of the two metals, creating movement that can open or close a switch.

Border light: A permanently installed overhead strip light.

Capacitance charging current: Initial high-current flow that quickly decays to zero after the insulation is charged to full voltage. Sometimes referred to simply as *charging current*.

Carrier frequency: In a pulse-width modulated (PWM) drive, the frequency at which the IGBT can be switched on or off to create an output waveform that mimics a sine wave of desired voltage and frequency. Carrier frequencies typically range from 500 Hz to 20,000 Hz, but need to be at least 10 times the maximum drive output frequency.

Ceiling: The upper surface of a space, regardless of height. Areas with a suspended ceiling would have two ceilings: one visible from the floor and one above the suspended ceiling.

Ceiling height: The height from the continuous floor of a room to the continuous ceiling of a room or space.

Certification: A systematic program that uses randomly selected follow-up inspections of a certified system installed under the program to verify for the listing organization that a fire alarm system complies with all the requirements of the NFPA 72® code. A system installed under such a program is identified by the issuance of a certificate and is designated as a certificated system.

Chime: A single-stroke or vibrating audible signal appliance that has a xylophone-type striking bar.

Circuit: The conductors or radio channel as well as the associated equipment used to perform a definite function in connection with an alarm system.

Closed-circuit transition: A method of reduced-voltage starting in which the motor being controlled is never removed from the source of voltage while moving from one voltage level to another.

Coded signal: A signal pulsed in a prescribed code for each round of transmission.

Communication: The process of exchanging facts, information, and ideas. Communication comes in many forms, including verbal, written, visual, and nonverbal.

Compressor: The component of a refrigeration system that converts low-pressure, low-temperature refrigerant gas into high-temperature, high-pressure refrigerant gas through compression.

Condenser: A heat exchanger that transfers heat from refrigerant vapor to air or water, causing the vapor to condense to its liquid state.

Condensing furnace: A gas furnace with two heat exchangers to extract the maximum amount of heat from the combustion process. It was named after its process, where the combustion byproducts are cooled to the point where water vapor condenses into a liquid.

Constant-wattage heating cable: A heating cable that has the same power output over a large temperature range. It is used in applications requiring a constant heat output regardless of varying outside temperatures. Zoned parallel-resistance, mineral-insulated, and series-resistance heating cables are examples of constant-wattage heating cables.

Construction safety plan: A document that outlines the procedures, rules, and regulations that are or will be put in place to protect workers during a construction project.

Control unit: A device with the control circuits necessary to furnish power to a fire alarm system, receive signals from alarm initiating devices (and transmit them to audible alarm indicating appliances and accessory equipment), and electrically supervise the system installation wiring and primary power. The control unit can be contained in one or more cabinets in adjacent or remote locations.

Cooling compensator: A fixed resistor installed in a thermostat to act as a cooling anticipator by creating a slight warming effect.

Core loss: The electric loss that occurs in the core of an armature or transformer due to conditions such as the presence of eddy currents or hysteresis.

Cost control: The process that helps keep expenses under control by managing labor, material, and other costs to ensure that the project finishes on budget.

CPR (cardiopulmonary resuscitation): A lifesaving technique that is used when someone's heartbeat or breathing has stopped.

Crew leader: A person appointed leader of a team or crew, usually an experienced craft professional who has demonstrated leadership qualities. Also known as *frontline leader*, *frontline supervisor*, *lead person*, or *foreman*.

Critical path: In manufacturing, construction, and other types of creative processes, the required sequence of tasks that directly controls the ultimate completion date of the project.

Dashpot: A device that uses a gas or fluid to absorb energy from or retard the movement of the moving parts of a relay, circuit breaker, or other electrical or mechanical device.

Deadband: A temperature range that separates the heating and cooling modes in an automatic-changeover thermostat, within which there is no system activity.

Dead leg: A segment of pipe designed to be in a permanent no-flow condition. This pipe section is often used as a control point for a larger system.

Dead-front type: Types of equipment or enclosures covered or protected to prevent exposure of energized parts on the operating side of the equipment.

Decision-making: The action or process of making a choice. Decision-making involves starting an action, stopping one, or choosing a different plan or action.

Dew point: The temperature to which a vapor must cool before it begins to condense into its liquid state.

Diac: A three-layer diode designed for use as a trigger in AC power control circuits, such as those using triacs.

Dielectric constant (K): A measurement of a material's ability to store a charge.

Dielectric strength: The maximum voltage a material can withstand before dielectric breakdown occurs.

Differential: The difference between the cut-in and cut-out points of a thermostat or pressure switch.

Digital alarm communicator transmitter (DACT): A system component at a protected premises to which initiating devices or groups of devices are connected. The DACT will seize the connected telephone line, dial a preselected number to connect to a digital alarm communicator receiver (DACR), and transmit signals indicating a status change of the initiating devices.

Distractions: Anything that disrupts the communication flow between sender and receiver. Also called *noise*.

Duty: A work task an employee is expected to perform.

Dwelling unit: A single unit providing complete and independent living facilities for one or more persons, including permanent provisions for living, sleeping, cooking, and sanitation. A multifamily dwelling is a building containing three or more dwelling units.

Eddy currents: The circulating currents that are induced in conductive materials by varying magnetic fields; they are usually considered undesirable because they represent a loss of energy and produce excess heat.

Electrical datum plane: Horizontal plane affecting electrical installations based on the rise and fall of water levels in land areas and floating piers and landing stages.

Electrolyte: A substance in which the conduction of electricity is accompanied by chemical action, such as the paste that forms the conducting medium between the electrodes of a dry cell or storage cell.

End-of-line (EOL) device: A device used to terminate a supervised circuit. An EOL is normally a resistor or diode placed at the end of a two-wire circuit to maintain supervision.

Equipotential ground plane: A mass of conducting material that, when bonded together, provides a low impedance to current flow over a wide range of frequencies.

Equipotential plane: An area in wire mesh or other conductive material embedded in or placed under concrete that may conduct current.

Estimating: The process of calculating the cost of a project.

Ethics: The moral principles that guide an individual's or organization's actions when dealing with others.

Evaporator: A heat exchanger that transfers heat from air or water to the refrigerant vapor/liquid mixture flowing through, causing the refrigerant to vaporize.

Exciter: A device that supplies direct current (DC) to the field coils of a synchronous generator, producing the magnetic flux required for inducing output voltage in the stator coils.

Expansion device: A device that provides the pressure drop needed to reduce the pressure and temperature of a refrigerant as it enters the evaporator; also known as a *metering device*.

Extra-hard usage cable: Cable designed with additional mechanical protection for use in areas where it may be subject to physical damage.

Fan Affinity Laws: The mathematical relationship between fan speed, airflow rate, power used, and torque. Airflow is directly proportional to speed. Torque is proportional to the square of speed. Power used is proportional to the cube of speed. For example, decreasing fan speed by 20% decreases the power used by about 50%.

Fault: An open, ground, or short condition on any line(s) extending from a control unit, which could prevent normal operation.

Feasibility study: An analysis that considers all of a project's relevant factors—including budget, technical elements, legal aspects, and scheduling— to determine the likelihood that the project can be completed successfully.

Feeder: A conductor that is not a service or branch circuit conductor and is located after the main disconnect switch but before the final branch circuit overcurrent device.

Festoon lighting: Outdoor lighting that is strung between supporting points.

Field-effect transistor (FET): A transistor that controls the flow of current through it with an electric field.

Fire rating: Time in hours or minutes that a material or assembly can withstand direct exposure to fire without igniting and spreading the fire.

First aid: Help given to a sick or injured worker on the worksite immediately after an injury occurs.

Flame detector: A device that detects the infrared, ultraviolet, or visible radiation produced by a fire. Some devices are also capable of detecting the flicker rate (frequency) of the flame.

Footlight: A border light installed on or in a stage.

Forward bias: A condition that exists when voltage is applied to a solid-state device in such a way as to allow the device to conduct easily.

General alarm: A term usually applied to the simultaneous operation of all audible alarm signals on a system to indicate the need for evacuation of a building.

Generator: A rotating machine that is used to convert mechanical energy to electrical energy. In a broader sense, it is general apparatus or equipment used to convert or change energy from one form to another.

Ground fault: A condition in which the resistance between a conductor and ground reaches an unacceptably low level.

Harassment: Unwelcome conduct that is based on race, color, religion, sex, national origin, age, disability, or genetic information. Harassment includes verbal or physical conduct that impacts a person's work performance or creates an intimidating, hostile, or offensive work environment.

Harmonics: Oscillations at frequencies that are integral multiples of the fundamental frequency.

Hazards: Conditions or activities that, if left uncontrolled, have the potential for harm.

Heat detector: A device that detects abnormally high temperatures or high rates of temperature rise.

Heat pumps: Refrigerant-based heating and cooling units that can reverse the direction of the refrigeration cycle to absorb heat from outdoor air or water and transfer it indoors.

Heat sink: A metal mounting base that dissipates the heat of solid-state components mounted on it by radiating the heat into the surrounding atmosphere.

Heat source: Any component that adds heat to an object or system.

Heat transfer: The movement of heat energy from a warmer substance to a cooler substance.

High-potential (hi-pot) test: A high-potential test in which equipment insulation is subjected to a voltage level higher than that for which it is rated to find any weak spots or deficiencies in the insulation.

Horn: An audible signal appliance in which energy produces a sound by imparting motion to a flexible component that vibrates at some nominal frequency.

Hysteresis: The time lag exhibited by a body in reacting to changes in the forces affecting it; hysteresis is an internal friction.

Impairment: The point where someone's intake of substances affects their ability to perform appropriately.

Impedance: The opposition to current flow in an AC circuit. Impedance includes resistance (R), capacitive reactance (X_C), and inductive reactance (X_L). It is measured in ohms (Ω).

Incidents: Unplanned events that result in property damage, fatalities, injuries, illnesses, or near misses.

Indicating device: See *notification appliance (device)*.

Initiating device: A manually or automatically operated device with a normal intended operation resulting in a fire alarm or supervisory signal indication from the control unit. Examples of alarm signal initiating devices are thermostats, manual boxes (stations), smoke detectors, and waterflow devices. Examples of supervisory signal initiating devices are water level indicators, sprinkler system valve position switches, pressure supervisory switches, and water temperature switches.

Initiating device circuit (IDC): A circuit to which automatic or manual signal initiating devices are connected such as fire alarm manual boxes (pull stations), heat and smoke detectors, and waterflow alarm devices.

Inpatient: A patient admitted into the hospital for an overnight stay.

Insulated gate bipolar transistors (IGBTs): A type of transistor that has low losses and low gate drive requirements. This allows it to be operated at higher switching frequencies.

Insulation breakdown: The failure of insulation to prevent the flow of current, sometimes evidenced by arcing. If the voltage is gradually raised, breakdown will begin suddenly at a certain voltage level. Current flow is not directly proportional to voltage. When a breakdown current has flowed, especially for a period of time, the next gradual application of voltage will often show breakdown beginning at a lower voltage than initially.

Insulation classes: Categories of insulation based on the thermal endurance of the insulation system used in a motor. The insulation system is chosen to ensure that the motor will perform at the rated horsepower and service factor load.

Insulation shielding: An electrically conductive layer that provides a smooth surface in contact with the insulation's outer surface. It is used to eliminate electrostatic charges external to the shield and provide a fixed, known path to ground.

Invar®: An alloy of steel containing 36% nickel and one of the two metals in most bimetal control devices.

Isolation transformer: A transformer that has no electrical metallic connection between the primary and secondary windings.

Job description: A description of the scope and responsibilities of a worker's job so that the individual and others understand what the job entails.

Job diary: A written record that a supervisor maintains periodically (usually daily) of the events, communications, observations, and decisions made during the course of a project.

Job safety analysis (JSA): A technique that focuses on job tasks as a way to identify hazards before they occur. It focuses on the relationship between the worker, the task, the tools, and the work environment. Also known as *job hazard analysis (JHA)* or *activity hazard analysis (AHA)*.

Junction field-effect transistor (JFET): A field-effect transistor formed by combining layers of semiconductor material.

Labeled: In the context of fire alarm control units (FACUs), tags that identify various zones and sensors by descriptive names. Units may include dual identifiers, one of which is meaningful to the occupants and the other to firefighting personnel.

Landing stage: A floating platform used for the loading and unloading of passengers and cargo from boats or ships.

Leakage current: AC or DC current flow through insulation and over its surfaces, and AC current flow through a capacitance. Current flow is directly proportional to voltage. The insulation and/or capacitance are considered a constant impedance unless breakdown occurs.

Level 4 schedule: A schedule that offers additional detail to provide working schedules to the crews doing the work, usually within three to six weeks of completing specific work.

Light scattering: The action of light being reflected or refracted off particles of combustion. Used for detection in a modern-day photoelectric smoke detector. This is called the *Tyndall effect*.

Listed: Equipment or materials included in a list published by an organization acceptable to the Authority Having Jurisdiction (AHJ) that is concerned with product evaluation, whose listing states either that the equipment or materials meets appropriate standards or has been tested and found suitable for use in a specified manner.

Lookahead schedule: For planning and scheduling work that is happening in the short term, usually within one to three weeks; used for anticipating material, labor, tool, and other resource requirements,as well as identifying potential schedule conflicts or other problems. Also called *short-term schedule*.

Maintenance: Repair service, including periodic inspections and tests, required to keep the protective signaling system and its component parts in an operative condition at all times. This is used in conjunction with the replacement of the system and its components when they become undependable or inoperative for any reason.

Mechanical refrigeration: The use of machinery to provide a cooling effect or, in the case of a heat pump, a heating effect.

Megohmmeter: An instrument or meter capable of measuring resistances more than 200 MΩ. It employs much higher test voltages than are used in ohmmeters, which measure up to 200 MΩ. A megohmmeter is also commonly referred to as a *megger*.

Mineral-insulated (MI) heating cable: A type of constant-wattage, series-resistance heating cable used in long line applications where high temperatures need to be maintained, high-temperature exposure exists, or high power output is required.

Morale: An individual's emotional outlook toward work and the level of satisfaction gained while performing the jobs assigned.

Motivate: To make someone feel determined or enthusiastic or to make someone behave in a particular way.

National Fire Alarm and Signaling Code®: This is the update of the NFPA standards book that contains the former NFPA 71, NFPA 72®, NFPA 74, and NFPA 1221 standards. NFPA 72® is revised every three years.

National Fire Protection Association (NFPA): The NFPA administers the development and publishing of codes, standards, and other materials concerning all phases of fire and life safety.

Nichrome: An alloy based on nickel with chromium added (10% to 20%), and sometimes iron (up to 25%). Nichrome is often used for high-temperature applications such as in the fabrication of electric heating elements.

Noise: A term used in electronics to cover all types of unwanted electrical signals. Noise signals originate from numerous sources, such as fluorescent lamps, walkie-talkies, amateur and CB radios, machines being switched on and off, and power surges. Today, equipment must tolerate increasing amounts of electrical interference, and the quality of equipment depends on how much noise it can ignore and withstand.

Non-coded signal: A signal from any indicating appliance that is continuously energized.

Nonverbal communication: Things the speaker and the receiver see or hear while communicating. Examples include facial expressions, body movements, hand gestures, tone of voice, and eye contact.

Notification appliance (device): Any audible or visible signal employed to indicate a fire, supervisory, or trouble condition. Examples of audible signal appliances are bells, sirens, electronic/manual horns, buzzers, and chimes. A visible indicator consists of an incandescent lamp, strobe lamp, mechanical target or flag, meter deflection, or the equivalent. Also called an *indicating device*.

N-type material: A material created by doping a region of a crystal with atoms from an element that has more electrons in its outer shell than the crystal.

Obscuration: A reduction in the atmospheric transparency caused by smoke, usually expressed in percent per foot.

Occupational Safety and Health Administration (OSHA): A national public health agency that is part of the US Department of Labor. To promote a safe and healthy work environment, OSHA issues standards and rules for working conditions, facilities, equipment, tools, and work processes.

Open-circuit transition: A method of reduced-voltage starting in which the motor being controlled may be disconnected temporarily from the source of voltage while moving from one voltage level to another.

Organization: A group of people working together.

Organizational chart: A diagram that shows how the various management and operational responsibilities relate to each other within an organization. Named positions are ranked top to bottom, from those functional units with the most and broadest authority to those with the least. Lines connect positions and indicate chains of authority and other relationships.

Outpatient: A patient who receives services at a hospital but is not admitted for an overnight stay.

Overhead service conductors: Conductors routed overhead between the utility service point and the first point of connection to the service-entrance conductors at the structure.

Parallel-resistance heating cable: An electric heating cable with parallel connections, either continuous or in zones. The watt density per lineal length is approximately equal along the length of the heating cable, allowing for a drop in voltage down the length of the heating cable.

Path (pathway): Any conductor, optic fiber, radio carrier, or other means for transmitting fire alarm system information between two or more locations.

Peer: Someone who is in a position or level in an organization equal or similar to yours.

Personal growth: Improving one's talents and potential, both in and out of the workplace.

Photoelectric smoke detectors: Detectors employing the photoelectric principle of operation using either the obscuration effect or the light-scattering effect for detecting smoke in its compartment.

Planning: The process of laying out all details of a construction project before construction begins.

Policy: A general statement establishing guidelines for a specific activity.

Portable switchboards: Movable lighting switchboards used for road shows and similar presentations, usually supplied by a flexible cord or cable.

Positive alarm sequence: An automatic sequence that results in an alarm signal, even when manually delayed for investigation, unless the system is reset. A positive alarm sequence must not be longer than three minutes (180 seconds) but can be adjustable to allow on-site personnel to check the alarm.

Positive locking device: A screw, clip, or other mechanical locking device that requires a tool or key to lock or unlock it.

Potting compound: An approved and listed insulating compound, such as epoxy, which is mixed and installed in and around electrical connections to encapsulate and seal the connections to prevent the entry of water or moisture.

Power supply: A source of electrical operating power, including the circuits and terminations connecting it to the dependent system components.

Power-limiting heating cable: A type of heating cable that shows positive temperature coefficient (PTC) behavior based on the properties of a metallic heating element. The PTC behavior exhibits a much smaller change in resistance in response to a change in temperature than that shown by self-regulating heating cables.

Problem-solving: A process used to identify possible solutions to a situation.

Procedures: Formal instructions to carry out and meet policies.

Production: The amount of construction materials put in place. It is the quantity of materials installed on a job.

Productivity rate: A measure of how much work gets done over a period of time, also called *output per labor hour*.

Professional growth: Gaining new skills and work experience that can help one to reach a goal in one's career.

Profit: The amount of money that the contractor will make after paying all the direct and indirect costs.

Project delivery methods: Different ways to organize the services of development, planning, and construction in order to execute a project.

Project manager: Person responsible for managing one or more projects.

Projected beam smoke detector: A type of photoelectric light obscuration smoke detector in which the beam spans the protected area.

Proscenium: The wall and arch that separate the stage from the auditorium.

Protected premises: Physical locations protected by a fire alarm system.

P-type material: A material created when a crystal is doped with atoms from an element that has fewer electrons in its outer shell than the natural crystal. This combination creates empty spaces in the crystalline structure. The missing electrons in the crystal structure are called *holes* and are represented as positive charges.

Public switched telephone network (PSTN): An assembly of communications facilities and central office equipment, operated jointly by authorized common carriers, that provides the public with the ability to establish communications channels via discrete dialing codes.

Rate compensation detector: A device that responds when the temperature of the air surrounding the device reaches a predetermined level, regardless of the rate of temperature rise.

Rate-of-rise detectors: Devices that respond when the temperature rises at a rate exceeding a predetermined value.

Reactance: The imaginary part of impedance; also, the opposition to alternating current due to capacitance (X_C) and/or inductance (X_L).

Reactor-type dimmer: A dimming system that incorporates windings or coils that are linked by a magnetic core, an inductive reactor that functions like a capacitor, and a relay. The reactor stores current from the source and reduces lamp power.

Recognition: Acknowledgement of an employee's accomplishments through verbal and nonverbal communications.

Rectifier: A device or circuit commonly used to change AC voltage into DC voltage, or as a solid-state switch.

Redline drawings: Marked-up versions of construction drawings documenting any changes made during construction or installation.

Refrigerant: A fluid that assists in the transfer of heat through the manipulation of its pressure, temperature, and physical state in various parts of an HVAC or refrigeration circuit.

Refrigeration cycle: The thermodynamic cycle through which a circulating refrigerant transfers heat from one location to another.

Remote supervising station fire alarm system: A system installed in accordance with the applicable code to transmit alarm, supervisory, and trouble signals from one or more protected premises to a remote location where appropriate action is taken.

Reset: A control function that attempts to return a system or device to its normal, non-alarm state.

Resistance-type dimmer: A manual-type dimmer in which light intensity is controlled by increasing or decreasing the resistance in the lighting circuit.

Responsibility: The act of accepting a task and completing it to the best of one's ability.

Reverse bias: A condition that exists when voltage is applied to a device in such a way that it causes the device to act as an insulator.

Rewards: Tangible items given to an employee as recognition for good work.

Rheostat: A slide and contact device that increases or decreases the resistance in a circuit by changing the position of a movable contact on a coil of wire.

Ribbon tape shield: A helical (wound coil) strip under the cable jacket.

Root cause: A core issue or fundamental reason for the occurrence of a problem.

Root cause analysis (RCA): A method of problem-solving used for identifying the root causes of faults or problem.

Scheduling: Involves defining which activities happen in what order and assigning dates and times to those tasks.

Scope: The list of the commitments and activities that all contractors, subcontractors, and suppliers are expected to do during a project. Also called *scope of work*.

Self-regulating heating cable: A type of heating cable that inversely adjusts its heat output in response to an increase or decrease in the ambient temperature.

Semiconductors: Materials that are neither good insulators nor good conductors. Such materials contain four valence electrons and are used in the production of solid-state devices.

Separately derived system: An electrical source, other than a service, having no direct connection(s) to circuit conductors of any other electrical source other than those established by grounding and bonding connections.

Series-resistance heating cable: A type of heating cable in which the resistance of the conductor provides the heat. The wattage output depends on the total circuit length and on the voltage applied.

Service: The conductors and related equipment for delivering electrical power from the utility to a structure's wiring system.

Service conductors: The conductors routed from the service point to the service disconnecting means.

Service drop: The overhead conductors between the utility electric supply system and the service point.

Service equipment: The necessary equipment, usually consisting of a circuit breaker or switch and fuses and their accessories, connected to the local utility or power provider. The service equipment serves as the primary means of disconnect.

Service lateral: The underground conductors between the utility electric supply system and the service point.

Service point: The point of connection between the utility conductors and the premises wiring.

Shield: A conductive barrier against electromagnetic fields.

Shielding braid: A shield of small, interwoven wires.

Shunt trip: A low-voltage device that remotely causes a higher voltage overcurrent protective device to trip or open the circuit.

Signal: A status indication communicated by electrical or other means.

Signaling line circuit (SLC): A circuit or path between any combination of circuit interfaces, control units, or transmitters over which multiple system input signals, output signals, or both are carried.

Silicon-controlled rectifier (SCR): A device that is mainly used to convert AC voltage into DC voltage. To do so, however, the gate of the SCR must be triggered before the device will conduct current.

Site-isolating device: A disconnecting means at the point of distribution that is used to isolate the service for the purpose of electrical maintenance, emergency disconnection, or the connection of an optional standby system.

Site-specific safety plan (SSSP): A safety plan that includes a focused set of information that accounts for a jobsite's unique hazards.

Situational leadership: A leadership style that involves adjusting to the specific situation or task and the leadership needs of the group.

Slip: The speed difference between the synchronous speed and the base speed. Induction motors develop their torque because of the slip. The amount of slip depends on motor design and motor load.

Smoke detector: A device that detects visible or invisible particles of combustion.

Soft foot: When the feet of a motor frame are forced to anchor against an uneven surface, resulting in distortion of the motor frame. This can cause misalignment of bearings.

Solid-state device: An electronic component constructed from semiconductor material. Such devices have all but replaced the vacuum tube in electronic circuits.

Solid-state overload relay (SSOLR): An electronic device that provides overload protection for electrical equipment.

Solid-state phase-control dimmer: A solid-state dimmer in which the wave shape of the steady-state current does not follow the wave shape of the applied voltage (that is, the wave shape is nonlinear).

Solid-state relay (SSR): A switching device that has no contacts and switches entirely by electronic means.

Solid-state sine-wave dimmer: A solid-state dimmer in which the wave shape of the steady-state current follows the wave shape of the applied voltage (that is, the wave shape is linear).

Spacing: A horizontally measured dimension related to the allowable coverage of fire detectors.

Splice: Two or more conductors joined with a suitable connector and reinsulated, reshielded, and rejacketed with compatible materials applied over a properly prepared surface.

Spot-type detector: A device in which the detecting element is concentrated at a particular location. Typical examples are bimetallic detectors, fusible alloy detectors, certain pneumatic rate-of-rise detectors, certain smoke detectors, and thermoelectric detectors.

Startup temperature: The lowest temperature at which a heat-tracing cable is energized.

Strand shielding: The semiconductive layer between the conductor and insulation that compensates for air voids that exist between the conductor and insulation.

Stratification: The phenomenon in which the upward movement of smoke and gases ceases due to a loss of buoyancy.

Stress: An internal force set up within a body to resist or hold it in equilibrium.

Subbase: The mounting base of a thermostat that houses the wiring terminals.

Subcooling: The measurable heat removed from a refrigerant after it has been converted to its liquid state (condensed) and continues to reject heat.

Substance abuse: The inappropriate overuse of drugs and chemicals, whether they are legal or illegal.

Superheat: The measurable heat absorbed by a refrigerant after it has been converted to its vapor state (vaporized) and continues to absorb heat.

Superintendent: An on-site supervisor who is responsible for one or more crew leaders or frontline supervisors.

Supervisory signal: A signal indicating the need for action in connection with the supervision of guard tours, the fire suppression systems or equipment, or the maintenance features of related systems.

Switchboard: A large panel, frame, or assembly of panels upon which switches, overcurrent and other protective devices, buses, and usually instruments are mounted. Devices can be mounted on the face, back, or on both sides since switchboards are generally accessible from the rear as well as from the front.

Synchronous generator: An AC generator having a DC exciter. Synchronous generators are used as stand-alone generators for emergency and standby power systems and can also be paralleled with other synchronous generators and the utility system.

System unit: The active subassemblies at the supervising station used for signal receiving, processing, display, or recording of status change signals. The failure of one of these subassemblies causes the loss of a number of alarm signals by that unit.

Tap conductors: Conductors, other than service conductors, with overcurrent protection located upstream from its point of supply that exceeds the value permitted for similar conductors that are protected as described in ***NEC Section 240.4***.

Thermal conductivity: The ability of a material or substance to transfer heat away from a given point of contact.

Thermistor: A temperature sensor that exhibits a predictable change in its resistance proportional to the temperature.

Three-way communication: A form of communication with an initial message from a sender, which is then repeated by the receiver to confirm accuracy, and then validated by the sender. Also called *repeat-back communication*.

Throwover: A transfer switch used for supplying temporary power.

Thyristors: Bi-stable semiconductor devices that can be switched off and on. Thyristors turn on with a quick pulse of control current. They turn off only when the working current is interrupted elsewhere in the circuit. SCRs and triacs are forms of thyristors.

Toolbox talks: Short, informal safety meetings held at the start of each day or shift. Sometimes referred to as *tailgate meetings* or *safety briefings*.

Totally enclosed (TE) motor: A motor that is encased to prevent the free exchange of air between the inside and outside of the case.

Trait: A distinguishing quality of a person.

Transmitter: A system component that provides an interface between the transmission channel and signaling line circuits, initiating device circuits, or control units.

Triac: A bidirectional triode thyristor that functions as an electrically controlled switch for AC loads.

Trouble signal: A signal initiated by the fire alarm system or device that indicates a fault in a monitored circuit or component.

Unbalanced load: Three-phase loads in which the loads are not evenly distributed between the phases.

Underground service conductors: The underground conductors between the service point and the first point of connection to the service-entrance conductors in a terminal bus.

Upskilling: A type of training that provides someone with more advanced skills through additional education.

Verbal communication: Messages that are sent using voice or other audible sounds. Also called *spoken communication* or *oral communication*.

Vessel: A container such as a barrel, drum, or tank used for holding fluids or other substances.

Visible notification appliance: A notification appliance that alerts by the sense of sight.

Visual communication: The process of using visual elements, such as photos, graphics, colors, and fonts, to convey messages.

Voltage gradients: Fluctuating voltage potentials that can exist between two surfaces or components and may be caused by improper or insufficient bonding or grounding.

Wavelength: The distance between peaks of a sinusoidal wave. All radiant energy can be described as a wave having a wavelength. Wavelengths serve as the unit of measure for distinguishing between different parts of the spectrum. Wavelengths are measured in microns, nanometers, or angstroms.

Wide area telephone service (WATS): Telephone company service that provides reduced costs for certain telephone call arrangements. In-WATS or 800-number service calls can be placed anywhere in the continental United States to the called party at no cost to the calling party. Out-WATS is a service whereby, for a flat-rate charge, dependent on the total duration of all such calls, a subscriber can make an unlimited number of calls within a prescribed area from a particular telephone terminal without the registration of individual call charges.

Work breakdown structure (WBS): A method of organizing the entire scope of work in a logical manner based on how the work will be executed.

Workers' compensation: Insurance that companies have to cover medical expenses, lost wages, and other costs for employees who are injured or become ill while completing work for their job.

Written communication: The process of sending messages or information using words, whether digitally or physically.

Zones: Defined areas within a protected premises. A zone can define an area from which a signal can be received, an area to which a signal can be sent, or an area in which a form of control can be executed.